D0856252

Israel:
Pluralism and conflict

Israel:
Pluralism and conflict

Sammy Smooha
Department of Sociology and Anthropology, University of Haifa
Foreword by Professor Leo Kuper

University of California Press
Berkeley and Los Angeles 1978

University of California Press
Berkeley and Los Angeles, California

ISBN: 0–520–02722–1
Library of Congress Catalog Card Number: 74–76390

Printed in Great Britain

To Adi, Shahar and Tsofiya

Contents

Foreword by Professor Leo Kuper   xiii

Preface   xvii

1   Introduction   1

2   A theoretical perspective: structural pluralism   6

3   Models of intergroup relations   21

4   Historical background   48

5   Current social contexts   70

6   Pluralism and inequality   110

7   Oriental–Ashkenazi inequality   151

8   Conflict and integration   183

9   Continuity and change   234

10   Conclusion   258

Table appendix   266

Notes   353

Cited references   411

Selected bibliography   436

Index   444

Tables

1 A conceptual scheme for the study of pluralistic divisions 269
2 Current social contexts by major division 271
3 Estimates of indicators of pluralism and inequality by major division 274
4 Estimates of features of pluralism and inequality by major division 276
5 Estimates of indicators and features of cohesion by major division 277
6 Features of change by major division 279
7 Estimates of relative size of pluralistic divisions, 1975 280
8 Estimates of Orientals and Sephardim in World and Israel (Palestine) Jewries, 1500 1975 281
9 Jewish immigration to Palestine and Israel, 1882–1975 281
10 Monthly family income (in current Israeli pounds), 1956–7 to 1975 282
11 Monthly family income (in current Israeli pounds) by education, 1974 283
12 Relative index of equality of income by period of immigration, 1956–7 to 1975 284
13 Gross and adjusted index of relative equality of income by period of immigration, male wage-earners, 1957–8 to 1969 285
14 Relative index of equality of income and consumption, 1959–60 to 1968–9 286
15 Relative index of equality in per capita expenditure on consumption by period of immigration, 1956–7 to 1968–9 286
16 Improvement in per capita expenditure on consumption, 1956–7 to 1968–9 (1956–7 = 100) 286
17 Percentages of families possessing durable goods and adequate housing, 1957–74 287

18 Percentages of families possessing durable goods and adequate housing by period of immigration, 1958–74   288

19 Gross income per standard equivalent adult by quintile, urban wage-earners, 1968–9   289

20 Percentage distribution of occupations by place of birth, 1975   290

21 Percentage distribution of occupations, 1954–75   291

22 Relative index of equality and index of dissimilarity of occupational categories, 1954–75   293

23 Percentage distribution of occupational categories by period of immigration, males, 1959–73   294

24 Chances to belong to top occupational categories by ethnic origin, period of immigration and education, males, 1961 and 1970   296

25 Percentage distribution of education of people aged 14 or over, 1961 and 1975   297

26 Percentage distribution of education of people aged 14 or over by period of immigration and sex, 1961 and 1969   298

27 Percentage of Oriental students and graduates by type of school and class standing, 1956–7 to 1975–6   301

28 Student rates in post-primary and higher education by type of school and place of birth, 1956–7 to 1976–7   302

29 Estimates of retention rates in primary and post-primary education, late 1960s   304

30 Culturally disadvantaged pupils in elementary schools by father's education, family size and type of school, 1971–2   305

31 Percentage distribution of 8th grade scholastic test (seker), 1956–7 to 1969–70   306

32 Percentage of pupils scoring 70 points or more in 8th grade scholastic test (seker), by father's education and family size, 1971–2   307

33 Percentage of success among pupils sitting matriculation examination, 1965–6 to 1971–2   308

34 Political representation in selected positions of power by rank and sector, 1955–73   309

35 Cabinet ministers, 1949–73   310

36 Cabinet ministers and front bench Knesset members by rank, 1971   310

37 Knesset members, 1949–73   311

38 Civil servants by rank, 1955–69   312

39 Supreme Court justices, 1950–73   313

40 Major-generals, 1951–73   313

41 Police officers, 1955–69   313

42 Heads of local authorities by type of settlement, 1955–72   314

43 Heads of local authorities by ethnic composition of settlement, 1969   315

44 Members of local authorities by type of settlement, 1955 and 1965   315

45 Members of executive of the Jewish Agency, 1951–73   316

46 Members of Zionist executive committee (Israelis only), 1951–73   316

47 Directors of departments in the Jewish Agency, 1951–73   316

48 Members of central committee of the Histadrut, 1949–73   316

49 Members of executive committee of the Histadrut, 1949–69   317

50 Delegates to 11th Convention of the Histadrut, 1969   317

51 Top-ranking officials in the Histadrut headquarters, 1971   317

52 General secretaries of national trade unions of the Histadrut, 1970 and 1973   318

53 General secretaries of workers' councils, 1957–73   318

54 General secretaries of workers' councils by type and ethnic composition of settlement, 1970   318

55 Local top positions (heads of local authorities and general secretaries of workers' councils) by type and ethnic composition of local authority, 1970   319

56 Steering committee and secretariat of the Histadrut industrial complex (Hevrat HaOvdim), 1973   320

57 Managers in the Histadrut industrial complex (Herrat HaOrdim) by rank, 1970   320

58 Members of governing bodies of the Mapam Party, 1948–73   321

59 Members of governing bodies of the Israel Labour Party, 1970 and 1973   322

60 Members of governing bodies of the Ahdut HaAvoda Party, 1958–73   323

61 Members of governing bodies of the Mapai Party, 1950–73   324

62 Members of governing bodies of the Rafi Party, 1965–73   325

63 Members of governing bodies of the Mafdal Party, 1956–73   326

64 Members of governing bodies of the Liberal Party, 1956–73   327

65 Members of governing bodies of the Herut Party, 1949–73   329

66 General secretaries of local branches of the Israel Labour Party by type and ethnic composition of settlement, 1969 and 1973   330

67 Members of local authorities by major political party and bloc, 1955 and 1965   331

68 Knesset members by major political party and bloc, 1949–73   333

69	Members of Zionist executive committee (Israelis only) by major political party and bloc, 1951–72	336
70	Members of executive committee of the Histadrut by major political party and bloc, 1949–69	337
71	Members of the board and executive of the Industrialists' Union, 1969–70	339
72	Percentage distribution of top managers in industry, 1961–7	339
73	Status hierarchies by rank, late 1950s and late 1960s	340
74	Percentage distribution of family size, 1975	342
75	Adjusted index of similarity in consumption patterns, 1956–7 to 1963–4	343
76	Percentage distribution, of foreign-born Jews by type of locality, 1967	343
77	Students in primary, intermediate and post-primary schools by percentage of Oriental students in class and types of school and locality, 1966–7 and 1972–3	344
78	People marrying, by bride's and groom's ethnic origin, 1955–74	345
79	Rates of convicted Jewish offenders by age, 1952–74	346
80	Method of election of Knesset members of major divisions, 1949–73	347
81	Participation of the religious parties in government, 1949–73	348
82	Demographic characteristics of Israeli Arabs and Jews (Asia–Africa, Europe–America), 1975	349
83	Socioeconomic status of Israeli Arabs and Jews (Asia–Africa, Europe–America), 1975	350
84	Political representation in selected positions of power of Israeli Arabs and Jews (Orientals, Ashkenazim), December 1973	351

Foreword

The theory of plural societies and of divisive pluralism has generated much controversy in the brief period of its development. This is to be expected since it raises critical questions for a certain type of dogmatic Marxism, and for functionalism, while it poses some rather intractable problems for liberal perspectives. Part of the response to the challenge, unfortunately inevitable in ideologically laden analysis, is to misrepresent the theory, so that the real theoretical issues are not joined.

The theory derives from the work of J. S. Furnivall, a colonial administrator and economist with experience in Burma and the Middle East, who applied the term 'plural society' to describe the medley of peoples in tropical dependencies held together by the colonial power. He saw that these societies would face serious problems of internal conflict on decolonization, and he tried to find the political and social basis for integration in the post-colonial world. There were some early applications and criticisms of his theory, but the main stimulus came from M. G. Smith in two theoretical formulations, emphasizing in an initial version cultural pluralism. The theory has been further developed in the work of Professors Pierre van den Berghe and R. A. Schermerhorn, and in my own writing, among others.

The theory deals with societies characterized by persistent cleavages between sections of the population, whether the cleavages are based on race, ethnicity or religion. Decolonization, the changed structure of international relations, and the greater militance of deprived minorities, have given an increasing contemporary salience to racial and ethnic differences (and to religious differences in some societies). In the three decades following the Second World War, there have been many greatly destructive internal conflicts in plural societies. A list of some of the more extreme conflicts would include

Hindu and Muslim in India following partition, Indo-China, Algeria, Zanzibar, Rwanda, Burundi, the Congo, Angola, Mozambique, Rhodesia, South Africa, Uganda, Sudan, Ethiopia, Cyprus, Northern Ireland, Israel, Lebanon, Vietnam, Bangladesh, Malaya, Ceylon. Societies with sharply defined plural divisions are a quite common setting for genocidal type conflicts.

The increased salience of racial and ethnic pluralism has stimulated interest in societies which are politically a unit, but which are sharply divided by internal differences. The theory of the plural society and of pluralism is only one of many formulations, which include communalism, communally fragmented societies, multiple societies, composite societies and segmented societies.

Dr Sammy Smooha contributes to the theory of pluralism at many different levels. He reviews the state of the theory, correcting some of the misrepresentations. He offers his own criticisms, develops his distinctive approach and introduces a number of theoretical refinements. He rejects the typological concept of the plural society as too rigid, basing his own analysis on the concept of pluralism as a variable factor. This gives flexibility, and provides a basis for relating degrees of pluralism to the social consequences in terms of conflict and integration. At the same time, it imposes the need to devise measures of pluralism, which Dr Smooha successfully accomplishes, though the nature of the data is such that only crude measures are available to him. Finally he tests his theoretical framework by applying it in an extremely interesting case study of Israel.

The study of plural societies and of pluralism calls for comparative analysis, and it has been largely concerned with societal units. Dr Smooha draws on this literature, finding also within Israel a variety of plural divisions which provide comparative material within a single society, almost an experimental situation. The combination of these two approaches yields a broad range of comparative material.

Israeli society seems almost the embodiment of every conceivable type of pluralism. Dr Smooha distinguishes five major plural divisions: Palestinian Arabs in the occupied territories versus Israeli Jews (a demographic ratio of 29 : 71), Israeli Arabs versus Jews (13 : 87), Druze versus Christian versus Muslim Arabs (9 : 16 : 75), religious versus nonreligious Jews (30 : 70), and Oriental versus Ashkenazi Jews (55 : 45). This pluralism is combined with inequality, yielding a four-tier status hierarchy, 'where the disfranchised Palestinian Arabs rank at the bottom, the subordinate Arab minority occupy the next lower layer, the disadvantaged Oriental majority take an intermediate position, and at the top the superior Ashkenazi minority outdistance all the non-European groups'.

Virtually every contrast or type of opposition is to be found. At the level of cultural pluralism, there is a range from differences in subculture within the Jewish population or within the Arab population to basic differences in core culture between non-Jews and Jews. At the level of social pluralism, there is a range of variation including separate and unequal, separate and equal, not separate and unequal. All the nondominant groups are nonassimilating minorities, with the exception of Oriental Jews who are an assimilating majority within the Jewish population. Conflicts over objectives show comparable variety. The most extreme opposition is that which challenges the right of Israel to exist. Other oppositions in goals relate to the issues whether Israel 'should remain Jewish and Zionist, whether the current compromises which shape its religious or secular character should be modified, and whether resources must be radically redistributed in order to do away with ethnic stratification'.

From this range of plural divisions, Dr Smooha selects three for close analysis – the Oriental–Ashkenazi division, the religious–nonreligious division (both within the Jewish population), and the Israeli Arab–Jewish division. To each of these he applies a different model of plural relations, making use of a typology of pluralism. Oriental–Ashkenazi relations are analysed in terms of a 'dynamic paternalism–cooptation model', religious–nonreligious relations in terms of a 'contested accommodation model' and Arab–Jewish relations in terms of an 'exclusionary domination model'. Dr Smooha rejects the nation-building approach, which views Israel as a successful, new nation state, and the colonial perspective, which characterizes it as a racist Zionist state, in favour of a much more complex patterning of plural relations. And whereas the nation-building perspective emphasizes integration, and the colonial perspective conflict, Dr Smooha analyses the operation of both these processes, and the reciprocal influence of the plural divisions. The result is a comprehensive, analytically stimulating and richly rewarding study, characterized by great integrity and a strong commitment to equality. It is an important contribution, offering new insights into Israeli society, and into the theory of plural societies and pluralism.

The problem of greatest urgency and threat is represented by the Israeli–Palestinian conflict, or more broadly the Israeli conflict with the Arab world. This is an overriding cleavage, profoundly affecting the whole range of plural relations within Israel. In the contemporary world, conflicts within plural societies have an international component. It is especially marked in the case of Israel, and one can only hope that international involvement will take the form of a search for an equitable solution with a minimum of destruction and suffering and loss of life.

Menlo Park, California, April 1977   Leo Kuper

Preface

This book is an outcome of personal and intellectual concerns with the pluralistic structure of Israel. To put it rather simply, Israel is known to have two major conflicting images. According to one view it is a unique Jewish state and a leading model in nation-building (a viable young democracy, a strong people's army, a dynamic mixed economy, advanced cultural renaissance, and a successful melting-pot). The opposing outlook portrays Israel as a white settler, neocolonial, theocratic *Herrenvolk*, an artificial entity which will not endure. Both these standpoints underlie writings on Israel. This study attempts to develop an approach that avoids the pitfalls in each of the two perspectives.

It is my pleasure to thank all those who helped me to produce this book. The help extended by Professor Leo Kuper, of the University of California at Los Angeles, cannot be overestimated. Kuper was the first to expose me to the new school of pluralism which is applied throughout this study. Only those who personally know his intellectual standards, endless patience and human touch can understand my great indebtedness to him. I had also the privilege of close association with Professor Pierre van den Berghe during my work at the University of Washington, Seattle. Van den Berghe contributed much in insightful, provocative reactions to my thinking and in personal encouragement as well. I have also benefited from comments and criticisms made by Professors Richard Schermerhorn, Joseph Cohen and Samuel Surace.

Among my Israeli colleagues, I wish to mention especially Dr Hayyim Cohen of the Institute of Contemporary Jewry in the Hebrew University, Jerusalem. I had also the benefit of numerous stimulating discussions on ethnic relations in Israel with Dr Yochanan Peres, of Tel-Aviv University, and chapter 7 on Oriental–Ashkenazi inequality draws on our joint work in this area. Not less beneficial were my exchanges on the issues of the relations between religious and nonreligious Jews with Dr Menachem Friedman from Bar-Ilan University, Ramat-Gan.

The assistance of Professor John Rex, the editor of this series of books, Mr Peter Hopkins and Mrs C. J. Raab from Routledge & Kegan Paul, and Mr Alain Hénon, from the University of California Press, and Mrs. Nicolette Fried is greatly appreciated.

I alone, however, assume full responsibility for the ideas and analysis in the study.

My wife, Tsofiya, typed previous drafts and helped to develop my ideas. She shared with me the pains of analysing one's own society while guarding against the great temptation of rationalizing the status quo.

This study was originally completed in 1973. It has been revised twice since then to apply up to 1975. The dynamics of Israeli society defy updating. It is my hope that the kind of analysis pursued throughout will make up for the gaps in updating.

University of Haifa, Israel,
April 1977

1 Introduction

Our era is marked by both diversity and strife, or, to use more technical terms, pluralism and conflict. Uniformity strikes like an exception, as evidenced in the existence of countless ethnic or racial groups all over the world, but only about 150 independent states, 90 per cent of which have at least one significant minority (Connor, 1973: 1). Along with this vast diversity disunity abounds: Mason (1970b: 46) talks about the age of 'a revolt against inequality' and 'a search for a pedigree' by subordinate groups; Horowitz (1972) speaks of an international system of stratification in which the Third World nonwhite peoples are at the bottom of an emerging world society; and Segal (1967) coins the term 'race war' to express widespread anxieties of rampant hostility within and among nations. Blacks versus whites in the United States, nonwhites versus whites in South Africa, Chinese and Indians versus Malays in Malaysia, Ibos versus Hausas and Yorubas in Nigeria, Turks versus Greeks in Cyprus, Christians versus Moslems in Lebanon, Catholics versus Protestants in Northern Ireland are only a few, rather dramatic, instances of intergroup heterogeneity and animosity today.

The growing prominence of pluralism and conflict the world over presents a great challenge to specialists in intergroup relations. A number of questions come to mind. How do nondominant and dominant groups, looked at as wholes, differ from and relate to each other? What are the conditions which promote accommodation and peaceful change as opposed to those which induce conflict and instability? How can unity be maintained amid diversity, or, more specifically, how can national integration and political democracy prevail in a society composed of ethnic or racial groups that exhibit appreciable value dissensus, institutional segmentation, gross inequality in distribution of resources and other virulent cleavages?

1

The term 'pluralism' is not used in the common way. In the popular literature it means the existence of cultural variations, their desirability, or the right of minorities to preserve their distinctive identities; and in the social sciences it usually implies a modern, massive social differentiation of society into many complementary and interdependent groups – the institutional base of democracy. Here it refers, rather, to heterogeneity in the broadest sense, i.e., significant differences in culture and social institutions which distinguish and isolate constituent groups in society.[1] Although it is explicitly intended to accord pluralism a neutral meaning and to divorce it of its regular 'positive' connotations of harmonious coexistence, democracy, gradualism and stability, the new structural usage might invoke, instead, 'negative' associations of intolerance, domination, violent change and disruption. At any rate, it is not assumed that pluralism necessarily leads to conflict (or alternatively – integration), but that the relations between the two are complex and problematic.

We face all these issues in studying Israel, which is a striking example of the enormous varieties of pluralism and conflict. The 4.6 million residents within the ceasefire boundaries of Israel at the end of 1975 are internally separated along five lines resulting in the following divisions: Palestinians–Jews, Israeli Arabs–Jews, Druze–Christian–Moslem Israeli Arabs, religious–nonreligious Jews, and Oriental–Ashkenazi Jews. Disregarding further divisions and subdivisions,[2] these five sets of intergroup relations are discernible on many accounts. (Table 7, in the Appendix, furnishes information on their demographic ratios.)

The Palestinian–Jewish division is the most internationally publicized. About one million Palestinians were placed under Israeli rule after the June 1967 War. The Palestinians are a disfranchised people subject to a military government. Over the years a new, more full-fledged and durable set of intergroup relations between Palestinians and Jews, with generalized statuses, has been evolving, but this process was abruptly interrupted by the October 1973 War. Since the future of the occupied territories has become precarious, postwar relations have correspondingly become transitory and unstable.

The second division is between the Israeli Arabs and the Jews. The Israeli Arabs, numbering 442,000 as against 2,960,000 Jews (or 13 per cent of the total Israeli population), are those Arabs in Palestine who remained in Israel after the 1948 War. They are a religious and cultural minority within the Jewish state and their right to a separate identity is respected. Unlike the Palestinian Arabs, the Israeli Arabs enjoy, by law, civil rights and hold more intricate contacts with the Jewish majority.

2

The third division splits the Israeli Arabs into two small minorities of Druzes (9 per cent) and Christians (15 per cent) and a majority of Moslems (76 per cent). All Israeli Arabs share in common the Arabic language, Arab culture and the status of a non-Jewish minority in a Jewish state. But they differ not only in religion and size but also in level of modernization and relations with the Jews. Compared with other Israeli Arabs, the Druzes are the Jews' most favoured group and the Christians are the most modernized. Each group constitutes a legally separate religious community and maintains strict endogamy as well as political solidarity and other communal ties.

Among the Jews themselves, the division according to degree of religious observance is politico-sectarian rather than ethnic. The religious Jews constitute a numerical minority of 30 per cent or fewer, make themselves identifiable by their dress, lead a distinct way of life, maintain separate schools and political parties, and endeavour to reside and marry within the group.

The fifth and last division is between the Oriental and Ashkenazi Jews. The Orientals are Jews from the Near East and North Africa, including descendants of Jews from Spain. Despite their numerical preponderance (about 55 per cent of all Israeli Jews), they occupy a subordinate position in the Jewish community. The Ashkenazim, European Jews, are the oldtimers who founded the new Jewish society, set up its Western or Eastern-European social institutions, and still run it.

All these truly distinct groups are squeezed within a small territory. They differ considerably in size, geographical concentration, culture, modernism, civil rights, power, socioeconomic status and other factors. All nondominant groups, except the Oriental Jews, are nonassimilating minorities. The Palestinians, Israeli Arabs and religious Jews are nondominant minorities who reject the status quo in principle and aspire to dominance. Yet the whole society is ruled by a minority of secular Ashkenazi Jews. These are only a few of the more conspicuous contrasts that characterize Israel's constituent groups.

Although there is a large and expanding literature on Israel, with one or two minor exceptions none of the works has focused on its multifaceted pluralistic structure.[3] Furthermore, the five pluralistic divisions are not given equal attention by Israeli sociologists. Palestinian–Jewish relations, notwithstanding the headlines they capture, are rarely studied because of their newness, sensitivity and, perhaps, inaccessibility. Since religious–nonreligious relations are overshadowed by the broader state–religion issue, they are scrutinized by jurists, political scientists and publicists, and only in the early 1970s did they start to come to the attention of sociologists.

3

Relatively more research has been done on relations between the Israeli Arab minority and the Jewish majority, but it leaves much to be desired. Whereas some works on each of the three Arab religious communities (Druzes, Christians and Moslems) are available, there is virtually none on the relations among them. In conerast, Oriental–Ashkenazi relations are the most intensively investigated. They are indeed a favourite topic in Israeli sociology, claiming an extensive literature after more than two and a half decades of empirical research.

This book is devoted to the pluralistic structure of Israeli society, but the greatly asymmetric distribution of knowledge makes it impossible to treat all the five pluralistic divisions equally. Because of the lack of data on Palestinian–Jewish relations and Druze–Christian–Moslem relations, I shall not treat them here. The much documented Oriental–Ashkenazi relations will receive special consideration, followed by religious–nonreligious relations and Arab–Jewish relations.

While existing information is an asset for making continuing research possible, it is, nevertheless, a liability for the analyst who takes a different view of a field already dominated by a given perspective. The dominant nation-building perspective conceptualizes Oriental–Ashkenazi relations mainly in terms of immigrant absorption and modernization, religious and nonreligious relations in terms of *Kulturkampf* and modernization, and Arab–Jewish relations in terms of nationalism and modernization. The rival colonial perspective uses a diametrically different conceptual apparatus in approaching these internal relations. In comparison, the present inquiry adopts the perspective of structural pluralism or the 'theory of plural society'. This shift in viewpoint encounters some difficulties. As Kuhn (1964) shows, not only do facts appear dissimilar from each different perspective but also wide gaps in knowledge – which are not perceived from a particular angle – come to the foreground in the light of the other. Missing evidence may make the new perspective appear at first to be inadequately grounded in established truths.[4]

The pluralist perspective takes a macrosociological and dynamic view of Israeli society. It sensitizes us to two questions. One refers to pluralism and inequality, i.e., the precise way in which Orientals and Ashkenazim, religious and nonreligious Jews, and Israeli Arabs and Jews are different, separate and unequal. The other relates to conflict and integration; namely how much strain or solidarity there is in relations between these groups. The two questions will concern us throughout the study as we try to shed light on the more central problem of Israel's national cohesion and stability: How does Israel manage to preserve a relative tranquillity? Is it because of its relatively minor and tractable pluralistic structure? Is it because of its carefully suppressed internal pressures? Or is it a result of other factors?

The analysis proceeds as follows. In the next chapter the perspective of structural pluralism is introduced. The reader whose prime interest is in Israel can skip this theoretical chapter and go directly to chapter 3 in which present and alternative models of intergroup relations in Israel are expounded. In the next two chapters the setting in which the various pluralistic divisions are anchored will be examined in detail: in chapter 4 the historical background, and in chapter 5 the current social contexts. In chapter 6 the major dimensions of pluralism and inequality are systematically explored. In chapter 7 Oriental–Ashkenazi inequality is singled out for an intensive investigation. Chapter 8 discusses patterns of conflict and bases of integration. In chapter 9 continuity and change are dealt with and in the final chapter the major findings are summed up.[5]

2 A theoretical perspective: structural pluralism*

The rate of growth of the literature of intergroup relations is catching up with the rapid and explosive developments in this sphere. At the researcher's command today there is a repository of concepts, ideas, theoretical orientations and methods to choose from. But the question is not one of quantity or variety but rather of adequacy – to what extent a theory helps to understand the dynamics (conflict and change) in minority–majority relations and in society as a whole, and to what degree it is applicable across the immense diversity of minority situations all over the world.

It is by these criteria that the 'theory of pluralism' lays some claim to validity. Starting in the 1940s with the pioneering writings by John S. Furnivall, this new approach gained momentum only in the 1960s. Its main current spokesmen are Michael G. Smith, Leo Kuper, Pierre L. van den Berghe and Richard A. Schermerhorn. While these pluralists do not share a uniform view, their works provide a critique of the field and a new theoretical direction.

1 Some criticisms of the literature

Among the theoretical weaknesses of the literature of intergroup relations is the preoccupation with prejudice and discrimination and their psychodynamic foundations (Schermerhorn, 1970: 6–8; Newman, 1973: 17, chapter 5). This is particularly true of many socio-psychological theories, such as those relating to frustration–aggression–displacement, the authoritarian personality, stereotyping, cognitive congruity, and transfer and reinforcement.[1] Such a myopic focus is even commended as a virtue[2] and is still the

* The non-specialist who is interested only in Israel may choose to go directly to the next chapter. Parts of this chapter are adapted from Smooha (1975).

6

organizing theme in such widely circulated textbooks as those by Simpson and Yinger (1972) and Vander Zanden (1972), and in theoretical formulations as that by Blalock (1967).

Conflict, power and change are still not recognized as pivotal concepts, although there has been some move in this direction (Horton, 1966; van den Berghe, 1967b: 36). Instead, the main emphasis is put on adaptation, accommodation, acculturation, assimilation, integration and the like (Blauner, 1972: 6-7).[3]

Descriptive studies on the one hand and small-scale studies testing limited empirical generalizations on the other are typical. To make things worse, another deficiency in recent years has been to depend more on updating the results of scientific studies in the field than on rethinking them (Schermerhorn, 1970: 9). Much of the impasse lies in the lack of a comparative perspective. Macrosociological comparative research – across cultures, periods or minority situations in the same society – is the exception rather than the rule (van den Berghe, 1967b: 148-9).[4]

Ideological factors add to the difficulty. The positivistic reluctance to admit the influence of ideological commitments on sociological analysis and policy applications impedes a search for better orientations and solutions. Both the use of concepts with moralistic overtones (e.g., oppression) or the misleading substitution of milder terms when stronger ones are called for are frequent. Schermerhorn warns against 'victimology', that is, the tendency to blindly support the 'underdog' minority under any circumstances (1970: 8-9). Van den Berghe claims (1972: 10-11):

> The stance of the liberal academic establishment on the issue of race was not only conservative and politically naive, it was also bad sociology, because it attacked mostly epiphenomena like attitudes, stereotypes, and discrimination rather than the underlying historical, economic, and political causes of racism. Ask trivial questions and you get trivial answers. And, at the policy level, trivial answers cannot solve fundamental problems . . .

2 Major formulations

The earlier formulations of the pluralist perspective focused on the special type called 'plural society'. This concept was introduced originally by Furnivall (1948) in his work on the colonial societies in South-East Asia. According to Furnivall, plural societies are artificial entities, created by Western imperialism, and maintained through political coercion for economic exploitation of nonwhite populations. They consist of a medley of peoples who share little more than the imposed economy and polity.[5]

Furnivall's economic theory was generalized and applied empirically by Smith in the early 1960s (1960; 1965a). Smith expanded the term 'plural society' to cover all societies, colonial or other, which satisfy at least two requirements – incompatible institutions (except the unifying state), and rule by a cultural numerical minority. Excluded are 'heterogeneous' societies like many Western states which possess a high degree of 'functional differentiation' (among occupational groups, city and countryside, etc.) and 'stylistic variations' but not cultural and social pluralism; homogeneous societies like many simple pre-industrial societies are also excluded.

In these early and later formulations the new perspective draws a sharp line between itself and traditional approaches to pluralism. Among the latter the best known is 'political pluralism', a school associated with de Tocqueville, Shils, Reisman, Dahl, Kornhauser and others who consider 'pluralism' as a basis for democracy in Western societies.[6] In the ethnic or racial area, 'cultural pluralism' or kindred conceptions are explicated and applied to the United States by Gordon (1964), Glazer and Moynihan (1970), and Laumann (1973), who all conclude that ethnic or religious groups have persisted beyond the third or later generation.[7]

The differences between the new and common interpretations of pluralism can be epitomized by contrasting a plural society such as colonial Burma and Java as depicted by Furnivall (1948), Jamaica and Grenàda by Smith (1965a; 1965b), South Africa by Kuper (1965) and van den Berghe (1967a), and British Guiana by Despres (1967) with nonplural societies such as West Germany or Denmark as they would appear in Parsons's and Dahl's theoretical frameworks. Plural societies are marked by cultural differences as against subcultural variations; a structural segmentation and pervasive segregation rather than separation in some voluntary activities; exceedingly disproportional distribution of resources compared to a more equitable allocation; integration through common values, cross-cutting affiliations and balance of power as opposed to asymmetric economic interdependence and political domination; and fundamental vulnerability to instability and violence in lieu of institutional capability for peaceful change. Whereas the theorists of the plural society speak 'unfavourably' of pluralism as a permanent source of disruptive conflicts with little hope for accommodation among the constituent groups, the conventional pluralists look 'favourably' on political pluralism as a prerequisite for democracy and expect the eventual assimilation of minorities into the mainstream to be the dominant trend.

The plural society theme played a historical role in expediting a shift from ethnographic studies to macrosociological analyses of multi-ethnic societies and in demonstrating the inapplicability of functionalism to plural societies,[8] but as so many pioneering ideas, it had to yield to a more sophisticated version. To mention some of the attacks: the notion of institutional incompatibility, itself Parsonian, was too obscure; class factors were largely played down; the differences between plural and nonplural societies were over-drawn; the necessary condition of dominance by an ethnic numerical minority became obsolete with the passing of colonialism.[9]

The 'theory of pluralism' replaced that of the plural society in the late 1960s. The proponents of the revised theory include Smith (1969a; 1969b; 1969c), Kuper (1969a; 1969b; 1974), van den Berghe (1967b: chapter 7; 1973), and Schermerhorn (1970) among others.[10] A brief statement of the theoretical formulation of each of them follows.

In his revised version, Smith suggests the new dimension of 'mode of incorporation', which he then relates to pluralism (1969b: 435–48). Mode of incorporation refers to the position of people in the political system. Three situations are distinguished: 'uniform incorporation' (persons obtain their equal civil rights directly as individuals); 'equivalent incorporation' (persons are divided into corporate groups through which they enter the public domain); and 'differential incorporation' (persons hold unequal legal status because they belong to mutually exclusive and unequal groups).

Smith associates the political mode of incorporation with 'cumulative' levels of pluralism. In 'cultural pluralism', cultural diversity exists without social segmentation and with uniform mode of incorporation (e.g., tripartite religious pluralism in the United States). In 'social pluralism', society consists of groups which are culturally diverse and socially separate but have equal access to public life (e.g., Belgium). In 'structural pluralism', society is differentiated into distinct groups which are different in culture, separate in organization and unequal in political participation (e.g., Northern Ireland). An additional special type is the 'plural society' where structural pluralism is exacerbated by minority rule (e.g., Rhodesia).

It can be suggested that the four-fold typology implies, perhaps, an ascending order of potentiality of conflict and disruption: minimal in cultural pluralism, moderate in social pluralism and maximal in structural pluralism and plural society. Smith himself is somewhat vague in this matter.[11]

Kuper draws on Smith's work and develops a more elaborate formulation. He makes the distinction between conditions and dimensions of pluralism. Among the conditions, Kuper (1969b: 469-73) includes certain characteristics of society at large, the history of intergroup relations, and demographic factors (the number, relative size and ecological distribution of the groups). These

9

conditions constitute the general social context in which ethnic or racial pluralism exists.

Kuper suggests four primary dimensions of pluralism (1969b: 473–9). The first, particularism–universalism, corresponds to Smith's 'mode of incorporation', but is expanded 'to include not only differentiation in the general political structure of the society, but also in the government of such institutional structures as industrial, educational, and religious establishments' (1974: 242). At the particularism end of the continuum, individuals relate to the society or acquire rights only through their membership in de jure or de facto separate ethnic or racial groups, and at the universalism end, they are directly incorporated into society as equal members. The other dimensions tap three fundamental lines of differentiation between groups: cultural ('cultural diversity–homogeneity'), associational ('segregation–assimilation') and stratificational ('inequality–equality'). This eclectic conceptualization of pluralism is unique because it comprises both vertical and horizontal dimensions.

Kuper proposes, further, that the four dimensions of pluralism may be combined into two summary measures. These measures are discontinuity–continuity which relates to the distribution of members of ethnic groups in the various structures of society, and superimposition–dissociation which refers to the extent that lines of cleavage between groups coincide or diverge throughout these structures.

In studying problems of conflict and change in highly pluralized societies such as Rwanda, Zanzibar, colonial Algeria and South Africa, Kuper finds Smith's 'differential incorporation' of primary significance (1974, *passim*). When groups are differentially incorporated, whether by conquest or other means, 'there develops, over the years, an elaboration of social relations between the races' (1974: 227). This elaboration spreads out endemically to various social institutions, creating inequality in economic participation and education as well as resulting in segregation, discrimination in amenities and contemptuous stereotypes. In consequence, generalized statuses of dominant and dominated groups emerge.

But beyond the point of generalization of statuses, 'there is no inexorable predetermination, by the initial differential incorporation, of the course of race relations' (Kuper, 1974: 234). Although the struggle tends to focus on political power, which is associated with the mode of incorporation, ethnic or racial challenge, given the diffuse statuses, can start anywhere in the social structure. Hence, along with the structural determinants, nonmaterial factors like status incongruity, relative deprivation, ideology and leadership style are important elements in the situation. But the main and novel conclusion is rather negative – there is a significant degree of indeterminacy. That is, ethnic or racial change can erupt unpredictably, proceed either rapidly and violently or gradually and peacefully.[12]

The significance of the thesis of certain indeterminacy in the occurrence and mode of ethnic or racial change can be fully appreciated only when contrasted with the great determinism of other schools. Kuper contends that the functionalist–Durkheimian theory of change – that modernization erodes ethnic communalism and increasing differentiation promotes stability and integration – is not applicable to plural societies. Nor does the competing Marxist theory of polarization in the economic area leading to class revolution offer a realistic explanation (1974: 243–8).

Another pluralist formulation is advanced by van den Berghe. He defines pluralism in terms of segmentation into corporate groups and institutional duplication (1967b: 34). Thus pluralism is primarily social, but it is often accompanied by cultural pluralism. Race is a special case of social pluralism and ethnicity of cultural pluralism, even though both tend to mix in real life. The two types of pluralism take various dimensions, among which are number, relative size, geographical dispersion and permeability of boundaries of constituent groups; objective cultural differences and public attitudes towards them; range of shared institutions and quality of group contacts; and ease and frequency of passing and mobility from one group to another (1967b: 140–4; 1969: 69–72; 1973: 967–70). Through this multiplicity of measures, a great many refinements and distinctions can be made in the analysis of pluralism in a world perspective.

Van den Berghe offers some specific and valuable observations about the implications of pluralism beyond the overall expectation that pluralism is conducive to conflict and change. First, he attaches little importance to the possibility of 'cultural pluralism with only minimal social pluralism' which is singled out by Smith (e.g., the Protestant–Catholic–Jewish division in the United States) and emphasizes, instead, the other possibility of 'social pluralism with only minimal cultural pluralism' which is absent in Smith's typology (e.g., the black–white division in the United States). The latter is very significant because it is rather invidious, unbearable and disruptive. As a corollary, intensification of conflict may be expected when a decline in cultural pluralism is not matched by a drop in social pluralism, as is the case in South Africa.

To indicate another point, unlike Smith and Kuper who view political domination as the mainstay of integration in pluralistic societies, van den Berghe puts 'equal stress on political coercion and economic interdependence (often of an exploitative nature) as necessary, sufficient, and *mutually reinforcing* bases of social integration of plural societies' (1973: 965).

11

Van den Berghe also disputes the political pluralists' contention that there is a direct relationship between pluralism and democracy. Although such an empirical correlation does exist, under certain conditions, 'moderately pluralistic societies have been fairly democratic' (1969: 79), as the case of India or Canada would demonstrate.[13] This observation is in line with Kuper's thesis of indeterminacy.

To complete this survey of major formulations of pluralism, Schermerhorn's work must be mentioned.[14] He gives a more complete framework for comparative analysis of intergroup relations than do Smith, Kuper and van den Berghe (1970: 12–17, 238–41). He distinguishes three independent variables: degree of enclosure (social and cultural pluralism), power differential, and intergroup sequence. The latter refers to the type of initial contact (e.g., colonization, immigration) which led to the emergence of a minority situation. The dependent variables are patterns of intergroup conflict or integration, which fall into three categories: objective factors pertaining to the subordinates' participation in spheres of institutional activity, particularly rates of vertical mobility for subordinates and superiors; subjective factors referring to subordinates' degree of satisfaction with their achievements; and conflictual or integrative behaviours reflecting hostility or harmony between the groups. Mediating and elaborating the relations between these two sets of factors are intervening variables, including a cultural–historical sector (e.g., West European, Caribbean), economic–political structure (economy is dominant, polity is dominant, mixed), and congruence–incongruence between minority goals and majority policies.

To illustrate his line of analysis, Schermerhorn posits that conflict is more intense when the objectives of minority and majority are incongruent than when they are congruent, regardless of whether these objectives are pluralistic or not. That is, the reciprocal collective goals of assimilation–incorporation and of pluralism–autonomy tend toward integration, as opposed to the divergent collective goals of forced assimilation with resistance and of forced segregation with resistance, which tend toward conflict (1970: 82–3). Schermerhorn also traces in detail how the various intergroup sequences differ in their impact on pluralism and, in turn, in their contribution to conflict. Thus imposed contact as a result of annexation, colonization or slavery tends, on the whole, to produce greater pluralism and conflict than voluntary immigration (1970: chapter 4).[15]

3 A conceptual scheme

A systematic effort to apply the pluralist perspective to a particular case requires the construction of a conceptual scheme. The above formulations furnish a good many variables, from which the interested researcher can select as he needs or sees fit. The scheme proposed below is based on the idea, common to all pluralists, that the best strategy to reach valid universal generalizations in the field and to come closest to what is really important and relevant in social life is through comparative, macrosociological studies guided by sensitizing conceptual schemes. This is to reject wasteful ethnographic and historicist approaches on the one hand, and pretentious, rigorous (propositional or deductive) theoretical methods on the other.[16] The suggested scheme aims to assist the user to make a systematic analysis of pluralistic societies or of a certain pluralistic division in them.[17]

The scheme (see Table 1 in the Appendix) consists of five parts, corresponding to the five major themes shared by pluralists: setting, pluralism, inequality, cohesion and change.[18]

Setting

Setting refers to the fundamental historical and social conditions in which current pluralistic divisions are anchored. The chief questions are as follows: How was contact between the groups under study initially established? What kinds of relations did they have up to the time under investigation? How is membership in them defined at present? What are their collective goals vis-à-vis each other? In what ways are they dependent on or unimportant to each other? How are the relations between any two groups affected by the presence of other sets of intergroup relations in the same society? And how does the structure of the society at large mould their relations? The list of factors implied by these questions is derived from various pluralist formulations.

Settings vary considerably. To illustrate, voluntary initial contact (e.g., free immigration) is expected to have a different impact from involuntary initial contact (e.g., conquest, enslavement). A legacy of centuries-old violent conflict would differ in its implications for the present from a history of co-operative co-existence. Various definitions of group membership might have different consequences (e.g., ethnicity, race, caste, racial caste, estate, religious observance). It also makes a difference whether the subordinate group is a minority or a majority, whether it faces the dominant group alone or along with other groups, and whether it operates in an authoritarian or a democratic state.

Pluralism

Pluralism is a central structural feature of total societies. It is a continuous, multidimensional phenomenon, manifested by two main

13

aspects, i.e., cultural diversity and social separation. Although these two dimensions tend to overlap, they should be distinguished because the degree of their divergence is quite significant.

Two refinements are made in the concept of cultural diversity. One follows van den Berghe's emphasis on the significance of the distinction between objective and subjective facets of cultural differences (1969: 70; 1971: 510–11). The other follows a common-sense, though often vague, distinction between core-culture and subculture. In a core-culture are included those fundamental and comprehensive values such as language, religion, nationality family structure and basic ideology as compared with subcultural variations such as consumption habits and public attitudes.

Social separation may extend to several levels. The first is legal and extra-legal differentiation between members of different pluralistic groups. Like Smith's mode of incorporation and Kuper's particularism–universalism, the legal or extra-legal aspect of separateness concerns the way individuals relate to the public domain, but it is more restricted in meaning here than these concepts which are too broad and difficult to operationalize. Legal differentiation refers, rather, to explicit state or local laws or regulations and rules of public organizations which distinguish or separate between groups; and extra-legal differentiation refers to the practical applications of neutral laws, regulations and rules to this effect. A second level is social separation in public facilities, schools, political parties and other voluntary associations. A third level is in intimate frameworks such as friendship and marriage, and the fourth level is the degree of mobilization. As Smith (1967: xvii–xviii), for instance, points out, it makes a difference if besides isolation in different spheres of life only the ruling group is mobilized (as in colonial Surinam, the Congo, Algeria and South Africa) or instead the various groups are largely organized (as in Cyprus, Guyana, Nigeria, and India during and after independence).

Societies' pluralism varies a great deal. Most societies today are pluralistic to a greater or lesser degree. At one extreme of the continuum are those such as South Africa where the social structure is segmented into groups which share little more than the economic and political institutions, and at the other end one finds homogeneous societies such as Portugal.

The neutral, descriptive meaning of pluralism in the scheme should be underlined. Cultural diversity refers to cultural and subcultural differences and it is meant to carry no normative import. The same is true for social separation.

I am proposing three summary measures of pluralism: magnitude, inconsistency and durability. Let us suppose a five-point scale is employed to estimate the degree of each dimension of pluralism.

14

Magnitude, as reflected in the average of the assigned scores, would refer to the degree of pluralism. Inconsistency, which is the amount of variation of the scores, would indicate the extent of superimposition or dissociation of lines of division. Durability may be measured by comparing the scores of dimensions in two or more time-periods, so that trends of persistence or change in the magnitude or inconsistency (or both) can be established.[19] While a linear relationship between each of these three overall features of pluralism and cohesion (intergroup conflict or integration) is not hypothesized, it is suggested that much can be gained by studying all of them jointly.[20]

Inequality

Inequality in distribution of resources between pluralistic groups takes two forms – socioeconomic gaps and power disparities. The distinction between the two is essential because of the frequent dissociation between power and other resources. For instance, in Northern Ireland, socioeconomic gaps are much smaller than power disparities (while the average income of Catholics is 80 per cent of that of Protestants, the Catholic minority is virtually excluded from national decision-making) (Rose, 1971). Minorities in the middle, such as the Chinese in Indonesia or the Jews in medieval Europe, hold a privileged socioeconomic status but are politically powerless (Blalock, 1967: 79–84, especially proposition 29; Bonacich, 1973). Such disjunctions between class and power are paramount and might be overlooked if the two are lumped together under 'inequality'.

Pluralists usually hold that the nonhierarchical divisions of pluralism and the hierarchical divisions of inequality should not be subsumed into one another, nor assigned any a priori precedence, but rather studied concurrently to reveal the extent of their convergence or disjunction. They also maintain that societies differ as to the primary forces operating in them, i.e., pluralism versus inequality. For instance, van den Berghe observes regional differences and finds overall that ethnic pluralism is a central force in Africa compared to class in Latin America.[21]

The three summary measures – magnitude, inconsistency and durability – suggested to characterize pluralism are applicable also to inequality.

Cohesion

The cohesion of the pluralistic groups and how it affects the broader society is the main concern of the pluralist perspective. The focus here is, therefore, much more comprehensive than the narrow preoccupation with prejudice and discrimination common in North

American literature. Furthermore, cohesion is conceived through two complementary viewpoints, i.e., patterns of conflict and bases of integration. Underlying this conceptualization of cohesion is the idea that the rival sociological models of equilibrium and conflict are reconcilable; hence van den Berghe (1963), Kuper (1969a), and Schermerhorn (1970: chapter 1) suggest a synthesizing approach which would overcome the one-sidedness of both functionalists and Marxists.

Pluralists hold that conflicts in pluralistic societies are greater than in homogeneous societies for several reasons. First, in addition to inequality, pluralistic societies are affected by gulfs of cultural diversity and social separation. Second, the source of the conflict is extrinsic to the system of social relations (as a rule pluralism and inequality have existed prior to the first imposed contact between the groups) and thus is largely independent of them. And, third, there is a tendency for conflicts in pluralistic societies to become generalized and to spread.

Intergroup conflict is conceived here in the broadest sense to comprise any manifestation of strain between groups struggling over resources and values, and not just the injuries they inflict on each other. Following to some extent Schermerhorn's list of dependent variables, four areas of conflict may be discerned. First, tensions arise when the groups fail to realize their collective objectives because of an inability to reconcile their initially incongruent goals or simply because of a lack of implementation of the congruent goals. Second, pluralism may give rise to invidious distinctions, i.e., prejudice and discrimination. Third, conflicts are assumed to appear on the subjective level as dissatisfactions with status in society, alienation from the regime, deviant behaviour, and militant perspectives on intergroup relations with a willingness to take action for effecting change. Fourth, conflicts are obviously manifested in protesting behaviours on the part of the subordinate group and in countermeasures taken by the dominant one.

Similarly, different bases of intergroup integration are spelled out. The important ones are value consensus as emphasized by functionalists, and as applied by Schermerhorn (1970: chapter 2) to intergroup relations (legitimacy of dominant group's power, cultural resemblance, group-goal reciprocity); cross-cutting affiliations via 'broker institutions' (the existence of national schools, political parties, etc., which cut across ethnic groups) as stressed by Despres (1967: 23, 270; 1968)[22] and via more intimate solidarity bonds; elite accommodation (the absorption of the nondominant group's elite in the national power structure or providing it with control over the nondominant group's separate institutions) (van den Berghe, 1975: 8–9); economic interdependence as underlined by Rex (1970: 23) and van den Berghe (1973: 965); political domination as emphasized by Smith, Kuper and van den Berghe; and external factors such as common enemies and ecological exigencies. Although conflict-management can draw on all these bases of integration, it is evident that a higher level of conflict is associated with greater reliance on the negative forces, i.e., economic interdependence, political domination and external factors.

In order to get an overview of cohesion, summary measures and cohesive models are used. The three proposed summary measures are strength, voluntariness and stability (see p. 230 for definitions).[23] Besides three distinct alternatives to political stability in deeply divided societies are identified, i.e. the consensus model, consociational model and control model (see p. 233 for characterizations).

Change

There is reference to change throughout the entire pluralist analysis, but in the last part of the scheme change moves to the foreground. The major concerns are past trends and future possible developments.

Pluralists hold that change in pluralistic societies is rather problematic. Although the potentialities for change are great, both its actual occurrence and nature are not certain. Sometimes it remains dormant and sometimes it erupts suddenly; often it is incremental and tranquil and often it is abrupt and violent. The regularities of either the linear evolutionary type or the dialectical revolutionary type do not seem to fit the complex and volatile realities of pluralistic societies. In studying change, pluralists pay special attention to inconsistencies within and between pluralism and inequality and to political factors which are considered central in effecting social change in pluralistic structures.

The main features of change can be abstracted by three summary measures. 'Direction' refers to the 'content' of change – that is, a shift in the overall pattern of intergroup relations as well as trends (and increase or decrease) in pluralism, inequality and cohesion over the years. 'Scope' concerns the degree to which change is partial or total. And 'mode' indicates the extent to which change is gradual and peaceful.

The proposed five-part scheme makes it clear that the research of pluralistic divisions should take five directions: understanding the 'setting' which constitute the broader sociohistorical conditions that shape the main forces of pluralism and inequality; the analysis of pluralism; the study of inequality; the examination of the problem of cohesion (conflict and integration); and the assessment of the actual and possible change. These conceptual distinctions are built into the

17

scheme and supply not only a guiding framework for analysing pluralistic social structures but also a tool for relating the various factors to each other.

Empirical applications of the suggested conceptual scheme would encounter the usual methodological problems of operationalization, that is, specifying indicators for each factor, determining their statistical properties, assigning scores and computing the summary measures. However, at this stage, with only limited knowledge and unrefined data, it must suffice to use crude measures, construct indices by simple addition, and even rely on intuitive impressions.[24]

4 A critical evaluation

Since its rise in the early 1960s, the pluralist perspective has been under fire. Functionalists, Marxists and specialists on the Caribbean and Africa where the school was applied have made various criticisms. The bulk of the critique has, however, only a limited historical value because it is levelled against Smith's earlier, already abandoned, theory of plural society, and not to current formulations.

To mention only the more recent criticisms, Cox finds gross inconsistencies in the usages of pluralism in the past and present, concluding that 'the value of the term *pluralism* for the study of race relations is quite limited' (1971: 398). Cross maintains that the theory of pluralism amounts to no more than a descriptive conceptual scheme and as such it is oversimple and static (1971: 484). Rex, while praising Smith's revised formulation, dismisses the treatment of pluralism as a set of variables by other pluralists (1972: 292). Adam considers the theory of pluralism to be 'a reified vocabulary' which has survived because of irrefutable ambiguity rather than established theoretical utility (1971: 20).[25] He, further, charges it with giving categorical precedence to cultural and social pluralism and belittling class, status and power. Magubane (1969; 1971) debunks pluralism as an ideology of despair for having presented ethnic cleavages as irreconcilable, and accuses it even of serving as a disguised neocolonial tool to divide and rule Third World nations and to discredit the Marxist sociology of conflict.[26] Bekker (1975), in a critical review of van den Berghe's contribution, concludes that the conflict pluralism approach remains unclear and devoid of an explicit theory of action and hence fails to account for stability and change in plural societies.

Smith (1969b), Kuper (1969b) and van den Berghe (1970; 1973: 970) have responded to some of these criticisms.[27] The central question emerging from the exchanges is how the pluralist perspective measures up as a theory and what is the ideology underlying it.

Pluralism can claim only a modest positive contribution to a theory of intergroup relations. The pluralists themselves do not make undue claims for their theoretical accomplishments. On the contrary, these claims have been 'too modest' (Katznelson, 1972: 51), as witnessed in this statement by van den Berghe: 'It is still premature to speak of a theory of pluralism, and indeed it is doubtful that any such distinct body of theory will even emerge, for pluralism is nothing more than a set of basic characteristics common to a great many of the world's societies' (1973: 961). Negatively stated, the school of pluralism is, nevertheless, valuable in casting a serious doubt on the utility of functionalist and Marxist approaches; and positively – in constituting 'a step toward the understanding of change and conflict in a great many of the world's large-scale societies' and in refocusing on 'the macroscopic level of analysis, which has the most far-reaching relevance to our very survival as a species' (ibid.: 970).

These characteristics of the school of pluralism may hinder or boost further developments. Although the charge that cultural and social pluralism overshadows class and power in pluralist works is certainly baseless, it is true that in the current formulations neither set of determinants is assigned a priori precedence.[28] A positive specification of the relative importance of these factors would be a step forward.[29] Moreover, given the little research in the field, Kuper's thesis of a wide margin of indeterminacy may prove untimely and inhibitive. His suggestion, on the other hand, that 'some combinations of continuities and discontinuities [between the different sections in structure and culture] may be particularly conducive to conflict' (1974: 251) can serve as a fruitful point of departure for the much needed theory of pluralism and conflict.

Similarly the application of conceptual schemes like the one suggested here runs the risk of settling for systematic description instead of delving into analysis. While variation in cohesion and change are accounted for in terms of setting, pluralism and inequality, more specific explanations are necessary. It is proposed, therefore, that theoretical models such as Smith's plural society (1965a), Blauner's internal colonialism (1972), van den Berghe's paternalistic–competitive patterns (1967b), Mason's dominant–paternal–competitive–fluid patterns (1970a), Lieberson's migrant–indigenous domination (1961), Bonacich's split labour market (1972), to name only a few, should be also used in explaining a particular situation or a certain number of cases.[30]

On the ideological level the pluralist perspective is sober and realistic. As Kuper keenly observes, it appears rather pessimistic against the backdrop of the great optimism of the competing functionalist and Marxist schools that believe in the transitional nature of ethnic divisions, intercommunal solidarity and equality, and progressive universalism.[31] Since no such vision does inform the pluralist perspective, it renders itself open to various ideological distortions.[32]

This completes the theoretical formulation of the pluralist perspective, and we can now turn to apply it to Israeli society. Pluralism is at its best in cross-cultural comparative research as exemplified by van den Berghe's study of Mexico, Brazil, the United States and South Africa (1967b). While ours is a single-society study, like most pluralist studies, it is in fact an intra-societal comparative study because internal comparisons will be made between the three sets of pluralism – Oriental–Ashkenazi, religious–nonreligious, and Arab–Jewish. It is, therefore, hoped that this study may share to some extent in the riches of insight and sophistication of a comparative perspective.

3 Models of intergroup relations

Two distinct views of Israel exist at present: 'the nation-building perspective' and 'the colonial perspective'. Through the nation-building prism Israel looks like a unique Jewish state and an exemplary modernizing country. It is overcoming a host of problems of institution-building and modernization; transition from a partial, ideological community to a total, routine society; cultural renaissance; preservation of a viable democracy and a mixed economy; melting of a mass of immigrants into a nation; and harmonizing group relations. This image underlies the dominant models used in analysing intergroup relations in Israel. An absorption–modernization model is applied to Oriental–Ashkenazi relations; a *Kulturkampf–*modernization model to religious–nonreligious relations; and a nationalism–modernization model to Arab–Jewish relations.

In contrast, critics, particularly those in the radical Left, project a colonial image of Israel. They depict it as a white settler, neocolonial, *Herrenvolk*, theocratic and artificial entity heading inescapably towards disaster.

The models of intergroup relations derived from the rival nation-building and colonial perspectives on Israel will be presented and critically evaluated below, and then the alternative models associated with the synthesizing pluralist perspective will be elucidated.[1]

1 The nation-building perspective

The absorption–modernization model of Oriental–Ashkenazi relations

The nation-building perspective conceives of the Oriental–Ashkenazi problem in terms of 'absorption' and 'modernization' of the mass influx of Oriental Jews from underdeveloped countries to modern

21

Israel. It assumes many-sided processes of initial immigrant absorption, acculturation, social mobility and eventual assimilation. Supported by a large literature, this functionalist model is widely used and highly respected. It has its variations in Israeli sociology but encounters no real challenge. S. N. Eisenstadt, Israel's most leading sociologist and a world authority, has figured prominently in establishing and perpetuating this dominant trend in the sociology of Oriental–Ashkenazi relations. In delineating the model I shall draw on his writings and the contributions of his close associates.

Continuing his work (1950) on Orientals,[2] which he had begun a few years before the creation of the state, Eisenstadt develops a more general framework in his book *The Absorption of Immigrants*, chapter 1. He considers therein the prestate Ashkenazi sector as the Israeli society and spells out the various conditions which facilitated or hindered immigrant absorption. He uses the terms absorption and assimilation interchangeably and incorporates into his scheme the common concepts in the literature of culture-contact. He suggests three indexes of absorption (1955: 11):

> These are: (a) acculturation, (b) satisfactory and integral personal adjustment of immigrants, and (c) complete dispersion of the immigrants as a group within the main institutional spheres of the absorbing society ... The assumption underlying all three is that the less the immigrant stands out within his own society as having a separate identity, the more fully is he merged into it and the more complete is his absorption.

The addition of the term 'modernization' becomes necessary in analysing the absorption of the Oriental immigrants (see, e.g., Eisenstadt, 1956). Bar-Yosef, Eisenstadt's collaborator, in a more recent definitive study tellingly entitled 'Absorption versus Modernization', makes this clear (1971: 3):[3]

> With regard to this group of Oriental immigrants, it is usually impossible to make a distinction between processes of absorption and processes of modernization. Even in cases in which no major differences in education and outlook existed between a certain individual immigrant and the absorbers, the disparity between conditions of life in a traditional pre-industrial society, and those of the Israeli society, which is modern and Westernized in its structure and aspirations, still constituted an important factor in the process of assimilation.

In an early paper, Ben-David (1970, originally written in 1951), another collaborator of Eisenstadt, provides a rationale for the application of the model specifically to the Oriental immigrants. Since the Oriental cultures and communities are asserted to have disintegrated before and after immigration, the ethnic problem in Israel has not become one of incompatible 'ethnic differences', but rather a matter of exposing Orientals to 'social change'. In other words, the question is how to accelerate adaptation to existing society. Reaffirming this theme twenty years later, Bar-Yosef (1971: 2) explicitly rejects a model of ethnic pluralism:

> The problem, well-known from the process of nation-building of new nations – that of providing a basis of legitimation for a social-national identity – was non-existent in Israel. This is also the reason that the Israeli–Jewish society never in any sense presented a picture of a pluralistic society and that no tendencies to regard it as such were evident. In the sense that pluralism was relevant to the Israeli situation, it referred solely to the relations between the Jews and the non-Jewish sectors in Israel.

In reviewing the situation during the last two decades, Eisenstadt and Bar-Yosef underscore the favourable institutional conditions in which absorption took place. The two major conditions have been positive value orientation and great investment in immigrant absorption (Bar-Yosef, 1971: 129–30):

> The acceptance of absorption as one of the major values in the value system of the society prepared the cultural climate for policy decisions allocating large parts of the nation's resources for this purpose. This was also the source which generated a basic solidarity encompassing the absorbers and the absorbed . . .
> The system of welfare services was an important defense device against the possibility of total destitution resulting from immigration. It seems these symbolized for the immigrants their rights as citizens of the new country in times when they were still outside the universal set of roles.

In a later re-formulation, Eisenstadt (1969) distinguishes three stages in the integration of immigrants in Israel. The initial stage was the absorption of immigrants by providing them with housing and jobs and incorporating them into primary schools, political parties and the defence forces. Upon the successful completion of this step, the second stage, that of merging of exiles, started at the end of the 1950s. This phase was more problematic because of some shortcomings in the policy of absorption. The absorbers failed to extend the assistance offered in the first stage (1967a: 198):

> Most administrative agencies dealt mainly with the preparation of immigrants for adjustment in Israeli society, but not with continuous help and guidance. The immigrants were first given

financial help, housing or easy terms, and some help in finding work – but after that they were left more or less to their own devices, with little continuous guidance or help.

Besides, 'The absorbing society and its agencies often acted on stereotypic assumptions without understanding the essence of the cultural differences' (Bar-Yosef, 1971: 130). This attitude used to cause some difficulties in absorption. However, the uniform universalistic policies of the 1950s were reversed in the 1960s 'to stress the cultural differences between Oriental and Western, this often emphasizing ethnic problems and symbols of ethnic distinctions and separateness' (Eisenstadt, 1967a: 197).

In her long and detailed survey of absorption of Oriental immigrants in the last two decades, Bar-Yosef points out some errors made in absorption policies, and failures of the Oriental immigrants to adapt to the Israeli society in some areas. At the end she, nevertheless, draws the following conclusion (1971: 128):

Seen in its generality the absorption of the Oriental immigrants was successful. Each facet of the absorption, the cultural, the personal and the institutional, has shown good adjustment. They participate actively in each area of role activity and did not crystallize into segregated minority groups. During less than a generation they changed their predominantly non-industrial attitudes, motives and behaviour into a moderately modern approach.

Similarly Eisenstadt (1972: 300) notes the possible pitfalls of the continued overlap between ethnic origin and socioeconomic status but, as the Six-Day War has shown, this does not significantly affect the overall positive picture of integration (1972: 303). His view is best expressed in the discussion of strains in developing an inclusive collective identity. He epitomizes the core of the Israeli identity, in spite of ethnic pressures to the contrary, as follows (1967b: 19):

Whatever the exact contours of Israeli self-identity in relation to the broad framework of Jewish tradition and Jewish communities, it no longer defines Jewish identity in terms of a minority group or culture. Being a Jew in Israel does not necessitate the definition of one's self-identity in relation to a majority group or culture and does not involve the various problems, uncertainties, and anxieties which have constituted such an important aspect of Jewish life and identity throughout the modern world.

In brief, Israel was presumed to have been successful in fulfilling her mission of eliminating dominant and subordinate statuses for the entire Jewish population.

The above characterization of the absorption–modernization model appears in one way or another in every sociological account of the position of Orientals in Israel.[4] Beyond this striking fundamental consensus, however, there are some variations among different sociologists and other observers in the selection of and emphasis on different elements in the ethnic situation. Several major variations in the widely accepted model warrant mentioning.

One variation capitalizes on cultural pluralism. The leading exponent of this position is the social anthropologist R. Patai (1970). He and others see cultural pluralism as a mixed blessing. On the one hand, it constitutes a serious impediment to ethnic integration. It is, on the other hand, a great opportunity for enriching the prevailing European culture or even for reaching cultural syncretism between West and East in Israel.[5]

Another variation stresses socioeconomic differences. M. Lissak (1969) is the leading spokesman for this point of view. The general problem of absorption and modernization of the Orientals is primarily evident in their disadvantageous class position and in the lack of social assimilation which expectedly accompanies it. A solution involves providing greater opportunity for the Orientals and closing the ethnic gap.[6]

A third variation places a special stress on prejudice. J. Shuval in a number of publications (1956; 1962) and more recently Y. Peres (1968; 1971) have become identified with this standpoint.[7] While cultural and class differences accompany hardships of absorption and modernization, they generate the complication of stereotyping, scapegoating and self-hatred. This added barrier, although expected in conditions of intergroup contact, must be removed if full integration is to be accomplished.

Finally an all-around interpretation is advanced by some. The American social anthropologist A. Weingrod (1962; 1965) may be considered representative of such an approach. In his summary statement, he integrates the themes of immigrant absorption, modernization, cultural and social pluralism, class and power inequality, and prejudice.[8]

The Kulturkampf–modernization model of religious–nonreligious relations

In contrast to the advanced sociology of Oriental–Ashkenazi relations, the sociological study of religious–nonreligious relations is just emerging.[9] Meanwhile the available literature, dominated by clerical and anti-clerical spokesmen, jurists and political scientists, is polemic and descriptive, concentrating on the relations between state (or law) and religion, not on religious–nonreligious relations. Below I shall abstract a model which I believe to underlie the average account and at least be compatible with most presentations.[10]

The *Kulturkampf*-modernization model suggests that there exists a situation of *Kulturkampf*,[11] though still restrained and undeclared, and that certain delays in the modernization of the state and in the religious group in particular are its prime mover. The clash between the religious and secular subcultures takes place mostly in the legal and political institutions and gives rise to numerous issues. These overlap, but can be grouped under three categories: collective identity and boundary-maintenance, freedom of religion and freedom from religion. Let us take each one in this order.

The problem of collective identity and boundary-maintenance is inherent in the very structure of Israel as a Jewish state. With minor exceptions, all Israeli Jews concur that Israel should be Jewish.[12] They disagree, however, on what this precisely means. Unlike other world religions, Judaism has remained a single-religion ethnicity (or a mono-ethnic religion) in which nationality and faith are intimately intertwined and proselytizing zeal is absent. In modern Jewish history there have been anti-Zionist attempts to reduce Judaism to nationality alone (e.g., 'Bund' socialism) or to a mere faith (e.g., Reform Judaism). In contrast, Zionism inherited and has remained loyal to both elements in Judaism and it bequeathed them later to the state of Israel. In the process it has shifted the historical emphasis away from faith to nationality and has secularized many religious traditions.

In Israel today the dual nature of Judaism poses little difficulty in certain spheres and causes much controversy in others. For instance, religious and nonreligious Jews are agreed in adopting the Sabbath and traditional holidays as official days of rest and in incorporating the study of the Bible in public education, despite their different attitudes towards them. This and many other issues reflect on the contours of the Jewish collective identity, but the most central dispute emanating from the duality in Judaism hinges on the definition of a Jew.

The issue of 'who is a Jew' is of great consequence. It has direct implications in matters of citizenship and personal status. The Law of Return, the raison d'être of the state, bestows automatic citizenship on Jewish immigrants alone. Personal status is placed under the exclusive jurisdiction of the separate religious communities whose continuation reinforces further the inseparability between nationality and faith in Israeli Judaism. It is thus of utmost practical importance to sort out a Jew from a non-Jew in order to determine who qualifies for Jewish citizenship and for the privileges involved, including the prerogative of marrying Jews.

The definition of a Jew is the single most crucial bone of contention between the religious minority and the nonreligious majority. The religious group insists on imposing a restrictive, halakhic definition of a Jew and on strictly religious marriage and divorce, whereas the nonreligious public would prefer an inclusive, 'national' definition and more liberal family laws. Both agree, however, on retaining the basic distinction and the above legislation to serve as multiple boundary-maintaining mechanisms: namely, to ensure a permanent Jewish majority (by maximizing Jewish immigration and minimizing non-Jewish immigration), to discourage intermarriage between Jews and non-Jews, and to eliminate barriers against mingling and marrying Jews of varying religious observance.

The second major area of controversy is freedom of religion, i.e., the liberty to practise religion as one deems fit. The Declaration of Independence promises freedom of religion and conscience. Since it is not legally binding and since there is no state constitution, religious liberties are safeguarded only in practice, not by law. Among these established liberties are the right to worship without disturbance,[13] to organize a religious community with jurisdiction over personal status, to hold a variety of religious services, to be entitled to equal opportunity in employment regardless of religious observance, to qualify for certain privileges associated with the exercise of religion, to be exempted from some duties prescribed by religion, and to have legal protection against public desecration of religion or defamation on grounds of faith.[14] Moreover, houses of prayer, religious councils, Rabbinic courts, religious schools, military chaplaincy and many other religious activities are publicly financed.[15] All these arrangements are not contested because of the common commitment to a Jewish state which precludes such a complete separation between state and religion as exists in the United States.

There are, nevertheless, significant loopholes in the freedom of religion. First, in certain matters state laws are incompatible with religious laws. The most outstanding of these laws is the Women's Equal Rights Law, 1951, which runs counter to the inferior status assigned to women by the halakha. Other laws prohibit immature and polygamous marriages which are valid by religion. Since private law is secular and mandatory, religious Jews are compelled to seek adjudication in civil courts, notwithstanding their duty to pursue religious litigation. The objection to these laws has diminished considerably over the years, however. Second and more important, in some areas state laws fail to provide protection. There is no state law against fraud in kashrut and the ritual articles, although municipal regulations furnish partial safeguards. Similarly the Anatomy and Pathology Law, 1953, is opposed as too liberal in that it over-exposes religious Jews to the risks of what they consider forced and humiliating autopsies. And third and most important, there is much resentment against the subordination of religious institutions to the civil legal authorities. Generally speaking, state law takes precedence over religious law, but as a rule the civil courts and the Supreme Court do not intervene in the substantive decisions of the Rabbinic courts and Chief Rabbinate unless it appears that their decisions are made on grounds other than halakha. The religious sector wants, instead, total autonomy for these religious bodies.[16]

The last series of issues concerns 'freedom from religion', that is, the freedom not to practise and not to be governed by religion. The fact that, strictly speaking, Israel does not have a state religion, and officially recognized non-Jewish communities enjoy equal footing with the majority religion of Judaism, makes it possible in principle (a) to renounce religion, and (b) to convert from one religion to another. In practice, however, these two fundamental rights are quite restricted and in consequence freedom from religion is appreciably reduced.

The difficulty with renouncing the Jewish faith is that one would face a legal lacuna in matters of personal status (especially marriage and divorce) where the Rabbinic courts are entrusted with exclusive powers. The current Rabbinic jurisdiction on personal status limits the human right of a Jew to marry certain categories of fellow-Jews and all non-Jews.[17] Furthermore, a Jew who gives up his religion would have to bear other inconveniences. For instance, he would have his Jewish status struck off his official record – no small burden in a Jewish state that requires every person to carry an identity card and to produce it on numerous occasions.

The other right, to convert to the Jewish faith, is also limited because Judaism is generally non-proselytizing and, more important, because the monopolistic Orthodox Judaism places excessive demands on non-Jewish candidates. The status of people converted by Conservative and Reform Rabbis is contestable – they would qualify for the state-administered Law of Return but would not be recognized by the religious authorities.

In addition to these general constraints, there is at least some hardship in pursuing non-Orthodox or nonreligious lifestyles. Conservative and Reform Rabbis and synagogues are denied religious authority and financial support by the ruling Orthodox establishment. Their congregations are paradoxically forced to side with the nonreligious majority in demanding greater freedom from Orthodox Judaism. Similarly it is exceedingly hard, if not impossible, for any Israeli Jew to conduct a totally secular way of life. To mention only a few of the hindrances, the shutdown of public transportation, shops and recreational facilities on Saturdays and holidays narrows the range of activities possible in these official days of rest. Kashrut practices (including a state law banning pigs), which are widely enforced, restrict the freedom of consuming foods. One is inevitably confronted daily by many religious symbols displayed and values propagated by the state schools, radio and television, army and other public agencies, and of course the official religious bodies themselves.

The great intricacy of the three sets of issues, which mar religious–nonreligious relations, is manifested in their entangling interrelations. It is obviously impossible to balance the national and religious components in the collective identity and ethnic boundaries of Israel without affecting the modus vivendi existing between freedom of religion and freedom from religion. For instance, the chief demand of the National Religious Party in the negotiations to form a coalition government in the aftermath of the Yom Kippur War was the amendment of the somewhat ambiguous legal definition of a Jew to recognize conversion to Judaism according to halakha only. These issues – which seem directly relevant to the dilemma of collective identity alone and scores of other issues – are questions of 'freedom of religion' for the religious, but at the same time they are subjects of 'freedom from religion' for the nonreligious – and this is indeed the crux of the matter.

The viewpoint of the nonreligious majority can be simply stated. Adhering to a democratic Jewish state, they allow the religious sector to conduct a religious lifestyle and support them in it, and, by the same token, they request equal freedom to lead a secular way of life.

From the standpoint of the religious minority, however, the restrictions on freedom from religion are no less than elementary guarantees of their own freedom of religion. To illustrate: if industry, commerce, services and entertainment are permitted on the Sabbath, religious Jews as employees, businessmen and consumers will be discriminated against because of their strict observance. Similarly, persons converted to Judaism by Conservative and Reform Rabbis are still considered Gentiles, and by appearing as Jews they constitute an absolute danger of intermarriage. Moreover, civil divorce, which is void by the halakha, may create an irremediable problem of 'mamzerim' (bastards), i.e., children born to a married woman from a man other than her husband, and, by implication, children from the next marriage of a civilly divorced woman. Mamzerim, the only illegitimate offspring in Judaism, are forever forbidden from marrying Jews.[18] The increase in the number of illegitimate converts and mamzerim will violate the human right to marriage of the religious. They would have to segregate themselves from the majority of fellow-Jews who are polluted by 'outcasts' passing as ordinary brethren.

Basically the problem of religious–nonreligious relations is one of *Kulturkampf*, a conflict between two value-systems: exclusionary ascriptive particularism versus a measure of humanitarian universalism, absolute halakha versus revocable law, religious authority versus liberal democracy, and recognition of only one lifestyle as legitimate versus acceptance of cultural pluralism. Stated differently, the existence of at least some degree of irreconcilability between these sets of values produces a condition where freedom of religion is religious compulsion for the nonreligious majority and, conversely, freedom from religion is anti-religious compulsion for the religious minority. To add fuel to the fire, the overall collective goal of the religious minority is to impose its own standards on the entire Jewish population, not only as a matter of self-defence but also as a divinely ordained ideal.

The problem is, further, diagnosed as one of modernization, or lack of it. Although Jewishness is no doubt a serious complicating factor, the young state of Israel is experiencing the strains most Western democracies endured a century or so ago in settling the church and state issue. Advanced modernization may gradually bring about a situation of coexistence if the religious group undergoes a significant transformation of values. Now the Orthodox community is in a deep crisis. It wants a Torah state but realizes that halakha is a corpus of religious laws originally intended to preserve Jewish life in the Diaspora, merely as an adjunct minority in a Gentile world and under former conditions. The current halakhic laws offer only meagre means for operating a sovereign, self-sufficient and modern Jewish state – a new society the halakha had not even envisioned. The religious minority rejects a *secular* Jewish state in principle but it has neither an alternative workable value system nor the coercive power to impose it. Meanwhile it settles for 'theopolitics',[19] hoping to achieve a theocratic state through cumulative piecemeal religious legislation.

The future of religious–nonreligious relations is not certain. On the one hand, it is possible to reach a peaceful accommodation through the disestablishment of religion and with the assistance of an innovative religious leadership that seeks legitimate answers to contemporary concerns. It is likely, on the other hand, that Israel is heading toward an open *Kulturkampf* whose fateful results are difficult to foretell.

The nationalism–modernization model of Arab–Jewish relations

There is a great variety of literature on the Arab minority in Israel, comprising journal and newspaper reports, ethnographic accounts and polemics.[20] The more scientific work includes contributions of specialists in the fields of Near Eastern studies, human geography, economics, psychology, political science, anthropology and sociology.[21] Although the impact of Arab exposure to the Jewish majority is examined in these diverse publications, the focus is by and large on the Arab minority rather than on the Arab–Jewish relations which are of prime interest to us. Since in Peres's writings an explicit effort to develop a framework for understanding Arab–Jewish relations has been made, the following model draws much on them.[22]

Israeli Arabs are under strong cross-pressures. The key to their predicament lies in the contradiction between the universalistic orientations of Israel (no state religion, equal rights for all) which make for accommodation, and the particularistic Jewish orientations which induce alienation. The opposing forces, of which nationalism and modernization are the most important, are more complex. They create a grave problem of 'identity' among Israeli Arabs.

Several adaptive factors are at work. Israeli Arabs constitute a small minority of 13 per cent who cannot gain dominance by regular channels. Their numerical weakness is expected to add to their reconciliation with a minority status. As an indigenous minority and a traditionally peasant society they have a strong personal and national attachment to the soil. They claim a mission for their uninterrupted stay in Israel – to preserve the land right of their exiled people. Such consciousness instils at least temporary resignation to life as a minority in a Jewish state. More important, Israeli Arabs are an ex-colonial, Third World people openly committed to modernization with its higher standard of living and new values. They recognize the Jewish majority as agents and models of modern man and society. Without the Jews the benefits of modernization would be significantly smaller. Modernization multiplies contacts between the two groups. Israeli Arabs are becoming increasingly integrated into the dominant economy, their elites are being incorporated into the main political parties and the younger generation is becoming by and large bilingual and acculturated into the Israeli mainstream. As modernization proceeds, Arabs and Jews draw nearer on the personal level.

These positive factors are countered, however, by a good many alienating forces. The Israeli Arabs are a new minority. Up until 1948 they were the majority, though not the dominant group, in Palestine. They have not had enough chance to get adjusted to a downward minority status. To complicate matters further, the Israeli Arabs feel the pinch of the involuntary position of an 'enemy-affiliated minority'. Their situation is in a sense worse than that of the American Japanese during World War II. The Israeli Arabs are an integral part of the surrounding Arab world in language, religion, nationality, traditions, kinship and even in location (proximity to the borders). The Arab neighbours refuse to recognize the right of Israel to exist and maintain a constant state of belligerency with it. They bombard Israeli Arabs with hostile propaganda to enlist their loyalty to the 'Arab cause'. The Jews fear a possibility of the Israeli Arabs turning into a fifth column. To avert the danger, the Israeli government imposed military administration on them (up to 1966), accompanied by other restrictive measures. The general public, and the deprived Oriental Jews in particular, react with much suspicion and repulsion toward them. Arab estrangement from the state can, therefore, feed on various sources.

Furthermore, modernization contributes on the whole more to discontent than to adaptation among Israeli Arabs. Along with its notable gains, modernization revolutionizes expectations far beyond what can be achieved by the lower skills and meagre resources of a population in transition to modernity. More important than the frustrating sense of relative deprivation is the tendency of modernization to shatter 'accommodating' (traditional, local, familial) identities and to clear the way for a rising 'militant' national identity. Hence the more modernized (i.e., urbanized, Westernized, better off) Israeli Arabs are, overall, more psychologically deprived, nationalistic and alienated.

It is no wonder that the Israeli Arabs experience an identity crisis. They are at once Israeli citizens and national Arabs. At best they are tolerated by the Jews in Israel and by brethren in Arab countries; at worst they are suspected by them as 'spies' and 'traitors' respectively. To cope with their compound and fractured identity, the Israeli Arabs use compartmentalization and other psychodynamic mechanisms. They identify themselves with Arab nationalism but obey law and order in everyday life. Their modal response is best described as 'being pro-Arab without being anti-Israel, and being pro-Israel without being anti-Arab'. This attitude of passivity, of partial commitment, of sitting on the fence, is compatible both with the Jewish majority's policy of demanding compliance with the law without expecting identification with the state and also with Arab propaganda of calling for support of Arab nationalism without insisting on active resistance.

The future of Arab–Jewish relations is tied with the Israeli–Arab conflict. The recurrent open hostilities have polarized the Israeli–Arab population and intensified their feelings of nationalism and alienation, but they have not altered the basic situation of ambivalence.[23] Only a permanent peace settlement can radically change the current strained relations.

2 The colonial perspective

In sharp contrast to the nation-building perspective, as it is reflected in the above models of intergroup relations, stands the colonial perspective. The conceptualization of Israel as a colonial state is the basis for a severe critique of Israel by Marxist intellectuals, a broad section of the New Left, Arab militants and sympathizers with the Arab cause who attack Israel from the outside. Within Israel there is a splinter group (Matzpen) of revolutionary socialists and anti-Zionists who also disseminate similar views. These circles differ in their degree of sophistication, articulation and criticism, but they share the same overall viewpoint about Israel.

Proponents of the colonial perspective offer more of an ideological exposé than a theoretical analysis of Israeli society. Given the frequent correspondence between ideology and theory, this is not a serious drawback were it not for the total absence of social scientists to theorize and test such an approach empirically. It also focuses primarily on non-Jewish–Jewish relations, and in many cases its relevance for the divisions within the Jewish population remains implicit. Despite these limitations, the colonial perspective does suggest a coherent, genuinely distinctive interpretation of Israel and intergroup relations there.[24]

The colonial perspective contains three broad themes: Zionism is a colonial movement, Israel is a neocolonial state and Israeli society is an oppressive social system. Since these defining structural features are interrelated and mutually sustaining, their impact on patterns of intergroup relations are all the more decisive.

The colonial nature of Zionism takes various shapes. In essence Zionism is a movement of white settlers displacing a native, non-European people. European Jews colonized Palestine during the era of colonialism in Europe. By encroaching on the local Arab majority, they betrayed the spirit of the time: 'In common with the dominant outlook of European chauvinism, Zionism considered any territory as "empty" and available if its indigenous population had not yet achieved national independence and recognized statehood' (Buch, 1973: 12).[25] Zionism also adopted the European supremist 'civilizing mission' of bringing the light of modernization to backward peoples. Its deep European roots are evident still in another peculiar way. Since the dispersed Jews are merely a faith, not a full-fledged nation,[26] the Zionist settlers did not have a particular metropolitan country. Europe as a whole, in effect, served as their mother continent and it disposed of them as it did of other undesirable elements by sending them to overseas colonies (Rodinson, 1973: 86).

With the political support of the great powers and the financial backing of the Jewish bourgeoisie in the Diaspora, the Ashkenazi settlers managed to build a new society in Palestine. In the process they dispossessed the native Arabs territorially and politically, although they did not exploit them economically. Political domination and territorial usurpation overrode economic exploitation in the Zionist colonization because the grand goal was to construct an exclusively Jewish community.[27] The newly found entity excluded Arabs on grounds of ethnicity (or race) and was modelled after the Western world in culture and social institutions. It has thus become a foreign body in the area.[28]

The other theme, that Israel is a neocolonial state, stresses the prior determination of the present situation by the above historical forces. To begin with, as a successor to the British colonial regime and like many other ex-colonial developing countries, the new state of Israel is essentially neocolonial. It is tied by an umbilical cord to the capitalist world on whose continuing military, political and economic assistance it is dependent for its very survival. Ample aid is extended to it for its reactionary role in the Cold War or in its transformed version of détente – as a dependable Western stronghold against communism in the strategic Middle East, serving as a countervailing force against revolutionary social struggles among the peoples of the region, and constituting a beachhead of capitalism in the developing world. Under these circumstances the spread of militarism and expansionism in Israel is to be expected.[29]

To perform the tasks of a client state and a multitentacled agent of imperialism, Israel must maintain internally a capitalist economy and a façade of democracy.[30] True, it has some structures of 'democratic socialism' such as collective settlements, co-operatives, Histadrut- and government-owned economic sectors and an egalitarian ideology. However, they are marginal to the overall bourgeois infrastructure and have inevitably been losing ground over the years.

Turning to the last and most pertinent theme for our analysis, internal oppression is an unavoidable outgrowth of the colonial Zionist movement and the current neocolonial situation. Israel is divided into a minority of dominant white Europeans and a majority of subordinate Third World peoples. Alternatively it is a three-tier society: the Ashkenazim are at the top controlling the Arab Jews (Orientals), who are below them, and the native Palestinians (both the Arab citizens and conquered aliens) who are at the bottom. The patterns of dominance in this ethnic stratification are pervasive – legal and illegal discrimination, economic exploitation, cultural suppression and other forms of oppression. The neocolonial Jewish state, itself established by Zionist colonialism, only continues the longstanding tradition by exercising internal colonialism on its non-European population and classical colonialism in the occupied territories.

Israel is oppressively sectarian as well. This is evident in the lack of separation between state and religion, in the discriminatory Law of Return and in the legal separation between non-Jewish and Jewish communities that results in the prevention of intermarriage and in de facto segregation. These legal provisions are instrumental in institutionalizing inferior and superior statuses for non-Jews and Jews, in denying the Palestinian refugees the right of repatriation while granting it to Jewish immigrants who are far removed from the area, and in making the Israeli–Arab minority strangers in their own homeland. Israel is, therefore, a *Herrenvolk* democracy like South Africa, where human, social and civil rights are, to all intents and purposes, reserved to the 'master race' of Jews, and to the 'more equal' among them – European Jews.[31] These diverse functions of the sectarian character of the state explain why the Ashkenazi elite, despite its secularism and even anti-clericalism, acquiesces in the theocratic demands of a small religious minority.

The scenario of Israel's destiny is predetermined by the cumulative effect of her complex colonial attributes. Whereas the precise nature of the revolutionizing forces is not certain, the end of the present Zionist structure will come sooner or later. It is likely that external factors will decide the future. Israel might be abandoned by the great powers in a world of *Realpolitik*, shifting global interests and expendable small states. She can be struck by the rising strength, emanating from a series of genuine socialist revolutions, of the new Arab world.

Endogenous sources of change may also play a role in shaping the forthcoming development. Under certain conditions internal power realignments might take place. At present the Oriental majority is put in check. Like the white proletariat in the United States who enjoy the status of an 'aristocracy of labour', the Orientals are bought off by similar privileges given at the expense of the Arabs. They are also misled by hopes of moving into the ruling Ashkenazi class. For the time being, they co-operate in maintaining the status quo. But eventually, following a prolonged economic squeeze or another setback, they will rid themselves of false consciousness and join forces with the Arabs whom they much resemble in class deprivation and cultural tradition.[32] Defection from the ranks by disillusioned elements in the Ashkenazi group as a result of religious compulsion, soaring costs of the Arab–Israeli conflict and the like, will usher the transition into the coming epoch.[33]

Whatever the sources of change will be, its direction is unmistakable. Israel is bound to become a truly democratic, secular, socialist and pluralistic society, an integral part of the region, and a country for the benefit of all concerned parties.[34]

3 The pluralist perspective

A synthesizing approach

As indicated in the theoretical formulation in the previous chapter, the pluralist perspective is a synthesizing approach which combines insights from both consensus and conflict perspectives. It analyses the overlaps and disjunctions among vertical and horizontal lines of group division, and explores the patterns of conflict among the groups and the bases for their integration. These general orientations will guide us in evaluating the nation-building and colonial perspectives on Israel and in developing an alternative to them.

Theoretically the existing perspectives are heavily oriented to the two general views of society (Horton, 1966). The nation-building perspective is biased toward an order–equilibrium approach and the colonial perspective is based on a Marxian variant of a power–conflict framework. One emphasizes the existence of a core of values, structural compatibilities and strains of institution-building, whereas the other stresses conflicts of interests, internal contradictions and manifest and disguised class exploitation. One approaches development in terms of transmutation of values and benevolent modernization, whereas the other approaches it in terms of redistribution of resources and malevolent dependency (Portes, 1976).

The ideological contrasts are equally striking. The nation-building perspective is Zionist. It defines Zionism as a Jewish liberation movement and legitimizes its central role in creating Israel. It accepts the Jewish character of the state, injects a basic sense of justice to group relations and seeks some liberal reforms. The colonial perspective, on the other hand, is anti-Zionist. It sees Zionism as a colonial movement and deplores whatever action it has taken. It rejects the idea of a Jewish state in Palestine, frowns upon the injustices inflicted on the non-Europeans and advocates a radical revolution.

Although these two mirror-images of Israel appear overdrawn, no major effort has been made to reconcile them. Israeli sociologists, subscribing by and large to the nation-building perspective, systematically ignore the opposing view. This categorical disregard of a rival explanation of Israeli society is readily understandable given the facts that the colonial perspective has emerged outside sociology (and as an ideology, not a theory), that it has far-reaching political implications, and that its Marxian slant lacks any appeal to non-Marxist sociologists.[35] Similarly the exponents of the colonial perspective are usually ideologists who tend to dismiss the 'bourgeois', 'Zionist' Israeli sociology. The only 'dialogue' between the two perspectives takes place on the ideological plane in pro- and anti-Israel exchanges.[36]

It is not our intention here to attempt to iron out the many differences between the two perspectives. Our primary interest is pluralism and what affects it. This is where we shall seek an alternative interpretation.

The general colonial perspective has paradoxically risen rather than fallen with the passing of colonialism. 'Neocolonialism' is introduced to characterize the post-colonial systems of most new underdeveloped states. 'Internal colonialism' is another form which is thought to prevail in South Africa, Canada, the United States and Latin American countries with large American-Indian populations. The 'sociology of imperialism and colonialism' (Rex, 1973: 195) is presented as the clearinghouse of all ideas of importance in race relations, combining the literatures on stratification, pluralism and minorities. However, the more colonial models have become fashionable, the greater is the danger of their misuse.

The conceptualization of Zionism and Israel in terms of colonialism carries so many consequences that it merits a specific comment. Essentially the implication is that the structure is so exploitative, unviable and rotten that only destruction ('decolonization') is the right remedy. It is clear, nevertheless, that the all-or-nothing way in which the question of colonialism is usually put is not fruitful.[37] Zionism can be more appropriately conceived as a complex phenomenon – a Jewish liberation movement that is imbued with some traces of colonial spirit.

Consider the following points in support of the idea that Zionism has not been an ordinary colonial movement:

(a) Judaism is a single ethnicity religion in which nationalism and religion are interwoven, and Zionism inherited Jewish nationalism through this age-old duality rather than manufacturing it.

(b) Zionism rose as a movement of national self-determination of a persecuted minority before reaching Palestine, not after.

(c) The choice of Palestine by Zionism as a Jewish homeland was grounded on legitimate rights (the land of Israel is at the centre of the Jewish religion; Jews used to maintain, before exile, a sovereign state in Palestine; a Jewish community never ceased to exist in Palestine and was aided by the Diaspora to validate Jewish rights there), not on expedient grounds (availability of space, opportunity, etc.).

(d) The policy of Zionist settlement was to build a Jewish state with a maximal disengagement between Arabs and Jews, rather than economic exploitation of and political domination over Arabs.

(e) Until the proclamation of the state, Jews recognized the right of Arabs to national self-determination and supported various plans of partition, and did not claim exclusive national rights in

Palestine nor did they pursue a practice of total displacement of Arabs.

The thesis that Zionism is a liberating rather than a colonial movement stands thanks to the pattern set by these considerations and does not fall with the refutation or qualification of any single one of them. The 'historical specificity' of Zionism makes it a peculiar, successful, separatist national movement rather than a classic or modified colonial endeavour.

Having said so, it would be too charitable to overlook the marks left on Zionism as a result of its rise at the peak of the era of colonialism. Although Zionism managed to escape European racism, against which it reacted, it itself became Europocentric. The sense of superiority over and disdain for non-Europeans, widespread in Europe at that time, touched Zionism. The manifestations of this ethnocentric thinking were many. Most important was the attitude towards the Palestinian indigenous population: ignorance and indifference, invocation of the civilizing mission, expectation of co-operation, gross underestimation of its resistance and lack of a major direct effort to deal with it. Perhaps these historical under-currents can sustain the deep-seated feeling among most Israeli Jews today that the Arabs in Israel simply do not belong to Israeli society. The attitude of Zionism towards Oriental Jewry was also reserved and negligent: Zionism did not expect much from it and cared little for its needs. To mention another offshoot, in reviving and creating a national culture, borrowing from the despised Arab or Oriental traditions was kept to a bare minimum.

The pluralist perspective also differs from the other two in treating pluralism as a central structural characteristic of Israeli society. By focusing on general problems of building of institutions, the nation-building perspective considers Oriental–Ashkenazi pluralism as a secondary question in stratification, and religious–nonreligious pluralism as one of the issues in the formation of cultural and political consensus, whereas Arab–Jewish pluralism is considered in isolation from the institutional analysis under 'minorities'.[38] Similarly the colonial perspective concentrates on 'class exploitation' and analyses the various sets of pluralism in terms of class dynamics only. While both perspectives do not ignore pluralism, they fail to give it the attention it deserves. The pluralist perspective studies the distinctions and relations between the groups, the group tensions and conflicts caused by them, and the difficulties they present to national integration and democracy in Israel.

It is true that today pluralism does not loom largest in Israeli society, but this is not a sufficient reason for denying it centrality. At present the peculiar political and economic conditions dull the sting of pluralism among the Jewish groups. The perpetual external threat and the world-wide isolation on the one hand and the heavily subsidized economy (making for sustained growth, full employment and non-zero sum competition) on the other provide Israel with unusually strong integrative forces. However, problems of pluralism do frequently surface and, with a change of conditions, the potentiality of pluralism for conflict will be certainly felt.

After making these general comments on the pluralist perspective, it is possible to turn now to its critical evaluation of the models of intergroup relations developed by the other perspectives and to its alternative models.

The alternative models

a The dynamic paternalism-co-optation model of Oriental–Ashkenazi relations. The absorption–modernization model and the colonial model stress different elements in Oriental–Ashkenazi relations. According to one model the problem stems, in the final analysis, from the cultural backwardness and class deprivation of the Orientals and the resultant prejudice which make it difficult for them to adapt to modern Israeli society. While the whole process of integration is presumed to involve personal and social tensions as well as occasional errors in policies, it is presented as essentially benevolent and entailing no real conflicts of interests. The rival model posits, on the other hand, that fundamental class conflicts prevail. The Orientals are exploited (though to a lesser extent than the Arabs) by the ruling Ashkenazi group, but they falsely experience their exploitations as ethnic rather than as class-based.[39]

These two models have their advantages and disadvantages. The absorption–modernization model aptly emphasizes absorption and modernization for the Orientals' integration into Israeli society. But of no less importance are the basic class deprivation of the Orientals, their intermediary position, and the political economy which moulds social and ethnic stratification in Israel as indicated by the colonial model. On the other hand, both models err in underplaying the ethnic factors. The absorption–modernization model sees no real barriers for eventual full assimilation of the Orientals in a society boasting of 'amalgamation of exiles' as a supreme national objective. This is also true for the colonial model, which often treats ethnicity as an epiphenomenon of class. A more realistic model should, therefore, build on the merits of the two perspectives and avoid the pitfall of belittling ethnicity.

Since the absorption–modernization model enjoys, within Israeli sociology, the status of an unchallenged paradigm that guides so much empirical research and bolsters up the dominant ideology and folk wisdom in the area of Oriental–Ashkenazi relations, it deserves closer examination. Its explanation of Oriental–Ashkenazi relations is not satisfactory for at least five reasons.

First, accounts utilizing the absorption–modernization model usually lack a proper historical perspective. They tend to overlook the implications of centuries of ethnic separation between Orientals and Ashkenazim, to disregard the significance of the Orientals' nonparticipation in the Zionist movement, and to gloss over the Yishuv period. The model is essentially ahistorical.[40]

Second, the existing literature accepts the official ideology of ingathering and merging of exiles at its face value. Instead of stripping it to its bare operative elements and examining its actual implementation, the official ideology is taken for granted as a strong favourable force for integration. Little effort is made to unveil ideological undercurrents which may have effects adverse to ethnic integration.

Third, the studies tend to neglect power factors. While the disparity in power between the Ashkenazi sector and the immigrant and Israeli-born Orientals is generally recognized, it has never been considered central. Power is admittedly missing, for example, in Bar-Yosef's statement of the absorption–modernization model (1971: 131). On the other hand, Lissak gives some attention to power. In a study of social mobility in Israel, he concludes that there exists discontinuity (in fact, a ceiling) in the social mobility of Orientals. Talking about the politically impatient Oriental elite, he writes (1969: 111):

> Those relatively mobile on the economic, educational and occupational levels are the ones who emphasize the political aspect of the struggle; they are extremely disillusioned by the impossibility of translating their achievements into real political power on the one hand and diffuse prestige on the other, and feel, more than others, the relative oligarchization of the power elite of Israeli society.

And finally he warns: 'It is not sufficient to raise the standard of education or to ensure economic security, without guaranteeing more practical integration in positions of power and prestige' (1969: 113). Lissak is fully aware of the power disparity and of invidious distinctions. He indicates them as he completes his analysis of economic, educational and occupational mobility as well as voting patterns, but he does not focus on them as he does on the other problems. He also avoids the issue, suggested by his own analysis, of why there is discontinuity in the social mobility of the Orientals.

Fourth, the phenomenon of discrimination is practically absent from Israeli sociological accounts of the ethnic situation. It emerges as a residual category in writings of some economic analysts who examine factors affecting income, but even then its impact is belittled. Apart from one exception (Inbar and Adler, 1977) ethnic discrimination has not been studied. In the absence of such studies, analysts of ethnic tensions deny its existence (e.g., Shuval, 1962: 327). As typical of order–equilibrium analysis, attitudinal prejudice, rather than behavioural discrimination, is focused on. More important, the wider and deeper ideological sources of prejudice are not only ignored but also explicitly brushed aside, so that prejudice appears as foreseeable individual reactions in situations of culture-contacts and class differentials.

Fifth, as a rule Oriental–Ashkenazi relations are analysed in isolation from other divisions. The relevance of the relations between religious and nonreligious Jews and the relations between Israeli Arabs and Jews for those between Ashkenazim and Orientals is not comprehended. The interplay between the various lines of cleavage, which is central in the colonial model, is nowhere ascertained. Peres (1971) made the first significant contribution in this direction by showing that prejudices of Ashkenazim and Orientals towards each other and towards the Arabs are influenced by the relative position of each one of the three ethnic groups in Israeli society. Peres's analysis is, however, confined to a social-psychological level of stereotyping, scapegoating and reference group behaviour which is far from exhausting the potential of such an analysis. The more crucial repercussions for distribution of resources and power alignments among the various groups remain unexplored.

Oriental–Ashkenazi relations can be better conceptualized in terms of 'a dynamic paternalism–co-optation model' than by either an absorption–modernization model or a colonial model. Briefly, the Orientals are co-opted into an Ashkenazi-dominated system, since they are still 'unqualified' they cannot move freely into higher echelons because of Ashkenazi paternalism, yet their status is changing with the erosion in the inhibitory forces.[41]

The proposed model takes the centuries-old separation of the two ethnic groups as its point of departure. The rift continued up to the proclamation of the state in spite of earlier historical opportunities – notably the emergence of Zionism as a national liberation movement of *all* Jews, and national rebuilding in the Yishuv for the *entire* Jewish people – to bridge it. The mass influx of 'forgotten' Oriental Jews after 1948 presented a problem to the established Ashkenazi group which viewed them as 'backward' non-Europeans. The Ashkenazim feared that the Orientals might downgrade the Ashkenazi–Western culture and disrupt the young political democracy. More positively, they desired to make the Orientals best serve the needs of the new state.

The policies of immigrant absorption and modernization were employed in a piecemeal, partial fashion in order to avert the possible hazards of overflowing the Western structure by Orientalism rather than to promote equality and integration. While professing the ideals of the ingathering and merging of exiles, the Ashkenazim looked down on the Orientals as 'a generation of the desert'. This paternalistic, strong though unofficial, ideology which conceives of the Orientals as impossible to be perfected practically has delayed full equality to the next generation or reserved it to the select few.

The common practices attest to the general attitude of the dominant group. The extension of minimal services to the immigrants was directed to prevent the destitution of the Oriental newcomers, but not to bring about equality. The system was opened up for the Orientals from the middle section down. Most Orientals entered lower and lower-middle positions, some obtained middle slots, and a few who enjoyed benign quotas reached higher token appointments. This wholesale co-optation of the Orientals did not only provide them with a stake in the society but also furnished the Ashkenazi group with large-scale upward mobility. The Orientals helped to settle the land, boost the economy, increase the armed forces and so on by occupying the less important roles. The better skilled and more powerful Ashkenazim moved upwards, benefiting from the expansion of the system, the large capital imports and the broad ethnic base underneath them. The existence of a rigid Arab–Jewish division, in which Oriental Jews were assured certain status, economic and power gains denied to Israeli Arabs, facilitated the dismantling of the Oriental culture and guaranteed Oriental backing of the regime.

These patterns of co-optation and paternalism have become eroded over the years, however. The process is somewhat inevitable when co-optation is applied to large groups. The costs of massive co-optation have risen steadily because more Orientals have become 'qualified' and pressed for full participation. After more than two decades of intergroup contact, the perils of cultural dilution and political instability have proved unrealistic or have been overcome, dispelling deep-seated Ashkenazi apprehensions. There has been an ongoing transition to a liberal competitive system where the Orientals can freely enter competition with fellow Ashkenazim but tend to lose out because of inferior skills and informal discrimination. This transformation marks continuing processes of weakening of ethnicity, heightening of class and power inequality, and an overall improvement in Oriental–Ashkenazi relations.

Ethnic calm is thus maintained by diverse cohesive mechanisms ranging from activation of Jewish solidarity and national consensus to neutralization and control.

b The contested accommodation model of religious–nonreligious relations. Unlike the mixed case of Oriental-Ashkenazi relations, religious–nonreligious relations follow the more familiar pattern of consociationalism dominant in certain western democracies like Holland (Lijphart, 1969, McRae, 1974).

There exists a need for examination of the diverse aspects of religious–nonreligious pluralism and for the development of a balanced view. At present the nation-building model focuses on *Kulturkampf* and consensus-formation and the colonial model merely 'debunks' the lack of separation between state and religion as a device for exclusion of the Arabs. There is, however, more to the relations between the religious minority and nonreligious majority. In addition to the legal and value disputes about the specific Jewish physiognomy of the state, they involve issues of quality of institutions, distribution of resources, and collective attitudes and interpersonal behaviours. It appears that 'a contested accommodation model', namely a religious status quo which is continuously challenged by persons on both sides, may sum up the type of religious–nonreligious relations.

As to social segmentation, although the religious group has managed to set up the necessary institutions for self-perpetuation, certain difficulties remain. The religious community maintains comprehensive socialization agencies, including separate kindergartens, elementary schools, post-primary schools, yeshivot, youth movements, a university, newspapers and publishing houses. It controls various publicly funded religious services, among which are synagogues, religious councils, Rabbinic courts, the Chief Rabbinate and the department for religious affairs in secular sectors (army, government, Histadrut, Jewish Agency and political parties). Separate neighbourhoods, housing projects, banking and credit unions and so forth provide extra insulation. While all these measures guarantee the survival of religious Jews as a group, the threats of the all-embracing secular institutions of the wider society and the relative ease of crossing over to the nonreligious camp present them with a continuing problem of accommodation. To illustrate, separate religious schools are not sufficient: different curricular and extra-curricular activities should be devised, and, more important, to be effectively attractive, religious education must be competitive in quality with nonreligious education. The existing institutional separation has to be consolidated, elaborated and deepened in order to be efficient.

The struggle for distribution of resources, though secondary to matters of cultural and social pluralism, plays some role in religious–nonreligious relations. A large number of religious people derive their livelihoods from the religious establishment, among whom are ritual slaughterers, kashrut supervisors, Rabbis, Rabbinic judges, and the staff of religious bureaucracies (Chief Rabbinate, Ministry of Religious Affairs, religious parties). The sizeable category of teachers in religious schools enjoys equal pay in a system of public financing of all streams of education. Religious politicians find it expedient to get political support by articulating religious interests and dispensing benefits to religious constituents. The religious public at large do not have to bear the costs of the religious services and are also protected against 'unfair' competition by the stoppage of work on days of religious observance. In other words, the standard of living and share in rewards of the religious minority are not unrelated to the religious status quo. In many ways religious Jews are organized as a strong interest group within the broad society.

Another totally neglected facet of religious–nonreligious pluralism is invidious distinctions and interpersonal relations. Although it is true that the religious way of life is legitimate and noninvidious, group prejudices and discriminatory practices cannot be ruled out. Nor can we ignore possible strains in person-to-person contacts, even though fluidity seems to distinguish religious–nonreligious relations on the individual level.

The religious status quo is acquiesced in by the overwhelming majority in the two sectors but is under fire from certain circles in both. Within the religious minority the militant semi-ultra-Orthodox or ultra-Orthodox groups press for greater religious compulsion in the public domain. They put on the defensive the compromising National Religious Party and the Chief Rabbinate – the major religious representatives – who react, in turn, with renewed aggressiveness. Similarly, within the non-Orthodox majority, different groups feel hurt by the present situation. They include some people who experience personal hardships in getting married or divorced and many who sympathize with them, the followers of the non-recognized movements of Reform and Conservative Judaism, anyone who wants more public services to operate on Saturdays and holidays, and some avowed secularists and libertarians. The resultant cross-pressures prevent the full institutionalization, i.e., acceptance, legitimacy and stability of the religious status quo.

A confrontation between the religious and nonreligious communities is also avoided. After all, the religious group is only a minority and lacks coercive power. It knows that the old halakha does not fit a modern Jewish state. Moreover, it is assured of its continuity and other fringe benefits by the current arrangements. On the other hand, the nonreligious majority is not discontented with the basically secular society. It condones the religious restrictions because they preserve the Jewish character of the state and because political stability necessitates the inclusion of religious parties in the coalition government. And both sides understandably try to refrain from full-scale crises as long as the Israeli–Arab conflict goes on.

The religious status quo has deep historical roots. It is as old as the Zionist movement itself, which recognized 'religious Zionism' as a full-fledged branch and supported the establishment of parallel religious structures alongside the main secular ones. Its concrete foundations were laid on the time-honoured Ottoman 'millet' system of separate religious communities that the British sanctioned when they took Palestine over. Since the early 1930s it has served as a basis for co-operation between the religious and labour parties and since 1948 it has been formalized as a special clause in the working principles of every Israeli government.

The religious status quo, therefore, lingers on. It has been repeatedly tested, punctured and patched up. Since stable settlement is beyond reach and all-out confrontation is feared, 'contested accommodation', 'ocmpromise politics' and 'consociational democracy' are institutionalized to regulate religious–nonreligious relations.

c The exclusionary domination model of Arab–Jewish relations. The plight of the Arab minority in Israel is generally recognized but is differently interpreted. The nation-building perspective stresses the Israeli Arabs' ambivalence and dual identity as Israeli citizens and Arab nationals. It expects the advancing processes of modernization and nationalism to exacerbate their already painful predicament. On the other hand, the colonial perspective views the Israeli Arabs as a segment of the Palestinian people – nationally suppressed and economically exploited. Their problem is, therefore, not a psychological marginality but an objective condition of dislodgment and oppression. In comparison, our pluralistic perspective specifies the status of the Arab minority as a quasi-caste and conceptualizes their relations to the Jewish majority in terms of an effective machinoy of control–exclusion, dependence and subordination.

Israeli Arabs and Jews qualify as ethnic quasi-castes according to a minimal definition of caste.[42] Their status is determined by birth and is legally binding. However, since people may theoretically switch membership via religious conversion, only quasi-castes obtain. Endogamy is the practice. Status-hierarchy is evidenced by the facts that Arabs do not usually have Jewish subordinates and that their positions gain less reward than those occupied by Jewish counterparts.

The religion–nationality quasi-caste structure was established and is sustained by the over-riding national objective of building a purely Jewish society in the land of Israel. Jewish settlers founded separate structures of their own, insisting on maximum disengagement from the indigenous Arabs. Reluctant to compromise Jewish exclusiveness, the founders of the state had to face the unwelcome reality of a defeated Arab minority which emerged as a result of the Jewish victory in the 1948 War. The pre-statehood tradition of complete separation was superseded by forced co-existence for both Arabs and Jews.

The mass of the Jewish people regard the Arabs as outsiders, and their feelings toward them range from hostility, through contempt and pity, to indifference. They opt out of any responsibility for the Arabs, entrusting a free hand to the authorities to deal with them. The authorities, being on the average more liberal than the general public, are interested in pacification and the compliance of the Israeli Arabs and in minimizing the potential costs of the presence of an Arab minority to the national goals of the Jewish character of the state, national security and democratic pluralism.

The compliance of the Arab minority is sought in a variety of ways. The Arabs are granted civil liberties as well as the right to a separate religious and cultural identity. They maintain their own institutions which ensure their separate existence. Their problems are handled through special departments for minority affairs.

The Arabs are heavily incorporated into and thereby strongly dependent on the Jewish economy. Most of them are wage-earners working for Jewish employers. The self-employed farmers and businessmen are dependent on the Jewish market. And, generally speaking, the Arabs are dependent on the Jews for the delivery of welfare state services and the funding of community development projects.

The Arabs' economic dependence is reinforced by political subordination. They do not have control of their own institutions – Jews run Arab education and mass media, manage the special Arab departments and intervene in Arab local government and state-wide politics. In order to weaken Arab national consciousness and avert national struggle, the Arabs are treated as a mere ethnic group, are denied the status of a national minority and even deprived of cultural autonomy. Extra restraints are imposed by barring Arabs from the armed forces and other sensitive institutions and by close surveillance over potential opponents and troublemakers.

These diverse measures had proved effective in securing the passive compliance of the Arab minority up until the end of the 1960s but have become increasingly ineffective in the 1970s. Jewish restrictions have been relaxed over the years – the abolition of military rule, the inclusion of Arabs in the Histadrut, the extension of the right to join Jewish political parties, etc. Arab conditions have greatly improved – a significant rise in the standard of living, better education, the emergence of a sizeable middle class and a small modern elite. A Palestinian national consciousness has engulfed the Arab masses. The cumulative effect of these and other changes is to make the Arabs impatient with the quasi-caste structure and with their subordinate position in society. Unrest has grown, and by the mid-1970s Arabs have already presented direct challenges to the ethnic status quo.

The status of the Arab minority in Israeli society is very problematic. It is quite difficult to make the Jewish state and national security compatible with democratic pluralism. Since the Arabs are regarded as outsiders and security risks, their demands for full equality can be easily ignored. And as a small minority and of little account in the social structure (unlike other subordinate groups such as the non-white majority in South Africa), the Arabs' negotiating power is weak.

4 Historical background

Both change and continuity stand out in the internal relations within the three major divisions in Israel. The 'Oriental problem' attracted attention only after the proclamation of the state, when the Orientals became a numerical majority. However, the effects of the age-old separation between the two ethnic groups are still felt. Although secularization created a rift between the religious and nonreligious communities, early in this century a pattern of accommodation was set that greatly influences their current relations. The reversal of the Arab status from a majority in Palestine to a subordinate minority in Israel was indeed critical. But so is the perpetual forced co-existence that has typified Arab–Jewish relations from the inception of the Zionist settlement.

In this chapter Oriental–Ashkenazi pluralism will be placed in a proper historical perspective, which is usually absent in the sociological writings in this area. In addition, brief historical reviews of religious–nonreligious division and Arab–Jewish division all provide the background to present-day relations.

1 Oriental–Ashkenazi relations

In 1964 Kalman Katzenelson, a veteran journalist and a self-declared 'Ashkenazi nationalist', published a book entitled *The Ashkenazi Revolution*. The author surveyed more than three thousand years of Jewish history and implied that the Jewish people have always been made up of tribes, ethnic groups, or nations. For the last millennium, the division has been between the 'Sephardo–Oriental nations' and the 'Ashkenazi nation'. These two nations have nothing in common except nominal religious ties. The superior 'Ashkenazi nation', although destined to rule, made a blunder in admitting inferior non-Ashkenazi Jews to Israel. It summarily has to assume formal control of the state to prevent the erosion of its domination and hence the destruction of Israel. These ideas and many others stirred a public storm. The 'theory' was slandered as anti-Jewish, anti-semitic, anti-Zionist and racist, and Katzenelson's book was soon banned by the government.

While Katzenelson carried his arguments to extremes and reached absurd conclusions, his analysis cannot be dismissed offhand. He reasoned that Ashkenazim and Orientals (Sephardim) are historically two different and separate peoples, and that the former have no obligation to promote equality for and integration with the latter. As one commentator on the book wrote, 'the book has not been written and produced in a complete vacuum – no book of this kind ever is' (Rejwan, 1964: 15). Stripped of its extremism, Katzenelson's thesis reveals some deep-rooted feelings or unstated thoughts of the Ashkenazim toward non-Ashkenazim during the period prior to their encounter in Israel.

The centuries-old ethnic separation

Ethnic separation among Jews had begun with their dispersion. Since Jews tend in many ways to resemble Gentiles in countries of their residence, the exiled Jewish people corresponded in a large measure to the different nations of the world in whose midst they settled. The territorial dispersal not only produced ethnic diversity, but also produced no problems as long as the Jews were scattered and had only very minimal contact with each other. But beginning with the ingathering of the exiles into Palestine, ethnic differences started to generate tensions.

Historically three ethnic branches evolved among the Jews, i.e., Orientals, Sephardim and Ashkenazim, who took turn in leading world Jewry.[1] Up to the eleventh century most Jews were Orientals, displaying few if any internal ethnic distinctions.[2] But since then the Jewish communities in Europe have been sufficiently large and culturally outstanding to take over as the main centre of world Jewry. Between the eleventh and the fifteenth centuries, the Sephardim (Spanish Jews) succeeded the Orientals as holders of the hegemony over world Jewry and from the sixteenth century on, the Ashkenazim have been the dominant Jewish group.

The Oriental Jews lived in almost all areas in the Middle East and North Africa after the destruction of the Second Commonwealth in AD 70 and even much earlier.[3] Their most enduring experience has been life under Islam, which conquered the entire region during the seventh and eighth centuries. Islam regards Jews and Christians as 'People of the Book' (Ahl al-Kitab), who are entitled to a status of a 'protected people' (Ahl al-Dhimmah) upon paying a special poll-tax (jizya). Their status as a subordinate minority to the Moslem dominant majority is manifested by various disabilities, including the prohibition to proselytize, to marry Moslem women, to witness against Moslems, to construct tall buildings or new houses of prayer without a permit, to ride horses, to bear arms and to hold public office. However, few of these restrictions were adhered to in most places, most of the time. The Oriental Jews maintained fairly symbiotic and cordial relations with the Arabs through the ages. They rose to eminence at the epoch of Arab renaissance and lost vitality thereafter. The deterioration in their conditions continued uninterruptedly until the nineteenth century, when some modernization was introduced by the reformist Ottomans and the expanding Western powers.

Life-situations varied appreciably from one country to another. By the middle of the nineteenth century Jews in Algeria, Tunisia, Libya, Egypt, Iraq, Lebanon, Syria and Turkey were granted civil rights. On the other hand, Yemenite Jews, who were treated as aliens, suffered a great deal from the above humiliating constraints on non-Moslems (and were even further abused by the forced conversion of orphans) up to the time of their immigration. The Persian Jews occupied a similar subordinate status officially till 1906 and practically till 1925 with the rise to power of the Pahlavi dynasty. The Moroccan Jews, too, were extended certain rights by the French in 1912 but were enfranchised only after Morocco's independence in 1956. These political handicaps were reinforced by economic deprivations. As opposed to other Oriental Jews who mostly resided in the main cities, the Yemenite, Persian and most Moroccan Jews were dispersed in many villages and small towns, enjoying little opportunity for social mobility, and were deprived of the educational and other services attended upon big urban Jewish communities. Great contrasts existed in some countries as well, like those between cavedwellers and city residents in Morocco or between the rural Kurds and sophisticated townspeople in Iraq.[4]

The Orientals expanded the spread of the Sephardic Jewry by migrating to the Iberian peninsula long before it fell at the hands of the Moors in the eighth century.[5] With the amicable contacts and spiritual cross-fertilization between Arabs and Jews, the Sephardim reached the cultural splendour called in Jewish history 'the golden Age of Spain' at the very time of the Dark Ages in Europe. The gradual Christian reconquest of Spain initiated a long process of Europeanization of the Sephardim. Between 1391 and 1492 Spanish Jews were compelled to migrate by persecution and final expulsion. These refugees (sometimes known as Levantine or Near Eastern Sephardim) settled mostly in Turkey and the Balkans, though some went to North Africa, Palestine and other parts of the Near East.

The forced converts who returned to Judaism (often called Western Sephardim) left some time later for Holland, England and the New World. Although some Sephardim became assimilated into both Oriental and Ashkenazi communities, most retained separate identities and independent organizations.

The Sephardim and Orientals have had much in common. They share the same religious style and follow the *Shulhan Arukh*, the religious corpus juris compiled by the Sephardic Rabbi Caro in Palestine in the sixteenth century. The resemblance between the Orientals and Near Eastern Sephardim is much greater. Both were under the rule of the decadent Ottoman Empire. This meant cultural, economic and political stagnation, and late exposure to modern ideas. In physiognomy, demography and culture, they were like their Middle Eastern non-Jewish neighbours.

The Sephardim and the Orientals differed, however, in certain important respects. The Sephardim spoke Ladino, a derivative of medieval Spanish mixed with Hebrew, whereas the Orientals spoke Judeo-Arabic and Judeo-Persian dialects. The Sephardim have also a tradition of elitism and self-pride (grandezza), which is hardly found among the Orientals. More significant differences separate, of course, the privileged Western Sephardim from the underprivileged Orientals.

The sixteenth century was the turning-point in the history of ethnic diversity within world Jewish society. By this time the Oriental and Sephardic Jews lost cultural dominance and subsequently even their numerical majority. It is estimated that non-Ashkenazim constituted two-thirds of the 1.5 million Jews in the world in 1500, two-fifths of the 2.5 million Jews in 1800, and only one-tenth of the 10.5 million Jews at the end of the nineteenth century (see Table 8). The dramatic natural increase of Ashkenazi Jewry during the nineteenth century reflects the transitional stage of a low deathrate and a high birthrate; at the time non-Ashkenazi Jews were still in the traditional phase of little population growth (i.e., high death- and birthrates).

At first, world Jewry was centred mainly in the German regions. For this reason European Jews have been called Ashkenazim, a term which means, literally, 'Germans'. Then it moved to Eastern Europe, and after the seclusion of Russian Jews behind the Iron Curtain and the Holocaust it was transferred to Western Europe, America and Israel.

Despite the cultural diversity within Ashkenazi Jewry, like that among German, East European, Anglo-Saxon and native Israeli Ashkenazim, they have some fundamentals in common.[6] In physical features Ashkenazi Jews resemble European Gentiles, not Mediterraneans. Their cultural heritage includes, above all, Yiddish, a

German-Jewish dialect spoken on the eve of World War II by as many as eleven million. They have a common liturgy and follow their own style of religious law, which differs in minor significant points from the Sephardic version (as institutionalized by an Ashkenazi halakha code assembled by Rabbi Isserles in Poland in the sixteenth century in reaction against the *Shulhan Arukh*).[7] In other cultural traditions, the Ashkenazim are quite part of Europe. In spite of tenacious persecution and anti-Semitism, they maintained cultural creativity as manifested in religious revitalization movements (Hasidism and Reform), Jewish philosophy, literature and the science of Judaism. Since the seventeenth century, many started to absorb the spirit of Europe which bestowed on them the fruits of enlightenment (haskalah), emancipation, assimilation, nationalism, other contemporary ideologies and social movements (liberalism, socialism), and abundant opportunities for social mobility (Patai, 1971f: 287–311).

In this study a rough distinction between Ashkenazim and non-Ashkenazim (or, more positively, Orientals) is adopted. This is not to overlook the differences in numerical strength, cultural tradition and socioeconomic status within each group. It is, rather, the intention to sharpen the focus on the more significant divergences and hence the relations between the two major Jewish groups in Israel. The Ashkenazim constitute the dominant in-group which is selectively open to Jews from other countries. Although the Sephardim can be best considered an intermediate group between Ashkenazim and Orientals, they are combined here with Orientals. This is because the Israeli Sephardim are Mediterranean (not Western) and are still defined socially as non-Ashkenazi outsiders.[8] Their small and dwindling numbers also do not warrant their treatment as a separate group. It is estimated that 17 per cent of the world Jewry of 14.1 million in 1975 are non-Ashkenazim, of whom only 4 per cent are Sephardim and 13 per cent are Orientals, and, more important, out of the Israeli Jewry of about 3 million, the non Ashkenazim amount to 55 per cent – only 7 per cent Sephardim and 48 per cent Orientals.[9]

Up to the twentieth century there was little contact between Ashkenazim and other Jews: they were, in practice, estranged. Where early encounters took place, such as in Holland, the United States and Palestine, they were strained and hardly ever resulted in the merging of the two communities. At the turn of this century, however, two interrelated and historically unprecedented opportunities for large-scale rapprochement between the two Jewish sections occurred. One was the world-wide Zionist movement, and the other was the building of a new Jewish society, which came to be known as the Yishuv, in Palestine.

The Zionist movement and the Orientals

Very few studies have been made of the relationship between the Zionist movement and non-Ashkenazi Jewry. Despite its stated goals of liberating Jews all over the world, the basic fact is well established that the Zionist movement was not active among Orientals. It did not set up chapters in lands where Orientals lived, and, with minor exceptions, did not send any emissaries among them until World War II – and very few afterwards. It did not recruit and train Oriental immigrants for Aliyot. As an Israeli Zionist wrote in 1950: 'Oriental Jewry is abandoned and left to itself, and that we content ourselves with sending them a few solitary emissaries without budgets and without the possibility of wide activity' (Zerubavel, 1950: 5, quoted by Patai, 1970: 292–3). This had far-reaching repercussions, namely, that Zionism failed to serve as a modernizing agent for the non-Ashkenazi Jews and to make them equal partners in the enterprise of nation-building.

In the absence of comparative studies of the activity of the Zionist movement in different countries, it is hazardous to speculate about the reasons for Zionist neglect of Oriental Jewry, yet some general factors may be suggested. First, Zionism was originally a response to the Jewish problem in Europe and as such it limited its activity to European Jewry. Expansion to the Near East or North Africa would have split its efforts and drained off its resources. Second, the non-Ashkenazi Jewry was small (only 10 per cent of world Jewry at the end of the nineteenth century), and it was poor and backward by European standards. As such it was not expected to contribute much in people and funds. Third, because of the limited contact between Ashkenazim and non-Ashkenazim, the Ashkenazi Zionist activists knew little about non-Ashkenazim and felt detached and remote from them. Barriers of language and culture added to these difficulties. And, finally, the Zionist movement was prohibited in some Moslem countries in the 1930s and 1940s and Oriental Jewish leaders did not encourage it because they feared being identified with the Jewish settlers in Palestine and with Zionists all over the world who were considered enemies of the Arabs.[10]

Patai may be right in speculating that 'the Ashkenazi Diaspora, and it alone of the three major divisions of the Jewish People, was ready for Zionism' (1971f: 310). Had the Zionist movement tried to expand to the Oriental and Sephardic Jewries, it might possibly have failed. My point is, rather, that its failure even to try signifies the gulf which separated Ashkenazim and non-Ashkenazim, and more specifically the unfavourable attitudes Ashkenazim as Europeans took towards non-Ashkenazim as non-Europeans. The aloofness and feeling of superiority of Ashkenazim in evidence at this time strained Oriental–Ashkenazi relations in the Yishuv and later in Israel.[11]

Since there are as yet no comparative studies, I must rely on the few case-studies of separate Oriental communities to illustrate my point.[12] H. Cohen (1969, especially chapter 9), in an extensive study of Zionist activity in Iraq, shows that Zionism emerged by local initiative. Iraqi leaders launched Zionist activities very early and intensified their efforts in the 1920s. They contacted the World Zionist Organization (WZO) but failed to get co-operation in sending agents and propaganda material, or in obtaining representation. The WZO refused to allocate certificates to Iraqi Jews who wished to immigrate to Palestine. It co-operated in one area only – receiving donations. Later, Zionism was prohibited by the Iraqi government, but the WZO did nothing through available British channels to help to make it legal. To quote one of the Zionist leaders in 1934: 'We have sent emissaries to Poland, Romania, Germany, America, etc., but not to Baghdad.' Emissaries were not sent to Iraq in the 1920s and 1930s, because 'it is difficult . . . to make investments while there are no chances for profits' (H. Cohen, 1969: 139).[13] After the pogrom of Iraqi Jewry in 1941, the Yishuv did send agents to Iraq and helped to establish a Zionist underground movement there. That was the only Zionist movement of any significance which operated among the Orientals. Though it was late, just seven years before the creation of the state, this movement played an indispensable role among Iraqi Jewry both in Iraq and Israel.

The failure of the Zionist movement to emerge in North Africa is also partially documented (Bensimon-Donath, 1970: chapter 3), but will not be considered here.[14] I would like, however, to mention an earlier attempt by the World Zionist Organization through its office in Palestine to attract Oriental immigrants – the Yemenite Jews.

After two independent waves of immigration of Yemenites in 1881 and 1907, an effort was made in 1910 to organize immigration from the Yemen. The full story of this exceptional endeavour is still to be told, but there is some interesting evidence. In 1907 'messianic' Yemenite immigrants became productive farmhands. On the other hand, the Ashkenazi newcomers were few and found it hard to adjust to agricultural work, lower wages and poor living conditions. It was feared that the slogan 'conquest of labour', i.e., replacement of Arab workers by Jewish ones, would fail. The Yemenites offered an expedient solution. They were 'a human element as modest in its demands as the Arabs of Palestine, as able or at least as willing to carry out heavy physical labour under the blazing sun of Palestine, and yet Jewish, hence constituting no danger to the Zionist plans for development' (Patai, 1970: 187–8). Or, as one of the Ashkenazi leaders of the time recalls the deliberations to send an emissary

54

to Yemen, an objection was in fact raised that 'it is an absolute prohibition to deliberately bring Jews to the land for servitude, to become hewers of wood and drawers of water in the farms of idle, noble Ashkenazim'. The over-riding justification for the plan was, however, that 'since these Yemenite Jews are used to poverty and are frugal people whose wants are modest, their immigration to Palestine and life as agricultural workers would be both a physical and a spiritual salvation' (Tsemah, 1967: 17).

The subsequent policies testify to this peculiar viewpoint. Among the immigrants who received public housing, the Yemenites got smaller houses than the Eastern Europeans (Bein, 1954: 102), although their families were no doubt larger. There was also a policy to keep the Yemenites as labourers instead of helping them to become peasant proprietors (Gluska, 1974: 110). They were settled in separate quarters and allotted only small, auxiliary farms, so that they had to be wage-earners in the near-by Ashkenazi moshavot, while Ashkenazi workers were assigned large parcels of land in order to become independent farmers.[15] Only after organized pressures and protests were these policies altered (Taviv, 1943).

The treatment of the Yemenite Jews makes it clear that Orientals were looked down upon as a different type of Jew, and that they were not expected to become full partners but rather 'assistants', if at all, in building the new Jewish community. The Yemenites themselves were so keenly sensitive to this attitude that one of their contemporary leaders complained at the 18th Zionist congress in 1933 that 'the members of his community were still second-class citizens in Palestine, like non-Aryans in Germany' (quoted by Lacqueur, 1972: 503).

I mentioned earlier that notwithstanding the fact that Zionism is a Jewish movement of national liberation, it demonstrated traces of contagious colonial spirit that prevailed in Europe at the time – feelings of superiority and paternalism of Europeans towards Asian and African peoples. The pervasive Ashkenazi ethnocentrism of Zionism had important consequences, one of which was indicated by Patai (1970: 27):

The old-fashioned and shortsighted view, which unfortunately is expressed only too often both orally and in writing in Israel, holds summarily that the Oriental Jews are in need of a complete re-education, that their entire being and thinking must be reshaped in the European Jewish image, and that, where this cannot be achieved by suasion and example, the situation calls for legislative measures.

This viewpoint was typical of the approach of the colonial powers to their subject peoples, the 'natives' of their colonies, in past centuries.

The Zionist modernizing mission in respect to Oriental Jews was carried out on a large scale only after the declaration of the state. During the pre-state period, it was invoked as legitimation of the Jewish settlement and was used to counteract Arab opposition, but it was not put into practice. The Ashkenazi settlers developed new separate institutions and did little to alleviate the conditions of Arabs or Orientals.

But beyond paternalism, the lack of activity on the part of Zionists in Moslem areas reflected a grave problem of Jewish identity. Centuries of near total separation between the two ethnic groups caused Ashkenazim to consider Orientals, if at all, as a marginal section of the Jewish people. As one notable writer put it in a press interview (Hazas in interview with Bashan, 1966, quoted by Rejwan, 1967: 101):

> Listen: We the Jews of Eastern Europe had thought, in our
> innocence, that the Jews who lived in Greater Russia . . .
> that it was these Jews who constituted the Jewish People, and
> no one else besides. True we had known that Jews were to be
> found in Germany; but as far as we were concerned this was a
> Jewry whose relevance was fast disappearing as a result of
> Reform and assimilation which greedily ate into its body. We
> also knew that there were Jews in France, England and overseas.
> But *Oriental Jews*! We simply forgot that such a thing existed.

Goitein confirmed this observation in his historical analysis (1964: 8):

> The Jews in Arabic-speaking countries, who at one time
> had formed both the majority of the Jewish people and its
> social and spiritual pivot, simply faded out of Jewish history.
> They were almost forgotten by the bulk of the nation, which was
> now concentrated in the Christian countries, taking its full
> part in their stupendous development in modern times.

Hence when the Ashkenazim started to spread Zionism and build a homeland in Palestine, they hardly thought of Orientals as Jewish equals or full members to be recruited to the Zionist idea, encouraged to immigrate to Palestine or to share in common in the new Jewish enterprise.

Orientals in the Yishuv

In retrospect, the failure of the Zionist movement – which professed the ideal of redeeming all Jews and forging them into one people – to operate among Orientals perpetuated the ethnic separation which already existed and missed a historical opportunity to overcome it. But the national rebuilding of Palestine offered another promising possibility.

The presence of the Orientals in Palestine was by no means insignificant. They constituted about 60 per cent of the Jews at the beginning of the Zionist settlement in 1882 and 23 per cent on the eve of Israel's birth in 1948 (see Table 8). In spite of a lack of Zionist encouragement in the pre-state period (1882–1948), more than 50,000 Orientals immigrated to Palestine (see Table 9). Some were driven by the traditional yearning to return to Zion and most were pushed by dire conditions and motivated by mundane aspirations toward upward mobility (H. Cohen, 1968). While they constituted only about 8 per cent of world Jewry, their average proportion among the immigrants to Palestine is estimated to have been 12 per cent (H. Cohen, 1968: 11) – even greater than proportions of Ashkenazim.[16]

The Oriental presence in Palestine seems to have been appreciable enough to have challenged the narrow Ashkenazi conception of the Jewish people and to have moved the Ashkenazim to attempt to bring the two communities together. It did not succeed.

The Old Yishuv[17] was also ethnically divided into Sephardic and Ashkenazi communities and even further subdivided into regions of origin. The Sephardim held a definitely dominant position. Jews were considered as a separate 'millet' (a religious community) in the Ottoman Empire and the Sephardic Chief Rabbi was the only officially recognized representative of the entire Jewish community in Palestine. The Old Yishuv was culturally traditional and economically backward, and virtually depended for its existence on charitable donations from abroad. The Ashkenazi pioneers of the New Yishuv viewed the predominantly Sephardic Old Yishuv as a satellite of the Diaspora against which they rebelled, and thus they either ignored it or tried to neutralize it as a social force. From an ethnic viewpoint, the history of the Yishuv is the story of a reversal of statuses. As we shall see below, the Orientals lost their majority status to the Ashkenazi newcomers and waged a hopeless battle for survival as an ethnic group.

The thirty years of the British mandate (1918–48) were the critical period during which nation-rebuilding was under way. During this period the Orientals suffered setbacks. Their proportion in the Jewish population dropped from 40 per cent at the beginning to 23 per cent at the end of the mandate period. In 1921 they lost their exclusive religious authority when the British established a dual Rabbinate based on an ethnic parity of Ashkenazim and Sephardim (HaCohen, 1971). Their political power steadily declined. They clearly occupied the lowest socioeconomic positions (Lissak, 1965). In addition to their disproportionately large crime-rate (Frankenstein, 1947), they deviated from the Yishuv mainstream in other ways such as in their

57

over-representation among rank and file members of the two secessionist underground movements, in their social and residential segregation, their high rate of illiteracy, and so forth.

In order to better understand the position of the Orientals during the pre-state period, we should examine the ideological and social structure of the nascent Jewish society at that time.[18] The Yishuv was highly ideologized and politicized, and it became fragmented into many groups. Three major sectors can be distinguished as the most influential: labour (Left), religious and right-of-centre. Each sector attempted to develop many separate self-sufficient institutions. Each sector mobilized its own resources, sent emissaries abroad to train and recruit immigrants and raised funds for its own purposes. Newcomers to Palestine were received by the organizations of the appropriate sector or, if uncommitted in advance, were brought under strong pressure to affiliate with a particular competing sector. The separate sectors had their own networks of service institutions such as schools, youth movements, health provisions, housing, trade unions, employment offices and recreational facilities. The strength of each sector was dependent on its ability to extend these services as well as on the attractiveness of its ideological claims. The labour sector supplied the most 'comprehensive' coverage, and the most 'marketable' ideology. It was, hence, the largest and the strongest.

There existed an intrinsic relation between the special structuring of the Yishuv and the situation of the Orientals. The considerable intersector rivalry within Jewish society and the position of Jews vis-à-vis the British administration and the Arab majority in the wider plural society diminished the significance of ethnic relations among Jews. Eisenstadt (1948: 6) talks about the 'neutralization' of ethnicity as both an ideology and a reality of the Yishuv. Newcomers were expected to give up their historical Diaspora-related, distinctive ethnic identities and to merge into the newly integrated society. Ashkenazi immigrants conformed to this pattern and became readily 'absorbed' thanks to their modernized background, willingness to change and other ideological commitments. Lacking all these characteristics, the Orientals failed to assimilate (Eisenstadt, 1950).[19]

While Eisenstadt is correct concerning the existence of processes of cultural change and anomie, his account of the failure of the Orientals to assimilate tends to explain this entirely on the basis of their shortcomings. He overlooks some important factors by taking the Yishuv ideology for granted without questioning its assumptions. Looking at the matter from the point of view of the dominant modern Ashkenazi Yishuv, as Eisenstadt does, the Orientals, both newcomers and natives, were deviants insofar as they failed to conform to the Ashkenazi pattern. The Orientals themselves and their elites, however, did not feel that way. Apart from general identification with the development of a new national homeland, they tried to preserve some of their social frameworks and traditions. Unlike the ultra-orthodox groups that officially seceded from the organized Yishuv, the Orientals stayed on and struggled to retain their deteriorating position in the expanding Yishuv.

As a matter of fact, the Sephardic leaders were aware of the division of the Yishuv into semi-feudal sectors and attempted in vain to establish a sector of their own. They did set up their own separate political ethnic parties, the Union of Pioneers of the Orient (Eliachar, 1970), the World Federation of Sephardic Communities (Attias, 1971) and the Sephardic Workers' Union (Elazar, 1970). These new organizations were formed in addition to local community associations. But all these undertakings failed to make the Orientals a sector of any significance because of denial of support and obstruction on the part of the Yishuv. The Orientals made abortive attempts to urge the Zionist movement to extend their activities to Oriental communities abroad, to allocate immigration certificates to the Orientals, to furnish funds for new settlements of Orientals in Palestine and to obtain resources to ease the hard conditions in the Oriental communities.

The justification for the withholding of assistance was the professed ideology of the neutralization of ethnicity which Eisenstadt mentions. In practice, however, other factors operated as well. The Yishuv was not an open, mobile society. It was not void of any ethnic particularism as Eisenstadt, following the official ideology, claims was the case.[20] True, it was so for East Europeans, less so for the German immigrants of the 1930s, and least of all for non-Ashkenazim.

The achievements of the Orientals who joined the three established sectors were insignificant. The neglect of the Oriental Jewry abroad by the Zionist movement was only duplicated by the East European establishment regarding Orientals in Palestine. Behind the lofty ideals of 'one people' and the neutralization of ethnicity there were the stark realities of superiority and paternalism of Ashkenazim towards Orientals which rendered impossible any meaningful relations between them. Orientals were looked upon as backward and incapable of contributing to the new society. They were considered marginal members of the Yishuv whose lack of adaptiveness was deplored, yet nothing was done to incorporate them as equal members. As Lissak points out, there was no systematic effort to bridge the ethnic split in the Yishuv. 'It is possible that the ideologists [the Ashkenazi establishment] felt confident that the ethnopolitical split was only temporary, a problem of the "generation of the desert", and the end seemed therefore close' (1969: 70).

The Ashkenazi immigrants were never thought of as a 'generation of the desert'. They were perceived as potential full partners; great pains were taken to 'absorb' them in informal groups, to settle them, to provide them with necessary services and to open opportunities to them. In contrast, the Oriental immigrants received little attention. Our discussion so far has made clear that the historical ethnic rift in the Jewish people was deep indeed and had serious implications. The failure of the Zionist movement and of the Yishuv to bridge it is a topic which commands even wider attention. The problem of Oriental–Ashkenazi relations has been shown to predate the establishment of the state. The sociological literature by and large concentrates on the state period and is oblivious to the impacts and lessons of its preceding history.[21]

The impact of statehood

Israel's independence was a turning-point in many ways. The plural society of Palestine in which Jews were a minority under indirect colonial rule was succeeded by a new state which is also plural, with Jews constituting the dominant majority. It is also a Jewish sectarian state as institutionalized in the Law of Return and in the legal separation in matters of personal status among religious communities. The Yishuv institutions, with appropriate adaptations, became the institutions of the new state, and understandably those who controlled the Yishuv came to power upon its creation. The practical significance of this continuity was that the Ashkenazi-modelled institutions and the Ashkenazi domination of the Yishuv were simply carried over to the state.

Beyond the transfer of power and institutions, however, several important changes took place. Previously the Zionist movement and the Yishuv had the character only of voluntary organizations and, thus, had neither mandatory authority over, nor formal responsibility for, Jews. But with statehood the Israel government became at once answerable in all state and social problems. By declaring itself a Jewish state, it assumed some indirect liability for Jews all over the world. As a result the ethnic problem became for the first time one for which the state had both power and accountability. Furthermore, the new Jewish state inspires a widespread expectation of normalizing every Jew's status by immigration, that is, a Jew supposedly alters his minority status in the Diaspora to a majority status in Israel when he becomes a citizen.

Israel strongly commits herself accordingly to Jewish immigration and she carried the burden of creating such conditions that make all immigrants, regardless of country of origin, full members of society. To put this into effect, Israel has made, directly as a government and indirectly through the Jewish Agency or subsidiary agencies, a historically unprecedented effort to maintain a large-scale, well-financed machinery for the immigration and absorption of Jews. She actively recruits immigrants, and upon their arrival she assists them in varying degrees in matters of housing, employment and in many other areas.[22]

Immigration also changed radically. It became massive and sometimes took the form of the transplantation of entire communities within a year or two. Since its birth, Israel has absorbed 1.6 million Jews and nearly quintupled her original Jewish population of 650,000 inhabitants. Large numbers of the new arrivals came with relatively limited skills. Over half of them hailed from the Middle East and North Africa. And more significantly, because of both their increasing representation among immigrants and their high birthrate, the Orientals achieved a majority by the early 1960s.

Statehood therefore affected Oriental–Ashkenazi relations in a number of ways. First, Orientals turned into a numerical majority who could no longer be so readily ignored. Second, as they properly sensed the meaning implied in the idea of the Jewish state (i.e., ridding Jews of a minority status and conferring upon them a majority status), they looked forward to becoming in Israel equal partners with their Ashkenazi brethren. And finally, being aware of the new reality of Jewish sovereignty, they considered the Israeli government empowered and responsible for their situation and expected it to ensure them full equality.

2 Religious–nonreligious relations

The division between religious and nonreligious Jews had started with secularization: a long process concomitant with emancipation, enlightenment and exodus from the ghetto. It lasted for more than three centuries among Ashkenazi Jews but started mainly after World War I among Oriental Jews. This time-lag had far-reaching effects. The Orientals have remained, overall, more religious or traditional than the Ashkenazim. The centuries-long exposure to secularizing forces gradually modernized Ashkenazi religious Jews in many respects. It stimulated them to form separate institutions that preserved the integrity of the religious style of life and served as a springboard to press for a greater role for religion in the Jewish public domain. In consequence, the religious minority succeeded precisely in those areas in which Orientals totally failed, that is, participation in the Zionist movement and the establishment of a separate sector in the Yishuv.[23]

The seed of the long-standing strained accommodation between the religious and nonreligious was sown during the early days of

Zionism. The founding fathers of Zionism were secular in their outlook. Herzl, the founder, pleaded for a separation of state and religion and modelled his visionary Jewish state on progressive, Western democracies. [24] He was equally convinced, however, that Zionism as a national movement should cater for the needs of all Jews, and, therefore, a compromise had to be worked out with religious Jews. The fact that the religious Jews who joined Zionism and settled in Palestine came almost exclusively from the ranks of Orthodox Judaism left a decisive mark on the nature of the compromise and the ensuing course of religious–nonreligious relations. Reform Judaism, being non-nationalist and assimilationist, opposed Zionism up to the early 1940s, whereas Conservative Judaism was fairly sympathetic but uncommitted. In hindsight, had Reform and Conservative Judaism been active in the Zionist movement, the Herzlian dream of separation of religion from state or a similar arrangement might have stood a better chance.

Orthodox Jews were, nevertheless, sharply divided over Zionism. On the whole all approved of the goal of a Jewish state but differed on the legitimate means to accomplish it. For many years the ideological and organizational dispute was embodied in two movements – the Mizrahi and Agudat Israel. [25] The backers of the Mizrahi were 'national-religious' people who held that Jews ought to have a hand in building their homeland and that religious Jews should strive to strengthen the religious character of the Jewish state. Supporters of Aguda, on the other hand, were 'ultra-Orthodox' people who maintained that the Jewish commonwealth would be restored by God, the attempt to hasten redemption through non-messianic political measures was a heresy, and that only a theocratic state was acceptable. The Mizrahi was by far the larger and it pushed its ideas by struggling within the Zionist movement. In contrast, Aguda counted on a small, militant minority and exercised pressure by fighting from without.

From the start religious Zionism was recognized as a major branch along with the two other political and cultural branches. The Mizrahi was formed in 1902, only a few years after the first Zionist Congress (1897). As an official party in the World Zionist Organization, it was represented in all the governing bodies and received its share of funds for the intensive activities it undertook. It appealed to Orthodox Jews to rally around Zionism, set up religious schools and organized the immigration of religious Jews to Palestine.

With the enormous financial and political assistance of the World Zionist Organization and the world Mizrahi movement, religious Jews established a separate sector in the Yishuv. At first the social base of the Mizrahi in Palestine consisted of middle-class small businessmen and people engaged in the services, but since 1920

Orthodox pioneers arrived with the intention to combine Zionism and the religious tradition of the Mizrahi with the socialism of the day. In 1922 they founded the Hapoel Hamizrahi (Mizrahi Worker). This religious labour movement soon overtook its parent Mizrahi in resources and constituents. There was much friction within the movement over the extent of structural separation from the nonreligious dominant institutions. Like the other major sectors in the Yishuv, the religious sector had its own agricultural settlements (religious kibbutzim and moshavim), schools, youth movements, sporting groups, periodicals, construction companies for building religious housing projects, banks and credit unions and many other voluntary associations. On the other hand, other functions were integrated. The Histadrut (General Federation of Labour) supplied the religious sector with health services (since 1927) and employment offices (between 1940 till their nationalization in 1957) and, after independence (since 1953), trade unionism. Instead of launching a separate underground, the religious sector encouraged its members to belong to the secular resistance organizations (within the Haganah, for instance, there were separate religious units).

In furthering its interests, the national-religious movement derived much power from the 'millet' system. This structural separation between the religious communities which are entrusted with sole authority over personal status traces its roots to the Islamic tradition of religious tolerance. The Ottoman rulers perfected it as a tool of religious freedom. They recognized the Jews as a separate religious community and the Chief Rabbi as its head. Following their policy of not interfering in the internal affairs of their colonies, the British perpetuated the arrangement with some modifications. Moreover, they seized upon it to define the legal status of the Yishuv as a religious community rather than as a national entity. While the continuation of the 'millet' system was certainly not an achievement of the political parties, it gave the religious sector a staggering lead in the struggle against the disestablishment of religion. Both the age-old status quo and the colonial administration which upheld it institutionalized the lack of separation of religion from the state.

Since Judaism is devoid of an ecclesiastical hierarchy, the religious sector widely used a host of functional substitutes to generate more power. The Chief Rabbinate became the central authority tightly controlled by the religious sector. So were the Rabbinic courts and the local Rabbinate and religious councils. Furthermore, departments for religious affairs in the national bodies were penetrated and dominated by members, nominees or sympathizers of the Mizrahi or Hapoel Hamizrahi parties. This network of organizations not only furnished essential religious services but also operated as a strong pressure group in assisting the religious sector, with its own independent organizations, to impose religion in public life. Aside from the reluctance of the ultra-Orthodox splinter groups to co-operate, the absence of the Conservative and Reform branches of Judaism contributed a great deal to the unity of goals and political mobilization of the religious sector and to effective concerted action by the various religious bodies.

In addition to the institutionalization of religion in the legal structure of the Yishuv and the broad organizational base of the religious minority, coalition politics was another unfailing source of power. In practice, the Yishuv was organized as a quasi-autonomous community ruled by an Elected Assembly (Assefat Hanevharim) and a National Council (Va'ad Leumi). Because of rampant factionalism, reinforced by the proportional method of elections, no one party could secure a majority of votes. The largest ruling party, which is nonclerical and socialist, had to get the co-operation of other parties in order to stay in power. The small national religious parties served as convenient partners. They bartered unqualified support to the ruling party in exchange for a greater say in religious matters. The coalition was facilitated by the dominance of the labour movement (Hapoel Hamizrahi) in the religious sector. This 'trade-off' had its beginnings in the early 1930s and this partly accounts for the fact that the political strength of the religious group usually exceeded its relative size.[26]

The other branch of Orthodoxy, the traditionalist Agudat Israel, fought against both secular and religious Zionism. Aguda was established in 1912 as a world movement. It accused the Mizrahi of complicity with the Zionist 'satan' and collusion with infidel Jews to create a sinful society not based on the Torah. At first, however, the ultra-Orthodox Jews of the Old Yishuv were persuaded to participate in the elections for the first Elected Assembly in 1920. But they soon broke away on the immediate issue of women's suffrage and on the more fundamental question of drawing up a secular constitution for the Yishuv.[27] The opposition of the traditionalists was vehement. They boycotted all the next elections (from 1925 on). They mourned the day of publication of the Yishuv constitution in 1928 and seceded from the Yishuv at once. Their request for the status of an independent religious community was denied by the administration but their community was de facto separate throughout the British mandate.

Agudat Israel gradually moderated its position toward Zionism and the Yishuv.[28] This was mostly due to its shifting constituency in Palestine. The immigration of progressive elements from Germany and Poland in the mid-1930s shattered the dependence of Aguda on the Old Yishuv. The new arrivals entered the modern economy and pushed for ideological reconciliation with the Zionist establishment.

In the 1920s Aguda founded its own labour movement (Poale Agudat Israel) whose branch in Palestine, starting in the 1930s, leaned heavily towards the Yishuv and was rewarded by funds and lands for settlement. Besides, the plight of the European Jewry and then the Holocaust convinced many of Aguda's followers that a Jewish homeland was a necessity. As Aguda drew nearer to the Zionists, it lost the support of some fundamentalist circles who withdrew into a separate militant community (N'ture Karta). On the eve of Israel's independence, Aguda co-operated with the Zionist religious parties in negotiating an agreement with the nonreligious parties about the role of religion in the new Jewish state. As a result Aguda joined the Provisional Council and Provisional Government and in the first national elections in 1949 it formed a united religious front with the other religious parties.

In spirit and substance the agreement sanctioned the pre-state religious status quo, no matter how unsatisfactory it was for all the parties concerned. More specifically, four provisions were formally stated: (a) the Sabbath and Jewish holidays to be official holidays; (b) kashrut to be kept in state kitchens; (c) religious law to continue to regulate personal status; and (d) all trends, religious and non-religious, of education to be recognized and funded by the state.[29]

The negotiated continuity in religious affairs was, however, impossible to implement in practice. New problems arose for which the agreement provided no guidance. For example, should the new government television station and the municipal subway at Haifa, both completely unforeseen eventualities, be allowed to operate on the Sabbath? More important, statehood ushered in two novelties. The enactment of the Law of Return stirred up a controversy over the definition of a Jew. The other notable development was the transformation of membership in the Jewish religious community from voluntary to compulsory. The safety valves established in the mandate period vanished, and all Jews (citizens and aliens, believers and nonbelievers) had to turn to the Rabbinic authorities in all matters of personal status. Since Israel's birth, many uncharted territories have been discovered to which the old regime could not lay claim. No wonder, then, that the religious status quo has continuously been contested, negotiated and compromised.

3 Arab–Jewish relations[30]

At the onset of Zionist colonization in 1882 the number of Arabs in Palestine is estimated to have been around half a million and that of Jews about 24,000. The Arabs had been the indigenous people in the area for centuries. Most were Moslems and all were Arab in language as well as in other cultural traits. The majority lived in an agricultural economy as semi-feudal farmers. They led a traditional way of life in small villages scattered all over the country. A sizeable minority were nomads (Bedouin). Only a fraction of the population was urban. The extended family (hamula) remained the cornerstone of Arab society throughout the period (up to 1947) although its central role declined steadily with the gradual shift from joint estates to private land-ownership and with urbanization. The country as a whole was poor, underdeveloped and badly managed. In consequence, the living conditions of the overwhelming majority of inhabitants bordered on destitution and insecurity.

The tiny Jewish minority at that time was later known as the Old Yishuv. It was by and large composed of religious Jews who resided in the four holy cities. Some worked as shopkeepers and craftsmen and most depended on charities from world Jewry. The majority were Orientals and Sephardim.

The relations between Arabs and Jews in Palestine before World War I resembled those in other parts of the Ottoman Empire. They maintained separate religious communities and had a 'live-and-let-live', friendly attitude toward each other.

The scene took a dramatic turn during the British mandate. Between 1882 and 1947 some 447,000 Jews arrived in five major waves of immigration, about 90 per cent of whom hailed from Europe (Table 9). They formed the New Yishuv. Jewish self-sufficiency in every sphere was their all-embracing goal. At the close of the mandate the Yishuv became a semi-autonomous, modern society with a separate territorial base, economic system, class structure, personal law, self-government, living language, and cultural and educational institutions. The endeavour of nation-building was so successful that Jews could live in a community of their own, almost isolated from Arabs and depending on them only partially in technical matters of land purchase, labour and farm products.

Arab society experienced tremendous transformations, and Arabs shared in the general progress. The eradication of malaria and the institution of public health measures halved the infant mortality rate (from 41.2 per cent in 1926–30 to 25.1 per cent in 1941–4). This and the continuing high birthrate and some migration doubled the population (about 600,000 in 1917 and 1,319,000 in 1947). Greater educational opportunities became available and progress was made, although in 1944 two-thirds of school-age children were not at school and three-quarters of the population were still illiterate. A transition from a virtually peasant society to a more differentiated one was initiated. The proportion of the population living in the 22 Arab towns increased to one-third, but still two-thirds resided in about 900 villages scattered all over Palestine. The majority of the rural population was employed in primitive agriculture. Around

75–80 per cent of the fellahim are estimated to lack 'a viable lot' (a parcel of land sufficient to make a living). A growing number of villagers turned into wage-earners taking odd jobs which became available in the cities. The proletarianization of a sizeable minority of villagers resulted in neither migration to the cities where life was precarious nor the urbanization of the villages.[31]

Arab society during the mandate was a four-tier society. Lowest in the class structure were the masses of poor villagers consisting of independent farmers, land tenants and migratory wage-earners. The second stratum consisted of the urban proletariat, i.e., labourers who stayed either permanently or temporarily in the cities, suffering from unstable work and life conditions and feeling restless. A middle class of professionals, clerical and managerial workers and small businessmen comprised the third stratum. And at the top were scores of aristocratic families who owned a good part of the land in the villages and the industrial and financial enterprises in the cities and vied for the leadership of the entire population.

The Arab national movement evolved early and grew rapidly. It was closely related to the emergent Arab nationalism in the Middle East. Nationalists from Palestine participated in the Arab congresses and caucuses from the outset. Since for many centuries Palestine had been administratively considered as 'southern Syria', the Arabs in Palestine thought of themselves as Syrians. Their representatives demanded the inclusion of Palestine in the promised new state of Syria before it was mandated to the French in 1920. Palestinian nationalism developed then as a resistance movement to Zionism and the Yishuv. The first official anti-Zionist association was founded in Jaffa as early as 1911. A series of Arab riots, which started to erupt in 1920, led to a progressive escalation of the strife. The Arabs' aims did not change throughout the period: cessation of Jewish immigration, a ban on land sales, an establishment of one state in Palestine under a majority rule. This uncompromising stance was espoused by the three major parties, i.e., the Palestine Arab Party (ruled by the Hussainis), the National Defence Party (ruled by the Nashashibis) and the small Independence Party (which drew on the intelligentsia). Even the Arab communists did not come up with an alternative programme.

Palestinian resistance reached its climax and its anti-climax during the Arab revolt of 1936–9. The increasing Jewish immigration from Europe after Hitler's rise to power alarmed the Palestinian community. For some time leaders co-operated in the all-Palestinian Arab Higher Committee. Their potential effectiveness was demonstrated in a well-observed general strike and a co-ordinated series of terrorist raids on the British and the Jews. However, old personal rivalries and family feuds among the leadership soon degenerated

67

into political assassinations, unleashed internal terror and terminated the short-lived unity. More important, the revolt was then crushed by the British with the assistance of the Jews.

The suppression of the Arab Revolt constituted a historical turning-point. It marked the dissolution of the Palestinian people as a major force, a quandary which lasted until the 1967 Six-Day War. It also concurrently dated the initial involvement of the Arab countries in the conflict. The exodus of the Arab leadership and intelligentsia had begun, and whatever armed forces the Palestinians had were soundly defeated. On the eve of World War II Britain announced plans to found a state with majority rule in Palestine, but by that time the Palestinians were too disintegrated to insist on implementation.

Oddly enough, the Zionist and Palestinian movements exhibited certain striking similarities. Both were separatist and exclusionist and neither took the other seriously. The Zionists, whom Amos Elon (1972: chapter 7) nicknamed 'innocents at home', were at first unaware of the numerical preponderance of the Arab population, then underestimated its resistance, and throughout failed to come to terms with it. The Palestinian Arabs were treated as a mere nuisance who stood in the way between the Jews and the colonial administration, and were not recognized as an independent force to be reckoned with.[32] Similarly the defeat of the Palestinian national movement was due not only to its failure to embark on large-scale nation-building on a par with that of the Yishuv, but also to its relative under-rating of the seriousness of Zionist intentions, the zeal of the Jewish immigrants and the ample resources at the disposal of the Yishuv. As most Israeli Jews denied Palestinian Arabs the right of peoplehood and statehood on the West Bank between the 1967 and 1973 wars, even the old asymmetry which distinguished their mutual attitudes seems to have disappeared (in the pre-state period, the Jews accepted the partition that Palestinians rejected, and in 1973 both opposed it).

Of all the three divisions, Arab–Jewish relations, while continuing to be characterized by forced co-existence, showed the greatest degree of discontinuity after Israel's birth. Whereas in 1917 Arabs made up 91 per cent of the total population and 68 per cent in 1947, their numbers dropped sharply to a record low of 14 per cent in 1949. The reversal of status from a majority to a minority was a painful shock to those Arabs who stayed behind. The severance of family and cultural ties with Arabs across the borders required a long adjustment. The near complete departure of the Arab elite (not just politicians but essential professionals such as teachers, clergymen, lawyers and doctors) and the inaccessibility of the Arab leadership of the large towns in the West Bank left the Israeli Arabs helpless, without services and lacking a sense of direction. The Arab economy immediately collapsed, and the Israeli Arabs were willy nilly brought within the Jewish economy. The military administration, the relocation of some Arabs from sensitive border regions to the interior, the expropriation of lands and their exclusion from certain institutions induced much resentment. The acceleration of the process of modernization and the continued rise in the standard of living imbued the younger generation with a frustrated nationalism.

After about two decades of strenuous efforts to adapt to their new status, the Arab minority entered another era of tribulations in 1967. The reunion with their Palestinian brethren did in the event produce tension. Israeli Arabs are citizens, whereas Palestinian Arabs are aliens. But both share the same nationality, language, religion and cultural heritage. The gap in socioeconomic conditions is too small to present a barrier. This situation poses many psychological and practical dilemmas for Israeli Arabs.

5 Current social contexts

The significance of pluralism and inequality in a given society is contingent on broader historical and social conditions. Depending on their specific nature, these contextual factors may either augment or lessen the problem of cohesion and potentiality for change of the existing group differences.

There is a variety of social contexts. Our selection for closer scrutiny includes the primary bases (initial contact, definition of membership and relative size) of the constituent groups, the degree of congruity of group goals, the unofficial attitudes and policies of the dominant group toward the subordinate groups, the effects of group interdependence, the implications of the existence of more than one pluralistic division and the repercussions of certain features of the society at large for intergroup relations. Examination of these factors assures an all-round perspective on pluralism and inequality by relating them to wider social forces.

To complete our analysis of the setting of the pluralistic structure of Israeli society, we now turn to review the current social contexts after surveying the historical background in the previous chapter. Table 2 provides an overview of our assessments of the varying favourability of the present Israeli contexts for Oriental–Ashkenazi relations, religious–nonreligious relations and Arab–Jewish relations.

1 The primary bases of major divisions

It is feasible to guardedly generalize from the literature in the field that intergroup relations which are involuntary in their historical origin, rigidly defined and based on a minority rule, are relatively more conflict prone than others.[1] By these criteria, Oriental–Ashkenazi relations are situated in mixed contexts, religious–nonreligious relations in favourable circumstances and Arab–Jewish relations in inauspicious conditions. This conclusion draws on the following observations.

Historically, Oriental-Ashkenazi relations originated with two consecutive patterns. The earlier contact took the form of 'migrant superordination' (Lieberson, 1961): namely, the Ashkenazi settlers established themselves as superordinates vis-à-vis the Oriental and Sephardic natives a long time before the creation of the state. The Ashkenazi newcomers had the advantages of numbers, skills and resources. They built a new society in which the Orientals of the Old Yishuv occupied lower positions. As Europeans, they took a paternalistic attitude toward the native Jewish population. Ashkenazi dominance was limited, though, because the New Yishuv was essentially a voluntary community in the broader colonial society. The Orientals, as subordinates, had several options: they could dissociate themselves from the Jewish community, they could appeal to the British administration in case of inequity and they were less vulnerable to intervention by the Ashkenazim in their affairs.

The early pattern was superseded by a newer one of 'migrant subordination'. The trickles of Oriental immigrants during the mandate period and their post-state overflow became subordinate in status to the established Ashkenazi group. This phenomenon is well known in the modern era: it is the fate of poor immigrants who enter the host society at the bottom. As immigrants, and in contrast to 'involuntary' minorities, the Orientals apparently had the advantage of geographical and socioeconomic mobility in the country.

Compared with the Ashkenazi immigrants and with most immigrants elsewhere, the Oriental immigrants did have some disadvantages. Although considered internationally free immigrants, many Orientals suffered from the closed options which characterize a refugee status.[2] Israel was by and large the only country to which they could go. Once arrived, they effectively had no hope of leaving. Unlike immigrants to other areas, the Orientals could neither retain the protection of their countries of origin nor enjoy the opportunity to return to them. Lacking linguistic and occupational skills, financial resources, or a formal status as refugees, they could not gain entrance to Western countries. As 'captive' residents of Israel, the Orientals were only minimally able to apply pressure by heading elsewhere or emigrating from Israel to other states.[3] Their impotence had an impact on the policies of Israeli authorities toward them.[4]

Extra burdens were the adverse conditions associated with the Oriental immigration. It came at a time of great hardship for Israel. In its first years, the newly founded state had to invest in post-war reconstruction and absorb mass immigration, shortages of public finances, food and housing notwithstanding, and despite lack of

71

experience in large-scale immigrant absorption (Shuval, 1963: 17–21). The mass influx of new arrivals presented yet another difficulty. Being limited in size and, more important, underprivileged in status, the pre-state Oriental-Sephardic community could not be of much help to the newcomers. Only a few Oriental immigrants found relatives or acquaintances upon arrival. As early as 1953 the number of immigrants from Asia and Africa who came after 1948 was already six times as large as their counterparts who had arrived before 1948.[5]

The Ashkenazi immigrants were, on the other hand, more fortunate than the Oriental immigrants. They had a wider range of choice of immigrating to and from Israel, higher skills, greater family connections and, above all, a large dominant group to which to relate.

As for the definition of group membership, of the three correlated criteria of descent, cultural background and socioeconomic status, descent is the most important determinant in placing people in one of the two ethnic groups. That is, country of origin of ancestors is the basis for classification. People born in Israel are categorized accordingly and cannot be considered to be a third group. Likewise, descendants of mixed marriages, whose number is increasing, do not constitute an independent social category, but their status is not at all clear. Usually people are readily identifiable by physical appearance, accent, surname and by many other signs. Passing off or crossing over to the other group are, however, possible, though difficult and infrequent. There was a slow and gentle shift over the years from stress on descent towards sociocultural criteria as the yardstick for status-assignment. The latter criteria, perhaps, play a crucial role in the identification of native Israelis, starting with the third generation, and of mixed offspring.

The fact that the dominant Ashkenazi group is no longer the majority is another potential strain on Oriental–Ashkenazi relations. The Orientals made up about 12 per cent of the total immigration before 1948 but 48 per cent between 1948 and 1975 (see Table 9). As a result, their weight in the Jewish population soared from a minority of 23 per cent in 1947, to parity in 1963 and to a majority of 55 per cent in 1975 (Table 8). According to one projection, they will reach a high majority of 75 per cent in 1985, when their birthrate is expected to drop to that of the Ashkenazim (Patai, 1971c). Given the immigration from the Soviet Union and possibly from the West, this predicted proportion will probably prove to be incorrect. It is, nevertheless, safe to say that the Orientals will remain the absolute majority for the foreseeable future. The loss of majority status in such a brief time was bound to make the Ashkenazim feel swamped by the Orientals.[6] The pre-existing common cultural ties (religion and nationality) between the incoming Orientals and the established Ashkenazim dulled the sting of the ominous sense of threat, but the basic situation of minority rule remains potentially problematic.[7]

Similarly the religious–nonreligious division is situated within a mixture of broader conditions. As to historical origin, it came about as a result of a secularization that differentiated between persons of the same community and even members of the same family. The contact between religious and nonreligious groups is, therefore, by no means an encounter between strangers but that between people who have been related to each other for generations.

Who is a religious Jew in Israel? There is much confusion about this question. Deshen (forthcoming), for instance, classifies Israeli Jews into four major religious types: Orthodox (Aguda-type), neo-Orthodox (Mizrahi-type), national (secular) and Oriental (traditional, secularizing). Others (e.g., Zuckerman-Bareli, 1975) apply a three-fold typology: religious, traditional and nonreligious. Although their classifications are useful for ethnographic and attitudinal studies, a division into religious and nonreligious Jews is much more appropriate for the analysis of the religious pluralistic structure. The major reason for this lies in the monopolistic hegemony of Orthodoxy on Israeli Judaism. Thus religious Jews, in the Israeli context, are Orthodox Jews; namely, Jews who accept the authority of the halakha as a divine law and do their best to observe it in their daily life. This definition of who is a religious Jew in Israel turns all nonreligious Jews into a residual category of atheists, secularists, traditionalists, Conservative or Reform Jews, and others who reject the authority of the halakha. The selective observance of religion by many nonreligious Jews does not make them Orthodox, because their orientation to the observed religious traditions remains secular (Don-Yihye, 1975b: 9).

The obvious polarizing tendency inherent in the dominant dichotomy between Orthodox and non-Orthodox Jews in Israel is, however, counterbalanced by the existence of two additional secondary criteria for religiousness. A criterion more inclusive than the test of Orthodoxy is lifestyle, which is under the influence of voluntary religion. A more restrictive standard is membership in 'the religious camp', which is operationally defined as belonging to or voting for the religious parties. The relative size of the religious group varies remarkably with each criterion. As a rough estimate, people who maintain a non-secular lifestyle constitute 75 per cent of the Jewish population, people who observe Orthodox practices 30 per cent, and people who are organizationally or politically affiliated with the religious sector only 15 per cent. These multiple yardsticks of religiousness indicate ambiguity and fluidity in the otherwise rigidly defined Orthodox group. Put differently, the partial overlap between the Orthodox group and its related smaller and larger groups contributes to flexibility in religious–nonreligious relations.

A further moderating factor is the variable nature of the Orthodox status. Orthodox Jews 'volunteer' their status by making themselves distinctive in appearance (e.g., wearing a skullcap) or by observing certain religious practices. But if they so wish, they can pass off as nonreligious Jews or defect to the nonreligious majority. Religious identity is, therefore, both fluid and not invidious; the exact opposite – a racial identity – is a system where 'descent rule' prevails (Harris, 1964: 37, 56, 59).

The minority position of religious Jews also has mixed effects. On the one hand, a minority status squares well with a nondominant status. On the other hand, religious Jews are not content with a nondominant minority status and aspire to dominance. But in political democracies, such as Israel, they do not have a chance to establish a minority rule. Religious Jews can, however, manoeuvre the democratic rules of the game to acquire disproportional power, but then their influence would appear illegitimate to many nonreligious Jews.

The Arab–Jewish division, in comparison, had its foundation in worse circumstances than the two Jewish divisions. In the pre-state period, Arab–Jewish contact was, strictly speaking, a relation between colonized peoples under a foreign rule. In practice, despite the fact the Jews were not classic colonizers, their encounters with the Arabs are reminiscent of European colonization elsewhere insofar as the Jewish settlers felt superiority and paternalism vis-à-vis the indigenous Palestinian majority, and the latter feared and resisted the Zionist 'invasion'. More important, the division between the Arab minority and Jewish majority came into existence after Israel's independence as a result of conquest – a very unfortunate start. Subsequently the victorious Jewish majority could impose restrictions on the physical and social mobility of the new Arab minority.

As for the definition of group membership, as indicated in chapter 3, the Arab–Jewish division is at present so rigid as to require a stronger term than the common notion of ethnicity. If we adopt the three minimal criteria of caste – i.e., ascriptive membership by birth, endogamy and status hierarchy – we may speak of Arabs and Jews as ethnic quasi-castes. This term parallels the term 'racial castes' used by Warner (1936) and Berreman (1960) for blacks and whites in the United States and by van den Berghe (1967a: 52–6) for Whites, Africans, Coloureds and Asians in South Africa. Ethnic quasi-caste implies, however, much less rigidity than racial castes, so that the simple equation of the status of Arabs in Israel as equal to the

74

status of blacks in the United States and non-Whites in South Africa is simply fallacious.[8]

The three minimal criteria of caste, however, do apply to Israeli Arabs and Jews to a large extent. As for ascriptive membership by birth, Arabs are assigned to a minority status when they are born. Membership is legally sanctioned. According to the latest (1970) legal definition, 'a Jew is he who was born to a Jewish mother or converted (to Judaism), but does not belong (at present) to another religion'.[9] The law enforces identity between religion and nationality, but since both law and custom recognize the possibility of conversion to Jewish religion–nationality, Arabs may become Jews.[10] For this reason it is not justified to speak of fully-fledged castes but rather quasi-castes. Conversions are rare, however, in practice. In spite of their physical and cultural resemblance to Oriental Jews, the Arabs are clearly identifiable by a special combination of appearance, accent, name and address and can rarely pass as Jews. Thus mobility between the groups is nil.

Endogamy holds even better than ascriptive membership. Because of the legal separation between the religious communities, Jews and Arabs (or Gentiles) may not marry, and marriage within the group is the rule. Intermarriage is tabooed and those who violate it are either marginal to the society or become so later (E. Cohen, 1969a).

Status-hierarchy is similarly well established. There is virtually no position in society in which Arabs exercise authority over Jews. The same role when occupied by a Jew carries much more prestige and privileges than when it is held by an Arab. In terms of education, occupation and income, Arabs have a much lower status than Jews.

The religion–nationality quasi-caste line between Israeli Arabs and Jews is quite solid and immutable. The fact that this line also rigidly divides the loyal Druzes[11] from the Jews shows that the gulf between Israeli Arabs and Jews is more fundamental than the changeable status of an enemy-affiliated minority that the Arabs are today. This yawning chasm is primarily religious and national, but it is linguistic, cultural and socioeconomic as well. Moreover, it has the invidious peculiarity of a quasi-caste structure.

Even the compatibility between the numerical minority and non-dominant status of the Arabs in Israel does not create the reconciliatory atmosphere one might expect. The Arabs have not become resigned to losing their majority status following the birth of Israel, and they have not entirely abandoned their hope of regaining it. Arabs and Jews are keenly aware of the fact that the Arabs are a nondominant minority in Israel but a dominant majority in the region. The repeated open warfare, with gains claimed by both sides, is a live reminder that the outcome is yet to be decided.

2 The congruity of group goals

Agreement on the collective goals of the ethnic groups is essential for harmonious relations between them. It is clear that fewer tensions exist when both minority and majority groups seek assimilation or separation than when their goals clash. Collective goals may be ascertained from public statements or overall ideologies expressed by spokesmen for each group. Publicly stated goals are important even if contradicted by unofficial pronouncements, 'hidden intentions' or incompatible policies, which will be taken up in section 3 (Undercurrents).

Three inter-related ideologies dominate in Israeli society: i.e., nationalism (Zionism), socialism and modernization, and all militate against the Oriental–Ashkenazi division. Following other European nationalist movements, Zionism aims at national unity and cultural homogeneity. For a long time the national slogan spoke of the creation of 'one people, one language, one culture'. The point of departure of Jewish nationalism is negation of the Diaspora. The dispersal of Jews and their adaptation to their countries of residence is conceived as the source of disunity and diversity. The return to the homeland is not just a political act but one which should also be accompanied by a cultural renaissance and nation-building. Negation of the Diaspora is synonymous with abolition of ethnicity, so that the ingathering of the exiles is presumed to be followed by the merging of the exiles. While Jewish ethnic pluralism is anathema to the Zionist ideology, it recognizes the objective problems of immigrant absorption associated with the return to Israel. Such problems are not ethnic, however, because they are inherent in the conditions of all immigrants and are transitional.[12]

While the socialist ideology cannot claim to have the substantial acceptance that Zionism has,[13] its Israeli watered-down version is fairly dominant. This is still the official ideology of the labour movement which has been in power since the 1920s.[14] The part of the socialist ideology relevant to Oriental–Ashkenazi relations amounts to class reductionism of the ethnic problem. As Mapam, the socialist Zionist political party of Israel, put it in one of its resolutions: 'There exists in Israel discrimination against Orientals, discrimination which is class based, but ethnic in form' (Mapam, 1963: 39). In other words, the overlap between class and ethnicity is deceptive, since ethnicity is an epiphenomenon. This class formulation, though in a less extreme form, is quite common. The Hebrew term for the Oriental–Ashkenazi division is 'pa'ar adati' ('ethnic gap'), which strongly implies socioeconomic differences.

Modernization is also a widely accepted ideology. Generally speaking, Israel, like other new nations, strives for development and progress. Ethnicity is frowned upon as a remnant of the past that hampers advancement. Modernization breaks old ethnic ties, removes obsolete divisive traditions and provides training for the underdeveloped sections of the population. It facilitates thereby their upward mobility and creates new loyalties which transcend ethnic particularism. The commitment of Israel to modernization is very firm. From this perspective the ethnic problem appears to be temporary and certain to vanish as soon as all parts of the population reach the same level of modernization.

The three ideologies converge at many points and sustain each other. In its broader interpretation, Zionism embraces all of them. The Zionist ideal, as expounded and implemented by the dominant left-of-centre political bloc in Israel, specifies a Jewish, socialist and modern state. All the ideologies share in common the withholding of legitimacy from ethnic pluralism and the denial of the existence of an ethnic problem. The problem is reduced to immigrant absorption, the socioeconomic gap or uneven modernization. This view is adhered to by all political parties, as an examination of their programmes for the national elections would demonstrate. Or, as the Israeli government indicates in its basic principles (1970: 27):

> The government will work systematically for the merging of all communities [Orientals and Ashkenazim], veterans and newcomers. All communities will be assured of equal opportunities for full integration in Israel's economy and society, in education, culture and social life, and steps will be taken to remove the economic gaps between communities.

The triple ideology which negates ethnicity has been so dominant over the last fifty years that one can look in vain for serious deviations from it among the Orientals. My survey of pronouncements by Oriental spokesmen, ethnic publications and programmes of ethnic election lists shows a broad consensus with the established ideologies. The stated target is definitely ethnic integration, and separatism is out of the question. The emphasis is on uniculturalism with minor subcultural pluralism.[15] The central problem is defined in terms of inequality in level of education, standard of living and distribution of power. The dispute is over tactics or short-term goals; i.e., whether to take independent ethnic action or to work within the establishment to achieve the agreed aim of ethnic integration. Even the two grass-root ethnic uprisings, the Wadi-Salib riots of 1959 and the Black Panthers of the 1970s, were integrationist.

Field studies document similar tendencies. In my state-wide survey of 121 Moroccan, Iraqi and Romanian leaders in 1970–1, 73 per cent of the Oriental leaders defined the aim of Oriental–Ashkenazi relations as equality and assimilation and only 23 per cent wanted equality with preservation of cultural differences. The comparable figures for the Ashkenazi leaders in the sample were 85 and 15 per cent respectively. In my more recent state-wide study of the leadership corps of the Black Panthers in summer 1975, the results were nearly identical: 72 per cent of the thirty-nine Oriental activists surveyed favoured equality and assimilation as a long-term objective and only 28 per cent endorsed the continuation of certain ethnic customs. About 90 per cent of the Panthers were in favour of complete ethnic integration of schools, neighbourhoods and marriages (though only 64 per cent supported the merging of religious institutions).

The commitment of the elite to ethnic equality and assimilation does not necessarily mean the rejection of minor subcultural variations such as folklore and even social and cultural relations within the ethnic group. On the contrary, the majority of people in the 1970s recognize the utility of retaining these harmless patterns. For instance, in a survey of the adult population in 1970, between half to three-quarters of both Orientals and Ashkenazim of different educational background were in favour of retention of special ethnic traditions and the promotion of social and cultural ties within the ethnic group (Katz and Gurevitch, 1973: 332).

The collective goals, as they are stated in the dominant ideologies of both Ashkenazi and Oriental elites and in the attitudes of the general public, are congruent. Minimization of ethnic pluralism is advocated. Integration is the final objective. The elimination of barriers to integration, such as disparity in levels of social class or modernization, is recommended as a solution. This fundamental consensus is conducive to the weakening of ethnic pluralism and hence to harmonious relations between Orientals and Ashkenazim.

The great correspondence in group goals that exists in Oriental–Ashkenazi relations is less in the other cases of intergroup relations. In fact, a conflict of collective objectives is at the very heart of the religious–nonreligious division. While there is a virtually full agreement that Israel must be 'Jewish', there is considerable disagreement about what is meant by 'Jewishness'. Rosenak (1971a) spells out five public attitudes regarding state and religion in Israel:

(a) *Jews who deny Israel's Jewish significance.* Some ultra-Orthodox Jews, especially Jerusalem's N'ture Karta sect and the right wing of Agudat Israel, hold the anti-Zionist idea that Israel is a manifestation of false Messianism. They see themselves as a Jewish community within a non-Jewish state.

(b) *Jews who consider the state a development of Divine Providence.* The Orthodox Jews who belong to the Mizrahi and the left wing of

78

Agudat Israel believe that Israel is the dawn of the redemption. Meanwhile they prefer to strengthen the Jewish character of the state by religious legislation.

(c) *Jews who seek new religious norms within a Jewish state.* The semi-observant Jews, including members of Conservative and Reform congregations, followers of Martin Buber and some Oriental Jews, oppose both traditional Orthodoxy and secular nationalism. They consider Israel a new phase in Judaism and search for a novel religious lifestyle.

(d) *Jews who view Judaism as a secular national culture.* The majority of nonreligious Jews subscribe to secular Zionism, according to which Israel is the carrier of the revived Jewish culture (Hebrew language, Hebrew literature, the Bible, etc.).

(e) *Jews who reject Judaism.* Some staunch non-Zionist secularists, including intellectuals, Canaanites and sabras who feel indifferent to religion, deny the spirit of Judaism even in its Zionist interpretation. They perceive Israel as the cradle of an indigenous ('Semitic' or 'Hebrew') culture to be developed by all natives of all persuasions.

Of the five ideologies, only two are dominant. The extreme two (the ultra-Orthodox anti-Zionist and the secularist non-Zionist) are subscribed to by a tiny fraction of the population. The third perspective, of the semi-observant Jews who look for a new religious style, is still in a formative stage and without an organizational base. The second stance is that of religious Zionism – the Mizrahi and that part of Aguda which accepts the Jewish state. The fourth outlook is that of secular Zionism of both left and right. More concretely, Mafdal (the National Religious Party) is the religious establishment speaking on behalf of most of the religious minority and the Israel Labour Party is the nonreligious establishment representing most of the nonreligious majority. Indeed, although both parties are accused of selling out and misrepresenting the interests of their constituents on religious issues, their objects as stated in official resolutions do reflect their general ambitions better than does their actual political activity.[16]

The resolutions of the 1973 convention of the National Religious Party affirmed the credo and stance on various religious issues. The encompassing principle was 'to prevent the separation of religion and state – a danger to the nation'. The religious status quo was claimed as an achievement by the religious public and as a basis for co-operation between the religious and nonreligious in order to forestall a *Kulturkampf*. The formulae for a continued collaboration were specified as follows:

(1) To apply the Torah law (halakha) to all state institutions.
(2) To assure equality of right and opportunity to religious Jews in employment and all economic branches.
(3) To guarantee an independent and superior status to the Chief Rabbinate Council as the highest halakhic authority in the state.
(4) To secure the independence and exclusive sovereignty of the Rabbinic courts in personal affairs and to grant them legal jurisdiction in other matters when all concerned parties voluntarily request them to adjudicate.
(5) To amend the Law of Return, explicitly specifying that 'a Jew is defined according to the halakha'.
(6) To safeguard the legal standing of religious education at all levels.

In addition, it was resolved to strive for further religious legislation, including a state-wide Sabbath law, a law against fraudulence in kashrut, amendment of the law concerning autopsies to make it more restrictive, and one banning the operations of Christian missionaries.

This statement of purpose by the major religious party implies long-term and immediate targets. The ultimate end is theocracy, or as it is put in the time-honoured slogan of the Mizrahi – 'Eretz Israel for the people of Israel according to the Torah of Israel.' The short-term goal is religious legislation and other concessions. It is hoped that legal provisions will add up ultimately to a halakha state and ensure 'religious freedom' (i.e., equal opportunity for a religious minority in a predominantly secular society).

The position taken by the ruling party (Mapai and later the Israel Labour Party) is of course different. In its 1971 convention the party refrained from adopting a stand, leaving the matter to its central committee. But the party platforms since 1949 (Aloni, 1970: 144–6) have reiterated the key points. The relevant plank in the platform of the Alignment to the 8th Knesset in 1973 reads as follows:

(1) National integration in a period of the ingathering of the exiles and the need to preserve normal public life and to respect all religions require that Israel be a constitutional state which guarantees freedom of conscience and religion, and religious tolerance, catering for the religious needs of the religious public and the prevention of religious and anti-religious coercion.
(2) The Alignment will act to ensure complete freedom to all religions, their denominations and ethnic groups.

80

(3) The religious institutions should discharge their legal authority, should apply no pressure to intervene in the way of life, and should not misuse their power to further nonreligious aims.

(4) The Alignment will continue to act – even through legislation if necessary – to resolve problems of personal status which cause hardships and suffering to Jewish women and men in Israel, prevent them from or make it difficult for them to establish families in Israel, and create a stumbling-block for the Aliyah (for people with mixed marriages).

(5) The Alignment considers essential the easing and speeding up of the conversion procedures which may save candidates – and especially seekers of conversion among immigrants – unnecessary hardships.

(6) The military drafting of yeshiva students will be examined. There will be also considered the possibility of implementing the National Service Act 1953, which requires that women exempted from the army on grounds of conscience or religion should perform civilian national service.

The aim of the nonreligious public, as presented by the non-religious dominant party, is a state which is Jewish in its Hebrew language, cultural heritage and ties with world Jewry, yet open to Western influences and also religious to the minimum extent necessary to avoid a *Kulturkampf*. The non-Orthodox majority confers on religious bodies an authority over personal status in order not to split the nation into two separate camps, while endeavouring to confine their sovereignty.

The ideological disagreement between the religious and non-religious sectors regarding the desired cultural identity of Israel is well documented in opinion polls. To illustrate from a typical one conducted on eleventh-grade pupils in the Tel-Aviv area in 1972, a near polarization of opinions was found regarding Judaism and the type of culture wished for Israel. Whereas 87 per cent of the religious pupils believed that Judaism could never be outmoded and was not in conflict with modern times, only 32 per cent of the nonreligious pupils concurred with this view and a majority of them thought Judaism to be either in need of renewal or outmoded. Furthermore (Zuckerman-Bareli, 1975: 61–2):

> Regarding the question as to which culture should be developed in Israel, the findings revealed that the more religious the subject, the greater his support of a 'national culture' which is not based on foreign influences. There seems to be a conflict of opinion and an emergence of polarization between the religious group on the one hand, and the non-religious and traditional groups, on the other. The absolute majority of religious

respondents (67%) favors a national culture with a minimum of influence by foreign cultures, while a minority (33%) wants a culture open to foreign influences. Among the non-religious group the situation is reversed. Eighteen percent of non-religious youth favors a national culture with a minimum of influence by foreign cultures and 82% wants a culture open to foreign influences.

This divergence in outlook is, however, counterbalanced by the well-documented fact that there is generally a greater support for religion in public life than in individual practice. In Antonovsky's (1963) survey of the Jewish population, 53 per cent opposed and 43 per cent favoured the idea that public life be conducted in accord with Jewish religious tradition (4 per cent did not reply), compared with 30 per cent who defined themselves as religious, 46 per cent somewhat observant and 24 per cent entirely secular. To put it differently, 22 per cent of the population were consistently clerical, 6 per cent were personally religious but did not wish to impose religion in community life, 19 per cent were clerical although themselves nonreligious, and 47 per cent were uniformly anti-clerical (4 per cent were not classified). It is evident that the endorsement given by the religious minority to the religious goals expressed by the major religious party is greater than the support of the non-religious majority for the goals of compromise projected by the major nonreligious party. This picture has not changed by the early 1970s. In a Harris poll in 1971, 47 per cent of the Israeli respondents rejected the idea of separation of religion and state (following the American model) and 46 per cent were in favour (8 per cent were uncertain), as contrasted with 13 per cent who identified themselves as religious, 47 per cent somewhat observant (masorti), and 49 per cent nonreligious (quoted by Eyal, 1971b: 17).[17] The same tendencies exist among the young generation. In a nation-wide survey of high school pupils in 1964–5, 25 per cent of them considered themselves to be religious, but 55 per cent felt it desirable for the Jewish religion to play an important part in the public domain (Herman, 1970: Tables 84 and 133). In another survey in the same year, overwhelming support was found for the religious goals among a representative sample of the pupils in the state religious high schools (Zuckerman-Bareli, 1970).

In brief, although there are extremists and moderates on both sides, running the whole gamut of aims from a theorcratic state to a nonsectarian one, the modal objective of the religious minority is a religious state in the long run and religious legislation in the short run, whereas that of the nonreligious majority is a secular state in the future and restrained religious influence for the time being. The irreconcilability of the final goals is enormous but there is only a moderate incompatibility of short-term targets.

Any rapprochement in the collective goals of Arabs and Jews is also lacking. Up to the establishment of the state, both national movements sought complete separation. The idea of an integrated or binational state, espoused by some intellectual and leftist circles, never got off the ground. The Zionist settlers wanted to found a state in part of Palestine, whereas the Arabs considered them to be foreign colonizers and insisted on possessing the entire territory. This is a case of incongruity of goals in its extremist form, leading to polarization and antagonism.

Although the fundamental contradiction inherent in forced coexistence continued in the post-state period, both sides had to reconsider their positions. The view of the Jewish dominant majority, as proclaimed in 'the basic principles of the government', is that 'the policy of the Government of Israel will aim towards the complete integration of the minorities in Israel into all spheres of life in the State, while respecting their religious and cultural individuality' (Israel Government, 1970: 35).

The major goal underlying the policy of the Jewish authorities towards the Arabs in Israel can be, however, more fully stated and better understood only in reference to three factors. One is national security. The Arabs are regarded as potential fifth-columnists, and the immediate task of any measure taken concerning them is to curb this menace. A second factor is the Jewish identity of the state. Any policy towards the non-Jewish minorities aims, therefore, at assuring a Jewish character and a Jewish majority for Israel. And the third factor is democratic pluralism. As a democracy, Israel grants civil liberties to its residents and respects the right to separate identity of recognizable pluralistic groups. Such a policy applies to the Arabs in Israel.

Officially it is believed that the three principles of national security, a Jewish state and democratic pluralism are compatible. Thus restrictions on national security and structural constraints on the Jewish state do not necessarily encroach on the Arabs' fundamental rights to full citizenship and separate identity. The general policy is to avoid cases of inconsistency between these considerations, but when contradictions do occur, unbiased pragmatic compromises are supposed to be worked out (e.g., the Arabs' exemption from the basic civil duty of military service is a way out of the apparent incongruity between the demands of national security and wholesale democracy).

To put it bluntly, the goal is to make the Arabs in Israel loyal citizens, resigned to their fate as a minority in a Jewish state, and acquiring a new consciousness and a new identity as Israeli Arabs.

More elaborately, the three official policies – each stated both positively and negatively – are as follows:

(1) *Loyal citizens.* To make the Arabs loyal, law-abiding citizens; to prevent them from becoming a security and political threat to the state (by turning to espionage, terrorism, guerrilla warfare, riots, irredentism, etc.).

(2) *Minority members.* To enable the Arabs to preserve and to encourage them to accept fully their status as an ethnic or cultural minority; to prevent them from jeopardizing the Jewish mould and majority of the state (by assimilating with or outnumbering the Jews, evolving into a national minority or by exercising pressure, to make Israel a bicultural or a binational state).

(3) *Israeli Arabs.* To recast the Arabs as a new minority espousing a fresh 'Israeli Arab' consciousness and identity; to dissociate them from the Palestinian people to whom they belong historically and to discourage Pan-Arab or Palestinian nationalism among them.

There is probably a near consensus on these policies among all the Jewish parties – left and right, in and out of the coalition government.

The declared aims of the Jewish-Zionist establishment vis-à-vis the Arab minority are, nevertheless, shared with less enthusiasm by the Jewish public. It seems that exclusion of the Arab minority, the historical sequel of the Zionist mission of establishing an exclusive Jewish state, is still the first choice. Peres (1971: 1039), for instance, reports that 91 to 93 per cent of the respondents in a sample of Tel-Aviv residents in 1967–8 felt that it would be better if there were fewer Arabs in Israel. Some Jewish nationalists openly advocate a policy of population transfer (the emigration of Arabs from Israel in exchange for the immigration of Jews from Arab countries to Israel) (Kokhavi, 1968) or a policy of giving incentives to any Arab who voluntarily opts out of Israel (Kahane, 1973: 49–53).

Similarly, the Arab minority's aspirations are not uniform or clear. Conflicting views prevail among them and it is doubtful whether they accept the above operative policies toward them. Some Israeli Arabs see their future as part of the state of Israel, aspire to attain a status of a recognized national minority, to take part in national policy-making and especially to have a say in decision-making affecting their own affairs, and to achieve full equality in the level of modernization and distribution of resources. The Arab accommodating leaders, among whom are non-Communist Knesset members, Histadrut functionaries, heads of local authorities, public officials and selected intellectuals, would probably concur. Among these are a few who advocate greater social integration, but stop short of assimilation. For instance, Bastuni (1973) has been the most outspoken Arab leader for integration, demanding complete desegregation of the schools and compulsory military service for Arabs;[18] Zubi appeals to the Arabs to adopt 'Israeli Arab consciousness' (see excerpts in Landau, 1969: 230–6); members of the Arab circle in the Israel Labour Party ('the Ideological Circle for Change and Coexistence') believe that Arabs can identify fully with Israel and that Arab–Jewish peaceful coexistence is possible; and Druze spokesmen are known to be the most pressing for greater incorporation into the Israeli mainstream.

Other Arabs in Israel, on the other hand, are not at all content with this goal of Arab–Jewish peaceful coexistence. They reject the Jewish-Zionist shape of the state, project a future of a Palestinian national minority in Israel, or look for new political and territorial arrangements in the region. The most articulate among them are some dissenting Arab intellectuals, professionals and university students. To illustrate, the outlawed Al-Ard group stated in 1964 that 'the Arabs in Israel are part of the Palestinian Arabs, who are an integral part of the whole Arab nation'. It called upon Israel to recognize the Arab national movement and to co-operate in implementing the 1947 partition plan for Palestine.[19]

Opinion polls taken in the last decade uncover the deep disagreement prevailing in the Arab community regarding its desired status in Israel. In a survey of Arab high school pupils conducted by Peres, about half (53 per cent) of them said shortly after the 1967 War that the political future of the Israeli Arabs should be as 'a separate but equal people within the state of Israel', as compared with 36 per cent of them who would prefer a separate state of their own or an Arab state in the undivided territory of Palestine (1971: Table 23). And in a more recent survey of the general Arab population in northern Israel taken a year after the 1973 War, Tessler reports that nearly half (48 per cent) thought that 'Israel should become a secular state where Jews and Arabs would have equal status' (1975a: Table 7).

To sum up, the reciprocity in goals between the Orientals and the Ashkenazim on the official ideological level contributes to their solidarity and mutual acceptance. The incongruity of the objectives professed by religious and nonreligious Jews tend to induce conflict between them. Polarization of aims strains Arab–Jewish relations. The contrasts in the ultimate ends are the sharpest. While the Orientals are an assimilating majority who want full equality within the existing institutional frameworks, both religious and Israeli Arabs are nonassimilating minorities who wish to reach a dominant status and to impose their radically alternative ideals of a good society on the entire population.

3 Undercurrents

By 'undercurrents', we refer to unofficial policies or widespread attitudes which shape the position of the dominant group vis-à-vis the subordinate groups. So our attention shifts now from the formal to the informal level.

The absorption–modernization model capitalizes on the positive contributions of the official ideologies of Zionism, socialism and modernization to the Oriental–Ashkenazi relations. It emphasizes the favourable atmosphere prevailing in Israeli society for the absorption of immigrants, i.e., equality, brotherhood, assimilation. While these factors are certainly important, at the same time there is some evidence for the presence of countervailing forces. The failure of the absorption–modernization model to recognize and incorporate other 'under-currents' reduces its validity.

Putting the lofty ideals of Jewish brotherhood and full equality aside, the climate in which the Oriental immigrants were received was far from cordial and enthusiastic. The predominantly Ashkenazi society was virtually unprepared for the 'unfamiliar', 'forgotten' or 'destitute' Orientals who suddenly flocked into the new state. In the thinking of the Ashkenazim, the Orientals belonged to a lesser order than their Ashkenazi brethren. Zionism, in neglecting the Oriental communities, sustained this fissure in Jewish identity, and so did the Yishuv's lack of effort to incorporate the Orientals into the building of the new society. The Orientals were also perceived as backward and, since they came mostly from Arab countries, were associated with the 'primitive Arabs' of Palestine. On the other hand, despite their resemblance in certain sociocultural respects to Arabs and despite the deprecatory Ashkenazi attitude towards them, the Orientals were recognized basically as Jews. As such, they were entitled to repatriation on the basis of the Law of Return and, upon arrival, to inclusion in the upper Jewish quasi-caste, whereas native Palestinian refugees were refused entry as non-Jews.

The Orientals were not Israel's first choice, but there was no other alternative than to accept them. The Ashkenazi immigrants came only in small numbers because of the depletion of the reservoir in Europe following the extermination of six million Jews and the ban on immigration from behind the 'iron curtain'. Further, there was an unwillingness of Jews from the Western world to migrate in spite of the desires of the Israeli Ashkenazim. At the same time the position of the Oriental Jews in Arab countries deteriorated with the intensification of the Arab–Jewish conflict in Palestine, and became untenable after the creation of the state. Israel could not avoid facing direct responsibility for the predicament of the Oriental Jews and indeed feared a 'second Holocaust'.[20] The country was not only officially committed to an open-door Jewish immigration policy, but it needed many immigrants to populate towns deserted by Arabs, to settle the land, to increase the armed forces, to expand the economy, and so forth, and could not afford losing potential manpower.

In such circumstances it is understandable that Oriental immigration should have been accepted, but not pursued with the same degree of zeal as Ashkenazi immigration. Quotas were imposed on newcomers from Morocco supposedly because of health deficiencies – which apparently existed to no lesser degree among the Ashkenazi survivors of the concentration camps who came at the same time. More serious were the anxieties about the galloping proportion of Orientals and the possible downgrading of Israel's high cultural quality that dominated the public scene in the early years of the state (Eliachar, 1948; 1950) and for years later (Tevet, 1966).

Many statements in the media and by public figures can be quoted to document these fears. Some are cited below as illustration. A journalist in an article entitled 'The truth about the human material', published in a respectable Hebrew daily, reported the following about the immigration of Moroccans to Israel in 1948–9 (Gelblum, 1949, quoted by Patai, 1970: 294–6):

A serious and threatening question is posed by the immigration from North Africa. This is the immigration of a race the like of which we have not yet known in this country . . .
    Here is a people whose primitiveness reaches the highest peak. Their educational level borders on absolute ignorance. Still more serious is their inability to absorb anything intellectual...
    But above all these there is a basic fact, no less serious, namely, the lack of all the prerequisites for adjustment to the life of the country, and first of all – *chronic laziness and hatred of work* . . .
    . . . Has it been considered what will happen to this country if this will be its population? And to them will be added one day the immigration of the Jews from the Arab countries! What will be the face of the State of Israel and its level with such a population?
    . . . They will 'absorb' us and not we them. The special tragedy of this absorption is . . . that there is no hope even with regard to their children; to raise their general level out of the depths of their ethnic existence – this is a matter of generations!

We do not know how widespread these views were among the general public. The article stirred public opinion and was instrumental in clearing the way for the decision to restrict Moroccan immigration.

87

In a rejoinder, one well-meaning Ashkenazi apologist for the Orientals wrote (K. Shabtai, 1950, quoted by Patai, 1970: 297):

> This is exactly the 'race' we need. We suffer from an overdose of intelligence, of brain-workers and of brain-work . . . We need, like air to breathe, sizeable 'injections' of naturalness, simplicity, ignorance, coarseness. These simpletons, these childish Jews, with their simple-mindedness and their natural intelligence . . . are a life-elixir against our over-intellectual worrisomeness . . .

Ben-Gurion is quoted as saying in the mid-sixties:[21]

> Those from Morocco had no education. Their customs are those of Arabs. They love their wives, but beat them . . . Maybe in the third generation something will appear from the Oriental Jew that is a little different. But I don't see it yet. The Moroccan Jew took a lot from the Moroccan Arabs. The culture of Morocco I would not like to have here. And I don't see what contribution present Persians have to make. (Moskin, 1965)

> We do not want Israelis to become Arabs. We are in duty bound to fight against the spirit of the Levant, which corrupts individuals and societies, and preserve the authentic Jewish values as they crystallized in the Diaspora. (Rouleau, 1966. Both quoted by Rejwan, 1967)

Eban wrote as late as 1969 (76):

> One of the great apprehensions which afflict us when we contemplate our cultural scene is the danger lest the predominance of immigrants of Oriental origin force Israel to equalize its cultural level with that of the neighbouring world. So far from regarding our immigrants from Oriental countries as a bridge toward our integration with the Arabic-speaking world, our object should be to infuse them with an Occidental spirit, rather than to allow them to drag us into an unnatural Orientalism.

Israeli spokesmen, when abroad, not infrequently hinted at these apprehensions in their appeal to Western Jewry to immigrate to Israel in order to balance the ethnic mix. For example, addressing leaders of the Zionist Federation of Great Britain in 1964, Golda Meir, then Foreign Minister, had the following to say (quoted by Rejwan, 1964: 17):

> We in Israel need immigrants from countries with a high standard, because the question of our future social structure is worrying us. We have immigrants from Morocco, Libya, Iran,

Egypt and other countries with a 16th century level. Shall we be able to elevate these immigrants to a suitable level of civilization? If the present state of affairs continues, there will be a dangerous clash between the Ashkenazim who will constitute an elite, and the Oriental communities of Israel. This is the most tragic thing that can befall us. We need greater equilibrium and immigrants from countries with a high level.

To be sure, counterstatements which profess beliefs in Jewish brotherhood and equality might also be quoted. It would be pointless to deny the existence of the official favourable ideologies which were discussed previously. My point is, rather, that along with the benign ideological mainstream there have been quite different undercurrents which were opposed to Oriental immigration and to their absorption.

The absorption–modernization model not only ignores these discordant undercurrents but also overlooks inequities in immigrant absorption concurrent with them. Eisenstadt does not use the term 'discrimination' and Bar-Yosef refers to the unduly frequent complaints of discrimination by Oriental immigrants as 'a myth of discrimination' (Eyal, 1971a). This stance corresponds essentially with the official view as stated in the final report of the Public Inquiry Commission set up to investigate the Wadi-Salib riots in 1959.[22]

While I am not prepared to argue that there was deliberate discrimination, I would like to point to other forms of differential treatment which contributed to the unfavourable undercurrents. These were institutional discrimination in standards of immigrant absorption and discriminatory practices in their application.

The official policy of the absorption agencies in the 1950s was to provide identical necessary arrangements for adjustment. But these seemingly universally applied practices turn out, upon close examination, to be based on a double standard. To illustrate, a common policy was to allocate a two-bedroom apartment to a typical Ashkenazi immigrant family of four and to a typical Oriental immigrant family of eight. This should not be surprising, since social institutions conformed with Ashkenazi standards and were geared to the needs of, and controlled by, Ashkenazim. Eisenstadt, on the other hand, explains (1967a: 197):

> For a relatively long period basic absorption policies which
> were undertaken within these frameworks were guided by
> 'homogeneous' approaches, rooted in basic official ideology.
> The strong tradition of rebellion against the Diaspora prevented
> full awareness of different cultural and social backgrounds
> and explains the initial tendency to treat all immigrants as a
> uniform whole.

What Eisenstadt calls 'homogeneous' or 'uniform' policies are in fact practices of institutional discrimination. One 'contradiction' in absorption policies, which Eisenstadt indicates, is that immigrants were given services and guidance at the initial stage but were then left on their own. There was, in fact, consistency here rather than contradiction. This policy was tailored to the needs of more Westernized Ashkenazi immigrants and it was immaterial to the absorbing agencies that it proved unsuitable to the special problems of Oriental immigrants. The policies that in a functionalistic absorption–modernization model appear to be uniform or contradictory turn out in a dynamic paternalism–co-optation model to be discriminatory and consistent.

The primary goal of the absorption policies was to make immigrants instrumental for obtaining national objectives, and their 'integration' was only a secondary matter. It was clear that the dispersion of population – in reality the settlement of Orientals in arid remote areas – was incompatible with integration (E. Cohen, 1969b), but it did not matter. It was also evident that the Orientals had neither practical nor ideological training for agriculture (especially not for its co-operative forms) but they were forced, nevertheless, into this type of absorption which was of a high value from the viewpoint of the absorbing society. The Oriental immigrants helped to expand the economy, the bureaucracy and the army, and the fact that they entered mainly the lower or lower-middle rungs was of little importance.

The official ideology of modernization was linked to the unofficial paternalist image of the Oriental immigrants as 'the generation of the desert'. They were considered backward, their needs primitive and their potential limited. The state was given credit for indications of improvement in their conditions, and they were reminded to be grateful. For example, in an interview with the editor of *Le Monde* (15 October 1971), Golda Meir, then Prime Minister, repeated the idea that the Oriental immigrants had brought 'discrimination', i.e., backwardness, with them from their countries of origin. She drew attention to immigrants who dwelled in caves, never wore shoes, had never seen a bathtub, and the like. Then she concluded: 'Therefore, when I see today what has been done for them, I can say that the progress we have achieved is spectacular.' In another interview, commemorating the twenty-fifth anniversary of the State of Israel, Mrs Meir acknowledged, however, as one failure of the state, the persistence of 'a group' of people in society who, while they are no longer hungry or without shoes, have yet to be 'integrated into twentieth-century society' (an inteview on 'Meet The Press', NBC television, taped on 4 May 1973).

It did not matter that the Oriental immigrants differed a great deal in their degree of 'backwardness', i.e., their deviation from

90

dominant Ashkenazi standards. The more modernized Jews from Iraq, Syria, Lebanon, Egypt and Turkey fared as badly as did the less modernized Jews from Kurdistan, Yemen and North Africa. The Oriental Jews from an urban background were not distinguished from those from rural communities.[23] The wholesale stereotyping reduced ethnicity to its bare minimum – country of birth rather than culture or behaviour patterns. This fundamental dichotomy sorted out European immigrants from an undifferentiated mass. The Ashkenazi immigrants were viewed as more valuable to the state; their absorption was considered more risky since they had the option of leaving for other countries; they were expected to have greater needs, and were thus entitled to, and were in fact given, better services.[24]

For illustrative purposes, one case of a double standard in immigrant absorption will be presented in some detail. In 1957–8 about 127,000 immigrants lived in ma'abarot (transit camps) and other temporary housing. Most of them were Orientals who had been living there since 1951. Instead of a crash programme for their quick total evacuation, the government built small housing projects here and there, presumably because of lack of funds. Meanwhile, unexpected immigrants started to come from Eastern Europe, and the treatment they received was much superior to that of the Oriental immigrants.

First, special concessions were established to meet the needs of the Eastern European immigrants, among which were exemptions from customs and income tax, social security payments for the aged and disabled,[25] and reservation of jobs. Second, they were sent in larger numbers to the highly desired coastal strip which had been hitherto closed to immigrants. Between October 1956 and April 1958, 22.5 per cent of Polish immigrants as compared with only 8.5 per cent of North African immigrants were assigned to the coastal strip (Jewish Agency, 1958: Table 8[26]). This was an explicit deviation from a policy of population dispersion directing all new immigrants to the newly-built development areas and to other immigrant towns. Third, since there was no public housing in the urban centres for new immigrants (precisely because of the same policy of absorbing the new immigrants elsewhere), apartments were purchased from private contractors; the budget for building low-standard housing units for those living in temporary accommodation was cut and reallocated to building high-standard apartments for the newcomers; and even units originally built for the former were reassigned to the latter. Funds were raised by special drives abroad and by levying an 'absorption tax'.

These discriminatory practices did not go unnoticed by the Orientals. They registered their disapproval in demonstrations in

91

1957–8 (Tevet, 1957). Driven by the widespread protest, Shlomo Hillel, an Oriental Knesset member at that time, spoke on behalf of the previous Oriental immigrants, 'who have been waiting for years for . . . departure from the Vale of Tears of the transit camps'. 'A dangerous attempt was made . . . Under no circumstances is it reasonable to conceive the possibility of pushing the newcomers ahead and skipping over the earlier arrivals' (Hillel, 1957).[27]

The 1958 protests had a bitter sequel in the Wadi-Salib rioting in 1959. Bar-Yosef (1970: 428) tried to account for the disorders. Among other factors, she mentioned the following:

> Inconsistency on the part of the establishment in almost all fields of contact with the immigrants confuses them and results in their complete disorientation . . . it is generally accepted that there is one People of Israel and that all immigrants are equal. Yet everyone knows that while transition camps still exist, special housing is allocated to immigrants from Eastern Europe, and 'special treatment' is given to college graduates who are almost all from Europe. Sometimes inconsistency, with the best of intentions, can have as bad results as no action at all.

Typically, the absorption–modernization model allows no leeway for the discordant ideological undercurrents which have nurtured ethnic discrimination. Instead, the blatant discriminatory practices were termed 'inconsistencies' in policies that, unfortunately, 'confused' the Oriental masses.

The reaction of the political establishment to the Oriental protest is no less revealing. The chairman of the Absorption Department in the Jewish Agency at that time defended the policy by a rationale that brought into the open the double standard in treating Oriental and Ashkenazi immigrants (Jewish Agency, 1957: speech by Bergenski of the Jewish Agency executive):

> At the beginning of our action in 1953 [when the Department for Western Immigrants was established in the Jewish Agency] we decided on differential treatment with regard to Jews from Western countries, whom we need for various reasons. First of all because of their work skills, second, because of their ramified connections with Jews from Western countries. These Jews are also not very eager to come to Israel – and because of this we decided to grant them other concessions. This was the 'first discrimination' – for the immigrants from the West.
> Has anybody said then that it was not right or not just? We have said that we had to attract them to the country, to create

for them conditions that would persuade them to stay. We are now confronted with the problem of immigration from Eastern Europe, which has already started and which has similar dimensions

Should not this be taken into consideration? Was there any need for these Jews to continue wandering, not having been given any permanent abode? There was thus no alternative. We took apartments designed for others and gave them to them. We admit this and will correct it in the near future.

Thus for a long time special preferential privileges were given to immigrants from 'affluent' (i.e., Western) countries as incentives to attract middle-class, highly skilled immigrants. People of similar qualifications who came from 'distressed' (i.e., Oriental) countries were accorded fewer of such privileges. But since the mid-1960s this policy was gradually modified to apply to qualified immigrants regardless of country of origin. However, the Russian Jews who started to come in 1970 have been given these special privileges as a group although not all qualify for them.

It is generally assumed that special terms must be offered in order to secure the immigration and permanent settlement of Jews who have wide options. This is how the better treatment, on the whole, to Ashkenazi immigrants is justified. The question is why this expedient approach has not been equally applied to qualified sections of the Oriental Jewry. Although it is true that the Orientals had on the average narrower choices than the Ashkenazim, there was some tendency among the more educated and better-off Oriental Jews from Arab countries (especially North Africa and Iraq) to go elsewhere directly, or after a sojourn in Israel. The striking case are the advanced Algerian Jews who opted almost en masse to migrate to France. The fact that this negative selection of Oriental Jews, compared with the potential threat that Askhenazi Jews would not come or settle unless granted special privileges, failed to ameliorate the policies of the government toward Oriental newcomers is itself significant. Among other reasons, the sifting out of the better qualified elements among the Oriental immigrants squares with the subordinate role they were expected to play in Israeli society. The Ashkenazi establishment frequently deplores this phenomenon, presenting it as a major stumbling block to Oriental progress, but until after the 1962 massive decline in numbers of Algerian Jews coming to Israel it has done little about it.

Let me conclude this section on the anti-Oriental undercurrents with highlights from a recent comparative survey which carefully documents the differential treatment in the absorption of Moroccan and Romanian immigrants in the 1950s (Inbar and

93

Adler, 1977: chapter 6). As to housing, 73 per cent of the Moroccans and 74 per cent of the Romanians benefited from government assistance, but since they were assigned standard apartments averaging 1.8 to 1.9 rooms, the larger Moroccan families had twice as many people per room as Romanian families. Only 12 per cent of the Moroccans as compared with 43 per cent of the Romanians were allowed to choose their locality of residence upon arrival, and the best educated Moroccans (i.e., those with twelve or more years of schooling) were accorded the same amount of choice as the least educated Romanians (i.e., those with up to only five years of schooling) (18 and 17 per cent respectively). It was also found that more of the Moroccans, as compared with the Romanians, had to turn to absorbing agencies for getting their first job, and they were given fewer job offers. In effect, when the last job abroad and the first job in Israel are compared, it turned out that 73 per cent of the Moroccans as against 31 per cent of the Romanians experienced a downward mobility. Overall, and in comparison with the Romanians, the Moroccan newcomers were sent to less urbanized areas where occupational and educational opportunities for themselves and their children were much worse. They suffered from both class and ethnic discrimination.[28]

The undercurrents which affect religious–nonreligious relations are rather mixed. With some oversimplification, it is safe to say that the general attitude of the nonreligious majority is one of ambivalence. On the positive side, for the nonreligious Jews, the religious Jews personify Judaism, i.e., Jewish religion, culture, tradition and nationhood. As such, the Jewish religion is credited with three paramount accomplishments: the preservation of the Jews as a nation in exile throughout history, the provision of a solid base for ties between Israel and the Diaspora, and the moral legitimacy for the state of Israel to exist in the historical land of Israel (Palestine). The distinctive part of Judaism is religious tradition, while most of the rest consists of cultural borrowings. On the negative side, nonreligious Jews associate religious Jews with lack of modernism, i.e., traditionalism, clericalism and intolerance. Religious Judaism is a legacy to which the Zionist principle 'Negation of the Diaspora' applies to some extent. This considerable ambivalence among the nonreligious group makes for both flexibility and rigidity in the situation.[29]

The undercurrents in Arab–Jewish relations are extremely unpropitious. The declared view that national security, Jewish state and democratic pluralism are reconcilable should be contrasted with the informal ideology which guides the authorities in their relations with the Arab minorities. Two observations can be suggested. One is that in cases of inconsistency, national security and the Jewish state usually take precedence over democratic pluralism, thus making Arab interests subordinate to other considerations. The other phenomenon is the extensive use of steps toward equality and integration of the Arabs as an instrumental means to obtain compliance and dependence rather than as an ultimate end or basic right. The authorities hope that by dispensing more benefits to the Arabs and by enhancing their incorporation into the Jewish-dominated system, they will be more accommodating. Equal treatment is thus conditioned by Arab conformity.

These unofficial policies are bolstered by a deeply rooted contempt and fear of the Arabs. The Ashkenazi Europeocentrism which hurts Oriental Jews hits the Israeli Arabs the hardest. In the statements cited above, Ben-Gurion spoke derogatively of Oriental Jews because of their Arab customs, and warned against the spread of 'the spirit of the Levant, which corrupts individuals and societies'. Eban expressed repugnance at the idea of Israel's 'integration with the Arab-speaking world' and the fear lest Oriental Jews drag Israel into 'an unnatural Orientalism'. Some Jews are also disturbed by anxieties of persecution and annihilation. They feel that they, not the Israeli Arabs, are the real underdogs.

The relegation of the Israeli Arabs to a de facto status as an inferior quasi-caste is very incapacitating. They are viewed as aliens by the Jewish majority, and are not expected to contribute to the state. This is why nothing has been done to broaden the Israeli identity to include them.

4 Interdependence

The nature of mutual dependence between groups and their exchange of services are important for the type of cohesion between them. The interdependence between the Orientals and the Ashkenazim is considerable, though somewhat asymmetric, and has mixed effects upon their integration.

On arrival in the state, the Orientals were exceedingly dependent on the Ashkenazim or on Ashkenazi-controlled institutions. They came with little capital, had not relatives to turn to, could not expect much assistance from the relatively small and powerless Sephardic community, and most had practically no choice of going elsewhere. The substantial Oriental dependence was further strengthened by the structure of Israeli society. Because of the voluntary nature of the Yishuv, the Jews had to set up many organizations as substitutes for ordinary services. After statehood, the government gradually took over various organizations (defence organizations, schools, employment offices, etc.), but the basic situation of an 'overorganized society' did not change. The state and other public agencies simply monopolized all kinds of services and made immigrants dependent on them.

The monopoly of services to the immigrants had divergent impacts. As exponents of the absorption–modernization model aptly indicate, the new immigrants were not left on their own but received the necessary services. They were assigned a place of residence, given housing accommodation, assisted in finding employment, offered membership in, and the protection of, the powerful trade union (Histadrut), provided with health coverage, instructed in Hebrew, etc. The new poor immigrants were not allowed to become destitute in Israel, unlike those in other states, because all newcomers were granted primary services.

But provision of services meant also pre-emption and dependence. New immigrants, and especially Orientals who came with few resources, became strongly dependent on the authorities (the state administration, the Jewish Agency, the Histadrut and the political parties) for these services. Under such circumstances immigrant organizations (*Landsmanshaften*) which generally tend to flourish among incoming ethnic or racial groups, as they did in the United States and Canada,[30] were insignificant in Israel. The pre-emptive, pervasive encroachment of the public bodies goes a long way in accounting for this. The ethnic associations became redundant, as they could not match the benefits forthcoming from the powerful established organizations.

The services did not, however, have the effect of making the Oriental immigrants independent. For instance, the government adopted a policy of full employment. To attain this goal many techniques were used, including the extension of free credit or grants-in-aid to economic enterprises which opened new positions regardless of their profitability, unrestricted trade union protection of immigrant workers irrespective of their productivity and the creation of public relief jobs with substandard pay. Objectively considered, the upshot of this policy was to appease the immigrant workers and keep them in a state of dependence on the established organizations; it did not have the result of upgrading their skills and thereby making them more competitive and independent.

The absorbing Ashkenazi group, on the other hand, relied on the new Oriental immigrants, though in a different way. The Orientals supplied manpower to the economy, to the armed forces and to the new settlements. They made possible the rapid expansion of the society. Their co-operation was necessary for the stability of the regime. Since they arrived in great numbers and were ill equipped to participate in a modern democracy, their pacification or acquiescence was essential. Their voting rights, given upon arrival, could be misdirected by 'demagogic' leaders: this might jeopardize the entire system. These real or apparent dangers posed by the Oriental immigrants were divulged in a semi-official document (Hebrew University, 1970: 14):

> This size and speed of the immigration posed two serious dangers for Israeli society. One was that a 'negative development' would occur, pulling the society towards an Oriental rather than Western culture. The other was, that if the new immigrants were not quickly integrated, the society might polarize, leading to ethnic division. The possibility of the accompanying social conflict, tension and unrest was all too clear. In the face of the constant security threat that is confronting Israel, it was essential to the preservation of the State that these dangers be averted.
>
> The single most important preventive measure in dealing with these dangers is the opening of tracks of social, political, cultural and economic mobility.

The active incorporation of the Orientals into the mainstream was, therefore, 'preventive' in nature. The primary goal was to avert the perils of growing Orientalism and ethnic unrest, and only secondarily, if at all, to set up conditions of full equality and integration. The solution was found in the wholesale co-optation of Orientals – by opening up many established Ashkenazi-controlled organizations and 'absorbing' most of them in the lower and lower-middle ranks. The better qualified or the elite were also 'integrated'. Many of them became civil servants, noncommissioned officers in the police and army, administrators in local government and local workers' councils, councillors, shop stewards, foremen and line managers in industry, members of the broader national governing bodies of political parties (or the central bodies of their local branches), and the like. Benign quotas (i.e., a practice that assures deprived groups of a minimal number of appointments, irrespective of candidates' qualifications) in some visible top political posts were set up to project an image of equality and full participation.

The opening up of the system from the middle echelons down was made under very favourable conditions. In a sense it was unavoidable because in a modern economy and a democratic state it is difficult to shut off the large lower-middle and middle sections of society. More positively, the limited opening of the structure partially fulfilled the manifest goals of equality and assimilation.

At the same time it was not at all costly to but rather beneficial for the Ashkenazi group. Contrary to popular misconceptions, the Orientals' immigration did not require any economic sacrifices on part of the Ashkenazim. The reverse is true: it furnished them with

97

ample opportunities for upward mobility. Klinov-Malul (1969) suggests that the mass immigration directly stepped up the inequality of income between the newcomers and the established residents to the great advantage of the latter. She further indicates that the economic relations between the newcomers and the established residents were of 'a complementary type'. In other words, since their skills were not interchangeable they did not have to compete, but could enter those positions for which they were better suited. Thus, there was mutual benefit. This 'harmonious' arrangement depicted by Klinov-Malul meant, in fact, the 'absorption' of the new-comers – practically all Orientals, not Ashkenazim – in lower niches and the advancement of the settled population, mostly Ashkenazim, to higher rungs. Such a peculiar situation did not make much difference as long as the main objective was the expansion of the economy and while there was no serious social unrest. It was certainly in tune with the minimalist preventive policy of the Ash-kenazi establishment and could not have possibly promoted equality and integration between the two ethnic groups.

The current state of Oriental–Ashkenazi dependence remains mutual and asymmetric, though less skewed than in the past. The surging proportion of Orientals in the Jewish population and especially in the more valuable younger age-groups, their spread into various fields and their greater familiarity with the system have made the Orientals more needed objectively by the Ashkenazi group and their contributions more recognizable. Most important, the ubiquitous and escalating Arab–Israeli conflict provides a perfect case of what K. Lewin calls 'interdependence of fate'. The conflict is obvious, real and pervasive, and experienced as a personal fatal threat. It is common knowledge that the Orientals compose about half of the security forces (the army, police and secret services), a fact that well demonstrates the need for them.

The patterns of interdependence between religious and non-religious Jews are deep and ramified. The above-mentioned recognition by the nonreligious public of the indispensable functions of religion in preserving the Jewish people, the unity of world Jewry, and the legitimacy of the Jewish state is quite important. Similarly, the religious minority 'yields' to the authority of a secular state not only because it has no other choice, but also because it acknowledges the inability of the outdated halakha to provide satisfactory solutions for the needs of a modern Jewish state. Furthermore, on an inter-personal level, the nature of the split cuts across families and friend-ship networks. Mutual dependence is thus an individual as well as a collective experience.[31]

The peculiar politicization of the religious conflict contributes, in a sense, to rapprochement. The religious political parties usually aggregate the interests of the religious sector and fight for concessions through the regular channels. Hence, popular participation in the struggle is often prevented. A greater institutionalization of it is achieved by the long-standing co-operation between the non-religious ruling party, which lacks a majority vote, and the religious parties. Political interdependence engenders a unique situation in which religious issues are decided between the political parties forming the coalition government without consulting the general public. This consociational arrangement enforces moderation and stability in religious–non-religious relations.

Arab–Jewish interdependence is the least symmetrical of the three sets of intergroup relations. The economic dependence of the Arabs on the Jews is substantial. The flight of Palestinian Arabs in 1948 resulted in the collapse of the Arab economy. The Israeli Arabs were gradually brought into the Jewish economy. Arab agriculture, which used to be the mainstay of the Arabs' productive life, was badly hit by the extensive loss of cultivable lands. It is estimated that 40 per cent to 60 per cent of the Arab land holdings were expropriated in the years 1948 to 1967 (Stock, 1968: 46). The Arab predominantly subsistence agriculture soon became cash oriented, thereby making the remaining Arab peasants excessively reliant on the Jews for farming technology and marketing. Many Arab villagers had to seek jobs in the Jewish sector. By 1975 most of the Arabs in employment worked outside their place of residence: these comprised mainly migrant workers who derived their livelihood directly from Jewish employers. The entire Arab community relied on Jews for manufactured goods, professional services and welfare assistance. The Arabs have virtually no industry or modern financial and commercial establishments. They are greatly dependent for employment opportunities and standard of living on economic decisions made by the Jewish majority.[32]

The Arabs' political dependence on the Jews is appreciable as well. Its deep roots go back to the military administration. This special state machinery was vested with broad powers, including the authority – which was widely exercised – to suspend all civil freedoms (movement, assembly, organization, and expression), to establish courts-martial and to expropriate land. The military administration was defended on security grounds, but opponents criticized it for its undue intervention in many matters with stratagems to maximize the political gains of the ruling party. Accommodating leaders were carefully selected and heavily backed up to serve as a base for a Jewish indirect rule along with and especially after the removal in 1966 of the military government. Knesset members elected on the client Arab lists lack any political independence. For instance, their decisive support of the government in 1962 in a close vote in the Knesset defeated a motion to abolish the military administration. Similarly Arab community development is very much affected by policies of the central administration whether to incorporate the locality into a municipal council and what subsidies to extend to it – and these decisions are taken with regard to the record of co-operation of the population.

The expendability of the Israeli Arabs adds to their economic and political dependence. The Arab minority is small and the Jewish economy does not rest on it. The building of an independent, exclusive society has always been the ideal and practice. Furthermore, the potential contributions of the Arab minority to the welfare of Israel are considered meagre. Drawing on a relevant comparison, Peres rightly observes (1971: 1046):

> Orientals contributed to Israel's survival and progress in ways that Israeli Arabs were in no position to do. Even the most moderate and loyal individuals among them could not fully identify with the country's Zionistic zeal, with its commitment to Jewish immigration, and, most important, with its struggle against the Arab world.

The Jewish public is well aware of the expendability of the Arab minority whose presence is judged undesirable, as Peres's survey shows.

The multi-faceted dependence of the Arab minority has been gradually reduced and counterbalanced over the years. The lifting of the military administration marked a continuous process of liberalization in policies toward the Israeli Arabs. Their civil rights are now better protected. The younger generation of Arabs is more vocal and critical. The concentration of Arab migrant labour in certain sectors of the Jewish economy produces significant pockets of Jewish dependence. In addition to its contribution to economic growth, Arab labour eases internal tensions within the Jewish society. This is made possible since they serve as a convenient scapegoat and, as we shall see shortly, since they boost the Orientals' upward mobility.

Whatever services the Arab minority renders to Israeli society, its dependence on and marginal value to the Jewish majority are still highly significant and they obviously do not foster harmony in Arab–Jewish relations.

5 Multiple rifts

Multi-pluralism opens up possibilities for power coalitions which are of course absent in a dyadic situation. The intensity of conflict would increase in some sets of intergroup relations and decrease in others, depending on the alliances made. It can be shown that, on the whole, the Oriental–Ashkenazi and the religious–nonreligious splits are mitigated by other divisions, whereas the Arab–Jewish rift is consolidated by internal Jewish conflicts.

The religious–nonreligious conflict splits both Orientals and Ashkenazim. Antonovsky (1963) reports the following to be religious in various groups: 30 per cent of the total Jewish population; 53 per cent of the North Africans, 44 per cent of Asians and 18 per cent of Oriental sabras; 18 to 28 per cent of various European groups and Ashkenazi sabras. These figures show that religious observance in the foreign-born generation is greater among the Orientals than the Ashkenazim, but the differences tend to level off in the Israeli-born generation. This is probably due to the cumulative secularization of the Orientals, especially those born in the country.

The large proportion of religious people among the Oriental immigrants created an important possibility of a power coalition between the highly mobilized religious Ashkenazi group and the passively religious Oriental masses.[33] This coalition could have turned the religious Ashkenazi minority into a dominant majority and changed the character of the state. Driven either by hope or fear of forming such a union, religious and nonreligious Ashkenazim fought the big 'battle for the immigrants' in the early 1950s. The nonreligious dominant group had much more patronage to dispense to the new immigrants as well as direct control over their absorption arrangements (where to settle them, what schools to set up for them, etc.). It used its power, therefore, to shield the Oriental immigrants from the religious political machine. The religious group, which co-operated at the same time with the nonreligious ruling group in the government and the Jewish Agency, was forced to accept a deal to divide the new immigrants into spheres of influence. In this way, then, the status quo in religious–nonreligious relations was preserved. Patai (1970: 370) is probably correct in making the following projection:[34]

> The political coalition hoped for by the religious parties
> between them and the Oriental Jews, which would have resulted
> in an Ashkenazi religious–Oriental Jewish majority dominating
> the Knesset and thus the government and the country, has not
> materialized, and cannot materialize in the future.

The religious–nonreligious split and the fateful results of the 'battle for the immigrants' constituted a decisive factor in preventing the Oriental immigrants from either forming an independent force or joining the ethnic political parties which operated in the early years of the state. The two rival established Ashkenazi groups shared a common interest in averting this 'danger'. The fear that the other side would seize upon the Oriental immigrants allowed them to be more forceful and induced them to adopt a policy of active recruitment, patronage and co-optation of the Oriental newcomers. The religious–nonreligious cleavage mitigates the Oriental–Ashkenazi division in yet another way. It obviously splits the Oriental group into religious and nonreligious categories, the co-operation between them being diminished.

Besides, the continued struggle between the religious and nonreligious Ashkenazim (the powerless Orientals are left out of the fight) serves to intensify the sectarian-Jewish character of the state and tends thereby to heighten the quasi-caste barriers between Arabs and Jews. Consequently, when Jewishness is the dividing issue, the Oriental–Ashkenázi line becomes blurred and insignificant. As religious observance itself is excessively noticeable and politicized among Jews, it dulls moreover the acuteness of the Oriental–Ashkenazi split.[35]

The Arab–Jewish quasi-caste division plays an even greater role in blurring the Oriental–Ashkenazi rift. The unrestricted inclusion of the Orientals in the Jewish quasi-caste had weighty consequences. Generally speaking, the theoretical significance of the term 'racial' or 'ethnic caste' (or 'quasi-caste') derives from the fact that caste or quasi-caste divisions are more rigid than are class or ethnicity. For instance, the racial caste structure in the United States hampers the joint alignment of the white and black proletariat against the bourgeoisie, and in South Africa it precludes the assimilation of the Cape Coloureds (who resemble the Afrikaners in language, religion and some other cultural traits) into the White caste. By the same token, despite similarity in social class, certain subcultural patterns (dialect, family size, values, manners and personality dispositions) and the physical appearance of Oriental Jews and Israeli Arabs, any alliance between them is unlikely as long as the religious–national quasi-caste line prevails. The colonial model of ethnic relations in Israel, perhaps because of its Marxian slant, fails to note this fundamental situation. The emphasis upon the sectarian Jewish character of the state has the function of solidifying the two quasi-castes, stressing the Oriental membership in the superior Jewish quasi-caste, and consequently playing down the Oriental–Ashkenazi division.

Membership in the Jewish quasi-caste ensures for the Orientals some symbolic and material gains. The status superiority of the Orientals qua Jews (majority members) over the Arabs (minority members) is not insignificant, but not less appreciated are the economic benefits. The separate facilities for the Arabs or the agencies for controlling them provide jobs and positions of power for Oriental Jews.[36] Since the Arabs are discriminated against in jobs for security and other reasons, the Orientals have an edge in employment over them. During an economic recession such as that of 1966–7, the Arabs are the first to be fired; during periods of full employment, as occurred after the Six-Day War, they take up the manual, low-paid jobs. They thus displace Orientals upwards in the occupational structure (Stock, 1968: 22–3). In 1975 half of the Israeli Arab workers and all of the 64,000 or so Palestinian migratory labourers were regularly engaged in the lowest jobs in agriculture, construction and menial services for Jewish employers. The increasing weight of the Arab labour in the Jewish economy is a definite boost to Oriental social mobility.

The Orientals have still another advantage over the Israeli Arabs. The various steps the government takes, either directly or indirectly through the Jewish Agency, to promote ethnic equality are more or less limited to Orientals. An equitable allocation of resources would require the diversion of some of the funds now apportioned to development towns, new agricultural villages (moshavim), slum clearance, compensatory education, etc., where Orientals enjoy the stronger vested interests, to corresponding Arab areas which are no less needy.[37]

The Arab–Jewish quasi-caste system, however, not only affords privileges to the Orientals but also inflicts penalties on them. Ashkenazi feelings of cultural superiority towards the Arabs are unavoidably carried over to the Orientals, who somewhat resemble the Arabs in subculture.[38] The Ashkenazim tend, fairly categorically, to reject cultural pluralism within the Jewish quasi-caste, but at the same time wish to retain it as an additional boundary between the two quasi-castes. Concurrent with this cultural intolerance is a considerable expression of stereotyping, prejudices, social distance and discrimination.

Ashkenazi ethnocentrism apparently complicates the identity problems of the Orientals and foments feelings of self-hatred among them (Shuval, 1966). Peres presents some data for the disproportionate intolerance of Arabs among the Orientals, and suggests the following explanation (1971: 1040):

> The Orientals feel that they must reject the remaining traces of their Middle Eastern origin to attain the status of the dominant European group. By expressing hostility to Arabs, an Oriental attempts to rid himself of the 'inferior' Arabic elements in his own identity and to adopt a position congenial to the European group which he desires to emulate.

The fact that the Orientals as a group express greater hostility toward the Arabs than do the Ashkenazim is well established, but it is not clear whether this is largely a result of their lower socioeconomic status. Peres, for instance, shows in a survey of high school pupils that the Orientals were more prejudiced and reserved than the Ashkenazim toward the Arabs, but this could reflect the differences in their family class background. Similarly, among adults, the Orientals who were judged to resemble Arabs by accent and appearance were slightly more prejudiced than other Orientals against Arabs – but this, again, might be the consequences of relative variations in social standing. It is possible that anti-Arab emotions and scapegoating are particularly intense among the Oriental lower class as a result of the interaction of poor education, deprived status and blocked mobility. Members of the Oriental lower classes are observed to lead attacks against Arabs in mixed cities and to manhandle Arab passers-by in incidents of sabotage. For instance, after the terrorist massacres in spring 1974 in the predominantly Oriental depressed development towns (Kiryat Shmona and Ma'alot), some Oriental residents beat up innocent Israeli Arabs who happened to be near by, and clamoured for retaliatory revenge against the Arabs across the borders.[39]

As for the implications of the Arab–Jewish quasi-caste system for the policies of the Ashkenazi majority towards the Orientals, the striking fact is that the Oriental immigrants have never been thought of as a security risk. Their allegiance to their own Jewish quasi-caste is never questioned. There was no apprehension that they would join forces with the Arabs on the grounds of cultural affinity or class solidarity. The quasi-caste structure serves as a watertight guarantee against such an eventuality. It has a double effect: it provides the Orientals with a basic stake in the system and the dominant Ashkenazi group with assurance against an adverse development;[40] and makes the full incorporation of the Orientals less urgent. By excluding the Arabs, concessions to the Orientals become less costly, and by stigmatizing their culture, the dismantling of it is much easier. In brief, the quasi-caste structure contributes to the effectiveness of the co-optation policy vis-à-vis Orientals, and at the same time makes a policy of full equality less imperative.

Similarly the religious–nonreligious split is mitigated by the cross-cutting Oriental–Ashkenazi and Arab–Jewish divisions. The Oriental–Ashkenazi pervasive division and its occasional coming to the forefront divert attention from the heated religious controversies. More importantly, the Arab–Jewish quasi-caste bar pulls the two Jewish sectors together.

The Arab–Jewish division is, on the other hand, hardened by those internally among the Jews. The tensions generated by the conflicts among Jews are partially dispelled by scapegoating the Arabs. Lower-class Orientals are seemingly disposed to enhance their status within the Jewish quasi-caste by taking a harder line than the Ashkenazim against the Arabs. The possibility that Jews living in their own country ('the holy land') might intermingle with Arabs, like their brethren in the Diaspora who assimilate into Gentile society, is anathema to religious Jews in particular, and they feel more animosity towards Arabs than do nonreligious Jews. The Oriental and religious Jews tend, therefore, to push for a more rigid quasi-caste structure in view of their relations with their rivals. This can only exacerbate the already uneasy Arab–Jewish relations.

6 The relevant features of society at large

Israeli society has certain characteristics, some of which were touched upon previously, that have important implications for its pluralistic structure. Among these relevant features are the Jewish–Zionist nature of the state, the Western make-up, the political-economic system, the Arab–Israeli dispute and the pragmatic disposition of the political elite.

Israel is a sectarian state grounded in Judaism and Zionism. It is Jewish in the name, emblem, flag, anthem, ceremonies, heroes and other national symbols of the state as well as in the official holidays and almost exclusive use of the Hebrew language. It is Zionist in its identification as a direct continuation of Jewish history, a carrier of Jewish culture, in its close links with world Jewry, and the Law of Return. Judaism and Zionism, which are the raison d'être of Israel, equip the Oriental and Ashkenazi Jews with a common core-culture and thus significant bonds of solidarity.

The Western make-up of Israel has several repercussions.[41] First, its origin as a society derived from Europe is of some consequence. As indicated earlier, the dominant Ashkenazi group, beginning with the Zionist settlers and continuing with the recent European immigrants, is imbued with European ethnocentrism, superiority feelings and paternalism towards the so-called Third World peoples or groups such as the Oriental Jews and the Arabs in Israel.

Second, the Western structure and orientation of the state give the Ashkenazim a decisive advantage over the less Westernized Orientals. The adoption of Western methods, patterns of behaviour and values makes the Orientals less competitive than the Westernized Ashkenazim. For instance, since the value and reward systems are geared towards a small family, the majority of Orientals with large families do not enjoy equal opportunities. Elite positions require distinctive European skills, as do a great many roles which are linked directly or indirectly with maintaining ramified diplomatic, economic and cultural ties with the Western world and with world Jewry. Had Israel had a structure which took into account the needs of both the European and non-European population, had it been more oriented to the Middle East and at least more balanced in its

105

orientation, and particularly had it established normal relations with the Arab world, the position of the Orientals in Israel would have been much better.

And third, among the many areas in which Israel borrows from the West, especially from the United States, are the developments in intergroup relations. The rising militancy of minorities in the United States, the civil rights movement, the Black Power movement and the resurgence of white ethnic groups have already reached Israel in the form of the Black Panthers. But in addition to the possible radicalization of the Orientals, the escalation of militant ethnic activity in the United States may serve as a spur to the dominant Ashkenazi group to reassess its ethnic policies in order to prevent further crises. No doubt, an increase of such influence with even more profound implications must be expected.

The political-economic structure of Israel has some noteworthy consequences. It is a stable democracy with considerable centralization of political and economic power. The democratic process enables the Orientals to press for reforms in the system. The Orientals, like all other Jewish immigrants, are enfranchised upon arrival and, in fact, have a voting rate not significantly different from the very high national average of 80 per cent (Central Bureau of Statistics, *Statistical Abstract of Israel*, 1974, 25:562).[42] The growing proportion of Orientals in the Jewish voting population, which was estimated at 42 per cent in 1970 (H. Smith, 1969: 25),[43] contributes appreciably to their political power. The highly competitive multi-party system makes their votes valuable.[44] The established parties have to make concessions such as benign quotas and material benefits in order to secure the Oriental vote. There are, however, some impediments to the full utilization of this large political potential. The major hindrances are the Orientals' lack of experience in democracy and poor organization on the one hand, and the proportional nonregional method of elections which stresses nonethnic national issues and which demands a state-wide political machine beyond the ability of the Orientals, on the other.[45]

The centralization of power is demonstrated in many ways. Although the economy is mixed – the public sector comprises two-fifths – the government exercises tight controls through regulations and allocation of subsidies. Since 95 per cent of Jewish employees are unionized, over three-fifths of whom are in the giant Histadrut, this body has substantial control over the labour force. Wages and work conditions are negotiated between the Histadrut and the Industrialists' Union and the government on a nation-wide basis. Not only the economy but also all other important matters concerning land settlement, population dispersal, regional development, housing, education, the nomination of candidates to top local positions, police conduct and the like are decided nationally. The Jewish Agency and the Ministry of Immigrant Absorption establish the basic policies towards immigrants. The Israel Labour Party, which controls all three centres of power, i.e., the government, the Jewish Agency and the Histadrut, takes the decisions on the crucial issues.

It is clear that in such a highly centralized system national policies and administrative measures are decisive for the course of Oriental–Ashkenazi relations. National decision-making and planning in Israel are less centralized than in socialist countries, but much more so than in Western capitalist countries. Since the government has the option of serious intervention in ethnic affairs, as in other matters, the potential for either the slowdown or the acceleration of ethnic integration depends a great deal on the national power centres.

Another key characteristic of Israeli society is sustained and marked growth. The scale of the society has been expanding through a large population increase (continuing immigration), capital imports and even the widening of the territorial base. The Jewish population rose from 650,000 in 1948 to 2,959,400 in 1975. Between 1950 and 1967 Israel received $9.3 billion of which only $1.3 billion were repaid.[46] These enormous capital imports are almost unparalleled.[47] In the same period the GNP rose at an annual rate of 9.3 per cent and GNP per capita was 3.4 per cent. 'Only a very few countries, notably Japan, exceeded this growth rate during the entire period' (Remba, 1971a: 265). With an annual per capita income of over $2,000 in 1973, Israel was doing even better than 'intermediate' European nations such as Austria, Italy and Ireland. The average standard of living has more than doubled since 1957–8, skyrocketing at an annual rate of 8.8 per cent (Public Inquiry Commission, 1971: 32). With 22.7 per cent of all employed persons in 1975 having at least some college education (Central Bureau of Statistics, *Statistical Abstract of Israel*, 1976, 27: 336) and 63.0 per cent of Jews being employed in white-collar occupations (ibid.: 314) (one of the highest percentages in the world), Israel is making considerable progress.

The tremendous growth has an overall favourable impact on Oriental–Ashkenazi relations. It makes it possible to maintain full employment and to expand services. It creates a situation of largely non-zero sum competition between the Orientals and the Ashkenazim, who both benefit from the boom. Ethnic tensions are, in consequence, reduced.

The security situation which seems unparalleled elsewhere can hardly be overemphasized as an integrative force. In fact, the problem of physical survival dates back to the early 1920s. The conflict between the Jews on the one hand and the Arabs and Palestinians or Arab states on the other has always been an integral element in the cohesion of Jewish society. The continuing belligerence distracts attention from internal tensions. Positively, the gravity of the situation creates an atmosphere of interdependence and more willingness among the Ashkenazim to integrate the Orientals and treat them as equals. Negatively, the external threat constitutes a structural substitute for internal mechanisms of ethnic integration and enables the establishment to avoid the ethnic problem. Overall, the Arab–Israeli conflict is definitely more integrative in its effects.

The dominant Ashkenazi group has certain qualities that tend to ease relations between Orientals and Ashkenazim. Apart from the undercurrents of European ethnocentrism, paternalism and anti-Orientalism, the Ashkenazim and the power elite are publicly and strongly committed to full equality and integration among Jews. All three prevailing ideologies of Zionism (nationalism), socialism and modernization, to which the Israeli power elite subscribes officially, are contributory factors in harmonizing relations between the two ethnic groups.

The Ashkenazi group also has a keen sense of historical experience as a minority. The Askhenazi Jews were the outcasts of Europe, suffered from blatant anti-semitism and were subjected to persecutions and pogroms for centuries. Zionism itself was based on the assumption that anti-semitism is an incurable disease. The more recent traumatic tribulations were the Holocaust and the omnipresent Arab threats to destroy the Jewish entity, beginning with the British mandate and reaching a peak in the 1967 and 1973 wars. These bitter ordeals make the Ashkenazim sensitive to criticism of prejudice and differential treatment against their Jewish brethren. An articulated, publicly accepted ideology of 'Ashkenazi supremacy' does not exist, again despite undercurrents to the contrary. [48]

Most important, the Ashkenazim may be described as an ethnic group with a fairly high political development. [49] The Eastern European power elite has rich political experience which started during participation in social movements in Europe and had developed in the nation-rebuilding during the Yishuv. The statehood period provided greater opportunities, yet it marked a waning in stamina. The Ashkenazi establishment is skilful, sophisticated, manipulative and flexible. It combines dogma with pragmatism. Its distinctive approach is well described by Eisenstadt as 'dynamic conservatism' (1972: 298). It is innovative in finding short-term piecemeal arrangements for basic issues but is conservative in avoiding radical, long-term solutions. The staggering blunders attendant upon the Yom Kippur War betrayed the weaknesses of the ageing Ashkenazi leadership. The measure of movements for political reform which mushroomed in the aftermath of the war hastened its replacement by the New Guard of a somewhat younger Ashkenazi generation.

As to the policies toward the Orientals, the Ashkenazi establishment excels in soliciting legitimacy for its power and in taking steps to put on at least a façade of responsiveness. Sympathetic observers would probably portray its approach towards the Orientals in terms of 'a controlled gradualism model'[50] instead of 'a dynamic paternalism–co-optation model'. This is the benevolent form in which the official policies are made public.

The above-mentioned features of Israeli society which mostly contribute to ethnic integration between the Orientals and the Ashkenazim have mixed effects on religious–nonreligious relations. On the one hand, the democratic structure and centralization of power, the fairly high political skills of the two sections which lead the struggle (the Ashkenazi religious and nonreligious power elites), and certainly the external threat pave the way for consociationalism, i.e. settlement of disputes not in the streets but through give-and-take within the national centres of power. On the other hand, the growing leaning of Israel towards Western Europe and to the United States in particular, which makes the American model of separation of religion and state more and more attractive, and the rapid modernization and economic growth of the country may overtax the patience of the nonreligious majority with the religious status quo and thus heighten the tensions between the two groups.

The same factors have quite unfavourable repercussions on Arab–Jewish relations. The critical handicaps are of course the Jewish-Zionist character of the state, which makes the Arabs a certain kind of outsiders, and the Arab Israeli conflict which places them in the indefensible posture of an enemy-affiliated minority. Under such circumstances, Israeli democracy while rewarding the Arabs in many ways can hardly provide them with institutionalized means for change (the Arabs constitute a small dissenting minority facing an organized dominant group). Although the centralization of power and resource of the dominant Ashkenazi group are instrumental in protecting the Arab minority against denial of basic civil rights, economic exploitation and physical assaults, they are also effective in keeping the Israeli Arabs in their place. Similarly, whereas the sustained economic growth benefits the Arabs by making more low-status jobs, evacuated by Jews, available to them, it may at the same time intensify Arab frustration by raising their expectations way beyond the actual opportunities. Furthermore, the Western structure of the state handicaps the Israeli Arabs more than the Orientals because of their relatively lower level of Westernization.

In conclusion, our discussion shows that current social contexts are both favourable and unfavourable for Oriental–Ashkenazi relations and religious–nonreligious relations, but are unequivocally and substantially unfavourable for Arab–Jewish relations.

6 Pluralism and inequality

Constituent groups of pluralistic societies usually differ in the two major areas of pluralism and inequality. In our conceptual framework, pluralism stands simply for cultural diversity and social separation, and inequality refers to socioeconomic gaps and power disparities. These four dimensions are the cardinal lines which separate pluralistic divisions. Whereas the two dimensions of pluralism are nonhierarchical, the two dimensions of inequality are hierarchical. Pluralism and inequality vary quantitatively and independently and can be averaged by a number of summary measures (magnitude, inconsistency and durability).

In a world perspective, pluralism in Israel is moderate. Haug (1967), using a limited number of indicators of pluralism,[1] compares 114 states which were independent in 1963. Of the maximum of 8 points in Haug's scale of pluralism, Israel scores 3 and is, therefore, classified within the moderate category along with the United States and Britain, in a higher category than Sweden, Argentina and Egypt, and in a lower category than Belgium, Canada, Switzerland, Lebanon, India and all the new African states (1967: 299). Van den Berghe also places Israel in the moderate category of pluralism together with India, and comments on the substantial reduction in the original high degree of pluralism in their transition to statehood, i.e., the flight of the Arabs from Palestine, and the partition of India, which contributed much to the stability of their democracy (1969: 74–8).

Compared with other countries, Israel is even lower on inequality. The Lorenz coefficient of inequality of income rose from 0.19 in 1950 to 0.28 in 1959 and then to 0.32 in 1969, namely, by 3.6 per cent annually, bringing Israel up to the highly industrialized Western states (Roter and Shamai, 1971: 57).[2] Similarly, Israel has developed an occupational structure which is strikingly like that of Western

110

economies. In 1973 44.7 per cent of all employed in Israel were white-collar workers, 35.9 per cent blue-collar workers, 12.4 per cent service workers and 7.0 per cent agricultural workers (CBS, *Statistical Abstract of Israel*, 1974, 25: 305) and in the United States the figures were 47.9, 35.2, 13.4 and 3.4 per cent respectively (Bureau of Census, American Almanac for 1974, no. 94: 233). Like other Western states, Israel is of course much more egalitarian than all developing countries.[3]

The class structure is still neither very strong nor rigid in Israel, because of a variety of factors. These include the continuing influx of new immigrants for whom ethnic origin is more significant than socioeconomic status, the expanding structure and the subsidized economy which make available ample opportunities for social mobility, the absence of a traditional aristocracy and the dominance of working-class organizations (the Histadrut and labour political parties) (Zloczower, 1972).

Against this background of relatively moderate pluralism and inequality in Israeli society as a whole, we wish to assess pluralism and inequality for each of the three pluralistic divisions. Cultural diversity, social separation, socioeconomic gaps and power disparities will be examined in detail for each division and, finally, summary measures will be applied in order to get a broader view. For a quick and schematic review of the findings, consult Tables 3 and 4 in the Appendix.

1 Pluralism

Cultural diversity

Conflicting images of Israel's cultural diversity prevail. On the one hand, Israel is widely known as a land of sharp cultural contrasts as demonstrated in such social types as a traditional Yemenite, an ultra-Orthodox Jew and an Arab fellah as against a sabra town-dweller, a woman soldier and a kibbutz member. The latter types foster, on the other hand, a stereotype of Israel as a super-modern state with an advanced technology and a Western way of life. While the first image was more valid two decades ago, the reverse holds true for the present. On closer examination neither image is justified today. Cultural pluralism reflects, of course, appreciable class differentials in addition to genuine cultural differences. The bulk of the available data, however, lack the refined comparisons of culture within equal socioeconomic levels.

If we make a rough distinction between a *core*-culture and a *sub*-culture, we may say that the Orientals and the Ashkenazim, like all Jews in Israel, share the same core-culture, i.e., language,

111

nationality, religion, family structure and basic ideology. Hebrew is the common language, and all the historical and present literature in Hebrew (the Bible, Mishnah, Talmud, Rabbinic works, philosophy and fiction) is a common heritage. Israeli Orientals and Ashkenazim are Jews by both nationality and religion. As part of the broader Jewish people and faith, they have a common past and a common fate. They share, further, the same fundamental kinship values, namely, a nuclear family structure and centrality of the family in private life. And, finally, they all subscribe to the ideological principles of Israel as a Jewish and a Zionist state, the integration of exiles, modernization, democracy and equality of opportunity.

Along with this common core-culture, the Orientals and the Ashkenazim differ greatly in subculture. Even the same basic commonalities turn into significant subcultural differences beyond a certain point. Although Hebrew is the agreed official language of Israeli Jews,[4] and in fact the majority of both ethnic groups speak it in the same proportion, the minority of non-Hebrew-speakers use various languages. More important, the Orientals and the Ashkenazim differ widely in their Hebrew accents.[5]

The Orientals and the Ashkenazim diverge in their national consciousness as well. Broadly speaking, Oriental nationalism is more traditional, diffuse and concrete than Ashkenazi nationalism. The Orientals feel and expect greater Jewish communal solidarity and warmer Jewish brotherhood in their dealings as Jews with fellow-Jews. This discrepancy in national orientations strains communications between the two groups, but harms the Orientals more for being more demanding.[6]

Ethnic diversity pervades Jewish religion, too. The 'Sephardic style' deviates from the 'Ashkenazi style' in many respects, including texts of prayers, melodies, dietary prohibitions, rituals, manners of festivity, certain family common laws and the like. Furthermore, the Oriental religious world-view diverges from the Ashkenazi one. Compared to religious Ashkenazi Jews, religious Oriental Jews have, overall, a deeper confirming and responsive religious experience, draw a much milder line between the sacred and the profane, and tend to be more tolerant and accommodating towards nonreligious Jews. The Orientals, sense of religion is to a great degree a part of a traditional way of life and thinking which is undergoing an intensive process of modernization. From the point of view of the dominant Ashkenazi religious group which considers its Orthodoxy a rational, conscious and modern religious lifestyle, Oriental religiousness in Israel today appears to some extent to be irrational, inconsistent and reformist. For instance, a sizeable number of Orientals who identify themselves as 'religious' or say that they practise religion also report engaging in activities proscribed by the halakha on the Sabbath (e.g., watching TV).[7] The incidence of religious observance among the Orientals is greater than among the Ashkenazim. In a state-wide survey conducted in 1962, 53 per cent of immigrants from North Africa and 44 per cent of immigrants from Asia said that they observed all or most religious duties, as compared with 30 per cent of the general Jewish population (Antonovsky, 1963). Similarly, while Orientals constituted 59.8 per cent of the pupils in all primary schools in 1972–3, their proportion in the state religious schools amounted to 80.8 per cent and in the independent religious schools 65.1 per cent (Table 77).

There is a clearcut trend toward secularization among the Orientals, as evidenced in intergenerational comparisons. Matras (1965: 100–8) showed that Oriental women were less observant than their mothers. Herman (1970: 121–5) in a large survey of high school pupils in 1965 also showed from his evidence that Oriental young people were less religious than their parents. In a follow-up study in 1974, 56 per cent of the Oriental pupils felt less religious than their parents, 37 per cent considered themselves to the same degree and 7 per cent more religious (Herman, Farago and Harel, 1976: 114).[8] In fact, since the Orientals' religious observance is a facet of the larger traditional pattern, modernization or social mobility is associated with secularization among the Orientals, but not among the Ashkenazim.

The Orientals not only have become less religious but also less Orientally religious. Oriental religious traditions are passing and new patterns of any significance have not yet emerged. Certain new or revived religious activities such as festivities and memorial celebrations reported in some Oriental communities (Deshen and Shokeid, 1974) are limited in meaning, scope and appeal and they do not amount to a new religious lifestyle. At the same time, those young Orientals who remain religious are acculturated into the Ashkenazi practices which dominate in the schools, youth movements, the army and the public domain in general.[9]

More significant are the subcultural variations in family life. Orientals have, on average, much larger families than Ashkenazim. In 1975 45.6 per cent of the Asian-African families as against only 11.6 per cent of the European-American families had 5 or more members, but the ethnic gap among the Israeli-born families is smaller, 30.4 and 20.0 per cent respectively (for more details see Table 74). The dissimilarity in the median age of marriage has already vanished.[10] There has also been a steady decline in the birthrate differential. In 1955 the gross reproduction rate, which represents the average number of female offspring born to a woman in her lifetime, for Asian- or African-born women was 2.77 compared to 1.28 for European- or American-born women, whereas in 1975 it was 1.83 and 1.37 respectively (CBS, *Statistical Abstract of Israel*, 1976, 27: 76). A rapid increase in family planning has been shown among Orientals (Matras, 1969: 141; 1973: 380-4). These indications are the basis for the expectation that the birthrates will equalize by 1985 (Patai, 1971c). Besides, the virtual disappearance of households based on extended families, the decline of parental authority and the growing democratization in respect to sex and age differentiation, which took place among Orientals during the last two decades, considerably diminished the ethnic divergences in family life.[11]

Variations in cultural consumption reflect, to a large extent, ethnic socioeconomic gaps and tend gradually to decline. In 1963-4 Oriental families spent half as much as Ashkenazi families of comparable size and income bracket on education, recreation and other cultural needs (Table 75). Had such a study controlled for the more relevant factor of education of the family's head and had it been conducted in the mid-1970s, the ethnic differences would have been greatly reduced. This reservation holds equally for the finding of a survey in 1965 that of Oriental literate adults 34 per cent read books and 49 per cent read newspapers, compared with 61 and 88 per cent respectively of Ashkenazi literate adults (cited by Patai, 1971e : 306).

A more comprehensive study of the culture of leisure in Israel conducted in 1970 concluded that ethnic origin is of much less significance than level of education. With increasing years of education ethnic differences diminish considerably, and in some cases disappear (Katz and Gurevitch, 1973: 17). Within the same category of years of schooling there were minor variations in reading books (pp. 229-31), watching TV and going to the cinema (pp. 100-3). On the other hand, substantial divergences still remained in theatregoing and concerts, which are distinctive Western patterns. The ethnic differences in attendance at concerts, for instance, ranged from ratios of 1:3 to 1:6 in various subgroups, being greater in the lower socioeconomic levels. Such differences are much smaller than they used to be. To illustrate, about one-quarter of the Orientals in the lower category of education and half in the higher category attended theatres at least several times a year (p. 104). Similarly in a 1971 survey of Oriental adult males, 25.2 per cent favoured Oriental music only, 16.8 per cent Oriental and other music, and over half preferred Israeli songs and Western music (Eshel and Peres, 1973). The significant proportion adopting the Western habit of theatregoing and the lack of strong preference for Oriental music – areas of legitimate options – demonstrate the enormous acculturation of the Orientals into the Israeli mainstream.

These general tendencies apply equally to the differences which still exist in social values. The Orientals are observed to be on the average lower in consciousness and appreciation of time, in rational planning and achievement motivation, and in general possess less of the so-called 'Protestant ethic' than the Ashkenazim. Many of these differences can be accounted for by the fact that the lower class in Israel is almost exclusively Oriental, where the spread of middle-class values is limited because of unequal opportunities and traditionalism. Indeed, several large-scale studies on high school pupils in the mid 1960s and in the 1970s have repeatedly shown the striking similarities between Orientals and Ashkenazim in a variety of attitudes and behavioural patterns (Herman, 1970; Herman, Farago and Harel, 1976; Levy and Guttman, 1974).[12]

The picture is similar with regard to personality and achievement. There is some evidence for dissimilarities in certain personality traits (Zadik, 1968; Preale, Amir and Sharan, 1970). Smilansky and Yam (1969) report the superior performance of Ashkenazi children even when the father's education and family size are taken into account, but also note that among children reared in kibbutzim no ethnic gap in performance was noticeable. Studies of intelligence have found differences in 'the level but usually not in the pattern of the subjects' scores. First-generation Oriental children performed relatively lower, but the gap between second-generation Israeli children of Oriental and Western origin is notably diminished' (Lieblich, Ninio and Kugelmass, 1972: 159; see also the earlier study by Ortar, 1953); we will return to this point in the next chapter. Orientals and Ashkenazim do not differ in the way they function mentally.

As for subjective aspects of culture, opinion polls show that the two ethnic groups share all the basic self-perceptions. Social-psychological studies of the identity of Jewish youth in Israel provide support for this observation. The broader Jewish and Israeli identities, which transcend communal (Oriental–Ashkenazi) sub-identities, were found to be central. In a state-wide survey of high school pupils in 1974, 81 per cent of the Orientals and 70 per cent of the Ashkenazim said that 'Jewishness' played a very important or an important part in their life, and 92 and 91 per cent respectively felt the same about their 'Israeliness' (Herman, Farago and Harel, 1976: 150). These self-identities are linked with a host of psychological attachments to Jews in the Diaspora, Jewish history and Israeli society. In an earlier study, 44 per cent of the Oriental pupils and 55 per cent of the Ashkenazi pupils said that they were barely aware of their ethnic origin, and 72 and 74 per cent respectively thought that their ethnic origin hardly affected their behaviour (Peres, 1968: Tables 35, 36). Most important are feelings of cultural resemblance. In the 1974 study pupils were asked about similarity between Israelis in several areas. They perceived a very high degree of similarity in cultural spheres: 71 per cent perceived Israelis as very similar or similar in customs and culture and 68 per cent did so with regard to character and behaviour (Herman, Farago and Harel, 1976: 37). In a sample of Tel-Aviv residents in 1967–8, 86 per cent of the Orientals and 81 per cent of the Ashkenazim expressed their belief that within twenty years substantial differences or even all differences between the two ethnic groups would have vanished (Peres, 1971: 1037). It is difficult to say to what degree this expectation is a realistic assessment of trends.

In concluding this discussion of Oriental–Ashkenazi cultural diversity, it must be emphasized that despite the growing Oriental acculturation significant objective and subjective subcultural differences still exist. Many of the quoted data underestimate their differences because they are based on opinion polls. These surveys tend to tap the more superficial layers of social consciousness which are dominated by the official anti-ethnic views. It is expected, for instance, that depth interviews of the general population would reveal much stronger ethnic identity and other ethnic subcultural affinities than the common fixed-choice questionnaires administered to high school pupils.

Turning now to cultural differences between religious and non-religious Jews, it is tempting to either exaggerate or underplay them. It is also difficult to generalize because of the diversity within each group. The religious sector is culturally subdivided into followers of the Mizrahi versus affiliates of Agudat Israel, Orientals versus Ashkenazim, and the intelligentsia versus the masses. Within the nonreligious majority, the semi-observant (masortyim) differ from the secularists. Despite these great variations, the major religious–nonreligious division is readily discernible.

Like the Orientals and Ashkenazim, the religious and non-religious Jews share the same core-culture, with the significant exception of basic ideology. They have in common the Hebrew language and heritage, Jewish nationality, the Judaic faith, the nuclear family as a central life-interest, and even certain elements in the basic ideology such as the idea of a Jewish state, Zionism and the democratic and egalitarian ethos. They disagree, however, on certain basic values which underlie the substantial and enduring divergences in their subcultures.

Since Orthodox Judaism regulates the entire round of everyday life and lays heavy emphasis on proper behaviour, religious thought and practice are distinct in many respects. Orthodox Jews (and religious Jews in Israel are Orthodox) accept the halakha as a divine revelation and as an absolutely binding religious legal system. Compared with nonreligious Jews, religious Jews also observe the Sabbath and holidays (i.e., refrain from work, travel, turning on electrical appliances, smoking, writing, etc.), keep a kosher kitchen, devote time to Jewish learning (the Bible and Talmud), have larger families, differentiate between and segregate the sexes more, dress more modestly, and spend their leisure time more at home than outside.

It is difficult to say to what extent the differences in outlook and lifestyle between the religious and nonreligious Jews are sharp and qualitative. Given the heterogeneity within each group, many tend to regard them as relative and quantitive. This question can be explored further by examining how all-inclusive are the religious and non-religious subcultures.

It is evident that, overall, most religious Jews no longer hold the traditional all-inclusive outlook. The forces of secularization compartmentalize their life and bring them nearer to nonreligious Jews. A study of pupils in religious high schools and yeshivot (Talmudic colleges), conducted in 1964–5 by Zuckerman-Bareli (1970), substantiates this generalization with regard to the dominant section, the moderate Mizrahi, in the religious minority. About 90 per cent of the youth could be described as conformist in the realm of man–God commandments (e.g., beliefs in the sanctity of the halakha, divine reward and punishment, and the resurrection of the dead; observances of daily prayers, kashrut and fast-days) and for them Orthodox belief and practices were mutually sustaining and consistently inter-related. The unity between faith and ritual points up the conspicuous dearth of non-practising believers among the Orthodox young generation. This assures Israel's Orthodoxy against the emergence of an internal reform movement and insulates its members from appeals by Conservative and Reform Judaism.

On the other hand, it was confirmed that in the area of attitudes to man, society and state, the consistency prevailing in the sphere of man and God disappears. Over half of the respondents thought, for instance, that boys and girls should attend separate classes, that only educational films should be viewed, and that the Sabbath and marriage laws should be kept intact. On the other hand, only a minority of them felt that a religious person should not undertake certain occupations (such as a professional combat officer, a biologist, or a nurse which do not perfectly square with the Orthodox way of life), that charity should be religiously motivated, and that means to adapt halakha to modern needs should not be discussed. Although there is no doubt that religious Jews share on the whole different

117

social attitudes from nonreligious Jews, the unanimity in specific matters of religious observance simply does not exist on other issues. The religious minority has neither a uniform set of social values to transmit to its members nor an apparatus with which to police conformity.[13]

The compartmentalization of the religious outlook and the secularization of certain sections of the religious lifestyle still lack full legitimacy and they are attacked both by the ultra-Orthodox as deviant and also by modernistic religious circles (the intelligentsia, kibbutzim and supporters of the Young Faction in Mafdal). The latter call for the restoration, with necessary adaptations, of the all-embracing religious world-view. They stress the dynamics of halakha and the necessity to find within it answers for Jewish political sovereignty and to many contemporary issues.

One of the central questions is how a modern Jewish state can maintain on the Sabbath and holidays essential services such as water supply, electricity, hospitals, police and army, diplomacy, merchant fleet, heavy industry, agriculture, etc., if it adheres to the Jews' strict principle of doing no work and does not resort to Gentile labour. The more conservative circles (the Rabbinic elite) fear, on the other hand, that a greater concern with current issues would result in some sort of reform and in a subtle erosion of Orthodoxy. Thus the powerful Rabbinic elite ends up by sanctioning the outdated traditions, making unsatisfying compromises and suspending judgment. To illustrate, the Chief Rabbinate prescribed special prayers for Independence Day but declined to equate it with a Jewish holiday that takes precedence over any personal mourning. It ruled against the drafting of women and yeshivot students. It sidesteps the obligation to remove hametz (any food not kosher for Passover) by arranging a fictitious sale of all hametz in the state to an Arab, and evades the precept of shemita (a fallow year) through a similar ruse. All these rulings and the many matters left unsettled indicate that the Rabbinic elite is reluctant to face the reality of Jewish sovereignty.

There are also no specific religious answers to pressing questions of public policy (national security, the occupied territories, economy, welfare, etc.). Since there is a tendency for the religious normative void to be filled by the prevailing secular norms, the results are continuing compartmentalization and secularization of the world-view of many religious Jews on the one hand, and increasing counter-vailing pressures to greater religious integrity by certain religious circles on the other.

The dominant nonreligious subculture, like the religious one, is neither uniform nor consistent. In the evolving national culture, elements from the traditional Jewish heritage are selectively adopted and in most cases they are also adapted. Many state symbols are religious (Liebman, 1975). The traditional festivities are national holidays celebrated religiously by a minority and nonreligiously by the majority. Many nonreligious Jews voluntarily observe the duties of circumcision and Bar-Mitzva as well as burial and mourning rituals. E. Katz stresses the continuity between the values of traditional Judaism and the secularized values of the dominant culture in Israel (1973: 17):[14]

> The threads of continuity are still clearly visible in Israeli culture. The Jewish values of collectivity-orientation, familism, learning, sense of purpose, and orientation to reality are all much in evidence. Some of these values seem to have remained intact. Others are undergoing transformation. Thus the People of the Book have become the people of reading; the religious festival is transformed in meaning; ethnicity and national identification appear to be dominating religious integration.

These continuities are unduly stressed. It must be emphasized, on the other hand, that even when the two sections share the same cultural element (e.g., the Bible, holidays), they attach a different meaning to it.[15]

Furthermore, studies of identity-formation and culture-building in Israel reveal significant divergences between the religious and nonreligious groups. Along with socioeconomic level, religious observances emerges in many studies as one of the strongest correlate or the best predictor of a variety of attitudes and behaviours. This was one of the conclusions of the above-mentioned comprehensive study of the culture of leisure in Israel (Katz and Gurevitch, 1973). Herman (1970), Hofman (1970), Herman, Farago and Harel (1976) and Levy and Guttman (1974) have shown in a series of studies on high school pupils in the 1960s and 1970s that while the majority in each group attach a central role to both Jewish and Israeli sub-identities in their life, Jewish subidentity is stronger among the religious youth and Israeli subidentity is stronger among the non-religious youth. For instance, when one survey asked them to choose between self-identification as a Jew, an Israeli or a human being, only 14 per cent of the nonreligious as against 86 per cent of the religious pupils opted for Jewish identity (Zuckerman-Bareli, 1975: Table 2).

Zuckerman-Bareli's study, which was conducted at the end of 1972, discloses additional substantial disagreements. As for the key issue of Judaism as the national culture of Israel, the majority of the nonreligious pupils thought Judaism needed to be brought up to date and advocated the development of a culture open to outside influences, whereas the majority of the religious pupils felt that Judaism needed no renovation and endorsed a Jewish culture with

119

minimal borrowings. The more nationalist orientations of the religious pupils were also manifested in their much stronger identification with the national goal of Aliyah (immigration to Israel) and their categorical denunciation of Yeridah (migration from Israel), their overwhelming support for 'hawkish' policies, lack of leaning towards socialism or the left, and related matters. Also particularly pronounced were the differences in leisure and fashion which are of prime importance for inter-relations among young people. While the majority of the nonreligious approved of trendy fashions and permissiveness (long hair, pop music and dress, discotheques, and sexual intercourse at high school age), the religious by and large rejected them. Even if differences in actual behaviour are smaller than the differences in expressed attitudes, they are sufficiently large to impede effective religious–nonreligious contacts.

Another study of high school pupils in 1973 by O. Cohen (1975) concludes that in many ways the religious are much more collectivist in orientation than the nonreligious. The religious young people exhibited a greater identification with Israel, Zionism, Jewry and Jewish history, as well as a greater willingness to volunteer for social and national causes.

The possible effects of the significant and enduring religious–nonreligious subcultural differences have been of some public concern, and as a result a direct effort has been made to reduce them. In 1959 the Ministry of Education and Culture launched the 'Jewish consciousness' programme in the state nonreligious schools, with the aim of strengthening ties with and knowledge of past Jewish history, present world Jewry and religious practices (prayers, rituals, oral law). While the programme has not had much success, it could narrow the gap between the religious and nonreligious in Israel (Goldman, 1964: 84–93; Zucker, 1973: 140–2).

Cultural diversity in Israel is at its most striking between Arabs and Jews. Israel's Arabs are explicitly differentiated from Jews in precisely the core-culture that is common to Jews. They are native Arabic-speakers; Arab or Palestinian in nationality; Moslem, Christian or Druze in religion; still largely oriented to the extended family; and alienated from the basic ideology of a Jewish and a Zionist state. These primary cultural differences are institutionalized and cannot be expected to weaken as a result of the Arabs' modernization or social mobility or of other developments.

In spite of the diversity within the Arab sector along lines of age, religion, religious observance and education, and within the Jewish sector along lines of age, ethnicity, religious observance and social class, the divergences between them as a whole are roughly the same as those between a society in transition and a modern one. (Kleif, Segalman and Rothstein, 1971; Habash, 1973).

The location of the Israeli Arabs around the middle transitional section of the traditional–modern continuum as compared with the location of Jews near the modern pole is best documented in the sphere of the family. The hamula as a marrying, political and solidifying unit is still the most important social group in the Arab community, whereas it plays little part in Jewish society (see, for instance, Rosenfeld, 1976; Abu-Gosh, 1969). Patriarchal authority, although declining, has a greater hold among Arabs than Jews. Patrilocal residence is much more widespread among Arab young couples than Jewish ones. The status of Arab women is still inferior and segregated compared with that of Jewish women despite the reduction in the initial gaps through legislation against polygamy, immature marriages and unilateral divorce on the one hand and the Women's Equal Rights Law on the other (Layish, 1975b). The Arab natural population increase (i.e., annual population growth), which is among the highest in the world, remains more than double that of the Jews (the annual rates were 3.7 versus 1.8 per cent in 1975). The proportion of families with six or more members among Arabs is four times as high as that among Jews (56.7 versus 13.0 per cent in 1975) (for this and other demographic comparisons, see Table 82).

The modernizing political culture of the Arab minority is still lagging behind the highly developed political culture of the Jewish majority. A study of the impact of local government in six Arab villages in 1970 concludes (Abu-Gosh, Shye and Hartman, 1972: 1562):

> The local council – and the elective system upon which it is based – provides the Arab village with an institution of government which has achieved a modus vivendi for two worlds: the modern and the traditional. Thus, for example, although the traits contributing to achieved status for the new elite positions have gained recognition, blood relationship still remains the most fundamental unit of social distinction. Similarly, the elective process is readily endorsed by the villagers, but party affiliation is still, to a large extent, based on family loyalties. Likewise much of the village political life seems to reflect an ambivalent state between two political worlds.

The clash between the new and old values is in evidence in many areas of Arab life. It is quite apparent in Arab education (Mar'i, 1974), leisure habits (Sarsour, 1971), food consumption, social values and personality characteristics. In a state-wide representative survey of villagers in 1969 a large majority reported observance of religious precepts (as compared with only 30 per cent of the Jewish urban population), the majority believed in predestination, about half were in favour of family planning, but a majority would not

121

allow unmarried young girls to attend college in the city or decide who to marry (Guttman, Klaff and Levy, 1971). The Arabs also display more of the friendliness, neighbourliness and hospitality than the Jews, but fewer of the individualistic values (the 'Protestant ethic').[16] To cite another example, although blood-feuds are on the wane, there are very many more of them among the Arabs, compared with the Jews, as statistics on murderers and their victims demonstrate (Landau, Drapkin and Arad, 1974; Landau, 1975), and in such cases the Arab customary law of compromise is still in force in the Arab communities along with the state criminal law (Nakhleh, 1974).

On the psychological level, the Arabs are found to score significantly higher than the Jews on the social desirability scale which correlates with conformity and other personality traits (Sohlberg, 1976). Distinct differences in the mental ability of Arab rural children and Jewish urban children are shown up in intelligence tests (using the WPPSI examination with all its verbal and performance subtests) (Kugelmass, Lieblich and Bossik, 1974), but they virtually disappear in urban matched samples (Lieblich, Kugelmass and Ehrlich, 1975). This demonstrates how different today are the sociocultural milieu of the majority of Arab and Jewish children.

Arab–Jewish cultural pluralism would have been even more marked but for the intermediate Oriental cultural position. Although the Orientals are quickly becoming assimilated into Ashkenazi culture, however, the overall cultural gap between the Arabs and the Jews still remains wide. For example, in 1955 the gross reproduction rate of Arabs was 3.55 and of Jews 1.77 (of Asian- or African-born 2.77 and of European- or American-born 1.28) and the comparative rates in 1975 were 3.31 and 1.55 (1.83 and 1.37) respectively (Table 82).[17] These figures are by no means atypical: the Orientals shifted over the years away from a similarity to the Arabs towards a similarity to the Ashkenazim in general cultural patterns.

In both Arab and Jewish thinking, the cultural diversity between Arabs and Jews is substantial and persistent despite the continuing inroads of modernization into the traditional Arab way of life. The cultural gulf is seen to be so immense that virulent prejudice is bound to exist. To illustrate, 76 per cent of the Jewish respondents in one survey in 1968 believed that 'the Arabs will never reach the level of progress of the Jews' (Peres, 1971: Table 15).

Cultural differences are manifested in the striking contrasts in the self-images of the Arabs and Jews. As indicated above, the overwhelming majority of Jewish young people define themselves as Israelis, Jews or Zionists, and all these images are central to their self-identity. Although the Israeli subidentity is more important than

the Jewish subidentity, for most Jews in Israel both are complementary rather than conflicting. The case of the young Arabs is
quite different. The Arabs' identity looks problematic against the
backdrop of the Jewish nature of the state and their perceived
status as a hostile minority in it. Some of them do feel the potential
conflicts between the national and civic components in their identification as 'Israeli Arabs', but some do not, so the overall picture in the
mid-1970s was that of independence rather than complementarity or
irreconcilability between the two subidentities (Zak, 1976).

The situation is changing rapidly, however. With the advance of
modernization the familial, regional and religious subidentities are
receding and the national subidentity is taking precedence (Peres,
1970; Hofman and Debbiny, 1970). National identity among the
Arab intelligentsia is more attractive than Israeli citizenship (Hofman
and Rouhana, 1976) and alienation from the state is even greater
among the more intellectually oriented elite (Benjamin and Peleg,
forthcoming). Furthermore, in the aftermath of the October 1973
War the shaky identity of the Arabs in Israel is undergoing
Palestinization (Nakhleh, 1975b), a process which will turn the
present independence between the civic and national subidentities
into a growing irreconcilability. In a survey conducted in 1974,
85 per cent of the Arab respondents said that the term 'Palestinian'
described them well, as compared with 53 per cent who thought the
same of the term 'Israeli' (Tessler, 1975b).[18]

Social separation

The other facet of pluralism is social, i.e., to what extent pluralistic
divisions are differentiated legally or isolated in separate ecological
and social units. Separation reflects the quantity and quality of
contacts between the groups. To be sure, it is affected by the collective goals of the groups involved (whether they seek assimilation
or not) as well as by the socioeconomic gaps between them. It can
be voluntary or enforced. But the scope and form of separation are
significant, regardless of the underlying causes.

The legal and extra-legal differentiation between pluralistic groups
is of special importance because it constitutes a crossroads where
cultural and social pluralism may meet. Laws and regulations, or
their applications by public bodies in which a distinction is made
between the groups, reflect the dominant attitudes towards the
kinds of intergroup contacts desired and, in turn, the separateness of
each group.

The Declaration of Independence in 1948 promised the adoption
of a Constitution which 'will ensure complete equality of social and
political rights to all its inhabitants irrespective of religion, race, or

sex; it will guarantee freedom of religion, conscience, language, education, and culture'. While civil liberties are universal, the continued failure of Israel to adopt a Constitution makes them somewhat vulnerable.[19] In a strict legal sense, civil rights are not contingent on ethnicity or any other criterion, but beyond this basic universalism, varying degrees of legal and extra-legal differentiation do exist in Israeli society.

The legal and extra-legal distinctions between Orientals and Ashkenazim are by and large few and moderate. The only legislation in existence is in the religious sphere. The Elections Law of the Chief Rabbinate Council, 1972, specifies the selection of 150 electors, half of them Orientals and half Ashkenazim, to elect two Chief Rabbis, one Oriental and one Ashkenazi, and ten members of the Chief Rabbinate Council, five Orientals and five Ashkenazim, who hold equal power. Other regulations provide also duality in the Rabbinates in cities and other large localities if one-third or more of the residents are of each ethnic group and there is a demand for two Rabbis.

The legal provision for a dual Rabbinate does not mean, however, that the law sanctions ethnic separation in all religious institutions. The reverse is true. Since the Jewish religion is 'churchless', the Orientals may, and indeed do, use Ashkenazi religious services or facilities and vice versa. Furthermore, ethnic duality is very limited in scope. It is confined to the Rabbinate. It is customary, but not legally required, in case of dayyanim (religious judges), shohatim (ritual slaughterers) and mashgihim (inspectors of kashrut). The law also leaves open the question of the ethnic composition of local religious councils (top authorities in charge of local religious affairs). Legally speaking, ethnic duality is totally absent in the religious state school system, the army chaplaincy and the Ministry of Religious Affairs. While the law of the dual Rabbinate contributes to the ethnic folklore mosaic, it has neither binding implications nor any spin-offs.

The circumstances which led to the enactment of the Elections Law of the Chief Rabbinate Council are quite significant. Until 1972 the ethnic duality in a Rabbinate was based on government regulations inherited from the days of the British mandate (Morgenstein, 1974). Since the creation of the state, various fruitless efforts were made to legalize the status of the Rabbinate. One crucial obstacle was the issue of ethnic duality. Most of the Knesset members, who are Ashkenazim, objected in principle to making a legal distinction between the Ashkenazim and the Orientals and insisted on a unified Rabbinate. The Oriental spokesmen, on the other hand, saw in duality a tool for parity, and resisted the change explicitly on grounds of expedience rather than ideology.[20] In 1970 the Minister of Religious Affairs announced his intention to submit a law to the Knesset in which no ethnic distinction would be made. It required a historically unique combination of concerted pressures by Oriental leaders from different parties, and the fear of further ethnic escalation after the Black Panthers' demonstrations in early 1971 to reverse the trend. Under these unusual conditions the new law of duality in the Rabbinate was approved.[21]

Whereas the distinctions in the area of religion aim to preserve the ethnic separation, the administrative distinctions in education intend to reduce it. Oriental pupils used to be given extra credits in a state screening scholastic test for high schools (seker) (this was eliminated in 1972). Now, students in preparatory courses for university education conducted by the army are usually Orientals; they are selected intentionally to increase the Oriental representation in higher education. Furthermore, the new reform, with the purpose of modelling education after the American system, provides for ethnic integration at the junior high school level. The Knesset approved the reform and the Supreme Court in a test case upheld it as a binding regulation even though it had not been legally enacted.[22]

The scarcity of legal distinctions between Orientals and Ashkenazim primarily reflects the official line of negation of ethnicity and the declared national goal of complete ethnic amalgamation. There are no public bodies or organizations, except certain religious and educational institutions as indicated above, which maintain an ethnic distinction. Seen from a different standpoint, the insignificant degree of legal differentiation echoes the Orientals' inability to secure protective or compensatory legislation. For instance, Israel still lacks a specific law against ethnic discrimination. Several private Bills were introduced by non-Ashkenazi Knesset members between 1959 and 1965 to this effect, but none succeeded (see, e.g., *Knesset Proceedings*, 30 January 1962). The rationale of the overwhelming opposition was that the proposed law might create a false problem of ethnic discrimination, that other laws give sufficient protection and, most important, that Israeli law should not make any mention of 'obsolete' ethnic divisions among Jews.

Turning to the geographical distribution of Orientals and Ashkenazim, separation is, overall, moderate. On the regional level there are minor variations.[23] The Orientals are not concentrated in any contiguous territory which can differentiate them as a separate unit or serve as an independent territorial base for a possible struggle.

More significant is the ethnic separation on the community level because it also influences equality of opportunity and chances to develop local power. While 90 per cent of each group live in urban settlements, their distribution varies among more specific types of locality. In 1967, 23 per cent of the Orientals compared with 39 per cent of the Ashkenazim lived in the three largest cities, which provide the best avenues for social mobility. On the other hand, 40 per cent of the Orientals and only 17 per cent of the Ashkenazim lived in new towns and other new urban settlements where opportunities are much poorer. The same pattern is found in the new rural communities, where 7 per cent of the Orientals but only 4 per cent of the Ashkenazim resided (Table 76). As for incorporated localities, I estimate that in 1970 the ethnic composition of the ninety-eight Jewish local authorities in Israel was as follows: in thirty-two, neither ethnic group constituted a clear majority (defined as 60 per cent or more of the foreign-born local population), in forty-one, Orientals constituted the majority, and the Ashkenazim in twenty-five (Table 55). These figures indicate that the socioeconomic disadvantages of the Oriental concentration in new towns, immigrant towns and development areas are offset by greater opportunities for achieving local power.[24]

Isolation on the residential level is moderate. Well-off neighbourhoods are by and large Ashkenazi as much as the urban slums are Oriental, but there are quite a few mixed residential areas. A random ethnic mix of the population of the three largest cities in 1965 would have required 35 per cent of the inhabitants of Jerusalem to move house, 35 per cent of Haifa's, and 41 per cent of Tel-Aviv's residents.[25]

Residential and community isolation leads to de facto segregation in the primary schools, which are organized on a neighbourhood principle. In 1971–2 three-fifths of all primary school pupils were Orientals, but two-fifths of them attended classes in which they constituted an overwhelming majority of at least 75 per cent, and one-fifth of them attended almost completely segregated classes (where 95 to 100 per cent of the pupils were Orientals). Segregation in the religious state schools was even greater, since 84.2 per cent of their pupils were Orientals and religious Oriental Jews tend to live in much more ethnically homogeneous settlements than non-religious Oriental Jews. And in post-primary schools, while Orientals constituted 35.6 per cent of the pupils in 1966–7, the majority (63.1 per cent) of them attended classes with a poor mix (where over 75 per cent or fewer than 25 per cent of the pupils were Orientals) (Table 77).

Nothing has been done so far to desegregate the primary schools, but one of the chief goals of the new school system is stated to be ethnic desegregation, starting at the seventh grade.[26] However, the available figures about the implementation of the reform in education show that ethnic integration has made only limited headway (Table

77) (Inbar, 1975). If optimal integration means mixed classes composed of a majority of 60 per cent of advantaged children and the balance disadvantaged, the Israel of the mid-1970s is a long way from this virtually impracticable target.

There is no distinction between Orientals and Ashkenazim in public facilities, business, the armed forces and various bureaucracies. Inter-ethnic contact here is, in fact, daily and extensive, but it is unclear whether or not it is conducive to personal or permanent relations. The schools and the army are viewed as the two major ethnic melting-pots and indeed intergroup contact in them occurs under quite favourable conditions (the youth of the participants, common goals, etc.). However, the basic barrier against establishing firmly based associations is that the Orientals and Ashkenazim, in many cases, do not meet as status equals but rather as employees versus employers, clients versus bureaucrats, noncommissioned officers versus officers, lower-class pupils versus higher-class pupils, and so forth.

The existing evidence about the effects of inter-ethnic contact in the schools and army is by no means clear cut, but it is mostly discouraging. One study of preschool children attending ethnically heterogeneous and homogeneous kindergartens shows few differences in the amount of inter-ethnic interactions between the two settings. The dissimilarities in social experiences seem to be too wide even at the age of three, and they hamper effective mixing (Feitelson, Weintraub and Michaeli, 1972). Initial findings from another study of ethnic integration in the new Intermediate schools 'showed very little overall change in ethnic attitude and preference as a result of one year of ethnic contact' (Amir, 1976). Hence Amir casts doubts on the success of the reorganization of the educational system in promoting effective integration. He then extends his argument to the Israeli army (1969: 340):

It is doubtful whether intergroup contact in the army
situation really changes and improves ethnic relations.
Findings from two unpublished studies seem to support this
negative evaluation. One of these studies was concerned with
sociometric choices and the other, on a different population,
was concerned with ethnic attitudes. Both of them point to a
lack of change in the above aspects resulting from long and
continued contact between ethnic groups in the army.

(For one of these studies, see Amir, Bizman and Rivner, 1973.)

In political life, on the other hand, ethnic separation is blurred. Isolation was substantial during the Yishuv, but it declined after the proclamation of the state. Up to 1944, the Orientals sent 25 per cent of the delegates to the National Council – all elected on separate

127

ethnic lists (Attias, 1949: Appendix IX–XXI). When they boycotted the elections in 1944 because their demand to change the election method to a regional one was rejected, their representation dropped to 3.5 per cent. In the years 1949–73 eight national elections were held in which twenty-two Oriental lists took part. Four lists managed to obtain at least one seat but all have failed since the 1955 elections. In the 1969 national elections only one ethnic list ran and it received only 2,116 votes, amounting to 0.15 per cent of the total vote. Counting on the ethnic agitation stirred by the Black Panthers, six Oriental lists (two of which were sponsored by the Panthers themselves) were registered for elections in 1973, a short time before the October War broke out. They received altogether 38,208 or 2.5 per cent of the votes cast, but none obtained the 1 per cent or more of the total vote necessary to be apportioned a Knesset seat.

The Oriental lists have some success in the Histadrut and local elections. In the Histadrut general elections in September 1973 five Oriental lists participated; they received over 27,000 or 3.6 per cent of the total votes. There are some Oriental lists in local government. The number of these lists and the number of councillors elected from them dwindled over the years and reached an insignificant level by the 1965 elections.[27]

The virtual failure of the separate Oriental lists marks the integration of politics at one level, but permits ethnic isolation at another. The established political parties themselves maintain special departments for ethnic affairs and ethnic circles for party members and activities. Such departments and circles have the latent function of short-term separation which has been, nevertheless, on the decline. Most important, ethnic politics within the parties are well under control.

As for membership in and voting for established political parties, there is evidence for certain ethnic patterns. 'The battle for the immigrants' in the early 1950s resulted in their massive political incorporation and in the failure of the independent Oriental lists. At first, the two ruling parties, i.e., Mapai (Labour) and Mafdal (National Religious), which had more benefits to dispense, received more than their share from the newcomers. However, the right-of-centre parties, especially Herut, gradually and steadily improved their position by winning over the Oriental immigrants through a combination of nationalist and protest appeals. By the 1970s the polarizing ethnic voting is showing the following tendencies: the dominant labour bloc has gained disproportionate support from the European- or American-born (the broad middle class); the religious section has obtained much more from the traditionalist Asian- or African-born (lower class); and the right-of-centre bloc has received well over the average from the Asian- or African-born (lower-middle class). Thus the Orientals vote, overall, more for the religious and right-of-centre lists and less for the left-of-centre stream.[28]

In other voluntary associations ethnic separation varies but, overall, it is moderate. In synagogues, segregation is very high, whereas in sporting activities it is minimal. In most organizations such as social clubs, professional societies, service associations and so on, isolation is moderate. In voluntary associations there is a minimal mixing of the ethnic groups, mostly because the Orientals tend not to join them.

Most personal relationships are naturally confined to members of the same ethnic group, although inter-ethnic personal contacts are increasing. A majority of 73 per cent of Oriental male adults in 1971 reported that the neighbour last visited was an Oriental (Eshel and Peres, 1973). A study of a mixed neighbourhood found that relatively few inter-ethnic neighbourly relationships had developed (Menachem and Spiro, 1974). As for friends, in the above survey 72 per cent of the Oriental adults said that at least two-thirds of their five closest friends were Orientals (Eshel and Peres, 1973). On the other hand, 80 per cent of the high school pupils in a 1973 survey indicated that two or more of their close friends were from the other ethnic group (Levy and Guttman, 1974: 236).

One of the best indices of close interpersonal relations is marriage patterns. To cite the representative figures, of all Oriental bridegrooms in 1968, 40 per cent married brides of the same country of origin, 43 per cent married other Oriental brides and 17 per cent married Ashkenazi brides. By comparison, of all Ashkenazi bridegrooms, 23 per cent married brides born in the same country of origin, 61 per cent other Ashkenazi brides and 15 per cent Oriental brides (Shelah, 1974: Table 11). These and the comparative percentages for the 1950s show that (a) there exist two separate melting-pots – one Oriental and one Ashkenazi; (b) assimilation within the Ashkenazi melting-pot is much greater than among the Oriental one; and (c) there is some increasing convergence between the two melting-pots.

As for the more significant phenomenon of mixed marriages, they rose from 11.8 per cent in 1955 to 19.1 per cent in 1974. Since the number of the people marrying in each group has been nearly equal during this period, one would expect that in a situation of random matching, about half the marriages would have been mixed. This means that the figure for the actual out of the expected mixed marriages was 24 per cent in 1955 and 39 per cent in 1974 (see Table 78). Thus there has been a definite trend towards less endogamy.

The rate of mixed marriages seems to be even higher in the broad middle-class levels. In the absence of a direct study, this observation is supported by figures which show a greater exogamy among the relatively more privileged groups, i.e., more among established residents as compared to new immigrants, more among Israeli-born than foreign-born and more among Jews born in Iraq, Egypt, Syria, Lebanon and Turkey than among Jews from the Yemen, North Africa and the rest of Asia and Africa (H. Cohen, 1972: 10; Peres and Shrift, 1975).[29]

Many find in the current rate and rising trend of mixed marriages a strong sign of impending ethnic integration. Patai (1970: 388) goes so far as to predict that within the next generation: 'If this trend continues, the resulting interbreeding will reinforce cultural intermingling, until Jews of Israel will not only become one un-differentiated gene pool but also constitute one people socio-culturally' (p. 378). Since mixed families now make up about 5 per cent of all Jewish families, and given the facts of the continued immigration of families already established abroad, the existence of significant subcultural and socioeconomic differences between the ethnic groups and the apparently almost complete endogamy among the disadvantaged and poor, it is hard to see how total assimilation can be achieved so soon.

Despite the moderate ethnic isolation, the level of independent group organization of the Orientals is low. They are internally divided along the major lines of country of origin, religious observance, social class, political orientation, regional interests and the 'generation gap'. They also lack sufficient resources, organizational skills and leadership experience. To these handicaps, the disapproval of independent ethnic activities, and co-optative measures by the Ashkenazi dominant group, should be added.

As for social separation between the religious and nonreligious, it is much more entrenched than that between the Orientals and the Ashkenazim. The question whether religious Jews should set up separate organizations or participate in the broader community organizations which are dominated by nonreligious Jews has divided Orthodoxy for a long time. The separatists argue that integration would tacitly legitimize non-Orthodox practices and dangerously expose Orthodox Jews to outside influences. The integrationists claim, on the other hand, that separation would jeopardize the unity of the Jewish people, that integration is the best tool to spread religious observance among the nonreligious Jews and that a struggle from within stands a better chance than secession to enforce religion in the public domain. The Agudat Israel camp leans toward isolationism. Before the creation of the state it seceded from the organized Yishuv and maintained a separate community; thereafter it continued to run independent schools with only some supervision by the Ministry of Education and Culture, independent Rabbinate and religious services, and to congregate in segregated neighbourhoods. By contrast, the predominant Mizrahi camp is predisposed toward integration but its self-imposed segregation is far greater than would be expected on the basis of its stated aims. In this case seclusion is justified in terms of self-defence.

The controversy within the religious sector and the inconsistency between the integrationist ideology and the separationist practice of the dominant nationalist-religious section are apparent in the most crucial area of legislation. Should the distinction between the religious and nonreligious be formally institutionalized and then enjoy the force of compulsory law? The position of the religious establishment on this issue is clear. In principle, it fights, first, for general laws which aim to impose religion on the entire population ('universalistic religious legislation' which equally or uniformly applies to religious and nonreligious Jews), but should this prove impracticable, it turns to legislation based on differentiation along the line of religious observance ('particularistic religious legislation').

The universalistic religious legislation provides for the exclusive Rabbinic jurisdiction over personal status, the Sabbath and Jewish holidays as official days of rest, kashrut in state kitchens, and the public financing of religious services.[30] Since these laws are imposed on all Jews, distinctions between Jews according to religiousness are rendered superfluous in areas to which these laws apply. Universalistic laws, therefore, promote integration and they are supported by the nonreligious establishment, among other considerations, for this reason. They are also a measure of success of the religious establishment by serving the ultimate cause of a halakha state.

By contrast, particularistic religious legislation sanctions separation. On the one hand, it signifies the failure of the religious minority to legalize its standard as a general duty and it marks, on the other hand, its power to exact important concessions from the nonreligious majority by achieving legal protection for a minority way of life.

The two key particularist laws which draw on the religious–nonreligious division are in the areas of education and military service. A group of laws regulate primary education. The primary schools are divided into state (nonreligious), state religious (Mizrahi), and independent religious (Agudat Israel) systems. The law provides for triple bureaucracies, supervision, curriculum and selection of the teaching staff in the religious schools according to standards of Orthodoxy. Teachers' seminaries and school programmes in the state educational television are regulated by law to conform with this separation. There is no legislation for post-primary education, but the situation is practically the same. Of course the triple educational system is not compulsory and the law specifically ensures freedom

131

of choice and ease of transfer from one type of school to another. It is obvious, however, that in contrast to the ethnic dualism in the religious institutions, the parallel educational systems serve as a solid base for the stable pluralism of the Jews along the lines of religious observance.

Israel tries hard to avoid making social distinctions within the armed forces but has had to make some concessions to the religious.[31] With two significant exemptions, military service is compulsory for all Jews. Girls are allowed to substitute a year of civilian 'national service' on grounds of religious Orthodoxy. Most religious girls opt for the exemption and, since the programme of national service is largely inoperative, they do not fulfil the required civilian duty.[32] Besides, in an extra-legal way, Orthodox male students in yeshivot can obtain draft deferments for indefinite periods of time.[33]

There are also quite a few laws and regulations which recognize the religious–nonreligious division. More precisely, laws often make special exemptions for religious Jews in order to avoid any interference in their lifestyle and to assist them to adhere to their standards. Among the legal dispensations are the provision in the police law to relieve religious personnel of duties on the Sabbath and holidays, the right to a yearly vacation from which days off work because of personal mourning are not deducted, religious organizations are granted tax exemptions, ritual articles are exempt from sales tax, the right not to swear but to affirm before witnessing in various courts, the right of religious women to obtain identification cards without having their photos taken, and so forth.

Public bodies do not usually make distinctions about religious observance, whereas the religious organizations often do. For example, while the nonreligious parties stipulate no religious requirement, the religious parties restrict membership to religious persons. Likewise, the universities are open to all, but the Orthodox Bar-Ilan University recruits more religious students and staff.

Legal and extra-legal distinctions are reinforced by widespread ecological separation, which is quite high except on the regional level. The religious Jews are dispersed throughout the country and this is the major reason why the religious parties vehemently oppose the proposed change of the election method to a regional one. On the other hand, isolation in communities and residential quarters is widespread. It may be roughly estimated that three-fifths of the large and small towns are 'unmixed', i.e., there is a disproportional concentration of either religious Jews in places such as B'nai Braq, Ganie Hatikva, Hazor, Netivot and Yeruham or nonreligious Jews in towns like Arad, Karmiel, Metula, Kiryat Haroshet and Kfar Shemaryahu.[34] And in most towns there are separate religious quarters whose number is on the increase due to sustained but quiet efforts by the Mizrahi to build housing projects for its members, notwithstanding its declared objection to religious segregation. Voluntary segregation is at a record peak in the closely-knit, small rural communities. In 1975, 273,600 Jews lived in nonurban localities, of which 85 per cent were incorporated in moshavim (including some collective moshavim) and kibbutzim. Since almost all these settlements are affiliated with politico-religious sectors, they are mostly homogeneous with regard to religious observance. The moshavim were divided into 72 religious and 306 nonreligious and the kibbutzim into 13 and 213 respectively (CBS, *Statistical Abstract of Israel*, 1976, 27: 30–1). Segregation in the religious rural communities is complete and in the nonreligious ones it is massive.

Separation varies outside the sphere of personal relations. Even though the religious sector has some corporations, hospitals, etc., the religious Jews are largely integrated into the economy and various institutions. At least some of this integration is indirect, as the case of the Histadrut shows. The two religious labour organizations had 121,000 members (not including children) in 1972 who received, through a special arrangement, health insurance and trade union protection from the Histadrut. The major institutional separation lies of course in the schools and political parties. It is less complete, however, than it appears. Educational isolation diminishes with increasing level – it is less in the post-primary schools and higher institutions.[35] Furthermore, the religious parties win only half of the religious vote and most of the remainder vote for the left and right nonreligious parties.

Although informal encounters between religious and nonreligious Jews are common in the public sector, offices and most places of work, it is doubtful whether they lead to closer interpersonal relationships. In one survey of high school pupils in 1973 (O. Cohen, 1975: 154–5) the majority of the nonreligious students reported having few religious family members, few religious residents in the neighbourhood, few religious neighbours and few religious friends, and they also said that they did not usually go out with or visit a religious friend. The majority of the religious respondents also reported isolation from the nonreligious, but to a lesser degree, because as members of a numerical minority they had greater opportunities for contact.

Unlike the largely unorganized Orientals, the religious minority excels in its capacity to act as a group. The established parties provide a solid institutional base and a dynamic leadership. Independent religious activities are considered legitimate. Despite the split between the Mizrahi and Agudat Israel and the further divisions along the lines of social ideology and ethnicity, the goal of unity between state and religion musters the active commitment of the

133

majority of religious Jews. As a corporate group, the religious minority can readily take concerted action when necessary.

Separation between the religious and nonreligious Jews, and even more that between the Oriental and Ashkenazi Jews, however serious it may be, is definitely moderate compared with the exceedingly deep gulf between Arabs and Jews. The Arab–Jewish rift takes extreme and diverse forms – legal, territorial, institutional and interpersonal. The realities of separation are in line with the accepted right of the Arab minority to a separate identity, but its extreme proportions clearly deviate from the official policies of integrating Israeli Arabs into all spheres of life in Israeli society.

The legal and extra-legal distinctions which separate Arabs and Jews are numerous and fundamental (Sabri, 1973; Stendel, 1973b). While Arabs enjoy the universal freedoms of speech, assembly, movement and election, they hold a separate legal status as a linguistic, religious and cultural minority. Arabic is the second official language. The official gazette of the Israeli government, *Reshumot*, appears in Hebrew and Arabic, and Acts, Bills and local government regulations are translated into Arabic by the Ministry of Justice. Arabs have the legal right to use Arabic in Parliament, the courts and in their dealings with the state administration. Most important, the law provides for a separate, Arabic-speaking, state school system with a different curriculum. The state also maintains separate radio and television channels in Arabic. Arabs have the legal right to observe their holidays on the prescribed dates.

Arabs and Jews are also recognized as four major separate religious communities; i.e., three are Arab religious communities (Moslems, Christians and Druzes) and one is a Jewish community.[36] Legislation concerning marriage, divorce and inheritance is officially assigned to these religious communities;[37] it is thus difficult for any citizen, Arab or Jew, to renounce his or her personal religious status, although one can cross over from one religious community to another. The law leaves thereby no legal provision for intermarriage between Arabs and Jews, though it does not, strictly speaking, make it illegal. The state finances the machinery (personnel, administration) of the various religious communities.

In addition to the legally instituted statuses of the Arabs and Jews as separate ethnic and religious communities, there are many other legal and extra-legal distinctions between them. The most important of all is the Law of Return, which grants the right of automatic citizenship to Jewish immigrants and to them alone. Although the Defence Laws (State of Emergency) of 1945 (which were inherited from the British) and the Emergency Laws (Security Areas) of 1949 make no mention of ethnicity, they have been used extensively to separate Arabs from Jews. These laws empower the government to impose military rule over any area in the country and to suspend common civil rights. The government has so far applied them to Arabs alone, regardless of where they live. Military rule was abolished in 1966, but since the laws have not been rescinded, they can be reactivated at any time – as they were during the 1967 War and to a certain degree during the 1973 War.[38] There are also various land control laws which are used mostly to expropriate Arab land.[39] With few exceptions, Arabs are not conscripted for military service. This extra-legal exemption of Arab citizens aims to prevent situations of extreme cross-loyalties.

Most public institutions apply a de facto distinction between Arabs and Jews. The Zionist Jewish parties, except Mapam, used to be closed to Arabs. They have recently liberalized their admission restrictions in order to permit certain categories of Arabs (e.g., army veterans) to join. Arabs are almost totally barred from most government offices and managerial and professional positions in the Jewish economy. Neither can 'Arab' be considered a neutral status for membership in some other voluntary associations.

Geographical isolation is similarly large in all its macro and micro planes. The overwhelming majority of Israeli Arab citizens in 1975 were concentrated in three regions: Galilee (57 per cent), the 'Little Triangle' (21 per cent) and the Negev (9 per cent), and only a minority (13 per cent) were dispersed in other parts of the country. This heavy concentration serves Arabs as a territorial base that has been an unceasing cause for alarm to the Jewish authorities. To prevent possible claims of irredentism or co-operation with the enemy, the Israeli government exercised its powers to relocate Arab border villages in the interior, to expropriate Arab lands and to increase the Jewish population in Arab areas. These preventive measures have reduced the Arab territorial base over the years.

Separation is even greater at the community and residential level. About 90 per cent of Israeli Arabs in 1975 lived in complete segregation from the Jews in the 2 all-Arab towns (Nazareth and Shefaram), in 103 all-Arab villages and in the 40 Bedouin encampments. A minority of about 10 per cent resided in the seven mixed towns (Western Jerusalem, Tel-Aviv–Yafo, Haifa, Lod, Ramle, Akko and Maalot–Tarshiha) characterized by a Jewish majority and a nearly absolute residential segregation of Arabs and Jews.

Segregation is pervasive in many institutions and organizations. These include the schools (except the universities), political parties (with the minor exceptions of Mapam and Rakah), armed forces and most voluntary associations. This institutional segmentation is furthered by the maintenance of special departments for minority affairs in most government ministries as well as the Histadrut.[40] On the other hand, it is important to note that the Histadrut trade

135

unions were desegregated officially in 1959 but in practice not until 1965. By 1974 48 per cent of all the 109,000 employed Arabs and 67 per cent of all the 78,000 Arab wage-earners were members of the Histadrut enjoying union protection and health and other services (Histadrut Arab Department, *Leket Yediot*, no. 36, January–March 1975, p. 22).

Impersonal contacts between Arabs and Jews are, however, quite frequent. About 65 per cent of Arab employees come into daily contact at work with Jewish co-workers or employers. The integration of public facilities such as public transportation, business, entertainment establishments and hospitals also provides for numerous casual encounters.

On the other hand, close personal contacts are rare and unstable. The near-complete residential segregation causes a virtual absence of the neighbourly relations which are of special importance in Arab society.[41] Similarly, friendships are infrequent[42] and 'dating' is taboo (E. Cohen, 1971: 223). As for intermarriages, it should be recalled that there is no provision in Israeli law for them[43] and hence no official statistics are gathered. One reliable estimate gives a figure of 400 for the entire 1948–75 period.[44] These mixed families constitute a negligible fraction of all families in Israel and they lack an acceptable public status. The man is usually Arab and the woman Jewish; they display other kinds of eccentricities and are confined to living in Arab quarters. Being marginal to both ethnic groups, the mixed couples do not serve as a bridge but rather as a deterrent and an aberrance which further hardens the quasi-caste line (E. Cohen, 1969a).

Despite their large-scale isolation, the Israeli Arabs are not well organized at present. They are divided by traditional hamula feuds, religious affiliations and local loyalties. Their resources are meagre. Apart from all these handicaps, the fear, grounded in past experience, that the Jewish authorities would not permit Arab independent organizations is in most cases sufficient to stifle any organized action.

2 Inequality

The scale of Israeli society has expanded dramatically since the early 1950s. The population, living standards, power and other positions, to mention only a few indications, trebled in this period. The tremendous growth and prosperity raise the fundamental question of inequality between the dominant and nondominant pluralistic groups. In what follows we will examine various manifestations of inequality in the distribution of resources and rewards between the groups at present, so that we can track down any levelling-off effects of the general developments on the large initial inequalities. Since the next chapter is devoted fully to a detailed analysis of Oriental–Ashkenazi inequality, we will treat them here only briefly in order to allow comparisons with the other pluralistic divisions.

Socioeconomic gaps

Generally speaking, the Ashkenazim are about twice as well off as the Orientals. In 1975 the annual per capita income of the Ashkenazim (IL 10,774) was twice that of the Orientals (IL 5,729) (CBS, *Statistical Abstract of Israel*, 1976, 27: 261). The gap in per capita expenditure, which is a rough index of standard of living, stands also at a ratio of 2:1. The same ratio appears in the occupational structure: in the top white-collar (professional, administrative and business) occupations, in which about half the Jewish labour force was employed in 1975, the proportional representation of the Ashkenazim (57.7 per cent) was twice that of the Orientals (33.1 per cent) (ibid.: 314–15).

The ethnic educational gap in both the general population and the student population is even more marked. While in 1975 the Ashkenazim had on average three more years of schooling than the Orientals (9.8 compared to 7.1), and the percentage of the Ashkenazim with at least some college education was about three times greater than that of the Orientals (22.9 compared with 7.0 per cent), the Oriental illiteracy rate (21.8 per cent) was eight times as high as that of the Ashkenazim (2.6 per cent) (ibid.: 589). The Ashkenazi superiority in school attendance rates is equally substantial. In 1975–6 70.8 per cent of Ashkenazi young people aged between fourteen and seventeen attended post-primary schools as compared with 52.2 per cent among Orientals, but in the more important academic high schools the Ashkenazi rate was 2·5 times as high (43.9 compared with 17.1 per cent) (ibid.: 608). And, most important, in higher education, the Ashkenazi attendance rate (9.3 per cent of the Ashkenazi foreign-born aged twenty to twenty-nine and 13.8 per cent of the Ashkenazi Israeli-born studied in universities in 1973) was five times greater than that of the Orientals (2.0 and 2.8 per cent respectively) (ibid.: 616).

These and other data which will be taken up more fully in the next chapter show that the overall socioeconomic gap between the Orientals and Ashkenazim is substantial and largely persistent. The Orientals have improved their conditions considerably over the years but given the proportional improvement in the living conditions of the Ashkenazim and the marked rise in the various socioeconomic standards in Israeli society as a whole, Oriental–Ashkenazi inequality has remained large indeed.

Material regarding socioeconomic differentials between religious and nonreligious Jews is scarce, but some circumstantial evidence suggests that the religious group is at some disadvantage. There is a correlation between religious observance, ethnicity, education and income (O. Cohen, 1975: 26). Overall, the religious tend to be disproportionally Oriental, less educated and poorer. In one national survey of the urban Jewish population taken in 1969, some 26 per cent of all respondents reported religious observance. In comparison, 44 per cent of the foreign-born Orientals, 38 per cent of all people with primary or less education, and 40 per cent of the underpaid were religious (Arian, 1973: 67). Much of the average disadvantage of the religious minority is, however, because of the overrepresentation of the poor Orientals among them. For this reason the socioeconomic inequality between the religious and nonreligious sectors should be considered as relatively small.

Compared with the socioeconomic differentials among the Jewish groups, those between the Arabs and Jews are usually greater. The ratio in the distribution of socioeconomic resources between the Arabs and Jews is higher on average than the 1:2 ratio between the Orientals and the Ashkenazim.[45] (The following figures are taken from Table 83, unless otherwise indicated.)

The Arab–Jewish gap is well in evidence in the area of material wellbeing. In 1975 the annual per capita income of the Jews (IL 8,289) was twice that of the Arabs (IL 4,651). Comparative figures regarding possession of durable goods, however, indicate an even larger gap in the standard of living. In 1975, 53.8 per cent of non-Jewish families as against 98.3 per cent of Jewish families owned electric refrigerators, but as to the more differentiating items – 7.0 compared with 52.2 per cent had telephones and 11.5 as against 27.6 per cent owned private cars. Similarly in 1975 only 13.9 per cent of Arab families compared with 52.5 per cent of Jewish families had decent housing accommodation (one or fewer people per room).

Employment shows a similar picture. In 1975, 19.2 per cent of the Arabs compared with 51.1 per cent of the Jews held top white-collar (scientific, professional, managerial, clerical and business) jobs, and 13.0 as against 5.2 per cent respectively were nonskilled workers. Furthermore, 40.3 per cent of Arab employees were concentrated in the low-status blue-collar branches of agriculture and construction as against 11.8 per cent of Jewish employees. The disparities between Arab and Jewish agriculture is considerable. In 1974–5 Arab peasants farmed 895,000 dunams (1 dunam = 0.247 acre), of which 7.6 per cent were irrigated. In comparison, Jewish farmers cultivated 3,425,000 dunams, of which 51.4 per cent were irrigated (CBS, *Statistical Abstract of Israel*, 1976, 27: 354). The Arab value of production totalled IL 380.0 million or IL 425 per dunam and the

Jewish value of production totalled IL 8,081.3 million or IL 2,360 per dunam (ibid.: 363). The Jewish output per dunam was, therefore, 5.5 times as high as that of the Israeli Arabs.[46] Because Jewish agriculture has the advantage of access to better land, superior irrigation, machinery, subsidies, markets and farming techniques, this gap is so wide.

The differences in the sphere of education between Arabs and Jews are equally substantial. In 1975 the median number of years of schooling among Arabs was 6.0 as against 9.6 among Jews, i.e., a Jew has on the average about three and a half more years of education than an Arab. The gap is much wider at the ends of the educational ladder. The Arabs had an illiteracy rate (22.9 per cent) three times as high as the Jews (7.6 per cent), but the proportion of Arabs with some college education (4.5 per cent) was only one-quarter of that of the Jews (17.7 per cent).

The differentials in school attendance are also substantial. Whereas almost all Jewish children (except for 1 per cent) attended the compulsory primary schools, there is still a high rate of non-attendance among Arab children. Out of all Arab six-year-olds in 1966–7, who were supposed to finish their primary education in 1972–3, only 66 per cent reached the eighth grade (some of them never started and most dropped out) (Israel, Ministry of Education and Culture, 1975: 7). In 1974–5 32.0 per cent of all Arabs aged fourteen to seventeen attended post-primary schools as compared with 60.9 per cent of the Jews, i.e., the Jew's, attendance rate in post primary education was twice that of the Arabs. And at the university level the gap is greater (as one would expect); the attendance rate of Jews in 1973 is estimated to be five to six times as high as that of Arabs.

A public inquiry Commission in 1973 defined three impeding factors: low education of the head of the family (seven or fewer years of schooling), inadequate housing (three or more people per room), and below average per capita income (Prime Minister's Commission, 1973: 15–18). The Commission determined that Israeli children who are raised in families suffering from two or more of the above drawbacks lack the necessary conditions for development. It estimated that 19 per cent of all Jewish children in 1968–9 fell into this category, but failed to assess the percentage of the Arab children similarly handicapped. An estimate that at least half the Arab children live in disadvantaged families is by no means far-fetched.

The asymmetric distribution of jobs, incomes and educational attainments as well as the overall inferior position of the Arabs as a semi-caste in Israeli society reveal a sharp discrepancy in prestige between Arabs and Jews. In the post-state period the Israeli Arabs turned from being peasants into semi-skilled or unskilled wage-earners. This change in status caused a dramatic reduction in the traditional class differentials. As 'a déclassé class' (Rosenfeld, 1964), the Arabs experienced a substantial decline in status in Israeli society. The average Arab in Israel today cannot expect high status on the grounds of his employment or training. And even when he works as a professional and has a higher education, he does not enjoy the same status as a Jew because social status in Israel is assigned not only by occupational and educational achievements but also by identification with the predominant goals of Israel as a Jewish-Zionist state and by contribution to its national security and Jewish immigration. It is clear that the Arabs as a status group are the lowest in Israeli society according to these criteria (Waschitz, 1975: 52).

The available figures do show, nevertheless, that the improvement in Arab conditions over the years has reduced Arab–Jewish inequality. The per capita income of an average Arab family rose from 35 per cent of that of an average Jewish family in 1956–7 (CBS, *Family Expenditure Surveys*, Special Publication Series 148, 1963) to 56 per cent in 1973. Only 8 per cent of Arab families in 1965 had electric refrigerators as compared with 54 per cent in 1975 (among Jews 84 and 98 per cent respectively). Some equalization of education is also discernible. The illiteracy rate dropped considerably from 49.5 in 1961 to 22.9 per cent in 1975 (among Jews from 12.6 to 7.6 per cent respectively) and the percentage of people with some higher education rose from 1.5 in 1961 to 4.5 per cent in 1975 (among Jews from 9.9 to 17.7 per cent). By the same token Arab attendance rates in primary, post-primary and post-secondary schools improved markedly, decreasing to some extent the Arab–Jewish gap.

Three conclusions can be drawn from the available data on the distribution of socioeconomic resources between Arabs and Jews. First, the divergences rather resemble those between the backward and modern sectors of nonindustrialized countries. They are thus considerable for Western countries such as Israel, where the inequalities between social strata are relatively small.

Second, despite the noticeable improvements in living conditions of the Israeli Arabs and the reduction in the Arab–Jewish gaps, they are still closer to the standards of the Palestinian population of the West Bank than to the Jewish population in Israel. Several comparative figures are sufficient to demonstrate this conclusion. In 1975, 48.4 per cent of the Palestinians on the West Bank were aged 0–14 years, 49.5 per cent of the Arabs in Israel and 29.9 per cent of the Jews in Israel (CBS, *Statistical Abstract of Israel*, 1976, 27: 40, 688). The respective percentages of overcrowded families (three or

more people per room) were 52.7, 43.5 and 4.2 per cent (ibid.:
273, 701), and possessing electric refrigerators (in 1974) – 22.6,
53.8 and 98.3 per cent (CBS, *Statistical Abstract of Israel*, 1975,
26: 275, 277, 698). Of all the employed in 1975, 21.0 per cent of the
West Bank Palestinians worked in the professions, administration
and business, 19.2 per cent of the Arabs in Israel and 51.1 per cent
of the Jews in Israel (ibid.: 287, 314, 714). And finally a comparative
study of higher education shows that the Palestinians on the West
Bank surpassed Israeli Arabs in attendance rates by a ratio of
6:1 or more (Mar'i, 1976:29).[47] In other words, whatever their
socioeconomic gains, the Israeli Arabs are still much below the
higher Western standards of the Jewish population and closer to
those of their parent Palestinian population (Peretz, 1970b: 100).

And third, there are indications among the Arab minority of a
heightening sense of relative deprivation. As far as socioeconomic
measures are concerned, the Israeli Arabs aspire to attain the higher
standards of Israeli society rather than deriving satisfaction from
comparison with their own former lower achievements (in or earlier
than the 1950s), with Arabs in Arab countries or Palestinians on the
West Bank or elsewhere.[48] The Israeli Arabs' tendency to make direct
and less favourable comparisons with the Jews conflicts sharply
with the Jews' emphasis on the progress the Israeli Arabs have made
in comparison with the past or with Arabs across the borders.[49]
Contrary to Jewish paternalist expectations, the Arabs have strong
aspirations. To illustrate, in one state-wide survey of villagers in
1969, 62 per cent of the men said that college education was suitable
for children of people like themselves (and an additional 18 per cent
thought that complete secondary education would be adequate) and
the majority wished their children to be professionals (Guttman,
Klaff and Levy, 1971: questions 16 and 165 in the Appendix).[50]

Power disparities

Power disparities in pluralistic societies may be assessed from two
viewpoints. On the one hand, it is possible to investigate inequalities
in the distribution of power between the constituent groups of the
society at large; namely, the extent to which they enjoy equal access
and proportional representation in the major power centres. On the
other hand, where there are institutionalized pluralistic divisions, it
would be equally appropriate to find out whether the minority
groups have a free hand to decide and manage their own affairs;
i.e., whether cultural diversity and social separation are properly
matched by cultural autonomy and community control. These two
aspects of approaching power disparities are inter-related. They
are relevant to the institutionalized religious–nonreligious, and

the Arab–Jewish divisions, but the second view is less applicable to the noninstitutionalized Oriental–Ashkenazi division.

Despite the Oriental penetration of many power positions, the distribution of power is still grossly unbalanced.[51] Despite the extent of the Orientals' participation in power, the Ashkenazim are at present in full control. All the national power centres which govern the society were Ashkenazi-controlled in 1973. These include the state government (two of the eighteen ministers were Orientals), the Jewish Agency (one Oriental out of thirteen executive members), the Histadrut (five of the twenty members of the central committee were Orientals), the top governing bodies of political parties (Oriental representation ranged from 0 to 25 per cent in the five major parties),[52] the Industrialists' Union (one Oriental out of fifteen board members), the managerial elite (3 per cent of the top-ranking officials in government and 3 per cent of the top managers in industry were Orientals), the mass media and national voluntary associations. A study of the Israeli national elite in 1972 shows that only 3 per cent of the elite members included in the sample were Orientals (Gurevitch and Weingrod, 1976: 363). It is then evident that the asymmetry in the distribution of national decision-making positions is reflected by Oriental–Ashkenazi ratios several times greater than the 1:2 ratio observed in the distribution of Oriental–Ashkenazi socioeconomic resources.

My extensive survey of the ethnic composition of power positions to be reported in the next chapter shows, however, that the Orientals' representation varies widely with the nature of the power positions. In some minor roles, such as councillors in the new local governments, the Orientals achieved near parity, whereas in other positions such as membership in the Steering Committee of Hevrat HaOvdim (the Histadrut industrial complex), they are still excluded. To generalize, the Orientals are better represented in the less powerful posts. Their relative share is greater in the lower grades of various power hierarchies, in weaker sectors of power such as the Histadrut rather than the state, in local rather than in national offices, and in positions which depend on electoral pressures rather than on oligarchic ones.

The survey also detects a significant trend in the shape of increasing Oriental representation over the years. The slow and consistent increase up to the mid-1960s was followed by a sharp rise in 1965 at the time of a political rift in the ruling party. By 1969 a standstill or even a downswing occurred as a result of expedient cuts in ethnic appointments in the guise of the alleged disappearance of ethnicity after the 1967 War. Since 1971, with the resurgence of dormant ethnicity in the form of the Black Panther demonstrations, the pendulum has been swinging up again. These 'seasonal' fluctuations attest to the fact that the Orientals lack a power base and a leadership of any stature. Their representation is vulnerable to transient strategies or the needs of the dominant Ashkenazi group.

It must be emphasized, on the other hand, that in spite of the modesty and precariousness of the Orientals' power achievements, especially against the foil of an Oriental numerical majority, the policy of assuring the Orientals a minimal number of positions in top levels and the open-door policy in lower levels have been successful in winning both strong support and high compliance from the Orientals. Their penetration of the system, though in its less important niches, gives them a stake in it and validates their sense of membership in the superior segment of the population.

As for the Orientals' cultural autonomy and community control, the question is of little relevance by the mid-1970s. The Orientals have never had the right to a separate identity, and during the last two decades they have lost much of their cultural distinctiveness. They have no separate schools, political parties or other organizations. In communities where the Orientals constitute a majority, they also occupy the top power positions although the significance of local power is quite limited in the Israeli centralized system.

The picture is quite different in the case of the power disparity between religious and nonreligious Jews. The case of religious Jews is striking in its internal contrasts, as they (a) are a numerical minority (no more than 30 per cent) of the Jewish population, (b) desire to model the entire society after their ideals, (c) are politically under-represented, (d) wield little influence on decision-making in nonreligious areas, and yet (e) enjoy rights of veto on religious issues, cultural autonomy and community control.

The religious Jews' political under-representation can be shown in various areas. It appears in all the four centres of power. As to the state positions of power, religious under-representation is manifested in the number of Orthodox Knesset members, which averaged 17 (ranging from 15 to 19) out of 120, corresponding to 15 or 16 per cent of the Jewish votes during 1949–73 (Table 80). The number of Orthodox cabinet ministers averaged 3 (ranging from 2 to 4) out of an average of 16 (ranging from 12 to 24) with a mean of 17 per cent representation in the fifteen governments in which they served during the same period (Table 81). A similar situation obtained in the Zionist executive committee, where the number of Orthodox members ranged from 4 to 7 out of the 39–52 Israeli delegates, with a mean proportion of 12 per cent during 1951–72 (Table 69) and in the Jewish Agency, where the religious parties had 2 members out of the 12 or 13 or a mean of 17 per cent during 1951–73. The religious Jews are not represented at all in the Histadrut, although some of them belong to it, and the majority subscribe to its health and

143

trade union services via the religious parties. There is in the Histadrut a tiny Religious Workers' Faction affiliated to the Israel Labour Party, whose head, the Rabbi of the Histadrut and Moshavim Movement, was the first to become an Orthodox member of the central committee of the Histadrut and then to be elected to the Knesset in 1973 on a nonreligious list (Israel Labour Party). This is, however, an exception to the rule in view of the fact that the religious Jews hold virtually no power in the nonreligious parties of the left or right despite their sizeable support for them.

The power of the religious group is quite limited in other nonreligious areas. Some religious Jews can be found among ranking government officials, but they are usually confined to the offices of religious affairs, interior and welfare, which have for long been under religious cabinet ministers. Religious Jews in positions of power exercise very little influence on foreign, security, economic or social policies. Only one of the ten justices of the Supreme Court in 1973 was religious. No Orthodox Jew has ever been appointed a major-general in the army or a top officer in the police. It is clear that the religious minority neither own nor dominate any sector of the national economy. Although the religious parties own banks, corporations and certain assets, and some Orthodox Jews are part of the bourgeois and managerial class, the religious group as a whole does not constitute a significant factor in the economic structure.

Under-representation is evident in local political roles as well. The religious parties usually obtain about 15 per cent of the votes in local elections and thus the same proportion of the representatives in local authorities are religious. For instance, in the 1969 elections 17.5 per cent of the 1,086 elected representatives in Jewish local authorities came from the religious parties and in the 1973 elections they gained 16.0 per cent of the votes. In contrast, only ten out of the ninety-seven (i.e., 10.3 per cent) Jewish heads of local governments were religious in 1969 and six (i.e., 6.2 per cent) in 1973 (Elazar, 1975: Tables 2–3).[53] Furthermore, hardly any of the sixty-five Jewish general secretaries of local workers' councils in 1972 were religious.

Yet it is true that the religious minority exercises power in religious matters to an extent which far exceeds its actual political representation or its size, and to a degree which is sufficiently large to ensure it cultural autonomy and community control. The religious Jews' effective power stems from three major sources.

The first bulwark of religious Jews are their strong political organizations. The religious Jews provide the religious political parties with a solid electoral bloc and a mandate to represent their well-defined interests. The nonreligious majority recognizes the legitimacy of the religious interests and agrees to take them into consideration in order to prevent clashes on religious questions. This is the firm social base for the historical co-operation between the religious and nonreligious parties in national and local governments. Over the years the National Religious Party has become the junior party in power along with the senior Israel Labour Party. The large number of splinter parties and the need for coalition governments adds to the power of the religious parties. [54] In practice, the religious parties have a decisive say in religious policy-making affecting the entire Jewish population, and on certain religious issues they often enjoy effective powers of veto at both national and local levels. [55]

Second, the religious group effectively controls or monopolizes all the religious institutions which are entrusted with jurisdiction over all Jews, including the nonreligious majority. These institutions are the Ministry of Religious Affairs, the Chief Rabbinate, the Rabbinic courts, the army chaplaincy, the local Rabbinates, and religious councils. The personnel of all these institutions is restricted to Orthodox Jews, and by and large to people affiliated to the National Religious Party. This means that Conservative or Reform Jews do not serve in these bodies at all. Furthermore, the non-religious members who participate in the election or appointment of the personnel of the religious institutions occupy a minority position. For instance, 80 out of the 150 electors of the Chief Rabbinate (i.e., 52.5 per cent) should by law be Rabbis, but in fact a good number of the other 70 'public representatives' are religious. And 45 per cent of the members of the local religious councils are appointed by the Minister of Religious Affairs, 10 per cent by the local Rabbi and 45 per cent by the local authority. [56] Although all these religious institutions are part of the state machinery and, as such, subject to supervision by nonreligious bodies, they have a great deal of autonomy and intervention in their rulings is usually initiated only in response to complaints of improper practices.

And, third, the religious group enjoys nearly complete autonomy in the specific religious institutions tailored to its needs. These include the religious political parties, religious education, religious settlements, religious periodicals and the religious voluntary associations. The religious political parties have an independent power-base and act independently rather than as client parties. State religious education is managed by a religious staff in a special department in the Ministry of Education and Culture. All the other religious institutions have freedom of action despite the partial subsidies which they often receive from nonreligious bodies such as the government and the Jewish Agency.

The weak position of the Arab minority contrasts sharply with the powerful status of the religious minority notwithstanding the basic similarities between them as recognizable pluralist groups. The Arab minority is impotent to participate in state-wide power positions and to control its own communities and organizations.

Because of their fewer members (13 per cent of the total population) and the informal excluding measures taken by the dominant Jewish majority, the Israeli Arabs are in practice excluded from national and even from middle-rank power positions (for details see Table 84). They usually have no representation in the top ranks of the four major national power centres; i.e., the state (cabinet ministers, directors-general, Knesset members, majors-general, Supreme Court justices), the Jewish Agency (members of the executive, directors-general, members of the Zionist executive committee), the Histadrut (members of the central committee, members of the executive committee, top officials), and the top governing bodies in the major political parties (Ma'arakh, Likud and Mafdal). There are a few exceptions, though, including 1 deputy minister out of 21 ministers and deputy ministers, 6 Knesset members out of 120, 5 members of the executive committee of the Histadrut out of 167, 10 members of the central committee of the Israel Labour Party out of 615, 11 members of the central committee of Mapam out of 340, 3 members of the central committee of Herut out of 251, and a number of top officials out of several hundreds.

The Arabs' share in the top administrative and economic bodies is meagre. They are absent from the governing bodies of the Industrialists' Union as well as of the publicly-owned corporations. The Israeli Arabs have neither a bourgeoisie which owns the means of production nor the control of any branch of the Israeli economy. There is hardly any Arab industry (except for scores of small workshops), and Arab agriculture is marginal (the value of its production amounted to 4 per cent in 1974–5 of the total agricultural value) (CBS, *Statistical Abstract of Israel*, 1976, 27: 363). The Arabs in employment comprised just 10 per cent out of 1.1 million employed persons in the economy, and their percentage exceeded this average in two spheres only – in agriculture (23 per cent) and in construction (27 per cent) (ibid.: 287). Doubtless, the proportion of Arabs among the unskilled and semi-skilled workers in these two areas is much greater. But the control of these branches is in the hands of the owners of the means of production and the trade union leaders, almost all of whom are Jewish.

Although 90 per cent of the Israeli Arabs live in all-Arab communities and two-thirds of them elect their representatives to local governments, it is doubtful whether they really have any community control. First, local power in Israel remains weak. Second, frequent interventions from the outside (the authorities, the Histadrut, the Zionist political parties) further weaken the power that Arab heads of local authorities can exercise. And, third, hamula feuds and intense struggles between kinship and religious factions hamper the emergence of a modern, efficient and nonaccommodating local leadership (Nakhleh, 1975a).

Nor do Israeli Arabs have control of their separate institutions. Most office-holders in the Arab religious bodies (Kadis, Moslem religious personnel, Wakf trustees, apart from certain Christian Arab officials) are appointed by the Jewish authorities and receive their salaries from the state. Jews head the Arab education section in the Ministry of Education and Culture: they determine the curriculum and appoint the employees (superintendents, teachers and ancillary educational staff), who work as civil servants. Other Arab departments, the most important of which are the Office of the Prime Minister's Adviser on Arab Affairs, the Arab Department in the Histadrut, and the Arab Department in the Israel Labour Party, are headed by Jews who are assisted by an increasing number of Arab functionaries and hamula elders at the local level. Decisions regarding the Arab sector are made after consultations with the heads of Arab departments who are nicknamed 'Arabists' (i.e., advisers to the authorities on Arab affairs).

The Israeli Arabs lack the organizational base to mobilize independent public opinion and support. They neither own nor control any newspaper, radio or television station, youth movement, university, industry, trade union or political party of their own. Rakah (the New Communist Party) attempts to fill the vacuum by supplying the Arab minority with an independent, ideological and state-wide leadership. Although it has scored a good deal of success in the last decade, its serious limitations are becoming more evident. Rakah's doctrinaire commitment to Soviet communism, its anti-bourgeois and anti-traditional orientation, the balanced Arab–Jewish composition of its leadership and its proclaimed desire to be an Arab–Jewish party curb its development into an Arab national party and deter traditional elements on the one hand and national elements on the other from supporting it.

Three conclusions can be drawn from this discussion of power disparity between the Arab minority and the Jewish majority. First, the distribution of power is exceedingly asymmetric. National positions of power are concentrated in the hands of the Jewish majority. The Israeli Arabs neither constitute a pressure group nor a veto group.

Second, the Israeli Arabs do not have cultural autonomy. Their separate culture, identity, territorial base, local government and religious and educational institutions do not constitute an independent power-base. Their important affairs, including Arab education, are determined by the authorities. Likewise they lack the essential organizational apparatus which is necessary to create power and guarantee independent action.

And, third, a trend towards a growth in the Israeli Arabs' power is discernible, especially in the context of the initial helplessness, disorientation and lack of control and leadership that characterized them when the state was established. The formation of Rakah in 1965 and the abolition of military government in 1966 created the basic conditions for organized Arab political activity. The growing class differentiation in Arab society since 1948 has given rise to an expanding new middle class which already constitutes the social base for the activities of a new sizeable elite of educated Arabs. In 1974 there were about 700 students in teachers' colleges, about 1,000 college students, about 4,000 people with post-secondary (though not complete university) education and about 2,000 with full academic education, i.e., about 8,000 educated Arabs compared with only several hundreds in the early 1950s.

3 Overall characterizations

After surveying in detail the cultural diversity, social separation, socioeconomic gaps and power disparities between each of the three divisions, it is possible to make an overall characterization of each one so that the similarities and differences between them would become clear.

I suggested earlier (chapter 2, section 3) three overall features of pluralism and inequality, namely, magnitude, inconsistency and durability. Magnitude is the amount of the differences between the groups. Inconsistency is the degree of convergence or divergence of the various group differences. Durability is the extent to which group differences gradually change, i.e., increase (or decrease) and converge (or diverge). Table 4 sums up our estimates of these features for each pluralist division.

Oriental–Ashkenazi pluralism is characterized as moderate, consistent and partly transitory, partly stable. In other words, the cultural diversity and social separation between Orientals and Ashkenazim are intermediate in magnitude, the moderate amount of social separation corresponds consistently with the moderate amount of cultural diversity, and over the years there is a definite trend toward diminishing cultural diversity and social separation without so far blurring the separate ethnic subidentities and subcultures.

On the other hand, Oriental–Ashkenazi inequality is considered substantial, inconsistent and stable. To elaborate, the ratio of 2:1 or more in the distribution of socioeconomic and power resources between the Ashkenazim and the Orientals is considerable for a

Western society with an egalitarian ethos such as Israel; the power disparities are disproportionately greater than the socioeconomic gaps and, despite certain equalization of resources, the dominant trend is one of persisting ethnic inequalities. Some insights can be gained from this profile of the Oriental–Ashkenazi division. First, the moderate extent of pluralism indicates that as far as the Oriental–Ashkenazi division is concerned, Israel faces a much easier problem than most developing countries where pluralism is maximal, but a greater difficulty than most Western European nation-states where pluralism is minimal. Second, there is a real problem of ethnic inequality and the crystallization of ethnic stratification. Third, certain disjunctions do exist in the Oriental–Ashkenazi division which have a mixture of effects. On the one hand, the growing acculturation and social mixing have the integrative effect of creating cross-cutting loyalties and solidarity bonds. On the other hand, a reduction in cultural diversity and social separation without a simultaneous, proportional reduction in inequality have the aggressive effect of heightening relative deprivation and intensifying group tensions.

The features of the religious–nonreligious division are different. Pluralism is moderate, very consistent and stable. This means that the distinct Orthodox subculture finds suitable and legitimate expression in separate institutions which successfully transmit it to the new generation. At the same time, inequality is relatively minor since much of the observed socioeconomic gap between the religious and nonreligious is accounted for by ethnicity; given the status of the religious as a group with the power of veto, there is practically no question of power disparities.

Such a sketch of the religious–nonreligious division shows how well balanced and potentially harmonious it is. It could be upset, however, for a number of reasons. First, the dynamics of Israeli society itself (continuing immigration, advancing technology, foreign influences, etc.) presents an enduring threat of secularization and constantly produces new issues for which there are no clear answers in the religious status quo. Second, the institutionalization of the religious way of life in a predominantly secular society is a continuing effort of high political awareness, closing loopholes in self-sufficiency and guaranteeing equality of opportunities and resources. And third, and most important, the goal of imposing religion on the entire Jewish population (both as a preventive measure to protect the religious subculture and as a general ideal) obviously leads to various manifestations of what is felt to be religious coercion in a society dominated by a nonreligious majority. Under these circumstances, the otherwise finely-balanced and peaceful religious–nonreligious division could turn into a battleground.

149

The features of the Arab–Jewish division differ greatly from those of the two Jewish divisions. Cultural diversity, social separation, socioeconomic gaps and power disparities between Israeli Arabs and Jews are more or less substantial, consistent and stable. The endemic and permanent convergence of lines of cleavage separating the two ethnic communities leaves little to hold them together. This involuntary co-existence between an Arab minority and a Jewish majority is potentially explosive, and it has so far been kept in check through economic dependence and political subordination.

The above summary descriptions also make clear the similarities and differences among the three pluralistic divisions. A focused comparison among the three nondominant groups would show that in many ways religious Jews and Israeli Arabs are similar. Both are nonassimilating minorities, are granted a right to a separate identity and separate institutions, and are in principle against the dominant character of society and their status in it as nondominant minorities. Of course the religious minority, being the 'most Jewish' in a Jewish state and enjoying a long tradition of effective organization, is more powerful than the Arab minority, and therefore strikes a far better deal with the majority.

By contrast, the Oriental majority presents a relatively narrower problem. It demands equality in distribution of resources in exchange for its gains in acculturation and assimilation. But precisely because progress is made in the reduction of pluralism, inequality becomes of prime importance. Since inequality is the key issue in Oriental–Ashkenazi relations, its dimensions and trends will be examined more fully in the next chapter.

7 Oriental–Ashkenazi inequality

Socioeconomic gaps and power disparities have become the most central factors in Oriental–Ashkenazi relations. Ethnic equality is, on the official level, a national goal and, therefore, the persistent ethnic inequality is of public concern. This is why the inequality between the Orientals and the Ashkenazim deserves the greatest attention.[1]

Although the issue of ethnic inequality is 'very likely *the* crowning question in our analysis of ethnic pluralism' (Schermerhorn, 1970: 267), not much is known theoretically or empirically about it. There is a lack of 'a valid measure of similarities and differences in socioeconomic situations' and 'a valid methodology for drawing conclusions as to their political significance' (Kuper, 1974: 183).

The three features which, as I suggested earlier, characterize pluralism as a whole, i.e., magnitude, inconsistency and durability, can be applied to ethnic inequality as well. Magnitude refers to the average amount of inequality in the distribution of the various resources; inconsistency concerns the degree of variation in inequalities; durability is the measure of the length of their persistence. The severity or potentiality for conflict of ethnic inequality is manifested in these overall features of it.

In studying all these three features of ethnic inequality, two major problems arise. One is the degree of coverage. Studies can focus on the distribution of one or more of the resources: material wellbeing (income, expenditure, property), occupation, education (cognitive skills, school attendance, educational attainment), or power (political, economic, other). Since distributions of these resources are independent, at least to some extent, selectivity of focus is of great consequence. The other problem is the amount of elaboration. The choice is between studying 'gross' and 'adjusted' ethnic inequalities. Adjusted inequalities are those which remain after introducing controls. Although they serve diverse functions,[2] gross inequalities best reflect ethnic reality as it is at a given time.

151

Apart from these general problems, each feature of ethnic inequality encounters specific difficulties. With regard to magnitude there is, first, a basic measurement question. The measurements most frequently used are of two kinds: relative indexes based on ratios (e.g., Oriental average income as a percentage of Ashkenazi average income) and absolute indexes based on differences (e.g., the difference in Israeli pounds between the average incomes of Orientals and Ashkenazim). The two sets of data tap different aspects of ethnic inequality, they are frequently inconsistent,[3] and there is no valid ground for preferring either.

A more fundamental issue is what should be regarded as slight, moderate or considerable inequality. In the absence of evaluative techniques, some criteria may be suggested. One is the amount of ethnic inequality compared to the overall level of social inequality in society. According to this criterion, the same amount of ethnic inequality is more conspicuous in the more egalitarian societies (e.g., more in the developed than in the underdeveloped countries). The second criterion is the relative magnitude of the dimensions of ethnic inequality compared with the dimensions of ethnic pluralism (e.g., the same degree of ethnic inequality is less tolerable when cultural diversity among the ethnic groups is minimal rather than maximal). The third criterion is the amount of stress laid by the dominant ideologies and public opinion on ethnic inequality – the greater the stress, the greater ethnic inequality is felt.

Even more problematic is the examination of the second feature of ethnic inequality; that is, inconsistency. There is still no satisfactory method for making internal comparisons between inequalities in economic, occupational, educational and power resources. One technique is to divide each status hierarchy into ranks (e.g., top income quintile, second top income quintile, and the rest), and to compare inequalities in each rank. Since indexes of equality are sensitive to the size of the ranks compared, ranks should be defined to maximize the equality of their size and thus their comparability. There is, in addition, a question of interpretation of disjunction between ethnic inequalities. The evidence for greater strains attendant upon status inconsistency is still inconclusive (cf. Laumann, 1973: 160–85). The type of incongruence itself (e.g., more education than occupational level, more power than income) is also significant.

The third feature, durability, refers to changes over time in the magnitude or inconsistency (or both) of ethnic inequality. The time span examined is important, since short-term trends may differ from long-term trends. As to the direction of the trends themselves, there are theoretical and empirical grounds to expect diminishing, rising, stabilizing and inconsistent trends. The trend of diminishing inequality can be derived from equilibrium models according to which industrial societies, as they become advanced welfare states, tend to move toward greater cultural homogeneity, social assimilation and hence equality of constituent groups.[4] The reverse trend of rising inequality can draw on the Marxian theory of growing polarization of the social classes and from the vicious circle or poverty cycle thesis.[5] The stabilizing trend may be the product of conflicting trends.[6] Inconsistent trends such as a sequence of upswing–plateau–downswing or downswing–upswing may also occur. Trends of ethnic inequality are a function of a good many factors, including size of the minority, policies of the majority, initial minority–majority inequalities and economic growth; thus it is doubtful whether any universal trend of ethnic inequality should be expected.

Trends differ in their impact on ethnic relations. A trend of decline in both the magnitude and inconsistency of inequality would contribute a great deal to peaceful accommodation among the ethnic groups. On the other hand, a trend of decrease in magnitude but rise in status inconsistency would disturb a sizeable section, the elite, of the subordinate group. A sequence of upswing–downswing may cause widespread ethnic unrest (Davies, 1969). Entrenched, stable inequalities in situations of rising expectations and egalitarian ethos would have adverse effects, too.

Given the diverse facets of the problem, the study of ethnic inequality must be as comprehensive as possible in order to avoid various biases of selectivity. In studying Oriental–Ashkenazi inequality, several steps are taken to collect and analyse the data to arrive at as complete a picture as possible. First, a broad coverage of areas of inequality, including both socioeconomic differences and power disparities, is made.[7] Second, trends are established by comparing the last two decades. This time-span represents the statehood era, and in a society of rapid growth it is long enough to allow trends to show up. Third, both measurements of equality (relative and absolute gaps) are examined. And fourth, whenever possible, an elaboration of ethnic inequalities is made to distinguish between 'gross' and 'adjusted' inequality. (Most data are arranged in the Tables at the end of the book. The magnitude and durability of ethnic inequality in material wellbeing, occupation, education and political representation will be, first, discussed and then the inconsistency between ethnic inequalities will be taken up.)

1 Socioeconomic gaps

Gaps in material wellbeing

Gross family income, despite many limitations, is a common measure of material wellbeing. The real income of the Jewish population more than doubled since the 1950s. Controlling for inflation, the gross income of 'a standard equivalent adult' in Israel in 1957–8 was, at 1970 prices, IL 2,050 and in 1970 IL 4,450, namely an increase of 114 per cent (Public Inquiry Commission, 1971: 32). The rise is much higher for the entire period 1956–75 under consideration. A comparison of the incomes of Orientals and Ashkenazim during this period suggests stability in the relative gap and some increase in the absolute gap (see Table 10). The index of relative inequality indicates that an Oriental family income ranged between 57 and 82 per cent of an Ashkenazi family income, but the mean was around 70 per cent. The index of absolute inequality, on the other hand, manifests a rise in the absolute disparity in the purchasing power of the two ethnic groups. Orientals earned (in 1975 prices) IL 1,258 a month in 1956–7 and IL 2,292 in 1975, whereas Ashkenazim earned IL 1,723 and IL 2,783 respectively – thus the gap increased from IL 465 to IL 491, although the relative index of equality rose in fact from 73 to 82 per cent.

An examination of the gross income differences by introducing controls leads to two major conclusions. First, the differences are genuine and not due to irrelevant factors such as variations in age or employment status, though they are slightly affected by them. Adjusted for the differences in education, the relative index of equality in 1974 rises from 77 to a maximum of 90 per cent among families whose heads have post-secondary education (Table 11). The most important factor which could have explained away the income gap is period of immigration, since the Orientals arrived more recently than the Ashkenazim. However, when controlled for years of residence in Israel, income disparities are usually reduced only to some extent (the relative index of equality does not exceed 80 per cent in most immigrant groups and in most years during the 1956–7 to 1975 period – see Table 12). Moreover, the ethnic gaps among the Israeli-born generation (statistics about whom have become available only since the late 1960s) not only persist but also tend to be greater than those among the foreign-born generation. Among the foreign-born in 1969, the Orientals earned 70 per cent of the Ashkenazi income but among the Israeli-born only 58 per cent (Table 13), and in 1974, 77 and 67 per cent respectively (Table 11).

The other conclusion is the existence of evidence of certain direct discrimination against Orientals in employment. There are a number of economic studies on gross and adjusted income inequality which point in this direction (the results are summarized in Table 13). In spite of some inconsistency in the findings, the overall pattern is quite clear.[8] Haim Levy's findings for 1963–4 are the most typical (they constitute the median indices reported). The gross relative index of income equality was 68 per cent and the adjusted index, after controlling for age, sex, employment status, period of immigration, occupation and education, was 87 per cent. In general, three-fifths of the differences (the 30 per cent short of full equality) are due to factors that are known to affect income, while the remaining two-fifths are attributable to direct economic discrimination in employment. In the light of this kind of evidence, the common complaints of Orientals and the general public awareness of the prevalence of discrimination, the virtual absence of sociological research on ethnic discrimination in Israel is striking.

Because of the larger family size among Orientals,[9] inequality in standard of living is expected to be greater than in income level. In 1969 Oriental family income averaged 69 per cent of Ashkenazi family income (Table 10), but per capita income was only 48 per cent and, more importantly, per capita expenditure was only 52 per cent (Table 14). The available figures suggest three tendencies.

First, using per capita income and per capita expenditure as rough summary measures of standard of living, it is evident that the average Ashkenazi maintains a standard of living twice as high as that of the average Oriental.

Second, it is significant that inequality in per capita expenditure on consumption is only slightly smaller than per capita income (the indices were 52 and 48 per cent in 1968–9).[10] This means that social policies are ineffective (and have lost effectiveness since 1959–60 when the indices were 63 and 52 per cent respectively) in equalizing the standard of living of the Jewish population.

Third, the trend is of rising disparity in the standard of living. During the decade, the relative index of equality in per capita expenditure dropped from 63 per cent in 1959–60 to 57 per cent in 1963–4 and 52 per cent in 1968–9. At 1968–9 prices, an average Oriental family that immigrated during 1948–54 spent IL 132 per capita in 1963–4 and IL 197 in 1968–9, compared with IL 204 and IL 325 by its Ashkenazi counterpart, i.e., the absolute gap in consumption doubled within five years (from IL 65 to IL 121).

And fourth, as in the case of family income, per capita expenditure on consumption is only slightly influenced by period of immigration. In 1968–9, the Orientals spent 52 per cent of the Ashkenazi expenditure per person; immigrants who arrived before 1955, 60 per cent, and immigrants who came after 1955, 51 per cent (Table 15). It is clear that inequality in material wellbeing cross-cuts all immigrant groups and does not significantly decline with longer residence in the country.

The persistence or even widening of the ethnic gap in economic conditions has taken place amid enormous betterment in the standard of living of both ethnic groups. When measured in per capita expenditure on consumption, the standard of living of the Orientals

155

rose by 85 per cent or 7.1 per cent per year between 1956–7 and 1968–9 and that of the Ashkenazim rose even faster – by a total of 106 per cent or an annual increase of 8.8 per cent for that period (Table 16). The increase is, no doubt, much higher because the inter-war (1967–73) great jump in the standard of living is not reflected in these figures.

An important indicator of the pronounced rises in the standard of living is consumption patterns as measured by the percentage of families that possess selected durable goods (see Table 17). Both ethnic groups enjoyed an enormous boom in the acquisition of household commodities for which comparable figures for 1958 and 1975 are available. Gas (or electric) cookers and electric refrigerators, which were not usually owned in the 1950s, became commonplace in the 1970s. The majority already have washing machines and television sets. The popularity of these consumer goods has turned them into poor differentiators between ethnic groups. The tremendous improvement in living conditions has turned the telephone, the private car and quality housing into more accurate indicators of the standard of living. In these items the Ashkenazim are still twice as well off than the Orientals, and the absolute gap is widening, despite some reduction in the relative gap. To illustrate, in 1965, 1.8 per cent of Oriental families had private cars compared with 9.9 per cent of Ashkenazi families, whereas in 1975 the figures were 15.2 and 31.2 per cent respectively. While the relative index of equality rose from 18 to 49 per cent, the absolute gap increased from 8.1 to 16.0 per cent. These appreciable disparities in the possession of consumer goods are not affected in practice by the family's length of stay in the country, and the Ashkenazi lead is equally great among oldtimers and more recent immigrants (see Table 18 for detailed comparisons). Once again, ethnicity overshadows the period of immigration in this area, as in others.

Another way of approaching inequality in material wellbeing is to compare patterns of poverty. If the poor are defined as people in the lowest quintile of income, then 30 per cent of the Orientals were poor in 1968–9 compared with only 12 per cent of the Ashkenazim (Public Inquiry Commission, 1971: 25). Similarly in 1974–5, the Orientals were represented about 2.3 times as much among the 156,000 families who received welfare assistance, and 3.6 times more among the 30,000 families who were hard-core welfare recipients (i.e., those who received a regular economic allowance) (CBS, *Statistical Abstract of Israel*, 1976, 27: 666).

The ethnic gap in material wellbeing is probably underestimated in the available statistics. During the period under consideration (1948–75), tax avoidance (legitimized by a variety of untaxable incomes)[11] and tax evasion were quite widespread among the middle and upper

156

classes in Israel, and, proportionally, the better-off Ashkenazim practise in fact more of both.[12] The Ashkenazim also benefited exclusively from the personal reparations paid by West Germany (every fifth Ashkenazi family received money), and being oldtimers, they disproportionately profited from the ownership of property and other assets whose value has been soaring. These sources of revenue are not reflected fully in the figures on the ethnic economic differences.

In conclusion, in spite of the substantial improvement in the living conditions of the Orientals, their overall material inequality has somewhat grown over the years.

Gaps in occupational distribution

Compared with the Ashkenazim, the Orientals are disadvantaged in the rate of participation in the labour force,[13] but the more serious ethnic discrepancies concern the kinds of jobs they hold. An examination of the occupational data shows that ethnic inequalities and trends are similar to those in the sphere of material wellbeing. The inequality ratio is around 1 : 2. Disparities in specific occupational categories in 1975 ranged widely, but were greatest in the scientific and academic occupations, where only 2.0 per cent of the foreign-born Orientals as against 13.0 per cent of the foreign-born Ashkenazim were employed, and in the major grouping of higher status white-collar jobs in which twice the number of Ashkenazim (57.7 per cent) were represented as compared with the Orientals (33.1 per cent). In all other occupations, which enjoy less prestige and reward, the Orientals were overrepresented (e.g., 8.9 per cent of the Orientals as against 4.3 per cent of the Ashkenazim were classified as unskilled workers in industry, building and transport in 1975). (For detailed comparisons, see Tables 20, 21 and 22.)

There were mixed trends in the occupational field over the last two decades. Although all benefited from the reduction in the weight of the blue-collar and agricultural sectors in the Jewish economy,[14] the overall ethnic gap remained unchanged (the 'indices of dissimilarity' in the occupational distributions were 0.249 in 1954 and 0.244 in 1975) (see Table 22 for a definition of the indices and more information). The relative gap in the top white-collar occupations decreased slightly, but the absolute gap remained unchanged. In 1954, 19.8 per cent of the Orientals and 42.9 per cent of the Ashkenazim were engaged in white-collar occupations; in 1975, 32.2 and 57.7 per cent respectively, thereby increasing the relative index of equality from 46 to 57 per cent and the absolute gap from 23.1 to 24.6 per cent. In blue-collar jobs both the relative and absolute gaps increased. In 1954, 45.6 per cent of the Orientals and 39.4 per cent of the Ashkenazim held blue-collar jobs, whereas in 1975 their proportions dropped to 42.0 and 28.9 per cent respectively, raising relative inequality from 116 to 145 per cent and absolute inequality from 6.2 to 13.1 per cent. In the same period the gap was reduced in personal services and in agriculture.

The above figures suggest that although the ethnic gap in the occupational sphere has not diminished, the Orientals enjoyed some social mobility. As a result of the decline in the percentage of the total labour force engaged in agriculture in the country in the last two decades, some Orientals migrated from rural settlements to urban centres and development towns and took up low-status jobs. Other Orientals moved from these low occupational categories into the professions, administration and business. But the Ashkenazim have enjoyed the same and even greater mobility. For instance, according to one survey, the proportion of Ashkenazi unskilled workers dropped dramatically from 41.4 per cent in 1957–8 to 18.9 per cent in 1963–4, compared with a moderate trend in the same direction among Orientals (a drop from 52.3 to 41.0 per cent) (Haim Levy, 1968: Table 19). This inequality in occupational mobility suggests the existence of a hard-core Oriental proletariat which includes a great many immobile, unskilled workers who are apparently uneducated, have large families and are heavily concentrated in underdeveloped areas. Two studies of inter-generational mobility in the 1950s (Matras, 1963) and 1960s (Zloczower, 1968) report that the rate of occupational mobility of the Ashkenazim is about twice that of the Orientals, and that inequality is even greater among sons of manual parents.[15] This latter finding provides a further sign of the presence of a hard-core Oriental underclass.

Data similar to income figures adjusted for various factors scarcely exist for occupations, but some information on the effects of period of immigration and education is available. The data confirm the previous findings that a longer stay in the country is not conducive to the disappearance of ethnic inequalities. The occupational disparities among oldtimers are as great as those among post-state immigrants, and those among Israeli-born are as great as those among foreign-born. The Ashkenazi representation in 1973 in white-collar jobs was about twice that of the Orientals in all these groups, whereas the Oriental proportion in blue-collar jobs was around 1.5 times that of the Ashkenazim among the immigrant groups and 2.5 times among the Israeli-born (see Table 23 for detailed comparisons). Whereas the Oriental sabras are struggling to catch up with their already underachieving older generation, Ashkenazi sabras, who already measure up to the high standards of their parents, are striving to reach greater heights.

A study of the occupational distribution in 1961 and 1970 conducted by Hartman and Eilon (1975) reveals a trend of consolidating ethnic stratification. Needless to say, the findings of this pioneering study (and the only one of its kind) require reconfirmation before they can be considered valid, but they are in line with what is known at present. It is found that the chances of belonging to the top occupational categories were unequal for Orientals and Ashkenazim of equal length of stay in the country and equal years of schooling. The advantage that Ashkenazim enjoyed was greater in 1970 than in 1961. In fact, during the decade, Ashkenazi chances improved, whereas those for the Orientals decreased, thereby widening the ethnic gap and increasing the net weight of ethnicity on status attainment (see Table 24). Furthermore, the occupational gap between Israeli-born Orientals and Ashkenazim is not smaller than that in the foreign-born generation. These findings correspond with the above-mentioned findings on gaps in the adjusted income, and both point to the existence of certain direct discrimination in employment and to increasing crystallization of ethnic stratification.

To conclude, as in the economic sphere, both ethnic groups have improved their occupational levels – but the gaps between them have not been reduced and in some senses have even worsened.

Gaps in education

There is a considerable gap in the educational level of the two ethnic groups. The Ashkenazim have on the average about three more years of schooling than the Orientals: in 1975 the median years of schooling of the Ashkenazim was 9.8 compared with 7.1 of the Orientals (Table 25). The gap somewhat declined over the last decade: the index of relative equality rose from 64 per cent in 1961 to 72 per cent in 1975 and the absolute gap was reduced by six months.

A closer examination, through breakdowns according to sex and period of immigration, reveals several tendencies (see Table 26). First, the ethnic gap is greater among women because of the traditional educational deprivation of Oriental women. Second, the gap cuts across all immigrant groups, though it is lower among the Israeli-born, thanks to compulsory primary education. Third, the largest ethnic disparities tend to lie at the extreme ends of the educational scale. The illiteracy rate among Orientals is nine times as high as the Ashkenazi rate, and the percentage of Orientals with higher education is only one-quarter of that of the Ashkenazim. Fourth, while there is a general trend of improvement in education, it is relatively higher among Orientals than Ashkenazim and among women than men. This reveals a general tendency that the lower the starting level of education of a group, the faster is its rate of improvement.[16] The initial reduction in educational inequality is achieved much more easily than are further reductions. If this

159

tendency is extrapolated to the overall Oriental–Ashkenazi inequality, it suggests that the ethnic gap in education will not be closed within the present generation at least. And, fifth, the absolute gap in the top category of people with college education not only did not diminish, but almost doubled over the past dozen years (the Ashkenazi lead rose from 8.8 to 15.9 per cent between 1961 and 1975; see Table 25).

The headway made in reducing the ethnic gap in education of the general Jewish population was due mainly to the better educational opportunities given to the young generation. The increasing weight of youth in the educational statistics (they are included in the statistics when they reach the age of fourteen) has the effect of showing a smaller gap. The contribution of programmes of adult education is, on the other hand, rather limited. Apart from some effort to teach elementary reading and writing in Hebrew to illiterates, adult education in Israel is neglected. The disparaging view of the Oriental adult population as the lost 'generation of the desert' militates against the expansion of adult education. In addition, the continuing flow of well-educated immigrants makes investment in adult education economically unnecessary.

The overall picture of the population at school or college is also one of considerable ethnic disparities. The most striking is the stable pyramid-shaped representation of the Orientals among the students. In 1972–3, Orientals constituted 59.9 per cent of all primary school pupils, 49.5 per cent of all students in post-primary education (in 1975–6), and 14.8 per cent of students in higher education (Table 27). This low representations among college students will restrict the entry of the Orientals, who constitute about 55 per cent of the Jewish population, into Israeli elites. This situation is especially grave, since higher education has increasingly become a prerequisite for entry to such positions.[17] At the same time, the weight of Orientals in the student population has grown appreciably since the 1950s: they constituted 17.7 per cent of all post-primary students in 1956–7 and 49.5 per cent in 1975–6, and 6.2 and 14.8 per cent respectively of college students (in 1972–3) (Table 27). This increase does not necessarily imply a diminishing educational gap, which can be established only by the figures of representation of age-groups.[18]

The inequality in school attendance rates is quite high. In 1976–7 every other Oriental youth aged fourteen to seventeen attended a post-primary school as against seven out of every ten Ashkenazi young people (53.8 versus 70.6 per cent; see Table 28). The ethnic gap in high school education is even greater if the chances of receiving a matriculation diploma (teodat bagrut), which is required for admission to a university, are considered. According to an official estimate, only 6 per cent of all Oriental first-graders ever reach and pass matriculation examinations, as against 35 per cent of the Ashkenazim (see Table 29 for figures on retention rates from the first grade to the bagrut). In 1972–3 7.4 per cent of Orientals and 31.7 per cent of Ashkenazim aged seventeen received matriculation diplomas, i.e., the disparity ratio is over 1 to 4 (Table 28). The inequality in higher education is even greater, reaching a ratio of 1 to 5: in 1972–3 2.8 per cent of all Israeli-born Orientals and 13.8 per cent of all Israeli-born Ashkenazim aged twenty to twenty-nine attended institutions of higher education; the figures for foreign-born were 2.0 and 9.3 per cent respectively (Table 28).

As for changes over the years, there is a trend of a diminishing relative gap and a counter-trend of a rising absolute gap. The decline of the gap in post-primary education as a whole was consistent (between 1956–7 and 1976–7, the relative equality rose from 32 to 76 per cent and the absolute inequality dropped from 27.9 to 16.8 per cent), but the trend was mixed in the more important academic high schools (the relative index improved from 19 to 42 per cent, but the absolute gap went up from 15.6 to 25.6 per cent). The same held true in the upper levels as well. In matriculation diplomas, the ratios rose from 15 per cent in 1966–7 to 23 per cent in 1972–3, but the difference widened from 20.6 to 24.3 per cent. Similarly, in the universities, the ratios increased from 9 per cent to 20–22 per cent, but the difference was up four- or five-fold from 2.1 per cent in 1956–7 to 7.3–11.0 per cent in 1972–3. Furthermore, whereas the reduction in the relative gap lost momentum in the mid-1960s, the trend of a growing absolute gap is continuing. The Oriental marked underrepresentation in the universities has remained unchanged, despite the enormous expansion in higher education after the Six-Day War in 1967, to the extent that Israel is already on a par with, or even better than, the European average.[19]

The moderate decline in the relative gap reflects a large-scale effort on the part of the government to incorporate the Orientals into the educational system – but often at the cost of lowering quality. Programmes of compensatory education (starting with pre-school children and ending with pre-academic preparatory schools) have not significantly reduced the considerable gap in achievements. The poorer Oriental performance can be indexed in various ways.

First, the majority of Oriental pupils in the primary schools are still officially defined as 'culturally disadvantaged' (teone tipouah), i.e., have less than 40 per cent chance to score 70 points on the seker scholastic test. Cultural disadvantage correlates highly with ethnicity, father's education and family size (Table 30). In 1974–5 47 per cent of all pupils were 'culturally disadvantaged', of whom 95 per cent were Oriental. So considered were three-quarters of the Orientals and this proportion was even higher in the religious schools, development towns, urban slums, and among the poor and the Moroccans (Table 32).[20]

Second, the Orientals' performance on intelligence and scholastic tests upon entering and completing the primary school is significantly lower than that of the Ashkenazim. Overall, Ashkenazi children averaged as much as 1 standard deviation higher than Oriental children, and within equal socioeconomic levels two-thirds of a standard deviation higher. In standardized tests with a mean of 100 and a standard deviation of 15, the Ashkenazi advantage is around 15 points and within the same socioeconomic groups around 10 points. This generalization is substantiated in a number of studies. Ethnic gaps in intelligence tests of such a scale were found in a random sample of 1,072 children aged four to six and a half years in the late 1960s (Lieblich, Ninio and Kugelmass, 1972). The same is true for performance in the 'seker', a scholastic test which was administered to all Jewish eight-graders in the years 1955–72. A follow-up by Ortar (1967) of twelve years of seker testing shows an overall ethnic gap of 1 standard deviation, which is somewhat reduced after the effect of the father's education is neutralized. In a study of the 1963 seker, the Oriental average score was 82 per cent of the Ashkenazi, but the ratio rose to 90.5 per cent after family size and father's education were held constant (Smilansky and Yam, 1969: 243). To cite from the 1971–2 seker, 55 per cent of all pupils scored a passing grade of 70 or more points, but only 35 per cent of pupils originating from Africa, 42 per cent from Asia and as many as 76 per cent of pupils from Europe. These ethnic gaps in the proportions of passes are smaller within the same categories of family size and father's education (see Tables 31 and 32 for more information).

The persistent ethnic inequality in knowledge and mental level is due not only to socioeconomic gaps and subcultural differences but also to the anti-Oriental biases inherent in the Ashkenazi-modelled educational system and the psychological tests based on it.[21]

Furthermore, the continual ethnic discrepancy in performance is an indicator of the failure of primary education to equalize achievements. The success is quantitative rather than qualitative. The wide gap in quality at the end of primary schooling was even carried a step further by administrative policies. Since the seker served as a screening test for entrance to high schools, it was decided in the late 1950s to lower the admission standards for Orientals, whose failure rate in the test averaged two to three times that of the Ashkenazim (Kleinberger, 1969: 296). In this way a mass entry of Orientals to post-primary education was implemented without improving their competitive skills.[22]

Third, high schools are thus the next level where Orientals perform much more poorly than Ashkenazim. To absorb large numbers of

Orientals, post-primary education had to be diversified. Continuation classes, evening schools and trade schools were set up, and vocational and agricultural high schools were expanded (Kahane and Starr, 1974). The Ashkenazim moved to the first-rate academic secondary schools, leaving room for the Orientals – who now dominate the deserted second-rate, non-academic schools. About two-thirds of the Orientals in post-primary education attend trade schools and only one-third attend academic schools, as against roughly reverse proportions among the Ashkenazim. It is, then, no wonder that the Oriental dropout rate is substantial. Oriental recipients of the governmental matriculation diplomas account for only one-quarter of the total number of Oriental entrants to post-primary education (Table 29). And out of those who in 1972–3 reached the final stage of the matriculation examinations, only 66 per cent of the Oriental students as against 82 per cent of the Ashkenazi students passed them, and the ethnic gap in performance has not narrowed since 1965–6 (Table 33).

And, fourth, the inferior achievement rates of the Orientals appear in higher education as well. The Orientals are underrepresented among magisterial and doctoral students. In 1972–3 Ashkenazi students were two to three times overrepresented at the graduate level (CBS, *Statistical Abstract of Israel*, 1974, 25: 633). They are also underrepresented in the high status fields of study; i.e., engineering, natural and mathematical sciences and especially medicine (CBS, *Students in Academic Institutions*, Special Series 418, Table 19).[23]

In conclusion, the balance of ethnic equality in education is quite mixed. The progress made by each group in a relatively short time is tremendous. The relative gap has diminished but the gains have been made at the cost of quality. At the same time, the absolute gap has grown wider and the remaining inequality is considerable.

2 Power disparities

Power in modern Western democratic societies can be classified roughly into three types: political, economic and other. Political power refers to decision-making by bodies such as central and local government, the military and police, the legislatures, judiciary and political parties. Economic power concerns decision-making associated with ownership of the means of production, management of the economy and control of the trade unions. Other forms of power, which are mostly parapolitical, pertain to the control of the mass media, voluntary associations, educational and religious institutions and recreational facilities as well as control of loosely organized social movements and action groups. The relative importance and interrelations of these sources of power vary from one society to another, and they should be determined empirically.[24]

Political power in Israel is the most crucial resource and thus the subject of intense competition. The relatively greater concentration of political power in Israel, compared with other Western democracies, makes political power a very strategic tool. There is so much at stake in Israel that political powerholding is essential. In addition to the common dispensation of patronage, national powerholders intervene a great deal in the economy and exercise much influence on many parapolitical organizations, distribute the enormous flow of capital and make historical decisions about the character of the new state. Competition is all the more intensified by the strong orientation of the Eastern European power elite to political power.

In these conditions the distribution of power between the ethnic groups is of prime importance. Power disparities have greater repercussions for other spheres, and for the course of intergroup relations. For instance, since the Israeli government has wide options to interfere in the ethnic area and to control the allocation of large capital imports, by action or by default, it assumes much responsibility for trends in the socioeconomic inequality between the ethnic groups. Greater participation in national policy-making would increase the ability of the Orientals to influence national priorities in favour of closing the ethnic gap.

Despite their importance, the power disparities between the Orientals and the Ashkenazim have hardly been studied, and the lack of readily available data constitutes a hindrance. The Central Bureau of Statistics or other public agencies do not usually collect and publish data on power disparities as they do on socioeconomic differences. But the failure of Israeli sociologists to study the power dimension of intergroup relations is by no means accidental. As stated in my earlier critique, it follows from preoccupations with problems of immigrant absorption and modernization and from other functionalist biases.

To fill the gap in knowledge, a field study was conducted to gather information on power disparities. Because of its centrality, political power was taken as the main focus, but not to the exclusion of other spheres of power. Table 34 summarizes the highlights of power disparities. Tables 35–72 include detailed information on the ethnic composition of a large number of power positions.

Trends

An overview of the available information (Table 34) shows an overall trend of reduction in power disparities over the last two decades. Oriental representation has gradually grown in many positions where it was virtually nil or small. In some areas, like the top and middle governing bodies of political parties, the reduction in the relative gap (i.e., the difference in the number of Oriental and Ashkenazi powerholders) is a result of an increase in the personnel in these positions and, thus, a deflation of the power vested in them.

A more detailed examination of the general trend (Tables 35–72) reveals that it is not unilinear but follows a significant sequence of 'pre-1965 slow rise – 1965 upswing – 1969 downswing – post-1970 slow upswing'. Up to the mid-1960s there was a slow but steady trend of growing Oriental representation which was followed by an upturn in 1965, and a standstill or even a downturn after mid-1967 (especially near 1969), and an upturn starting in 1971. While this is not a universal trend, it is the average pattern.[25]

It is highly significant that the changes in Oriental representation coincided with the turning-points in the overall political and ethnic situation in Israel. The upswing in 1965 was caused by political instability as a result of a serious challenge to the ruling party by its splinter party (Rafi) (Medding, 1972) and the political bloc established between the two major opposition parties (Gahal). At this particular time the support of the Orientals was crucial and concessions were made to attract them. The economic recession after the 1965 elections hit the Orientals hard, creating an effective deterrent against a standstill or a reduction in ethnic representation. The 1967 War altered the entire situation, since the recession was replaced by full employment and prosperity; the intense competition for power was sharply diminished through the formation of a wide coalition government and by mergers of several parties, and by the spirit of national unity during the War of Attrition (1969–70). Under these circumstances some cuts were made just before and after the 1969 elections. By 1971, the pendulum of Oriental representation had swung upward again, following the ethnic unrest.

The years 1971–3, in which the Black Panthers were most active, were characterized by Oriental pressures and Ashkenazi concessions. In April 1971, several months after the Panther uprisings, delegates to the national convention of the Labour Party held a historically unprecedented Oriental caucus demanding across-the-board 35 per cent Oriental representation. Although the demand was, not surprisingly rejected, it marked an unusual show of power on the part of the accommodating Oriental politicians. The Oriental caucus in the Israel Labour Party has there after continued to operate despite threats and obstructions.

The Orientals did score some achievements during this period. In 1971 for the first time an Oriental was elected as a secretary-general of the Israel Labour Party, and he soon became the first

Oriental to be elected Speaker of the Knesset. A series of accomplishments ushered in the 1972 World Zionist Congress. The World Federation of Sephardic Communities, which had been denied recognition since 1925, was suddenly recognized as an official representative body of Orientals and Sephardim and was granted representation. A department for Sephardic Communities was established in the Jewish Agency and was apportioned a budget. A Sephardi was for the first time elected to the top position of chairman of the Zionist executive committee. An Oriental was also co-opted as a member of the board of directors of the Jewish National Fund, a Zionist body which had been exclusively Ashkenazi since its inception in 1901. Serious deliberations were under way in choosing the new President of the state in spring 1973 and although an Ashkenazi was finally chosen, the odds were in favour of a Sephardi.

The rise in Oriental representation, however, once again slowed down and was even stopped at the end of 1973. The turn for the worse was caused by two developments. Towards the time of the national elections, originally scheduled for November 1973, a political merger of several right-of-centre parties took place (Likud), thereby lessening the competition for votes. The October 1973 War constituted, however, a stronger blow to the Oriental ability to apply political pressure. No doubt it was a decisive factor in the failure of all six of the Oriental lists to gain a seat in the Knesset.

The overall trend of reduction in power disparities and the ups and downs in Oriental representation are significant in a number of ways. First, they disclose a growing incorporation of Orientals into the Ashkenazi power structure. This is in line with the overall pattern of Oriental–Ashkenazi relations, namely, the co-optation rather than the exclusion of Orientals. Since the Orientals' entry into power has been spaced over a period of two decades, the general pace amounts to 'controlled gradualism', a strategy which prevented the Orientals from accumulating power and from affecting the system. Second, the special sequence reveals the vulnerability of Oriental political achievements. The Ashkenazi establishment effectively controls Oriental representation, and it can raise or lower it as seems expedient. As our 'dynamic co-optation–paternalism model' of Oriental–Ashkenazi relations suggests, the establishment seeks neither greater ethnic equality nor power-sharing but, rather, neutralization and the appeasement of the Orientals. And third, the turning-points in Oriental representation demonstrate political flexibility and tactics of 'gamesmanship' on the part of the Ashkenazi establishment. Concessions are made at the right time and for the most conspicuous positions. This show of responsiveness is valuable in keeping the support and compliance of the Orientals.

166

Differentials

Power disparities vary widely (Table 34). Oriental representation ranges from zero in some positions such as mayors of large or middle-sized long-established cities to near parity in cases of local councillors (44 per cent). The wide range is not random but falls into a significant pattern of increasing power disparity with higher levels. This generalization, i.e., the more powerful the position the smaller the Oriental representation, is confirmed by examination of differentials in power disparities. More specifically, it can be shown that the Orientals are relatively better represented in the lower ranks and worse in the higher ranks, more in the weaker spheres and sectors of power and less in the stronger spheres and sectors, more on a local level and less on a national level, more in non-executive roles and less in executive roles, and more in positions that depend on electoral pressures and less in those that are relatively independent of constituents.

Lower versus higher ranks. Every power sphere is internally stratified into ranks. Higher ranking persons make the more important decisions and leave little power to those lower down. The representation of a given group in the various echelons of the power hierarchy may be symmetrical, that is, constant for all ranks, or asymmetrical, i.e., variable with rank. Asymmetrical, or, more precisely, pyramidal, representation is a sign of special weakness on the part of the subordinate group.

Oriental representation is pyramid-shaped. It is relatively wider at the base of lower ranks and narrower at the middle and higher ranks. When cabinet ministers and front-bench Knesset members are classified into five ranks, Oriental representation ranges from 28.9 per cent in the lowest rank, 12.1 per cent in the next lowest, zero in the middle, an exceptional 18.2 per cent in the next to the top, and zero in the top rank (Table 36). This pattern appears consistently in the governing bodies of political parties: on average, Oriental representation in the lower-rank bodies is 23.7 per cent, in the middle rank 16.7 per cent, and in the top rank 10.8 per cent (Table 34). The same holds in the civil service: in 1967 Oriental representation was 40.1 per cent in the lower ranks, 20.8 per cent in the middle ranks, 6.6 per cent in the higher ranks and 3 per cent at the top (Table 38).[26] By the same token, the pyramidal representation stands out in the armed forces; i.e., the police – in 1969 47.3 per cent of all policemen but only 20.4 per cent of the police officers were Orientals (Table 41) – and the army – up to 1973 there has been no major-general of Oriental origin as against an Oriental majority among enlisted soldiers (Table 40). The same pattern is repeated in the managerial staff of Hevrat HaOvdim (The Histadrut industrial complex) – in 1970 31.4 per cent of all managers, but only 3.6 per cent of top managers were Orientals (see Table 57). Likewise, Oriental representation is much greater among members as against heads of local authorities – in 1965 the Oriental proportions were 36.6 and 44.2 per cent respectively (Tables 42 and 44).

Weaker versus stronger spheres and sectors. Power spheres and sectors vary in strength. As indicated above, in Israel the political sphere is comparatively stronger than the economic and parapolitical spheres, and within the political sphere, the state sector and Zionist organizations are stronger than the Histadrut. The power of an ethnic group is reflected in its penetration into all spheres and sectors of power and in its relative representation in the more powerful ones. The available evidence indicates that Orientals are almost entirely excluded from the economic and parapolitical spheres, that their generalized inefficacy is not alleviated by their modest entry (which is made possible by their electoral weight) to the political sphere, and that they are disproportionally underrepresented in the more powerful state sector and Zionist organizations.

The Orientals have little control of the economy as owners of means of production, trustees and managers. The non-private sector in the Israeli economy is among the largest in non-Communist states. One-fifth is public (owned by the government, Jewish Agency, or their subsidiary enterprises), another one-fifth is Histadrut-owned, and three-fifths are private (Barkai, 1964: 25). There is no Oriental presence in the non-private sectors. While there are no exact figures on the ethnic composition of boards of directors of publicly-owned corporations there are strong indications that the Orientals are virtually absent.[27] The evidence available for Hevrat HaOvdim shows that its steering committee and secretariat are strictly Ashkenazi – with one token nomination (Table 56), and its top management is almost exclusively Ashkenazi – only 4 out of 139 top managers included in one survey were not Ashkenazim (Table 57).

The Orientals are similarly powerless in the private sectors. With a few exceptions (the Discount Bank and the Eliahu Insurance Company are notable ones), they do not hold key positions in the economy.[28] Basic research is still needed to look into the ethnic disparities in ownership and other forms of control of the private economy. There is one piece of information, however, that may well anticipate the general finding of the required studies. The most important political organ of the private economy is the Industrialists' Union, which includes not only the financial magnates but also represents *all* employers (and indirectly and paradoxically even the state and the Histadrut as employers) engaged in collective bargaining with the Histadrut in its capacity as a trade union. Of the fifteen board members of the Union, only one is not Ashkenazi and of the fifty-five executive members, all are Ashkenazim (Table 71). At the middle and top levels of industrial management, Oriental representation is low. According to a number of surveys, 3 per cent of the top managers in industry are Orientals (Table 72).

The key positions in the parapolitical spheres of power – namely the media, the intellectual and scientific ruling elite, semi-political action groups and numerous voluntary associations – are monopolized by the Ashkenazim. The media, whose power in a democratic society such as Israel is by no means insignificant, are Ashkenazi-controlled. Few, if any, Orientals are found among the board of directors of the Public Broadcasting Authority which is in charge of the monopolistic radio and television networks. The editorial staffs of both independent and aligned newspapers, as well as most journalists, are Ashkenazim. Orientals staff the state-controlled Arabic-speaking media which cater for Arabs, and have a few low-circulation ethnic publications. An Oriental is rarely to be found among the fifty-one members of the Israeli Academy of Sciences and Humanities, the highest scientific body, or even in the Hebrew Language Academy, the Council for Higher Education, the central committee of the Union of Writers, and so forth. Few Orientals man positions of power in the universities and research institutes. The few that do tend to concentrate on the area of Near Eastern studies such as Arabic language, literature and history.

The Orientals wield little power in the national semi-political action groups and voluntary associations. Israel enjoys a large number of these because of the legacy of the Yishuv, whose voluntary nature required the formation of a variety of organizations. The power of these parapolitical bodies stems not from their independence but rather from their ramified connections with political sectors of power. They participate in one way or another in forming public opinion and in mobilizing and allocating resources in society. They include the Movement for Greater Israel, the Movement for Peace and Security, the Israeli New Left, the various lodges (the Freemasons, B'nai B'rith, etc.), many professional societies, service organizations (e.g., the Israeli branch of WIZO, the Magen David Adom, which is the Israeli equivalent of the Red Cross) and other associations. Even in view of the absence of statistics, it will not be risky to speculate that, throughout the country, hardly a single Oriental is to be found in any key position in a national organization. An exception to the rule is the Black Panther Movement, whose power in the aftermath of the October War is fairly limited.

The Orientals do maintain, however, some national immigrant associations. These ethnic associations are either client organizations

169

of the major political parties or dependent fully for their existence on the financial support of the government or the Jewish Agency. They have so far proved to be ineffective as vehicles of influence for Orientals, apart from serving as a stepping-stone for a handful of ethnic bosses in making token political careers.

Turning to the political sphere, the differences in power between the sectors within it need a brief mention. The most striking change accompanying statehood was the growing power of the state sector at the expense of all other sectors. The expansion of the state functions and power positions hit the Histadrut the hardest. The Histadrut lost its informal control over local affairs to the state (Weis, 1968: 167), its power to conduct collective bargaining with management was curtailed by the counterbalancing intervention of the state, and its public image became much less attractive. The direction of political mobility was one way: from the Histadrut to the state, not the other way round. While the state encroached also on the Zionist bodies, they managed to maintain a good deal of power because their base was international or outside Israel (raising money through the United Jewish Appeal and mobilization of manpower through immigration offices). For these reasons the state and Zionist bodies can be considered more powerful than the Histadrut political organs.

The data show that Orientals penetrated the Histadrut much more than the state and Zionist organizations. The picture is all the more clear when these sectors of political power are compared at their highest levels. Out of eighteen cabinet ministers only two were Orientals in 1973 (Table 35), and out of thirteen members of the executive of the Jewish Agency only one was Oriental (Table 45), compared with five Orientals out of twenty members of the central committee of the Histadrut (Table 48). The same results obtain when the top elective, non-executive bodies of these sectors are compared. In the early 1970s Oriental representation in the Knesset was 15.8 per cent (Table 37) and in the Zionist executive committee 11.8 per cent (Table 46), as against 20.9 per cent in the executive committee of the Histadrut (Table 49). The same holds also for the top-ranking officials. The Oriental proportion in the state civil service were 3 per cent (Table 38) and 5.9 per cent in the Jewish Agency (Table 47), compared with 15.8 per cent in the Histadrut administration (Table 51). [29] And, finally, this pattern is repeated at the local level, where Oriental representation among the heads of local authorities was 33.7 per cent (Table 42), as against 56.9 per cent among general secretaries of workers' councils (Table 53).

Local versus national levels. Local positions are obviously less important than national ones. There are some indications that local feeling is particularly weak in Israel because of the small size of the country, overriding national issues and the proportional non-regional system of elections (Weingrod, 1964). This limited significance of local power in Israel, along with the ethnic ecological concentrations, tends to open up local positions for the Orientals much more than national offices.

The greater representation of Orientals at local levels cuts across all sectors of power. In the mid-1950s 23.6 per cent of the members of local authorities (Table 44) as against 8.3 per cent of Knesset members (Table 37) were Orientals and, in 1965, 44.2 and 17.5 per cent respectively. Similarly in 1956–7 Oriental representation among general-secretaries of (local) workers' councils was 20.9 per cent (Table 53), whereas among the members of the Histadrut executive committee it was 8.8 per cent (Table 49) and, in 1969–70, 42.9 and 20.9 per cent respectively. The same holds for the political parties. In 1973 45.1 per cent of the general secretaries of local branches of the Israeli Labour Party (Table 66) but only 26.0 per cent of the members of the central committee (Table 59) were Orientals.

A more systematic examination is possible by comparing, within each political party or bloc, the inequality of representation among members of local authorities on the one hand, and among members of the Knesset, the Zionist executive committee and the Histadrut executive committee on the other. The available figures (Tables 67–70) indicate clearly and consistently that, in each party or bloc, Oriental representation at the local level is much higher than at the national level. To illustrate from the left (alignment) bloc, Oriental representation in the mid-1960s was 43.1 per cent among members of local authorities (Table 67) as against 15.6 per cent among Knesset members (Table 68), 13.6 per cent among members of the Zionist executive committee (Table 69) and 16.8 per cent among members of the Histadrut executive committee (Table 70).

The greater equality in political representation at the local level can be further demonstrated by detailed examination of the local positions themselves. Local positions vary in strength according to type of settlement and sector of power. When localities are classified according to the combined criteria of size and time of foundation, it is clear that the Orientals achieved power in the least important places. In 1969–70, the Oriental representation among mayors of large or middle-sized long-established cities was zero (i.e., none of the nineteen mayors was Oriental), among heads of other established authorities, 19.4 per cent and, among heads of new local authorities, 53.2 per cent (Table 42). The same pattern holds for members of local authorities – in 1965, 20.9, 39.4 and 61.9 per cent respectively (Table 44), general secretaries of workers' councils – 15.4, 27.8 and 59.0 per cent respectively (Table 54) and general secretaries of local branches of the Labour Party – 7.1, 35.0 and 60.5 per cent respectively (Table 66). When localities are classified according to ethnic composition, this tendency is even more pronounced. Oriental representation among heads of local authorities in which the Ashkenazim constitute a majority of 60 per cent or more of the population is 4.0 per cent, in ethnically mixed authorities, 15.6 per cent and in local authorities where Orientals are the majority, 63.4 per cent (Table 43). This also holds true for general secretaries of workers' councils (Table 54) and local branches of the Israel Labour Party (Table 66).

Oriental local political achievements are more restricted to the less important positions of power. At the top of the local power hierarchy stands the head of the local authority, followed by the general secretary of the workers' council and the general secretary of the major political party. The most recent figures show that the Oriental representation in these positions was 33.7 per cent (Table 42), as against 56.9 (Table 53) and 45.1 per cent (Table 66) respectively.

If we examine the joint distribution of the two top local positions we find the following distribution in 1970: in forty-four of the ninety-eight local authorities both the municipal heads and the general secretaries of the workers' councils were Ashkenazi, in twenty-two the heads were Ashkenazi but the general secretaries were Orientals, in seventeen the heads were Oriental but the general secretaries were Ashkenazi and in fifteen both positions were staffed by Orientals (Table 55). Put differently, in 45 per cent of the local authorities, Orientals controlled none of the two key positions, as against only 15 per cent of the local authorities in which the Ashkenazim had no control. It seems that the process of increasing equality in local representation takes two stages. At first, the two key positions become ethnically bifurcated (with some tendency for the Ashkenazim to concede first the weaker position, i.e., that of general secretary of the workers' council, to the Orientals), and then, if at all, the Orientals take over local power. This sequence most often occurs in the new and immigrant towns, and especially in areas where the Orientals constitute a majority. In only 15 per cent of the localities where Orientals are in the majority do they still not have any control, as against 44 per cent of the mixed localities and 80 per cent of those with an Ashkenazi majority (Table 55).

The increased political power of the Orientals is more confined to local than to national levels; at the local level it is restricted to settlements which are poorer, more dependent on power centres for resources and, quite predictably, to settlements in which the Orientals are the majority of the population. No doubt, these achievements may seem modest, but they do constitute significant progress compared with the 1950s, when even these new settlements were controlled by Ashkenazi emissaries sent from the national power centres.

Non-executive versus executive roles. The growing bureaucratization of modern societies is accompanied by a shift of power from the legislative to the executive branch of government. This is due to the better efficiency of the administrative staff, to its greater expertise and to its control over vast resources. A director-general of a ministry, for instance, usually exercises more power on policy-making than a member of parliament.

It is to be expected that the Orientals would penetrate more into the less influential, i.e., non-executive, positions. The data confirm this expectation. Oriental representation in the Knesset (15.8 per cent, Table 37) is greater than in the government (11.1 per cent, Table 35), greater than in the top state administration (3 per cent, Table 38) and greater than in other key state posts such as nominated Supreme Court justices (10 per cent, Table 39) and major-generals (zero, Table 40).[30]

The same is true for the top ranks of the Zionist organizations. Oriental representation is greater in the Zionist executive committee (a misnomer for the highest elective body of the World Zionist Organization) (at 11.8 per cent Table 46) than in the top decision-making bodies – the Jewish Agency (7.7 per cent, Table 45) and directors of departments (5.9 per cent, Table 47).

The situation is not significantly different in the Histadrut. Oriental representation is greater among delegates to the Histadrut convention (23.7 per cent, Table 50) and members of the top elective body (again misnamed as the executive committee) 20.9 per cent (Table 49) than among top officials (15.8 per cent, Table 51), greater than among general secretaries of national trade unions (zero, Table 52), and greater than among top administration of the Histadrut industrial complex: steering committee (zero) and secretariat (4.3 per cent, Table 56), and top managers (3.6 per cent, Table 57). On the top decision-making body of the Histadrut (the government of the Histadrut which is modestly called the 'central committee'), the Oriental representation is, however, relatively higher (five of the twenty members are Orientals, i.e., 25 per cent, Table 48). But on close examination this turns out to be an exception that upholds rather than refutes the general rule.[31]

The same pattern holds true for local power as well. More representation existed in 1965 among regular members (i.e., councillors 44.2 per cent, Table 44) than among chief executives (heads) of local authorities (36.6 per cent, Table 42).

Elective positions that are devoid of executive powers are more open to the Orientals not only because of their weakness but also because of their vulnerability to electoral pressures, the significance of which is taken up next.

Electorally dependent versus independent positions. Power positions which depend on the electorate are expected to be more open to the Orientals than ones that are electorally independent because of the increasing weight of the Oriental vote. However, because of the proportional method of election, in which all the population in national elections and all residents in municipal elections make up one constituency, there is no direct accountability of elected office-holders to constituents. This, no doubt, curtails the effectiveness of Oriental political pressure. At any rate, greater Oriental representation in electorally dependent offices implies that political concessions are made when they are politically expedient and take the form of the less influential elective, nondecision-making roles.

Various evidence exists to confirm the observation that Oriental representation is greater when the Oriental electorate cannot be disregarded. The fact that equality in power at the local level is larger than that at the national level is at least partly due to this factor, even though in both cases the method of election is proportional. This is because local elections are less immune to electoral pressures and must take into consideration the personal standing, including the ethnic origin, of the candidates.

While the Orientals' vote is important, it is limited as an effective power tool because the Orientals constitute neither a solid voting bloc to be negotiated with nor a pool of floating voters to be persuaded by attractive offers. Notwithstanding these limitations, certain token nominations are made in response to diffuse electoral pressures and with the explicit intention of gaining legitimacy for the regime. In the 1950s one Oriental minister was included in all government cabinets. In the 1960s the benign quotas were raised: two cabinet ministers, one member in the executive of the Jewish Agency, a few members in the Histadrut central committee and even one Supreme Court justice. All these nominations are strictly ethnic and symbolic.[32] The Oriental representatives are given the least important offices within these top power centres and in fact their presence there has no effect on Oriental social conditions. There are no benign quotas in the more significant decision-making appointments such as top administrators in government and other political sectors.

In the absence of electoral pressures, among other factors, the monopolization of power is next to absolute in the Zionist organization. Instead of holding elections in Israel, the World Zionist Organization takes the distribution of seats in the Knesset as a basis for giving representation to the Zionist Jewish parties. For this reason the Oriental vote is hardly relevant. The WZO is independent of the

Orientals in other ways as well. The Oriental Jews make up a small percentage (17 per cent) of world Jewry, and since most of them are already concentrated in Israel they contribute little in immigrants and funds. This is why the monopoly the Ashkenazim have had over organized Zionism since its inception at the end of the last century could continue virtually uninterrupted until 1972, in spite of the fact that the Jewish Agency handled the arrival and then the absorption of about 750,000 Orientals to Israel since 1948. Some changes took place in 1972, however. The World Federation of Sephardic Communities was officially admitted into the WZO, and it was then assisted in forming the Sephardic Zionist Organization in the United States. The Federation is being increasingly co-opted into the Ashkenazi-controlled WZO in matters of funding, representation and policy.

Likewise, the Hevrat HaOvdim, which in 1968 employed 23.5 per cent of Israel's labour force and accounted for 20.8 per cent of the domestic product (Executive Committee of the Histadrut, *Report to the 11th Convention*, 1969: 272, 274), has had no special reason to accommodate the Orientals since no elections are held to choose the people in charge of it.

Oligarchization of power of the same absolute scale exists in the national trade unions of the Histadrut. The Histadrut is a Federation of Labour. As such, it consists of trade unions whose political structures resemble the Histadrut itself, i.e., convention, council, executive committee, central committee and general secretary. While each trade union organizes workers of the same trade (such as the union of construction workers), the Histadrut as a whole, through its trade union department, is the central body which represents all workers vis-à-vis management. The various trade unions can, however, exercise much power indirectly through the Histadrut trade union department, or directly by dealing with the workers' specific problems in each particular trade. More than twenty years have passed since it was decided to set up national trade unions, but only in a few cases were elections held. The turnover of the general secretaries of these national trade unions is minimal. In the light of such an entrenched oligarchy, it is not at all surprising to find in 1973 that all the forty-one general secretaries were Ashkenazim (Table 52).

The political parties are more sensitive to electoral pressures than other power centres, yet close examination of variations in representation between them once again confirms the above observations.

Seligman suggests a classification of the Israeli political parties into pluralist, sectarian and populist. He assigns Mapai, the moderate socialist party, and Mafdal, the major religious party, to the pluralist type (1964: 92–3). These two are ruling parties and as such they have to represent the interests of various groups and to appeal to a wider constituency, including the Orientals. Pragmatism and moderation are their distinguishing features. Pluralist parties are thus the most dependent on the electorate. In contrast, the so-called 'sectarian' parties such as the Communists, Mapam (a left-of-centre party) and Agudat Israel (the ultra-Orthodox party), owing to their dogmatic ideology, show little enthusiasm to compromise with special interests of segments of the electorate. The populist parties, of which Herut (a nationalist right-of-centre party) is the prime example, have a similar tendency, since they claim to represent 'all the people' regardless of social class, religious observance or ethnic group, and as such they are less susceptible to sectional or ethnic pressures. For these reasons, Oriental representation is expected to be greater in Mapai and Mafdal as ruling, pluralist parties than in other parties, since the former are more electorally dependent than the latter.

The data only partially support this expectation. On the one hand, Oriental representation in the governing bodies of Mapai and Mafdal is better than that in other parties, as manifested in the following percentages of Orientals in the broad central committees: Mapai, 29.1 per cent (Table 61) and Mafdal, 32.5 per cent (Table 63) as against 14.7 per cent for Mapam (Table 58), 14.2 per cent for Ahdut HaAvoda (Table 60), 29.1 per cent for Herut (Table 65), 6.1 per cent for the Liberals (Table 64), and while no exact figures are available on the small sectarian dogmatic parties (the Communists, Agudat Israel and Poale Agudat Israel), it is common knowledge that the Orientals are almost entirely unrepresented in them. On the other hand, no consistent pattern is noticeable when the allocation of patronage (seats in the Knesset, Zionist executive committee and Histadrut executive committee) is compared between the parties (Tables 68–70).

More conclusive evidence, nevertheless, comes from another but related angle. The dependence of political parties on voters is not only structural but also dynamic. Generally speaking, party splits increase dependence on the electorate because both the parent and the splinter parties appeal to the same constituency. The splinter party as a new party also appeals for support – by offering better representation to the discontented elements (whose votes tend to be more volatile), and in reaction the parent party matches the offer to counterbalance a loss of votes. On the other hand, mergers of political parties operate in the reverse direction. In a multiparty system like that of Israel, it decreases the competition and thereby diminishes the dependence on voters.

On the basis of these general considerations it can be predicted that Oriental representation would go up in cases of political splits and down in cases of mergers. The data clearly confirm this expectation. In 1955 the Mapam party split. In consequence, Ahdut

HaAvoda, the splinter party, gave an exceedingly large representation to the Orientals, unprecedented in the history of ethnic politics in Israel (Table 60). However, after its failure in the 1959 elections to capture the Oriental vote which it had counted on winning, it drastically cut the Oriental representation. To match the challenge, Mapam made a slight increase in Oriental representation between 1955 and 1959 (Tables 58, 68–70). Rafi seceded from Mapai in 1965 and gave a high representation to the Orientals (Table 62). In response to the Rafi threat in the 1965 elections, Mapai increased the Oriental representation but slightly decreased it after the establishment of the Labour Party in 1968 (Table 61). A similar development is evident in the Liberal Party. At its 1968 convention, realizing that the political bloc it formed with Herut had passed the test of time, it reduced the Oriental representation (Table 64). As a result of the consolidation of the left and right political blocs, each reduced its Oriental representation in the 1969 and 1973 Knessets (Table 68.)

These ups and downs testify to the precarious nature of the Oriental representation and its vulnerability to opportunist manipulation by Ashkenazi political bosses.

Proportionality of political representation

The significance of the figures on power disparity can be ascertained by checking them against an independent criterion of proportionality of political representation.

The simplest and most fundamental criterion is the ethnic composition of the general population. Since the Orientals constitute 55 per cent of the Jewish population, equality would amount to a reversal of status of the Orientals and the Ashkenazim. By this standard, the Orientals are represented in the top and middle ranking positions at an average of three or four times less than their numerical strength (see Table 34).

A second and related criterion is the demographic ratio in the voting population. Since the Orientals make up about 42 per cent of the eligible Jewish voters,[33] their representation falls much short of this measure.

A third criterion of proportionality is the allocation of patronage. Since the political parties are the distributors of patronage, we can adopt Oriental representation within political parties (since no figures are available on membership of them) as a standard for the Orientals' due share. Such a test is obviously most relevant for the ruling parties Mapai and Mafdal. If we take the percentage of Orientals in the central committee of Mapai, i.e., 29.1 per cent (Table 61), as the yardstick for an equitable distribution of patronage, we find that Mapai assigns to the Orientals only 21.4 per cent of its seats in the Knesset (Table 68), 23.1 per cent in the Zionist executive committee (Table 69) and 14.6 per cent in the Histadrut executive committee (Table 70). Mafdal has an Oriental representation of 32.5 per cent within the party (Table 63), 20.0 per cent in Knesset (Table 68) and 33 per cent in the Zionist executive committee (Table 69).[34] The allocation of decision-making positions such as cabinet offices (11.1 per cent, Table 35) and key ranks in the administration (e.g., only 3 per cent of the top officials are Orientals, Table 38) for which these two parties are responsible is much less favourable.[35]

Generally speaking, while Oriental representation in the broader governing bodies of the political parties averages 23.7 per cent, the percentage in the middle-rank bodies averages 16.7, and in the top bodies, 10.8 (Table 34). By the same token, if we take Oriental representation in the Histadrut convention as the criterion for allocation of Histadrut patronage, we see that the representation of 23.7 per cent (Table 50) is not fairly matched by the 15.8 per cent among top officials (Table 51), zero among general secretaries of national trade unions (Table 52), or 0–4.3 per cent in the steering committee and secretariat of the Hevrat HaOvdim (Table 56), with the exception of 25.0 per cent in the central committee (Table 48).

Finally, there is the question whether the political parties differ in proportionality of Oriental representation. There is no party in which the Orientals have equitable representation but, relatively speaking, they fare better in the labour bloc. There is evidence to show that the Orientals disproportionally vote more for the right-of-centre bloc (Likud) and the National Religious Party, and less for the labour alignment (Ma'arakh). In representation within the parties (Tables 58–65) and in power positions allocated by them (Tables 68–70), it is evident that the Orientals by no means have a greater (often lesser) representation in the right and the religious parties.[36]

Our data, therefore, suggest that the Orientals hold less power than their proportion as members of the Jewish society, as voters, or even as active participants in political parties.

To conclude, while power disparity has declined, Oriental political achievements tend to concentrate in the less influential positions.

3 Some implications

Oriental–Ashkenazi inequality is severe by all the summary measures (magnitude, inconsistency and durability). It is substantial, inconsistent and stable.

To mention quickly the highlights of the current ethnic inequalities in the Jewish population of Israel today: the Ashkenazim maintain a standard of living twice as high as the Orientals, they have double the representation in the higher-status white-collar occupations of the Orientals, and they have on the average three more years of schooling than the Orientals. Their attendance rate in academic high schools is 2.4 times as high, and it is five times as high in universities. The Ashkenazim also dominate all national centres of power; i.e., the state government, the Zionist organization, the Histadrut and the political parties. While the Orientals are not excluded from power, their representation tends to be relatively higher in the less influential (especially local) power positions.

These ethnic inequalities should be considered substantial, for three reasons. First, ethnic inequality is noticeably significant against the background of social inequality in wider society. Roughly speaking, Israel is more like the United States and some European states than the developing countries, in the magnitude of both social and ethnic inequality.[37] This means a relatively small class and power differentiation, in view of which the comparatively small ethnic inequality is hard to tolerate.

Second, the growing centrality of ethnic inequality compared with ethnic pluralism makes it more significant and less tolerable. The advancing acculturation and social assimilation of the Orientals into the Ashkenazi mainstream strengthen their awareness of inequality. Furthermore, by the early 1970s a new Israeli-born generation of Orientals had come of age. This generation resembles widely and interacts intensively with its Ashkenazi counterpart, and is thus becoming more and more impatient with its increasingly inferior socioeconomic and power achievements.

And, third, ethnic inequality is becoming a social issue. The dominant ideologies in Israel, i.e., socialism, nationalism (Zionism) and modernization, have always frowned upon the ethnic gap and defined ethnic equality as a national goal. Although counter-ideological undercurrents operated against giving top priority to this cause and even condoned ethnic inequality, the emergence of the Black Panther movement in 1971 attracted much public attention to the problem and sharpened the sense of relative deprivation among the Orientals.

As to the inconsistency between ethnic inequalities, a rough cross-rank comparison (Table 73) shows that there is a striking imbalance between the socioeconomic gaps in material wellbeing, occupation and education on the one hand, and power disparities on the other. While in the late 1960s the Orientals constituted between 22 and 34 per cent of the two top ranks of the class hierarchy, they constituted only 16 to 17 per cent of the two top ranks of the power hierarchy. This discrepancy was even sharper in the 1950s (20 to 29 per cent against 5 per cent, respectively) because most Orientals were new immigrants at that time. The marked power disparities are particularly outstanding when checked above against the various independent criteria of proportionality of political representation. The Orientals have a sizeable socioeconomic 'elite', defined in broad and relative terms, which is appreciably underrepresented in power positions. In view of the radicalizing potential of the status inconsistency of elites (cf. Lenski, 1966: 88, 409–10), this disjunction is rightly regarded as an important source of possible ethnic unrest (Lissak, 1969: 111).

An examination of the changes over time reveals mixed trends. First, compared with their conditions in the 1950s, the Orientals have made substantial headway. Their standard of living has more than doubled, their proportion in the professions and administrative jobs has also doubled and their attendance rates in post-primary schools and universities have more than trebled. By 1973, they had entered almost all the positions of political power from which they were excluded in the 1950s and their representation in the lower and lower-middle positions of power is quite appreciable.

Second, these impressive Oriental achievements in the last two decades were only partially effective in reducing the relative ethnic gaps (as measured by percentage ratios). In the areas of education and political representation, the rates of improvement of the Orientals exceeded the Ashkenazi rates, increasing the relative equality between them to some extent. On the other hand, in the economic and occupational spheres, the paces of change of the two ethnic groups equalized more or less – leaving intact the gap which separates them.

Third, despite the immense improvement in the Oriental situation and the fact that it sometimes surpassed that of the Ashkenazim, the absolute gaps (as measured in differences) between them have widened considerably. The gaps in purchasing power, standard of living, possession of the better jobs and attendance at academic high schools and colleges have grown wider over the years.

And fourth, the betterment in the living conditions of the Orientals is not uniform. Class divisions within the Oriental population have increased as the Orientals in the broad middle class moved forward, leaving behind a great number of immobile persons. As a result the sharpest Oriental–Ashkenazi gap exists at the lower end of the socioeconomic scale. Jewish society has a sizeable underclass which is almost exclusively Oriental (and predominantly Moroccan) and held back by multiple handicaps including large families, substandard housing, 'cultural' deprivation, lack of skills, religious observance, concentration in urban slums and development towns, and inheritance of poverty.

These conflicting trends reflect the complicated dynamics of ethnic inequality in Israel. The Orientals' progress is a result of the general growth and prosperity prevailing in the state since its creation. The partial reduction in the relative gap was due to the lower starting-point of the Orientals, which tend to make initial advances relatively easy to achieve – as was the case in the spheres of education and political power. The widening absolute gaps are similarly due to the pre-existent inequality in the take-off point – so that the Ashkenazim, by taking advantage of the expanding opportunities in society, have made gains which were absolutely greater, though at times relatively smaller, than those of Orientals. The emergence of an Oriental immobile proletariat was facilitated by the particularly low education and poor skills which distinguished a certain stratum of Oriental new immigrants, the services to the state it rendered and the expansion of opportunities for social mobility to other groups it made possible, and consequently the lack of effort on the part of the Ashkenazi establishment to deal with its problems.

The end result of the countervailing trends is perhaps a mixture which led to stabilizing and entrenching Oriental–Ashkenazi inequality rather than consistently diminishing or rising gaps. In consequence, by the mid-seventies, an ethnic stratification has already taken shape. It is firmly grounded in a correlation between class and ethnicity and in the exclusive restriction of poverty to the Orientals, and both phenomena are institutionalized, as their persistence across generations may indicate.

The analysis of ethnic inequalities lends general support to the model of dynamic paternalism–co-optation of Oriental–Ashkenazi relations. The limited equalization in allocation of resources between the two ethnic groups is due, to a large extent, to the piecemeal measures taken by the Ashkenazi establishment to achieve equality. The assumption that the primary goal was to neutralize and appease the Orientals rather than to promote equality and integration is compatible with the findings. The greater efforts made in the area of education aimed to avert the danger of dilution of Western Ashkenazi culture. Political concessions were made as a preventive measure. The paternalistic strategy of 'controlled gradualism' corresponds to a trend of stability or slow decline in the ethnic gaps. In this way the Orientals are slowly incorporated and assimilated into the system without jeopardizing or changing it. Meanwhile, they are presumably prepared, step by step, for more active participation in society some time in the future.

The discrepancy between class and power reflects similar tendencies. It is clear that a massive entry of Orientals into politics or power positions could have blocked policies which were not designed to obtain equality and integration. The modest power achievements of the Orientals could hardly be used to press the Ashkenazi national power-holders to take special action to reduce the socioeconomic differences.

The benevolent element in the 'controlled gradualism' strategy is equally clear. Since the goal is not continued Ashkenazi domination, the Orientals are allowed to compete and assimilate into the mainstream and to share in the general prosperity without encroaching on the interest of the dominant group.

Although the progress the Orientals have made in the last quarter-century was not sufficient to reduce the ethnic gaps, it contributed a great deal to a continuing process of changing Oriental–Ashkenazi relations from a paternalistic to a more truly competitive pattern and of shifting the emphasis from primarily 'ethnic' to 'class' factors.

In conclusion, the significance of the findings regarding the trend of ethnic inequality should be emphasized. If these findings can be sufficiently generalized, it can be suggested that in industrial societies ethnic or racial inequalities tend to show opposing trends and, on the whole, to stabilize.[38]

Among the most pertinent features of industrial societies are the growing provision of social services, the availability of opportunities for social mobility and a relatively high general standard of living. These characteristics are associated with the idea of a welfare state. Welfare states can aptly claim two important and interrelated achievements in the ethnic or racial area. The 'positive' achievement is the steady improvement in the living conditions of disadvantaged ethnic or racial groups (as of all lower strata in the society). The 'negative' achievement is to prevent the relative ethnic or racial gaps from widening. Minorities are not left behind, but are given their share in the general prosperity of society.

Welfare states have so far shown, however, only a modest success in redistributing social resources, curbing the widening absolute gaps in significant spheres and doing away with ethnic or racial inequalities (Girvetz, 1968). The expansion of social services or opportunities has not significantly levelled out the socioeconomic differences and power disparities. At the same time, the absolute improvement in living conditions tends to revolutionize expectations, and the growing absolute inequality becomes more and more noticeable. Paradoxically, advanced welfare states might become a scene of severe ethnic tension.

Finally, if the elimination of ethnic inequalities at a rapid pace is desired, radical means beyond the policies of Western welfare societies seem to be necessary. It does not suffice to 'raise the floor' by subsidizing the underprivileged while the ceiling is determined by free competition. Ethnic equality can be approached only if the deprived progress *faster* and *at the expense of* the privileged.

8 Conflict and integration

Despite the problems associated with pluralism and inequality, Israel up to the mid-1970s has been observed to be a land of relative tranquillity where both group harmony and open struggle are absent. In order to examine this observation, patterns of conflict and bases of integration for each pluralistic division will be reviewed in detail below. Group conflicts may be manifested in various ways: the major ones are failures of collective goals, invidious distinctions (prejudice and discrimination), dissatisfactions and protests by the nondominant group and countermeasures by the dominant group. On the other hand, possible sources of integration include value consensus, cross-cutting affiliations, elite accommodation, economic interdependence, political coercion and external factors. After surveying the evidence bearing on conflict and integration, an all-round picture of group cohesion will be presented by applying certain summary measures.

Table 5 provides a summary of the findings.

1 Conflict

Failures of group goals

Group goals may fail under two different circumstances. In the case of congruence in goals, their actual materialization may still leave much to be desired. In the more serious case of incongruence, failure of goal-achievement, by at least one of the contending parties, is an inevitable outcome. In a situation of compromise, partial implementation of the discrepant aims reduces the intensity of conflict. In the contrasting condition of polarization, full attainment of the objectives of one party heightens the conflict because it means the denial of the other's wishes. The severity of the failures of group-goals also depends on the relative importance of the goals themselves. Both circumstances under which group-goals fail prevail in Israel.

While the Orientals and Ashkenazim agree that their ultimate total merger is desirable, full equality is the short-run, more urgent target, and complete assimilation is the long-range, remote goal. The socialist ideology of the ruling political party naturally leads to the doctrine that reduces the ethnic problem to one of class inequality. This is in fact the official interpretation given by national leaders. In a national 1970–1 study of Oriental (Moroccan and Iraqi) leaders and a sample of Ashkenazi (Romanian) leaders, I made some enquiries into this matter. When asked to characterize the ethnic situation, 99 per cent of the Oriental leaders and 86.5 per cent of the Ashkenazi leaders indicated socioeconomic gaps as problematic as against only 49 and 40.5 per cent respectively who felt thus about cultural diversity.

Overall, both objectives are still unfulfilled, but Israel has done much better in eradicating cultural and social pluralism than in eliminating socioeconomic and power inequality. This is probably because the equalization of the resources of the two ethnic groups would directly hurt the privileged Ashkenazim whereas the Orientals' acculturation and social mixing would cause them less harm.

Our previous analysis in chapter 7 clearly shows that the immediate goal of equality is far from becoming realized. Ashkenazi socioeconomic status is roughly double that of Orientals, and the overall trend is toward stability rather than closing the ethnic gap. Power disparities are even greater. This situation must, therefore, be viewed as a gross failure of short-run goals, at least as far as the Orientals are concerned. From the viewpoint of the dominant Ashkenazi group the failure is part of the total official record according to which ethnic equality is a national goal. However, given the practices of paternalism and co-optation, this 'failure' is neither serious nor frustrating from an Ashkenazi perspective.

The Orientals have paid the price of making progress towards cultural homogeneity by a unilateral movement towards the Ashkenazim. The official melting-pot has remained what it is – a myth. The Orientals had hoped to have at least some element from their cultural heritage incorporated into the evolving Israeli culture. On the other hand, the Ashkenazim have feared cultural dilution, popularly known as the 'Levantinization' of the state. Both sides have proved, however, unrealistic in their expectations.

During the last two and a half decades, changes in the cultural situation have been remarkable. Writing in 1952, at a time when Oriental mass immigration was still under way, the anthropologist Patai advocated a cultural synthesis between East and West.

Re-evaluating the situation in 1969, he said that 'the Westernizing process had indeed reached the point of no return' (1970: 377), and 'Israel has thus succeeded by the late 1960s in making the Western culture of Ashkenazi veteran settlers the dominant one in the country . . . However, by achieving this in a brief period, it has practically excluded the possibility of a true cultural synthesis between East and West' (ibid.: 385).

Not only has a cultural synthesis not been accomplished, but also the fulfilment of the much more modest target of mixing Oriental elements into the nascent Israeli culture is deficient. Patai finds the Orientals' contribution to be negligible in all but one of the five 'crucial focal complexes of traditional Oriental culture' (1970: 55; 381–3).[1] The Orientals have contributed nothing in the religious realm – religion has not become more central in Israel because of them nor have their liturgy and other religious customs acquired any currency. Similarly their spontaneous, humanistic world-view has taken little hold. Their family patterns – i.e., of larger families, broader households and stronger kinship ties – have set no example. Nor can they be credited with relaxing the heavy emphasis on achievement and competition in Israeli society. Only in the aesthetic field have Orientals had some minor influences, mainly in folk music and dancing, arts and crafts (by and large Yemenite embroidery and jewellery), foods and – most important – pronunciation. In fact, the only significant general Oriental contribution has been in speech, although the widespread belief that modern Hebrew follows the Oriental pronunciation is fallacious.[2] On the other hand, this does not mean that the present Israeli culture is Ashkenazi in the historical and specific sense of continuing Eastern European Jewish traditions. It is in many respects a new culture which has been developed by the Ashkenazim and which fits their strong orientation toward the West.

From an Oriental standpoint, the lack of cultural variegation, not to mention synthesis, can be considered a failure, whereas from an Ashkenazi angle this does not matter. Of greater significance to the Ashkenazim is the fact that their unofficial apprehensions have not eventuated. As Weingrod (1965: 76) observes:

> The possibility of a 'Levantine future' is very slight. The overwhelming direction of culture is to the West, not to the East, and Middle Easterners adopt many of the habits and aspirations of their European brethren. There is no basis for concluding that changes are merely 'skin deep'.

The noticeable movement toward ethnic assimilation instils some sense of achievement in the Jewish population. Thus in a representative sample of high school pupils taken in summer 1975,

57 per cent said that Israel was relatively successful in amalgamating the exiles as compared with only 37 per cent who thought that it was doing well in constructing a society based on social justice.[3] The public is certainly aware of Israel's failure to approach ethnic equality.[4]

In the case of religious and nonreligious Jews, group goals cannot be more than moderately achieved because of their initial incongruence. There is little doubt, however, that the religious minority have fully accomplished the short-range, minimalist goals of cultural autonomy and nonseparation between religion and state. More specifically, religious Jews maintain separate institutions which guarantee their continued existence as a separate-but-equal group. They control their institutions and communities. They hold a right of veto in religious matters, have a monopoly over religious expression (by denying any public recognition and support to non-Orthodox streams of Judaism) and enjoy a freedom of action to propagate Orthodox religion and to strengthen its institutionalization in the public domain. They have made significant contributions to the national culture which by now incorporates numerous religious elements, although not all in their original forms.

These great accomplishments of the religious minority fall short, nevertheless, of the long-range, maximalist goal of a halakha state in which religious practices will be mandatory. The nonreligious majority not only reject this religious ideal but also object to certain present religious arrangements. Thus both sides have grounds to believe that their collective goals are only partially fulfilled.

Public opinion surveys reveal reservations and disagreements about the religious status quo. In the 1975 national survey of high school pupils, a majority of 71 per cent said that the religious status quo was not good and religious and nonreligious respondents did not differ in the percentage of their negative evaluations. As to more specific arrangements, the general public accept some and reject others. On the one hand, in a 1970 survey, 77 per cent of all respondents were in favour of the current television broadcasts on the Sabbath, 74 per cent approved of the present practice that government offices close on holidays, and 72 per cent agreed that public kitchens should continue to keep kosher (Gurevitch and Schwartz, 1971: 71). On the other hand, in a 1971 survey, the majority favoured amending the status quo to allow public transport on the Sabbath (64 per cent) and to open entertainment halls on Friday evenings (63 per cent). With regard to more crucial matters, the prevalence of a small majority endorsing the status quo along with a sizeable minority which opposes it points to a fundamental controversy. To illustrate from the same survey, while 54 per cent of the respondents opposed civil marriage, 39 per cent favoured it (7 per cent were not certain). Similarly 58 per cent were in favour of a law defining a Jew according to the halakha only, whereas 31 per cent were against it (11 per cent had no opinion). (All the above figures were cited by Eyal, 1971b.) The discord between the religious group and at least a minority in the nonreligious group is sharp indeed.[5]

While the discrepant aims of religious and nonreligious Jews are moderated and partially implemented through a mutual compromise, the conflicting ends of Arabs and Jews are hardly reconciled and, in consequence, the failure of the subordinate Arab minority to achieve its goals is much greater than the Jewish failure.

No matter how Arabs differ among themselves on specific desires, they seek the still unfulfilled short-range goals of cultural autonomy and equality of resources. Although the Arabs are assured, like religious Jews, of their collective survival, they are denied, unlike religious Jews, the recognition of their full collective identity and control over their separate institutions. The Arabs are recognized as a cultural minority but not as a national minority.

They lack truly independent organizations. Even Arabic-speaking media and schools are in Jewish hands. The Jewish control of appointments of the staff, supervision and curriculum of the Arab schools is a good example of the policy of denying the status of a national minority to the Arabs. A study of the curriculum in Arab schools (Peres, Ehrlich and Yuval-Davis, 1970: 161) shows that[6]

> It has fallen to a tendency to blur Arab nationality and to educate the Arab student towards self-disparagement vis-à-vis the Jewish majority. These tendencies are revealed, in the main, in two ways: (a) the goals of various subjects are formulated with a disregard of the nationalist elements in the Arab pupil's consciousness; (b) a wide and profound knowledge of purely Jewish subjects (for example, Jewish history, Bible) is demanded of the Arab students at the expense of their own culture. This tendency is even more conspicuous against the background of an almost total absence of the Arabic language and culture in the Jewish pupil's education.

Nor can the Israeli Arabs be said to enjoy equality of socio-economic status, a proportional share of power and equal opportunities.

To these failing operative goals, the unrealized ultimate end of the Israeli Arabs of doing away with their minority status in a Jewish state should be added. The Arabs would like first-class citizenship, the right of repatriation for Palestinian refugees and, perhaps, the de-Zionization of Israel. These goals are, of course, far from realization.

In contrast, the Jews have made more progress than the Arabs in carrying out their own goals. The danger of Arabs becoming an active fifth column or a threat to the Jewish-Zionist nature of the state has not occurred, or, from the Jewish perspective, has been successfully averted by effective policies. The compliant Arabs do not constitute a real challenge to Israel's culture and identity which remain Jewish or Western and devoid of Arab influence.

The Jews have failed, on the other hand, to achieve broader objectives vis-à-vis the Arabs. Contrary to the Jews' first preference for an exclusively Jewish state, the Arabs have become a permanent and significant minority (they have not left the country en masse nor can they be expected to do so in the future). Alternatively, the Arabs have not acquired the new identity of 'Israeli Arabs' which implies the wilful acceptance of a new cultural (but not national) minority status in the Jewish state as well as the severence of ties with Palestinian nationalism and peoplehood.

Of all the three nondominant groups, the religious Jews are comparatively the most successful in approaching their collective goals, and the Orientals have made some headway, whereas the Arabs' aims remain remote. On the other hand, the strains stemming from the failure to attain group goals for Oriental–Ashkenazi relations are smaller in the long run than in the other pluralistic divisions. This is because the Orientals and Ashkenazim officially concur on equality and assimilation as national goals, though the Ashkenazim are less happy about this in practice. The question is thus reduced to goal attainment; i.e., to have the assimilating Oriental group dissolved as assimilated individuals. In the other cases, goal incongruity presents a constant obstacle which causes perpetual frictions and frustrations because both religious Jews and Arabs are nonassimilating minorities, opposed in principle to certain elements in the status quo, and vying for dominance in the long run. While various factors allow the religious and nonreligious Jews to seek a compromise, the forces leading to a rapprochement between the Arabs and Jews are quite unfavourable and volatile.

Invidious distinctions

Invidious distinctions are the central theme in the conventional literature of ethnic relations. Prejudice, discrimination and involuntary segregation, to mention just a few forms, are considered to be major symptoms of intergroup conflicts.

In discussing the unfavourable undercurrents underlying Oriental–Ashkenazi relations (see chapter 5, section 3), I mentioned the high level of institutional discrimination which existed in the early years of the state. The dominant Ashkenazi majority simply extended their own 'ready-made' social frameworks over the incoming Orientals without significant adjustments. This was common in many spheres.

Oriental immigrants were dispatched to become Yishuv-type pioneers and farmers in remote settlements for which they had no practical or ideological training (Weingrod, 1966). Many of them were settled in new development towns where living conditions were poor, and opportunities to find suitable jobs and to move up- wards were slim indeed (Spilerman and Habib, 1976). Nationally, there has been a reluctance to switch to a regional method of elec- tions which might give a better chance to Orientals, who are in- experienced in national politics and are concentrated in some areas, than the existing proportional method. The Ashkenazi religious style was imposed in the schools, the army and the rest of the public sector. Schools were geared to predominantly middle-class Ashkenazi children, welfare services disregarded the special needs of large (Oriental) families, and immigrant absorption policies were heavily biased in favour of the Ashkenazi immigrants.[7] These and many other measures reveal the narrow perspective from which the dominant Ashkenazi group viewed the special needs of the Oriental newcomers.

Whereas most of these practices have survived to this day, a marked reduction in institutional discrimination against the Orientals has, however, taken place. This substantial improvement was made possible by both the Orientals' adjustment to society and the state's greater consideration of their needs. To illustrate the basically static situation, one might look at current conditions in the schools, which still operate on the assumption that the family is very much re- sponsible for a child's education. This assumption is realistic for children from small Ashkenazi, education-oriented, middle-class families. In a larger sense, schools generally educate towards a monolithic ideal of an Israeli person without making any allowance for a degree of cultural pluralism (Shuval, 1969: 183). There is still in the schools little, or even token, mention of the history, literature or other achievements of the Orientals during the last five hundred years (Shtal, 1976: 10–14). On the other hand, the educational system has demonstrated a remarkable flexibility, initiative and investment in developing compensatory education programmes and adopting preferential treatment policies for underprivileged Oriental children (Kleinberger, 1969: 295–307; Adler and Peleg, 1975).[8]

Despite a continuing decline in paternalism and anti-Oriental feelings, there are still serious problems. No doubt, the stereotype of the Oriental immigrant as a second-rate newcomer who threatens to 'Levantinize' the established Ashkenazi, Western culture has diminished. Under the pressure of new realities, the belief that generations will be needed to overcome centuries-old 'backwardness' has also waned. Much stereotyping still lingers, though it has now taken subtler and more disguised forms.

A good illustration can be taken from the military sphere before the Six-Day War, when doubts were expressed about the capabilities of Oriental soldiers. Israel's first Chief of Staff, General Y. Dori, declared that 'the spirit which enabled the country to win two wars is not possessed by immigrants from the depressed countries' (*Jewish Chronicle*, 20 December 1963: 12).[9] Pronouncements made after the Six-Day War confirm these deep-seated anxieties. A top army officer made a statement, which was not retracted, that the Israeli army officers' 'After Me' slogan was intended 'to prevent, so to speak, a collapse of the front, or the retreat, under harsh conditions and confronted by dangerous tasks, of Oriental soldiers, who, without the personal example of a courageous officer, would not be willing, as it were, to advance in the face of shell fire and overpower the enemy' (quoted by Shaki, 1967: 52).[10] The praise the Ashkenazim lavished on the Orientals for the latter's unexpected performance in the war also revealed a prior basic lack of confidence (Tsoriel, 1967; Fein, 1968: 331).[11] Such views are on the decline, however, as the absence of similar utterances in the aftermath of the 1973 War may show.[12]

The dominant 'somatic norm image', to use Hoetink's concept,[13] is definitely Ashkenazi rather than Oriental or 'mixed'. A high premium is placed on European physical traits such as a fair complexion and light-coloured eyes, which are much more frequent among Ashkenazim than Orientals. Although the Orientals are further from these standards of beauty,[14] the 'somatic distance' between the two ethnic groups is not appreciable and, in consequence, practices such as skin-bleaching, which are common among minorities in racially stratified societies, are not widespread in Israel.[15]

Opinion polls confirm the observation that the Ashkenazi image is preferable. In a study of national stereotypes held by children, a clear trend to perceive the Oriental photos as non-Israeli is discernible (Rim, 1968). Other studies, using the semantic differential technique, document the superiority of the Ashkenazi image. One study shows that Ashkenazi respondents attached better evaluations to 'a typical Ashkenazi' than to 'a typical Oriental' (Rim and Aloni, 1969). In another study of eleventh-graders, the distance between the ideal self and the image of 'a typical Ashkenazi' was found to be much smaller among Ashkenazi students than the distance between the ideal self and the image of 'a typical Oriental' among Oriental students. More specifically, the hierarchy of ethnic images presented by the Ashkenazi respondents appeared to follow the order: self-image, country-of-origin compatriot, Ashkenazi, typical Israeli, Yemenite, Oriental, Moroccan and Arab. The rank-order found among Oriental respondents was not very different: self-image, typical Israeli, country-of-origin compatriot, Ashkenazi, Oriental, Yemenite, Moroccan and Arab (Peres, 1968: 154).

The negative stereotyping of the Orientals is well evident in two studies in which the more valid, indirect research techniques were applied. In one study a select sample of 'liberal' Ashkenazim (in their twenties, with at least some higher education, nonreligious) were asked to assess the traits of people on the basis of their appearance. The naive judges attributed more favourable characteristics such as intelligence, industriousness and pleasantness to Ashkenazi photos than to Oriental ones. In fact, the Ashkenazi portraits were judged to be substantially more favourable in their qualities than the Oriental ones (Yinon, Abend and Chirer, 1976).

A similar experiment demonstrates the great vulnerability of Orientals to stereotypes in education. A group of schoolteachers were asked to grade an examination. Half of them were told that the paper was written by a typical Ashkenazi student from a privileged family, whereas the other half were told that it was written by a typical Moroccan student from a culturally disadvantaged background. Although the examination papers of the two hypothetical students were identical, the naive teachers assigned very much lower grades to the 'Orientally named' student (for this finding and other evidences of virulent prejudices among educators, see Shtal, Agmon and Mar-Haim, 1976).

Other studies show that there is a great deal of prejudice against the Orientals, that prejudice is asymmetrical (i.e., greater among the Ashkenazim towards the Orientals than vice versa), and that the Orientals also share the prejudices of the Ashkenazim towards themselves. For instance, in a sample of adults, 43 per cent of the Ashkenazim and 43 per cent of the Orientals agreed that for prejudices to be abolished Orientals must rid themselves of their shortcomings. Twenty-five per cent of the Ashkenazim and 34 per cent of the Orientals believed that even though the Orientals might make much progress, they would never reach the level of the Ashkenazim (Peres, 1971: Table 7). On the other hand, 11 per cent of the Ashkenazim as against 27 per cent of the Orientals believed the Ashkenazim to be emotionally cold and unresponsive (ibid.: Table 8), demonstrating a milder stereotyping of the Ashkenazim by the Orientals.[16]

Some evidence of discrimination in the access to socioeconomic resources was discussed earlier (see chapter 7, section 1). Several studies indicate that, on the average, Oriental income remains equal to about 85 per cent of that of Ashkenazim after eliminating the major factors affecting income, such as occupation, education, period of immigration, age and sex. Sizeable inequalities in occupational distribution still exist even after the major factors of education and period of immigration are accounted for. In the absence of any study, the actual mechanisms of ethnic discrimination in employment are not documented.

In spite of official denials, the Israeli public are well aware of widespread discriminatory practices against the Orientals. According to various surveys of the Jewish urban population made periodically since 1967, about three-fifths of the respondents usually concede the existence of ethnic discrimination. For instance, in a national survey in June–July 1972, the proportion was 61 per cent, and in a similar survey of high school pupils in summer 1975, 65 per cent said that too often Jews from certain ethnic groups suffered because of their ethnic origin.[17]

It is interesting to note, however, that the Hebrew term of Eastern European provenance, 'proteksia', is perhaps one of the most common words in the modern Israeli vernacular. It means 'favouritism' or 'good connections', and it implies a great measure of particularism in taking on employees, in dealings with bureaucrats and in obtaining various benefits. Proteksia is widespread in Israeli society. In a public survey in 1968 a majority of 69 per cent reported the use of proteksia from among those who had access to and need of it, although only a minority approved of it (Danet and Hartman, 1972: 432). The highest proportion of users was recorded among Israeli-born Ashkenazim (82 per cent) and Israeli-born Orientals (76 per cent), but most of the others were also proteksia users. The symmetric distribution of proteksia between members of the two ethnic groups is the result of the massive penetration of the Orientals into lower and lower-middle power positions. Nevertheless, the considerable favours accruing to the higher-status Ashkenazim cause much greater inequity than the relatively minor favours obtained by Orientals.

In an earlier study in 1963–5, North African immigrants were asked about the treatment they received, and the majority refused to answer. Or, to put it positively, only 10–12 per cent said that they received 'just' or 'equal' treatment, 23 per cent noticed 'differences' in treatment and 50 per cent complained of proteksia (Bensimon-Donath, 1970: 461). The extremely high rates of refusal to answer these questions (ranging from 48 per cent to the question of proteksia to 88 per cent to that of justice in treatment) were due to the taboo against complaints of ethnic discrimination that North Africans, the most likely victims, were afraid to violate.

Some Oriental spokesmen present invidious distinctions as a central problem in Oriental–Ashkenazi relations. The theme of discrimination is the leitmotif in the two main ethnic publications *Bamaarkha* and *Afikim*. One author who used to be affiliated with the committee of the Sephardic community in Jerusalem described Orientals as 'the outcasts of Israel' (Selzer, 1965), and then spoke of the 'Aryanization of the Jewish State' (1967). The former president of the Sephardic community warned against 'Jewish racism in the Jewish state' (Eliacher, 1967) and another writer denounced Israeli

'Europocentrism' (Rejwan, 1967). Another Oriental advocate, a dissenting voice within the Ashkenazi establishment, attracted much attention when he made public his 'Reflections on the Third Destruction' (i.e., the downfall of Israel). To quote some of his statements (Nini, 1971: 58–9):

They [Oriental soldiers] fell in order to have Abramovitches and their like, the descendants of merchants of notions, clothes, and shemitta appointed as public leaders. The civil service is in Ashkenazi hands. Statistics show that there are Oriental civil servants, but let us examine which positions they fill. They are located on the lowest rungs, among those who serve tea, the clerks, and the cleaning personnel. I do not despise these jobs, only the policy which creates the two classes . . .

Is there a conspiracy? No. There is no document or evidence designed to effect discrimination against Orientals. Public pronouncements even call for their encouragement. This is the official line, but it is not implemented. The truth is not obvious but is divulged by everyday practices. The only true document published in Israel which reflects the real attitude toward Orientals is found in Kalman Katzenelson's book – *The Ashkenazi Revolution*.

(On the extreme anti-Oriental overtones of Katzenelson's book, see chapter 4, section 1.)

In my study of ethnic leadership in 1970–1, 70 per cent of the Oriental leaders, as against only 3 per cent of the Romanian leaders, mentioned invidious distinctions as a problem in Oriental–Ashkenazi relations. And in my study of Black Panther activity in summer 1975, 95 per cent made explicit charges of anti-Oriental discrimination; when asked more specifically to compare the chances of an Oriental youth with those of an Ashkenazi youth of similar relevant traits (both young, educated, energetic and Israeli-born), 67 per cent said that Ashkenazi young people have better chances to make good in Israeli society.

Oriental origin handicaps access to power, especially power beyond the lower or lower-middle ranks; ethnic particularism is perhaps highest in politics and in assignment to positions of trust, and ethnic quotas prevent free competition for power. By setting them too low, quotas become benign for the lucky few but work against the majority of Orientals. By confining them to visible, mostly nonexecutive, appointments, they become no more than token measures. Our analysis of power disparities documents the pyramidal form of Oriental representation. Such distribution patterns strongly suggests the existence of barriers against Oriental upward mobility, and the Orientals do receive less than their proportional share of patronage dispensed by their respective political parties (see the section 'Proportionality of Political Representation' in chapter 7).

In the absence of studies on differential treatment in areas of power, some attitudinal evidence can be cited from my ethnic leadership study. Forty-five per cent of the Ashkenazi (Romanian) leaders in the sample expressed the prejudicial view that an increased Oriental representation in government would lower the standards of state administration. In comparison, 18 per cent of the Oriental leaders gave an exceedingly qualified endorsement of this view. The majority of Ashkenazi leaders also believe that Oriental origin is an asset in political life, whereas the majority of Orientals believe it is a burden. More specifically, 70 per cent of the Ashkenazi leaders and only 30 per cent of the Oriental leaders considered Oriental origin to be as favourable in obtaining positions of power, 12.5 and 1 per cent saw it as neutral and 17.5 and 69 per cent felt it to be unfavourable.[18] These figures lend credence to the contention that ethnicity is pervasive in Israeli politics, since there is nearly complete agreement that Oriental origin does count, one way or another. Oriental politicians often feel bitter about their power positions and make many complaints against discriminatory practices. This is despite the fact that they are by and large a privileged elite, are given entry into the Ashkenazi power structure and serve as an extension of the establishment.[19]

Surveys of social distance attitudes among Jewish adults and young people reveal three tendencies: (a) The Ashkenazim reject contact with the Orientals more than vice versa, (b) some self-rejection and self-hate exist among the Orientals and (c) the rejection of the Orientals by the Ashkenazim, and perhaps by the Orientals themselves, has declined significantly over the years. To cite some of the available evidence: in a study of four development centres in 1959 reported by Shuval (1962: Table 1), 33 per cent of the Europeans, 33 per cent of the North Africans and 37 per cent of people of Near Eastern origin indicated dislike of having North Africans as neighbours, and 22, 25 and 27 per cent respectively would rather not have Near Eastern neighbours. In comparison, only 10, 11 and 7 per cent rejected the idea of European neighbours. Self-rejection by the Orientals is thus as high as rejection by others, suggesting the existence of an implicit norm of prejudice (Shuval, 1966). In surveys reported by Peres, 37 per cent of Ashkenazi high school pupils in 1965 regarded neighbourhoods shared with Orientals unfavourably, while only 12 per cent of the Oriental pupils felt similarly about sharing neighbourhoods with Ashkenazim (1971: Tables 3 and 4). In the adult sample, 23 per cent of the Ashkenazim in 1967–8 were not in favour of renting a room to Orientals, while 10 per cent of the Orientals did not favour renting a room to Ashkenazim (ibid.: Tables 5 and 6). In a more intimate area, marriage, 60 per cent of the Ashkenazi pupils in 1965 and 43 per cent of the adults in 1967–8 viewed marriage to Orientals with disfavour while only 18 per cent and 6 per cent respectively of the Orientals disapproved of marriage to Ashkenazim (ibid.: Tables 3–6).[20] Surveys in the 1970s show, however, much less rejection of Orientals. In the survey of high school pupils in 1975, only 21 per cent expressed unwillingness to marry a Jew of a different ethnic origin – 23–32 per cent of the Ashkenazi subgroups as compared with 13–15 per cent of the non-Ashkenazi subgroups. The drop in the percentage of high school pupils who have reservations or objections to mixed marriages from 60 per cent in 1965 to 21 per cent in 1975 is quite significant.

In closing this discussion on anti-Oriental invidious distinctions, the preferential treatment of Orientals should be mentioned. A feeling that the Orientals are publicly granted privileges over the Ashkenazim in access to education and political openings is observed to be quite widespread among the Ashkenazim, especially Ashkenazi sabras. This feeling is readily invoked and voiced as soon as a case is mentioned of the prevalence of discrimination against Orientals. In recent years informal Oriental benign quotas were established in some institutions of higher education in addition to the longstanding Oriental quotas in certain political posts. The conspicuous nature of these quotas has the consequence of appeasing the Orientals, concealing the token effect of these measures and inculcating the Ashkenazim with a sense of self-righteousness (for an Oriental view, see Research Team, 1973).

Compared with the Oriental–Ashkenazi ethnic division, the religious–nonreligious division is predominantly noninvidious, even though intolerance and differential treatment are by no means absent.

The question of institutional discrimination is subject to a heated controversy. Clerical activists complain of infringement of freedom of religion or anti-religious compulsion and make charges that there is a continuing erosion in the religious character of the state (Meron, 1973). Anti-clerical spokesmen, on the other hand, protest against the lack of freedom from religion or religious compulsion, and allege that mounting religious coercion is engineered through the state (Aloni, 1970; Tamarin, 1973).[21] (See chapter 3, section 1B for details about the conflicting viewpoints.) However, the status quo in religious matters, with its endless fluctuations, strikes a balance between the two factions and even slightly favours the religious group.

There is no doubt that prejudice does colour religious–nonreligious relations. The substantial subcultural diversity and social separation breed at least some estrangement, rejection and stereotyping. The more secular Jews within the nonreligious majority feel much resentment against the religious Jews to whom they attribute outdated traditionalism, Galuth mentality, fanaticism and religious coercion. Likewise the more Orthodox within the religious minority harbour much disdain for secular Jews, whose way of life they consider sinful, undisciplined and wasteful.

Some empirical evidence for prejudice is documented in a pioneering study of eleventh-graders conducted in 1973 by O. Cohen (1975). It is found that social distance between the two groups is substantial and symmetrical (p. 64). Of the nonreligious respondents 65 per cent were unwilling to have a religious close friend, 72 per cent to marry a religious mate and 81 per cent to have a religious neighbour, and most of them felt that the attitudes of the nonreligious majority were the same. The rejection of the religious respondents was equally strong: 68 per cent were unwilling to have a nonreligious close friend, 71 per cent to marry a nonreligious mate and 65 per cent to have a nonreligious neighbour, and most of them attributed these attitudes to the religious minority as well. This considerable unpreparedness of both sides for personal contact is, however, only partially prejudicial. It is primarily based on legitimate differences in lifestyle and on the need to refrain from the strains associated with mixed relations.[22]

The other clue for religious–nonreligious prejudice is the prevalence of group stereotypes. Religious Jews are stereotyped as a more homogeneous group than nonreligious Jews. About half (45 per cent) of the respondents (47 per cent of the religious and 44 per cent of the secular) thought that 'all religious Jews are alike or very alike', as compared with only one-quarter (24 per cent) of the respondents (26 per cent of the religious and 18 per cent of the secular) who thought that 'all secular Jews are alike or very alike' (O. Cohen, 1975: 169). An examination of the contents of these stereotypical perceptions reveals that different characteristics were imputed to the two groups. While both were viewed as equally loyal to the state, intelligent, industrious and tolerant, religious Jews were positively perceived as much more moral but also negatively as much more stubborn, physically weak and cowardly, whereas nonreligious Jews were more favourably seen as sociable and sporting (ibid.: 171). The broad agreement among various sections of the population on these stereotypes suggests that they have become social norms in Israeli society and that the religious group as a nondominant minority does accept the derogatory stereotypes directed against itself.[23]

As to discrimination in access to income, employment, education, power and housing, observations point to counterbalancing directions. The religious group control their own resources and dispense them to their members, and religious persons also have access to resources under nonreligious control. For instance, a religious applicant has a better chance of being admitted to the religious university than a nonreligious applicant, but has an equal chance of acceptance by nonreligious universities. Religious circles sometimes charge that their people are discriminated against in jobs in the Foreign Office, the Broadcasting Authority, merchant fleet and certain private industries. These jobs often require occasional unofficial work on Saturdays and holidays, non-working days which are strictly observed by religious Jews. The halakha has yet to resolve the question of operating the essential services on holidays. For instance, the public electricity company would face a problem in taking on a religious engineer whose refusal to work on holidays would mean giving him preferential treatment over nonreligious engineers. On the other hand, there are many positions which are reserved for the religious group and paid for by the general public, such as the staff of the Chief Rabbinate, supervisors of kashrut and staff in the religious educational system. As to political power, it is true that religious Jews have little chance of making good in nonreligious parties and thereby participating in the patronage dispensed by them. Their effective political organizations, especially the religious parties, are mainly responsible for the handicap, but they provide reasonable compensation for whatever is lost by religious persons this way. And with regard to housing, a religious person will experience little difficulty in buying or renting a flat in a nonreligious neighbourhood if he is prepared to endure the personal hardship involved in living there. At the same time, in many religious neighbourhoods there is no open occupancy and nonreligious Jews are not allowed in at all.

Invidious distinctions are most marked in Arab–Jewish relations in all their forms – institutional, prejudicial and discriminatory. Institutional discrimination against the Arab minority is built into the very structure of the Jewish sectarian character of the state. The exclusionary Law of Return, which grants citizenship to foreign-born Jews but fails to extend the right of repatriation to native Palestinian refugees, establishes the favourable status of a Jew in Israel.[24] This is also the effect of the extensive incorporation of Jewish symbols in Israel's public domain. Furthermore, in many policies, the state and other public bodies favour the Jewish population. This is made possible mostly through the special departments for minority affairs which apply to Arabs standards which are different from the general ones. Special projects to assist the poor, disadvantaged children and underdeveloped areas (through measures such as low-interest loans and grants-in-aid to investors, subsidized public housing, income tax deductions and compensatory education)

197

are limited to the Jewish population.[25] In addition, Arabs are obviously ineligible for a great deal of public assistance that is channelled through the Jewish Agency.

Public inquiry commissions reveal some of the institutional differential treatments. One commission (Israel, Ministry of the Interior, 1973) which looked into the predicament of the Arab local authorities pointed to their poor standard of services. But despite their greater needs, they received one-fifth or less of the funds given to comparable Jewish local authorities by the Ministry of the Interior in 1973. This inequality in subsidization was to some degree redressed during the 1974–5 fiscal years in reaction to pressure by the Arab local governments. Another inquiry commission (Israel, Ministry of Education and Culture, 1975) showed how inadequate present Arab education is in preparing the Arabs for life as a national minority in a Jewish state and for bridging the considerable Arab–Jewish gap in achievements. Arab education does not enjoy the attention and support given to Hebrew education. Even the Druzes, who are generally granted better treatment than other Arabs, are subject to double standards, as two public commissions have reported (Israel, Prime Minister's Office, 1974; Israel, Knesset, 1975).

Israel's land policy vis-à-vis the Arab minority is a case in point. The government has taken a variety of measures to reduce the extent as much as possible of lands owned or claimed by Arabs. This policy is motivated by considerations of national security, Judaization of Arab-populated areas, and regional development, but in most cases it runs counter to Arab interests. The transfer of land is from Arab to Jewish hands, hardly ever the other way round. Development plans usually disregard the Arabs' needs, even in areas such as Galilee and Acre where the Arabs are numerically superior. It is estimated that during 1948–67 between 40 to 60 per cent of Israeli Arabs' land was confiscated (Peretz, 1958: 142; Stock, 1968: 46). Since then more land has been taken over. Compensation for the lost holdings has been unsatisfactory (Oded, 1964: 17–18). A significant portion of the expropriated lands belonged to Arabs who became 'absentees' by a legal technicality because they left or were forced to leave their homes during the 1948 War. These internal Arab refugees, numbering about one-fifth of all Israeli Arabs, were resettled in other Arab villages and their lands were handed over to Jews.

A trend of reducing institutional discrimination against Israeli Arabs is, however, discernible, although the decline is much smaller than that in the case of Oriental Jews. Policies have become more and more liberal over the years. Military government has been lifted, two five-year plans for Arab village development have been carried out, the protection of Arab civil liberties has been improved and the government and Histadrut pay attention to the Arabs' special needs much more now than they used to. There are certain limits to the adoption of more liberal policies by the authorities, the most restrictive ones being the conception of Israel as a country of Jews, and for Jews, and the strong anti-Arab attitudes of the Jewish public. The fact is that in a survey of high school pupils in 1972, 76 per cent of the nonreligious, 89 per cent of the partly observant and 94 per cent of the religious thought that the Israeli government did much or too much for the Israeli Arabs (Zuckerman-Bareli, 1975, an earlier draft), despite the realities of differential treatment. This fact is related to informal deep-seated expectations among the Jewish population for double standards in catering for the needs of the two groups.

Anti-Arab ethnocentrism takes extreme proportions. Paternalism against Arabs is much more pervasive than that against Orientals, and the Arabs are viewed with contempt and pity. (See chapter 5, section 3, for anti-Oriental statements by Israeli leaders, that imply rejection of the Arab culture and people.) The common Hebrew slang term for a shoddy performance is 'Arab work'. In the minds of many Israeli Jews, the Arabs are inferior. To cite from public surveys, 76 per cent of adult Jews in the Tel-Aviv area in 1968 believed that Arabs would never reach the level of Jews (Peres, 1971: Table 15) and 60 per cent of adult Jews and 58 per cent of Jewish high school pupils, in two state-wide samples taken by the Israel Institute of Social Applied Research in summer 1975, felt the same.

Arab–Jewish stereotypes are overgeneralized and distorted images of the status of Arabs as a hostile, underdeveloped, separate and unequal minority as against the superior status of the Jewish majority (Peres and Levy, 1969). The image of the Arab is, overall, negative. In a study of young people in 1965 and 1968 (Benyamini, 1969), the Arabs were unfavourably stereotyped as old-fashioned, rigid, selfish, ungrateful, bad, ugly, slow, passive, failing, unimportant and emotional. The image of the Israeli, who was identified as a Jew in the minds of the Jewish respondents, was a negative mirror-image of the Arab, with the exceptions of manhood, warmth and emotionalism attributed to both Arabs and Jews. This asymmetric perception was reconfirmed by other surveys. Whereas both Arabs and Jews in 1970 evaluated the 'Israeli Jew' in positive terms, the Arabs rated the 'Israeli Arab' much more favourably than the Jews (Hofman, 1972). When Jews are presented with a number of images, they usually place the Israeli Arabs in the lowest and least preferred rank (e.g., in the study by Peres, 1968: 154). Similarly Arabs, too, feel themselves to be distant from Jews (Hofman, 1974), and they are observed to stereotype Jews as haughty, materalistic and lacking certain traditional Arab social graces such as honour, hospitality and neighbourliness.

It is clear that Jewish evaluations of Israeli Arabs are overshadowed by the Israeli–Arab conflict. There is a tendency in Israel (and in the West) to 'psychologize' the dispute and to place the blame on imperfections in the 'Arab personality', including such irrational traits as authoritarianism, suspiciousness, lack of reality-testing, hostility, fatalism and the prominence of shame as a motive (Beit-Hallahmi, 1972: 23). These stereotypes of the Arabs, no doubt, shape the Jewish majority's perceptions of the Arab minority. This is, of course, in addition to the widespread suspicion that every Israeli Arab is a potential fifth columnist.

Contrasted with the deep-seated prejudice of Arab inferiority is the notorious myth of the 'sabra superman', namely, the typical Israeli-born (usually of European extraction) who is alleged to be superior, invincible, patriotic, resourceful, aggressive and arrogant, and at the same time a social success and a man of warm emotions.[26] The 1973 October War, which boosted Arab morale and self-confidence and has stirred soul-searching and misgivings among the Israeli Jews, may somewhat correct these false images.

Social distance between Arabs and Jews is mutual, though somewhat asymmetrical. Given the institutional separation, it is understandable why there is more reservation towards or rejection of mixed neighbourhoods than mixed friendships. In a state-wide sample of the adult urban population in June–July 1970, 85 per cent of the Jews expressed unwillingness to live in a neighbourhood shared by Arab families. In an earlier sample of Tel-Aviv residents, 67 per cent of the Jews did not want to have an Arab as a neighbour and 86 per cent would not rent a room to an Arab (Peres, 1971: Table 15). The Arabs' unwillingness to live close to Jews is also great: 70 per cent were unwilling to live in an apartment house with Jews and 58 per cent were unwilling to live in a Jewish quarter (ibid.: Table 16). Whereas large majorities on both sides reject living close to each other, about half do not mind having friendly contacts. For instance, 51 per cent of the Jewish adults and 51 per cent of Jewish young people in two national surveys in summer 1975 were willing to have Arab friends. In the 1967 Arab sample, 58 per cent were receptive to friendship with Jews (Peres, 1971: Table 16).

Other studies on preparedness for Arab–Jewish contacts reveal a number of tendencies. First, by big majorities, both Arab and Jewish young people consider inter-ethnic contact possible and desirable. Second, a majority of Arabs consider contact essential and try to foster it, as against only a minority of Jews. And, third, a sharp drop in Arab readiness for contact with Jews took place between 1971 and 1975, indicating greater disappointment with and lesser dependence on Jews, and greater self-assertiveness among Arabs two years after the October 1973 War (Hofman, 1972; and for a summary of recent data see Smooha and Hofman, 1976–7).

Individual discriminatory practices, reinforced by poor skills, weaken the Arabs' competitive potential for socioeconomic and power resources in Israeli society. While equal wages are paid thanks to Histadrut union protection and manpower shortages, the Arabs have less chance of obtaining a good job or gaining promotion. With few exceptions, only manual and lower-status service jobs which usually allow little upward social mobility are open to Arabs in the Jewish economy. The backward Arab sector cannot provide compensation because its demands for white-collar and higher-status jobs are limited.

As a result, Arabs with post-primary or higher education are deprived of fair employment opportunities. Arabs with post-primary education usually lack marketable trades (in 1973–4 only 15 per cent of pupils in Arab post-primary education attended vocational and agricultural schools compared with 57 per cent of puplis in Hebrew post-primary education). They can get very few clerical or other white-collar jobs in the private and public Jewish economy. On the other hand, at the higher education level, precisely those, such as engineers, with special skills face the toughest problem because they are refused employment in the developed Jewish sector and are not needed in the underdeveloped Arab sector. Teachers, doctors and lawyers who cater for their own communities had been easily absorbed until the mid-1970s, but with the growing numbers of university graduates they will have increasing problems in finding jobs. All other graduates are encountering difficulties already. [27]

The near-total exclusion of Arabs from middle and higher ranking power positions in society-at-large also points to unfair practices.

Along with these indications for the existence of a variety of invidious distinctions against the Arabs in Israel, counter-arguments which are widespread among the Jewish population should be considered. It is claimed that the Arabs enjoy full equality except in sensitive areas related to national security. To be an Arab in Israel, it is often said, is more beneficial than being an Israeli Jew. To cite some of the often-mentioned advantages of the Arabs, compared with the Jews, the Arabs are relieved from the burdens of the years of compulsory military service and periodical calls to the reserve for many years thereafter; they pay less local and state taxes (one estimate puts the Arab share of state taxes at 1.5 per cent compared with their 13 per cent proportion in the population) but get a great deal more in social security payments; they build illegally and squat on state lands much more often; they avail themselves more of reductions in high school fees and of benign quotas in admission to the universities, etc. These and similar contentions are either inaccurate or taken out of context. They, in fact, can be taken as further evidence for the prevalence among Jews of the patronizing thinking that Arabs are untrustworthy outsiders who do not deserve equal treatment and should be grateful for whatever good opportunities are made available to them.

To conclude, invidious distinctions between Orientals and Ashkenazim are moderate, those between religious and nonreligious Jews are relatively minor and those between Arabs and Jews are substantial.[28]

Dissatisfactions

Disharmony in group relations can be further examined on a subjective plane. The greater the conflict between the groups, the greater will be the dissatisfaction of the nondominant group members compared with the dominant group members. There are many manifestations, direct and indirect, including alienation, status dissatisfaction, criminality and militant attitudes.

The available evidence regarding Oriental dissatisfactions indicates two tendencies. On the one hand, within equal socioeconomic categories, the Orientals differ from the Ashkenazim only slightly in overall level of satisfaction or wellbeing. They do not feel miserable or alienated from the state. At the same time, in specific and concrete spheres, and in ethnic matters in particular, they have views and feelings significantly different from those of the Ashkenazim. Thus as Orientals they experience a significant degree of deprivation and rejection, and lack the sense of being full partners in Israeli society.

Various state-wide opinion polls of Jewish young people and adults, conducted periodically by the Israel Institute of Applied Social Research since the 1967 War, provide supporting evidence for the above observations. Of central interest are the findings on the subjective evaluation of 'wellbeing' (Levy and Guttman, 1975). Respondents are asked, first, to assess their 'overall happiness' ('Generally speaking, are you happy these days?') and then to indicate the degree of their satisfaction with specific areas of life. While there is rather more overall unhappiness among the Orientals (for instance, in summer 1975, 37–39 per cent of the high school pupils originating from different Oriental subgroups as compared with 21–28 per cent of the Ashkenazi students felt unhappy) much of it is due to the Orientals' inferior socioeconomic status. As a matter of fact, the Orientals report much greater dissatisfaction with material wellbeing (for instance, in the above sample 46 to 57 per cent of the

Oriental young people said that their family income was not sufficient, as against only 17 to 21 per cent of the Ashkenazi youth), even within same levels of education of head of family.

Similarly, other findings indicate that while the Orientals do not differ from the Ashkenazim in general political alienation, they do show a certain alienation in the ethnic sphere. For instance, roughly half of the youth and half of the adults in the 1975 surveys felt that the government did not do a good job in coping with the problems of the state, and three-fifths of the youth and three-fifths of the adults did not believe official announcements. The Orientals and Ashkenazim do not differ on these and other general questions. Yet in a survey of Oriental male adults in 1971, 40 per cent said they would support an Oriental political party for the municipality, 39 per cent for the Histadrut and 32 per cent for the Knesset (and 28, 28 and 30 per cent respectively were undecided) (Eshel and Peres, 1973). It is, therefore, clear that the significant disenchantment with the Ashkenazi political establishment as far as Oriental interests are concerned does not spill over and injure the strong identification the Orientals feel with Israeli society and its power structure.

At least some of the Orientals' much greater status-dissatisfaction, compared with Ashkenazi dissatisfaction, surfaces in the criminal records. To be sure, reported crimes are heavily biased against the lower classes and especially against the low-status ethnic groups, whereas a disproportionately greater number of white-collar crimes of the higher classes go unheeded. However, there is more to the Oriental lead in court convictions than this. In 1970, comparable rates of convicted adult offenders per 1,000 were 11.4 for Israeli-born, 7.8 for Asian-born, 17.4 for African-born and only 3.0 for European–American born, and the corresponding rates for convicted juvenile offenders were 8.2, 4.8, 21.8 and 4.8 (see Table 79; for a comparative analysis of crime rates of different ethnic groups in Israel in 1960–5, see Schmelz, 1969). The 1974 figures also demonstrate that the Orientals are three to five times more represented among convicted criminals than the Ashkenazim. As a matter of fact, 78 per cent of all adult Jewish offenders (CBS, *Criminal Statistics 1970*, Special Series 417, Table B) and 93 per cent of all juvenile Jewish offenders in 1970 were of Oriental origin (CBS, *Juvenile Delinquency*, Special Series 408, Table E). The much larger crime rate among Orientals, and especially Moroccan Jews,[29] reflects greater relative and actual deprivations in addition to greater ethnic and class discrimination in the administration of justice and lack of full acculturation.

The crucial question is to what degree Oriental dissatisfactions are specifically channelled into the ethnic sphere. Do the Orientals and

Ashkenazim share similar perspectives on the ethnic question? Do the Orientals feel ethnically deprived? What solutions do they see to the problem? What actions are they willing to take to improve their conditions? There is little evidence to allow adequate answers to these questions, and I can only suggest that while the Orientals probably do not hold the same views on the ethnic issue as the Ashkenazim, they seek accommodation with them. They would, therefore, avoid any extreme action that might hamper the existing accommodating relations between the two groups.

My study of ethnic leadership in 1970–1 provides information that supports the suggested generalization. The Oriental leaders are by and large integrated within the Ashkenazi establishment, and have thus pursued an accommodating style, and cannot be considered extremists by any criterion. Intensive interviews with them disclose, nevertheless, a significant amount of militancy, i.e., a deviation from the views of the dominant group in the ethnic area. While Romanian leaders, who speak for the establishment, defined the ethnic problem in terms of varying degrees of Oriental sociocultural maladjustment (backwardness) and socioeconomic disadvantages, only 45 per cent of the Oriental leaders held such views. The majority (55 per cent) emphasized that in addition to class handicaps, the crucial elements are ethnic deprivations such as prejudice, discrimination or malign neglect by the state.

In identifying factors which account for the present ethnic gaps, 31 per cent of the Oriental leaders, compared with 12.5 per cent of the Romanian leaders, found the dominant group to be the most blameworthy, and 48 and 17.5 per cent respectively found it to be the second most blameworthy. A majority of 70 per cent of the Oriental leaders, and only 3 per cent of the Romanian leaders, mentioned invidious distinctions as a problem area. Similarly, 63 and 3 per cent respectively regarded power disparities as problematic and 37 and 10 per cent expected future Ashkenazi opposition to Orientals obtaining more power positions.

The majority of the Oriental leaders doubted the sincerity of Ashkenazi adherence to the official goals of ethnic equality and melting-pot assimilation. Thirty-six per cent accused the establishment of trying to assimilate the Orientals into Ashkenazi culture, and an additional 21 per cent accused it of perpetuating the status quo of inequality and lack of assimilation. Forty-two per cent and 21 per cent respectively attributed these two adverse intentions to the Ashkenazi public. The Romanian leaders, on the other hand, admitted no such intentions, though 20 per cent of them said that the establishment had no clear policy and 59 per cent explained that the Ashkenazi public is divided on the specific goal of ethnic integration.

The willingness of the Oriental leaders to adopt non-accommodating strategies of ethnic change falls significantly short of their non-accommodating views. They agree on the need for ethnic organizations – 47 per cent considered them to be an integrative catalyst while 49 per cent considered them a necessity for improving Oriental conditions (52.5 and 17.5 per cent of the Romanian leaders also concurred). But they primarily endorsed accommodating ethnic organizations (such as self-help societies and ethnic circles in established political parties which are reminiscent of the immigrant associations) that operate as auxiliary tools for the establishment. Only 12 per cent favoured local ethnic lists, 16 per cent national ethnic lists and 12 per cent an ethnic protest movement – organizations which are all militant by Israeli standards. Asked about the hypothetical situation of an escalating ethnic struggle the overwhelming majority agreed only with the use of persuasive means as a pressure tactic, and as a last resort – 30 per cent would accept forming a separate list for the Knesset, 12 per cent demonstrations (including sit-ins), 9 per cent mass protest movement and 7 per cent more drastic means. Eighty-seven per cent maintained that the ethnic problem should be handled with moderation. These perspectives on ethnic change are very close to those of the establishment, as expressed by the Romanian leaders, albeit somewhat less accommodating.

Although we do not know to what extent the Oriental leaders represent the views of the Oriental group and the Romanian leaders the Ashkenazi group, we should expect greater differences in the same direction among the two groups. The Oriental masses are by and large less contented in ethnic affairs than their 'leaders', who have had to pass the test of accommodation in order to survive. Compare, for instance, the above-mentioned proportions of Orientals willing to support an Oriental political party: for the municipality 40 per cent of the constituents as against only 16 per cent of the power-holders, and for the Knesset 32 and 12 per cent respectively.[30] The slim support given to the ethnic lists in the 1973 national elections was due to the poor state of Oriental candidates and to the self-restraint exercised by the Orientals.[31] The Oriental group is, no doubt, more critical of the present patterns of ethnic relations than the Ashkenazim. Most importantly, the Ashkenazi group is quite wary of the escalation of ethnic tension and will probably make significant concessions to avoid it. Both sides are inclined to compromise.

In concluding this discussion of Oriental dissatisfactions, it is important to note that the Orientals are ultimately quite ambivalent about their status in Israeli society. On the 'skin deep' psychological plane, expressions of general satisfaction with living in a Jewish state predominate. These accommodating feelings are in accord with

205

the formal norms of ethnic equality and Jewish brotherhood as well as with the realities of the Israeli–Arab conflict and the beneficient national economy. Some of the opinion polls reflect this more superficial layer of Oriental psychology. Such surveys fail, however, to penetrate the more profound layer of Oriental consciousness which is overloaded with pent-up emotions of detachment, estrangement, inadequacy, disenchantment, deprivation and indignation. While the shallow psychological level is valid in the present situation, it is expected that the deeper level will become more relevant following an easing of the Israeli–Arab dispute, an economic depression or a related alteration of the institutional context.

The limited evidence indicates little difference between religious and nonreligious Jews in dissatisfaction with general life areas and, more importantly, with the religious sphere. State-wide surveys of both young people and adults in 1975 reveal no significant differences in feelings of overall wellbeing ('happiness') and dissatisfaction with specific life situations (family income, health, neighbourhood, etc.). And in the most relevant area of religious observance, 90 per cent of all the adult respondents in the February–April 1973 survey reported contentment with the degree they personally observed (or rather did not observe) religious traditions, and more of the religious than the nonreligious were happy on this crucial point. This shows that both the religious and nonreligious, despite the disagreements and inconveniences, are generally satisfied with their respective religious and secular lifestyles and that there is ample leeway in Israeli society today for both freedom of religion and freedom from religion.

While no hard data are available on comparative crime-rates of the religious and nonreligious, it may be suggested that one by no means finds among religious Jews the disproportional criminality through which Oriental Jews apparently channel some of their frustrations. On the contrary, the religious Jews are observed to have a lower incidence of court convictions, perhaps because of a greater conformity or a more favourable stereotype of higher moral standards as compared with nonreligious Jews.

What is characteristic of religious–nonreligious relations, however, is the existence of minorities on both sides who do not share the accommodating posture of the majorities in each group. Some religious Jews hold strong convictions and are ready to go to any extremes to live up to them. They still do not grant legitimacy to the Jewish state, let alone religious legitimacy. Should the state deviate from some basic religious principles, such as legislating civil marriage and divorce, it is not at all inconceivable that a sizeable section of the religious group would withdraw support from the regime. Some sections among the nonreligious group are equally committed to their ideas and will not hesitate to escalate the struggle.

Dissatisfactions are greatest in Arab–Jewish relations, although there is no evidence for significant differences between Arabs and Jews in self-reported general wellbeing. For instance, 84 per cent of the Arab male villagers in a representative sample in 1969 expressed satisfaction with their life in the village and 87 per cent of them said they would not leave their village (Guttman, Klaff and Levy, 1971). In another study of Arab villagers in 1970, 70 per cent felt satisfied with local government (Abu-Gosh, Shye and Hartman, 1972: 1543). While no comparative figures are available for the Jews, it is unlikely that they would feel a greater general satisfaction.

The strains focus, however, on group relations or the status of Arabs and Jews vis-à-vis each other. The alienation of most Arabs from Israeli society and the state should not be underestimated. Their status as an involuntary minority, as a publicly perceived hostile group and as an inferior quasi-caste is obviously not gratifying. For instance, the overwhelming majority of Israeli Arabs reject Israel's basic ideology – Zionism. The feeling that Zionism is a racist movement rather than a national liberation movement of Jews is widespread among them. Most Israeli Arabs also think that Israel should withdraw to the 1947 borders, a demand that almost none of the Jews would accept.

The deep Arab alienation surfaces even in the superficial opinion polls, not to mention the personal accounts of dissident Arabs (e.g., Jiryis, 1969; El-Asmar, 1975). Quite a few Arabs question the right of Israel to exist: 69 per cent in a 1967 general survey (Peres, 1971: Table 13), 60 per cent in a 1974 general survey (Tessler, 1976a: Table 3) and 43 per cent in a 1974 student survey (Zak, 1975: 57). Similarly for a large proportion of Arabs, Israel is not a place where they feel at home. In 1967 57 per cent of the Arab respondents said that they would feel more at home in an Arab country, 12 per cent felt it would make no difference and 31 per cent stated that they would feel more at home in Israel (Peres, 1971: Table 22); in 1974 45, 30 and 25 per cent respectively felt the same (Tessler, forthcoming).[32] In two other surveys of Arab high school pupils, 46 per cent of them were sceptical about their chances to fulfil their occupational aspirations in Israel in 1971, and 78 per cent expressed such doubts in 1975 (quoted by Smooha and Hofman, 1976–7).

The disproportional Arab crime-rate reflects this alienation to some extent. The adult crime-rate among Arabs in 1970 was about two and a half times greater than the Jewish crime-rate (21.9 and 8.4 per thousand, CBS, *Criminal Statistics 1970*, Special Series 417, Table 8).[33] Direct evidence for the prevalence of an element of alienation in the Arab crime statistics is the Arabs' over-representation in infractions of public order and offences against the administration of lawful authority (CBS, *Statistical Abstract of Israel*, 1972,

23: 563). The correlation between Arab deviance and cultural anomie (as a result of advancing modernization) (Shoham, Segal and Rahav, 1975) is probably another clue.

The Jewish majority is equally dissatisfied with its relations with the Arab minority. Underlying the Jews' alienation from the Arabs is a profound sense of distrust. The Arabs are perceived as a constant potential threat to both national security[34] and to the Jewish character of Israel. From the Jews' viewpoint, the Arabs are not indispensable (in a 1968 survey, 80 per cent of the Jews maintained that it would be better if there were fewer Arabs; Peres, 1971: Table 15). This is why the Jewish public is unprepared to make significant concessions to the Arabs in Israel.[35]

Protests and countermeasures

The amount of harmony between ethnic groups can be further manifested in acts of protest by the subordinate group and in countermeasures by the dominant group. Protests and countermeasures may be classified into the categories of 'legitimate' and 'illegitimate'. Although the line between the two is often blurred, especially because of the dominant group's power to manipulate the definition of legitimacy, the distinction is helpful for evaluating the intensity of the intergroup conflict.

It must be emphasized from the outset that there is virtually no intergroup violence in Israeli society. There are no pogroms, terror, serious police brutality, riots with fatalities or significant property losses, or other collective outbursts. Tamarin, who rightly makes this observation, also notes: 'In everyday Israeli prose, although official ideals of cooperation and social justice coexist with cut-throat competition, aggressiveness, lack of courtesy and so on, physical violence is condemned' (1973: 172). This is despite the legacy of political violence by dissident groups during the British mandate and the continuing Arab–Israeli warfare.

The striking feature of Oriental–Ashkenazi relations is the relative lack of Oriental protest. Reference is seldom made to protest in the mass media, letters to the editor, commentaries or articles. A number of ethnic publications usually voice protests but they reach a very limited audience. The Oriental leaders, who are politically incorporated into the establishment, make low-key critical speeches in infrequent meetings of ethnic circles in political parties.

Protest voting is limited, too. Many consider the Oriental vote for the traditional opposition Herut party to be a protest vote and there is no doubt that the broader right-of-centre opposition bloc gains disproportionate Oriental support at least partly for combining protest with nationalism. The Orientals also register their protest by voting for local ethnic lists. But the failure of the national ethnic lists since 1955 and, more significantly, the failure of the Communist Party and other radical splinter parties to receive any Oriental backing shows how modest and inconsequential the Oriental voting protest is.

Other avenues of protest are also rarely used by Orientals. There is not even a single case in which the Orientals have gone to the courts for adjudication of ethnic discrimination or defamation, or to protest against unfair laws or regulations. With a few exceptions, notably the Committee of the Sephardic Community in Jerusalem, the Orientals have no independent organizations that can bring pressure upon the establishment in any significant way. The various Oriental immigrant associations can be considered, to all intents and purposes, as satellite organizations of the establishment.

Two frequently mentioned protest movements disrupted the restrained and non-violent Oriental–Ashkenazi scene – the Wadi-Salib riots of the late 1950s and the Black Panther demonstrations of the early 1970s. A brief comment on them may be helpful.

The Wadi-Salib riot was triggered by the shooting of a Moroccan drunkard by a policeman in a Haifa slum in July 1959. In reaction, local Moroccan slum residents attacked the police. A day later a large crowd marched out to protest against police brutality, unemployment, worsening housing conditions and ethnic discrimination. The Union of North Africans, which had been established in the Wadi-Salib slum a few months earlier as a counter-organization to the co-opted North African national immigrant association, provided militant leadership. The demonstration quickly turned into a riot as the marchers stormed the Ashkenazi business and residential sectors of the city, attacking passers-by and looting stores. In several days the riot spread out to a number of predominantly Moroccan development towns, but the damage caused there was smaller. The government convened in an emergency session and set up a Public Inquiry Commission. The Commission (Public Inquiry Commission, 1959) filed a report a month later that documented problems of ethnic integration but denied the charges of ethnic discrimination. The press dealt with the matter intensively and the issue received some attention in the national elections held a few months later. The movement's leader, who headed the Union of North Africans, ran for the Knesset on an ethnic list while in prison, but he lost (for commentaries see Patai, 1960; Bar-Yosef, 1970).

The Black Panthers are a more significant manifestation of ethnic protest. They have gone through two stages: in the earlier stage (March 1971 through March 1973) they tried to change from a street gang to a protest movement (Bernstein, 1976; E. Cohen, 1972; Smooha, 1972; Sprinzak, 1973), and in the later stage (from March

209

1973 on) they made an effort to change from a protest movement to a political party. Both attempts were only partly successful.

Originally the Black Panthers were youths of mostly Moroccan extraction who lived in the slums of Jerusalem and who neither studied nor worked. Because of heavy criminal records they were also army rejects. Frequent contact with American students studying at the Hebrew University, as well as with some Israeli leftists, provided them with the means of ideological articulation. The great relaxation in security tension that followed the ceasefire of August 1970 and the special treatment given to the new Russian immigrants also helped to radicalize them. In March 1971 they started a series of demonstrations which went on intensively till August 1971 and sparsely since then. The Panthers demanded better education, standard housing, greater public support for large families, privileges similar to those extended to the new immigrants, job training for unemployed youths, qualification for the draft, rehabilitation, and integration of schools and neighbourhoods. The Panthers' demands and demonstrations, and especially their accusations of ethnic discrimination, drew much public attention.

After two years of activity the strengths and weaknesses of the Black Panthers became clear. The Panthers managed to propagate their protest demands through skilful manipulation of symbols and resort to street demonstrations.[36] But beyond a successful communication of their message, they proved ineffective, failing to build a mass base, to form a permanent organization or to mould an internally acceptable and publicly respectable leadership corps. In fact, the Panthers have never become a mass protest movement, nor an Orientals' movement, not even a movement of the underprivileged. By spring 1973 the Panther movement reached a dead end and was saved from virtual extinction through an opportune merger with a leftist splinter group ('the Israeli Democrats' headed by S. Cohen and N. Giladi who broke away from the HaOlam Haze movement). The intent of the union was to found a party and to run for the forthcoming elections in summer 1973.

Just as the Panthers failed to institutionalize themselves as a mass protest movement, they similarly failed to institutionalize themselves as a political party. The union provided the Panthers with money, organization and political experience but exacerbated factionalization. The Panthers participated in the Histadrut elections in September 1973 and scored some achievements. In December 1973 they ran in thirty-five (out of ninety-eight) Jewish local elections and for the Knesset, and suffered a defeat. During the following two years the Panthers acted in three directions: to become a publicly recognized spokesman for the poor, to develop a regular party apparatus (governing bodies, an administrative staff and branches) and to gain the support of diverse groups (ethnic organizations, leftist circles and even the establishment). All these targets were reached only to a limited extent.

My state-wide survey of forty Panther activists and my observations on the first convention of the Black Panther Party in 1975 reveal deep cleavages. Overall, there is a wide gap between the Panther leadership and its potential following. On many issues the Panthers take a much more radical or militant stand than those usually taken by the poor, or by Orientals in general. Furthermore, intense personal rivalries and ideological dissensions split the Panther ranks. The Panther activists disagree on the very conditions necessary to transform the Panthers from a protest movement to a political party. Only 26 per cent of the activists in the survey wished the Panthers to become a party as compared with 44 per cent who favoured a self-help organization and 31 per cent who desired a mass protest movement. A majority of 64 per cent wanted the Panthers to restrict their activities to social or ethnic issues, whereas a minority of 36 per cent felt that they should address themselves to all political matters. The Panther activists were more or less evenly divided on questions of ethnic versus class solidarity. A majority still refused to commit themselves exclusively to ordinary democratic politics, and approved of resorting to extra-parliamentary steps such as un-licensed demonstrations, seizures of public buildings, threats and even 'more extreme means if necessary'.

The Panthers' accomplishment lies, however, in their very survival as a splinter opposition group in the Israeli political system and in their continued presence as a potential threat to the ethnic status quo in crisis situations.

The Wadi-Salib riots and the Black Panther demonstrations shared much in common. The protesters came from the lowest stratum in Jewish society and from the most disadvantaged section in the Oriental group (Moroccans). While the themes of protest blended class with ethnicity, the class element was much more emphasized in the mass media. The demands for full equality and integration were received with sympathy, but the 'unrespectable' lower-class leadership proved ineffective in gaining broader support. Both protests were relatively short lived, and they failed to become more permanent mass protest movements. The two generated a similar reaction from the establishment and can thus shed light on the countermeasures taken by the dominant group.

After the failure of initial efforts of suppression,[37] official policy moved to a show of responsiveness. Protesters were listened to. Public inquiry commissions were set up.[38] The social, nonethnic, demands were stressed and given legitimacy. Oriental leaders in service of the establishment were despatched to mediate and to calm

211

down the unrest. An increased ethnic quota in political power positions was granted, and the protest leaders were gradually bought off by individual benefits and by other means.[39] Public spokesmen lavished rosy promises of reform, and some funds were promptly budgeted to cope with the immediate causes of the trouble.[40] When order was restored, certain measures of change, though in a somewhat watered-down form, were implemented.[41]

The Wadi-Salib and the Black Panthers' ventures did not change the basic picture of passivity and accommodation by the Oriental masses. The situation was usually under control. There was almost no compelling need to use oppressive means.[42] Ethnic conflicts caused little disruption in the economic, political and other spheres of the system.

The factors accounting for the lack of realization of a much greater potential of ethnic unrest will be discussed shortly (under 'Integration'). Here let me mention only the more salient and immediate causes, namely, the absence of an independent Oriental leadership of any stature and the enormous political skill shown by the Ashkenazi establishment in handling ethnic tensions.[43]

Protests and countermeasures are a more enduring feature of religious–nonreligious relations. They take different forms. The main arena of strife is religious legislation. While the ethnic problem is kept out of politics and the judiciary, the religious issue appears there time and again. There is a distinctive pattern of legal struggle. Nonreligious Jews suffering from religious restrictions turn to the courts for relief; favourable decisions upset the religious status quo and religious circles seek corrective legislation; law amendments are retested in the courts by new cases, which, in turn, lead to another round of legislation; etc. The full stories of the various battles are dramatic. Among the well-known controversies are the cases of Brother Daniel (a monk, born a Jew, who applied for citizenship as a Jew by nationality), Shalit (a navy officer, married to a Gentile woman, who wanted to have his children registered as Jews by nationality and of no religion), Bene Israel (Indian Jews who demanded equal status in matters of marriage), the Marbek slaughterhouse and Shalom Zim passenger ship (two different cases of embittered struggles to obtain kashrut certification) and Reform Jews (who sought to rent public halls to hold services). (Details of these and other affairs can be found in most books on state and religion in Israel such as Zucker, 1973; Aloni, 1970.)

The predominance of legitimate means in the conflict between religious and nonreligious Jews is related to the resilience of the religious status quo. This is both a set of pragmatic arrangements in controversial religious matters and a set of democratic procedures for settling issues. Underpinning its success to prevent all-out

212

confrontations is the general rule of not deciding in questions of principle and of letting each party seek a practical remedy for problems as they arise (Don-Yihye, 1971). To illustrate, after a long series of court rulings and legal amendments, the compromise definition of a Jew, adopted in 1970, is 'a person born to a Jewish mother or has converted to Judaism but is not a member of any other religion'. This definition leaves open the crucial issue whether conversions by Reform and Conservative Rabbis are binding. Other clauses in the law grant non-Jewish children, grandchildren and spouses of Jews all Jewish privileges (including automatic citizenship) without registering them as Jews. These inconsistencies give partial relief to each side. To cite from the area of marriage and divorce, unmarriageable persons may contract private marriages (most are religiously valid), arrange civil marriage abroad (in person or by post) or become 'an unmarried spouse' (a legal status which establishes most of the duties and rights of marriage).[44]

Along with the legitimate, orderly struggle between the majority of the religious sector and the nonreligious sector, there is the continuing religious fanaticism on the part of the religious circles not affiliated with the dominant Mizrahi. They attack both the 'selling-out' religious establishment and nonreligious Jews. The growing number of incidents includes abuse of immodestly dressed persons, the stoning of intruding cars and the blockage of near-by streets on days of rest, harassment of pathologists for conducting autopsies, violent interference in the work of Christian missionaries, zealous actions against liberal Rabbis, hiding and aiding girls whose request for exemption from military service is denied, setting fire to a shop selling sex aids and even one serious case of child kidnapping (the 'Yossele affair'). Religious zealotry, i.e., verbal outbursts or violent actions against deviants from traditional religion or their perceived accomplices, is quite common in Israel (M. Friedman, 1975).[45] Despite its limited scope, it gives a clue to the great potential for conflict between religious and nonreligious Jews.

Small action groups which do not hesitate to resort to confrontation exist on both sides. For instance, Havaad Lehaganat Kudshe HaOma, an ultra-Orthodox political group, is quite active in the 1970s. In the secularist camp, in the 1960s the League against Religious Coercion held demonstrations and clashed with religious circles. Showdowns between religious and nonreligious Jews are, nevertheless, local and sporadic.

Acts of protest and countermeasures are more common in the case of Arab–Jewish relations than in the relations between the Jewish groups. Arab protest is manifested by both legitimate and, to a lesser extent, illegitimate means. The Arabs make extensive use of verbal protest which is the major channel of protest in Western

213

democracies. Anti-Israeli pronouncements by Israeli Arabs of various ages, education and affiliations are commonplace. In fact, in the mid-1970s, verbal protest is so universal that one should carefully examine nuances in order to distinguish between moderate and militant Arabs. Arab–Palestinian nationalism and charges of differential treatment are the leading themes in the protest. Arab literature is highly politicized and is full of vehement criticisms of the authorities (Yinon, 1965; Landau, 1969: 59) along with a critique of Arab traditionalism (Yinon, 1966).

The rising, substantial protest voting is another outlet. In Israel it takes the form of disproportional Arab support of the Communists. The Communists, Arabs and Jews, have been consistently non-Zionist and also willing to fight for the Arabs' equal status in Israeli society (Czudnowski and Landau, 1965; Bailey, 1970; Nahas, 1976). Until 1965, Maki (the Israeli Communist Party, a Jewish–Arab party) operated. In 1951, 16.3 per cent of the Arab vote was cast for Maki as compared with only 4.0 per cent in the country as a whole; in 1961 the respective percentages were 22.0 and 4.2 per cent.

In 1965 Maki split and Rakah (the New Communist Party) has emerged as the major party identified with the Arab cause and 'perhaps the only immediately available means of registering a protest' (Landau, 1972: 258). While accepting the legitimacy of the state, Rakah opposes Zionism, advocates the repeal of the Law of Return, calls for the foundation of a Palestinian state alongside Israel and the recognition of the Palestine Liberation Organization as the representative of the Palestinian people and demands absolutely equal treatment for Arabs and Jews in Israel. Such a platform obviously appeals to Israel's Arabs. It is estimated that 29 per cent of the Arab voters in the 1969 national elections voted for Rakah as compared with 2.8 per cent in the total population. The estimate for the 1973 national elections is 37 per cent among Arab voters against only 3.4 per cent nationally. Given the greater frustration and militancy of the younger Arab generation, it can be safely assumed that most of them and of the intelligentsia cast their ballots for Rakah. In 1973 Rakah also won a majority in twenty Arab villages (compared with only seven in 1969), usually the more developed ones, and it also carried the Arab city of Nazareth.

The formation of protest organizations is a further way to express discontent and to press for change. Till the early 1970s there was, however, hardly any significant Arab protest organization with the exception of Rakah. Even the struggle against the military administration imposed on Arabs in the years 1948–66 was mostly staffed and led by Jews. One very important abortive attempt to establish a nationalist protest organization was made in 1958–65 – Al-Ard (The

Land). The Al-Ard group is an offshoot of the Popular Front formed in 1958 in response to the resurgence of Pan-Arabism following the union between Egypt and Syria. The rift between the Communists and nationalists that swept the Arab world in 1959 affected the Front. The nationalists seceded to create Al-Ard. They endeavoured to represent truly the interests of the Arab minority (to fight against military administration, expropriation of lands, etc.) and to work for a united Palestine. The new movement had to face the crippling resistance of the authorities and their subservient Arab leaders and traditional structures. The group was first denied a permit to issue a periodical, then an application to form a voluntary association, and finally in 1965 a request to have an election list. Following the Supreme Court's ruling that Al-Ard negated Israel's territorial integrity and Zionist mission, the government declared it illegal. [46]

During the 1970s several new Arab organizations were founded. They maintain an increasing measure of independence and militant posture. They include local associations of Arab university graduates, a state-wide council of Arab high school pupils, national committees of Arab university students, of heads of Arab local governments and for the defence of Arab lands (to fight against government policies of expropriating lands of Arab citizens). All these organizations claim to represent Arab interests, air Arab grievances and demands publicly and take protest actions.

Another means of protest is litigation. In the past, Israeli Arabs frequently turned to the courts for protection of their civil liberties, especially in matters of land expropriations, restrictions imposed by the military administration and the like. Since the courts could not be of much help, Arabs no longer use them so often, but continue to seek relief through them.

Illegitimate protest actions exist as well, though they are not common. Demonstrations or riots without permits are infrequent. The May Day 1958 disturbances in Nazareth (see Schwarz, 1959: 15–34 for a description) were an exception. On the other hand, co-operation with the enemy in cases of espionage and sabotage is not rare. A sizeable number (about 400 during 1967–75) of court convictions of Arab collaborators with the enemy is one indicator. Another is the relatively large number of Arab youths who have crossed the borders since 1967. Some have returned for clandestine activities and a few even joined the suicide squads responsible for the massacre of Jewish schoolchildren in Kiryat Shmone and Ma'alot in spring 1974.

It must be emphasized, on the other hand, that the Arab minority as a whole has remained law-abiding and loyal. The Jewish fear that the Arabs would turn into a fifth column has not materialized. The

Arabs refrained from hostilities during all the four Israeli–Arab wars and the terrorist raids.[47] They adopt the neutral attitude that the conflict is between states or national movements, and that they are neither a party to it nor a force which can affect it.

The stringent countermeasures exercised by the Jewish authorities attest to the intensity of the conflict and, as will be shown below, account at least partly for the relatively few serious eruptions. The relocation of Arabs from border to interior regions reduced the Arabs' accessibility to outside hostile pressures. The long military administration made possible the effective selection of an accommodating elite and leadership. The opportune use of preventive detention for suspected agitators leaves smouldering discontent unorganized. Finally, the close surveillance by the security authorities serves as a strong deterrent.

2 Integration

The above survey of manifestations of conflict emanating from the pluralistic structure of Israel's society presents a picture of subdued strife or even relative calm rather than open struggle. Although comments were occasionally made above to clarify specific reasons for the moderation, I turn only now to explore more systematically the bonds that integrate the constituent groups. The relevance of certain integrative factors, known to be central in Israel or elsewhere, will be examined below for each of the three pluralistic divisions. These factors include value consensus, cross-cutting affiliations, elite accommodation, economic interdependence, political coercion and external factors.

Value consensus

Value consensus as a base of social integration, according to functionalists, is quite problematic in pluralistic societies. In looking into this possible integrative force, special attention will be paid to the following questions: How wide is the agreement between the groups on values and goals and what are the issues which divide them? Are the dominant culture and dominant identity closely associated with the dominant group or are they, rather, neutral and all-inclusive? How widespread is institutional and personal biculturalism? And are there specific value-orientations which bear directly on intergroup solidarity?

Overall, considerable value consensus makes the Orientals and Ashkenazim similar and close to each other. The two groups share a common core-culture (Judaism, Zionism, Hebrew language, nuclear family structure, past heritage) and, with the Orientals'

216

growing acculturation, they share a common subculture more and more (mainly a middle-class Western lifestyle) as well. Furthermore, the full acceptance of the national ideal of ethnic amalgamation adds the essential cohesive element of reciprocity of collective goals. Beyond these basic agreements there are, however, two issues. One concerns the failure to produce a melting-pot or even a meaningful subcultural variegation. As indicated above, the Orientals alone bear the cost of cultural assimilation by giving up their own traditions. Although the current dominant culture is not, strictly speaking, Ashkenazi, it is definitely linked to the dominant Ashkenazi group which has been singly responsible for its adoption and adaptation. The Orientals, therefore, feel left out and would like to have a greater impact on Jewish institutions. A more crucial issue by far is the exceedingly asymmetric distribution of resources. The Orientals have not as yet withdrawn legitimacy from the dominant group's power but they might do so if present inequalities persist.

A certain degree of similarity in subcultures is obtained through bi-subculturalism which is predictably restricted to members of the nondominant group. Many Orientals conform to the dominant norms but preserve different styles inside their homes or communities. Bi-subculturalism is, however, subsiding with diminishing Orientalism.

Another contributory force is the Orientals' sharp sense of nationalism. They exhibit a strong collectivistic orientation which encourages moderation and transcends ethnic sectional interests. To appreciate this point fully, it must be recalled that according to many specialists constituent groups in new or underdeveloped states are characterized by divisive primordial commitments which hinder political integration. The Orientals, in contrast, possess a countervailing collectivistic orientation alongside common ethnic communalism.

Value consensus plays an integrative role in religious–nonreligious relations, but to a much lesser extent. The two sectors have in common a core-culture and elements of a subculture. They concur, further, on the right of religious Jews to a distinct lifestyle and separate institutions. The controversies are deep, however. Although religious Jews, with the exception of extremist circles, recognize the state of Israel, they differ markedly about the religious meaning of the Jewish state. A sizeable number of religious Jews deny Israel a religious legitimacy which is very significant in their world-view. The religious minority also withhold legitimacy from the way of life of the nonreligious majority and feel responsibility, in principle, to revolutionize it. Its final end is to enforce the halakha in public and private life as much as possible. On the other hand, the religious status quo serves as a social contract. It requires that both sides seek reconciliation instead of clear-cut principled decisions and use parliamentary procedures instead of mass actions to sort out their differences. Consociational democracy is accepted as a binding norm.

The dominant culture is neither secular nor Orthodox but a blend of religious and nonreligious patterns. The interweaving of religious and secular elements in national Hebrew culture precludes the identification of the dominant culture with the dominant group and thus strengthens the sense of belonging to the broader society by the religious minority. The symbols of political integration in Israel ('civil religion') draw a great deal from 'traditional religion' (Liebman, 1975).

Related to this cohesive factor is the widespread bi-subculturalism among both religious and nonreligious Jews. Most religious Jews, especially the Mizrahi Ashkenazi section, lead a modern way of life. By the same token, most nonreligious Jews keep certain religious traditions and feel a strong attachment to Judaism. This is true not only for individuals but also for institutions. The significant degree of individual and institutional bi-subculturalism contributes, no doubt, to interpersonal accommodation between religious and nonreligious Jews.

The religious Jews possess contradictory value-orientations that are relevant to social integration. On the one hand, the larger Mizrahi segment is imbued with a moderating collectivistic orientation (national unity as a top value) (O. Cohen, 1975). Zealotry characterizes, on the other hand, a smaller segment (M. Friedman, 1975). But there is also a coercive component in the religious sense of collectivism – a self-righteous conviction that it is all right to impose the good (religious) life on the entire population. It is not clear at what point collectivism shifts from reconciliation to sectarianism apart from the obvious cases of vested self-interest (i.e., a perceived threat to one's own religious way of life).

Value consensus is at its lowest in Arab–Jewish relations. It narrows down to the merest reciprocity in collective goals; i.e., the Arabs' right to be culturally different and socially separate. But beyond this agreement to disagree, the Arabs and Jews differ in fundamentals. Most Arabs reject the Jewish-Zionist nature of the state and would prefer a reversal in minority–majority statuses.

The dominant culture is strictly identified with the Jewish dominant group. One can find hardly any Arab cultural symbol or tradition incorporated into the national culture. Likewise, Israel's identity is usually limited to members of the Jewish majority. Under these circumstances, Arab alienation from Israeli society is unavoidably profound.

The Arabs shoulder the burden of bi-culturalism (including bilingualism). They are heavily exposed in the schools, media and daily routine to the dominant values and lifestyles. Since most Arabs come into contact with Jewish employers, customers or bureaucrats, a certain degree of bi-culturalism is a necessity for them. Jews, on the other hand, make no effort to acquire the stigmatized Arab cultural traits. It is thus understandable why bi-subculturalism is waning among foreign-born Orientals and vanishing among the Oriental Israeli-born generation.

The value orientations relating to integration between Arabs and Jews are very unfavourable. In both Judaism and Islam (and most Arabs in Israel are Moslem), politics is not separated from religion and religion is the basis for the political community (Tessler, 1975b: 178–84). For the Jews, the Arabs are thus outsiders in Israeli society, and for the Arabs, a minority status in a non-Moslem society is incomprehensible and objectionable. The strong nationalistic attachments add another dimension of mutual rejection. Hence it is clear that in the absence of true secularism it is as difficult for Jews to accept Arabs as equals and partners as for Arabs to resign themselves to their fate as a minority – let alone a minority in a Jewish state.[48]

Cross-cutting affiliations

Cross-cutting affiliations serve as a major source of integration because they create conflicting loyalties within individuals. People who are under cross-pressures are most likely to choose a moderate source of action (Coleman, 1956). Yet in the reverse situation of overlapping affiliations which divide individuals into rival camps, conflict can be contained through separation (Newman, 1973: 157). In applying the double principle below, the following queries will be considered: How much do affiliations cross-cut or overlap? How significant are the 'broker institutions' which tie people to the broader society? Is there separation in areas of superimposed conflicts? What is the capacity of the nondominant group to activate its members?

The overall contribution of cross-cutting affiliations to Oriental–Ashkenazi solidarity is fairly good. As mentioned earlier, the superordinate loyalties of nationality, religion, language, basic ideology and quasi-caste cross-cut the Oriental–Ashkenazi division. At the same time, the partial overlap between ethnic origin, religious observance and socioeconomic status have mixed effects. While the Orientals are roughly evenly split into religious and nonreligious, they are disproportionately religious. And more importantly, although the Orientals are widely scattered throughout the socioeconomic scale and fall into one-third poor and two-thirds non-poor, as a whole they occupy the ranks of the lower strata, furnish almost all the Jewish poor and disadvantaged and wield little national power.

Oriental–Ashkenazi solidarity is firmly reinforced, nevertheless, by a variety of broker institutions. The most central ones are schools, trade unions, political parties, the police and army – all are national, non-ethnic organizations in which the Orientals are incorporated as individuals and not as a separate ethnic group. Of course some degree of de facto ethnic separation can be found in all these complex bureaucracies (e.g., ethnic concentrations in the schools, ethnic circles in political parties), but it is of definitely secondary importance.

As a result, Oriental ethnicity has to compete very hard with other bases of solidarity. Its most likely ally is social class, even though the class polarization within the Oriental group imposes a limit on ethnicity–class as a base of solidarity. Besides, the activation of ethnicity is checked by countervailing commitments to higher values and ideologies and by counterbalancing memberships in powerful national organizations. Widespread stigmatization cripples, furthermore, independent ethnic solidarity. It must be emphasized, on the other hand, that below the surface there is a large reservoir of ethnic attachment and discontent on which ethnic militant movements can draw if and when a radical change in the situation takes place (e.g., an economic crisis).

Cross-cutting affiliations are of much less significance as a solidarity mechanism for the religious–nonreligious division than for the Oriental–Ashkenazi division. At first sight it appears that numerous cross-cutting affiliations help to unite religious and nonreligious Jews. These include the basic loyalties shared by all Jews (religion, nationality, language, quasi-caste), the factionalization of the religious sector along lines of ethnicity and Orthodox trend (Mizrahi, Aguda, ultra-Orthodoxy) and the dissociation between class and religious observance within the same ethnic groups. Yet, upon closer examination, it turns out that the apparent criss-crossing of cleavages does not yield an individualization of the religious Jews who tend, instead, to cluster in a number of viable corporate groups.

The limited effectiveness of cross-cutting affiliations is well in evidence in broker institutions. On the one hand, the religious Jews are, in practice, directly incorporated into the economy, state bureaucracy, army, the national radio and television networks and the public health insurance schemes. They are, however, differentially incorporated via separate schools, youth movements, political parties, newspapers, rural settlements and a variety of other voluntary associations. Yet this wide institutional separation serves an integrative latent function by averting tensions in controversial areas. To illustrate: school separation prevents the educational system from becoming a battleground where religious and nonreligious Jews fiercely fight over values, curriculum and extra-curriculum content, and appointments.

220

Religious observance is thus a solid base for co-operation. Orthodox religion is a central interest in the life of Israeli religious Jews. Despite internal differences, the religious Jews lead a similar way of life, have clear-cut interests and congregate in separate corporate social units. Their organization rests on a firm foundation of cultural autonomy. They constitute not only a solid voting bloc but also a dependable social base ready for activation in relevant religious matters. The existing cross-cutting affiliations have, no doubt, moderating effects and account for the reduced 'completeness' of the religious sector (manifested in facts such as that only about half of the religious Jews vote for religious parties), but in no sense undermine the great ability of the religious Jews to organize and apply pressure.

Cross-cutting affiliations contribute little to the integration between Arabs and Jews. Cardinal loyalties tend to overlap, thereby intensifying the potential for conflict. Against the backdrop of the Arab–Jewish quasi-caste structure, intergroup tensions mount as a result of the growing class differentiation within the Arab community. Arabs who reach middle-class status become less tolerant of inequalities and deprivations. Only the traditional kinship and religious subdivisions still cut deeply into the Arab minority and weaken their overall solidarity.

By the same token the integrative part played by broker institutions is meagre. The Arabs are differentially incorporated into Israeli society. They maintain separate institutions – schools, settlements, local governments, mass media, election lists, etc. They indirectly relate to state bureaucracies, the Histadrut and most voluntary associations via special departments for Arab affairs. They are, further, excluded from the armed forces which constitute a pivotal integrating broker institution in Israeli society.

On the other hand, the considerable institutional segmentation saves the Arabs and Jews from much friction by curtailing the number of contact situations where sharp disagreements prevail. The Arabs are placed in a kind of quarantine which assures the Jews that the Arabs gain no access to sensitive information and positions of trust, lend themselves to close control and have little opportunity to develop personal relations with Jews. Concurrently the Arabs are guaranteed a separate group identity.[49]

Arab ethnicity is, however, only moderately mobilizable. One check against their ability to function as a group is the internal split. A severer stumbling-block is the lack of cultural autonomy. With the exception of Rakah, Arabs do not control their separate institutions and thus can hardly count on them as independent bases of power. The Jews regard Arab group activity as a national threat and take steps to curb it.

221

Elite accommodation

The stable integration of pluralistic divisions necessitates reasonable accommodation between their elites. Dominant groups follow different policies in order to prevent nondominant elites from supplying a militant leadership for disaffected nondominant groups. These policies may include assimilation, co-optation, co-operation and negotiation, suppression or physical elimination. In democratic societies the range of possibilities is of course smaller. One effective option is to absorb the nondominant elite into the dominant power structure (either by neutralization or power sharing). A more pluralistic strategy is to accord a nondominant elite control of its group's separate institutions. Either one or both of these solutions may be attempted, as is the case of the nondominant elites in Israel.

The general policy adopted by the dominant Ashkenazi group toward the Oriental elite is co-optation and neutralization. Channels of social mobility are kept wide open up to the middle rungs and then they narrow rapidly. Through 'positive discrimination', selected Orientals are co-opted to the top. The Oriental ranks are then drained of potential leadership. The continued movement upwards of some Orientals demonstrates that the Orientals can make good in the present system, and the conspicuous placement of a few of them at the top projects an image of goodwill and progress toward the national end of ethnic assimilation. The disgruntled members of the Oriental elite who try any independent organized action quickly discover its futility. They fail because of the stigma attached to ethnic solidarity, lack of an institutional base, poor resources, inexperience – and tempting offers by the establishment. It is, therefore, not surprising that by the mid-1970s the Oriental leadership is by and large integrated, dependent and accommodating, and that the independent leadership is tiny and insignificant.

Consociational democracy, which regulates religious–nonreligous relations, leads to a sharply different kind of elite accommodation. Instead of neutralization, one finds co-operation and negotiation. The clear advantage of the religious minority is attributable mostly to their powerful position, beginning with initial group contacts. Historically and today the nonreligious majority must agree to the demands for cultural autonomy by the nonassimilating religious minority in order to avert the danger of a mass alienation of the religious minority from Zionism and Israel.

The extensive self-sufficiency partly accounts for the unparalleled, almost exclusive independent leadership of the religious minority, i.e., its leaders are part of the religious community and only a few religious people occupy leadership roles within the nonreligious community. Autonomous institutions prevent elite defection by

222

making available a good many respectable power positions to ambitious religious Jews. At the same time the nonreligious majority usually refrain from setting up rival religious institutions and also conform in not recognizing a non-Orthodox religious elite. They respect an essential, tacit understanding underlying the religious status quo according to which the religious establishment is the sole representative of both the religious minority and religion in Israel (Liebman, 1975: 25). [50]

There are two types of independent leaders in the religious group: Rabbinic and political. The Rabbinic leaders are by and large non-accommodating. They are trained in the strictest Aguda-controlled yeshivot, are oriented to religious colleagues, are bound by the halakha and are relatively shut away from outside pressures. Even Rabbis who are state functionaries do not tend to be liberal, because their immediate constituency is the religious minority rather than the entire Jewish community whom they are supposed to serve. [51]

Elite accommodation is thus limited to the more secularized and politically motivated religious political leadership. The latter speak for the religious minority in general and for the Rabbinic leadership in particular. The religious and nonreligious national political leaderships do their utmost to settle disputes among themselves and to minimize the involvement of their respective constituents.

Coalition politics is actively sought by both sides as an auxiliary device of elite accommodation. Contrary to popular belief, the religious minority's veto powers in religious matters are not due to coalition politics but rather to their institutional capability to resort to mass dissent and disruption if necessary. Paradoxically the National Religious Party has participated in almost all coalition governments (see Table 81), even though in most cases a winning coalition could have been established without it or an alternative, ideologically closer partner could have been found. [52] Coalition politics stems, therefore, from a social necessity to create a 'trading-post' where controversial religious interests can be bargained in a congenial atmosphere of national politics in lieu of violent mass confrontations.

In the present conditions of substantial disagreements between the religious and nonreligious groups, the politicization of religion is more integrative than disruptive. It supplies institutional mechanisms of conflict-resolution. It also encourages moderation by giving rise to a reconciliatory religious political leadership whose perspectives are broader than those of the militant Rabbinic leadership. However, the politicization of religion perpetuates rather than resolves conflicts.

In contrast to the Jewish pluralistic divisions where arrangements of elite accommodation are made, in the area of Arab–Jewish relations the dominant pattern is *control* rather than the accommodation of elites. The Arab minority is not granted cultural autonomy because the Jews fear that autonomy would result in a security risk as well as a menace to the Jewish character of the state. Yet the Arabs lack the power, which the religious Jews do have, to enforce their will on the majority. Neither do the Arab elite enjoy the benefits (which do accrue to the Oriental elite) of upward social mobility, co-optation and 'positive discrimination'.

Three categories can be discerned in the Arab elite: an accommodating leadership, a militant leadership and an intelligentsia The Arab accommodating leaders (including office-holders in special departments for minority affairs, most heads of local governments, religious functionaries and hamula elders) are directly dependent on the Jewish authorities. Like all accommodating, leaders, their power within the minority community rests on a widespread belief that moderation prevents the danger of a helpless showdown and the bestowing of concessions. Since the authorities and traditional hamula heads are responsible for the final selection, more often than not these leaders are the less qualified candidates or the ones who do not command the respect of the more advanced section in the Arab population.

The militant leaders cluster around Rakah and a number of other organizations, such as student committees. They express the social and national interests of the Arab minority and protest strongly against manifestations of differential treatment. The Jewish authorities are well aware of the tension-release function of verbal protest, and as long as these militant leaders neither call for nor engage in subversive activities, they are allowed to act.

Accommodation with the Arab intelligentsia is seriously neglected by the Jewish majority. As indicated earlier, there is a problem of suitable employment. Job openings are restricted because of the closure of the Jewish economy and because the accelerating number of new Arab graduates far exceeds the demands of the backward Arab labour market. Another issue concerns the educated Arabs' status in the Arab community and in Israeli society. Education yields prestige, but not yet power. Suspected of Arab nationalism, educated Arabs are not admitted into the Jewish power structure and are denied support to obtain positions of power in the Arab minority.

The accommodation with the nationalist Arab elite is the most problematic. In 1975 there was no Arab national party or any other nationalist organization. Since the disbandment of the Al-Ard group in 1965, no further attempt to form a nationalist political organization has been made. Some Arab nationalists are active in Rakah and other non-nationalist organizations, but many stay away. The nationalists are usually inactive because they fear suppression by the government. The authorities would, no doubt, ban any Arab national organization which supported the Palestine cause, identified itself with the Palestine Liberation Organization and denied the legitimacy of Israel's Zionist-Jewish character and territorial integrity.

In the mid-1970s the shaky Arab-Jewish elite accommodation has become a social problem. The accommodating leaders have lost much credibility and, to prevent a collapse, many radicalized their styles. The militant leaders are on the offensive. The intelligentsia is restive and leaning toward the nationalists. The atmosphere seems ripe for a rise of an Arab national or resistance movement.

Economic interdependence

Participation in a common economy engenders firm integrative bonds. Economic interdependence can be an effective base of integration even if value consensus and cross-cutting affiliations are weak. It varies a great deal in symmetry – from 'positive' symmetric economic interdependence to 'negative' asymmetric economic dependence of the nondominant group on the dominant group.

The conscious manipulation of the economy by the Israeli power elite for reducing group tensions and enhancing integration is remarkable. It dates back to the 1920s, when a voluntary Jewish community was established in Palestine and the emergent political elite, lacking coercive powers, looked for a viable base of authority. The chief solution was found in the capability of the elite to import and allocate economic resources and in making groups dependent on it for these resources (Horowitz and Lissak, 1970). Similarly, political parties owed much of their power to their capacity to dispense services and benefits (Shapira, 1975).

The integrative underpinnings of the Israeli economy lie deep in its political and ever-expanding (non-zero-sum) nature. The fact that the economy is under political control enables the Israeli dominant elite not only to restrain economic conflicts but also to harness the economy for promoting internal peace. This is done by directing the high rate of economic growth, made possible by the enormous import of capital, to attain the following targets:

Full employment. The government, the Jewish Agency and the Histadrut have done their best to assure every able person of gainful employment by building or aiding labour-intensive plants, irrespective of their profitability. In fact, they overreached this target. In 1975 there was in Israel a surplus of labour (compared with 6–10 per cent unemployment in Western countries) which backfired against the national goal of economic independence.

Improved standard of living. A large portion of the national budget is spent on direct or indirect subsidies to the population. The average standard of living is about one-third higher than average economic production. It has probably trebled since the early 1950s. All sectors of the Israeli population benefit from improved, heavily subsidized conditions of life.

Expanded opportunities for social mobility. Economic growth is an essential factor in the general expansion of the scale of society through population increase, more job opportunities, development of education, etc. As a result, more opportunities for upward social mobility have become available.

The cumulative contribution to social integration of the above fulfilled targets is not difficult to comprehend. To put it simply, everyone in Israel is gaining, no one is losing. The disruptive effects of destitution and zero-sum competition are thus minimized. Although the basic problems of persistent intergroup inequality and relative deprivation have remained unaffected, the social balance of the Israeli economy is quite positive.

All pluralistic divisions gain from the integrative characteristics of Israel's political economy. The nondominant Orientals, religious Jews and Arabs avail themselves of full employment, an improved standard of living and expanding opportunities for social mobility without inflicting any cost on the dominant group members who enjoy the same benefits. Yet beyond this fundamental similarity, certain differences between the divisions are noticeable.

The economic interdependence between the Orientals and Ashkenazim is extensive but somewhat asymmetrical. It is impossible to envisage the Israeli economy without Oriental labour. Yet the Orientals, as the poorer nondominant group, are devoid of an independent economic base that is essential for waging an ongoing struggle. At the same time, the mass introduction of less skilled Oriental immigrants into the economy in the 1950s, and the continuing entry of undereducated young Orientals every year since then, prevent a threat to the Ashkenazi advantageous and secure status and gives them a definite edge in obtaining the expanding better vacancies. This explains why, among other things, blatant direct discrimination against Orientals is not widespread, since the main economic benefits to be gained from discrimination are already accruing to the Ashkenazim.

In comparison, the economic interdependence between the religious and nonreligious Jews is strong and more or less symmetrical. Although the religious Jews do not control any branch of the economy, their economic status, within the same ethnic groups, is not very different from that of the nonreligious Jews. Furthermore, they control substantial independent resources, including publicly owned corporations and agricultural settlements, and can rely on continuing support from Orthodox communities abroad. Hence their capability to disrupt the system, if necessary, should not be under-rated.

Arab–Jewish economic integration is quite different, taking the form of asymmetrical economic dependence of Arabs on Jews. The economic incorporation of the Israeli Arabs into the national economy made them almost totally dependent on the Jews. The Arab village economy nearly collapsed and was not superseded by modern industry. The Arab breadwinner is dependent for his livelihood on Jewish employers, Jewish clients and Jewish-controlled welfare and social services. While the Jewish economy is also dependent on low-status, manual Arab labour and on Arab agricultural produce, this dependence is relatively small. In a situation of confrontation, the Arab family would undergo severe privation, whereas the national economy can easily replace Arab workers by the redeployment of Jewish (in practice, Oriental) manpower.

The significant material benefits the Israeli Arabs derive from participation in the national economy, their lack of an economic base, their great economic dependence on the Jews and the fact that they can be dispensed with (if they cause serious disruptions to the economy) are the single, most central, base of Arab–Jewish integration in Israel.

Political coercion

Political coercion is a universal source of integration. The potential or actual use of violence is a common means of making dissidents compliant. Overall, the spread of coercion in political democracies is smaller than in authoritarian regimes, but it is widely used against dissidents.

To date, political coercion has not loomed large in the integration of the Jewish groups. The effectiveness of other integrative factors and the lack of serious dissidence account for the near-absence of violence within the Jewish pluralistic community. Certain minor exceptions exist here and there, such as the exercise of some force by the police at the beginnings of the Wadi-Salib and Black Panther protests and against some unpermitted demonstrations by ultra-Orthodox Jews.[53]

Moderate political coercion serves, however, an integrative function in Arab–Jewish relations. Two legal arrangements underpin the political regulation of Arab behaviour in Israel: the defence Laws (State of Emergency) 1945 and the Emergency Laws (Security Areas) 1949. These regulations aim to assist the authorities to combat subversive activities. They empower the government to declare 'closed areas', the entry into and exit from which require a written permit; to administer censorship; to make administrative arrests; to place a person under police supervision; to impose a curfew; to deport; to control arms; to court martial, etc. These regulations constituted the legal base for the military government until its termination in 1966. The laws are, however, still in force and can immediately be reactivated if necessary. For instance, some Israeli Arabs suspected of agitation are ordered out of certain areas and from time to time preventive arrests are made.

The counter-intransigence and certain other functions of the defunct military government were transferred to the security services. Special departments for minority affairs operate in the two branches of the Israeli intelligence charged with internal security; i.e., the Department for Special Duties (known as Matam) in Israel's police, and the General Security Service (known as Shabac). The security services have a record of efficiency in the Arab sector with regard to ongoing information-gathering, surveillance, prevention, detection and final conviction. Their deterrent power is thus considerable.

Political coercion of the Arab minority is effective because of its judicious use and calculative application. Jews object to violence in interior affairs. The authorities employ force as a last resort and then act with discretion and restraint. Collective punishment and random terror, which are characteristic of fascist-type regimes, are virtually absent in Israel. The police provide Arabs with good protection against Jewish mob attacks on occasions of terrorist acts or a war.[54] The extensive manipulation of rewards and sanctions encourages compliance. Law-abiding Arabs are not harassed but are allowed to live peacefully in their villages and to take advantage of the general material prosperity. In contrast, defiant Arabs will endure a hard life and offenders will in all probability be brought to justice. Arab conformity definitely pays off.

External factors

We turn now to the last factor bearing on the integration of pluralistic groups: namely, the impact of the outside world. The nature of extra-societal forces varies from one society to another. In Israel two related factors can be spelled out. One is the relations of Israel with its neighbours, i.e., the Arab–Israeli conflict. The other are the relations of Israeli society with wider communities in the world over. Generally speaking, the effects of these external relations are integrative for the Jewish divisions and disintegrative for the Arab–Jewish division.

The centrality of the Arab–Israeli dispute in the integration of the Jewish groups cannot be overemphasized. The common enemy is felt as an immediate and fatal threat to the lives and statehood of the Jews. Personal involvement in the conflict is direct and intensive through lifelong military duties, first-hand knowledge of casualties and daily exposure to the media.[55] The dispute is in fact an ever-present and constant factor with only minor ups and downs. It sharpens the feeling of the interdependence of fate among all Israeli Jews. It restrains divisiveness by overshadowing and even freezing internal issues. As long as the entire Jewish community is mobilized to fight for its survival, nondominant Jews would prefer not to rock the boat.

The connections of Israel with world Jewry and the Western world furnish additional solidarity bonds for the Israeli Jews. The Jews in Israel recognize the Jews in the Diaspora as their wider membership group with which they identify. They also take the Western countries as a reference group, i.e., a model for comparisons and an ally.[56] These common positive orientations are reinforced by the reciprocal attitudes of world Jewry and the Western world toward Israel.

The impact of these external relations on the Arab–Jewish cleavage are different. The Arab–Israeli conflict has mixed effects, but the balance is negative. It is obvious that the conflict is an endless source of mutual alienation. For some Israeli Arabs, their country (Israel) is at war with their people, and for others Israel is to blame for much of the injustices involved. For most Jews, the Israeli Arabs cannot be trusted as soldiers or as workers in security-related jobs. On the other hand, the stablizing element in the Israeli Arab conflict applies equally to Arabs and Jews. The conflict tends to freeze all internal problems, including the Arab–Jewish one. It provides a latent and pragmatic legitimacy to the inferior status of the Arabs in Israel by impairing the face-validity of their demands for full equality as long as they are regarded as a liability to national security.

The divergence in the wider membership and reference frameworks exacerbates Arab–Jewish disunity. Unlike the Jews, the Israeli Arabs do not see the Jews outside Israel as brethren but perceive them, perhaps, as potential rivals. They are also ambivalent toward the West. They relate, instead, to the Arab world, Moslem peoples, the Third World, Arab countries and the Palestinian nation to which most Jews do not feel attached. The empirical ramifications of this basic dissimilarity in orientations include separate allies and enemies, mass communications, cultural borrowings and symbols.

The Arab–Jewish disharmony caused by external factors has intensified considerably since the June 1967 War. Up to that time the Israeli Arabs were to a large extent cut off from the outside world, with the exception of radio transmissions. They were also suspected of collaboration with the Zionists and hence were not incited by Arab propaganda to take an active part in the Arab–Israeli conflict. In 1967 the Israeli Arabs resumed familial, social and cultural ties with the Arabs on the West Bank and, through them, with the Arab world which, in turn, has gradually restored its trust in them. By 1975 the Israeli Arabs were almost rehabilitated – their identity as Palestinian Arabs was reinstated, several ex-Israeli Arabs were co-opted to the council of the Palestine Liberation Organization to represent them, and their role in the struggle against Israel was emphasized. These developments have certainly widened the gulf in Arab and Jewish orientations in Israel.

3   The problem of national cohesion

After reviewing the various patterns of conflict and bases of integration relating to the three pluralistic divisions, it is possible to take a more general view of the problem of cohesion. Three summary measures can be helpful. 'Strength' of cohesion is reflected in the range and intensity of the controversies as well as in the diversity and effectiveness of the bases of integration. 'Voluntariness' refers to the relative weight of 'positive' versus 'negative' integrative forces. And 'stability' indicates the extent of continuity in the intensity of conflict and in the relative importance of the same bases of integration over time.

The cohesion between the Orientals and the Ashkenazim is strong, fairly voluntary and stable. The conflict is moderate, nonviolent, depoliticized and mostly restricted to questions of resource competition – socioeconomic and power inequality. Integration is quite diverse and well balanced by extensive value consensus and cross-cutting affiliations on the one hand, and elite co-optation, economic interdependence and the external conflict on the other. Over the years cohesion had remained essentially unchanged – there were neither severe crises nor significant shifts in the balance of the integrative forces.

The overall cohesion between religious and nonreligious Jews is similarly fairly voluntary and stable, but not quite so strong. Although both the religious and ethnic cleavages are single-issue based, the religious conflict is more intense because of its tendency to spread. The religious Jews raise questions about the legitimacy of the system, but the Orientals do not. They are equipped with an independent leadership, an institutional base and resources to disrupt society, a capability that the Orientals still lack. Co-operative, stable cohesion does prevail, however, because of a special mix of a shared core-culture, cultural autonomy, politicization of religion, economic interdependence and a common enemy.

Arab–Jewish cohesion has been hitherto not strong, very involuntary, yet stable. In the absence of positive solidarity bonds, its relative strength stems from the considerable economic dependence, political subordination and separation without cultural autonomy which characterizes the Arab minority in Israel. The Arab–Jewish cohesion which is sustained by these negative forces, is paradoxically as strong and stable as the well-balanced religious–nonreligious cohesion, but this is where similarity between these two non-assimilating minorities ends. Unlike the voluntary nature of religious–nonreligious relations, coexistence between Arabs and Jews is imposed on both sides. Arab–Jewish cohesion is, however, slowly and steadily diminishing as a result of both a weakening of the economic and political controls over the Arabs and an escalation of Arab protest since the 1967 War.

If the three divisions are ranked according to their overall cohesion, there is no doubt that Oriental–Ashkenazi relations are comparatively the most cohesive, followed by religious–nonreligious relations; Arab–Jewish relations are by far the least cohesive. This assessment corresponds very well with feelings of solidarity of the Jewish public. Jews are observed to be aware of the fact that Arab–Jewish relations are the most troublesome, and as for the Jewish divisions, they feel, according to available survey data, that religious–nonreligious relations are the least close, as compared with other group relations such as those between Orientals and Ashkenazim, newcomers and oldtimers, employees and employers and the young and adult generations. For instance, in a survey of the Jewish urban population taken a short time before the October 1973 War, only 44 per cent regarded Ashkenazi–Oriental relations as good, 33 per cent felt so about immigrant–veteran relations, as compared with only 16 per cent who defined religious–nonreligious relations as good. During the war and for some time after, public perceptions of group relations were improved, but then slowly dropped to their pre-war level. But beyond temporary fluctuations, surveys repeatedly show that a majority of various sections of the population (defined in terms of age, education, religious observance and ethnic origin) think that religious–nonreligious relations are not good and are the most unsatisfactory within the Jewish community.

Notwithstanding Israel's asymmetric pluralistic–hierarchical structure (i.e., rule by a dominant minority of nonreligious Ashkenazi Jews) and widespread feelings of group tensions, Israeli society has so far managed to keep internal peace. Although pressures continuously build up, confrontations are usually avoided. Israel does not have a record of extreme phenomena such as *Kulturkampf*, extensive legislation of discrimination, biological racism, involuntary segregation, imposed assimilation, pogroms, repression, deportations, extermination, resistance movements, riots, mass emigration, irredentism, an active fifth column or civil war which appear from time to time in the relations between groups in multi-ethnic or multi-racial societies.

The relative calm in group relations in Israel should be attributed mostly to a special combination of a pre-existing Jewish core-culture, a heavily subsidized political economy and the Arab–Israeli conflict that have greatly assisted the power elite in handling the nondominant groups. Israel's Jewish-Zionist core-culture is seized upon as a basis of co-operation and unity among Israeli Jews. Enormous capital imports are distributed throughout society to create stakes in the system, to dispel disaffection and to pay in exchange for conformity. The fateful and continuing Arab–Israeli dispute contributes a great deal to preventing tensions from erupting, short-cutting all-out show-downs and freezing internal problems.

Greatly buttressed by these three pillars of national cohesion, the Israeli power elite have shown resourcefulness in coping with nondominant groups. Their reactions have varied considerably from one group to another. The Orientals have been brought into the mainstream and bought off. They have been too poor and dis-organized to resist. Alien Arabs have been excluded; given their numerical and organizational weaknesses as well as their potential threat to the entire system, they have been neutralized through coercive economic and political means. Only with the powerful religious minority have the power elite had to make a very significant compromise. Religious Jews have been granted substantial cultural autonomy and the evolving national culture has been adapted to their special values and needs.

It is evident that the involuntary Arab–Jewish coexistence is the most problematic. In a democratic and dynamic society such as Israel, there are constraints on how much compliance can be achieved through economic dependence and political subordination. This is why Arab–Jewish relations have reached a critical point in the mid-1970s.

On the other hand, co-operative relations have continued among the Jewish groups. This continuity highly correlates with the stability in the above three unchanging integrative forces: namely, the crystallization of a Jewish national culture, the viability of an economy without depressions and losers, and the need to close ranks in order to fight a common enemy.

Stable national cohesion has its own shortcomings, however. Since the problems are not faced and attacked but are counteracted and sidetracked, group tensions remain pent up. The Arab minority pay a heavy price in inferior status and alienation. The Orientals bear the cost of considerable inequality. Religious and nonreligious

Jews suffer from the patchy religious status quo. Effective measures to reach national economic independence are not taken because it is feared that group relations are not cohesive enough to withstand economic dislocations attendant upon the cessation of vast capital imports. And to these, and related social costs, moral imponderables have to be added.

Let me conclude with a brief comment on the main cohesive models. Along with other deeply divided societies, Israel has faced the dilemma of how to maintain political stability. Theoretically there are three options. One is to create a national consensus by blurring group boundaries, multiplying cross-cutting ties, and forming overarching values and an all-inclusive collective identity. The other path to internal peace is to recognize the right of the constituent groups to a separate identity, to provide them with some autonomy and to institutionalize politics of compromise between their elites to reconcile group differences. Still another solution is to set up a machinery of control over the nondominant groups.

These three ways to obtain national cohesion in fragmented societies are identified in the literature as a consensus model, a consociational model and a control model respectively. Although they do not exhaust all the range of possibilities, Smith (1969b: 440–8) has shown that they are the chief distinct alternatives. He also relates them to the nature of the pluralistic structure of society and indicates their weaknesses as cohesive mechanisms. However, if successfully applied, they all prevent social instability but with different benefits and costs for the nondominant groups. In the consensus arrangement, the nondominant groups merge with the mainstream and reach power and privilege, in consociationalism they preserve their independent existence and protect their interests by participating in decision-making, and in the control situation they are subordinated but saved from persecution, bloodshed and chaos.

Israel has had a remarkable record for keeping law and order since 1948. It should be clear from the foregoing analysis that Israel has managed to escape unrest by skilfully resorting to all the above three models of social stability – applying simultaneously and visibly different policies toward its nondominant groups. Consociational democracy has been at work to maintain the balanced accommodation between religious and nonreligious Jews. The control apparatus has been imposed to ensure the compliance of the Arab minority. And a mixture of consensus, consociational (yet mostly pseudo-consociational) and control mechanisms has been used to obtain the acquiescence of the Oriental majority. Although these diverse strategies have not resolved the internal tensions, they are and will be effective in averting any large-scale national crisis as long as the current military, political and economic conditions in the state continue.

9 Continuity and change

Despite numerous and large-scale developments since 1948, continuity definitely predominates over change in Israel. In the period between 1948 and 1975 the population quintupled, the territory expanded, the economy grew quite fast, the standard of living more than trebled, social diversity increased greatly and there were four all-out Israeli–Arab wars. Yet social and political stability has been preserved.

Similarly, continuity is greater than change in the pluralistic structure of Israeli society as it appears from our recurrent observations so far. In this chapter we will piece together our cross-time comparisons in order to establish trends for the years 1948–75 for each pluralistic division (for an overview, see Table 6). Likely future developments will then be discussed, and ideological solutions to Israel's pluralistic problems will be presented as a conclusion.

1   Past trends

Although continuity is, on the whole, greater than change for all the three major pluralistic divisions, trends vary a great deal from one division to another.

A review of Oriental–Ashkenazi relations from the beginning of the 1950s to the mid-1970s reveals several trends. First, during this period the Orientals have risen in number from a minority of about a quarter to a majority of over a half. This demographic shift has complicated the Oriental problem by adding an inconsistency between a socially nondominant status and a majority status.

Second, over the years, Oriental–Ashkenazi pluralism has diminished substantially. The Orientals have lost many of their traditions and become acculturated, instead, into the mainstream. Concurrently as they have become culturally more like the

234

Ashkenazim, the social separation between them has lessened. The significant attenuation of pluralism is exemplified by the growing similarity in birthrates and in the rising rate of mixed marriages among the young generation. Cultural diversity and social separation have declined in all spheres with the exception of the religious area, where ethnic pluralism is institutionalized.

Third, Oriental–Ashkenazi inequality has diminished only to a limited degree and has remained appreciable. The Orientals, like others, have enjoyed a continuing betterment in life conditions, but the ethnic socioeconomic gaps have persisted. They have penetrated all centres and positions of power, but their representation in national management and decision-making posts is still insignificant.

Fourth, over the years the Ashkenazim have become much more alike than have the Orientals. The distinct cultural heritage, endogamy and class-differentiation among Ashkenazi sub-groups (e.g., Russians, Poles, Germans, Western Europeans) have dwindled enormously, making the Ashkenazim a more solidly dominant group in the 1970s than in the 1950s. In contrast, pluralism and inequality among the Oriental subcommunities (e.g., Moroccans, Iraqis, Yemenites, Turks) are still striking. In fact, the sharpest differences between the traditional and modern and between the poor and rich are within the Oriental community. Since the Ashkenazim are conspicuously absent from the quarter of the Jewish population who can be called poor, the Orientals are divided into one-third poor and two-thirds non-poor. As a group, the Orientals have yet to overcome serious communal and class barriers in order to achieve concerted action.

Fifth, anti-Oriental ethnocentrism has dropped appreciably. In the 1950s the Ashkenazim felt estranged from the Oriental new-comers, fearing that they would be swamped, their Western culture diluted and political democracy undermined. Prejudice and dis-crimination against the Orientals were thus widespread. As a result of the advancing Oriental acculturation and the persistent lack of threat to the Ashkenazi dominant status, anti-Oriental feelings and practices have either subsided or taken subtler forms.

Sixth, ethnic calm has continued throughout the post-state period. The ethnic problem has never become a national issue on which the major political parties are divided. The Orientals have registered their protest in various ways, including sporadic demonstrations during the 1950s, the Wadi-Salib riots in 1959, the Black Panther activities in the 1970s and separate lists in all elections, but none has risen to a protest movement on any scale. Protest has remained non-violent and largely unorganized.

And, seventh, public awareness and consideration of ethnic pluralism and inequality have increased over the years. While the complete assimilation of all ethnic groups is still a national goal, cultural uniformity is no longer pursued with the same zeal as in the past. During the 1965–75 decade there has been a growth of Oriental cultural expressions, mostly with the encouragement of the Ashkenazi establishment that feels secure in its cultural dominance. In the 1970s public opinion became sensitive to poverty and ethnic inequality. The government, on its part, has shown a willingness to take these social problems into account in national policy-making. The standing Ministers' Committee on Social Affairs and the Black Panther Party, however weak they might be, are unparalleled new bodies which serve as watchdogs in the ethnic situation.

These developments have modified and weakened the dynamic paternalism–co-optation model of Oriental–Ashkenazi relations, but have not been sufficient to phase it out. The offshoots of various trends is a shift from ethnic to class elements in the relations between Orientals and Ashkenazim.[1] There is more and more open competition, where Orientals tend to lose out less because of Ashkenazi paternalism than because of their own inferior competitive skills. However, the deep-seated view of the dominant group that the Orientals do not measure up to the standards required and hence cannot share fully in running the country still exists. In addition, the Ashkenazim continue to apply mechanisms to neutralize the Orientals rather than to bring them up to par. In this way the basics of the dynamic paternalism–co-optation model have been preserved.

Quite different trends are discernible in religious–nonreligious relations. First, the religious Jews have remained a minority. In the 1950s the dominant nonreligious group prevented the religious sector from taking over the mass influx of tradition-observing Orientals and thus from winning majority status. On the other hand, the religious community has managed to keep its original numerical strength. It has overcome its continuous attrition rate[2] by maintaining a higher natural increase and by receiving a proportional share of the new immigrants.

Second, religious–nonreligious pluralism has become more institutionalized over the years. The religious cultural heritage has flourished. The number of religious cultural activities has multiplied. One manifestation of the religious cultural vitality is the expanding volume of publications issued every year in the areas of the halakha, Jewish philosophy, religious literature, religion and medicine, and general religious affairs. Another sign is the enormous diversification and the innovations in religious education. The most outstanding new institutions are the high school yeshiva for boys ('yeshiva tikhunit'), high school yeshiva for girls ('olpaniya'), military yeshiva ('yeshivat hesder'), and the quasi-Rabbinic seminary at Bar-Ilan University. These novel educational frameworks combine old with

236

new forms and aim to produce the ideal person who is both a religious scholar ('talmid hakham') and a modern man. Their graduates are both more Orthodox in thinking and practice, and more secularized, in certain respects, than their parents.[3] Along with the blooming religious subculture, separate religious institutions have expanded. Over the last two decades the religious Jews have intensified their development of residential ghettoes and 'from cradle to grave' organizational encapsulation.

Third, the religious minority has maintained its nearly equal status in Israeli society. Its position as a highly mobilized pressure group and as a part of the governing elite have ensured it a proportional share in the socioeconomic and power resources. Some drop in average socioeconomic status occurred, however, concomitant with the increased weight of low-status Oriental immigrants within the religious minority.

Fourth, the cohesion between religious and nonreligious Jews has been well preserved. There have been a great many controversies and frictions, but they have been either ironed out, disregarded, or a compromise has been reached. None has led to a serious crisis, mass unrest or violence. The consociational machinery of conflict-resolution known as 'the religious status quo' has proved workable.

And, fifth, the growing involvement of the religious sector in nonreligious matters has been marked since the 1967 War. A dramatic sign of this trend is the rise of Gush Emunim, a militant social movement of religious Jews for unlimited settlement of the occupied territories. This is a case of a movement dealing with a problem which is not religious per se, but the activists define it in halakhic terms. Another indication is the pressure exercised by the Young Faction in the National Religious Party to become a fully-fledged party which fights for general causes such as national security in addition to religious ones (Oren, 1973). The justification given for this move is the duty to apply the tenets of the halakha to all areas of life. The diversification of interests and the willingness to commit resources to different issues are an indication of the religious minority's added strength and self-assurance, but the overall implications of this development are not clear yet. It is possible that the shift towards a multi-issue pressure group will detract from the centrality of the religious issue and thus promote moderation. It is more likely, however, that it will radicalize positions by adding sectarianism (and, for that matter, anticlericalism) as a prime factor in nonreligious matters.[4]

It is evident that the dominant trend in religious–nonreligious relations is continuity and stability. The 'contested accommodation pattern' has persisted. The religious minority has managed to consolidate its distinctive subculture and separate institutions. In fact, it has gained so much self-confidence that it can afford to channel some of its resources to spheres outside the circumscribed religion–state relations.

Turning to the Arab–Jewish division, the following continuities and transformations are noticeable.[5] First, the Arabs have remained a small but increasingly significant minority in Israeli society. Hopes or fears on both sides regarding a change in the basic demographic situation have proved unrealistic. On the one hand, proportionally the Arabs should have decreased in numbers by the continuing flow of Jewish immigrants to Israel, the voluntary mass emigration of the Arabs from Israel[6] and an Arab exodus during the periodic eruption of the Arab–Israeli wars. On the other hand, the Arabs' percentage should have increased as a result of their exceedingly larger natural increase, which is twice as high as that of the Jews (in 1975 1.8 versus 3.7 per cent). Instead, the relative weight of Arabs in Israel's population has remained around 13 per cent because of a balance between the Jewish immigration and the greater Arab net natural increase. At the same time the dimension of the Arab problem in Israel has become aggravated as the absolute number of Arabs grew from 156,000 in 1948 to about 450,000 in 1975 (excluding Arabs in East Jerusalem).

Second, the overall position of the Arab minority vis-à-vis the Jewish majority has been changing since the 1967 War. The Israeli Arabs resumed their familial, social and cultural ties with the Palestinians in the occupied territories. In consequence, they have become more Palestinian in their orientation and identity. Palestinization has been intensified by the reorientation of the Palestinian people towards the Arabs in Israel. The degrading perception of the Arab minority as Arab collaborators with, or hostages of, the Jews before 1967 has been superseded since then by the more honourable view of the Israeli Arabs as equal Palestinian Arabs who are expected to contribute their share in the struggle for the Palestinian cause.

Third, Arab–Jewish pluralism has somewhat decreased but has continued to be substantial and institutionalized. The initial divergences in culture and social structure have been reduced by different factors, such as: the growing standardization of certain elements (e.g., consumption, media exposure) in the lifestyle of all Israelis, the increasing biculturalism and bilingualism of Israeli Arabs, the massive incorporation of Arabs into the Jewish economy and the Histadrut, the urbanization of most Arab settlements and the piecemeal entry of Arabs into various public bodies. However, these developments have by no means impaired the accepted, permanent and vast cultural diversity and social separation between the two ethnic groups.

Fourth, like Arab–Jewish pluralism, Arab–Jewish inequality has somewhat diminished but has remained appreciable and institutionalized. The Arabs' gains in employment, education, a higher standard of living, and better life conditions in the villages have curtailed the wide socioeconomic gaps which existed in the beginning but have not brought them up to the level of the dominant modern Jewish sector. The basic services (roads, electricity, sewage, telephones, housing, health, education, etc.) in Arab settlements, despite improvements (Shidlowski, 1965; Bar-Gal, 1975), have remained backward. At the same time as the Arab economy almost collapsed due to greatly unequal regional developments, the gap between the Arab and Jewish sectors as producing regions has widened considerably (Gottheil, 1973). Similarly, the achievements of Arabs as manifested by the abolition of military government and the increased representation in political institutions have not significantly modified their subordinate status.

Fifth, the Arab population has undergone a significant differentiation of their class structure. In the transition from mandatory Palestine to the state of Israel the Arabs have lost their upper strata and been absorbed as an undifferentiated 'déclassé' class at the bottom level of Israeli society. The amelioration of Arab life conditions over the years has gradually engendered certain distinct variations within the Arab community along the lines of education, occupation and influence and the concomitant lines of lifestyle. More specifically, a sizeable middle class, amounting to about one-fifth of the Arab population, as well as a small elite of professionals, intellectuals and politicians, have emerged from the Arab masses.

And, sixth, Arab unrest has been in abeyance throughout the period but it has recently become more and more difficult to contain. The major cohesive forces of economic dependence and political subordination have weakened with the rise in the Arabs' standard of living, the extension of trade union protection for Arabs, the abolition of the military administration and the acquisition of political awareness and experience by the Arabs. The Arabs are now able to launch a more effective protest.

These various trends have weakened but not destroyed the exclusionary domination pattern of Arab–Jewish relations. Although these relations have become less stereotyped and more democratic, the Arabs have essentially remained an involuntary and a separate-but-unequal minority in the Jewish state.

How can the major variations in the past trends among the three pluralistic divisions be accounted for? As for the dynamics in cultural and social pluralism, it is evident that the Orientals have proved to be an assimilating group, whereas the religious Jews and Israeli Arabs are nonassimilating groups. The Orientals lack all the essentials which have sustained the cultural distinctiveness and social separation of the other two nondominant groups, i.e., the publicly recognized right to a separate identity, institutional arrangements (such as legal distinctions, schools and political parties), and large-scale voluntary concentration in separate communities.[7]

With regard to changes in the distribution of resources, it appears that while the Orientals and Israeli Arabs have continued to share the heavy burden of socioeconomic and power inequality, the problem has always been less in the case of the religious Jews. Basically the situation is one of an encounter between a dominant European sector and a nondominant Third World sector. The sharp discrepancies which predated the initial group contact have become blurred over the years because of the extension of welfare state services to the entire population, but in the absence of a tough policy of redistribution, inequalities have persisted. The problem of the Arab minority is even further exacerbated by its institutionalized unequal status.

When the cohesion of the three groups is compared, it turns out that the relationship between the two Jewish groups has continued to be mostly united and voluntary as against the alienated and involuntary relations between Arabs and Jews. The reason is that Arabs and Jews have more controversial issues and fewer conflict-resolving frameworks.

2 Future developments

During the 1948–75 period Israel has managed to overcome the difficulties associated with the various conflict-ridden pluralistic divisions and to preserve national cohesion, and the question now is: How well will Israel manage in the next two or three decades? Before considering this point, a word of caution is in order. To the usual reservations about the limited ability of the social sciences to make sound predictions at this stage, a special qualification should be added. The pluralist perspective, which is applied here, insists that developments in pluralistic societies do not usually follow consistent and generalizable patterns. It is stressed that there is a significant degree of indeterminancy and ambiguity that render future forecasts in pluralistic societies quite risky.

Given the difficulties in predicting trends in pluralistic social structures, it is important to specify the conditions in which these predictions should apply. In the Israeli case the projections are based on the assumption that the current setting will prevail. That is to say, Israel will preserve its Jewish-Zionist character and remain a sovereign state, free of foreign intervention. There will be no large-scale population and territorial shifts (attendant upon a natural disaster, a war or a mass immigration), the regime will continue to be a political democracy, the economy will still be largely subsidized and with full employment, and the Arab–Israeli dispute will continue. A drastic alteration in any of these dimensions may invalidate the expectations for the future.

If these conditions persist, it is expected that past trends will essentially continue. More specifically, Israeli society will remain a pluralistic and therefore problematic society but there will be no large-scale crisis such as an emergence of a mass protest or resistance movement, breakdown of democracy, *Kulturkampf* or civil war because of it. The above-mentioned societal contexts, especially the Arab–Israeli conflict and the subsidized economy, will continue to short-circuit tensions generated by the pluralistic structure.

Notwithstanding the overall continuity, several major changes are apparent. There will be significant transformations in the dominant patterns of intergroup relations: the general direction will be of greater liberalization or relaxation of present constraints. The Israeli–Palestinian division (i.e., the conflict between the Israeli citizens and Palestinian Arabs in the occupied territories) will have a deeper impact on the pluralistic divisions in Israel proper. This is true whatever the fate of the Palestinians: violent resistance to Israeli military government, home rule, the creation of a separate state, economic integration with Israel, or whatever. The Arab–Jewish division will move to the foreground in the Israeli pluralistic scene. The neglected Arab problem will become the most pressing and the Arab minority will change from being the most passive to the most active nondominant group in Israeli society.

The continuation of past trends into the future will bring about the following developments in Oriental–Ashkenazi relations. First, cultural diversity and social separation will continue to decline up to a certain point and then will stabilize. The Orientals will continue to lose their most distinctive subcultural attributes (such as non-Hebrew mother tongues and a higher birthrate) while preserving some of their folk variations (such as food and music). Thus they will more and more resemble the Ashkenazim and will draw nearer to them. But notwithstanding the Israeli ideal of amalgamation of the Jews, Oriental ethnicity will not fade away. Like nondominant ethnic groups elsewhere, it will continue to rest on de facto separation of community life, restricted opportunities for the poor, the ethnocentrism of the dominant group as well as the desire of the nondominant group to keep some separate identity.[8]

Oriental–Ashkenazi inequality will continue to be the most central issue. The large Oriental non-poor strata will acquire more political representation and prestige. The lot of the Oriental poor will also improve, perhaps enough to prevent them from falling further behind the rest of society and slow down their chronic cultural drift. However, the overall socioeconomic and power disparities will still be appreciable in Israeli society as long as it adheres to the egalitarian ethos and the national goal of ethnic assimilation. As a result of the constant erosion of ethnicity, however, these inequalities between Orientals and Ashkenazim will become socially defined as more and more class-based and less and less specifically ethnic.

The cohesion of the Orientals into Israeli society will continue to be based upon a mixture of positive and negative forces and – given a lack of change in the broader social conditions – will be sufficiently strong to curb the rise of a radical mass protest movement. If an Oriental-based movement were to be radicalized, this would manifest itself in the desire to reverse the trend of diminishing ethnic pluralism and to secure for the Orientals the right to a separate identity, demanding a redistribution of resources as an immediate target, and rejecting basic values (the Zionist ideology, Jewish solidarity or the democratic means of struggle). It is unlikely that such radical movements would receive enough mass support to disrupt the ethnic status quo. Nor should we expect recurrent violent riots, which, unlike isolated eruptions, characterize a social movement.

More generally, past tendencies in Oriental–Ashkenazi relations present Israel with the dilemma of either preserving the dynamic paternalistic–co-optation pattern as much as possible or moving towards a competitive–fluid pattern. The old course is based on the conception that the Orientals are still inferior and a threat and therefore must be contained by restrictions such as informal quotas, co-optation and neutralization. The new alternative requires, on the other hand, a radical change in Ashkenazi thinking, acceptance of the fact that the Orientals are, like the Ashkenazim, equal, free to compete, and can be depended upon to run the country. It also requires an upgrading of the Orientals' average competitive skills to ensure their full participation in the newly liberalized system.

The transition towards a competitive–fluid pattern of Oriental–Ashkenazi relations has been made possible by the weakening of the dynamic paternalism–co-optation pattern, and the smoothness of this transition is affected by countervailing forces. Among the favourable factors is the increasing importance of the non-Jewish–Jewish division. The rise of the non-Jewish population (both Israeli and Palestinian Arabs) from 12 per cent in 1966 to 36 per cent in 1975 has broadened the narrow base of the Arab–Jewish quasi-caste structure. The predictable growing prominence of this division will make the internal Jewish divisions less relevant, but at the same time the perpetuation of Jewish domination will require stronger cohesion within the Jewish quasi-caste. Such developments will contribute to greater equality between the Orientals and Ashkenazim. Second, the more convinced the Ashkenazim become that full Oriental participation would not lower the high quality of the Jewish society, the more receptive to change will they become. Past experience operates, therefore, as supporting evidence that, contrary to long-standing Ashkenazi fears, the Orientals are an assimilable element, not an agent of Levantinization, and a group incapable of damaging the Ashkenazi–Western character of the state.

Third, the Orientals are increasingly becoming impatient with paternalism, co-optation and an inferior status, and will thus increase pressures to achieve change. Despite the persistent ethnic gaps, more and more Orientals are adopting the dominant values and behaviours of the Ashkenazim. They are reaching their material and educational standards and acquiring political consciousness. Their expectations are rising and their protest is becoming more vocal. Because of these gains the inconsistency between what the establishment says and what it in fact does is more and more apparent to the Orientals. The strategy of the Black Panthers is quite clear in this context. They take the stated goal of full equality and assimilation at its face value and challenge the establishment to be faithful to its own ideals. In this respect, they certainly speak not just for the Oriental hard-core poor but for all Orientals.

Fourth, the recent change of powerholders in the Ashkenazi establishment is also a positive force. The new guard that has come to power since the 1973 War is much less paternalistic than its predecessor.[9] For many Ashkenazi sabras, within and outside the new establishment, free competition with the Orientals seems 'natural' and ethnic quotas objectionable. Furthermore, the Ashkenazi establishment, new or old, excels in highly developed political skills, pragmatism and responsiveness. It would be capable of diagnosing the Orientals' disaffections and, if these disaffections became transformed into constant pressures, of responding favourably. This propensity of the Ashkenazi establishment favours the possibility of switching to more liberal ethnic policies.

The negative factors are, however, equally weighty. First of all, the omnipresent external menace to national security will continue to freeze internal problems and to provide a convenient functional alternative to positive mechanisms of ethnic integration.[10]

Second, demographic considerations, which are seldom discussed openly, are also involved. The Orientals make up 55 per cent of Israeli Jewry and in all probability will remain in a majority position in the near future. But from another viewpoint, akin to the Ashkenazi establishment, the Oriental numerical preponderance

243

appears quite different. Since Israel is considered as the homeland of all Jews, the demography of world Jewry, of which the Orientals constitute less than one-fifth, is more relevant than the demography of Israeli Jewry. Oriental proportional representation in all walks of life in Israel would presumably mean over-representation and cause tensions in the relations between Israel and the predominantly Ashkenazi Diaspora.[11] Israel's strenuous efforts to encourage immigration from Europe and the Americas are, among other things, motivated by this global consideration. At any rate these efforts tend to counterbalance the pressures towards full equality.[12]

Third, since the Orientals are still not fully Westernized, the paternalistic ideology of 'the generation of the desert' can be prolonged for some time. They do not supposedly yet measure up to Ashkenazi standards and hence cannot be admitted as full members of society.

Fourth, the Ashkenazim have strong vested interests in the existing system. In the past they profited considerably from the expansion of opportunities and state services and at present they enjoy some protection in the competition for resources, but the effort to bridge the ethnic gaps will damage their interests. Although crash programmes to stamp out poverty, to construct public housing for not-so-recent immigrants, to train the unskilled and to invest more in compensatory education can be at least partially funded by importing capital, the established Ashkenazi section will have to assume the lion's share of the prohibitive costs of achieving more ethnic equality. Furthermore, the Ashkenazim will be the natural victims of any successful reduction in ethnic inequality. They will have to compete harder, and sometimes even lose. Freer competition for power, which is certainly a more zero-sum resource than socio-economic resources, will inflict on them losses in a sensitive area.

Fifth, it is difficult to open up the system to full Oriental participation without creating, in addition to crash programmes, some structural changes such as greater democratization of the political process and reorganization of the social and welfare services. Although public support for such measures exists, it is not clear whether they will be finally implemented and how effective they will be.

Sixth, the continuing flow of immigrants impedes ethnic equality. Since 1957, with the exception of a few years, the majority of newcomers have been Ashkenazim who came with good training, earning ability and money.[13] To attract and to help them to settle permanently, Israel lavishes special privileges on them. The steady middle-class Ashkenazi immigration harms the Orientals in two ways. The typical Ashkenazi immigrant, with his skills, resources and enormous government aid, enters – after a few years of adjustment – Israeli social structure at the middle section or higher. This of course has the direct effect of holding down Oriental upward mobility. The situation is almost the reverse of the pattern known from United States history where each wave of immigration, entering the system at the bottom, pushed the earlier arrivals upwards. Israel's needs for technological, scientific and military progress are satisfied both by the continuing importation of highly skilled manpower from abroad, and by training the socially mobile Ashkenazi population. The self-sufficiency of the Ashkenazi group in highly trained labour has the far-reaching indirect impact of neglecting the unnecessary, greatly untapped, potential of the Orientals. The under-utilization of Oriental talents not only presents no problem to the national economy, but actually helps the Ashkenazim to avoid competition with the Orientals and therefore to perpetuate their superior position. These inauspicious side-effects of immigration, for ethnic equality, are expected to last for years to come.

Seventh, the Arab–Jewish quasi-caste structure, and the expansion of its base after the Six-Day War, while serving as a positive force by pressing for greater solidarity among Jews, has also the indirect effect of inhibiting a radical solution of the ethnic problem. Despite the Zionist–socialist ideal of ending the traditional Jewish occupational 'inverted pyramid' in the new Jewish society,[14] the Ashkenazi group in Israel has been undergoing serious processes of embourgeoisement which are fairly similar to those of Ashkenazi world Jewry. Under such circumstances the elevation of the status of the Orientals to that of the Ashkenazim will create an enormous vacuum in the lower levels of the economy. A possible remedy to such a problem – i.e., opening up the Jewish economy to non-Jewish workers, regardless of their current or future political status – is not acceptable to the Ashkenazi dominant group which still supports traditional exclusionary policies against the Arabs. Since the early beginnings of the new Yishuv at the turn of the last century, the Jews have insisted on a Jewish society and economy and have taken various measures to avoid dependence on Arab labour, and to prevent the creation of a split labour market of unequal wages and work conditions. For this reason the Ashkenazi governing elite and public would probably prefer the status quo; where the Orientals fill the low-status and manual jobs instead of the Arabs taking over these jobs and the Orientals moving up to higher-status positions.[15]

Eighth, and finally, the growing class differentiation within the Oriental group will transform the ethnic conflict into a social problem and weaken the Orientals' ethnic solidarity and efficacy. The Oriental poor appear more as poor than Oriental. They are denied a leadership from the more educated and better off Orientals. For the time being the more ambitious of these Orientals are siphoned off into the Ashkenazi segment. If the dominant Ashkenazi group feels threatened by a possible coalition between a rising disenchanted Oriental elite and the underprivileged Oriental masses, they will intensify this process of absorption.

Whatever the net balance of the various counteracting forces, Israel is moving towards more liberal and more competitive Oriental–Ashkenazi relations. Even if paternalism and co-optation survive cross-pressures, the costs of maintaining such a system will rise steadily. Whether or not the opening up of the occupational and power structure from the middle section down has so far been sufficient, now the more urgent necessity is to open the next higher level in order to meet demands for more egalitarian relations. For instance, it is significant that Orientals were nominated to the positions of Secretary-General of the Israel Labour Party, chairman of the Zionist Executive Committee and Speaker of the Knesset; also important are the proposing of a Sephardi as a candidate for the Presidency, entrusting a Sephardi with the chairmanship of the top-ranking Knesset Committee on Defence and Foreign Affairs, and the appointment of three cabinet ministers. While all were made 'in good faith' as pacificatory measures in the old tradition of ethnic quotas, they have, nevertheless, the latent function of eroding paternalism and co-optation. As Gamson (1968: 135) observes, co-optation is a double-edged sword – it neutralizes opponents but it does so at the cost of power-sharing. In the mid-1970s the Orientals have reached the stage at which significant concessions must be made in order to buy them off. Power-sharing will be increasingly important until neutralization ceases to be a goal.

As to the relations between religious and nonreligious Jews, the following developments are expected. First, the process of institutionalization of religious–nonreligious pluralism will go on. The religious minority will become more encapsulated and segregated. It will expand its present separate institutions and communities and build new ones. Younger religious Jews will be more Orthodox and more consciously so than their parents. Gaining self-confidence they will feel less threatened by the secular society. They will invest the additional gains of resources such as money and leisure time in perfecting their religious lifestyle; e.g., sending children to yeshivot instead of schools and spending more time on religious studies. At the same time they will be more involved in areas of wider interest, but as religious people with religious views.

Second, more concessions to promote mutual understanding and adjustment will be made by both sides. On the religious minority's side, such a development will be occasioned by the rise of a new Rabbinic elite which will be self-confident, dynamic, modernizing and problem-solving. This elite will be willing to cope with the

246

problems of adapting the halakha to the realities of modern life in a Jewish state. For instance, the procedures for Orthodox conversion to Judaism will be simplified and speeded up, and special solutions will be found within the religious law for certain categories of unmarriageable persons. Mounting pressures on the part of the nonreligious majority will force the religious minority to make a sharper distinction between essential and nonessential matters. For example, allowing public transport and entertainment on the Sabbath will interfere much less with religious Jews' practices and their relations with nonreligious Jews than instituting civil marriage and divorce. The religious minority will stand fast, however, against demands for concessions on the more essential questions. Nonreligious Jews, on their part, will respect more the sharply drawn distinction between the essential and nonessential and therefore will exercise less pressure in areas essential to the religious minority. They will also acquiesce in new legislation, such as a kashrut law, that is considered necessary to safeguard the religious way of life.

And, third, the two internal subdivisions within the religious minority, i.e., the national–political and the ethnic–class, will become exacerbated. Liberal reinterpretations of the halakha and greater freedom from religion which will be ushered in by the dominant Mizrahi section will be opposed vehemently by the conservative wing in Aguda and perhaps by some in the Mizrahi. These traditionalist circles will be further alienated from the state and will resort to growing religious fanaticism on the one hand and to segregation in separate ultra-Orthodox communities on the other. The ethnic–class split will widen as well. The desertion of the religious camp by socially mobile Orientals will continue. The predominant Mizrahi section will be smaller, more ethnically balanced and more sharply divided between a privileged, modern section of Ashkenazim and a small number of religiously 'Askhenazied' Orientals on the one hand and an underprivileged, traditionalist section of Orientals on the other. The divergences in the religious world-view, lifestyle and socioeconomic status between the two will be so immense that within the religious minority ethnic relations will be highly strained and ethnic assimilation will be exceedingly problematic.[16]

Beyond these future developments, the most crucial question is whether Israel will keep the religious status quo or move towards separation between state and religion. The continuation of the religious status quo means that Orthodox Jews will remain a numerically nonassimilating minority who fight to strengthen their cultural autonomy and reinforce the Jewish-religious character of the state. The nonseparation of religion from the state will preserve the existing arrangements of the monopoly of the Orthodox stream

247

of Judaism, halakhic jurisdiction of personal status and other religious legislation, public financing of religious services and the machinery of the Chief Rabbinate, Rabbinic courts and local religious councils. The religious political parties will continue to play the role of guardians of the religious status quo. The alternative pattern of separation of state and religion would mean that religious status would become private and the state would refrain from regulating it in any way. Marriage and divorce will be handled by civil courts. All the current official institutions will be either abolished or will become private. The religious minority will have to organize its voluntary self-contained communities which will cater for the religious needs of their members, including education, the Rabbinate and the Rabbinic courts.

The separation of state and religion will end the present consociational democracy. Mutual accommodation will cease to be contested and strained. The battle over the religious character of the state will be over. Private religion will gain more support than politically negotiated religion. The cessation of religious coercion will make nonreligious Jews more amenable to religious influences and less resentful of religious Jews. Freed from state intervention in religious affairs and from their own impossible task of imposing religion on the state, the religious Jews will lead a much more satisfying life in their autonomous and self-supporting communities. They will withdraw some religious legitimacy from the state and, with the introduction of civil divorce, will have to enforce endogamy strictly. Contacts between religious and nonreligious Jews will be less frequent and less personal but more official and peaceful.

The chances for harmonizing religious–nonreligious relations by a shift towards the new pattern are slim indeed. Such a radical change will come about only after a confrontation or an open *Kulturkampf,* which both sides are and will be careful to avoid.[17] The considerations for keeping the present contested accommodation pattern are so overwhelming that it is unlikely that in the foreseeable future either side will tamper with the religious status quo. To begin with, the Arab–Israeli conflict is a definite deterrent. The disestablishment of the religious status will deny the centuries-old overlap in Judaism of ethnic origin, nationality and religion, and create then a possibility of Israeli Jewish nationals who follow a non-Jewish religion. The divorce of religion from nationalism will dilute Israel's Jewish identity and culture in which religion is a basic component. It will cause even more harm to Jews all over the world, for whom Judaism is primarily religion. Intermarriage and assimilation will be therefore licensed in Israel and abroad. Israel will gradually loosen its ties with the Diaspora and develop, instead, a new, less Jewish, but more inclusive, local identity.

In addition to these long-range considerations, there are no strong reasons to expect that the nonreligious majority will launch a serious struggle for remodelling the religious status quo, and the religious minority will yield. After all, religious pressure on most nonreligious Jews is relatively light because of the selective incorporation of religion into public life. The religious minority for its part is well organized and hence capable of disrupting the system if a major change were to be unilaterally imposed. It is a permanent political force whose interests must be considered even if it stays out of the coalition government. Since about half of the religious vote goes to nonreligious parties, the major labour and right-wing blocs cannot afford to undercut whatever votes they usually obtain from religious Jews. The ongoing process of becoming a floating coalition partner instead of a traditional ally of the ruling Labour Party will add to the negotiating power of the religious parties.

Given the present conditions, Israel will probably not choose to separate state and religion. The existing pattern of contested accommodation will persist, with the above-mentioned developments, which will perhaps make life somewhat easier for both the religious and nonreligious groups.

While the two Jewish divisions might become weaker in the future, Arab–Jewish relations will become more acute and pronounced. The following developments are expected. First, a certain reduction in the considerable cultural and social pluralism between Arabs and Jews is to be expected. As the modernization of the Arab minority advances, more and more Arabs will become bilingual and will incorporate in their subculture some elements from the dominant middle-class lifestyle. More Arabs will be admitted into the state and Histadrut administration, industry and other Jewish-controlled white-collar branches of the economy. The special Departments for Arab Affairs will be gradually phased out.[18]

Second, the piecemeal decrease in Arab–Jewish inequality will continue. The government and Histadrut will invest in the improvement of services in the Arab settlements and the creation of jobs near to them. The average standard of living of the Arabs will continue to rise. The class differentiation within the Arab sector will increase as the middle class and elite grow in size.

And, third, tensions between Arabs and Jews will escalate. The Arabs will lose patience with the slow pace of change, second-class citizenship and the denial of their nationalistic feelings. They will form independent organizations, a national party and, perhaps, a resistance movement to further their causes.

These projections imply a continuing erosion in the present exclusionary domination pattern of Arab–Jewish relations. Does Israel have any alternative? In principle, Israel can take one of three major alternative directions on the 'approach–avoidance' continuum in order to reach a more co-operative coexistence. These are 'maximal incorporation', 'a status of a Palestinian national minority' and 'an individual choice between incorporation and separation'.

'Maximal incorporation' consists of incorporating Arabs as individuals into Israeli society as much as possible without assimilating them. These Arabs will develop an Israeli Arab identity which is distinguishable from the Palestinian identity. They will see themselves as an integral part of Israel, and the Jews, on their part, will regard the Arabs as equals and partners. Although Israel will remain a Jewish-Zionist state, bilingualism and biculturalism will be fostered, and new, shared cultural traits will emerge. Civil rights and duties, apart from the Law of Return, will be fully equalized and applied universally: namely, army service will be compulsory for Arabs as well as Jews, the special Departments for Arab Affairs will be abolished, free entry for Arabs into all occupational and political spheres will be assured, and perhaps even a legal provision for mixed marriages will be made.[19] The creation of common social frameworks such as bilingual schools and mixed neighbourhoods will also be encouraged. Likewise, great efforts will be made to reduce the disparities in the level of modernization and in the distribution of resources between Arabs and Jews. A special law will be enacted against discrimination, and it will be strongly enforced. Government agencies and other public bodies, including the Jewish Agency, will have to avoid double standards or any ascriptive distinction.

In contrast, the second direction could establish the Arabs' status as that of a Palestinian national minority. The Arabs will publicly identify themselves as Palestinian Arabs who are part of the Palestinian nation living in Israel and will be recognized as a national minority by the state. They will gain control over their present cultural, religious and educational institutions as well as the Arab Departments. They will also establish new independent organizations such as a national political party, communications media and a university. They will demand, and receive, large investments for creating Arab-owned and Arab-managed industrial plants, bringing services in the Arab settlements up to the high Israeli standards, and narrowing the socioeconomic gaps between Arabs and Jews. While remaining a part of a Jewish-Zionist state, the Palestinian Arab minority will promote cultural and other ties with the Arab world, including the option of acquiring citizenship of an Arab state in addition to Israeli citizenship.

The third direction could offer the Arabs a choice between the above two alternatives. A selective implementation of elements from both alternatives will create a situation in which Arab individuals will have a meaningful freedom of choice between a greater personal incorporation into Israeli society or a greater separation as members of a recognized Palestinian national minority. The Israeli Arabs will enjoy the right religious Jews have today, namely, integration as individuals into wider society or continued membership in largely self-contained communities.

These three options are similar in some respects. All are serious attempts towards co-operative Arab–Jewish coexistence in Israel instead of the declining pattern of Arab exclusion and subordination. They intend to preserve the Jewish-Zionist character of the state. The Arabs are accorded much better opportunities and rights than they now have, but not an absolutely equal status.

The differences between these possible future developments are, however, marked, especially those between the first two alternatives. To sharpen the dissimilarities, the 'maximal incorporation' regards the Arabs as a cultural minority only, whereas the other alternative accords them 'the status of a Palestinian national minority'. The former offers the Arabs greater equality but less expression of their Palestinian nationalistic feelings. It seeks to atomize and neutralize the Arabs, while the second one seeks to pacify them with the status of a separate-but-not-so-equal national minority. The two differ in the nature of the threat they pose to the Jewish-Zionist character of the state: the former is liable to dilute Israel's Jewish identity by making citizenship the central factor and thereby creating an all-inclusive Israeli identity, while the latter emperils Israel's Jewish identity by encouraging de facto binationalism, transferring too much power to the Arabs and running the risk of Arab irredentism.

As far as the Jewish majority is concerned, the 'maximal incorporation' direction is the lesser evil. It may be viewed as a preventive measure against the dangerous polarization inherent in the status of a Palestinian national minority provided by the other two options. If a Palestinian state is established alongside Israel, maximal incorporation will provide better protection against a resistance movement or irredentism than Arab cultural autonomy. There is even a chance that the creation of a new Palestinian state will satisfy the Arabs' national aspirations and they will be content with life in the Jewish state, given fuller civil rights, an open access to institutions and a proportional share of resources. In fact, the Arab minority will agree to maximal incorporation, although it would prefer the status of a national minority if Israel were to consent to a Palestinian peoplehood and statehood.[20]

The possibility of Israel taking one of the three directions to achieve a more co-operative coexistence between the Arabs and Jews is not very realistic. The advisers on Arab affairs, who are alarmed by the rising Arab unrest in the years following the 1973

251

War, press for greater incorporation of Arabs into Israeli society, but they do not go beyond tinkering with the status quo in which incorporation is used only as a mechanism of control. Since the authorities will not introduce any significant change in their policies as long as the Arab–Israeli conflict exists and the state remains Jewish-Zionist in character, only limited improvements in the Arabs' status in Israel can be expected. Essentially, more economic departments and public bodies will be open to Arabs, and Arabs will be allowed to compete with Jews in certain jobs. Such concessions, however, will not appease the Arab population who will fight against the continued efforts by the government to salvage a new sugar-coated version of the ever-present exclusionary domination pattern.

In concluding this part it should be recalled that all these future projections assume the continuation of the current broader parameters of Israel's social structure, notably the Arab–Israeli conflict, the Jewish-Zionist character of the state, the highly subsidized economy, political democracy and the demographic ratios, among other conditions. Any major alteration in any element of this setting, such as a settlement of the Arab–Israeli conflict or a severe economic crisis, would require, therefore, these predictions to be altered.

3 Utopias and new directions

After a long and detailed analysis of the pluralistic structure of Israeli society in the past, present and future, the time has finally come to turn to the question of what should and can be done to make Israel a better society. Since I do not believe that social scientists can divorce science from ideology (although social science can in the abstract), the ensuing discussion should be viewed as a shift in emphasis rather than as a shift in ground. For this reason readers and critics of studies of controversial topics, such as the present one, are entitled to know the author's biases.

As a point of departure let me examine, first, the existing utopias pertaining to Israel's pluralistic structure. Utopias are portraits of an ideal society, overall solutions to current problems and, by implication, social critiques of the status quo. There are five major utopias of this kind: an exclusive Jewish-Zionist state, a halakha state, a Canaanite state, an Arab Palestinian state and a democratic secular state. They are all live ideas, not dead dreams, which are sincerely advocated by groups of people for resolving the pluralistic problem of Israel.[21]

Of all utopias, the utopia of an exclusive Jewish-Zionist state is the most widespread and influential idea in Israel. It consists of a nation-state for Jews only, a complete bringing together of all the

Jews who are dispersed in the world, the revival of Jewish national culture in a modern society on the lines of a Western democracy, with a harmonious nonseparation between state and religion. This ideal is one of outright uniformity – a society of one ethnicity, one religion, one nationality, one language and one culture. The pluralistic status quo of Israeli society is anathema to this vision. The implications are: bringing home as many Jews as possible, excluding the Arabs, assimilating the Orientals and compromising with the religious. The solution simply lies in the virtual elimination of all pluralistic divisions.

The halakha state utopia can count of course on religious adherents only. The ideal society is conceived of as a community of Jewish believers for whom the halakha is their legal system and the Rabbis their ruling elite. Nonpractising Jews are treated as deviant members and non-Jews as tolerated nonmembers. Pluralism is to be restricted considerably and, inasmuch as it survives, it would constitute the criterion for a status-hierarchy. Hence implementation will imply advancing the religious minority into a dominant position, doing away with democracy and imposing the halakha in private and public life.[22]

The Canaanite utopia can claim the fewest supporters, perhaps only a few scores of intellectuals, but they are the most articulate. An entirely new nation-state is envisioned. It is a Hebrew society, both in language and nationality. Religion is absolutely separated from the state and made utterly private. The Hebrews are of diverse religions (Jews, Moslems, Christians and others) and ethnic origins (Arabs, Jews, Armenians and others). The final homeland of the new nation, a revived ancient country, would cover the present lands of Israel, Jordan, Lebanon, Syria and Iraq. The free immigrants and annexed groups must accept the Hebrew language, nationality and culture. The greater Hebrew nation-state is projected as democratic, secular, non-Jewish, open and oriented to the Middle East. The Canaanites advocate the de-Judaization and de-Zionization of Israel, separation of state and religion, conversion of Arabs into Hebrews and territorial expansion.[23]

The above utopias have only Jewish followers, whereas the next two appeal mostly to Arabs. The idea of an Arab Palestinian state in the entire territory of Palestine was developed in mandatory Palestine in reaction to Jewish colonization and became utopian with the proclamation of Israel. Greater Palestine is Palestinian in nationality, Arabic in language and culture, but multi-ethnic. It is part of the Arab world. The rights of religious, ethnic and cultural minorities are protected. This utopia, which is popular among Arabs in and outside Israel, forecasts the de-Judaization and de-Zionization of Israel, the Palestinization of its nationality, the Arabization of its culture and the promotion of Palestinian Arabs to a dominant status.

The last utopia of a democratic secular state is quite recent. It is espoused by the Palestine Liberation Organization, by the small Israeli Matzpen group and by their backers the world over. The complete secularization and democratization of a greater Palestine means an exclusively individual incorporation of all the 'legitimate residents'[24] into the state as full and equal citizens. Such a state is presented as an open and humanistic society where people relate to each other as humans rather than as members of collectivities. To carry this ideal through, it would be necessary to de-Judaize and de-Zionize Israel, to separate state from religion and to eradicate the dominant status of the Jews.[25]

The above sketch of utopias is instructive in a number of ways. The great divergence of these utopias from Israeli realities highlights the deep dissatisfaction of certain groups with the present situation. The sharp contrasts among them disclose the enormous potentiality for conflict among the constituent groups. It is also significant that the religious and Arab nondominant minorities have their own self-serving utopias but the Oriental nondominant majority does not. The Zionist utopia of negation of ethnicity is not challenged by the Orientals.

Since these utopias are broad frames of reference in Israeli society, my stand on them may clarify my general position. My first bias is to reject all of them in toto. To name one objection only, I do not like the strict and exclusionary uniformity in the Zionist utopia, the theocratic totalitarianism in the halakhic utopia, the Hebrew supremacy and imperialism in the Canaanite utopia, the simplistic reversal of statuses of Arabs and Jews in the Palestinian utopia, and the denial of national self-determination in the democratic secular utopia.

If, however, I have to select one from among the above five, I would opt for the Zionist utopia. Several convictions underlie this enforced choice of mine. I do believe in the legitimacy of both the Zionist and Palestinian national movements and I am convinced that their separatist nature makes the redivision of Palestine the most just and expedient solution for the historical antagonism between them (Smooha, 1974). I hold that the Jewish-Zionist character of the state of Israel is irreversible for the foreseeable future and that any remedy for Israel's problems, both external and internal, should take it for granted. It is my conviction, therefore, that, given the status quo, the implementation of the Zionist utopia would cause injustice to many fewer people than any other.

A non-utopian Zionist idea is, in my opinion, compatible with the desires of most of the concerned parties. It accords with the wishes of the overwhelming majority of the Jews in Israel. It is compatible with the aspiration of the Palestinian people for statehood. The Zionist idea is also right in seeing full ethnic equality and fusion as an answer, in the mid-1970s, to the Oriental problem. It is similarly correct in opposing, for the time being, the separation of state and religion because such a major digression from the religious status quo might be fateful for religious–nonreligious relations and for the very Jewish identity of Israel. And although the Zionist idea is inconsistent with an equal status for Arabs in Israel, it is congruous with alleviating the Arabs' predicament by letting them choose between maximal incorporation into Israeli society or the status of a national Palestinian minority.

My further biases are laid bare in a number of steps that I strongly feel Israel should take in the foreseeable future. My suggestions will be justified by referring to four principles prevalent in Israeli society: namely, a Jewish-Zionist state, democratic pluralism, equality of resources among pluralistic groups and national security. The inconsistencies and tensions which exist among these principles will be clarified in my following proposals.

First, Israel should recognize the right of the Palestinians to a state in the occupied territories. This is indispensable for reducing the appalling magnitude of Israel's pluralistic structure where a semi-colonial situation is taking shape. Zionism runs the risk of falsification, undermining the moral base of Israeli society and the continuation of bloodshed if it resists Palestinian sovereignty in a part of Palestine. A Palestinian state alongside Israel hopefully would provide normalization of the status of Israel in the region and the improvement of the status of Arabs in Israel.

Second, Israel should recognize its pluralistic structure. It must rid itself of the Zionist dream of an exclusive Jewish state. The Israeli Arabs and religious Jews are permanent nonassimilating minorities whose right to a separate identity has to be fully respected. This fundamental resemblance also suggests a similar strategy of conflict-resolution. The delicate issue of the Arab minority should be treated in the same manner as the religious minority issue. In other words, the right of religious Jews to choose between maximal incorporation or cultural autonomy should be extended to the Israeli Arabs.[26] On the other hand, it must be emphasized that, by the mid-1970s, the Orientals are already embarked upon the irreversible course of assimilation and, as an assimilating group, they should not be offered a similar choice.

A full recognition of the pluralistic structure implies that Israel should end its identification with the Ashkenazi dominant minority and face the reality of the existence of diverse groups with different needs. While remaining a Jewish-Zionist state, Israel has to open its national culture to diverse influences (including Middle Eastern ones) and to let all its constituent groups (Orientals and Arabs included) take part in the culture-building process.

Third, Israel should recognize the overlap between its pluralistic and stratificational structures and do its utmost to reduce it. Today Israel of the pre-1967 borders is a three-tier society in which Arabs are at the bottom, Orientals in the middle and Ashkenazim at the top. The Ashkenazi minority controls the entire state and benefits from a vast superiority in jobs and material wellbeing. These structural inequalities are perpetuated from one generation to another. The redistribution of resources and opportunities is essential in order to redress past and present inequities and to avert unrest.

Fourth, Israel should recognize the danger to democracy of having the resolution of conflicts on values or interests between pluralistic groups always to the advantage of the same side. This is applied most appropriately to the Arab minority for whom the odds are low that the principle of democratic pluralism will prevail when it is in real or apparent contradiction with other principles. For example, the Arabs' rights to an open job market and to form independent organizations are frequently denied because they ostensibly stand in conflict with the principle of national security. The national programme of 'development of the Galilee' has turned into a programme of 'Judaization of the Galilee' because the principle of a Jewish state takes precedence over the principle of democratic pluralism. Israeli democracy faces, indeed, a clear-cut situation of 'the tyranny of the majority' (de Tocqueville, 1969: 250–4) and possesses deplorable features of 'a *Herrenvolk* democracy' (van den Berghe, 1967b: 18) in the case of the Arab minority. The Arabs, who find themselves permanent losers in all issues, may become disillusioned with the democratic rules and may resort to violence.

The Orientals encounter a similar problem, but to a lesser degree. For instance, the continuing middle-class Ashkenazi immigration frustrates efforts to narrow the ethnic socioeconomic gaps, but the principles of national security and a Jewish state prevail. As a matter of fact, such considerations never even come into the open owing to the dominant group's effective control of national decision-making.

Religious Jews, on the other hand, avail themselves of 'the beneficial consociational democracy' which assures that their values and interests are taken into account in policy-making. Enjoying the status of a strong pressure group, they negotiate the terms of a modus vivendi with the dominant majority. They sometimes win and sometimes lose, but almost always exercise a veto on decisions which they define as detrimental to them. Israeli democracy will be strengthened if some of the protection religious Jews have is extended to the other nondominant, Oriental and Arab, groups.

Fifth, and finally, Israel should recognize the necessity for nondominant groups to become organized and to fight for their interests. Since it is unconceivable that dominant groups would ever give up power and privilege voluntarily, counter-pressures are vital. In seeking effective measures, the Orientals, religious Jews and Arabs are entitled to use, among other means, their identities as legitimate bases for group solidarity. Conflict is thus unavoidable if significant change is to be effected. [27]

10 Conclusion

The overwhelming majority of societies today are internally divided into ethnic, racial, linguistic and other groups that lead distinctive lifestyles or maintain separate institutions. In most cases cultural diversity and social separation between constituent groups are reinforced by socioeconomic gaps and power disparities. These cleavages of pluralism and inequality vary in magnitude, overlap to a greater or lesser degree, and change over time, thereby producing a variety of intergroup situations.

Pluralistic and inequality structures augment the potentiality for authoritarianism and instability. In extreme cases, such as colonial societies and South Africa, sharp conflicts prevail and cohesion is achieved through political domination and economic interdependence. The vulnerability to disorder of highly pluralistic societies has been frequently manifested in the internal wars which have plagued Rhodesia, Nigeria, Northern Ireland, Iraq, Pakistan, Cyprus and Lebanon, to name a few and the most recent instances. Virtually all ex-colonial, new African and Asian countries as well as Latin American states experience the tensions of structural pluralism and inequality. Countries such as Belgium, Canada and Yugoslavia, where pluralism and inequality are moderate, have managed so far to preserve national cohesion by exercising much flexibility, but they still face the hazards of disintegration. Against the background of unstable or undemocratic pluralistic societies, the case of Switzerland is very striking. For over a hundred years, social solidarity has not been shattered despite a fairly high degree of ethnolinguistic pluralism. The Swiss exception proves the rule, but more important, by its mere existence, suggests that under certain conditions peaceful coexistence among pluralistic groups is a viable possibility.

The theoretical perspective of structural pluralism takes as a central problem the near-universality of 'pluralistic–inequality

258

structures', i.e., social structures consisting of pluralistic groups which in most cases make up a hierarchy of status groups. It differs in this respect from the common approaches of cultural and political pluralism. These approaches focus on a limited number of states, mostly Western, in which pluralism and intergroup inequality are relatively unproblematic and political democracy is sustained by, among other things, checks and balances among competing interest groups. On the other hand, the more widely applicable pluralist perspective treats pluralism and intergroup inequality as problematic.

The pluralist perspective aims at studying systematically the ways and degrees to which constituent groups are different in culture, separate in organization and unequal in resources. It proceeds in two directions. One examines the setting in which pluralism and inequality are anchored; namely, how they historically emerged and what are the broader social conditions at present which affect them. The other direction traces the consequences of pluralism and inequality for the cohesion (conflict and integration) of the groups under study and of society-at-large.

It is the main thesis of this book that Israel possesses a pluralistic–inequality structure whose study is important per se and is also indispensable for the understanding of wider Israeli society. Israel's post-1967 population is divided into five major pluralistic divisions: Palestinian Arabs in the occupied territories versus Israeli Jews (the demographic ratio is 29:71), Israeli Arabs versus Jews (13.87), Druze versus Christian versus Muslem Arabs (9:16:75), religious versus nonreligious Jews (30:70), and Oriental versus Ashkenazi Jews (55:45). These divisions make two significant cleavages in Israeli society, one of structural pluralism and another of intergroup inequality.

Pluralism covers wide variations indeed. It ranges from differences in subculture (lifestyle) and partial separation within the Jewish population or within the Arab population, to divergences in core-culture (ethnic origin, language, religion, nationality, family structure, basic ideology) and in institutional frameworks between non-Jews and Jews.

Considerable inequalities are superimposed on the nonhierarchical pluralistic divisions. A four-tier status-hierarchy prevails where the disfranchised Palestinian Arabs are at the bottom rank, the subordinate Arab minority occupies the next lower layer, the disadvantaged Oriental majority takes an intermediate position, and at the top the superior Ashkenazi minority outdistances all the non-European groups.

The significance of the pluralistic–inequality structure of Israeli society is, further, demonstrated by its institutionalization. All

259

nondominant groups, with the exception of Oriental Jews, are nonassimilating minorities whose right to separate identity is publicly recognized, and institutional arrangements prevail to guarantee their separate existence. Although intergroup inequalities are not formally institutionalized, they are perpetuated in practice from one generation to another.

The importance of the pluralistic–inequality structure is also reflected in its effects. There are conflicts among the pluralistic groups over whether Israel has any right to exist, whether it should remain Jewish and Zionist, whether the current compromises which shape its religious or secular character should be modified, and whether resources must be radically redistributed in order to do away with ethnic stratification.

Yet Israel has preserved a stable order. Several broad conditions contribute to the relative quiet. They include the overwhelming Arab–Israeli dispute which overshadows all internal dissensions; the highly subsidized economy which supplies full employment, a minimal standard of living and short-range upward mobility for all; and political democracy which accords universal civil rights to all Israelis and respects the right of nonassimilating groups to a separate identity. Disruptions are also averted by the common cultural factors of language, religion, nationality, and the Zionist ideology shared by members of the Jewish majority on the one hand, and the technological superiority of the Jewish sector as a European transplant vis-à-vis the underdeveloped Arab sector.

The state of Israel is doing better than the new and developing countries, but compared to most Western states where it belongs, it experiences greater hardships and scores more modest achievements. To grasp the complexities of the pluralistic–inequality structure, a close examination of three of its components, i.e., the Oriental–Ashkenazi division, the religious–nonreligious division and the Arab–Jewish division, has been undertaken throughout this study.

Oriental–Ashkenazi relations are analysed in terms of 'the dynamic paternalism–co-optation model'. The Ashkenazi majority in world Jewry formed the Zionist movement in order to solve its own problems in Europe. Centuries of separation and discrepancies in level of development led the Ashkenazim to ignore the Orientals as equal participants in the rebuilding of the Jewish homeland. The post-state mass influx of Oriental immigrants was received with mixed feelings. The Zionist dream of the ingathering of the exiles was coming true, but it was feared that the 'backward' Orientals would dilute the Western culture and upset the political democracy of the newly founded state. To forestall these dangers, the dominant Ashkenazi group has taken the countermeasures of providing minimal services for the Oriental arrivals in order to prevent destitution, admitting them into the lower and middle rungs of society and neutralizing them as an independent force.

Over the years a conflict-laden uneven development of ethnic pluralism and inequality has transpired. The Oriental subculture was dismantled and the Orientals were pressed to adapt to the mainstream. Significant headway has been made in assimilating the Orientals into the Ashkenazi lifestyles and social frameworks. At the same time, considerable ethnic disparities in the distribution of resources have persisted despite appreciable improvements in the Orientals' living conditions. Tensions between the two communities have thus mounted as a result of the sharp contrast between the official objectives of full ethnic equality and amalgamation on the one hand, and the realities of anti-Oriental paternalism, entrenched inequality and the failure to take the necessary steps to implement the official objectives, on the other.

The dynamic paternalism–co-optation pattern of Oriental–Ashkenazi relations has been declining. Class is superseding ethnicity. Competitive relations are becoming more and more frequent. Ethnic stratification has, nevertheless, remained a sticky problem. Hence it is expected that Israel will run into an ethnic crisis if current policies continue and if the Arab–Israeli dispute and the subsidized economy cease to be the mainstay of ethnic cohesion.

In comparison, religious–nonreligious relations are conceptualized in terms of 'the contested accommodation model'. With the advent of secularization, this division has crystallized within every Jewish community. The Mizrahi, the dominant section in the Ashkenazi Orthodox branch of Judaism, developed a modernized Orthodox subculture in reaction to the exigencies of life in the last two centuries in Europe. It then participated, from the very beginning, as a separate sector in the Zionist movement and the Yishuv. The mutual adaptations worked out during the mandate have mostly been carried over to Israeli society.

In many respects the religious Jews constitute a separate-but-equal minority. They have all the necessary institutional arrangements to maintain a distinct lifestyle such as separate schools, political parties, neighbourhoods and localities, media, and the like. Various legal provisions (including exclusive religious jurisdiction of personal status, the exemption of religious girls from army service, and the appointment of the Sabbath and other religious holidays as national days of rest) enable religious Jews to mix and compete with non-religious Jews on an equal footing, without threatening their separate identity. The religious Jews' minor socioeconomic disadvantage is partially due to their larger families and partially to the over-representation of poor Orientals among them. In fact, they enjoy cultural autonomy, a proportional share of resources and even a right of veto in religious matters.

The pattern of relations between religious and nonreligious Jews is accommodation, which has been constantly contested by both sides. Living as a religious minority in a secularized society, the religious Jews have continuously to fight in self-defence for cultural autonomy and equal opportunity. But of greater consequence is their missionary zeal to impose the halakha on the entire Jewish population. The nonreligious majority acquiesces in the selective incorporation of religion into different areas of life through fear that a sundering of the centuries-old unity among ethnic origin, nationality and religion in Judaism might undermine the legitimacy of Zionism and Israel. It also fears that the religious minority might disrupt the system if any large-scale change in the status of religion in the public domain is attempted. On both sides there are large majorities who are resigned to the religious status quo alongside militant minorities who are prepared to resort to a confrontation.

Against the backdrop of the internal Jewish divisions, the Arab–Jewish division looks the most problematic and fits 'the exclusionary domination model'. The initial intergroup contact took the form of animosity between European settlers and traditional natives. Later on it turned into a violent clash between two separatist national movements which fought for the same territory in a colonial system. In the aftermath of the Jewish victory in 1948, a small segment of the vanquished Palestinian people stayed on. Since then, the Arabs have had to put up with the status of an involuntary minority, and the Jews, inspired by their separatist Zionist ideology, have had to be resigned to the status of an involuntary majority.

The Arabs are a separate-but-unequal minority in Israeli society. Numerous institutional arrangements shore up their continued cultural distinctiveness and social separation. These are the law of separate religious communities which makes each group endogamous, the contiguous concentration of Arabs in three major geocultural regions, separate localities and neighbourhoods, separate schools and media, and the special Departments for Arab Affairs. The Arabs are granted full civil liberties and their right to a separate identity is honoured. Yet they are incapacitated by institutionalized inequalities. Israel's majority and institutions are Jewish and the raison d'être of the state. As such, the state is identified with its majority group, and members of the Arab minority as well as many Jews feel that the Arabs are outsiders. Regarded as a security risk, the Arabs as a whole are exempted from compulsory military service, denied free access to white-collar jobs in the civil service and other branches of the national economy, and deprived of control of their separate institutions. They are, further, handicapped by underdevelopment like other Third World groups in Western societies.

The exclusionary domination pattern of Arab–Jewish relations has recently been whittling away the cumulative transformations and strains in the Arab sector. The Arabs have increasingly become bilingual and bicultural. Their standard of living has risen appreciably. A sizeable middle class and a small elite have emerged. Palestinian nationalism has gained rather wide acceptance. In consequence, the Arabs are losing more and more patience with the irreconcilable contradictions between the democratic pluralism to which Israel is committed and the reality of an institutionalized inferior status. Their economic dependence and political subordination to the Jews have been diminishing. Therefore, unrest is in the offing.

The similarities and differences among the above three pluralistic divisions are marked. With some simplifications, the following points should be clear. The Orientals are poor immigrants, the religious Jews are internally differentiated members and the Israeli Arabs are defeated enemies. The Orientals are a nondominant majority, whereas the religious Jews and Israeli Arabs are nondominant minorities. The religious Jews are strengthened by a dominant, politically sophisticated section of Europeans, whereas the Orientals and Israeli Arabs are not. The Orientals are an assimilating group, whereas the religious Jews and Israeli Arabs are permanent nonassimilating groups. The Orientals have a right to neither a separate identity nor a cultural autonomy, the Israeli Arabs have a right to a separate identity but not cultural autonomy, and religious Jews have both. The Orientals are not-separate-but-unequal, the religious Jews are separate-but-equal, and the Israeli Arabs are separate-but-unequal.

The Orientals do not yet question the legitimacy of the Israeli social structure, whereas the religious Jews reject in principle the legitimacy of a secular Jewish state, and the Israeli Arabs deny Israel's right to exist as a Jewish-Zionist state. The Orientals present no ideological dilemma for Israeli society, whereas the religious Jews and Israeli Arabs do. The Orientals do pose a formidable practical problem of ethnic inequality; the religious Jews, a grave ideological and practical problem with regard to religious–nonreligious pluralism; and the Israeli Arabs, an unsurmountable ideological and practical problem concerning Arab–Jewish pluralism and inequality.

The Israeli Arabs are not essential to Israeli society, whereas the Orientals and religious Jews are. Within the crucial context of the Arab–Israeli conflict, the Orientals and religious Jews are assets and

263

allies, whereas the Israeli Arabs are liabilities and perhaps expendable. The religious Jews muster the power to disrupt the system, whereas the Orientals and Israeli Arabs in the meantime do not. The Orientals and religious Jews are integrated into the broader society voluntarily, whereas Israeli Arabs are integrated involuntarily. Israeli political democracy is a reconciliatory 'consociational democracy' for the religious Jews, a restricted democracy for the Orientals and a failing '*Herrenvolk* democracy' for the Israeli Arabs. That is, it is most serviceable to the strong religious group, it is less beneficial to the Orientals because of paternalism and co-optation, and it is least helpful to the Israeli Arabs who are victimized by democracy's weakest point – 'the tyranny of the majority'. All in all, the religious Jews get the best deal in Israeli society, the Israeli Arabs the worst and the Orientals something in between.

This partial listing of focused points of comparisons among Oriental–Ashkenazi relations, religious–nonreligious relations and Arab–Jewish relations makes evident the sensitivity of the theoretical perspective of structural pluralism to intergroup relations in complex societies. The utility of our pluralist analysis throughout this book can be further and better assessed relative to the contributions of the existing nation-building and colonial perspectives on Israel.

The nation-building perspective, which is dominant in the social scientific literature on Israel, views Israel as a successful new nation-state. It is a society which has already overcome its major difficulties of institution-building, consensus-formation, collective identity and social solidarity. Pluralism and conflict are not cardinal, the basic needs of the constituent groups are satisfied, and there is no real menace to national integration. The future has in store consolidation of the current processes and amelioration of certain structures.

On the other hand, the rival colonial perspective, which is prevalent in leftist critiques of Israel, conceives of Israel as a vicious, artificial entity. It is a white settler society, created by the displacement of the indigenous Palestinian people, and maintained by the support of the Western superpowers. The inherently racist Zionist state is ruled by a minority of Ashkenazim who mystify their exploitative control over the Oriental Jews and Arabs through exclusionary Jewish nationalism and clericalism. Growing internal pressures will finally force Israel to follow the right lead of decolonization, de-Zionization and de-Judaization.

The alternative pluralist perspective rejects both these points of view. It regards Israel as a pluralistic state, neither a nation-state nor a neocolonial state. It recognizes the centrality of genuine pluralism and pluralism-based conflict, which both perspectives deny. The pluralist perspective agrees with the nation-building perspective that nation-building, modernization and democracy are far advanced

264

in Israeli society, but they have so far failed to reduce the pluralistic–inequality structure significantly. It concurs with the colonial perspective that the potentiality for conflict in Israel is great indeed, but at the same time it observes strong cohesive forces which prevent turmoil and it predicts more continuity than change for the future as long as these forces endure. The pluralist perspective avoids the sweeping generalizations in the other two perspectives by studying in detail how the situation varies a great deal from one pluralistic division to another.

This study will serve its purpose if it draws a more balanced, realistic and convincing picture of Israeli society than the views in existence today. Hopefully, it would add to the dozen or so studies of complex societies which have demonstrated the greater explanatory power of the structural pluralist perspective compared with other approaches. The cumulation of such theoretically grounded research is paving the way for the emergence of a theory of pluralistic divisions and societies.

A more valid analysis would also call attention to Israel's neglected pluralistic–inequality structure. The founders of Israel have sought to make the state as homogeneous and egalitarian as possible. They have dreamed of a society composed of Jews, Jewish in its institutions, where ascriptive distinctions of ethnicity, religious observance and gender make no difference, and democratic freedoms apply to all citizens. This unpluralistic vision has for a long time sustained the ostrich-like denial of the pluralistic reality. The time is overdue for Israel to come to grips with its structural pluralism, intergroup inequality and conflict and to do justice to its disadvantaged groups. Israel's most cherished political stability and national cohesion are in danger unless firm measures are taken to redress structural inequities.

Table appendix

Introductory comments on the tables

An effort has been made to assemble in this Appendix anything of importance available on Oriental–Ashkenazi, religious–nonreligious and Arab–Jewish divisions in Israeli society. Because of space limitations, material from opinion polls has been left out (but reported in the text); thus only firm or behavioural data are tabulated. Most tables (72 out of the 84, i.e., Tables 8 to 79) concern the Oriental–Ashkenazi division – which reflects the scarcity of information on the other two divisions. They are further restricted mainly to Oriental–Ashkenazi inequality because of the paucity of factual knowledge on Oriental–Ashkenazi pluralism. For this reason all tables refer to the Oriental–Ashkenazi division, unless the title indicates otherwise.

The tables fall into four categories: the pluralistic divisions scheme and its application; population and immigration; Oriental–Ashkenazi inequality (socioeconomic gaps and power disparities) and other information.

The pluralistic divisions scheme and its application (Tables 1–6)

This group of tables presents the conceptual scheme to the study of pluralistic divisions and its application to three major divisions in Israel. Table 1 furnishes a list of indicators, measures and overall features needed for empirical investigation of pluralistic divisions. Tables 2–6 provide an overview of Israel's pluralistic structure.

A five-point scale is used as a rough scoring guide (0 = low, 1 = below average, 2 = average, 3 = above average, and 4 = high). Scores are impressionistically assigned to each indicator and then are aggregated to arrive at summary measures. The use of scores (more precisely, ranks) is not intended to create a false sense of precision but to stress the multidimensional and continuous nature of pluralistic divisions and to sharpen comparisons.

Population and immigration (Tables 7–9)

These tables contain figures on the demographic ratios of the three pluralistic divisions and details on historical trends in population size and immigration of Orientals and Ashkenazim.

Oriental–Ashkenazi inequality (Tables 10–73)

Socioeconomic gaps (10–33)

The tables in this section are chiefly taken from official publications of Israel's Central Bureau of Statistics. The CBS is among the few in the world (the United States Bureau of Census is another notable agency) which continuously collects and publishes reliable, systematic and sociologically relevant statistics on ethnic groups.

The official statistics distinguish between people born in Asia or Africa and those born in Europe or America, and sometimes in recent years also between Israeli-born, according to the continent of birth of the father. Such distinction is a rough approximation of the Oriental–Ashkenazi division.

In order to simplify and standardize comparisons, two indexes of equality are used: relative and absolute. If A = the Oriental statistic, and B = the Ashkenazi statistic, then:

$$\text{relative index of equality} = \frac{A}{B} \times 100$$
$$\text{absolute index of equality} = A - B$$

Mathematically, the relative index is a ratio, whereas the absolute index is a difference. For example, Oriental average income as a percentage of Ashkenazi average income is a relative index of equality, and the difference in Israeli pounds between the average income of the two ethnic groups is an absolute index.

Most of the reported indexes of equality are 'gross', but they are occasionally 'adjusted' when computed from data on comparable groups (e.g., income discrepancy between Orientals and Ashkenazim of the same educational level).

The relative and absolute indexes apparently measure different aspects of equality, which are difficult to pinpoint. Their statistical properties are little known. They often disagree, yet there is no methodological rationale to choose between them.

Oriental–Ashkenazi power disparities (34–72)

There is little material on Oriental–Ashkenazi power disparities. To fill the gap in knowledge, a field study was conducted. Because of its centrality and relative accessibility to research, political power was taken as the main focus, but some information on other spheres of power was also gathered.

To determine the weight of Orientals in a certain political office, a complete roster of current and former occupants of that office was secured. The roster was presented to at least two knowledgeable authorities or political leaders for independent identification of ethnic origin. Panellists had little difficulty or disagreement in identifying the names. To identify 'obscure names', a larger network of informants was consulted, personal files were examined if possible and extra steps were taken to complete the record. As a result, the common category of 'unknown' was eliminated. The reliability of data is believed to be reasonably high, although minor errors probably still exist.

The use of the dichotomy 'Oriental–Ashkenazi' instead of the specific place of birth facilitated the identification of officeholders and added to its reliability. Considered as Orientals are not only people born in Asia and Africa (except South Africa), but also the Israeli-born of non-Ashkenazi origin, Jews from Bulgaria, Greece and Soviet Georgia, and some Sephardic Jews from Italy, Latin America and elsewhere. This definition corresponds to the broader term 'Oriental' as it is used throughout our study and which best fits ethnic politics.

Political representation is reported by absolute numbers of Oriental and Ashkenazi officeholders and by the index '% Orientals'. This index is the percentage of Orientals in the total number of people holding a position at a given time.

In Table 73 an attempt is made to compare the magnitude of Oriental–Ashkenazi inequality across various status hierarchies (income, occupation, education and political power). Each status is divided into three in such a way that the top category in all statuses compared approaches equality in size, and so do the middle and lower categories. This tentative technique suggests clues as to the degree and type of status incongruity of the ethnic group as a whole.

Other information (Tables 74–84)

In this section, several tables on cultural diversity and social separation between Orientals and Ashkenazim are presented. In addition, some tables sum up data on the political strength of the religious parties, and others condense what is available on differences in demographic characteristics, socioeconomic gaps and power disparities between Israeli Arabs and Jews.

TABLE 1 *A conceptual scheme for the study of pluralistic divisions*

1 Setting

  1.1 Historical background (origins, developments and patterns of the pluralistic divisions up to the period under study)

  1.2 Current social contexts

    1.21 Primary bases of pluralistic divisions (nature of initial group contact, definition of group membership, relative size of nondominant groups)

    1.22 Congruity of group goals

    1.23 Undercurrents (unofficial attitudes and policies of the dominant group)

    1.24 Interdependence

    1.25 Multiple riffts (implications of the existence of more than one pluralistic division)

    1.26 Relevant features of society at large (cultural–historical or economic–political type of society, etc.)

2 Pluralism

  2.1 Cultural diversity

    2.11 Objective cultural differences (core-culture, sub culture)

    2.12 Subjective cultural differences (perceived size and expected durability of cultural diversity, self-identity)

  2.2 Social separation

    2.21 Legal and extra-legal distinctions

    2.22 Isolation in ecological location

    2.23 Isolation in impersonal frameworks

    2.24 Isolation in personal contacts

    2.25 Mobilization of the nondominant group

Summary measures: Magnitude, inconsistency and durability.

TABLE 1—*continued*

---

3 Inequality

  3.1 Socioeconomic gaps
    3.11 Gaps in material wellbeing
    3.12 Gaps in occupational distribution
    3.13 Gaps in education
  3.2 Power disparities
    3.21 Disparities in economic power
    3.22 Disparities in political power
    3.23 Disparities in parapolitical power
  Summary measures: Magnitude, inconsistency and durability.

4 Cohesion

  4.1 Patterns of conflict
    4.11 Failures of group goals
    4.12 Invidious distinctions (institutional invidious distinctions, prejudice, discrimination)
    4.13 Dissatisfactions (psychological and political alienation, status dissatisfaction, deviance, militant views)
    4.14 Protests and countermeasures ('legitimate' and illegitimate means)
  4.2 Bases of integration
    4.21 Value consensus
    4.22 Cross-cutting affiliations
    4.23 Elite accommodation
    4.24 Economic interdependence
    4.25 Political coercion
    4.26 External factors
  Summary measures: Strength, voluntariness and stability.
  Cohesive models: consensus, consociational and control.

5 Change

  5.1 Past trends (continuities and transformations in intergroup relations)
  5.2 Future developments
  Summary measures: Direction, scope and mode.

TABLE 2 Current social contexts by major division[a]

Context	Oriental–Ashkenazi	Religious–nonreligious	Arab–Jewish
1.21 Primary bases			
1.211 Initial group contact	Immigration (poor immigrants or refugees from Near Eastern underdeveloped countries came in contact with mostly established European group)	Secularization (a minority of religious Jews came in contact with a majority of secularized or nonreligious Jews)	Conquest (Arabs who remained in areas conquered by the Jews became a minority in the new Jewish state)
1.212 Definition of group membership	Ethnic origin; visibility; possible, mild passing	Lifestyle or affiliation with the religious sector (via schools and parties); visibility; easy, quick and frequent passing	Ethnic quasi-caste (based on religion–nationality); visibility; possible but difficult, and rare passing
1.213 Relative size of nondominant group	Majority	Minority	Minority
1.22 Congruity of group goals	Reciprocal goals (full equality and mutual assimilation on the official level)	Moderately incongruous goals (agreement on the idea of Jewish state and disagreement on the role of religion in public life)	Fairly high incongruous goals (agreement on separate identity of Arabs and disagreement on cultural autonomy and status of national minority for Arabs and disagreement on fundamental issue of Israel's right to exist and to keep its Zionist character and Jewish majority)

TABLE 2—continued

Context	Oriental–Ashkenazi	Religious–nonreligious	Arab–Jewish
1.23 Undercurrents (unofficial attitudes of dominant group)	Paternalism, co-optation	Preservation of the status quo in religious matters	Exclusion (expulsion of Arabs), continued domination
1.24 Interdependence	Considerable, but somewhat asymmetric	Considerable	Some, appreciable dispensability of Arab minority despite its services to Jewish majority
1.25 Multiple rifts	Other cleavages cross-cut and weaken division	Other cleavages cross-cut and weaken division	Other cleavages consolidate and strengthen division
1.26 Relevant features of society at large			
1.261 A Jewish–Zionist state	A base of integration	Both a base of integration and a central issue	The most critical issue and main source of Arab alienation
1.262 Western state	Perpetuates pre-existing and present differences and inequalities	May disrupt status quo by growing modernization and emulation of the model of separation between religion and state	Institutionalizes pre-existing and present differences and inequalities

1.263 Democracy and centralization of power	Turns subordinates into a potential pressure group and makes possible a large-scale solution of the problem	Facilitates peaceful settlement of disputes	Provides protection for minority but keeps it in place ('tyranny of the majority')
1.264 Sustained and marked growth	Supplies ample opportunities for upward mobility for all, with non-zero sum allocation of rewards	May disrupt status quo by drifting towards secularization as a result of social mobility	Furnishes improvement in living conditions for all, but heightens expectations beyond possibilities
1.265 External threat	Serves as a unifying force, but 'freezes' ethnic problem	Serves as a unifying force, but prevents basic and permanent solution of controversial issues	Serves as a divisive force and provides prima facie legitimacy for continued domination (fear of a fifth column)
1.266 Political development of dominant group	Promotes legitimacy of power and helps to find pragmatic solutions for ethnic problem	Facilitates avoidance of intense conflict by innovative search for 'endless' compromises	Reinforces domination by increasing the minority compliance through manipulation of rewards

a This table corresponds to part 1.2 (Current social contexts) in Table 1.

273

TABLE 3 *Estimates of indicators of pluralism and inequality by major division*[a]

Dimension	Indicator	Oriental–Ashkenazi	Religious–nonreligious	Arab–Jewish
2 Pluralism	2.1 Cultural diversity			
	2.11 Objective cultural differences			
	2.111 Core-culture			
	2.1111 Language	0	0	4
	2.1112 Nationality	0	0	4
	2.1113 Religion	0	0	4
	2.1114 Family structure	0	0	3
	2.1115 Basic ideology	0	2	4
	2.112 Subculture			
	2.1121 Language background and habits	1	0	2
	2.1122 Nationalist consciousness	1	1	4
	2.1123 Religious style and observance	1	3	1
	2.1124 Family life (number of children, age and sex differentiation, familial values)	2	2	3
	2.1125 Other sub-cultural variations (consumption habits, dress, folklore, public attitudes, personality traits)	2	2	3
	2.12 Subjective cultural differences			
	2.121 Public perception of size of cultural diversity	2	2	4
	2.122 Public perception of durability of cultural diversity	1	3	4
	2.123 Self-identity	2	2	4
	2.2 Social separation			
	2.21 Legal and extra-legal distinctions			
	2.211 Legal distinctions	1	2	3
	2.212 Extra-legal distinctions	1	1	3

2.22 Isolation in ecological location			
2.221 On territorial–regional level	0	0	3
2.222 On community level	1	1	4
2.223 On residential level	2	1	4
2.23 Isolation in impersonal frameworks			
2.231 Economy	0	0	1
2.232 Public facilities	0	0	0
2.233 Bureaucracies (state, local government, Histadrut)	0	0	3
2.234 Armed forces	0	0	4
2.235 Schools	2	3	4
2.236 Political parties (membership and voting)	1	3	3
2.237 Other voluntary associations	2	2	4
2.24 Isolation in personal contacts			
2.241 Neighbourliness	2	2	4
2.242 Friendship	2	2	4
2.243 Marriage	2	2	4
2.25 Mobilization of the nondominant group	1	3	2
3 Inequality 3.1 Socioeconomic gaps			
3.11 Gaps in material wellbeing	2	1	3
3.12 Gaps in occupational distribution	2	1	3
3.13 Gaps in education	3	1	4
3.2 Power disparities			
3.21 Disparities in economic power	3	1	3
3.22 Disparities in political power	3	0	4
3.23 Disparities in parapolitical power	2	0	3

a This table corresponds to parts 2 and 3 in Table 1 (Pluralism and Inequality). A 5-point scale is used: 0 = low, 1 = below average, 2 = average, 3 = above average, 4 = high.

275

TABLE 4 Estimates of features of pluralism and inequality by major division[a]

Feature	Oriental–Ashkenazi	Religious–nonreligious	Arab–Jewish
a Magnitude			
Pluralism—overall	2 (intermediate)	2 (intermediate)	4 (very substantial)
Cultural diversity	2 (intermediate)	2 (intermediate)	3 (substantial)
Social separation	2 (intermediate)	3 (substantial)	4 (very substantial)
Inequality—overall	3 (substantial)	0 (very minor)	4 (very substantial)
Socioeconomic gaps	2 (intermediate)	1 (minor)	3 (substantial)
Power disparities	3 (substantial)	0 (very minor)	4 (very substantial)
b Inconsistency			
Within pluralism (between cultural diversity and social separation)	1 (consistent)	0 (very consistent)	0 (very consistent)
Within inequality (between socioeconomic gaps and power disparities)	3 (inconsistent)	0 (very consistent)	1 (consistent)
Between pluralism and inequality	3 (inconsistent)	0 (very consistent)	1 (consistent)
c Durability			
Pluralism—overall	2 (partly transitory, partly stable)	3 (stable)	3 (stable)
Inequality—overall	3 (stable)	3 (stable)	3 (stable)

a This table corresponds to the summary measures in parts 2 and 3 in Table 1. A 5-point scale is used: 0 = low, 1 = below average, 2 = average, 3 = above average, 4 = high.

TABLE 5 Estimates of indicators and features of cohesion by major division[a]

Dimension	Indicator	Oriental–Ashkenazi	Religious–nonreligious	Arab–Jewish
4.1 Patterns of conflict				
	4.11 Failures of group goals			
	4.111 Failures of short-range group goals	3	0	2
	4.112 Failures of long-range group goals	2	3	4
	4.12 Invidious distinctions			
	4.121 Institutional invidious distinctions (prejudice and discrimination)	2	0	3
	4.122 Prejudice	2	1	3
	4.123 Discrimination	2	0	3
	4.13 Dissatisfactions			
	4.131 Alienation	1	1	3
	4.132 Status dissatisfaction	1	0	2
	4.133 Deviance	2	0	2
	4.134 Militant views	1	2	3
	4.14 Protests and countermeasures			
	4.141 'Legitimate' means	1	2	2
	4.142 'Illegitimate' means	0	2	2
4.2 Bases of integration				
	4.21 Value consensus			
	4.211 Range of agreement	3	2	1
	4.212 Inclusiveness of culture and identity	1	2	0
	4.213 Spread of personal and institutional biculturalism	2	2	1
	4.214 Implications of some specific value orientations	3	1	0

TABLE 5—*continued*

Dimension	Indicator	Oriental–Ashkenazi	Religious–nonreligious	Arab–Jewish
	4.22 Cross-cutting affiliations			
	4.221 Range of cross-cutting affiliations	2	1	0
	4.222 Spread of broker institutions	3	2	1
	4.223 Prevalence of separation in areas of disagreement	1	3	3
	4.224 Immobility of nondominant group	3	0	2
	4.23 Elite accommodation			
	4.231 Nondominant elite's absorption into the dominant power structure	3	2	0
	4.232 Nondominant elite's control of nondominant group institutions	0	4	1
	4.24 Economic interdependence			
	4.241 Nondominant groups' indispensability to the national economy	4	4	1
	4.242 Nondominant groups' unilateral economic dependence	2	1	4
	4.25 Political coercion	0	0	3
	4.26 External factors (implications of extra-societal relations)	4	4	0
Cohesion	Strength	3	1	1
	Voluntariness	2	2	0
	Stability	3	3	1
	Model	Mixed	Consociational	Control

278

[a] This table corresponds to part 4 in Table 1 ('Cohesion'). A 5-point scale is used: 0 = low, 1 = below average, 2 = average, 3 = above average, 4 = high. Since higher scores are assigned to greater conflict and greater integration, the two sets of scores tend

TABLE 6 *Features of change by major division*[a]

Feature	Oriental–Ashkenazi	Religious–nonreligious	Arab–Jewish
a Direction			
Intergroup pattern	Weakening of the dynamic paternalism-co-optation pattern; increase in the internal contradictions within the Oriental status; shift from ethnicity to class	Continuation of the contested accommodation pattern; increase in religious minority's self-confidence, cultural autonomy and involvement in broader social issues	Weakening of the exclusionary domination pattern; increase in the Arab minority's independence and willingness to challenge the status quo
Pluralism	Decreased to a moderate degree	Increased to some extent	Decreased to some extent
Inequality	Decreased to a limited degree	Remained minor	Decreased to some extent
Cohesion	Increased to some extent	Unchanged	Decreased to a moderate degree
b Scope	Partial; more continuity than change	Minor; more continuity than change	Partial; more continuity than change
c Mode	Nonviolent; gradual (rapid in pluralism, slow in inequality)	Nonviolent; piecemeal	Nonviolent; gradual

[a] This table corresponds to part 5 in Table 1 (Change).

TABLE 7 *Estimates of relative size of pluralistic divisions, 1975*

Division	Numbers	Percentage
Total[1]	4,605,400	100
Non-Jews (Palestinians and Israeli Arabs)	1,646,000	36
Jews	2,959,400	64
Palestinians[a]	1,204,200	29
Jews	2,959,400	71
Israeli Arabs[b]	441,800	13
Jews	2,959,400	87
Israeli Arabs[c]		
Moslems	335,800	76
Christians	66,300	15
Druzes	39,700	9
Jews		
religious[2]	887,800	30
nonreligious	2,071,800	70
Jews		
Orientals[d]	1,627,700	55
Ashkenazim	1,331,700	45

[a] Arabs in Gaza strip and North Sinai, West Bank of Jordan, Golan Heights and East Jerusalem who were placed under Israeli occupation after the Six-Day War in 1967.

[b] Excluding about 92,000 Arab residents in East Jerusalem.

[c] This estimate excludes Arabs in East Jerusalem and thus gives greater weight to non-Moslems among Israeli Arabs because they are underestimated in the official statistics which include East Jerusalem.

[d] Including 'Sephardim' and Israeli-born Jews of Oriental–Sephardic parentage.

Sources: 1 CBS, *Statistical Abstract of Israel*, 1976, 27: 19, 43, 687.

2 Based on self-identification in a 1962 nation-wide public opinion survey (Antonovsky, 1963). The reported figure of 30 per cent religious Jews corresponds to 29 per cent found in a nation-wide survey of the urban population taken in February–April 1968 and to 31 per cent in another survey in February–April 1973 (*Current Surveys*, nos. 1 and 16, Jerusalem: Israel Institute of Applied Social Research and Hebrew University Institute of Communications) and to 29.3 per cent of the Jewish children attending religious schools in 1974–5 (CBS, *Statistical Abstract of Israel*, 1975, 26: 612).

TABLE 8 *Estimates of Orientals and Sephardim in World and Israel (Palestine) Jewries, 1500–1975*

	World Jewry		Israel (Palestine) Jewry	
Year	Total	Thereof: % Orientals and Sephardim	Total	Thereof: % Orientals and Sephardim
1500	1,500,000	67	5,000	80
1800	2,500,000	40	8,000	60
1882			24,000	60
1895	10,500,000	10	47,000	40
1914	13,000,000	8	85,000	30
1930	15,900,000	8	174,000	27
1936	16,500,000	9	355,000	23
1947	11,300,000	12	630,000	23
1952	11,600,000	13	1,629,500	40
1957	12,035,000	14	1,763,000	48
1963	13,121,000	15	2,155,000	50
1975	14,145,000	17	2,954,000	55

Sources: CBS, *Statistical Abstract of Israel*, 1–27; *American Jewish Year Book; Encyclopedia of Social Sciences* (in Hebrew), 2: 665; *Megamot*, 10 (4), March 1960: 367; Tartakower (1959: 30); Raphael Patai (ed.) (1971f: 79 (Table 1)).

TABLE 9 *Jewish immigration to Palestine and Israel, 1882–1975*[a]

Wave of immigration		Total	Thereof: Orientals and Sephardim Numbers	Percentage
First Aliyah	1882–1903	25,000	1,000	4
Second Aliyah	1904–14	40,000	2,000	5
Third Aliyah	1919–23	35,000	2,400	7
Fourth Aliyah	1924–31	82,000	9,800	12
Fifth Aliyah	1932–48	265,000	36,200	10
Post-state Aliyah	1948–75	1,570,000	751,000	48
	1948–51	687,000	331,000	50
	1952–4	54,000	41,000	76
	1955–7	165,000	112,000	68
	1958–60	75,000	27,000	36
	1961–4	228,000	137,000	60
	1965–8	81,000	44,000	54
	1969–75	279,000	59,000	21

[a] Estimates include immigrants and tourists settling; totals include people whose ethnic origin is not known; in the pre-state period, Orientals and Sephardim include Jews from Bulgaria and Greece; afterwards, Jews from Asia and Africa only.

Sources: Hayim Barlas, 'Immigration to Palestine and Israel', in Raphael Patai (ed.), *Encyclopedia of Zionism and Israel*, p. 538 (Table 8); CBS, *Statistical Abstract of Israel*, 1976, 27: 125.

281

TABLE 10 *Monthly family income (in current Israeli pounds), 1956-7 to 1975*

	1956-7[1]	1957-8[2]	1963-4[2]	1963-4[3]	1965[4]	1966[4]	1967[4]	1968[4]	1969[4]	1970[4]	1971[4]	1972[4]	1973[4]	1974[4]	1975[4]
Asia–Africa	219	172	402	477	517	567	558	642	692	808	893	1,067	1,192	1,717	2,292
Europe–America	300	304	640	671	717	825	925	908	1,000	1,100	1,200	1,433	1,608	2,217	2,783
Index of equality															
relative	73	57	63	71	72	69	60	71	69	73	74	74	74	77	82
absolute	−81	−132	−238	−194	−200	−258	−367	−266	−308	−292	−307	−366	−416	−500	−491

Sources: 1 CBS, *Family Expenditure Surveys, 1956-7* and *1959-60*, Special Series 148, pp. cxxiv–cxxv.
  2 CBS, *Saving Survey, 1963-4*, Special Series 217 p. xxix (Table 5).
  3 CBS, *Family Expenditure Survey, 1963-4*, Special Series 200.
  4 CBS, *Statistical Abstract of Israel*, 1971, 22: 182; 1973, 24: 271; 1976, 27: 261.

TABLE 11   *Monthly family income (in current Israeli pounds) by education, 1974*

	Total	Years of schooling				
		0	1–4	5–8	9–12	13+
Foreign-born						
Asia–Africa	1,717	1,375	1,475	1,567	1,858	2,558
Europe–America	2,217	a	1,292	1,775	2,200	2,842
Index of equality						
relative	77	a	114	88	84	90
absolute	−500	a	+183	−208	−342	−284
Israeli-born						
Asia–Africa	1,733	a	a	1,458	1,725	a
Europe–America	2,583	a	a	1,817	2,442	2,808
Index of equality						
relative	67	a	a	80	71	a
absolute	−850	a	a	−359	−717	a

a Since this category is infrequent, sample figures are not reliable.

Source: CBS, *Income of Employees' Families*, 1972–4, Special Series 510, Table 11.

283

TABLE 12   Relative index of equality of income by period of immigration, 1956–7 to 1975

	1956–7[1]	1959–60[1]	1963–4[2]	1965[3]	1966[3]	1967[3]	1968[3]	1969[3]	1970[3]	1971[3]	1972[3]	1973[3]	1974[3]	1975[3]
Immigrated														
up to 1947	73	74	69	75	68	68	73	70	75	74	82	76	67	79
1948–54	79	76	79	78	80	68	76	78	77	77	79	78	87	84
1955–60				80	74	63	72	65	78	76	80	71	81	87
1961+			74	74		78	72	73	81	77	69	79	80	85

Sources: 1 CBS, *Family Expenditure Surveys*, 1956–7 and 1959–60, Special Series 148, pp. 16 (Table 4) and 164 (Table 25).
2 CBS, *Family Expenditure Survey*, 1963–4, Special Series 200, Table 5.
3 CBS, *Statistical Abstract of Israel*, 1971, 22: 182; 1973, 24: 271; 1976, 27: 261.

TABLE 13 *Gross (G) and adjusted (A) index of relative equality of income by period of immigration, male wage-earners, 1957–8 to 1969*

	1957–8 Hanuch		Levy		1963–4 Klinov-Malul		Levy		1969 Peres	
	G	A	G	A	G	A	G	A	G	A
Total	64[1]	92[2]	63[3]	84[4]	73[5]	95[6]	68[3]	87[4]	70[9]	83[a]
Immigrated up to 1947	75[1]	97[2]			71[7]					
Immigrated 1948+	68[1]	77[2]								
Immigrated 1948–54					80[7]	98[8]			75[9]	
Immigrated 1955+					68[7]	91[8]				
Immigrated 1955–60									68[9]	
Immigrated 1961+									71[9]	
Israeli-born									58[9]	74[a]

a Adjusted for age, sex, employment status and education.

Sources: 1 Hanuch (1961: Tables 21 and 22).
2 Hanuch (1961: Table 22). Adjusted for age, sex, employment status, period of immigration and education.
3 Levy (1968: Table 17).
4 Levy (1968: 35 (text)). Adjusted for age, sex, employment status, period of immigration, education, and occupation.
5 CBS, *Family Expenditure Survey*, 1963–4, Special Series 200, p. 41.
6 Klinov-Malul (1969: 103 (text)). Adjusted for employment status, period of immigration and education.
7 Klinov-Malul (1969: Table 3).
8 Klinov-Malul (1969: Table 4).
9 Hana Peres, unpublished MA Thesis, New York: Columbia University, 1971.

TABLE 14 *Relative index of equality of income and consumption, 1959–60 to 1968–9*

	1959–60	1963–4	1968–9
Net per capita income	52	51	48
Per capita expenditure on consumption	63	57	52

Source: Family expenditure surveys, quoted by Raphael Roter in Public Inquiry Commission, Report of the Committee on Income Distribution and Social Inequality (duplicated), Tel-Aviv, 1971, p. 54.

TABLE 15 *Relative index of equality in per capita expenditure on consumption by period of immigration, 1956–7 to 1968–9*

	1956–7	1959–60	1963–4	1968–9
Immigrated up to 1947	60	59	59	60
Immigrated 1948–54			64	60
	55	57		
Immigrated 1955+			55	51

Sources: CBS, *Family Expenditure Survey*, Special Series 148, Table 25; 200, Table 5; 290, Table 6.

TABLE 16 *Improvement in per capita expenditure[a] on consumption, 1956–7 to 1968–9 (1956–7 = 100)*

	1956–7	1959–60	1963–4	1968–9
Asia–Africa	100	136	141	185
Europe–America	100	136	144	206

[a] Per capita expenditure is standardized in May 1956 prices so that the improvement trends indicate a real rise in standard of living.

Sources: as for Table 15.

TABLE 17 Percentages of families possessing durable goods and adequate housing, 1957–74

Commodity		1957				1974			
		Asia–Africa	Europe–America	Index of equality Relative	Absolute	Asia–Africa	Europe–America	Index of equality Relative	Absolute
Gas range	1958	14.0	48.9	29	−34.9	66.2	60.1	110	+6.1
Electric refrigerator	1958	8.2	51.4	16	−43.2	97.3	98.9	98	−1.6
Washing machine	1958	3.1	12.0	26	−8.9	69.2	57.1	121	+12.1
Television set	1965	1.9	2.5	76	−0.4	81.4	84.4	96	−3.0
Telephone	1969	12.4	45.7	27	−33.3	31.3	63.6	49	−32.3
Private car	1965	1.8	9.9	18	−8.1	15.2	31.2	49	−16.0
Adequate housing, total[a]						29.3	68.8	43	−39.5
Immigrated up to 1947[b]	1957	24.6	57.4	37	−42.8	56.5	87.9	64	−31.4
Immigrated after 1947[b]	1957	26.7	41.8	64	−15.1	49.4	83.4	59	−34.0

a Defined as density of 1 or fewer persons per room.
b Defined as density fewer than 2 persons per room; 1969 instead of 1974.

Source: CBS, Statistical Abstract of Israel, 1975, 26: 273; 277–8; 1970, 21: 181; 1961, 12: 164.

TABLE 18 Percentages of families possessing durable goods and adequate housing by period of immigration, 1958–74

| | Immigrated up to 1947 | | | | | | | Immigrated since 1948 | | | | | | |
| | 1958 | | Index of equality | | 1974 | | Index of equality | | 1958 | | Index of equality | | 1974 | | Index of equality |
Commodity	Asia–Africa	Eur.–Amer.	Rel.	Abs.	Asia–Africa	Eur.–Amer.	Rel.	Abs.	Asia–Africa	Eur.–Amer.	Rel.	Abs.	Asia–Africa	Eur.–Amer.	Rel.	Abs.
Gas range	31.0	60.9	51	−29.9	68.1	62.2	109	+5.9	10.2	37.0	28	−26.8	66.0	59.2	111	+6.8
Electric refrigerator	21.8	68.2	32	−46.4	97.9	99.3	99	−1.4	5.2	34.7	15	−29.5	97.3	98.9	98	−1.6
Washing machine	(7.7)[a]	15.9	48	−8.2	65.3	58.4	112	+6.9	(2.1)[a]	8.2	26	−6.1	69.5	56.5	123	+13.0
Television set					81.3	86.3	94	−5.0					81.4	83.5	97	−2.1
Telephone					48.2	80.3	60	−32.1					29.5	55.3	53	−25.8
Private car					18.6	36.0	52	−17.4					14.9	28.8	52	−13.9
Adequate housing[b]	24.6	67.4	37	−42.8	56.5	87.9	64	−31.4	26.7	41.8	64	−15.1	49.4	83.4	59	−34.0

[a] Based on small samples and may be unreliable.
[b] Defined as density fewer than 2 persons per room; for 1957 and 1969.

Source: CBS, Statistical Abstract of Israel, 1975, 26: 277–8; 1970, 21: 181; 1961, 12: 164.

TABLE 19   *Gross income per standard equivalent adult by quintile, urban wage-earners, 1968–9*

	Total	Lowest quintile	Second quintile	Third quintile	Fourth quintile	Highest quintile
Asia–Africa	100.0	30.1	27.8	19.8	14.3	8.0
Europe–America	100.0	11.9	11.7	19.9	24.4	32.1
Index of equality						
relative		253	238	100	59	25
absolute		+11.8	+16.1	−0.1	−10.1	−24.1

Source: Public Inquiry Commission, Report of the Committee on Income Distribution and Social Inequality (duplicated), Tel-Aviv, 1971, p. 25.

TABLE 20 *Percentage distribution of occupations by place of birth, 1975*

	Israeli-born				Foreign-born			
			Index of equality				Index of equality	
Occupation	Asia–Africa	Europe–America	Rel.	Abs.	Asia–Africa	Europe–America	Rel.	Abs.
Total	100.0	100.0			100.0	100.0		
Scientific and academic workers	2.0	13.0	15	−11.0	2.1	10.3	20	−8.2
Other professional, technical and related workers	9.4	24.4	39	−15.0	7.6	13.4	57	−5.8
Administrators and managers	1.1	4.7	23	−3.6	1.9	4.7	40	−2.8
Clerical and related workers	22.2	24.2	92	+2.0	13.7	18.8	73	−5.1
Sales workers	5.3	4.9	108	+0.4	7.8	10.5	74	−2.7
Service workers	11.5	6.2	185	+5.3	19.8	8.9	222	+10.9
Skilled workers in industry, building, transport, etc.	36.8	16.0	230	+20.8	33.1	24.6	135	+8.5
Other workers in industry, transport, building, etc.	5.7	1.5	380	+4.2	8.9	4.3	207	+4.6
Agricultural workers	4.0	7.1	56	−3.1	5.0	4.5	111	+0.5

Source: CBS, *Statistical Abstract of Israel,* 1976, 27: 314–15.

TABLE 21 *Percentage distribution of occupations, 1954–75*

	Total	Professionals, scientific, technical	Admin., executive, managerial	Traders, agents, salesmen	Service, sports and recreation	Transport and communications workers	Construction, crafts and prod. workers	Farmers, fishermen
1954[1]								
Asia–Africa	100.0	3.4	7.3	9.1	11.9	2.4	43.2	22.6
Europe–America	100.0	12.5	18.7	11.7	7.5	4.2	35.2	10.2
Index of equality								
relative		27	39	78	159	57	123	222
absolute		−9.1	−11.4	−2.6	+4.4	−1.8	+8.0	+12.4
1959[2]								
Asia–Africa	100.0	4.5	7.0	6.5	16.3	3.3	40.0	22.4
Europe–America	100.0	13.5	17.6	11.6	12.4	4.5	31.4	9.0
Index of equality								
relative		33	40	56	131	73	127	249
absolute		−9.0	−10.6	−5.1	+3.9	−1.2	+8.6	+13.4
1964[3]								
Asia–Africa	100.0	5.1	9.2	6.9	16.6	3.9	43.9	14.4
Europe–America	100.0	15.5	21.2	11.5	11.3	4.8	28.6	7.1
Index of equality								
relative		33	43	60	147	81	153	203
absolute		−10.4	−12.0	−4.6	+5.3	−0.9	+15.3	+7.3

TABLE 21—continued

	Total	Professionals, scientific, technical	Admin., executive, managerial	Traders, agents, salesmen	Service, sports and recreation	Transport and communications workers	Construction, crafts and prod. workers	Farmers, fishermen
1968[4]								
Asia–Africa	100.0	6.1	11.0	8.0	18.0	5.2	39.9	11.8
Europe–America	100 0	16.3	21.4	12.1	11.1	4.6	28.2	6.3
Index of equality								
relative		37	51	66	162	113	141	187
absolute		−10.2	−10.4	−4.1	−6.9	+0.6	+11.7	+5.5
1973[5]								
Asia–Africa	100.0	8.5	13.5	7.3	18.6		44.9	7.2
Europe–America	100.0	21.5	23.5	10.7	9.9		29.8	4.6
Index of equality								
relative		40	57	68	188		151	157
absolute		−13.0	−10.0	3.4	+8.7		+15.1	+2.6
1975[6]								
Asia–Africa	100.0	9.7	15.6	7.8	19.8		42.0	5.0
Europe–America	100.0	23.7	23.5	10.5	8.9		28.9	4.5
Index of equality								
relative		41	66	74	222		145	111
absolute		−14.0	−7.9	−2.7	+10.5		+13.1	+0.5

Sources: 1 CBS, Labour Force Survey, Special Series 56, Table 24.
2 ibid, Special Series 162, Table 49.
3 ibid, Special Series 243, Table 42.
4 ibid., Special Series 305, Table 44.
5 CBS, Statistical Abstract of Israel, 1974, 25: 334–5.

TABLE 22   *Relative index of equality and index of dissimilarity of*
            occupational categories, 1954–75

	1954	1959	1964	1968	1973	1975
White collar[a]	46	42	44	50	53	57
Personal services	159	131	147	162	188	222
Blue collar[b]	116	121	143	138	151	145
Agriculture	222	249	203	187	157	111
Index of dissimilarity[c]	0.249	0.259	0.279	0.247	0.264	0.244

[a] Combination of professionals, scientific and technical workers,
administrative, executive and managerial workers, and traders, agents and
salesmen.
[b] Combination of construction, crafts and production workers, and transport
and communications workers.
[c] Index of dissimilarity is defined as $D_{ij} = 1/2 \sum_g /P_{ig} - P_{jg}/$

P_{ij} = Proportion of persons in group i employed in occupation g.
P_{ig} = Proportion of persons in group j employed in occupation g.
(Put differently, the index equals half the sum of the absolute differences
between ethnic groups in each occupation divided by 100.) The index ranges
from 0, when the two occupational distributions are identical, to 1, when they
are totally different. The indexes are computed from the percentage
distribution of occupations in Table 21.

Sources: as for Table 21.

TABLE 23 Percentage distribution of occupational categories by period of immigration, males, 1959–73

	1959				1964			
	White collar	Personal services	Blue collar	Agri-culture	White collar	Personal services	Blue collar	Agri-culture
Immigrated up to 1947								
Asia–Africa	31.9	13.2	45.1	9.8	34.8	10.7	39.4	5.1
Europe–America	46.6	6.7	38.9	7.8	52.9	6.1	35.1	5.9
Index of equality								
relative	68	197	116	126	66	174	112	87
absolute	−14.7	+6.5	+6.2	+2.0	−18.1	+4.6	+4.3	−0.8
Immigrated 1948–54[a]								
Asia–Africa	14.5	10.0	49.1	26.4	20.1	10.2	55.6	14.1
Europe–America	32.3	9.3	48.4	10.0	39.4	7.6	45.5	7.5
Index of equality								
relative	45	108	101	264	51	134	122	188
absolute	−17.8	+0.7	+0.7	+16.4	−19.3	+2.6	+10.1	+6.6
Immigrated 1955–60[b]								
Asia–Africa					13.8	10.2	55.1	20.9
Europe–America					37.4	(8.9)	43.8	(9.9)
Index of equality								
relative					37	115	126	211
absolute					−23.6	+1.3	+11.3	+11.0
Immigrated 1961 +[c]								
Asia–Africa								
Europe–America								
Index of equality								
relative								
absolute								
Israeli-born								
Asia–Africa								
Europe–America								

Asia–Africa	30.9	12.3	49.6	7.2	40.1	18.9	37.7	3.3
Europe–America	45.0	7.1	41.5	6.4	60.6	7.7	24.8	6.9
Index of equality								
relative	69	173	120	113	66	245	152	48
absolute	−14.1	+5.7	−8.1	+0.8	−20.5	+11.2	+12.9	−3.6
Immigrated 1948–54[a]								
Asia–Africa	23.6	11.7	52.6	12.1	29.4	19.1	43.6	7.9
Europe–America	40.0	8.3	45.9	5.8	53.9	10.1	32.3	3.7
Index of equality								
relative	59	141	115	209	55	189	135	214
absolute	−16.4	+3.4	+6.7	+6.3	−24.5	+9.0	+11.3	+4.2
Immigrated 1955–60[b]								
Asia–Africa	19.5	12.2	51.0	17.3	27.8	18.1	44.7	9.3
Europe–America	41.3	7.8	44.3	6.6	54.7	10.7	32.1	2.5
Index of equality								
relative	47	156	115	262	51	169	139	372
absolute	−21.8	+4.4	+6.7	+10.7	−26.9	+47.4	+12.6	+6.8
Immigrated 1961+[c]								
Asia–Africa	20.8	13.6	50.1	17.5	23.0	18.2	53.3	5.5
Europe–America	33.6	9.5	48.6	8.3	50.9	12.6	32.8	3.7
Index of equality								
relative	62	143	103	211	45	144	163	149
absolute	−12.8	+4.1	+1.5	+9.2	−27.9	+5.6	+20.5	+1.8
Israeli-born								
Asia–Africa					36.6	12.4	46.6	4.4
Europe–America					65.3	7.7	17.9	9.1
Index of equality								
relative					56	161	26	48
absolute					−28.7	+4.7	+28.7	−4.7

a This group is defined in 1959 as 'immigrated 1948+'.
b This group is defined as 'immigrated 1955+' in 1964.
c The last year for this group is 1972 instead of 1973.

Sources: CBS, Labour Force Surveys, Special Series 162, Table 49; ibid. Special Series 243, Table 42; ibid. Special Series 305, Table 44; CBS, Statistical Abstract of Israel, 1974, 25: 334–5.

TABLE 24   Chances to belong to top occupational categories[a] by ethnic origin, period of immigration and education males, 1961 and 1970

Years of schooling	Asia–Africa		Europe–America		Rel. index of equality	
	0–8	9+	0–8	9+	0–8	9+
1961 Census						
Immigrated before 1948	0.311	1.743	0.446	2.500	70	70
Immigrated in 1948 or later	0.150	0.839	0.215	1.204	70	70
Standardized figures for the 1961 Census[b]						
Immigrated before 1948	0.207	1.162	0.297	1.667	70	70
Immigrated in 1948 or later	0.100	0.559	0.143	0.803	70	70
1970 Labour Force Survey						
Immigrated before 1955	0.129	0.678	0.329	1.724	39	39
Immigrated in 1955 or later	0.088	0.461	0.224	1.172	39	39
1970 Labour Force Survey						
Immigrated before 1961	0.151	0.788	0.297	1.552	51	51
Immigrated in 1961 or later	0.090	0.471	0.177	0.927	51	51

a The higher the figure, the greater the chances. Chances are computed according to Leo A. Goodman's formula ('A general model for the analysis of surveys', *American Journal of Sociology*, 77 (6), May 1972: 1035–86).
b Figures are standardized in order to make the 1961 and 1970 data comparable, because overall chances declined during the decade.

Source: Hartman and Eilon (1975: Table 3).

TABLE 25 *Percentage distribution of education of people aged 14 or over, 1961 and 1975*

Years of schooling	1961				1975			
	Asia–Africa	Europe–America	Index of equality Rel.	Abs.	Asia–Africa	Europe–America	Index of equality Rel.	Abs.
0	31.5	3.2	984	+28.3	21.6	2.6	831	+19.0
1–4	10.1	7.6	133	+2.5	6.6	5.9	112	+0.7
5–8	36.2	37.9	96	−1.7	33.3	28.6	116	+4.7
9–12	19.2	38.5	50	−19.3	31.5	40.0	79	−8.5
13+	3.0	12.8	23	−8.8	7.0	22.9	31	−15.9
Median	5.4	8.6	64	−3.2	7.1	9.8	72	−2.7

Sources: CBS, *Population and Housing Census*, 1961, Languages, Literacy and Educational Attainment, no. 15, Table 28; CBS, *Statistical Abstract of Israel*, 1976, 27: 589.

TABLE 26 Percentage distribution of education of people aged 14 or over by period of immigration and sex, 1961 and 1969

Total (males and females)	1961						1969					
	0	1–4	5–8	9–12	13+	Median	0	1–4	5–8	9–12	13+	Median
Total												
Asia–Africa	31.5	10.1	36.2	19.2	3.0	5.9	25.5	8.9	37.2	24.1	4.3	6.7
Europe–America	3.2	7.6	37.9	38.5	12.8	9.1	2.7	9.0	33.3	38.8	16.2	9.5
Index of equality												
relative	984	133	96	50	23	65	944	99	112	62	27	71
absolute	+28.3	+2.5	−1.7	−19.3	−9.8	−3.2	+22.8	−0.1	+3.9	−14.7	−11.9	−2.8
Israeli-born												
Asia–Africa	4.2	4.4	52.3	34.6	4.5	8.2	1.6	1.6	41.0	51.4	4.4	9.5
Europe–America	0.6	0.7	14.5	64.5	19.7	10.1	0.4	0.2	10.0	64.6	24.8	11.4
Index of equality												
relative	700	629	361	54	23	81	400	800	410	80	18	83
absolute	+3.6	+3.7	+37.8	−29.9	−15.2	−1.9	+1.2	+1.4	+31.0	−13.2	−20.4	−1.9
Immigrated up to 1947												
Asia–Africa	30.0	9.0	37.1	19.9	4.0	5.2	27.7	8.5	37.3	19.6	6.9	6.5
Europe–America	2.3	3.0	33.3	45.4	16.0	10.0	2.1	3.8	32.5	42.9	18.7	10.1
Index of equality												
relative	1304	300	111	44	25	52	1319	224	115	66	37	64
absolute	+27.7	+6.0	+3.8	−25.5	−12.0	−4.8	+25.6	+4.7	+4.8	−23.3	−11.8	−3.6

Immigrated 1948–54											
Asia–Africa	31.7	10.4	36.4	18.9	5.9	25.9	9.1	38.3	22.4	4.3	6.6
Europe–America	4.1	11.3	41.9	33.7	8.3	3.2	11.9	36.2	35.6	13.1	8.9
Index of equality											
relative	773	92	87	56	72	809	76	106	63	33	74
abstract	−27.6	−0.9	−5.5	−14.8	−2.4	+22.7	−2.8	+1.9	−13.2	−8.8	−2.3
Immigrated 1955–60											
Asia–Africa	32.0	9.7	34.9	19.7	6.0	22.3	7.7	37.5	29.6	2.9	7.1
Europe–America	3.5	9.7	38.9	32.6	8.8	2.3	8.3	28.5	42.4	18.5	10.0
Index of equality											
relative	914	100	90	43	68	970	93	132	70	16	71
absolute	+28.5	0	−4.0	−12.9	−2.8	+20.0	−0.6	+9.0	−12.8	−15.6	−2.9
Immigrated since 1961											
Asia–Africa	27.0	10.1	33.6	25.1	4.2	6.5					
Europe–America	3.0	15.2	31.0	33.7	17.1	9.1					
Index of equality											
relative	900	66	108	74	25	71					
absolute	+24.0	−5.1	2.6	−8.6	−12.9	−2.6					

TABLE 26—continued

Males

	1961						1969					
	0	1-4	5-8	9-12	13+	Median	0	1-4	5-8	9-12	13+	Median
Total												
Asia–Africa	19.7	10.5	41.2	24.1	4.5	6.9	13.4	9.8	42.9	28.3	5.6	7.5
Europe–America	1.8	7.2	35.2	38.7	16.1	9.6	1.2	8.4	32.1	38.9	19.4	9.9
Index of equality												
relative	1094	146	117	62	28	72	1117	117	134	73	29	75
absolute	+17.9	+3.3	+6.0	−14.6	−11.6	−2.7	−12.2	+1.4	+10.8	−10.6	−13.8	−2.4

Females

	1961						1969					
	0	1-4	5-8	9-12	13+	Median	0	1-4	5-8	9-12	13+	Median
Total												
Asia–Africa	43.6	9.6	31.2	14.1	1.5	3.7	37.6	8.0	31.6	19.9	2.9	5.6
Europe–America	4.7	8.0	39.6	38.3	9.4	8.8	4.2	9.5	34.5	38.7	13.1	9.2
Index of equality												
relative	928	120	79	37	16	42	895	84	92	51	22	61
absolute	+38.9	+1.6	−8.4	−24.2	−7.9	−5.1	+33.4	−1.5	−2.9	−18.8	−10.2	−3.6

Sources: CBS, *Population and Housing Census,* 1961, Languages, Literacy and Educational Attainment, no. 15, Table 28; CBS, unpublished figures for 1969 based on labour force survey 1969, obtained from survey 1969, obtained from the Labour Section of CBS.

	1956–7[1]	1963–4[2]	1966–7[3]	1969–70[4]	1970–1[5]	1971–2[6]	1975–6[7]
Primary education							
Total		55.1	59.3	61.2			59.8c
1st grade		61.1	63.2	63.0			59.6c
8th grade	35.5	45.5	53.6	57.4			53.9c
Post-primary							
Total	17.7a	25.9	35.6	42.6	43.6	46.1	49.5
9th grade	22.1a	31.7	45.3	49.9	51.1	54.8	54.3
12th grade	8.8a	17.1	18.9	30.2	31.9	35.0	43.8
Academic							
Total	12.6	17.8	25.4	30.5	32.0	32.8	36.2
9th grade	15.8	20.6	32.0	35.0			
12th grade	7.8	13.6	15.3	24.7			
Vocational: Total	25.1	35.9	47.0	58.2	58.1	60.9	63.3
Agricultural: Total	26.7	38.6	52.4	61.1	61.5	60.4	64.0
Total passing matriculation				18.7	20.0	21.7	23.8c
Higher education							
Total	6.2b	12.8	12.5	13.2	13.8	14.1	14.8c
BA		13.7	12.9	14.2	14.9	15.3	16.4c
MA and PhD		3.3	8.4	9.0	10.1	10.3	10.1c

a These figures are conservative estimates. They do not include evening schools and continuation classes.
b This is an estimate for 1956–7. It exceeds Smilansky's estimate by 1 per cent, since it includes Israeli-born Orientals and students in all institutions of higher education.
c These figures are for 1972–3.

Sources: 1 Moshe Smilansky, 'The social implications of the educational system in Israel' (in Hebrew), Megamot, 8 (3), July 1957.
2 CBS, Bulletin of Educational Statistics, 17, January 1968: 96–8; CBS, Statistical Abstract of Israel, 1965, 16: 597–598.
3 CBS, Statistical Abstract of Israel, 1967, 18: 53–, 544.
4 ibid., 1971, 22: 557, 561, 568.
5 ibid., 1972, 23: 589, 599; 1973, 24: 639, 642.
6 ibid., 1974, 25: 622; 1973, 24: 647.
7 ibid., 1974, 25: 622, 633; 1976, 27: 606.

TABLE 28 Student rates in post-primary and higher education[a] by type of school and place of birth, 1956–7 to 1976–7

	1956–7	1964–5		1966–7	1969–70	1970–1	1971–2	1972–3
	Foreign-born	Foreign-born	Israeli-born	Israeli-born	Israeli-born	Israeli-born	Israeli-born	Israeli-born
Post-primary education								
Total								
Asia–Africa	13.0	26.3	38.3	37.9	44.2	45.9	49.9	53.8
Europe–America	40.9	48.7	70.0	68.6	77.5	77.9	79.7	70.6
Index of equality								
relative	32	54	55	55	57	59	63	76
absolute	−27.9	−22.4	−31.7	−30.7	−33.3	−32.0	−29.8	−16.8
Academic secondary								
Asia–Africa	3.3	8.2	14.8	12.5	14.6	15.3	16.4	18.2
Europe–America	18.9	27.6	37.4	37.6	44.3	44.6	46.6	43.8
Index of equality								
relative	19	30	39	33	33	34	35	42
absolute	−15.6	−19.4	−22.6	−25.1	−29.7	−29.3	−30.2	−25.6
Vocational secondary								
Asia–Africa	2.2	9.9	12.9	15.3	23.0	24.5	28.4	35.6
Europe–America	6.6	12.4	14.3	16.7	21.3	22.0	24.3	26.8
Index of equality								
relative	91	107	79	118	132	138	125	133
absolute	−0.4	+0.2	−0.9	+0.5	+0.9	+1.0	+0.7	+8.8

Matriculation diplomas													
Asia–Africa					3.7								7.4c
Europe–America					24.3								31.7c
Index of equality													
relative					15								23c
absolute					−20.5								−24.3c
Higher education													
Asia–Africa	0.2b	0.7	1.2	0.9	1.7	1.6	2.5	1.7	2.3	1.9	2.5	2.0	2.8c
Europe–America	2.3b	6.7	7.9	6.5	9.4	9.8	12.5	9.8	12.4	9.7	13.4	9.3	13.8c
Index of equality													
relative	9	10	15	14	18	16	19	17	19	20	19	22c	20c
absolute	−2.1	−6.0	−6.7	−5.6	−7.7	−8.2	−10.0	−8.1	−10.1	−7.8	−10.9	−7.3c	−11.0c

a Student rates in post-primary education equal the number of students per 100 14–17-year-olds. Rates for matriculation diplomas are for all 17-year-olds. In higher education, rates are of all students for the age-group 20–29 in the corresponding population.

b These are estimates based on various sources (exact figures on higher education are available only for the years since 1964–5).

c For 1972–3

Sources: For post-primary education, CBS, Statistical Abstract of Israel: (for 1956–7), 1964, 15: 513; (for 1964–5), 1965, 16: 585; (for 1966–7), 1967, 18: 533; (for 1969–70), 1971, 22: 558; (for 1970–1), 1972, 23: 590; (for 1971–2), 1974, 25: 625; (for 1976–7), 1977, 28: 616) Figures for matriculation diplomas were obtained from the Planning Department, Ministry of Education and Culture. For higher education, CBS, Students in Academic Institutions: (for 964–5), Special Series 249, Table 4; (for 1966–7), 296, Table 4; (for 1969–70), 354, Table 4; (for 1970–1), 418, Table 4; (for 1971–2 and 1972–3), CBS, Statistical Abstract of Israel, 1973, 24: 646; 1974, 25: 612; (for 1956–7, see note b).

TABLE 29   *Estimates of retention rates in primary and post-primary education, late 1960s*

Percentage reaching a given level	Orientals	Ashkenazim
1st grade	100	100
5th grade	96	99.5
8th grade	90	95
9th grade academic	24	55
10th grade academic	19	52
11th grade academic	14	47
12th grade academic	11	42
Matriculation	6	35

Source: Figures released by the Deputy Minister of Education and Culture, quoted by the Prime Minister's Commission on Disadvantaged Children and Youth, Report, 1972, Appendix 5, p. 8.

TABLE 30 *Culturally disadvantaged pupils in elementary schools by father's education, family size and type of school, 1971–2*

	Percentage of all pupils	Percentage of culturally disadvantaged pupils	Percentage of culturally disadvantaged pupils in category
Father's continent of birth			
Total	100.0	100.0	44.0
Africa	27.2	52.9	80.2
Asia	29.3	41.8	58.6
Europe	33.0	4.1	5.1
Israel	10.5	1.2	4.8
Father's education			
Total	100.0	100.0	44.0
Uneducated	11.6	26.8	100.0
Primary	49.8	62.1	54.9
Post-primary	35.9	11.1	13.6
College	8.7	0	0
Number of children in family			
Total	100.0	100.0	44.0
1–2	44.5	2.8	2.6
3	13.2	7.8	24.2
4	9.0	15.4	70.2
5	8.7	18.1	85.2
6	7.5	16.7	91.5
7	6.2	14.1	93.1
8+	10.9	25.1	95.1
Type of school			
Total	100.0	100.0	44.0
State	72.9	55.2	33.3
State (religious)	27.1	44.8	72.9

Source: Planning Department, Ministry of Education and Culture, quoted by Algarebly (1975: Tables 1–4 in the Appendix).

TABLE 31 *Percentage distribution of 8th grade scholastic test (seker), 1956–7 to 1969–70*

	Total	Test score				Median test score
		0–59	60–9	70–9	80–9	
1956–7[a]						
Asia–Africa	100.0	62	25	12	1	48.4
Europe–America	100.0	26	32.5	33.5	8	67.4
Index of equality						
relative		239	77	36	13	72
absolute		+36	−7.5	−21.5	−7	−19.0
1964–5						
Asia–Africa	100.0	39.9	28.0	20.5	11.7	62.6
Europe–America	100.0	10.6	17.6	28.1	43.8	77.0
Index of equality						
relative		376	159	73	27	87
absolute		+29.3	+10.4	−7.6	−32.1	−14.4
1969–70						
Asia–Africa	100.0	37.0	25.5	21.9	15.7	64.1
Europe–America	100.0	10.7	16.0	25.5	47.9	78.3
Index of equality						
relative		346	159	86	33	82
absolute		+26.3	+9.5	−3.6	−32.2	−14.2

[a] The distribution presented by Smilansky is given for boys and girls separately. These figures are estimates for both the boys and girls assuming 0.50 sex ratio.

Sources: For 1956–7, Moshe Smilansky, 'The social implications of the education system in Israel', *Megamot*, 8 (3), July 1957, p. 242 (Table 9). For 1964–5 and 1969–70, files in the Ministry of Education and Culture, Jerusalem.

TABLE 32   *Percentage of pupils scoring 70 points or more in 8th grade scholastic test (seker), by father's education and family size, 1971-2*

Father's education and continent of birth	Number of children in family							
	Total	1-2	3	4	5	6	7	8+
Grand total	55	75	57	42	36	33	30	28
Total								
Asia	42	60	51	39	35	32	31	27
Africa	35	55	42	38	33	29	27	26
Europe	76	79	72	56	51	50	46	50
Israel	76	83	69	59	54	55	50	50
Uneducated								
Asia	27	35	35	27	27	24	27	23
Africa	24	30	27	30	22	23	22	19
Europe	30	36	32	a	a	a	a	a
Israel	31	a	a	a	a	a	a	a
Primary school								
Asia	41	52	51	40	36	35	31	28
Africa	34	49	38	38	34	31	28	28
Europe	65	69	60	38	32	32	44	23
Israel	58	67	58	42	39	38	44	25
Vocational high school								
Asia	40	54	54	24	22	24	23	15
Africa	32	60	38	26	34	18	24	18
Europe	75	79	65	42	25	a	a	a
Israel	82	86	70	66	a	a	a	a
Academic high school and yeshivot								
Asia	57	72	55	48	43	48	43	39
Africa	47	62	57	48	40	38	32	35
Europe	80	86	78	73	63	67	60	65
Israel	81	84	72	72	76	88	65	76
University								
Asia	80	88	77	68	58	a	a	a
Africa	68	85	55	54	a	a	a	a
Europe	91	91	88	88	a	a	a	a
Israel	95	96	91	81	a	a	a	a

ᵃ Indicates that percentage is not computed because of an insufficient number of cases in category.

Source: as in Table 30.

TABLE 33   *Percentage of success among pupils sitting matriculation examination, 1965–6 to 1972–3*

	1965–6	1967–8	1968–9	1969–70	1970–1	1971–2	1972–3
Asia–Africa	60	58	58	63	64	62	65
Europe–America	76	80	81	81	79	80	82
Index of equality							
relative	78	73	73	78	81	78	80
absolute	−16	−22	−23	−18	−15	−18	−18

Source: files in the Ministry of Education and Culture, Jerusalem.

[...] representation in selected positions of power by rank and sector, 1955–73

Top rank

Sector	Position	Total	Orientals	Ashkenazim	% Orientals
State	Cabinet ministers				
	1955	12	1	11	8.3
	1973	18	2	16	11.1
	Knesset members				
	1955	113	10	103	8.8
	1973	114	19	95	16.7
Zionist organizations	Members of executive of the Jewish Agency				
	1955	12	0	12	0
	1973	13	1	12	7.7
	Members of Zionist executive committee				
	1955–60	52	1	51	1.9
	1972–3	51	6	45	11.8
Histadrut	Members of central committee				
	1956	13	0	13	0
	1973	20	5	15	25.0
	Members of executive committee				
	1956	91	8	83	8.8
	1970	163	34	129	20.9
Parties	Members of top governing bodies in 5 major parties[a]				
	1950s	104	8	96	7.7
	1973	130	14	116	10.8

Middle rank

Sector	Position	Total	Orientals	Ashkenazim	% Orientals
State	Top-ranking governmental officials				
	1961	100%	3%	97%	3.0
	1965	100%	3%	97%	3.0
	Mayors of large or middle-sized veteran cities				
	1955	19	0	19	0
	1972	19	0	19	0
	Supreme Court justices				
	1955	9	0	9	0
	1973	10	1	9	10.0
	Major-generals				
	1955	6	0	6	0
	1973	21	0	21	0
Zionist organizations	Directors of departments in Jewish Agency				
	1955	21	1	20	4.8
	1973	17	1	16	5.9
Histadrut	Top-ranking officials in Histadrut headquarters				
	1971	234	37	197	15.8
	Top managers in Histadrut industrial complex				
	1970	100%	4%	96%	4.0
	General secretaries of workers' councils in large, middle-sized veteran cities				
	1970	13	2	11	15.4
Parties	Members of middle governing bodies in 5 major parties				
	1950s	216	19	197	8.8
	1973	353	59	294	16.7

Lower rank

Sector	Position	Total	Orientals	Ashkenazim	% Orientals
State	Civil servants (total)				
	1961	100%	28%	72%	28.0
	1967	100%	28%	72%	28.0
	Heads of local authorities (total)				
	1955	96	11	85	11.5
	1972	98	33	65	33.7
	Local councillors				
	1955	652	154	498	23.6
	1965	951	421	530	44.3
	Police officers				
	1955	386	16	370	4.1
	1969	728	181	547	24.9
Histadrut	Delegates to 11th convention				
	1969	990	235	755	23.7
	Managers in Histadrut industrial complex (total)				
	1970	100%	31%	69%	31.0
	General secretaries of workers' councils (total)				
	1957	67	14	53	20.9
	1970	70	30	40	42.9
Parties	Members of broad governing bodies in 5 major parties[a]				
	1950s	663	63	600	9.5
	1973	1562	370	1192	23.7

a Figures refer to simple combinations of governing bodies of the five major parties (Israeli Labour Party, Mapam, Mafdal, Liberals, and Herut).

Sources: Tables 35, 37–42, 45–54, 57, 58–9, 63–5 below.

TABLE 35 *Cabinet ministers, 1949–73*

Government[a]	1st 10 Mar. 1949	2nd 1 Nov. 1950	3rd 8 Oct. 1951	4th 23 Dec. 1952	5th 26 Jan. 1954	6th 29 June 1955	7th 3 Nov. 1955	8th 7 Jan. 1958	9th 17 Dec. 1959	10th 2 Nov. 1961	11th 6 June 1963	12th 22 Dec. 1964	13th 1 Jan. 1966	14th 17 Mar. 1969	15th 16 Dec. 1969	As of 31 Dec. 1973
Total	12	13	13	16	16	12	16	16	16	16	15	15	18	22	24	18
Orientals	1	1	1	1	1	1	1	1	2	2	2	2	2	2	2	2
Ashkenazim	11	12	12	15	15	11	15	15	14	14	13	13	16	20	22	16
% Orientals	8.3	7.7	7.7	6.3	6.3	8.3	6.3	6.3	12.5	12.5	13.3	13.3	11.1	9.1	8.3	11.1

a At the beginning of each term.
Sources: Asher Zidon, *The Knesset* (in Hebrew), Tel-Aviv: Achiasaf (6th ed.), 1971, Appendix; Israel, *Government Year Book*; Israel, *Knesset Proceedings* (in Hebrew).

TABLE 36 *Cabinet ministers and front bench Knesset members by rank, 1971*

Rank and position	Total	Orientals	Ashkenazim	% Orientals
Total	103	14	86	13.6
Rank A (highest), senior cabinet ministers: Total	7	0	7	0
Rank B, other cabinet ministers: Total	11	2	9	18.2
Rank C, Speaker of Knesset: Total[a]	1	0	1	0
Rank D, Total	69	7	60	12.1
Deputy ministers	9	1	6	11.1
Chairmen of top Knesset committees[b]	3	0	3	0
Members of Defence and Foreign Affairs committee	19	2	17	10.5
Members of Finance committee	19	2	17	10.5
Members of Constitution, Law and Justice committee	19	2	17	10.5
Rank E (lowest) – Total	15	5	9	28.9
Deputy Speakers of Knesset	9	3	5	33.3
Chairmen of other Knesset committees	6	2	4	33.3

TABLE 37   *Knesset members, 1949–73*

Knesset[a]	*1st* *1949*	*2nd* *1951*	*3rd* *1955*	*4th* *1959*	*5th* *1961*	*6th* *1965*	*7th* *1969*	*8th* *1973*
Total[b]	118	112	113	113	114	113	113	114
Orientals	8	7	10	14	14	21	17	19
Ashkenazim	110	105	103	99	100	92	96	95
% Orientals	6.8	6.3	8.8	12.4	12.3	18.6	15.0	16.7

[a] At the beginning of each term; for the 8th Knesset, those elected on 31 December 1973 elections.
[b] Excluding Arab members.

Sources: as in Table 35.

TABLE 38   *Civil servants by rank, 1955–69*

	Total	Lower rank[a]	Middle rank[a]	Higher rank[a]	Top position[b]	Profes- sionals
1955						
Total	100.0					
Israel	18.1					
Asia–Africa	14.3					
Europe–America	67.6					
1961						
Total	100.0c	100.0c	100.0c	100.0c	100.0	100.0c
Israel	—	—	—	—	20.4	—
Asia–Africa	27.9	39.0	19.5	5.4	3.1	31.0
Europe–America	72.1	61.0	80.5	94.6	76.5	69.0
1967						
Total	100.0	100.0	100.0	100.0		100.0
Israel	22.3	20.2	24.7	22.8		24.1
Asia–Africa	27.6	40.2	20.8	6.6		11.8
Europe–America	50.1	39.6	54.5	70.6		56.1
1969						
Total				100.0d	100.0e	100.0f
Israel				23.8	21	40.0
Asia–Africa				4.6	3	5.7
Europe–America				71.6	76	54.3

a Ranking changed several times during the period under study, so it was necessary to redefine rank categories.

b Top position is defined as the two highest executive levels under a director-general of a ministry, or a comparable lower level which maintains a direct contact with a minister. See Gloverzon (1970: 24).

c 100 per cent refers to Asian-African-born and European–American-born, excluding Israeli-born.

d As of July 1968; ranks 17–19 in the general grading scale; excluding civil servants in the Foreign Office and in the Defence Ministry.

e Mid-1969; position as in note b.

f As of December 1969; ranks A and B in the Academics' Scale; excluding professionals in the Foreign Office and in the Defence Ministry.

Sources: Civil Service Commission, *Comparative Study of the Composition of the Civil Service in the Years 1953, 1955, 1960, 1967* (in Hebrew); Civil Service Commission, *Researches and Surveys*, F. The Senior Civil Servants in the General Grading Scale 1968, G. The Senior Civil Servants in the Academics' Scale (Humanities and Social Sciences), 1969 (in Hebrew); CBS, *Survey of Civil Servants*, 1961 (quoted Bar-Yosef and Padan (1964); Gloverzon (1970)).

TABLE 39   *Supreme Court justices, 1950–73*

	1950	1955	1960	1965	1969	1973
Total	7	9	8	10	9	10
Orientals	0	0	0	1	1	1
Ashkenazim	7	9	8	9	8	9
% Orientals	0	0	0	10.0	11.1	10.0

Source: Israel, *Government Year Book.*

TABLE 40   *Major-generals, 1951–73*

	1951	1955	1960	1965	1970	1973
Total	12	6	6	12	17	21
Orientals	0	0	0	0	0	0
Ashkenazim	12	6	6	12	17	21
% Orientals	0	0	0	0	0	0

Source: Israel, *Government Year Book.*

TABLE 41   *Police officers, 1955–69*

	1955	1960	1965	1969
Manpower				
Total	5,988	5,882	6,727	9,408
	100.0	100.0	100.0	100.0
Israel	17.5	18.9	19.9	26.3
Asia–Africa	36.3	42.6	46.3	47.3
Europe–America	46.2	38.7	33.8	26.4
Officers				
Total	444	497	652	886
	100.0	100.0	100.0	100.0
Israel	13.1	12.5	14.1	17.8
Asia–Africa	3.6	7.0	13.6	20.4
Europe–America	83.3	80.5	72.2	61.7

Source: data received from Personnel Division, Israel Police, Jaffa
     Headquarters.

313

TABLE 42   *Heads of local authorities by type of settlement,*[a] *1955–72*

	1955	1965	1969	1972
Total	96	93	98	98
Orientals	11	34	32	33
Ashkenazim	85	59	66	65
% Orientals	11.5	36.6	32.7	33.7
Mayors of large, middle-sized veteran cities				
Total	19	17	19	
Orientals	0	0	0	
Ashkenazim	19	17	19	
% Orientals	0	0	0	
Heads of authorities of other veteran settlements				
Total	45	33	36	
Orientals	2	9	7	
Ashkenazim	43	24	29	
% Orientals	4.4	27.3	19.4	
Heads of new authorities				
Total	32	43	47	
Orientals	9	25	25	
Ashkenazim	23	18	22	
% Orientals	28.1	58.1	53.2	

[a] Classification of local authorities follows one used by Weis (1968: ch. 8) with some modifications (combining the original 6 categories into 3 and reclassification of several authorities in 1969).

Sources: For 1955 and 1965, Weis (1968: p. 365); for 1969, Ben-Zion Michaeli, *Heads of Local Governments in Israel* (in Hebrew), Tel-Aviv: Merkaz Hashilton Hamkomi, 1971.

TABLE 43   *Heads of local authorities by ethnic composition of settlement,*[a] *1969*

	Total	*Oriental majority*	*Mixed*	*Ashkenazi majority*
Total	98	41	32	25
Orientals	32	26	5	1
Ashkenazim	66	15	27	24
% Orientals	32.7	63.4	15.6	4.0

[a] Oriental majority is defined as 60% or more Asian–African-born, Ashkenazi majority – 60% or more European–American-born, and mixed – all other settlements. Classification is based on 1965 figures, CBS, *Population in Settlements*, 1965 and 1966, Special Series 267.

Source: Ben-Zion Michaeli, *Heads of Local Governments in Israel* (in Hebrew), Tel-Aviv: Merkaz Hashilton Hamkomi, 1971.

TABLE 44   *Members of local authorities by type of settlement,*[a] *1955 and 1965*

	1955	*1965*
Total	652	951
Orientals	154	421
Ashkenazim	498	530
% Orientals	23.6	44.2
Councillors in large, middle-sized, veteran cities		
Total	211	230
Orientals	27	48
Ashkenazim	184	182
% Orientals	12.8	20.9
Councillors in other veteran settlements		
Total	251	327
Orientals	51	129
Ashkenazim	200	198
% Orientals	20.3	39.4
Councillors in new local authorities		
Total	191	394
Orientals	76	244
Ashkenazim	115	150
% Orientals	39.8	61.9

[a] See note a to Table 42. 'Orientals' here include 'non-Ashkenazim miscellaneous' in Weis's table.

Source: Weis (1968: 356).

TABLE 45   *Members of executive of the Jewish Agency, 1951–73*

	1951	1955	1960	1965	1970	1973
Total	12	12	12	12	12	13
Orientals	0	0	0	1	1	1
Ashkenazim	12	12	12	11	11	12
% Orientals	0	0	0	8.3	8.3	7.7

Source: Israel, *Government Year Book.*

TABLE 46   *Members of Zionist executive committee (Israelis only), 1951–73*

	1951–5	1956–60	1961–4	1965–8	1968–72	1972–3
Total	39	52	49	41	51	51
Orientals	0	1	3	5	4	6
Ashkenazim	39	51	46	36	47	45
% Orientals	0	1.9	6.1	12.2	7.8	11.8

Source: World Zionist Organization, *The Zionist Congress.*

TABLE 47   *Directors of departments in the Jewish Agency, 1951–73*

	1951	1955	1960	1965	1970	1973
Total[a]	29	21	21	22	13	17
Orientals	1	1	0	1	0	1
Ashkenazim	28	20	21	21	13	16
% Orientals	3.4	4.8	0	4.5	0	5.9

[a] All people who appear in the list of 'directors of departments', which sometimes includes directors of sections and other top officials.

Source: Israel, *Government Year Book.*

TABLE 48   *Members of central committee of the Histadrut, 1949–73*

	1949	1955–9	1960–5	1966–9	1970	1973
Total	9	13	23	18	18	20
Orientals	0	0	2	5	5	5
Ashkenazim	9	13	21	13	13	15
% Orientals	0	0	8.7	27.8	27.8	25.0

Sources: Histadrut, *Year Books*; file of the Executive Committee Resolutions in the Histadrut Archives (resolutions on elections of members of the central committee on 7 July 1949; 28 July 1956; 16 December 1969).

TABLE 49   *Members of executive committee of the Histadrut, 1949–69*

	1949	1956	1960	1966	1969
Total[a]	51	91	107	130	163
Orientals	3	8	12	22	34
Ashkenazim	48	83	95	108	129
% Orientals	5.9	8.8	11.2	16.9	20.9

[a] Excluding non-Jews.

Source: File of the Histadrut Council Resolutions in the Histadrut archives (64th, 69th, 73rd and 83rd councils).

TABLE 50   *Delegates to 11th Convention of the Histadrut, 1969*[a]

Total	990
Orientals	235
Ashkenazim	755
% Orientals	23.7

[a] The number of delegates was 1,001, of whom 990 were estimated to be Jews. Only 882 replied to the inquiry and indicated their country of birth. In making the estimates it is assumed that the ethnic composition of nonrespondents is the same as that of respondents, and that the ethnic composition of the Israeli born (excluding non-Jews) equals that found among members of the executive committee of the Histadrut; i.e., about 15%. As in other tables, Greeks and Bulgarians are reclassified as Orientals and South Africans as Ashkenazim.

Source: Yosef Lavon, *Survey of Delegates to the 11th Histadrut Convention,* Tel-Aviv: Institute for Economic and Social Research of the Histadrut, 1971.

TABLE 51   *Top-ranking officials in the Histadrut headquarters, 1971*

Total[a]	234
Orientals	37
Ashkenazim	197
% Orientals	15.8

[a] Excluding one non-Jew, effective January.

Source: Data received from the Technical Secretariat of the executive committee of the Histadrut.

TABLE 52 *General secretaries of national trade unions of the Histadrut, 1970 and 1973*

	1970	1973
Total	42	41
Orientals	0	0
Ashkenazim	42	41
% Orientals	0	0

Source: Data received from Trades Union Department of the executive committee of the Histadrut.

TABLE 53 *General secretaries of workers' councils, 1957–73*

	1957	1960	1967	1970	1973
Total[a]	67	69	70	70	65
Orientals	14	22	24	30	37
Ashkenazim	53	47	46	40	28
% Orientals	20.9	31.9	34.3	42.9	56.9

[a] Excluding non-Jews.

Source: Data received from the Technical Secretariat of the Organization Department in charge of workers' councils, Histadrut headquarters.

TABLE 54 *General secretaries of workers' councils by type and ethnic composition of settlement,*[a] *1970*

	Total	Orientals	Ashkenazim	% Orientals
Total	70	30	40	42.9
Type of settlement				
Large, middle-sized, veteran cities	13	2	11	15.4
Other veteran settlements	18	5	13	27.8
New settlements	39	23	16	59.0
Ethnic composition				
Oriental majority	14	2	12	14.3
Mixed	24	7	17	29.2
Ashkenazi majority	32	21	11	65.6

[a] For classification of settlements, see notes to Tables 42 and 43.

Source: as in Table 53.

TABLE 55 *Local top positions (heads of local authorities and general secretaries of workers' councils) by type and ethnic composition of local authority,[a] 1970*

Pattern[b]	All local authorities					Local authorities with independent workers' councils					Local authorities with workers' councils under jurisdiction of adjacent workers' councils				
	Total	+/+	+/-	-/+	-/-	Total	+/+	+/-	-/+	-/-	Total	+/+	+/-	-/+	-/-
Total	98	15	17	22	44	69[c]	14	10	16	29	29	1	7	6	15
Type of settlement															
Big or middle-sized, veteran cities	15	0	0	2	13	13	0	0	2	11	2	0	0	0	2
Other veteran settlements	36	0	7	10	19	18	0	5	5	8	18	0	2	5	11
New settlements	47	15	10	10	12	37	14	4	9	10	10	1	6	1	2
Ethnic composition															
Oriental majority	41	15	11	9	6	32	14	6	7	5	9	1	5	2	1
Mixed	32	0	5	9	18	25	0	3	7	15	7	0	2	2	3
Ashkenazi majority	25	0	1	4	20	12	0	1	2	9	13	0	0	2	11

[a] For classification of settlements see notes to Tables 42 and 43.

[b] Four patterns of division of power are distinguished. The top sign refers to head of a local authority and the lower sign to the general secretary of a workers' council. + means Oriental and − Ashkenazi. For instance, the pattern ± designates a settlement in which the head of local authority is Oriental and the general secretary of the workers' council is Ashkenazi.

[c] Excluding one settlement in which there is a workers' council but not a local authority.

Sources: Ben-Zion Michaeli, *Heads of Local Governments in Israel* (in Hebrew), Tel-Aviv: Merkaz Hashilton Hamkomi, 1971; for general secretaries, as in Table 53.

TABLE 56 *Steering committee and secretariat of the Histadrut industrial complex (Hevrat HaOvdim), 1973*

	Steering committee	Secretariat
Total	11	33
Orientals	0	1
Ashkenazim	11	32
% Orientals	0	3.0

Source: Data received from the Director of the Bureau of Hevrat HaOvdim, Histadrut headquarters. Figures include all people serving during the 1969–73 term.

TABLE 57 *Managers in the Histadrut industrial complex (Hevrat HaOvdim) by rank, 1970*

	All managers	General directors and top managers
Total	440[a]	139[b]
Orientals	138	5
Ashkenazim	302	134
% Orientals	31.4	3.6

[a] Excluding 72 (70 Israeli-born and 2 others) whose ethnic origin is unknown.
[b] Excluding 8 whose ethnic origin is unknown.

Source: Unpublished survey of managers in Hevrat HaOvdim, Institute for Economic and Social Research of the Histadrut, 1971.

TABLE 58   *Members of governing bodies of the Mapam Party,*[a]
1948–73

	1948	1951	1958	1963	1968	1973
Steering Committee[1]						
Total						9
Orientals						0
Ashkenazim						9
% Orientals						0
Secretariat[2]						
Total	20		27	16	30	51
Orientals	0		1	1	2	3
Ashkenazim	20		16	15	27	48
% Orientals	0		3.7	6.3	6.7	5.9
Political Committee[3]						
Total	37	38	74	58	82	118
Orientals	0	0	4	4	5	12
Ashkenazim	37	38	70	54	77	106
% Orientals	0	0	5.4	6.9	6.1	10.2
Central Committee[4]						
Total[b]	99	152	246	151	230	340
Orientals	1	5	17	10	24	50
Ashkenazim	98	147	229	141	206	290
% Orientals	1.0	3.3	6.9	6.6	10.4	14.7

a Mapam (United Workers' Party) is a leftist Socialist Zionist party. It
received 6.6% of the votes in the 1965 national elections. It formed an
alignment bloc with the Israel Labour Party and they ran in a united list in
1969 and 1973. For details, see 'Mapam' in Raphael Patai (ed.) (1971a).
b Excluding non-Jews.

Sources: 1 Members were elected in the 6th Convention (December 1972),
Bashaar, 16 (109–11), March–August 1973.
2 Members were elected in the 1st Convention, *Al Hamishmar*,
25 Jan., 1948. No data are available on members elected in the
2nd Convention. Members were elected in the 3rd Convention,
Al Hamishmar, 23 Jan. 1958 (this list is somewhat erroneous; the
corrected list is filed with the Tel-Aviv District Officer of the
Interior Office, File 27/99). Members were elected in the 4th
Convention, 4th Convention – Resolutions, April 1963. Members
were elected in the 5th Convention, 5th Convention – Resolutions,
March 1968. Members were elected in the 6th Convention, see
above.
3 Members were elected in the 1st Convention, *Al Hamishmar*,
25 Jan. 1948. Members were elected following the 2nd
Convention, *Al Hamishmar*, 2 August 1951. Members were
elected in the 3rd Convention, *Al Hamishmar*, 23 Jan. 1958.
Members were elected in the 4th, 5th and 6th Conventions, see
above.
4 Members were elected in the 1st Convention, *Al Hamishmar*,
25 Jan. 1948. Members were elected in the 2nd Convention, *Al
Hamishmar*, 22 June 1951. Members were elected in the 3rd
Convention, *Al Hamishmar*, 9 Jan. 1958. Members were elected in
the 4th, 5th and 6th Conventions, see above.

TABLE 59 *Members of governing bodies of the Israel Labour Party,[a] 1970 and 1973*

	1970	1973
Bureau		
Total	33	27
Orientals	4	3
Ashkenazim	29	24
% Orientals	12.1	11.1
Political Committee of the Alignment		
Total	22	29
Orientals	2	5
Ashkenazim	20	24
% Orientals	9.1	17.2
Secretariat		
Total	186	151
Orientals	33	32
Ashkenazim	153	119
% Orientals	17.7	21.2
Central Committee		
Total	432	605[b]
Orientals	102	157
Ashkenazim	330	448
% Orientals	23.6	26.0

a The Israel Labour Party was founded in 1968 by the merger of Ahdut HaAvoda, Mapai and Rafi (see note a in Tables 60–2). It is the largest party, receiving (with Mapam) 39.6% of the votes in 1973. For details see 'Israel Labor Party' in Patai (ed.) (1971a).
b Excluding 10 Arab members.

Source: Lists obtained from the office of the general secretary of the Israel Labour Party.

TABLE 60 *Members of governing bodies of the Ahdut HaAvoda Party,*[a] *1958–73*

	1958–62	1962–8	1970	1973
Bureau				
Total			7	5
Orientals			0	0
Ashkenazim			7	5
% Orientals			0	0
Political Committee of Alignment				
Total			5	5
Orientals			0	0
Ashkenazim			5	5
% Orientals			0	0
Secretariat				
Total	13	33	40	30
Orientals	5	5	7	5
Ashkenazim	8	28	33	25
% Orientals	38.5	15.2	17.5	16.7
Central Committee				
Total	n.a.[b]	105	93	120
Orientals	n.a.[b]	19	13	17
Ashkenazim	n.a.[b]	86	80	103
% Orientals	n.a.[b]	18.1	14.0	14.2

a Ahdut HaAvoda (United Labour) is a Zionist Socialist workers' party. It received 6.6% of the votes in the 1961 elections. In 1965 it established a bloc with Mapai and in 1968 they and Rafi merged to found the new Israel Labour Party. Figures after 1968 refer to the Ahdut HaAvoda division within the Israel Labour Party. For details see 'Ahdut Avoda-Po'ale Zion' in Raphael Patai (ed.) (1971a).

b Data for the 1958 central committee are not available. On 16 April 1958 the party council confirmed a central committee of 95 members and on 27 August, 1959 it resolved to give at least one-third representation to Orientals and women (Between Convention and Convention: 1958–1962, submitted to the party Convention on 12 September 1962). It follows that Oriental representation was relatively high, as the available figures for the secretariat indicate.

Sources: Members of the secretariat elected in 1958, *Lamerhav*, 5 May 1958. Other data were obtained from the office of the secretary general of the Israel Labour Party.

TABLE 61 *Members of governing bodies of the Mapai Party,*[a] *1950–73*

	Early 1950s	Late 1950s	Early 1960s	1966–8	1970	1973
Bureau[1]						
Total	17	22	18	16	19	18
Orientals	2	2	2	2	1	2
Ashkenazim	15	20	16	14	18	16
% Orientals	11.8	9.1	11.1	12.5	5.3	11.1
Political Committee of Alignment						
Total					9	16
Orientals					1	2
Ashkenazim					8	14
% Orientals					11.1	12.5
Secretariat[2]						
Total	20	35	40	55	107	94
Orientals	2	4	4	11	18	18
Ashkenazim	18	31	36	44	89	76
% Orientals	10.0	11.4	10.0	20.0	16.8	19.1
Central Committee[3]						
Total	131	197	257	251	244	406
Orientals	8	33	50	67	63	118
Ashkenazim	123	164	207	184	181	288
% Orientals	6.1	16.8	19.5	26.7	25.8	29.1

[a] Mapai (the Israeli Workers' Party) is a Socialist Zionist party. This is the largest ruling party ever to operate in Israel. In 1961 it received 34.7% of the votes. In 1965 it established a political bloc with Ahdut HaAvoda. In 1968 it joined Ahdut HaAvoda and Rafi to found the Israel Labour Party, which received with Mapam 39.6% of the votes in 1973. Figures after 1968 refer to the Mapai division within the Israel Labour Party. For details see 'Mapai' in Raphael Patai (ed.) 1971a, and Peter Medding (1972).

Sources: 1 For the 1950s, file 10/7 in Mapai Archives in Bet-Berl includes two undated lists, but informants identify them as of the early and late 1950s. For the early 1960s, 1966–8 (list dated 7 May 1967), and 1969–70 (list dated 27 July 1970), lists were obtained from the office of the general secretary of the Israel Labour Party.

2 For the early and late 1950s and the early 1960s, file 10/7 in Mapai Archives in Bet-Berl includes a list dated 25 March 1954, another dated 23 September 1956 and another marked 1959–65. For 1966–8, list dated 3 May 1966 and list dated 29 April 1970 were provided by the office of the general secretary of the Israel Labour Party.

3 For the early and late 1950s and early 1960s, file 10/7 in Mapai Archives in Bet-Berl includes a list dated 20 August 1950, another dated 30 August 1956 and another 23–25 March 1960. For 1966–8 and 1969–70, list of members of central committee elected in the 10th Convention, and a list dated 14 June 1970 were supplied by the office of the general secretary of the Israel Labour Party.

TABLE 62   *Members of governing bodies of the Rafi Party,*[a] *1965–73*

	1965–8	1970	1973
Bureau[1]			
Total		7	4
Orientals		3	1
Ashkenazim		6	3
% Orientals		42.9	25.0
Political Committee[2]			
Total	29	4	4
Orientals	5	0	2
Ashkenazim	24	4	2
% Orientals	17.2	0	50.0
Secretariat[3]			
Total	32	39	27
Orientals	8	9	9
Ashkenazim	24	30	18
% Orientals	25.0	23.1	33.3
Central Committee[4]			
Total	206	94	79
Orientals	60	26	22
Ashkenazim	146	68	57
% Orientals	29.1	27.7	27.8

[a] Rafi (Israeli's Labour List) is a splinter party (headed by Ben-Gurion and Dayan) which seceded from Mapai in 1965 and merged with Mapai and Ahdut HaAvoda to found the new Israel Labour Party in 1968. Figures after 1968 refer to the Rafi division within the Israel Labour Party. It received 7.9% of the votes in 1965. For details, see 'R'shimat Po'ale Yisrael' in Raphael Patai (ed.) (1971a) and Natan Yanai, *Rift at the Top* (in Hebrew), Tel-Aviv: Levin–Epstein, 1969.

Sources: 1 List dated 27 July 1970 was obtained from the office of the general secretary of the Israeli Labour Party.
2 Lists dated 1965–8 and 2 February 1970 were obtained from source (1).
3 Lists dated 1965–8 and 24 September 1970 were obtained from source (1).
4 Lists dated 1965–8 and 14 June 1970 were obtained from source (1).

TABLE 63 *Members of governing bodies of the Mafdal Party,*[a] *1956–73*

	1956–63	1963–9	1969–71	1973
Secretariat[1]				
Total	17	10	14	16
Orientals	0	1	2	4
Ashkenazim	17	9	12	12
% Orientals	0	10.0	14.3	25.0
Directorate[2]				
Total	19	40	48	51
Orientals	1	6	12	14
Ashkenazim	18	34	36	37
% Orientals	5.3	15.0	25.0	27.5
Executive Committee[3]				
Total	34	29	47	51
Orientals	2	6	15	18
Ashkenazim	32	23	32	33
% Orientals	5.9	20.7	31.9	35.3
Broader Executive Committee[4]				
Total	67	140	173	200
Orientals	6	31	55	65
Ashkenazim	61	109	118	135
% Orientals	9.0	22.1	31.8	32.5

[a] Mafdal (the National Religious Party) is a Zionist religious party. It was formed in 1956 as a result of a merger between socialist and non-socialist religious factions. It is the largest ruling religious party. It obtained 8.3% of the votes in 1973 national elections. For details, see 'Mizrahi' in Raphael Patai (ed.) (1971a).

Sources: 1 For 1956–63, the secretariat consisted of two separate bodies. The list of the Hapoel Hamizrahi is printed in Between Convention and Convention, 1963; that of Hamizrahi was supplied by the office of the party spokesman. The two lists are combined in the table. For 1963–9, Toward a Summary of a Period: Report Submitted to the 3rd Convention of the Mafdal, 1968. For 1969–71, a list, effective to 13 January 1971, was provided by the office of the secretary of the executive committee. For 1973 the list of members elected in the 4th Convention of Mafdal appeared in Hatsofe, 8 March 1973.

    2 For 1956–63, two lists, of an earlier and a later date were combined. Both were obtained from the office of the party spokesman. For 1969–71, as in source (1), and also Resolutions of the 3rd Convention, 1969. For 1969–71 and 1973 as in (1).

    3 For 1956–63, Between Convention and Convention; for 1963–9 on, as in (1).

    4 For 1956–63, The Constituent Convention of the Mafdal (20 June 1956). This list was compared with other lists which were supplied by the office of the party spokesman. It seems that no new names were added to the later lists, but names were struck off due to deaths and resignations. For this reason the 1956 list can be considered as complete. For 1963–9 on, as in (1).

TABLE 64 Members of governing bodies[a] of the Liberal Party,[b] 1956-73

	1956	1957	1960	1961-3	1963-8	1968-71	1973
Steering Committee[1]							
Total		11	17	16	19	11	5
Orientals		0	1	2	3	1	0
Ashkenazim		11	16	14	16	10	5
% Orientals		0	5.9	12.5	15.8	9.1	0
Chairmen and Directors of Departments[2]							
Total		20		21	20	19	
Orientals		0		2	1	1	
Ashkenazim		20		19	19	18	
% Orientals		0		9.5	5.0	5.3	
Executive Committee[3]							
Total	32	43	47	52	52	33	33
Orientals	1	2	3	4	8	1	1
Ashkenazim	31	41	44	48	44	32	32
% Orientals	3.1	4.7	6.4	7.4	15.4	3.0	3.0
Central Committee[4]							
Total	131	119		89	154	88	115
Orientals	8	5		9	20	6	7
Ashkenazim	123	114		80	134	82	108
% Orientals	6.1	4.2		10.1	13.0	6.8	6.1

TABLE 64—*continued*

a The names of the governing bodies have changed. The executive committee is usually called 'the directorate' (Hanhala), and the English terms are used to improve inter-party comparisons.

b The Liberal Party is a right-of-centre, middle-class-based party. It received 6.2% of the votes in 1959 elections, running as a General Zionist Party. In 1961 the Progressive Party and the General Zionist merged to form the Liberal Party. In 1965, the Progressives seceded and the party established a political bloc with Herut known as Gahal. This bloc is the stronghold of the nonsocialist stream as against the dominant Socialist Alignment stream of Israeli politics. The two blocs received 30.2 and 39.6% respectively of the votes in the 1973 national elections. For details, see 'General Zionists' and 'Liberal Party' in Raphael Patai (ed.) (1971a).

Sources: 1 For 1957, members were elected on 27 June 1957, 'A Meeting of the Delegates of the 21st Convention of the General Zionists, 1958'. For 1960, members were elected on 10 July 1960, the list was received from the Organization Department of the Liberal Party. For 1961–3, Report to the 1st National Convention of the Liberal Party, 1963. For 1963–8, Report to the 2nd National Convention of the Liberal Party, 1968. For 1968–71, Report to the 3rd Convention of the Liberal Party, 1971. For 1973, a small group assumed the functions of the previous steering committee, and are known as 'chairmen of party institutions'.

2 Sources as in (1). List provided by party headquarters.

3 For 1954, *Haboker*, 27 June 1954. For 1957, as in (1). For 1960, Protocols of the 22nd Convention of the General Zionist Party, July 1960. For 1961–3 on, as in (1).

4 For 1954, members were elected on 22 June 1954, Protocols of the 20th Convention of the General Zionist Party, 1954. For 1957, members were elected on 25 June 1957, Protocols of the 21st Convention of the General Zionist Party, 1957. For 1961–3, as in (1). The central committee was called the directorate. The list on pp. 12–13 of the quoted source includes the members of the Progressive Party as well, but they are excluded from the computation. For 1963–8, as in (1). For 1968–71 on, as in (1).

TABLE 65 Members of governing bodies of the Herut Party,[a] 1949–73

	1949–51	1951–4	1954–6	1956–8	1958–9	1959–61	1961–3	1963–6	1966–8	1968–70	1971–2	1973
Executive Committee												
Total	9	6	20[b]	14	15	11	11	10	14	16	28	31
Orientals	0	0	3	0	3	0	2	2	3	5	4	4
Ashkenazim	9	6	17	14	12	11	9	8	11	11	24	27
% Orientals	0	0	15.0	0	20.0	0	18.2	20.0	21.4	31.3	14.3	12.9
Central Committee												
Total	29	20	20[b]		45	48	79	67	74	127	182	251
Orientals	2	1	3		8	10	11	14	19	25	47	73
Ashkenazim	27	19	17		37	38	68	53	55	102	135	178
% Orientals	6.9	5.0	15.0		17.8	20.8	13.9	20.9	25.7	19.7	25.8	29.1

[a] The Herut (Freedom) Party is a right-of-centre, nationalist party which is strongly supported by the working class. It is the largest opposition party. It received 13.8% of the votes in 1961. Since 1965 it forms part of the electoral and political bloc named Gahal which received 21.7% of the votes in 1969. For details, see 'Herut' in Raphael Patai (ed.) (1971a).

[b] In September 1954 the Executive and Central Committees were identical.

Sources: Reports submitted to national conventions of the Herut Party, Jabotinski archives, box 9/27. For 1973, a list was obtained from the Herut Party headquarters.

TABLE 66   *General secretaries*[a] *of local branches of the Israel Labour Party by type and ethnic composition of settlement,*[b] *1969 and 1973*

	Total	Orientals	Ashkenazim	% Orientals
1969				
Total	75	33	42	44.0
Type of settlement				
Large, middle-sized, veteran cities	14	1	13	7.1
Other veteran settlements	20	7	13	35.0
New settlements	43	26	17	60.5
Ethnic composition				
Oriental majority	35	25	10	71.4
Mixed	27	7	20	25.9
Ashkenazi majority	15	2	13	13.3
1973				
Total	82	37	45	45.1

[a] The position of a general secretary of a local branch is in most cases a full-time paid job. The general secretary is the chief executive of the party in local affairs, but not the local chairman (the leader) of the party.
[b] For classification of settlements, see notes to Tables 42 and 43.

Source: Data obtained from the office of the general secretary of the Israel Labour Party.

TABLE 67 *Members of local authorities by major political party and bloc, 1955 and 1965*

	1955	1965
Total		
Total	653	951
Orientals	154	421
Ashkenazim	499	530
% Orientals	23.6	44.3
Mapam		
Total	49	52
Orientals	4	21
Ashkenazim	45	31
% Orientals	8.2	40.4
Ahdut HaAvoda[a]		
Total	46	
Orientals	7	
Ashkenazim	39	
% Orientals	15.2	
Mapai[a]		
Total	234	391
Orientals	66	165
Ashkenazim	168	226
% Orientals	28.2	42.2
Rafi		
Total		81
Orientals		40
Ashkenazim		41
% Orientals		49.4
Religious parties[b]		
Total	110	169
Orientals	35	89
Ashkenazim	75	80
% Orientals	31.8	52.7
Liberals[c]		
Total	76	
Orientals	7	
Ashkenazim	69	
% Orientals	9.2	
Herut[c]		
Total	58	144
Orientals	12	73
Ashkenazim	46	71
% Orientals	20.7	50.7

331

TABLE 67 *continued*

	1955	1965
Other lists[d]		
Total	80	122
Orientals	24	62
Ashkenazim	56	60
% Orientals	30.0	50.8
Left (Alignment)		
Total	329	524
Orientals	77	226
Ashkenazim	252	298
% Orientals	23.4	43.1
Religious[e]		
Total	110	169
Orientals	35	89
Ashkenazim	75	80
% Orientals	31.8	52.7
Right (Gahal)		
Total	134	144
Orientals	19	73
Ashkenazim	115	71
% Orientals	14.2	50.7

[a] Ahdut HaAvoda is included in Mapai in 1965.

[b] Religious parties include Mafdal (the major religious party) and two other splinter parties.

[c] The Liberals are included in Herut in 1965.

[d] Other lists include the Independent Liberal Party and local and ethnic lists.

[e] The figures for the religious bloc equal those for the 'religious parties' (see note b).

Source: Weis (1968: 360–1).

TABLE 56 Knesset members by major political party[a] and bloc, 1949–73

Knesset[b]	1st 1949–51	2nd 1951–5	3rd 1955–9	4th 1959–61	5th 1961–5	6th 1965–9	7th 1969	8th 1973
Total								
Total	127	123	125	128	126	124	113	114
Orientals	12	12	12	14	16	25	17	19
Ashkenazim	115	111	113	104	110	99	96	95
% Orientals	9.4	9.8	9.6	10.9	12.7	20.2	15.0	13.6
Mapam								
Total	21	14	9	9	9	7	6	5
Orientals	1	0	1	1	1	1	0	0
Ashkenazim	20	14	8	8	8	6	6	5
% Orientals	4.8	0	11.1	11.1	11.1	14.3	0	0
Ahdut HaAvoda								
Total			11	8	8	10	8	8
Orientals			2	1	1	3	2	1
Ashkenazim			9	7	7	7	6	7
% Orientals			18.2	12.5	12.5	30.0	25.0	12.5
Mapai								
Total	51	58	46	48	47	40	33	28
Orientals	4	7	5	8	8	10	6	6
Ashkenazim	47	51	41	40	39	30	27	22
% Orientals	7.8	12.1	10.9	16.7	17.0	25.0	18.2	21.4
Rafi								
Total						10	8	9
Orientals						3	4	4
Ashkenazim						7	4	4
% Orientals						30.0	50.0	44.4

TABLE 68—*continued*

Knesset[b]	1st 1949–51	2nd 1951–5	3rd 1955–9	4th 1959–61	5th 1961–5	6th 1965–9	7th 1969	8th 1973
Mafdal								
Total	10	10	11	12	14	12	12	10
Orientals	0	0	1	1	2	2	1	2
Ashkenazim	10	10	10	11	12	10	11	8
% Orientals	0	0	9.1	8.3	14.3	16.7	8.3	20.0
Liberals								
Total	8	21	16	8	13	12	12	14
Orientals	0	1	1	1	1	2	1	1
Ashkenazim	8	20	13	7	12	10	11	13
% Orientals	8	4.8	6.3	12.5	7.7	16.7	8.3	7.1
Herut								
Total	14	11	15	18	18	15	14	16
Orientals	2	1	2	2	3	3	2	4
Ashkenazim	12	10	13	16	15	12	12	12
% Orientals	14.3	9.1	13.3	11.1	16.7	20.0	14.3	25.0
Other Lists								
Total	23	21	19	15	17	18	20	24
Orientals	5	3	0	0	0	1	1	1
Ashkenazim	18	18	19	15	17	17	19	23
% Orientals	21.7	14.3	0	0	0	5.6	5.0	4.2

Left (Alignment)								
Total	72	72	66	65	64	67	55	50
Orientals	5	7	8	10	10	17	12	11
Ashkenazim	67	65	58	55	54	50	43	39
% Orientals	6.9	9.7	12.1	15.4	15.6	25.4	21.8	22.0
Religious (Mafdal)								
Total	10	10	11	12	14	12	12	10
Orientals	0	0	1	1	2	2	1	2
Ashkenazim	10	10	10	11	12	10	11	8
% Orientals	0	0	9.1	8.3	14.3	16.7	8.3	20.0
Right (Gahal, Likud)								
Total	22	32	29	26	31	27	26	39
Orientals	2	2	3	3	4	5	3	6
Ashkenazim	20	30	26	23	27	22	23	33
% Orientals	9.1	6.3	10.3	11.5	12.9	18.5	11.5	15.4

a The three major blocs are the Socialists, organized politically as the Alignment (Israel Labour Party, Ahdut HaAvoda, Mapai, Rafi and Mapam), Likud (Liberals, Herut and other splinter parties), and the Religious (taken here as Mafdal – the Religious National Party; the other two religious splinter parties are not included). In 1973 elections these three blocs received 78.1% of the votes, i.e., 39.6, 30.2 and 8.3% respectively.

b In the 1st to 6th Knesset, all members who served during the term; in the 7th and 8th Knesset, new members only. Non-Jewish members are excluded.

Source: as in Table 37.

335

TABLE 69 *Members of Zionist executive committee (Israelis only) by major political party and bloc, 1951–72*

	1951–5	1956–60	1961–4	1965–8	1969–70	1972
Total[a]						
Total	39	52	49	41	51	41
Orientals	0	1	3	5	4	5
Ashkenazim	39	51	46	36	47	36
% Orientals	0	1.9	6.1	12.2	7.8	12.2
Mapam						
Total	9	4	5	5	4	4
Orientals	0	0	0	0	0	0
Ashkenazim	9	4	5	5	4	4
% Orientals	0	0	0	0	0	0
Ahdut HaAvoda						
Total		4	4	3	5	4
Orientals		0	0	0	0	0
Ashkenazim		4	4	3	5	4
% Orientals		0	0	0	0	0
Mapai						
Total	17	20	22	14	14	13[b]
Orientals	0	0	3	3	2	3
Ashkenazim	17	20	19	11	12	10
% Orientals	0	0	13.6	21.4	14.3	23.1
Mafdal						
Total	7	7	4	5	4	6
Orientals	0	0	0	1	0	2
Ashkenazim	7	7	4	4	4	4
% Orientals	0	0	0	20.0	0	33.0
Liberals						
Total	4	10	3	4	5	5
Orientals	0	1	0	0	1	0
Ashkenazim	4	9	3	4	4	5
% Orientals	0	10.0	0	0	20.0	0
Herut						
Total	2	7	7	7	5	4
Orientals	0	0	0	1	1	0
Ashkenazim	2	7	7	6	4	4
% Orientals	0	0	0	14.3	20.0	0
Other lists						
Total			4	3	14	5
Orientals			0	0	0	0
Ashkenazim			4	3	14	5
% Orientals			0	0	0	0

TABLE 69 *continued*

	1951–5	1956–60	1961–4	1965–8	1969–70	1972
Left (Alignment)						
Total	26	28	31	22	23	17
Orientals	0	0	3	3	2	3
Ashkenazim	26	28	28	19	21	14
% Orientals	0	0	9.7	13.6	8.7	17.6
Religious (Mafdal)						
Total	7	7	4	5	4	6
Orientals	0	0	0	1	0	0
Ashkenazim	7	7	4	4	4	6
% Orientals	0	0	0	20.0	0	0
Right (Gahal)						
Total	6	17	10	11	10	9
Orientals	0	1	0	1	2	0
Ashkenazim	6	16	10	10	8	9
% Orientals	0	5.9	0	9.1	20.0	0

a Up to 1972, members who served during the term and in 1972, members
elected in the 28th Zionist congress in January 1972 only.
b Including several Rafi members.

Source: as in Table 46.

TABLE 70 *Members of executive committee of the Histadrut by
major political party and bloc, 1949–69*

	1949	1956	1960	1966	1969
Total					
Total[a]	51	91	107	130	163
Orientals	3	8	12	22	34
Ashkenazim	48	83	95	108	129
% Orientals	5.9	8.8	11.2	16.9	20.9
Mapam					
Total	17	11	15	18	18
Orientals	1	0	2	3	3
Ashkenazim	16	11	13	15	15
% Orientals	5.9	0	13.3	16.7	16.7
Ahdut HaAvoda					
Total		13	18	20	20
Orientals		3	3	4	3
Ashkenazim		10	15	16	17
% Orientals		23.1	16.7	20.0	15.0

TABLE 70 *continued*

	1949	1956	1960	1966	1969
Mapai					
Total	31	53	59	47	48
Orientals	2	5	7	7	7
Ashkenazim	29	48	52	40	41
% Orientals	6.5	9.4	11.9	14.9	14.6
Rafi					
Total				16	16
Orientals				3	5
Ashkenazim				13	11
% Orientals				18.8	31.3
Liberals					
Total		1	4	9	13
Orientals		0	0	1	3
Ashkenazim		1	4	8	10
% Orientals		0	0	11.1	23.1
Herut					
Total				11	15
Orientals				4	4
Ashkenazim				7	11
% Orientals				36.4	26.7
Other lists					
Total	3	13	11	9	33
Orientals	0	0	0	0	9
Ashkenazim	3	13	11	9	24
% Orientals	0	0	0	0	27.3
Left (Alignment)					
Total	48	77	92	101	102
Orientals	3	8	12	17	18
Ashkenazim	45	69	80	84	84
% Orientals	6.3	10.4	13.0	16.8	17.6
Right (Gahal)					
Total		1	4	20	28
Orientals		0	0	5	7
Ashkenazim		1	4	15	21
% Orientals		0	0	25.0	25.0

a Excluding non-Jews.

Source: as in Table 49.

TABLE 71   *Members of the board and executive of the Industrialists'*
Union, 1969–70

1969–70	Board	Executive
Total	15	55
Orientals	1	0
Ashkenazim	14	55
% Oriental	6.7	0

Source: List provided by the office of the Industrialists' Union.

TABLE 72   *Percentage distribution of top managers in industry, 1961–7*

	1961[1]	1966[2]	1967[3]
Total	100	100	100
Israeli born[a]	11	10	26
Orientals	3	3	3
Ashkenazim	86	87	71

a The ethnic origin of the Israeli-born is either not reported or not known.

Sources: 1 Ozi Peled, 'The Climate of Management in Israel' (in Hebrew),
Jerusalem: Israel Institute for Applied Social Research, 1964.
2 Mathew Radom, 'Management Development in Israel', Haifa:
Industrial and Management Engineering, Israel Institute of
Technology, 1967.
3 Ya'akov Blecher and Ora Ben-Yisrael, 'The Position of Managers
in Public Plants' (in Hebrew), Tel-Aviv: Labour Productivity
Institute and the Hebrew University, 1968.

TABLE 73 *Status hierarchies by rank, late 1950s and late 1960s*

	Late 1950s		Index of equality		Late 1960s[a]		Index of equality	
	Asia–Africa	Europe–America	Rel.	Abs.	Asia–Africa	Europe–America	Rel.	Abs.
Income[1] (standard equivalent adults, 1963–4 and 1968–9)								
Total	100.0	100.0			100.0	100.0		
Rank A[b]	5.4	31.3	17	−25.9	8.0	32.1	25	−24.1
Rank B[b]	14.2	24.1	59	−9.9	14.3	24.4	59	−10.1
Others[b]	80.4	44.6	180	+35.8	77.7	43.5	179	+34.2
Occupation[2] (males, 1959 and 1969)								
Total	100.0	100.0			100.0	100.0		
Rank A[c]	10.3	28.8	36	−18.5	15.2	36.3	42	−21.1
Rank B[c]	10.7	16.3	66	−5.6	14.4	16.6	87	−2.2
Others[c]	79.0	54.9	144	−24.1	70.4	47.1	147	+23.3
Education[3] (males, 1961 and 1969)								
Total	100.0	100.0			100.0	100.0		
Rank A[d]	4.5	16.1	28	−11.6	5.6	19.4	29	−13.8
Rank B[d]	24.1	38.7	62	−14.6	28.3	38.9	73	−10.6
Others[d]	71.4	45.2	158	+26.2	66.1	41.7	159	+24.4

Political representation[4] (late 1950s and 1960s; total = 100)

Rank A[e]	5	95	5	−90	17	83	20	−66
Rank B[e]	5	95	5	−90	16	84	20	−68
Others	20	80	25	−60	37	63	59	−26

a In the late 1960s in the top two ranks, 40% of standard equivalent adults are included in case of income, 43.4% of the males in occupation, and 54.6% of the males in education.

b Rank A (20% of standard equivalent adults of urban Jewish families in 1968–9) is defined as the highest quintile; rank B (20%) as the second highest quintile; and others, the remainder.

c Rank A (27.8% of male workers in the population in 1969) includes professional, scientific and technical workers as well as executive and managerial workers. Rank B (15.6%) includes traders, agents and salesmen as well as transport and communications workers. Others = all other categories.

d Rank A (13.8% of males aged 14 or over in 1969) refers to people with 13 or more years of schooling; rank B (40.8%) to 9–12 years, and 'others' to those with 8 or fewer years.

e Rank A refers to the tops of three power centres; i.e., the state government, the executive of the Jewish Agency and the central committee of the Histadrut. The reported percentage is computed from a simple combination of the Oriental representation there: Rank B refers to a representative governing body of the various parties. The reported percentage is computed from a simple combination of the Oriental representation in the following bodies: political committee in Mapam, secretariat in Ahdut HaAvoda (only in the late 1960s; for the late 1950s this party is not included in the computation), bureau of Mapai in the late 1950s and secretariat of Rafi (late 1960s only), directorate of Mafdal, steering committee of the Liberal Party in the late 1950s and executive committee in the late 1960s, and executive committee of Herut. The category 'others' refers to local power; i.e., heads of local authorities and general secretaries of 'workers' councils.

Sources: 1 Public Inquiry Commission (Horowitz Commission), Report of the Committee on Income Distribution and Social Inequality (duplicated), Tel-Aviv, 1971. p. 25.
2 CBS, Labour Force Survey, Special Series 162, Table 49.
3 CBS, Population and Housing Census, 1961, Languages, Literacy and Educational Attainment, no. 15, Table 28.
4 For Rank A, Tables 35, 45 and 48; for Rank B, Tables 58, 60–5; and for 'others', Tables 41 and 43.

TABLE 74 *Percentage distribution of family size, 1975*

	Number of people in family								Average size of family[a]
	Total	1	2	3	4	5	6	7+	
Asia–Africa	100.0	9.1	14.1	13.2	18.0	17.0	10.4	18.2	4.5
Europe–America	100.0	17.6	34.6	18.9	17.4	8.2	2.4	1.0	2.8
Israel-born, total	100.0	12.7	16.0	21.2	26.4	14.8	5.3	3.5	3.5
Father born in Israel	100.0	13.7	16.7	21.0	22.7	15.0	8.0	3.0	3.5
Father born in Asia–Africa	100.0	9.3	16.4	21.3	22.7	15.4	6.4	8.6	3.8
Father born in Europe–America	100.0	14.0	15.6	21.1	29.4	14.6	4.1	1.3	3.3

[a] Including single persons.

Source: CBS, *Statistical Abstract of Israel, 1976,* 27: 49.

TABLE 75 *Adjusted index of similarity in consumption patterns, 1956–7 to 1963–4*

	Adjusted index of similarity[a]		
Item	1956–7	1959–60	1963–4
Food	102	100	104
Clothing	138	138	114
Furniture and household appliances	111	127	136
Education	42	45	48
Culture (recreation)	52	43	48

[a] Adjusted index of similarity equals the average monthly expenditure of an Oriental wage-earning family on a given item as a percentage of average monthly expenditure of an Ashkenazi wage-earning family of equal income and size on the same item.

Source: Yaaqov Parush, 'Differences in consumption among population strata' (in Hebrew), *Riv'on Lekalkala*, 49–50, June 1966, Table 4.

TABLE 76 *Percentage distribution of foreign-born Jews, by type of locality, 1967*

Type of settlement	Total	Asia–Africa	Europe–America
Total	100.0	100.0	100.0
Urban, total	90.3	90.4	90.2
The three major cities	31.6	22.6	39.3
Other veteran towns and urban settlements	30.8	27.7	33.3
New towns and urban settlements	27.8	40.1	17.5
Rural, total	9.7	9.6	9.8
Veteran	4.3	2.4	5.9
New	5.2	6.9	3.7
Not known	0.2	0.2	0.2

Source: CBS, *Population in Settlements*, 1967–1969, Special Series 339, Table 22.

TABLE 77 Students in primary, intermediate and post-primary schools by percentage of Oriental students in class and types of school and locality, 1966–7 and 1972–3

	Total number of students	Thereof: % of Oriental students	Percentage of Oriental students in class									
			Total	up to 4.9	5.0–14.9	15.0–24.9	25.0–34.9	35.0–64.9	65.0–74.9	75.0–84.9	85.0–94.9	95.0–100.0
Primary education 1972–3												
Total	361,726	59.8	100.0	2.3	6.2	8.5	10.0	26.3	7.2	8.8	10.3	20.5
Thereof: culturally deprived	106,963	90.0	100.0	0.2	0.3	0.1	0.4	5.7	5.7	12.3	20.6	54.7
State	250,800	51.8	100.0	2.5	7.2	10.4	12.3	32.6	8.6	10.1	9.6	6.6
Thereof: culturally deprived	47,437	84.2	100.0	0.1	0.2	—	0.4	9.0	10.8	22.7	30.3	26.4
State-religious	91,199	80.8	100.0	1.3	2.5	3.0	4.1	12.7	4.3	5.8	11.7	54.5
Thereof: culturally deprived	59,526	94.7	100.0	0.2	0.4	0.2	0.4	3.1	1.7	3.9	12.8	77.3
Independent (ultra-religious)	19,727	65.1	100.0	5.8	10.0	9.1	7.7	8.0	2.6	5.6	11.6	39.5
New urban settlements	89,620	80.9	100.0	0.5	0.8	1.2	2.6	16.6	8.0	13.0	18.1	39.2
New rural settlements	22,249	75.0	100.0	5.1	4.4	4.4	4.6	11.3	4.0	4.3	10.3	51.6
Intermediate education 1972–3												
Total	38,542	58.6	100.0	1.8	5.8	10.7	12.8	24.7	5.2	7.4	9.6	22.0
State	26,831	46.7	100.0	2.4	7.4	14.4	17.1	31.8	6.2	8.1	7.0	5.5
State-religious	11,485	85.6	100.0	0.5	2.0	2.2	3.0	8.6	3.1	5.6	15.1	59.8
Other religious	226	95.6	100.0	—	—	—	—	—	—	—	43.4	56.6
New urban settlements	11,860	83.7	100.0	0.5	0.4	0.6	2.5	14.4	7.6	12.0	16.2	46.0
New rural settlements	3,832	74.2	100.0	—	1.6	4.6	8.1	20.8	2.0	9.9	12.0	40.9
Post-primary education 1966–7												
Total	116,259	35.6	100.0	10.3	21.5	16.4	10.4	21.6	4.9	4.9	4.8	5.2
Academic	53,577	25.4	100.0	12.6	30.5	20.8	11.6	14.7	2.9	2.5	2.7	1.7
Vocational	35,234	47.0	100.0	3.7	11.2	13.8	11.0	30.8	7.0	6.8	6.5	9.2
Agricultural	7,062	52.4	100.0	3.6	9.9	10.4	6.1	33.9	8.1	11.1	7.7	9.2

TABLE 78 *People marrying, by bride's and groom's ethnic origin,*[a] *1955–74*

	1955	1960	1965	1970	1974
Groom from Asia–Africa					
Bride from Asia–Africa	39.8	42.4	45.2	39.6	43.7
Bride from Europe–America	4.3	5.0	7.0	9.3	8.7
Groom from Europe–America					
Bride from Asia–Africa	7.5	9.5	6.8	8.3	10.4
Bride from Europe–America	48.4	43.1	41.0	42.8	37.2
Total	100.0	100.0	100.0	100.0	100.0
Actual percentage of mixed marriages	11.8	14.5	13.8	17.6	19.1
Expected percentage of mixed marriages if choice is random[b]	49.7	50.1	49.9	50.0	49.4
Ratio (percentage) of actual to expected	23.7	28.9	27.7	35.2	38.7

a Before 1965 statistics refer to foreign-born only, for 1965 onwards they include Israeli-born classified according to continent of birth of father.
b Computed as follows

$$\frac{(a \times b) + (c \times d)}{(a+c) \quad (b+d)} \text{ where}$$

a = number of Ashkenazi grooms
b = number of Oriental brides
c = number of Oriental grooms
d = number of Ashkenazi brides.
This computation is suggested by Yochanan Peres and Ruth Shrift (1975).

Source: CBS, *Statistical Abstract of Israel,* 1976, 27: 69.

TABLE 79 *Rates of convicted Jewish offenders by age, 1952–74*[a]

	1952		1960		1970		1974	
	Juveniles	Adults	Juveniles	Adults	Juveniles	Adults	Juveniles	Adults
Israeli-born	7.3	13.8	5.0	10.0	8.2	11.4		
Thereof: Father born in Asia–Africa					8.7			
Foreign-born								
Asia	7.4	16.8	12.1	13.7	4.8	7.8	} 10.7	6.8
Africa	13.8	24.2	18.0	23.9	21.8	17.9		13.1
Europe–America	3.4	6.6	5.3	4.3	4.8	3.0	2.2	2.9

[a] Rates are per 1,000 specific population. In 1970 juvenile delinquents were defined as boys aged 9–16 and girls aged 9–18, and adult delinquents as men over 17 and women over 19.

Sources: For 1952 and 1960, O. Schmelz and D. Salzman, *Criminal Statistics in Israel 1949–1962,* vol. 2, Jerusalem: Hebrew University, 1964, p. 47 (quoted in Rivkah Bar-Yosef (1971: Table 17)). For 1970, CBS, *Juvenile Delinquency,* 1970, Special Series 408, p. xvi (Table E), and CBS, *Statistical Abstract of Israel,* 1973, 24: 615–16. For 1974, CBS, *Statistical Abstract of Israel,* 1976, 27: 577–8.

TABLE 80   *Method of election of Knesset members of major divisions,*
 1949–73[a]

	1st 1949	2nd 1951	3rd 1955	4th 1959	5th 1961	6th 1965	7th 1969	8th 1973
Total	120	120	120	120	120	120	120	120
Orientals, total	8	7	10	14	14	21	17	19
Thereof: elected on Oriental lists	4	2	0	0	0	0	0	0
Religious, total	16	15	17	19	18	17	19	17
Thereof: elected on religious lists	16	15	17	18	18	17	18	15
Arabs, total	3	8	7	7	6	7	7	6
Thereof: elected on Arab lists	2	5	5	5	4	4	4	3

[a] At the beginning of each term.

Sources: Asher Zidon, *The Knesset* (in Hebrew), Tel-Aviv: Achiassaf (6th ed.),
 1971, Appendix; Israel, *Government Year Book*; Israel, *Knesset
 Proceedings* (in Hebrew).

TABLE 81 *Participation of the religious parties in government, 1949–73*

Government[a]	Number of Knesset members supporting the government			Number of Cabinet Ministers		
	Total	Thereof: religious[b] Number	religious[b] %	Total	Thereof: religious[b] Number	religious[b] %
1st, 10 March 1949	73	16	21.9	12	3	25.0
2nd, 1 November 1950	73	16	21.9	13	3	23.1
3rd, 8 October 1951	67	15	22.4	13	4	30.8
4th, 23 December 1952	87	10	11.5	16	2	12.5
5th, 26 January 1954	87	10	11.5	16	2	12.5
6th, 29 June 1955	64	10	15.6	12	2	16.7
7th, 3 November 1955	80	11	13.8	16	2	12.5
8th, 7 January 1958	80c	11c	13.8c	16c	2c	12.5c
9th, 17 December 1959	86	12	14.0	16	2	12.5
10th, 2 November 1961	68	14	20.6	16	3	18.8
11th, 6 June 1963	68	14	20.6	15	3	20.0
12th, 22 December 1964	68	14	20.6	15	3	20.0
13th, 1 January 1966	75	13	17.3	18	3	16.7
14th, 11 March 1969	106	13	12.3	22	3	13.6
15th, 16 December 1969	102	12	11.8	24	3	12.5
As of 31 December 1973	76	12	15.8	18	3	16.7

a At the beginning of each term.

b Including members of all religious parties which supported the government.

c Between July 1958 and December 1959 the National Religious Party stayed out of the government because of the 'Who Is a Jew?' controversy. This did not cause the resignation of the government. An independent Rabbi was nominated as a Minister for Religious Affairs and continued in the 9th government for some time till his death.

Sources: as in Table 35.

TABLE 82   *Demographic characteristics of Israeli Arabs and Jews (Asia–Africa, Europe–America), 1975*

Demographic characteristic	Arabs	Jews Total[a]	Asia–Africa	Europe–America
Births and deaths				
rate of live births[b]	42.7	25.0		
rate of deaths[b]	5.7	7.4		
rate of infant mortality[b]	39.5	17.9		
rate of natural increase[b]	37.0	17.6		
gross reproduction rate[c]	3.31	1.55	1.83	1.37
life expectancy (of newborn)				
male[d]	68.5	70.9		
female[d]	71.8	74.5		
Age distribution				
percentage of people under 15[e]	49.5	29.9	33.6	16.8
median age[e]	15.2	25.7	21.7	35.8
Family size				
Percentage of families with 6 or more persons[f]	56.7	13.0	28.6	3.4
Average size (including single persons)[f]	6.3	3.5	4.5	
Type of locality				
Percentage urban[g]	50.7	90.6	90.4	90.2
Percentage rural[g]	49.3	9.2	9.6	9.8

a 'Total' refers to the entire Jewish population, including Israeli-born (whose figures are deleted).

b pp. 59–60 (in source below).

c p. 76. The gross reproduction rate represents the average number of female offspring born to a woman in her lifetime (regardless of mortality).

d p. 89. Arab figures are averages for the years 1973–5.

e pp. 44–5. In computing the measures of the Jewish groups, figures for Israeli- and foreign-born are combined.

f p. 50.

g p. 29. The 50.7% Arab urban in the table is smaller than the official figure of 59.2% because of the exclusion of the 92,000 Arab residents of East Jerusalem. The figures for Asia–Africa and Europe–America are for 1967, taken from CBS, *Population in Settlements*, 1967–9, Special Series 339, Table 22.

Source: CBS, *Statistical Abstract of Israel*, 1976, 27 (page numbers are indicated in notes above).

TABLE 83   *Socioeconomic status of Israeli Arabs and Jews (Asia–Africa, Europe–America), 1975*

Socioeconomic measures	Arabs Total[a]	Jews Asia–Africa	Europe–America
Material wellbeing			
Annual per capita income in Israeli pounds[b]	4,651	8,289 5,729	10,774
% of families possessing electric refrigerator[e]	53.8	98.3 97.3	98.9
% of families possessing telephone[c]	7.0	52.2 31.3	63.6
% of families possessing private car[c]	11.5	27.6 15.2	31.2
% of families living in decent housing (one or fewer persons per room)[d]	13.9	52.5 31.3	70.1
Occupation			
% in scientific, professional, managerial and clerical jobs[e]	12.8	43.0 25.3	47.2
% in unskilled jobs[f]	13.0	5.2 8.9	4.3
% in agriculture and construction[g]	40.3	11.8	
Education			
Median number of years of schooling[h]	6.0	9.6 7.1	9.8
% illiterate[h]	22.9	7.6 21.6	2.6
% with at least some college education[h]	4.5	17.7 7.0	22.9
% of youths aged 14–17 in post-primary schools[i]	32.0	60.9 52.2	70.8
Students in higher education per 100 people aged 20–9 of the population[j]	1.4	8.5 2.6	13.6

a 'Total' refers to the entire Jewish population. Since Israeli-born, whose figures are deleted, are better off than Asia–Africa, the 'total' is closer to the Europe–America data than to the Asia–Africa data.
b p. 261 (in source below).
c For 1974; CBS, *Statistical Abstract of Israel*, 1975, 26: 275–8.
d p. 273.
e pp. 287, 314–15. First four (top) categories of occupation. Arab figures were obtained by taking the difference between totals and Jews.
f As in note e. Last category of occupation.
g p. 287.
h p. 589.
i For Jews, refined rates, p. 608. For Arabs, a crude rate computed on basis of figures on pp. 40 and 598.
j Crude rates for the 1972–3 academic year; CBS, *Statistical Abstract of Israel*, 1974, 25: 46–8, 633.

Source: CBS, *Statistical Abstract of Israel*, 1976, 27 (page numbers are indicated in notes above).

TABLE 84 *Political representation in selected positions of power of Israeli Arabs and Jews (Orientals, Ashkenazim), December 1973*

Position and year	Arabs	Total[a]	Jews Orientals	Ashkenazim
State				
President (1973)	0	1	0	1
Cabinet ministers (1973)	0	18	0	16
Deputy ministers (1973)	2	6	0	6
Knesset members (elected on 31 December 1973)	6	114	19	95
Supreme Court justices (1973)	0	10	1	9
Major-generals (1973)	0	21	0	21
Directors-general (1973)	0	18	0	18
Top officials (1968)	0[a]	496[a]	23[a]	355[a]
Zionist organization				
Executive of Jewish Agency (1973)	0	13	1	12
Zionist executive committee (1973)	0	51	6	45
Directors-general of departments in the Jewish Agency (1973)	0	17	1	16
Histadrut				
Central committee (1973)	0	20	5	15
Executive committee (1969)	4	163	34	129
General-secretaries of national trade unions (1973)	0	41	0	41
Top-ranking officials (as of January 1971)	1	234	37	197
Secretariat of Hevrat HaOvdim (1973)	0	33	1	32
Parties				
Israel Labour Party				
Bureau (1973)	0	27	3	24
Central committee (1973)	10	605	157	448
Mapam				
Steering secretariat (1973)	0	9	0	9
Central committee (1973)	11	340	50	290
Mafdal				
Secretariat (1973)	0	16	4	12
Broader executive committee (1973)	0	200	65	135

TABLE 84—*continued*

Position and year	Arabs	Total[a]	Jews Orientals	Ashkenazim
Parties—*continued*				
Herut				
Executive committee (1973)	0	31	4	27
Central committee (1973)	3	251	73	178
Liberal Party				
Executive committee (1973)	0	33	1	32
Central committee (1973)	0	115	7	108
Localities				
Heads of local authorities (1973)	48	98	33	65
General secretaries of workers' councils (1972)	2	65	37	28
General secretaries of local branches of Labour Party (1973)	0	82	37	45

[a] With one exception, 'Total' refers to the entire number of officeholders (Israeli-born are classified according to their ethnic origin). Only in the category of state top officials, there are 118 Israeli-born whose ethnic origin is not reported. They are probably Ashkenazim, but might include several Orientals and one or two Arabs.

Sources: as in Tables 35, 37–40, 42, 45–9, 51–3, 56, 58–9, 63–6.

Notes

1 Introduction

1   For a survey of the various meanings of pluralism, see Schermerhorn (1970: 122–8); Cox (1971).

2   The additional pluralistic divisions concern other small culturally distinct or socially separate minorities, including Karaites (non-Rabbinic Jews, numbering about 12,000), Samaritans (members of a sect related to Judaism, about 200 in Israel proper), Circassians (members of a Moslem, partially Arabized sect, fewer than 2,000 members) and Bahais (about 200) (for some details on these and other small Israeli minorities, see Cohen and Gronau, 1972). Subdivisions pertain to extra subgroupings within the five major divisions mentioned above. For instance, the Orientals and Ashkenazim are internally divided among people hailing from about a hundred countries of origin.

3   For books which provide a comprehensive introduction to or an analysis of Israel, see the list under the heading Israel (general) in the Selected Bibliography at the end of the book. Weingrod (1965) has remained the only book dealing with the various aspects of pluralism in Israel, although the treatment of religious–nonreligious and Arab–Jewish relations is very sketchy. Patai (1970), which first appeared in 1953, is another exception.

4   There is of course also a problem of the impingements of ideology on scientific social analysis. Even if theory and ideology can be totally separated in the abstract, they are hardly divorced in practice. I will comment later on the ideological underpinnings of the present perspectives on Israel. Here let me clarify one relevant point. Groups' names are often used not just for simple identification but also as symbols of desired identities and as weapons in intergroup struggles (note the shift from 'Negroes' to 'Blacks' in the United States). In choosing names social scientists have to balance the demands for clarity and doing justice to social reality. The appellation 'nonreligious Jews' is preferred to 'secular Jews' because the majority of

this group keep some religious traditions and identify themselves as semi-observants rather than secular. By the same token the term 'Orientals' is used instead of 'Sephardim' because Orientals are the large majority of non-Ashkenazi Jews. It is more difficult to justify the names 'Israeli Arabs' and 'Arab minority', which quite a few Arabs reject. Recent surveys have shown that the Palestinian identity is gaining more and more acceptance among them, but they have not managed yet to enforce their renewed identity on the Israeli public. Thus the technical consideration not to confuse Arabs in Israel proper with Palestinian Arabs in the post-1967 occupied territories took precedence in the final selection of the name 'Israeli Arabs'.

5   Tables 1–6 in the Appendix provide a quick synopsis of the conceptual scheme of analysis used and the main findings of the study.

2   A theoretical perspective: Structural pluralism

1   For useful propositional summaries, see LeVine and Campbell (1972: Part 3); Ehrlich (1973).

2   Westie, in a summary statement of the field, writes: 'This discussion of research and theory does not include such concepts as "social solidarity", "integration", "harmony" and their opposites. Instead it is built around the concepts of *prejudice* and *discrimination*, with greater emphasis on the former than the latter. Both of these concepts refer to phenomena which can be specifically conceptualized and observed. This is probably the reason why more research in this area has been built around the concepts of prejudice and discrimination than all the other concepts in the area combined' (1964: 581).

3   Barth and Noel distinguish four problems in intergroup relations and four sociological frameworks to tackle them. 'Although each of the frameworks has relevance for more than one of these empirical problems, it is concluded that the race cycle is most useful in explaining the emergence of ethnic differentiation, consensus is most useful vis-à-vis persistence, interdependence vis-à-vis adaptation, and conflict vis-à-vis change' (1972: 333). The overwhelming majority of studies fall under the first three categories. There is also a tendency, as in Park's classical model and even in Shibutani's and Kwan's theory (1965), to overlook the fact that the emergence of ethnic differentiation is due to involuntary contact (e.g., conquest, slavery) resulting in conflict.

4   Van den Berghe maintains that this holds true of sociology in general. Maintaining that 'sociology, as a nomothetic enterprise, cannot be anything but comparative', he charges that 'Much of what has hitherto been passed off as theory in sociology textbooks has in fact been North American ethnography overlaid with a thick crust of functionalist jargon' (1972: 14).

5   Furnivall describes the plural society as follows: 'In Burma, as in Java, probably the first thing that strikes the visitor is the medley of peoples – European, Chinese, Indian and native. It is in the strictest sense a medley, for they mix but do not combine. Each group holds

by its own religion, its own culture and language, its ideas and ways. As individuals they meet, but only in the market place, in buying and selling. There is a plural society with different sections of the community living side by side, but separately, within the same political unit. Even in the economic sphere there is a division of labour on racial lines' (1948: 304).

6 Kornhauser (1959), among others, offers a statement of political pluralism.

7 Although concurring with this conclusion, Newman (1973) criticizes these and other models of American pluralism and, drawing on a power–conflict framework, he offers a different interpretation. His approach to pluralism does not fall, however, within the limits of the new school.

8 Smith's Caribbean studies (1965a; 1965b) and van den Berghe's study of South Africa (1967a: chapter 11) provide formal, negative tests of the functionalist approach. It has been clearly shown that these societies do not have and thus are not held together by common values as functionalism would claim.

9 For summaries of criticisms see Smith (1969b: 419–37, including his responses) and Rex (1970: 21–4).

10 Many scholars have contributed to the new school of pluralism. For listings see Smith (1969b: 418) and van den Berghe (1973: 962–5).

11 Cross (1971: 482–5) criticizes Smith's ambiguity with regard to the repercussions of pluralism for conflict and change.

12 Kuper concludes: 'the processes of political change in plural societies should be seen as indeterminate' (1974: 252).

13 For other criticisms of the political pluralists' stance by van den Berghe, see also 1967b: 146–7; 1973: 959 61.

14 Schermerhorn is a late-comer to the new pluralist school after being long associated with a power–conflict framework (1970: 53). He is not known as pluralist, but his important volume, *Comparative Ethnic Relations*, fits clearly into this perspective.

15 Another conceptual scheme is suggested by Despres (1967: 21–9). He distinguishes between *local* institutions (dialects, family and kinship, religion, work, socialization, recreation, voluntary associations, and local government) and *broker* institutions (markets, corporations, labour unions, governmental agencies, political parties, school organizations, social and civic associations, national ethnic alliances). Society is homogeneous to the extent to which no group differentiation can be discerned; heterogeneous to the degree there is group differentiation in local institutions alone; and plural to the amount constituent groups maintain separate or parallel national broker institutions. Despres emphasizes that in order to understand conflict and change in plural societies one should study both cultural. pluralism and nationalist politics – thus ideologies and leadership styles are important factors in channelling pluralism into either conflict or integration.

Mason (1970a; 1970b), Rex (1970), and Hoetink (1967; 1973), while themselves not pluralist and even critical of pluralism, have suggested theoretical frameworks which are compatible with and often close to pluralism. Mason, for instance, has proposed a conceptual scheme consisting of six sets of factors: numerical proportions; nature of initial intergroup contact; sexual attitudes of the dominant group; territorial factors; characteristics of the dominant group; and characteristics of the subordinate group (1970a: chapter 8; 1970b: Part II). Although Mason does not take pluralism as a cardinal parameter, he offers some determinants that pluralists can incorporate in their own schemes.

16 For a discussion of the various strategies, see Schermerhorn (1970: 237–55) who recommends the 'inductive typology' method that pluralists are predisposed to.

17 It must be emphasized that this scheme, as the others, falls far short of what Merton calls a paradigm (like his paradigms of deviant behaviour and functionalism). According to Merton, paradigms 'provide a compact parsimonious arrangement of the central concepts and their interrelations as these are utilized for description and analysis', supply pragmatic guides 'for avoidance of *ad hoc* hypotheses', 'advance the cumulation of theoretical interpretations', 'suggest the systematic cross-tabulation of presumably significant concepts and may thus sensitize the analyst to types of empirical and theoretic problems which might otherwise be overlooked', and finally serve as tools for codification of theories (1957: 13–16). Conceptual schemes are, on the other hand, more modest. They list strategic variables and provide certain rationales for analysis. Their usefulness should be demonstrated by fruitful or insightful empirical applications.

18 Cohesion (conflict and integration) and change are dependent variables. Setting factors are either independent variables affecting pluralism and inequality (as they appear in Kuper's scheme) or intervening variables which channel the effects of pluralism and inequality (as they are conceived by Schermerhorn). Pluralism and inequality are independent variables in relation to cohesion and change, or dependent variables when setting factors are taken as independent variables.

19 All these three features of pluralism can be found in the pluralists' writings. Van den Berghe (1967b: 142–3) and Schermerhorn (1970: chapter 4) treat magnitude of pluralism as a variable. Kuper (1969b: 478) suggests superimposition–dissociation, following Dahrendorf, as a summary measure. Van den Berghe (1967b: n. 4 on p. 150; n. 11 on p. 81) makes the distinction between transitory and stable pluralism, which implies durability. (Kuper also proposes discontinuity–continuity as another summary measure, but since it does not lend itself readily to operationalization it is excluded from the scheme.) None of them, however, has explicitly distinguished among all the three suggested features nor has examined the interplay among them.

20 Elsewhere I have illustrated the utility of the three features of pluralism (Smooha, 1975: 81–4). For their application in this study, see the last section in chapter 6.

21 Personal communication to the author.

22 See n. 15 above.

23 All these three summary measures refer to overall cohesion rather than to conflict or integration separately. It must be noted that whereas several summary measures of conflict are well established in the sociological literature (e.g., frequency, intensity and violence are suggested by Newman, 1973: chapter 4), nearly none is available regarding integration or cohesion.

24 There is not as yet any study which quantifies the components in our scheme. In two studies reported by Haug (1967) and Bagley (1972), simple scores are used to measure 'pluralism', which is defined differently.

25 Adam counsels pluralists: 'Instead of reifying cultural heterogeneity as a quasi-natural state of affairs, ethnic identifications should be seen as the result of efforts by underprivileged groups to improve their lot through collective mobilization; conversely, the efforts of a superordinate group to preserve the privileges they enjoy by exploiting subjected groups' (1971: 22).

26 According to Magubane: 'An attempt to substitute the idea or theory of plural society for the Marxist sociology of conflict is a manifestation of the ideological struggle going on between the defenders of the old order and those who are trying to break loose from the economic and political chains of neocolonialism' (1971: 442).

27 In launching their attacks, critics are often selective in their references to pluralist formulations. In referring to Smith's original statement of the plural society only, Rex makes the criticism that pluralism neglects economic interdependence (1970: 23–4) and thus is deficient in accounting for race relations in South Africa (1971). As indicated above, Furnivall and van den Berghe do emphasize economic factors. Cross (1971) also limits his critical discussion to Smith's earlier and present formulations, but since in concluding his paper he exonerates Kuper, van den Berghe and perhaps Schermerhorn, his criticism is misleading in its generality.

28 In our scheme inequality is as important as pluralism. What is peculiar to the pluralism school is, therefore, not negligence of important structural factors but its rejection of unideterminism.

29 Such specifications are occasionally made. For instance, as mentioned above, van den Berghe regards ethnic pluralism as more central in Africa than in Latin America. Or Kuper admits to 'have come to question the universality of the class struggle' (1974: 203), yet he considers differential incorporation emanating from vast inequality in political power the major determinant in highly pluralized societies.

30 These theoretical models are often contradictory and only partially informative. In referring to some of them, Bonacich is correct in saying that 'one is generally struck by the absence of a developed theory accounting for variations in ethnic antagonism' (1972: 548).

31 As Kuper puts it: 'Intrinsic to both Marxist and Durkheimian perspectives is a moral conception; in Marxist theory, a conception of progress toward equality by a revolutionary dialectic of change, and in Durkheimian theory, a conception of increasing contact,

harmonious interrelationship and progressive withering away of racial inequality, by a process of evolutionary change. At the political level, these perspectives correspond to communist and liberal ideologies' (1974: 234).

32 Among these distortions are the interpretation of pluralism by dominant groups as part of the social order justifying their domination; subordinate groups may find in it encouragement for unrestrained expression of ethnic antagonism; and others would deduce from the theory that ethnic conflict is inevitable. Kuper comments: 'The interest in plural societies may indeed develop out of strong moral commitment to the avoidance of destructive social conflicts, and to the search for methods, of peaceful change to harmony and equality' (1974: 238). No doubt, such interest is shared by Smith, Kuper, van den Berghe and Schermerhorn. A commitment to a liberal inter-racial strategy is advocated by Kuper (1974: 273–4) and perhaps appeals to the others as well.

3 Models of intergroup relations

1 The term 'model' is used here simply to mean a capsule statement or a succinct account of a phenomenon, not a precise presentation as implied by terms such as path or mathematical models.

2 Eisenstadt's analysis of ethnicity in the prestate period will be taken up in the next chapter.

3 In another formulation, Bar-Yosef (1968) conceptualizes the adjustment of immigrants as the complementary processes of desocialization and resocialization.

4 Similar explanations are offered by Teller (1965), Deutsch (1969) and Adler (1969).

5 Either one of these themes is stressed by educationists such as Shumsky (1955), Simon (1956) and the anthropologist Willner (1969).

6 This idea is expressed also by Antonovsky (1964), Bar-Yosef and Padan (1964) and by social critics like Ben-Chaim (1967); and numerous press commentators throughout 1971 and 1972 at the time of the Black Panthers' activities. These commentaries are echoed in the report published by the Minority Rights Group: 'The problem is, rather, partly a cultural one but principally a socioeconomic one' (Friendly, 1972: 3). The World Sephardic Federation chooses to stress the theme of inequality in its publications (see Abbas, 1959; Geffner, 1972).

7 The question of prejudice and stereotyping is also raised by P. Cohen (1963), and Adar and Adler (1965).

8 P. Cohen (1967; 1968) also gives similar explanation.

9 This is evinced in a number of dissertations completed in the Sociology Department of the Hebrew University (Zuckerman-Bareli, 1970; Friedman, 1973; O. Cohen, 1975; Fishman, 1975). A Reader was published (Samet, 1973) and courses are taught in the departments of sociology in the Hebrew University and Bar-Ilan University.

10 In sketching this model I draw on extensive literature. The references are listed in the selected Bibliography and here I wish to mention only the most useful sources: Guttman (1971), England (1966; 1968), Rubinstein (1957a; 1967b), Meron (1973), Goldman (1964), Liebowitz (1975), Eisenstadt (1967a: *passim*), Leslie (1971), Birnbaum (1970) and Zucker (1973).

11 Segre (1971: 195) argues that the term *Kulturkampf* which is commonly used to describe the strife between the religious and nonreligious in Israel is misleading because the issue is not separation between church and state and because the religious hierarchy of Judaism is too weak to present a challenge to the state. The first point is well taken and the second is only partially correct but neither objection holds against applying the term to refer to a conflict of values or cultures.

12 The opposition to the idea of a Jewish state is now confined to tiny groups. At one extreme are the Canaanites ('the quintessential secularists') and at the other are N'ture Karta ('the quintessential religionists') (Zucker, 1973: 213). The Canaanites comprise scores of writers and intellectuals who declare an attachment to the land and disavow any connection with Judaism, Zionism and world Jewry. The N'ture Karta, on the other hand, are a thousand or so ultra-Orthodox Jews in Jerusalem who believe in a Messianic redemption only and consider the secular Jewish state an aberration (see entries in Patai, 1971a: 173–4, 851–3).

13 The Police Law, 1971, provides for a ban on rallies, demonstrations, etc., which may disturb worship at near-by houses of prayer. The Supreme Court has upheld blocking of roads by police for this purpose.

14 More details on religious legislation will be given in the first section of chapter 6.

15 The religious organizations, services and personnel of non-Jewish communities are equally supported by the state.

16 The Chief Rabbinate is also not fully autonomous. In summer 1974 its request to expand its departments was denied by the Minister of Justice. The reason given for the decision was a need to prevent functional duplication or overlap of authority between the Chief Rabbinate and the Ministry of Religious Affairs. Religious spokesmen criticized the move as anti-religious.

17 Three prohibitions are worth noting:
   (a) A Cohen (a man of a priestly descent) may not marry some 'tainted' kinds of women: a divorcee, a proselyte, a childless widow (who has to get halitzah – see below), a prostitute, a halallah (a woman born to a Cohen married in any one of these illegitimate ways).
   (b) An agunah is a woman whose husband has disappeared. She is not allowed to remarry. (A related status is that of agun, a man whose wife has disappeared. Since Judaism recognizes polygamy, this case is minor because an agun can get special permission to remarry.)
   (c) Halitzah is an ancient ceremony which releases a childless widow to marry a man other than her brother-in-law. Problems arise

when the brother-in-law is a minor, cannot be reached, is reluctant to perform the ceremony on principle, or blackmails her for his consent.
For details on marriage and divorce in Israel, see Shiloh (1970).

18 The case of mamzerim is worse than that of Gentiles because as Jews they may not legitimize their status by conversion or in any other way. They are allowed, however, to marry other mamzerim, proselytes and barren persons.

19 This term is borrowed from Zucker, who defines it as 'the attempt to establish a Torah state by means of legislation' or 'the attempt to attain theological ends by means of political activity' (1973: 2, 46).

20 Cohen's (1974) bibliography lists many such references.

21 Typical examples of these publications are by, respectively, A. Layish, G. Golani, Y. Ben-Porath, J. Hofman, J. Landau, H. Rosenfeld and Y. Peres.

22 The best source is Eisenstadt and Peres (1968 – the report was prepared by Peres) which appeared later as a series of articles (Peres and Yuval-Davis (1969), Peres (1970), Peres, Ehrlich and Yuval-Davis (1970), Peres and Yuval-Davis (1970)). Also relevant are Peres and Levy (1969), and Peres (1971).

23 Peres observes a serious imbalance in the Israeli Arab identity caused by the 1967 War, but ambivalence has remained as its defining characteristic.

24 The following exposition of the colonial perspective is a composite picture, whose parts and nuances vary in the literature. Instead of recording the exact arguments actually made (some of the inconsistencies are indicated in the notes), I find it more instructive to develop a general explanation of the Israeli scene which is in line with the colonial approach. The two best sources are Bober, 1972 (a collection of essays by members of the Israeli Socialist Organization, Matzpen) and Rodinson, 1973 (an independent, French Marxist scholar). Lumer provides a doctrinaire Marxist version with specific references to intergroup relations (1973: 15–24). The Palestinian national charter states the case conclusively (Palestine Liberation Organization, 1973). These four sources will be the base for our discussion. Other relevant references are El Kodsy and Lobel (1970), Jansen (1971) and Nikitina (1973).

25 Rodinson (1973: 39) speculates that had the Jewish ancestral homeland been already settled by a European group (French, Germans, etc.), the Zionists could hardly have taken the callous attitude they did. In judging the Zionist indifference, Buch takes issue with Rodinson: 'Rodinson balances this harsh description of the early Zionists by pointing out that their racist prejudices and assumptions were no worse than those prevailing among their contemporaries, and might even be excused on that account as products of their time. This judgment can be questioned as overly charitable, in view of the existence – also among contemporaries – of alternative movements for socialist and anti-imperialist liberation which were attracting far more of the Jewish youth than was Zionism' (1973: 12).

NOTES TO PAGES 33–5

26 The definition of Jews as only a faith is generally accepted for past and present world Jewry, but is disputed for current Israeli Jewry. In the official Palestinian national charter both are denied nationhood: 'Judaism, being a religion is not an independent nationality. Nor do Jews constitute a single nation with an identity of its own; they are citizens of the states to which they belong' (Palestine Liberation Organization, 1973: clause 20). On the other hand, the Matzpen group distinguishes between world Judaism as a religion (Bober, 1972: 203) and the 'Hebrew nation' which emerged in the process of Zionist colonization: 'The argument that this nation has been formed artificially and at the expense of the indigenous Arab population does not change the fact that the Hebrew nation now exists. It would be a disastrous error to ignore this fact' (Bober, 1972: 211).

27 This is another way in which Zionism differs from classical colonialism: 'While the nature of "classical" colonialism is primarily to *exploit*, Zionist colonialism *displaces* and *expels*' (Bober, 1972: 11). This exclusionist feature of Zionism is the cause for the creation of a new Hebrew nation in Palestine (Bober, 1972: 211).

28 The idea that Israel is alien to the region is laboriously elaborated by Jansen (1971: *passim*, and especially in chapter 6).

29 The Palestinian national charter claims: 'Zionism is a political movement organically associated with international imperialism and antagonistic to all action for liberation and to progressive movements in the world. It is racist and fanatic in its nature, aggressive in its methods. Israel is the instrument of the Zionist movement, and a geographical base for world imperialism placed strategically in the midst of the Arab homeland to combat the hopes of the Arab nation for liberation, unity and progress' (Palestine Liberation Organization, 1973: clause 22).

30 The Mazpan ideologists put a stress on these structural continuities: 'These three aspects of Israeli–Jewish society and the Zionist state – the settler-colonial character, the imperialist client state offering the services of a counterrevolutionary army to imperialism, and the bourgeois nation with its internally repressive state apparatus – are interrelated in an exceedingly complex fashion' (Bober, 1972: 196).

31 Regarding the parallels and ties between Israel and South Africa, Lumer notes: 'The roots of Israeli–South Africa relationships go deeper, however, than immediate, political, or military interests. They lie in the racist, reactionary character which these two states have in common today' (1973: 51). See similar statements in Bober (1973: 189) and others.

32 The status and allegiance of Oriental Jews are at issue among proponents of the colonial perspective. The Palestinian national charter states: 'The Jews who had normally resided in Palestine until the beginning of the Zionist invasion will be considered Palestinians' (Palestine Liberation Organization, 1973: clause 6). Since nearly all Orientals arrived after the 'Zionist invasion', they will be excluded from the future state of Palestine. However, in an interview in 1969, Yasser Arafat considered the Oriental Jews to be 'Arabs of the

Jewish faith' along with Arabs of the Moslem or Christian faith – all sharing 'a common culture, a common language, and a common background' (quoted by Segal, 1973: 105). As such, Orientals are expected to co-operate with the Arabs and will be allowed in the new Palestine. The better-informed Matzpen spokesmen, on the other hand, explain that Orientals tend to support the most nationalistic elements in Israel and that it is unrealistic to conceive 'a future alliance of Arab Palestinians and Oriental Jews, whether on the basis of their common exploited condition or on the basis of their cultural affinity, a result of the Oriental Jews having come from Arab countries' (Bober, 1972: 93).

33 There seems to be a broad consensus that despite its inherent structural contradictions, Israeli society can be held together with the continuous help of Western imperialism. Change will probably come from without rather than from within (see, for example, Bober, 1972: 196, 200).

34 This is the slogan of the Palestine Liberation Organization. The programme of the Israeli Matzpen calls for the de-Zionization of the state. It includes the following measures: a worker-controlled economy, separation between religion and state, abrogation of the Law of Return, repatriation of the Arab refugees, the end of all relations of dependence on imperialism, and rupture of the ties between Israel and the Diaspora (Bober, 1972: 202–4).

35 Social background also plays a part. The majority of Israeli sociologists are observed to be well established socioeconomically, oldtimers (or Israeli born), from East or Central European backgrounds, liberals to moderate leftists in outlook, and with a Zionist world-view already formed by the time Israel was born. The minority are sociologists who immigrated, probably out of a Zionist commitment, after 1948 from English-speaking countries (mostly the United States). All share a non- or anti-Marxist approach. It is interesting to note that despite the spread of Marxian ideology and thought in the Yishuv and to a lesser degree in Israel, Israeli sociology has not yet developed a Marxian branch.

36 For arguments in defence of Israel and against the colonial perspective see Newberger (1970, especially Lectures 1, 6, and 7), Curtis (1971, the contributions by Halpern, Syrkin and, in particular, Avineri), Chertoff (1971), Howe and Gershman (1972), Talmon (1970), and Gal (1973).

37 Kinloch (1974: 156) presents a continuous colonial model of race relations and applies it to four countries with descending amounts of colonial characteristics: South Africa, the United States, Brazil and Hawaii.

38 This is the way Eisenstadt handles pluralism in his book on Israeli society (1967a).

39 The spokesmen for the Mazpen group write: 'However, such social divisions and differences are interpreted by the Orientals in ethnic terms; they do not say, "I am exploited and discriminated against because I am a worker" but "I am exploited and discriminated against because I am an Oriental"' (Bober, 1972: 93).

40 Eisenstadt takes historical factors into consideration in two ways. One is his interest in the social conditions of immigrants' countries of origin. This interest is, however, confined to elements conducive to adaptability of immigrants to Israeli society. The other is his historical analysis of the pre- and post-state periods. In regard to this analysis Matras makes the following criticism: 'The analysis of S. N. Eisenstadt of the change in social structure of the Jewish community in Palestine which accompanied achievement of independence and the mass immigration of Jews from both Europe and the Islamic countries of Asia, North Africa, and the Middle East falls short both of being an adequate sociological description of the Yishuv and of describing adequately the ensuing changes in social structure . . .

'The notion that economic differentiation in the *Yishuv* was independent of social prestige, of political power, of country of origin and duration of residence in Palestine and that successive waves of immigrants to the *Yishuv* were promptly absorbed into all social, economic, and political spheres of the organized Jewish community without segregation and discrimination seems consistent enough with Zionist ideology and with assertions emanating prior to independence from the organized Palestinian Jewish political institutions. But this notion is nowhere supported by any systematic data. To be sure neither is it contradicted by any systematic data; but the post-independence data suggesting ethnic origin and period of immigration, social differentiation and residential and economic segregation could as readily and as reasonably be interpreted as reflecting continuation of a pre-statehood pattern rather than as they have been interpreted: as reflecting very strong and abrupt changes' (1965: 197–8).

My own analysis is in line with the thesis of continuation of the pre-state conditions.

41 This and the other models suggested below draw on Mason's typology (1970a: 143–6) of patterns of intergroup relations. Mason spells out four patterns: dominant, paternal, competitive and fluid.

The dominant pattern is a situation of continued domination: 'here one group has a monopoly of political power, and enormous advantages in wealth, education, esteem, and opportunity. It has no intention of sharing these advantages with the subordinate group.' The paternal pattern is, in comparison, temporary and benevolent: 'paternalism is the relationship of a father to a son, who will one day be independent; it is intended to benefit the son and the relationship can be healthy unless it is prolonged after the son comes of age. Dominance on the other hand is the relationship of master to servant or slave; it is frankly for the benefit of the master and is permanent.'

In the dominant and paternal situations, members of the subordinate group are not allowed to enter into free competition with members of the superordinate group, whereas in the competitive and fluid models they may compete but under unequal conditions. In the competitive pattern, the minority 'wish, on the whole, to obtain a place in a competitive industrial society and are prevented from complete success, not by regulation but by lack of training, opportunity, and incentive; by varying forms of discrimination, sometimes by parental upbringing.' Finally, in the fluid situation, a minority member may change his group membership and his social position in different stages of his life.

The following examples may illustrate the various types: South Africa and the Deep South – dominant pattern; British India and Uganda – paternal; contemporary northern United States and Britain – competitive; and Mexico and Brazil – fluid (Mason, 1970a: p. 146, Table 1).

Intergroup relations in Israel do not fit these patterns precisely and thus qualifications must be made. The Oriental–Ashkenazi situation can be best understood not just in terms of a change from a paternal to a competitive pattern, but in terms of co-optation as well. Co-optation in the broader sense, i.e., as a majority 'policy' towards minorities, is the mechanism by which the dominant group attempts to prolong domination by granting various concessions to the subordinate group. Unlike 'exclusion', which is associated with domination, co-optation involves limited entry and is not a foolproof control technique. As Gamson aptly notes, co-optation is a double-edged sword that 'invariably involves some mixture of outcome modification and social control and the exact mix is difficult to determine in advance' (1968: 137).

42 The three minimal criteria of caste are ascriptive membership by birth, endogamy and status hierarchy. Fuller justification of the application of this term to Israeli society and its wider implications will be discussed in chapter 5.

4 Historical background

1 For useful surveys of these branches of Jewry and discussion of particular Jewish communities see Patai (1970: chapter 1; 1971f) and Tartakower (1969). The Yemenites are sometimes distinguished as a fourth section but as a matter of fact they are an integral part of the Oriental branch.

2 According to one estimate, 93 per cent of the 1.5 million Jews in the world in 1070 were Oriental or Sephardic (Patai, 1971f: 79).

3 For sociohistorical sketches of Oriental Jewry and particular communities see Patai (1970), Tahon (1957), Ben-Zvi (1957), Goitein (1964) and especially H. J. Cohen (1973), on which most of the following discussion is based.

4 There is a controversy in the emerging historiography of Jews in Arab lands. Some historians tend to emphasize the status of Orientals as a persecuted minority not very different from the outcast status of Ashkenazi Jews in Europe. Others lay more stress on the peaceful coexistence between Arabs and Jews, which was conspicuously absent under Christianity. The dispute is by no means academic. It is directly relevant to the crucial issue whether the current manifestations of animosity against Israel in the Arab world are a situational response

to the Israeli–Arab conflict or an outgrowth of ingrained hatred of the Jews comparable to the age-old anti-Semitism in the Christian world. For a review of the two stances, which have different political implications for the settlement of the conflict, see Rejwan (1973; 1974), who underscores the basic dissimilarity in attitude toward the Jews between Islam and Christianity.

5 For reviews of the history and culture of Sephardic Jewry see Bernardete (1952) and Barnett (1971).

6 Any standard history of the Jews in the modern era deals almost exclusively with Ashkenazi Jewry. There are, therefore, countless sources, of which only several can be singled out here. In a series of sociological studies J. Katz (1961a; 1961b; 1972; 1973) makes a penetrating analysis of the transition to modernity of Ashkenazi Jews and their changing relations with Gentiles from the end of the Middle Ages through to the nineteenth century. Zborowski and Herzog (1962) give a vivid anthropological reconstruction of the culture of the shtetl (a small town which was the centre of Jewish life in Eastern Europe until World War II).

7 For the religious differences between Ashkenazim and non-Ashkenazim, see Zimmels (1958).

8 The ethnic dichotomization into Orientals and Ashkenazim that is used throughout raises the basic question of ethnic boundaries. The common structuralist position that ethnic groups are differentiated clearly by distinctive cultures and diacritical social structures, and the rival subjectivist position represented by F. B. Barth (1969: 13–14) that self and social categorizations are the most significant, are both untenable. More realistic is the view that objective and subjective factors are important in drawing ethnic boundaries (van den Berghe, 1970: 512–13; LeVine and Campbell, 1972: 81–113). On both objective and subjective bases there is a dichotomy between Ashkenazim and non-Ashkenazim in Israel at present, though each group is further subdivided by countries of origin.

9 These estimates are based on Table 8 and on Patai (1971b; 1971c; 1971d).

10 Nini (1973: 49–50) explains that Zionism as a secular national movement was geared to rescue Jewish communities that were under threat of physical destruction. Hence it ignored Oriental Jews who were not threatened in Arab lands up to the 1940s.

11 Patai presents no evidence for the following statement: 'That Zionism did extend an urgent invitation to Sephardic and Oriental Jews to join it was in keeping with the Herzlian idea of Zionism as a political movement of the Jewish people as a whole and of the Herzlian conception of national unity extending to all Jews irrespective of their ethnic background' (1971f: 310). It is exactly this point I would like to dispute.

12 The *Encyclopedia of Zionism and Israel* (Patai, 1971a) includes short articles which deal with Zionist activity in most Oriental communities ('Syria and Lebanon, Zionism in', 'North Africa, Zionism in', etc.). The descriptions are very sketchy, however, and, as expected,

tend to give a false impression of intensive Zionist activity in Oriental countries.

13 While this was partially true in absolute terms, it was totally false in relative terms. In 1920–5, Iraqi Jews contributed to the National Fund £4,060 sterling compared with £63,416 by Polish Jews who were thirty times as numerous. The Iraqi contribution was proportionately twice as much as the Polish contribution. Similarly Iraqi Jews bought 7 times as many sh'kalim (golden tokens serving as membership dues) per capita, and contributed much more than their share for other Zionist activities. In the Third Aliyah (1919–23), about 1,000 Iraqi Jews and 11,000 Polish Jews immigrated to Palestine and in the Fourth Aliyah (1924–31) about 2,500 and 37,000 respectively. Proportionally speaking, the Iraqi Jewry contributed three times as many immigrants as the Polish Jewry. All this despite the double standard of the Zionist movement in treating these two Jewries – refusal to support Zionist activities and immigration from Iraq, as against enormous support for Polish Jewry. For some details see Mendelsohn and Cohen (1973 – the quoted figures are from p. 14).

14 The lack of interest of the Zionist movement in North African Jewry is undisputed (e.g., Chouraqui, 1968: 293). This is not even denied in the semi-official *Encyclopedia of Zionism and Israel*: 'Before World War II, Zionism made comparatively little headway in North African countries owing to French inspired assimilation as well as to a lack of interest on the part of the Zionist movement in attracting North African Jewry. During the early decades of the 20th century the World Zionist Organization (WZO) did little to disseminate the ideas and ideals of modern Zionism in this region. Such efforts as the WZO did make along these lines were mostly inadequate. Sometimes, for example, sh'lihim (emissaries) who spoke only Yiddish, German, Polish, or Russian were sent to North Africa, where the Jews spoke only Arabic and French. It was only after the war, and especially after the creation of the State of Israel, that the worldwide Zionist movement "discovered" North African Jewry' (Hirschler, 1971: 842).

15 When the first smallholders' settlement (Nahalat Yehuda) was founded in 1914, a total of 360 dunams were available, of which 60 dunams were offered to thirty Yemenite families, or 2 dunams for each, whereas 300 dunams were earmarked for thirty East European families or 10 dunams per family. When the Yemenites complained about the double standard, they were told that they could supplement their income by wage-labour in the surrounding settlement. The Yemenites decided to settle only six families, providing each one with the 10 dunams given to Ashkenazi families (M. Taviv, 1962).

16 This is a little higher than the official figure of 10.5 per cent because many Oriental illegal immigrants were not counted. But even the official percentage refutes the common false conception that Orientals were under-represented in pre-state immigration. In fact, the reverse is true. From some countries the rate of immigration was exceedingly high: one-third of the Yemenite and Syrian Jews and one-sixth of the Kurdish and Turkish Jews immigrated between 1919 and 1948.

None of the Ashkenazi communities had such high rates of immigration during the same period (H. J. Cohen, 1974: 23).

17 The Old Yishuv is the Jewish community in Palestine before 1881, which retained a separate existence from the New Yishuv (or just the Yishuv), composed of the new Zionist immigrants.

18 For more detailed analysis of the internal structure of the Yishuv, see Eisenstadt (1948; 1967a: chapter 4).

19 Eisenstadt writes in this regard: 'It is significant that the Oriental Jews in Israel have not developed any "nativistic" movements of the kind that quite often develop in situations of "culture change". This is due chiefly to the fact that there is no basic ideological or political bar to their possibilities of advancement and participation within the general Jewish community in Israel. Both the new community and the Oriental Jews insist on basic mutual identification within the general framework of revived Jewish nationhood. The undermining of the security of the traditional social structure by the impingement of the social process emanating from the new community was not accompanied by a denial of the possibility of advancement and participation within that community' (1950: 219).

20 See n. 40 in chapter 3.

21 Minor exceptions are Eisenstadt (1950, cited above); Deutsch (1969).

22 For informative surveys of immigration and absorption in Israel, see Jewish Agency (1964); Israel, Government (1970).

23 For reviews of the pre-state relations between the religious and non-religious groups, see Rubinstein (1967b), Patai (1970: chapter 9), Marmorstein (1969: chapter 4), Leslie (1971: chapter 2), Bentwich (1971), Abramov (1971) and Oren (1973: 36–40).

24 Herzl wrote in *The Jewish State*, outlining his programme: 'Are we eventually going to set up a theocracy? No! Belief holds us together, science makes us free. We are not going to allow our rabbis even to think about theocratic ideas. We are going to know how to restrict them to their synagogues just as we are going to retain our army within their bases. Army and Rabbinate shall be honored as deeply as is becoming to their high function and merits. They have no word to say in the affairs of the state which has thus honored them because they would bring about internal and external complications' (quoted by Rubinstein, 1967b: 108).

25 Mizrahi is an acronym for 'merkaz ruhani' (spiritual centre) and it means phonetically 'Easterner' (i.e., the European Jew who goes back east to Palestine). The meaning of Agudat Israel is 'union of Israel'. For a survey on the Mizrahi see the biography of Rabbi Reines, its founder (Wanefsky, 1970); and Y. Cohen (1973). On Aguda, see Friedman (1971) and his sources. The biography of Rabbi Kook (Yaron, 1974) sheds much light on the historical controversies.

26 The Mizrahi lists won 11 out of 314 (i.e., 3.5 per cent) seats in the first elections in 1920 to the Elected Assembly of the Yishuv. In the second elections in 1925 they obtained 15 out of 221 (or 6.8 per cent). In the third elections in 1931 there was only one list, which received

5 out of 71 (or 7.0 per cent). And in the last fourth elections in 1944 five lists got 30 out of 171 (or 17.5 per cent). The strategic position of wielding a balance of power in the Elected Assembly was far more important than the small proportions. These figures are computed from electoral rolls published in Attias (1949: 332f.).

27 The ultra-Orthodox made an impressive showing in the elections for the first elected Assembly. Their main list (Mifleget Haharedim) won 53 out of the 314 (or 16.8 per cent) seats. They could, further, count on a large number of Mizrahi, Sephardic and Yemenite delegates for support. In fact nearly half of the delegates of the elected Assembly walked out of the meeting in 1925 when their objection to the enfranchisement of women was not sustained. Their participation in the first elections was made possible by a temporary agreement to double the votes they received to compensate for the absence of female voters. See Attias (1949: 332f.) for election returns; and pp. 93–4 for the dispute over women's political rights.

28 For a sociological account of the changes in structure and politics of the Old Yishuv and Aguda during the crucial period 1917–36, see Friedman (1973).

29 The agreement was formalized in a letter dated 19 June 1947 to Agudat Israel signed by David Ben-Gurion – the chairman of the executive of the Jewish Agency, Yehuda Fishman (Maimon) – the leader of the Mizrahi, and Yitzhak Gruenbaum – the representative of the General Zionists. For the full text of the letter, see Marmorstein (1969: 86–8).

30 Comprehensive historical accounts of Arab–Jewish relations in Palestine are given by Aharon Cohen (1970), Shimoni (1947), Waschitz (1947) and Assaf (1967; 1970). Brief surveys are offered by Carmi and Rosenfeld (1974), Peretz (1970a), Abner Cohen (1965: chapter 7), Peres (1971: 1028–31), Shimoni (1971) and Landau (1971). For more information on Palestinian nationalism and its clash with Zionism, see Lesch (1973) and Lobel (in El Kodsy and Lobel, 1970: 63–137).

31 It is estimated that the Jews invested £115 Palestine (P) million (i.e., £ sterling) in Palestine between 1920 and 1941. Of this sum £P30 million went to the Palestinian Arabs as payments for land sales, compensation of sharecroppers, agricultural produce, wages, building material, industrial products and rent. The economic boom caused a disproportionate rise in the standard of living of the Arab population compared with other Arab countries. The annual per capita income of Arabs in Palestine was £P0.10–0.12 in 1920 and soared to £P0.27 in 1937 at a time when the respective figures were £P0.12 in Egypt, £P0.16 in Syria and Lebanon and £P0.10 in Iraq. In comparison, the annual per capita income of Jews in Palestine in 1936 was £P0.49. These figures are taken from Aharon Cohen (1970: 225–6), who provides more information (in chapter 6) about the mutual benefits of Jews and Arabs in Palestine.

32 Segre observes: 'The Jews dressed, ate, spoke, behaved differently from the Arabs. Their conception of society, honour, feminine beauty,

music, and the very meaning of life was different. It was not a question of a European dislike for Oriental life, as has been so often intimated. It was something very different and perhaps more dangerous: it was indifference. The Jews built their society as if the Arabs did not exist' (1971: 100). Upon arrival, Jewish settlers were, perhaps, 'innocent' or 'indifferent', but without the European mentality of disdain for the natives one can hardly understand how they managed for so long to ignore the numerous Arabs and to build their society as though these defiant people did not exist.

5 Current social contexts

1 These generalizations refer to three primary bases of divisions: namely, historical origin, definition of group membership and relative size of the dominant group. They can be stated as follows:

(a) Intergroup relations which emerge out of 'involuntary contact' (conquest, colonization, annexation, enslavement, indentured labour, displaced refugees) are more conducive to conflict than those subsequent to 'voluntary contact' (free immigration, certain cases of endogenous differentiation). This generalization can be deduced from the brief discussion by Lieberson (1961) and the more elaborate analysis of 'intergroup sequences' by Schermerhorn (1970: chapters 4 and 5). An excellent application to the divisions in the United States is made by Blauner (1972: chapters 1–3, and especially pp. 36–41).

(b) Intergroup relations which rest on relatively rigid ascriptive membership (race, caste, racial caste, descent rule) are more conflict laden than relations based on moderate group definitions (nationality, religion, language), and much more so than those grounded on criteria susceptible to personal achievement or control (lifestyle, regional residence, organizational affiliation). This generalization appears in the discussions by Harris (1959); Yinger (1965: 21–7); van den Berghe (1967b: 135 – the distinction between race and ethnicity).

(c) Intergroup relations in which the dominant group is numerically a minority tend to lead to greater conflict than in a situation of lack of clear majority, and than where the dominant group is also a majority. This generalization is derived from Williams (1947: 57–8), Mason (1970b: 64), Bonacich (1972: 558), M. G. Smith (1960 – the type of plural society) and others.

It must be emphasized that these generalizations merely indicate tendencies and that the operation of other factors too often restricts their validity. For instance, intergroup conflict in Nazi Germany, Northern Ireland and the United States is very intense despite the favourable conditions of majority rule.

2 Israeli officials often argue that Jews who came from Arab countries after 1948 were 'refugees' comparable with the Palestinian refugees who fled to Arab countries in 1947–8. As a result a de facto exchange of population (refugees) took place between Israel and the Arab world

and in conclusion it is baseless to demand a right to repatriation for the Palestinian refugees. It is difficult to say if this line of reasoning is sincere or opportunist. At any rate, it demonstrates that the idea that Oriental newcomers were some kind of refugees was not foreign to the Israeli authorities.

3 Since 1948 about 1.5 million Jews immigrated to Israel. It is estimated that during the same period about 250,000 emigrated, of whom only a small percentage were Orientals or Israeli Arabs. Between 1948–63, 3.1 per cent of the Asian–African immigrants and 12.7 per cent of the European–American immigrants left Israel (official figures, quoted by Ben-Chaim, 1967).

4 Some Jews from Arab countries came to Israel and left, and others opted to go elsewhere. But even this fact did not persuade the government to give the Orientals a better deal. I shall touch on this point later (in the section on 'Undercurrents').

5 The comparable ratio of newcomers to old-timers among Jews from Europe and America was 0.67, so that the old-timers remained a majority (computed from figures given in Central Bureau of Statistics, *Statistical Abstract of Israel*, 1955, 6: Table 12, p. 15).

6 Williams makes the following pertinent generalization: 'Migration of a visibly different group into a given area increases the likelihood of conflict; the probability of conflict is the greater (a) the larger the ratio of the incoming minority to the resident population, and (b) the more rapid the influx' (1947: 57–8). Both hold for the Oriental migration and even more so because in this case they eventually became the majority.

7 I wish to thank R. A. Schermerhorn for his suggestion that I explore further the implications of the shifting demographic ratios in the Jewish population. He perceptively notes that the Israeli case has only few historical parallels in two respects: (a) that the incoming group became the absolute majority and did so in a very short period, and (b) that pre-migration cultural ties bound the incoming group and the resident population.

8 It must be emphasized that the term 'racial' or 'ethnic' caste expressly does not imply more than the three defining features. Thus, contamination by contact, inheritable occupational roles, religious legitimacy of the status hierarchy and other characteristics attendant on the Indian classic caste system are explicitly not presumed to exist in racial or ethnic caste structures.

9 This is Amendment 2 to the Law of Return, which was approved by the Knesset on 10 March 1970.

10 According to the Religious Community (Change) Ordinance, a person who seeks reclassification of his status has to secure written approval from the head of the religious community which he wants to join. This means, in essence, a religious conversion.

11 The Druzes are a small community comprising 9 per cent of all Israeli Arabs. They are an offshoot sect of Islam, culturally Arab, nationally undefined, but loyal to Israel. (For a general survey of the Druzes in Israel, see Falah, 1974, and for a political study see Ben-Dor,

1974.) In a study of social distance, attitudes and prejudices among Jewish youths, the Druzes did not fare better than other Israeli Arabs (Peres, 1968: 73–7). Druzes are drafted into the army, but serve in separate units and take orders from Jewish commissioned officers. It is also significant that Druze soldiers were beaten by some Jewish civilians in development towns in the aftermath of the terrorist attacks in spring 1974.

12 It is interesting to note that Jews, and Zionists in particular, are dedicated champions of cultural pluralism abroad and, concurrently, its adamant opponents for Jews of different ethnic origins in Israel. There is no inconsistency in this attitude, since pluralism is viewed as a device against Jewish assimilation into the Gentile world which has no place in the Jewish state. By the same rationale, pluralism between Arabs and Jews in Israel is insisted upon.

13 In state-wide surveys taken by the Israel Institute of Applied Social Research in summer 1973, 82 per cent of Jewish adults and 66 per cent of Jewish high school pupils defined themselves as Zionist (Levy and Guttman, 1974: 249). Most of those who failed to do so can be considered as unclear about the current meaning of Zionism to Israeli Jews. And in fact 36 per cent of Jewish adults in an earlier survey said so when asked (Levy and Guttman, 1971: question 19 in the Appendix). Similarly 52 per cent of youth expressed little interest in Zionism (Levy and Guttman, 1974: question 67b in the Appendix). More important, Zionism is the ideology of the Israeli political parties except Rakah (the Arab-based New Communist Party) and to some extent Agudat Israel. Certain small factions reject Zionism, including the HaOlam Haze Movement (Avnery, 1971), Caananite circles (Kurzweil, 1953), and Matzpen (Bober, 1972).

14 Arian (1968) documents the persistence and power of the socialist ideology even up to the mid-1960s. It is, however, on the decline. In one survey, 54 per cent supported socialism, 26 per cent capitalism, 1 per cent a mixture of both, and 19 per cent did not answer (Antonovsky, 1963).

15 The most militant and ideologically articulate spokesman for the Oriental cause is Mr Eliahu Eliachar, who served as the leader of the Sephardic community in Jerusalem for many years. While advocating independent ethnic organizations, he expresses his anti-ethnic national ideas with equal rigour: 'We do not have races – all of us are from one race and one people. All of us are descendants of Abraham, Isaac and Jacob, and we must remember that all of us are Jews and Israelis' (1967: 15). He, nevertheless, reacts against the goal of 'integration' (mizug) not in principle but because it amounts in practice to the assimilation of the Orientals into 'the Ashkenazi shtetl culture' and, therefore, as an alternative tactic he suggests 'partnership' (shituf) (1970: 76).

16 The attitude of political parties in Israel toward religion varies a great deal. Among the religious parties, Poali Agudat Israel and Agudat Israel take a much harder religious line than Mafdal. And of the secular parties, Herut and to a great extent the Liberals take a

more moderate stand, and the Independent Liberals, the Civil Rights Movement, Mapam, Moked and Rakah take a much firmer secular stand than the Israel Labour Party. Most of the latter advocate the separation of state and religion which, in the Israeli context, means the liberalization of religious restrictions rather than separation in the strictest American sense of the term. (See Oren, 1973 and Milstein, 1975 on the parties' positions on religion.)

17 According to a Gallup survey taken in Israel in August 1971, 55 per cent opposed the separation of religion and state, 36 per cent were in favour and 9 per cent were undecided (cited by Zucker, 1973: p. 236, n. 20). The breakdown of personal religious observance was not reported.

18 Rustum Bastuni is a Christian Arab architect who served as a Knesset member on behalf of the Mapam Party in 1951–5. He heads the Arab Committee for Israel whose goal is to foster Arab–Jewish understanding and integration. For an essentially similar position before the Six-Day War, see his article in the *Jerusalem Post*, 25 September 1964 (excerpts in Landau, 1969: 221–4). Landau (231–6, 251–2) reproduces further pronouncements by accommodating Arab representatives.

19 These aspirations were expressed in Al-Ard's memorandum to the United Nations. For excerpts, see Landau (1969: 223–30), and for other militant views see also pp. 226–7 (a speech by an Arab Communist Knesset member).

20 Ben-Zvi, Israel's second President, spoke seriously of fears of an Arab holocaust after World War II. He said that given the Nazi extermination, the slaughter of Armenians (in Turkey) and the decimation of Assyrians in Iraq – which all encountered little condemnation by the West – Arab rulers could have done the same to Oriental Jews. However, 'Israel's victory [in 1948] was followed by an armistice; those who had intended following in the footsteps of their Nazi masters had no time to carry out their nefarious designs, and the Jewries in Moslem lands had a respite' (1957: 8). It is a moot question whether the Orientals were really under a threat of annihilation. The question is, unfortunately, obscured by current interpretations of opposition to Israel today in the Arab world. See in chapter 4, n. 4.

21 Maurice Samuel, Weizman's secretary, criticized Ben-Gurion for allowing the unselective immigration of Orientals to Israel: 'There were men in the Israeli government who understood the dangers of this course. They protested privately to the man in control – to Prime Minister Ben-Gurion.' Samuel also said that Ben-Gurion himself did not feel at ease concerning this matter (1953: 64–8, quoted by Rejwan, 1972): 'In the midst of the operation of *Kibbutz Galuyot* (Ingathering of Exiles) Prime Minister Ben-Gurion cried out that the country was in danger of Levantinization because the flood of primitive panicky Oriental Jews was not matched by a comparable flow of volunteer Jews from the trained West. But the Arabs were beaten precisely because they are Levantinized, and if there was no prospect of compensating contribution from the West,

the tide of Eastern immigration into Israel should have been controlled as far as it could be, and not whipped up artificially. We are weaker, not stronger, because of that unnecessary addition to the natural and inevitable influx.'

22 The Commission concluded (1959): 'While in the lower ranks of administration there exist in practice situations of deprivation and discrimination, in the planning bodies and in policy-making not only is there no trace of deliberate discrimination but also there are many cases of goodwill, clear inclination and increasing tendency toward affirmative action of special and preferential treatment of Orientals, as well as the aspiration to integrate them in all Israeli public spheres.' That is, while the Commission conceded the existence of some informal practices of discrimination against the Orientals, it emphasized the preferential treatment given to the Orientals, and dismissed ethnic discrimination as a social problem.

23 H. Cohen (1965; 1973; 1974) discusses important differences between Oriental Jews who hailed from different countries.

24 For tentative inquiries by Oriental spokesmen in this matter see Elia (1964) and Yisraeli (1971).

25 In comparison, immigration from Morocco was restricted in the years 1949–56 for supposedly these reasons – the high incidence of aged and disabled.

26 The Oriental immigrants were despatched in greater proportions to development towns and new agricultural settlements than the Ashkenazi immigrants. 'Between May 15th, 1948 and May 22nd, 1961, a total of one million immigrants came into the country but at the time of the population census in 1961 only 17.5% of these lived in the new towns, of European immigrants 10.5%, of Orientals 23%' (Spiegel, 1967. 30). From October 1956 to December 1967, 36.5 per cent of the European–American immigrants as against 57.1 per cent of the Asian–African immigrants were assigned to the unpopular development areas (Jewish Agency, 1968: Table 18). The justification sometimes given for this double standard is that more jobs were available in established cities for the better trained Ashkenazi immigrants. This is not true, because more jobs were equally available in the cities to the less trained Oriental immigrants. The rate of unemployment in the early years in development towns was so high that relief works had to be artificially created. More serious were the impediments in the way of modernization of the Orientals to which the government was supposedly committed. The Moroccan Jews were the most affected by these policies. In Morocco they had been in the process of urbanization, so their allocation to rural settlements and development areas in Israel reversed the sought-for trend and damaged their ability to rise from the lowest stratum of Jewish society which they entered upon arrival (Weingrod, 1960: 326).

27 It is believed that this speech constituted an important factor in the non-renewal of Hillel's term in the next Knesset and his relegation to a minor post as consul in an African country. In 1969 he was called to fill the Oriental benign quota as a Minister of Police. He has been

careful since then not to say anything offensive. In April 1971, however, he attended the Oriental caucus in the Israel Labour Party convention and was held responsible for not calming the Caucus down. For some time later rumours were circulated in the press concerning his dismissal.

28 This pioneering study by Inbar and Adler is the first sociological study to examine charges of discrimination by the use of survey methods. As such, its value cannot be overemphasized, although self-reporting is only one way, and not the best, to investigate discriminatory practices. It is also a pity that the functionalist perspective of immigrant absorption often confuses interpretations. To illustrate, with regard to the policy of allocating uniformly small apartments to Romanian small families and Moroccan large families, the authors write: 'Such a policy is indeed the official tenet in Israel and has its roots in the pre-state phase of the Jewish society in Palestine, particularly its prevalent egalitarian ideology. To the extent that this policy has been enacted . . . it would appear from the density figures that while uniform policies might have been appropriate for a small, highly selective and socioculturally homogeneous population, they may have become less functional under changed conditions of immigration, in particular for immigrants with large families' (1977 : 48–9). The authors do not question the official egalitarian ethos, do not raise the possibility of anti-Oriental ideological undercurrents, speak stereotypically of a homogeneous population during the Yishuv, and refer to the discriminatory practices as 'less functional'.

29 Rosenzweig and Tamarin (1971: 38–9) explain the ambivalence toward religion by the Eastern European power elite in Israel in terms of their youthful revolt against 'the religious fanaticism of their parents and grandparents' which later, with advancing age, changed into regret about past rejection of religion and into new religious romanticism. 'While endless acquiescence to the demands of the orthodox parties is rationalized in political terms it really fulfills a basic psychological requirement of the Israeli ruling class.' This simplistic psychological explanation is inadequate, since ambivalence is much more widespread and is anchored, rather, in current realities.

30 For the United States see Glazer and Moynihan (1970); for Canada, Royal Commission on Bilingualism and Biculturalism (1970: Book VI).

31 This adds a great deal to the fluidity of the religious–nonreligious division when compared to common ethnic divisions. In the same continuum the female–male division may be considered as almost a pure case of full interdependence and cross-cutting of loyalties. Incidentally this is essentially why some militant feminists today advocate Lesbianism and single-sex relationships as a way out of the inherent female dependence.

32 For changes in the economic structure of Israeli Arabs in the 1950s and early 1960s see Abner Cohen (1965: chapter 2); Rosenfeld (1964); Zarhi and Achiezra (1966). Cohen (1965: 41) draws the following conclusion from his economic survey of the Arab rural communities: 'The village has thus reached a point of no return in its

dependence on the general Israeli society. The whole of its livelihood is now tied to the Jewish economy, and is thus unavoidably involved in the major Arab–Israeli strife. In time of serious tension on the border, the military authorities in affected areas can, in principle, easily withdraw recent concessions and practically pin Arab labourers to their villages.'

33 If, in 1962, 44 to 53 per cent of the Oriental immigrants were religious (Antonovsky, 1963), it is safe to say that the percentages were at least as high, and probably higher, also during the mass immigration of the early 1950s.

34 The immigrants were neither won over by one party nor divided proportionately among the parties. The religious parties have received more votes from the Orientals than from the Ashkenazim (although never the votes they hoped for from the majority of Orientals). The right-of-centre parties, especially the Herut Party which was in opposition and had no patronage to offer, won many less than their proportional share from the Orientals during the 1950s. But over the years Herut caught up and has gained disproportionately more support from the Orientals than from the Ashkenazim by serving as a channel of protest. Ethnic patterns of voting behaviour will be discussed in the next chapter. For details on the government crisis precipitated by the religious parties in the early 1950s with regard to the education of the Yemenite immigrants' children, see Birnbaum (1970: 120–9).

35 These integrative functions of the religious observance split are checked to some extent by counter-trends. Ethnic origin cuts across the religious minority as it does the nonreligious majority. The religious Orientals and Ashkenazim have quite different styles of religious observance and, in consequence, maintain dual religious institutions. There is some, though declining, overlap also between the two lines of division since the Orientals still tend to be more religious than the Ashkenazim.

36 These include various departments of Arab affairs in the government, in the Histadrut and in the political parties; the Arabic-speaking schools and mass media; the internal security services; and the military apparatus which was expanded considerably after the Six-Day War for the administration of the occupied territories.

37 It is significant that the outcry of 'pa'ar adati' ('ethnic gap') is exclusively confined to inequality between Orientals and Ashkenazim. The Committee on Income Distribution and Social Inequality (Public Inquiry Commission, 1971) and the Prime Minister's Committee on Disadvantaged Children and Youth (Prime Minister's Commission, 1973), not surprisingly, excluded the Israeli Arab minority, although they were commissioned to investigate the entire population. The latter, the most serious effort ever to confront problems of deprivation in Israeli society, acknowledged this omission and recommended the setting up of a separate public-professional body to assist in formulating socioeconomic policies toward the Arab minority (Prime Minister's Commission, 1973: chapter 2: 9). Such

an Arab public commission was finally appointed in 1975.

38 For a long time the invincibility of Israel in her warfare against her Arab neighbours has been accounted for by the cultural superiority of the Western Ashkenazi system which implies Arab, and hence Oriental, 'backwardness' (see the quotation in n. 21 above). The shattering of the myth of Israel's invincibility after the Yom Kippur War is bound to undermine this attitude.

39 There is inconclusive evidence regarding the extent the Orientals' origin and socioeconomic status contribute to the lack of tolerance towards Arabs. In one national survey in June–July 1970, 63 per cent of the Orientlsa compared to 55 per cent of the Ashkenazim opposed living in mixed Arab–Jewish neighbourhoods. Within the same educational levels, the percentages were as follows: 78 versus 68 per cent among people with 0–4 years of schooling, 64 per cent equally among people with 5–8 years, 57 and 52 per cent among people with 9–12 years, and 43 versus 51 per cent among people with 13 or more years of schooling (Adi and Froilich, 1970b). While this may bear out the interpretation that in the lower socioeconomic level the Orientals are more anti-Arab than the Ashkenazim, the findings are not consistent.

40 There has been over the years no co-operation between the Orientals and the Arabs. The Orientals channel their protest vote, if at all, to the most Jewish nationalist parties whereas the Arabs register their protest by voting heavily for most 'Arab' nationalist party, Rakah (the New Communist Party). Oriental ethnic lists and protest movements (the 1959 Wadi-Salib riots and the 1971 Black Panther demonstrations) neither extended the demand for equality and the complaint of discrimination to the Israeli Arabs nor appealed to them for support. The Black Panther leaders were, at first, indecisive on this point because of the influence of Ashkenazi leftist backers who wished the movement to spread to all the underprivileged, but then followed the traditional course of ignoring the Arabs.

In this connection the first Arab–Jewish espionage ring discovered in December 1972 may be mentioned. The discovery caused a public storm because this was the first time that quasi-castes had formed an alliance against the Jewish state and also because the main Jewish figure was an Ashkenazi sabra who was raised in a kibbutz. Among the four Jews convicted, there was one college-educated Oriental who received little attention. He was reported to have expressed disgust at 'the racist-Ashkenazi state'. In reference to this case, one leading left-of-centre intellectual wrote that it indicated 'the failure of Israeli society to serve as a home in which the Orientals can be absorbed . . . the question is how to prevent a repetition of such cases [of espionage among Jews] not among the Left movements but among those Orientals who are frustrated by the current structure of Israeli society. The security services or the condemnation of certain ideologies will not help in this matter. We need, instead, internal reform. The question must be addressed to ourselves, because we are all guilty' (Avineri, 1972). The doubt raised by Avineri only confirms the public confidence that the Orientals are not likely to side with the Arabs. In fact, the number of Jews, including Orientals, who have been indicted for espionage since 1948 is negligible.

41 In his world-wide classification of societies, Schermerhorn assigns Israel to the 'Western European nations and the derivative neo-European complex', which includes not only the nations of Western and non-Communist Europe, but also Canada, the United States, Australia and New Zealand. In addition to being a European settler society, Israel shares with all these nations many features including a stable democracy, a capitalist or mixed economy, a relatively high GNP, high degrees of urbanization and industrialization, a high rate of literacy, a very broad middle class, and a moderate to high measure of value consensus (1970: 167–8).

42 This is one of the highest voting rates in democratic countries. In comparison, the rate in presidential elections in the United States is around 60 per cent.

43 This proportion comprises 37.7 per cent of first- and second-generation Orientals and an estimate of the Orientals of the third or more generations in Israel. Because they are younger, the Orientals are not a numerical majority in the Jewish voting population (aged eighteen or over), though they are a majority (55 per cent) of the Jewish total population.

44 Between 1949 and 1965 the numbers of lists which contested seats in the Knesset ranged from seventeen to twenty-four; eleven to fifteen won at least one seat, and eleven to twelve political parties are permanently represented, of which none has received more than 40 per cent of the votes (H. Smith, 1969: 13–14). As a result of a trend to set up bigger party blocs since 1969, this pattern has changed. The largest list received a record peak of 46.2 per cent of the votes in 1969 and 40.1 per cent in 1973, and the second largest list 21.7 and 31.0 per cent respectively. In 1973 twenty-one lists ran, but a record low of only ten of them gained seats.

45 These obstacles are declining in importance as the Orientals acquire more experience and in view of the expected switch to a predominantly regional method of elections.

46 Of the $9.3 billions received, 53 per cent were unilateral transfer payments (28 per cent from world Jewry, 21 per cent from West Germany and 3.5 per cent from the United States government), 36 per cent were loans and 11 per cent came from foreign investments (official figures quoted by Remba, 1971a).

47 'Israel indeed received substantially more aid than the vast majority of developing nations. According to a United Nations study, Israel received $113.20 per capita in net long-term capital and official donations in 1961; this figure was exceeded only by the $151.70 received by Puerto Rico. All underdeveloped countries combined received $4.70 per capita' (Remba, 1971b: 268).

48 Katzenelson's (1964) attempt to formulate an ideology of Ashkenazi supremacy, as mentioned in chapter 4, was fiercely condemned by all public political circles.

49 Enloe (1973: 208) characterizes the following dominant ethnic groups as 'currently crippled by political underdevelopment': Malays in Malaysia, Protestants in Ulster, Afrikaners in South Africa, Sinhalese in Sri Lanka, Negroes in Trinidad and Anglo-Saxons in the United States. All these dominant groups play plain ethnic politics, fail to seek legitimacy from their subordinate groups and do not use their political superiority to solve ethnic problems.

50 The concept, 'controlled gradualism', which indicates a strategy of dominant groups, is used and illustrated by Enloe (1973: 209–10).

6 Pluralism and inequality

1 These indicators are language, race, religion, sectionalism and interest articulation by non-associational groups (i.e., the extent to which kinship, lineage, ethnic-regional and religious groups are involved in political life).

2 These coefficients refer to the distribution of personal income of urban wage-earners' families. Because of standardization, which improves comparability, they differ slightly from those reported by the Central Bureau of Statistics (*Statistical Abstract of Israel*, 1972, 23: 270) and by the Public Inquiry Commission (1970: 33). The latest comparable coefficients available are: for Israel 0.33 in 1968–9, for the United States 0.33 in 1966, for Canada 0.30 in 1965 and for Britain 0.37 in 1964.

3 In a study of income distribution in forty-four developing states by Adelman and Morris in 1971 (quoted by Nwaneri, 1973: Table 1), Israel was found to be the most egalitarian. The averages for all countries in the study were as follows: the poorest 20 per cent of the population received 5.6 per cent of the total national income, the lower middle 21–39 per cent received 8.4 per cent, the middle 40–60 per cent received 12.0 per cent, the upper middle 61–79 per cent received 17.7 per cent and the highest 20 per cent received 56.0 per cent (the top 5 per cent received 30.0 per cent). The respective percentage shares for Israel were 6.8, 13.4, 18.6, 21.8 and 39.4 per cent (11.2 per cent). The 39.4 per cent share received by the highest quintile (or 11.2 per cent by the top 5 per cent) is the smallest in all the developing countries compared.

4 According to a linguistic authority: 'In 1967, it was estimated that about 76% of the Jewish population used Hebrew as their main language of communication. It was also estimated that of the 2,496,000 Jews living in Israel at the end of 1969 about 95% could carry on their daily business in Hebrew, though many still spoke other languages at home and read daily papers in languages other than Hebrew' (Rabin, 1971: 9). According to the 1972 census, 88 per cent of people aged fourteen or over use Hebrew as a daily spoken language and only 12 per cent use foreign languages as their first or only everyday speech (CBS, *Statistical Abstract of Israel*, 1974, 25: 731). In a state-wide sample of Oriental adult males taken in 1971, the majority reported the use of Hebrew in free and personal situations: 51.1 per

cent said they spoke only Hebrew with their wives and an additional 34.4 per cent used a combination of Hebrew and a foreign language; 70.9 per cent reported the exclusive use of Hebrew with friends and an extra 23.1 per cent used a combination (Eshel and Peres, 1973).

5   The most important ethnic differences lie in the pronunciation of the Hebrew letters resh, a'yin, het, koof, and tet (Rabin, 1971: 16). In the above-mentioned survey, 72.8 per cent of the Oriental respondents were judged by the interviewers to have a distinctive Oriental accent (Eshel and Peres, 1973).

6   According to a Jewish saying, 'Jews are responsible for one another.' The Jews in Israel make excessive claims for warmth, sympathy, permissiveness and mutual help from fellow-Jews and they are thus bound to be disappointed (Weingrod, 1965: 38). This holds, however, more for Oriental Jews.

7   To illustrate, in a state-wide survey conducted in 1970, 39 per cent of those who defined themselves religious and 17 per cent of those who identified themselves as very religious reported watching television on the evening of the Sabbath, which ought to be strictly observed. 'This inconsistency between religious attitudes and behaviour is, however, more apparent than real, because a brief examination of the characteristics of the "religious" and "very religious" viewers reveals that most of them are of Asian and North African origin. Since the interpretations of religious observance among these ethnic groups differ from those of the Ashkenazim, for many of them television viewing (as well as some other activities) on the Sabbath is not considered to be a breach of any religious injunction' (Gurevitch and Schwartz, 1971: 70–1).

8   The respective figures for Ashkenazim are 30, 59 and 11 per cent. The trend of secularization among the Ashkenazim is less marked. Two other surveys show that religious retention as indexed by non-travel on the Sabbath or wearing a skullcap is less among the Orientals (quoted by Don-Yihye, 1975b: 100).

9   A study of 11th-graders in religious high schools in 1964–5 shows no differences between Oriental and Ashkenazi students in behavioural and nonbehavioural aspects of religious observance and in many other religious attitudes. The explanation given for this unexpected similarity is that 'Oriental youths who did not drop out until the eleventh grade in academic high schools have strong leanings towards Ashkenazi culture' (Zuckerman-Bareli, 1972: 34).

10   The median age of marriage in 1974 was 25.1 years for Oriental grooms, 25.4 for Ashkenazi grooms, 22.4 for Oriental brides and 22.5 for Ashkenazi brides (CBS, *Statistical Abstract of Israel*, 1976, 27: 71).

11   Although the family plays a central role in the life of both Orientals and Ashkenazim, it has declined as a source of personal contacts. One survey shows that 72 per cent of all respondents in 1970 saw their parents at least once a week and the two ethnic groups did not differ in this regard (Katz and Gurevitch, 1973: 164–5). According to another survey, 63.4 per cent of Oriental men in 1971 reported

none of their closest friends to be a relative and 83.4 per cent stated that two-thirds or more of their intimates were unrelated to them (comparative figures for Ashkenazim were not reported) (Eshel and Peres, 1973).

12 Antonovsky and Arian (1972: chapter 7) report significant ethnic differences even within equal educational-occupational levels. Yet their data were gathered in 1962 and they emphasize that more recent studies show a trend for social class gradually to supersede ethnicity (p. 174).

13 The religious curriculum is still full of gaps and inconsistencies. A study of moral education in elementary schools found no differences between religious and nonreligious schools except in the emphasis put on religious values (Adar and Adler, 1965: 131). Another study confirmed that religious and secular values were separately taught in state religious high schools and yeshivot: in only 6.1 per cent of the cases observed did the teachers present various economic, moral, family, etc., values in religious terms (Zuckerman-Bareli, 1970: 91). Shneller (1974) shows that the apparent conflicts between secular and religious studies in the state religious schools (e.g., the story of the creation of man as it is in fact taught in Bible and biology classes) are usually left unresolved, and suggests methods to strengthen a sense of religion by a greater integration of teaching.

14 To illustrate, the traditional value of learning is manifested in the finding that 77 per cent of all Israeli Jews read at least one book a year compared with 69 per cent of all adults in Switzerland, 63 per cent in England, 56 per cent in France, 24 per cent in Italy, etc. (Katz, E.1973: 21). While the values are perpetuated, their religious content is not. Thus in this instance most people read translations of literature, not holy books.

15 The convergence of the worlds of the religious and nonreligious may be explained through the development of 'secular religion' by the latter. However, these secularized Jewish traditions of the non-religious majority are far removed from the traditional religion adhered to by the religious minority. Nationalism and statism are not the same as divine authority. Yom Kippur as a day of atonement is quite different from a day of soul-searching. The special dinners and exchange of gifts as family rituals in the secular religion are not comparable with the family celebration of the Sabbath and holidays in traditional religion (Shelah, 1972).

16 Of course, adjustments are made to the highly cherished values. Zaid (1973: 16) observes with regard to hospitality: 'The tradition of hospitality, for instance, continues to head the list of fine customs in Arab society. None the less, today as the host makes plans to receive his guests, who in most cases advised him of their visit, he no longer fears that he will be considered a miser if he wants to know the number of portions to prepare and does not invite the leaders of the neighbourhood to dine along with his guests.'

17 Some of the contrasts in trends in family life between Oriental Jews and Israeli Arabs are noted by Matras (1973: 385–6): 'Thus, universal

marriage persists among the Oriental Jewish and the Moslem Arab population groups despite the demographically-based and social-change-based marriage squeezes. Among the Oriental Jews this has taken place concomitantly with the breakup of the traditional marriage regime, the expansion of marriage markets for virtually all origin groups, and the passing of initiative and control of marriage from the parents' generation to the couples themselves. Among Moslem Arabs universal marriage has persisted alongside the return to, and strengthening of, the traditional marriage regime, including lineage endogamy and parental control of mate selection. The breakup of the traditional marriage regime is associated, in the Oriental Jewish population, with rationalization of family formation and intervention to control numbers of pregnancies and births. The persistence of the traditional marriage regime in the Moslem Arab population is associated with continued high, uncontrolled fertility.'

18 Zak (1976) demonstrated, on the basis of a factor analysis of attitudes of 532 Arab university students in a survey taken shortly before and after the October 1973 War, that the Arab and Israeli identities constituted independent factors (technically they are said to be orthogonal rather than bipolar). The correlation between the two factors was −0.22 and it disappeared after controlling for several points of disagreement between Arabs and Jews (e.g., Israel's right to exist). Zak's generalization about the divergence between Israeli and Arab identities should be qualified for a number of reasons: (a) Arab, not Palestinian, identity was examined; (b) a negative correlation was found and its statistical partialling out begs the question; (c) the incompatibility between the two identities was felt more among the Arab activists and intellectuals and less among the general population of university students, many of whom were schoolteachers employed by the state; and (d) the situation has changed since the winter of 1974.

19 Israel failed to adopt a Constitution mainly because of the opposition of the religious parties which held that no secular constitution may supersede halakha. In 1974, under the pressure of social movements for political reform, the government announced its intention to introduce a constitutional Bill of Civil Rights.

20 An editorial in the most outspoken Sephardic publication concluded (*Bamaarakha*, March 1971, p. 5): 'The majority of the people in Israel are Sephardim and Orientals and they will insist strongly on their right to a Sephardic Rabbinate. The abolition of the duality of the Rabbinate will achieve one and only one goal which the Minister of Religious Affairs has wished for for so long, i.e., making the Rabbinate in the country an Ashkenazi Rabbinate.' Earlier, the Israeli Executive of the World Federation of Sephardic Communities made a public statement in Israel (published in *Haaretz*, 6 June 1970) and abroad denouncing the proposed law as 'a scheme to rob the Sephardic public of its influence in religious and state institutions'. The Executive warned that 'the destruction of the Sephardic Rabbinate might endanger national unity'.

21 Reacting to pressures from the Sephardic Faction in his own party (the National Religious Party), the Minister of Religious Affairs backed down from his original plans already in 1970. The government debated the question, and General Dayan made an unusual move in opposing the continuation of ethnic duality. The final decision to sanction the status quo was made by the government in August 1971 and by the Knesset in January 1972. The Black Panthers' agitation was behind these historic decisions.

22 The Knesset approved 'The recommendations of the Commission to investigate the educational systems of primary and post-primary schools in Israel' on 29 July 1968 (*Knesset Proceedings*, 52, 36: 3037–9). The two stated goals of the reform are improvement in the quality of schools and their ethnic integration. On 13 June 1971 the Supreme Court rejected the plea of a group of parents to allow their children, who were assigned to an integrated school in Jerusalem, to attend a private school.

23 Orientals are more concentrated in the Northern, Southern and Jerusalem districts; Ashkenazim more in the Haifa and Tel-Aviv districts; both are equally distributed in the Central district (Matras, 1969: 134–5).

24 The Orientals have already gained control of many local authorities. In 1972 34 per cent (33 out of 98) of the heads of Jewish local governments and 57 per cent (37 out of 65) of the general secretaries of Jewish local workers' councils were Orientals.

25 Matras (1969: 138) reports a greater isolation in Jerusalem in 1961, when refined categories of countries of origin were used rather than a dichotomous division into people born in Asia or Africa and persons born in Europe or America.

26 In the detailed planning of the educational reform designed by the Ministry of Education and Culture, ethnic integration is to be implemented by the following measures: the transfer of all primary-school-leavers to the newly established junior high schools, the remapping of educational zones to maximize the ethnic mix in schools, the formation of ethnically mixed classes, and the introduction of ethnically mixed extra-curricular social activities (Israel, Ministry of Education and Culture, 1969: 16).

27 It is difficult to know the exact figures, since many ethnic lists are disguised as local (non-partisan) lists. Of the total number of lists in 1950, 8.2 per cent were specifically ethnic and 14.1 per cent local, but in 1965 the figures were 1.9 and 16.3 per cent. Of the total number of councillors elected in 1950, 3.2 per cent ran on ethnic lists and 14.1 per cent on local lists, and in 1965 1.0 and 10.0 per cent respectively (Weis, 1968: 293).

28 The available evidence for these ethnic voting patterns is still not sufficient. Lissak (1969: chapter 4; 1972) has analysed the election returns for ethnic ecological concentrations. He discerns a continuous trend among Orientals to vote for the right-of-centre parties and among Ashkenazim to vote for the left-of-centre parties. Arian (1973; 1975), in returns from pre-election polls, examines the class

and ethnic base of the three political streams. Peres, Yuchtman and Shafat (1975), drawing on a pre-election poll taken in August 1973, demonstrate clear voting preferences. The Alignment (labour bloc) is backed by the older, European- or American-born, and oldtimers, whereas the reverse is true for the Likud (right-of-centre bloc). Of the Orientals, 32 per cent said they would vote for the Alignment and 43 per cent for the Likud, whereas the Ashkenazim reported 47 and 20 per cent respectively (Table 6). Or to take the extreme categories, only 13 per cent of the Ashkenazim who arrived before 1947 and were thirty-six or older indicated support for the Likud as against 43 per cent of the Orientals who arrived after 1947 and were thirty-five or younger.

29 In 1968 24.5 per cent of Israeli-born Orientals married Ashkenazim as against 15.4 per cent of the foreign-born Orientals. Also 20.4 per cent of the Jews born in Iraq, Egypt, Lebanon, Syria and Turkey married Ashkenazim, compared with 13.0 per cent of Orientals hailing from other countries in Asia and Africa (CBS, *Vital Statistics*, 1967–8, Special Series 318: 34–5, quoted by H. Cohen, 1972: 10).

30 The laws and statutes in the area of religion and state in Israel are compiled in England and Shelah (1973). For a full commentary, see Elon (1968).

31 Two steps were taken to achieve complete integration between the religious and nonreligious in the army. One is a specific state law requiring exclusively kosher food to be served in the army (the army is the only state body where such a law exists). The other is the formation of a military Rabbinate which is entrusted with the powers to supervise the observance of religion in the army's public domain, to cater for the religious needs of the soldiers and to try to solve conflicts between the military and the religious life.

32 The religious parties oppose the draft of women. They hold that military service is incompatible with the traditional role of women as potential wives and mothers and it does not offer the protection of the home against the hazards of secular life (especially intensive contacts between the sexes). The compromise of civilian national service (mostly teaching and community service in remote areas) was not put into effect because of continued religious opposition for the same reasons. Liberal circles in the National Religious Party agitated in 1971–2 to revive the programme, but were blocked by stronger traditional factions within and outside the party.

33 Full-time religious studies at grand yeshivot for men in their twenties are considered by many religious people to be so essential to the spiritual welfare of the nation, and more particularly to the training of a Rabbinic elite, as to justify exemption from military service. The nonreligious majority resent the present illicit avoidance of the draft by yeshiva students. Lately a new type of yeshiva is emerging, known as 'yeshivat hahesder', which integrates religious studies with military training.

34 In the absence of studies on segregation between religious and nonreligious Jews, this crude estimate is based on circumstantial

evidence, i.e., the percentage of total votes won by all religious parties in the 1973 local elections. Since the religious parties obtained an average of 15 per cent, localities in which 10 to 20 per cent of the votes were cast for the religious parties are considered as largely mixed communities and the rest as largely unmixed. An analysis of the election results shows that out of the ninety-seven local authorities in which elections were held, only thirty-seven (or 38 per cent) were mixed and a majority of sixty (or 62 per cent) were unmixed (subdivided into twenty-nine with more than 20 per cent of votes for the religious and thirty-one with fewer than 10 per cent for the religious) (Elazar, 1975: Table 1).

35 In a state-wide survey of high school pupils in 1973 it was found that around one-fifth of the pupils in the religious schools were non-religious and around one-fifth of those in the nonreligious schools were religious (Levy and Guttman, 1974: 25). The percentage of pupils attending post-primary education which does not fit their religious observance is, however, much smaller than one-fifth, because yeshivot where religious standards are strictly imposed and which impart nearly half of the religious post-primary education were not included in the survey.

36 In the strict legal sense, there are about a dozen religious communities (including several for various small Christian denominations and one for the Bahai faith), but the major ones are those of Jews, Moslems, Christians and Druzes.

37 Several civil laws were enacted, however, to counteract undesirable religious laws in these areas. For instance, the law against premature marriages is incompatible with the Moslem religious law that allows minors to marry.

38 Military government was fully restored during the Six-Day War. During the Yom Kippur War it was not restored, but scores of Israeli Arabs, suspected as potential agitators or communist activists, were put under administrative detention.

39 There are three laws:
    1 The Land Transfer (Acquisition for Public Purposes) Ordinance of 1943, which was passed on from the British, is the general law entitling the government to expropriate lands for public purposes. It has been used especially since 1953 to expropriate lands mainly from Arabs, but also from Jews.
    2 The Absentee Property Law of 1951 regularizes the confiscation of the lands of Arab refugees, including the lands of Israeli Arabs who were technically 'absent' (i.e., outside Israeli territory or who had left their homes during and after the 1948–9 War).
    3 The Land Acquisition (Validation of Operations and Compensation) Law of 1953 authorizes the government to take over lands which were not in the possession of their owners on 1 April 1952. It legalizes the de facto post-war confiscation of lands of Israeli Arabs against some compensation.
    Whereas the first law applies to all, though in practice it is mostly imposed on Arabs, the last two laws are directed exclusively against

the Arabs (for a brief review see Stock, 1968: 45–6; Oded, 1964).

40 The 'trustworthy' Druzes are subject to less segregation than the other Arabs. They serve in the army (though mostly in separate units) and border police and since 1967 they have been gradually granted direct access to the same channels as Jews in their dealings with the Israeli government and the Histadrut.

41 Since Jews usually do not trust Arabs and since the Orientals supply the domestic help needed, Arab–Jewish relations lack even the physical proximity and direct paternalism common elsewhere.

42 There are various organizations that try to encourage Arab–Jewish social relations (see Rosen, 1970: 10–114 for an extensive survey), but they make little headway.

43 The typical case of a marriage between a Moslem man and a Jewish woman is acceptable in Islamic law and the couple may be married by a Kadi and be legally registered. The problem is, however, that Rabbinic law does not recognize such unions. The legal adjudication in matters of divorce, alimony, inheritance, etc., will largely depend on the religious court chosen. Moreover, the status of the offspring is in limbo because both religions claim them as their own.

44 This estimate is based on an explorative field survey by Yosef Ginat (*Ma'ariv*, 3 March 1975). Other speculations range from several hundreds to several thousands (quoted by E. Cohen, 1969a; Rubinstein, 1973: 452).

45 The Jewish figures consist of Oriental and Ashkenazi components which differ widely. In most cases, the Orientals are much closer in socioeconomic status to the Arabs than to the Ashkenazim. Because of the large variation in measures it is difficult to compute summary ratios between Arabs, Orientals and Ashkenazim, but the average is perhaps around 1:2:4 respectively.

46 The discrepancy in productivity prevails in every field crop. To cite some of the available comparisons, in 1971–2 the average yield of wheat (unirrigated) in non-Jewish farms was 135 kilograms per dunam compared with 315 in Jewish farms and, respectively, barley (unirrigated) 130 and 265, sorghum for grain (unirrigated) 170 and 290, winter hay (unirrigated or partly irrigated) 360 and 430, sunflower seeds (unirrigated and irrigated) 80 and 130, and sugar beet (in non-Jewish farming unirrigated and in Jewish farming irrigated) 2,045 and 5,600 (CBS, *Statistical Abstract of Israel*, 1973, 24: 373).

47 Mar'i discusses higher education in three Arab villages which during 1948–67 were split into two by the Israel–Jordan border and were reunited in 1967. It was found that the proportion of students and university graduates per 100,000 residents in 1972 was 472 among the Israeli villagers as compared with 2,797 among the Palestinian villagers on the West Bank (the ratio is 6:1). More generally, in 1971 the rate of university students per 100,000 residents in Jordan (including the West Bank) was 1,210, among Israeli Arabs 130, and among Israeli Jews 1,300; i.e., the rate of Jordanian Palestinians was nine times as high as that of Israeli Arabs and the Jewish rate ten times as high. (See Mar'i, 1976: Tables 1 and 3).

48 Opinion polls in which Israeli Arabs were directly asked to compare themselves with Arabs in the West Bank yielded inconsistent results. Compare, for example, Peres (1970: 488) with Zak (1975: 57–8).

49 This Jewish view is commonly put forward in publications of the Israeli government; see, e.g., Stendel (1970; 1973a); Shemesh (1975). This observation is noted by Stock (1968: 49). As for the Arab view, it is best expressed by the Arab intelligentsia. Israeli Arab students, for instance, argue that despite substantial progress, 'Arab education is not what it should be; again, one hears the same claim regarding the Arab village; Arab education in Israel ought to be absolutely equal to the Jewish' (Landau, 1969: 52).

50 The distribution of the men's answers was as follows: 54 per cent said that their children should work in whatever jobs they wanted, 38 per cent wanted all the children to be professionals, 8 per cent thought that some of the children should be professionals and some labourers, and only 1 per cent wished their children to become labourers.

51 Oriental–Ashkenazi power disparities are discussed here only briefly. A fuller account and documentation will be given in the next chapter: Table 34 summarizes the main findings.

52 In 1973, Oriental representation in the bureau of the Israel Labour Party was 11 per cent (three out of twenty-seven), none in the steering secretariat of nine of Mapam, 25 per cent in the unified secretariat of Mafdal (four out of sixteen), 13 per cent in the executive of Herut (four out of thirty-one) and 3 per cent in the executive of the Liberal Party (one out of thirty-seven).

53 Of the 244 Jewish heads of local authorities in the years 1950–67 only 21 or 8.6 per cent came from the religious parties (Weis, 1973: 127).

54 The number of Knesset members supporting the government during the 1949–73 period ranged from 67 to 106, of whom between 10 to 16 came from the religious parties (for more details see Table 81). In half of the governments, the withdrawal of the religious parties from the coalition could have deprived it of its majority in the Knesset. Moreover, the backing of the religious parties was essential in all the coalition governments in order to give the leading party a wider base or a counterbalancing force against the other coalition partners.

55 What the religious parties fail to attain at national level (for instance, a nation-wide Sabbath law), they make up for at local level (e.g., municipal Sabbath bylaws). Since political splintering pervades both political levels and the centre controls the periphery, deals can be made between the religious and nonreligious Jews in positions of national power which may apply nationally or just locally. For religious politics in state government see Birnbaum (1970); in local government see Weis (1972: 149–55) and for an interesting case study see Aronoff (1973).

56 The religious Jews seriously fear, however, that the nonreligious majority might use its numerical superiority to take over religious

institutions or to elect people who will be accountable to the non-religious power structure and make religious reforms in defiance of the halakha. While such a possibility cannot be dismissed, it has so far proved to be unrealistic. In fact, the religious group has been quite successful in instituting measures against this development. These considerations are apparent in the account by Friedman (1972) of the Chief Rabbinate.

7 Oriental–Ashkenazi inequality

1 This chapter draws on Smooha and Peres (1975). I would like to thank Dr Y. Peres, from Tel-Aviv University, for his co-operation. Needless to say, the responsibility for the entire chapter is mine alone. Here, only the inequality between the Orientals and the Ashkenazim will be discussed. The few available data on inequalities between religious and nonreligious Jews and between Arabs and Jews were summarized in the previous chapter.

2 Among other things, adjusted inequalities serve the following objectives: a neutralization of the effects of irrelevant factors such as age and sex; an assessment of the relative contributions of different factors to a given inequality (e.g., how much of the variance in income is accounted for by variance in occupation and education respectively); an estimation of direct ethnic discrimination indicated by the most refined inequality possible; and finally a prediction of the degree of inequality which could have been expected if certain factors (i.e., the controls) could be actually removed.

3 Inconsistency occurs especially in the common case of a high initial inequality and increasing opportunities in society. For instance, suppose the Orientals have IL 250 and the Ashkenazim IL 600 per capita per month in a given year. Because of a steady rise in the standard of living, suppose the two groups a decade later to have IL 350 and IL 750 respectively (after allowing for inflation). In this case, the relative equality increases from 42 to 47 per cent, but the absolute gap also rises from IL 350 to IL 400. Such an inconsistency of findings obtained from the use of absolute and relative measures of inequality is demonstrated for the United States. Miller, for instance, concludes: 'The figures shown above pertain to the relative income gap, which has narrowed. But what about the absolute gap – the dollar gap? This gap between whites and nonwhites has widened since 1947' (1971: 78). Jencks and his associates drew the same conclusion after a rigorous analysis (1972: 216–17).

4 Modernization is conceived of as a tremendous ethnic leveller. The processes of industrialization and urbanization, and the rise of a welfare state, directly increase social equality and indirectly ethnic equality. Lenski (1966: 401) generalizes in this direction: 'Viewing status group stratification in a broadly comparative perspective, it appears that the general trend in most advanced industrial societies is toward a reduction in the degree of inequality between such groups. Weber recognized this half a century ago and explained it as a result

of the rising rate of economic change. Though he did not say so, we may infer that he saw rapid economic changes as disruptive of established patterns of social relations, and thereby destructive of the important practice of status group segregation.' Lenski considers the rise and spread of the democratic-egalitarian ideology to be another factor, not less important than economic growth, in enhancing ethnic equality.

While studies of long-term trends of ethnic inequalities are scarce, the evidence of impressions and some hard facts indicate a trend of increasing ethnic equality. There is both an absolute and a relative improvement in the conditions of ethnic and racial groups. This is demonstrated in the United States for the Japanese and Chinese Americans (Schmid and Nobbe, 1965), the Mexican-Americans (Grebler *et al.*, 1970: 189–93), and the blacks (Miller, 1971: 80). The acculturation and social mobility of the poor white immigrant groups is, however, a model case for the diminishing inequality thesis.

5 Blumer's critique of the idea that modernization necessarily results in diminution of ethnic inequality lends support to the rising inequality thesis. Drawing on industrialization in the American Deep South and South Africa, Blumer shows (1965: 245) that 'when introduced into a racially ordered society, industrialization conforms to the alignment and code of the racial order' rather than undermining it. While 'industrialization will continue to be an incitant to change', political pressures remain more important in reshaping ethnic relations.

The basic rationale for the rising inequality thesis is, however, that competition between initially unequal groups widens the pre-existing inequalities between them. The phenomenon of structured inequality has many aspects, including the principle of cumulation or the vicious circle (Myrdal, 1944: 75–8), the continuation of inequality in the next generation, 'the culture of poverty' (Lewis, 1966) as an impediment of social mobility and the presence of stereotypes and discriminatory practices which hold back underprivileged ethnic groups. For instance, Porter (1965: 402) shows a growing occupational disparity during 1931–61 between French and British Canadians and, according to another study (cited by Royal Commission, 1970: 40), the trend of a widening ethnic gap is even more marked in Quebec.

The broader perspectives of colonial domination in all its types (overseas, new and internal colonialism), also imply rising inequalities. Pre-existing inequalities between the ethnic or racial sections (e.g., the 'white' and 'nonwhite' nations) not only do not decrease, but increase because of initial discrepancies present when development begins as well as the various forms of exploitation that appear as development proceeds.

6 This thesis fully recognizes the conflicting processes in industrialized societies which are selectively emphasized by the above two theses. On the one hand, ample opportunities are available, but the ethnic groups differ to some extent in their access to them. A poverty subculture is a hindrance, but not an incapacity. Prejudice and discrimination are not uncontested but are, rather, attenuated by

universalistic values and practices. By granting everyone the same rights and services, the welfare state creates basic equality between all citizens, regardless of ethnicity or race. At least some of its policies serve, however, the latent function of increasing inequality. The privileged groups benefit relatively more than the under-privileged from the expansion of social services. For instance, they take greater advantage of free higher education, or they dispro-portionately staff positions in service institutions such as education, welfare and the health services.

While welfare state services raise the standard of living of the entire population, and considerably improve thereby the conditions of the lower strata, they do not necessarily reduce the gaps between the groups. By raising the 'floor', new distinctions, smaller in magnitude but not in significance, are introduced. Compulsory primary educa-tion, for example, makes primary schooling an obsolete differentiating criterion, and at the same time higher education becomes the real cut-off point between the ethnic groups.

Because of the simultaneous operation of trends and counter-trends, the reduction in ethnic inequality is expected to be small, slow and piecemeal at best, and stability or the entrenchment of ethnic inequality is foreseen at the worst.

7 Lack of adequate coverage characterizes many studies in social and particularly ethnic inequality (Schermerhorn, 1970: 268) and the previous studies in Israel betray the same deficiency. The surveys of Hanuch (1961), Levy (1968), Klinov-Malul (1969), and the Public Inquiry Commission (1971) are limited to the economic field. The studies by Bar-Yosef and Padan (1964), Lissak (1969) and the Prime Minister's Commission (1973) are more comprehensive, but they barely touch on power disparities.

8 There is no correlation between the number of controls and the degree of increase in the relative index of equality. For instance, for the year 1963-4 Klinov-Malul obtains an average index of 95 per cent as against an index of 87 per cent reached by Levy, who counts a greater number of variables as constant (see footnotes to Table 13).

9 In 1973 Oriental families averaged 4.5 members compared with 2.8 members in Ashkenazi families (see Table 74).

10 There are two major reasons to explain why inequality in per capita expenditure is somewhat smaller than inequality in per capita income. One is negative taxation. In 1968-9 the gross average monthly income per family was IL 900 and IL 744 after tax deductions, i.e., the average income was taxed at a rate of 17.3 per cent. The lowest-income decile of urban families was taxed at a rate of 1.5 per cent of gross income, the fifth decile at 7.9 per cent and the upper decile 26.2 per cent (CBS, *Statistical Abstract of Israel*, 1972, 23: 269). Transfer payments have similar effects: in 1969-70 allowances for large families constituted 7.9 per cent of the average wage of employees with four children, 10.0, 12.4 and 14.9 per cent for employees with five, six and seven children respectively (ibid.: 624). The other reason is the negative balance of Oriental family budgets

as compared with positive savings by Ashkenazi families. In 1968–9 the total monthly income of the average Oriental family was IL 796.5 and its consumption expenditure totalled IL 818.1, compared with IL 1,116.5 and IL 970.2 respectively of the average Ashkenazi family (ibid., 1970, 21: 164).

11 Untaxable incomes include full or partial reimbursements for private telephone, car, professional books, insurance and similar expenses; loans with nominal interest rates and grants-in-aid; and so forth. These and many other untaxable incomes were investigated by a special inquiry commission (Commission on Tax Reforms, 1975) and they were eliminated by the 1975 tax reform.

12 On the other hand, the incomes of some Oriental small entrepreneurs (such as building contractors and subcontractors), proprietors of small businesses, independent artisans and domestics are also under-reported. Their impact is, however, too small to counterbalance the more general advantages enjoyed by the Ashkenazim. For a journalist's exposé of tax evasions in Israel, see Nadel (1975).

13 In 1975 72.2 per cent of men and 25.9 per cent of women aged fourteen or older and born in Asia or Africa, as against 72.3 and 36.0 per cent of men and women born in Europe or America, respectively, were in the labour force (CBS, *Statistical Abstract of Israel*, 1976, 27: 294–5). Oriental women, who must take care of larger families and who are undereducated, go out to work less than Ashkenazi women.

In 1969, 9 per cent (18,000 out of 207,000) of Jewish young people aged from fourteen to seventeen neither studied nor worked (66 per cent studied, 18 per cent worked and 7 per cent studied and worked) (Prime Minister's Commission, 1973, Appendix 5, p. 5). The over-whelming majority of them were Orientals. Their number was quite high in a society which places heavy emphasis on education and in an economy experiencing full employment.

14 The blue-collar jobs (i.e., construction, craft, production, transport and communications) in the Jewish economy declined from 40.9 per cent in 1954 to 31.9 per cent in 1975, and agricultural jobs from 13.5 to 5.2 per cent (CBS, *Labour Force Survey*, Special Series 56, Table 23; CBS, *Statistical Abstract of Israel*, 1976, 27: 314). In the same period the proportion of white-collar and service occupations increased.

15 Matras (1963) reports that 6 per cent of the Oriental grooms whose fathers were manual workers and new immigrants held nonmanual jobs in 1955, compared with 13 per cent of their Ashkenazi counter-parts (sons of nonmanual workers did better: 22 and 37 per cent respectively). The proportions found in Zloczower's (1968: 52) study in 1964 were 20 and 34 per cent respectively (and 38 and 50 per cent). The ethnic gaps in mobility among oldtimers were somewhat smaller.

16 This tendency is more pronounced when measured in ratios rather than in differences.

17 In 1973, 19.3 per cent of all employed persons in Israel had at least some college education; among Jews only, it was somewhat higher

(CBS, *Statistical Abstract of Israel*, 1974, 25: 336). This is one of the highest percentages in the world.

18 The available figures of age-specific representation are somewhat deficient. Figures for post-primary education up to 1966–7 refer to foreign-born only, and accurate figures for higher education exist only since 1964–5. These shortcomings affect, however, the exact indices and trends of equality in the proportional representation but not the overall findings.

19 In 1970 20.6 per cent of all persons aged twenty to twenty-four in Israel (22.8 per cent of the Jews and 3.1 per cent of the Arabs) attended an institution of higher or post-secondary education. In comparison the average in European countries in the same year was 17.3 per cent (Israel, Ministry of Education and Culture, 1974, Table 28).

20 The 1974–5 figures were released by the Committee for the Planning of Education in the 1980s. See Tables 30 and 32 for the 1971–2 figures. Algarebly (1975) provides details about the definition and measurement of the percentage of culturally disadvantaged pupils

21 Of course there is the theoretical possibility of a biological inequality in ability. The biogenetic thesis re-emerged in the late 1960s in the United States to account for the IQ disparities between blacks and whites (see the exchange between Jensen and his critics in *Environment, Heredity and Intelligence*, 1969). The weakness of the alternative biological explanation in the Israeli case is quite evident, as is shown in the following findings. In a comprehensive longitudinal study, the mental development of infants from the prenatal period up to the age of four from Moroccan and Ashkenazi groups was compared. Up to eighteen months, the Moroccan children developed better than Ashkenazi children, but at three and four the Ashkenazi children scored considerably higher. 'However, all the differences in IQ at these age levels were accounted for by parents' educational level. No ethnic effect was found' (Smilansky, Shephatia and Frenkel, 1976: 7). The investigators suggest that Moroccan socialization patterns are more favourable for child development for the first year and a half, whereas Ashkenazi practices are superior for later years (ibid.: 74–5). In another study of pre-school children, a notable decline in the ethnic gap in IQ scores in the second generation compared with the first generation is found (Lieblich, Ninio and Kugelmass, 1972). In still another study, no significant differences in scholastic achievement between Oriental and Ashkenazi children in kibbutzim were found (Smilansky and Yam, 1969: 270). This is because in kibbutzim the Oriental children enjoy good education, high socioeconomic standards and full Westernization.

22 The tendency for educational systems to do well in quantitative measures but poorly in qualitative terms in dealing with disadvantaged groups is quite general. This seems to apply to American education during the recent decade and also to the expansion of education in developing countries (e.g., see Szyliowicz, 1973, for education in the Middle East).

23 On the other hand, a survey of third-year students at Tel-Aviv University shows that Oriental and Ashkenazi students do not differ in their academic success. Given the less demanding fields of studies they enter and the multi-step selection they pass until they reach the third year, this finding is not surprising (Shapira and Etzioni-Halevy, 1973: 100–1).

24 This classification into three analytically independent types of power implies, of course, a rejection of the Marxist approach which assumes the primacy of economic power. The old school of political pluralism which stresses the independence of political power is also rejected as a general theory of Western democracies. In applying the suggested classification, some reclassifications of power positions are necessary. For instance, trade unions in Israel are reclassified as 'political' rather than 'economic', because they are built into the Histadrut which is a predominantly political sector.

25 This pattern appears in the Knesset, the Zionist executive committee, local authorities and so on, but is absent in the Histadrut executive committee and several other bodies.

26 The 3 per cent weight of Orientals in the top ranks was for 1969, but it was also found for 1965–6 (Gloverzon, 1970: 38, Table 5). A top position is defined as the two highest executive levels under a director-general of a ministry, or a comparable lower level executive who maintains a direct contact with a minister (p. 24).

27 I have a list of members of boards of directors of all governmental corporations in 1970. Only a few have Oriental surnames. For technical reasons I was unable to identify systematically the ethnic origin of the powerholders in the list.

28 The Orientals took up to a great extent the lucrative branch of construction, mainly as small contractors and subcontractors. Though some have personally profited, this prosperity has brought no control over the building market.

29 The 15.8 per cent of Orientals in the Histadrut top administration is somewhat inflated due to a loose definition of 'top official' in the Histadrut but, even so, equality in the Histadrut administration is greater than that in the administrations of the state and the Jewish Agency.

30 Brichta and Ben-Dor, in a study of the social background of Knesset members and cabinet ministers in Israel in the years 1948–69, concur that (1974: 236–8): 'Immigrants of European origin are consistently overrepresented, while those born in Africa and Asia, along with the population born in Israel, are consistently underrepresented. It is noteworthy that in all these cases misrepresentation is greater on the governmental than on the parliamentary level.

'This misrepresentation is a most significant phenomenon since in Israel, as in other Western parliamentary regimes, there has been a definite process of the transfer of power from the legislative to the executive branch of government ... By allowing for a symbolic increase in the representation of the distinctly underrepresented sectors in the legislature, the [East European] elite has been successful in gaining continuous support and acceptance even from the mis-represented groups, without decreasing its control over, the major decision-making process emanating from the cabinet.'

31 In 1973 five members of the Histadrut Central Committee were non-Ashkenazi as against thirteen Ashkenazim. After the split of the ruling Mapai Party in 1965, the splinter party Rafi nominated a Moroccan as a representative to the Histadrut Central Committee. In this situation Mapai had no alternative but to nominate also a Moroccan representative in order to match the offers of Rafi to Oriental politicians and voters. A third Oriental was assigned willingly or unwillingly to the Histadrut Central Committee after having been sidetracked from another important post, and was also denied a promised compromise seat in the Knesset. On the other hand, a fourth member is only nominally non-Ashkenazi: he is of Sephardic rather than Oriental origin, does not identify himself as an 'ethnic repre-sentative', and reached the top post not on grounds of ethnic quotas. Statistically he is counted as a non-Ashkenazi, but Oriental politicians usually leave him out. The circumstances of the nomination of the fifth member are not clear. Besides, the Oriental members of the Histadrut Central Committee were in charge of relatively unimportant departments and their power was much smaller than suggested by their number. One of them conceded in an interview: 'I have asked time and again to change my assignment. The resources are so limited that I am not able to do anything. I just fill a chair and spread empty slogans. It is trivial' (Ben-Simhon in interview with Goldstein, 1971).

32 The ethnic nature of these quotas is well reflected in the 1961 agree-ment between David Ben-Gurion, then Prime Minister, and Eliahu Eliachar, the President of the Sephardic community in Jerusalem. Ben-Gurion committed himself to increase the quotas and perform other reforms in exchange for Eliachar's pledge of support in the 1961 national elections. For the full text of the agreement and other exchanges on ethnic matters, see Eliachar (1973).

33 This is an amended estimate which includes both foreign- and Israeli-born Orientals (based on figures in Smith, 1969: 25).

34 Mafdal does not belong to the Histadrut, so no comparison is possible.

35 Precisely against these inequities in representation and patronage, the above-mentioned Oriental caucus during the Labour Party convention in 1971 demanded across-the-board representation of 35 per cent in all positions of power in all ranks and sectors.

36 Brichta (1974), analysing representation in the Knesset and the cabinet, reaches a similar conclusion.

37 If social inequality is indexed by income distribution, comparative figures quoted earlier show that in the 1960s Israel had approached in income inequality capitalist English-speaking societies such as the United States, Britain and Canada, but was more egalitarian than the developing non-European states (Mexico, India and Ceylon) (Roter and Shamai, 1971: 60–2; Nwaneri, 1973: 19). Similarly, ethnic

socioeconomic differences in Israel and the English-speaking societies average at a ratio of 2 to 1 in income, less than 2–3 to 1 in occupation and 2–4 to 1 in education. To illustrate, in the 1960s, the Orientals' income was about 70 per cent of that of the Ashkenazim, in 1961 the French Canadians' income was 80 per cent of the British Canadians' (Royal Commission, 1969, *Report*, vol. 3, parts 1–2: 18), in 1968 the Catholics' income was 80 per cent of the Protestants' income in Northern Ireland (Rose, 1971: 289), in 1969 American blacks' income was 61 per cent of that of the whites (US Bureau of the Census, 1973: 29), etc. In developing countries the ratios are much higher. For example, in distribution of income as well as in education and other resources between non-black and black groups in Jamaica of the 1940s, ratios often exceeded 10 to 1 (Broom, 1954: Table 3).

38   There is a striking similarity in the dynamics of Oriental–Ashkenazi inequality in Israel and black–white inequality in the United States in spite of the marked differences in the patterns of intergroup relations and the societal contexts in these two countries. In both cases the underprivileged (blacks, Orientals) received their share in the general prosperity, the relative gaps declined, the absolute gaps widened and a sizeable underclass composed mainly of members of the subordinate group was perpetuated. (For summaries of data on blacks see, inter alia, Miller, 1971: chapter 5; Jencks *et al.*, 1972: *passim*; US Bureau of the Census, 1973.)

8 Conflict and integration

1   While I am following here Patai's classification, my interpretation of the categories is somewhat different.

2   It is still not clear why the Ashkenazi settlers in Palestine were strongly influenced by Oriental speech habits despite their negative attitudes towards Oriental culture. The fact that the Oriental dialect is the historically authentic one and that the Ashkenazi revivers of Hebrew managed initially to get the co-operation only of the Sephardim of the Old Yishuv in speaking Hebrew, no doubt favoured the adoption of the Sephardic pronunciation. Modern Hebrew pronunciation has become mixed, not Oriental-dominated. It differs from that of the Ashkenazim in the following details only: (1) 'qamatz gadol' is 'a' (e.g., kasher, not kosher); (2) 'holam' is 'o' (e.g., oved not oived); (3) 'tav' without 'dagesh' is 't' (e.g., brit, not bris); and (4) in most words there is an ultimate stress (*Encyclopedia Judaica*, vol. 16, 1971: 1646). Although not numerous, these differences are significant. At the same time, in Israel today the Oriental Hebrew accent, despite its authenticity, is viewed pejoratively.

3   The survey was conducted by the Israel Institute of Applied Social Research. Since 1967 the Institute takes a survey of the urban adult Jewish population at least three times a year. In 1973 and 1975 it took national surveys of Jewish high school pupils. I shall cite findings from the various surveys and identify them by the population

and date of the survey. Unless otherwise indicated, the survey was conducted by the Institute.

4   In my 1970-1 ethnic leadership study, 93 per cent of the Oriental leaders and 92.5 per cent of the Ashkenazi leaders expressed their dissatisfaction with the pace of bridging the ethnic gap. Looking to the future, 86 and 70 per cent respectively felt that the ethnic gap would not be reduced at a reasonable pace but would disappear slowly, reach a standstill, or even grow wider.

5   The dispute between the religious and nonreligious groups can be illustrated by reference to two issues. The two sides take conflicting positions towards the desired character of the Sabbath. Most of the nonreligious Jews in a 1970 survey were in favour of public transport and entertainment on the Sabbath, whereas the majority of the religious were opposed (Katz and Gurevitch, 1973: 43-5). In another survey taken in October–November 1972 a question was asked about ways to solve the problem of the discontented category of religiously unmarriageable persons (for example, the proscribed union of a male Cohen and a divorcee). On the whole, 87 per cent favoured some sort of solution: 38 per cent suggested a civil marriage in Israel for them; 25 per cent, a change of the halakha by an authoritative Rabbinic body; 19 per cent, handling the matter religiously and on an individual basis; 4 per cent, civil marriage abroad; 1 per cent, some other arrangement. Polarization is evident along lines of religious observance. Only 9 per cent of those defining themselves as observant favoured civil marriage in Israel compared with 26 per cent of the largely observant, 35 per cent of the somewhat observant and 63 per cent of the secular.

6   Reform of the Arabic curriculum was promised on several occasions by the Ministry of Education and Culture, but nothing has been done to change the situation.

7   The biases and inequities in the area of immigrant absorption were many. The personnel of the absorption bureaucracies neither spoke non-European languages nor understood the mentality and special problems of Oriental immigrants. The standard of public housing was modelled on the needs of small families. Services to immigrants were limited to a brief length of time sufficient for absorbing a typical Ashkenazi immigrant but not sufficient for an average Oriental immigrant. Special privileges were provided for immigrants from Western countries only.

8   The special efforts made in the area of education are also reflected in research and planning. During 1972-5, large-scale research projects on educational opportunity in the primary schools (the Israeli counterpart of Coleman's study in the United States) and the effects of ethnic integration in the junior high schools were under way. Likewise a commission of experts was working on an ambitious project to draw up a master plan for education in the 1980s.

9   A question about this declaration was raised by Knesset member M. Bibi. The official reply given by the government was that the statement was taken out of context and the original one referred to all

immigrants – who supposedly lack the fighting spirit that all old-timers presumably possess. However, General Dori himself did not deny the statement (*Knesset Proceedings*, 39, 23 March 1964).

10　In the same vein another unidentified Israeli officer from the air force made the following statement in 1970: 'We are part of Western technological civilization. The Arabs do not have the feeling for sophisticated machinery. Even in Israel, those Jews who have come from countries such as the Yemen and Iraq are not good material for pilots. And they are the elite of these places, and sons of doctors and engineers – so you can imagine what the lower ranks of people are. And this difference extends beyond just flying. It includes planning, maintenance, all that goes into an air force' (*Look*, 30 June 1970).

11　Fein writes in this regard: 'Although the thought itself was patronizing, Westerners were impressed with the Eastern response. They had feared panic in the civilian population and some uncertainty among the eastern soldiers. Instead, save as the officer corps was disproportionately Western, it was difficult to distinguish between East and West. Once more, there was the appreciation that for all they might, in Western eyes, be wanting, the Easterners had shared the dangers and the casualties and hence deserved the state and all its fruits' (1968: 331).

12　The question of prejudice and discrimination against Orientals was raised publicly during the ethnic unrest in 1971–2. Among countless communications on the subject, a series of articles by the journalist Donevitz (1971) is worth mentioning. He wrote about the Moroccans in the same respectable *Haaretz* daily in which the journalist Gelblum wrote in 1949 on the same subject. While Oriental spokesmen found virulent prejudice in Donevitz's articles (Chouraqui in a letter to the editor, *Haaretz*, 29 June 1971; Eliachar, saying that Donevitz follows in Gelblum's footsteps, *Bamaarakha*, no. 125, August 1971, p. 10), one is rather struck by the changes in tone that occurred over the period. Donevitz is much more restrained, and is subtler and much less prone to wholesale stereotyping than his predecessor. Paternalism is, to be sure, pervasive in both. Compare, for instance, the following quotation by Donevitz with that by Gelblum (on p. 000 above): 'I have too often heard two words in the slums and development towns – "They owe me", or "I deserve it". Ethnic groups and whole communities arrived in the new, sought-for country, and started to *receive*. Houses and apartments were given for almost nothing. So were beds and mattresses, food for the first days, and cash. Do you want a farm? Take one. Welfare is extended. Medical insurance is supplied. Education is provided. Not everyone paid and not all pay for all these services. But everybody, even those who do not pay, knows how to request and demand more. A welfare case who immigrated as a welfare case and has continued to be so cried out: "I deserve it"' (*Haaretz*, Weekly Supplement, 25 June 1971).

13　Hoetink introduces two new, related concepts to intergroup relations. One is the 'somatic norm image', which is 'the complex of physical (somatic) characteristics which are accepted by a group as its norm and ideal' (1967: 120). The other is 'somatic distance', which refers to the perceived difference between one's own somatic norm image and another physical type (ibid.: 153). These concepts were originally used by Hoetink to analyse Caribbean race relations, but they are broad enough to apply to racial and ethnic relations in general. It must be emphasized that both pertain to social definitions rather than to actual realities.

14 The popular derogatory name for Orientals is '*shehorim*' or '*schwartzes*' (meaning blacks).

15 The images Israel projects abroad are correspondingly of a 'white' society. This backfires against Israel because it is associated with white settler societies such as South Africa in the minds of radical critics as well as ill-informed people (cf. Rubinstein, 1970).

16 In a sample of 800 Oriental adults taken in 1971, 35 per cent endorsed the prejudice that the Orientals would never reach the level of progress of the Europeans and 40.5 per cent thought the Europeans had more capacity for learning and progress than people of other origins (Eshel and Peres, 1973). On the other hand, the derogatory term for Ashkenazim is '*vouz-vouz*', a neologism alluding to the clicks in the Yiddish dialect incomprehensible to Orientals.

17 On the other hand, when the question on discrimination was phrased in personal, direct terms, only 8 per cent of the pupils said that they personally suffered because of their ethnic origin. The projective form of the question is the valid one, because to complain of personal discrimination is to violate a taboo and to disparage oneself. Besides, the personal form of the question is less relevant because in the 1970s discrimination is no longer individual, direct and blatant, but quite subtle and grounded in public policies and practices.

18 With regard to Romanian origin, 27.5 per cent of the Romanian leaders viewed it as having a positive effect for political mobility; 57.5 per cent, no effect; and 15 per cent, a negative effect.

19 When asked to assess the impact of their ethnic origin on obtaining present positions or on chances of obtaining further leadership roles, the Oriental leaders gave much more favourable answers. Eighty-one per cent viewed their ethnic origin as a positive factor in the past and 50 per cent expected it to operate on their behalf in the future; 14 and 16 per cent considered it to be irrelevant; and 4 and 36 per cent evaluated it as negative (the comparative figures for Romanian leaders were 40, 52.5 and 7.5 per cent in the past and 25, 72.5 and 2.5 per cent for the future). It is quite significant that 4 per cent of the Oriental leaders saw their own origin as a handicap in the past, 36 per cent expected it to present an obstacle to their prospective promotion and 69 per cent regarded Oriental origin in general as a handicap in getting ahead in public life. This increase in percentage suggests that the existing Oriental leaders are the fortunate few who enjoyed the quotas and other support from the establishment. They are less optimistic about their prospects because their promotion means moving to higher positions which are less open to

Orientals. But according to their own testimonies, they are still personally much better off than 'regular' Orientals.

20 In the above 1971 sample of Oriental adults, only a few rejected mixing with Ashkenazim: only 3.5 per cent would not accept an Ashkenazi of a comparable occupational-economic level as a close friend, only 9 per cent would not agree to live in a dominantly Ashkenazi neighbourhood, only 3 per cent would not want an Ashkenazi family as a next-door neighbour and only 4 per cent would not allow their children to marry an Ashkenazi (Eshel and Peres, 1973).

21 Aloni subtitles her book, 'From a Legal State to a Halakhic State'. Tamarin makes a similar charge of theocracy. In order to taste the flavour of the arguments, it will be sufficient to cite Tamarin's justification for branding the religious law of marriage and divorce, prevalent in Israel, as 'the most reactionary'. To paraphrase his reasons (1973: 31–3), this law

(a) Results in 'apartheid' by preventing mixed marriages between Jews and non-Jews (this is reminiscent of the Nuremberg Laws), and also between different kinds of Jews, thereby violates Paragraph 16 of the United Nations Declaration of Human Rights.

(b) Creates a special category of Rabbinic judges who do not swear to judge according to the state laws; discriminates against women and non-Orthodox Rabbis who may not be appointed as Rabbinic judges; and discriminates against some lawyers who may not appear in Rabbinic courts.

(c) Endorses the principle of inequality of women, who cannot obtain divorce without the consent of the husband (the Women's Civil Rights Law, 1951 is explicitly not applicable in matters of marriage and divorce).

(d) Causes uncertainty as to the validity of mixed (and other) marriages (and divorces) contracted abroad in civil courts or by non-Orthodox Rabbis.

(e) Approves the principle of inequality between Jews and non-Jews (non-Jews may not bear witness in Rabbinic courts) and between 'kosher Jews' and 'bastards'.

(f) Produces inequality concerning unions between people belonging to recognized religious communities and others (including atheists).

(g) Violates freedom of conscience by forcing non religious people to undergo religious ceremonies.

(h) Denies the right of the Supreme Court to rule concerning the validity of marriages forbidden by religious law (like those between a divorcee and a Cohen).

(i) Prevents the possibility of remarriage for some widows, deserted women and divorcees (to their marriage-breaking lovers).

(j) Leads to legal and social absurdities such as that a child of a Moslem father and a Jewish mother is both a Moslem and a Jew, or that Gentile fathers and sons in mixed families do not have the same religion, etc.

22 In an earlier 1965 study by Herman (1970: Tables 64 and 65) each group felt very close to its own members, but different in its feeling toward the other – the religious felt 'close' to the nonreligious, whereas the nonreligious did not feel at all close to the religious. This asymmetry can be explained by the greater collectivistic orientation among the religious.

23 O. Cohen also interprets the religious Jews' acceptance of negative stereotypes against themselves as symptoms of self-hate. He points to another symptom of self-rejection: 40 per cent of the religious students had reservations or objections to considering N'ture Karta (ultra-Orthodox Jews who oppose Israel as a false redemption) as members of the Jewish people, and 46 per cent thought the same about anti-religious Jews who do not maintain ties with other Jews in the Diaspora (51 and 31 per cent respectively of the nonreligious respondents answered similarly) (1975: 142). In this case, the religious respondents denied the halakha tenet that Jews remain Jews irrespective of their attitudes or behaviours and thereby adopted the secular view that membership in the Jewish people is national rather than religious (ibid.: 176).

24 For the opposing view that by international standards the Law of Return is not discriminatory because it is akin to immigration laws based on categories of preference prevalent in other countries, see Rubinstein (1967a: 413); and that it is not discriminatory simply because it negates none of the rights of the Israeli Arab citizens, see Stendel (1973b: 187). These legalistic arguments disregard the social contexts and consequences of the Law of Return.

25 These double standards reach extreme proportions in the local council of Ma'alot-Tarshiha which was established in 1963 by a municipal union of the Jewish development town of Ma'alot and the Arab village of Tarshiha. The aim was to design a model of co-operation on an equal basis between Jews and Arabs, but the reality has proved different. Despite the fact that the local council has a common budget, the Jewish Ma'alot enjoys preferential treatment from the government since it is classified as a development town, a border settlement and a locality with a needy population, whereas Tarshiha does not receive any special assistance. The Arabs of Tarshiha define this situation as discriminatory and have a strong feeling of deprivation (Benjamin, 1975: 18).

26 For a study bearing on this stereotype, see Tamarin (1973: 113), who also maintains that the myth of the sabra superman was developed in opposition to the myth of the inferior Diaspora Jew. For a debunking of the national mythology of the sabra superman, see Avineri (1972). Like most stereotypes, the sabra stereotype is partially correct but it is erroneous in its selectivity, categorical applicability and frailty against contradictory evidence. For instance, sabras are observed to be on the average resourceful; middle-class Ashkenazi sabras are observed to be disproportionately resourceful; and sabra resourcefulness is observed to be manifested in mixed traits such as problem-solving orientation and ingenuity as well as in

399

excessive use of personal connections and 'white-collar' law avoidance.

27 Rekhess (1974) made an extensive survey of Israeli Arab university graduates. He reports that the majority of the university-educated Arabs at the time of the survey in 1972 were fully employed and all were white-collar workers. Their job opportunities were restricted, however, since 54 per cent of them were schoolteachers, most of whom were dissatisfied with their conditions of work. It must be emphasized that the small number of graduates in the total Arab population could be absorbed in the Arab sector during the 1960s. In the 1970s the number of Arab graduates is increasing rapidly, much faster than the capacity of the underdeveloped Arab sector to absorb them and the willingness of the Jewish sector to employ them.

28 The answer to the question of whether racism exists in Israel depends very much on the definition of racism adopted. If we adopt van den Berghe's view (1967b: 11) that the term racism must be restricted to beliefs that a given biological make-up, attributed to groups of people, predetermines their behaviour and other socially relevant characteristics, then ethnocentrism rather than racism should be considered to exist in Israel.

According to Rex's broader definition, racism refers to a belief that membership in a given group determines behaviours or qualities of given categories of the population. 'It doesn't really matter whether this is because of men's genes, because of the history to which their ancestors have been exposed, because of their culture or because of divine decree' (1970: 159). The view, held by some at least of the Israeli public, that the Orientals and Arabs are behind the Ashkenazim by several centuries of development and that it will take generations to get rid of their backwardness, if indeed this is possible at all, has a racist flavour.

In this connection the positive response in the Israeli press to the upgrading of Israel–South Africa relations by establishing the rank of ambassador in March 1974 should be mentioned. A journalist who prides himself in liberalism rejoiced and confessed his long-standing feelings about the 'disgusting' African states. He then quoted from a new study that compares 'Negroes' and Jews in New York City and shows that 'there is a hereditary difference in the intellect of a person whose father lived in a jungle and a person whose "ancestors were priests in the Temple" – as Disraeli put it' (Lapid, 1974). It is unknown to what extent these views can be generalized and how widespread these pent-up feelings may be.

It must be emphasized, however, that there is no study on the question of racism in its strictly biological determinist sense. Some militant Arab and Jewish writers make the charge of racism, but they use the term in a very loose way (e.g., Eliachar, 1967; Jiryis, 1969). The definition of a Jew is religious and clearly not racist. The rejection of the 'Black Hebrews' by Israeli authorities was on religious-nationalist, not racial, grounds (the Black Hebrews themselves do not claim to be Jews in the common sense). The hardships

Indian Jews (Bene Israel) used to have in marrying other Jews in Israel were purely halakhic and had nothing to do with their darker skin. The Falashas of Ethiopia still face a similar problem. While the norms are unequivocably non-racist, some racism may exist in the population. For instance, in one public opinion survey taken in June–July 1971, 32 to 35 per cent of the religious said that it was difficult to treat a proselyte the same way as a Jew by birth, and 29 per cent of the somewhat observant Jews, and 17 per cent of the secularists, felt the same.

29 The exceedingly high crime-rate among Moroccan Jews is a glaring symptom of their acute status-dissatisfaction with the lowest position which they occupy in Israeli Jewish society. The Moroccans have the largest proportion of unskilled and uneducated individuals because of the negative selectivity of their immigration and because of structured poverty. They populate the development towns and city slums in the highest percentages. Their public image is notoriously bad and they serve, next to the Arab minority, as a scapegoat for most Israeli Jews. Their disproportional criminal behaviour corresponds well with their disproportional deprivation.

30 Some of the difference is due to the timing of the survey: the general Oriental sample was interviewed in 1971 at the time of the Black Panther demonstrations, whereas the leaders were interviewed in 1970 at the time of the War of Attrition with Egypt.

31 Of course the October 1973 War hit the ethnic lists in the national elections held later in December. However, in the pre-war September elections to the Histadrut, the Oriental lists received only 3.6 per cent of the votes as compared with the 39 per cent in the Oriental survey in 1971 who said they would vote for an Oriental party in the Histadrut general elections (and 28 per cent were undecided).

32 In Tessler's survey (1975a: Table 7), 67 per cent said that they would possibly or definitely move to a Palestinian state were it to be established alongside Israel.

33 Schmelz (1969) offers a detailed analysis of Arab–Jewish crime-rates for the years 1960–5. Among juveniles the Arab rate was twice as high as the Jewish. However, no differences in juvenile crime-rates for Arabs and Jews were reported for 1970 (they were 9.4 and 9.6 respectively, CBS, *Juvenile Delinquency 1970*, Special Series 408, Table B). It is not clear if this indicates a significant change or a temporary fluctuation.

34 In a survey of the Jewish urban population taken in June–July 1970, 56 per cent of the respondents felt that the loyalty of the Arab minority had declined since 1967. This feeling has probably sharpened since 1970.

35 The reluctance of the Israeli authorities and public to seek accommodation with the Israeli Arabs can be illustrated in the case of Biraam and Ikrit. The Arab residents of these two villages were evacuated temporarily during the fight in 1948 but have been barred from them since that time. This is despite the Supreme Court ruling in their favour. During 1972 these residents held demonstrations and

won the sympathy of some circles in Israel. The government refused any compromise and a public opinion survey taken in October–November 1972 showed that 80 per cent of the Jews opposed the return of these refugees to their villages. Similarly 89 per cent objected to the return of other Israeli Arabs who were evacuated or left their villages during the War of Independence.

36 By effective manipulation of symbols, the Panthers managed to capture the attention of the media and the general public. Among the symbols or symbolic activities are included the name 'Black Panthers', which provokes the associations of extreme militancy and anti-semitism in the minds of Israeli Jews; the conduct of a burial ceremony for 'ethnic discrimination'; stealing milk bottles from residents of a privileged neighbourhood and distributing them free to slum-dwellers, etc.

37 In the case of the Black Panthers, the police refused to give a permit to the first rally and arrested their leaders a day before the prohibited rally was scheduled to take place.

38 The government first nominated a Public Inquiry Commission to investigate trends in income inequalities, and then formed another Commission to study the matter more thoroughly. The second Commission produced a voluminous report recommending various social and economic measures (Prime Minister's Commission, 1973).

39 The leader of the Wadi-Salib riot was paroled, given a new flat outside the slum and assigned a good job in a public corporation. Attempts at co-optation of the Panther leaders were made at various stages of the struggle (e.g., see Ben-Simhon's criticism in Goldstein, 1971; the Panthers' own testimony in Ronen, 1971: 13). A good measure of success was achieved by training the activists as youth leaders and sports coaches and by drafting some into the army (as the Panthers originally demanded). A large number of social workers were hired to 'rehabilitate' the Panthers, to find them jobs, etc.

40 Special funds were allocated for slums clearance on both occasions. In the Panthers' case, some money was granted for the rehabilitation of disturbed youths.

41 After the Wadi-Salib riots numerous programmes of compensatory education were launched and then a special adviser on ethnic integration to the Prime Minister was nominated. Following the Panther demonstrations, the government promised to implement the recommendations of the Prime Minister's Commission on Disadvantaged Children and Youth. A special adviser to the Prime Minister was appointed and a public advisory council was nominated, both to assist in implementation of the recommendations. A committee of cabinet ministers was also formed for this purpose.

42 The abuse of protesters by the police is common. Other oppressive means might include the infiltration of the Union of North Africans, which was involved in the Wadi-Salib riots, and the infiltration of the ranks of the Black Panthers by security agents (both were likely, though they cannot be documented. In 1963 obscure leaflets, using extremist ethnic slogans and signed by an underground organization

('The Front for National Equality'), appeared in a number of places (*Bamaarakha*, no. 25, July 1963: 18–19). The organization has either vanished or it has probably been put down quietly by the efficient security authorities.

43 Etzioni-Halevy, analysing the Young Couples and Panther protests, reaches similar conclusions. She sums up the establishment's counter-measures as follows (1975: 514):

(a) Protest is allowed to a certain degree rather than being sup-pressed.

(b) Some symbolic reassurances are given to the aggrieved groups (establishing a committee, announcing ameliorative actions, etc.).

(c) Some devices are employed to attenuate the demands by dis-pensing benefits or buying off the protest leaders.

(d) Some of the aggrieved group's demands are actually fulfilled.

(e) The basic allocative patterns and power structure of Israeli society are left more or less as they were.

Etzioni-Halevy also suggests that ethnic protest groups in Israel have been deprived of their leaders because of upward social mobility and co-optation (p. 516).

44 The institution of 'unmarried spouse' (or, as it is commonly known, unmarried woman) usually serves certain categories of religiously unmarriageable Jews. It refers to a man and a woman who live as a family in a joint household without a marriage contract. Various legislation provides for naming offspring after their reputed father, inheritance and alimony rights for the woman, and many social and material benefits. The religious sector seeks to abolish this arrange-ment although they tacitly recognize the pragmatic solutions it supplies. For details and conflicting views, see Elon (1968: 119–54); D. Friedman (1973); Shava (1973).

45 Fanatic acts are usually perpetrated by young Ashkenazi males belonging to extremist groups (M. Friedman, 1975: 93–4, and for a sociological account of religious zealotry in Israel). Tamarin observes that the 'extreme religious (and ideological) fanaticism is the speciality of people raised in the *Shtetles* and of their sons' (1973: 174).

46 For a sympathetic story of Al-Ard told by one of its leaders, see Jiryis (1969: 129–40). Jiryis concludes: 'As to the future, it can be assumed that the official Israeli policy of suppressing any manifesta-tion of the nationalist movement amongst the Arabs resident in Israel, and of combating any organization that claims to defend their rights, will continue unchanged' (p. 140). For a critical account by a political scientist who brands Al-Ard as 'extremist', see Landau (1969: 92–107).

47 Israeli Arabs locked themselves in their localities during the 1967 War and most expected an Arab victory (Peres, 1971: Table 20). During the 1973 War, conflicting reactions were in evidence: some rejoiced at Israel's 'calamity', whereas the moderates went out of their way to show goodwill by contributing money, volunteering labour, etc., to assist in the war effort.

48 It is also true that both Judaism and Islam recognize the possibility

of religious minorities. Judaism is tolerant of a non-Jewish minority and Islam is tolerant of Jewish and Christian minorities. However, for both religions, minorities are not fully equal members of the community. In addition, Jews, as a minority persecuted for centuries, are motivated to demonstrate a liberal treatment of minorities. This tendency, however, is offset by their inexperience and immaturity as a *new* dominant majority.

49 The conflict-reducing function of separation between Arabs and Jews can be shown, further, in the problems encountered in the few cases of desegregated frameworks. The mixed towns of Acre and Ma'alot are cases in point. In Acre an attempt has been made to solve the housing shortage in the Arab old city by placing about forty Arab families in a public Jewish housing project in the northern part of the city. Although neighbourly relations are good, this living accommodation makes for difficulties for the Arab families who are forced to receive cultural, educational and even commercial services from the Arab quarter which is located a number of kilometres away in the southern section of the city (E. Cohen, 1973). Similarly, a follow-up study in 1974 on the state of the municipal union of Ma'alot-Tarshiha concluded that the experiment was unsuccessful and that both sides would probably benefit more by the dissolution of the mixed local council (Benjamin, 1975: 18).

50 The monopoly of the Orthodox leadership in Israel in representing the religious minority and religion was achieved after a long struggle and it is still unfinished. In the early 1950s, for instance, the ruling Mapai Party started to open religious schools of its own in order to compete with the Mizrahi and Aguda schools in registering immigrant children. The religious parties left the coalition government in protest and the Mapai stopped. As a rule, nonreligious organizations neither engage in religious activities nor attract religious people. Two minor exceptions may be mentioned. The Israel Labour Party has an affiliated religious election list in the Histadrut whose head, a Rabbi who favours the separation of religion from state, was elected as a Knesset member on the general Alignment list. He was the second religious man to become a Knesset member on a nonreligious list (the first was elected in 1965 on behalf of the Liberal Party). See Table 80 for complete figures on the partisan affiliation of religious Knesset members since 1949.

51 Friedman (forthcoming) analyses the historical changes in the role and status of the Rabbinic leadership following the transition from a traditional, religious community to a modern, secular society. It is true that the Rabbinic leaders have lost their absolute authority and have, like all professionals, to compete in a market situation for a clientele. They became less powerful but have essentially remained independent. More structurally problematic is, nevertheless, the position of those Rabbis whose authority is enforced on all Israeli Jews.

The Chief Rabbinate is the most typical and crucial example (Friedman, 1972). It does not enjoy full acceptance among the non-religious majority who reject the halakha as binding, and it is not recognized at all by the more radical Agudat Israel and N'ture Karta. It is thus under cross-pressures. On the one hand, the nonreligious majority and the religious intelligentsia expect it to make reforms in the halakha or at least reach liberal rulings. Its hands are tied, on the other hand, because of the definite limit to the flexibility of Orthodoxy, the counter-pressures of the Council of Tora Sages (of Agudat Israel) and other top halakha authorities in Israel and abroad whose views the Chief Rabbinate respect and fear, and the possible reactions of a sizeable militant Orthodox sector. The authority of the Chief Rabbinate is additionally undermined by its deficient ecclesiastical structure. Since Judaism is churchless, the Chief Rabbinate cannot in the final analysis impose its decisions down the Rabbinic line. To make and sustain innovative resolutions, it depends on the moral and practical backing of Rabbis at various levels. The fact that the Supreme Court can and does issue injunctions against it weakens it further. Despite these structural weaknesses and ambiguities, the Chief Rabbinate maintains, overall, an independent position.

52 Don-Yihye (1975a) shows that the coalition theories of a 'balanced coalition', 'ideological proximity' and 'intensivity differences' cannot account for the quasi-permanent participation of the National Religious Party in the government. On the other hand, the theory of consociational politics does explain the situation. According to this theory, coalition government is a tool to preserve democracy in pluralistic societies by enabling the cultural majority and minority to work out pragmatic solutions. The alternative is *Kulturkampf*. To some extent the politics of accommodation is used vis-à-vis the Oriental Jews as well by appointing leaders for them and taking the wishes of these leaders into consideration. Accommodation with the weak Oriental majority takes the form of neutralization, however, whereas that with the strong religious minority takes the form of a true compromise. As it will be shown shortly, little accommodation is sought with the Arabs, apparently because they are a weak minority and because they fall far outside the national consensus.

53 In fact there is an undeclared status quo between the small ultra-Orthodox community and the dominant majority. Although these extremist religious Jews do not recognize the state of Israel (refuse to have Israeli identity cards, avoid the draft, etc.), the authorities ignore them as long as they do not violate public order. Their unapproved demonstrations, if they remain nonviolent, are not put down. In recent years the industrialization of food and other processes have made them more dependent on the wider society. In order to preserve communal autonomy they need the goodwill of the authorities for concessions and 'benign neglect'. It is expected that this dependence would moderate them (Friedman, 1975).

54 There have been only a few incidents of attacks against innocent Arabs. The most notorious one is the Kfar Kassim massacre. A curfew was imposed in Arab areas during the day before the Suez Campaign in 1956. Forty-seven villagers from Kfar Kassim who

returned from the fields at the evening and were not aware of the curfew were ruthlessly gunned down by the Israeli guards, who were later found guilty. The Kfar Kassim massacre became a symbol of Israeli Jewish brutality against Israeli Arabs, although it was an isolated incident. The Hebrew press at the time condemned it, even though its coverage left much to be desired (Linenberg, 1972: 60–1). See Jiryis (1969: 91–118) for a detailed story of the whole affair and its significance from an Arab nationalist's perspective.

55 National concerns, and especially questions of peace and war, loom largest in the phenomenological world of Israeli Jews. In a public opinion survey of the Jewish urban population taken in September 1975, over three-quarters of the respondents said that they were worried or very worried about Israel's security, political relations and economy, and a majority expressed anxieties about terrorist activities in their immediate surroundings.

56 Along with the solidarity bonds which it supplies to the Israeli Jews, Israel's Western orientation puts the Orientals at a disadvantage and religious Jews on the defensive (see chapter 5, section 6).

9 Continuity and change

1 Deshen (1972; 1974) holds that 'political ethnicity' has declined, whereas 'cultural ethnicity' has intensified during the 1960s. But he tends to overstate the case. As for politics, he puts an undue emphasis on a statement by one of his informants that 'the business of ethnicity is finished'. Nor can the rise in Oriental festivities be taken seriously as evidence of Oriental cultural growth.

2 Defection from the religious camp is best evidenced in the declining weight of religious education. For instance, in 1959–60, 33.1 per cent of all Jews in primary education attended religious schools, as compared with 29.3 per cent in 1974–5. The Orientals are over-represented among these defectors.

3 Chen (1975) argues that religious education exhibits less diversification in kind and quality of institutions than nonreligious education. Being elitist, it has become over the years less accommodating to the student population, which is mostly composed of disadvantaged Orientals. However, as a whole, religious education is more diversified than nonreligious education, but Chen is correct in branding it elitist. This is not the result of any orientation toward sponsored mobility patterns but rather because of its greater investment in catering to the needs of a select minority of Ashkenazi students.

4 Both opposing tendencies are found in Gush Emunim. The Gush's commitment to the settlement of the densely Palestinian populated Samaria is motivated by messianic convictions and carried out fanatically in defiance of government policies. But religious sectarianism is mitigated by the appeal to sections in the non-religious majority. In fact, the Gush refrains from identification with the National Religious Party or with religion–state issues in order not to alienate nonreligious supporters.

5 Layish (1975a) provides a detailed survey of social change in the Arab minority.

6 Between 1948 and 1974 about 1.5 million Jews immigrated to Israel as compared with about 25,000 Arabs (as a result of the Israeli–Jordanian agreement to annex the Little Triangle to Israel in 1949 and of a limited number of family reunions). It is estimated that about a quarter of a million Jews and about 20,000 Arabs left the country during this period.

7 The contrast between Oriental Jews and Israeli Arabs with regard to their different geographical mobility is striking. The Oriental Jews are immigrants who lost contact with their countries of origin, whereas the Arabs are natives who resumed ties with their people. The Orientals have a large degree of internal migration, whereas the Arabs almost none. In fact, the Arabs are strongly attached to their communities and for various reasons they do not move to the urban centres where they work (proletarianization without urbanization). The Orientals' high geographical mobility has contributed a great deal to their cultural change, while the Arabs' stable residence has sustained their cultural continuity.

8 These are also the factors which account for the continuity even in the third generation of the white ethnic groups in the United States (cf. Yancey, Ericksen and Juliani, 1976). White ethnicity has, however, become diluted a great deal from one generation to another (Laumann, 1973: 206–7).

9 The old guard of foreign-born Eastern European Jews was very paternalistic. It can boast of accomplishing its two missions in the ethnic area – averting the 'dangers' of downgrading Orientalism and political instability following the Oriental mass immigration. The policies of paternalism and co optation, which can be equated with a strategy of 'controlled gradualism' from the benevolent standpoint of the establishment, were successful, but they are also no longer essential.

10 The Israeli establishment realizes how much national security contributes to ethnic cohesion. It is also aware of the possibility that the settlement of the conflict may aggravate the ethnic problem and expose the Orientals to 'contagious Levantinization' as contacts with Arabs become freer. It is difficult to say whether such fears are taken into account when questions of peace and war with the Arabs are discussed. At any rate, the government uses national security as a device for downgrading the ethnic problem. Statements by General Dayan, then Defence Minister, are the most explicit in this regard. At the peak of the Panther agitation in 1971 he declared: 'It is impossible to raise simultaneously the flag of war and the flag of social reform . . . Israel cannot support two flags – the flag of war and the flag of all these reforms and improvements for the workers, and the young and not so young Panthers. Those two flags cannot exist together in the state of Israel . . . Those flags are contradictory' (*Yediot Aharonot*, 7 November 1971, quoted by Bober, 1972: 34). In another speech, Dayan said that Israel's primary problems were

security and immigration. Then he added: 'I know that there are other problems such as social gaps or housing. However, in Israel people do not starve or sleep under bridges. If we will manage to tackle these problems, too, this would be fine, and if not – this would not constitute a great disaster' (*Ma'ariv*, 8 February 1973).

11 In the selection of people for top posts such as Prime Minister, Foreign Minister and the Chairman of the Jewish Agency, the candidate's standing in world Jewry is taken into consideration. The Orientals have, of course, lower chances in this case.

12 The Wadi-Salib riot and especially the Black Panther demonstrations helped to some extent to publicize the Oriental cause abroad. However, the effectiveness of the internationalization of the Oriental–Ashkenazi problem as a pressure for change is not encouraging. Appeals to world public opinion by Oriental protesters may cause embarrassment to the Israeli government and can be a factor in forcing it to reconsider its policies. Rather limited are appeals to world Jewry, although they appear more pertinent and could have been considerably more effective. This is because of the close links between the power elites in Israel and the Diaspora. The existing power elite which controls the Jewish communities abroad owes much of its power to the support of the Israeli power elite and to the links between various Jewish activities and Israel. It lacks both the interest and the ability to influence Israel's internal affairs. No strings are attached to the financial contributions whose volume depends more on Israel's security needs than on any other factor. These hard facts plus the increasing conservatism and embourgeoisement of world Jewry have been 'discovered' only in the 1970s by Jewish, radical, Zionist students in the United States who have tried in vain to institute changes in their Jewish communities (some of them speak of the 'Stalinization' of the Zionist movement; e.g., Berson and Brent, 1972). Furthermore, the co-optation in 1972 of the World Federation of Sephardic Communities into the World Zionist Organization, while it is a remarkable achievement, has, nevertheless, the unintended function of undercutting the Orientals' ability to protest abroad.

13 By 1974 the proportion of immigration from Asia and Africa dropped to a record low of 10 per cent of all Jewish immigrants that year.

14 The traditional occupational distribution of Jews in the Diaspora has consisted mostly of white-collar occupations and the revolutionary Zionist ideal was to build 'a society of workers'.

15 Despite the ideological objections, the economic integration of non-Jews is expected to continue because of the uneven development of the region (the same holds true for foreign labour in contemporary Europe). Israel will absorb more Arab labourers because it needs them economically and because it uses employment as a mechanism of control. The Arabs, for their part, will seek jobs in the Jewish market out of necessity. This process will continue to ease the ethnic problem by supplying the Orientals with some opportunities for social mobility.

16 To mention one portent of this development, the ethnic integration of the new religious intermediate schools is already much smaller than that of the nonreligious intermediate schools (see Table 77). The situation will probably worsen.

17 Zucker prophesies what he terms 'the coming crisis in Israel' involving state–religion issues, but he is aware of the forces which operate on behalf of the religious status quo (1973: 58–9). The reasons he cites do not justify his expectation of an imminent *Kulturkampf*.

18 The Arabs are more willing to participate in the mainstream of Israeli society than the ultra-Orthodox Jews, although both live at present outside the wider society. This is established in a comparative study of an ultra-Orthodox Jewish community and an urban Arab community (Simon and Gurevitch, 1971). The ultra-Orthodox young people wish to continue their fathers' traditional lifestyle and to preserve separate community organizations, whereas the Arab youth want to break away from their fathers' traditionalism and isolation and seek greater acculturation and incorporation into the larger society. Since the Arabs will encounter barriers, they will present a harder problem for Israel than the ultra-Orthodox Jews who choose to be segregated.

19 This provision stands a good chance, for reasons which are not related to Arab–Jewish relations. In the 1970s a Bill was introduced in the Knesset to allow certain couples who are unmarriageable according to the halakha (e.g., a Cohen and a divorcee) to marry in a civil ceremony. Such legislation would also provide for mixed marriages.

20 There is also the contingency of the emergence of a chauvinistic Palestinian state which will meddle in the process of maximal incorporation of the Arabs into Israeli society and will try to incite them to demand annexation to it.

21 The discussion of utopias is limited here to those aspects of them which are of direct relevance to the pluralistic structure, while ignoring other dimensions. Because of this selective focus, class-based utopias (such as an egalitarian, socialist or kibbutz-like society) and abandoned ones (such as the binational state) are excluded. It is also not the intention to furnish an accurate and detailed description of each utopia, but to draw a brief sketch of their skeletal elements as perceived by the general public. For instance, the utopia of an exclusive Jewish–Zionist state is abstracted neither from Herzl's utopian writings nor from the works of other Zionist thinkers. It is, rather, the image of Zionism held by the dominant Jewish public.

22 In fairness to religious Jews it must be emphasized that they do not expressly advocate the idea of a halakha state as it is portrayed here. As a matter of fact, the term 'halakha state' was coined only recently by secularists to embarrass the religious political parties (cf. Aloni, 1970), and religious people do not use it. As indicated elsewhere, since the halakha takes for granted Jewish life under Gentile regimes, it lacks provisions for life in a Jewish state. The true utopia in Orthodox Judaism is the messianic 'Torah Kingdom', for which

Jews are supposed to wait passively. By using the term 'halakha state' here instead of 'Torah Kingdom' I wish to stress the actual hopes of certain religious circles for and the fears of their opponents of some kind of a state whose laws are halakhic and rulers are Orthodox.

23 An earlier account of the Canaanite ideology and programme was provided by an alarmed opponent (Kurzweil, 1953). A good sample of the Canaanite ideas can be found in the founder's book (Ratosh, 1967) and an edited anthology (Ratosh, 1976).

24 It is not clear whether all Jews who live in Israel today are considered 'legitimate residents' and will be allowed to remain in the new democratic secular Palestine. According to one version, Jews who arrived after the 'Zionist invasion' in 1917 will be excluded; according to another version, only Jews who came after 1947 will have to leave.

25 A fair critical scientific presentation of the most controversial utopia of a democratic secular state is furnished by Tessler (1975b).

26 It must be emphasized that the two major alternative directions for the future of Arab–Jewish relations (i.e., maximal incorporation and the status of a Palestinian national minority) are not mutually exclusive. It is my position that Israel should take the third optional direction as outlined above. In other words, the Arabs should be presented with a real choice between the first two alternatives. It is, then, to be expected that some Arabs will opt for one possibility and some for another as is the case with religious Jews (some of them are affiliated with the autonomous religious institutions and some prefer direct and individual incorporation into the dominant nonreligious institutions).

27 Lova Eliav, a former Secretary-General of the Israel Labour Party and a Knesset member, has recently written the most penetrating social critique to date of Israel's pluralistic-stratificational structure from a leftist Zionist perspective (Eliav, 1976). Eliav's critique and proposals and my own account and suggestions are similar in some respects.

Cited references

Note: (H) following a publication indicates that it was written in Hebrew.

ABBAS, ABRAHAM (1959), *From Ingathering to Integration: The Communal Problem in Israel*, Jerusalem: Council of the Sephardic Community.

ABRAMOV, ZALMAN S. (1971), 'Yishuv, self-government in the', in Raphael Patai (ed.) (1971a: 1246–50).

ABU-GOSH, SUBHI (1969), 'The Politics of An Arab Village in Israel', Jerusalem: unpublished (duplicated).

——— (1972), 'The election campaign in the Arab sector', in Alan Arian (ed.), *The Elections in Israel – 1969*, Jerusalem: Jerusalem Academic Press, pp. 239–52.

———, S. SHYE, and H. HARTMAN (1972), *The Impacts on the Elective Local Council System on Arab Traditional Society in Israel*, Research Report, Ford Foundation. Project No. F–IX, pp. 1513–627.

ADAM, HERIBERT (1971), *Modernizing Racial Domination: The Dynamics of South African Politics*, University of California Press.

ADAR, LEA, and CHAIM ADLER (1965), *Education for Values in Schools for Immigrant Children In Israel*, Jerusalem: Hebrew University and Ministry of Education and Culture (H).

ADI, PESAH, and DANIELA FROILICH (1970a), 'Attitudes towards Political and Security Affairs and Public Morale', Publication no. 208, Jerusalem: Israel Institute of Applied Social Research (H).

——— (1970b), 'Attitudes towards Political and Social Affairs', Publication no. 211, Jerusalem: Israel Institute of Applied Social Research (H).

ADLER, CHAIM (1969), 'The role of education in the integration of ethnic groups in Israel', in *The Integration of Immigrants from Different Countries of Origin in Israel*, Jerusalem: Magnes Press, pp. 17–31 (H).

———, and RACHEL PELEG (1975), 'An Evaluation of the Effects of Studies and Experiments in Compensatory Education', Jerusalem: Hebrew University (duplicated) (H).

ALGAREBLY, MORDECHAI (1975), 'Indices for the characterization of the social composition of schools and a system for the allocation of budgets to schools with disadvantaged pupils', *Megamot*, 21(2) (Feb.): 219–27 (H).

411

ALONI, SHULAMIT (1970), *The Arrangement: From a Legal State to a Halakhic State*, Tel-Aviv: Otpaz (H).

AMIR, YEHUDA (1969), 'Contact hypothesis in ethnic relations', *Psychological Bulletin*, 71 (May): 319–42.

—— (1976), 'The role of intergroup contact in change of prejudice and ethnic relations', in Philips A. Katz (ed.), *Towards the Elimination of Racism*, New York: Pergamon Press, pp. 245–308.

——, AHARON BIZMAN, and MIRIAM RIVNER (1973), 'The effects of interethnic contact on friendship choices in the military', *Journal of Cross-Cultural Psychology*, 4(3) (Sept.): 361–73.

ANTONOVSKY, AARON (1963), 'Israeli political-social attitudes', *Amot*, 1(6) (June–July): 11–22 (H).

—— (1964), 'The integration of ethnic groups', *Amot*, 2(13) (Sept.–Oct.): 35–9 (H).

——, and ALAN ARIAN (1972), *Hopes and Fears of Israelis: Consensus in a New Society*, Jerusalem Academic Press.

ARIAN, ALAN (1968), *Ideological Change in Israel*, Press of Case Western Reserve University.

—— (1973), *The Choosing People: Voting Behavior in Israel*, Press of Case Western Reserve University.

—— (1975), 'Were the 1973 elections critical?', in Asher Arian (ed.), *The Elections in Israel – 1973*, Jerusalem Academic Press, pp. 287–308.

ARONOFF, MYRON (1973), 'The politics of religion in a new Israeli town', *Eastern Anthropologist*, 26(1) (Jan.–March): 145–71.

ASSAF, MICHAEL (1967), *The Arab Awakening and Flight*, Tel-Aviv: Tarbut Vehinukh (H).

—— (1970), *Arab–Jewish Relations in Palestine 1860–1948*, Tel-Aviv: Tarbut Vehinukh (H).

ATTIAS, MOSHE (1971), 'World Federation of Sephardic Communities', in Raphael Patai (ed.) (1971a: 1230–1).

—— (ed.) (1949), *Knesset Yisrael – Book of Documents: 1918–1948*, Jerusalem: National Council (H).

AVINERI, SHLOMO (1972), 'Sabras and spies', *Ma'ariv* (22 Dec.) (H).

AVNERY, URI (1971), *Israel Without Zionism*, New York: Collier.

BAGLEY, CHRISTOPHER (1972), 'Racialism and pluralism: a dimensional analysis of forty-eight countries', *Race*, 13(3) (Jan.): 347–54.

BAILEY, CLINTON (1970), 'The Communist Party and the Arabs in Israel', *Midstream*, 16(5) (May): 38–56.

BAMAARAKHA (1963), 'Ethnic underground?' (editorial), *Bamaarakha*, 3(25) (July): 18–19 (H).

BAR-GAL, YORAM (1975), 'Changes in the structure of the minority villages in Israel: outlines and reasons', *Sociologia Ruralis*, 25(3): 173–88.

BARKAI, H. (1964), 'The public sector, the Histadrut sector and the private sector in the Israeli economy', in *Sixth Report, 1961–3*, Jerusalem: Falk Project for Economic Research in Israel (H).

BARNETT, RICHARD D. (ed.) (1971), *The Sephardi Heritage: Essays on the History and Cultural Contribution of the Jews of Spain and Portugal*, New York: Ktav.

BARON, HAROLD M. (1968), 'Black powerlessness in Chicago', *Transaction* (6) (Nov.): 27–33.

BARTH, ERNEST A. T., and DONALD NOEL (1972), 'Conceptual frameworks for the analysis of race relations: an evaluation', *Social Forces*, 50(3) (March): 333–48.

BARTH, FREDRICK B. (ed.) (1969), *Ethnic Groups and Boundaries*, Boston: Little, Brown.

BAR-YOSEF, RIVKAH (1968), 'Desocialization and resocialization: the adjustment of immigrants', *International Migration Review*, 2(3) (Summer): 27–43.

—— (1970), 'The Moroccans: background to the problem', in S. N. Eisenstadt, Rivkah Bar-Yosef, and Chaim Adler (eds), *Integration and Development in Israel*, Jerusalem: Israel Universities Press, pp. 419–28.

—— (1971), 'Absorption Versus Modernization', Jerusalem: Department of Sociology, Hebrew University (duplicated).

——, and DORITH PADAN (1964), 'Orientals in the class formation of Israel', *Molad*, 22(195–6) (Nov.): 504–16 (H).

BASHAN, RAPHAEL (1966), 'An interview with Hazaz', *Ma'ariv* (14 Sept.) (H).

BASTUNI, RUSTUM (1973), 'The Arab Israelis', in Michael Curtis and Mordecai Chertoff (eds), *Israel: Social Structure and Change*, New Brunswick, N.J.: Transaction Books, pp. 408–18.

BEIN, ALEX (1954), *A History of the Zionist Settlement* (3rd ed.), Tel-Aviv: Masada (H).

BEIT-HALLAHMI, BENJAMIN (1972), 'National character and national behavior in the Middle East conflict: The case of the "Arab personality"', *International Journal of Group Tensions*, 2: 19–28.

BEKKER, SIMON (1975), 'The pluralist approach of Pierre van den Berghe', *Social Dynamics*, 1(1) (June): 11–17.

BEN-CHAIM, EFRAYIM (1967), 'The gap between ethnic groups', *Ott*, 1(2) (winter): 62–75 (H).

BEN-DAVID, JOSEPH (1970), 'Ethnic differences or social change?', in S. N. Eisenstadt, Rivkah Bar Yosef, and Chaim Adler (eds), *Integration and Development in Israel*, Jerusalem: Israel University Press, pp. 368–87.

BEN-DOR, GABRIEL (1974), 'The Druzes in Israel: A Political Study', University of Haifa (duplicated).

BENJAMIN, AVRAHAM (1975), 'Experiment in Existence – Ma'alot-Tarshiha', Jerusalem: American Jewish Committee (duplicated).

——, and RAHEL PELEG (forthcoming), *The Arab Student and the University*, Tel-Aviv: Am Oved.

BENSIMON-DONATH, DORIS B. (1970), *Immigrants D'Afrique du Nord en Israel*, Paris: Editions Anthropos.

BENTWICH, NORMAN (1971), 'Religion and state in Israel', in Raphael Patai (ed.) (1971a: 944–6).

BENYAMINI, KALMAN (1969), 'National stereotypes of Israeli youth', *Megamot*, 16(4): 364–75 (H).

BEN-ZVI, ITZHAK (1957), *The Exiled and the Redeemed*, Philadelphia: Jewish Publication Society of America.

413

BERNARDETE, MAIR JOSE (1952), *Hispanic Culture and Character of the Sephardic Jews*, New York: Hispanic Institute.

BERNSTEIN, DEBORAH (1976), 'Contradictions and Protest in the Process of Nation-Building: The Black Panthers of Israel: 1971–2', unpublished PhD thesis, University of Sussex.

BERREMAN, GERALD D. (1960), 'Caste in India and the United States', *American Journal of Sociology*, 66(3) (Sept.): 120–7.

BERSON, JEREMY, and S. BRENT (1972), 'Zionism betrayed', *Jewish Liberation Journal*, no. 11 (summer–fall).

BIRNBAUM, ERVIN (1970), *The Politics of Compromise: State and Religion in Israel*, Cranbury, N.J.: Fairleigh Dickinson University Press.

BLALOCK, HUBERT M. (1967), *Toward a Theory of Minority-Group Relations*, New York: Wiley.

BLAUNER, ROBERT (1972), *Racial Oppression in America*, New York: Harper & Row.

BLUMER, HERBERT (1965), 'Industrialization and race relations', in Guy Hunter (ed.), *Industrialization and Race Relations: A Symposium*, Oxford University Press.

BOBER, ARIE (ed.) (1972), *The Other Israel: The Radical Case Against Zionism*, Garden City, N.Y.: Anchor Books.

BONACICH, EDNA (1972), 'A theory of ethnic antagonism: the split labor market', *American Sociological Review*, 37(5) (Oct.): 547–59.

—— (1973), 'A theory of middleman minorities', *American Sociological Review*, 38(5) (Oct.): 583–94.

BRICHTA, ABRAHAM (1974), 'The Knesset by ethnic origin and period of immigration of members', *Megamot*, 20(4) (Sept.): 452–66 (H).

——, and GABRIEL BEN-DOR (1974), 'Representation and misrepresentation of political elites: the case of Israel', *Jewish Social Studies*, 36(3) (July–Oct.): 234–52

BROOM, LEONARD (1954), 'The social differentiation of Jamaica', *American Sociological Review*, 19(2) (April): 115–25.

BUCH, PETER (1973), Introduction, to Maxime Rodinson, *Israel: a Colonial-Settler State?*, New York: Monad Press, pp. 9–26.

CARMI, SHULAMIT, and HENRY ROSENFELD (1974), 'The origins of the process of proletarianization and urbanization of Arab peasants in Palestine', *Annals of the New York Academy of Sciences*, 220(6) (March): 470–85.

CBS (Central Bureau of Statistics) (1950–76), *Statistical Abstract of Israel*, 1–27, Jerusalem: Government Printer.

CHEN, MICHAEL (1975), 'Sponsored and contest mobility in religious and secular state education in Israel', *Megamot*, 22(1) (Nov.): 5–19 (H).

CHERTOFF, MORDECAI (ed.) (1971), *The New Left and the Jews*, New York: Pitman.

CHOURAQUI, ANDRE (1968), *Between East and West: A History of the Jews of North Africa*, Philadelphia: Jewish Publication Society of America.

COHEN, ABNER (1965), *Arab Border Villages in Israel*, Manchester University Press.

COHEN, AHARON (1970), *Israel and the Arab World*, New York: Funk & Wagnall.

414

COHEN, ERIK (1968), 'Social images in an Israeli development town', *Human Relations*, 21: 163–76.

—— (1969a), 'Mixed marriage in an Israeli town', *Jewish Journal of Sociology*, 11(1) (June): 41–50.

—— (1969b), 'The dispersion of population and amalgamation of exiles as conflicting goals', in *The Integration of Immigrants from Different Countries of Origin in Israel*, Jerusalem: Magnes Press, pp. 143–57 (H).

——(1970), 'Development towns: the social dynamics of "planted" communities in Israel', in S. N. Eisenstadt, Rivkah Bar Yosef, and Chaim Adler (eds), *Integration and Development in Israel*, Jerusalem: Israel Universities Press, pp. 587–617.

—— (1971), 'Arab boys and tourist girls in a mixed Jewish Arab community', *International Journal of Comparative Sociology*, 12(4) (Dec.): 217–33.

——(1972), 'The Black Panthers and Israeli society', *Jewish Journal of Sociology*, 14(1) (June): 93–109.

—— (1973), 'Integration vs. Separation in the Planning of a Mixed Jewish–Arab City in Israel', Jerusalem: Hebrew University (duplicated).

—— (1974), *Bibliography of Arabs and Other Minorities in Israel*, Givat Haviva: Centre for Arab and Afro-Asian Studies.

——, and Hermona Gronau (1972), *A Survey of Israeli Minorities*, Jerusalem: Hebrew University (H).

COHEN, HAYYIM J. (1965), 'Further aspects on the education of the Oriental Jews', *Molad*, 23 (Dec. 1965 and Sept. 1966): 208–10 (H).

—— (1968), *20th Century Aliya From Asia and Africa*, Jerusalem: Institute of Contemporary Jewry, Hebrew University (H).

—— (1969), *Zionist Activity in Iraq*, Jerusalem: Hasifria Hatzionit and Hebrew University (H).

—— (1972), 'Integrating Israel's underprivileged immigrants: the Jewish migration from Africa and Asia', *Wiener Library Bulletin*, 25(3–4): 3–12.

—— (1973), *The Jews of the Middle East, 1860–1972*, New York: Wiley.

—— (1974), 'The problem of absorbing the Jews from Asia and Africa in Israel', *Haoniversita*, 19(1) (March): 23–37 (H).

COHEN, OVED (1975), 'The Conflict between Religious and Non religious Jews in Israel: Solidarity and Social Distance among High School Students', doctoral dissertation, Jerusalem: Hebrew University (H).

COHEN, PERCY S. (1963), 'Ethnic hostility in Israel', *New Society* (28 Feb.). 14–16.

—— (1967), 'Israel's ethnic problem', *Jewish Journal of Sociology*, 9(1) (June): 100–7.

—— (1968), 'Ethnic group differences in Israel', *Race*, 9(3) (Jan.): 301–10.

COHEN, YONA (1973), *Chapters in the History of the National Religious Movement*, Tel-Aviv: Information Department, National Religious Party (H).

COLEMAN, JAMES S. (1956), 'Social cleavage and religious conflict', *Journal of Social Issues*, 12(3): 44–56.

Commission on Tax Reforms (1975), *Recommendations for Changing the Direct Tax*, Jerusalem: Government Printer (H).

CONNOR, WALKER (1973), 'The politics of ethnonationalism', *Journal of International Affairs*, 27(1): 1–21.

COX, OLIVER (1971), 'The question of pluralism', *Race*, 12(4) (April): 385–400.

CROSS, MALCOLM (1971), 'On conflict, race relations, and the theory of plural society', *Race*, 12(4) (April): 477–94.

CURTIS, MICHAEL (ed.) (1971), *People and Politics in the Middle East*, New Brunswick, N.J.: Transaction Books.

CZUDNOWSKI, MOSHE M., and JACOB M. LANDAU (1965), *The Israeli Communist Party*, Palo Alto, Calif.: Hoover Institution, Stanford University.

DANET, BRENDA, and HARRIET HARTMAN (1972), 'On "Proteksia": orientations toward the use of personal influence in Israeli bureaucracy', *Journal of Comparative Administration*, 3(4) (Feb.): 405–34.

DAVIES, JAMES (1969), 'The J-curve of rising and declining satisfactions as a cause of some great revolutions and a contained rebellion', in Hugh D. Graham and Ted R. Gurr (eds), *Violence in America*, New York: Bantam, pp. 690–730.

DESHEN, SHLOMO A. (1969), 'Changing patterns of religious traditions: the ethnic synagogue', in *The Integration of Immigrants from Different Countries of Origin in Israel*, Jerusalem: Magnes Press, pp. 66–73 (H).

—— (1972), '"The business of ethnicity is finished!"?: the ethnic factor in a local election campaign', in Alan Arian (ed.), *The Elections in Israel – 1969*, Jerusalem Academic Press, pp. 278–302.

—— (1974), 'Political ethnicity and cultural ethnicity in Israel during the 1960s', in Abner Cohen (ed.), *Urban Ethnicity*, London: Tavistock, pp. 281–309.

—— (forthcoming), 'Israeli Judaism: introduction to the major patterns', *International Journal of Middle Eastern Studies*.

——, and MOSHE SHOKEID (1974), *The Predicament of Homecoming: Cultural and Social Life of North African Immigrants in Israel*, Cornell University Press.

DESPRES, LEO (1967), *Cultural Pluralism and Nationalist Politics in British Guiana*, Chicago: Rand McNally.

—— (1968), 'Anthropological theory, cultural pluralism and the study of complex societies', *Current Anthropology*, 9(1): 3–26.

DE TOCQUEVILLE, ALEXIS (1969), *Democracy in America*, Garden City, N.Y.: Anchor Books.

DEUTSCH, AKIVA (1969), 'The Israeli "melting pot" and its social background – sociologically reviewed', in *Bar-Ilan Volume in Humanities and Social Sciences*, Ramat-Gan: Bar-Ilan University, pp. 82–105.

DONEVITZ, NATHAN (1971), 'Moroccans: deprivation, care, and annexation', *Haaretz*, Weekly Supplement (11, 18 and 25 June) (H).

DON-YIHYE, ELIEZER (1971), 'The status quo solution in the religion–state area in Israel', *Medina Vemimshal*, 1(1): 100–13 (H).

—— (1975a), 'Religion and coalition: the National Religious Party and coalition formation in Israel', in Asher Arian (ed.), *The Elections in Israel – 1973*, Jerusalem Academic Press, pp. 255–84.

—— (1975b), *Religion in Israel*, Jerusalem: Merkaz Hehazbara (H).

——, and CHARLES LIEBMAN (1972), 'The separation of religion and state: slogan and content', *Molad*, 5(25–6): 71–89 (H).

EBAN, ABBA (1969), *Voice of Israel*, New York: Horizon Press.

EHRLICH, HOWARD J. (1973), *The Social Psychology of Prejudice*, New York: Wiley-Interscience.

EISENSTADT, S. N. (1948), 'The Sociological structure of the Jewish community in Palestine', *Jewish Social Studies*, 10(1) (Jan.): 3–18.

—— (1950), 'The Oriental Jews in Israel. (A report on a preliminary study in culture-contacts)', *Jewish Social Studies*, 12(3) (July): 199–222.

—— (1955), *The Absorption of Immigrants*, Chicago: Free Press.

—— (1956), 'Sociological aspects of the economic adaptation of Oriental immigrants in Israel: a study in process of modernization', *Economic Development and Cultural Change*, 4(3).

—— (1967a), *Israeli Society: Background, Development, Problems*, New York: Basic Books.

—— (1967b), 'Israeli identity: problems in the development of the collective identity of an ideological society', *Annals of the American Academy of Political & Social Science*, 370 (March): 116–23.

—— (1969), 'The absorption of immigrants, the amalgamation of exiles and the problems of transformation of Israeli society', in *The Integration of Immigrants From Different Countries of Origin in Israel*, Jerusalem: Magnes Press, pp. 6–13 (H).

—— (1972), 'Change and continuity in Israeli society', in Jacob M. Landau (ed.), *Man, State and Society in the Contemporary Middle East*, New York: Praeger, pp. 294–311.

——, and YOCHANAN PERES (1968), *Some Problems of Educating a National Minority; A Study of Israeli Education for Arabs* (report prepared by Yochanan Peres), Project no. OE-6-21-013; ERIC Document no. Ed-033-867, Washington, D.C.: US Department of Health, Education and Welfare.

EL-ASMAR, FOUZI (1975), *To Be An Arab in Israel*, London: Frances Pinter.

ELAZAR, DANIEL (1975), 'The local elections: sharpening the trend toward territorial democracy', in Asher Arian (ed.), *The Elections in Israel – 1973*, Jerusalem Academic Press, pp. 219–37.

ELAZAR, YAACOV (1970), 'The Sephardic Workers' Union', *Bamaarakha*, 10(109) (April) (H).

ELIA, DAVID (1964), 'The Situation of the Sephardic Communities in Israel', Tel-Aviv: unpublished (H).

ELIACHAR, ELIAHU (1948), 'Lest they multiply? On the question of rescuing the Oriental Jews', *Hed Hamizrah* (19 Nov.): 3 (H).

—— (1950), 'The ethnic problem in Israel', *Hed Hamizrah* (13 Oct.) (H).

—— (1967), *We Must Prevent Jewish Racism in the Jewish State*, Jerusalem: Council of the Sephardic Community (H).

—— (1970), 'The status of the Sephardic Jews since the Balfour Declaration', *Shevet Vaam*, 1: 67–84 (H).

—— (1973), 'Correspondence with David Ben-Gurion on "One People"', *Shevet Vaam*, no. 7 (April): 3–56 (H).

417

ELIAV, ARIE LOVA (1976), *Israel's Ladder: The Dream and its Meaning*, Tel-Aviv: Zmora, Bitan, Modan Publishers (H).

EL KODSY, AHMAD, and ELI LOBEL (1970), *The Arab World and Israel*, New York: Monthly Review Press.

ELON, AMOS (1972), *The Israelis: Founders and Sons*, New York: Bantam Books.

ELON, MENACHEM (1968), *Religious Legislation*, Tel-Aviv: Hakibbutz Hadati (H).

ENGLARD, IZHAK (1966), 'The relationship between religion and state in Israel', in Studies in Israel Legislative Problems, *Scripta Hierosolymtana*, vol. 16, Jerusalem: Magnes Press, pp. 254–75.

—— (1968), 'The problem of the Jewish law in a Jewish state', *Israel Law Review*, 3(2) (April): 254–78.

——, and HANAN SHELAH (eds) (1973), *Religion and State: Selected Sources*, Jerusalem: Academon (H).

ENLOE, CYNTHIA (1973), *Ethnic Conflict and Political Development*, Boston: Little, Brown.

Environment, Heredity and Intelligence (1969), *Harvard Educational Review*, Reprint Series, no. 2.

ESHEL, SMADAR, and YOCHANAN PERES (1973), 'The Integration of a Minority Group: A Causal Model', Sociology Department, Tel-Aviv University (duplicated).

ETZIONI-HALEVY, EVA (1975), 'Protest politics in the Israeli democracy', *Political Science Quarterly*, 90(3) (fall): 497–520.

EYAL, ELI (1971a), 'Wadi-Salib – again? Perhaps after a reduction in security tension', *Ma'ariv* (12 March) (H).

—— (1971b), 'Religious–secular relations: the dialogue which is lacking', *Ma'ariv* (27 Aug.) (H).

FALAH, SALMAN H. (1974), *History of the Druze in Israel*, Jerusalem: Prime Minister's Office (H).

FEIN, LEONARD J. (1968), *Politics in Israel: A Country Study* (2nd ed.), Boston: Little, Brown.

FEITELSON, DINA, S. WEINTRAUB, and O. MICHAELI (1972), 'Social interactions in heterogeneous preschools in Israel', *Child Development*, 43(4) (Dec.): 1249–59.

FISHMAN, ARYEI (1975), 'The Religious Kibbutz: A Study in the Interrelationship of Religion and Ideology in the Context of Modernization', doctoral dissertation, Jerusalem: Hebrew University (H).

FRANKENSTEIN, KARL (1947), *Neglected Youth*, Jerusalem: Szold Foundation (H).

FRIEDMAN, DANIEL (1973), 'The "unmarried wife" in Israeli law', *Tel-Aviv University Law Review*, 3(2) (Sept.): 459–83 (H).

FRIEDMAN, MENACHEM (1971), 'Agudat Israel', in *Encyclopedia Judaica*, vol. 2, Jerusalem: Encyclopedia Judaica Jerusalem and New York: Macmillan, cols 421–6.

—— (1972), 'The Chief Rabbinate – dilemma without solution', *Medina Vemimshal*, 1(3) (spring): 118–28 (H).

—— (1973), 'The Old Yishuv During the British Mandate, 1917–1936', doctoral dissertation, Jerusalem: Hebrew University (H).

—— (1975), 'Religious zealotry in Israeli society', in Solomon Poll and Ernest Krausz (eds), *On Ethnic and Religious Diversity in Israel*, Ramat-Gan: Bar-Ilan University, pp. 91–111.

—— (forthcoming), 'Religious Leadership in a Secular Society', Ramat-Gan: Institute of Contemporary Judaism and Thought, Bar-Ilan University (duplicated) (H).

FRIENDLY, ALFRED (1972), *Israel's Oriental Immigrants and Druzes*, Report no. 12, London: Minority Rights Group.

FURNIVALL, J. S. (1948), *Colonial Policy and Practice: A Comparative Study of Burma and Netherlands India*, Cambridge University Press.

GAL, ALON (1973), *Socialist Zionism*, Cambridge, Mass.: Schenkman.

GAMSON, WILLIAM A. (1968), *Power and Discontent*, Homewood, Ill.: Dorsey Press.

GEFFNER, EDWARD (1972), *Sephardi Problems in Israel*, Jerusalem: World Sephardic Federation.

GELBLUM, ARYE (1949), 'The truth about the human material', *Haaretz* (22 April) (H).

GIRVETZ, HARRY K. (1968), 'Welfare state', *Encyclopedia of the Social Sciences*, vol. 16: 512–21.

GLAZER, NATHAN, and DANIEL MOYNIHAN (1970), *Beyond the Melting Pot* (2nd ed.), MIT Press.

GLOVERZON, ARYE (1970), *The Managerial Elite in Israel's Civil Service*, Tel-Aviv: Midrasha Leminhal (H).

GLUSKA, ZECHARIA (1974), *On Behalf of Yemenite Jews*, Jerusalem: Ya'akov Ben David Gluska (H).

GOITEIN, S. D. (1964), *Jews and Arabs: Their Contacts Through the Ages*, New York: Schocken.

GOLDMAN, ELIEZER (1964), *Religious Issues in Israel's Political Life*, Jerusalem: Mador Dati, Jewish Agency.

GOLDSTEIN, DOV (1971), 'The interview of the week with Shaul Ben-Simhon', *Ma'ariv* (28 May) (H).

GORDON, MILTON M. (1964), *Assimilation in American Life*, New York: Oxford University Press.

GOTTHEIL, FRED M. (1973), 'On the economic development of the Arab region in Israel', in Michael Curtis and Mordecai Chertoff (eds), *Israel: Social Structure and Change*, New Brunswick, N.J.: Transaction Books, pp. 237–48.

GREBLER, LEO, *et al.* (1970), *The Mexican American People*, New York: Free Press.

GUREVITCH, MICHAEL, and ALEX WEINGROD (1976), 'Who knows whom? Contact networks in the Israeli national elite', *Megamot*, 22(4) (Sept.): 357–78 (H).

——, and GILA SCHWARTZ (1971), 'Television and the Sabbath culture in Israel', *Jewish Journal of Sociology*, 13(1) (June): 65–72.

GUTTMAN, EMANUEL (1971), 'Religion in Israeli politics', in Jacob M. Landau (ed.), *Man, State and Society in the Contemporary Middle East*, New York: Praeger, pp. 122–34.

GUTTMAN, LOUIS, CHAIM KLAFF, and SHLOMIT LEVY (1971), 'The Histadrut and Its Activities in the Arab Sector: a Study of the Attitudes, Opinions and Behaviours of Arab Villagers in Israel', Report no. 224, Jerusalem: Israel Institute of Social Applied Research (duplicated) (H).

HABASH, AWNI H. (1973), 'Society in Transition – a Social and Political Study of the Arab Community in Israel', doctoral dissertation, Cornell University.

HACOHEN, MORDECAI (1971), 'Rabbinate of Israel', in Raphael Patai (ed.) (1971a: 927–9).

HANUCH, GIORA (1961), 'Income differentials in Israel', in *Fifth Report, 1959 and 1960*, Jerusalem: Falk Project for Economic Research in Israel, pp. 37–135 (H).

HARRIS, MARVIN (1959), 'Caste, class, and minority', *Social Forces* (March): 248–54.

—— (1964), *Patterns of Race in the Americas*, New York: Walter.

HARTMAN, MOSHE, and HANNA EILON (1975), 'Ethnicity and stratification in Israel', *Megamot*, 21(2) (Feb.): 120–39 (H).

HAUG, MARIE R. (1967), 'Social and cultural pluralism as a concept in social system analysis', *American Journal of Sociology*, 73(4) (Nov.): 294–304.

Hebrew University (1970), 'The function of education in social integration in Israel: Summary of experience and research activities', memorandum prepared by the Hebrew University, in *Education in Israel* (Report of the Select Subcommittee on Education and Labor), House of Representatives, 91st Congress, 2nd Session, Washington D.C.: U.S. Government Printing Office.

HERMAN, SIMON N. (1970), *Israelis and Jews: The Continuity of an Identity*, New York: Random House.

——, URI FARAGO, and YA'AKOV HAREL (1976), 'Continuity and Change in the Jewish Identity of High School Youth in Israel (1965–1974)', Jerusalem: Eshkol Institute, Hebrew University (duplicated) (H).

HILLEL, SHLOMO (1957), Speech in the Knesset debate on the budget law of 1957–8, *Proceedings of the Knesset* (1 April), Jerusalem: Government Printer (H).

HIRSCHLER, GERTRUDE (1971), 'North Africa, Zionism in', in Raphael Patai (ed.) (1971a: 842–5).

HOETINK, H. (1967), *Caribbean Race Relations: A Study of Two Variants*, Oxford University Press.

—— (1973), *Slavery and Race Relations in the Americas*, New York: Harper & Row.

HOFMAN, JOHN E. (1970), 'The meaning of being a Jew in Israel: an analysis of ethnic identity', *Journal of Personality and Social Psychology*, 15(3): 196–202.

—— (1972), 'Readiness for social relations between Arabs and Jews in Israel', *Journal of Conflict Resolution*, 16(2): 241–51.

—— (1974), 'National images of Arab youth in Israel and the West Bank', *Megamot*, 20(3) (July): 316–24 (H).

——, and s. DEBBINY (1970), 'Religious affiliation and ethnic identity', *Psychological Reports*, 26: 1014.

——, and NADEEM ROUHANA (1976), 'Young Arabs in Israel: some aspects of a conflicted social identity', *Journal of Social Psychology*, 99: 75–86.

HOROWITZ, DAN, and MOSHE LISSAK (1970), 'The Yishuv as a political society', *Megamot*, 13(2) (April): 108–40 (H).

HOROWITZ, IRVING L. (1972), *Three Worlds of Development: The Theory and Practice of International Stratification* (2nd ed.), New York: Oxford University Press.

HORTON, JOHN (1966), 'Order and conflict theories of social problems as competing ideologies', *American Journal of Sociology*, 71(6) (May): 701–13.

HOWE, IRVING, and CARL GERSHMAN (eds) (1972), *Israel, the Arabs and the Middle East*, New York: Bantam Books.

INBAR, DAN (1975), 'Structural aspects and trends in the operation of the reform in Hebrew education', *Megamot*, 21(3) (May): 295–305 (H).

INBAR, MICHAEL, and CHAIM ADLER (1977), *Ethnic Integration in Israel*, New Brunswick, N.J.: Transaction Books.

Israel, Government (1970), 'The basic principles of the new Government', in *Israel Government Year Book*, 1969–1970, Jerusalem: Keter Publishing House.

Israel, Knesset (1975), *A Joint Report on the Druzes Submitted by the Knesset Committee on Education and Culture and the Knesset Committee on the Interior* (20 May), Jerusalem: Knesset (H).

Israel, Ministry of Education and Culture (1969), *The Intermediate Division*, Jerusalem: Ministry of Education and Culture (H).

—— (1974), 'The Educational System in Figures', Jerusalem: Ministry of Education and Culture (duplicated) (H).

—— (1975), Report of the Committee on Arab Education, Jerusalem: Planning Project of Education for the 1980s, Ministry of Education and Culture (duplicated) (H).

Israel, Ministry of the Interior (1973), Report of the Committee to Determine the Structure of Expenditure and Sources of Revenue in the Local Councils of the Minorities, Jerusalem: Ministry of the Interior (duplicated) (H).

Israel, Ministry of Social Welfare (1969), 'Social Policies in the Platforms of Political Parties to the Seventh Knesset', Jerusalem: Ministry of Social Welfare (duplicated) (H).

Israel, Prime Minister's Office (1974), 'Committee Report on Investigation of the Druze Problems in Israel', Jerusalem: Office of the Prime Minister's Adviser on Arab Affairs (duplicated) (H).

—— (1975), 'Report of the Committee on Arab Affairs: Some Problems in the Arab Sector', Jerusalem: Office of the Prime Minister's Adviser on Social Affairs (duplicated) (H).

JANSEN, G. H. (1971), *Zionism, Israel and Asian Nationalism*, Beirut: Institute for Palestine Studies.

JENCKS, CHRISTOPHER, *et al.* (1972), *Inequality*, New York: Basic Books (London: Allen Lane, 1973).

Jewish Agency (1957), Absorption Department Information, *Yediot Makhleket Haklita*, nos. 9–10, Tel-Aviv: Jewish Agency.

—— (1958), *Summaries of Ten Years of Immigration and Absorption*, Jerusalem: Jewish Agency (H).

—— (1964), *Sixteen Years of Immigrant Absorption*, Jerusalem: Jewish Agency.

—— (1968), *Twenty Years of Immigration and Absorption*, Jerusalem: Jewish Agency (H).

JIRYIS, SABRI (1969), *The Arabs in Israel: 1948–1966*, Beirut: Institute for Palestine Studies.

KAHANE, MEIR (1973), *The Challenge: A Chosen Land*, Jerusalem: Hamerkas Letodaa Yehudit (H).

KAHANE, REUVEN, and L. STARR (1974), 'Education under cross pressures: an analysis of the dilemmas facing vocational education in Israel', in Reuven Kahane and Simha Koppstein (eds), *Israeli Society 1967–1973*, Jerusalem: Academon, pp. 261–87.

KATZ, ELIHU (1973), 'Culture and communication in Israel: the transformation of tradition', *Jewish Journal of Sociology*, 15(1) (June): 5–22.

——, and MICHAEL GUREVITCH (1973), *The Culture of Leisure in Israel*, Tel-Aviv: Am Oved (H).

KATZ, JACOB (1961a), *Tradition and Crisis: Jewish Society at the End of the Middle Ages*, New York: Free Press.

—— (1961b), *Exclusiveness and Tolerance: Studies in Jewish–Gentile Relations in Medieval and Modern Times*, Oxford University Press.

—— (1972), *Emancipation and Assimilation: Studies in Modern Jewish History*, Farnborough: Gregg International Publishers.

—— (1973), *Out of the Ghetto: The Social Background of Jewish Emancipation, 1770–1870*, Harvard University Press.

KATZENELSON, KALMAN (1964), *The Ashkenazi Revolution*, Tel-Aviv: Aanakh (H).

KATZNELSON, IRA (1972), 'Comparative studies of race and ethnicity (review article)', *Comparative Politics*, 5(1) (Oct.): 135–54.

KINLOCH, GRAHAM C. (1974), *The Dynamics of Race Relations: A Sociological Analysis*, New York: McGraw-Hill.

KLEIF, BAHEOJ, RALPH SEGALMAN, and EDWARD ROTHSTEIN (1971), 'The Arab–Israeli encounter within Israel: a study of Gemeinschaft-Gesellschaft in culture-conflict and social change', *Sociologia Internationalis*, 9(2): 167–78.

KLEINBERGER, AHARON F. (1969), *Society, Schools and Progress in Israel*, New York: Bergman Press.

KLINOV-MALUL, RUTH (1969), 'Immigrant absorption and income differentials between immigrants and oldtimers', in *The Integration of Immigrants from Different Countries of Origin in Israel*, Jerusalem: Magnes Press, pp. 97–108 (H).

KOKHAVI, S. Y. (1968), *Coexistence or Population Transfer*, Tel-Aviv: Authors' Publishing House (H).

KORNHAUSER, WILLIAM (1959), *The Politics of Mass Society*, Chicago: Free Press.

KUGELMASS, SOL, AMIA LIEBLICH, and DORIT BOSSIK (1974), 'Patterns of intellectual ability in Jewish and Arab children in Israel', *Journal of Cross-Cultural Psychology*, 5(2) (June): 184–98.

KUHN, THOMAS S. (1964), *The Structure of Scientific Revolutions*, University of Chicago Press.

KUPER, LEO (1965), *An African Bourgeoisie: Race, Class and Politics in South Africa*, Yale University Press.

—— (1969a), 'Plural societies: perspectives and problems', in Leo Kuper and M. G. Smith (eds) (1969: 7–26).

—— (1969b), 'Ethnic and racial pluralism: Some aspects of polarization and depluralization', in Leo Kuper and M. G. Smith (eds) (1969: 459–87).

—— (1974), *Race, Class and Power*, London: Duckworth.

——, and M. G. SMITH (eds) (1969), *Pluralism in Africa*, University of California Press.

KURZWEIL, BARUKH (1953), 'The new Canaanites in Israel', *Judaism*, 2(1) (Jan.): 3–15.

LACQUEUR, WALTER (1972), *A History of Zionism*, New York: Holt, Rinehart & Winston.

LANDAU, JACOB M. (1969), *The Arabs in Israel: A Political Study*, Oxford University Press.

—— (1971), 'The Arab population', in *Encyclopedia Judaica*, vol. 9, Jerusalem: Encyclopedia Judaica Jerusalem and New York: Macmillan, cols 1023–7; 'Arabs in Israel', in Raphael Patai (ed.) (1971a: 62–4).

—— (1972), 'The Arab vote', in Alan Arian (ed.), *The Elections in Israel – 1969*, Jerusalem Academic Press, pp. 253 63.

LANDAU, SIMHA F. (1975), 'Pathologies among homicide offenders: some cultural profiles', *British Journal of Criminology*, 15(2) (April): 157–66.

——, ISRAEL DRAPKIN, and SHLOMO ARAD (1974), 'Homicide victims and offenders: an Israeli study', *Journal of Criminal Law and Criminololgy*, 65(3): 390–6.

LAPID, JOSEPH (1974), 'For South Africa I would not keep silence', *Ma'ariv* (14 March).

LAUMANN, EDWARD (1973), *Bonds of Pluralism*, New York: Wiley-Interscience.

LAYISH, AHARON (1975a), 'Social and political changes in Arab society in Israel', in Michael Curtis *et al.* (eds), *The Palestinians*, New Brunswick, N.J.: Transaction Books, pp. 81–7.

—— (1975b), *Women and Islamic Law in a Non-Muslim State*, New York: Wiley.

LENSKI, GERHARD E. (1966), *Power and Privilege: A Theory of Stratification*, New York: McGraw-Hill.

LESCH, ANN M. (1973), 'The Palestine Arab nationalist movement under the Mandate', in William B. Uuandt, Fuad Jabber, and Ann M. Lesch, *The Politics of Palestinian Nationalism*, University of California Press, pp. 5–42.

LESLIE, CLEMENT S. (1971), *The Rift in Israel: Religious Authority and Secular Democracy*, London: Routledge & Kegan Paul; New York: Schocken.

LEVINE, ROBERT, and DONALD CAMPBELL (1972), *Ethnocentrism: Theories of Conflict, Ethnic Attitudes and Group Behavior*, New York: Wiley.

LEVY, HAIM (1968), 'Changes in wage differentials by occupational groups, 1957–8 to 1963–4', *Bank of Israel Bulletin*, no. 30 (May): 50–78.

LEVY, SHLOMIT, and LOUIS GUTTMAN (1971), 'Zionism and the Jewish People in the Public's Eye in Israel', Publication no. 266, Jerusalem: Israel Institute of Applied Social Research (duplicated) (H).

——, and —— (1974), 'Values and Attitudes of High School Youth in Israel', Publication no. 438, Jerusalem: Israel Institute of Applied Social Research (duplicated) (H).

——, and —— (1975), 'On the multivariate structure of well-being', *Social Indicators Research*, 2(3) (Dec.): 361–88.

LEWIS, OSCAR (1966), 'The culture of poverty', *Scientific American*, 215(4): 19–25.

LIEBERSON, STANLEY (1961), 'A societal theory of race and ethnic relations', *American Sociological Review*, 26(6) (Dec.): 902–10.

LIEBLICH, AMIA, ANAT NINIO, and SOL KUGELMASS (1972), 'Effects of ethnic origin and parental SES on WPPSI performance of school children in Israel', *Journal of Cross-Cultural Psychology*, 3(2) (June): 159–68.

——, SOL KUGELMASS, and CHEDVA EHRLICH (1975), 'Patterns of intellectual ability in Jewish and Arab children in Israel: urban matched samples', *Journal of Cross-Cultural Psychology*, 6(2) (June): 218–26.

LIEBMAN, CHARLES S. (1975), 'Religion and political integration in Israel', *Jewish Journal of Sociology*, 17(1) (June): 17–27.

LIEBOWITZ, YASHAEIHU (1975), *Judaism, the Jewish People and the State of Israel*, Tel-Aviv: Schocken (H).

LIJPHART, AREND (1969), 'Consociational democracy', *World Politics*, 21(2) (spring): 207–25.

LINENBERG, RON (1972), 'Attitudes in the Israeli press towards the Kfar Kassem affair', *Medina Vemimshal*, 2(1) (winter): 48–64 (H).

LISSAK, MOSHE (1965), 'Patterns of change in ideology and class structure in Israel', *Jewish Journal of Sociology*, 7(1) (June): 46–63.

—— (1969), *Social Mobility in Israeli Society*, Jerusalem: Israel Universities Press.

—— (1972), 'Continuity and change in the voting patterns of Oriental Jews', in Alan Arian (ed.), *The Elections in Israel – 1969*, Jerusalem Academic Press, pp. 264–77.

LUMER, HYMAN (1973), *Zionism: Its Role in World Politics*, New York: International Publishers.

MCRAE, KENNETH (ed.) (1974), *Consociational Democracy: Political Accommodation in Segmented Societies*, Ottawa: McClelland & Stewart.

MAGUBANE, BERNARD (1969), 'Pluralism and conflict situations in Africa: a new look', *African Social Research*, 7 (June): 529–54.

—— (1971), 'A critical look at indices used in the study of social change in colonial Africa', *Current Anthropology*, 12(4–5) (Oct.–Dec.): 419–45.

MAPAM (1963), The Fourth Convention – Resolutions, Tel-Aviv = Mapam Headquarters (H).

MAR'I, SAMI K. (1974), 'School and society in the Arab village in Israel', *Eyonim Bahinukh*, 4(2) (June): 85–104 (H).

—— (1976), 'Higher education in three Arab villages in Israel and the West Bank', *Hamizrah Hehadash* (26(1–2): 27–36) H).

MARMORSTEIN, EMILE (1969), *Heaven at Bay: The Jewish Kulturkampf in the Holy Land*, Oxford University Press.

MASON, PHILIP (1970a), *Race Relations*, Oxford University Press.

—— (1970b), *Patterns of Dominance*, Oxford University Press.

MATRAS, JUDAH (1963), 'Some data on intergenerational occupational mobility in Israel', *Population Studies*, 18(2) (Nov.): 167–86.

—— (1965), *Social Change in Israel*, Chicago: Aldine.

—— (1969), 'Demographic perspectives on the amalgamation of exiles in Israel', in *The Integration of Immigrants from Different Countries of Origin in Israel*, Jerusalem: Magnes Press, pp. 131–42 (H).

—— (1973), 'On changing matchmaking, marriage, and fertility in Israel: some findings, problems, and hypotheses', *American Journal of Sociology*, 79(2) (Sept.): 364–88.

MEDDING, PETER (1972), *Mapai in Israel: Political Organization and Government in a New Society*, Cambridge University Press.

MENACHEM, GILA, and SHIMON SPIRO (1974), 'The effects of ethnic origin and geographical distance on neighbouring relations in an Israeli city', *Megamot*, 20(4) (Sept.): 445–51 (H).

MENDELSOHN, EZRA, and HAYYIM, J. COHEN (1973), *Zionism in Countries of Jewish Distress – Poland and Iraq*, Jerusalem: Institute of Contemporary Jewry and Hebrew University (H).

MERON, SIMHA (1973), 'Freedom of religion as distinct from freedom from religion', *Tel-Aviv University Law Review*, 3(2) (Sept.): 414–32 (H).

MERTON, ROBERT K. (1957), *Social Theory and Social Structure* (rev. ed.), Chicago: Free Press.

MILLER, HERMAN P. (1971), *Rich Man, Poor Man* (new ed.), New York: Crowell.

MILSTEIN, URI (1975a), 'Ideological views of political parties in the religion-state area in Israel', *Medina, Mimshal Veyehasim Benleumiyim*, 7: 95–106 (H).

—— (1975b), 'The religious plea in the formulation of Israel's declaration of independence', *Rivon Lemehkar Hevrati*, nos 9–11 (Aug.): 27–40 (H).

MORGENSTEIN, ARIE (1974), *The Chief Rabbinate in the Land of Israel*, Tel-Aviv: Moreshet (H).

MOSKIN, ROBERT J. (1965), 'Prejudice in Israel', *Look* (5 Oct.): 67–72.

MYRDAL, GUNNAR (1944), *An American Dilemma*, New York: Harper & Row.

NADEL, BARUKH (1975), *Nadel Report: Everything on the Income Tax in Israel*, Tel-Aviv: Authors' Publishing House (H).

NAHAS, DUNIA HABIB (1976), *The Israeli Communist Party*, London: Croom Helm, Portico Publications.

NAKHLEH, KHALIL (1974), 'Multiplicity of legal systems in Israel: the case for legal heterogeneity', *Third World Review*, 1(1) (fall): 28–38.

—— (1975a), 'The direction of local-level conflict in two Arab villages in Israel', *American Ethnologist*, 2(3) (Aug.): 497–516.

—— (1975b), 'Cultural determinants of Palestinian collective identity: the case of the Arabs in Israel', *New Outlook*, 18(7) (Oct.–Nov.): 31–40.

NEWBERGER, BENJAMIN (1970), *Speaker's Manual*, New York: Israeli Students' Organization in the United States and Canada.

NEWMAN, WILLIAM M. (1973), *American Pluralism: A Study of Minority Groups and Social Theory*, New York: Harper & Row.

NIKITINA, GALINA (1973), *The State of Israel: A Historical, Economical and Political Study*, Moscow: Progress Publishers.

NINI, YEHUDA (1971), 'Reflections on the "Third Destruction"', *Shedemot*, 41 (spring): 54–61 (H).

—— (1973), 'Ingathering of the exiles', *Betefutsot Hagola*, 15 (65–6) (summer): 48–55 (H).

NWANERI, V. C. (1973), 'Income distribution criteria for the analysis of development projects', *Finance and Development*, 10(1) (March): 16–19, 37.

ODED, YITZHAK (1964), 'Land losses among Israel's Arab villagers', *New Outlook*, 7(1) (Sept.): 10–25; 7(9) (Nov.–Dec.): 45–52.

OREN, STEPHEN (1973), 'Continuity and change in Israel's religious parties', *Middle East Journal*, 27(1) (winter): 36–54.

ORTAR, GINA (1953), 'A comparative analysis of components of intelligence between ethnic groups', *Megamot*, 4(2) (Jan.): 107–22 (H).

—— (1967), 'Educational achievements of primary school graduates in Israel as related to their sociocultural background', *Comparative Education*, 4(1) (Nov.): 23–34.

Palestine Liberation Organization (1973), 'The Palestinian national charter' (endorsed in Cairo in 1968), in *The Middle East and North Africa, 1973/74* (20th ed.), London: Europa Publications, pp. 61–2.

PATAI, RAPHAEL (1960), 'The riots of Wadi Salib', *Midstream*, 6 (winter): 5–14.

—— (1970), *Israel Between East and West* (2nd ed.), Westport, Conn.: Greenwood.

—— (ed.) (1971a), *Encyclopedia of Zionism and Israel*, New York: Herzl Press and McGraw-Hill.

—— (1971b), 'Ashkenazim', in Raphael Patai (ed.) (1971a: 85–6).

—— (1971c), 'Orientals', in Raphael Patai (ed.) (1971a: 864).

—— (1971d), 'Sephardim', in Raphael Patai (ed.) (1971a: 1019–20).

—— (1971e), 'Ethnic groups and problems in Israel', in Raphael Patai (ed.) (1971a: 304–7).

—— (1971f), *Tents of Jacob: The Diaspora Yesterday and Today*, Englewood Cliffs, N.J.: Prentice-Hall.

PERES, YOCHANAN (1968), 'Ethnic Identity and Ethnic Relations', doctoral dissertation, Jerusalem: Hebrew University (H).

—— (1970), 'Modernization and nationalism in the identity of the Israeli Arab', *Middle East Journal*, 24(4) (autumn): 479–92.

—— (1971), 'Ethnic relations in Israel', *American Journal of Sociology*, 76(6) (May): 1021–47.

——, AVISHAI EHRLICH, and NIRA YUVAL-DAVIS (1970), 'National education for Arab youth in Israel: a comparative analysis of curricula', *Jewish Journal of Sociology*, 12(2) (Dec.): 147–64.

——, and ZIPPORAH LEVY (1969), 'Jews and Arabs: ethnic group stereotypes in Israel', *Race*, 10(4) (April): 479–92.

——, and RUTH SHRIFT (1975), 'Patterns of intermarriage: a comparative study', Sociology Department, Tel-Aviv University (duplicated).

——, EFRAIM YUCHTMAN (YAAR), and RIVKA SHAFAT (1975), 'Predicting and explaining voters' behavior in Israel', in Asher Arian (ed.), *The Elections in Israel – 1973*, Jerusalem Academic Press, pp. 189–202.

——, and NIRA YUVAL-DAVIS (1969), 'Some observations on the national identity of the Israeli Arab', *Human Relations*, 23(3) (July): 219–33.

PERETZ, DON (1958), *Israel and the Palestine Arabs*, Washington, D.C.: Middle East Institute.

—— (1970a), 'The historical background of Arab nationalism in Palestine', in Don Peretz, Evan M. Wilson, and Richard J. Ward, *A Palestine Entity?*, Washington, D.C.: Middle East Institute, pp. 1–55.

—— (1970b), 'Forms and projections of a Palestine entity', in Don Peretz, Evan M. Wilson, and Richard J. Ward, *A Palestine Entity?*, pp. 78–105.

POLL, SOLOMON (1972), 'A functional analysis of religious diversity in Israel', *Bar-Ilan Annual*, 10(2): 29–66.

PORTER, JOHN (1965), *The Vertical Mosaic: An Analysis of Social Class and Power in Canada*, University of Toronto Press.

PORTES, ALEJANDRO (1976), 'On the sociology of national development: theories and issues', *American Journal of Sociology*, 82(1) (July): 55–85.

PREALE, ILANA, YEHUDA AMIR, and SHLOMO SHARAN (SINGER) (1970), 'Perceptual articulation and task effectiveness in several Israeli subcultures', *Journal of Personality and Social Psychology*, 15(3): 190–5.

Prime Minister's Commission (1973), Report of the Prime Minister's Commission on Disadvantaged Children and Youth, Jerusalem: Prime Minister's Office (duplicated) (H).

Public Inquiry Commission (1959), 'Wadi-Salib: Background of a Social Problem', Tel-Aviv: unpublished (H).

—— (1971), Report of the Committee on Income Distribution and Social Inequality, Tel-Aviv: unpublished (duplicated).

RABIN, CHAIM (1971), *The Revival of Hebrew* (rev. ed.), Jerusalem: Israel Digest (*Israel Today*, no. 5).

RATOSH, YOUNATHAN (1967), *Shalom Ivri*, Tel-Aviv: Hermon (H).

—— (ed.) (1976), *From a Victory to a Defeat*, Tel-Aviv: Hadar (H).

REJWAN, NISSIM (1964), 'Israel's communal controversy – an Oriental appraisal', *Midstream*, 10(2) (June): 14–26.

—— (1967), 'The two Israels: A study in Europocentrism', *Judaism*, 16(1) (winter): 97–108.

—— (1972), 'Israel: The two kinds of Jews', in Irving Howe and Carl Gershman (eds) (1972: 125–34).

—— (1973), 'Arab–Jewish relations through the ages: a problem for the historian', *Dispersion and Unity*, 19–20: 87–105.

—— (1974), 'Arab aims and Israeli attitudes: a critique of Harkabi's prognosis of the Arab–Israeli conflict', *New Outlook*, 17(3) (March–April): 44–53; 17(4) (May): 18–27.

REKHESS, ELI (1974), *A Survey of Israeli Arab Graduates from Institutions of Higher Learning in Israel (1961–1971)*, Shiloah Centre, Tel-Aviv University; Jerusalem: American Jewish Committee.

REMBA, ODED (1971a), 'Economy of Israel', in Raphael Patai (ed.) (1971a: 265–71).

—— (1971b), 'Standard of living in Israel', in Raphael Patai (ed.) (1971a: 1068–72).

Research Team (1973), 'A myth named discrimination in favour of Orientals', *Afiqim*, 9(48–50) (March, May, August) (H).

REX, JOHN (1970), *Race Relations in Sociological Theory*, London: Weidenfeld & Nicolson; New York: Schocken.

—— (1971), 'The plural society: the South African case', *Race*, 12(4) (April): 401–14.

—— (1972), 'Review of Kuper's and Smith's Pluralism in Africa', *Sociology*, 6(2) (May): 289–92.

—— (1973), *Race, Colonialism and the City*, London: Routledge & Kegan Paul.

RIM, YESHAYAHU (1968), 'National stereotypes in children', *Megamot*, 16(1) (Oct.): 45–51 (H).

——, and R. ALONI (1969), 'Stereotypes according to ethnic origin, social class and sex', *Acta Psychologica*, 31(4): 312–25.

RODINSON, MAXIME (1973), *Israel: A Colonial-Settler State?*, New York: Monad Press.

RONEN, MATTI (1971), 'The Panthers at the crossroads (symposium)', *Bamaarakha*, 11(127) (Oct.) (H).

ROSE, RICHARD (1971), *Governing Without Consensus: An Irish Perspective*. London: Faber; Boston: Beacon Press.

ROSEN, HARRY (1970), *The Arabs and Jews in Israel*, New York: American Jewish Committee.

ROSENAK, MICHAEL (1971a), 'Religion and religious attitudes in Israel', in Raphael Patai (ed.) (1971a: 940–4).

—— (1971b), 'Sabbath and holidays in Israel', in Raphael Patai (ed.) (1971a: 987–90).

ROSENFELD, HENRY (1964), 'From peasantry to wage labor and residual peasantry: the transformation of an Arab village', in Robert A. Manners (ed.), *Process and Pattern in Culture*, Chicago: Aldine, pp. 211–34.

—— (1968), 'Change, barriers to change and contradictions in the Arab village family', *American Anthropologist*, 70(4): 732–52.

—— (1976), 'Social and economic factors in the explanation of the increased patrilineage endogamy in the Arab village in Israel', in J. G. Peristiany (ed.), *Mediterranean Family Structures*, Cambridge University Press, pp. 115–36.

ROSENZWEIG, RAFAEL, and GEORGES TAMARIN (1971), 'Israel's power elite', *Transaction* (July–Aug.): 26–42.

ROTER, RAPHAEL, and NIRA SHAMAI (1971), 'The distribution of personal income in Israel: The trends of the sixties', *Social Security*, 1(1) (Feb.): 55–62 (H).

ROULEAU, ERIC (1967), Interview with Ben-Gurion, *Le Monde* (9 March).

Royal Commission on Bilingualism and Biculturalism (1970), *Voluntary Associations*, vols 5–6, book VI, Ottawa: Queen's Printer.

RUBINSTEIN, AMNON (1967a), 'Law and religion in Israel', *Israel Law Review*, 2(3) (July): 380–414.

—— (1967b), 'State and religion in Israel', *Journal of Contemporary History*, 2(4) (Oct.): 107–21.

—— (1970), 'Israel is not white', *Haaretz* (23 Oct.) (H).

—— (1973), 'The right to marriage', *Tel-Aviv University Law Review*, 3(2) (Sept.): 433–58 (H).

SABRI, MAHSAN (1973), 'The legal status of Israeli Arabs', *Tel-Aviv University Law Review*, 3(2) (Sept.): 568–81 (H).

SAMET, MOSHE (ed.) (1973), *State and Religion*, Jerusalem: Academon (H).

SAMUEL, MAURICE (1953), *Level Sunlight*, New York: Knopf.

SARSOUR, SA'AD (1971), 'Leisure and Patterns of its Use: a Study of Patterns of Spending Leisure Time by Students of the Arab High Schools in the Triangle Area', M.A. thesis, Ramat-Gan: Bar-Ilan University (H).

SCHERMERHORN, R. A. (1970), *Comparative Ethnic Relations*, New York: Random House.

SCHMELZ, USIEL O. (1969), 'Differentials in criminality rates between various groups in Israel's population', in *Scripta Hierosolymitana*, vol. 21, Jerusalem: Magnes Press, pp. 264–319.

SCHMID, CALVIN F., and CHARLES E. NOBBE (1965), 'Socioeconomic differentials among non-white races', *American Sociological Review*, 30(6) (Dec.): 909–22.

SCHWARZ, WALTER (1959), *The Arabs in Israel*, London: Faber.

SEGAL, RONALD (1967), *The Race War*, New York: Bantam Books.

—— (1973), *Whose Jerusalem? The Conflicts of Israel*, London: Cape.

SEGRE, V. D. (1971), *Israel: A Society in Transition*, Oxford University Press.

SELIGMAN, LESTER G. (1964), *Leadership in a New Nation: Political Development in Israel*, New York: Prentice-Hall.

SELZER, MICHAEL (1965), *The Outcasts of Israel: Communal Tensions in the Jewish State*, Jerusalem: Council of the Sepharadic Community.

—— (1967), *The Aryanization of the Jewish State*. New York: Black Star Book.

SHABTAI, K. (1950), 'Those for whose children "there is no hope"', *Davar* (3 March) (H).

SHAKI, AVNER (1967), 'Thoughts following the war', *Gevilin* (Dec.) (H).

SHAPIRA, RINA, and EVA ETZIONI-HALEVY (1973), *Who Is the Israeli Student?*, Tel-Aviv: Am Oved (H).

SHAPIRA, YONATHAN (1975), *The Historical Ahdut HaAvoda: The Power of a Political Organization*, Tel-Aviv: Am Oved (H).

SHAVA, MENASHE (1973), 'The "unmarried wife"', *Tel-Aviv University Law Review*, 3(2) (Sept.): 484–515 (H).

SHELAH, ILANA (1972), 'The Family Ritual as One Manifestation of "Secular Religion" in Israel', M.A. thesis, Jerusalem: Hebrew University (H).

—— (1974), 'Patterns of mixed marriage in Israel in 1952–1968', in Reuven Kahane and Simha Koppestein (eds), *Israeli Society 1967–1973: Anthology of Papers* (B), Jerusalem: Academon, pp. 333–59 (H).

SHEMESH, EZEKIEL (1975), 'Israel's Arabs – 1975', *New Outlook*, 18(7) (Oct.–Nov.): 24–30.

SHIBUTANI, TAMOTSU, and KIAN M. KWAN (1965), *Ethnic Stratification: A Comparative Approach*, New York: Macmillan.

SHIDLOWSKI, BENYAMIN (1965), 'Transformations in the development of the Arab village in Israel', *Hamizrah Hehadash*, 15 (1–2): 25–37 (H).

SHILOH, ISAAC S. (1970), 'Marriage and divorce in Israel', *Israel Law Review*, 5(4) (Oct.): 479–98.

SHIMONI, YAAKOV (1947), *The Arabs of Palestine*, Tel-Aviv: Am Oved (H).

—— (1971), 'The Arab population', in *Encyclopedia Judaica*, vol. 9, Jerusalem: Encyclopedia Judaica Jerusalem and New York: Macmillan, cols 1021–3.

SHNELLER, RAPHAEL (1974), *The Religious Youth in Israel in the Face of Faith and Science Questions*, Ramat-Gan: Bar-Orian, Bar-Ilan University (H).

SHOHAM, S. GIORA, ESTHER SEGAL, and GIORA RAHAV (1975), 'Secularization, deviance and delinquency among Israeli Arab villagers', *Human Relations*, 28(7): 661–74.

SHTAL, ABRAHAM (1976), *Cultural Fusion in Israel*, Tel-Aviv: Am Oved (H).

——, TAMAR AGMON, and MATATHIA MAR-HAIM (1976), 'Teachers' attitudes towards the culturally disadvantaged', *Eyonim Bahinukh*, 11 (May): 45–58 (H).

SHUMSKY, ABRAHAM (1955), *The Clash of Cultures in Israel*, Columbia University Publications.

SHUVAL, JUDITH T. (1956), 'Patterns of inter-group tension and affinity', *International Social Science Journal*, 8(1): 75–123.

—— (1962), 'Emerging patterns of ethnic strain in Israel', *Social Forces*, 40(4) (May): 323–30.

—— (1963), *Immigrants on the Threshold*, New York: Atherton.

—— (1966), 'Self-rejection among North African immigrants to Israel', *Israel Annals of Psychiatry and Related Subjects*, 4(1) (spring): 101–10.

—— (1969), Concluding discussion, in *The Integration of Immigrants from Different Countries of Origin in Israel*, Jerusalem: Magnes Press, 180–4 (H).

SIMON, ORIEL (1956), 'East and west – towards understanding the ethnic dissimilarity in Israel', *Hahinuch*, 28(4–6): 423–33 (H).

SIMON, RITA J., and MICHAEL GUREVITCH (1971), 'Some intergenerational comparisons in two ethnic communities in Israel', *Human Organization*, 30(1) (spring): 79–87.

SIMPSON, GEORGE E., and MILTON M. YINGER (1972), *Racial and Cultural Minorities* (4th ed.), New York: Harper & Row.

SMILANSKY, MOSHE, and YOSEF YAM (1969), 'The relationships between family size, ethnic origin, father's education and students' achievement', *Megamot*, 16(3) (July): 248–73 (H).

SMILANSKY, SARA, LEAH SHEPHATIA, and EVA FRENKEL (1976), *Mental Development of Infants from Two Ethnic Groups*, Jerusalem: Szold Institute.

SMITH, HANUCH (1969), *Everything About the Elections in Israel*, Tel-Aviv: Adi (H).

SMITH, M. G. (1960), 'Social and cultural pluralism', *Annals of the New York Academy of Sciences*, 83(5): 763–85.

—— (1965a), *The Plural Society in the British West Indies*, University of California Press.

—— (1965b), *Stratification in Grenada*, University of California Press.

—— (1967), Foreword to Leo A. Despres, *Cultural Pluralism and Nationalist Politics in British Guiana*, Chicago: Rand McNally, pp. vii–xxvi.

—— (1969a), 'Institutional and political conditions of pluralism', in Leo Kuper and M. G. Smith (eds) (1969: 27–65).

—— (1969b), 'Some developments in the analytic framework of pluralism', in Leo Kuper and M. G. Smith (eds) (1969: 415–58).

—— (1969c), 'Pluralism and precolonial African societies', in Leo Kuper and M. G. Smith (eds) (1969: 91–51).

SMOOHA, SAMMY (1972), 'Israel and its Third World Jews: Black Panthers – the ethnic dilemma', *Society*, 9(7) (May): 31–6.

—— (1974), 'On behalf of a Palestinian entity', *New Politics*, 11(2) (spring): 44–51.

—— (1975), 'Pluralism and conflict: a theoretical exploration', *Plural Societies*, 6(3) (autumn): 69–89.

——, and JOHN E. HOFMAN (1976–7), 'Some problems of Arab–Jewish coexistence in Israel', *Middle East Review* 9(2) (winter): 5–14.

——, and YOCHANAN PERES (1975), 'The dynamics of ethnic inequalities: the case of Israel', *Social Dynamics* 1(1) (June): 63–79.

SOHLBERG, SHAUL C. (1976), 'Social desirability responses in Jewish and Arab children in Israel', *Journal of Cross-Cultural Psychology*, 7(3) (Sept.): 301–14.

SPIEGEL, ERIKA (1967), *New Towns in Israel*, New York: Praeger.

SPILERMAN, SEYMOUR, and JACK HABIB (1976), 'Development towns in Israel: the role of community in creating ethnic disparities in labor force characteristics', *American Journal of Sociology*, 81(4) (Jan.): 781–812.

SPRINZAK, EHUD (1973), 'Beginnings of Politics of Delegitimation in Israel in 1967–1972', Jerusalem: Hebrew University (duplicated) (H).

STENDEL, ORI (1970), *Arab Villages in Israel and Judea-Samaria*, Jerusalem: Israel Economist.

—— (1973a), *The Minorities of Israel*, Jerusalem: Israel Economist.

—— (1973b), 'Rights of minorities in Israeli law', *Tel-Aviv University Law Review*, 3(2) (Sept.): 556–67 (H).

STOCK, ERNEST (1968), *From Conflict to Understanding*, New York: American Jewish Committee.

SZYLIOWICZ, JOSEPH (1973), *Education and Modernization in the Middle East*, Cornell University Press.

TAHON, CHANA H. (1957), *Ethnic Groups in Israel*, Jerusalem: Reuben Mass (H).

TALMON, JACOB L. (1970), *Israel Among the Nations*, London: Weidenfeld Nicolson.

TAMARIN, GEORGES R. (1973), *The Israeli Dilemma: Essays on a Warfare State*, Rotterdam University Press.

TARTAKOWER, ARIEH (1959), *The Israeli Society* Tel-Aviv, Masada (H).

—— (1969), *The Tribes of Israel*, vols 1–3: Tel-Aviv: Yavneh (H).

TAVIV, AVRAHAM (1943), *The Immigration and Settlement of Yemenite Jews in Palestine*, Tel-Aviv: Yemenite Union (H).

TAVIV, MORDECHAI (1962), 'The forgotten', *Min Hayisod* (11 October) (H).

TELLER, J. L. (ed.) (1965), *Acculturation and Integration: A Symposium by American, Israeli and African Experts*, New York: American Histadrut Cultural Exchange Institute.

TESSLER, MARK A. (1975a), 'Israel's Arabs and the Palestinian problem', paper presented at annual meeting of the Middle East Studies Association of North America.

—— (1975b), 'Secularism in the Middle East? Reflections on recent Palestinian proposals', *Ethnicity*, 2: 178–203.

—— (forthcoming), 'Identity of religious minorities in non-secular states: Jews in Tunisia and Morocco and Arabs in Israel', *Comparative Studies in Society and History*.

TEVET, SHABTAI (1957), 'The blacks and whites', *Haaretz* (22 September)(H).

—— (1966), 'Israel acquires an Oriental character', *Haaretz* (15 July) (H).

TSEMAH, SHLOMO (1967), *Amongst People and Ethnic Communities*, Jerusalem: Council of the Sephardic Community (H).

TSORIEL, YOSEF (1967), 'The good people have proved themselves to be . . . good', *Ma'ariv* (29 Nov.).

United States Bureau of Census (1973), *The Social and Economic Status of the Black Population in the United States, 1971*, Current Population Reports P-23, no. 42, Washington, D.C.: U.S. Government Printing Office.

VAN DEN BERGHE, PIERRE L. (1963), 'Dialectic and functionalism: toward a theoretical synthesis', *American Sociological Review*, 28(5) (Oct.): 695–705.

—— (1967a), *South Africa: A Study in Conflict*, University of California Press.

—— (1967b), *Race and Racism: A Comparative Perspective*, New York: Wiley.

—— (1969), 'Pluralism and the polity: a theoretical exploration', pp. 67–81 in Leo Kuper and M. G. Smith (eds) (1969: 67–81).

—— (1970), 'Pluralism and conflict situations in Africa: a reply to B. Magubane', *African Social Research*, 9 (June): 681–9.

—— (1971), 'Ethnicity: the African experience', *International Social Science Journal*, 23(4): 507–18.

—— (1973), 'Pluralism', in John J. Honigmann (ed.), *Handbook of Social and Cultural Anthropology*, Chicago: Rand McNally, pp. 959–77.

—— (1975), 'Integration and conflict in multinational states', *Social Dynamics*, 1(1) (June): 3–10.

—— (ed.) (1972), *Intergroup Relations*, New York: Basic Books.

VANDER ZANDEN, JAMES W. (1972), *American Minority Relations* (3rd ed.), New York: Ronald Press.

WANEFSKY, J. (1970), *Rabbi Isaac Jacob Reines: His Life and Thought*, New York: Philosophical Library.

WARNER, LLOYD W. (1936), 'American class and caste', *American Journal of Sociology*, 42(4) (Sept.): 234–7.

WASCHITZ, YOSEF (1947), *The Arabs in Palestine*, Merhavia: Sifriat Poalim (H).

—— (1975), 'Commuters and entrepreneurs', *New Outlook*, 18(7) (Oct.–Nov.): 45–53.

WEINGROD, ALEX (1960), 'Moroccan Jewry in transition', *Megamot*, 10(3): 193–208 (H).

—— (1962), 'The two Israels', *Commentary*, 33(4): 313–19.

—— (1964), 'Immigrants, localism, and the political regime', *Amot*, 10(2) (Feb.–March): 15–22 (H).

—— (1965), *Israel: Group Relations in a New Society*, London: Pall Mall Press for Institute of Race Relations.

—— (1966), *Reluctant Pioneers: Village Development in Israel*, Ithaca, N.Y.: Cornell University Press.

WEIS, SHEVA (1968), 'Local Government in Israel and its Leadership', doctoral dissertation, Jerusalem: Hebrew University (H).

—— (1972), *Local Government in Israel*, Tel-Aviv: Am Oved (H).

—— (1973), *The Politicians: Representation, Positions and Recruitment Patterns*, Tel-Aviv: Achiassaf (H).

WESTIE, FRANK (1964), 'Race and ethnic relations', in Robert E. L. Faris (ed.), *Handbook of Modern Sociology*, Chicago: Rand McNally, pp. 576–618.

WILLIAMS, ROBIN M. (1964), *Strangers Next Door*, Englewood Cliffs, N.J.: Prentice-Hall.

WILLNER, DOROTHY (1969), *Nation-Building and Community in Israel*, Princeton University Press.

WILSON, WILLIAM J. (1973), *Power, Racism, and Privilege*, New York: Macmillan.

YANCEY, WILLIAM L., EUGENE P. ERICKSEN, and RICHARD N. JULIANI (1976), 'Emergent ethnicity: a review and reformulation', *American Sociological Review*, 41(3) (June): 391–403.

YARON, ZVI (1974), *Rabbi Kook's Teachings*, Jerusalem: World Zionist Organisation (H).

YINGER, MILTON J. (1965), *A Minority Group in American Society*, New York: McGraw-Hill.

YINON, AVRAHAM (1965), 'Some themes in the literature of Israeli Arabs', *Hamizrah Hedadash*, 15(1–2): 57–84 (H).

—— (1966), 'Social themes in the literature of Israeli Arabs', *Hamizrah Hehadash*, 16(3–4): 349–80 (H).

YINON, YOEL (1975), 'Authoritarianism and prejudice among married couples with same or different ethnic origin', *Journal of Marriage and the Family*, 37(1) (Feb.): 214–20.

——, ARIE ABEND, and AMOS CHIRER (1976), 'Prejudice towards Israelis of Oriental origin among Israelis of Western origin', *Journal of Social Psychology* 99: 171-8.

YISRAELI, YAIR (1971), 'Absorption policy – a principal cause of the ethnic gap', *Afiqim*, 4(40) (Sept.): 12–14 (H).

ZADIK, BARUCH (1968), 'Field-dependence-independence among Oriental and Western school children', *Megamot*, 16(1) (Oct.): 51–8 (H).

ZAID, KASSIM (1973), 'Israel's Arabs after twenty-five years', *New Outlook*, 16(6) (July–Aug.): 11–16.

ZAK, ITAI (1975), *Arab–Israeli Identity and Readiness for Social Relations between Young Arabs and Jews in Israel*, Research Report, Ford Foundation.

—— (1976), 'Structure of ethnic identity of Arab–Israeli students', *Psychological Reports*, 38: 239–46.

ZARHI, SHAUL, and A. ACHIEZRA (1966), *The Economic Conditions of the Arab Minority in Israel*, Givat Haviva: Centre for Arab and Afro-Asian Studies.

ZBOROWSKI, MARK, and ELIZABETH HERZOG (1962), *Life is with People: The Culture of the Shtetl*, New York: Shocken.

ZERUBAVEL, Y. (1950), 'A turning point in Zionist work', *Yalqut Hamizrakh Hatikhon* (Jan.–Feb.) (H).

ZIMMELS, HIRSCH J. (1958), *Ashkenazim and Sephardim: Their Relations, Differences, and Problems as Reflected in the Rabbinical Responsa*, Oxford University Press.

ZLOCZOWER, AVRAHAM (1968), 'Social Mobility Patterns and Images of Stratification in an Urban Population of Israel', doctoral dissertation, Jerusalem: Hebrew University (H).

—— (1972), 'Occupation, mobility and social class', *Social Science Information*, 11(50): 329–57.

ZUCKER, NORMAN (1973), *The Coming Crisis in Israel*, MIT Press.

ZUCKERMAN-BARELI, CHAYA (1970), 'The Structure of Religious Conceptions of Youth in Israeli Society', doctoral dissertation, Jerusalem: Hebrew University (H).

—— (1972), 'The world view of religious youth in Israel', in *University of Bar-Ilan Yearbook*, Ramat-Gan: Bar-Ilan University, pp. 21–36 (H).

—— (1975), 'The religious factor in opinion formation among Israeli youth', in Solomon Poll and Ernest Krausz (eds), *On Ethnic and Religious Diversity in Israel*, Ramat-Gan: Bar-Ilan University pp. 53–89.

Selected bibliography

Note: The literature on Israel is enormous. This bibliography is limited to some important publications which are relevant to the pluralistic structure of Israeli society. It consists of four parts: Israel (general), Oriental–Ashkenazi division, Religious–nonreligious division and Arab–Jewish division. More publications are listed in Cited References.

Israel (general)

This section includes general writings on Israel from diverse perspectives.

ARIAN, ALAN (1973), *The Choosing People: Voting Behavior in Israel,* Press of Case Western Reserve University.

BEIN, ALEX (1954), *A History of the Zionist Settlement* (3rd ed.). Tel-Aviv: Masada (H).

BOBER, ARIE (ed.) (1972), *The Other Israel: The Radical Case Against Zionism,* Garden City, N.Y.: Anchor Books.

Central Bureau of Statistics (1950–76), *Statistical Abstract of Israel,* 1–27. Jerusalem: Government Printer.

CURTIS, MICHAEL, and MORDECAI CHERTOFF (eds) (1973), *Israel: Social Structure and Change,* New Brunswick, N.J.: Transaction Books.

EISENSTADT, S. N. (1967), *Israeli Society: Background, Development, Problems,* New York: Basic Books.

——, RIVKAH BAR-YOSEF, and CHAIM ADLER (eds) (1970), *Integration and Development in Israel,* Jerusalem: Israel Universities Press.

ELIAV, ARIE LOVA (1976), *Israel's Ladder: The Dream and its Meaning,* Tel-Aviv: Zmora, Bitan, Modan Publishers (H).

ELON, AMOS (1972), *The Israelis: Founders and Sons,* New York: Bantam Books.

Encyclopedia Hebraica (1957), 'Eretz Israel', vol. 6, Tel-Aviv: Encyclopedia Publishing Company (H).

—— (1967), 'Eretz Israel', Tel-Aviv: Encyclopedia Publishing Co., cols 400–550 in Supplementary Volume to vols 1–16 (H).

Encyclopedia Judaica (1971), 'Israel', vol. 9, New York: Macmillan, cols 107–1045.

FEIN, LEONARD J. (1968), *Politics in Israel: A Country Study* (2nd ed.), Boston: Little, Brown.

FRIEDMANN, GEORGES (1968), *The End of the Jewish People?*, Garden City, N.Y.: Anchor Books.

HERMAN, SIMON N. (1970), *Israelis and Jews: The Continuity of an Identity*, New York: Random House.

Israel, Government (1949–76), *Government Year Book*, Jerusalem: Government Printer.

KATZ, ELIHU, and MICHAEL GUREVITCH (1973), *The Culture of Leisure in Israel*, Tel-Aviv: Am Oved (H).

KLEINBERGER, AHARON F. (1969), *Society, Schools and Progress in Israel*, New York: Bergman Press.

LACQUEUR, WALTER (1972), *A History of Zionism*, New York: Holt, Rinehart & Winston.

LEVY, SHLOMIT, and LOUIS GUTTMAN (1976), 'Values and Attitudes of Israel High School Youth', 2nd Research Project, Jerusalem: Israel Institute of Applied Social Research (H).

LUMER, HYMAN (1973), *Zionism: Its Role in World Politics*, New York: International Publishers.

MATRAS, JUDAH (1965), *Social Change in Israel*, Chicago: Aldine.

PATAI, RAPHAEL (ed.) (1971), *Encyclopedia of Zionism and Israel*, New York: Herzl Press and McGraw-Hill.

RATOSH, YOUNATHAN (ed.) (1976), *From a Victory to a Defeat*, Tel-Aviv: Hadar (H).

RODINSON, MAXIME (1973), *Israel: A Colonial-Settler State?*, New York: Monad Press.

SEGRE, V.D. (1971), *Israel: A Society in Transition*, Oxford University Press.

SHUVAL, JUDITH T. (1963), *Immigrants on the Threshold*, New York: Atherton.

SICRON, MOSHE (1957), *Immigration to Israel, 1948–1953*, Jerusalem: Central Bureau of Statistics (Special Series 60) and Falk Project for Economic Research in Israel.

SPRINZAK, EHUD (1973), 'Beginning of Politics of Delegitimation in Israel in 1967–1972', Jerusalem: Hebrew University (duplicated) (H).

WELLER, LEONARD (1974), *Sociology in Israel*, Westport, Conn.: Greenwood.

Oriental–Ashkenazi division

Note: Cohen and Yehuda (1976) provide an extensive annotated bibliography.

BAR-YOSEF, RIVKAH (1970), 'The Moroccans: background to the problem', in S. N. Eisenstadt, Rivkah Bar-Yosef, and Chaim Adler (eds), *Integration and Development in Israel*, Jerusalem: Israel Universities Press, pp. 419–28.

—— (1971), 'Absorption versus Modernization', Jerusalem: Department of Sociology, Hebrew University (duplicated).

——, and DORITH PADAN (1964), 'Orientals in the class formation of Israel', *Molad*, 22(195–6) (Nov.): 504–16 (H).

BEN-DAVID, JOSEPH (1970), 'Ethnic differences or social change?', in S. N. Eisenstadt, Rivkah Bar-Yosef, and Chaim Adler (eds), *Integration and Development in Israel*, Jerusalem: Israel Universities Press, pp. 368–87.

BERNSTEIN, DEBORAH (1976), 'Contradictions and Protest in the Process of Nation-Building: The Black Panthers of Israel: 1971–72', unpublished PhD thesis, University of Sussex.

COHEN, ERIK (1969), 'The dispersion of population and amalgamation of exiles as conflicting goals', in *The Integration of Immigrants from Different Countries of Origin in Israel*, Jerusalem: Magnes Press, pp. 143–57 (H).

COHEN, HAYYIM J. (1968), *20th Century Aliya From Asia and Africa*, Jerusalem: Institute of Contemporary Jewry, Hebrew University (H).

—— (1973), *The Jews of the Middle East, 1860–1972*, New York: Wiley.

——, and ZVI YEHUDA (eds) (1976), *Asian and African Jews in the Middle East 1860–1971: An Annotated Bibliography*, Jerusalem: Ben-Zvi Institute and Hebrew University.

DESHEN, SHLOMO A. (1974), 'Political ethnicity and cultural ethnicity in Israel during the 1960s', in Abner Cohen (ed.), *Urban Ethnicity*, London: Tavistock, pp. 281–309.

EISENSTADT, S. N. (1955), *The Absorption of Immigrants*, Chicago: Free Press.

ELIACHAR, ELIAHU (1967), *We Must Prevent Jewish Racism in the Jewish State*, Jerusalem: Council of the Sephardic Community (H).

FRANKENSTEIN, KARL, *et al.* (1951–2), 'A discussion of the problem of ethnic differences (symposium)', *Megamot*, 2: 327–38, 261–84; 3: 50–64, 158–83, 319–29 (H).

HARTMAN, MOSHE, and HANNA EILON (1975), 'Ethnicity and stratification in Israel', *Megamot*, 21(2) (Feb.): 120–39 (H).

INBAR, MICHAEL, and CHAIM ADLER (1977), *Ethnic Integration in Israel*, New Brunswick, N.J.: Transaction Books.

Israel, Knesset (1965), 'Debate on ethnic integration', *Proceedings of the Knesset* (Dec. 1964 and Jan. 1965), Jerusalem: Government Printer (H).

KATZ, ELIHU, and A. ZLOCZOWER (1961), 'Ethnic continuity in an Israeli town: relations with parents', *Human Relations*, 14(4) (Nov.): 293–309.

LISSAK, MOSHE (1969), *Social Mobility in Israeli Society*, Jerusalem: Israel Universities Press.

MATRAS, JUDAH (1973), 'On changing matchmaking, marriage, and fertility in Israel: some findings, problems, and hypotheses', *American Journal/ of Sociology*, 79(2) (Sept.): 364–88.

ORTAR, GINA (1967), 'Educational achievements of primary school graduates in Israel as related to their sociocultural background', *Comparative Education*, 4(1) (Nov.): 23–34.

PATAI, RAPHAEL (1970), *Israel Between East and West* (2nd ed.), Westport, Conn.: Greenwood.

PERES, YOCHANAN (1976), *Ethnic Relations in Israel*, Tel-Aviv: Sifriat Poalim (H).

Prime Minister's Commission (1974), Report of the Prime Minister's Commission on Disadvantaged Children and Youth (2nd ed.), Jerusalem: Prime Minister's Office (duplicated) (H).

Public Inquiry Commission (1959), 'Wadi-Salih: Background of a Social Problem', Tel-Aviv: unpublished (H).

REJWAN, NISSIM (1967), 'The two Israels: A study in Europocentrism', *Judaism*, 16(1) (winter): 97–108.

SELZER, MICHAEL (1967), *The Aryanization of the Jewish State*, New York: Black Star Book.

SHTAL, ABRAHAM (1976), *Cultural Fusion in Israel*, Tel-Aviv: Am Oved (H).

SHUMSKY, ABRAHAM (1955), *The Clash of Cultures in Israel*, Columbia University Publications.

SHUVAL, JUDITH T. (1962), 'Emerging patterns of ethnic strain in Israel', *Social Forces*, 40(4) (May): 323–30.

SMOOHA, SAMMY, and YOCHANAN PERES (1975), 'The dynamics of ethnic inequalities: the case of Israel', *Social Dynamics*, 1(1) (June): 63–79.

WEINGROD, ALEX (1965), *Israel: Group Relations in a New Society*, London: Pall Mall Press for Institute of Race Relations.

YINON, YOEL, ARIE ABEND, and AMOS CHIRER (1976), 'Prejudice towards Israelis of Oriental origin among Israelis of Western origin', *Journal of Social Pychology* 99: 171-8.

SELECTED BIBLIOGRAPHY

Religious–nonreligious division

Note: Zucker (1973) provides a broader bibliography.

ALONI, SHULAMIT (1970), *The Arrangement: From a Legal State to a Halakhic State*, Tel-Aviv: Otpaz (H).

ANTONOVSKY, AARON (1963), 'Israeli political-social attitudes', *Amot*, 1(6) (June–July): 11–22 (H).

BIRNBAUM, ERVIN (1970), *The Politics of Compromise: State and Religion in Israel*, Cranbury, N.J.: Fairleigh Dickinson University Press.

COHEN, OVED (1975), 'The Conflict between Religious and Nonreligious Jews in Israel: Solidarity and Social Distance among High School Students', doctoral dissertation, Jerusalem: Hebrew University (H).

COHEN, YONA (1973), *Chapters in the History of the National Religious Movement*, Tel-Aviv: Information Department, National Religious Party (H).

DESHEN, SHLOMO A. (forthcoming), 'Israeli Judaism: introduction to the major patterns', *International Journal of Middle Eastern Studies*.

DON-YIHYE, ELIEZER (1975), *Religion in Israel*, Jerusalem: Merkaz Hehazbara (H).

ELON, MENACHEM (1968), *Religious Legislation*, Tel-Aviv: Hakibbutz Hadati (H).

ENGLAND, IZHAK, and HANAN SHELAH (eds) (1973), *Religion and State: Selected Sources*, Jerusalem: Academon (H).

FISHMAN, ARYEI (1975), 'The Religious Kibbutz: A Study in the Inter-relationship of Religion and Ideology in the Context of Modernization', doctoral dissertation, Jerusalem: Hebrew University (H).

FRIEDMAN, MENACHEM (1972), 'The Chief Rabbinate – dilemma without solution', *Medina Vemimshal*, 1(3) (spring): 118–28 (H).

—— (1973), 'The Old Yishuv During the British Mandate, 1917–1936', doctoral dissertation, Jerusalem: Hebrew University (H).

GOLDMAN, ELIEZER (1964), *Religious Issues in Israel's Political Life*, Jerusalem: Mador Dati, Jewish Agency.

GUTTMAN, EMANUEL (1971), 'Religion in Israeli politics', in Jacob M. Landau (ed.), *Man, State and Society in the Contemporary Middle East*, New York: Praeger, pp. 122–34.

KATZ, ELIHU (1973), 'Culture and communication in Israel: the transformation of tradition', *Jewish Journal of Sociology*, 15(1) (June): 5–22.

KATZ, JACOB (1973), *Out of the Ghetto: The Social Background of Jewish Emancipation, 1770–1870*, Harvard University Press.

KNAANI, DAVID (1975), *The Working Second Aliyah and its Attitude towards Religion*, Tel-Aviv: Institute for Labour and Social Relations, Tel-Aviv University (H).

LESLIE, CLEMENT S. (1971), *The Rift in Israel: Religious Authority and Secular Democracy*, London: Routledge & Kegan Paul; New York: Schocken.

LIEBMAN, CHARLES S. (1975), 'Religion and political integration in Israel', *Jewish Journal of Sociology*, 17(1) (June): 17–27.

LIEBOWITZ, YASHAEIHU (1975), *Judaism, the Jewish People and the State of Israel*, Tel-Aviv: Schocken (H).

MARMORSTEIN, EMILE (1969), *Heaven at Bay: The Jewish Kulturkampf in the Holy Land*, Oxford University Press.

MERON, SIMHA (1973), 'Freedom of religion as distinct from freedom from religion', *Tel-Aviv University Law Review*, 3(2) (Sept.): 414–32 (H).

MORGENSTEIN, ARIE (1974), *The Chief Rabbinate in the Land of Israel*, Tel-Aviv: Moreshet (H).

OREN, STEPHEN (1973), 'Continuity and change in Israel's religious parties', *Middle East Journal*, 27(1) (winter): 36–54.

ROSENAK, MICHAEL (1971), 'Religion and religious attitudes in Israel', in Raphael Patai (ed.), *Encyclopedia of Zionism and Israel*, New York: Herzl Press and McGraw-Hill, pp. 940–4.

RUBINSTEIN, AMNON (1967), 'Law and religion in Israel', *Israel Law Review*, 2(3) (July): 380–414.

—— (1967), 'State and religion in Israel', *Journal of Contemporary History*, 2(4) (Oct.): 107–21.

SAMET, MOSHE (ed.) (1973), *State and Religion*, Jerusalem: Academon (H).

TAMARIN, GEORGES R. (1973), *The Israeli Dilemma. Essays on a Warfare State*, Rotterdam University Press.

WEILER, GERSHON (1976), *Jewish Theocracy*, Tel-Aviv: Am Oved (H).

ZUCKER, NORMAN (1973), *The Coming Crisis in Israel*, MIT Press.

ZUCKERMAN-BARELI, CHAYA (1970), 'The Structure of Religious Conceptions of Youth in Israeli Society', doctoral dissertation, Jerusalem: Hebrew University (H).

—— (1975), 'The religious factor in opinion formation among Israeli youth', in Solomon Poll and Ernest Krausz (eds), *On Ethnic and Religious Diversity in Israel*, Ramat-Gan: Bar-Ilan University, pp. 53–89.

Arab–Jewish division

Note: Cohen (1974) provides an extensive bibliography; Smooha and Cibulski (1978) provide an annotated bibliography of scientific publications.

BENJAMIN, AVRAHAM, and RAHEL PELEG (1978), *The Arab Student and the University*, Tel-Aviv: Am Oved.

CARMI, SHULAMIT, and HENRY ROSENFELD (1974), 'The origins of the process of proletarianization and urbanization of Arab peasants in Palestine', *Annals of the New York Academy of Sciences*, 220(6) (March): 470–85.

COHEN, ABNER (1965), *Arab Border Villages in Israel*, Manchester University Press.

COHEN, ERIK (1973), 'Integration vs. Separation in the Planning of a Mixed Jewish–Arab City in Israel', Jerusalem: Hebrew University (duplicated).

—— (ed.) (1974), *Bibliography of Arabs and Other Minorities in Israel*, Givat Haviva, Israel: Centre for Arab and Afro-Asian Studies.

EISENSTADT, S. N., and YOCHANAN PERES (1968), *Some Problems of Educating a National Minority: A Study of Israeli Education for Arabs* (report prepared by Yochanan Peres), Project no. OE-6-21-013; ERIC Document no. Ed-033-967, Washington, D.C.: US Department of Health, Education and Welfare.

HARARI, YECHIEL (ed.) (1976), *The Arabs in Israel: Statistics and Facts*, Givat Haviva, Israel: Centre for Arab and Afro-Asian Studies.

HOFMAN, JOHN E. (1972), 'Readiness for social relations between Arabs and Jews in Israel', *Journal of Conflict Resolution*, 16(2): 241–51.

——, and NADEEM ROUHANA (1976), 'Young Arabs in Israel: some aspects of a conflicted social identity', *Journal of Social Psychology*, 99: 75–86.

Israel, Ministry of Education and Culture (1975), Report of the Committee on Arab Education, Jerusalem: Planning Project of Education for the 1980s, Ministry of Education and Culture (duplicated) (H).

Israel, Ministry of the Interior (1973), Report of the Committee to Determine the Structure of Expenditure and Sources of Revenue in the Local Councils of the Minorities, Jerusalem: Ministry of the Interior (duplicated) (H).

JIRYIS, SABRI (1976), *The Arabs in Israel* (2nd ed.), New York: Monthly Review Press.

KIPNIS, BARUCH (1976), 'Trends of the minority population in the Galilee and their planning implications', *Aeer Veaeezor*, 3(3): 54–68 (H).

LANDAU, JACOB M. (1969), *The Arabs in Israel: A Political Study*, Oxford University Press.

MAR'I, SAMI K., and NABIH DAHER (1976), 'Facts and Trends in the Development of Arab Education in Israel', University of Haifa (duplicated) (H).

MARX, EMANUEL (1967), *Bedouin of the Negev*, Manchester University Press.

NAKHLEH, KHALIL (1975), 'The direction of local-level conflict in two Arab villages in Israel', *American Ethnologist*, 2(3) (Aug.): 497–516.

442

OPPENHEIMER, JONATHAN W. S. (1976), 'The Social Organization of a Druze Community in Israel', unpublished Ph.D. thesis, University of London.

PERES, YOCHANAN (1971), 'Ethnic relations in Israel', *American Journal of Sociology*, 76(6) (May): 1021–47.

PERETZ, DON (1958), *Israel and the Palestine Arabs*, Washington, D.C.: Middle East Institute.

REKHESS, ELI (1974), *A Survey of Israeli Arab Gradates from Institutions of Higher Learning in Israel (1961–1971)*, Shiloah Centre, Tel-Aviv University; Jerusalem: American Jewish Committee.

—— (1976), 'The Arabs in Israel After 1967: the Exacerbation of the Orientation Problem', Shiloah Centre, Tel-Aviv University (duplicated) (H).

ROSENFELD, HENRY (1964), 'From peasantry to wage labor and residual peasantry: the transformation of an Arab village', in Robert A. Manners (ed.), *Process and Pattern in Culture*, Chicago: Aldine, pp. 211–34.

—— (1968), 'Change, barriers to change and contradictions in the Arab village family', *American Anthropologist*, 70(4): 732–52.

SHIMONI, YAAKOV (1947), *The Arabs of Palestine*, Tel-Aviv: Am Oved (H).

SMOOHA, SAMMY (1976), 'Arabs and Jews in Israel: minority-majority group relations', *Megamot*, 22(4) (Sept.): 397–423 (H).

——and ORA CIBULSKI (1978), *Social Research on Arabs in Israel, 1948–1976: Trends and an Annotated Bibliography*, Tel-Aviv: Turtledove Press.

——, and JOHN F. HOFMAN (1976–7), 'Some problems of Arab–Jewish coexistence in Israel', *Middle East Review*, 9(2) (winter): 5–14.

STENDEL, ORI (1973), *The Minorities of Israel*, Jerusalem: Israel Economist.

STOCK, ERNEST (1968), *From Conflict to Understanding*, New York: American Jewish Committee.

WASCHITZ, YOSEF (1947), *The Arabs in Palestine*, Merhavia: Sifriat Poalim (H).

YALAN, EMMANUEL, CHAIM FINKEL, LOUIS GUTTMAN, and CHANOCH JACOBSEN (1972), *The Modernization of Traditional Agricultural Villages: Minority Villages in Israel*, Rehovot: The Settlement Study Centre.

ZAK, ITAI (1975), *Arab–Israeli Identity and Readiness for Social Relations between Young Arabs and Jews in Israel*, Research Report, Ford Foundation.

Index

Abbas, Abraham, 358, 411
Abend, Arie, 191, 434, 439
Abramov, Zalman S., 367, 411
Absentee Property Law, 384
Absorption–modernization model,
    4, 21–5, 39–41, 86, 89, 92,
    96, 164
Abu-Gosh, Subhi, 121, 207, 411
Achiezra, A., 374, 434
Adam, Heribert, 18, 357, 411
Adar, Lea, 358, 380, 411
Adi, Pesah, 376, 411
Adelman, I., 378
Adler, Chaim, 41, 93, 189, 358,
    374, 380, 411, 421, 439
Agmon, Tamar, 191, 430
Agudat Israel, 62–5, 73, 78–9,
    130–1, 133, 176, 220, 223,
    247, 359, 367–8, 371, 404–5
Aguna, 398
Ahdut HaAvoda Party, 176–7,
    323, 331, 333, 336–7
Al-Ard, 85, 214–15, 224, 372, 403
Algarebly, Mordechai, 391, 411
Algerian Jews, 50, 93
Alienation: Israeli Arabs, 207–8,
    218, 229; Oriental Jews,
    202–3; religious Jews, 206, 222
Alignment (Ma'arakh), 146, 178,
    332, 335, 337–8, 383, 404
Aloni, R., 190, 428
Aloni, Shulamit, 80, 195, 212,
    398, 409, 412, 440

Amir, Yehuda, 115, 127, 412, 427
Anatomy and Pathology Law,
    27–8, 80
Anti-religious compulsion, see
    religion, freedom of
Antonovsky, Aaron, 82, 101, 113,
    358, 371, 375, 380, 412, 440
Arab–Jewish division, 3, 52, 241,
    354, 365, 371; Arab–Israeli
    conflict affecting, 47, 75,
    83–4, 94–5, 100, 109, 200,
    224, 252, 374–5; bases of
    integration, 218–19, 221,
    223–33; comparisons with
    other divisions, 140–1, 259,
    262–4, 271–9; congruity of
    group goals, 82–5, 218;
    countermeasures by the
    dominant group, 216, 277;
    cross-cutting affiliations, 221,
    404; colonial perspective of,
    35, 45; cultural autonomy, 46,
    146–7, 187, 221, 224, 250;
    cultural diversity, 120–3, 238,
    249, 274, 349; discrimination
    against Israeli Arabs, 35,
    102–3, 197–9, 201–2, 224,
    250, 277, 399;
    dissatisfactions, 122, 141,
    202–8, 218, 229, 401; elite
    accommodation, 99–100,
    223–5; ethnocentrism against
    Israeli Arabs, 38, 46, 75,

86-8, 95, 103, 105;
exclusionary domination
model of, 45-7, 239, 245,
249, 252, 262-3; external
factors affecting, 229-30;
failures of group goals, 187-8;
features of society-at-large
affecting, 109; future
developments, 32, 35, 241,
249-52; gaps in education,
139-41, 350, 385; gaps in
material wellbeing, 138-41,
202-3, 250; gaps in
occupational distribution,
138-41, 250; historical
background, 65-9; identity,
31-2, 84, 122-3, 150, 188,
250, 255, 354, 360-1;
inequality, 187, 239, 249-52,
256, 259-60, 262, 350-2;
interdependence, 46, 99, 100,
227; intermarriage, 27, 29, 45,
75, 134, 136, 248, 250, 385,
409; literature on, 4, 30-1,
360, 368, 441-3; multiple
cleavages in Israel affecting,
41, 104-5; nationalism-
modernization model, 4, 30-2;
new directions, 250-2, 255-7;
past trends, 46-7, 238-40;
paternalism vis-à-vis Arabs,
103, 141, 199; patterns of
conflict, 187-8, 197-202, 207-8,
213-16; pluralism, 120-3,
134-6, 238, 249-50, 347, 349;
political coercion, 45-6, 150,
227-8; power disparities,
145-8, 351; prejudice against
Israeli Arabs, 41, 199-201,
277, 376; primary bases of,
74-5; protests of nondominant
group, 213-16, 224, 277;
social separation, 27, 29, 31,
45, 75, 134-6, 221, 238, 248,
250, 347, 385, 404, 409;
socioeconomic gaps, 138-41,
202-3, 239, 250, 350, 385;
statehood affecting, 68-9;
statistics on, 347, 349-52;

undercurrents, 94-5, 199;
value consensus, 120-3, 218-9,
249, 274; in the Yishuv, 54,
65-9; and Zionism, 38, 68,
207, 230
Arab-Israeli conflict, xv, 32, 86,
98, 107, 208, 241, 365, 406;
repercussions for Arab-
Jewish relations, 47, 75, 83-4,
94-5, 100, 109, 200, 224, 252,
374-5; repercussions for
integration in Israel, 38, 108;
repercussions for Oriental-
Ashkenazi relations, 98, 108,
206, 228-9, 232, 243, 407-8;
repercussions for religious-
nonreligious relations, 45,
228-9, 232, 248
Arabists, 147
Arab Revolt, 67-8
Arad, Shlomo, 122, 423
Arian, Alan, 138, 371, 380, 382-3,
412, 423, 427, 436
Army chaplaincy, 27, 124, 145, 383
Aronoff, Myron J., 386, 412
Ashkenazim, 34, 49, 51-7, 235,
364-5
Ashkenazi supremacy, 108, 377
Assaf, Michael, 368, 412
Attias, Moshe, 59, 128, 368, 412
Avineri, Shlomo, 362, 376, 399,
412
Avnery, Uri, 371, 412

Bahais, 353, 384
Bagley, Christopher, 357, 412
Bailey, Clinton, 214, 412
Bar-Gal, Yoram, 239, 412
Bar-Ilan University, 132, 236
Barkai, H., 168, 412
Barnett, Richard D., 365, 412
Barth, Ernest A. T., 354, 413
Barth, Fredrik B., 365, 413
Bar-Yosef, Rivkah, 22-4, 40, 89,
92, 209, 358, 389, 413, 438
Bases of integration, 16-17, 36,
216-30, 227-8, 233, 356; see
also cross-cutting affiliations,
economic interdependence,

elite accommodation, external factors, political coercion, value consensus
Bashan, Raphael, 56, 413
Bastuni, Rustum, 85, 372, 413
Battle for the immigrants, 101–2, 128
Bedouin, 66, 135
Bein, Alex, 55, 413, 436
Beit-Hallahmi, Benjamin, 200, 413
Bekker, Simon, 18, 413
Ben-Chaim, Efrayim, 358, 370, 413
Ben-David, Joseph, 22–3, 413, 438
Ben-Dor, Gabriel, 370, 392, 413
Bene Israel, 212, 400–1
Ben-Gurion, David, 88, 95, 368, 372, 393
Benjamin, Avraham, 123, 399, 404, 413, 441
Ben-Porath, Yoram, 360
Ben-Simhon, Shaul, 393, 402
Bensimon-Donath, Doris B., 54, 192, 413
Bentwich, Norman, 367, 413
Benyamini, Kalman, 199, 413
Ben-Zvi, Itzhak, 364, 372, 413
Bergenski, Yehuda, 92
Bernardete, Mair Jose, 365, 414
Bernstein, Deborah, 209, 414, 438
Berreman, Gerald D., 74, 414
Berson, Jeremy, 408, 414
Bibi, Mordekhai, 395
Biculturalism, 31, 216–19, 249–50
Biraam and Ikrit, 401–2
Birnbaum, Ervin, 359, 375, 386, 414, 440
Bizman, Aharon, 127, 412
Black Hebrews, 400
Black Panthers, 77–8, 106, 125, 128, 142, 165, 169, 179, 193, 209–12, 227, 235–6, 243, 376, 382, 402–3, 407–8
Blalock, Hubert M., 7, 15, 414
Blauner, Robert, 7, 19, 369, 414
Blumer, Herbert, 388, 414
Bober, Arie, 360–2, 371, 407, 414, 436

Bonacich, Edna, 15, 19, 357, 369, 414
Bossik, Dorit, 122, 423
Brent, S., 408, 414
Brichta, Abraham, 392–3, 414
British mandate, see Yishuv
Broker institutions, 16, 220–1
Broom, Leonard, 394, 414
Brother Daniel case, 212
Buch, Peter, 33, 360, 414

Campbell, Donald, 353, 365
Canaanite state, utopia, 253, 410
Canaanites, 79, 359, 371
Carmi, Shulamit, 368, 414, 442
Central Bureau of Statistics (CBS), 106, 111, 114, 133, 137, 140–1, 146, 156, 163, 203, 207, 370, 378–9, 383, 385, 389–91, 401, 414, 436
Change, 17, 234–57, 279, 357–8; see also future developments, new directions, past trends
Chen, Michael, 406, 414
Chertoff, Mordecai, 362, 414
Chief Rabbinate, 28, 43–4, 63, 124–5, 145, 197, 248, 387, 404–5
Chief Rabbinate Council, 80, 124–5
Chirer, Amos, 191, 434, 439
Chouraqui, Andre, 366, 396, 414
Christianity, 80, 364–5
Cibulski, Ora, 441, 443
Circassians, 353
Civil religion, 218, 380
Civil Rights Movement, 372
Civilizing mission, 33, 38
Class, 38–9, 76–7, 102, 120, 130, 181–2, 220, 242, 380; see also 'disparities in . . .', 'gaps in . . .', inequality
Coalition politics, 64, 99, 101, 145, 223, 249, 386, 405
Cohen, Abner, 368, 374, 414, 442
Cohen, Aharon, 368, 414
Cohen, Erik, 75, 90, 136, 209, 353, 385, 404, 415, 438, 441–2

Cohen, Hayyim J., 54, 57, 130, 364, 366–7, 373, 383, 415, 425, 438
Cohen, in Judaic law, 359, 395, 398, 409
Cohen, Oved, 120, 133, 138, 196, 218, 358, 399, 415, 440
Cohen, Percy S., 358, 415
Cohen, Shalom, 210
Cohen, Yona, 367, 415, 440
Cohesion, 15–17, 183–233, 277–8, 356–7; see also bases of integration, patterns of conflict
Coleman, James S., 219, 395, 415
Colonial perspective, 21, 33–9, 41, 45, 102, 264–5, 360, 388
Commission on Tax Reforms, 390, 415
Communist Party (Maki, Rakah), 67, 135, 147–8, 176, 209, 214, 221, 224, 371–2, 376
Conflict, 1, 7, 9, 11–12, 15–16, 18, 36, 39, 70, 208, 219, 277–8, 356, 369–70; see also patterns of conflict
Congruity of group goals: of Israeli Arabs and Jews, 82–5, 218; of Orientals and Ashkenazim, 76–8, 85, 217; of religious and nonreligious Jews, 78–83, 85
Connor, Walker, 1, 416
'Conquest of labour', 54
Conservative Judaism, 28, 44, 62, 64, 73, 79, 117, 145, 186, 212
Consociationalism, 17, 43, 45, 99, 109, 145, 218, 222, 233, 237, 248, 256, 264, 405
Contested accommodation model, 43–5, 98–9, 222, 232–3, 237, 249, 261–2
Controlled gradualism, 109, 166, 181–2, 378, 407
Conversion, religious, 28–9, 45, 50, 75, 81, 247, 370
Core-culture, 14, 259; Israeli Arabs and Jews, 120, 218, 274; Orientals and

Ashkenazim, 105, 111–12, 216–17, 219, 232, 274; religious and nonreligious Jews, 116–17, 217–18, 232, 274
Countermeasures by the dominant group: against Israeli Arabs, 216, 277; against Orientals, 211–12, 277, 402–3; against religious Jews, 212–13, 277
Cox, Oliver, 18, 353, 416
Cross-cutting affiliations: among Israeli Arabs, 221, 404; among Orientals, 149, 219–20; among religious Jews, 220–1
Cross, Malcolm, 18, 355, 357, 416
Cultural autonomy, 141; and Israeli Arabs, 46, 146–7, 187, 221, 224, 250; and Orientals, 143; and religious Jews, 43, 143, 145, 149, 186, 221–3, 386–7, 405
Cultural diversity, 9–11, 14, 111, 269; Israeli Arabs and Jews, 120–3, 238, 249, 274, 349; Orientals and Ashkenazim, 112–16, 234–5, 274; religious and nonreligious Jews, 116–20, 236–7, 241, 246, 274
Cultural synthesis, 25, 184–5, 217–18
Current social contexts, 13, 70–109, 271; see also congruity of group goals, definition of group membership, features of society-at-large, historical background, initial group contact, interdependence, multiple cleavages, relative size of nondominant group, undercurrents
Curtis, Michael, 362, 416, 436
Czudnowski, Moshe M., 214, 416

Daher, Nabih, 442
Dahl, Robert, 8
Dahrendorf, Ralf, 356
Danet, Brenda, 192, 416

Davies, James, 153, 416
Dayan, Moshe, 382, 407–8
Debbiny, Sami, 123, 421
Defence Laws (State of
    Emergency), 134–5, 227–8
Definition of group membership:
    Israeli Arabs, 74–5;
    Orientals, 72; religious Jews,
    73–4
Delinquency, see deviance
Dependence, see interdependence,
    economic interdependence
Deshen, Shlomo A., 73, 113, 406,
    416, 438, 440
Despres, Leo, 8, 16, 355, 416, 431
de Tocqueville, Alexis, 8, 256, 416
Deutsch, Akiva, 358, 367, 416
Development towns, 91, 103–4,
    189, 373, 399, 401
Deviance: among Israeli Arabs,
    122, 207–8, 401; among
    Orientals, 57–8, 203, 401;
    among religious Jews, 206
Diaspora, 30, 33, 37, 57, 60, 66,
    76, 88–9, 94, 105, 115, 175,
    196, 227, 229, 244–5, 248,
    399, 408
Discrimination, 6–7, 231, 363,
    387–8; against Israeli Arabs,
    35, 102–3, 201–2, 224, 250,
    277; against nonreligious
    Jews, 44; against Orientals,
    40–2, 76, 89–94, 125, 154–5,
    159, 191–5, 203–4, 209–10,
    226, 277, 285, 373–4, 397–8,
    402; against religious Jews,
    196–7; see also
    ethnocentrism,
    paternalism, prejudice,
    quotas–benign, racism
Discrimination, institutional:
    against Israeli Arabs, 197–9,
    399; against Orientals, 55, 87,
    89–94, 188–9, 366, 373–4,
    395; against religious Jews,
    195, 399
Discrimination, positive: of Israeli
    Arabs, 201–2, 224; of
    Orientals, 195; of religious

Jews, 196–7; see also
    quotas–benign
Disparities in economic power:
    between Israeli Arabs and
    Jews, 146; between Orientals
    and Ashkenazim, 142–3, 168,
    339; between religious and
    nonreligious Jews, 144
Disparities in parapolitical power:
    between Israeli Arabs and
    Jews, 147; between Orientals
    and Ashkenazim, 142–3,
    169–70; between religious and
    nonreligious Jews, 145
Disparities in political power:
    between Israeli Arabs and
    Jews, 146, 351; between
    Orientals and Ashkenazim,
    40, 142–3, 164–81, 241–2,
    309–38, 351; between
    religious and nonreligious
    Jews, 143–5, 237, 331–6, 348
Dissatisfactions, 202–8, 277; see
    also alienation, deviance,
    militant views, status
    dissatisfaction
Donevitz, Nathan, 396, 416
Don-Yihye, Eliezer, 73, 213, 379,
    405, 416, 440
Dori, Yaacov, 190, 395–6
Drapkin, Israel, 122, 423
Druze–Christian–Moslem Arab
    division, 3–4, 134, 221
Druzes, 3–4, 75, 85, 134, 198,
    370–1, 385
Dual Rabbinate, 57, 124–5, 381–2
Dynamic paternalism–
    co-optation model, 39–42, 90,
    109, 166, 181, 236, 242,
    260–1, 364

Eban, Abba, 88, 95, 417
Economic interdependence:
    between Israeli Arabs and
    Jews, 46, 99–100, 150, 227;
    between Orientals and
    Ashkenazim, 97–8, 226;
    between religious and
    nonreligious Jews, 226–7, 405

Economy: Israeli, 39, 106–7, 110–11, 168, 225–6, 232, 241, 377, 390, 244–5, 252; Israeli Arab, 66, 69, 99, 138–9, 239, 250, 374–5, 385
Education: adult, 160; compensatory, 161–2, 189, 197, 244, 402; see also gaps in education
Ehrlich, Avishai, 187, 360, 427
Ehrlich, Chedva, 122, 424
Ehrlich, Howard J., 353, 417
Eilon, Hanna, 158, 420, 439
Eisenstadt, S. N., 22–4, 58–9, 89–90, 108, 358, 359–60, 362–3, 367, 417, 436, 438, 442
El-Asmar, Fouzi, 207, 417
Elazar, Daniel, 144, 384, 417
Elazar, Yaacov, 59, 417
Elections Law of the Chief Rabbinate Council, 124–5, 381–2
Elia, David, 373, 417
Eliachar, Eliahu, 59, 87, 192, 371, 393, 396, 400, 417, 438
Eliav, Arie Lova, 410, 418, 436
Elite, 153, 160; Ashkenazi, 34–5, 108–9, 164, 166, 243, 392, 407, Israeli Arab, 31–2, 123, 148, 222, 224–5, 239, 249, 381, 386; Oriental, 142, 160, 180, 245–6; religious, 118, 222–3, 246, 253, 383, 404–5
Elite accommodation: Israeli Arab elite, 99–100, 223–5; Oriental elite, 97, 222; religious elite, 222–3, 404–5
El Kodsy, Ahmad, 360, 368, 418
Elon, Amos, 68, 418, 436
Elon, Menachem, 383, 403, 418, 440
Emergency Laws (Security Areas), 134–5, 227–8
Encyclopedia Hebraica, 436–7
Encyclopedia Judaica, 394, 430, 437
Enemy-affiliated minority, 31–2, 75, 109, 207
England, Izhak, 359, 383, 418, 440
Enloe, Cynthia, 378, 418

Ericksen, Eugene P., 407, 433
Eshel, Smadar, 114, 129, 203, 379–80, 397–8, 418
Espionage, 215, 376–7
Ethnic amalgamation, see Mizug Galuyot
Ethnicity, 39, 74, 76–7, 102, 120, 124, 133, 138, 181–2, 220, 242, 380, 407; see also Arab–Jewish division, Oriental–Ashkenazi division
Ethnocentrism: against Israeli Arabs, 38, 46, 75, 86–8, 95, 103, 105; against Orientals, 38, 53–5, 59, 86–92, 103, 105, 192–3, 235, 372–3, 376, 395–7; against religious Jews, 94; see also discrimination, paternalism, prejudice, quotas–benign, racism
Etzioni-Halevy, Eva, 392, 403, 418, 429
Exclusionary domination model, 45–7, 239, 245, 249, 252, 262–3
Exclusive Jewish-Zionist state, utopia, 84, 188, 252–3, 409
External factors, 17, 229; affecting Arab–Jewish relations, 229–30; affecting internal Jewish divisions, 228–9; see also Arab–Israeli conflict, diaspora
Eyal, Eli, 82, 89, 187, 418

Failures of group goals: of Israeli Arabs and Jews, 187–8; of Orientals and Ashkenazim, 184–6; of religious and nonreligious Jews, 186–7
Falah, Salman H., 370, 418
Falashas, 400
Family, 14; among Israeli Arabs, 120–2, 380–1; among Orientals, 112–13, 379–81; among religious Jews, 117; see also intermarriage, marriage and divorce
Farago, Uri, 113, 115–16, 119, 420

Features of society-at-large:
    affecting Arab–Jewish
    relations, 109; affecting
    Oriental–Ashkenazi relations,
    105–9; affecting religious–
    nonreligious relations, 109
Fein, Leonard J., 190, 396, 418, 437
Feitelson, Dina, 127, 418
Finkel, Chaim, 443
Fishman, Aryei, 358, 418, 440
Fishman, Yehuda (Maimon), 368
Frankenstein, Karl, 57, 418, 438
Frenkel, Eva, 391, 431
Friedman, Menachem, 213, 218,
    358, 367–8, 387, 403–5,
    418–19, 440
Friedmann, Daniel, 403, 418
Friedmann, Georges, 437
Friendly, Alfred, 358, 419
Froilich, Daniela, 376, 411
Functionalism, xiii, 11, 16, 18–19,
    36, 41, 152–3, 164, 216, 355,
    357–8, 387–8
Furnivall, J. S., xiii, 6–8, 354–5,
    357, 419
Future developments, 240–1, 252;
    in Arab–Jewish relations, 32,
    35, 241, 249–52; in Oriental–
    Ashkenazi relations, 35,
    241–6; in religious–
    nonreligious relations, 30, 35,
    246–9

Gahal, 165, 332, 335, 337–8; see
    also Likud
Gal, Alon, 362, 419
Gamson, William A., 246, 364, 419
Gaps in education: between
    Israeli Arabs and Jews,
    139–41, 350, 385; between
    Orientals and Ashkenazim,
    137, 159–63, 297–308;
    between religious and
    nonreligious Jews, 138
Gaps in material wellbeing:
    between Israeli Arabs and
    Jews, 138–41, 202–3, 250;
    between Orientals and
    Ashkenazim, 137, 153–7,

282–9; between religious and
    nonreligious Jews, 138
Gaps in occupational distribution:
    between Israeli Arabs and
    Jews, 138–41, 250; between
    Orientals and Ashkenazim,
    137, 157–9, 290–6; between
    religious and nonreligious
    Jews, 138
Geffner, Edward, 358, 419
Gelblum, Arye, 87, 396, 419
German Jews, 51–2, 59
Gershman, Carl, 362, 421, 428
Giladi, Naim, 210
Ginat, Yosef, 385
Girvetz, Harry K., 182, 419
Glazer, Nathan, 8, 374, 419
Gloverson, Arye, 392, 419
Gluska, Zecharia, 55, 419
Goitein, S. D., 56, 364, 419
Golani, Gideon, 360
Goldman, Eliezer, 120, 359, 419,
    440
Goldstein, Dov, 393, 402, 419
Gordon, Milton, M., 8, 419
Gottheil, Fred M., 239, 419
Grandezza, 51
Grebler, Leo, 388, 419
Gronau, Hermona, 353, 415
Gruenbaum, Yitzhak, 368
Gurevitch, Michael, 78, 114, 119,
    142, 186, 379, 395, 409, 419,
    422, 430, 437
Gush Emunim, 237, 406
Guttman, Emanuel, 359, 419, 440
Guttman, Louis, 115, 119, 122,
    129, 141, 202, 207, 371, 384,
    420, 424, 437, 443

Habash, Awni H., 120, 420
Habib, Jack, 189, 431
HaCohen, Mordecai 57, 420
Halakha, 27, 29–30, 44, 73, 80,
    98, 117–18, 217, 223, 236–7,
    247, 253, 262, 381, 385, 395,
    399, 404–5, 409–10
Halakha state, utopia, 30, 62, 80,
    82, 131, 186, 252–3, 360, 398,
    409–10

Halitzah, 359–60
Halpern, Ben, 362
Hamula, 66, 136, 147, 221, 224
Hamizrahi, *see* Mizrahi
Hanuch, Giora, 389, 420
HaOlam Haze Movement, 210, 371
Hapoel Hamizrahi, 63–4
Havaad Lehaganat Kudshe HaOma, 213
Harari, Yechiel, 442
Harel, Ya'akov, 113, 115–16, 119, 420
Harris, Marvin, 74, 369, 420
Hartman, Harriet, 121, 192, 207, 411, 416
Hartman, Moshe, 158, 420, 439
Haug, Marie R., 110, 357, 420
Hazaz, Chaim, 56
Hebrew, pronunciation of, 112, 185, 379, 394
Hebrew University, 97, 420
Herman, Simon N., 82, 113, 115–16, 119, 399, 420, 437
Herrenvolk democracy, 21, 35, 256, 264
Herut Party, 128, 146, 176–7, 208, 331, 336, 338, 371–2, 375, 386
Herzl, Theodor, 62, 367, 409
Herzog, Elizabeth, 365, 434
Hillel, Shlomo, 92, 373–4, 420
Hirschler, Gertrude, 366, 420
Histadrut, 43, 63, 106–7, 111, 128, 133, 135–6, 142–4, 146–7, 168, 170, 174–6, 178, 199, 201, 210, 221, 225, 238, 249, 385, 392–3, 401, 404
Historical background: Arab–Jewish relations, 65–9; Oriental–Ashkenazi relations, 48–61; religious–nonreligious relations, 61–5
Hoetink, H., 190, 355, 396, 397, 420
Hofman, John E., 119, 123, 199, 201, 207, 360, 420–1, 431, 442–3
Holocaust, 51, 65, 86, 108, 372
Horowitz, Dan, 225, 421

Horowitz, Irving L., 1, 421
Horton, John, 7, 36, 421
Howe, Irving, 362, 421, 428

Ideology, 10; as a component of core-culture, 14, 58, 76–7, 86, 179; and science, xiii, 7, 18–20, 33, 36, 40, 252, 353, 357–8; underlying the study of Israel, 33, 36, 353–4, 363
Identity, 24, 249, 353; of Israeli Arabs, 84, 150, 188, 250, 255; of Jews, 24, 26, 56, 361; of Orientals, 58, 241, 361–2; of religious Jews, 74, 150, 255; right to separate identity, 46, 83, 134, 150, 233, 255; *see also* self-identity
Immigrant absorption, 21–4, 42, 58, 60, 76, 86, 89–98, 189, 244–5, 367, 395
Inbar, Dan, 127, 421
Inbar, Michael, 41, 93, 374, 421, 439
Independent Liberal Party, 372
Inequality, 1, 4, 15, 110–11, 136–82, 184, 187, 217, 235, 237, 241–6, 249–52, 256, 258–62, 274–6, 279, 282–344, 350–2, 356–7, 385–94; *see also* 'gaps in . . .', 'disparities in . . .'
Initial group contact: between Arabs and Jews, 74; between Orientals and Ashkenazim, 71–2, 369–70; between religious and nonreligious Jews, 73
Integration, *see* bases of integration, social separation
Intelligence, 115, 122, 162, 391; *see also* seker
Interdependence: between Israeli Arabs and Jews, 46, 99–100; 227; between Orientals and Ashkenazim, 95–8, 108, 226; between religious and nonreligious Jews, 98–9, 226–7

Intergroup relations, 70, 369; criticisms of the literature on, 6–7, 354; patterns of, 363–4

Intermarriage: between non-Jews and Jews, 27, 29, 45, 75, 134, 136, 248, 250, 385, 409; between Orientals and Ashkenazim, 129–30, 235, 345, 383; between religious and nonreligious Jews, 27, 133

'Inverted pyramid', 245, 408

Invidious distinctions, see discrimination, ethnocentrism, paternalism, prejudice, racism

Iraqi Jews, 50, 54, 91, 93, 130, 184, 366, 396

Islam, 49–50, 63, 219, 364–5, 385, 403–4

Isolation in ecological location: between Israeli Arabs and Jews, 135, 404; between Orientals and Ashkenazim, 125–6, 343, 382; between religious and nonreligious Jews, 132–3, 383–4

Isolation in impersonal frameworks: between Israeli Arabs and Jews, 31, 135–6, 221; between Orientals and Ashkenazim, 126–9, 220, 282–3, 344; between religious and nonreligious Jews, 43, 63, 133, 220–1, 384

Isolation in personal contacts: between Israeli Arabs and Jews, 31, 136, 385; between Orientals and Ashkenazim, 129–30; between religious and nonreligious Jews, 133

Israel, government, 83, 367, 421, 437

Israel Labour Party, 79–81, 85, 107, 144–7, 165, 177, 246, 249, 372, 386, 404, 410

Israel, Ministry of Education and Culture, 382, 421, 442

Israeli Socialist Organization (Matzpen), 33, 254, 360–2, 371

Israel, state of: centralization of power, 106–7; as colonial state, 33–5; constitution issue, 123–4, 381; culture, 38, 105, 118–19, 217–18, 248; Declaration of Independence, 27, 123–4; democracy, 38, 83, 94–5, 106, 109–10, 241, 244, 252–3, 264; economy, 39, 106–7, 110–11, 168, 225–6, 232, 241, 377, 390, 244–5, 252; Herrenvolk democracy, 21, 35, 256, 264; images of, 21, 111, 376, 397; Jewish-Zionist state, 60–1, 78–9, 83–5, 94–5, 102, 105, 109, 112, 116, 120, 150, 197, 199, 218, 224–5, 232, 240, 248, 250–2, 254–5; literature on, 436–8; local power, 106, 125–6, 143, 146, 170–3, 382; pluralism in, xiv–xv, 2–4, 110–36, 148–50, 258–65, 274–6, 280, 353; political development of dominant group, 108–9; sociology in, 3–4, 25, 36, 39–40, 155, 164; Western state, 105–6, 109, 243, 377

Jacobsen, Chanoch, 443

Jansen, G. H., 360–1, 421

Jencks, Christopher, 387, 394, 422

Jensen, Arthur R., 391

Jewish Agency, 43, 91–2, 103, 107, 142–3, 145–6, 166, 170, 174–5, 198, 225, 250, 367, 373, 422

Jewish consciousness programme, 120

Jiryis, Sabri, 207, 400, 403, 406, 422, 442

Judaism, 26, 37, 78–9, 81–2, 94, 105, 119, 124, 218–19, 248, 262, 403–5; Conservative and Reform, 26, 28, 44, 52, 62, 64, 73, 79, 117, 145, 186, 212–13

Juliani, Richard N., 407, 433

Kahane, Meir, 84, 422
Kahane, Reuven, 163, 422
Karaites, 353
Kashrut, 27, 29, 65, 80, 117, 124, 131, 186, 197, 212, 247, 383
Katz, Elihu, 78, 114, 119, 379–80, 395, 422, 437, 439–40
Katz, Jacob, 365, 422, 440
Katzenelson, Kalman, 48–9, 193, 377, 422
Katznelson, Ira, 19, 422
Kfar Kassim Affair, 405–6
Kinloch, Graham C., 362, 422
Kipnis, Baruch, 442
Klaff, Chaim, 122, 141, 207, 420
Kleif, Baheoj, 120, 422
Kleinberger, Aharon F., 162, 189, 422, 437
Klinov-Malul, Ruth, 98, 389, 422
Knaani, David, 440
Kokhavi, S. Y., 84, 422
Kook, Rabbi Abraham Isaac, 367
Kornhauser, William, 8, 355, 423
Kugelmass, Sol, 115, 122, 162, 391, 423–4
Kuhn, Thomas S., 4, 423
Kulturkampf, 26–7, 30, 43, 80–1, 231, 241, 248, 359, 405, 409
Kulturkampf-modernization model, 4, 25–30
Kuper, Leo, xiii–xv, 6, 8–12, 14, 16–19, 151, 355–8, 422, 431–2
Kurzweil, Barukh, 371, 410, 423
Kwan, Kian M., 354, 430

Lacqueur, Walter, 55, 423, 437
Ladino, 51
Land Acquisition (Validation of Operations and Compensation) Law, 384
Landau, Jacob M., 85, 214, 360, 368, 372, 386, 403, 416, 423, 442
Landau, Simha F., 122, 423
Land expropriations, 135, 198, 215, 384–5
Land Transfer (Acquisition for Public Purposes) Ordinance, 384

Language, 105, 111–12, 116, 134, 216, 378–9; pronunciation of Hebrew, 112, 185, 379, 394
Lapid, Yoseph, 400, 423
Laumann, Edward, 8, 152, 407, 423
Law of Return, 26, 28, 35, 60, 65, 80, 86, 105, 134, 197, 213–14, 250, 362, 370, 399
Layish, Aharon, 121, 360, 407, 423
Leadership, 10; Israeli Arab, 84–5, 147–8, 215–16, 224–5; Oriental, 77–8, 130, 184, 193–4, 204–5, 208–12, 222, 245–6, 395, 397; religious, 133, 222–3, 404–5; Romanian, 77, 184, 193–4, 204–5, 222, 395, 397–8
League Against Religious Coercion, 213
Legal and extra-legal distinctions, 14, 123; between Israeli Arabs and Jews, 134–5; between Orientals and Ashkenazim, 124–5; between religious and nonreligious Jews, 131–2, 384
Leisure, 114–15, 120–1
Lenski, Gerhard E., 180, 387–8, 423
Lesch, Ann M., 368, 423
Leslie, Clement S., 359, 367, 424, 441
LeVine, Robert, 354, 365, 424
Levy, Haim, 154, 158, 389, 424
Levy, Shlomit, 115, 119, 122, 129, 141, 202, 207, 371, 384, 420, 424, 437
Levy, Zipporah, 199, 360, 423, 427
Levantinization, 88, 95, 184–5, 189, 243, 372, 407
Lewin, Kurt, 98
Lewis, Oscar, 388, 424
Liberal Party, 176–7, 327, 331, 334, 336, 338, 371–2, 386, 404
Lieberson, Stanley, 71, 369, 424
Lieblich, Amia, 115, 122, 162, 391, 424
Liebman, Charles S., 119, 218, 417, 423–4, 441

Liebowitz, Yashaeihu, 359, 424, 441
Lijphart, Arend, 43, 424
Likud, 146, 166, 178, 335, 383; see also Gahal
Linenberg, Ron, 406, 424
Lissak, Moshe, 25, 40, 57, 59, 180, 225, 382, 389, 421, 424, 439
Lobel, Eli, 360, 368, 418
Lumer, Hyman, 360, 424, 437

Ma'abarot (transit camps), 91–2
Ma'arakh (Alignment), 146, 178, 332, 335, 337–8, 383, 404
Mafdal Party, see National Religious Party
Magubane, Bernard, 18, 357, 424, 433
Maki Party, see Communist Party
Mamzerim (bastards), 29, 360, 398
Mapai Party, 80, 128, 175–8, 331, 336, 338, 393, 404
Mapam Party, 76, 135, 146, 176–7, 331, 336–7, 372, 386, 425
Marbek slaughterhouse, 212
Mar-Haim, Matathia, 191, 430
Mar'i, Sami K., 121, 141, 385, 425, 442
Marmorstein, Emile, 367–8, 425, 441
Marriage and divorce, 26, 28–9, 44, 65, 75, 81, 187, 213, 247–8, 250, 395, 398, 403, 409; see also family, intermarriage
Marriage, mixed, see Intermarriage
Marx, Emanuel, 442
Marxism, xiii, 11, 16, 18–19, 33, 36, 102, 153, 357–8, 360, 388, 392
Mason, Philip, 1, 19, 355–6, 363–4, 369, 425
Matras, Judah, 113–14, 158, 363, 380–2, 390, 425, 437, 439
Matzpen (Israeli Socialist Organization), 33, 254, 360–2, 371

McRae, Kenneth, 43, 424
Medding, Peter, 165, 425
Meir, Golda, 88, 90
Menachem, Gila, 129, 425
Mendelsohn, Ezra, 366, 425
Merger of Exiles, see Mizug Galuyot
Meron, Simha, 195, 359, 425, 441
Merton, Robert K., 356, 425
Michaeli, O., 127, 418
Militant views: among Israeli Arabs, 207; among Orientals, 204–5, 210–11, 401; among religious Jews, 206
Military government, 99–100, 135, 148, 198, 214–16, 228, 239, 384
Miller, Herman P., 387–8, 394, 425
Millet system, 45, 57, 63
Milstein, Uri, 372, 425
Ministry of Religious Affairs, 44, 124–5, 145, 359, 381–2
Minority, Arab, see Arab–Jewish division
Mizrahi, 62–4, 73, 78–80, 117, 131, 133, 213, 218, 220, 247, 261, 367–8, 404
Mizug Galuyot, 23, 39–40, 42, 58, 77–8, 80, 86, 89, 94, 125, 184, 186, 204, 217, 222, 241–4, 253–5, 260, 371
Mobility, social, 12, 107, 226, 388; of Israeli Arabs, 46, 224, 226, 239, 249; of Orientals, 40, 42, 97–100, 103, 142, 154–63, 165–6, 180–2, 193–4, 222, 224, 226, 235, 244–7, 390, 408; of religious Jews, 226, 237, 247, 406; see also Poverty
Mobilization of the nondominant group: Israeli Arabs, 136, 221; Orientals, 130, 220, 222; religious Jews, 64, 133–4, 221, 249
Modernization: ideology of, 76–7, 86, 90, 108, 179; of Israel, 264; of Israeli Arabs, 4, 30–2, 120–2, 249; of

Oriental Jews, 4, 21–2, 39, 50, 56, 61, 90; of religious Jews, 4, 26, 30, 61, 94, 246–7, 404–5; theory of, 36
Moked, 372
Morgenstein, Arie, 124, 425, 441
Moroccan Jews, 50, 87–8, 91, 162, 180, 184, 190, 203, 209–11, 373, 391, 393, 396, 401
Morris, C. T., 378
Moskin, Robert J., 88, 425
Moynihan, Daniel P., 8, 374, 419
Multiple cleavages: affecting Arab–Jewish relations, 41, 104–5; affecting Oriental–Ashkenazi relations, 41, 101–4, 375; affecting religious–nonreligious relations, 104, 375
Myrdal, Gunnar, 388, 425

Nadel, Barukh, 390, 425
Nahas, Dunia Habib, 214, 425
Nakhleh, Khalil, 122–3, 147, 426, 442
National Religious Party (Mafdal), 29, 44, 79, 118, 128, 145–6, 175–8, 223, 237, 331, 335–6, 371, 382–3, 386, 393, 405–6
National minority, status of, 46, 84, 187, 198, 250–1, 255
Nationalism, Palestinian, 67–8, 84
Nationalist consciousness or identity: among Israeli Arabs, 32, 46–7, 123, 219, 224, 250–1; among Orientals, 112, 217, 362, 379; among religious Jews, 120
Nation-building perspective, 21, 36–9, 264–5
Negation of ethnicity, see Mizug Galuyot
Newberger, Benjamin, 362, 426
New directions, author's proposals, 254–7
Newman, William M., 6, 219, 355, 357, 426
Nikitina, Galina, 360, 426
Nini, Yehuda, 193, 365, 426

Ninio, Anat, 115, 162, 391, 424
Nobbe, Charles E., 388, 429
Noel, Donald, 354, 413
N'ture Karta, 65, 78, 359, 399, 405
Nwaneri, V. C., 378, 393, 426

Oded, Yitzhak, 198, 385, 426
Oppenheimer, Jonathan W. S., 443
Oren, Stephen, 237, 367, 372, 426, 441
Oriental–Ashkenazi division, 3, 354; absorption-modernization model of, 4, 21–5, 39–41, 86, 89, 92, 96, 164; Arab–Israeli conflict affecting, 98, 108, 206, 228–9, 232, 243, 407–8; bases of integration, 216–17, 219–20, 222, 226–9, 233; colonial perspective of, 35, 39; comparisons with other divisions, 259–64, 271–9; competitive-fluid pattern, 242, 246; congruity of group goals, 76–8, 85, 217; countermeasures by the dominant group, 211–12, 277, 402–3; cross-cutting affiliations, 149, 219–20; cultural autonomy, 143; cultural diversity, 112–16, 234–5, 274; cultural synthesis, 25, 184–5, 217; discrimination against Orientals, 40–2, 55, 76, 87, 89–94, 125, 154–5, 159, 188–95, 203–4, 209–10, 226, 277, 285, 366, 373–4, 395, 397–8, 402; dissatisfactions, 57–8, 202–6, 210–11, 401; dynamic paternalism–co-optation model of, 39–42, 90, 109, 166, 181, 236, 242, 260–1, 364; elite accommodation, 97, 222; ethnocentrism against Orientals, 38, 53–5, 59, 86–92, 103, 105, 192–3, 235, 372–3, 376, 395–7; external factors affecting, 228–9;

failures of group goals, 184–6; features of society-at-large affecting, 105–9; future developments, 35, 241–6; gaps in education, 137, 159–63, 297–308; gaps in material wellbeing, 137, 153–7, 282–9; gaps in occupational distribution, 137, 157–9, 290–6; historical background, 48–61; identity, 58, 115–16, 241, 361–2; inequality, 178–82, 184, 217, 235, 241–6, 256, 259–61, 282–341, 350–2; interdependence, 95–8, 108, 226; intermarriage, 129–30, 235, 345, 383; literature on, 4, 60, 358, 438–9; multiple cleavages in Israel affecting, 41, 101–4, 375; new directions, 255–7; past trends, 42, 234–6, 239–40, 406; paternalism vis-à-vis Orientals, 41–2, 59, 103, 184, 244, 246, 396; patterns of conflict, 183–6, 188–95, 202–6, 208–12; pluralism, 111–16, 124–30, 234–5, 241, 261, 343–5, 347, 349; political coercion, 227; power disparities, 40, 142–3, 164–81, 235, 241–2, 309–42, 351; prejudice against Ashkenazim, 41, 108, 191, 194, 397–8; prejudice against Orientals, 24, 39, 41, 108, 189–91, 194–5, 204, 277, 358; primary bases of, 71–3; protests of nondominant group, 208–12, 277, 402–3, 408; social separation, 124–30, 220, 235, 282–3, 343–5, 382; socioeconomic gaps, 25, 137, 153–63, 235, 241–2, 282–308; statehood affecting, 60–1, 363; statistics on, 267–8, 280–347, 349–52; undercurrents,

40, 86–94, 188; value consensus, 105, 111–16, 122, 216–17, 219, 232, 261, 274; in the Yishuv, 40, 56–60, 66, 127–8, 366–7, 394; and Zionism, 38, 40, 53–6, 59, 86, 365–6
Oriental caucus, 165, 374
Orientals, 49–61, 66, 79, 86, 235, 245, 364–6, 370, 372; and Arabs, 49–50, 102–4, 242–3, 361, 364–5, 376, 407–8; see also Sephardim
Ortar, Gina, 115, 162, 426, 439

Padan, Dorith, 358, 389, 413
Palestinian Arabs, 3, 34, 38, 65–9, 86, 103, 107, 110, 140–1, 187, 230, 238, 253–4, 262, 362, 369, 385–6
Palestinian–Jewish division, 2–4, 35, 140–1, 241, 385
Palestinian Liberation Organization (PLO), 214, 225, 230, 254, 360–2, 426
Park, Robert E., 354
Parsons, Talcott, 8–9
Past trends: in Arab–Jewish relations, 46–7, 238–40; in Oriental–Ashkenazi relations, 42, 234–6, 239–40, 406; in religious–nonreligious relations, 45, 236–40
Patai, Raphael, 25, 51, 53–5, 72, 87–8, 101, 114, 130, 184–5, 209, 353, 359, 364–5, 367, 394, 426, 428, 437, 439
Paternalism: vis-à-vis Arabs, 103, 141, 199; vis-à-vis Orientals, 41–2, 59, 103, 184, 244, 246, 396; see also discrimination, ethnocentrism, prejudice, quotas–benign, racism
Patterns of conflict, 16, 183–216, 277; see also dissatisfactions, countermeasures by the dominant group, discrimination, failures of group goals, prejudice,

protests of nondominant group

Peleg, Rachel, 123, 189, 411, 413, 441

Peres, Yochanan, 25, 31–2, 41, 84–5, 100, 103, 114, 116, 122–3, 129–30, 187, 190–1, 194–5, 199–200, 203, 207–8, 360, 368, 371, 379–80, 383, 386–7, 397–8, 403, 417–18, 426–7, 431, 439, 442–3

Peretz, Don, 141, 198, 368, 427, 443

Persian Jews, 50, 88

Pluralism, xiii–xiv, 4, 258; Arab–Jewish, 120–3, 134–6, 238, 249–50, 347, 349; conceptual scheme of, 12–18, 267–70, 356; critical evaluation of, 9, 18–20, 355; Despres on, 355; distinguished from other perspectives, xiii, 2, 8, 11–12, 36–9, 259, 355; Furnivall on, xiii, 6–8; and ideology, xiii, 19–20, 358; indeterminacy, 10–12, 19, 240, 355; in Israel, xiv–xv, 2–4, 38–9, 63–4, 76, 110–36, 235–8, 241, 246, 249–50, 254–5, 259–65, 343–5, 347–8, 353; Kuper on, 8–11; meanings, 2, 14, 353; Oriental–Ashkenazi, 111–16, 124–30, 234–5, 241, 261, 343–5, 347, 349; plural society, 7–9, 19; religious–nonreligious, 63–4, 116–20, 130–4, 236–7, 241, 246, 347; Smith on, 8–9; Schermerhorn on, 12; summary measures of, 14–15, 356–7; theory of, 9, 19, 258–9, 357; van den Berghe on, 11–12

Poale Agudat Israel, 65, 176, 371

Policies: towards Israeli Arabs, 46, 83–4, 197–9, 375; towards Orientals, 71, 77, 109, 375

Police Law, 359

Political coercion, 45–6, 150, 227–8

Political parties, 175–6, 225; see also Herut party, Israel Labour Party, etc.

Poll, Solomon, 427

Porter, John, 388, 427

Portes, Alejandro, 36, 427

Poverty, 23, 42, 138, 156, 158, 162, 180–1, 197, 210–11, 219, 226, 241, 243–7, 261, 401, 408; see also mobility, social

Power disparities, 15, 141–8, 163–81, 309–42, 351, 392; see also 'disparities in . . .'

Preale, Ilana, 115, 427

Prime Minister's Commission, 139, 375, 389, 390, 402, 427, 439

Prejudice, 6–7, 388; against Askhenazim, 41, 191, 194, 397–8; against Israeli Arabs, 41, 199–201, 277, 376; against Orientals, 24, 39, 41, 108, 189–91, 194–5, 204, 277, 358; against religious Jews, 44, 195–6, 277, 399; see also discrimination, ethnocentrism, paternalism, quotas–benign, racism

Primary bases of pluralistic divisions, see definition of group membership, initial group contact, relative size of nondominant group

Proteksia, 192

Protestant ethic, 115, 122

Protests of nondominant group: Israeli Arabs, 213–16, 224, 277; Orientals, 208–12, 277, 402–3, 408; religious Jews, 212–13, 277

Public Inquiry Commission, 89, 154, 156, 198, 209, 373, 375, 378, 389, 427, 439

Public perception of cultural diversity, 116, 122, 236–7

Quasi-caste, 45, 47, 74–5, 86, 95,

102–5, 136, 139, 219–21, 242, 245, 370, 376

Quotas, benign, 42, 97, 106, 143, 174, 193, 195, 212, 222, 224, 243, 246, 373, 393, 397; *see also* discrimination, ethnocentrism, paternalism, prejudice, racism

Rabbinic courts, 27–8, 43, 63, 80, 124, 145, 248, 398
Rabin, Chaim, 378–9, 427
Racism, 38, 192, 231, 264, 360–1, 376, 400–1; *see also* discrimination, ethnocentrism, paternalism, prejudice, quotas–benign
Rafi Party, 165, 177, 331, 333, 338, 393
Rahav, Giora, 208, 430
Rakah Party, *see* Communist Party
Ratosh, Younathan, 410, 423, 427, 437
Reform Judaism, 26, 28, 44, 52, 62, 64, 73, 79, 117, 145, 186, 212–13
Reines, Rabbi Isaac Jacob, 367
Reisman, David, 8
Rejwan, Nissim, 49, 56, 88, 193, 365, 372, 427–8, 439
Rekhess, Eli, 400, 428, 443
Relative size of nondominant group: Israeli Arabs, 75; Orientals, 72–3; religious Jews, 74
Religion, freedom from, 28–30, 195–6, 206, 248, 398
Religion, freedom of, 27–30, 80, 124, 195, 206
Religion, separation from state, 27, 35, 43, 62–3, 79, 82, 133, 186, 219, 247–9, 253–5, 367, 372, 404
Religious attitudes, beliefs and values, 30, 78–9, 117–21, 186–7, 380
Religious compulsion, *see* religion, freedom from

Religious councils, 27, 43, 63, 124, 145, 248
Religious legislation, 26–30, 80, 82, 131–2, 212–13, 247–8, 383, 386
Religious–nonreligious division, 3, 353–4; Arab–Israeli conflict affecting, 45, 228–9, 232, 248; bases of integration, 217–18, 220–1, 222–3, 226–9, 233; colonial perspective of, 35, 43; comparisons with other divisions, 259, 261–4, 271–9; congruity of group goals, 78–83; 85; consociationalism, 43, 45, 109, 218, 222, 232, 237, 248, 256, 264, 405; contested accommodation model of, 43–5, 98–9, 222, 232, 237, 249, 261–2; countermeasures by the dominant group, 212–13, 277; cross-cutting affiliations, 220–1; cultural autonomy, 43, 143, 145, 149, 186, 221–3, 386–7, 405; cultural diversity, 116–20, 236–7, 241, 246, 274; discrimination against religious Jews, 195–7, 399; dissatisfactions, 206, 222; elite accommodation, 222–3, 404–5; external factors affecting, 229; failures of group goals, 186–7; features of society-at-large affecting, 109; future developments, 30, 35, 246–9; gaps in education, 138; gaps in material wellbeing, 138; gaps in occupational distribution, 138; historical background, 61–5; identity, 74, 119, 150, 255; inequality, 138, 143–5, 237, 261; interdependence, 98–9, 226–7; intermarriage, 27, 133; *Kulturkamf-* modernization model of, 4, 25–30; literature on, 3, 25–6,

358–9, 440–1; multiple cleavages in Israel affecting, 104, 375; new directions, 255–7; past trends, 45, 236–40; patterns of conflict, 186–7, 195–7, 206–7, 212–13; pluralism, 63–4, 116–20, 130–4, 236–7, 241, 246, 347; political coercion, 227; power disparities, 143–5, 237, 331–6, 348; prejudice against religious Jews, 44, 94, 195–6, 277, 399; primary bases of, 73–4; protests of nondominant group, 212–13, 277; social separation, 27, 43, 63–4, 130–4, 220–1, 237, 241, 249, 347, 383–4; socioeconomic gaps, 138, 237; statehood affecting, 65; statistics on, 347–8; undercurrents, 94; value consensus, 117–20, 217–18, 232, 274; in the Yishuv, 63–5, 124, 130, 261, 367–8; and Zionism, 45, 61–5, 78–9, 261

Religious observance, 73–4, 101–2, 113, 119, 130–1, 138, 180, 206, 219–21, 375, 379, 406

Religious status quo, 43–5, 65, 79, 101, 109, 149, 186–7, 195, 212–13, 217–18, 223, 233, 237, 247–9, 255, 262, 368, 409

Religious style, 51–2, 112–13, 185, 189, 365, 375, 379

Religious Workers' Faction, 144, 404

Religious zealotry, 213, 218, 247, 403

Remba, Oded, 107, 377, 428

Research Team, 195, 428

Rex, John, 16, 18, 37, 355, 357, 400, 428

Rim, Yeshayahu, 190, 428

Rivner, Miriam, 127, 412

Rodinson, Maxime, 33, 360, 428, 437

Romanian Jews, 93–4; leadership, 77, 184, 193–4, 204–5, 222, 395, 397–8

Ronen, Matti, 402, 428

Rose, Richard, 15, 394, 428

Rosen, Harry, 385, 428

Rosenak, Michael, 78, 428, 441

Rosenfeld, Henry, 121, 140, 360, 368, 374, 414, 428, 442–3

Rosenzweig, Rafael, 374, 429

Rothstein, Edward, 122, 422

Roter, Raphael, 110, 393, 429

Rouhana, Nadeem, 123, 421, 442

Rouleau, Eric, 88, 429

Royal Commission on Bilingualism and Biculturalism, 374, 388, 394, 429

Rubinstein, Amnon, 359, 367, 385, 397, 399, 429, 441

Russian Jews, 72, 93, 210

Sabra superman, the stereotype of, 200, 399–400

Sabri, Mahsan, 134, 429

Samaritans, 353

Samet, Moshe, 358, 429, 441

Samuel, Maurice, 372, 429

Sarsour, Sa'ad, 121, 429

Schermerhorn, R. A., xiii, 6–7, 9, 16, 151, 353, 355–8, 369–70, 377, 389, 429

Schmelz, Usiel O., 203, 401, 429

Schmid, Calvin, 388, 429

Schwartz, Gila, 186, 379, 419

Schwarz, Walter, 215, 429

Secular religion, 218, 380

Segal, Esther, 208, 430

Segal, Ronald, 1, 362, 429

Segalman, Ralph, 120, 422

Segre, V.D., 359, 368–9, 429, 437

Segregation, see Social separation

Seker, 115, 125, 161–2, 306–7; see also intelligence

Self-identity: of Israeli Arabs, 31–2, 122–3, 354, 360; of Jews, 122–3, 371, 381; of Orientals, 115–16; of religious Jews, 119; see also identity

Seligman, Lester G., 175, 429
Selzer, Michael, 192, 429, 439
Sephardic Workers' Union, 59
Sephardim (Sephardic Jews),
    49–53, 57, 59, 66, 166, 365,
    368, 393–4; see also Orientals
Setting, 13, 269, 356
Shabtai, K., 88, 429
Shafat, Rivka, 383, 427
Shaki, Avner, 190, 429
Shalit case, 212
Shalom Zim passenger ship, 212
Shamai, Nira, 110, 393, 429
Shapira, Rina, 392, 429
Shapira, Yonathan, 225, 430
Sharan (Singer), Shlomo, 115, 427
Shava, Menashe, 403, 430
Shelah, Hanan, 383, 418, 440
Shelah, Ilana, 129, 380, 430
Shemesh, Ezekiel, 386, 430
Shephatia, Leah, 391, 431
Shibutani, Tamotsu, 354, 430
Shidlowski, Benyamin, 239, 430
Shiloh, Isaac S., 360, 430
Shils, Edward, 8
Shimoni, Yaakov, 368, 430, 443
Shneller, Raphael, 380, 430
Shoham, S. Giora, 208, 430
Shokeid, Moshe, 113, 416
Shrift, Ruth, 130, 427
Shtal, Abraham, 189, 191, 430,
    439
Shumsky, Abraham, 358, 430, 439
Shuval, Judith T., 25, 41, 72, 103,
    189, 194, 430, 437, 439
Shye, S., 121, 207, 411
Sicron, Moshe, 437
Simon, Oriel, 358, 430
Simon, Rita J., 409, 430
Simpson, George E., 7, 431
Six-Day War, 2, 24, 68–9, 103,
    108, 135, 142, 161, 165, 190,
    229, 231, 237–8, 245, 360,
    375, 384, 403
Smilansky, Moshe, 115, 162, 391,
    431
Smilansky, Sara, 391, 431
Smith, Hanuch, 106, 377, 393,
    431

Smith, M. G., xiii, 6, 8–12, 14,
    17–19, 233, 355, 357–8, 369,
    423, 431–2
Smooha, Sammy, xiv–xv, 6, 201,
    207, 209, 254, 356, 387, 431,
    439, 441, 443
Social class, see class
Social conflict, see conflict,
    patterns of conflict
Socialism, socialist ideology, 34–5,
    76, 86, 108, 179, 184, 245,
    371, 409
Social separation, 14, 123–37,
    219; see also intermarriage,
    isolation in ecological
    location; isolation in
    impersonal frameworks;
    isolation in personal contacts,
    legal and extra-legal
    distinctions, mobilization of
    the nondominant group
Socioeconomic gaps, 15, 39,
    137–41, 153–62, 178–82, 267,
    282–308, 350, 385; see also
    'gaps in . . .'
Sohlberg, Shaul C., 122, 431
Somatic norm distance, 190, 397
Somatic norm image, 190, 396–7
South Africa, 1, 8, 10–11, 14, 20,
    35, 37, 47, 74–5, 102, 258,
    355, 357, 361, 364, 378, 388,
    397, 400
Spiegel, Erika, 373, 431
Spilerman, Seymour, 189, 431
Spiro, Shimon, 129, 425
Sprinzak, Ehud, 209, 431, 437
Starr, L., 163, 422
Status dissatisfaction: among
    Israeli Arabs, 207–8; among
    Orientals, 202–3, 205–6;
    among religious Jews, 206
Stendel, Ori, 134, 386, 399, 431,
    443
Stock, Ernest, 99, 103, 198, 385–
    6, 432, 443
Subculture, 14; Israeli Arabs and
    Jews, 120–3, 218–19, 249,
    274, Orientals and
    Ashkenazim, 112–16, 122,

217, 261, 274; religious and nonreligious Jews, 117–20, 217–18, 274
Supreme Court, 28, 125, 144, 146, 173–4, 215, 359, 398, 401, 405
Syrkin, Marie, 362
Szyliowicz, Joseph, 391, 432

Tahon, Chana H., 364, 432
Talmon, Jacob L., 362, 432
Tamarin, Georges R., 195, 208, 374, 398, 399, 403, 432, 441
Tartakower, Arieh, 364, 432
Taviv, Avraham, 55, 432
Taviv, Mordechai, 366, 432
Teller, J. L., 358, 432
Tessler, Mark A., 85, 123, 207, 219, 401, 410, 432
Tevet, Shabtai, 87, 92, 432
Theopolitics, 30, 360
Torah Kingdom, 409–10; see also halakha state
Tscmah, Shlomo, 55, 432
Tsoriel, Yosef, 190, 432

Undercurrents: in attitudes towards Israeli Arabs, 94–5, 199; in attitudes towards Oriental Jews, 40, 86–94, 188; in attitudes towards religious Jews, 94
United States, 1, 9, 11, 20, 37, 52, 74, 102, 106, 109–11, 179, 245, 353, 362, 364, 377–8, 383–8, 391, 393–5, 407–8
United States Bureau of Census, 394, 432
Union of Pioneers of the Orient, 59
Utopias, 252, 254, 409; Arab Palestinian state, 353–4; binational state, 409; Canaanite state, 253, 410; democratic secular state, 254, 410; exclusive Jewish–Zionist state, 84, 188, 252–3, 409; halakha state, 253, 409–10; Matzpen's, 362; socialist state, 409

Value consensus: Israeli Arabs and Jews, 120–3, 218–19, 249, 274; Orientals and Ashkenazim, 105, 111–16, 122, 216–17, 219, 232, 261, 274; religious and nonreligious Jews, 117–20, 217–18, 232, 274
van den Berghe, Pierre L., xiii, 6–9, 11–12, 14–20, 74, 110, 254–8, 365, 369, 400, 432–3
Vander Zanden, James W., 7, 433
Violence, 17, 208, 227–8, 405–6
Voting: Israeli Arabs, 214, 376; Orientals, 106, 128–9, 177, 203, 205, 208–9, 376–7, 382–3, 401; religious Jews, 133, 221, 249

Wadi Salib riots, 77, 89, 92, 209, 211–12, 227, 235, 376, 402, 408
Wakf, 147
Wanefsky, J., 367, 433
Warner, Lloyd W., 74, 433
Waschitz, Yosef, 140, 368, 433, 443
Weber, Max, 387–8
Weiler, Gershon, 441
Weingrod, Alex, 23, 142, 171, 185, 189, 353, 373, 379, 419, 433, 439
Weintraub, S., 127, 418
Weis, Shevah, 170, 382, 386, 433
Welfare state, 153, 182, 388–9
Weller, Leonard, 438
Westie, Frank, 354, 433
'Who is a Jew' issue, 26–7, 29, 65, 75, 80, 186–7, 213, 400–1
Williams, Robin M., 369–70, 433
Willner, Dorothy, 358, 433
Wilson, William J., 427, 433
Women's Equal Rights Law, 27, 121, 398
World Federation of Sephardic Communities, 59, 166, 175, 381, 408
World Zionist Organization (WZO), 54, 62, 174–5, 366, 408

Yalan, Emmanuel, 443
Yam, Yosef, 115, 162, 391, 431
Yancey, William L., 407, 433
Yaron, Zvi, 367, 434
Yehuda, Zvi, 438
Yemenite Jews, 50, 54–5, 91, 130, 185, 190, 364, 366, 368, 375, 396
Yeshivot, 43, 117–18, 132, 223, 236, 246, 380, 383–4
Yiddish, 51–2
Yinger, Milton, 7, 369, 431, 434
Yinon, Avraham, 214, 434
Yinon, Yoel, 191, 434, 439
Yishuv, 58–60, 63–4, 66, 95, 108, 169, 208, 225, 245, 363, 367; Arabs in the, 54, 65–9; Orientals in the, 40, 56–60, 66, 127–8, 366–7, 394; religious Jews in the, 63–5, 124, 130, 261, 367–8
Yom Kippur War, 2, 108, 123, 128, 135, 166, 169, 190, 200–1, 231, 243, 251–2, 376, 381, 384, 401, 403
Yuchtman (Yaar), Efraim, 383, 427
Yuval-Davis, N., 187, 360, 427
Yisraeli, Yair, 373, 434

Zadik, Baruch, 115, 434
Zaid, Kassim, 380, 434
Zak, Itai, 123, 207, 381, 386, 434, 443
Zarhi, Shaul, 374, 434
Zborowski, Mark, 365, 434
Zerubavel, Y., 53, 434
Zionism, 262, 371, 408; and Arabs, 38, 68, 207, 230; and colonialism, 33–4, 36–8, 55, 360–1; as a national ideology, 76, 86, 108, 179, 207, 245, 262, 409; and Orientals, 38, 40, 53–6, 59, 86, 365–6; and religious Jews, 45, 61–5, 78–9, 261; World Zionist Organization, 54, 62, 174–5, 366, 408
Zimmels, Hirsch J., 365, 434
Zloczower, Avraham, 111, 158, 390, 434, 439
Zubi, Sef Al-Din, 85
Zucker, Norman, 120, 212, 359–60, 372, 409, 434, 440–1
Zuckerman-Bareli, Chaya, 73, 81–2, 117, 119, 199, 358, 379–80, 434–5, 441

Love, Amy

Love, Amy

THE SELECTED LETTERS OF AMY CLAMPITT

Edited by Willard Spiegelman

COLUMBIA UNIVERSITY PRESS   NEW YORK

Columbia University Press
Publishers Since 1893
New York   Chichester, West Sussex
Copyright © 2005 Columbia University Press
All rights reserved

Library of Congress Cataloging-in-Publication Data
Clampitt, Amy.
   Love, Amy : the selected letters of Amy Clampitt /
edited by Willard Spiegelman
      p.   cm.
   Includes index.
   ISBN 0-231-13286-7 (alk. paper)
      2. Clampitt, Amy — Correspondence. 2. Poets,
American — 20th century — Correspondence.
   I. Spiegelman, Willard. II. Title.

   Ps3553.L23Z48 2005
   811'.54 — dc22
                                          2204065669

Casebound editions of Columbia University Press books
are printed on permanent and durable acid-free paper.

Printed in the United States of America
c 10 9 8 7 6 5 4 3 2 1

*For the family, friends,
and fans of Amy Clampitt*

Contents

A Poet's Life in Letters   *ix*

Acknowledgments   *xxiii*

The Letters of Amy Clampitt   *1*

Index   *291*

Illustrations appear following page 45

A Poet's Life in Letters

It is a sad but undeniable truth that the age of letter writing, among the literati as well as ordinary people, has probably come to a close. Some future scholar may have access to "The Complete E-Mails of Mr. or Ms X," but by the end of the twentieth century the great epistolary tradition had begun to wither following its vast flowering in the nineteenth. Lewis Carroll is said to have written ninety-seven thousand letters. Darwin's projected correspondence will require thirty volumes. After 1871, the year of *The Descent of Man,* he wrote approximately four letters a day (fifteen hundred a year), and he installed a mirror in his study window to catch sight of the postman when he walked up the drive. Still, bulk is not everything. In roughly seven years' worth of letters before his death at twenty-five Keats presented as full an autobiography of a young writer as has ever existed.

Because we like acquainting ourselves with people even at a distance, the draw of letters as a means of getting to know their author remains strong. Their allure requires little explanation: reading correspondence is one way of constructing or reimagining a life, like assembling a jigsaw puzzle slowly out of various mosaic pieces. And letters by literary figures (like Keats, Byron, George Eliot, and, in the century just past, Virginia

Woolf, Hart Crane, Elizabeth Bishop, and James Merrill) offer double in-sight, or open a double window, into a writer's work as well as his or her life. Like ordinary readers, scholars and biographers persist in wanting to have access to writers' letters as a possible way of explaining their authors' inner and outward selves. But even letters by careful stylistic craftsmen will frustrate as well as satisfy because the reader gets only a single possi-ble picture among many. There will always be missing pieces, of course; all accounts will be partial.

Amy Clampitt offers challenges to a would-be editor. Her literary life, at least her *public* literary life, absorbed only the last decade-and-a-half of her seventy-four years. Like her life, her letters can be divided, somewhat simplistically, between the years before her fame and the years of her celebrity, especially after the 1983 publication of *The Kingfisher*, the first of five commercial volumes published before her death in 1994. (In 1973 Clampitt had gathered together and published her early poems in a small volume entitled *Multitudes, Multitudes*. A second apprentice work, *The Isthmus*, appeared as a chapbook in 1981. None of these collected poems was ever reprinted.) Elizabeth Bishop, Robert Lowell, and James Merrill, the first two slightly older, the last slightly younger than Clampitt, all pub-lished their first poems when they were young. They became parts of the literary scene, even Bishop in far-off Brazil, and they wrote to other liter-ary people as well as to family and friends, all of whom suspected they were dealing with someone "important" or soon-to-be important. Clampitt, however, lived in quiet obscurity for sixty-three years. She nev-er became a part of a poets' community. She wrote few literary letters even after she became well-known, in part because she lacked the time to do so and in part because she had nothing to gain from it. In her sixties Clampitt had already established her styles and ideas, and she did not need to curry favor with other poets or editors or with the general public. Dur-ing her first foray into a poetry writing class, at the New School in 1977, she came up against an amiable young instructor named Dan Gabriel "who I think disapproves of the kind of thing I do" but who seemed to offer her bemused tolerance. In her first letter to the poet Mary Jo Salter (June 5, 1979) she observes that "a whole generation has been so deadened by rock music that an ear for the music of words may be obsolescent. 'You're in love with words,' I was told (by a poet, yet) in a tone of accu-sation. What he meant, I guess, was that I tend to use too many of them."

With regard to "words," their "music," and so many other poetic habits, Clampitt's "presiders" (to use Keats's term for Shakespeare) had been Keats,

Dorothy as well as William Wordsworth, Coleridge, Hopkins, Dickinson, Whitman, and George Eliot, not her contemporaries. Like all great poets, she was always addressing her departed masters as much as her living and future readers. In a 1990 letter about a George Eliot project to Jennifer Snodgrass at the Harvard University Press, Clampitt speaks to the combined isolation and community that all writers maintain: "Writers are all to some degree conscious of being lonely people; they crave a company they do not always find except in the vicarious company of those whose imaginative power has electrified their own." The nineteenth century came alive—electrically, vicariously—in her. Once she found her medium (poetry rather than fiction) and developed sufficient self-confidence to recite her poems in public and to submit them to journals, in the late 1970s, she was "discovered" and championed by Howard Moss at the *New Yorker*, by the young Mary Jo Salter, who mistook Clampitt for a contemporary when she was reading the slush pile of poems at the *Atlantic*, and by various critics, especially Helen Vendler, who reviewed her favorably and supported her for Guggenheim and MacArthur grants. With the exception of Clampitt's exchanges with Salter and Vendler, however, most of the literary correspondence in 1978–1994 is of a strictly business sort, essentially unexciting. One irony of Clampitt's sudden appearance on the literary scene was the dismissal of her work by certain feminist critics who scoffed at her bookish and intellectual temperament, her commitment to "high" culture, and her exuberantly descriptive style. And not only ideologues of her own gender made fun of her: James Dickey once observed, while seated next to her at dinner, that she wrote poems about flowers. She suffered from the same condescension from men that Dickinson and Bishop also received. Clampitt's letters—as well as her poetry—will prove, I hope, that she was an exemplary, determined, woman with strong political convictions as well as independent tastes.

The external shape of Clampitt's life before the decade of renown is clear in its outlines. (See Salter's vibrant, informative introduction to Clampitt's *Collected Poems*.) Born in Iowa to a Quaker family on June 15, 1920, the eldest of five children, bookish and slightly eccentric from an early age, she was graduated from Grinnell College in 1941 and immediately made a beeline to New York. She had a fellowship for graduate school at Columbia in English, dropped out before the year was up, soon went to work at Oxford University Press as a secretary, and rose to the post of promotions director for college textbooks. In 1949 she won an essay contest, sponsored by OUP, for which first prize was a trip to England. A bit after her return she left the press (1951) to write a novel. When no publisher accepted it, or two subsequent ones, she went back to work, this time as a reference librarian for the National Audubon Society. Birds, like cats, weather, and landscape remained perennially fascinating to Clampitt the woman and the writer: "She was galvanized by nature," remembers her oldest New York friend, Phoebe Hoss. (Indeed, in her mature poetry nature often stands in—as it did in her life—as a surrogate for any direct treatment of personal relations.)

In the sixties and seventies she came into her own in several ways. She started working as a freelance editor, then went to Dutton, began writing poetry with greater earnestness, and became involved in antiwar and other political pursuits. Is it coincidental that she took up poetry-writing for the first time since adolescence when she began to feel the attraction of the Episcopal Church in the mid-1950s? Or that her major poetry coincides with her abandonment of the church in the late 1960s and early 1970s in favor of political activism? In 1968 she met her longtime partner (whom she married several months before her death; she had always opposed marriage, on principle), Harold Korn, a law professor at NYU and later at Columbia University, through their shared political activity and work with the Village Independent Democrats. She moved in with Hal in 1973 (keeping this cohabitation something of a secret from her more conventional relatives) but also kept the small walk-up apartment in a Greenwich Village brownstone that remained the Woolfian "room of [her] own" until she was forced to give it up in the last year of her life when the building was converted into co-ops. Her poems began appearing in magazines, and she rose like a comet, praised by many and derided by some, on the literary scene in the late seventies. A MacArthur prize in 1992 gave her the first real money she ever had; with it she purchased a small cottage in Lenox, Massachusetts, between Tanglewood on one side and Edith Wharton's The Mount on the other. In the spring of 1993 she was diagnosed with ovarian cancer; she died in Lenox eighteen months later.

* * *

A literary editor is left with Clampitt's correspondence to family and friends mostly from the previous, precelebrity, decades. Even here lacunae inevitably appear. Trying to assemble the letters of someone born in 1920 means realizing that many people who may have saved her letters died before an editor could contact them. In addition, others did not know that their friend or relative would become "Amy Clampitt" and did not save her correspondence. There are no letters from the 1940s. The earliest letter I have found is a polite thank-you, and a report on recent activity, to her English host, Barbara Blay, from 1950. It is a model of etiquette and poise.

What was it like to be a young career woman in Manhattan, with a war going on, with soldiers and sailors shipping out and then, in 1945, returning to postwar American prosperity? Did Clampitt ever meet Madeleine L'Engle, or Leonard Bernstein, both of whom also lived on West 12th Street in the early 40s? Did she run with the Village crowd described by Anatole Broyard in *Kafka Was the Rage*?: "Nineteen forty-six was a good time—perhaps the best time—in the twentieth century. The war was over and there was a terrific sense of coming back, of repossessing life. Rents were cheap, restaurants were cheap, and it seemed to me that happiness itself might be cheaply had." What was Clampitt's version of Wordsworth's "Bliss was in that dawn to be alive, / But to be young was very heaven"? We shall never know unless we come upon new letters. (The husband of Barbara Clark, a Grinnell friend, threw out all of Clampitt's pre-1968 letters in an excess of housecleaning zeal.) And we confront more than just chronological omissions. Amy Clampitt and Hal Korn were inseparable most of the time; "being around him has the effect of expanding who I am, rather than diminishing and curtailing it as close associations so often do," she wrote to Barbara Clark in August, 1971, after Hal set out, solo, for a European trip. When they were apart they usually communicated with one another by phone. They seldom wrote. I have seen three of Clampitt's letters and several cards to Korn, written when she was at the Djerassi Foundation in the early 1980s and then visiting friends and relatives out West. She addressed him as "Lion" and signed herself with a "Prrrr" and a cat's face. The letters are reportorial rather than intimate.

What of earlier lovers? We know that she had them. The title poem of *The Kingfisher* deals somewhat opaquely in a third-person narrative with a love affair gone awry, which friends say was Clampitt's own. There was a broken engagement in the early fifties. Clampitt refers to several "young men" and serious love affairs in letters to her youngest brother, Philip, in the 1950s, but there are no "love letters" per se to anyone. She discusses Peter Marcasiano, a painter she met on a park bench in Paris in 1955, with whom she had an intense but (according to her friend Mary Russel) platonic relationship until 1958 when Marcasiano returned to Paris. There were also European men—one who married someone else, one who died—say Mary

Russel and Phoebe Hoss, her companion at the Oxford University Press between 1947 and 1949, but specific identities seem to have been lost. Amy was determined to remain private, resolute not to breach confidences in her letters. Instead, we have the meditative reflections of someone who has known love, in several forms and at various levels of depth, without the kind of specific details that would today be grist for gossip magazines. Reticence and self-revelation go hand in hand. What she withholds from the letters only adds to the luminous dignity of the writer's introspection.

A degree of circumspection, especially with regard to personal matters, must surely constitute one part of Clampitt's heritage from her Quaker parents. Her father, Roy J. Clampitt (1888–1973), wrote an autobiography, *A Life I Did Not Plan*, in 1966, and he is equally reserved on certain matters—the private life in general, the sexual life in particular—like many people of his generation. His daughter eventually came to share what she referred to (in a 1984 letter to Helen Vendler) as his "shy eminence." She also shared the bookishness of her grandfather, Frank Clampitt, who wrote a little autobiographical memoir, privately printed in 1919, about *his* father (Amy's great-grandfather), in which he proudly remembers a small room in their renovated Iowa farmhouse (1881) "which I furnished myself and which with its single book case seemed to my book obsessed fancy at the time a near approach to literary paradise."

In her father's book Amy receives less attention than practically anyone else in the family. Roy joyfully announces the birth of his firstborn; soon we learn that she is off at college, then in New York on a fellowship; she makes periodic visits home, especially when she moves back to Des Moines for six months to live with her sister Beth (who had been diagnosed with schizophrenia during her senior year at college and who spent most of her adult life in health care facilities); she takes up photography; the parents occasionally see her in New York or at the house of her brother Larry (1923–) outside Boston. We have little idea of what she does or of who she is. Rather like Anne Elliot in Jane Austen's *Persuasion*, Amy seems to be taken for granted. Being ignored, however, is not the worst thing that can happen to an artist. Even a person who seems to have support from, and community within, a family, can experience the profound kind of isolation that inspires creativity as self-expression, compensation, or even (though not in Clampitt's case) revenge.

How does one take the measure of a literary life? Clampitt always knew she was a writer. The letters, especially the extraordinary early ones to her youngest brother, prove her capacity even before she alit upon the right genre for its expression. In *The Cyclone*, the Grinnell College yearbook for 1940, her junior year, there are several photos of her looking largely like the other well-coiffed girls in one of the last classes before the beginning of World War II. In a group shot of the staff of *Tanager*, the literary magazine ("the most serious publication issued on campus"), seven of nine people (three faculty, six students) are smiling and looking off to one side. One unhappy girl seems to scowl at the camera. The last has her head cocked and looks straight ahead both seriously and skeptically. That's Amy. Literature defined her—and affected her work, her inner life, and her love life—from the start to the finish. In a letter to Philip (March 17, 1956) she says with the confidence of the young and hopeful: "I feel as if I could write a whole history of English literature, and know just where to place everybody in it, with hardly any trouble at all. The reason being, apparently, that I feel *I am in it.*"

Her sense of her literary calling ("a writer is what I was meant to be," she admits to Philip) coincided with, or was temporarily eclipsed by, her flirtation with the Anglican Church *nel mezzo del cammin*, in her thirty-sixth year. She complemented her commitment to "the hidden power of language" with a religious zeal that allowed her, for a while, to find harmony and wholeness in spiritual observances, to find a place in a religious community, which she later abandoned for a place in political activism. Almost sixty, coming out of obscurity well beyond the age when one might hope to do so, she sounds a different note in her first letter to Mary Jo Salter, who has just written her a fan letter: "I don't greatly enjoy the company of literary types—the more literary they are, the more miserable they seem as human beings. . . . I've yearned secretly for a poet I could write to." If she was born to be a poet, it certainly took her a long time to discover that fact. Her vocation was always clear, but the right genre was not. Not only did she try her hand at fiction when young but near the end of her life, fascinated with the place of Dorothy Wordsworth in the circle that included her brother and Coleridge, Clampitt wrote and rewrote a play about the Romantics, which displayed virtually no gift for the conflict and dialogue inherent in drama in the same way her earlier novels, one about life on an Iowa farm, another about religious controversies, were thick with description and commentary but thin on plot and characterization.

From the start Clampitt committed herself to her literary vocation as a consumer, that is, as a reader. In her letters her voice is that of a custodian of literature, a keeper as well as a sharer of property. Even more than the writing of letters, her long life of reading bespeaks a dedication to learning and to a solitary, contemplative temperament that looks increasingly old-fashioned in the third millennium. In a 1959 letter to her New York friend Mary Russel she refers to "solitude—that dangerous luxury—or is it a necessity after all?" Earlier that same year, to the same correspondent, she allows that "I made a real try at not wanting to be a writer. . . . The curious thing about this kind of voluntary relinquishment—or anyhow attempt at relinquishment—is that one emerges with renewed confidence: not in oneself, precisely, so much as in the nature of things." She was well aware of her "vocation"—which she admits "is a curious thing"—well before she experienced any success in it. Virtually every letter makes some mention, even in passing, of a new discovery, or of some book that she brings to the attention of her correspondent. Books called to her, and she responded.

Reading aloud, a common custom in the nineteenth century, has connected contemporary couples such as Donald Hall and Jane Kenyon. Likewise, it was always part of Hal and Amy's routine, especially during summer holidays in Maine and, at the end, in Lenox, when they would work their way through Dickens, Eliot, and Balzac, with no television in sight (although they were fans, in their Manhattan apartment, of Masterpiece Theater). In the country Clampitt and Korn had a life similar to the one Virginia Woolf describes as her routine with Leonard in the country: in the morning they wrote, in the afternoon they walked, in the evening they read.

Many of the external circumstances of Clampitt's life, though hardly her personality or character, changed after fame and notoriety caught up with her. She loved her laurels but never rested on them. The success of *The Kingfisher* made her work harder. She said yes to invitations to read and to give classes. She accepted teaching posts at Amherst, Smith, and William and Mary. She continued to travel everywhere, whenever possible by train or bus, preferring to see the landscape from inside a Greyhound. (The majority of her European trips were managed via boat, almost until the end.) Buses appealed to the Quaker in her: "It's a way of having solitude without feeling like a recluse" she writes to Rimsa Michel in 1974. No other contemporary poet has expressed so keenly the complementary feelings of separateness and togetherness, selfhood and community, as she does. Travel had always brought out her congenital, almost giddy, eagerness and joie de vivre: at forty-five, traveling in Naples, she says she is mistaken for twenty-five and feels fifteen.

Once eminent, she offered suggestions on the work of friends and strangers alike. She accepted honors, from virtually everyone, everywhere.

But she also knew when to say no. She had second thoughts about guest-editing a volume of *The Best American Poetry* (see her letter to David Lehman of April 3, 1989). She made a fuss in 1992, when William and Mary commissioned Clampitt to compose and deliver a poem in honor of the college's three hundredth anniversary. The authorities thought that her "Matoaka,"—about Pocohantas—might offend the sensibilities of Prince Charles, who would be on the same platform, and asked her to read it on a separate occasion. Her icy formal letter to Martha Hamilton-Phillips shows the same steel in her spine that was evident in her earlier letter to Henry Kissinger and in her deeply felt, Quaker-inspired resistance to perceived injustices and social inequities during her years of political activism. When she acted indignantly, she always did so on behalf of a higher, or impersonal cause, and never out of vanity or mere self-righteousness. Her fierce integrity matched her unsentimental generosity.

The literary culture had changed by the time Clampitt made her appearance in it. In the era of poetry workshops, degrees in creative writing, not to mention open-mike readings in coffee houses and church basements, being "a poet" conferred a certain modest cachet. In a June 30, 1990 letter (not included here) to Barbara Blay Clampitt reports on a trip to the Midwest:

> There were several poetry readings, and at one of them half a dozen relatives from my hometown—the last ones I would have expected at a *poetry reading*—turned up. Another occasion brought out a group from my old college, along with a different crew of relatives. Times have changed, from when admitting to being a writer was an embarrassment. (What do you do? I'm a writer. What do you write? Poetry, said with a slow blush. What kind of poetry? Oh . . . well . . . I don't really know . . . And so on.)

The letters from the decade of celebrity evince surprise as well as gratitude: Clampitt always maintained an unworldly naïveté in addition to her political commitments and fierce Quaker willingness to speak out and act against social injustice. Even as she threw herself into the world she gave the impression that at least part of her (is this not true of every writer?) was not *of* it. She was delighted to see new things, to meet new people and audiences all across the world—from Cambridge to Williamsburg to Lake Charles, Louisiana, to California, and beyond to Britain and Bellagio—and to the extent that her schedule permitted she remained in touch with the new friends (Edward Hirsch, John Wood, Eileen Berry) as well as the older ones (Barbara Clark, Rimsa Michel, Mary Russel). At the end of her life she was as excited by poetry slams as she was by readings in bohemian Village coffeehouse backrooms decades before.

* * *

What do we expect from a writer's letters? Information about literary activity, certainly, which in Clampitt's case meant (for the most part) reports of reading. Although she was always a writer, she came into her poetic maturity late, after her misguided efforts at writing fiction that no one ever wanted to publish. We don't read about her poems until she had already mastered the art of writing them. In her exchanges with Salter, Vendler, and Craig Raine (her English editor) she discusses the nuts and bolts of her poems and others'; although she is willing to accept editorial advice she clearly knows her own mind and does not seem to fret excessively over potential missteps and errors.

More broadly, we want reportage of the Frank O'Hara "I do this, I do that" sort. Clampitt loved weather, as she admits to her brother early on; the landscape in general as well as its particular flora and fauna always engaged her observant, Darwinian eye for detail. One of the strongest legacies of her devotion to nineteenth-century literature was her patient looking: Ruskin and Hopkins, as much as Darwin, are major precursors. She shared with Dorothy Wordsworth an enthusiastic delight in the daily trivia that constitute the largest part of anyone's life. Clampitt shopped for clothes; she sewed! We get a recipe for homemade granola and descriptions of Amy and Hal in jogging outfits working out with their handsome trainer. (Even close friends would be amused, I suspect, to picture the two of them jogging around the Central Park reservoir.) Observation extended to human beings as well. Because she had tried her hand at novels before she succeeded as a poet, many of her longer poems have a narrative or anecdotal base. As do her letters. She tells stories deftly, describing a boat of tourists bound for Europe, a peace protest, a night in jail, a tipsy dinner party, a trip to the secondhand bookstore. As a writer about place—whether the Midwest, Maine, Manhattan, or Europe, which she visited with a renewal of giddiness, balanced by her spiritual profundity about place, on each successive trip—she opens our eyes by focusing her own. Her prose is limpid, clear, classic in its simplicity—the exact opposite of the sinuous, swirling, baroque exuberance we find in her poems. It's as if she not only meticulously crafted each letter with an eye to its recipient (as any writer sensitive to her audience will do; we notice how much simpler her letters to Beth are than those to Philip) but also maintained two different styles, one for her epistolary examinations and reports and the other for poetic invention.

Finally, although she seldom used the letter as an occasion for "mere" self-analysis, she lets us into her life and mind, most notably in the letters to her youngest brother in the fifties (which constitute roughly one third of the pages here), when she could play the role of wiser sibling, "Dutch Aunt," and didactic counselor because of the ten years between them. ("I start out analyzing and end up delivering a sermon," she admits.) In these letters we watch her grapple with the affective life, the political life, and the spiritual one. Clampitt remained in touch with a Benedictine nun in England well after the decade of her high Anglo-Catholic phase and after she left the Church, disappointed in its refusal to speak out on political matters. (Intransigent with regard to the Church's refusal to be as radical as she wanted it to be, she had a private interview with Paul Moore, the liberal bishop of New York, and could not understand that the Church encompassed a wide spectrum of opinions, tastes, and views.)

Above all, we sense a temperament that encompasses polarities: fierce intelligence and exuberant, childlike wonder, assertive self-confidence and timidity, austerity and sensuousness. Writing to Helen Vendler in 1985, Clampitt refers to her inability to grasp the poetry of Wallace Stevens except "in bits" and proceeds to a lovely metaphor for her own creative and mental instincts: "A barnacle is what I sometimes think I really am, seizing on any passing thing that may be tempting, but unequipped to deal with the whole of anything. Ideas do interest me, but I can't hold onto a whole idea long enough to understand it." We may legitimately infer an analogy to her beloved Keats, with his "negative capability" and his innate sympathy with the sparrow pecking in the gravel outside his window. And, like wonder, gratitude was one of her mainsprings, a legacy from her Quaker simplicity. At the end of a 1982 letter to Mary Jo Salter Clampitt modestly apologizes for a slight, and uncharacteristic, querulousness in her tone: "I'm not complaining about anything really. . . . I simply regard myself, in spite of everything, as one of the fortunate people who happen to be around." It seems likely that she would have been a happy woman even without literary success; she possessed—from nature or genetic inheritance? from training?—an unaffected enthusiasm for the things she loved and an unself-contained ardor the world could not squelch.

A WORD ON METHOD

This volume offers a selection of correspondence rather than a complete collection. Owing to restrictions of space, I have had to leave out many interesting, long letters to persons who are already so well represented in this volume that I feel I have done neither them nor Clampitt herself a disservice. Like numerous short notes, post cards, thank-yous, and letters about business matters, also omitted here, these letters will ultimately find a place among the Clampitt papers in the Berg Collection of the New York Public Library. To save time, space, and my own eyesight, I have passed over the occasional lengthy handwritten letter that future scholars may try to decipher and transcribe. (Clampitt's spidery handwriting will baffle and provoke these scholars in equal measure.)

The second kind of omission comes *within* letters, especially longer ones. I have tried to make, where appropriate, judicious excisions: these occur mostly at the start and the end of letters, when the writer tends to clear her throat (saying something like "forgive me for not writing sooner" or "I don't know where the time has flown since the last letter") or to bid a formulaic farewell ("please try to visit next summer," "make sure to give my regards to . . . "). I have also cut sections that repeat information, tones, or feelings that recur elsewhere. Omissions and occasional amplifications are marked by bracketed ellipses: [. . .]. Clampitt was scrupulous with regard to niceties of punctuation, spelling, and syntax. Still, the letters contain an understandable, though small, number of obvious errors, which I have taken upon myself to correct silently.

I have dropped New York return addresses. (Letters from Iowa, Maine, or abroad retain the addresses.) Until 1979 all letters are addressed from 354 West 12th Street; after, from 160 East 65th Street, #4F. Although she was living with Harold Korn before 1979, she maintained at least the fiction of keeping her mailing address in the Village.

For the first twenty years or more Clampitt dated her letters in the European way (day/month/year). Beginning in 1978 she began to revert to the American mode (month/day/year), which she retained until the end. One wonders whether the change had anything to do with her coming into her own as a poet. Perhaps the shift was purely coincidental, but it is tempting to find a correlation between a vocational confirmation as an American poet and even a modest stylistic gesture such as this one.

The number of correspondents in the following pages is a relatively small one. In addition to several letters (from abroad) addressed to the entire Clampitt family, the recipients are Philip Clampitt (1930– ; occasional letters are addressed as well to his wife Hanna); Beth Clampitt (1928–1994), her only sister; Barbara Blay, the Englishwoman Amy visited on and off from 1949 until her death and who at some point came to live with her friend Joan Goom; Barbara (McClenon) Clark, a 1942 Grinnell graduate and dorm mate, who lived in Washington and worked for *U.S. News and World Report* before retiring to Florida in 1984; Rimsa Michel, Amy's assistant at the Audubon Society, who left New York for Alabama; Mary Russel, a New York painter and one of the few New York friends who received and saved letters from Amy; Henry Kissinger, secretary of state under Richard Nixon (and one of many recipients of formal letters of political protest that Clampitt wrote in the 1970s on international and local matters); Mary Jo Salter; Robert Quint, the college friend of Amy's favorite nephew, David Clampitt; Sister Mary John (née Anne Marshall), abbess of St. Mary's Abbey in Kent, England, the Benedictine nun whose order forbade her to save letters after she read them (how three have survived is unclear); Helen Vendler; John Wood, professor at McNeese State University in Lake Charles, Louisiana; Eileen Berry, a student of Clampitt's at a Florida writers' retreat; the poets George Bradley, Edward Hirsch, current head of the Guggenheim Foundation, David Lehman, and Craig Raine; Dorothy Blake, one of many writers who sent her work to Clampitt for evaluation and commentary; Jennifer Snodgrass of the Harvard University Press; Libby Braverman (another Grinnell dorm mate); and Martha Hamilton-Phillips of William and Mary. For the letters addressed to Barbara Blay I have inserted her last name in brackets [Bray] to distinguish one "Dear Barbara" from another (Barbara Clark).

I have chosen to end this volume with a letter from Phoebe Hoss, one of Clampitt's oldest New York friends, a coworker at the American OUP, to Barbara Blay, her old OUP friend on the British side. The obvious analogy to Joseph Severn's letter after Keats's death would, I hope, please Amy, whose sequence "Voyages: A Homage to John Keats" (*What the Light Was Like*) ends with a weaving together of Keats, Hart Crane, and Osip Mandelstam, all poets who dreamed of being warm, as did she. The poem's last line—"Letters no one will ever open"—testifies to everything not done, not accomplished, not acknowledged, in anyone's life, especially that of a poet cut off before the right time, whenever that may be.

The letters that follow open us up to and open to us a remarkable woman who, although not young when she died, was nevertheless still a young poet.

Acknowledgments

Assembling a book of letters is a way of reimagining or reconstructing a life, and, like constructing an actual life, it requires many participants. Although I edited this collection, I did not work alone on it. The following individuals provided letters that I could not include in this selection as well as leads to other friends and correspondents of Amy Clampitt: Helen Korn Atlas, Cecile Starr Boyajian, Julia Budenz, Sharon Chmielarz, Joan Clampitt, Eleanor Cook, Alfred Corn, William and Carole Doreski, Oriole Feshbach, Florence and Robert Fogelin, Laurence Goldstein, Joseph Goodman, Bruce Hainley, Donald Hall, Henry Hart, Sherrey Hutchison, Hugh Kennedy, James Kissane, Rozanne Knudson, Jeanne Hanff Korelitz, Peter Kybart, Linda Lovejoy, J. D. McClatchy, Doris T. Myers, Cynthia Nadelman, Alice Conger Patterson, Alice Quinn, Stephen Sandy, Grace Schulman, Kent Shaw, Susan Sheridan, Marjorie Clampitt Silletto, Warren Allen Smith, Ben Sonnenberg, Suzanne S. Szalay, John Tagliabue, Susan Tiberghien, Pauline R. Utzinger, Siri von Reis, Baron Wormser, and David Yezzi.

The staff of the Houghton Library at Harvard made copies of the letters that Clampitt wrote to Helen Vendler. For permission to reprint Clampitt's letters to Dorothy Blake, Martha Hamilton-Phillips, David Lehman, Craig Raine, and Jennifer Snodgrass I am grateful to the Berg

Collection of English and American Literature (where all of Clampitt's papers and letters will eventually land) at the New York Public Library and to the Astor, Lenox, and Tilden Foundations.

In Dallas I profited from the aid of two graduate assistants, Diana Howard and Jacob Rinehart, who helped to decipher Clampitt's spidery handwriting and who assembled lists for me from her address books. Once I had collected the letters, Kim Conley, Anneliese Finke, and Kim McDonald, in Lenox, served as more than capable amanuenses and proofreaders.

I did not know Amy Clampit very well when she was alive (having met her a half dozen times), but over the course of the past several years I have come to know her very well indeed. For ten months I lived in the Lenox cottage that Clampitt and her partner Harold Korn bought in 1992, two years before her death. Nestled among the Berkshire hills, with Tanglewood on one side and Edith Wharton's the Mount on the other, I felt immediately at home and imbued with the spirit of the woman whose possessions—especially her books—surrounded me. The hospitality, warmth, and good services of the following local people increased my sense of belonging: Robert and Ilona Bell, Michael Bissaillon, Karen Chase and Paul Graubard, Peter Filkins and Susan Roeper, Tim Geller and Robin Raphaelian, and Matthew Tannenbaum.

The staff of the Berkshire Taconic Foundation, especially its director Jennifer Dowley, supported my work in more ways than I can recall. I owe special thanks to Alexcia WhiteCrow, communications expert *extraordinaire*, who saved me many times from computer emergencies, problems, and general anxiety.

At Columbia University Press Jennifer Crewe oversaw the entire project and Susan Pensak performed the task of copyeditor with a light but steady hand. Bonnie Costello and William Logan, the formerly anonymous readers of my proposal to the press, wrote encouraging and helpful letters that guided the book through to its completion.

My greatest debts are to Amy Clampitt's literary executors and her family. Karen Chase, Ann Close, and Mary Jo Salter invited me to deal with this project, and as the first recipient of a grant from the Amy Clampitt Trust (established at his death by Harold Korn to promote the work of poets and scholars of poetry) I enjoyed time away from teaching as well as gracious living in the Berkshires. David and Cynthia Clampitt, Larry and Jeanne Clampitt, and Philip and Hanna Clampitt aided in many ways. To Phil Clampitt in particular I am deeply grateful for his overseeing and typing and for his providing countless kinds of information. I trust that his late sister would be happy with the results of our joint efforts.

Love, Amy

The Letters of
Amy Clampitt

5 March 1950
Dear Barbara [Blay]—
How very nice of you to send the little purse, which arrived with remarkable promptness. You are right about the popularity of plaids, but the clever design is quite unlike anything I ever saw here—it's so thoroughly Leak-Proof, and what could be more important! I had great fun carrying it shopping with me yesterday, and I'm so pleased to know of your thoughtfulness in finding it for me.

As you can imagine, England has been a good deal in everybody's mind lately, and the English people in the United States have found it vastly amusing to see our excitement on the day the election returns came in. As it happened, Charles Johnson was down from Toronto (what a surprise it was to learn that he was there!) on that very day, when we were taking turns phoning up the *New York Times* every hour to hear the latest figures—and I must say that he appeared to have far greater equanimity than the rest of us! At any rate, it is a disappointment that it could not have been more decisive, one way or another; but I suppose it does prove what ties there are between the countries, that we should find your election nearly as exciting as our own back in 1948. It happened that about a week beforehand I went to a showing of British information films, and I was particularly delighted with one about what it is like to be a new M. P., with all the traditions that have been going for centuries. There was also one about London's water supply, with lovely shots of the New River and the source of the Thames in the Cotswolds, and as you may have heard, it could not have been more *apropos*—because although the heart of New York is an island, the city water supply is in dire danger of being used up! I can't possibly explain how it happened, but the emergency has its comic aspects. Every Thursday all and sundry are expected to refrain from bathing, shaving, and all water-consuming activities. But the funniest development has come with the Mayor's announcing that he had called in a rain-making expert for consultation—no, I'm perfectly serious, they can create rain by sprinkling dry ice out of an airplane or something. And immediately there were protests from the mayor of Albany, that this would constitute pilfering from his city's water supply! So far as I know, the argument has so far not been settled, and meanwhile Dry Thursday continues.

It was pleasant to think of you seeing Moira Shearer dance so soon after I had seen her here. Unfortunately I didn't see *Cinderella*, but I did see her in *Façade* and, as you may know, I saw her in *Coppelia* at Covent Garden last spring. And I have also been to *The Red Shoes*, which has been playing steadily in New York for over a year. If you have seen it, you can imagine how exciting I found the opening scenes of the opera house—I very nearly caused a disturbance in my enthusiasm. Naturally I was interested to hear of her marriage, especially since the chapel at Hampton Court was on my itinerary and I remember it vividly.

It has just been announced that one of our native companies, the New York City Ballet, will be performing in England next summer. This is an enormous honor for them, as everybody who saw the Sadler's Wells company in New York well knows, and I am already a little nervous for them. But they do some delightful things, the best of which is *Firebird*, with new choreography and costumes to the Stravinsky music. I saw it a week ago; but I'm sorry now that I wasn't at the performance a couple of evenings ago, for the premiere of a new ballet, *Illuminations*, with music, choreography and costumes all by Englishmen—Britten, Ashton and Beaton. A friend of mine tells me that it was really gala, with the British Ambassador in the audience and the orchestra playing "God Save the King" along with "The Star-Spangled Banner."

You asked whether I had done any more sewing. Actually I am now in a position to do an enormous amount, because my parents surprised me with a portable sewing machine for Christmas! But somehow I have been so occupied with various other things that I haven't used it a great deal so far, though I did made myself some new curtains and have the material to make a blouse when I can settle down to it. At least I did launch the thing with something of a flourish—one evening I had a sewing-machine-warming, like a house-warming, you know, to which everybody was required to bring something to sew on. And though a good deal of the work was done by hand, since only one person could use the machine at a time, it seems to have been a success.

Do give my best wishes to everybody, and to Mr. Norton especially, and tell them how often I think of you all and the wonderful time I had. Again, my thanks for such a charming present, and I hope you'll write again when you have time.

Yours,

Amy

. . . .

13 February 1952
Dear Philip—

[. . .] I congratulate you on finishing *Paradise Lost*. I decided a while back that I was going to read it again, but it turned out to be as dull and pompous as the first time, and I haven't succeeded in getting very far. I always seem to turn to it just when I'm about to go to sleep, which I suppose isn't fair, but all it seems to do is to put me to sleep entirely. However, one of these days I still mean to tackle it properly. I also intend to read the Bible all the way through. These intentions are prompted by, of all things, an interest in religion which dates, as nearly as I can remember, to my reading of Toynbee just after I got back to New York from Iowa, and which is related to all the cathedrals and altarpieces and religious festivals that puzzled me in Europe. I have just finished, after my own fashion, with looking into the matter of St. Francis, and have written a chapter on Assisi which ends up, somewhat to my own surprise, with the assertion that the tradition of his receiving the Stigmata is a logical necessity! Of course, just when I think I understand religion, I meet up with a real believer who says I am talking nonsense. This happened again just yesterday, when after a couple of martinis Joe Goodman and I and a girl friend of his got into a terrible argument, in which I maintained that religious feeling was everything, the girl that dogma was everything, and Joe took the more complicated position of the skeptical believer. None of us convinced the others of anything. Of course I have a different idea about every week. To follow the process you will have to read my so-called book, in which I am now about to start Chapter Six and thus am about halfway through.

It doesn't seem likely that the book is going to be published. A literary agent to whom I sent the first three chapters said it was well written but that there was no market for it. The curious thing is that I don't care very much. It would be nice to make some money, of course, but I have gone ahead writing it and having the time of my life. I haven't gotten a job and haven't even looked for one, but though the money is beginning to run rather low even that doesn't bother me. I can always go to work at Macy's or something, and probably will, because the idea of a good job in which I should have to work hard chiefly at flattering people and pushing them around now seems too awful to contemplate, and I have discovered that I am really happier with a very little money than I was when I could buy things just for the fun of buying. Of course, I have had my spending jag and have all the clothes I need for a while—I haven't even had to buy nylons, since I wear them only when I go out—and I can take books out of the public library. I wouldn't feel this way, either, if I hadn't first proved that I *could* hold a job and gotten enough self-respect thereby to make my present frugal existence an act not of defiance but of transcendence. I have the feeling now that I may be going to write a good book—not the one I'm working on, which is simply groundwork and a process of thinking a few things out that has to be gone through first—and that even if I don't I shan't feel too badly, because I will have found out that I didn't have it in me, and if I hadn't tried I never could be sure.

So far I've enjoyed myself so much that it isn't as if I had given anything up. I've never been in a better frame of mind, day after day. Of course Iowa gave me the fidgets, and so, even, did Boston. I suppose I've gotten so used to my little spot on West Twelfth Street that I don't feel at home anywhere except in New York. It's a wonderful place. I never know any more who is going to appear or what is going to happen. The other evening I got into an argument with a painter, which started out innocently enough and ended up with questions of the condition of the artist in Russia, and what is really the function of the painter. The fellow turned out to be a Marxist, and I hadn't met any of them for so long that I had almost begun to consider the species extinct. He thought a painter could say something that had nothing to do with painting; that the truth was simple; and that the deep-freeze was no more but no less important than paintings to put on the wall. I thought exactly the opposite: that no good painting could make a simple declarative statement; that the deep-freeze was of less importance than paintings; and that the truth cannot be simplified without being turned into lies. However, there were so many things neither of us were sure about that we didn't come to blows, but ended up quite amicably, both grateful for the work-out. When I left I had a headache from sheer mental exertion. What was still more interesting was going to look at an exhibition of this same artist's paintings. They were wonderful! And if any of them made simple declarative statements, these were denied by the richness of the colors and the brushwork. All of which proves nothing except that artists are of all complicated people the most complicated.

Then there was the evening when I listened to a poet reading Yeats aloud, and practically floated out of the window, the effect was so intoxicating. And the party that Joe gave after a performance of his flute sonata, at which I had planned to stay half an hour but actually got home at half-past nine the next morning! We had drifted, half a dozen of us, from Joe's mother's to the apartment of a White Russian journalist who believes in absolutely nothing but has a wonderful collection of objects—figures out of Egyptian tombs, Turkish fezzes, Persian shoes and a Mohammedan prayer rug, books in all languages, and musical instruments including African drums, a snake-charmer's pipe, a musical gourd, and Maracas. I took a lesson in the latter and found them a good deal more difficult than I had supposed they would be, but the musicians in the crowd were presently playing a little concert on the various instruments against a background of Zulu chanting from the phonograph. I found myself drinking brandy and eating cheese-and-baloney sandwiches for breakfast and feeling fine. When it began to be light we got into the journalist's car and were delivered to various points—one girl to her office, somebody else to Penn Station, and me home. Joe had another, more genteel party the other evening—really a musical soiree, organized around a rehearsal of his new string trio (flute, cello and piano). After they had played it once we listened several times to a tape recording. After that—chamber music in its proper setting—the performance in Town Hall yesterday was something of an anticlimax, but exciting. I found that I was—almost as nervous as the composer himself. [. . .]

Love,

Amy

. . . .

13 January 1953

Dear Barbara [Blay]–

[. . .] As for the book, it has been finished and revised and looked at rather kindly—so far as I can make out—by several publishers, but none of them has gone so far as to offer a contract. A literary agent is taking care of it for me, so I hear only the nicer comments, of course! I have my doubts about its ever getting published but don't care too much. The main thing was to have written it, and I'm hoping to get myself organized sufficiently one of these days to write another one. No, the subject is no secret, though it's a little difficult to explain. The setting is New York, and in general it's about young people with jobs. Of course there is a love story—there always is, no doubt. *If* it ever sees print you shall have a copy, and I shan't even require you to like it!

I imagine Mrs. Jepp told you that I got a new job. It had become a matter of necessity—I had holes in my shoes and approximately twenty-five dollars to my name. It's with the Audubon Society, a foundation

concerned with wildlife conservation, birds in particular, and I work in the reference library with a delightful, unbusinesslike Frenchwoman who is no more of an ornithologist than I am—so in looking up the answers to people's questions, piecemeal we find out all kinds of odd things about birds. The people who come in are often slightly crazy too, but frequently very nice—like the man who spends most of his time these days camping out in the Bahamas and Yucatan watching the habits of flamingoes. Before that he was watching the whooping cranes, huge magnificent birds of which there are now only about thirty in existence, and the Society had just published a thick book all about what he learned. Aside from the fact that he usually wears a blue suit with a bright yellow pullover, he *looks* a good deal more normal than you would expect. There is also a man who is, I am told, the leading authority on bats in the United States, and *he* looks like any nice young businessman, or perhaps a professor of political science—very difficult to imagine climbing around in caves with a flashlight (if indeed that is what bat specialists do). Then there are bird artists and bird photographers, and once in a while the warden of a bird sanctuary who comes in and immediately engages you in a conversation about the behavior of the reddish egret. You just look very knowing and nod your head a few times and it seems to be all right. [. . .]
Love,
Amy

. . . .

16 February 1953
Dear Philip—
Your letter arrived on a day when I had given up coping with broken boilers and fifty-degree temperatures at the new Audubon house and gone to bed with a galloping sore throat. It presently turned into a quite conventional cold, thereby upsetting my theory about seasonal immunities, and since the boilers still weren't fixed I spent four days in bed. I almost said four wonderful days, but they weren't really, in fact I was so disinclined to get up that I began to wonder uneasily whether I was ever going to; the wonderful thing was that when I did totteringly pull myself together in the middle of Friday afternoon the cold was practically gone. The Kleenex supply had run out, I just remember—that was really why I had to get up. Matthias had meanwhile very kindly gone to the grocery store for me, and on the day before another friend of mine had dropped in and shared a hot

toddy—whiskey and lemon juice with boiling water and two cloves—which didn't do me a bit of good.

But you must be quite bored with bedridden people and their symptoms by this time. I didn't mean to go into so much detail about the fascinating common cold. The one thing I did that isn't usually done was to discover Gilbert White. Maybe you know about him—the eighteenth-century Englishman, a clergyman evidently, who wrote *The Natural History of Selborne*. I read the whole thing, and when I had finished I had the rare feeling of being sorry that there wasn't any more. He made it his business to note down everything like the habits of cockroaches, the rainfall, the dew, the growth of trees, and the appearances and disappearances of birds, at a time when there was still some doubt about whether migration really occurred. He never did decide for certain whether swallows and swifts actually left the country or merely hibernated somewhere or other. He had a friend who went out with a pitch-pipe and discovered, or thought he had, that all the owls hooted in B-Flat; but then one of them went down to A, so the generalization had to be abandoned. He was the most patient curious man who ever lived, I do believe, and that is his great charm. The one time he seems to [have] been even slightly inclined to pass moral judgments on animal behavior (he was always looking for explanations of why the cuckoo should lay its egg in another bird's nest, but he never found one, though for a while he thought he had) [. . .] the one creature that seems to have incensed him the least little bit was an old tortoise, and I suppose that was because he had gotten fond of it. He saw it first in another town, where it had been living for a good while, and watched it digging in for the winter, with the speed, he said, of the hour hand on a clock.

Eventually, after a series of references to it, he notes that "the old Sussex tortoise is now become my property." He dug it up before the end of the hibernation season, carried it back to Selborne, and dug it into his own garden, where he noted that on one day of unseasonable warmth, in February or March, it came out for a while but then retired underground. He noticed that it was as fussy as an old lady about being caught in the rain, and would go for cover though heaven knew that it was as well protected already as one would suppose necessary. And then he exploded that it did seem odd that a creature so torpidly oblivious to delight of any kind should be permitted to drag out so long an existence on earth. Later on he seems to have made amends by noting a few more positive qualities, such as that it did have sense enough to keep from falling down a well when it came to the edge of it. Well, you can see that I have been pretty much obsessed with that tortoise ever since. I have already told one person whom I quite liked but found somewhat exasperating that *he* was an old Sussex tortoise. The upshot was that I managed to get him to unearth some enthusiasms—Adlai Stevenson, and the ballet, and some novel by John O'Hara, and some other girl who hadn't anything to say. Of course the last exasperated me all over again, but that was no doubt what I deserved. Anyhow, for the time being "Don't be an old Sussex tortoise" seems to be my rallying cry. Why are people so afraid of being enthusiastic? I don't think it's so much laziness as the fear of turning out to be wrong. But who knows what is right, anyway? If one only feels the *right* things one might as well not feel anything. Of course one usually is wrong. I've been being enthusiastic and getting knocked down and proved wrong for some time now, so that I'm practically used to it.

Now what all this has to do with anything I don't quite know. I think it was brought on by your *almost* confessing to envy me for enjoying [Suzanne Langer's] *Philosophy in a New Key* and then taking it back, *almost* and all. I don't see anything wrong with that—it's probably healthy, and besides, at your age I would have found the whole thing impenetrable. I've forgotten the logical framework already, in fact I had before I finished the book. What I understood I understood through things that had affected me, and I've had ten more years to be affected in than you have. You have a far better brain than I do, and you use it. What needs paying attention to now is your feelings, which are undoubtedly there somewhere though you seem to do a wonderful job of traveling miles in order to circumvent them. Does this make you mad? It ought to.

Well, here you are, twenty-three years old tomorrow. I'm late with birthday wishes, but then I always am. These are about the queerest I ever sent anybody, but you see it's all on account of that old Sussex tortoise.
Love,
Amy

. . . .

22 April 1953
Dear Philip—
Your letter was indeed appreciated. I found it so stimulating, in fact, that my impulse was to sit down and answer it right away; but if I hadn't restrained myself the result would have been more than usually incoherent, with all the ideas you had set in motion. You have certainly got down to

the real issues, from minority rule and majority rights (i.e. the dictatorship of the vegetariat) on to Ole Debbil Sax (as you will remember Bloody Mary was pleased to pronounce it), and I was especially pleased with your story of bringing a little air-clearing doubt into the smug confusion of the would-be professional pacifists. Than which I think there are few people more tiresome: I know one or two bigots who are actually delightful, but pacifist bigots never are. They are, as somebody once pointed out that free love is, a contradiction in terms, or in other words self-defeating. I doubt that organized pacifism can ever get far, except under the leadership of a saint like Gandhi, because as soon as they constitute a bloc they tend to become belligerents. The thing that saved Gandhi's movement was the man himself: he didn't simply have ideas, he *was* his ideas, as only that great rarity, the true saint, ever completely is. In a real saint thinking, feeling, and doing all follow the same straight line, while the rest of the human race spends most of its time getting tied up in knots.

The whole thing, as I see it, is very closely related to the problem of individual relationships, which is really the problem of expressing one's feelings, which in turn involves the problem of dominating or being dominated by other people, of hurting and getting hurt. It's a problem that shows no sign of getting solved; and the terrible, eternal irony is that when one is young and trying to find one's way around in the shambles of human society, when one is least capable of satisfactory personal relationships is just when one needs them most. The usual short-cut seems to be to avoid getting hurt (a) by being aggressive, and hurting other people first or (b) by being recessive, just letting things slide by. Of course the two can overlap, and I'm not sure which is more common or which is worse. But they both lead to misery, of the most terrible, blind, self-perpetuating kind—a worse misery, really, than the one they were supposed to circumvent. What I am trying to say, of course, is that suffering of one kind or another is not to be avoided, and that honest suffering is much less worse, finally, than any substitute. The day I woke up and really knew this was so—and it wasn't so terribly long ago, either—I began finally, in a very small way, to be a responsible adult. I'm not sure that the fairly long chronicle of mistakes and emotional crises that went into, and led up to, this private triumph would sound worth while to anybody else, but they were so far as I'm concerned. About the only thing I can be proud of is that I never made the same mistake twice—it was always a new one, and I always emerged knowing a little more than I did before. One has to live with one's mistakes, either by hiding them away in a closet somewhere or making some use of them. The only alternative to the process of education by trial and error is to take somebody else's word for everything—I tried that too, with ludicrous consequences—and in the present confused state of things that alternative is probably satisfactory only for an imbecile. Now what all this may or may not have to do with you and Virginia, or any other girl, I haven't any very clear idea. The thing I had in mind about the old Sussex tortoise was, I guess, to caution you against becoming paralyzed by the fear of injury, either inflicted or received. If you find you are discussing a relationship as a substitute for the relationship itself, and can't do anything else, then there is probably no point in pursuing the will-o'-the-wisp, but if on the other hand you really do enjoy each other's company then it ought to be worth while to find some modest basis for continuing it. All of which you perfectly well know already. You have the advantage of an exceptionally good mind. I don't think the fact makes you really any lonelier than other people, it just makes you more aware of the loneliness which is the fate of absolutely everybody.

There was a whole lot more I meant to say about how I seem to have turned out to be a pacifist in spite of myself—though I do hate the word. That accounts for my finding it impossible to go back into business of any kind, where so much energy, at least of mine, was used up in fights of the most trivial kind. It used to be that a day wasn't complete if I didn't lose my temper, less and less privately as time went on. I walked all over people and had quite a few of them scared of me, and for a while it was fun of a perverse sort; but there were also quite a few people I was scared of. The difference now is that I don't think I'm really scared of anybody; and the people I can't like I'm mostly just sorry for. Of course people hate having anybody genuinely sorry for them (as distinguished from just feeling guilty about them, as if their plight were one's own fault), so the only thing I have found to do is avoid them. Fortunately, the Audubon Society makes that pretty easy. It's not an ideal solution but it seems to be the best I'm capable of, for the time being anyway. It means a certain sense of isolation, but that is only sad instead of being bitter and having to blame somebody. I think I understand that as the essence of pacifism—well, say Christianity, which is the same thing really—not blaming anybody. But it's a thing that can't be imposed from the outside; it just has to happen. But I'm getting too tired to follow these observations much further. You're right; letter-writing can be exhausting. [. . .]
Love,
Amy

. . . .

31 January 1954

Dear Philip—

One of the few disadvantages of living alone, it has just occurred to me, is that when one thinks one may have lost one's voice there is no way to find out except by talking to oneself. At a quarter past two this morning, though I find the recollection slightly incredible, I was shouting my head off in Pooh-Bah's lament from *The Mikado* while skipping up Bleecker Street in the company of several people who had a similar inclination to shout their heads off, though at the party we had just come from we had been doing exactly that for at least an hour. I now suspect that the singing had gone on too long and merrily, because when I finally got up a while ago and felt the inclination to burst into song (a Burl Ives lament I had just thought of), all I could raise was a hoarse squeak. The question now is, can I talk? Evidently I am not going to find out until this evening when I go out to dinner, because I simply cannot bring myself to say anything out loud with nobody but me around to hear it. This dilemma, aggravated by not being able to sing, has produced an irresistible urge to communicate. All of which is the long-drawn-out explanation of this letter. I am not sure which of us owes the other one one at this point, and that being the case I might just as well break the deadlock. I enjoyed your letter and I'm glad you enjoyed *Gatsby*, for sending which I had no particular reason except that it's a good story and one which (unlike the majority of novels which on first reading you can barely put down) stands up under repeated reading. The usual critics' explanation for the fascination of the character of Gatsby—and he is, of course, fascinating just because he is convincing and incredible both at the same time—is that he represents the American Dream, that peculiar mixed faith in romantic love and the power of money. He is a kind of mythical character, like Faust or Oedipus or the Little Mermaid, and the critics these days are very fond of myths. And so am I.

Though for slightly different specific reasons, I think I have been getting the same feeling lately that you seem to have about psychologists—or at any rate about psychoanalysts. And they are all involved, so far as I can make out, in the creation of another Great American Myth. Since I don't believe that myths are necessarily lies, this is not so much a condemnation as a rather weary, even wistful objection; because the psychoanalytic myth seems to be that There Is No Sin. Now it is fairly easy to trace the genesis of this proposition which may or may not be true: first there is the idea, which can make things quite messy, that Sex is Sin; so in order to make things less messy, this idea must be rooted out and disposed of, like a stand of poison ivy in a fencerow; and behold, the arduous labor completed, if Sex is not a Sin, there is no Sin. My trouble just now, I suppose, is that I have been reading the Inferno, which is concerned with nothing but sin; and be it noted that in Dante's system Paolo and Francesca, along with Cleopatra, Dido, and Helen of Troy, whose transgressions were all carnal, are regarded as the least guilty, and their punishment is the exact equivalent of their earthly condition—namely to be driven about eternally by the winds, like a flock of birds, a situation which, if wearisome, is infinitely to be preferred to lying forever in the rain, like the gluttons, or burning forever, like the false counsellors, or being locked forever in the ice, like the traitors. So I suppose the trouble is not with the psychoanalysts alone, but with the nineteenth-century preoccupation which made such a Thing out of sex. But the awful thing that seems to have happened, whosever fault it was, is that the psychoanalyst's couch has become the lazy sinner's confessional, where on payment of a large fee excuses are found for all the things one ought not to have done (and they are always the same excuse: that one felt guilty about being human, or in other words one felt, though one knew better, that Sex was a Sin). I had it explained to me again last night that the purpose of psychoanalysis is to make people Accept Themselves; the inference being that they are incapable of change. ("Except a man be born again he shall not enter the kingdom of heaven"—or did I make that up?) The terrible thing is that being Born Again became such a cliché that it had to be rooted out too—oh that terrible nineteenth century, for which, nevertheless, I am coming to have a certain affection, if only in reaction against the reaction against it.) There is something to this effect in [David Riesman's] *The Lonely Crowd*, as I remember, in connection with homosexuals, whom psychiatrists often do not try to "cure" but merely to accustom to their inverted habits. It is all very discouraging, anyhow, if one persists in believing in free will. The thing I hold against psychology just now is that by explaining too much it explains nothing, that it becomes, unreal as it is, a substitute for reality, and its version of life is nothing but a lot of empty nutshells and squeezed orange rinds. And more and more I find that the disparity between the way I see these people, believing as I do in the existence of free will, sin and damnation, and the way they see themselves, believing in nothing special, is so great that I can barely communicate with them, except by a kind of wig-wag semaphore conducted in two different languages. Neither of us knows what the other is talking about. There are times when I feel closer to the flamingos, isolated in their salty fastnesses where nothing else can live except the minute plant and animal forms they feed upon; it is as though they had more life in them than most of the people one sees. But of course that is unfair, whether to the people or to the flamingos I'm not quite sure.

Space here to indicate that I did go out to dinner and that I *had* lost my voice. My whispers got more attention than my normal tone of voice, but I had to choose my remarks carefully and the fact that people hung upon them, and even began talking in whispers themselves, did not make them profound.

The mad Pole I told you about, who made me laugh so much on the train from Boston last spring, was in town this week and called me up. We arranged to meet at the Metropolitan Museum on my lunch hour, carrying respectively, for purposes of identification, the *Inferno* and the *Journal of the British Interplanetary Association.* Yes, by golly, there is such a thing, and there was even an article in it about the air-conditioning of space ships! However, on inquiring I was told that an emigration to Mars within at least the next fifty thousand years is not likely, even if anybody wanted to go, for the reason that the expenditure of energy to get a single person there would be more than that required to keep a city in operation here—which is self-evident enough when one thinks about it, but about physics my credulity is boundless. I certainly never met anybody so learned on a train, or just possibly anywhere, and indeed such learning in somebody whose profession is designing rockets to beat the Russians with in the next war is rather disconcerting. However, it was quite easy to keep off that subject while surrounded by the relics of the Italian Renaissance, the portraits and the carved furniture and the altarpieces; they have re-opened the European painting galleries at the museum, and I am there practically every lunch hour. There are times when it seems to me that without these evidences of its potentialities I should despair of the human race altogether. This, undoubtedly, is what [Bernard] Berenson's famous "life-enhancing" label is about; when there is real life behind a work of art, there is the power in it of lifting the spectator beyond himself and into some community of human experience which is beyond time and space; but this is a power which can only be tapped through a process which cannot be taught or entirely explained. I suspect, however, that at bottom it is simply a respect for life in all its forms. I read somewhere about a man who acquired a belief in God, or immortality, or the soul—they all mean approximately the same thing—from watching a "wave" of migrating war-blers, and I think I understand this perfectly. Once you really sense the life behind a mass movement like that, or behind a single bird, or behind a single human being, no matter how stupid or miserable, then you know that all the science in the world can never explain it, and you do not ask to have it explained. And implicit in all art, I think, is a respect for this mystery; it is a homage to the inexplicable. Perhaps science is too in its purer forms, but it seems to me that just as often it exploits the mystery without even recognizing that it is mysterious, and that—in the case of psychology—it lays destructive hands on a principle it does not even recognize; it devalu-ates life by burying the inexplicable under a load of explanations. But I'm becoming indignant, and it's late, so I'll stop for now anyway.

Love,

Amy

. . . .

10 April 1954

Dear Philip—

It's startling to discover that your last letter is already a month old. My impulse was, as it always is when I get a letter that says something, to sit down and answer it right away; but not having done that, I find that the time has slid past without being properly accounted for. Your adventures with St. Thomas Aquinas and Machiavelli and the philosopher with a ma-terialist base interested me very much. I haven't read either of the for-mer—certainly not the latter!—though both have been on my tentative list of people to be read sometime. Since I find St. Thomas's almost-contemporary Dante so congenial—I'm on the *Purgatorio* now—I can imagine I would share your sympathies on that score, and the comments on Machiavelli as you report them only substantiate my own feelings about the thinness and confusion of popular ideas these days. If you are going to explain away Machiavelli by saying his moral ideas were wrong, or by blaming his environment, you end up by explaining away all of western civilization. Of course the way he was brought up, and the polit-ical conditions of fifteenth-century Florence—which is the Florence of the high Renaissance, of Raphael and Michelangelo and Pico della Mirandola and Lorenzo the Magnificent—entered into his idea of human nature, and certainly there was vice and cruelty and horror tangled up with all the magnificence of that time; but if you are going to pay attention to histo-ry at all, you can't just pick out the parts you like and ignore the rest. I have come to the conclusion, and not a very original one at that, that history is a conflict of interests because human nature is a conflict of interests. We're all subject to contrary pulls and pressures from without and from within. Probably the most powerful of these pressures are exactly those of which we are least aware. The advantage of a chaotic time like this one—and like so many advantages it is also pretty terrifying—is that to avoid being smothered on the one hand or torn limb from limb on the other, one is forced to examine one's own assumptions, and to try to understand where they came from. That's the significance of a book like Suzanne Langer's, as I understand it: she makes a brief for intuition, which is the living kernel of any system of philosophy. One man's logic is as good as another's; I don't see how it is possible to choose among sets of ideas on the basis of logic alone. In the end, it is what one feels to be true that matters, not the plausibility or the force of the arguments that develop out of what one feels. But as T. S. Eliot pointed out, the hardest thing in the world is to know what one feels: there are so many things one is supposed to feel, that one has been told one is going to feel, that certain people are said to have felt, and so on and on. The whole basis of Roman Catholicism, as I understand it, is that certain things have been felt by certain people which an ordinary believer may never feel except at second hand; again quoting Eliot, we can endure only just so much reality; hence the ritual, which preserves these feelings and keeps them in operation even though they are not individually revived in each worshiper each time the mass is sung. It is pretty hard to argue with this; in a sense it may be considered a more democratic idea than the orthodox democratic notion that everybody has a right to get ahead (and maybe lose his soul in the process). But the truth is, I don't really believe it. I still believe that it is still possible to discover what one feels, and that until that happens one is not quite alive. There are just too many different systems now, all clamoring to be adhered to, to settle down comfortably with any one of them. One compromises, one acquiesces, one keeps one's mouth shut—but if one goes on thinking one is not quite defeated. The wear and tear involved is something terrific, but it is better than never having been quite alive.

And the same thing applies to people individually. It is more and more my melancholy observation that in any close relationship either one person dominates with the more or less complete assent of the other, or each tries to dominate the other. The more we are attached to people for what they are, the more we also try to change them. But how much better than that there should have been no relationship at all! When people are grown up enough to recognize the danger in people they like, they are perhaps also grown up enough to sort out what is to be valued from what is a threat to their own integrity. And as far as I'm concerned, recognizing the value of another person is the fundamental human experience. If I didn't believe that people do reach each other once in a very great while, in spite of all the anguish that is usually mixed up in the process, I don't suppose I would see very much in Dante, or Rembrandt, or Bergson, or even things in which people aren't directly involved, such as hearing a song-sparrow in a high wind or finding snowdrops in bloom, as I did one brisk day when I paid a visit to the Cloisters a few weeks back. Otherwise existence would be a treadmill, as it seems to be for a good many people—all labels and no contents. As it is, no day is quite like any other; one doesn't know exactly where one is going—that seems to rest these days in the hands of the makers of international policy, who don't know where they're going either—but at least one is not standing still.

However, I make an effort not to meditate on the H-Bomb, and if I do find myself getting indignant about Senator McCarthy, I try to remember that he has a possible analogue in the Hebrew prophets: he too is a product of his times, a malignant growth which gets its sustenance from the fact that there are a few thousand people too scared to think. Not that I think the Hebrew prophets were all bad, but they certainly were fanatical. If you haven't read *The True Believer*, you really should. (I know, I hate having books prescribed to me too; but at least this one is short.)

We had a party, a very civilized party, at the Audubon Society a couple of days ago—an opening, more properly, what the French call a *vernissage*, of a show of rather insignificant flower paintings by one Redouté, who was court flower painter to Marie Antoinette and who weathered the Revolution to become ditto to the Empresses Josephine and Marie Louise. Most of the people who came were Luxembourgers, including the Envoy Extraordinary and Minister Plenipotentiary to Washington from that country, a Monsieur Le Gallais. He looked exactly as such an official from a very small country might be expected to look—rather bald, not very tall, and not so much solemn as expressionless, as though he was afraid all dignity might disappear if he noticed anything to provoke a smile. The other Luxembourgers whose responsibilities weighed less heavily proved quite delightful, and that the Minister's heart is in the right place I am sure because he thoughtfully provided two cases of Luxembourg wine for the occasion. He didn't drink any of it himself, as I remember, but that was again probably because the dignity of Luxembourg was too much on his mind. Anyway, it turned out to be a fine party. For one thing the weather favored us—sunny, and rather headily in the seventies, all of a sudden, so that it was possible to open the window onto our little balcony. And there were roses on the tea-table and roses on the mantelpiece and roses—mostly, mixed in with humbler growths such as a thistle and a twig of *Ribes*, I'll have you know, which looked so real you could practically smell it—all around the walls. And then there was the wine, a Moselle, very light and with a flowery bouquet, exactly right for a warm spring afternoon. It arrived in the morning, brought by the Luxembourger who had arranged the show and the head of the consulate in New York, and they came back into the serving pantry and found me polishing the silver tea-service (really the maid's job, but we weren't sure the maid would have time or even if she would show up). No ceremony about them. In fact, they pried open the cases with a pair of scissors and insisted that we must open a bottle right away to see how it tasted. Even before lunch, it tasted fine. When the party began I was put in charge of it, to see that everybody had enough and nobody was permitted to drink too much. There turned out to be only one offender—he had that abject, alcoholic look around the eyes, and after about the tenth glass I began pointedly evading him. Everybody else—and long after the Minister had made his speech and departed there were people who stayed and stayed—was drinking for fun, not from necessity. I didn't ever realize until I got home at around eight o'clock that I was completely exhausted—too tired to eat, though all I had had since lunch, besides the wine, was a tea sandwich and a cookie or two. Monica and I had agreed just beforehand, when the third in a succession of maids contracted for and then incapacitated, came down at the eleventh hour with acute appendicitis and sent a message from the operating table, that we would never go through with another exhibition. The final substitute maid, located for us by a catering establishment, luckily arrived—a stately creature named Rose, who asked me if this was going to be a Social Register affair or just people who liked the birds, and confided that her girl-friend had been waitress the other evening at an affair which included the Duke and Duchess of Windsor. He was, according to the girl-friend, Just Charming. The girl-friend had wanted Rose to help her, but unfortunately she was working somewhere else, and she was so sorry. I told Monica about the Duke and Duchess afterward. "Those *cockroaches!*" she said. In her set, the famous pair are deplored as parasites and publicity-seekers. The real quality don't need to have their names in the papers, is the idea; it is only the pseudo-society one hears anything about.

It is a little like the story Henry James told about the Henry Adamses, who, living in Washington, decided to give a party and said, "Let's be vulgar—let's invite the President!" However, nothing makes Monica more furious than to be introduced as the Countess de la Salle—her own self-esteem is sufficient, so I guess she has a right to look down on the Duke and Duchess if she wants to.

I will send off to you very shortly a copy of Pettingill's *Guide to Bird Finding West of the Mississippi,* a sort of un-birthday present which really isn't from me but from my friend Leona, at whose apartment you may remember having dinner, and who gets copies of all Oxford books by virtue of her job editing them. There are a number of interesting things about Iowa—though I notice that a review in *Iowa Bird Life* complains about the McGregor district being left out—such as directions about seeing the piece of authentic prairie near Cherokee: nobody allowed in without the permission and the company of the owner: and a vivid summary of the changes in the landscape since the white man moved in.

It's rather chilly again, which is a nuisance. In Central Park the robins seem to be pairing up, and I've seen a flicker and a couple of phoebes, but the weather is all wrong for catching birds on their way through. A couple of months back I saw a small flock of what turned out to be American mergansers on the Reservoir—both males and females, scudding and bobbing along at a great rate. There are always gulls, up until sometime in May when they will all go off to breed, and lately they have become very vocal—I even hear them at work with the windows closed, and from that distance they sound rather like killdeers. Niko Tinbergen, the student of instinct and animal behavior who is an expert on the three-spined stickleback as well as the herring gull, and who is almost as good a writer as David Lack, has a new book out on the herring gull's world, which I intend to read. Peterson's guide to the birds of Europe is also out and seems to be universally admired, though one English reviewer complains mildly that this is the third book in a year whose jacket claims it to be illustrated by the greatest living bird artist. I happen to know that Peterson was greatly set up by this bit of blurb-writing; whether he believes it or not I don't know, but I certainly don't, though he is unquestionably the greatest living bird-popularizer. Anyhow, it is certainly a good book to have around, and was just what I needed the other day when Joe Goodman called up to ask what kind of bird the *zumaya* was; it was in a Lorca poem he had set to music and which was now being translated. Turned out to be a night-heron—I found this equivalent in a French book, lacking Peterson. Joe was busy turning out Lenten motets at the time; I suppose he still is. He said he had sent Mamma some piano pieces he had recently composed. I owe the Goodmans an invitation; must call them up. [. . .]

Love,

Amy

. . . .

13 May 1954

Dear Philip—

Your letter arrived yesterday, and of course I am concerned. Not that I have any intention of trying to dissuade you from going to the psychiatrist; the decision is yours and I am not honestly entitled to an opinion about it. What concerns me is your situation, and the fact that some things I have made bold to say from time to time at least appear to have influenced it. I don't take them back, of course, and I don't really believe that I am a bad influence. But it is possible that I have made things difficult for you, and even that I have misled you by tossing out fragments of a credo without giving you much idea of what it was based on. So if I mention things I have not brought up before and which are not brought up ordinarily, that is because I feel I owe it to you.

My adverse feelings about psychoanalysis are based on what I know of it at second hand. In New York it has become a cult; there are all those jokes about it only because it is taken so seriously. In certain sections of the career world it is hardly normal not to be in the process; it becomes no longer a cure but a way of life. I tried very hard to believe that it could be beneficial, mainly because of a particular instance—Cecile. You remember her, I am sure. She is an extremely gifted and likable girl and I owe her a great deal; for a long time I had considered her my closest friend, at least of my own sex, and I think she considered me likewise. But a day came, a few months back, when to my horror I saw all the things coming back which I had excused in her as part of her neurosis, and I could no longer excuse them. I could not excuse them because her very friendship had become a threat. I won't go into the details, which on the surface were so trivial that they explain nothing anyhow, but I saw that we disagreed fundamentally. We disagreed about what was real. And the only way I could go on being a friend of hers was to agree with her. Conversely, if I insisted on my own version I could no longer be her friend. It was the first absolute defeat I had met with since I began thinking for myself, and it was a terrible thing. How can I explain it? I saw that she was no less miserable than she had been five or more years ago, when she began her analysis; she had not changed; she was, if anything, more riddled by the envy and self-pity that had been there all the time; she hadn't learned a thing, and she had spent heaven knows how many thousands of dollars without even finding this out. For this I don't think her analysts were to blame; she has had two of them, the first of whom gave up and the second of whom, so far as I can make out, simply lowered the sights. She wanted to change, possibly, but not very much. I don't say this is what is in store for you; your problem is not in the least like hers, and I think you are capable of more honesty, which is a prime requisite if one is to be helped by a professional man concerning one's private difficulties. But having in a sense lived through this ordeal, and come to the shocking conclusion that I had lent my support to a worthless cause, I suppose I tremble a little at the thought of anyone's embarking upon it. For myself, the alternative is preferable. I am pretty sure I have been through the alternative, and I am not sorry; but it seems to me quite possible that some people, perhaps most people, would not envy me the experience, and that they would recommend the third possibility, which is inertia, conformity, capitulation, security, etc., in short a quiet form of self-annihilation, as the most satisfactory answer to the immemorial problem of what to do with one's life.

But the alternative? It is less systematic than the methods of the analyst, but as I understand those methods it is the same thing. It consists of being broken, smashed, shattered, torn apart—whatever words you like, none of them is too strong—and then, if the process is to have any significance, made whole. He that loseth his life shall find it; except a man be born again he shall not enter the kingdom of heaven—it's a biblical matter, only biblical terms quite express it. It is exposing the live kernel which, at any rate according to Christian theology, exists at the center of every human being. I am not certain whether I think this live kernel is actually in some people killed or perverted very early and thus rendered past redemption—which is a modification of the Calvinist notion, I suppose, and there is something to be said for the realism of their gloomy scheme of things—and that this possibility of early destruction or perversion explains a failure like Cecile's. (Of course it is possible that in the months since I removed myself from her life something has happened.) But the live kernel—it can be given all kinds of names, but I prefer the simplest one: love. What I mean by it is not passion, not sentiment, not altruism; they are all substitutes for the real thing, which I can only describe as a kind of stillness before the unknown. This sounds like mysticism, and I guess it is; but life is a mystery, despite all the brazen know-nothing-know-it-alls who keep telling us otherwise.

However, I didn't really mean to start on a disquisition. I really meant to try to tell you about me. Being the older sister, and having both an inordinate pride and an inordinate wish not to offend anybody or to get in anybody's way, I have gotten into the habit of keeping my own counsel. If I seldom give advice, knowing how unwelcome it generally is, as well as how useless, I still more seldom ask for it. This does not mean, though, that I have not many times been bewildered, miserable, and desperately alone, or that I have not done any number of things I was ashamed of. I am not so ashamed of them as I used to be—in fact I have pretty well forgiven myself once I began to understand why I did them, and however painful and costly my various mistakes may have been—there were all kinds of them—none of them was ever fatal or, indeed, useless; I learned something every time, and so far as I can make out I never made quite the same mistake twice. So perhaps they were not mistakes—call them experiments, part of the process of becoming educated. Out of all this welter has evolved, only half consciously, a set of principles. They will probably sound pretty negative, since they constitute a reaction against prevailing tendencies, all of which I recognize in myself: never to exert power for its own sake; never to cultivate anybody or anything for the sake of a possible future advantage; never to blame anybody without assuming a share of the blame myself; never to make claims on anybody else; to yield gracefully and with equal grace to be firm, and not to be swayed by other people's ideas of what is important. But to act on such a set of principles one has to know what is important to oneself; and one has to know that the right thing to do very frequently turns out to be the thing that is supposed to be wrong. This is particularly true of the most private relationships. Generosity, sincerity, spontaneity, according to the going canon are to be avoided, since they make you vulnerable; somebody is liable to take advantage of you, you are going to get hurt. But you forget the prevailing canon, because being yourself seemed temporarily more important; and of course the wiseacres were right all along—you do get hurt. Being yourself is not the way to get ahead. If you really want to get ahead, you had better stop wanting to be yourself. It's too bad, but—the truth is, it costs too much. This is the theme of any number of novels: the lament for the life that was lost by saving it.

Well, I don't know exactly how it happened, but I had some latent ambitions that did not consist in getting ahead. It is true that I very much wanted to make a fairly impressive marriage, in order to have seemed to have arrived, in the eyes of other people—and what other people thought has always been of great importance, odd as it may seem. On the other hand, I wanted a great romance; I wanted to know what it felt like to be tragic; I wanted the impossible. And the extraordinary thing is that without calculating in the least, I got it. I got two big romances, plus a number of small interludes that were in various degrees exciting, amusing and painful, plus a couple of more extended involvements that were none of these and were the hardest of all to get out of. That, I suppose, is what is meant by having been around. It would probably not have been possible anywhere else but in New York. I still vaguely thought, up until quite recently, that I would end up settling down like anybody else. Now I don't suppose that is very likely. The great romance turned out to be too wonderful. It proved something I wanted to believe without quite supposing I ever would—namely that people are not interchangeable; for certain rare ones there are no substitutes, and rather than the substitute that might be possible one would prefer nothing at all. This is all very much on my mind because I read your letter on the subway on the way back from Grand Central, where I had just put the uninterchangeable young man on the train. This has been going on for quite a while, and I thought I knew all there was to know about farewells on station platforms, and all about being tragic, and all about love; but by this time we had even got past the tragedy and the histrionics. I don't understand it at all. There is nothing quite like it in any of the books I have read, so it isn't simply a matter of life trying to be like literature. But it is something that must have no official existence, since officially it would be nothing but a social outrage. The label means nothing only because what lies behind it is so much more real—it's the whole mystery and tragedy of discovering what it means to reach another human being. Of course the whole thing is a risk; it always was; but so is life, if one is to find out anything about it. There is still the chance that I shall end up being beaten and embittered, though there seems less chance of it the more things go on developing unexpectedly, as they continue to do. From what I have observed I know more about being happy than most people; but the direct corollary is that I also know more about what it is to suffer. And, though I do my best not to offend more conventional people, I am not conventional. So whatever wisdom I may have to offer comes out of having done the wrong things. And there is a good deal to be said for abiding by the conventions, unless one is prepared for all kinds of anguish and even trouble. I really don't know what to tell anybody, except that thinking and feeling as a separate human being instead of letting society think and feel through one, is hard work, and one cannot expect to be thanked for doing it.

Perhaps you had guessed something like this; I have never known exactly what the accepted version of myself was, if there is such a thing. Anyhow, my standards are severe, if peculiar, and according to them I rate you very highly. It seems to me possible that this spent and invaded feeling which you seem to have is a step forward, even though it may seem like the opposite. Nothing needs to be a step backward; it is simply moving in a new direction, and you can never know in advance what it may lead to. As I said at the beginning, I am not in the least qualified to say whether you ought or ought not to get psychoanalyzed. It is bound to be disagreeable, but so are so many other things.

There were barn swallows in Central Park the other day—beautiful sight. Heaven knows where they came from. Also, there is a scarlet tanager which I have seen on four different occasions, and the warblers are passing through, so I spend my lunch hours in the open these days when it isn't pouring rain. The horse-chestnuts are in bloom, and precisely on Shakespeare's birthday I finally succeeded in finding the Shakespeare garden, where there were violets and even one rather spindly little Iowa sort of bluebell, along with bluebells of the English sort, and narcissus, and a mulberry tree from Stratford. The gulls are still making a lot of noise, but I learned from Peterson when he was in the other day the reason why— they're laughing gulls, which moved in about the time the herring gulls left. We hear them screaming maniacally every afternoon through our open window. "Listen to the laughing gulls," I remarked to a girl who came down to the library the other day. "What are they laughing at?" she wanted to know. Monica had the answer: "Human stupidity." And sometimes, watching them cruise over the reservoir, having the time of their lives, I almost believe it. Well, do write, and if you feel like coming to New York for your vacation, or part of it, please come—I can put you up some way, even if it means mending that old camp cot.

Love,
Amy

P.S.

15 May, Saturday. I have just been reading some essays by that dangerous, often tiresome, and often superb maverick, D. H. Lawrence, and will copy

out some passages that pleased me especially: [Extended quotations follow, taking up three quarters of a page.]

The book was lent me by an Italian-American painter whom I met in Paris, and who fined me five hundred francs at the time because I told him I guessed he was a genius. I hadn't heard from him since, but he turned up one day a few weeks back and now I am buying on the installment plan (the five hundred francs was the first installment, retroactive) a painting I haven't yet seen because so far as I know it isn't even started; and meanwhile we are trading books—he has my Toynbee, Volume Three. . . . Today I bought three pink peonies from a little boy who sells them by the subway; the smell reminds me of wet June days in Iowa, just after school was out. Then I went into a second-hand bookstore and bought the Confessions of St. Augustine in a paperback edition, and a Greek grammar. I have decided to see if I can't learn enough to be able to read Sophocles in a Loeb parallel edition, the way I have been reading Dante. I'm well into the Purgatorio—and after all, D. H. Lawrence isn't necessarily the last word. You might, though, look into *Sons and Lovers*. It's beautiful, dreadful, and finally infuriating, but probably very great. Oh, and there is also Stendahl—I just finished *The Red and the Black*—but I advise you to leave him alone. He ain't healthy.

A

. . . .

2 October 1954

Dear Philip—

[. . .] Of course I very much appreciated your letter, on which I won't comment further since I'm hardly qualified in the circumstances. What moves me to write is a conclusion I have gradually been coming to for years and years and which now strikes me more forcibly than ever—namely, that people are a lot stupider than practically anybody thinks they are. Maybe it would be more precise to say, than *I* used to think they were. And by stupidity I mean not the inability to think but the refusal to, on the assumption that other people know what they are talking about. The most striking example I can think of is what has happened over the last several months to people's opinions of Senator McCarthy. I distinctly remember, early in the year, reading one of Rovere's Letters from Washington in the *New Yorker*, and shuddering at the statement from this very intelligent reporter that in the minds of many people McC. was "perhaps the most original and daring politician since Franklin Roosevelt." The implication was that if Rovere himself hadn't invented the opinion (I almost suspect he did), he at any rate shared it; he sounded very gloomy indeed, away last January. At the time I was still maintaining (not having read enough in the newspapers to be carried away by the despair that seemed to grip everybody well-informed) that McCarthy was a stupid man. I remember saying this to my friends Leona and Phoebe (you met them), and they said oh no, McCarthy was smart—as though stupidity and evident paucity of intellect were two different things entirely, and there was just no hope of triumph over that kind of smartness. Well. A couple of weeks back, in an exceptionally moving as well as delightful Letter from Washington, Rovere described what was going on in the meetings of the Senate committee appointed to consider the move to censure McC. From the tone and the details of the description of McCarthy's appearance before that committee it was clear that Rovere thought the Senator was stupid, and the implication was very close to being that stupidity and paucity of intellect were the same thing after all. Did Rovere remember that eight or nine months [ago] or earlier he had characterized this odious but stupid man as "perhaps the most original and daring politician since Franklin Roosevelt"? There is no way of knowing, but one is certainly entitled to wonder. A further Well. A few evenings ago Leona was here; the McCarthy issue was already so dead that we mentioned it only in passing, but clearly she no longer thought McCarthy was smart. I didn't bother to remind her that she had once thought so, so I don't know whether she remembered that she ever had; but I wonder. And Leona is an extremely intelligent girl, as quick as anybody I know to detect a cant phrase in most quarters; but she reads the papers, which I begin to think is the best way of keeping oneself confused about what is going on in the world. Anyhow, we sat here agreeing that people are stupid, and that we had been stupid ourselves to believe what most of them said most of the time. (While we were agreeing, my mouse came right out into the open, and sat there in the space between the stove and the icebox, looking at us; no doubt it was thinking the same thing, since on the kitchen shelf sat a trap delectably baited with Swiss cheese; as if people thought any self-respecting mouse couldn't see right through that one!) And yet it isn't that the world is made up of stupid people. Look at those six Senators who had hardly been heard of, and who were thus supposed to be the easiest thing in the world for McCarthy to make mincemeat of. They were not stupid. On the contrary, they are the first proof we have had for quite a while that there is any intelligence in the Senate, or maybe even in the whole Government.

Eisenhower's trouble isn't stupidity—it's fear. And it was his fear that gave everybody else an excuse for being afraid. When one looks back on this year, it seems an extraordinary one—and yet the same kind of demonstration of fear of thinking for oneself has been going on for years: people being so scared of being wrong that they don't let themselves know when they are right. I suppose there is no cure for the majority: self-interest breeds fear, and fear breeds snobbery and a closed mind, and at that self-interest is probably a solider hub for society to turn on than self-denial, though either one is dangerous without the other. I guess what moves me now is mainly indignation at my own stupidity: that I should have listened for so long to the gospels of a frightened, pious snobbery when all the time I knew better, if I had only had the courage to see with my own eyes! The East is full of snobs and bluffers and advertising men, and the Midwest takes orders from the East, all the time quaking in the boots of an imaginary inferiority. In my now fairly extensive acquaintance the number of people who give any sign of confidence in the brains they were born with is outrageously small. You are one of that small number. Now I am going to sound like an exhorter, though I have no wish to be one (anybody so ill-advised as to attempt to follow in my footsteps would deserve everything that happened to him, and would enjoy none of it; and happily I have no desire to found a cult, though at moments I wonder whether I am not the happiest person in the world)—I am going to stick my neck out and say, as one believer in free inquiry to another, that I think you would make a very good teacher. This is not a piece of advice, it is simply an opinion; it is conceivable that the same statement might be made to me (though I can't recall that it ever has) but it would not send me back to finish up my master's degree.

A chickadee just now flew up and perched on the fire escape, announced its identity, and flew away. There have been chickadees in the garden underneath my windows for the last week now. I don't recall having seen any there before, and this was certainly the first time one has come as close as the fire escape while I was around—though I have seen kinglets, myrtle warblers and thrushes down there after a big night in the migration season. The migration in Central Park has gone somewhat ker-flooey because of peculiar weather: after a warm night there never seems to be much doing, and for the last week the nights have been unseasonably, indeed almost disagreeably warm. However, one day I saw young black-throated green warblers by the dozen in one tiny area—perching all over trees and bushes, running all over the ground, chasing grasshoppers and butterflies, and letting me get so close that I could see every detail of their immature plumage. I don't think they knew the difference between a human being and a tree, though none of them actually used me for a perch—I couldn't stand still long enough, too much to see. I also got my first good look at a Parula warbler—beautiful little thing—and at a red-breasted nuthatch.

I've been too busy writing (I'm on chapter nine now, something like seventy thousands words written and the half-way mark only just coming into sight) to do a great deal of reading, and Greek has had to go entirely by the boards though I expect to get back to it some day. However, I've managed a few snippets from the Greek historians as translated by Toynbee (another paperback), a novel of dreadful precocity called *Bonjour Tristesse*, written by an eighteen-year-old girl and currently a best-seller in France, which I sailed through with no trouble, and the first few poems in the *Fleurs du Mal* of Baudelaire—here I look up absolutely every word I'm not sure of, the only way to read poetry in a foreign language and a good way of increasing one's vocabulary besides; and, for exercise of a different kind, a couple of books by extreme conservatives. The first was a thing called *Ideas Have Consequences* by Richard M. Weaver, published in 1948 by the University of Chicago Press, and it was not only one of the most literate, it was one of the most serious, and thus impressive, books of recent vintage I have read. His contention is that the world went wrong back around the end of the fourteenth century, with William of Occam and the doctrine of nominalism. (To be sure I had this right, I have just consulted Webster, who says "the doctrine that there are no universal essences in reality, and that the mind can frame no single concept or image corresponding to any general term," and the Concise Oxford, which puts it more succinctly, "doctrine that universals or abstract concepts are mere names.") From the denial of any transcendent reality, he says, come the evils which riddle our culture: with the kind of detached moderation which only makes them seem more awful, he catalogues them as Fragmentation and Obsession, Egotism in Work and Art, the Great Stereopticon (by which he means the popular press and all the other means by which the vested interests of the age perpetuate selected images of life which they wish to have imitated), and the Spoiled-Child Psychology ("the scientists have given him the impression that there is nothing he cannot know, and false propagandists have told him that there is nothing he cannot have. . . . The spoiled child has not been made to see the relationship between effort and reward. He wants things, but he regards payment as an imposition or as an expression of malice by those who withold for it. . . . He has been given the notion that progress is automatic, and hence he is not prepared to understand impediments; and the right to pursue happiness he has not unnaturally translated into a right to have happiness, like a right to the franchise. If all this had been couched in terms of spiritual insight, the case would be different, but when he is taught that happiness is obtainable in a world limited to surfaces, he is being prepared for that disillusionment and resentment which lay behind the mass psychosis of fascism. . . . The Stereopticon has so shielded him from sight of the abysses that he conceives the world to be a fairly simple machine, which, with a bit of intelligent tinkering, can be made to go. . . . But the mysteries are always intruding, so that even the best designed machine has been unable to effect a continuous operation. No less than his ancestors, he finds himself up against toil and trouble. Since this was not nominated in the bond, he suspects evildoers and takes the childish course of blaming individuals for things inseparable from the human condition. The truth is that he has never been brought to see what it is to be a man.") All of which seems to me very profoundly true, the more because, until the repeated intrusion of the mysteries shook me loose, I was at least halfway committed to the Spoiled-Child Psychology myself. As might be expected, this man is so thorough-going a conservative that he sees nothing good in jazz or non-objective painting, that he believes more than half seriously that women should not smoke or drink, and that he is committed to the institution of private property. And there is no doubt that, simply because he means what he says, this is a much solider book than the one I wrote you about before, *The Uses of the Past*, which was in itself a much more serious book than most books which attempt to set forth the point of view of liberalism are. I even wondered whether I was turning out to be a conservative, in spite of my private conviction that the institution of private property is a pernicious nuisance; for private convictions are based on private experience, and private experience is not universal. I thought, in short, that what is best for one not being best for all, I perhaps ought to set aside my own romantic individualism as too special to mean anything. This may or may not be so; however, I followed Mr. Weaver with a book by another writer of a similar stripe—but oh, what a different color! This was *God and Man at Yale*, which I promised Monica I would read after having admitted that what other people said about it was really not sufficient basis to condemn its author on. I read it, striving to keep an open mind, though that was a dull and disagreeable task. Buckley quotes

Weaver at one point, but it is clear that he does not understand his own sources of authority, if indeed he has read them. It is a terrible tattle-tale sort of book, by a young man who does not believe in free inquiry, and certainly would not agree with the following statement, also by Weaver: "The virtue of the splendid tradition of chivalry was that it took formal cognizance of the right to existence not only of inferiors but also of enemies. The modern formula of unconditional surrender—used first against nature and then against peoples—impiously puts man in the place of God by usurping unlimited right to dispose of the lives of others. Chivalry was a most practical expression of the basic brotherhood of man. But to have enough imagination to see into other lives and enough piety to realize that their existence is a part of beneficent creation is the very foundation of human community. There appear to be two types of whom this kind of charity is unthinkable: the barbarian who would destroy what is different because it is different, and the neurotic, who always reaches out for control of others, probably because his own integration has been lost. However that may be, the shortsightedness which will not grant substance to other people or other personalities is just that intolerance which finds the different *minderwertig.* . . . Not until we have admitted that personality, like nature, has an origin that we cannot account for are we likely to desist from parricide and fratricide." If this is not liberalism, that is because most liberals are incapable of such open-mindedness. Certainly that Buckley fellow is no liberal; he is no gentleman either, he is a barbarian. If private property has no more graceful defenders than Mr. Buckley, there is no hope for it that I can see. It occurs to me that these days most reactionaries are barbarians and most liberals are neurotics, and neither one of them has any self-confidence. I guess there is no use trying to decide whether I am a liberal or a conservative. I am not quite sure but that I am more nominalist than realist: there may be universals, but all I am sure of is that there are individuals and that each one is unique because it is an individual, though back of it there must be some transcendant reality from which they unfold as the leaves on a tree.

Well, this has gone on long enough. I am not totally preoccupied with the eternal verities—the other day I at least took time off from them long enough to buy a new dress I had happened to see in an ad (black, very chic, very svelte, and the first real dress I've bought in years and years) and which I suppose I shall wear when I go to hear the *Rosenkavalier,* finally, a couple of weeks hence. Also, I sent the *New Yorker* a remark I overheard at the pier when I went to see Annabel and Arthur off ("He keeps oysters. He puts in a thing so it doesn't come out pearls, it comes out diamonds"—I swear it, that's what the man *said*), and the *New Yorker* has sent me a check for five dollars. And this seems to be a most satisfactory achievement.

Love,

Amy

. . . .

3 February 1955

Dear Philip—

All this talk about the polar ice cap breaking up is premature, I've decided. I'd begun to think so yesterday, when I woke up to find it snowing, and at eight o'clock this morning, when the Weather Bureau reported a reading of zero, I was sure of it. There wasn't a proper amount of heat at work, but it could have been worse so I didn't bother to go out to lunch; and after lunch I spent an hour or so writing a letter to a little girl in Guttenberg, Iowa, who wrote in asking us to settle an argument about whether or not man was descended from the ape. This is probably going to be my favorite answer-to-a-question for a while. In the first place, it was going to be a letter for Monica, who is a Catholic, to sign, and it also had to be a letter whose contents I myself approved of; in the second place, I had never before so much as looked inside the *Origin of Species*. Well, if I do say so the finished product wasn't bad; Monica found nothing in it to quarrel with, and I had looked at the *Origin of Species* and even quoted a couple of sentences each from the first and last chapters—discovering in the process that Darwin got the idea of writing it during the voyage of the Beagle, spent five years collecting and meditating on facts before setting down an outline of his theory, and fifteen more writing the book itself, and finished it in a spirit of audacity tempered by reverence. Of course the substance of the letter, which ran to two pages, was that we do not know. What the little girl in Guttenberg may make of it is, of course, another matter, but I feel as if I had put in a good day's work on that letter alone.

Yesterday it snowed all day long. Since I had brought a sandwich I wasn't going to go out at noon then either, until Monica dared me to because I say I believe in principle in getting a little fresh air in the middle of the day. And of course the principle is absolutely right. I went stamping through the snow into Central Park, watched the gulls riding white-on-white through the snow over the reservoir, heard the noise of water gurgling against the fringes of an open patch in the ice, and thought of Thoreau describing the spring thaw on Walden Pond. One understands perfectly, hiking through the snow on one's lunch hour, what Thoreau was up to. One also understands why people go to church, though one prefers, oneself, to continue staying away (which is why it is possible for a non-conformist born and bred and confirmed by any amount of experience, to write a letter on the origin of species which a Catholic will sign). The most delightful and startling part of that twenty minutes' tramp, however, was more specific—it had to do with the color red. In the midst of all the degrees of white and gray and no-color that you get in a snowstorm, here was this little gray tree with a few red berries on it—some kind of hawthorn or holly. It was pretty enough in itself, but it happened that I had just been reading Bob Allen's flamingo manuscript (for the purpose of straightening out the commas and the thats and whiches, ostensibly) and had just come to the discussion of the difference in intensity of color between the European and the West Indian species—a question I had wondered about and had tentatively supposed, as it turned out Huxley had suggested, must be one of diet (more carotene in West Indian shrimps, or something). It turns out, though, after all the researches into stomach contents, et cetera, that the diet theory doesn't hold up. Why the European bird should be pale pink and the West Indian one bright scarlet, they simply don't know. Actually, sober scientific monograph though it is, with no effort to dress it up for lay consumption, the flamingo manuscript is not only fascinating—in all its painstaking accuracy it is fundamentally poetic. This is partly because it is very well-written, mainly because it is the product of an imagination that sees not only facts but meanings and relations, all part of some marvelous whole. The purpose in gathering all these facts was to find out what might be done, if anything, to save the few remaining West Indian flamingo colonies from extinction; and the conclusion is, not much. The problem turns out to be a human almost more than an ornithological one: one reason the flamingos in the Bahamas have been nearly wiped out—aside from things like being buzzed by low-flying planes, which have been known to scare away several thousand incubating birds from their nests—is that since some kind of disease attacked the sponge fisheries off which the natives made their living heretofore, they have been so nearly reduced to starvation that they kill or catch (very difficult, this latter) the birds, which aren't very good eating, simply to keep alive. It's sad, but it's real. Well, you see why I like working for the Audubon Society.

On my way home from work in the snow I paused in front of the second-hand bookshop which opened up a year or so back in a little hole-in-the-wall on Twelfth Street—the one where I bought my Greek grammar, and, more recently, a set of Gibbon for three-fifty, and where one usually gets into a very intense literary discussion every time one wanders in, though I don't know who these people are at all. I didn't have it in mind to buy anything, but there was a window display on Henry James—a couple of minor first editions, a couple of pictures, and some lovingly selected quotations about him from Conrad and T. S. Eliot and F. R. Leavis; and since for years I have regarded Henry James as a sort of private guiding light as well as probably the greatest American novelist, there was nothing to do but drop in and pay my respects (almost the way a properly brought up Catholic will bend the knee before the altar every time he enters a church). There was nobody there but one of the partners, and pretty soon (he is, whoever he is, exceedingly learned, and I had hitherto thought, rather pedantic—but I guess I was wrong) we were talking about historians and I was realizing that after I finish Trevelyan's *History of England* (which has sent me straight back to Shakespeare—the two Richards and both parts of Henry IV so far) I have got to read Macaulay and Carlyle—not for the facts, which I never retain in any detail for very long, but for the qualities of their minds. Presently we had got around to James again, and to the inexhaustibility of *his* quality of mind—every time I reread anything, as I have just reread *The Wings of the Dove*, I have the feeling that I hadn't really understood it before, and this seems to be the experience of everybody who cares for him at all. (One of those lovingly selected quotes, I forget from whom, called him the most intelligent man of his generation—a queer kind of superlative, but possibly true.) Then the phone rang—somebody telling the partner to get a move on, dinner was getting cold. I made my apologies, to the partner and the cook, and bolted into my Italian greengrocer's (easier to say than fruit-and-vegetable store), where there was the usual conversation: Che dice? Fa freddo, no? Lei piace il neve? Quando scendi, si, ma non doppo. . . . Due pampelmi. . . . Pampelmi? Si, si, you know, grep*froot* . . . Ah! pampelmi! E che ciu'? (This, I guess, is Sicilian, and what Italian I know is Florentine. Sometimes I wish I had never started all this, or else that I knew the words for a few things besides vegetables; it isn't conversation, it's a ritual.)

By the time I got in—the conversation in the bookstore had gone on for at least forty-five minutes, it turned out—I was about ready to call it a day, in fact I was so tired that I read Shakespeare until half-past eleven because I was too lazy to close the book and go to bed.

The night before I had been at a party and hadn't got to bed until one—a very decorous and really rather dull party, where I didn't know very many of the people, most of whom were English; and I always forget, such are the manners of well-bred English people when one meets them at such affairs, that it is just their way of self-defense, that really I love the English and that really I consider theirs the only civilized country in the world. The only conversation I had all evening that deserved the name—conversation, as distinguished from chitchat and showing off—turned about the Salinger story in the then current *New Yorker*, the one about the girl named Franny who had gone in for religious exercises. One of the people who had read it, and who professed a great admiration for Salinger, said he just didn't get it; several other people considered it an inferior sample, with too much talk and not enough happening; one girl, rather to my surprise—and I think she had understood the story better than anybody else—said, "Yes, of course there are girls who go to pieces like that—and who wouldn't, with that awful guy!" I hadn't thought of the guy as awful myself, but simply as the victim of something awful—which is hardly a distinction. Anyhow, it's a very good story, and a very symptomatic, if frantic one—one always has the feeling about a story by Salinger that he doesn't understand what is happening very well himself, he is simply compelled to set the thing down, and whenever he sets anything down it is with such helpless anguish and outraged innocence that by the end of it he has you tied up in knots and gasping with indignation too. The interesting thing to me about this Franny story is that it deals with the same thing precisely that Henry James invariably deals with—the search for a pure heart. What makes James a great writer and Salinger a merely touching one is a matter of intelligence, of seeing things whole. Read James sometime. Not now. He makes great demands on your attention, as a great writer should, and there are still people who say he never really dealt with Life.

You see what's the matter. I'm defending myself against the success of a writer like Salinger, whose appeal consists precisely in that he feels confusion, communicates confusion, and in a sense justifies it; he doesn't ask you to think, but asks you, on the contrary, to feel along with him how utterly useless it is to think at all. Now I deliver a large chunk of manuscript to my agent and am told, in effect, that it is cold and detached and lacking in feeling—good writing, oh yes, beautiful writing, but he very much doubts that it would sell. One has to fight rather hard for a little while against this unhappy prognosis, knowing that the feeling is there, else there would have been no incentive to write in the first place, and that intelligence and self-control are in effect being condemned as defects, that depth has been written off as mere detachment. Well, enough of this. My friend Peter, the one I bought the painting of, came around the other evening and listened to a couple of chapters. He is as Latin as I am Anglo-Saxon and so touchy that he is likely to take offense at the most innocent statement, such as that perhaps—just perhaps, since I had been reading Shakespeare—the English Renaissance was more wonderful even than the Italian. He got so excited that I had to say immediately that I wasn't sure I thought so, simply to avoid a pointless argument. But when it comes to art we respect each other, and if he knows the real thing when he sees it, that's the important satisfaction—or *an* important one. The main one is still that I know what I am doing, and I have to do it, for quite other than market considerations. In fact, I'm fidgeting now because there have been too many distractions all week to leave any energy for writing, and the weekend was shot to pieces because of a birthday party that didn't break up until half-past three—to everybody's astonishment, because it was such a very good party that the entire conception of time had simply evaporated. But such parties are few and far between, and too many of them would leave no energy for anything else.

I haven't said a word about your letter, which I was very happy to have and which made perfect sense in spite of your professed anxiety about it. As for your not knowing whether you prefer being alone or with other people, I doubt whether anybody ever does except for a few very rare souls who are entirely contemplative and a few others who either can't stand to be alone a minute or who end up flagellating their sociability by turning hermit (and that last is a rather dubious analysis which I have no business making). So far as I can make out, solitude sharpens and refines one's taste for company, and just so much company renews the taste for solitude— Toynbee's theory of withdrawal-and-return, which he got from the Chinese—and the balance between them is something that works itself out as one goes along. The main thing is not to be anxious about it, or if one is anxious to translate the anxiety into something more positive. [. . .]
Love,
Amy

P.S.
Tell Mamma and Daddy I was sorry to hear that the trip left them under the weather. To tell the truth, I was pretty tired myself from the amount of rushing around I let us all in for. And as for lame knees, I know about

them from Paris—I had to stop climbing to the tops of towers, and when one knee began to improve only to have the other one give way, I had visions of the wheelchair for the rest of my life!

. . . .

26 March 1955
Dear Philip—
[. . .] It's a great relief to know that you've stopped seeing the psychiatrist. In my rasher moments, as you know, I'm opposed to the whole business, or anyway I'm likely to say I am. Actually what opinion I have is mainly prejudice, and though prejudices are generally based on something real, if irrational, when one looks at them closely one discovers that one is simply emphasizing one thing at the expense of something else. What bothers me about psychiatry, or one thing that bothers me (aside from the pious quackery that goes on, after all, in any profession) is that it is one more artificial manipulation, like enriched bread, homogenized milk, personalized whiskey bottles . . . I've just thought of a new slogan they might use: Your shirt is sanforized [*sic*]; are you psychoanalyzed? Of course the analogy with medicine is more reasonable: the introduction of an artificial process in order to prevent a natural one from becoming fatal. One can't quarrel with the theory. But in nine cases out of ten, I suspect, what medicine is able to do has no essential bearing on the outcome: the course of the disease may be speeded up, the discomfort may be alleviated, and there is a certain security for the patient in the fact that he is being attended to, but that is really all. But if the behavior of viruses and bacilli is complex and full of mysteries, the metabolism of a particular human personality is a thousand times more so; and whether psychotherapy, which so far as I can make out is simply an attempt to reproduce in the laboratory the very complex and mysterious process of change from helpless egotism to responsibility—or in old-fashioned terms, of having one's soul saved, of being born again— whether psychotherapy has ever actually accomplished anything of the sort, I have my doubts. The really bad cases I suspect are past cure, and the milder ones are probably cured mainly by natural processes. But so long as you have seen for yourself that there are limits to what the artificial process is able to solve, it's probably a good thing to have found out about. It's like that thing Emerson said about going to Harvard College, which I am so fond of quoting: it's a good thing to have gone there, if only to see for oneself how little it amounts to.

As for your not wanting to go into the teaching profession, I can understand it very well, since I think I feel pretty much the same way about it. One doesn't want to be pushing other people around, with so much pushing-around going on already all over the place. It was the same thing that made me decide I couldn't go back into the publishing business, or any other business: I didn't want to go on telling people to buy books I wouldn't have bought myself. The only redeeming feature about the job I did at the Oxford Press—aside from the people I met, and the fact that it sent me to England, both of which had incalculable effects on the entire course of my life—was that there was a certain latitude for creativeness. I set my own standards for the kind of thing I turned out, but I finally had to admit to myself that however much the result might be admired, there was no proof that those standards had any effect on what I was supposed to be doing, namely to sell more books. All the good taste and originality were just trimming, and they were costing money which, whether the people who paid my salary cared or not, I felt guilty about; so either it was a matter of turning completely cynical or simply pulling up stakes and starting over. Of course I didn't have this all thought out when I left to go to Europe, or even after I came back; but I see now that this is what it amounted to. And it isn't that I don't believe in the publishing business, since anybody who cares about literature as I do has to believe in it; nor do I doubt that there are people in it who care as sincerely, and who have the satisfaction of accomplishing something in cooperation with other people—which is, after all, the only real satisfaction. But I had, as I still have, a horror of turning professional, of having a label stuck on me which sooner or later might have eaten in and become more then skin-deep. It is one my own peculiar difficulties that while on the one hand I don't want to push other people around, on the other, and even more intensely, I don't want to do what I'm told unless I myself see a reason for it. And it isn't just that I can't conform; there was a time, in fact, when I conformed all too easily, with the result that I was usually conforming to several totally different patterns at once. Most incapacitating. Then there was a period when I made a real effort to pull myself together and to be like all the other middle-class young people I knew. It was fun while it lasted, but it didn't last very long, because I soon discovered that most of them were even more confused than I was, and that the pattern I thought was there simply didn't exist. This is why I found *The Lonely Crowd* so interesting; I'd been through it, and I knew what Riesman was talking about. Still, it was a painful thing to have pulled out of it, since being lonely by oneself, though it has its ultimate rewards, is much more acute than being lonely along with a lot of other people who are too bewildered to know how lonely they actually are. Now, though I have stopped being quite so belligerent about it most of the time, since vague masses and blocs of people don't scare me any longer, I am a non-conformist through and through and I don't see how I could have been happy being anything else. Within limits, I do pretty much as I like. For instance, I like being poor, relatively speaking; and it is a great victory not to have been made to find a job where I would simply be pushing other people around for no reason except the money and the prestige attached. There are very few people in this country, I honestly believe, who value money for itself; or for the purely material advantages it can buy, half as much as for the purely ideal effect it has in the eyes of other people. I couldn't have seen this, I suppose, without having earned enough to buy a few clothes, see a few plays, and go abroad; and I suppose I might feel hampered by my present relative poverty if I didn't regard it as poverty by choice. But then I am a nonconformist. If one is going to bring up a family it is not so easy. Then, if one's children are not to grow up puzzled, defensive, perhaps miserable, one has to pay more attention to what other people think—how much attention I really don't know, and I doubt whether anybody knows.

But I didn't mean to go on at such length about my own brand of nonconformity, which ought not to be taken as a model even supposing anybody wanted to try. (It's not an entirely negative attitude, in fact it is positively based on what I owe to quite a number of very different people. I don't consider myself a rebel, but a small, oddly shaped, not quite dispensable buttress in the architecture of society.) (Second parenthetical note: in the middle of the last sentence my friend Peter called up to say that while sitting in a cafe with some people at two o'clock in the morning he had had a revelation. It was almost exactly the same thing.) What I started out to say was that sooner or later you are going to have to come to a decision about what you want and what you can do without. There is not much point in giving advice, since such decisions are largely unconscious and are generally made, I suspect, long before we know anything about them. This does not mean that I doubt the existence of free will, or the enormous part that chance can play in what becomes of us; I think each of us is born with some essential nature, which is not mechanistically determined, which may be shaped to some degree by outward circumstances and even ruined by them, but is not governed by them altogether; even being ruined, I think, involves a certain choice.

I am a fatalist in that I believe we become what we are; but I am also not a fatalist, because I also believe that we are what we become. I suppose this is pretty close to Bergson's Creative Evolution. An organic interpretation of things makes more sense to me than a purely mechanistic one; but even the physicists, or one school of them, seem to believe now that there is not an absolutely demonstrable connection between cause and effect—which I take to mean that there must be some kind of free will even within the atom. But I keep getting off the track. You are going to have to decide, sooner or later, such things as a) the relative importance of what you think compared with what other people think, or seem to think; b) where you want to live; c) whether you would rather deal mainly with people—as you would in business, teaching, law, medicine, or almost any of the professions—or with things—as you would in engineering, scientific research, or farming. Your particular problem, of course, is that you don't want to specialize, and while I see no hurry about it unless the thing you want to do more than anything else is to settle down and start raising a family, the fact remains that you will have to specialize eventually. Santayana said, talking about Goethe, that one can't be anything without being something in particular, though I suppose that the longer one is allowed to postpone specializing, the less chance there is of getting stuck in the wrong niche. In thinking about the things you might do, my first thought was that the ideal recommendation would be for you to go to Europe for several months, just to wander around and get your bearings; but on second thought I am not sure this would solve anything. In my own case it worked because it threw me back on my own critical powers, whose functioning up to then had been obstructed by timidity and a lot of rather mixed-up enthusiasm; whereas your own very exceptional critical faculty doesn't appear to be obstructed by enthusiasm, but quite the reverse. (I may be entirely wrong about this last statement.) Europe opened a whole new dimension for me: it cured me finally of the belief in material progress which denies reality to the past, with the result that I stopped trying to live entirely in the present, which, as the Red Queen told Alice, is a pretty poor, thin way of doing things if one is inclined to think at all; and since all my ideas seem to come out of concrete, first-hand experience, I don't see how this could have happened in any other way. I see no reason why you shouldn't simply float around for a while, if you can find the means and that is what you feel like doing; though if you combined the floating with some private project, such as reading every word somebody like Thoreau or Jane Austen or Milton or Shakespeare ever wrote, or bringing your list of birds past the six hundred mark, I should think it would be more satisfactory, since some of the discipline of specialization would be involved. Until one imposes some limits on one's freedom one is not really free at all; and there has got to be freedom if existence is to make any sense. [. . .]

The other day during my lunch-hour wanderings in Central Park I saw a chickadee fly down off a limb and eat out of a man's hand. (I should have asked him whether he was a card-carrying member of the Human Ornithological Perch Society, or H.O.P.S. as it is more generally referred to, but I didn't think to do it at the time.) Actually, the man was trying to interest a cardinal which happened to be singing from a branch rather higher up, and which would have none of him, when the chickadee flew down. Of course, all the squirrels and even the English sparrows in the immediate vicinity were exceptionally tame, and were all running around every which way, along with a lot of singing grackles and one magnificent mallard duck that was swimming around a little pond; the green-necked bird in the water, the red one in the tree, and all the iridescent blue and purple grackles with their yellow eyes, were as astonishing a sight, if one really saw them, as could be imagined. The laughing gulls are back on the reservoir, and despite a cold rainy day yesterday and really fierce windy one today, the cherry trees along the reservoir should be out before the end of the week. I am also keeping track of things in the Shakespeare Garden, which I had never been able to discover until last year on, by a happy coincidence, Shakespeare's supposed birthday, the twenty-third of April; by which time the daffodils had finished blooming and the violets and bluebells were out. The daffodils are up out of the ground now, but the last time I looked there was no sign of bloom yet. They have a mulberry tree there which is a scion of another mulberry in Stratford; whether it was there in the sixteenth century or not I don't know for sure. [. . .]
Love,
Amy

. . . .

16 July 1955
Dear Philip—
[. . .] Your letters have a way of arriving with a timing that seems almost fatal now and then, and this latest has been one of those. In fact, there is nobody I would rather have heard from, since it found me in one of those states of exaltation when I would like to communicate, if there

were anybody around to whom I could make sense; but since there generally isn't, all I can do is contain myself. If I can't get a book published, I sometimes think it may be because I have already lived one—and however much I believe in literature, I still put life first. About ten days ago, just at the moment when it was the thing I wanted most, my young man—I mean *the* young man; he isn't really mine, he's just himself— phoned me from Vancouver, and the next thing I knew here we were again, riding the Staten Island Ferry, sitting in a bar and putting to rest the ghost of some awful thing more fundamental even than a quarrel that had been haunting the place since we last sat there a couple of years ago. I took a day off from work and we hired a car and went to the beach, but otherwise there was no signal to the world at large that for a few days I was leading that absolutely romantic existence that everybody wants but that even I, romantic as I am, had never quite believed could happen. One can't keep it up for very long at a time, and one wouldn't want to, I guess, even if one could; there are, after all, other things in the world than being completely, serenely happy in the company of one other person. But so much has gone into this—so many separations, hundreds and even thousands of miles, and so much misery which somehow never quite turned bitter, with moments and even hours when I wondered how I was going to keep from throwing myself out of the window, and simply so much time, during which we have seen each other change from a couple of scared, uncertain children into something like self-respecting adults—so much has gone into it since a particular instant, years ago now, when I had a rather frightened presentiment that something was happening that I couldn't help, and that I would never be the same again, (of course one can have such a presentiment only if one wants or at least halfway expects it)—so much has happened, I keep trying to say, that having at last discovered how to be happy seems a privilege that is warranted. Otherwise the implicit disapproval of the world at large would get in the way. One has to be very sure of what one wants, and one has to be very fortunate besides, if one is to be happy while breaking all the rules. I don't know what all this proves; the only advice to be drawn from it seems to be not to break the rules if one can possibly avoid it; but if I had the choice to make over again, I would still have broken the rules. The thing I am most conscious of sacrificing is any possibility of explaining myself to other people. Perhaps it is the inevitable price one pays, whatever the circumstances, for finding the one person with whom one can be completely oneself. The result is that people, consciously or unconsciously, tell me things about themselves; I don't think they know why they do it, but I know—it's because they feel safe with me. It's an enormous compliment, of course, though it still leaves one rather solitary. So here I am confiding in you. I can't tell you what a comfort it is to be able to do that, since as you know there is nobody else in the family who has any notion—unless, which I think doubtful, they have simply guessed—and it would only worry them if they did. I sometimes have the feeling that it is my career to put together the broken halves of something that seems to have split apart because of growing too fast—if it didn't sound so presumptuous, I would call that thing our national consciousness: on the one hand the old, rigid, fatalistic sense of evil and damnation, and on the other the reckless and frantic effort to smash it, kill it, get away from it somehow which only ends up in a sense that nothing means anything after all. If I have succeeded after a fashion, and by what I almost think must be the grace of God, in becoming a whole person, maybe that is all I can hope to do. Of course I would still like to carry it over into a book that a few hundred people might read with appreciation, but it begins to appear that in the book I have been working on anyway it simply isn't going to work. Scribner's turned it down with the most lukewarm half-praise ("intelligent and sensitive, but needs something to give it urgency"), and now there is a letter from Knopf which says the same thing, though with a more percipient editorial conscience: they wish it had more pace, more of an outward story line; as it stands (and no doubt for the author's purposes it is right as it stands) it is not likely to engage a sufficient number of readers to encourage them to take it on. I suppose it may be flattering myself somewhat, but I take what solace I can in thinking that this is close to an admission that the fault is less mine than it is all those unengageable readers'. ("Why dost thou pine within and suffer dearth, Painting thy outward walls so costly gay?" in the words of that sonnet of Shakespeare's which has been ringing in my ears for almost as long as I can remember. After all, it isn't enough to be personally happy; one still wants to *do* something.) If I knew how, I suppose I would give up fiction and try writing theology instead. But nobody pays any attention to that either, unless there is a prescription in it, Norman Vincent Peale fashion. The only prescription I can see right now is to use one's head, and seeing the pass some people have come to by doing presumably that, I'm not sure but that this is also bad advice at times. [. . .]

Love,

Amy

. . . .

28 November 1955

Dear Philip—

This will, I hope, be more in the nature of a reply to your letter, as well as an effort to make amends for that rather egotistical outburst of last week. If I had been born a Catholic, I should be doing penance; in fact, I think at moments I rather wish I had been, but since I wasn't, I have made do with reading some ten cantos of Dante. Oh, you know how I exaggerate things. But the truth is, I needed taking down a peg. I was getting smug about my own unique and fascinating existence, and when I wrote you—though partly it was to share an experience with a sympathetic auditor—I was showing off a little, I'm afraid, and I was also, more than a little, whistling in the dark. I think I already knew that my protests at being put, slightly drunk, on the subway, were really against the operation of ordinary human laws, from which even my unique and fascinating self is not exempt. Getting what one wanted, even when one pays a pound or two of flesh for it in advance, and particularly when it turned out to be more wonderful than one had dreamed it could be, is something one goes right on paying for, in one way or another. It's nobody's fault, and the anguish is the more acute because nobody can be blamed. Things change; one's self changes; other people change; and none of it can be stopped. I know just what Shelley meant with his *O world! O life! O time!*—and he was younger than I am when he said it. Fortunately, that wonderful sonnet of Shakespeare has also been echoing in my mind—"O no, it is an ever-fixed mark"—even while I was reminding myself that Paolo and Francesca were placed in hell, and rightly so. Disillusion is one thing, but cynicism is quite another. But here I go getting solemn again. I am not offering any moral precept about romance, and certainly not in the manner of Mr. Herman Wouk's *Marjorie Morningstar*, which spends something like six hundred pages telling a soggy and frowzy tale which arrives at no better conclusion than that none of it should ever have happened. It was almost enough to smother any wish one might have to join the company of the successful novelists. I was sore enough about *Bonjour Tristesse*, but at least that one was short. No, I still stick to romance; it hurts, but it also sharpens one's moral wits, if one has any to begin with.

Actually, there has been a lot else to think about besides one's very private affairs. Just now I had a call from a girl whom I took an immediate liking to, the first and only time I saw her, several weeks ago. I don't know very many girls any more; I get fidgety in their company, and have trouble finding anything to talk about. But this girl, Mary [Russell], is an artist;

she is just back from three years abroad, and she comes from Nebraska. She is a friend of my friend Peter's [Peter Marcasiano, the painter whom Amy met in Paris the previous year], from the time they were at the Art Students' League together, and since he had read me some of her letters from Baghdad and Florence and Amsterdam and such places, I had already a little the feeling that I knew her. Anyhow, just after she came back he brought her around for dinner, and it was an eminently satisfactory occasion. I made a soufflé which, I have to confess, was better than I thought a soufflé could be, and after the strawberry tarts and espresso coffee we sat around talking and talking until two o'clock in the morning, mostly about painting but about a good deal, at least in snatches, besides. And it wasn't just intellectual talk, than which there is nothing more unsatisfactory. Such evenings don't happen very often. Anyhow, I'm having lunch with Mary tomorrow. Peter tells me she is usually rather shy and silent, and I only hope my chatter won't scare her back into it again. [. . .]

I re-read *Wuthering Heights* the other day. Marvelous. For certain moods anyhow. And there is the Brancusi sculpture show, to which I have been five times, so now when I go I have to chat like a habitué with the guard. He told me it was much the most successful show the Guggenheim Museum has yet had—you remember, we went there during lunch when you were last here; there was a Cézanne then, I forget what else. I wandered in the first time by accident, not having any particular interest in Brancusi, and discovered by degrees that I was being astonished as I never had been by anything modern, or any sculpture, before. I have recommended the show to several people, and they all seem to have had the same experience. It's hard to describe precisely what its effect is, or how it happens; but when I came out of it the first time I felt as if I could fly. A great deal of smoothing and simplifying and polishing has gone into it; there are often several versions, differing only slightly, of the same thing; and the materials, which have been treated with such care, are delicious— polished brass, alabaster, yellow marble; and then there are some things made out of old pieces of wood that are in some ways the most marvelous of all. And yet this is the first real museum show Brancusi has ever had; for years, it seems, he has been working away in Paris, bitter at being neglected. He must be close to seventy by now. [. . .]

Love,
Amy

. . . .

1. Amy, with cat, as a teenager.

2. Amy (*right*) at Grinnell College, 1940, with two classmates.

3. Amy with her parents, at Grinnell, 1941.

4. Amy in Riverside Park, near Columbia, c. 1942.

5. Amy with Barbara Blay, London, 1949.

6. Amy, as Phi Beta Kappa poet, at Harvard University, June 1987, with President Derek Bok.

7. Amy among the "Literary Lions" at the New York Public Library, November 9, 1989: (*left to right, front row*) Edward Albee, Tess Gallagher, Amy Clampitt, Bharati Mukherjee, Eve Merriam, William Zinsser; (*second row*) Mordecai Richler, Avery Corman, Carl Bernstein, Elmore Leonard, Joseph Mitchell, Hunter S. Thompson; (*top row*) William Arrowsmith, Lucille Clifton, Jay McInerney, Garry Wills, Robert Giroux, Kate Simon, Nat Hentoff.
Photo: Mary Hilliard

8. Amy, c. 1990.

9. Amy and Harold Korn, on the day of their wedding,
June 10, 1994, in their Lenox cottage.
Photo: Karen Chase

13 February 1956

Dear Philip—

This is the end of a three-day weekend and it finds me fuming, but if I don't write you now there will be absolutely nothing to show for it and besides I should be getting around to wishing you a happy birthday. So if I sound cranky I hope you will make the proper allowances.

It all started out with having to come down with a cold in the head just in time to collapse miserably into bed on Friday night. There I stayed all day Saturday. I got myself up yesterday, only to discover that my brains were like tallow, and that there was nothing to be done but to go on reading. So by today, with the cold nearly gone except for two queer hollow patches somewhere behind the cheekbones, I was simply gorged and sated with literature. Really, books can be quite tiresome. Besides, my kitchen tap is dripping again, and the apartment next door is inhabited by a vivacious creature who the minute she comes in turns on the radio and starts calling people up on the telephone, and her voice is just penetrating enough so that the intonations all come through the wall but the words remain behind and so there is the eternal mystery of whether it is always the same person or one of fifty different people at the end of the wire, and what on earth is so merrily, or so indignantly (for one can't be sure either of the intonations themselves) being talked about. Of course, it is also possible that there is somebody else there whose voice doesn't penetrate the walls, or that she is an actress rehearsing, or that she is simply mad and talking to herself. One could go similarly mad with such speculations. So, remembering hungrily the cowslips and bluebells growing under medlar trees at the Cloisters, and likewise the snowdrops blowing in a March wind under an apple tree, I thought this morning that the thing for me to do would be to get on the subway and go up there. Then I thought of the chilly tapestry corridors one has to pass through before one reaches the gardens, and it hardly seemed worth while. Then I thought of taking along Book One of *The Faerie Queene* for the subway, to get me into a proper mood to look at the tapestries too, and decided I must go after all. Then I remembered that this was Monday, and the Cloisters would be closed. It was all exceedingly frustrating. I went out anyhow, forgetting my library card though I had it in mind to see if I could get the first volume of the letters of Katherine Mansfield, having finished the second, and discovered that anyhow the library was closed so I could not even see if the first volume was on the shelves. The only other real mission I had was to buy some buttons to sew on a little yellow dress, originally intended for

Joe Goodman's daughter Meredith, which I have ended up making for her little sister Alison since Meredith has gotten too big meanwhile for the amount of material there was (I'm not even sure, in fact, that Alison won't have outgrown it by the time it is delivered, at this rate). I found these in a dime store, along with a lot of demented parakeets and forced azaleas in pots too small for them and floorwalkers shrieking at sassy salesgirls, and sassy salesgirls talking back to impatient customers, and squalling children being shouted at by their mothers, and shriveled old women shuffling along in somebody else's shoes. I also went into a female haberdashery, since I remembered that I needed some stockings, and there was a Negress six feet tall, with her hair dyed red, behind the counter. A sale was going on, and the place was full of pawing women, for any one of whom, I suppose, hairdressers, foundation garments, and eyebrow tweezers are indispensable, whether or not the rent is paid or their souls are their own or in a hockshop somewhere. I also went into a bookstore, not because I really wanted to, and bought a paperbound book of thirty translated Spanish poems for seventy-five cents, because this seemed a venture calling for support, and for ninety-five cents another paperback of Dylan Thomas's *Portrait of the Artist as a Young Dog* for I'm not quite sure what reason, since now that he is dead it is a little late to be lending one's support, and they collected a fairly tidy sum, I understand, to take care of his widow and three children. I have never read any of his poetry. Once I went to hear him read it; he was already quite rumpled and roly-poly and not at all romantic-looking any more, with red wine spilled down the front of his seersucker jacket, and he said he was sick of everybody's poetry including his own, so what he read was prose—and that is what P.O.T.A. etc. turns out to be, more of same. But oh, how he read it! He had the true voice of the bard. A girl I met not long afterward had been there, and she and her girl-friend got up and walked out in indignation, as though he had meant to shock them personally. I forget now just what it was that made them so indignant, but the prose anyway is all very much in the same key, in fact it is almost all on the same note, a rather monotonously cavorting exuberance, with human figures, very much alive but about the size of sand-fleas hopping through the waves along the shore. According to the jacket of this book I just bought, he didn't believe in New York but he loved Third Avenue. Poor man, it may be just as well that he died when he did; the bars are still there, but now that they have taken the El down you can't tell it from any other avenue. He used to hang out at a place called the White Horse, where I used to go, but I never saw him there, and I still remember

the week he died, and the appropriately dismal and alcoholic surroundings in which I heard the news. The reason *I* don't believe in New York right now, though—and how furious it makes me to have to admit that I don't believe in it, even as a place for *me*—is the flowers. Not being able to see snowdrops under an apple or cowslips under a medlar tree, I walked past a flower market, hoping to find a little slip of something I might take home as a substitute. But it was the same thing all over again, and that gets worse every season: hybridized monsters such as never belonged in nature, raised under glass and fed on hormones. Not only are they determined to produce a blue carnation if it kills them, just because there is no such thing in nature and thus is certain to be hideous; but even the natural colors have become quite unnatural. Daffodils and mimosas are only technically distinguishable, otherwise they are the same—mealy and bloated, and approximately the hue of dried egg yolk. Freesias and cyclamens have had all the scent inflated out of them, and violets are an enormous, flat, meaningless purple. There is no sense of fitness, no art, no respect for life. Really, I do feel ready to blow my top. I suppose when things start sprouting in the open air I'll get over it, and that the trouble, aside from a cold in the head and a three-day weekend wasted, is simply impatience to have the winter end. [. . .]
Love,
Amy

. . . .

17 March 1956
Dear Philip—
Something quite astonishing has occurred. No, I haven't fallen either in or out of love, in any literal sense; I haven't changed jobs; I haven't been offered a contract for my novel. On the contrary, just about a month ago I wrote a letter to the agent, asking him to put the manuscript on the shelf—and this decision, which I was able to arrive at only little by little and at the cost of some slight ego-mortification, appears to have precipitated what was to follow. Launched it, rather—it wasn't a plunge but simply a casting-off, in the nautical sense and possibly the theological as well. I had not only admitted that the novel would have to be rewritten from the beginning if it were ever to satisfy me; I had also admitted that though I knew to a certain extent what needed to be done, I was not at all sure that I was, or ever would be, capable of doing it.

This was a pretty hard admission, but once I had brought myself to the point of making it, it no longer seemed painful, but almost a kind of relief. Since the new year began I had found myself so unaccountably happy, so confidently sociable, that I had come to wonder whether my particular talent was for writing at all, whether it wasn't something far more modest but probably more satisfying, and just possibly somewhat less usual—a talent for living, for being happy. (I begin to think now that such a talent is after all much more prevalent than I suspected—but this is to anticipate. But I see you skipping lines already, or at least wishing the creature would come to the *point*. But the creature is garrulous, you know, and besides the point, if you skip at all, is likely to become invisible. Patience and forbearance, I pray—I threatened a long letter, and it is barely started.) [. . .]

New paragraph. It was a beautiful Sunday afternoon. Having written my letter, I signed, sealed and stamped it and deposited it in a corner mail-box to forestall any temptation to backslide, procrastinate and possibly change my mind. Then I took the subway to Overlook Terrace, to pay that visit to the Cloisters which I wrote you, I think, about being frustrated from paying earlier in the week. I forget if you have ever been there. If not, the next time you come to New York a visit is absolutely required. It's a beautiful place, both in its contents and in its location. On a sunny afternoon, as this one was, its location high on a bluff above the Hudson, facing the Palisades, is bathed in light, both direct and reflected. There are ramparts where you can walk in the open, and inside there are gardens where, just as I had hoped, some hothouse daffodils and crocuses and narcissus were already in bloom—the Cloisters proper. Or rather, not proper—a true cloister does not exist in any aggregate, but is simply an enclosed courtyard, quite generally, if not always, open at its center to the elements, and attached to a church or a monastery—a place not for formal worship, but simply for walking and meditation. Rockefeller money has made a museum of various elements of a number of cloisters, most of them from different regions in France, and there are odd pieces of painting, sculpture, stained glass, metalwork, enamel, and so on, dating to the middle ages. These, and above all tapestries. The really glorious treasure is a roomful of these which have to do with the mythological hunt for the unicorn. I have always loved them—everybody does—but on that afternoon I felt that I had discovered them for the first time. Before then I had been inclined to regard tapestry, even so marvelous a specimen of it, as a minor art, a sort of inferior brand of painting. But on that afternoon, while I wandered in and out, visually speaking, among the little wild strawberries, the bluebells and daisies and periwinkles and dozens of other flowers (so faithfully rendered that nearly all have been botanically identified) which are woven into the background of each of the scenes of the hunt, for the very reason that it was a composite work rather than that of a single individual—and not only composite but anonymous; not only the weavers, but the designer and even the place of origin are unknown, and even for whom it was commissioned is a matter of conjecture—I found it more satisfactory than painting. I don't know that I was intellectually conscious of any reason for this preference; I don't know that I was intellectually conscious of anything except thorough enjoyment. The place was full of people, most of whom had cameras and who appeared to have come primarily for the purpose of taking snapshots of each other; even so, I didn't mind them in the least. When it came time for the regular Sunday program of transcribed medieval music, I found myself a stone, instead of a chair, to sit on, and watched them file in. And after a while, when the first *Kyrie* started, I stopped watching the people and simply concentrated on listening to the music and watching the sunlight come in at a thirteenth-century window. The *Kyrie*, which of course is a cry for mercy, and the sun on the stone, a purely physical phenomenon, seemed while I listened to have some affinity, almost to be one and the same thing. After a while, when the music changed to something else, I was mildly aware that while this was going on I had—perhaps for no more than an instant, but there is no measuring this kind of experience—entirely forgotten my own existence. It is the sort of thing that has happened to me a few times in my life, but always before in moments of great excitement and with a kind of incredulity surrounding it like an iron ring. This time there was no iron ring, no excitement, no surprise even, but a serenity so complete that I hardly thought about it just then, I simply took it for granted. Possibly this is what is supposed to take place at baptism—but if baptism it was, it wasn't of water, but of light. By this time it was late afternoon, and with the reflection from the river so bright that you could barely look at it directly, the whole hilltop, the whole world was fairly brimming with radiance. I walked around for a while, looked at the people, and walked to the subway, rather tired, and yet rested too, and pleased with everything.

New paragraph. That evening my friend Peter called, full of things he wanted to talk about, and I told him to come by. You almost met him once; on that evening when we went to the concert in Washington Square, and I had no idea he was around, he spotted us walking, too far away to be hailed. Perhaps it was just as well, at the time. Since our extremely odd first meeting in Paris, when we sat in cafes, engaged in a sort of double monologue, a contest to see who could out-talk the other, both more interested in our own thoughts than in the other's, and since his sudden reappearance in New York, when—both of us somewhat older and surer of ourselves, though not so very sure at that—we resumed the double monologue, we have gradually arrived, through a number of rather tense and quarrelsome vicissitudes, at something approaching that living equilibrium that is perfect friendship. So long as a relationship is alive I suppose new tensions must arise and be resolved, but it appears that since the new year began—significantly, he came by for a while on New Year's Day—the last lingering traces of distrust have disappeared. Not being involved in any romantic sense, we have been able to share each other's fears and frustrations, and, more and more, each other's enthusiasms; but behind all this, until very recently, there still lurked a suspicion on my part that he might be nothing more, after all, than a somewhat promiscuous, irresponsible and pretentious, working-class-Italian ne'er-do-well (God!), and on his, I rather suspect, that I was nothing more than a priggishly literary, pretentious, white-collar-middle-class American fraud (wow!) Just before Christmas, in fact, we arrived at a kind of deadlock. I forget exactly the terms of the argument, but I went on secretly fuming at him, even though I appeared to have won, until he did something so characteristic and so perfect that all the fuming simply went out of me: I had been reading the letters of Keats, which sent me back to the poetry; I remarked that I had never read all of *Endymion*, and couldn't, because I didn't own the complete poems. A few days later he appeared with a *Poetical Works* of Keats, dated 1865, which he had picked up in a bookstall in Florence. It had cost him only a few *lire*, and it was certainly no sacrifice for him to give it away, but it was his own purely spontaneous gesture; and besides, between the leaves were some pressed flowers—a piece of red may and a magnolia petal he had picked up in Lerici, and also a violet, some sprigs of lilac, and what appears to have been a carnation, which has left its ghost printed on the pages, and dating to when and where nobody, now, will ever know. . . . Well. Peter was full, that evening, of a strange book about Quattrocento stone-carving which I had lent him, though I haven't yet read it. It came from the girl in England who owned half of the antique taxi in which I went south through France, and to make connections with whom I had come back to Paris when I met Peter (how the connections and interconnections do multiply! I hadn't thought of that one until just now); she has since married the owner of the other half of the taxi, though the taxi itself was long since sold, and they now have a Bugatti (Italian racing model) and a baby, and ever since I saw the book in her apartment in London and was fascinated by it she had been trying to get around to send me a copy of it. And the odd thing is that though I haven't actually read the book myself, I seem already to know it better than if I had, from hearing Peter talk about it. He knows it now practically by heart, and something from it must have been behind, or in, my feeling about the affinity between the music of the *Kyrie* and the light on the stone. Do you begin to see what I mean about weavers and tapestry? I think I only begin to see it myself. Anyhow, we both talked, that evening, and we both listened, though my main enthusiasm was still for the tapestries and his for Quattrocento stone carving; and I read him some of the letters of Katherine Mansfield, with which I had for a while been almost excruciatingly involved, simply because they are so beautiful, and were both so carried away by her description of a nightmare journey to Marseilles, a sea-storm on the Riviera, and the morning when she first coughed up blood, read Keats, and knew she was going to die, that we came out of it blinking, not quite sure where we were. The fear of death is what more than anything else gives her letters their beauty, and I had found myself almost envying the intensity even of her fear—though the truth is that I have felt something like it at times, and it is not a thing one ought to envy. But it was as though, that afternoon, any possibility of envy like this had been obliterated. It was only by degrees that I began to be able to describe to myself the experience which was not a temporary extinction of personality, but the opposite: for the first time in my life, without even knowing that I knew it, I had been without fear. This is the negative way of stating it. The positive statement has ramifications which are still unfolding, and for all I know they will go on unfolding forever. I did not know that this was what had happened until I began to describe my afternoon in the journal which I have been keeping (Peter's suggestion) faithfully but spasmodically since New Year's. Before I had finished the entry it interested me so much that I decided to try to make a short story out of it, purely for the exercise. And then something happened which I could absolutely never have predicted: I have not altogether recovered yet from the surprise, though I suppose I shall get used to it in time. Quite as though they had a will of their own, the sentences broke in a way that was not my usual style at all. Rather frightened, I must admit, for the moment, I let them break. The next thing I knew, they had begun to reach out for rhymes. This frightened me almost more, until I discovered that finding a rhyme could be almost as natural a process as the resolution of a dominant chord: I didn't have to look for them, they simply came. Now I have not even so much as thought of wanting to write poetry since I was about sixteen and produced the usual sixteen-year-old effusions. I associated writing in verse with adolescence; there was a time, even, when I stopped reading poetry, though that was terminated a good while back. So here I am, writing a long poem. It is already something like five hundred lines, and though the end appears to be in sight, I am not sure. When it is finished—as I now feel it absolutely must be by Easter at the latest—you shall see it, if you want to. What I am to do with it otherwise, I haven't the faintest idea. What it appears to be, anyhow, is a kind of natural history of belief—religious belief, which is after all the only real kind. Because, having discovered what it was to be without fear, I also discovered that everything, in a way that is complex but entire and simple, made sense.

At which point, you will not be surprised to learn (if indeed you have not long ago done likewise) I did fall by the wayside. It is now Monday, and there has intervened an absolute mountain of snow. It snowed all day yesterday and all day today, and the way it leans, banked a foot deep, against the window-panes, is straight out of Emily Brontë Clampitt misquotes slightly]:

Cold in the earth! the snow piled deep above thee,
Far, far removed in the cold of the dreary grave,
My only love, have I forgot to love thee . . .

Not that I echo any such sentiment. The Brontës are a kind of family apotheosis of the death-wish, and Emily was the apotheosis of the apotheosis—*Wuthering Heights* is one long cry to be buried and reunited with the earth. So of course she had to die early—it was her wish. This just came to me. I feel as if I could write a whole history of English literature, and know just where to place everybody in it, with hardly any trouble at all. The reason being, apparently, that I feel *I am in it*. This will be true whether or not I am recognized now, or remembered later—and though (however many rash *statements* I may make) I don't think I ordinarily make rash predictions, I feel that this may happen too. I suppose you can preserve this as a piece of documentary evidence, whichever way it turns out. But I have been walking around in places familiar to Blake and Shelley, and I don't know who else. I have a vague idea that I may share a family resemblance with those two, though they are not my masters. I think I know now who those masters are: Thoreau is the first and Dante the last, and in between, oddly, and yet not so oddly, there is Henry James; and they are, all three, of the kingdom of heaven. But this is something I don't really ask anybody else to understand, and it doesn't especially matter.

I have finished my poem. I finished it early last evening—there will be lines that need tidying up here and there, but otherwise it is complete—flat on my back, because I was simply too done in to go on sitting up. There was something quite uncanny about winding it up in the middle of a driving snowstorm, since it is a poem about light and the end of winter, and here was the season, quite unaccountably and quite unpredicted, reversing itself; it seemed like a conscious and deliberate challenge to what the thing I was doing had to say. Of course this is pure subjectivity, but it is still uncanny, the more so since the storm appears to have been purely local—people were skiing in bright sunlight in the Catskills. And at about four a.m. I was awakened—as any number of other people seem to have been (no, I exaggerate—I heard of two, and I make three)—by what must have been something like the crack of doom. Because there was thunder along with this blizzard. We had the first installment of it on Friday night (respite on Saturday for the St. Patrick's Day parade), and in the middle of the snow there came a really blinding flash (I know of three people besides me who saw *that*), which I halfway believed, in the split second before thunder ensued, and the return of common sense, might be the beginning of the end of the world. You must really be sure now that I have gone mad. I am just as sure that I haven't. I went into this production a quasi-reactionary, quasi-obscurantist, quasi-orthodox half-believer, and I have emerged a heterodox total believer in the unity of being, in grace, in ultimate human progress, and the absolute freedom of the will. This last was the most surprising discovery—I didn't really know what I thought until I found it coming out this way:

But let light speak:
Know that the will
Is, and was ever, free:
Free at the verge of time, free in the weak,
Primeval, floating cell,
For whom the urge to be
Came not as a command, but as a call.

I looked up what Rachel Carson had to say about the presumed origin of life, and found the intuition confirmed—not that anybody really knows, of course. But it now seems to me that the whole notion of command is [a] piece of human machinery—I would almost say *masculine* machinery, since the intuition is an extremely feminine one. It seems to me absolutely clear that the beginning of organic existence could not have willed, or imposed on the inorganic, but that it was simply a response to light:

Light, not whose ordination
But whose slow touch slowly awoke
Life, from the dim, the slumbering, the scarcely dreaming sea—

all of which seems highly extraordinary, not because I invented it, but because I didn't invent it—it simply came to me as something which must be so. I also find that I believe, though I could never explain it, the Christian doctrine. I don't mean the dogma. That is machinery that came later. It started with St. Paul, I suppose. Jesus himself had no interest whatever in dogma—what dogma already existed, he seems to have been against. All of which isn't quite fair—I am showing you the horse before the cart, and the cart is after all what one has to see first, since anything of this sort must be approached from behind—otherwise one would be moving backwards. I must sound devilishly witty, but if it is wit, I assure you it isn't devilish—it is simply that I have come upon, all of a sudden, the hidden power of language. The poem hasn't been properly copied out yet, so I can't send it to you now. Anyhow, it is powerful long for any poem written in the twentieth century—something like fourteen single-spaced typewritten pages, or somewhere near seven hundred lines, if I estimate it correctly. How, and even whether, it will manage to get published, I haven't the faintest idea, and so far I don't much care. It can be passed around in manuscript. Nobody buys or reads poetry by living authors, except Eliot, anyhow. The critics get copies sent to them free.

Meanwhile, I am absolutely tuckered out, and to make matters still more tuckering, I am absolutely seething with ideas. The revision of the novel is only one of them. I would like to go to bed for a week, and read about nothing but geology—I have just begun devouring a textbook on the subject whole, in between re-reading, mainly on the subway, the *Purgatorio*—but I doubt if I actually would, even if it could be managed. Simply living is much too exciting. In the midst of all this—scribbling out lines on little scraps of paper on the subway and during my lunch hour, and even in between answering letters at work—I have been seeing all kinds of people, talking about everything under the sun, hearing the first song sparrow and spotting the first robin and tracking a whick-whick-whicking cardinal to its perch in the top of a tree, discovering spaghetti with green sauce (fresh basil leaves simmered in butter) at an honest-to-goodness workingman's *trattoria* south of Washington Square, cooking what I must say was a marvelous meal for Peter and his friend Mary (my friend now too, in remarkably short order—the girl who lived in Baghdad, about whom I think I wrote you). What a time we had! The pièce de resistance was a rare roast beef, and we opened a thirty-year-old Burgundy that had, as it happened, just begun to turn to sugar—but it was the kind of calculated risk that only adds a fillip to the occasion by being a fiasco—and we made collages (little framed, pasted-up pictures, you know) out of some pressed leaves and flowers that I had brought back, tenderly preserved between the pages of guidebooks, from Austria and the south of England, and we talked and talked and talked until one o'clock in the morning, and I read them as far as I had got with the then work in progress (with one exception, a gloomy young friend from of old, who tempered and improved it by challenging it with his own uneasy unbelief, nobody else even knows about it so far). But I can't go on like this. I have to go to bed and get ten hours' sleep, and *you* have already been detained overtime, if you have got this far.

I do wish you would tell me, though, what on *earth* is going on at that church at Des Moines. If it is really as odious a piece of power-jockeying as Daddy quite unwittingly makes it sound, I should think he would be well out of it. It begins to sound as though none, absolutely none, of these people cared for what the truth about anything might be, but only for holding onto the driver's seat. I suppose I am much too impatient with internecine squabbles, but what good does any of it do anybody? They talk about the mote and the beam, but do any of them actually go off and sit in a corner and let the still small voice have its say? Are any of them really honest with themselves? I feel somehow that Daddy may be letting himself be used. And of course I can't say so—I can't seem to say anything to him lately that I really mean, in fact. The trouble is probably that my feelings have not got over being hurt—not my feelings really, but my tiresome ego, which I really ought to know better than, but which I don't always seem quite able to manage—my ego has not got over being given that book by Milton Mayer for Christmas. I cannot be charitable toward the fellow. He is a charlatan, a show-off, a journalist who dresses up a perfectly voracious, scared, mixed-up need to think well of himself in the costume of—oh, I don't know what: liberalism, humanitarianism, it's hard to make out what kind of motley he even thinks it is. He is dishonest. He is so dishonest that he even has to confess to his readers on the other side of the Atlantic that he did not confess to those Germans he went to pry into the psychoses of that he was a Jew, simply because somebody advised him not to—and thinks this makes him honest. And yet, for some inscrutable reason, Daddy approves of him. And I can't tell him in so many words what I really think, though I am convinced that it is true, because it would wound his ego. In fact, I already have, by simply hinting at disapproval. Of course it's complicated still further by my own absolute perverseness in sending him that naughty *I, Claudius* book for Christmas. Poor man, he read it. He can't for the life of him see why I sent it to him. I know why, now that the damage is done: it's the same thing on both sides, we're still trying to make each other over. You see, apprehending the unity of being doesn't solve one's problems, it only makes one see how many problems there are. Ought one to wound the ego of one's own parent, of whom one is deeply fond and to whom one is endlessly beholden, in the interest of impartiality? Terrible dilemma. I begin to sound as though I wanted you to function as the conciliating intermediary—a burden that should be imposed only on somebody who has no problems, so please don't think I expect you to attempt any such thing. Actually, I just want to unburden myself concerning a subject I don't know how to handle. Maybe, if I stop being impatient, it will come to me, all in good time. Because another part of this queer revelation I seem to have had is that haste, impatience to accomplish anything, is simply the product of fear, and fear is the root of every evil—what I call the primordial sin.

But now this absolutely must not go on any longer. Do please write sometime, whether what I have heaved in your direction like a ton of bricks is assimilable or not. It's a great comfort, as I have said before, to have a brother one can heave things in the direction of. You know, I have to talk—it helps me to think (a joke Eliot put into a dialogue of critics once, but it happens to be perfectly true). I have probably been tedious, but I have a practically unshakable confidence that if so I shall be forgiven. Is it spring out there yet? I have pussy-willows on my mantel now, by the way, which helps.

Love,

Amy

. . . .

Easter 1956

Dear Philip—

[. . .] I have just been through one of the strangest weeks in my life, one which I could never have predicted and which nevertheless seems to have been foreshadowed by a thing I discovered several years back, and which I suppose has never quite been out of my mind since. This was a footnote to the first volume of Toynbee, which in turn was taken from what I believe is only a footnote to William James's *Varieties of Religious Experience*, anyhow, it came from a letter which a woman, a personal friend of James's, had written describing her sensations during an operation for which she had not been given a sufficient anesthetic. I can't quote it, but it was a very beautiful, almost Biblical image of intense pain, which became visual, a kind of wheel of fire. I was struck by it, as Toynbee evidently also had been, and when shortly afterward I found myself involved in a minor but extremely uncomfortable sort of betrayal, the passage seemed to catch fire in my own mind, and I thought something like this: *My vocation is to stand just a little more than one is supposed to stand.* And that seems to be what has happened ever since. Joined with what turns out to be the Categorical imperative, it is what might be called a philosophy. Of course one can't speak of it really, and I don't know that I have ever tried to in so many words. But I assure you it has no connection whatever with what is called a Martyr Complex—a thing I despise. It is only the corollary of very great and increasing happiness, and I do not regard myself as martyred but as privileged, to an extent I could not have imagined in advance.

There is probably some connection between all this and a feeling I have had more and more distinctly—odd as it may sound from a professed believer in science and ultimate human progress—that one day I might be going to join a church. I'm not sure what church, or whether the feeling is anything more than a temporary manifestation, but I have noticed a faint wish to observe the fasts and a kind of thirst for liturgy, which is no doubt partly just from being around people like Monica, who is a devout Roman Catholic, and the Goodmans, who are equally devout Anglo-Catholics; one respects their observances, after a while, to the point where one would like to share them. Last Sunday afternoon I went to St. Luke's, the little Anglican church a few blocks south of me, where Joe's mass—specially composed for them—was being sung, along with one of Mozart. I was in rather too exultant a mood, the lingering effect of having finished the poem apparently, to listen in the proper spirit to this mass of Joe's, which is a very tense, difficult, I would say almost painful composition; I have listened more worshipfully to recorded masses, such as the Mozart *Requiem.* In short, I was a little, and quite unjustifiably, puffed up with my own accomplishments. But since that afternoon I have been to church five times, not counting dropping into a couple where no services were going on, yesterday. I don't yet know exactly what all this means, if anything. It might not have happened at all if I had not found myself involved in a terrible and totally unexpected new argument with Peter. Just when I thought an equilibrium had been reached! One never knows, that's all.

This happened on Monday evening. It wasn't an ordinary argument, and neither of us lost our tempers; I simply found myself sitting perfectly still for fifteen minutes, not even consciously angry, while he did the same. It is impossible to say what I then thought it was about; the truth seems to be that each one of us had somehow become an absolutely implacable threat to the other. I didn't even realize how furious I was until the next day, and by the end of it I was so worn out from sheer rage that I went to bed at eight o'clock and was still tired out the next morning—tired, and no less in a rage. That was when I started going to church, hoping that might straighten me out. It didn't: all I could see was how tyrannical, irresponsible and utterly egotistical Peter was, and how furious *I* was that *he* couldn't see it too. It is like living in hell—I've been through states like this before, for totally different reasons, which I can only describe as being in a state of mortal sin. The thing that makes it so terrible is one's own helplessness—one is in a trap with the door shut, apparently from the outside. By Thursday, after seeming to diminish, it had only got worse, and though I don't make a practice of discussing my own affairs with Monica, I tried to tell her about it, partly to explain why I had been so cross all week. She has a very low opinion of artists—having been married to an intellectual with analogous characteristics, she feels that they are incapable of really experiencing anything, and that they prey upon those whose experience is genuine, and so, though her sympathy was of the most intelligent kind (really, she is one of the most intelligent, as well as generous, people I have ever known), she was hardly the one to defend Peter against my rage. And I couldn't possibly explain to her that it has been very necessary for me to believe in art, and in artists whatever their shortcomings, and that this, and not any personal attachment, was what made my state of mind so terrible. I didn't care, for myself, whether I ever saw him again; his attention is nothing my self-esteem requires; and moreover I knew I probably would see, or hear from, him very shortly, and the problem of what I would do or say was there, staring me in the face. After work that afternoon, in a pouring rain, I went with Monica to a very beautiful, very crowded church; she lent me her little French prayerbook, more to amuse me than anything else, but even in French the prayers seemed to help— plus the stained glass, plus the liturgy, though we were behind a column and couldn't see anything that was happening directly in front of the altar. I left just as the communion was beginning, and on my way home, on the subway, the solution came to me. The next time I heard from him I would simply say that before I saw him I wanted him to do one thing for me—I wanted him to go into a Catholic church and say a good Catholic prayer for my state of mortal sin. It came to me as a perfectly honest way out of a predicament, though in no time it had come to seem almost diabolically clever—Peter being one of those pagan Latin Catholics who say they are Catholic, and are, but who haven't been to confession in years and years and don't seem to feel in the least guilty about it. I gloated a little, but still I felt better. The next day, Good Friday, I went twice to church, as well as to the dentist, but I was in a much more cheerful mood. That is, until Peter called.

This was at nine o'clock or so, just as I was about to go to bed. I had been reading George Fox's Journal, trying to find my bearings from a different quarter, and planned to go on reading it until I went to sleep. But that call changed everything. If I was still furious with him, my fury was nothing to his with me. It was that slow kind of thing that seeps out like pitch, a little at a time, so that at first I didn't even realize what it was. The conversation was rather long; we both acknowledged being in a rage all week, but this in no way cleared the air; it only made everything ten times worse; until finally, when I told him what I wanted him to do, he answered in a voice that was as near pure hate as anything I ever had directed against me, that he wouldn't—my state of mortal sin wasn't his problem. Nothing was his problem, it seemed, not even his own sins. He was a humanist. He wasn't interested in—At which point I said goodbye, and hung up. For a few minutes after that I was as near going literally out of my mind as has ever happened. I felt as if I had just engaged in a battle with the devil himself, and that the devil had won. I, who was determined to believe that evil is not real, but simply, in the fashion of St. Thomas and Dante, that it was good gone astray, had come to the point where evil seemed not only real, but a positive force. I knew that weakness had made him talk in this way, and still this weakness had beaten me. But I also realized that I was no longer angry; there was simply a kind of vacuum where the anger had been, in which I seemed to feel nothing at all. Then I fell asleep.

When I woke up again, sometime after midnight, my state of mind had changed in a curious way. I was puzzled by the paradox of having benefited in so many ways from knowing Peter, of being surrounded by all kinds of mementoes of our friendship, none of which I had any urge to destroy. There was a book which I would have to send back, and I began composing a letter to go along with it, in which I would acknowledge that there was no mending this breach, but which would also be a kind of requiem for an association which, it now appeared, must inevitably have ended in one way or another, and a statement of indebtedness for past favors. If this was only a partial victory, at least it wasn't a defeat—I was out of my state of mortal sin. This seemed to me to be an almost miraculous achievement. And while I was thinking this, the phone rang. It was Peter. He had been to church; he had said a prayer; he wasn't mad any more. I could hardly believe my ears, and I still wasn't sure, until I saw him today, that either of us had got through the battle unscathed. But apparently we have, until another one comes along—except we may be both chastened enough to avoid any further head-on collisions. Is this not strange? One might argue that the argument, since we got past it, meant nothing; on the contrary, it meant everything. But now I have to stop. Time for bed. I'll add a postscript later.

Wednesday.
I'm not sure how much sense any of this may make. Possibly it is the kind of thing one ought to set down in a journal and let it go at that—but somehow I don't feel inclined to talk to myself about such matters any more. I am no less certain that there is a very real significance behind what took the outward shape of a private quarrel and reconciliation; and the best single word I can find for that significance is Grace. Where does the strength to overcome one's hate and anger come from? One can say that it comes from within, but ultimately this is not true at all; alone one can do nothing; ultimately it must come from without. If there had been no Roman Catholic church in the background, to which one could refer, not for moral authority—moral authority is not enough—but as a kind of reservoir of the strength and patience one did not possess alone—if there had been no such reservoir to draw upon when one's own resources gave out, then I should have lost this particular struggle with Peter and, more

important, with myself, and something would have died or, at the very least, gone into a kind of paralyzed cold storage. It is because of experiences like this—there have been several, though none of them quite so violent or concentrated before—that I have begun to find myself able to believe that a phenomenon such as St. Francis receiving the stigmata, could have occurred, and that the Resurrection itself could have occurred, entirely within the framework of natural law; and since it is possible to believe that such things *could* occur, the next step is surely to believe that they *did* occur. I have never read Aquinas, but I imagine this is pretty much what he says. The thing that gets in the way is simply an insufficient faith—not so much on the part of the honest doubters, who after all serve truth—but insufficient faith on the part of the self-styled faithful. I think this is what is wrong with organized religion generally, both Catholic and Protestant, but I suspect it is worse in the latter. The world is full of organizers wanting to hurry a lot of converts into the fold, apparently in order to convince themselves that what they say is what they believe. If they really believed, they would not require any phalanx of cohorts and allies, because they would no longer have any reason to fear an enemy. I am quite sure that my own long, proud, stubborn resistance to anything bearing the name of religion can be explained as an unconscious determination not to be, *me*, accessory to what looked from the outside like a total fraud. George Fox was bothered by the same thing—the difference being that he was a mystic from his childhood on up; and though he was perhaps a little too quick to judge the sincerity of absolutely everybody else, at bottom he was right—outward form alone can never create an inward certainty, though as a reforming radical he could not recognize that there can be great virtue and great satisfaction in the observance of outward forms also.

Maybe this is all part of the same thing, but from what you say about Beth, for the first time in a long while I begin to think there may be hope for her recovery. I didn't quite dare to write this to the folks, but this gradual kind of improvement somehow sounds as if it might be the real thing.

The weather has gone foggy and nondescript again, and foghorns are wailing on the river. However, this noon I was cheered to hear a song sparrow, gracing a particular spot between Fifth Avenue and the reservoir where I have listened for it from February to August for the last two or three years. Whether it was the same bird this time I'm not quite sure; the song was not the one I remembered, but of course most of these birds have several songs; possibly it may be a descendant re-establishing claim to an

ancestral freehold. Last spring for a while I listened to it or its predecessor, as the case may be, asserting itself against a rival newcomer, a few trees down the cinder path, but it is my impression that the original squatter won out. Now I must really end this. Keep the poem for the time being anyway; I might ask for the copy back sometime, but no hurry.
Love,
Amy

. . . .

20 May 1956
Dear Philip—
[. . .] Since I last wrote you I have finished a critical essay on Henry James and started another poem—in strict *terza rima*, the scheme used in the *Divine Comedy* and I must say a very difficult one—which I'm not sure how soon I may be able to finish. Sometime, I hope. I have also seen a blue-gray gnatcatcher (first one for me) and three scarlet tanagers. There are scarlet tanagers all over, for some reason to me entirely inexplicable. I wish I had kept track of all the phone calls we have had from people who have seen one or several, imagined it to be some rare and exotic species, and have called up to find out what it was. Oh, the calls—they are odder and odder, and more and more delightful, or perhaps it is only my own state of mind. Also, I might mention that Eugene Kinkead, who wrote that profile on the microbiologist for the *New Yorker*, was in a couple of times this last week to do research for some kind of article on birds around Manhattan. I didn't ask just what—one feels one oughtn't, as though this were one of the mysteries—but I did find a few things for him which he seemed not to have known about previously, and was most politely thanked. He is a rather beefy, red-faced, blue-eyed fellow with a somewhat worried look, which I rather imagine all *New Yorker* writers have. (I have found out, if you care for such incidental intelligence, that Our Man Stanley is a fiction, but that one of their research staff, one Stanley Eichelbaum by name, who calls us up occasionally about this or that, is introduced as Our Man Stanley at parties, furthermore that, having a doctorate in French from Columbia and feeling accordingly somewhat frustrated, he doesn't like it.) I have been on one bird-watching picnic in Central Park with this very organized girl I have gotten to know, and who does about three times as much as most people, in spite of (perhaps also because of) having had polio and wearing a brace. Most extraordinary. She has been to England, where she saw a most astonishing

amount, and is now arranging herself for a trip to Sweden one of these years—a part of the arranging being a course in Swedish, in which she seems to have done so well that the instructor, himself a Swede, has invited her to collaborate with him on a beginning textbook in the subject. She takes extraordinarily good color photographs and one of her projects has been a day-by-day canvass of the birds in a small area of the park near where she lives—where, most astonishingly, she saw what must have been the same blue-gray gnatcatcher that I saw in an entirely different part of the park—at least we both think so, since both times it was in the company of a magnolia warbler. We didn't do too badly in our count, though the warbler season was only just beginning.

The truth is, I can't now remember all the things I had it in mind one time or another to tell you about. One of them was that I found your name in the April issue of *Audubon Field Notes*, which carries the report of the Christmas Bird Count. Things have been happening so fast, and even for me so surprisingly, that details come and go without being entirely kept track of. Today, anyhow, two things of particular significance have occurred—I finished reading the *Paradiso*, and I took the first definite step toward becoming a member of the Anglican communion, that is, I spoke to the Vicar at St. Luke's about an appointment with somebody on the staff some time this week. Actually, I feel as though I were already a member, but I suppose it isn't as simple as that. In fact it isn't simple at all, in one sense. Whatever has been happening to me, as far as I can understand it, is from a psychological point of view no doubt extremely complex, but that there is a psychological point of view bothers me very little, if at all. I believe I have really begun to cease to feel complicated. Since Easter I have been to St. Luke's every Sunday, and in that time it may be that I have changed even more than I am myself entirely aware. What I do know is that I have never been happier, and that I look forward to Sunday morning, and in particular to that point in the mass (the *Agnus Dei*) at which, if I understand it properly, the Crucifixion takes place all over again. I suppose it may be still that I dwell too much on the Crucifixion—after all, I haven't yet taken communion, which is the real culmination of the service. The only instruction I have had is from reading Dante, from listening to any number of recorded masses or parts thereof, and from human experience—my own, I mean, and some of that seems (I mean this in all humility) to have involved something more than human. You have heard from me quite a bit about the experiences I especially have in mind. The quarrel with Peter was no doubt the immediately crucial one. It appears now (I hope I may be wrong, but I have no confidence any more that this may be so) that the aftermath of that quarrel and reconciliation is a sad one. I'm not at all sure I shall see Peter again, and the saddest part of it is that I hardly care any more. This may sound callous, though I don't think it is so much that as it is simply exhaustion and disillusion. It was very important for me to believe in him so long as I didn't believe in something that transcended either one of us. And if it wasn't altogether wrong to do so, it wasn't altogether right either—it was a kind of heresy, a substitution of a part for the whole. The truth is that Peter hates the poem, after having been enthusiastic about it—which wouldn't matter if it weren't that he hates it for the implications, which I didn't myself see entirely until after it was finished. And since he hates the poem for its implications, it follows that he must hate me. Of course the boundary between hatred and affection in people who have been very close is a very tenuous one always, and there comes a point at which both parties must work very hard to keep from trying to destroy each other. *Both* parties—I see now that one can rarely if ever do it alone. I believe I can honestly say that I did my best; I cared as long as I could, and then I simply had to stop caring. Of course he may change yet—what I have to guard against now is assuming that he is done for because there was nothing more I could do, and becoming merely self-righteous about it. It may seem odd that with this kind of problem before me I should still be able to speak of my own happiness—it may even sound sinful. I don't believe it really is. To try to do anything more would be, I think, to try to impose my own will on another person who is, in fact, free, though a central part of our quarrel is that I believe in freedom and he doesn't—mainly, so far as I can make out, because he doesn't wish to. However, the end of this may be not yet—I see more and more how little one is able to predict about anybody.

This conversion of mine—you see I have no doubt that it is a conversion in the radical meaning of the word—has its somewhat comic aspect, I shall hasten to say before anybody else does. Aside from Peter, and aside from what I have written you about the preliminary events, I hadn't mentioned it to anybody until a week ago, when I saw Annabel and Arthur for the first time since their return from three months in South Africa and Europe. And there all of a sudden at the dinner table I found myself telling Arthur that I thought I was going to join the Church of England. I could do it without sounding too silly since Arthur is Church of England himself, and has moreover a brother who is very High Church indeed. But Annabel was quite astonished, and the Australian who was sitting next to me and whom I had never seen before in my life was simply bewildered. There ensued a conversation, full of interruptings and confusion, about the differences between the Catholic and Apostolic Church of the Anglican creed and the Church of Rome—a matter which used to puzzle me but in which at the moment I am not even very much interested, since it is what all the creeds have in common, rather than their differences, that really matters. I hope it won't shock you very much if I say that I seem to regard myself as at least a proto-Catholic. It isn't an intellectual matter at all. I supposed at first that I would find the articles of the Creed, as it is given in the prayerbook and as it is sung by both choir and congregation, an intellectual stumbling-block; but without being able to explain anything, I find myself joining in when it is sung, by a wish that also seems to be a necessity. I think I was sure of this a couple of weeks back, when the sermon—I listen to every word of the sermon, which to be sure is only a not very long part of a long service—had to do with precisely what it was that made one a member of the church, and not simply a person who believed, who followed the Christian teachings and who hoped for better things. The difference, the priest said, was prayer. Without prayer—and incidentally one is on one's knees for a large part of the service in the Anglican church—one who behaved well would become merely self-righteous, and one who believed and hoped for better things merely a utopian. And the entire liturgy, he went on to say, is prayer—the one prayer, really, since it embraces in one community undertaking all individual prayers. I have come to realize that for a good deal of my life I have been praying, or at least trying to pray, without quite knowing it. I suppose that the patient on the psychiatrist's couch, if he is being helped at all, is trying to pray. It isn't words at all, but an attitude of mind, of waiting and hoping. I never could stand hearing people pray aloud because it always sounded insincere and self-righteous—not that it necessarily was, I suppose. But if I have come very near to regarding all of protestantism as a heresy, it is because most protestant churches seem to be more interested in persuading more people that what they say is so than in anything else. It is as though the only way they could prove that what they say is so was by getting converts. In other words, protestantism seems more a religion of despair, of fear and gloom, than of joy and thanksgiving. A good deal of this impression may be subjective, I imagine, dating as it does to a time when I regarded religion as an interference with my own most egotistical intentions. But the fact remains that I have found what I must have been looking for for a very long time in the liturgy and nowhere else. It is one of the mysteries that somehow joy should come out of pain and suffering. I do hope I'm not being tiresome about this. You must know that I mean every word of it. I don't do things by halves, it seems—which is presumably why all this has been so long in coming.

It is quite clear to me that it has come to a large extent by way of that long love-affair which you have heard a little bit about. Nobody can know very much about me who doesn't know about that—and since for most people it would have to be explained, and I can't explain it even to myself altogether, I suppose nobody ever will know very much, or at least not very many people. There is no doubt some sin in being so secretive so far as the rest of the world is concerned, but curiously enough—curious at least from the protestant point of view—the sin isn't hypocrisy. It is pride. I don't know yet how this is finally to be dealt with, or solved, if it ever is. Because what I thought might be true—that what has been happening was what the psychologists call, with just a faint sneer, Sublimation—(not that I minded the sneer in the least, you understand)—isn't the whole explanation. This last week I have seen the young man again. Of course I told him what had been on my mind, and moreover he believed me—because it has always been that we both told the truth and there was always this mysterious trust of each other, in spite of seeing each other only two or three times a year, very briefly, and in spite (on my side at least) of having been almost unendurably hurt. Almost, but not quite. There was always, even at the very worst, something that kept what I felt from turning into bitterness. The strange and quite unexpected thing was that these latest developments didn't come between us, as they seem to have between Peter and me—on the contrary, they brought us closer than ever before. I don't know quite where what is wrong about this leaves off and what is right begins. Graham Greene, I believe, is supposed to have had something to say on the subject, but I don't like Graham Greene and refuse to read him. All I know is that love is the only name I can give to the unseen unifying principle in which by a kind of necessity I seem to have come to believe, and that if it hadn't been for this particular love, which though I am quite sure now that it isn't mainly carnal and never was, is even now, or at any rate expresses itself as, partly that—if it hadn't been for this particular love I find it impossible to imagine that I should ever have found what lay beyond it. Again, I hope you'll forgive me if I am being tiresome. I feel somehow that this needs to be put on record, though I'm not exactly sure just why. [. . .]

Love,

Amy

. . . .

14 July 1956
Dear Philip—

[. . .] First of all, thanks so much for introducing me to the Baileys. One grows provincial here in New York, and needs to be reminded that there are just as many, if not more, lively, inquiring spirits operating beyond the metropolis as there are within it, and that on the whole these are probably healthier than what one encounters here in the way of intellect. For a good while now I have been coming to the reluctant but inescapable conclusion that literary people are not a very admirable lot these days. Possibly the fact that they are actually *worse* than most people, and hence more actively unhappy, is what makes them literary. Possibly it always was so. The conclusion was not an easy one to swallow when one was as determined as I have been to believe in the printed word as something good in itself. Of course I still do believe in it, and I expect to go on reading more, rather than less, even though I am not so eager as I was to see anything of my own get into print. Talking with somebody like Mabel, anyhow, makes me feel better about being interested in literature, and I'm eternally indebted to you for making it possible. I hope you'll be able to keep track of them, and that maybe even my path will cross theirs again someday or other.

Since I got back I have re-read *The Scarlet Letter* (as well as *Young Goodman Brown*), and found it an extraordinarily satisfactory accomplishment. It is the sort of thing one can hardly quarrel with or raise objections to, so complete and self-contained a thing it is, and so wonderfully compressed. I tried to read it with particular attention to the style, but even that is hard to isolate and so to characterize at all. It has been suggested that its sociable tone comes not from genuine sociability but simply from the fact that it is one half of a divided soul talking to the other half. The question of whom the author is addressing, and in what spirit, is anyway an interesting one to consider. Probably most writers these days do talk to themselves—usually in an almost violently hostile tone. Now take St. Augustine, whose *Confessions* I am reading—his whole account is a sort of open letter to the Creator. When I tried reading the *Confessions* a couple of years back, I found these continual apostrophizings distracting and hysterical, and finally gave up after a chapter or two. But the truth is, the sum total of what he had to say could be addressed nowhere else, without some falseness getting in the way. A great sinner had become a saint, and his attitude toward the sum total of reality had become, one can only suppose, that of continual and uninterrupted prayer. I find it one of the most engrossing documents I have ever read. He seems absolutely contemporary, partly because he is dealing with eternal matters, also because he was probably as acute an analytical psychologist as ever lived—an analytical psychologist with the advantage of knowing what Eternity consisted of.

I have had another visit with Father Morralee, and I am still astonished that there should have been such people around in this day and age (and I am ready to believe now that there must be many like him) without my ever suspecting it. He appeared this time in khaki shorts and Norfolk jacket, which did startle me a little—he was just back from a day in the country, and hadn't had time to change—the very picture of an English sporting gentleman, full of wry good humor. But inside half an hour he had gone from the subject of transubstantiation, on which I asked to have the Anglican position cleared up, into some of the mysteries. Without his explicitly saying so, or my asking, it became clear, really luminous, that he is certain of personal immortality. In the *Sursum corda* (Lift up your hearts, etc.), and the *Sanctus* that follows, and which he evidently regards as the climax of the mass, he said that on certain occasions there is what he calls a tremendous *pressure*—the actual presence of spirits gone before. I listened both astonished and enthralled, really too humbled to ask, Do I believe this? But the answer seems to be that I must—not because such a proposition can be proved, but neither simply because (as Tertullian is supposed to have said) it is impossible. The truth is, I was beginning to act, long before I was aware of believing anything of the sort, as though it might be so. I had enough experiences of a telepathic sort, which I was never able to assign to mere coincidence, to pave the way for a more radical extension of consciousness. I do not think anything of the sort will ever be proved in a laboratory, for all of Mr. J. B. Rhyne, and I devoutly hope not. The laboratory is not life. No matter how conscientious an effort is made to reproduce all the analogous conditions, the effort will fail. There is something about the purely scientific attitude which precludes its dealing with anything more than the attributes (the "accidents" of St. Thomas Aquinas) of reality. It seems to me curious how the timid materialist superstitions should have persisted in the prevailing attitude of an age which lives under the hypothesis that matter and energy are inseparable, that matter, indeed, *is* energy, and that this depends more desperately than ever in history upon what it has never seen, touched, tasted, or experienced except as a report of a completely incredible explosion. The difficulty seems to be that the world has no faith in an unknowable power which it has nevertheless had to accept, and so it sits shivering while the human aspect of this same formula of matter-equated-with-energy twists itself in all sorts of contortions of hate and envy and despair which are only, as Dante observed, defects of love—and so, since it *thinks* things are hopeless, it makes them so. Not that it really does altogether. I have also just read a brief history of the church, from which it seems clear to me that in many ways things are still better than they ever were, even in this miserable civilization. [. . .]

It was very good to have all the scattered pieces of information pulled together in a single narrative that puts them into proportion and relation with each other. I feel more strongly than ever how right T.S. Eliot was to emphasize Tradition, as a thing that at the same time remains, continually growing and being added to while remaining unchanged in substance. It seems the only way I could feel that I *belonged* to anything was to reach back into the past, really to become immersed in it. There seemed really no other way of coming to be a part of the present. So I don't feel in the least estranged or cut off from my immediate Quaker inheritance. I see the church now as all one, including all the denominational offshoots. Each of them no doubt served and still serves a purpose, and what they have in common is one and the same thing, and that is what really counts.

I am to be confirmed as soon as an appointment with the Bishop can be arranged. Meanwhile, I can also say that what I didn't think could happen has happened, quite naturally—Peter and I have made peace. He came to see me just after I got back, for the first time in a couple of months, and we were perfectly candid with each other without any necessity for quarreling. We can't be friends any more on the old pagan terms, but at least I have stopped feeling indignant with him and he has stopped trying to battle with the Holy Spirit; so far as I am concerned, the Holy Spirit has won and he will let it be so. I do hope I don't sound sanctimonious about this—it really is the truth. [. . .]
Love,
Amy

. . . .

3 November 1956
Dear Philip—
[. . .] Well, I have got this far without saying a word about religion—at least I don't think I have, and if I haven't it must be some kind of a record. From now on I fear you won't hear much about anything else. Since I last wrote you I have finally been confirmed; Father Morralee has gone back to

England and has been missed by me, I dare say, more than by anybody else, though he is one of those people whom everybody loves; and I have been paid a pastoral call by Father Moore, the young curate whose sermons I have admired so much and whom I despaired of ever telling so, and whom I now regard as an old friend. Between him and the nuns, who used to scare me rather but with whom I am now on the most sociable terms, I feel very much looked after, even without Father Morralee around, and it is a kind of being looked after that is not in the least intrusive or even, in any ordinary sense, very personal. The very satisfactory thing about St. Luke's is being able to come and go without saying a word to anybody, or even having anybody notice that you happen to be there; it's understood that whoever is there, is there for other reasons than sociability. However, since I have been helping the sisters in the sacristy on Saturdays, I now know the ins and outs of getting the chalice and vestments and altar candles ready for the Sunday services, and the other day I *finally* found out what their names were. They flattered me very much one week by asking me if I could be at the church at half-past six one weekday morning—too complicated to explain, but what it amounted to was substituting for one of them so that another one could make a retreat. That was before the time changed back, and when my alarm went off at six it was pitch dark. I was so afraid of sleeping through it that of course I woke up a couple of times before it did. It was barely beginning to be light when I slipped into the church, and the whole thing was as much an adventure as if it had been Paris in the middle ages. But of course that is true of every one of the services—all the centuries are your next-door neighbors when you are in the presence of eternity. I have now discovered the evening service which is said every day at six p.m., which is very English, and which is meditative instead of being dramatic like the morning mass. There is a psalm for each day, and two passages from the Bible are read—one from the Old Testament, one from the New. I now realize that, exactly as with poetry, the way to develop a feeling for the Bible is not to read it but to hear it read. For some reason which probably wouldn't be too difficult to explain psychologically, the ear is closer than the eye to direct intuition—another way of saying why even the churches that eschew gorgeous vestments and throw up their hands in horror at the idea of incense, do not dispense entirely with music. In this the Conservative Quakers are at least consistent, and it is a consistency I respect the more I think of it, though I doubt that it is conducive to success with any but a very small minority. From my observations I would say that the *forte* of Quakerism has become largely secular—which is fine for those who would rather be busy doing things, but which leaves no outlet for the less matter-of-fact side of human nature except a kind of emotional restlessness which can do all kinds of mischief. [. . .]

It is now Wednesday, and a good deal of the foregoing must sound pretty stale by this time. I didn't like so many things popping one after the other, but it wasn't until Monday morning's news from Hungary that I felt really shaken—even though I seemed to have known all along that this was exactly what would happen. I cast my vote for [Adlai] Stevenson—though without any very profound conviction—and otherwise followed the editorial recommendations of the *New York Times* (in fact I bought three papers on Monday, and discovered that the *Times* is the only paper around that has anything in it), with the result that there was a good deal of hopping back and forth across party lines on my ballot. It still makes me nervous to vote, and I never quite believe that I haven't done something to keep my vote from counting at all; but at the same time the idea of all these people standing solemnly in line waiting to exercise their franchise, and of being one of them, I find quite thrilling—and always did, even in my most pessimistic days. Monica rented a television set especially to be able to watch the post-election vigil, and stayed up until three a.m.; I went to bed at midnight, with no excitement whatever, though today I felt as worn out as though I had been through it all myself. I did talk to Annabel, whom you may remember meeting at the U.N., during the evening. She and her husband both still work there, and have recently moved into an apartment practically next door. She said that since things started to happen there has been a steady stream of people working until all hours and then dropping in to sleep on the floor; of course at the U.N. nobody talks or thinks of anything else these days. But I could hardly feel more in it if I were there myself. If I ever thought I had withdrawn from the world—the world, that is, where headlines happen—the result seems to have been that I now find myself inextricably interconnected. There is a woman who helped us half-days in the library, up until August, when she left because her husband had taken a professorship at the university in Jerusalem. She is Russian-Roumanian by birth, educated in Paris, Jewish by tradition though (she confessed to me) without any beliefs; her husband, who is very orthodox, does the praying. As a result she is what I would call the unhappiest sort of materialist; the only thing she really seemed to care about was clothes; and the state of her waistline—and flowers. This last I could almost say was her redemption. While Monica was away I got to know her quite well; it took some effort, since she was rather a touchy sort, but in an odd way I became quite fond of her, and promised to write to her. I was just about to get around to it when all this started to happen, and now it seems really imperative, if I can think just what to say, to let her know that the connection is there. Having known her, it is easier to sympathize with the curious mixture of stubbornness and scrupulosity that makes Israel behave in the however tiresome way it has these last few days. And on the other hand there is Mary Russel, my friend Peter's friend (I ran into him on the street last night, by the way, as I knew I was bound to do sooner or later, and was relieved to discover how fond I still am of him in spite of all the hard thoughts I have had about him). Mary is the girl who lived in Baghdad; her parents are still there, and of course I thought of her immediately when the news came from the Middle East. I went by the Metropolitan Museum, where she works part time, to see how she was; she wasn't alarmed about her parents just yet, but she was obviously quite worked up and declared that she didn't care what the British and French did, *she* was pro-Arab. She also turned out to be almost violently pro-Stevenson; in short—being an artist and an emotional girl generally, though it doesn't always show, and with a real feeling for the Middle East which it isn't fair to discount just because one doesn't have it oneself—she was very much involved, and in a state. And then there is Monica, who said rather softly, while everybody was talking bitterly about how impossibly the British and the French had behaved, that though *we* absolutely had to stay out, after all the French built the Suez Canal, and she couldn't help sympathizing. I had just got off the bus, that rainy morning last week, with some mention of the English umbrella I had left at home, and the Irish-American woman from the Audubon staff who happened to be on it had exploded, "Oh, don't speak of the English *this* morning!" I said it was all a dreadful, dreadful shame; but of course I was thinking of the people in England who in different ways, more or less personal, are dearer to me than almost anybody else. In view of all this, one neither needs nor can afford, as an individual and a U.S. citizen, to have a distinct and separate point of view. It occurs to me that this is the one country left in the world where national self-interest, as a thing in itself, simply has no meaning. Maybe that is our hope. Monica—though she talks like what used to be labeled an isolationist—seems to think so. I never saw an adopted citizen who loved this country the way she does; and it may be that she has a better idea of what it is like than the people who were born here.

There is one more thing to be said, and I was reminding myself of it when I realized that there was no possibility of hiding from the headlines any more, whether I read the papers or not. Whatever ingenious and frightful new forms of violence the human race may dare to use, it cannot do anything more unthinkable than it has already done, not quite two thousand years ago, when once and for all time it attempted no less than to kill God. The attempt was a success; and like all destructive successes it failed. The attempts go on being made, in the form of materialism, nationalism, and plain ordinary selfishness, but there is no possibility now that any of them can succeed. There is something more real than matter, and anybody who has ever cared about anything—which must include everybody— knows that it is so, whatever he may think he thinks to the contrary; and the louder and more insistent the arguments against any such supreme reality, the less weight they actually carry. The only way to make sense out of anything is to know that it is only a part of something that contains it all, and from which the only separation is self-destruction. But there is no point in explaining the self-explanatory. Besides, if I am to get up and go to mass in the morning it is time for bed. If I sound pontifical, please excuse it—and do write soon.

Love,

Amy

. . . .

20 April 1957

Dear Philip—

[. . .] It was also nice to hear about the weather. I love weather, as I have said before, and can never hear enough about what it is doing. So long as the news doesn't arrive in the form of a complaint anyhow, as yours certainly didn't. Oh dear, you've gone and seen another sparrow hawk, and I, who would like to get within nodding distance of one almost as much as I would of a screech owl on the branch of an evergreen, that answers when one calls to it, have never so much as been sure of seeing one from a distance. I have this predilection for owls—related, I expect, to my ancient one for cats—and it keeps on growing. I don't know quite what it is about them. I no longer regard owls as horrid hooting things or as mopers that do to the moon complain (leave it to the English poets of the graveyard-and-belfry school to put such notions into one's literary head) but rather as the Greeks must have—birds of Athena, with those great knowing luminous orbs, alert and at the same time so soft and so mutedly gorgeous in coloring. Now, I have really gone off the deep end on the subject, this time. Part of this stems from having seen Don Eckelberry, the artist for the

Pough guides and various other things, who does owls possibly better then any other bird—having seen Eckelberry *act* like an owl. He can also act a boat-billed heron, or a groove-billed ani, or practically anything avian. Which of course explains why his work is so pixyishly satisfactory. He comes around the Audubon Society quite often, and immediately all work is set aside and the occasion becomes a picnic. As an artist he is better than Peterson (Peterson himself wistfully says so) but since he is of my own generation I've never regarded him with the same kind of awe and so it is still more delightful to realize what a gift he has and to see it developing on the spot, as it were. By the way, they've discovered a nineteen-year-old named Fenwick Lansdowne, up in Victoria, British Columbia, who goes around on crutches and paints with his left hand because of an attack of polio when he was a baby, and who has been painting pictures of birds, and selling them to the neighbors, since he was about six; and already he is being compared with Audubon. Even from reproductions, his stuff is astonishing, and completely original; so I dare say they may be right about him. Also, the other day somebody presented the Audubon Society with an original Audubon Elephant Folio—a beautiful set, each of the four volumes so heavy that it takes two men to lift it, so that for several days it was just sitting there on the library table—insured for twenty-five thousand dollars, to be sure, but all the same I rather trembled until we finally got it moved to a somewhat more sequestered spot. They are beautiful things, those plates—every time I look I am overwhelmed all over again. Also, while I am on such subjects, I should mention that Bob Allen, the one and only Robert P., and still the pick of all the bird people, has a book out which will not get the attention it deserves, I suppose—*On the Trail of Vanishing Birds* is the title. Look at it if you have a chance. You met him, I think. They don't come more genuine, and he is the chief reward, I do believe, in being connected with the Audubon Society. [. . .]

But I have a thousand things to communicate, and all this last just got in on the spur of [the] moment, without prior intention. I started to talk about the weather. I meant to go on to say that spring here has been late, as I gather it has been out there too (after all, they do tell me a thing or two)—the cherry trees all of ten days behind schedule, and rain, rain, rain, occasionally mixed with and turning into snow. However, after all this chill and dank tail-end of more westerly blizzards and tornadoes, it would seem that spring has arrived, just in time for Easter. According to my own private time-table it arrived, in fact, yesterday, Good Friday, sometime between twelve and three. At least, when I emerged from three long florid hours (most of them spent standing) of the Passion According to St. Matthew as amplified by Bach, interspersed with some equally florid and far less commendable preaching, I found it for the first time this year too warm for a coat; the sun had come out; the cherry-trees along the Central Park reservoir were in full bloom, the Norway maples likewise; robins were singing all along the block, and laughing gulls laughing their heads off from a blue sky—and for sheer joy, mind you, not in derision. Add the fact that one is slightly light-headed from fasting—or one's slightly modified version thereof—and that Holy Week has been a week of drama such as one never imagined being both witness of and participant in, and the impression of a sudden emergence from winter into spring, given any encouragement at all, is no doubt explained. I have to set it down before I forget what it was like, and though it is the kind of thing that might seem more fittingly set down in a journal, I neither can nor, I am pretty sure, should keep a journal. One of the things I have realized while Lent was in progress was that I enjoy solitude so much that it becomes something very like self-indulgence for that very reason. I've almost forgotten what it feels like to be lonely, and this somehow makes it a responsibility to be sociable. Which, again, is an aside. Do bear with me if you can. You have heard about Holy Week, that fantastically black and furious week I spent a year ago, and so now there is nothing for it but that you should hear the sequel. How intelligible it may be I have no idea, but I have to set it down. I hardly supposed I was still capable of such astonishment, but it all goes to prove that one never knows.

Actually, one has to go back a little and to speak of Lent in general. I can tell you, as it would not be quite proper to tell anybody else, that in addition to giving up sweets I resolved to go to mass every morning, and managed to do it. Even the priests don't know—or anyway I trust they don't—since there are four of them conducting the services, one at a time on weekdays; and if they did know they wouldn't be particularly impressed. It's a thing people do, and that's about all. It meant going to bed rather earlier than usual, and though it wasn't really hard there was a point when I debated with myself about whether I should give it up. That was when I discovered that a cold I thought I had licked had taken its revenge in the form of post-nasal drip (very fashionable these days) and low blood pressure, and though I woke up feeling fine I could hardly drag myself home at the end of the day, and moreover wasn't getting things done out of sheer lassitude. Well, I was prescribed some reeking vitamin capsules, and they turned the trick just in time. (I would *not* ask any doctor's advice about getting up an hour earlier and going half a dozen blocks and back before breakfast, out of sheer stubbornness, I suppose.) And I learned something, whether or not there was any point in this particular form of discipline. (As for giving up sweets, I didn't lose weight, I gained; and as for no meat on Wednesday or Friday, I ate more meat than I ever did before in between; and even when I was tired I was never freer from aches and pains of any description. So much for the hazard to one's health.) What I learned had to do with the letter and the spirit of discipline. If one does things only when one feels like it, even though the thing itself is commendable, there is nothing especially commendable in doing it. Yet it is often argued, and I have argued myself, that only spontaneous acts are genuine. I don't think so any more. On the other hand, if one does a thing, finishes something one started, mechanically, because it is required by somebody or something else (and thus is regarded as a means to an end), or because one has decided to require it of oneself (and thus it comes to be regarded not as a means but as an end), one has done nothing particularly commendable either. Somewhere in between incoherently spontaneous behavior—which is bound to be irresponsible—and absolute inflexible rigor—which is at least apt to be just as irresponsible, and more dangerously so, since it makes no response to change, and there is always change—there is, of all things, the Golden Mean. One begins to see how much there is in Aristotle, after all, and why people like St. Thomas Aquinas referred back to him again and again. I have been reading Aquinas again these past few days, and what impressed me this time was the flexible instrument he made of his logic. I suppose logic is nothing more, really, than a way of expressing relations, and of arranging ideas in some kind of perspective so they come out undistorted and whole. But I am getting sidetracked again. What I am trying to say does have some bearing, I think, on theological matters in general, and on why denominations, and congregations, and individuals, go stale, or ossify, or simply fall to pieces. One must commit oneself, but if even within the commitment one does not go on growing, one is in a worse state than before—like that terrifying parable of the one devil that was driven out and the seven devils that stepped in and took its place. This is the thing that makes evangelical protestantism so dangerous, and I dare say that the same thing threatens the church of Rome; the one banks everything on a single individual act of commitment, and the other banks everything on a sort of machine for making people good. But I must *not* get sidetracked. At this rate it will be Holy Week a year from now before I get around to the one just past.

Anyhow, up until Palm Sunday I was so doggedly carrying out discipline that I had practically forgotten what I was supposedly doing it for. It's true that on Sundays there was a penitential procession to remind one, and two Sundays ago presto! all the crucifixes and other images veiled in purple. And then on Palm Sunday one suddenly woke up. There were palms for everybody, and then there was a procession—*the* procession, really. It went up to the altar, doubled back a couple of times, disappeared through a side door; a long wait; and then thump! thump! thump! three loud knocks at the back. Everybody looks around; the verger opens up; in they come, singing what is known as the *Vexilla regis*, the most magnificent of all the processional hymns. It would look silly, of course, if it weren't for the procession with palms into Jerusalem whose nineteen-hundred-and-somethingth anniversary was being commemorated; and of course if one doesn't believe that there was any such procession there is no reason to pay any attention to Palm Sunday at all. Well, that was one surprise; but there was more to come. After the *Kyrie*, as at every high mass, came the reading of the Epistle and the Gospel for the day. Ordinarily both are sung in what I think would be called plainchant; all on one note except for a change of pitch at the end of a quotation or a question. This time, when the procession of acolytes with candles and censers moved down from the altar into the choir for the gospel (a little ritual all in itself) I was astonished to realize that something different was going on: instead of one priest reading the account of the passion from St. Matthew, all three of them were taking part—the senior priest as narrator, one of the two curates reading the words of Pilate, Judas, and the other disciples, and the other the few words of Christ—and these few were sung softly, almost expressionlessly, which is really the only way such words ought to be rendered, and makes the drama all but unbearable. And when the choir joined in with the voices of the mob, a chill went down my spine. After that, Bach's St. Matthew Passion could only be an anti-climax. The thing about it is, you can listen to the whole thing, and be quite enraptured by all the gorgeous airs and choruses, particularly when they are sung well, without paying the least attention to what they are about; and no matter how well the Christus is sung, that part is all but smothered under the interpolations. That is the baroque for you; it takes up a lot of space, it commands a lot of attention, but it has puffed itself hollow. And meanwhile, the Palm Sunday gospel has gone on quietly being sung, year after year, by priests who are not professional musicians and so, happily, they do not collect an audience for the wrong reasons. Well, maybe on Easter they do. And not only the grandest choral music, of course, is a more or less direct off-shoot of the liturgy, but also the entire theater. Everybody knows this but nobody remembers it, until a thing like being in church on Palm Sunday shocks him into realizing for the first time how far the prodigal hath strayed without the faintest recollection whose offspring it is. I tell you, things are all, all, all mixed up and out of proportion for having forgotten their origin and been brought up imagining that they made themselves. Literally. Self-made men. People who change their names. Children ashamed of their parents. But I didn't mean to begin a sermon. I must get on.

Well, after Palm Sunday there were the gospels for Monday and Tuesday, which were just about as long. Among other things, I learned more about the Bible in this last week, just from listening and following in the prayerbook, than in my whole career up to now. Things begin to swallow you up; the whole world seems to have gone liturgical. Even the weather cooperates. It rains and rains. On Wednesday night there was a service for the whole of Trinity Parish, of which St. Luke's is just one of anyway half a dozen chapels, downtown at St. Paul's, the oldest church on Manhattan. Of course I got lost, though I have been past the place any number of times on pagan weekend prowls, and arrived late, but that didn't prevent the service from having its effect. If Lent in general is penitential, that was nothing to what one has become by the time that hour was over. Inside, St. Paul's is full of antique crystal chandeliers that tremble every time a subway train rumbles underneath (why they didn't all shatter long ago I can't imagine); outside, there is a churchyard full of slate headstones fallen sideways. Everything is dripping; people carry umbrellas; one's feet are slightly damp. And yet there is no gloom; the odd thing about penitence is that it is exactly the opposite; it is only when one is ashamed of being ashamed, or afraid of making a blunder (not of committing a sin, mind you—the prevailing fear is of being made a fool of, not of doing harm), that the gloom enters in. People are saying hello, though I recognize hardly anybody; I find myself with a little knot of them heading toward the subway, walking next to a girl who tells me her name is Hazel Johnson and that she is from Illinois. She has a face as plain as her name, but with something so engaging about it that she is one of those people it is literally a pleasure to meet.

Then comes Maundy Thursday, as the Anglicans call it—the day of the washing of the disciples' feet and the institution of the Eucharist at the last supper. This is a day of continuous vigil beside the altars, which are a last blaze of light before the darkness of Good Friday. White flowers; seven-branched candlesticks; after six weeks of purple, the priest comes out in a vestment of white brocade, and the sight is like a drink of water after a long drought. And of course the excitement is the more intense, and the effect the more startling, because of the absolute pitch-black that is about to fall. In the evening, up until ten o'clock, the candles on the little side altar are still blazing; but the lamps in front of the main altar have gone out, and the darkness there yawns like the mouth of a cave—almost, I would say, like the Pit itself. This evening the service is non-liturgical; the priest doesn't even enter the pulpit, but sits at the head of the center aisle, and after a hymn or two, simply talks—meditates aloud, really. The vicar at St. Luke's, being the kind of person he is, never really does any other kind of preaching, even from the pulpit. He never wags his head or waves his arms; he scarcely even raises his voice, and quite often he speaks with his eyes closed. It is a style that takes some getting used to, since it has no formal organization that you can follow; but once one is used to it, the sort of thing that passes for preaching in most places sounds hollow and frantic by comparison. I have no idea what he said, except that he quoted from Dr. Samuel Johnson and that he talked about charity, and that there could be no mistaking that he wasn't just using the word, he was communicating the meaning behind it. There must be many such people, quietly going about their business in places that don't get into the papers, and having an effect that doesn't show; it is, after all, what churches are for.

And then, Good Friday. In the morning the altars are bare; the gospel is read, but there are no masses, no candles, no sign of life; man has condemned God, mocked at Him, spat in His face, and hung Him up to die as a malefactor. For the three hours before the final "It is finished," in churches all over town there is preaching of one sort or another, or such substitutes as the Bach St. Matthew Passion I happened to hear; and again in the evening, there is the singing of the Reproaches: O my people, what have I done unto thee? The altars are still dark, but the veils have been torn from the crucifixes, and a great scarlet one is lying on the steps in front of the main altar; this is carried in procession about the church during the service, while a strange hymn, almost like a ballad, is sung, and then it is put back in the same place. By the time I left after this service, being in church had come to seem the normal condition of existence; I had gotten so accustomed to it, in fact, that (it is now the day after Easter, by the way) the normal, i.e. unecclesiastical, existence still seems rather strange. I got up early on Saturday morning for another altar service, at which, besides the priest, only the three nuns attached to the parish and one other girl were present; and after that, as prearranged, the other girl and I followed the nuns back to their house for breakfast. They were keeping the silence which is part of their rule at that hour, so they could only smile and nod and point out the daffodils and the one red tulip in their back yard. Inside, they showed us into the front room, where a little table was laid for two. We weren't quite sure whether we ought to break the silence ourselves, and not being so adept at signs, compromised by passing the butter in whispers. When the nuns had finished saying the office at their own little altar, and having their own breakfast, we washed the dishes while they went to say another office—a good deal of the life of people in religious orders seems to be spent in this way—and then we all headed for the sacristy, where we spent the morning polishing all the silver, laying vestments, and arranging the multitudes of flowers. The odd thing is that on the Saturday before Easter a year ago, after the look into the pit of hell that literally hurled me into the church, I wandered into St. Luke's in the middle of the afternoon and saw these same nuns and this same girl putting the lilies into place. When I told them this they said "Why didn't you come up? We certainly could have used you!" Very odd. They haven't very much sense of time—it comes from being used to a sense of eternity, I expect—and hardly remembered that a year ago they didn't even know me. We finished just as Lent officially came to an end, at noon, and Ann and I were sent home with an armload apiece of white carnations and snapdragons left over from Maundy Thursday. After I had had lunch, cleaned house and gone to the grocery store I went back for confession, and stayed for the lighting of the Paschal candle, a ceremony just as startling, and possibly still more ancient than the Palm Sunday procession; it is based, so far as I can understand, on the Old Testament prophecies, and is full of references to fire. Immediately after that came the blessing of the baptismal font, which again is full of Old Testament references, all of these to water. It is all elemental in much the same way as the idea of sacrifice and the spilling of blood—the function of the altar that seems to be universal in all primitive religions, and is so old that it may be regarded as prehistoric—and as recurrent as the myth of the slain youth, Tammuz, Adonis, Attis, Osiris, or however he Is called, whose death and rebirth was regarded as intimately connected with, or as a personification of, the cycle of the seasons and the death and rebirth of vegetation. If one wants to use such analogies to destroy the validity of religion in general, and Christianity in particular, well, then one will do it; but the paradox is that all these analogies can equally well be regarded as substantiating it. This I believe is the view of Jung, if that makes any difference; so far as ultimate validity goes, I don't suppose for a minute that it does. There are some things that are truer than any late-comer's gloss upon what they mean; when they *are*, what they mean doesn't matter.

Space to indicate the passage of time. It is now Friday after Easter, which day took a gorgeous leap forward from spring straight into summer. The temperature rose to the eighties, and the retarded trees sprang into leaf overnight. I don't know that I've ever seen a more glorious day, and the celebration at St. Luke's, for all that it was crowded with people in new spring wardrobes—I had new clothes myself, for that matter, and for the first time I saw how right the symbolism is, however it may be misused by vanity—the whole service was yet one more culminating astonishment. There is no doubt in my mind now that the forty days of discipline are a great piece of wisdom on the part of the church, and if I was not quite convinced before of the value of confession, I am now. The last lingering suspicion that it might be merely self-manipulation, and the last tight little fear of playing into the hands of authority, of having one's individuality crushed by the weight of the priestly hierarchy, seems to have vanished. Absolution is not an imaginary event; it *happens*, one doesn't know just how and one doesn't need to know. One only knows that it [is] nothing willed from within; it comes from without; it isn't willed at all, it is simply given. One makes no bargain, one asks nothing, one simply admits the truth, and the truth, once admitted, comes as a totally unexpected radiance of certainty. Even memory, which is a kind of holding on to what one cherishes and fears to lose because it is cherished, no longer seems important; one can let go even of that, and the letting go becomes one more step toward immortality: he that loseth his life shall find it. But probably there is no use trying to put into one's own feeble words what the saints of all the ages have been saying, that there is a benevolence at the heart of reality which only fear keeps anyone from experiencing directly.

But now I really must bring this to an end. All week I have been—for me—exceedingly social, which in this case means having people to dinner; hence the interruption in this all but interminable report. There are all kinds of things I had it in mind to mention, but they can wait for another time. Do write.

Love,

Amy

. . . .

15 June 1957

Dear Philip—

[. . .] Of course I don't object to the psychotherapy. In the first place I don't really know a thing about it, but if it can help anybody to get over being afraid, which is chiefly what prevents people from putting first things first and makes them feel pointless and thwarted as a consequence, so far as I can make out—then I can't be otherwise than in favor of it. The way I feel about it is a little the way I feel about Mr. Norman Vincent Peale and his Positive Thinking—I'm all in favor of positive thinking, and I don't know that Mr. Peale is as stupid as his detractors make him out to be; what I object to is Peale-ism, that glib sort of rubbish that gets thrown around by mixed-up people who are always running after the Latest Thing. (Did you, by the way, read that latest Salinger story that took up practically a whole *New Yorker* about a month ago? One ferocious tidbit in a generally ferocious piece, I don't know if you can call it story, is a passing reference to one Claude Vincent Smathers or something, who has just written a book called *God Is My Hobby*. That's what I mean.) But really now, about this Autoconditioning business. The title is enough: it belongs in the trash basket with all the other gimmicks that look so shiny and are no use whatever. As if the Latest Thing were really the Latest Thing to end All Latest Things (Now we're getting eschatological.) Won't the human race ever learn? Doesn't it want to learn? Anybody who issues a testimonial about a system called Autoconditioning is not interested in putting first things first, but only in putting the latest thing first. Excuse all this fulmination, but REALLY! The trouble with Democracy is that if a thing gets into the papers, or even onto a book jacket, it immediately becomes immutable. This being because after all one man's opinion is as good as another's; the main thing is to have the Latest one. Of course those stupid things don't do any direct harm; the harm they do is devaluative. If a thing goes over, then it must be a Latest Thing; therefore it has Status, until something else supersedes it; Has Status having superseded Is Good as a form of approbation. Now I know Daddy knows better, but there are people who have been gimmicked out of taking anything but keeping up with the Latest Thing seriously, by our wonderful all-embracing system of advertisement and so-called communication. Do you remember Dr. T. J. Eckleburg in *The Great Gatsby*? Actually that was the only thing I remembered, when I went back to it the other day. After the poor car dealer's wife has been killed on the highway, he looks out of the window and sees "the eyes of Doctor T. J. Eckleburg, which had just emerged, pale and enormous, from the dissolving night." "God sees everything," he says, and the man with him assures him that it's just an advertisement. And really this is the crucial passage in the whole book, whether Fitzgerald meant it to be or not.

To get back to psychotherapy and to Norman Vincent Peale's positive thinking, what is generally wrong, I suspect, is the motivation. Everybody ought to think positively, and everybody ought to know about a complex that has tied a knot in him somewhere, but if he undertakes any such thing with an idea of what he is going to get out of it, ten to one he isn't going to get what he wants or if he does, he'll find that it wasn't worth wanting. Everything is so *calculated* these days. So manipulated. Things are done not as things worth doing in themselves, but as means to something else. People all sitting around feeling their own pulses, getting outside themselves so they can look back in and see where they've been. People trying to make themselves over. People ashamed of being what they are. People so anxious about what other people think that they can't perform an honest act or think an honest thought. I've been through it; I know. It's terrible. Terrible!

Really, I don't know what's come over me. On rather, I do, but I didn't expect it to burst forth in quite this way. No, it isn't a theological crisis; the Incarnation never seemed to me more of a fact, however frantic I may sound. But I have quite suddenly gone to pieces in a rather complicated way, and I find myself in the midst of coming to a decision just possibly as crucial as any I ever made. The awful part is that one can never be sure at the time just how crucial it is. The whole thing is thrilling, and one has no wish to run away from it, but all the same it is a good deal of a strain.

A strain, apparently, is what I have been under for the past several weeks. One can't go around having religious experiences, taking a night course, getting ready to take over a new job, working at least mentally on a novel, and all the while thinking one is equal to everything, indefinitely, and have it otherwise, whether one is aware of the fact or not. I wasn't. I'm not sure whether I wrote you, but you may have heard, that Monica is going back to France—permanently, so far as she knows. I'd known that there was the possibility for a year or so, and while (as she perfectly well knew) I had no wish to see her go, it was understood that I would take over her job if it should happen. There really was no discussion, and there was no question in my own mind but that this was the right and normal thing for me to do. I'd handled things in her absence, after all, to everybody's satisfaction, for months at a time, and after five years I know my way around the library pretty nearly as well as she does. I'd also proved to my own satisfaction, since we took on a half-time clerical worker about a year and a half ago, that I could give directions quite adequately, and I can say without boasting that these people (we've had a series of three, and have just taken on a fourth), by the time they left (always for reasons of their own that had nothing to do with the job) were quite fond of me. I realize now that it wasn't easy, and it contributed to the strain that I put getting along with them as individuals above efficiency. I still think this is right, but whether it is good administration I'm not sure. Besides which, patience is not my strong point. But with Monica in charge, I managed a sort of detachment that made it a lot easier, and when I did get exasperated I'm afraid I was inclined to take it out on her. We have been through so many arguments, large and small, and have gotten to know each other so well, by this time, that being simply polite to each other, day in and day out, would have been both absurd and impossible. Well. A couple of weeks ago the bottom fell out of everything. I discovered that for no very distinct reason I was as cross as a bear; all day long I kept telling everybody I was, and not to pay any attention to what I said, but this didn't prevent me from being rude and perverse to absolutely everybody; until without any warning, late in the afternoon, I broke down entirely and started to cry. This sort of thing has happened to me once before in my life, and then I knew exactly why it was, so that I wasn't really surprised; but this time, since there didn't seem to be any particular reason, I was horribly startled and quite scared. Monica, who fortunately was the only one around just then, began consoling me and telling me she had been every bit as scared as I was when she started in at the Audubon Society. But I couldn't believe the job had anything to do with it; when I finally concluded that it must have a good deal, I realized that being equal to everything is not only a matter of volition, and that there are times when volition itself gives way—rather a shock to one's determination to be self-sufficient. I was pretty shaky over the whole weekend that followed, but it appeared that I had pulled myself together by Monday morning. All during the week I was interviewing prospects for the job as my assistant. I did a pretty good job of it, but by evening I was generally so tired that it was all I could do to wash up the dinner dishes before I went to bed. On Friday Monica was out, and all day long I was talking to people or listening to them talk—candidates for the job, garrulous visitors, and the senior vice president, a man whom I cannot like or respect and whose job it is to butter people up, either to get rid of them or to get something out of them. In my interview with him I permitted myself to be buttered out of taking an extra week without pay along with my vacation, which was to begin that day. Since he is a man who has no real authority, it doesn't much matter why he performed that little act; but in the terms he used, there was nothing to do gracefully but bow down and accept it. And with such people one must be graceful at all costs; one can't tell the truth, since for them there is no such thing. The upshot was that I was to come in on the next Monday after all. I had said I wanted the extra week because I was tired; it would have been stupid to mention that I also hoped to make some progress on the novel, which for weeks now has been at a complete standstill because I was too tired by the time the weekend came around. It seemed, at the time of the interview, a concession of no importance, and I was quite startled to find myself in tears again as soon as I had a minute to myself. All during the weekend it was like that; I had wild thoughts of handing in my resignation, which I couldn't believe were serious—until late on Sunday it came to me, with almost the shock of a revelation, that quite possibly they were. When that dawned upon me, for the first time in weeks I felt like myself again; I felt tired, but relieved and quite at peace.

Since then I have talked about this with Monica, with a doctor, and with a priest—nobody else. So until I have committed myself, one way or the other, this is going to be another of those confidences with which I seem compelled to burden you from time to time. Burden, of course, isn't quite the right word, since a burden is a thing one minds, and I seem to feel quite sure that you won't. When she had heard the story and seen how agitated I was—I still get agitated when I start thinking the decision isn't final, and that I might stay on after all—Monica ordered me home to calm down and rest up. Before I went, I saw a doctor, who found nothing wrong except nerves, prescribed a mild sedative (though there was nothing wrong with either my sleep or my appetite), and congratulated me on the promotion. When I saw him a second time—of course doctors can be quite obliging, and I suspect them of telling the patient mainly what the patient wants to hear—he granted that I had been trying to do too much, and that I would have to give up something. Which thing? The job? The novel? Helping the nuns, and going to mass twice or three times during the week? Well, no doctor can tell one that. In fact, nobody can. Nevertheless, after two days of being lazy, and hating myself during every minute, I went to see a priest. Not that I expected him to make a decision for me—I should have had no respect for him if he had—but I did want to hear what he would say on the question of whether the idea of giving up the job was simply an evasion of responsibility. There is a school of thought, after all—a very protestant one—which identifies the right thing with what is hardest or most distasteful. Father Weed didn't for a minute think so. He is a very remote man, even an abrupt one—I don't know that I ever saw anybody who was personally so shy. Which is probably why he is so good a priest—he puts everything into his function. He talked, of course, about the will of God, as priests do and must—but then I used the term myself before I was quite aware that I believed in it. And he said he would pray over the matter. Now the reason I decided to talk to him was that he had said in a sermon that in praying for people one must guard against being possessive—every individual soul has a destiny with which it is no one else's place to interfere, and all one can do is to care about that soul, as it were, in the presence of the truth, or the highest good, or however one chooses to refer to what is eternal. That, after all, is what charity means—anything else is spurious and out of proportion. You see how much such an attitude has in common with the true scientific one—not to demand, but without any constricting preconceptions simply to wait and see. And as far as I am concerned, that is what prayer is, and all it is— simply doing one's best to drop all preconceptions, and trusting what comes by way of illumination. Anything else is putting pressure on, and trying to bend the will of God to one's own. I think the reason I held out so long against Christianity was that I couldn't see the distinction between the will of God and doing what other people expect. I had got it into my head that to be Christlike was to be pliant and ineffectual—always give in, be nice, tell everybody the lies they want to hear. In other words, to be a conventional prig. Christ himself, of course, was nothing of the sort. He said what was true, and most of the time it wasn't at all what people wanted to hear. The confusion, of course, is between pretending to love everybody, which only comes out as interference, and *really doing it*; and about the nearest one can come, as a selfish human being, most of the time is to restrain oneself from interference, even mentally. It is devilish hard.

What has this to do with the question that has been exercising me this last week? Nothing directly, perhaps, but it is related somehow to the question of vocation. When I joined the church I was ready to give up all my notions of being a writer. I no longer regard writers as glamorous and enviable people; in general, I would say that they are vain, silly, and above all unhappy. Fame and success, if they come, are no satisfaction except to a rapacious vanity; and if one has more serious aims than simply being no-

ticed, the disappointment is perhaps more painful still. The really important work is mostly done, I suspect, by people whose names never get into
the papers. And yet, if the developments of the last couple of weeks mean
anything, they must mean that a writer is what I was meant to be. It seems
to me now that I have lulled myself with the notion that I could straddle
the issue, and follow two professions at once. Some people have done it,
and I guess I thought that what some people have done, I could do too.
All the time, I have been putting money in the bank, with the idea of making a trip abroad without giving up the job or the novel either; and for two
springs in succession that plan has come to nothing. Now I see that even
a week's leave of absence is something I can't arrange, and to finagle which
I have no aptitude and still less desire. I have enough now to live on, in
my own frugal way, for six months and more. If I handle a job as a department head, even so minor a one as this, successfully, I shall have to
put that first, with the prospect that I shall have very little energy for anything else. I'm not a born administrator; I'd even rather write my own letters than dictate them. I'm pretty good at needling a superior, and at keeping calm while she gets upset; but I now see that that doesn't mean I
wouldn't find myself getting just as upset in her place. I haven't interviewed anybody yet who really seemed fitted for the job as my assistant except one little girl who happens to be colored and toward whom I should
probably feel protective and compunctious, even should the president
think it advisable to risk the complications that might ensue. This may
sound priggish and hypocritical; so far as I can make out, it isn't. There
are people who enjoy creating issues of this sort, and flinging themselves
in the face of possible prejudice; I'm not one of them. I've even discovered
that my judgment has ceased to function, and that interviewing prospects
is harder and harder to carry off decisively. And the thought of all the
projects of cataloging and arranging, which I was eager to get at, has become simply suffocating when I bring myself to face it at all.

On the other hand, I foresee the reaction—just as she was settling
down to be respectable, *look* at her! The whole thing all over again. Whatever did she join the church for, then? Since the whole idea came like such
a bolt to me, I sympathize, and can hardly expect any other kind of reaction. And the only answer I can give is that this is what comes of putting
first things first. Is it self-indulgence, after all? I have gone to mass three
times over it, and each time I have come out certain that I cannot do otherwise than turn in my resignation and risk whatever follows. It's nothing
rational; but the really important decisions I have ever made were none of

them conscious. I've never tried so hard before to think a thing through, but it seems no use.

As I say, I don't complain; I find the whole thing very alive-making. When it's settled, I'll let you know.

All right, be different and don't join the family reunion this fall! No, that's wrong of me—it's putting on pressure in reverse, which is the very worst kind. All the same, it would be fun if you came. Whatever you do do, anyhow, please write. And good luck with the psychotherapy!
Love,
Amy

. . . .

10 January 1959
Dear Philip—

If I don't hurry, I shall have finished reading both your Christmas books before I've even thanked you for them. As it is, I began the *Letters to Young Churches* on New Year's eve and was well into them before the year was very many hours old; and this week, mainly while riding the subway to and from work, I have read the Barzun book all the way through. You don't know—or maybe you do—how clever you were to pick that one out. After being surrounded by Darwinian dogma day in and day out at the Audubon Society, it is most refreshing to read an anti-Darwinian for a change, and it is also illuminating—and reassuring—to look back at the mechanistic-materialist determinism that I spent so many years madly fighting against. The book was originally published the year I came to New York, and there are topical references that bring back the mood of those confused, gloomy, desperate days when nothing, either within or without, made any sense. Considering the circumstances, it seems to me a remarkably level-headed book, and I also found it fascinating. You are very nice to take my mention of *The Golden Bowl* so seriously, but I am very happy with the substitute you chose—the more because it was your choice.

As for the *Letters*, they are even better than I expected. I find St. Paul hard to read in the King James version, partly because of the oxlike stupor of long familiarity dating back to sermons half-heard under duress, and a long-standing notion of a distinctly unpalatable personality behind them. Here, they sound like—they *are*—real letters, and they are exhilarating and sometimes startling to read. To take for a sample, from the first letter to Corinth: "Are you really unable to find among your number one man with enough sense to decide a dispute between one and another of you, or must one brother resort to the law against another and that before those who have no faith in Christ? It is surely obvious that something must be seriously wrong in your Church for you to be having lawsuits at all. Why not let yourself be wronged or cheated? For when you go to law against your brother you yourself do him wrong, for you cheat him of Christian love and forgiveness." Dynamite—and as true as when it was written in spite of the different, and particular, circumstances that called forth this advice. It is a wonderful book to have, and I am indebted to you for it.

Christmas was beginning to seem rather a long time ago, but I have just come from a most extraordinary pageant that sent one straight back into the mood of the holiday. This was a twelfth-century work called *The Play of Daniel*, which until last year, when it was done at the Cloisters, had not been done for centuries. It is sung in Latin, with an added narration by W. H. Auden, and the production altogether can only be described as a labor of love. This year it has been revived in a Gothic-style church uptown, which must seat a couple of thousand people, and it was packed, with standees in the aisles. It is the sort of thing that can only be done, really, in a church, since that was where it was originally done. The remarkable thing about it is the attitude of naive wonder which is the only way one can respond to it at all, and it would be very difficult not to respond; and one feels that this is the way it felt to be burghers of Beauvais back in the thirteenth century. The whole Daniel story is there, beginning with Belshazzar's feast, and the dancing lions that try to maul him and are a comic touch that seems exactly right, and at the very end comes the prophecy, with a gorgeous angel which seems to have stepped out of a painted annunciation scene and to be just about to retreat into it again as the final Gregorian *Te Deum* ends and the play is over. I don't think I ever saw more beautiful costumes, ever.

It is now Sunday, and in a little while I shall be going up to the Carnegie Recital Hall to hear a flute concert featuring Bach, Mozart, Poulenc, and Goodman. Joe says this will be the first time he will hear his own flute-and-piano sonata; it has been done several times, but always with him as the pianist. He is very busy these days with teaching, private pupils, and commissions—the latest a cycle of songs for tenor and chamber orchestra, to be performed abroad next summer. I went out there for dinner on Twelfth Night, and found the tree still up and the children clamoring to be read aloud to before I was quite inside the door. Meredith is growing tall, has her hair shorn, and is missing some front teeth—six is an awkward age generally; but she goes to dancing school and is unmistakably musical. Alison, who used to run and hide when I came, is now as affectionate as the others; and Christopher is such a cheerful little boy that it is hard to believe that he is temperamental too. We had one of those sybarite meals—chicken under a luscious sauce made with *whipped cream,* if you please, and the most magnificent white Burgundy wine I ever drank (Chassagne-Montrachet, if you will excuse a touch of the connoisseur).

Don't tell anybody, but I think I may be working up to leaving my job one of these days. The old urge began to recur last fall, was shelved temporarily because there was too much else to do, but now I find it cropping up again. And now it begins to seem pointless, if I am ever going to finish that novel, to postpone taking the time off to do it. Do you have any idea what the family reaction would be? Because I really don't wish to defy anybody, though braving a little mild disapproval would probably be bracing. Things at the Audubon Society are almost too easy, and there is beginning to be just enough prestige to spoil me a little. The chief deterrent is a combination of plain ordinary timidity with the idea which is dinned into one constantly by priests and members of religious orders (more by implication than accusation, but all the more effective for that reason) that too much solitude is unwholesome, frivolous, and even downright wicked—and of course having a job to which one has to go daily is a rigorous guarantee against solitude. However, I begin to be surrounded by such guarantees from other quarters—the church above all, and the Community of St. John Baptist of which I am now formally an associate, and more and more people of various sorts and conditions. As you can see, I am still mulling the thing over in my mind, but one of these days I have got to make it up, before the indecision begins to be wicked in itself. [. . .]
Love,
Amy

. . . .

13 May 1959
Dear Philip—
[. . .] I'm sorry about your state of mind, and only wish (in spite of your explicit statement that you didn't want advice) that I had some nice, sparkling remedy to propose. A tendency to states of depression is probably partly constitutional, I suspect, and it appears to run in the family—

in fact it is so common that one could almost as well say that it runs in the human race. (I swear the play on words was not intentional—it just happened.) There is something, after all, in that old theory of the humors—did you ever look into *The Anatomy of Melancholy*? If you remember, Grandpa described in his memoir an acute state of depression he once went through. I suppose knowing it is not uncommon doesn't make the condition any less real, but perhaps it may make it a little easier to live with. I am reminded, somehow, of a piece of advice which the author of *The Cloud of Unknowing* gives his would-be contemplative, to the effect that one way of coping with distractions is simply to stop struggling with them, to "cower down under them as a captive, or a coward overcome in battle, to feel yourself overcome forever." And it is remarkable how well it works. When I see myself getting irritated or upset over things that happen, I say, "that isn't really me, out there, reacting like that; whoever it is, I'm just going to ignore it." I realize that ignoring depression isn't so simple a matter; it's like a load of lead by comparison with a pinprick. But still I think there may be something in the idea of total non-resistance, even when the adversary weighs a ton. My guess is (and it can only be a guess) that this sense of a burden coupled with feelings of panic—which I gather is what you are referring to—must come from some accumulated pressure, partly environmental, partly inherited, which says you *have* to accomplish something, you *have* to have something to show for it, you *have* to justify your having been brought into the world at all. Whereas the truth of the matter is, you don't *have* to do any such thing. Your existence is justified already, whatever you do or don't do. And the worst thing in the world that can happen is to be continually afraid of what might happen, either because of or in spite of what you do or don't do. Nothing anybody does is really that important. There—I start out analyzing and end up delivering a sermon. Please excuse. I have no idea, of course, whether it applies at all.

My friend Gene from across the hall is dead. This happened less than a month ago. A couple of months before that he had gone to Baltimore, where he married for the third time (first in this country)—an old friend of his who used to live in New York and whom I knew slightly. Everything seemed to be fine, and then one Sunday he had a heart attack, and died before his wife finished phoning for the doctor. Matthias and the younger boy, Hannes (who came over from Austria something over a year ago and has the apartment now) drove down to Pennsylvania, where they had the funeral, and took me along. It was somehow more like an escapade than anything so solemn as a man's last rites—we got up at three a.m. to start out, because Matthias was sure we would get lost, and since I had been to the ballet (of which more later) that evening I had only a couple of hours of sleep. As it turned out, we had the turnpikes practically to ourselves, and we didn't get lost, so it was only five, and just beginning to be light, when we pulled into the Philadelphia suburb where we were expected to appear at around eight. So we had breakfast of hot cakes in a diner and then drove around listening to the birds singing in the early morning—cardinals, robins, song sparrows, and in one enchanting place where we stopped, dozens of white-throats, each one singing its wistful, dreaming little song—a perfect rain of little flute-notes, the like of which I never heard before. Then we went to Gene's niece's house, and from there we drove out into Chester County, which is Pennsylvania Dutch country, full of rolling hills and tidy, settled-looking farms. The funeral, such as it was, was in one of those farmhouses, the in-laws' family place, where he had been for the weekend when he died. It was a heavenly place, with flowers blooming everywhere—apple-trees, dogwood, violets, blue-bells, buttercups, narcissus—and all dripping, and all the more fragrant, from a rain in the night. Since I hadn't been to a funeral in about twenty-five years, I had forgotten the excruciating embarrassment which is about the only feeling possible under the same roof with the mortal remains of one deceased. Ceremony is the only thing that can possibly mitigate the embarrassment—one is embarrassed, precisely, because of the absence of any suitable form to follow. Some records of Bach were played on a phonograph which there was some trouble in persuading to warm up properly, and then two of the numerous brothers-in-law made little speeches which were all the more embarrassing because they were in such desperately sincere good taste. At the grave it was better. The sun had finally come out, for one thing, and then there was a minister who read from the book of Job and the Psalms and the Epistle to the Romans, which make the act of mourning bearable. Afterward there was an enormous lunch at the niece's house, and much gay conversation with the numerous in-laws, and after they had gone Hannes and Matthias and I sat in the back yard under a dogwood tree, soaking up sunshine, before we finally started back. The truth is, it had been a delightful day, and it proved to me that to sorrow and to rejoice at the same time are not incompatible, they are actually part of the same thing; and as for the escapade-like character of taking a day off from work and getting up at three in the morning and driving around listening to white-throated sparrows, the whole thing was eminently fitting because it was so like Gene himself. The strange thing continues to be that I can't really grasp the idea that he is dead.

For the past few weeks it has been just one musical event after another. First there was the Bolshoi Ballet, whom [*sic*] I saw twice—and can count myself fortunate, even though the great Ulanova wasn't dancing either time. There is no company in the world to compare with it, whatever quibbles and qualifications occur to the reviewers, and there hasn't been a public response to compare with what happened here, ever—S. Hurok, who brought them over, finally hired Madison Square Garden for an extra week, and people were standing in line all day long for chances, at opera-house prices, to see them there. I suppose it is because my musical memory is so vague and fuzzy that I find ballet more exciting than pure music in a concert-hall—it is music in visible human form. And as for theater, a dancer can be as eloquent in a single gesture as most actors are in a thousand words—it's the dispensing with speech (a clumsy business, words, after all) that makes the language of pure movement so expressive. However, I go on liking music, and hearing a good deal of it—a harpsichord concert and a new opera, *The Ballad of Baby Doe*, on a single Saturday, and then a couple of evenings ago I heard the Handel oratorio *Israel in Egypt* at Carnegie Hall, with a contralto soloist who had a voice like Marian Anderson's, and a chorus of a hundred or so, plus harpsichord (which you couldn't hear) and organ (which could be heard now and then, such as in the passage where the Red Sea rolls over the pursuing Egyptians). It is certainly not much like the *Messiah*, and I was startled by some very graphic passages, such as the hissing and humming that describes the plague of flies. Most exciting, though, was hearing Joe Goodman's new trio for piano, flute and violin, which he and a couple of his colleagues played last Saturday at the Union Theological Seminary, to a small-but-select audience in a little auditorium somewhere among the labyrinthine passages of that hive of Presbyterianism, Niebuhrianism, and neo-Calvinism (if that is what it is). Anyhow, Joe has some pupils up there, and so the concert was arranged. The new trio is really brilliant—a somber theme that somehow works itself up into a most electrifying tarantella, and then a slow movement; but it's all of a piece, and very satisfying. Connie thinks it's the best thing he has done yet, and I agree. And the audience obviously liked it. [. . .]

Love,

Amy

. . . .

4 August 1959

Dear Beth—

This may sound most unlikely, but I swear it's true: there is a new tenant in my building whose name is Mary CRAMBLITT. You can imagine how confused the postman is by all this. Sometimes I get her mail, sometimes she gets mine, which we leave out for the other one to pick up. We haven't yet introduced ourselves—after all, to say "Miss Cramblitt, I am Miss Clampitt" or vice versa might only complicate matters further—but I think I know her when I see her, and she has a shaggy dog, just to make the whole thing completely unbelievable. Shaggy dog story, you know—if you know what one is, that is!

Love,

Amy

. . . .

13 August 1959

Dear Mary [Russel],

Few things delight me more than a letter-in-installments. The suspense!—Yours read practically like a novel, one by Henry James I think; your two-day search through Venice is straight out of one he never got around to writing, but would have, I dare say. I forget whether you ever read *The Wings of the Dove*, but Venice is in that. It is also in *The Aspern Papers*, whose plot turns on a lost manuscript; but what H.J. would have done with a Lost Gorgione—! As you can see, I was enthralled. You have a wonderful way of making one see and feel the mood of things and places and seasons, including the ones I missed. I missed the Giorgione *Cristo portacroce*, for instance. I was at San Rocco, but all I remember from there are the Tintorettos. And to think of you making obscure discoveries on the island of Murano! I remember pausing there aboard the chugging, oil-smelling non-tourist ferry that took me on one memorable afternoon to Torcello, but that was as near as I came to it.

But I must assure you before I go any further that Renée is still snug and safe in your apartment and the roof is still intact. She came down for dinner the other evening, your letter having spurred me to call her as I had been intending to do for weeks. I read her some parts from your letter, about "Zozzo" and your itinerary through the north of Italy—which reminded her of a tour she and a friend took through the region, staying mainly in convents, and her mention of some sisters in Verona reminded me in turn that I had caught a glimpse of those same sisters on my brief visit there, and then we were off: oh to be in the north of

Italy, bathing in the peacock-crystalline waters of Lake Garda, smelling the grapes and the peaches and gathering wild blackberries along the roadsides! I dug out my old journal and managed to decipher the following from the entry for Verona: " . . . at lunch in the vacant dining room a garrulous waiter with a red nose told me positively there would be a *temporale* before evening . . . and sure enough, when I came down at five after another nap, a leaden bank of cloud was rolling up behind the hills to the east; but the sun still shone, and eventually nothing came of it. I followed the Corso Cavour vaguely and found my way across a temporary bridge over the gray-green, swirling flood of the Adige, then up zigzagging flights of steps past the Roman theatre, under an aisle of cypresses and to the crest of the hill of San Pietro. Some nuns with white butterfly headdresses were leading a procession of small boys with shaven heads somewhere or other. Over a low stone wall the town spread out, cloven by the curving river, with red roofs and the sharp peaks of Lombard towers and campaniles, striped rose and white with alternate stringcourses of brick and limestone. I passed a farmhouse with dahlias in bloom and walked along a quiet road under the old fortress walls, where tangles of greenish-flowered clematis grew and I could smell but not see the ripening grapes on the terraces beyond the wall. It was very still, very rich with late summer growth. Coming back, I heard the treble voices of choir boys rehearsing, over and over, a chant I found myself recalling afterward at Dezenzano . . . " Oh, to hear that chant again!—but just what it was is now past remembering (though strangely prophetic) and so I shall never know. Gregorian, no doubt. I could spend my life listening to Gregorian chants. Music is a complete mystery to me, a closed door technically, and yet it opens the very gates of paradise in a way nothing else quite does. Especially sixteenth-century music and Gregorian chant.

I know that feeling of panic you speak of, about places left behind and what has become of them in one's absence. In Perugia, I think it was, after weeks of seeing no newspapers, I bought a Paris Herald, and was appalled. The amours of Hollywood stars, sex orgies among high school students in Indiana—that was all that seemed to be left of the U.S.A., and I could hardly believe it was my own country and never wanted to go back at all.

As for New York being a mess, it always has been and I can't see that things are much different, or any worse, than they ever were. There has been a great but (to me) incomprehensible hullabaloo over contracts for public housing—it would appear that even Robert Moses is involved in it somehow, and the mayor is full of wrath but can't get to the bottom of it either. A little earlier, there was another and even noisier hullabaloo when this same Moses, for some reason that was never clear, decided that there should be no more free Shakespeare in Central Park. Finally, though, that young fellow Joseph Papp, who produces the plays if you remember, took the matter to court, and one happy day the Daily News carried the headline: LET BARD IN, COURT TELLS MOSES. So now they are doing *Julius Caesar*, and the crowds are bigger than ever. I haven't been to any of the summer performances, but last winter I saw them do *Antony and Cleopatra* indoors, and found it better than the production I once saw with Katharine Cornell. . . . Also, the Monday evening concerts in Washington Square are on again, though I haven't been there either so far. At the first there was a large to-do, with much speechmaking and such gymnastics as perching a quartet on the top of Washington Square monument (where nobody could see them, according to the newspaper account I happened to read), in honor of the official closing of the Square to traffic last winter. There has been a strike at the A. & P.—of which I have gradually become a part-time customer—but it has now been settled, and the reopening was attended with about as much pomp and glee as a coronation and the news that Queen Elizabeth is expecting her third, combined. The Weather Bureau, when you call, now gives what is called a temperature-humidity index; originally it was given the name of Discomfort Index, but as you can imagine, that was received with universal indignation. The purpose of this innovation is said to be to let employers in non-air-conditioned places know when their employees are entitled to be sent home early. As for the weather—well, you know summer in New York, only some summers are more so. This one has been wet. It rained just about every day for something like two weeks—and often not once a day, but several times, in violent tropical downpours, with wind and lightning. As a result of one of those storms, a tree I was fond of is no more; it was a locust or acacia, the kind with many rounded feathery leaves and those drooping creamy clusters of blossoms, late in May, and it was in the garden a door or two down from me, so that I had to lean out on my fire escape to see it. Alas. I planted a windowbox with nasturtiums and they grew and have even, with great effort, produced a few somewhat stunted flowers. But life on a fire escape is hard, and the odds are against them. They are always either too wet or too dry, and a couple of times, after a night-long, pouring rain, I had to drain off the water in which they were standing up to their necks, poor things. There have been some hot days, not too many, and there have been at least two really spectacular sunsets— the kind with vast arching fans of cloud, rose and violet, that stretched for miles, and made me wonder how far one would have to travel to get from one end to the other of what was going on overhead. As you know, the amount of accessible sky here on Twelfth Street is a never-ending delight and satisfaction, and the view of chimneys and windows and rooftops and of that small jungle of a garden underneath is the sort of thing that grows, like a garden, the more intensively it is cultivated.

Oh, and I have slightly redecorated the apartment. It is gayer than it was, with a new couch-cover printed all over with Italianate arches and doorways in black and white, and a couple of rose-red cushions to set them off. This happened because by what seemed a ghastly mistake at the time, the walls got painted a sort of mauve, and since I hadn't the fortitude to make an issue about it the situation could only be retrieved by getting all the old browns and greens out of sight. And in the end, of course, it is much improved.

I have been having a wonderful four weeks of being right here, enjoying the décor within and the view without, cooking dinner for somebody now and then, and—writing. Yes, after having once again finally abandoned the novel as a dead duck and a lost cause, I found that it hadn't heard the death sentence after all. With some trepidation I got the Audubon Society to let me take a two weeks' leave of absence in addition to the two of paid vacation, and except for a weekend at the convent in New Jersey at the very beginning, I have spent it all right here. I must say that the life agrees with me—an ordered, early-rising, industrious but unhurried existence, with one's main energy going into the work to be done but still capable of being diverted to quite different considerations without—or at least very little—sense of rupture or strain. The book is now, if I keep it to the volume and symmetry it has in my mind, about two-thirds finished. I am over the hump; the stumbling-block which kept me writing and re-writing the same episode over and over without getting it right, and which led me to think it had already been worked over too long, simply evaporated, and one morning, in the space of perhaps ten minutes, the resolution I had despaired of achieving simply opened up like a map, as though it had always been there. Sometimes it scares me. A couple of days ago I found myself immersed in a broth of such sheer frightfulness and misery that I thought both the story and I would drown in it, and hardly dared to go on. But the next morning saw us both safely through. I don't know yet, but I think I shall most probably leave my job to finish it; after which, if all goes well, I shall head—at last, at last—for Europe. But that could hardly be before you are back here—probably not before spring.

As I think I wrote you, I made a real try at not wanting to be a writer, and that was pretty certainly a good thing. I am not as afraid now as I was (I suppose without quite knowing it) of one day having to admit that I *wasn't* one; and not being afraid now goes for the possibility of failure too. The curious thing about this kind of voluntary relinquishment—or anyhow attempt at relinquishment—is that one emerges with renewed confidence: not in oneself, precisely, so much as in the nature of things. It is something like going to confession, which basically is nothing but an exercise, a rigorous one, in seeing things not the way they might or ought to be but simply as they are. It seems to me, or has seemed a good deal of the time these last four weeks, that writing fiction is simply the job in which whatever working energy I have finds itself most at home, which is perhaps another way of saying it is the job I can do best. Well, one never knows. Vocation is a curious thing. A girl I know, who came to New York determined to be an actress, after four or five years of trying, had no sooner given up the idea and gone back to Minnesota than she discovered what seems to be a vocation to a religious order. It has been a most astounding thing to see happen, and quite humbling, really, and I suppose along with the excitement there is bound to be a little twinge of wistfulness about seeing, or rather not seeing, one's own way so clearly. Anyhow, at moments I catch a glimpse of Another Novel, piling up like a thunderhead behind the one I am working on now. Actually, the germ of it is not new; it has been lying there, more or less dormant, for several years, and it necessitates another look at Europe before it can be begun. Well, we shall see.

I am very eager to see your new paintings, and I am also delighted to know that "you-know-who" has sold some of his work and done some new ones. As for your seeing him, I hardly supposed you would fail to, sooner or later—later rather than sooner, though, I would have said. As for his knowing nothing about the blessing of apartments, either his memory or my imagination—or both—is being unreliable. I could have sworn that he had told me about being at home when the priest came to bless the house in Jersey City. Anyhow, it is fine that he has been to Greece. . . . As for the lost Giorgione, I imagine you thought of going to Berenson (he *is* still alive, isn't he?) and decided against it. No doubt at his great age he would be capricious as well as formidable. But there must

be somebody. This is all most exciting, and I shall be waiting to hear of further developments. [. . .]
Love,
Amy

. . . .

29 September 1959
Dear Philip—
Weird weather! It is almost as hot and sticky as when you were here. Well, not quite, but eighty-degree temperatures and eighty percent relative humidity are not what one has any reason to expect at this stage of the calendar, and that is what it was doing today. Mostly it has been beautiful, with a golden, hazy look over everything, and mainly I'm not complaining much.

I can't remember what I may have been doing, except that I have been seeing quite a lot of people, have been to a movie ("Wild Strawberries," which is in Swedish), and have formally resigned my job. I told them I planned to leave the middle of November, and I have written Beth that I thought I would come out to Iowa right after that and stay at least over Thanksgiving. The people at the Audubon Society whom I have told understand that my reason for leaving is a family matter, and that really is what it turns out to be, even if I hadn't quite planned it that way. I think it was your letter that decided me finally. I don't know what, if anything, I may be able to offer in the way of comfort and assistance, but having already made up my mind to leave the job, I at least can come feeling free and unpressed for time, as well as—quite strongly—that this is what I should be doing.

I have now had letters from both Mamma and Daddy, both mainly about Beth, and all that is clear is that the situation at home is too complicated to go on with everybody there at once. Possibly I am wrong, but I think Beth's erratic ups and downs may be a good sign, however hard they undoubtedly are on everybody else. Certainly it is more normal to *have* such ups and downs, and to express them, than to remain in a state of apathy and submission, while heaven only knows what is shoved down into the subconscious regions. Apparently part of any mental illness involves some kind of attrition of the normal inhibitions of reason and social pressure, so that the patient goes around deprived of the social "skin" worn by people who have not suffered this attrition; so things he does often look funny to people for whom the "skin" is second nature. The question would seem to be whether Beth can learn to reason, or to accept the reasoning of other people. The reason she can't accept Mamma's kind of "reasoning," I think, is that it *isn't* reasonable—that is, it is dictated by anxiety, and for some reason disturbed people are quicker to detect and exploit anxiety, even, than normal ones. And of course a clear-cut disagreement about how she is to be handled leaves the door wide open to an impossible situation. Mamma is a dear, good person who in some ways is easier to sympathize with than Daddy, but she can be maddeningly irritating—and I say this as one who has been around rarely, and then mainly in ideal circumstances. She is irritating because she is anxious; anxiety is what keeps her awake at nights, that keeps her from paying attention to what is said, so she asks silly questions, and then one gets impatient, and she gets defensive. Anyhow, this is what has happened to me, and so far as reason and social inhibitions are concerned I guess I am fairly normal. It is the failing of anxious people to be always trying to control things they can't control; actually, I think, they suffer from a kind of infection of the social skin, a hypertrophy rather than an atrophy, so it is no wonder that they and people who are just the opposite make life unbearable for each other.

All of which is sheer theorizing, and perhaps both mistaken and useless. I'm not sure that I agree with Daddy's hands-off, let-her-learn-by-her-mistakes-policy either; if her reasoning power is permanently impaired, I suppose she can't be expected to learn. But I do think his attitude is right. If she can be handled firmly, well and good; but if not, then above all she must not be fussed at.

And who ever heard of a mother who didn't fuss at her daughters? I've certainly had at least a dose of it in my day, and it wasn't until I had enough self-confidence to stop trying to be formidable that it ceased to bother me.

What I have in mind, anyhow, may turn out to be completely impractical, but my idea in coming out is to at least explore the possibility of taking an apartment somewhere in Des Moines, not too near but not too far from Grand Avenue, and having Beth live there with me. I don't plan to mention this to Mamma or Daddy until I've had a chance to see how Beth reacts to the idea, and in general I want to avoid discussing her with them as much as I can. I think one of her troubles may be the endless discussing of her case while she is in the house, of which she can't but be aware whether she actually overhears it or not; and I know I have been a party to discussions of her at which she was visibly present, simply because

Mamma and I didn't agree about something concerning her. It may turn out that I can't get along with her myself, but I can't be sure without seeing her and finding out. It occurred to me that sharing an apartment, if one could be found that I could afford, might even have advantages both ways: if she is able to go on working, she might be able to contribute something, which might give her more incentive to go to work regularly, and that would give me just that much more leeway to finish my novel. She would be out of Mamma's hair, but they would be near enough so I could call on them if I had to. What I have no idea about is whether a small furnished apartment with a short lease, or no lease at all, would be easily found in Des Moines, and what kind of rent I would have to pay. If you know anything about such things, I do wish you would let me know.

Love,

Amy

. . . .

18 October 1959

Dear Mary—

How wonderful to think of you in England, walking on a moor! Those particular moors I missed, alas, though I was in Yorkshire and got the feel of that strange, wild, treeless upland country, with its mists and its rough stone and that sullen, romantic sense of doom and fatality—so pagan really, but so totally different from pagan Italy—that Emily Brontë expressed so exactly. And what an extension of oneself, one's identity, to visit ancestral places! If I could just find the homes of my own Welsh great-greats, I fancy I should really begin to understand the wild streak in my own disjointed makeup. Also, I might begin to understand Dylan Thomas—maybe.

It must be interesting to see Italy again, after England, and to observe what difference it makes in one's point of view. Or perhaps, knowing Italy as you do, you were not troubled by the sense of being pulled in opposite directions, of having to make up one's mind which one *really* loved. A most childish internal conflict, no doubt—as though one could have only one Real Friend. It sounds rather like those dormitory sessions in which it was solemnly debated whether one could Really Be In Love with more than one boy at a time. All the same, it bothered me, until one sad, sad autumn day when I stood in Oxford, with the leaves falling and a fine rain misting down, and missed my train back to London because looking at the Radcliffe Camera I suddenly thought of Rome, and burst into tears at the very complicatedness of things—whereupon the conflict was resolved.

All of which does seem quite far away and long ago. Things here have been happening so fast that there is scarcely time to think, much less brood or give oneself over to nostalgia. I am definitely leaving my job, probably around the middle of November. There is a great sense of relief about having that settled, though I have even less idea than I expected to of what may be in store. My first move will be a trip out to Iowa, where the question of what is to be done about, with, or for my sister has now become a bit urgent. It seems clear that having her at home is simply too much of a burden on my mother, who, poor dear, has borne the strain so nobly all these years; and it has occurred to me that a possible solution, at least temporarily, would be for me to find an apartment in Des Moines and have my sister stay with me while I finish the novel. Whether there is a chance that such an arrangement might succeed, I won't know until I have gone out there, talked to the doctors, et cetera. It occurred to me that if I did leave New York for six months or longer, Renée might take my apartment—that is, if you had returned to your own apartment in the meantime. I haven't mentioned this to Renée (though the thought of her staying here when and if I went abroad did come up, a couple of months back), but I expect to see her this week and will probably talk with her about it then. It would be a great comfort to have her here, if I did leave.

In the meantime, there has been a series of autumnal visitations—fun, but exhausting: my brother Philip early in September, my mother last weekend, my Boston brother with his wife and their eight-year-old next weekend. And now Monica, my old boss, is here from Paris—more madly exhilarating to be around than ever, and now, her mother having died early this year, she is in her own words Filthy Rich, and so—in addition to giving an ornithological cocktail party or two, as of old—she is going to take me to lunch at Twenty-One—which means that I must calm my nerves and recoup my appetite, if all that food is to be done justice to. New York seems fuller and fuller of people to try to keep up with, which means less and less time for solitude, that dangerous luxury—or is it a necessity after all? I read when I am too tired for anything else, but there is no energy for writing, at this present pace. The weather has been weird— day after day the summer holds on, trees are still green, and it would be, if it weren't for the shortening days and southering sun, hard to remember what part of the year it is supposed to be. My mother and I saw *La Traviata*, which gave me to think again of Italian gesture and bravura, but before I could puzzle out and predicate the thought, whatever it was, I was caught up in the next preoccupation. And so it goes. I see you strolling by the Arno in the Italian autumn, of which (I suddenly realize) I know nothing except that passage out of Milton which describes the legions of fallen angels,

> Thick as autumnal leaves that strow the brooks
> In Vallombrosa, where t 'Etrurian shades
> High overarch't imbower . . .

Now I am off to a choral Evensong—altar thick with candles, scarlet-vested-and-cassocked priests and acolytes in procession, choir singing plainsong responses, and the most delicious sense of high festival—in honor of St. Luke, whose day it is.

Life had a picture story about Tuscany some weeks back. Perhaps you saw it. All a bit melodramatic, but then I suppose the Renaissance was that way. Must collect that elusive thought—the one *La Traviata* scared out of hiding. I suspect it must have been somewhat theological. [. . .]
Love,
Amy

. . . .

20 October 1959
Dear Beth—
[. . .] The other morning, I got up before the sun and went to church, and I walked back up the street afterward with the most delightful old priest who told me his name was Father Flye (he is actually quite famous in the vicinity, and I had heard about him but never met him until he introduced himself), who left me feeling so cheerful, in spite of its having started out a gray, sullen sort of day, that when I got back here to Twelfth Street and saw (first) a French steamship, the Liberté, moving up the Hudson without making a sound, and then (second) a tiny little bird with a yellow stripe on its head—to get back to the beginning, or something like the beginning, of this interminable sentence, I felt that it was somehow all Father Flye's doing. I mean the golden-crowned kinglet (for it was none other) was down below my fife escape, hopping and lisping in that faint little voice, in the top of one of the catalpa trees—not actually indoors. But the next thing I realized was that the catalpa trees were alive

with birds—kinglets both golden and ruby-crowned, nuthatches, white-throated sparrows, brown creepers, a woodpecker (downy, I think), juncos, and I forget what else. When I got to work I phoned a friend of mine who patrols a piece of Central Park, and told her to be sure to go out that day. In the evening there were some people here to dinner—non-bird-watchers—and while we were just getting ready for dessert the bird-watching friend called to report. At the mention of brown creepers, the non-bird-watchers at the table became vastly amused, and the next thing I knew they had invented a game involving brown creepers. I couldn't see very well what they were doing, but I gather their idea of a brown creeper was a very stealthy military maneuver that sneaks up from behind. It is just about as odd that there should be a brown creeper, I suppose, as that there should be a priest named Father Flye. At least a man in a hospital, whom he went to call on, thought it was so odd that he said he had to get up to see a man named Flye. Around the same church, it was pointed out to me, there are all sorts of natural history references—a Father Weed and a Father Leach. But I don't know that any of this is any odder than that there should be a Mary Cramblitt and an Amy Clampitt in the same apartment house. [. . .]

Love,
Amy

. . . .

17 December 1959
Dear Mary—
[. . .] You must be on your way to becoming an expert on spending Christmas in foreign parts—as I anyhow must still call them. There is something to be said, anyhow, for spending Christmas away from the rush and general short-temperedness that mark it here. (Or is it the same even in Florence?) I shan't be having a family Christmas myself this year, as it turns out—I'm here in New York, will go to midnight mass on the eve, and on the day itself to the convent in New Jersey, there to stay overnight; then back to New York for an hour or so, and then I am off for Iowa. Yes, I am going, with the idea of staying for six months, after which I have no idea what may happen. So Renée will take my apartment here, and I shall be sharing one in Des Moines with my sister—presumably, though she has said neither yes nor no to the suggestion, but is waiting, I think, to be sure I really mean it. I spent Thanksgiving out there, finding her much

better than I had been led to expect, and having a fine time generally. This was the first time I had seen Iowa in winter since 1951, and it seemed almost strange, and strangely beautiful. The very things I fled from are now attractive, and I think I can be happy there, though at moments I am still torn at the thought of leaving the east, Manhattan, and West 12th Street behind. But one must go back to one's native heath, prairie or back alley and set foot thereon once again, and I feel singularly fortunate in having such ground to set foot on. [. . .]
Love,
Amy

2838 Forest Drive
Des Moines 12, Iowa

. . . .

24 February 1960
Dear Mary—
[. . .] As you can see, I have an address of my own (or rather my sister and I have it together), in which I am not only quite settled but very happily so. Des Moines itself is so strange to me in some ways that I might almost be visiting a new country. Living first in rural and then in the most metropolitan of surroundings does not prepare one for life in a medium-sized city—which may possibly be why, happy as I am day after day, I continue to have an almost uncanny sense of detachment. Partly I suppose it is the blissful fact of not having to go to an office every day; partly it is the almost unbelievable quietness of my particular location; but I find myself wondering from time to time whether I shall ever again feel as though I *lived* anywhere the way I came to feel, in all those years, about West Twelfth Street, which is still so vivid to me, whenever I choose to think of it, that I am hardly conscious of missing it. The things I miss are relatively inconsequential. Who would have supposed that one could hunger and thirst as I have, simply for the pleasure of being in a bookstore filled with paperbacks most of which one has not and moreover never will read, most likely? And yet when I found myself in Iowa City, seeing my brother Philip get his Master's degree, a few weeks back, it was to such a bookstore that I made a bee-line, dragging sister, brother, and brother's brand-new fiancée (a lovely girl, and so exactly the right one that I occasionally marvel, even now) in the peremptory fashion for which I am known among my family, if not outside it, and where—to get back to the Iowa Book and

Supply Company—I spent an afternoon of bliss. Iowa City, being a university town primarily, seems to me much less strange than Des Moines, and in certain ways more attractive, though I have no real yearning to live there either. For one thing, it contains and in a gentle way is dominated by the Old Capitol, which so far as I know is the architectural gem of a state otherwise notorious for barns, silos, windmills and public monstrosities—a modest, almost eighteenth-century building (it is like New York City Hall on a smaller scale) in native limestone, built above the river from whose bluffs the limestone came. And the limestone has a golden tinge which might almost be Italian. Also, in a university town pedestrians are still not quite the solitary oddity they are here. Nobody walks; one has the feeling that feet are about to become vestigial, like the appendix. Sidewalks already are. Crossing a main thoroughfare is, in a somewhat different way, almost as formidable an undertaking as around the Étoile—the difference being in the utter solitariness thereof. But as you will understand, this is more in the nature of a gloss than a complaint. Inconveniences—such as those posed by being a dogged Anglo-Catholic in a family of Quakers, in a city of "low" churches (which means Communion only at eight a.m., most Sundays) and buses which operate, if at all, on a schedule I have yet to comprehend—have a way of turning into adventures and of heightening one's delight in what one would otherwise take for granted: being offered a ride on a morning of zero weather, with frost making halos about every least plume of smoke, and falling from every tree in a Dantean shower, and cardinals caroling from the branches thereof as though spring were already come, and after that the vestments, the candles, the cross, and the words of the prayerbook, and then the sacrament itself. . . . We are living in a three-room apartment above a garage, overlooking a wooded ravine which in turn slopes down toward the Raccoon River. Through the trees—mainly oak, ash, and catalpa—we have a view in three directions toward the hills on the opposite bank. Rock Island trains pass through the valley, and to me they sound almost invariably like tugboats on the Hudson, hooting before one is quite awake on a foggy morning in New York. And I have discovered, this morning when I went out to refill the bird feeder, that on a still day one can hear bells. They come, presumably, from the Roman Catholic cathedral downtown, and it is a commentary on the taste of that edifice and of R.C. piety in general that they should be followed by chimes playing "The Bells of St. Mary's." All the same, bells are bells. Do you remember Redentore, in Venice, that played Three Blind Mice, all out of tune, at five a.m. of an

already blinding summer day? My friend Anne, whom I mentioned, I think, in my last letter, wrote me from Zurich of the bells there, bells all over the city ringing at nightfall, and that reminded me of bells in Oxford and bells in Florence, where the campanile of Santo Spirito was part of the view from my pensione window. She is still in Italy, or somewhere about Europe; she told her parents at Christmas that she planned to join a religious order in June, and so her parents persuaded her to stay and she is now being shown the World with a vengeance by a baffled father. Her address is Anne Marshall, Villa Serbelloni, Bellagio, Lago di Como, if you should happen to find yourself in the vicinity. She is a blessedly lovely girl. [The story of Anne Marshall is the basis for "Rain at Bellagio" in *The Kingfisher*.] As for the novel: it goes, to date, better than I hoped it might. The quiet and the detachment are ideal for that; or perhaps it is the novel which accounts for the detachment. There is hardly any struggle; it just comes, like grace—which is, I suppose, what being able to do it at all amounts to. I believe it may be finished in the six months I gave myself. After that, I have no plans, no distinct ideas of plans even. My brother is to be married on the 12th of June. After that, sooner or later, I shall probably be back in New York—but for how long, at present there is no way of telling. [. . .]
Love,
Amy

2838 Forest Drive
Des Moines 12, Iowa

. . . .

4 May 1960
Dear Rimsa—
It was the first day of spring when you wrote, and though at the time it seemed highly improbably, spring here has now blossomed into a riotous and incontrovertible fact. Here on the banks of the Raccoon River whole hillsides, whole front lawns are carpeted with bells and stars and minute, embroidered, sky-blue faces. It has been the Iowa spring I remembered from my childhood, only more so. Such blossoming, such bird-song— across my typewriter this morning come the voices of veeries and white-throated sparrows (such wistful notes of linked-sweetness-long-drawn-out that I decline to believe they could really be construed as avian no-trespassing signs), of robins, mourning doves, cardinals, bubbling-over

wrens, and whicking flickers, among others. Those flickers, in fact, had me on the point of addressing a dickey-bird letter to the Audubon Society, asking whether it would be lawful for me to shoot the starling which has been engaging in a campaign to dislodge the new-wedded whicking pair from a certain nesting hole which I with my own eyes saw papa flicker excavating, with admirable energy and persistence, of a period of several days. I tell myself, as the Audubon Society would no doubt do, that the starlings merely know a good thing when they see it, and were not themselves witnesses to the excavation thereof. However, it appears that the flickers are going to win, and that truth, justice, and prior property rights may yet prevail.

I have become so preoccupied what such goings-on that one would expect progress on the manuscript to suffer. All the same, I am now within fifty pages of retyping and revising the first draft, which was done on the first of April, and now I must go down and buy some more Corrasable Bond before I can proceed further. I was even able to take a week's holiday from the manuscript while I went to visit Doris in Lincoln. From there we drove to Kansas City early on the morning of Good Friday, and there wound up Holy Week in the high-church style to which St. Luke's had accustomed me, and which is one thing I miss in Des Moines. We also explored, also feasted, and now I am crazy about Kansas City. Nobody told me it had any charm, but it turns out to be full of it. Also, it has a magnificent art gallery with a magnificent collection of Italian paintings, among other things which we never got around to looking at. Also, a church in the shape of a fish, which nevertheless has something of the soaring architectural grandeur of the Popes' palace at Avignon. Also, the best steaks anybody could ask for, at astonishingly low prices—I never ate a better filet mignon, and the whole dinner came to two dollars. Also, one can order cocktails in a restaurant—and the exhilaration of that fact can only be appreciated by one who has been living some three months in a dry state: you feel civilized and cosmopolitan, a certified adult. As a piquant touch, the city's tornado warnings were going off just as we finished our dinner—all the civil defense sirens wailing overhead, squad cars patrolling the streets and shooing pedestrians indoors, and over it all is an ominous dead calm, and one sits drinking a brandy, quite calmly except for a queer feeling at the pit of one's stomach, and looking out now and then to see whether the debris has started to fall. In the end the funnels that had been sighted never touched ground, and one had all the excitement with none of the discomfort of disasters and acts of God.

Back in Lincoln, I got a taste of graduate-school atmosphere for the first time in years, and found it vastly preferable to Columbia's. One thing that would have entertained you, I think, was a faculty round table at which it was announced that a member of the philosophy department was to discuss Wittgenstein. You know who he was—the ex-Logical-Positivist who taught at Cambridge and had such an influence, though he published next to nothing. What this Professor Bousma proceeded to do, however, was to read, first, an excerpt from Berkeley on knowledge-derived-via-sensation (a constellation of vagueness, that phrase, at which Wittgenstein would have shuddered, but you know what I mean), and after that, a longer excerpt from Boswell's *Life of Johnson*, in which the Berkleyan theory was refuted, in the opinion of Johnson himself, by his proceeding vigorously to kick a stone. From these two excerpts he then proceeded to read a paper in which, in words largely of one syllable, the Berkeleyan theory was delicately but at great length pummeled, kicked, trounced, and rolled over and over and over. At the beginning everybody laughed, but by the end of twenty-five minutes of this people were starting to get mad. There was an intermission, and the meeting was thrown open for discussion. It was almost impossible to open one's mouth without being delicately, even gaily, strung up and hanged by one's own slightly ill-chosen words. Having prudently abstained from opening my own mouth, I found it all vastly entertaining, and even those who got themselves strung up admitted that they had learned thereby something about the method of Wittgenstein. The next day, the English department coffee room, where people seem to spend a remarkable amount of time, buzzed all day long with some of the best talk I ever heard anywhere, and all of it stemming from the performance of the night before, and I went away much cheered at the state of at least one sector of the academic world.

Love,

Amy

. . . .

14 July 1960

Dear Philip and Hanna—

It's pouring rain here—almost exactly as it did on a certain day back in June—and I have spent the morning talking to people on the phone, playing the recorder, and mildly mourning the outcome of last night's shindig in Los Angeles. For the first time I watched a convention on t.v.—my tenant has added one, along with stacks of books, a record-player, a coleus plant, and morning-glory vines crawling up the curtains—and I would never have managed that if Arthur Tyrrell hadn't told me over the phone just how to turn it on. He had called to tell me (as strictly speaking an international civil servant has no business doing) to wire the New York delegation telling *them* to nominate Stevenson. Which I did. Alas and alas! I cannot bring myself to care for Kennedy.

Anyhow, it did seem that the time had come to be writing you. I apologize for having to do it by hand—my typewriter being yet in Iowa, while I continue to try to collect my thoughts. You will probably have heard that at the last minute I let the Forest Drive apartment go, after Dr. Sands told Daddy that Beth should not live with me. Dick [their brother] seemed rather of the same opinion. Poor Beth! I don't know whether I helped her at all—but she wrote me such a sweet letter, even before she got one from me, that I could have cried. It is literally heart-rending to stand by and see her so unhappy, and through no fault of her own, and not be able, seemingly, to do anything for her. But at least I'm glad I tried.

After [visiting their brother Lawrence and his family in suburban Boston] I came to New York for a few days with the St. John Baptist Sisters, and from there went out into the New Jersey hills for a week at their home convent. I stayed in the white building—the window where I *think* I was is marked—and let myself be thoroughly pampered. It is an almost unbelievably lovely place, even more picturesque than the postcard gives any idea. Deer come up out of the woods and browse under the apple-trees, birds sing night and day, and the sunlight and the moonlight on the white cloister walls are exactly the way one would imagine a convent to be. There is also a frog pond, beside which I practiced on the recorder in the mornings. It was delightful to lay down one's pipe and discover the frogs floating just under the surface, with only their eyes above water, and a lone, small, bobbing sandpiper going daintily about its business quite as though pipe and piper were no more than a part of the scenery.

I have finally learned how to make a recorder *sing*! It just came to me, the other day while I was trying out a sonata my tenant left behind (oh yes, she also plays), and instead of *blowing* I suddenly found myself warbling away like a thrush. It was hearing your cousin-in-law Bob, Hanna, that inspired me. We got him to play on Joan's recorder, out in the kitchen, after the reception, and hearing him I realized how I ought to sound, and had something to aim for. Such fun!

The news on the ms. is that the agent thinks it should be put aside while I try something more salable. Too many long, involved sentences, too many characters, too many demands on the reader's sensitivity, and so on, is his verdict—that is, for a first novel anyhow. It is the old story. What I shall do about it next I haven't yet decided.

Meanwhile, I have *about* decided to go to Europe in September, and have committed myself to the extent of booking passage to Naples (U.S.S. Constitution, sailing on the 2nd) and applying for a new passport. And while it must sound prodigally wild, I still have it in mind to come out to California before then—that is, unless another traveling companion has materialized. [. . .]

Love,
Amy

. . . .

S.S. Constitution
8 September 1960
    (I think)
Dear Family—

Tomorrow we'll have been a whole week on the ship, but I long ago lost all track of time and I can hardly remember anything before I came aboard. It is all very lively, the weather day after day has been beautiful, and even at night it is so warm that you can go out on deck without a coat and look at the full moon. This southern route is altogether something different from the northern one—besides which, this is a cruise ship, and so the atmosphere is quite gala—a party of some sort every night, with crazy hats and a band playing, and last night there was a passenger show which was really professional. Tourist class is fairly swarming with Fulbright fellowship people going to study music in Rome or Vienna, and you are likely to hear one of them practicing scales almost any time of the day. The star of the show turned out to be a baritone, Peter Binder, who brought down the house with his singing of *Largo al factotum* from Rossini's *Barber of Seville.* Of course the Italians loved it, and the ship swarms with them. So I am getting practice in Italian, and whenever there is a group of them, things are sure to be popping. Before we had been at sea more than a couple of hours I was startled to find myself being proposed to, in the wildest mixture of English and Italian; one of my table-mates has an admirer who swears he is ready to die for her; and altogether things are pretty operatic. (Both suitors are bricklayers, or were in Canada, where they worked.)

My cabin-mates are just as entertaining. One of them is a Georgian belle on her way to meet her Navy husband in Sicily; one is a blonde from

Chicago, named Margie, who always has half a dozen young men following her about, and who is going to Madrid to study Spanish, very logical-
ly; and one is a Canadian lady of seventy-one, who spends most of her
time traveling and living abroad, and is full of entertaining stories.

Yesterday (it already seems weeks ago) we passed through the Azores—
lovely green, volcanic islands, with terraced hillsides and little white houses. They raise olives and grapes and vegetables there, and there is usually
mist hanging over them; we were rained on for the first time during the
trip. Now we are in sight of land again—to the left (port—or I think
that's right) Spain, and Trafalgar Bay, where Nelson fell; to starboard
(right) are the Atlas Mountains of Africa! This evening we arrive in Algeciras, just next door to the Rock of Gibraltar; dock there an hour or two,
and say goodbye to the Spanish people headed for Madrid—including an
enchanting Spanish missionary priest to whom I promptly lost my heart.
If even a few people in Spain, and especially in the Church, are as forward-
looking and thoughtful as he is, there must be hope for that sad country.
Tomorrow night we arrive at Palma, on the island of Majorca, and spend
Saturday there—so at last I shall be setting foot on Spanish soil.

Later—9 September, Palma harbor

It seems a century or two since yesterday, when we came into the harbor at Algeciras and saw the Rock of Gibraltar. It rises in the middle of a
half-moon bay—a huge ship-shaped rock, with modern buildings at the
bottom and a cloud cover hanging perpetually above its top, from which
rain falls every day—or more precisely, every morning a new cloud forms,
exactly in the shape of the one the day before, it rains, and at sunset the
cloud disperses again. Algeciras itself is a white city at the foot of bare
brown mountains, which turn misty-looking in the blinding sunset light.
In the distance you can also see, across the Strait, the towering cliffs of the
Atlas Mountains on the coast of Africa. There, while we watched, ships
were coming and going; a tender arrived to pick up the debarking passengers—Margie among them, with dozens of admirers all waving her a frantic farewell—and in fact the ship isn't quite the same without her. Then
a little rowboat came toward us, with four boys singing and waving back
when we waved at them. Since then things have become steadily more romantic. The plot of the opera thickens, with go-betweens and confidants
popping up all over the place, everybody interceding for his friend, in this
fashion: "I think Carlo going to die soon. He say he loave you verray
moch, you no loave him, he joump overboard"—and so on and on. What

to make of it? The young man walks away forever, furious and broken-hearted, several times a day, and that seems to be the end of that—until next morning, or half an hour later—you never know.

—Still later—September 10, en route to Cannes

Now I can hardly remember yesterday. I have been ashore twice since the last installment—last evening just at sunset, for a three-hour exploration, and again bright and early today for a longer one by daylight. It is a beautiful town, the old part built of rosy-gold stone, with a vast, towering cathedral with Gothic towers and buttresses dominating it, and a Moorish castle at the top of a hill covered with bright green pines. Along the quay are gardens full of pink oleanders and plots of calla lilies; there are little white doves with pink eyes nesting in the walls, and bats flying about at dusk, and red-and-yellow carriages drawn by black Spanish horses clopping along the boulevards, which often have a promenade along the middle; also fountains playing, and curving narrow streets with doors opening into lovely courtyards with wrought-iron screens and palms planted inside. The cathedral is simply vast, with red-yellow-and-blue stained glass; and we heard the most wonderful singing of the mass there, by a whole choir of priests, that I ever heard anywhere. Everywhere we went, also, there were minor adventures, mostly revolving around not being able to sort out the few Spanish words one ever knew from the Italian one is so busily chattering on shipboard. But Spanish people are basically courteous, as well as beautiful to look at; I never saw so many flashing smiles as we met among these dark-eyed, long-lashed, gentle people. Getting to the Moorish castle was something of an expedition, which we finally managed by bus and on foot; and when we came down we dropped into a tiny restaurant for a glass of Spanish sherry and a sandwich (which incidentally was wonderful, as food in Palma seems generally to be). It turned out to be full of British expatriates, and the proprietor first took us for English people; when he found out where we really came from, we had a lecture on U.S. Foreign policy—and learned, incidentally, that people over here don't like Nixon and consider Eisenhower a failure, and, ergo, think Kennedy will be elected. I found it quite flattering to be addressed so frankly, though my cabinmate from Atlanta was, apparently, just a bit startled.

—Much later—September 13, at a pensione in Naples

The *Constitution* is still in the harbor, but we came off it yesterday afternoon—in the midst of a longshoremen's strike, so I found myself carrying my own bag. Since the last installment we have anchored at Cannes, on the French Riviera, for a day. I can't say I cared for the place, which is more like Miami Beach than anything else. But Naples, strike or no strike, is something else. Ginny, the girl from my table, is staying with me, and we have a room with a balcony overlooking that famous Bay—which is just as beautiful as reputation makes it—a perfect half-circle of blue water, full of boats, with tiers of tall houses, tawny yellow and brick-red, rising along the slope, and Vesuvius in the background. By night the slopes are like a nest of fireflies. The traffic is fierce—buses, taxis, big and little cars, and dozens of hornet-voiced motor scooters, rushing past all night long. All the same, I slept well, and after having spent the afternoon getting off the pier and the evening putting one of our Italian friends, who goes on to Genoa, back on the ship, I hope today will bring some proper sight-seeing.

Love, Amy

. . . .

Villa Serbelloni, Bellagio,
Lago di Como

17 September 1960
Dear Family—
Do pardon the pencil, which is all I have with me in this perfect spot—a tiny cabin, really a kind of cell, perched some five or six hundred feet directly above the deep-green water of Lake Como, with a view through pine trees of the cliffs which form the opposite shore. I arrived here yesterday afternoon, in pouring rain, and even then it was, I think, the most beautiful place I have ever seen. And as if the beauty of the view were not enough in itself, I find myself living in the midst of all but incredible luxury. The Villa itself has a long history—before the Rockefeller Foundation took it over, it was the property of a princess, Ella della Torre (?) (née Walker), and before she bought it, it was a luxury hotel. There are maids to press one's clothes, do one's personal laundry, bring one's breakfast, and turn down the covers at night; the food (as one would expect of a place with John Marshall in charge) is exquisite; and I have a room at least the size of the dining-room at Friends House, with a bath the size of an ordinary bedroom, and a view from its balcony of both arms of Lake Como. (If you look on a map, you will see that Bellagio is on a peninsula where the two arms of the lake [which is very deep and narrow, almost

like a fjord] branch off. Tonight we shall be eighteen at dinner (normal for weekends here, I am told); last night we were just five (Anne and I and three Italian professors), but afterward we went down the hill to join a party of lawyers and philosophers who have been having a conference, and had a fine, lively, bi-lingual time playing "What's my line?" before a wood fire, while outside the lightning flashed and torrential rain came roaring down. Today I woke to the sound of church bells all up and down the lake.

This was interrupted, as always seems to be happening. I am now in Pavia, a university town a few miles south of Milan, and it is now Sunday evening, and I am just about to settle down to sleep off all the wining and dining of the last forty-eight hours. The dinner party for eighteen proved so delightful that I scarcely took proper notice of the sweet soufflé and champagne with which it ended, what with the sparkling conversation of the Italian legal philosophers on either side of me, and the Oxford graduate and the teacher from Ohio State just down the line. Dining at the Villa Serbelloni is a real experience. One comes down a long marble hall and a deeply carpeted flight of marble stairs, at the foot of which Vincenzo, the butler, is waiting to direct the guests to the column room—a sort of glassed-in verandah—where there are drinks beforehand. (And it is not good form there to be late.) Presently Vincenzo comes in to announce that dinner is served, and shows the way. Outside the vast paneled and silk-hung dining room there is a seating plan, to make finding places easier. At each place last night there were three glasses—one for the mineral water which is used for drinking purposes at the Villa, one for red wine, with the roast duck, and the other for the champagne. After dessert the party moved to one of several drawing-rooms for coffee and liqueurs, and the conversation goes on. Last night, after the dinner guests had gone, Anne and I and two Americans went down the hill to another house (once a monastery) on the villa grounds, where we joined a party consisting of the director's secretary, a Greek girl brought up in Italy, and two young Italians from Milan. One of them works, of all things, in the Supermarket business—there are already two in Milan, and one will open soon in Florence. I expressed proper shock, in my stumbling and gesticulating brand of Italian, but he couldn't see why I objected. It was after midnight before we could get away, and the bells on the lake had struck 2 a.m. before I had myself packed and could go to bed; and Anne and I were up again before seven to catch a ferry across the lake, where there was an English church. It was pouring rain again—

after gorgeous September weather on Saturday—and we were the only passengers. We came back in a still heavier downpour, and went to mass at the church in Bellagio, where a handsome priest delivered an elegantly impassioned sermon of which I could make neither head nor tail, and Anne herself said she couldn't follow. Before lunch Anne's father showed us the wine-cellar—the first honest-to-goodness one I ever saw. There were seven at lunch, including an Italian professor and his American-born wife, and a Rockefeller Foundation geneticist and agronomist from Mexico City, with his wife, who turned out to be from Iowa! In their honor we were served corn-on-the-cob from the Villa gardens, and I have seldom eaten better. The Villa gardens also produce pears, apples, and quantities of grapes—these latter are just now ripening, and there was great fun raiding the vines on our way up and down hill—as well as a profusion of flowers, which decorate every room in the house. Altogether, I never stayed in any place so magnificent. It was a rather strange occasion, since when Anne and I left together this afternoon she was on her way to England, probably never to come back, possibly never to see her father again. (Her mother is already in England.) We had a wonderful time, exploring the Villa gardens, the woods above and the little fishing village below, and playing duets on our recorders in a ruined castle at the very top of the Villa grounds. Coming up from Naples to Milan, incidentally, was an adventure in itself. We splurged and came by *Wagons-lits*—the deluxe European Pullman which is hardly less than a hotel on wheels, but instead of eating in the diner we carried aboard a shopping-bag *full* of bread, wine, and cheese, and made merry over those in picnic style. The afternoon before we headed north—to continue proceeding backward—we went south to Paestum, where there is a splendid Greek temple, wonderfully well preserved. [. . .]
Love, Amy

. . . .

Rome

26 September 1960
Dear Family—
I found Daddy's letter when I went to call for mail this morning. I do hope that by now you will have received my letter from Naples, also one mailed from Pavia a week ago. Also that you have been able to read them, more or less! About this one I have doubts; I have just come in, pleasantly

addled from a fine lunch, with the wine of the region (Frascati) which in itself was almost reason enough to come to Rome, and Rome turns out—as did Florence, once the sun deigned to shine—to be more beautiful than I remembered, and so I am in a highly cheerful frame of mind, but somewhat incoherent.

Coming back to Italy is less of an adventure than the first visit, but in a way that makes it more interesting. In Florence I went back to my old pensione of nine years ago—run, that is, by the same plump, effusive little lady, and the same star boarder, one Signor Dino, on hand, but now at a new and grander address, with maids and a boy to serve the meals, and with more hot water, so a bath is less of a project, though on the other hand it is less picturesque and I preferred the old location. Anyhow, it was an experience to be welcomed back with open arms, and mealtimes were always lively—what with French, German, Swiss, and Italian people—and me—conversing in whatever common languages they were able to discover. I find that I understand both French and German fairly well, but whenever I open my mouth to speak in anything but English, it comes out Italian! The food at the pensione was, if anything, better, and I discovered that, as before, in Italy I am always hungry. Actually the cooking is quite simple—soups, spaghetti or some other form of *pasta*, beefsteak or veal cutlet cooked in olive oil, lettuce and tomato salad (you mix your own oil-and-vinegar dressing at the table, and the olive oil is superb), crusty Italian bread, and a first course of pears and grapes (these are wonderful, just now), and sometimes cheese. The famous lunch of this noon consisted of a Roman specialty, *saltimbocca*, which turns out to be veal skewered together with thin slices of ham, with some green herbs (basil or sage) in between, and a butter sauce over all. Delicious!

My impression of Italy by this time is that it is much more prosperous than nine years ago, and much more casual about tourists. Also, at this season, there are relatively few Americans. The language one hears most often, aside from Italian, is German, and I am taken for German or Swiss almost constantly—American never. I don't know what that means. Anyhow, they know I'm not Italian because I wear my skirts so long. Here, they are literally up to the knees. Also, Italian girls now go around without any lipstick but a great deal of black about the eyes, and what with the hair-styles in vogue (which are indescribable) they mainly look as though they had neither slept nor combed their hair for at least forty-eight hours. The effect is undeniably striking, but hardly becoming—so I dare say it will pass ere long.

I am so glad to hear that Beth is liking her job—that is just about the best news I could have. Thanks again for forwarding the various messages. The postcards from my elusive friend Mary are most tantalizing—I keep on missing her, it would seem, but she has postponed leaving Italy so often by this time that I may connect with her yet, I suppose. As for the letter from Barbados, it could hardly be from anybody but my old friend Father Morralé—the English priest who instructed me before I was confirmed—and so I would dearly love to have it, if you will send it on. Evidently he has moved, and I suppose the mimeographed letter is by way of bringing his friends up to date.

The rains, happily, appear to be over, and one could not ask for more perfect weather than the last three days in Florence and now here in Rome—bright and warm in the middle of the day, with just a hint of a nip in it, and pleasantly cool at night. There has been so much rain all summer that in the Po Valley and around Florence the countryside is as green as in spring. Only the grapes ones sees ripening everywhere give the season away.

29 September—Rome goes on being exhausting—I've just come from another expedition, on foot, which must have taken me five or six miles—to St. Paul's-Outside-the-Walls, a disappointment in itself, despite the ancient associations, but on the way I found the little cemetery where Keats and Shelley are buried, and that was very much worth finding. Tomorrow I leave for Assisi; after that Ravenna, and thence northward by way of Salzburg. But probably c/o American Express in Paris will be the safest address to write to, say, through the 15th of October.
Love,
Amy

. . . .

Paris (Place St.-Sulpice)

12 October 1960
Dear Family—
Wonderful, wonderful to find letters waiting! I arrived here this morning via the Orient Express, a romantic cross-continental train that starts out somewhere the other side of Budapest and winds up in Paris—and made a bee-line, as nearly as one can make a bee-line in a city as confusing as Paris, after nine years, for American Express, where I was rewarded with news, after a long dearth. It begins to be a long time since I last wrote—

though perhaps Beth will have shared my letter to her from Assisi. After I wrote, things there became increasingly more exciting, on account of the feast of St. Francis, which commemorates the day of his death, on the 4th of October. For a couple of evenings beforehand there were two-hour-long vesper services, with wonderful choirs of Franciscan monks, augmented by a boys' choir as well—singing and singing and singing I don't know what all, with a small forest of candles lighting up the frescos on the walls of the low-ceilinged, vaulted church which has been built just above the tomb of the saint; and afterwards throngs and swarms of people, pilgrims and sightseers, milling around outside, but still not spoiling the serene and peaceful atmosphere that is part of the town, and makes it unlike any other I ever saw. On the eve of the feast there were also torches lighted and blazing above the medieval gates, and from the walls of the fortress on the hill above the town; and the bells simply rang and rang and rang, a veritable orchestra of bells, for I don't know how long without stopping. Later that evening there was a midnight mass—again with a Franciscan choir—in the great church down the hill from Assisi itself, which has been built above the little chapel where St. Francis died. I went down for it on foot—though it is in the neighborhood of three miles each way—with a Swiss girl who was also staying at the convent. It was a perfectly beautiful night, very still and mild, and with a full moon in a dark-blue sky—and to look up from the road down into the valley and see Assisi, all white and still, perched there on its hillside—was worth the trip in itself. The next day there were more festivities, with a cardinal celebrating mass, and dressed in the most sumptuously jeweled vestments I ever saw—all of which may seem an odd way to remember the saint who fell in love with Lady Poverty, but then, what is one to do? Once again, the church and the whole town were swarming with visitors; but still I was able to walk out through the city gates, along a road lined with cypresses, and have the whole stupendous landscape, as undisturbed as ever, spread out like a map at my feet. I never wanted so much to be a painter as at Assisi. It is certainly one of the most enchanting places I ever visited, and I was never more reluctant to leave than I was that day when I gathered my belongings together and caught a train for Florence—a bit of backtracking which was necessary to get to Ravenna, where I had made up my mind to go. Actually, I was in Florence only overnight, and once again missed my friend Mary, it now appears—she was there looking for me, while I thought she was already on her way back to New York.

Anyhow, early the next morning I took a bus from Florence over the Appenines, up a long series of loops and curves, very wild and picturesque, through oak and chestnut forests and high cleared spaces, now and then, where sheep and goats were grazing with a shepherd on hand to see that they didn't go over a cliff. Then gradually down on the other side, into the plains where the Po and Adige and other rivers drain into the Adriatic. Ravenna, where I made an overnight stop, is some miles inland, but the feel of the sea is there, even though what you see are mainly canals and fields of sugar beets, and here and there a grove or avenue of the bright-green, round-topped pines which are characteristic of the coastal region. Ravenna is a very ancient town, going back to pagan times; Theodoric the Ostrogoth is buried there, as is Dante, who went there as an exile from Florence; and what I found wonderful to think of is that the mosaics for which the town is chiefly noted were already there, and already old (they date to the sixth century, he lived in the thirteenth) when Dante was there—and he saw them! They are one of the most astonishing sights I ever met with—still bright and fresh, and hardly restored at all, after well over a thousand years. The loveliest mosaics, and the loveliest of the churches, were once again a three-mile hike out into the country, and since the excursion buses had stopped running I started out on foot. As it happened, a kindly man gave me a lift part of the way in his car going out; but coming back I walked all the way, in the midst of a constant procession of passing cars, trucks, and bicycles—the latter still being the commonest mode of travel there, and indeed in most of Italy. As if the mosaics and the tomb of Dante weren't enough, Ravenna also offered the best eating (if you except the Villa Serbelloni, which is a category all by itself) I met anywhere in Italy. A wonderful place—and to think I debated whether to go there at all!

From Ravenna I proceeded to Padua, also a very ancient town, with I think the oldest university in Italy (though Italian towns are very jealous of their antiquity in this respect, and I believe more than one lays claim to that superlative). I had been there before, for part of a day when Joe Goodman and I made an excursion from Venice to look at the Giotto frescos for which it is famous, and wonderful as those were in themselves, I had thought I didn't care for Padua itself. This time, though, I quite fell in love with it, and with the people there, who seemed to me the most exquisitely courteous, even courtly, of all the cities I ever visited. Things like a little girl sharing her umbrella with me in the drenching downpour I found myself caught in; and the girl in a shop I went into, who seemed to be showing me what was for sale—beautiful, expensive Venetian glass, and Italian, French and English porcelain—not in order to sell me anything, but simply because it was so beautiful; and the man in a bank who noted on my passport, when he changed a traveler's check, that I had put myself down as a "writer," and wished me success. Part of this may be the fact that Padua is not a tourist town, in the way Rome and Florence are, and so their attitude toward the occasional stranger is to regard him as a sort of guest rather than a source of income. It is also, I decided this time, very beautiful, with many arcaded streets—I suppose intended to keep off the sun in summer, but useful also when one is caught in a downpour. Actually, that rainy night I didn't stay in Padua, but deposited my heavy luggage at the station and then caught a local bus up-country to Asolo, a little hill town about which I had learned from one of the postcards you forwarded, from the elusive Mary. Going up there was really an adventure. By the time the bus pulled up the long hill leading to the town it was after eight o'clock, my feet were soaked, I had no hotel reservation and the one place I knew the name of turned out to be closed; so there was some floundering about in the rain before I found a room—always a slightly weird experience in a town you have never seen, and all the more so in a town so medieval that it had no streetlights, *and* in pouring rain. However, I did finally find where to lay my head, and even cajoled a meal out of the kitchen, late as it was; and when morning came, I discovered that the view beyond the shutters of that otherwise dismal room was too stupendously, romantically beautiful, almost, to be believed. Once again, this is a very old town, also with arcaded streets, and built on the slopes of a hill radiating outward and down rather like the rays of a starfish, on dozens of different levels, so that there are views, views, views, in every direction. All sorts of people have come there through the centuries—Robert Browning was one, and his poem *Asolando* (which I have never read) was one of them. I spent the morning exploring Asolo, then caught the bus back to Padua, where I wandered around until dark; then to a hotel for my last night in Italy, and up in the morning at five to catch a train over the Alps to Salzburg. I arrived there (after a delightful ride, ten hours long, but hardly tiring, through mile after mile of mountain landscape) late in the afternoon on Saturday, and stayed until Tuesday evening (last night, though now it seems an age away. [. . .] I think after a month or so I would have been fairly chattering in German—it began to come back to me after a bit of the habit of talking Italian wore off—but here I am, once again, having to switch to French! More later, must stop now.

Love,

Amy

. . . .

Chepstow, Monmouthshire, England? Wales?
nobody seems to know

13 November 1960
Dear Philip and Hanna—

It really is time I wrote you a letter, and now I have the most impromptu, unexpected, one-thing-after-another day of the whole journey to report, and that was a Sunday at that. I find it hard even to remember the name of this town, which I hadn't so much as heard of until the day before yesterday, and which in fact I have hardly seen, in the tourist sense of the word, even now. I came here from Oxford—another story, except that it is every bit as wonderful as I always thought—yesterday afternoon on a bus, which arrived after dark, in streaming rain, and set me down at the door of a pub, where I stood dripping for a minute or two before darting out and, happily, finding the entrance of what turned out to be a very nice hotel, where they did have a room, charmingly furnished, where you put sixpence in a slot to turn on a gas fire, and where they put a hot water bottle into the bed for you. This morning, happily, the rain seemed to be over, and I headed for the parish church, where two kindly ladies took me in hand and set me down with them. It was like that all day long, most improbably. After I had had a good solid English breakfast—porridge, bacon, sausage, tomato, toast and marmalade—I put on my boots and set out on foot for the real reason for my coming to Chepstow—Tintern Abbey. I hadn't even known exactly where it was, until a nice young man at the bus headquarters in Oxford looked it up for me; but on a map in the hotel lobby I found the route to take to Tintern—a distance of some five miles, but I have walked so much in the last several weeks that it no longer sounds formidable. What I didn't know, until I was actually in it, was that the road led through Tintern Forest, a wild, steep, lovely region which has been set aside as a national reserve. It made me think, a bit, of the redwood forest we drove through that Sunday on our way to

San Francisco—though in place of the redwoods and Douglas firs there were yew trees, mixed with beech, and with here and there a holly tree, and ferns and ivy covering the ground and often the trunks of the trees. There were also still some flowers in bloom—there has been no frost to speak of—and to give you an idea I enclose a few botanical specimens. By the time I came out of the forest the sun had gone, and it was definitely raining again. I had just caught sight of Tintern Abbey itself when a car slowed down and the very nice-looking woman at the wheel asked if I would like a lift. I told her I had just come out to see the Abbey, but she said why didn't I come along first and have a drink with her and her husband; so I did, and in the end they also gave me lunch, and a most delightful time. She turned out to be an ex-entertainer (piano) who had met her husband, a civil engineer, while she was playing for troops in Korea; and they had traveled a good deal, and had last lived in Somaliland, but a few months ago they had bought this house, which was—part of it— three hundred years old. It had a lovely view of wooded hills, and the valley of the Wye River, which was just below their terrace. There were swans on the river (one sees them everywhere in England at this time of year) and I looked at them through binoculars to find out from the bills, which kind they were. After feeding me an enormous lunch of steak and chips (as they call French-fries over here), green peas, tomatoes, apple pie and custard, with a mug of excellent beer brewed by the hostess herself, she drove me back to the Abbey, and since it was literally pouring rain by then, waited in her car while I looked round, and then drove me back to Chepstow. The abbey itself is indescribably lovely—roofless and vast, with great pointed windows, the glass long gone but some of the stone tracery still remaining. The stone a warm, rosy tone, encrusted with green and gray lichens, and with bunches of ferns growing high up in the angles of some of the mouldings, and against a background of wooded hills on either side of the Wye, altogether one of the most thrilling places I have ever seen, and romantic even in pouring rain.

Since all this is on the very border of Wales proper, it occurred to me that I still might have a chance to hear Welsh people singing. The man at the gateway to the Abbey told me I would probably have to go to Newport, a matter of fifteen or so miles from Chepstow, so go to Newport I did, after having told the man in the bus station what I wanted to do there and being shown the church notices in Saturday's newspaper. To make sure I was getting off at the right place, I asked a girl on the bus, who immediately recognized from my accent that I was American (they always do), and volunteered to show me to wherever I was going. She didn't know where the Ebenezer Welsh Presbyterian Church might be, but brought a policeman into the inquiry, and as it turned out that she and a friend were going in the same direction, she invited me under her umbrella, we all hopped aboard a bus and then off again and into a coffee bar which turned out to be directly across the street from the Ebenezer chapel. The chapel itself was still dark, and the man behind the counter at the coffee bar was then enlisted to keep watch and let me know when the lights went on. Well, they didn't go on and they didn't go on, and meanwhile everybody in the vicinity knew that I had come down to Newport on purpose to hear people singing in Welsh, and since all the pubs are closed on a Sunday in this part of Britain, there was no chance to go and hear them singing there, as they do when they get drinking, and I was beginning to fear the expedition had been in vain. However, there was an unexpected diversion: a very handsome boy suddenly appeared, and almost before he sat down with us I learned that he was Italian! Finding an Italian is always a pleasure, because trying to talk to them in Italian is such fun; and the next thing I knew, here came another Italian, and another, and immediately they also had to be told that I was American and had come down to Newport to go to the Welsh church, and they thought I must be very religious, and I said no, it wasn't that, it was that I wanted to hear people singing in Welsh, and this bewildered them still more, but it didn't prevent them from being very friendly, and I learned that they came to England to become apprentices because jobs are still relatively scarce in Italy, but of course they talk all the time about *bella Italia* and how in England it always rains—and outside it was pouring harder than ever. Among all the Italians who kept coming in were two very good-looking Negroes, one of whom was soon drawn into the conversation, and it turned out that he was from Somalia, and so we all sat counting up the nationalities, and marveling over them, and there was the question of whether the girl who had brought me here, and who was Monmouthshire-born, was properly English or properly Welsh (she said she was English, but the others said no, Welsh), and this is what always happens when Monmouthshire is mentioned, and the Italians started telling me all the Welsh words they knew, and then, finally, lights were seen in the Ebenezer chapel, and I shook hands all round, and the Italians said I should pray for them, and I darted across the way and into the church, where I was handed a hymn-book which, sure enough, was all in Welsh, and I slipped into a pew and waited for things to start. There was an organ directly behind the pulpit, which wheezed whenever it was turned on, but no choir, for the reason that in a Welsh church the congregation is the choir. It really is true that they all sing, without direction, and in wonderful polyphonic harmony, as naturally, almost, as a baby cries or a flower grows. After a couple of hymns and a *very* long prayer by the minister, a ruddy and portly man in a clerical collar, and another hymn, the sermon began, and as I had suspected in advance, it turned out to be just about the longest sermon I ever listened to. And I really did listen, even though it was all in Welsh with an English phrase thrown in now and then for emphasis, but from those English phrases and the very graphic gestures of the preacher, I understood quite well that he was talking about the prophet Amos, and how he said, "I will put a plumbline among my people Israel." How many times over I saw that plumbline being suspended from the pulpit I did not try to count—that would have been rude anyhow—but I began to think a little uneasily of the hotel back in Chepstow, and to wonder whether I should be getting back there before its doors closed for the night, as they do at a quite early hour in these provincial towns, and I am afraid I began to fidget. But slowly, circuitously, and with more suspending of plumblines, eloquent pauses, vehement gestures, shutting of Bible, shutting of prayerbook, at last, somehow, the preaching came to an end; and bang! after one more hymn (in which, surreptitiously, I joined in) the service was over. Immediately all the ladies in my vicinity converged and addressed me in Welsh. I explained that I did not speak Welsh, but that I had come down from Chepstow—"From Chepstow! This lady's come down from Chepstow!"—and then ventured to add that I was from the United States. For once I had the satisfaction of seeing people register surprise. Before I got out of the church I must have shaken hands with half the congregation, while the word went buzzing around, and by the time I got to the door I found myself confronted by the pastor—"I hear you came from the United States"—and so I admitted that I did, and that I had wanted to hear people sing in Welsh, and I was highly satisfied, indeed I had loved it; and as far as I could see nobody was offended, though the pastor was amazed that I should have found my way down here, and how had I done it, and as I told him, I left him still shaking his head in amazement; and I did get back to Chepstow before the hotel doors closed, and now—it is Monday morning by this time—I am about to head for Dorchester, and so abruptly I shall end this breathless bit of illegibility.

Love, Amy

. . . .

Mendham, New Jersey

26 May 1961

Dear Philip and Hanna—

Do please pardon the handwriting. I'm out here for a weekend of peace and quiet (and also to see the reception of a novice into the Community of St. John Baptist), and my typewriter has stayed at home, but with congratulations of several sorts in order, what can I do? I *am* right about a birthday round about now? Here, anyhow, is to a happy one, and many more of same. And as for the comprehensives—I am quite bowled over with admiration and delight. I had not, somehow, got it through my head that they were to be so soon.

So physids are snails! I allowed as how they might be, from a reference some time back. I find it a bit hard transferring allegiance to them from the amphipods, but I suppose that is a matter of not having met them personally. On the other hand, I once wrote a story in which the central character (in a manner of speaking) was a snail, so you see I am not unacquainted with their peculiar molluscan charm.

Thank you so much for the blue, blue hepatica—my favorite hue of that delectable species, and to think of a whole hillside of them! *And* bloodroot! I have had moments of feeling nature-deprived, there on 12th Street, and of missing spring in Iowa most acutely. Spring in New York has been as cold and dank as it possibly could be, and the wonder is that the green things managed to come out at all. Out here, I am being consoled by dogwood in full bloom, not to mention jack-in-the-pulpits, sweet williams, and wood thrushes. There is also said to be a sandpiper down by the pond, but I haven't seen it yet.

To justify a long weekend in the country, I've brought along some books to review for the Audubon Society. One of them is a treatise on the monarch butterfly, by one of my favorite entomologists—he was the man who, in the interests of science, had various volunteers *eating* butterflies and comparing their taste sensations. He admits that the experiment doesn't prove decisively that the theory of Batesian mimicry either is or is not valid, but I do love its thoroughgoing-ness. Of course there is a good deal in this book about the butterfly trees at Pacific Grove, including a mention of *Sweet Thursday* and Steinbeck's charming (but erroneous) notion of monarchs drunk on Monterey-pinesap brew. As to the whole vexed question of whether or not monarchs migrate *back*, I am still in suspense and darkness, but hope to find out before I find myself assigned an encyclopedia article on the subject.

In that project I have progressed part-way into the B's. Picture me struggling to digest Simpson, Tiffany, and Pittendrigh in order to turn out a thousand-word essay on *Biology*! It is the biochemical part that really gives me trouble. I loved doing Bees, and of course with Birds I felt quite at home. Do remember that this is a simple-minded sort of Encyclopedia. [. . .]

The new novice was received yesterday, in a very thrilling ceremony, and there was a party (or as near as a convent ever gets to a party) afterward, with punch and coffee and doughnuts. Later, wandering about the grounds, I met the novice, who told me of her difficulties with the new costume—long sleeves that get into things, bonnet and collar that make chewing and swallowing precarious, and so forth. We had a long conversation about all kinds of things; from now on, I learned, she is not supposed to talk to "seculars" until she is a full-fledged sister. This morning, after dishwashing, she couldn't find her veil! (It comes off for household chores.)

Did I tell you that I have started a new novel? A first draft of a first chapter is now extant.

Love,

Amy

. . . .

5 January 1963

Dear Barbara [Blay]—

[. . .] The news of your new location sounds enchanting, and I can't think of a more interesting place to be working than a summer theater— especially one directed by Sir Laurence Olivier. I do hope I can accept your invitation to come and see it, one of these days. It will be interesting to compare it with the Shakespeare Festival Theater in Central Park, which became one of my favorite haunts last summer. Shakespeare-in-the-Park had been going on for several years, but previously there had been only a makeshift stage, and people sat on the grass or on folding chairs. Now there is an open-air amphitheater that holds nearly three thousand people, and a splendid stage with a little lake and a rocky bit of landscape in the background. All the seats are free, and in order to get in you take along a picnic and sit down on the grass to eat it while you wait in line—which is fun in itself. Even seeing a production of *King Lear* begin bravely after one downpour and finally give up when a second one blew up, was a gay sort of adventure—and a couple of evenings later I tried again, and the weather couldn't have been better. The whole institution is quite wonderful—the director, a young man named Joseph Papp, simply believed that there ought to be free Shakespeare in the park, and persuaded enough people to support the project that now it is a going concern, with gorgeous costumes and sets, specially composed music, and some really excellent acting.

Your letter arrived just after my return from a somewhat extended holiday, which once again took me across the continent. It all came about because I had promised a friend that I would stand up with her at her wedding—which for various reasons had to be in Berkeley, California, where she and her husband were to be living. So late in August I headed west, stopping to see a brother in Minnesota and my parents and sister in Iowa, and then joining my friend and her then fiancé in Nebraska. From there the three of us started out by car on what may have been a unique sort of expedition—a wedding trip before the wedding, with me acting as bridesmaid, duenna, and I don't know what else. We took along sleeping bags (no tent) and camped out, building fires to cook over, tucking sagebrush under our pillows, nearly freezing one night high in the Colorado mountains, and eating one last picnic in the middle of a Nevada dust storm. It was all a bit crazy, but just the sort of traveling I love, in spite of the discomforts, and since we were all still speaking to each other by the time we got to Berkeley it was clearly a success. The wedding went off happily, and when it was over I headed south for my first look at Los Angeles. I didn't see a film studio or go to Disneyland, but I did walk in an orange grove, and was taken for a swim in one of those backyard pools you hear about—a particularly delightful swim since I was just about to board a train after a hot, dusty day of sightseeing. That part of California is really a desert, and much of it is rather frightful—but even the frightful part of it is interesting, and thanks to some cousins who entertained me, I had a fine time. But the best part of the trip, so far as sightseeing goes, was still to come. I traveled back by way of the Grand Canyon, a truly magnificent sight—I spent a whole day there, tramping about the rim of the canyon and even going a little of the way down into it, and even after a night on the train it was so exhilarating that I left feeling happy and rested. After another night on the train, I stopped off again at Santa Fe, New Mexico— a very old town where I stayed a couple of days, and wished I didn't have to leave at all. I didn't know there was a town like it in the United States. People there still speak Spanish, but it isn't at all like Spain or even much like Mexico. All the architecture is adobe, in the style of the Indian pueblos, and there are many trees even though that is desert country, and the air is wonderfully clear and sparkling, with deep blue skies and great towering clouds. It's seven thousand feet up, but there are still higher mountains all around. I made an excursion to an Indian pueblo, where things go on much as they have for hundreds of years—nobody knows how old it is—and though the Indians drive cars they still wrap themselves in blankets like Arab burnooses, and speak their own language among themselves. If you ever come to the U.S., you *must* see the Southwest!

Altogether the trip lasted nearly five weeks, and after that I was mostly in a great dither, trying to catch up with things—and in what now seems hardly any time at all, I was heading back for Iowa once more. This came about because of a great family reunion at my parents' house—all three of my brothers and their families, my sister and I were all in the same place at the same time for the first time in longer than we can remember— twenty years or more, it must be, even though we had all seen each other at various times and we number sixteen—the youngest being an enchanting baby girl of six months, who quickly became everybody's favorite (but all the children are delightful). Somehow, room was found for all of us in my parents' house, and there was much chatter and playing of recorders— those little wooden flutes I may have mentioned, of which there are now at least five among us—and singing around the piano, and a certain amount of confusion in the kitchen, where preparing meals for so many was generally a cooperative project. On the Sunday before Christmas the crowd was swelled to forty-five (I'm told—I never got around to counting) when a great horde of aunts and uncles and cousins appeared from various places. They brought the trimmings; we did the turkeys—two fifteen-pound ones—and the mashed potatoes and the dessert. After attending to that operation, Christmas dinner for the sixteen plus three guests was a simple matter! Most of the crowd left the day after, but since my mother has been troubled with a lame back and was rather exhausted afterward, I stayed on until just after New Year's, madly finishing up a piece of ghost-writing (yes, I've even gotten into that sort of thing!) that was due, in between trying to invent new ways of serving up left-over

turkey. Except for a quart or so of broth made from the bones, it had finally all been used up by the time I left. [. . .]
Love,
Amy

. . . .

Aboard T.S.S. Olympia

30 April 1965
Dear Family,
This will be only an installment, but if I don't begin now I'll have lost track of things completely. The fourth day at sea, it's hardly possible to remember when the trip began, with all there is to take in. This is a fascinating ship, and in lots of ways the best I ever traveled on. After all, the Greeks have been sailors for a very long time, so they should know how to run a ship! And my impression of the Greeks, from being surrounded by them, is of a charming people, warm-hearted and dignified at the same time. One of my cabin mates is a grandmother, returning from a visit to her children in the States, who speaks nothing but Greek—literally. I think I know more Greek words than she does English ones. We manage to communicate somehow, and get along very well. Another cabin mate is a Russian exile, also a grandmother, who also speaks Greek and knows a very few words of English—a beautiful woman, the sort one imagines a grand duchess would be. The third cabin mate is a lady from Naples who speaks some Greek and some English; she is very lively and chic, and we communicate in a wildly haphazard mixture of French, English, and Greek phrases when they happen to come out (she has a Greek father, I believe). We are all crammed together in the smallest cabin for four imaginable, where we stumble over each other's luggage, and each other, and where there is only one ladder between the two of us in upper berths (I traded my original lower with the Russian lady, and it is fine once I am up there, but so high that I am marooned without the ladder). Fortunately, the weather has been quite calm (though there are a good many people who have been seasick), and we have been spared hearing moanings and groanings from the other berths. We have a delightful cabin steward named Giorgos, who speaks English and is very encouraging about one's stumbling efforts at Greek. ("Kalimera-sas," for Good morning; "Efkaristo" for thank you, "Ti kanis?" for How are you? "Poli-kala," for Very well, and so on.) And every afternoon there is a half-hour Greek

class, where we learn phrases and are being taught to sing "Never on Sunday" in Greek! I never saw a ship so organized; there are even something called Social Discussions—and an Iowa-born man and his wife told me they went, and the first one was about the benefits of the unpolished-rice diet! There are also classes in Hebrew, French, Italian, and Spanish. Since the ship goes to Haifa, there are many Israelis and American Jews aboard—many of them orthodox, with full beards and skullcaps (yarmulkas) on the backs of their heads. They have a staff rabbi, a kosher kitchen, and a synagogue of their own; today at lunch there was an announcement in Yiddish (or maybe Hebrew) about the Sabbath eve services.

Also, of course, there are many Greek orthodox people, including a wonderful patriarch who wears a black cassock, a handsome silvery beard, and long hair, done up in a knot—one of the most splendid-looking men I ever saw. On Sunday I am hoping to go to the Greek orthodox church service with my Greek cabin mate—if I can manage to explain to her! And who knows? Maybe the patriarch will conduct it—or maybe there are still other Greek orthodox priests aboard.

By some chance or other, I am at the captain's table—not the ship's master, but the staff captain who presides over tourist class. Most of my table mates are Greek-American girls, some of them quite beautiful and all very nice. There is also a young Greek-American who has a Greek wife waiting for him in Athens, and who is growing a beard. Also, an American couple from California, who are very funny and keep things lively; and *he* is growing a beard too. The captain himself, I am sorry to say, is so solemn that he is really quite dull; but he isn't always there, and besides we have a wonderful waiter, by the name of Demetrios, who is called Jimmy. There is about three times as much food as most of us can eat—except for the Greek-American, who was a cook in the Navy, and who orders seconds of everything, and winds up with *four* portions of ice cream! He told me at the beginning that he was going to Greece to climb mountains, but there begins to be some question whether he will have any wind left! He has a cabin mate who is about twenty-one and also a cook, and who makes puns at a rate that would leave Daddy behind in the dust. For a couple of hours last night he had all of us convulsed; and this morning while I was dozing in my deck chair there he was again, with more of the same.

Bringing my borrowed typewriter into the writing room turns out to be as infallible a way of meeting people as going out to walk the dog or take the baby for an airing. People under the impression that I was some kind of public stenographer have come by, and thus far I have obliged with notes to relatives in Cliffside, New Jersey, an itemized list of things a nice little man from Hollywood had had stolen from his luggage, to be witnessed by the purser, and two long letters dictated by a polylingual Israeli to friends in the U.S., one of them a strip-tease dancer in Dallas! This young man is writing down everything he sees going on in a huge diary—in Hebrew. There is obviously material enough there for a book, and from what he has to say it would be fascinating to read.

3 May 1965

So much has gone on since the previous installment that I hardly know where to begin. For one thing, after several gray days the sun began coming out, and it began to be warm enough even after dark to go out on deck and stay there for hours—so since then the typewriter has been less occupied. But the Greek lessons are progressing—not only the afternoon class, but private sessions with *three* teachers, no less, who by sheer chance have deck chairs next to mine. I don't mean they are professional teachers; but they are all Greeks, and full of enthusiasm about helping their pupil along. Also, there was the costume ball on Saturday night. I hadn't planned to go at all, but late that afternoon the Greek-American and his cabin mate (both of whom, for some unfathomable reason, are called Pat) summoned me with a plan; they would go dressed as doctors, and they would carry me in on a stretcher with a sheet over me, and a life jacket under that, as a corpse hauled in from overboard! Well, we didn't win a prize, but people laughed and laughed, and so did we. The next morning I went to a two-hour Greek Orthodox service, complete with incense and a choir of officers and waiters. Even in a crowded ship's auditorium, with a makeshift altar set up on the stage, it was a wonderful and thrilling occasion and every-now-and-then I picked out a word of liturgical Greek. Yesterday, after a week at sea, we docked at Lisbon, where we went ashore for a few hours. I went on a conducted tour which was rather a disappointment; we spent most of it sitting in the bus, and got into only one church; but the afternoon was redeemed at the last minute by a dash along the waterfront with a Turkish girl, the ship's Italian hostess, and one of the Pats. We found a wine shop where we drank Port and Muscatel straight from the wooden casks, and were given a sample of *calimares* (squid, and very good). We barely made it back to the ship in time to sail! This morning we came within sight of Africa and then passed through the strait of Gibraltar, in beautiful calm, bright weather. By now I am just sunburned enough that I have to come in for a while. The company is better and better, now that people are getting to know each other, and I get less and less sleep, but feel fine, and make up for it by eating. The food also gets better and better—more and more Greek dishes, which are the best on the menu. At my table the captain has ceased to appear, but the *esprit* is better than ever, and our waiter promises to take us all on a picnic after we reach Athens.

We docked this morning, and I am now established in my hotel room and have even made a two-or-three-mile walking tour, getting lost in my usual fashion, in order to get my bearings. During that time I discovered that I could order lunch, have a cup of coffee in a tiny place in the shadow of the Acropolis, and purchase a bunch of sweet peas (great pink, scarlet, and crimson ones, which along with all sorts of other flowers are for sale in stalls all over town—all of them in blazing colors) with no trouble whatever. My Greek teachers have served me well—and while I was waiting for my luggage to come off the ship I learned the numbers from twenty to a hundred, which I suddenly realized I hadn't bothered to do.

But I mustn't get started on Greece until I've retraced my steps a bit—or I'll have forgotten what went before. Without doubt this has been the most thoroughly delightful crossing I ever made. Things went on getting better and better when it began to seem that they *couldn't* be any more enchanting. That fabulous day when we entered the Straits of Gibraltar and found ourselves in a blue, calm Mediterranean, ended with a Mediterranean sunset—all rose and indigo with glowing bands of clouds across the west after the sun went down. The day ended, but the night went on and on, and a good deal of it was spent on deck, singing under the stars, with an interlude below, in a part of the ship where the fun didn't begin until midnight, when a Greek band started playing and the Greeks danced in their own exuberant fashion—a kind of blend of English country dancing and Russian gymnastics. I finally turned in around three, but was up again by eight and on deck before breakfast. With the Mediterranean all around, and the blue Mediterranean sky overhead, it seemed a pity to be indoors even for meals. As a result, by this time I am browner than I've been in years.

The sequence of days is a bit scrambled in my mind, but the fun went on, especially at meals—which also got better and better. We had filet mignon once and sirloin steak another time, both times with champagne in addition to the mild white wine that was always on the table. In Lisbon, just before I returned to the ship I bought a bottle of tawny Port, which we had the next evening with our dessert. On the evening after that, one of the

Greek girls had a birthday, and a couple of other people contributed Lancers, a sparkling Portuguese rosé which is delightful. In fact I believe that night we had champagne too! This begins to sound like the diary of an alcoholic, but for some reason the sea air kept all the alcohol from doing any noticeable damage. To add to the ship's attraction the bars on the ship had the cheapest drinks imaginable—twenty cents for a glass of Ouzo, the Greek anise liqueur which costs about $7 a bottle in the States. That is, sometimes it was twenty cents; sometimes thirty or forty if the bartender thought you could afford it—the Greeks were a bit inscrutable about it. But for whatever reason, I usually got charged the minimum. A single Ouzo, sip by sip, would last me through a two-hour conversation.

Fairly early on Thursday, the 6th, absolutely everybody was on deck as we came in sight of the Italian coast. We hadn't seen much of Spain except the Rock of Gibraltar (with schools of porpoises following us as we came into the Strait), and it had been dark when we came within sight of the coast of Sardinia. In the usual confusing manner of approaching coastlines, what I was sure must be Vesuvius turned out to be isle of Ischia, a somewhat less famous twin of Capri—rocky, barren and sparsely inhabited, with terraced vineyards and with a fortress guarding the approach to the Bay of Naples. We saw Capri too, but not at such close range. I begin to wonder whether the sky over that bay ever is the bright blue you hear about. When I last approached it—from a more northerly direction, five years ago—it was September, and it was hazy. A Fulbright scholar who came aboard at Lisbon told me that it was generally hazy in the summer, but that in spring it ought to be clear. Well, it was, but we could just make out the great cone of the volcano looming above the crescent shape of the bay, and there were clouds that led me to wonder whether it might even be going to rain. There were debates about what to wear, and a second thought decided me to put on the one coat I have with me, namely my raincoat. Dorothy Bereny, my table mate from Los Angeles, appeared in a very Californiesque costume, topped off by a wonderful hat made entirely of great floppy flowers. As it turned out, that hat made the entire afternoon an adventure for the six, seven or eight of us—the number varied from time to time—who decided to join forces. We started out as six, and at the quay (my idea) we hired two carrozzas, those clopping horse-drawn carriages that tourists ride in in every European city. I was the only one in the party who claimed to know any Italian, and trying to learn Greek had made that little pretty dim, so the bargaining was not very expert; but for a dollar apiece we were jounced and jolted along the main thoroughfares, including the curving street along the bay, for an hour or so. But if we were rubberneckers, the flowery hat caused us to be rubbernecked at in turn, in the most gratifying fashion; and since Dorothy is quite beautiful even without the hat, there were second looks as well. Or maybe it's just that Neapolitans aren't blasé about parties of tourists. Anyhow, we left the carrozzas and set out in search of a café that looked right; and before we found it we had added two more people to our party—one of them an elderly Englishman named Olly who joined us at Lisbon, the other our waiter, Jimmy. We found a sidewalk café, where we were accosted by the usual collection of Neapolitan beggars, and where we ate *sfogliate*, a kind of pastry which is a specialty of the region (I remembered it from the last time), and drank vermouth and Campari and Strega and such like (though I am afraid that one of the Pats ordered Coca-Cola). While we were sitting there, lo it began to rain. So we moved inside the café, where we found a couple of very black Moroccans wearing white-and-gold leather fezzes and speaking French—and also a cat. I seemed to remember that in Italy all cats are called Bobby (or it may be all dogs—I wish I could remember), and when I tried it, it did seem to work! Finally it stopped raining, and I asked the waiter whether there was a bus to the *Funiculare*, an underground railway leading to the top of one of the two peaks that are a part of the city of Naples. He said that the *Funiculare* itself was only five or six minutes away on foot, so we started out. The idea was to get to the top of the hill, where there is a fortress and also a monastery, for the view of Vesuvius and the bay. We inquired once or twice, and it stood to reason that if one headed up, it could hardly be anything but the right way. After five or six minutes we hadn't found the *Funiculare*, but we were unmistakably going up. The streets had turned into flights of steps, with cross streets intersecting them, narrower than most alleys in any other city. We looked into doorways and saw how people lived; and the people who lived there came out to stare at all of us, but chiefly at Dorothy and her flowery hat. Old women came up and touched it, and children danced all around and called out "Money, money"—but we didn't give them any, except to the ones who told us the way to the *Funiculare*. As somebody said, it was like the Pied Piper of Hamelin. We were a bit giddy in the first place after so many days on a rolling ship, and as we climbed things got gayer and gayer, even though we had been climbing for twenty minutes with no sign of the *Funiculare*. Since I was the one who had gotten everybody into this, there were a good many remarks flung in my direction; but if the rest of them were having half as much fun as I was, there was nothing to regret—and at least some of the party were, I am pretty sure. Finally we got to what was unmistakably a station of the *Funiculare,* and I had the fun of buying round-trip tickets for everybody. The train itself turned out to be a cross between a subway and a San Francisco cable car—it travels at such a steep angle that the cars are built in steps. At the end of the line we got out, and began asking people the way to the view. We found one view, in what was now a very respectable middle-class residential section, but it wasn't *the* view—Vesuvius was out of sight. So we began inquiring again, and a very small boy who was passing out handbills for a movie house or something volunteered to be our guide. I found out that his name was Maurizio and that he was eleven years old; he looked about seven. We conversed about the beautiful city of Naples, and whether America was as beautiful, and I told him sadly that it wasn't. Italians almost invariably talk like this; unlike Americans, the word *beautiful* comes naturally to them—and not without reason. I had forgotten how utterly beautiful, and even more how utterly full of life, Naples was. Being in Italy again had the same effect on me as before. (I am afraid that most of the people I have met on the ship take me for about twenty-five, if that—and mostly I felt about fifteen. All of which made for some amusing but harmless complications.) Somewhere along the way we were joined by another guide—a full-grown one this time, who explained that he was employed by the cameo factory. I was dubious about this, but he was very eager, and also Maurizio by now was farther and farther from home; so finally we dismissed Maurizio with a couple of hundred lire, and proceeded with the new guide to the cameo factory. It wasn't really a factory—just a tiny place with one man at work and some showcases full of finished wares. They were pretty but hardly inexpensive, and none of us bought anything, but the detour was made worth my own while because the salesman was one of those blonde, blue-eyed Italian boys I found so irresistible in the north of Italy—and he seemed to know all about that, and greeted me accordingly. He was a Neapolitan, too—or anyhow he said he was. Most of them are olive-skinned and dark-haired. Finally we got away from the cameos, and walked along under the castle wall, where swallows were skimming about, and a few boys playing ball on the steep grassy slope just above our heads. The view, when we finally came to it, had Vesuvius, the bay, and the roofs of the city lying below us, and just below our feet was a tangle of grapevines, on a very steep slope, an orange tree with ripe fruit among the leaves, and—a somehow typically earthy touch—a large pig tethered to a tree. By then the sun had just set, and it had begun to rain a little once more. Our new guide—who told us that his name was Johnny, and that he had helped the Americans during the German occupation, when he was about fifteen—showed us the way to a different station on the *Funiculare*, which took us all the way down to where we should have caught it in the first place. By then it was nearly half-past seven, and the ship was scheduled to sail at eight; but we went back to the pier on foot, and just made it aboard—all of us pretty exuberant over our adventure. By then it was almost dark, and we were treated to a spectacular view of the Bay of Naples. Up at the top of the peak of Vomero the monastery was floodlit, so that it stood out and showed exactly where we had been. And the great crescent curve of the beach was a necklace of lights about the water of the bay. As if that weren't enough, there was a new moon half hidden but every now and then breaking through the clouds. The effect was indescribably grand and romantic all at once. Naturally, we found ourselves breaking into *Santa Lucia* and *Funiculi Funicula* (which incidentally, according to our guide Johnny, was written about that very *Funiculare*). Then we had to go down to dinner; but between courses I ran out on deck for another look, and while I stood there all choked up, somebody called from the deck above, "Put a coat on!" There isn't much privacy on an ocean liner, for anybody who wants to go and have a little private cry over things being just too beautiful to be quite believed!

During the night we passed the volcanic island of Stromboli. A few passengers either got up or stayed up all night to see it; but I wasn't one of them, alas. One of the enterprising ones told me about the red glow that proved it was in eruption. When I got up, around seven, we were already docked in the harbor at Messina, on the Sicilian side of the strait known mythologically as Scylla and Charybdis. The passengers for Messina had already disembarked, and the rest of us had no chance to go ashore; but at least we had a good view of the town, with its domed churches and tawny facades, rising steeply against a mountain backdrop dotted with umbrella pines and monasteries, whose bells could be heard clanging in the distance. The Sicilians have a look of their own—small, brown people with leathery faces. For a while after we pulled out we had a view of the coast of Italy—still green in places with spring vegetation, and with terraces of vineyards here and there. On deck the day was the warmest and brightest yet, though it turned chilly around sunset. I was exhausted from the Naples expedition, and had every intention of going to bed directly after dinner; but what with an Ouzo after dinner, and turning the clocks up an hour, it was half-past eleven when I turned in. Even so, I asked the night steward to wake me at five, so as not to miss the earliest possible view of the isles of Greece. Some of us had talked about staying up all night, and one Greek-American I found on deck in the morning apparently had—or was that the Harvard boy on his way to Haifa? Anyhow, at half-past five I was looking at a sunrise that explained all those repeated references in Homer to Rosy-fingered Dawn. (Incidentally, to give an idea of the mood aboard, one day I took my Greek anthology up on deck and read aloud from the *Odyssey*—the part about Odysseus and the Cyclops and his cave full of cheeses and wineskins and his flock of sheep; it applied remarkably well to the fare on board.) Some unnamed island stood silhouetted against that rosy sky, and there were other rocky shapes rising from the sea—all the work of Poseidon the earth-shaper, as those of us who were seeing them for the first time couldn't help but tell each other. A flock of gulls followed screaming in the wake of the ship, and every now and then (ever since we entered the Mediterranean, in fact) there would be a stray swallow flitting about. The first identifiable island turned out to be Hydra (the Greeks pronounce it Idthra), and while we watched I read in my guidebook that its wealthy families got their start, several centuries ago, as pirates. After a while the Peloponnesus itself came into view, and Rosy-fingered Dawn was at work on its highest peaks—which, astonishingly, had snow on them. I hadn't realized that the Taygetos were quite so high. Then we passed Poros and Aegina, and the harbor of Salamis where the Persians were defeated, and finally, in the somewhat hazy distance, the harbor of Piraeus came into view. I had a hill all picked out that I was sure must be the Acropolis, but once again it turned out to be one of those mistaken notions. We did finally have an exceedingly hazy view of a hill, standing out against a higher, darker one, and with a blotch of white, which I was told was the Acropolis and the first sight of the Parthenon; but it was far too remote and dim to be at all spectacular. The excitement that morning was so great that I could hardly eat, and if my table mates hadn't urged me on I might not even have tried. By the time we pulled into the harbor, the ship's band was playing with a fervor that would have stirred the most sluggish pulse, and people were screaming from the deck to other people on the tugs that pulled us in, and there were more screams and waving from the pier, with a good many tears shed.

I think I had better bring this to an end. It's now Sunday afternoon; I've been in Athens only a little over twenty-four hours, and there is already so much to tell that it had better be saved for a separate installment.

I'll just say that the Acropolis is harder to see than you might think; about seven miles of walking all around it has given me my bearings and a pretty good idea of the city, but I'm saving the Acropolis itself—working up to it by easy stages as it were. Also that wild poppies are everywhere, great splashes and splotches of red among the grass and under the pines and cypresses; and nearly everywhere you go, the air has a whiff of orange blossom. Now I must stop.

Love,

Amy

. . . .

28 August 1965

Dear Rimsa—

[. . .] You wanted to know what prompted my fiery mutterings, some months back, about a general exodus from this gritty metropolis. Well, those mutterings were simply the culmination of everybody's getting more and more scared to go anywhere on the subway, for fear of getting murdered. Then they put policemen into all the trains and on all the station platforms, and they put more policemen on the streets—and here most of us still are, and here I am again. As usual, while I was away from New York I couldn't imagine why I had ever lived here; and as we pulled in aboard the *France* at four a.m. on a smoggy day in July, the red dawn looked like Sodom and Gomorrah, and I had the impression that the whole country had been burning down in my absence. Well, after a bit it didn't seem so bad. It was just that knocking about Greece, in reckless disregard of danger to life and limb on whose wild mountain roads, was a form of taking one's life in one's hands that could also be enjoyed. I expected to be killed from minute to minute, and I never was happier anywhere in my life.

Where to begin and how to tell about it all! I hope, anyhow, that you got my card from—I think it was Delphi. It probably said that that was the most beautiful place in the world—which is what I thought and which it may indeed be—a stupendous place, awesome as an oracle should be, and at the same time peacefully idyllic, with olive groves, barley fields, donkeys coming clop-clop ting-ting-ting underneath the balcony of one's hotel room twice a day, on their way to and from the mountain pastures; soaring cliffs, pine groves, wild flowers everywhere, and the music of the Castalian spring, sacred to Apollo and the Muses, cascading down from the snows of Mt. Parnassus. Another couple of thousand feet down—a breathtaking drop—was the sea, or more precisely the Gulf of Corinth. On a ferry across the gulf, bound I didn't yet know quite where, I was so immediately surrounded by a busload of students from Salonika, who descended like a flock of birds from nowhere and were my constant companions for the rest of the trip—though not one of them spoke a word of English—that I hadn't even a chance to notice the scenery. They were on a class tour with three of their teachers, likewise non-English-speaking, and in no time they had invited me to ride in their bus to Olympia. They also adopted a German couple, with whom I got to be great friends. Well, in Olympia I rode a donkey, listened to the nightingales and the frogs (which in Greece do indeed say "Brek-ek-ek-ek-ex co-ax, co-ax," just as Aristophanes said they did), said goodbye to the students and then to the German couple, and set out for what was supposed to be Mycenae on a local bus. Local buses in Greece being an inscrutable and unpredictable phenomenon, I wound up instead at Nauplia, on the coast—where lo and behold, there again were the students from Salonika! After a gleeful reunion and more farewells on the quay, I went out at dinnertime (which in Greece isn't until around nine), and the next thing I knew, there was another reunion, in a tavern under a grape arbor. I wound up having dinner with the whole crowd, and buying wine for them all; and they gave me a rose, and there were toasts upon toasts, and things got merrier and merrier, until they had simply taken over the place, and people gathered round outside and came to lean out of their windows to watch while they [sang] and did the dances of Macedonia. It was one of those unforgettable things that simply happen; but there is something about Greece, that makes for happenings, I can't say just what. Just the other day I had a letter, in beautiful French, from one of the crowd, an eighteen-year-old whose name—honestly—is Calliope, recalling the whole adventure, and with a snapshot taken in the ruins at Olympia that brought it all back.

Well, things went on happening. I went island-hopping; I mean really—for eight days I spent a good deal of my time getting on and off boats, and they weren't cruise ships; just the ordinary everyday ones that the Greeks get about on. I went first to Mykonos, and from there over to Delos for half a day, and it was all wild, improbable and romantic. I found a room in a house by a windmill, overlooking the water; it cost me a dollar a day, and was lined with family ikons, and there were lilies in a vase underneath them, and a terrace shaded by giant geraniums (California-like, as things can be in Greece) just outside the window, where I ate my breakfast. Beginning on Delos, there was a brief, confused, forever unforgettable sort of romance with somebody who turned out to be called Vassilis, involving skylarks and scrambling around among rocky little farms and talking (of all things) about etymology. But he went back to Athens, and I went to Samos, where I stayed for a day, riding about on the local buses, and saw the coast of Turkey, rising blue and unlikely across the water from a lonely plain where a single column remains standing of what was once a great temple of Hera. Then I decided to go to Naxos—because of the Ariadne story, because the guidebook said it had "no tourist amenities," and also because it was hard to get to. The complications that ensued would take too long to relate; but finally, at five o'clock in the morning, from the porthole of an old tub with a starboard list, which I halfway expected to sink before it landed, I had my first view of a white town, rising out of the Aegean in the rosy light of dawn, against a wild backdrop of mountain scenery, and it was almost too romantic to be believed. After that, even Crete, which is pretty wild itself, was a bit of a letdown. I had only a day and a half on Naxos, and it never ceased to be strange. The roads were the worst yet, and after an all-day expedition in a hired car to look at fallen statues in the middle of nowhere, abandoned Byzantine churches, and ancient towers where people still live, and mile after mile of plunging mountain scenery, the miracle was that any of us were still alive. Well, I could go on and on. I spent four days in Crete; finally got to Mycenae and also to Epidauros, where I watched a rehearsal in the ancient theater; and then headed north, via Salzburg and Paris. For a couple of days I lived in luxury at Monica's; then on to London, where I arrived in pouring rain during Ascot Week, with no roof over my head. But I had a great time, even being stranded. From there I went to Cambridge, Norwich, Lincoln, Oxford— still my favorite city of them all—visited my friend who is now a Benedictine nun at her abbey in Kent; and wound up on the Sussex coast, visiting two sets of old friends; and sailed from Southampton at the beginning of July. Before I'd quite settled down again, I made a frivolous expedition to Maine, where my brother had a house for a month, in an enchanting spot not too far from the Audubon Maine Camp (which I didn't see). And since then, a month-long writing jag—interspersed with a few editorial jobs that had to be done—has brought me to the end of the novel I'd been working on at odd times for the past couple of years. There is still the revising and copying on the final chapters; Lippincott has the first fifteen, and what may happen there is no telling. [. . .]

Love,

Amy

. . . .

17 May 1966

Dear Rimsa—

[. . .] The latest gossip concerning Audubon House is that John Vosburgh has resigned. I learned this from Mrs. Finney, whom I met by accident in the ladies' room at Altman's. Hadn't seen her in years, and I had just gone hog-wild and bought myself a pair of thirty-dollar shoes—French, with buckles, very something-or-other and possibly a mistake. Probably as a result of a long lunch with my book-designing friend Janet, at which we laid plans for a welcome-back celebration for our friend Annabel and her husband, who have been in Australia for two years and will be here for a month. Well, you see how one thing leads to another. I had really gone in there to buy something for my newest niece—that makes four, I think, though by now I've pretty much lost count—and before I got out I had also succumbed to a sort of hat with a Sally Victor label, much reduced, and not quite such an extravagance as one might suppose. But still. And not that I'm making that kind of money. But that is what happens when one hasn't been near a department store in months. Also, one runs into people like Mrs. Finney. She is just the same. She didn't know anything about the news she told me; she'd only seen it in the paper. So I can't give any details. I hadn't been around Audubon House since before Christmas, having concluded that I had done reviews for long enough, and served notice to that effect. The atmosphere had become quite weird. We are both of us well out of there, I can assure you—as if you needed assuring.

Well, so much for that sort of thing. My agent entered the novel I finished last fall in a contest sponsored by Putnam, McCall's, Fawcett Publishing, and Warner Brothers—total take guaranteed at about $210,000. I told her I thought it was pretty silly, but to go ahead. I was right. The ms. came back; so did thirty-five hundred others. Nobody won the prize. Can *you* imagine a novel that would satisfy all those customers and still sound like literature? So my heart isn't broken.

The last I heard, my agent had had a brainstorm and sent the thing to Henry Fonda, who seems to be producing movies these days. Well, anyhow *she* likes the book. At best the audience for it is probably quite small, so whether any publisher will care to bother remains to be seen. Meanwhile, in time available from making a sort of living I'm onto something rather different, about Greece—travel sketches I guess one would call them for lack of a better name, vaguely in the manner of Freya Stark. It all started when I decided to find out who Apollo was, and what he had to do with Dionysus. The result was a foray into mythology that started with buying Robert Graves's Penguin books on the subject, and has led deeper and deeper into all sort of odd byways—such as the amber route and woodpecker-gods and the magic bird-wheel and the mountain dancers of the *Bacchae*. I'm reading Euripides and Pindar and Hesiod and Theocritus and having a great time with them all. But of course the whole thing is a bit far out, so whether it can really be called a travel book at all remains to be seen. I've got it about half finished, anyhow, and never had more fun writing anything.

My latest adventure, if one can call it that, has been standing in line for tickets to the Bolshoi Ballet *for five hours*. I'm on S. Hurok's mailing list, and it wasn't until I'd offered to send off a check so that a little cousin of mine, new in New York, could go with me, that I looked again and saw that he wasn't accepting mail orders. What he did offer was a little private sale for his customers at the Metropolitan's box office. Well, his mailing list is a long one, and the little private sale had attracted a line that went pretty far around the block by the time I got there. But once in the line, the longer one stayed the harder it became to give up and drop out—so there I was, stuck. By the end of five hours a certain amount of cama-raderie had developed, and we began to realize that we hardly knew any more what we were there for. Most odd. The most distinguished of the people I talked to, in my opinion, was a boy in a fisherman's sweater who had just come from waiting in line for a Horowitz concert. I'm not sure how long he'd been in it, but it had started forming on Saturday after-noon, and this was Monday. Truly, there are all kinds of madness. Any-how, I got my two tickets; they were for *Don Quixote*, which turned out not to have much of the Don in it but was a great show all the same. It is sad to think that that was my last visit to the old Met, ever. I'd become a real opera buff, this last season. I even braved *Parsifal*—and do you know, I loved it! [. . .]
Love,
Amy

. . . .

8 March 1968
Dear Barbara—
[. . .] It is just conceivable that I may be in Washington a week from to-day. If so, it will be only for the day, most probably, and it will be a day of high-minded skullduggery. This time the gathering is to be in front of Internal Revenue Service headquarters, where various people who aren't

paying all or a piece of their tax plan to hand in incomplete returns and/or letters explaining that they're Agin the War. I sent in my tax return at the end of January minus twenty-three percent of the total due, and if it can be arranged I rather fancy standing and being counted. The penalty, should the Government choose to enforce it, is up to a year in jail and/or ten thousand dollars fine. I took my text from Thoreau, as being a part of the American Tradition.

I have gone on working for David Schoenbrun, who is getting out a book and various articles and every now and then asks for some raw material for a speech as well. And I have also gone into politicking, to the extent of joining the local Reform Democratic club and spending hours at headquarters attending to the various drudgeries of getting a canvassers' list together. This week, for the first time, I went canvassing. I was terrified of the prospect, but it turns out to be a great adventure. People invite you in and will hardly let you go, and the voices that growl "Not interested" from behind the door are no more than one out of ten. There are now fifteen New York City Democratic clubs that have voted to back Senator McCarthy, and needless to say the one I've thrown my lot in with is one of those. And the people are about as far removed from my old notion of a clubhouse gang as any lot of people can be. As a result, though I follow the war new with a horrified fascination (I never thought I would have a clue about military strategy, and now look) as what looks like a re-play of the French debacle in the 1950's unrolls—as a result, I am more cheerful than I was a year ago, when I was too busy being upset to follow very much of what was happening. I've just finished reading the Kennan memoirs, which I recommend as one of the best things I've ever read on U.S. foreign policy, as well as a fascinating look into the inner workings of a personality that would have baffled me totally, met face to face. Aside from that and a novel of sorts called *The Maze Maker*, on the myth of Daedalus—very good, and indeed totally relevant, as I already knew Greek myth, properly approached, to be—my reading these last months has been mostly the *New York Times* and reference stuff on the National Liberation Front and the people in Hanoi (e.g., a biography of Ho Chi Minh in French, and a very good book too). The opera and the ballet are too much trouble to get to, and I've been rushing about so that I've almost forgotten how to cook. [. . .]
Love,
Amy

17 June 1968
Dear Rimsa—

[. . .] Among the McCarthy people the chief enchanted has been an authentic flower child named Bill, who is twenty-one and was my canvassing companion, night after night, for something like five or six weeks. He offered faintly to get himself barbered and Clean for Gene, but I told him nonsense; the truth is, I liked him too much as he was to want to think of it. We acquired a certain fame as the team who brought in not only more signatures than any other (though in the end one of the old pros in the club outdid our total) but also totally unsolicited financial contributions, and also for being the last to appear with our evening's haul. This was because we got into the habit of stopping for a beer at the White Horse to talk, as we did about everything under the sun. I suppose the name of the game could be Bridging the Generation Gap, but in some ways I felt about the same age, and now and then—when he was delivering one of his austere judgments, which he did with wonderful articulateness—I felt even younger. It was with him that I saw [Godard's] *La Chinoise*. We had been on the April peace march, and I was very tired, and I am still not sure what to think of it. Visually it is an extremely beautiful picture, in a spare, clean-cut, almost painful way. It is about some very young Maoists who have an apartment in Paris for the summer, and a great deal of it consists of their conversations and debates about political theory, which sometimes take the form of little dramas, with masks and props. It isn't like anything I can think of. Bill and I disagreed about what the intent of it all was; he thought I laughed at things that were not to be taken irreverently. It meant a good deal more to him than to me (he'd seen it once before and wanted to go back); that is where the generation gap comes in, perhaps.

Anyhow, partly because of the effect it had on him, he has since defected from the McCarthy ranks. We had a long, long ambulatory conversation on the subject the night of the California primary. So I was already in a state of upset when I heard the news [of Robert Kennedy's assassination] the next morning, and it was days before I could bring myself to go near headquarters again. I finally went back, and found that everybody had been badly shaken, so things can never be as they were before the terrible things started happening. But the campaign goes on. I'm to "open the polls" for the primary tomorrow at my own polling place—whatever that means. I suppose as a poll-watcher or something. Tonight there is a meeting to find out.

Then after the primary, on Wednesday morning early, I'm taking a bus to Washington with the Poor People's Campaign people. And on Thursday I'm to fly to Iowa for ten days in those parts. I have to be back again by the first of July, and will be tied here by an assignment until the end of August. I've never seen a year rush past as this one has—I can hardly remember what month it is, most of the time. [. . .]

Love,

Amy

. . . .

2 December 1968

Dear Barbara [Blay]—

[. . .] As you know, things in this country have been in a pretty distressing state all year, and on that score I have had nothing to be cheerful about. But strangely enough, in the midst of all sorts of despair and forebodings about what is to become of things, I can say that in some ways I never had a better year. It all started after Senator McCarthy announced that he was running for President, and I decided to join the campaign. As you know, I had been more and more distressed over the war in Vietnam, and it was a relief to have something to do besides joining demonstrations and writing letters to Congressmen. My first step was to join a neighborhood political club that had just voted to support McCarthy for the nomination—and from then on my whole way of life was suddenly transformed. I found myself doing things I'd never supposed I could do, such as handing out buttons and collecting money on street corners, and going from door to door to collect signatures so as to get the candidate's name on the ballot. In fact, for five weeks in April and May, nearly all my evenings were spent ringing doorbells, rain or shine—usually with a delightful unbarbered youngster from whom I learned more than I could have any other way about what his generation were thinking. In the process, I also got to know my own neighborhood as I never had before. We were so successful, or so dogged anyhow, that we were then sent into other districts—but my own remained the friendliest, the most varied, and the most fun. Besides, I spent a good many of the daylight hours as a volunteer researcher, reading and taking notes on reams of Congressional testimony and back issues of the *New York Times.* Looking back, I still can't understand how I managed to make a living— but even if I hadn't, I wouldn't have missed the campaign. Of course the spectacle of the Democratic convention in Chicago was pretty traumatic— the more so for me since I kept seeing people I knew hauled off the convention floor, or protesting something or other that somebody had done. Some people I knew were jailed, and I talked to one staff member who had been in the McCarthy suite at the hotel when the police arrived at 5 a.m. and started beating people up. It was all pretty grim, but I think most of us had the same feeling—that it was worth being involved in, and there will be more to be involved in. Meanwhile, anyhow, I found myself elected to the executive committee of the local political club, and no sooner was the convention over than I went to work for Paul O'Dwyer, who was running for the Senate, and for another candidate the club was supporting. So once again, up until the election in November, I found myself running around night after night, trying to get out the vote. This time I was given two districts to take charge of, which meant rounding up a team, getting them together, stuffing literature under doors of apartment houses, and more doorbell-ringing. O'Dwyer lost very badly, which grieved me since he was a sort of heir of the McCarthy campaign; but our other candidate won, and so there was some celebrating to do—in fact, I think I never drank so much champagne in one evening! Even better than the champagne party, though, was another post-election festivity which I had more of a hand in: one member of my team, a law professor with a big apartment on Fifth Avenue [Harold Korn], who likes to give parties, and I decided to get our people together just for the sake of getting together. He supplied the liquor and I took care of the food, and together we produced a Sangria punch, among other things. In the middle of the evening I brought out a *quiche Lorraine*, straight from the oven, which was promptly devoured; and there were cheeses and a paté which I'd put together earlier. By the time we finished inviting people, the guest list had grown to about forty, and there were a couple of crashers neither of us could account for—but whom I couldn't really object to, since their presence seemed to be a tribute. If my own experience is any gauge, the affair was a success—I had a great time, though I'd expected to be too anxious for that. I finally got home at half-past four a.m., after we'd washed up all the glasses and otherwise disposed of the debris—and even so, the next day I went out and handed out leaflets about the California grape strike, the latest cause around here. Through all of this, as you can imagine, I've gotten to know any number of people, the like of whom I'd never have met any other way, and some of them very much worth knowing. I've also gotten involved in some fierce intra-party squabbles—this is what happens when you get into politics—and there have been some angry scenes, with the satisfaction of being able to kiss and make up afterward—at least with some of the squabblers. [. . .]

Love,

Amy

Christmas, 1968

Dear Barbara—

This won't be the letter I meant to write, but at least it's typed—the day having arrived when I admit to being unable to read my own scrawl when it's more than half a day old. First of all, condolences over the Constitution. I can imagine what that must have been like, better than I might have before, as a consequence of something like total immersion in politics—this being the latest phase in my ever-changing career, or more precisely education. What I mean is, I'm in it enough to have gotten into some fierce internecine disagreements, and lost one of them— over whether or not to endorse, even tepidly, Humphrey-Muskie over Nixon-Agnew. I guess I shall have to explain that I was against—stubbornly enough that I actually voted for Dick Gregory. You see what a radical I'm turning into—or more precisely, to use a word that already begins to sound faintly obsolete—an unreconstructed dove. From a quasi-recluse as late as a year ago, when I was immersed in reading and note-taking on Vietnam for David Schoenbrun, I've become a nighttime gadabout, and do you know what, it agrees with me! Imagine me as an election captain in not one but two E.D.'s, launching a sort of guerrilla operation to stuff literature under doors in a building I'd once been thrown out of, and succeeding. Or imagine me, after the election, throwing a party along with another member of my team, an N.Y.U. law professor, for no very precise reason except to bring a few of the dissidents together (but in the end including people from the opposite faction) and [here it turns] out a huge success. But that isn't all. In the midst of all the running around at night—which goes on even now, with the election all but forgotten, but things like the grape boycott and rent control rising up in its place—I'm also on the biggest poetry-writing binge in my history. Behind it all is the great love of this mad year, with whom I rang doorbells in the spring but who has since defected from the whole thing—very, very young, but articulate as the young seldom know how to be, and likewise gentle, and at the same time radical as only the young are, perhaps, even nowadays. In sort, I never felt more alive. I enclose a sample of what's been coming out of all this—one of a series of memorials to people I'd been fond of, and one that was a joy to write as such things aren't always. I hope you might like it. [. . .]

Love,

Amy

17 October 1969

Dear Beth—

There are golden-crowned kinglets in the catalpa trees underneath my fire escape again. They have been there several mornings lately, on their way through to wherever they go for the winter, making little lisping sounds that keep bringing me to the window to look. It's finally fall, though we still haven't had any frost; the leaves are falling and the days are getting shorter. In some ways it's hard to believe that it's now nearly two months since we all converged out there. So much has been happening that I've hardly been able to keep track of what day it is.

This week especially. I've been involved in the Moratorium, as you probably won't be surprised to hear, and there have been meetings and telephoning to plan and round up volunteers. Last Saturday we were already on street corners, handing out leaflets and buttons; and I could tell that it was going to be a big thing, because the buttons kept running out. It was like the beginning of the McCarthy campaign, only bigger. On Wednesday my job was to send out crews of people with leaflets and buttons and black armbands to set up card tables around the Village—and already at eight that morning I had almost more volunteers than I could give assignments to. We ran out of black armbands almost immediately, and a volunteer went off to look for black ribbon; by noon there wasn't any more to be had anywhere in the neighborhood—and we'd taken in about $350 in contributions. Counting out the change and depositing it in the bank took us about an hour. There were rallies all day long, all over town. I got into the one where Senator McCarthy and Mayor Lindsay spoke; an hour before it began, the park was already full, and we kept being packed in tighter and tighter. It wound up just at sunset, with the cast of *Hair* taking their place on the speakers' platform. Judy Collins was there, and Peter and Mary of Peter, Paul and Mary, and a lot of other people.

At the end of that rally I came downtown and joined a sort of straggling procession into Washington Square Park, with everybody carrying lighted candles. Under the arch, people were reading the names of American soldiers killed in Vietnam. It was very quiet and strange, with a little sliver of new moon just about to go down in the background. After a while the whole procession started uptown to Rockefeller Center, carrying candles and pretty much stopping traffic. I wanted to go too, but after having been on my feet all day I concluded that I'd never make it. [. . .]

In the midst of everything else, a Black and Brown Caucus has appeared at St. Mark's, and a couple of Sundays ago they startled all the rest of us by getting up and reading a list of demands and asking those who supported them to walk out of the service. Most of the congregation finally did, and ever since then there have been meetings and telephone calls and a lot of confusion and noise, and nobody knows when, if ever, things are going to settle down again. I think it was a good thing, but some people are still hurt and angry and wanting to know why it happened.

[According to Philip Clampitt, this event may have signaled the beginning of the end of Amy's active involvement with the Episcopal Church. She had been a fervent church-going Anglo-Catholic for a number of years, but eventually became disillusioned because of her opposition to the Vietnam War. This event might have helped make the break inevitable. See her letter to David Quint, October 25, 1980]
Love,
Amy

. . . .

30 November 1969
Dear Barbara—
[. . .] I was in Washington two weeks ago, and had it in mind that I might at least talk to you on the phone, but didn't manage even that. It was a beautiful thing altogether. Were you in for any of it, I wonder? I came down with a busload from St. Mark's, arriving around four a.m. on the Saturday, and almost immediately we joined the March Against Death. While we were en route it was dawn and then sunrise flaming gold behind the Capitol. I walked with a little girl, a tenth-grader whose last name I never learned, and I carried the name of one Norman Livingston of Michigan. The mood and ambiance of the whole thing were very strange—a funeral march that was also a celebration, lighthearted on the surface but with a solemnity that went down, down—and all day long it was like that. Woodstock, only cold, I had pronounced before the big march got under way. The thought was a cliché before the day was over. Late in the afternoon I wandered into a church—Epiphany, at 13th and G—that was indeed a kind of epiphany. Marchers were sleeping, sitting, quietly talking, sharing wine from a jug and cocoa from a vat in the kitchen, everywhere. The sanctuary was all very churchy with stained glass and Tudor beams and polished candlesticks and flowers on the altar for Sunday, and it had marchers sleeping in the pews. When I settled into one myself, a young man raised himself from the one in front to ask if I had a cigarette. I was never so sorry not to be able to oblige, but then again it

didn't matter. It was like a vision of paradise; it was also like rats or refugees taking over—in flight from a catastrophe yet to come. What I mean to say is that no questions were asked, nobody was subjected to any ordeal of acceptance or rejection, there was no ego any more. Outside, in that freezing weather, roses and camellias were still in bloom. I came back to New York and wept, telling Hal about it. It's the kids, I kept saying—what is to become of them?

All sorts of things have been going on, of course. The Lindsay campaign. The grape boycott, again. Black Power (also Brown) rising up at St. Mark's, in the shape of a minority caucus that one Sunday morning invited sympathizers with a list of demands to walk out of the service with them. It took me about a second to know what to do, and in a way it was a relief to be asked to take a position. But the congregation is still trying to pick up the pieces, and those of us who would like to lend our support to the caucus are having a hell of time getting together enough to do it. (The way white people turn on one another in times of upheaval is really scary; we trust each other so little—which is one reason that epiphany in Washington upset me so.) Personally I go on finding all kinds of satisfactions. (Like starting to wear pants to dress up in—I mean to church and the theater, yet. It's a real emancipation, for some reason, and not because I've joined the Women's Liberation Movement either.) The main one is being with Hal. It wouldn't be quite accurate any more to say that we've each kept our independence, I suppose, since we're together a good deal these days. But there is such ease and harmony that it feels like freedom, and by some miracle we don't get on each other's nerves the way people who are close so often do. We went to hear the Incredible String Band just after I got back in September, and expect to hear them again in a couple of weeks—this time in the company of a friend of his who is now hooked, as a result of an evening here when we built a fire and sat on the floor looking at it and listening to records for hours and hours. [. . .]
Love,
Amy

. . . .

4 January 1970
Dear Barbara [Blay]—
Your Christmas parcel arrived well in advance, but I didn't open it until just before leaving to spend the holiday with my brother's family in Boston—or you would have heard before now how enchanted I am with

the silver slippers. Besides being so pretty, they fit precisely, and altogether are much more elegant than anything of the sort I ever owned before. I've not only worn them happily at home, but also Out in Society; on New Year's Eve, when there were quantities of snow and slush underfoot, I took them along to slip into after taking off my high boots. With pants and a low-cut blouse and a silvery sash (my favorite costume these days), they were exactly right for a gay evening of two parties, with champagne at midnight. I wish you could have been here to see and share the fun. IT was one of the best New Year celebrations I've had, and left me less gloomy than I'd been over everything—a gloom reflected in my Christmas greeting, if you were able to make it out at all.

Altogether, the year just past has been one of the busiest ever for me. I can't remember what I may have written about such things as working to re-elect Mayor Lindsay (and meeting the man himself, one sweltering summer afternoon, when a group of us were invited to let him know our views; I let other people do the talking, but it was fascinating to watch him, sitting at the head of the table, rumpled and sweating in his shirt-sleeves, and I came away liking him very much; also, incidentally, he is even better-looking in person than in photographs). On election day I worked from six a.m. until after the polls closed, and then was foolish enough to make the journey uptown to Lindsay headquarters, where thousands of campaign volunteers were already crowding around the doors and there obviously wasn't a chance of getting in without being trampled or trampling someone else; so, again, foolishly, I wound up watching television until the small hours instead of calling it a day and going straight to bed. Almost immediately, of course, those of us who supported the Mayor began finding things we were unhappy about his having done or not done. But at least it was nice to work for a candidate and have him win for once.

In August my parents celebrated their golden wedding anniversary, and there was another gathering of the Clampitts in Iowa for that occasion. As always, it was fun being together and seeing the younger generation under one roof and getting along remarkably well; and the big celebration, with about a hundred people there, went off happily and was fun in itself. There were people I hadn't seen since I was a child, and whom I would never have recognized but who knew me. One special pleasure for me was having the assignment of arranging the flowers—and thanks to my father's thriving garden, there were bowls and vases of them on every table and in every nook by the time I'd finished! From Iowa I traveled west to

Colorado, for a few days with some good friends who live in sight of the Rockies. It's another world out there, and New York seemed really far away, under that deep blue sky where every afternoon great masses of white clouds would pile up, ending sometimes with a thunderstorm at sunset, and with sprinklers going to keep the grass green in the back yard, and a grape arbor to sit under. One afternoon we got into the car and drove into the mountains, along a winding track through evergreen and aspen forest and then above timberline, where there were glaciers and stupendous views and the air is thin but exhilarating as wine. [. . .]
Love,
Amy

. . . .

14 January 1970
Dear Rimsa—
[. . .] Did I write you that I went to Washington for the November march? It was one of the unforgettable experiences of my life, of a poetic kind that I used to associate with far-off foreign places (such as I've largely lost the wish to go to any more). I went with a busload that left from St. Mark's Place at midnight (whiffs of pot being wafted from the back, and the clergyman who was our marshal taking that in perfect stride), and was lucky enough to sleep a good deal of the way. We got to Arlington cemetery around four a.m., and very soon had taken our names and candles and were making the four-mile hike across the Potomac and past the White House. It was freezing cold as it can be in Washington, and there was a wind like a knife of ice, but the marshals who were posted along the way, wrapped up in blankets and shivering but beaming, kept the mood buoyant above the solemnity. I was carrying the name of one Norman Livingston, of Michigan. Walking beside me was a little girl, a tenth-grader who had come down with her parents and another couple, and who needed a partner, since by the time we got there the number of marchers exceeded the number of men killed and villages destroyed. Walking through the nation's capital at dawn, with the name of a person you know nothing else about, and with lines of people all doing the same thing, is simply an experience not quite any other. When we'd finally deposited the names in the coffins at the foot of the Capitol, we went another mile or so to a church, where volunteers were ladling out coffee and there was a place to get warm and nap for a few minutes (in a chair, or propped against the wall—though there were so many people that nobody

was supposed to stay very long). By half-past nine or so we were on our way again, to join the big march; and by then all of Washington was a march. Already I was saying it was like Woodstock, only cold; and the thought had soon become a cliché, because everybody had the same thought—but that was part of the experience. Hanging over us all was the possibility of tear gas and a stampede; but somehow that made us cheerful and relaxed, as we huddled together or linked arms to keep with the people we'd come with, and also just to keep warm. We were on the Mall for a couple of hours before joining the march, and it was well after noon before we got to the Monument. By then there were so many people that we were too far away from the loudspeakers to hear anything, and anyhow the rally seemed an anticlimax.

Around three I left, intending to look for a cab to take me to some friends whom I'd spoken to over the phone while we were at the church. There weren't any, and neither were there any policemen to tell me which bus to take, and so eventually I found my way to another church—having heard a marcher's remark, just ahead of me, that suggested it was open to such as we. It was a place I'd never seen before, with a kind of sheltered garden walk leading to the entrance to the parish house, a few yards back from the street, and even in that bitter cold there were roses and camellias still in bloom, and a little fountain, and I remember stopping to sniff the camellias, which were pale pink and somehow dreamlike. There was a sign on the door that said "Full-Sorry" but I concluded it had been put up the night before, and went inside, and from then on it was a scene from a painting that you may have seen at the Metropolitan Museum, a Giovanni di Paolo version of paradise. There were people everywhere, sitting on the steps, and in little groups in corridors and hallways (one group with a jug of wine), or sleeping curled up or stretched out in what must have been a Sunday school classroom, and ladling out coffee and cocoa in the kitchen. I had thought I might find somebody I might ask directions of, but clearly we were all strangers together, and it was so unnecessary to speak to anyone to explain who you were and what you might be doing there, that I didn't want to break the spell. In the main part of the church, everything was set up for Sunday morning—candlesticks polished, flowers on the altar—and people were sleeping in the pews. I suddenly realized that what I needed was a nap; and as I settled down with my handbag for a pillow, somebody in the one just ahead raised his head and asked if I had a cigarette. It was once that I wished I hadn't quit smoking. I don't know whether I've conveyed the sense of community, but it was in such contrast to the up-tight propriety of the arrangements, and so exactly in tune with what being a believer ought to be, that I still haven't stopped marveling. It was also weirdly like a refugee camp—a thought that didn't become explicit until afterward, when I was trying to explain the scene. If there hadn't been so much since to keep me on the move, I might have put it into a poem—but it's there anyhow.

Now I'm involved in so many things that may or may not have any effect—plans to have perpetual reading of the names of men killed in Vietnam at the Church of the Ascension, as they're already doing at Riverside; plans for a local Friends of Welfare Rights, and a marching on Albany to demand that cuts in the welfare budget last year be restored—that I'm out more evenings than I'm in, and the result is, among other things, that I don't get letters written. The whole inflation thing is blowing up into what may become a taxpayers' revolt; for example, there are protests against the latest increase in the subway fare that consist of having people hold the exit doors open while hundreds go through (some of whom, of course, but not all, get arrested). And as a result of the research project I'm on now as a way of earning a sort of living, it becomes clearer and clearer that the inflation is simply the result of pouring money, manpower and resources into fighting and preparing for wars and more wars. Everybody knows it in a vague way; but what to do? I agree with you about the ex-poor boy in the White House. Your budget figures aren't far from the one I tried for a week in July. What impressed me most about the experiment was that it took so much time deciding what I could afford and what to do with that little bit. My own good fortune continues to be that I pay so little rent; otherwise my whole style of life would have to be revised. Most people I know have stopped buying steak because of inflation; but it is a pleasure nobody should have to be without altogether, and there is something wrong with an economy where it is happening to so many. [. . .]
Love,
Amy

. . . .

12 June 1970
Dear Barbara—
[. . .] Everything here seems to have been accelerating and escalating, even since I saw you. I did manage to pull together the position paper on the environment (though so far as I know, it hasn't been released), and thereby added a new one to my list of things-even-worse-than-I-thought.

But education of any kind is somehow exhilarating, and I enjoyed pulling together a set of recommendations—e.g., a Survival Corps, to pay a living wage to the kind of young people who are already trying to Do Something about pollution.

Ditto the trip to Washington, as an educational venture if for no other reason. The driver of the VW Microbus is one of those ageless contemporaries one meets on such ventures, and we yakked all the way down on the front seat, while the law students we took along did the same in the back. On the return journey things got more homogenized, with various interesting developments; for half an hour or so I found myself taking on all three of them about the need for radical change (young people can be so *conservative*, I find), and in a Howard Johnson's they took the two of us on, the way males will, at the testing-of-equanimity game. I guess we passed; anyhow everything wound up friendly. There was some agreement over whether going down there had really accomplished anything, since Congress seems to be one of those self-perpetuating institutions that are just about incapable of doing anything more than perpetuate themselves. The ones who agree congratulate you and caution against rocking the boat too much; the ones who don't remain intractable. The greatest single satisfaction, for me, was in so infuriating a hawk from Illinois that he kicked over the waste basket—saying, as we sailed out that if we were under the spell of the *New York Times* there wasn't much he could do.

I was not much more than back, and beginning to feel depressed over the pointlessness of that kind of satisfaction, when I stumbled into a new thing—giving aid and comfort to a squatters' movement. Six families had been taking refuge in vacant apartments in buildings a hospital wants to demolish to make way for a nurses' residence; and to ward off the cops, a crew of volunteers were rounded up to stay with them around the clock. As a result, I became part of a kind of floating household, consisting of a very young couple, the Rodriguezes, and their black-eyed year-old daughter, and a dozen or so supporters. We sat around on mattresses donated by kindly neighbors (the Rodriguezes had been robbed three times, and the last time had cleaned them out entirely), and rapped about all sorts of things—women's lib, collectives, child care, and characters in the peace movement—while a fairly steady procession of reporters, tape recorders, TV cameras, and other visitors more or less sinister passed through. What is going to happen finally, nobody knows; but the hospital officials remain adamant despite all pleas, so next Wednesday the squatters are presumably to be evicted; and so it may be that this time, after a good many misses, I may get arrested. For criminal trespassing. I'll let you know.

As if that weren't enough, there was a traumatic evening in which an old friend/enemy of Hal's used his immunity as a psychiatrist to play the hostility game, and afterward it took twelve hours of groping misery and rage to establish just what had been done, and to whom, and why. Once that had been done, I was my silly self again. It was a close call, and to emerge finally unscathed a kind of miracle. Having been through it, I marvel that anything ever goes right. Rage is in the air we breathe, and to be free after twelve hours' imprisonment is to know what that kind of freedom really means. [. . .]

Love,
Amy

. . . .

22 August 1970
Dear Rimsa—

[. . .] My main concern lately has been with the housing crisis—trying to stop evictions for speculative purposes, and most recently getting arrested with a group of squatters whom he helped move into a vacant building on Fifteenth Street. There is nothing like getting arrested together to bring a feeling of unity, and though extremely exhausting (I had very little sleep for three nights running before we were all thrown out), it was also a lot of fun. We may have won a victory in spite of being thrown out (the squatters are now in another vacant building owned by the city, where they are being allowed to stay for the time being), but in order to keep negotiations open there have to be repeated demonstrations, plus meetings almost every evening to plan new actions. I'm also going to briefing sessions on the new rent control law, so called although it appears to herald the end of rent control and of what may turn out to be administrative chaos so far as housing is concerned.

It's a little bit like living a page out of Camus—or I think that's what it's like, having had *The Myth of Sisyphus* for years without being able to get through it: everything that could go wrong seems to be doing so, and you don't expect to accomplish much, but there is a peculiar happiness in banding together and refusing to take it all lying down. So much has been going on that I haven't gotten out of the city—unless you count a bus trip one night out to Far Rockaway, to picket a recalcitrant landlord on his own doorstep—since early June, when I joined a lobbying trip to Washington and spent a couple of days telling Congressmen what we thought of the invasion of Cambodia. It may be that I'll get away for a couple of days at the beach this next week, to get some sun and have another go at Camus. Thanks very much, meanwhile, for the issues of the *Atlantic*; I read the article about Kissinger, which was interesting, and will get to *Mr. Sammler's Planet* one of these days.

Love,

Amy

. . . .

25 September 1970

Dear Barbara—

[. . .] You guessed it. I've now been in jail, the honest-to-God lockup, and what's more that was my second arrest. The first time, there were so many women with children that they herded us all into a City bus and kept us there all morning (three helmeted policemen in the back looking silly, plus a couple of policewomen looking mean) while they made up the papers. It's the squatters' movement I'm into these days, and the main satisfaction is the feeling that it's doing something positive, if temporary, on behalf of people who have been officially pushed around for years. The building I first helped people move into is now the subject of negotiations with the City and the landlord, and it begins to seem that the squatters are going to be allowed to live there. The other is a different scene; the landlord is part of a really rotten outfit who are buying up buildings all over the Village and emptying them of tenants by all sorts of ugly means simply as a speculative operation. So there have been no negotiations, and we are probably going to have a full-scale trial in December (charges against most of us the first time were dropped). Also, that second time, I got the feel of what jail is like—we were there only part of a day, but that is long enough and grim enough, even for a high-spirited crew. We were joined toward the end by four prostitutes, one of whom was a good-natured sort who was feeling good and soon had us all listening in fascination to her account of how they do business. There were several Women's Lib types in the crowd, and they get along well with prostitutes. Meeting people is a great thing about all these operations. There is more education going on than in four years of college, just getting into things. So I can well understand Joanie's dissatisfaction. I hope she can find her way into something satisfying.

Reading over the quotation from my letter, I don't wonder that it made no sense. It *was* important, though, and it was on my mind when I wrote and so it got in in that cryptic form. What happened was that Hal and I had dinner with a couple he knew and I hadn't met—an old school friend of his who is now a psychiatrist up in the suburbs, and the friend's wife. I knew nothing at all about the background or anything more than this; but feeling very relaxed and open, I promptly got into some kind of political argument with the psychiatrist, the exact sequence of which I've now forgotten—except that at one point Hal echoed a remark by his friend to the effect that I was biased, whereupon I felt cornered and angry and showed it without saying a word. At this point we were on the sidewalk on our way to a restaurant, and Hal, who is very sensitive about such things, fell back with me to ask what was the matter and I told him I was hurt. So he told the two others to go on to the restaurant, and we walked around the block while I told him I thought he had been unfair, and he acknowledged that it was so. This was the first time I can remember that I've produced such an incident in the company of people I'd never met before. Quite naturally, the other two were put on edge by it, even though we were both composed and shrugged the whole thing off when we went to join them. And from then on the evening was one unmitigated misery. By the time we left the restaurant I was close to tears again, after another attack by the psychiatrist, in which his wife sided with him—earlier she had seemed to take my side in the arguments, or anyhow I had felt she agreed with me in a general way—an attack followed by one of those absolutely crushing *coups de grâce*—"Amy, we need *more* people with your idealism" (read, as targets and scratching-posts for other people's hard-nosed-realist aggression) that only hostile people know how to deliver. By this time Hal was totally on my side, and I knew it, but by the time we were finally rid of the other two and had breathed a sigh of relief, we were also both so upset that we ended up quarreling. The thing was, or seemed to be, finally resolved— but the next day it broke out again, in a form that took on the camouflage of my being so depressed over the state of the world that I simply couldn't stop crying. I remember Hal's saying maybe it was time I went to a psychiatrist, and my wondering if it had come to that while declaring that he *knew* I couldn't afford it. It wasn't until I was on my way out to a party I had said I would help with, where he was supposed to join me later, and to which neither of us now had any wish to go, that we got down to what the trouble really was. I finally deciphered my depression as unassuaged anger, and the tears as the mode the anger took in paying him back for hurting me—even though I already knew he acknowledged that he had done it and was genuinely sorry. (This is one of the many beautiful things about Hal—that he can be sorry without any defensiveness, any urge to hit back.) And then, finally, he told me several things which his natural discretion—another beautiful thing about him—had kept him from mentioning. One was that the same kind of thing had happened a few years ago, when his psychiatrist friend had made the same kind of attack on a young girl whom Hal had brought to meet them. That led to the conclusion that his friend really had some kind of thing against women, and also that attacking a woman companion was in fact an indirect attack on Hal himself, for reasons that don't need to be gone into for purposes of this discussion. Having cleared away that much emotional confusion, we were finally both calm enough to go to the party together, have a good time, and discover afterward that harmony had been restored. What I had discovered so vividly was how hard it is to be entirely truthful, even with the best will and with those one cares most about. What so often seems to happen is that unassuaged anger goes on festering for weeks, months, even years. That was what my remark about rage being in the air we breathe was all about. I have lived through several long sieges of that kind of rage, and I know other people who have. Truthfulness between people is so very seldom complete; and yet if there is not complete truthfulness, there can hardly be complete trust. And the reason truthfulness between people is so rare is that it is even harder to be completely honest with oneself. I never really expected to meet and be close to anyone who made truthfulness easier, the way Hal does. This isn't to say that we don't quarrel, or that it isn't painful when we do; but thus far the quarreling has been bearable because there has been some way of resolving it other than mere armed truce.

The switch in typewriters indicates a lapse of forty-eight hours, during which the newsletter has been run off, the weather has changed from unseasonably hot to seasonably cool, and a busload of us have made an odd Sunday-afternoon expedition into the borough of Queens to picket the five bad brothers whose real-estate firm had us thrown out of the last building we moved squatters into. We took along a coolerful of Sangria, Pepsi and milk for the kids, a hamperful of sandwiches, and a sheaf of signs, and on the way out we composed new lyrics to our repertory of housing-action songs—e.g.

There are five bad landlords
Kalimian is their name;
Elias lives in this house—
SHAME, SHAME, SHAME!

The song originated with one of the crew as he was climbing into the paddy wagon the day we were arrested, and begins:

> We want decent housing,
> At rents we can afford,
> And if we don't get it,
> OFF THE LA-ANDLORD!

We'd sung it all the way to the precinct house, inside the precinct house, and all the way down to criminal court where we were locked up, to what we like to think of as the discomfiture of the cops.

We discovered that two of the five villains had moved to grander places, farther out on Long Island, and the other three were conspicuously not at home; but the neighbors were surprisingly sympathetic. One told us that the landlord family next door had been expecting us (there had been a story in *The Village Voice* mentioning our plans, among other things) and had fled to avoid a confrontation; one actually made a contribution to our treasury. It was a demonstration—if that is even the word—totally unlike any other I've been a party to. Everything was so quiet among those winding suburban roads, those masses of trees and shrubbery and pseudo-Tudor architecture nesting among them, that it subdued even us; there was hardly a soul to be seen (for one thing, the day had turned cool and rainy), and we had the feeling that we were the first real excitement to intrude since the houses went up. [. . .]
Love,
Amy

. . . .

29 December 1970
Dear Rimsa—
Thank you very much for *Soul on Ice*. It would be an interesting document even if he weren't as good a writer as he is—and at his best he is also very much my own kind of writer. Prison documents in general have acquired a particular meaning for me, I think since I last wrote; anyhow, as a result of another move-on, I have had the experience of spending several hours in jail. Relatively speaking, we were well treated—the women's section of the Criminal Courts building is far less crowded than the men's, and for most of our stay the twelve of us females who'd been arrested together had no company but our own. Toward the end we were joined by

four hookers, one of whom was smart and cheerful and soon had us all listening with rapt attention to her account of how things go in that trade. Since several of the people in our party were into Women's Liberation, whose hallmark is solidarity with anything female, the rapport was excellent. We were there long enough to sample the fare, and it was so dreadful that I wonder anyone survives; and even in those four hours the sense of being cut off from the world was acute and did something to our attitudes, the result of which was that we behaved and felt generally like kids in the second grade being kept after school. Seeing forty or fifty people we knew when we were finally led into the courtroom was sweet, and made it easier for our attorneys to get us off on our own recognizances, with no bail. The case finally came to court just a couple of weeks ago, and we got off unscathed—guilty of a reduced plea, with no criminal record or anything like that. In the meantime there have been more actions, though the policy now is not to get arrested—and at least some of the people we helped move in are apparently going to be allowed to stay, or anyhow be given some kind of decent housing. The official policy has now reached the proportions of a scandal, with hundreds of families being put up, on taxpayers' money, in firetrap hotels that charge by the head, $5.50 per day. As a result of his handling of this, and of the situation in the city jails, I've lost all faith in Mayor Lindsay. For the time being, though, I'm deeper into politics than ever: the insurgent faction is pretty much in control of the Reform Democratic club I joined back in the days of the McCarthy campaign and have been involved with ever since—you remember the party I took you to; it's those people—and the arch-housing-activist has just been elected president, which means that a good deal of my spare time for the next year will be going in that direction. So there hasn't been much time for writing or reflection—though I did manage a piece of verse that I'll send along—or even for planned-ahead entertainment such as going to the theater. The main thing in that department lately was being taken to hear Beverly Sills in *Lucia*—an absolutely gripping performance, quite aside from the ravishing things she does with her voice. [. . .]

For Christmas I finally got as far as Boston, where it snowed almost continually and it was a pleasure to be inside watching it come down, or out walking through the lovely muffled stillness of it. There was also the pleasure of finding out that the younger generation, even out in suburbia, are just as *simpatico* as I like to imagine, and as Charles Reich finds them. He—though most of us have only read the excerpt from *The Greening of America* in the *New Yorker*, if that—and Kate Millett and Ramsey Clark

are the writers people I know are talking about these days. I met Ramsey Clark, as a matter of fact; he has taken an apartment in the Village, and there are people promoting him as a presidential candidate. He seemed to me very genuine, and his book confirmed the impression. [. . .]
Love,
Amy

. . . .

12 February 1971

Mr. Henry Kissinger
The White House
Washington, D.C.

Dear Mr. Kissinger:
This letter is prompted by an acute sense of distress, and of foreboding amounting almost to despair, over the extension of the Indochina war into Laos. It is addressed to you rather than to the President—to whom I have written on other occasions, and received no more than the standard acknowledgement from someone in the Department of State—because of a statement of yours which I have just now come across, quite by accident, in a volume entitled *No More Vietnams?*, and consisting of statements made at a meeting in June 1968 by a number of distinguished scholars and former government officials. To refresh your memory further, I take the liberty of quoting:

"It is a source of infinite wonder to me how General Westmoreland, for example, could continue to come back every time repeating exactly the same phrases, impervious to the lessons that were learned. The official military line for as long as I can remember is that the Viet Cong meant to cut the country into two pieces. Now, why should they want to do that when they already have cut it into fifty pieces? . . . Our blindness here really reflects the predominance of our traditional concepts, under which you measure success and failure by the control of territories. . . . Vietnam is more than a failure of policy. It is really a very critical failure of the American philosophy of international relations. . . . When one is asked for advice, the constant American tendency has been to respond by looking for a gimmick. Every year we had a new program in Vietnam, and we have carried out each program with the obsessive certainty that it was the ultimate solution to the problem. . . . I feel that we have to make a really prayerful assessment of what we went in there for, not to pin blame on any people or particular set of conditions but to assess the whole procedure and concepts that us involved there. . . . "

It is hard not to wonder, given the continued programs of destruction in Vietnam and the accelerated destruction in Laos—not to mention the entry into Cambodia and the suffering inflicted there on the people of a neutral country—given that continued destruction, is it possible that the "prayerful assessment" of which you spoke has in fact been made, now that you are in a position to deal with the matters of policy? And if it has been made, why have our troops not been withdrawn—or, at the very least, why has no timetable of withdrawal been offered? Since recent public opinion polls indicate that a majority of Americans now favors some such timetable, even the argument that the problem is one of public reaction at home seems hardly applicable. Is it asking too much to wonder whether you even remember what you once said about a failure of the American philosophy of international relations? Or to wonder whether, as an intellectual, you have encountered the kind of thinking offered by Lewis Mumford when he observes that " . . . unfortunately our time has produced many . . . who have been willing to do at a safe distance, with napalm or atom bombs . . . what the exterminators at Belsen and Auschwitz did by old-fashioned handicraft methods. The latter were slower in execution, but far more thrifty in carefully conserving the by-products—the human wastes, the gold from the teeth, the fat, the bone mean for fertilizers—even the skin for lampshades. In every country, there are now countless Eichmanns in administrative offices, in business corporations, in universities, in laboratories, in the armed forces: orderly obedient people, ready to carry out any officially sanctioned fantasy, however dehumanized and debased . . . "

It has been suggested by some observers that one of the reasons for the accelerated bombing of Laos since November 1968 is simply that with the bombing of North Vietnam at an end, it gave pilots who would otherwise have been unemployed something to do. I am not being facetious about this. If there was a better reason, I should like to know what it was—once the bombing of Laos was admitted to taking place at all—that it was necessary to interdict the flow of supplies along the Ho Chi Minh trail. Now we are told that a ground invasion is necessary because the supplies were still getting through—in short, the bombing had not achieved its objective. It is very hard to be patient with this kind of reasoning. And it would never have occurred to me to write one more letter to a high public official had it not been for your thoughtful assessment in 1968 of the problem that is now your especial concern.

What is the concept that guides our policy in Vietnam? Is there a new policy? Or is there a policy at all to explain what has been done to the people of Vietnam and Laos and Cambodia? If there is some member of your staff who is not content to be one of Mr. Mumford's administrative Eichmanns, I should deeply appreciate the courtesy of a reply.
Sincerely Yours,
Amy Clampitt

. . . .

1 August 1971
Dear Barbara—
[. . .] Hal sailed for Europe about ten days ago, and I'm discovering what it's like to miss the simple presence of somebody. (It's ironic, isn't it, after years of being really On One's Own.) He didn't want me to go with him, and I really didn't want to go—or I would have, on my own. The idea of being a tourist has ceased to be attractive, and there are just too many of us over there anyhow. But he hadn't been abroad since his honeymoon, sixteen years ago, and needed to be dislodged, and will probably have a good time. It's not so much a matter of being dependent that makes me miss him—at least I hope it's not—as that being around him has the effect of expanding who I am, rather than diminishing and curtailing it as close associations so often do. That is what is so marvelous about him. And so I'm feeling vaguely amputated, and not liberated one bit. [. . .]

Guess what—my father was given an Honorary Doctorate of Humane Letters at Grinnell! This spring was his sixtieth commencement reunion—and my thirtieth, horrid thought. I went out for Commencement itself, to see him get the degree. It was for his work with the American Friends Service Committee, especially with resettling refugees. Joe Wall read the citations, and I had a chance to talk with him briefly afterward. He was looking really better than when we were students. Also I saw Henry Laden, who is librarian there now. My nephew David was just winding up his second year there—taking Math and Russian, doing a special project on Camus, and earning money playing violin in the Des Moines symphony—and it was a joy to see him. There were several nonconformists who didn't wear caps and gowns, others (my father spotted them in the procession, or I wouldn't have known) who went barefoot, and altogether a prettier lot of girls I think I never saw.

I didn't stick around for the class reunion, which I'm not sure I would have been up to anyhow—though having reported going to join as my contribution to society has brought up my stock in a perverse sort of way. I really think it was that that finally got me over *my* inability to get up and say anything to an audience. As though it were a shorthand kind of identity: Oh, she's the one that keeps getting arrested. I forget if you will have heard about the third arrest, but I guess not. It was relatively unpremeditated—happened back in February, when some welfare families took over a not-quite-finished apartment building intended for middle-income residents, and a couple of us who'd come in with them discovered five black mothers who weren't leaving (they'd been living in one of those Welfare Hotels, which you will have heard about) and decided they could use some company. We never went to jail, thank goodness, but were kept at the police precinct for long enough that I got pretty obstreperous. When the case finally came up in courts, we got off again with minor guilty pleas, free to get into more mischief whenever we chose—and the defense attorney gave a statement that made the whole courtroom sit up and take notice. Eventually the mothers got apartments in public housing, but not without a long sojourn in a church basement that I won't go into because it is so depressing.

I have been reading Lewis Mumford's *Pentagon of Power*—a project that occupied me piecemeal over more than six months—and think he has more to say than just about anybody else who is writing these days. More recently, I've discovered the poetry of Sylvia Plath. Very disturbing but also very, very good. Do you know her, I wonder? I may include a copy of a piece I wrote to get the disturbance out of my system. The last one before that dates to January, and goes like this:

AT THE WELFARE HEARINGS

In other ages too, men were afraid
of her, and hid her image in a shrine
they said was holy. She was Hera then
or Mary—goddess or mother of a god,
not this lost object found and exhibited
to score a point before the microphone
where scurrying bureaucrats assemble. On
her lap her youngest looks already old.

Unjeweled ikon, scandal at the heart
of splendor's ruin, worn expressionless
by the long fraud that spans the centuries,

she sits and holds her baby. Others shout,
"They're using her!" Past hope, past righteousness
she endures, too tired even to accuse.

[This poem found its way into Clampitt's small chapbook, *Multitudes, Multitudes*, published in 1973.] That was a particular welfare mother, at hearings called by Congressman Koch. Not all of them are so passive.

The gloom is closing in outside again, for the third time today. Do write.
Love,
Amy

. . . .

14 November 1971
Dear Barbara—
I guess my friends Sara and Steve Clapp gave you a general idea of what happened on Tuesday. I'd tried to phone you that morning, but no luck, and on Wednesday we were on our way back to New York before the working day ended—free on condition that we get out of Washington and stay away until December 10, when we're scheduled to go on trial. The only way to avoid that would be to send in $25 collateral between now and the first of December, which I have no intention of doing—so I'll hope to have better luck seeing you then. The Clapps will put me up— they have a spare bed, and Sara will be hurt if I don't accept their hospitality. But there ought to be time to see you. This time I'm planning ahead, instead of just appearing.

The whole experience proved eminently worth going through—including a night in the D.C. jail, sleeping four in a four-by-eight-foot cell. Altogether there were about forty of us women, and a somewhat larger number of men. The morale was still bubbling next morning, when they transferred us to the courthouse lockup to wait for arraignment. The Park Police who arrested us were generally decorous and even friendly. The worst moment came during the processing—altogether, it took six hours to dispose of the whole crowd—and I realized that I was about to have my fingerprints taken. After that, even the mug shot—full face and profile, with the numbers around your neck—wasn't too upsetting. (New York criminal courts are less efficient and also much more disagreeable.) And the thing we got arrested for—lying as if dead for half an hour in front of the White House gate, surrounded by other bodies, and watching the cloud formation overhead—was restful and even happy. It wasn't until I'd been back in New York overnight that I discovered how tired I was. A lovely, lovely lot of people were what made the difference.

Did I write you that the *New York Times* published my "Existential Choice" poem? I got twenty-five dollars for it—the check was waiting in my mailbox when I got home. [. . .]

Love,

Amy

. . . .

9 January 1974

Dear Rimsa—

[. . .] My father died on the 16th of December, quite serenely after dictating a farewell message to my youngest brother. Since there was no hope of his recovery, it was better this way; toward the end, he simply stopped eating. Though he must have been in considerable pain, and undoubtedly was when I saw him the last time, his way of dealing with the end made it much easier for the rest of us. My mother is now settled in a home for the elderly which appears much less dreadful than such places in this part of the world, and having three brothers made all the necessary arrangements less burdensome. The memorial service, done Quaker fashion as a silent meeting, had its cheerful recollections along with the solemnity.

But as a result, I got back to New York after the second trip to Iowa in less than a month (all the way by bus both times) with a large index to finish and an editing job behind schedule because of that. I finally caught up only yesterday, having worked fairly steadily through both holidays—which was just as well, since I found that I wasn't in the mood for celebrations. But I did enjoy the trips by bus. It's a way of having solitude without feeling like a recluse—in fact, when the weather turns snowy and schedules get fouled up, things aboard become very sociable indeed.

Some of my best ideas seem to come while I'm traveling somewhere. [. . .]

Love,

Amy

. . . .

8 January 1975

Dear Rimsa—

[. . .] For me, 1975 began in something of a whirl of being sociable. I spent Christmas very quietly in New York, roasting a duck for Hal, who is my chief companion nowadays, and playing records. (I'd gone to Boston earlier in December to help my brother and his wife celebrate their twenty-fifth wedding anniversary, with a reunion of the original wedding party, or most of it, and a little side trip to join a demonstration in downtown Boston—almost like the old peace movement days, but not quite.) After going to a series of parties, Hal and I gave one ourselves on New Year's Eve—just eight people, but we fed them so it was something of a project, with my first try at Chinese cooking (shrimp with onions, celery, green peppers, and carrots, stir-fried, and a great success), a salad of endive, watercress, and walnuts, and a frozen lemon soufflé. The mixture of guests was a bit experimental too—a civil court judge and his wife, a cousin of Hal's and her schoolteacher husband, who happens to be black, a very young friend of ours who's studying philosophy at Brown and a friend of hers whom we hadn't met, who'd spent a year studying classics in Athens and hopes to go back. It turned out to be a successful evening. Then, just a few days later, we gave an after-concert party for Igor Kipnis, the harpsichordist whose wife is an old friend of mine, and who was making his debut with the New York Philharmonic. Since Hal's apartment is just across Central Park from Lincoln Center, it seemed a logical place to gather afterward. The artist got a steak (he doesn't eat dinner before a concert) and for the rest, there was spinach quiche (my own recipe) and something called Esau's Mess of Pottage, which I found in a Metropolitan Museum cookbook—lentils, rice, and onions all cooked up together, with raw vegetables around the edge. That's the kind of cooking I'm into these days—lentils, salads, home-made granola. The concert was a success, with good reviews all round—the Fifth Brandenburg Concerto, with a long, rarely played cadenza for the harpsichord, a de Falla concerto for harpsichord, flute, oboe, and I forget what else, and finally a Bartok symphony without harpsichord—but Avery Fisher Hall is bad acoustically, and we were in one of the worst spots.

Just before the holidays, I acquired a long black cape with a red silk lining, made for me by a friend who has a dressmaking shop on the Lower East Side—or what people now call the East Village. We'd gotten to know each other in one of my series of short-lived group projects—the neighborhood government one—and have kept in touch. The cape is pretty spectacular, and great fun to go swooping around in. To go with it, I found a pair of purple suede boots on sale—last year's style, apparently—and now I have all the clothes I need for a while. Except that I may try making a patchwork skirt out of scraps I never discarded, and having made a series of patchwork pillows for various people, I'm intrigued by the notion of doing something more complicated. I'm also in the process of getting ready to repaint my apartment—patching plaster, scraping old paint, et cetera. After mid-January, I go back to work on the Franklin project; meanwhile, I'm earning a living with a couple of editing jobs. I'm going to the country tomorrow to work on them while Hal grades exam papers.

So that's what I've been into lately. I can't remember exactly what I wrote before Christmas, but it was probably gloomy because I always am around that time. As soon as the days begin getting longer, I begin feeling better, though there certainly can't be any objective reason, these days. My rent has gone up again and prices in the supermarkets are dreadful, but thus far my own fortunes haven't suffered the way some people's have. I haven't read nearly as many books lately as you have. The latest recent one has been *All God's Dangers*, an Alabama sharecropper's memoirs as taped and edited by Theodore Rosengarten—a marvelous piece of history. I'm writing to a prisoner in Florida. My first prison correspondent, a native of Brooklyn, is now out on parole and at last word had a couple of part-time jobs and was pretty together. [. . .]

I enjoyed hearing about Xanthippe. I love cats and a lot of people I know own them, so I have the fun of being around them without the responsibility of another mouth to feed.

Love,

Amy

. . . .

6 February 1975

Dear Barbara—

[. . .] The visit to my Congressman was rather more appalling than I'd expected. My companions were three rather shaggy young men, and that one was a veteran and another had an Italian name and an impeccably working-class background didn't help in the least—the Congressman's distaste was evident from the moment he let us in, after letting us wait for half an hour while he conferred with an aide. The conversation was all non sequiturs, but the burden of it was that he supports Henry Kissinger and the Pentagon, recession or no recession. I'd halfway expected him to have concluded enough had gone to Indochina by now, but no such thing. From there we went to a gathering on the Capitol steps, where the sunshine only added to the same feeling of militant coziness at the church the night before. Pete Seeger was there, and I happened to be near enough to see him and people like Joan Baez and her ex-husband David Harris, and a whole raft of Congresspeople, really well. We wound up singing *Kumbaya*—or however in the world you spell it—and holding hands and swaying, row by row, in the best Sixties-rally fashion. Then I caught a bus back to New York, and I don't know where the time has gone since then, except for seeing *Scenes from a Marriage* and another expedition to Chinatown with Hal and Oriental friends. I came away with some ginger and a bagful of bean sprouts, and my experiments with stir-fry cooking continue. [. . .]

Love,

Amy

. . . .

12 May 1975

Dear Rimsa—

You're quite right about being entitled to something a little more explicit about Hal. How to categorize what's going on isn't easy, though, partly because we're both just wary enough of institutionalizing not to have settled on a category. I guess we mainly think of ourselves as Best Friends. He was married once and hated it, and (like more and more women nowadays) I realized some time ago that I really don't want to be anybody's wife; also, his parents are Orthodox Jewish and there is a terrible mishegass about their notion of the way things should be. But we seem to be together more and more of the time. He teaches at Columbia Law School and is working in his spare time on a massive scholarly opus, and in June we'll be going to Maine again, for the entire month, to work on our respective projects and keep track of the tide.

About lentils: I've discovered that cooked with onion, carrot, celery, and tomatoes, with a bay leaf and a few cloves for seasoning, they're delicious; and there are various other permutations. I've never yet done them with the standard ham bone, but sometimes boil the broth out of leftover chicken bones and use that as a base. Combined with brown rice, they become a better source of protein. Esau's Mess of Pottage is very simple: you boil a cup or so of lentils for fifteen or twenty minutes in a quart or more of water, add an equal amount of brown rice and boil the whole thing for another half hour or more, or until the ingredients are done, cook a cupful of chopped or sliced onions in a generous amount of oil until they're transparent, mix the whole thing together and chill it well (salt and pepper to taste). There are all kinds of seasoning possibilities in the way of herbs and spices, and you could add lemon juice and make a sort of salad.

About granola: it never comes out twice the same, but the general idea goes like this: you pour about a third of a cup of peanut or corn oil into a large baking pan with an equal amount of honey, add a generous pinch of salt and a teaspoon of vanilla extract, and heat and stir the whole thing over a flame until it gets thin; then you stir in (in approximately that order) a cupful of sesame seeds; a cupful of sunflower seeds; a cupful of soy grits or soy nuts (for nutritional purposes; I don't think they add anything to the flavor); two cups of untoasted wheat germ; a cupful of unsweetened grated coconut (*or* sweetened, but it's expensive); a handful, around 1/4 cup, of chopped raw cashew nuts (I've used almonds and walnuts too, but cashews taste best); and around four cups of rolled oats. Mix it ingredient by ingredient, so that the first dry ones in are fairly well coated with the wet ingredients, and bake in a 350 oven for around an hour, taking the pan out to stir everything carefully, so as to brown it evenly, every ten or fifteen minutes. The cape isn't quite as fluid as the picture, being quite heavy, but I'm flattered to be imagined in anything so dashing. One of these days I'll have a snapshot of me in it so you can get a less romantic idea of the actuality. Meanwhile, I'll enclose a new poem, just hatched. It's about an aunt of mine who died not long ago.

You're more into new books than I am. The latest I've gotten to have been *Sphere* by A. R. Ammons—a real discovery—and *Zen and the Art of Motorcycle Maintenance* by Robert Pirsig, which is unclassifiable and in fact indescribable, a real trip in more than one sense of the word. [. . .]
Love,
Amy

. . . .

Ship Chandlery
Corea, Maine

23 June 1975
Dear Rimsa—
The parcel containing the record arrived just as I was getting ready to leave for Maine, and I brought it along unopened. As it happens, we also brought along my portable stereo, so we were able to listen to it when the day arrived, with Hal exclaiming over what a nice present it was, and me concurring. We especially liked e.e. cummings and Allen Ginsberg—

cummings as being the most stylish reader and Ginsberg because whatever he does, he is completely himself. Some people say he's not a poet for this reason—the definition of poetry having lost all coherence these days—but even though I am rather in sympathy with the school of thinking that produced the judgment, I do like Ginsberg most of the time, and in the poem on the record he is absolutely at his best. Thank you very much.

It's just after eight a.m. on this Monday morning, and breakfast is long over, the housekeeping chores attended to, such as they are, and I've been outside to gather daisies, buttercups, orange hawkweed, red clover, and assorted other things growing just outside the door. It's like that up here—the exceptional thing about this morning being that it's already warm. Up until the middle of last week, fog, rain, and chilly weather in various sequences had been the rule, and layers of sweaters the obligatory costume. When the sun came out for a while, we would venture off on a small expedition in the immediate vicinity—to Cranberry Point, which is all wind and surf and exposed rock, with a stretch of tundra behind it, or to a small uninhabited island that can be reached only at low tide, via a strip of sand and shingle beach, where we've found a delightful little moss-cushioned perch underneath a lone spruce tree that is perfect for picnics, with a view of the sandbar so we won't forget and find ourselves marooned. On less inviting days, we've made short expeditions by car, exploring side roads and the little towns up the coast. This past weekend, we took the ferry across the Bay of Fundy to Nova Scotia and did some exploring over there. The high point was Grand Pre, which is so totally unlike anything I'd seen or been expecting hereabouts that I found myself thinking of Paestum and the ruined temple of Hera on the island of Samos. It's actually below sea level, with dikes holding off the sea at high tide, very still and a bit sad. It's also very French, with a little church built of dark stone rising among alleys of neatly clipped hedge, poplars and very old willow trees, with an apple orchard and the most gorgeous flowering borders I ever saw. The whole thing is a national monument, and whoever maintains it must really love the place. All around are prosperous-looking farms and more orchards, and what looked like local people were coming with picnic baskets just to stretch out on the grass and relax, as we did for an hour or two before reluctantly moving on. We stayed overnight and spent part of a day in Halifax, which is a real city and very attractive, but the best thing about the whole trip was getting back to Corea—where to a series of astonishing light effects, including the spectral one on foggy nights when the almost-extinguished lights across the inlet reminded me of an Albert Ryder moonscape, we now added our first sight of the open sea glimmering in the distance in the light of an actual full moon.

In the midst of all this, I've been getting work done, believe it or not. There are no distractions other than those of the place itself, and there are times when spending a day indoors at the typewriter is the pleasantest thing imaginable—such as the day when a southeast gale blew all day long, making the house creak like a ship at sea. The one local event since we got here has been a rummage sale last week, at which a food counter was featured. Remembering your report of finds at rummage sales—I hadn't been to one in I don't know when—as well as seeing it as offering a glimpse of the working of the community, I made a point of going. Though I arrived too late for the home-made pies—it seemed somehow a bit forward to be waiting outside the Grange Hall when the doors opened—I did find a couple of shirts in my size (one of them a boy's, and those are the best kind) and a cotton velour pullover for all of $1.40, as well as a brief look at a local function.

Meanwhile, we hear rumors that the heat in New York is breaking all records—not to mention the fiscal crisis, which people up here do tend to bring up, but which to us seems quite unreal and certainly not worth discussing—and it is hard to believe that we're ever going back there. We've gotten a week's extension of our stay, since the next tenants aren't arriving until later, so we'll be here until July 7! [. . .]
Love,
Amy

. . . .

19 December 1975
Dear Rimsa—
A parcel from you has arrived safely, and I hope for the same for a small one for you mailed from St. Cloud, Minnesota, while I was visiting my brother out there, earlier this month. My brother took care of it, at one of those twenty-four-hour do-it-yourself post office windows that seem to proliferate out there. I suppose the reason I don't quite trust them is that I saw how the latest in computerized banking worked in that town: you put a card into a slot, punch some code letters, and supposedly have money delivered to you—only the money wasn't forthcoming until some scurrying bank employees were called upon. Otherwise, though, it's a nice town—prairie landscape, lots of snow, ranch-style houses, healthy kids—and it's only a little over an hour from Minneapolis, which looks good and is vouched for by all kinds of people. I only saw it from the window of a Greyhound bus. Minnesota was the second stop on a little tour of the Midwest, catching up with various branches of the family. The first was

in Ferndale, Michigan, a suburb of Detroit, where my youngest brother and his family live—including my niece Holly, who is now nine and a great personality—loves trolls and penguins, has strong opinions on just about everything (purple, orange, and pink are her favorite colors, and the day I arrived she had managed to get them all into one ensemble), composes impromptu on the piano, and was quite equal to a tour of the Hermitage paintings from Leningrad, which happened to be at the Detroit museum, and, wonderful in a Clampitt, isn't at all shy. I don't know what in the world she is going to grow up into, but I am finding her as (the youngest Clampitt) interesting as her cousin David, who is now in New York studying violin at Manhattan School of Music.—Anyhow, from Minnesota I took another bus to Des Moines, for a visit with my mother and sister. My mother isn't very well, and living in a nursing home isn't the greatest life imaginable; but her friends are there, including a couple of great people she's gotten to know right there. Since I came back, it seems that the house where my parents lived in Des Moines, which is a regional headquarters of the American Friends Service Committee, has been blown up, presumably by a bomb—though who can have planted it isn't at all clear. Things do get weirder and weirder. But while I was out there, the Midwest seemed quite peaceful, and I enjoyed riding buses through that wide-open landscape.

The New York Public Library Christmas card isn't an accident. It occurred to me that because a good deal of my working life over the past year and a half had been spent there, this was a cause worth supporting to that extent. The main event of the past six months was finally winding up the Franklin project; the research is finished, the book is written, and all would be well except that there has been some sort of shakeup at Simon & Schuster and there is no telling whether they will publish it or not, notwithstanding the auction and the whopping advance involved. Publishing is in a bad way these days, and conglomerates are buying up publishing houses right and left; Gulf & Western now owns S&S. It's a good book, though, so it would be nice to have the whole thing straightened out. When and if, anyhow, it's to be called *Benjamin Franklin: Agent of the Revolution*, and David Schoenbrun is the author.

Hal has a half-year sabbatical beginning very shortly, and if current plans go forward, we are going to Europe in the spring. We have space on the *Leonardo da Vinci* —one of the few transatlantic liners still operating, and then only for a few crossings—for the 28th of March, and if it's not too expensive we may spend a couple of months over there, revisiting

places like Italy and England and exploring others new to both of us, such as Vienna and Amsterdam. But given the times, one never knows. [. . .]
Love,
Amy

. . . .

5 January 1977
Dear Rimsa—
The first letter of the new year—which may suggest the kind of holiday season it's been, and why I've been so long in acknowledging your Christmas remembrance. The parcel arrived safely some time ago, just as I was about to leave for Iowa on a visit to my mother—though I waited until Christmas eve to open it. I was reminded of the bow you were wearing in your hair the day you first came to Audubon House. No, I know it's not the same one, but it does look like you, as it does like me. Very becoming, in fact, and I'm pleased to have it. Thank you very much. [. . .]
Once I was back in New York, I found myself just a little bit busier than I needed to be, if not busier than I've ever been in my life, with a couple of editing projects. The result was that the holidays went next to ignored. Hal came down here for supper on Christmas Eve, and we built a fire and read aloud from Isaiah, as a sort of Jewish-Christian compromise. On New Year's Eve he read to me from *Little Dorrit* (reading aloud from Dickens is a sort of continuing project, since we spent a winter doing *Bleak House*, several years ago). But I was asleep by ten-thirty from sheer fatigue, and back at work on my manuscript early the next day. The current one is a big book by Peter Farb, whom you may remember from Audubon Society days, called *The Human Equation*. It has just about everything imaginable in it, and is a sort of natural history of the human species. The editing still isn't finished, but I'm near enough to the end to risk taking some time off to write letters. When that's done, I have some relatively small research projects to attend to before plunging into the next big one—reading about the French Underground during World War II for a new Schoenbrun Book. It will mean spending at least some weeks in Washington, going through documents from the OSS that are now in the National Archives. I wish I were more enthusiastic about spending all that time down there—it turns out that I'm just not keen on being away from New York, so I'll probably be coming back here for weekends. Arrangements for a place to stay remain be be made, though I have a few leads.

On the subway, and when snatching a free few minutes, I'm reading *The Mediterranean* by Fernand Braudel—a marvelous, dense, vivid, sweeping piece of history interwoven with geography. I've also read most of *Humboldt's Gift*, and liked it much the best of the Bellow novels I've read; *very* funny. I've hardly been to the theater or anything of that sort— partly because for a good deal of the fall I was still recuperating from the trouble in July (I think I wrote you about that), and then there was just too much to do. But Hal and I did see the National Theater of Greece when they were here in November, doing *Oedipus at Colonus* in modern Greek. Very grand and strange. [. . .]

Love,

Amy

. . . .

April 21, 1977

Dear Barbara—

I keep thinking of you, and wondering how the Sufis and the trees in Rock Creek Park are doing, and whether you've gone on any more expe- ditions to Sugar Mountain, and things like that—which spurs me finally to pull myself out of the vaguely disorganized ways I've fallen back into, at least to the extent of writing you a letter. We did have fun! The way I feel, is that I have another home to come back to. I hope that's all right.

How soon I'll be back in Washington remains unclear, since the xe- roxing at the Archives is evidently proceeding at its usual pace; I've got- ten just one small package, naturally of material I least need just now. Meanwhile, in my old disorganized way, I'm working on and off at the New York Public Library—as I explained to Mr. Newman over the phone when he begged to know where in the world I'd been. I've also done some wandering around, buying a lavender T-shirt and a new plant with pink-and-green leaves, and encouraging Hal in his long-deferred project of getting a little thinner around the middle. But after those clear- cut days of catching the bus with all the government people, morning and evening, I find it a bit difficult to account for where the time has gone. Understand, I'm not feeling guilty, just vague. Today I met with my man at Dutton, and the terms of the agreement have been set to everyone's satisfaction. I did say, on my own initiative, that I'd keep a record on my calendar of the days I put in for him; but at least I don't have to tot up totals of hours, as I've always had to do (or nearly always) in working for publishers.

The day after I got back, Hal and I went out to New Jersey (Milburn, to be precise, on the other side of Newark) to a dinner party. I found myself sitting next to what I understood was a famous constitutional lawyer, who was carrying on alarmingly about rounding up all the *animals* that are ripping off the little old ladies. After a while he put his arm around me and said, 'What do you think?" (From across the table, he'd been taken on by a vigorous opponent.) I said, "I'm a liberal," which disposed of that subject. Later, somebody told us that the noted constitutional lawyer had been, and perhaps still was, a Marxist. Which explains some of him, perhaps. He's also married to an Englishwoman who struck me as one of the most consummate snobs I ever met up with—which grieved me still more, since I don't like anybody giving England a bad name. Last Saturday we went to a rather different sort of party. It was given by one of Hal's law students, who is so rich that she simply took over a restaurant for the occasion, a place called Crawdaddy's, just west of Grand Central Station. There was a bar and you could get oysters at one end and Mexican food at the other; but we'd just had dinner, so I settled for a glass of white wine which I didn't finish. There was also a band, and pretty soon the place was so crowded that conversation became impossible. We stayed long enough to greet an old friend—the only person there I really knew—and got ourselves away. What I rather like about it is that I was wearing my espadrilles, and there were all these dressy people. (It's that New York thing I told you about; being underdressed is the best way of keeping one's perspective.) [. . .]

I've started reading *Simone Weil: A Life* by Simone Petrement—partly because Simone Weil had some small part in the French Resistance, mainly because I've been curious about her for a long time and came across a copy of the book at half price in the Strand Bookstore. I've also tidied up the poem I was struggling with on your typewriter when you came in on Palm Sunday. Here is the non-carbon copy:

PALM SUNDAY

Between the seasonal anarchies of upper air
and, underfoot, the sown constellations
of violet and periwinkle, the wild
tulip, poignant and sanguinary,
and dandelions blowsily unbuttoning,
grew up somehow, side by side

with order—the gardener's imperative—
the cultivated, peculiarly human taste
for committing martyrdom. Now, hardened
and lapidary, it embalms
the torturer's ingenuity, renders adorable
the horrid instruments of the Passion: never mind
whose howls, still not quite trembled under
by the feet of choirboys (sing,
my tongue, the glorious battle, sing
the winning of the fray) go on
out there among the olives,
applebloom, clipped boxwood, yew,
whitethorn, wych elm,
the gallows tree.

[One should compare this earlier version with the final, somewhat simpler, fourteen-line poem that appeared in *The Kingfisher.*]

But since getting it down, I've heard Elizabeth Bishop reading her poems and being interviewed on the radio—and she is so wonderful in a plain-as-an-old-shoe kind of way that I don't think so much of what I do. She has a new book, *Geography III*, which I've got to get, obviously. [. . .]

Love,
Amy

. . . .

Corea, Maine 04624

July 8, 1977 (I think)

Dear Barbara—

There is no excuse for this not writing you—none. The cartoon and clip-ping, with your characteristically self-effacing note, arrived safely, and there was no excuse then either. Especially since I think of you so much and so fondly, and a piece of me is still permanently lodged there on Con-necticut Avenue. We've been here nearly a week now, and are so settled in that it's as though we'd always lived here—though it's only this morn-ing that I've made myself get out the typewriter and open up communi-cations. For one thing, we're not getting any mail. Not even the *New York Times*, which we're *paying* to have sent. And it is a bit sheepish-making to arrive at the post office, beaming hopefully, and be told that there isn't anything. Better at least to bring something to be mailed. Of course the walk is good for us, and the weather has been so persistently bright and breezy that it's a crime *not* to be out walking. We're in what turns out to be a rather small house, very snug and busy with fishnet and the skeletal remains of starfish and sea urchins, plus all manner of what Hal refers to as Little Chotchkas (spelling probably off a little). Also oil paintings in large numbers; among many other things, our landlady does them. She also brings over things such as fresh-baked peanut-butter cookies and homemade wine. She is what her husband refers to as a "full-blooded Italian." He on the other hand is pure Yankee, and reminds me in many ways of my father. They have, of all things, a couple of goats. I could hardly believe it when, our first evening, I heard that small bleat from somewhere in the back. We're in sight of water, including a lighthouse and various islands, with woods at our back. There are lots of mosquitoes, but thus far no blackflies, the real horror of these parts. We've already pulled off a small adventure. Very early in the week, we started off on a walk and ended up crossing the exposed sandbar that turns our picnic island into a temporary peninsula. Discovering that the sandbar that connects it still more temporarily with yet another island, known as the Outer Bar, was above water, we achieved our ambition of getting onto it. After climbing around for a while, we suddenly realized that the tide was coming in and that our second sandbar was under water. For a few minutes we debated whether to stay and wait for the next low tide, subsisting on such wild strawberries as we might find, but then decided on getting our feet wet. For anybody else, all this may sound tame, but we're both so easily alarmed that we felt exceedingly intrepid. And our landlord made us feel more so by admitting that he'd been to the Outer Bar only twice himself. [. . .] We're reading *Little Dorrit*—still!—aloud, and I'm just about to finish the biography of Simone Weil that I've been reading off and on for weeks. I don't know of any twentieth-century figure I admire more. Do you know of her at all?

Actually, despite the bright weather I've gotten some work done— mainly editing a Dutton manuscript. Tonight we're going in to Ellsworth, the nearest real town, for a performance of *Così fan tutte*—after not being near the opera in New York for years. We seem to be living mainly on such things as blueberry pie, strawberry shortcake, and crabmeat—as being less bother than lobster and just as good. . . .

Love,
Amy

19 December 1977

Dear Rimsa—

Just how long ago it was when I wrote last, I can't be sure. Anyhow, in the meantime a package from you has arrived but not yet been opened, and one from me is on its way to you. I *hope* it may reach you in time for Christmas, and likewise that this will too—but mainly I hope that you're entirely recovered from you ordeal with shingles, and that things in general are as cheerful as may be for you and your mother. It is so hard to be old. My mother is eighty-six now, and remarkably well considering; but there is just no consolation possible for all the kinds of incapacitation that go with age. I saw her in August, when there was one of those super-family reunions—seventy people all told, and my mother the oldest one there. I made a hasty trip out to Iowa on the bus for the occasion, and enjoyed myself in spite of everything.

Hal and I spent the month of July in Corea, our hideaway on the coast of Maine—in a different house since the one we stayed in first has been sold—and have already spoken for still another one for next June. It was beautiful there in July, and what was a heat wave elsewhere meant simply a lot of bright, warm days—also a lot of wild blueberries to be had for the picking, so we lived on them, most notably in blueberry pancakes. But in many ways I still prefer June, when the summer people haven't yet arrived, and the spring flowers are still in bloom.

All through the fall, I was just busy enough—mainly with reading manuscripts for Dutton and editing a few of them—but not too busy to do something I'd been thinking about but never quite dared to, namely enroll in a poetry workshop at the New School. One is naturally a little uneasy about being cut down or in some way mortally wounded by such a thing; but it turned out not only to be fairly painless but stimulating in a way I would never have predicted. The instructor is a very young poet who is a bit of a jock and who I think disapproves of the kind of thing I do; we argue a lot, but there is enough mutual respect so we may manage to wind up the course as friends. He also writes plays, and last Saturday I went to hear a reading by a group who are considering one of his for a production—the first such thing I'd ever been to, and extremely interesting. The whole class also went to a poetry reading a few weeks back—Mark Strand was the featured reader, and very good indeed—and I'm wondering whether I may finally get up courage enough to try exposing my own work when there's occasion for it. Anyhow, I've been writing great quantities, even when there wasn't really time. I'll enclose a couple of samples.

"Cut Flowers" is from a series about my stay in the hospital a year and half ago. It's a sample of the kind of thing the workshop instructor doesn't really like: but some people do, and I hope you may be one of them. [. . .]
Love,
Amy

. . . .

31 December 1977
Dear Philip—
It was very good to have both your letters, and since there's a lull between holidays, I'll write while the inspiration is still fresh. I have problems with Christmas—for reasons which are partly given in a little thing I wrote the other day, and which I'll enclose—and have come to look forward with dread to the onset of December since I almost always find myself angry and depressed around that time. This year there were so many preoccupations beforehand that the letdown didn't get to me until Christmas day itself, and then my total gloom was to a considerable degree the result of total gloom in the weather. Such celebration as there was consisted of cooking supper on Christmas eve for Hal and another friend, and building a fire in my fireplace, opening presents, and reading a little from the book of Isaiah. A couple of days later Hal and I were hosts to a more elaborate evening—a custom we got into several years ago, and which we groan about, of putting together an elaborate meal and exchanging gifts all round. The irony is that we hardly see any of these people except at this one occasion (one of them is the judge who will be swearing in Ed Koch, the new New York City mayor, tomorrow), and a fifth couple got added to the roster this time. Hal and I were responsible for the main course, and having lately acquired a wok, we'd decided it would be Chinese—which meant a morning's shopping expedition to Chinatown, which in some circumstances ought to have been fun, but which I fumed about because I felt somehow roped-in. But despite forebodings, it all went off better than I'd thought possible. For one thing, I was able to turn the execution over to one of the guests who is truly an expert; I'd done all the chopping and measuring out beforehand, and the teamwork turned out to be good.

First there was chicken with cashews and various vegetables; then a steamed sea bass with ginger, scallions, and black beans; and then Szechuan pork, a somewhat peppery dish. We wound up with a *buche de Noël* somebody else had brought. Stir-fry cooking is so much fun that Hal and I are really into it now; I'm going to do a moo-shu pork this evening before we go off to a New Year's Eve party in New Jersey.

A couple of evenings ago I did something entirely new for me—namely, read my own poetry to an audience of strangers. I would never have gotten up courage, I imagine, if it hadn't been for the workshop I've been in. My instructor was to be the featured reader at one of these things, which go on all over town, mainly in the back room of pubs or restaurants, and had mentioned that there would be what's called an "open reading" afterward. So I made up my mind that now was the time. Hal went with me, and beforehand I did a little practicing with the help of his tape recorder. As a result, I wasn't in the least anxious, I apparently could be heard, and the applause at the end surprised me. Now that I've gotten a taste of becoming a performer—which is what reading one's own stuff amounts to—I expect I'll look for more occasions. And since the workshop was so stimulating, I may also look for another one to join for the spring semester. [. . .]

Love,

Amy

. . . .

January 7, 1978

Dear Barbara—

[. . .] Hal and I went to a New Year's Eve party in New Jersey, just over the George Washington Bridge. A big party with mainly Columbia Law School faculty plus a few students (the daughter of the household is one, and brought along some of her crowd), with noisemakers and flapper-ostrich-feather headbands and shiny hats distributed just before midnight. The high point for me is one I think you'll understand. I wasn't as dressed-up as most of the women there, but I did have on some black satin ballerina slippers with ribbons that cross around the ankles. So when one of the students said to me, "Excuse me, but are you a dancer?"—my answer was, "Oh, those things—no, I just wear them because I can't stand up in high heels"—to which the student said that it wasn't the shoes that made her ask, "It's the way you move." But like wow! Me, that gave up hope of ever measuring up because she couldn't *dance*! I'm still going around savoring the notion, though the fact is that I still can't dance, except in totally improvised cavortings about the living room that only Hal ever sees.

Which leads me to the thought of you being in two plays at once, and your mention of the fun it is even to try out. I can appreciate the feeling much more vividly now than I would have before December 29, when I did what I'd hardly quite believed I was going to go through with, namely reading my own poems to a roomful of strangers. Barbara, I did it! I may have mentioned that my poetry workshop man was to be the featured reader in the back room of this pub, and had mentioned that there would be an open reading afterward. (These things go on all over town, it appears.) To prepare myself, I practiced with Hal's tape recorder, got myself to slow down and keep my voice up, in other words to develop a performance. I read just three poems, but I could feel the attention—and Hal said afterward he thought I got more applause than anyone after the featured reader. I know the amount and duration of it surprised me. And I wasn't in the least agitated, before, during or after. It's a heady pleasure all right, and ever since I've been casting about for the prospect of doing it again. So it was all the more delightful to think of you rehearsing for two plays at once!!

And now I'm writing like crazy—six new poems in the first seven days of the new year, including two of them written on the same day. [. . .]
Love,
Amy

. . . .

9 March 1978
Dear Rimsa—
It was very good to have your letter, the recipe (which does sound great), and the Valentine poem. I think the influence is probably mainly Elizabeth Bishop, who is a great inspirer. Robert Lowell is quoted as attributing his change of style (beginning with *Life Studies*, about which I have to confess that I'm still of two minds) to her influence. He dedicated "Skunk Hour" to her. It's the *particularity* of her poems that's somehow liberating. I do think you're a bit hard-hearted about the poor old thing who sent the Valentine—but that's not important really. The important thing is to be writing again; there's some kind of momentum that can get generated, once the ice-jam gets broken. I was the more delighted to have your Valentine poem since, by sheer coincidence, I'd done one myself. Not everybody likes it, but I feel obliged to pass it on in the circumstances.

I'm still writing new things, though not at the same dizzy pace. I'll send one of two recent ones. The news is that one of the January poems is going to see print—in the *New Yorker*! It was my boss at Dutton's doing really—

he sent a few to Howard Moss, who sent them back with a very thoughtful letter asking to see more; so Jack sent another one I'd left with him, and that's the one they've accepted. It's called "The Sun Underfoot Among the Sundews"—I can't remember whether it was one I sent you, though I don't think so, and since there are going to be some changes in punctuation I don't have a good copy just now. Meanwhile I've sent them another batch, and we'll see. Incidentally, I'm going to take your advice and try "Dancers Exercising" on *Poetry.*

It snows and snows. Hal and I have taken up jogging and isometric exercises, as led by an out-of-work actor. I even got running shoes and a leotard! We had a musical afternoon on Sunday—my nephew and three other string players, doing Schubert for a select few of us. It's a very heady experience, like going back to the days of Count Esterhazy, and altogether different from hearing it in a concert hall or on records.

Love,

Amy

. . . .

20 March 1978

Dear Sister Mary John—

It was a great joy to have your letter of what seems now to have been just the other day, but was in fact somewhat longer ago than that, and to know that *The Art of the Fugue* did arrive safely, at last. Of course I'm delighted that you and the others are enjoying it. I understand very well what you say about becoming continually more sensitive to music. I'm sure that living a life of silence does add to that sensitivity, but even in my own noisy existence (relatively speaking), music comes to mean more all the time. There was a period in my life when I tended to shy away from listening to music—I'm still not sure exactly why—but being around Hal, who listens to it every minute he can, even while he's writing or preparing for class, has changed all that. He knows a great deal more about it than I do (which is ironic, since in grade school he was designated a "listener" and told not to sing with the group—a form of discrimination that has now, mercifully, been abolished from the New York City school system), but listening together tends to sharpen the appreciation on both sides. A couple of Sundays ago, we had the special privilege of listening to a Schubert quartet played by my nephew and three fellow students, in Hal's own apartment! The occasion turned into a small party, which was even happier than such occasions tend to be when Hal is the host. Next month

David gives his third-year recital, and we're planning another party to celebrate afterward.

You mentioned, in your previous letter, Arthur Mitchell and the Dance Theatre of Harlem. I've never seen the group perform in person, but I did see a television program about the school where the dancers are trained, a year or so ago. The dancing was very fine. Of course I remember Arthur Mitchell himself from the earlier days of what's now the New York City Ballet. Since I wrote last, Hal and I have been twice to see it. On the first of those evenings, we happened onto a premiere of a new Balanchine work, to the *Kammermusik No. 2* (I think) of Hindemith. It was very exciting, and is still being discussed by the dance critics. The audience that evening was full of dancers, and "Mr. B" himself finally came onto the stage to take a bow—the first time, so far as I can remember, that I've seen him do that. On the more recent evening at the City Ballet, along with some newer works there was *La Valse*, which I first saw with Tanaquil Leclerq, all those years ago, doing the part of the Girl in White, and have seen I don't know how many times since; and the magic was still there, though what I saw in the ballet itself this time was somewhat different from the other times. I wrote a poem about it which I'm venturing to send, hoping that you won't be offended by the little excerpt concerning St. Audrey at the beginning (according to my own book on the lives of the saints, her career was entirely given over to piety, quite unlike the dictionary version). In fact, I'll send a couple of others having to do in one way or another with dancers. Perhaps—though I can't be sure—they'll make more sense than the long one about the Jersey meadows. I'm not sure I can clarify that one, but possibly an account of how it came to be written may help. The idea first came to me last spring, when I was making weekly trips to and from Washington, and each time found myself looking with a mixture of loathing and fascination at a scene which I think must have been familiar to you once—the lowlands between the Hudson and the Watchung Ridge, into which the train emerges almost immediately after leaving the tunnel from Penn Station. Eventually, I suppose, the waterways will be filled entirely with a sort of soil—what they call landfill, which always seems to contain a large proportion of compacted garbage. For the time being, there are still fairly large patches of reeds, for which the botanical name is *Phragmites*—tall, dense, and graceful in their own way, with great tufted plumes that linger through the winter. All the ugliness and waste that seem an inescapable part of urban living appeared to be concentrated in those lowlands—chemical plants, refineries, junkyards—and this made the gracefulness of the reeds somehow precious, and it seemed to me, week after week, that something was there waiting to be said. When I suddenly woke up to the realization that reeds of the genus *Phragmites* were the ones used in antiquity to make simple pipes, and that such pipes were originally used to accompany elegiac poetry, I seemed to know in a vague way what it was that wanted to be said, or perhaps more accurately that I myself wanted to say—it was to lament the waste and ugliness, and in the process to say something about what poetry might do but somehow doesn't. I don't know how successfully I did any of this, but it was satisfying to have gotten some of those things set down. I haven't read it over lately, and haven't yet ventured to send it anywhere.—Oh yes, one more thing: the scene in Milburn is a dinner party I went to one weekend, and transcribes fairly accurately what in fact took place—as well as the kind of thing one hears sometime so-called liberals saying these days.—In the meantime, I've been writing more poetry than ever before. For a while, even though I had a good deal of work to do, I was writing one or more pieces every day. Lately they've come more slowly, but there still seem to be more ideas than I can quite catch up with. And sometime before too long, I don't yet know just when, one of these new things is going to appear in the *New Yorker.* This has just happened, and my boss at Dutton is really responsible for bringing it to the attention of the poetry editor there, who's asked to see more (having also turned down several others); and that of course is an encouragement.

I was greatly interested to hear about your correspondence with the Polish nun, and about her fascination with nineteenth-century English novels and "lost causes." I'm wondering whether George Eliot would be one of her favorites. Last summer while we were in Maine, Hal read *Middlemarch* for the first time, and was so eager to talk about it that I re-read it myself. It seemed to me more than ever, in its own sober and patient way, one of the greatest novels ever written. No one has ever written more powerfully of the drama of the inner life or of the complexity of human character ("a process and an unfolding," she called it). And there is this extraordinary passage which you may know, but having just lately copied it out, I pass it along: "If we had a keen vision of all ordinary human life, it would be like hearing the grass grow and the squirrel's heart beat, and we should die of that roar which lies on the other side of silence."—Again thanks to Hal's company, I've come to an appreciation of Dickens that I didn't always have. I may have mentioned that one winter several years ago we read *Bleak House* aloud to each other. Last summer we finished *Lit-*

tle Dorrit, which in some ways I liked even better. We have *Our Mutual Friend* and *Martin Chuzzlewit* waiting for whenever there is leisure to begin a new reading project.

I hadn't realized how easily one slips into jargon—which is what "spring list," which you found puzzling, really amounts to. I didn't even use it correctly; what I should have been talking about was the "fall list"— in less cryptic terms, the books that are scheduled to be published between September and the end of the year. The printing process seems to take longer and longer, with the result that if a book is to be out by September, the manuscript needs to be edited and ready for the printer by January. Hence the rush around the Christmas holidays to get manuscripts that have just come in edited in time. Something like a lull may be about to descend, and it will be welcome.—As for the snowy weather that was reported from New York, I welcomed the first big storm with a certain glee; there's still a child in me that enjoys watching the snow come down and the prospect of the total disruption that comes in the wake of a blizzard. By the time the biggest snowstorm of the year arrived, and lasted something like thirty-six hours, I was somewhat bored by it all. There was no hardship for me; for some, the cold became a problem. Now, I can report the very first crocuses already in bloom in a Village garden. And I send my very best wishes, as always, for a blessed Easter
Much love,
Amy

. . . .

Easter 1978
Dear Barbara—
Yes, you did send off the earlier installment, and then came your postcard from Florida, and then the concluding installment—and it is now time I did *something*. I'm sorry about the difficulties you mention. I would imagine that Gladys is simply accustomed to expressing herself freely around those she's close to, and that you as (I gather) her closest friend simply have to absorb the shocks now and then. But I don't know how one is to deal with the situation when it's at close quarters. I think, like me, you dislike scenes and friction even more than people generally. Hal and I are both that way, with the result that when there's a fight it's a relentless painful operation that can't be set aside until it's settled, even if it takes all day. But between women it's not the same. Maybe it would be better if you could air your own dismay more freely. Oh dear.

I don't think I've made a single concrete suggestion. But you do know I'm concerned. Gladys is such a great person, but I wouldn't enjoy having her irritated with *me*. And I feel quite sure that the problem isn't you at all.

This has been what Hal and I speak of as a *Grum* Easter Sunday, all day long—with the result that we've stayed in all day. Otherwise we would have been out—can you believe this?—*jogging*. Yes, we're really into it. We go twice a week, once privately as a pair, and the other time with a larger group, for exercises followed by running, as led by an out-of-work actor one of Hal's former students discovered. I wouldn't care for the whole thing quite as much if the leader weren't so sunny and patient and beautiful to look at. I'm learning a whole new set of ways to get that great muscle tone your doctor exclaimed over, as I remember; we do pliés and relevés and various stretching exercises, for which I even bought a leotard. Also running shoes. Nobody believes this when I tell it.

There is other news. I forget whether I mentioned that Jack, my boss at Dutton, volunteered to send some poems to Howard Moss, the poetry editor at the *New Yorker*. Well, anyhow he did, and the upshot is that they're going to publish one of them! It's called "The Sun Underfoot Among the Sundews" and I don't believe I've sent it to you; it's fairly recent, and has to do with a bog in Maine. The other day the check came, and it appears that they must pay by the word: one hundred eighty-two smackers for one little poem! It now becomes clear why everybody wants to get into that magazine. They've asked to see more and sent those back, saying send still others—which I'm about to do. I don't know yet just when I can expect to see the one they accepted in print, but since they apparently send out proofs beforehand to the author, I'll let you know beforehand.—No, I never had a chance to read the long Jersey Meadows poem to the class or anywhere, except to my nephew and his roommate one night when they were at Hal's. It's a good one to sort of cut loose with, and it appeared to go over well with them. I haven't yet sent it anywhere, but am getting ready to try some magazine that runs long things soon.

Most of the time I find it hard to believe it's close to a year since, for instance, that day when you and the diffident Mr. Cork went out looking for wild flowers. The new crop will be appearing soon, I suppose—likewise all those wonderful fragrant pale yellow jonquils at Johnny and Sandy's little house in the woods. It grieved me, as though I were entitled to any such reaction, to hear that they've left it for Florida. Of course I

don't know Florida. But I've seen the little house, and loved it for being so absolutely one-of-a-kind . [. . .]
Love,
Amy

. . . .

May 30, 1978
Dear Barbara—
[. . .] I do wish I could have been down there for the cherry blossoms. I did miss that gradual cavalcade of things unfolding, as seen from the bus. It's true that there are some flowering things hereabouts, even including some cherry trees in Riverside Park, which I had a few glimpses of on running days. The last of those for a while was on Saturday, when there were fond good-byes to Bob, our exercise master, who's going back to Missouri to work on his running. Too many people throwing beer-cans at him in Brooklyn, where he'd been living, and other obstructions; but he promises to be back, and we've all become so devoted to him that there was an awful lot of hugging and kissing, that last day. To make it all the more exciting, the prime mover in the group had a jealous husband to contend with. She's Chinese, but as American in just about every way as anybody I know; whereas her husband is very Chinese, and pretty scary when provoked. So there was this tense scene, and all sorts of consultations about whether it would be safe for Simone to be in the same apartment without a third party. What made her husband so furious, though, was mainly that after a dozen or so years of being married, and two kids, she's finally decided it's time to separate—and the ignominy of it has turned him violent. I can sympathize a little, in fact, with any husband's anxiety about having anybody as beautiful, sweet, but *muscular* as Bob for a possible rival. Now that we've got the routine worked out, Hal and I vow that it's going to be exercise every day—well, nearly every day anyhow—and lots of running. The running really is nice. Even Hal, who resisted longer than I did, has been weaned into liking it.

Domesticity around here got a little complicated for a while, when we began having visitations, all unannounced, from an old girlfriend of Hal's who either is in the process of going crazy or has been that way all along. She has no means of support, and lately has been going through a pattern of appearing unannounced on the doorsteps of various friends and relatives and, it would seem, staying put until they're provoked into throwing her out. She even did something of the sort with her psychiatrist—who, according to her own account, finally called the police. She brings little presents—bialys, a bottle of Perrier water—and talks plausibly enough, in a muted sort of way; and she drives around in a car that belongs to a long-suffering friend who took her into her household in a radical feminist community up in New Hampshire. Hal has a number of somewhat crazy friends—he likes people who're just a bit crazy, or he wouldn't put up with me—and for a long time he didn't see this one as any crazier than the rest of us. For the moment the visitations have stopped, but if she appears in Maine I won't be surprised.

Our friend from Harvard, whom one might imagine to be sanity personified but who is full of quirks, was down a few weekends back, and we had another of those magical Sunday brunches—asparagus hollandaise, croissants, and strawberries. I can't remember now much of what was talked about, except that I'd just gotten a proof of my poem from the *New Yorker* and read him some others, which he responded to most satisfactorily. For a while it seemed as though they were about to take another poem; they professed to like it enough to ask me to revise the ending, which they thought was wrong; so I did, but the revised ending didn't please them either, though they continue to ask to see more things. Now I'm not sure whether I think the original or the revised ending is better, and I'm about to impose on you to the extent of sending both for your opinion. Eventually I'll send it somewhere else, once I decide which version. [. . .]
Love,
Amy

. . . .

October 12, 1978
Dear Barbara—
Well, it seems not to be summer any more—though from the temperature you'd never know it—and that must mean that it's time I wrote you a letter. In fact, that weekend in July begins to seem a long time a go. I can't remember whether I wrote you that I went to the August production of Shakespeare in the Park, which was *The Taming of the Shrew;* anyhow, I can assure you that you saw the one worth seeing. Come to think of it, I seem never to have seen a production of that play before, and I discovered on the spot that I did not like that play. When Petruchio got to that "my goods, my chattel, my house, my land" speech, or however it goes, I let out a low groan, and in the next minute everybody around me was booing. I half thought I'd unleashed the boos, but apparently it went on

every night. They had some fancy interpretation that was supposed to make Kate's final groveling less offensive, but it offended me all the same. The picnic beforehand was nice, though not quite as ebullient as the one when you were here. Sharon came for lunch the other day—you remember Sharon, I dare say—with the manuscript of a children's book she's written and plans to illustrate, all about atoms and the universe. She's really turned on about cosmology.

I've just written Alfred, who sent me this funny Peanuts congratulations card back in August. The mail has been coming in from all over, surprisingly—in fact, it turns out that the best thing about getting into print is hearing from people. From the likes of Stuart Gerry Brown, for instance. Remember him? He's now emeritus at the University of Hawaii. And one of my high school classmates, whose son-in-law came across the poem and passed it along. and I just this week got word from the *New Yorker* that they're taking "The Cove"—I think it was in the set I sent you. If you'll excuse me, I'll throw diffidence aside and mention what the poetry editor said. He said deciding on that one was a matter of "winnowing the gold from the gold." Thus bolstered, I've sent off some things to the *Atlantic*—including an updated version of the penguin poem. Your comment about the previous ones persuaded me that something had to be done, and just the other day I came up with something. I hope you'll approve, never mind what the *Atlantic* does.

I'm still struggling with the manuscript I was groaning over when you were here. The author has been to China and come back, and we're now waiting for something like revision number four of the final chapter. Also, nobody can agree on a title. It's been a long haul, but not quite as tedious as having to deal with another author, more recently. The other day, when he raised questions that could have been cleared up weeks ago if he'd been paying attention, I told him over the phone that I was finding things "a little bit tiresome." How about that for assertiveness? He clearly hadn't expected such insubordination from a mere copy editor (which is what he sees me as). But I think that one is all attended to, and for the first time in weeks I'm feeling close to caught up—hence getting down to letter-writing is in order. [. . .]

Hal is fine, aside from struggles with the revision of the famous Article. A couple of weeks ago we both thought it was finished. Now he decides it isn't—not finely enough crafted, has to be developed. On the other hand, there is a Supreme Court case coming up which bears directly on his subject, so he's *got* to get it into print. But he has his own ineffably high standards, and it's no use telling a scholarly type that his standards are possibly *too* high—it's worse than telling an artist such a thing, I suppose.

Well, and how is Mr. Newman, and how is John Edgerton, and how, indeed, is the diffident Mr. Cork? But above all, how are you?

Love,

Amy

P.S.

I ran two miles the other day, in fact I've done it several times lately. Our angelic exercise master is back, and Hal and I meet with him twice a week for a workout, which gets harder and harder all the time. A week from Sunday is the New York marathon, for which Bob has been fanatically training, so of course Hal and I have to be on hand at the finish line to see him come in. We run along the East River, right next to the water, and I do believe I've never been in such good shape.

. . . .

December 3, 1978

Dear Sister Mary John—

Your letter of away back in April was so full of specially meaningful things, to which my delayed response was that I must answer it as soon as possible—and now I'm dismayed to realize how much time has passed, and what I'm writing is a Christmas letter as well as the answer I intended! You wrote, anyhow, a lot about dancing, and how as a "responding motion" it is also an expression of religious feeling. This is a thought I've had more and more lately—I remember saying to Hal, as one of those jokes that underneath are perfectly serious, "*Life* is dance." As I've mentioned, I think, we listen to a great deal of music, and often we start moving around the room in response to it—an unstiffening, on my part, that has been a long time in taking place but is not too late, even so. What you wrote about the young girl with whom you danced to Vivaldi, fluttering and spinning to the flute imitating the gold-finch, is specially poignant because that discovering of muscles, and feeling the discovery translated into joy, is so real for me. I have a trace of regret, I suppose, that I didn't unstiffen soon enough to study ballet—an art I've admired most intensely ever since I watched Tanaquil Leclerq and others like her in those very early days, before Balanchine was a household word, and long before his works were being done on television (as some of them were just a few evenings ago— "The Prodigal Son," with an extraordinary performancec by Mikhail

Baryshnikov, and a newer production to a Gluck "Chaconne"). Anyhow, as the next best thing, you may be surprised to hear that I've moved a step in that direction. Twice a week, these days, Hal and I do exercises—mainly limbering-up, Yoga-like stretching ones, but with some things such as pliés and relevés thrown in—with a delightful young man whom we've gotten to know, after which we put on runners' shoes and run for a mile or two, along the East River or the drives in Central Park. Physical fitness has become a kind of mania around here in recent months, and it's a bit embarrassing to find oneself caught up in a fad; but we look on the fad as simply a coincidence. (Did you know, by the way, that back in October, something over ten thousand people, both men and women, took part in a marathon run around New York City? It wasn't the first such marathon, but it was the first with such numbers—and still hardly believable, though I watched a little of it from one spot on the East Side. The runners went through all kinds of neighborhoods, including Harlem, and seem to have been welcomed everywhere.) Anyhow, among other things I've been shown how to "turn out" for a proper arabesque—and as a result I have all the more respect for the training a dancer must go through.

All this being so, you can see why images of dancers or submerged references to dancing have a way of cropping up when I write poetry—as I've gone on doing fairly regularly over the past few months. I'll enclose one I wrote in Maine this summer, called "The Tides," that's an example of what I mean—along with a photocopy of the one the *New Yorker* had accepted when I wrote you last. (They've since bought three others—and the *Atlantic Monthly* and the *American Scholar* have each bought one—all very gratifying, of course.) I must confess to a twinge of dismay at your reference to the sarcasm you found in some things I've sent, as not fitting in with your own picture of me. Of course you're quite right to speak of this, and I'm not in the least offended, just a bit bemused. It may have been some effort to build up a somewhat artificial demeanor, thereby suppressing a more mischievous side that's always been there, that's at fault. It may also have been some idea that I was grown up now, and not allowed to play any more. Anyhow, the mischief is always lurking—pointing to incongruities and the unacknowledged gaps in what's supposedly grown-up behavior, and recently I guess I've felt freer to let it emerge for what it is. What troubles me is that *you* seem to be troubled (or even offended? I hope not, but can't be sure) by what I hadn't really thought of as sarcasm, but rather as a sort of playful truth-telling. Doris, I seem to remember, called it "sly humor" and seems to regard it as a sort of trademark. Or are we referring to different things? Anyhow, I'm grateful to you for plain speaking, and look forward to more of it.

I'll include one poem, anyhow, which contains (I think) no sarcasm and hardly any playfulness. It's called "Letters from Jerusalem" and I'm prompted to send it by your mention of the Reformed Rabbi who had recently visited the Abbey, and your comments on the discipline of living according to the law that is implicit in all of Judaism. This, once again, thrilled me all the more because that subject was just then vividly in my mind, and I think I may in fact have been working on this poem when your letter arrived. For several years now I've corresponded with a young man, a friend of my nephew David, who is living in Israel. He comes from a Jewish background but had lived as a secularized Jew, not a religious one, and evidently felt the lack of something more searching and rigorous. We met only a couple of times but felt an immediate affinity (he writes poetry), and there is a certain challenge in trying to account for oneself to something leading a very different kind of life—something I feel whenever I sit down to write to you. (You're there in my mind, but more than a casual note is called for; there must be time to sit down and take stock, enter into a state of recollection, in fact.) He doesn't write very often; but last spring, knowing that he was somewhere with a tank division—the great hurdle having been crossed, of having to go into the army, otherwise he couldn't stay there any longer—I began to be alarmed about what might have happened to him. I got out all of his letters that I could find, and the poem was the result. I've since heard from him; he's back in Jerusalem, studying the Talmud, teaching English and music to earn a living, and troubled by the divisions within Judaism (having opted for the strictest Orthodoxy himself). I was struck, of course, by the parallel of the kind of strictness that he feels drawn to with the life of a Christian religious. I hope what I've written will convey some of all this for you. (I sent my friend the poem, and he absorbed it without comment—but with, I suspect, a certain modest chagrin.) [. . .]
Much love always,
Amy

. . . .

January 8, 1979
Dear Rimsa—
[. . .] I'm in my usual good shape now, after being laid low over the holidays by the most disagreeable of viruses—for a couple of days I was as sick as I've been since I had my appendix out, though at least there was the re-

lief of knowing it couldn't be *that*. I spent a good deal of the time it took to recuperate reading a biography of George Eliot by Gordon Haight, an Oxford book originally published ten years ago, and just lately out in paperback (a Galaxy book). It's so good that it was almost worth being sick so as to have the leisure to finish it; and for once, a really inspiring subject besides. Hal took care of me, and read aloud from a new collection of John Cheever stories. So things could have been a great deal worse.

Otherwise, there is not much news, except that I've finally had a poem accepted by a "little" magazine—actually, it bulks as rather a tome, pays a little, and appears to circulate outside the U.S. It's called *Antaeus*, and the thing they took was a bit of whimsy called "Agreeable Monsters." Just lately I've been reading Adrienne Rich's new book, *The Dream of a Common Language*. It's all off-the-deep-end feminist, including a sequence on a lesbian love affair, but less off-putting than I'd expected, and in fact quite beautiful. For Dutton, just lately, I've been reading a couple of manuscripts on remote and exotic places, one about Ladakh, a mountainous enclave between Tibet and Kashmir, full of Tantric Buddhist monasteries, where the old ways have pretty much survived until now, and the other an autobiographical book by Wilfred Thesiger, who lived with the Arabs and explored desert and mountain places no European had seen, and escaping with his life by a hair's-breadth of sheer luck maybe half a dozen times. That's fun, but not so a real basket case of a manuscript about Edward Weston, for which I've been given the assignment of redoing one chapter to show how it might be salvaged—though my own conclusion is already that it can't be. Even so, working for Dutton is about as pleasant as a job could possibly be.

In Iowa, I found my mother reasonably well for anyone of eighty-seven; there was snow on the ground everywhere but the weather was beautiful, and I managed to get in a three-mile hike, jogging part of the way, meeting one pedestrian the whole time and getting derisive comments from people behind the wheel of cars. We've finally gotten some genuine snow hereabouts; it was coming down in big flakes and every tree was outlined in white when I woke up this morning, but it's already beginning to drip and look sodden by now. Bit by bit, with my exercise man, I'm learning about demi-pointe and rond de jambe and how to "turn out" for a proper ballerina plié. I'll never go far with any of this, but it's wonderfully satisfying to be doing it at all.

Love,

Amy

. . . .

May 16, 1979

Dear Rimsa—

A small parcel by way of a birthday greeting is on its way to you, and I'm hoping it may have reached you on time—as I fear this letter won't. I'm getting vaguer and vaguer about what day it is, it seems. Anyhow, I hope it finds you feeling better and as cheerful as may be, in these more and more harrowing times. I occasionally feel like putting on a sandwich board and walking the streets with a message about the end of the world being at hand. I'd bought a bus ticket for the anti-nuke rally in Washington earlier this month, but then caught a nasty cold and didn't go, and sat drinking the whole thing in on TV. In the middle of the winter, I did get myself to Washington on the day Grace Paley and ten others were being sentenced for stepping onto the White House lawn and unfurling an anti-Nuke banner. They were charged with Unlawful Entry and the trial took seven days. They hadn't expected anything like that, but were mainly worried about their counterparts in Moscow, a group of U.S. citizens who unfurled a banner in Russian and after being arrested were simply let go with a talking-to. There were something over two hundred of us milling around in the corridor of the courthouse while the sentences were handed down—a hundred-dollar fine or thirty days I think it was, with probation. Then we proceeded along Pennsylvania Avenue in the snow to the White House, and it was almost like old times.

My mother died early in March. She'd just had her eighty-eighth birthday, and was very frail and tired, and altogether it could have been very much worse. I spent several days in Des Moines, and things were made much easier by a wonderful group of Quakers who had been her friends for years, and whom I now think of as my friends too. After that it seemed as though spring would never come, but today is lovely, and I've just finished editing a manuscript I'd been groaning over, and feeling liberated for the moment.

A couple of weeks ago I did, of all things, a poetry reading for a class of art students—actually it was a writing course, at the School of Visual Arts—and had a wonderful time. Everyone was so totally unthreatening that it was almost magical—for which credit must go to the teacher, who has some kind of genius for encouraging people to be themselves. I'd never met her before, but she'd heard about me from my friend Mary, and so the reading was arranged. They even paid me a little something, and there was talk about doing it again sometime. [. . .]

Love,
Amy

. . . .

Corea, Maine 04624

.June 5, 1979

Dear Mary Jo Salter—
Your letter pleased me more than you can possibly imagine. Since you're
a poet, I wouldn't be able to say such a thing if it weren't for our belonging to different generations—and to have evoked such friendliness from
a younger poet amounts to nothing less than a milestone. Few things
could please me more than to trade poems with someone sympathetic,
and so I'm sending along perhaps more than you'll feel like coping with.
I hope you won't feel swamped, and of course you're not obliged to read
everything in the little book. If you do, you'll find lots of exercises, throes
of self-expression, and all the weight of the grand tradition. *Milton*, yet!
The book [*Multitudes, Multitudes*] came about mainly because I got to
know a young man who was trying, against the tide, to be a letterpress
printer; he's since become a casualty of the economy, and gone back to
working for someone other than himself. At the time, though I sent out
things occasionally (and got them back), I wasn't quite ready to go out on
a limb and commit myself to being a pro. I think that happened when I
read some things in the back room of a pub (an "open reading," needless
to say) and discovered how heady a pleasure it can be to have an audience.
One thing that had held me back, I must admit, was that I don't greatly
enjoy the company of literary types—the more literary they are, the more
miserable they seem to be as human beings. This isn't just a complaint,
it's a *lament* in the elegiac manner. I've been fortunate in my friends, and
since I earn my living bookishly (half-time editor for E. P. Dutton, free-
lancing the rest of the time) I have no illusions about authors. My best-
friend-and-severest-critic—with whom I've shared a house up here in
Maine for several summers now—is a lawyer with an ear for music, who
takes pleasure in words as much as I do. A very old friend teaches English
in Colorado, and we correspond. I couldn't have gone on writing without those two. But I've yearned secretly for a poet I could write to. Editors, it turns out, are too busy—of course, with all those hordes of poets
sending in manuscripts, more poets writing than there are readers, it
would appear.

Is it W. C. Williams who's to blame for the current monotony of manner? This is what Howard Moss says, in a nice thing I just came across in *The American Poetry Review* (where, it strikes me, monotony tends to predominate unduly). Or is it something more pervasive, a general pulling inside oneself because the environment is so bad out there? The other day it occurred to me that a whole generation has been so deadened by rock music that an ear for the music of words may be obsolescent. "You're in love with words," I was told (by a poet, yet) in a tone of accusation. What he meant, I guess, was that I tend to use too many of them. So you can see why your letter, with its sweet and generous compliments for what in some quarters is evidently seen as a defect, meant so much.

As for data: I come from the Midwest, went to Grinnell College a long time ago, and have gone through lots of changes, some of them documented in *Multitudes, Multitudes*. I'm here in this delectably silent and foggy lobstering village ("The Cove" and "Fog" were written here, and the sundew poem's subject was discovered here) for six weeks, with some manuscripts to edit but also time for other things. The best-friend-and-severest-critic is writing a scholarly article. We listen to lots of music, and once we've settled in we'll probably be reading aloud to each other. One summer it was Dickens—we finished *Little Dorrit* here, and were almost too broken up by it to speak. This summer it may be George Eliot. Just at the moment I'm reading *Silas Marner* for—can you imagine?—the first time. Best-friend-and-severest-critic read it in high school! Before that it was *The Mill on the Floss*, and before that *Adam Bede*. While I've been writing this, the fog that has been moving in and out since we arrived has been dissipating, the water has turned from no-hue to just faintly blue, and Petit Manan lighthouse has shown itself for the first time. Thank you so much, once again, for writing as you have. I do hope you'll write again, and send *your* poems.
Gratefully Yours,
Amy Clampitt

. . . .

November 24, 1979
Dear Rimsa—
[. . .] The *New Yorker* has bought another poem, written while we were in Maine—and I've met Howard Moss! He is kindly, unassuming, pleasant company, and on the strength of a common fondness for Mozart, especially *Così fan tutte*, I'm getting up courage to invite him to dinner with

Hal and me one of these days. The other new connection by way of writing is that I had a letter from the young woman who reads for the *Atlantic*, and we've become friends on the strength of more common interests than I would have thought possible in anybody just twenty-five. She studied with Elizabeth Bishop at Harvard, and had an especial reason to grieve on hearing that E. B. was dead: a few months back, she'd gone to hear her read, went up to speak to her afterward, was urged to come pay a visit, but diffidently put it off—until it was too late. The other evening I went to a memorial reading of E. B.'s work at the Y—one oddity of which was that only one woman poet was on the roster, namely Grace Schulman of the *Nation*, who organized the thing. Otherwise, Howard Moss, Mark Strand, James Merrill (who must have flown over from Athens for the occasion), John Ashbery, and so on.

Along with "The Edge of the Hurricane," I'll send something brand new, at least in what I hope is more or less its final form. It had its genesis back in the summer, when I stayed overnight in New Haven with my old friend Doris—you might have met her back in Audubon days—who was at Yale on a summer fellowship, and we made the rounds of the museum exhibitions, including one of rare books. I'll also enclose a clipping I'd been intending to send, from the Times about your old home town, just in case it hadn't come your way. I did see the Calvin Trillin piece about Fairhope, and wondered how accurate it was. Your hints about the discussion at the Men's Club are, to say the least, intriguing. Nothing like a small town for that kind of intensiveness. [. . .]

Love,

Amy

. . . .

December 9, 1979

Dear Robert [Quint]—

Your letter written in August must have crossed paths with mine of around the same time, which I hope did reach you safely. I certainly intended to answer it before now; but this fall has been harrowing in some ways, with the result that taking time out for some intensive thinking before sending off a letter has been postponed unduly. I always feel that I can't simply dash off a note to you—that there must be something like the Composition of Place recommended by St. Ignatius Loyola beforehand. (It's no accident, this referring to the Jesuits—though in a weird way I can't help feeling the similarity of that structured life with your continued devotion to yeshiva studies.) I've just been reading a new biography of Gerard Manley Hopkins, by a woman named Paddy Kitchen, who is apparently an agnostic herself, and so the demands and strictures of the life he chose to follow are fresh in my mind. There is a passage in it that I'll pass along, as having struck me especially:

> In one letter to (Robert) Bridges, written after the 1871 Paris Commune had murdered five Jesuit Fathers among their hostages, he stated his very simple and clear views on communism. Efforts have been made to establish that he did not really mean what he said, that they are the views of a politically-naive young man; but there is nothing especially idealistic or extravagant in what he says. He just states a commonsensical view with elementary clarity. There would be, he felt, a great revolution in the not too distant future. He deplored the violent means by which it inevitably would be carried out, but considered that its causes were sadly justified. The nation's riches depended on the majority of her people living in poverty and without dignity. The majority were also deprived of education so could not be expected to respect, or wish to preserve, the monuments of civilization. The future was, Hopkins decided, black; but it was "deservedly black," and although he found it a horrible thing to say, he was in some respects a communist himself.

It occurred to me, in thinking about all this, that somewhere the future is always black—*deservedly* black for one group or another, and that what we in the U.S. are witnessing is what that blackness can look like when great tectonic shifts in the centers of power are taking place. Thus far it's only prestige that's threatened, but a threat to prestige is like the first rumble of an earthquake in prospect. People here tend not to think in such terms; in fact, it seems to me that there is less and less a long view of anything. (So I do understand, I think, the powerful attraction those studies must have for you, and how painful it must be to have to justify them to other people.)

One reason I intended to write before now is to urge you, if you can possibly find the time, to translate the Hebrew parts of your army journal into English—and in any event, if you can spare a copy, I would love to see the parts that I'm able to read. It seems to me that a record of your experiences might be of interest to many readers, if we can devise some way of getting it into print.

David is getting along well, with an orchestra job that guarantees him an income for a least a year or so. His group is to give a concert at a new hall in Lincoln Center next week, and Hal and I are planning to gather a few people for a party beforehand. Hal is working on a big piece of legal scholarship, and I have gone on writing poetry, having had enough encouragement (three poems in the *New Yorker* so far, with two others to appear sometime, three in the *Atlantic*, and a few others coming out in "little" magazines) that there is more energy to keep going. I've revised "Letters from Jerusalem," and plan to send it out one of these days; I'll put in a copy of the new version, along with one of several other war-and-fire poems I've done lately.

I'm afraid this won't reach you in time for Hanukkah (which I'm going to celebrate along with Hal and his parents this year), but in any event my best wishes for the holiday go with it. Please also convey my best wishes to Adina.

Ever,

Amy

P.S.

The address at the head of this letter is Hal's, and after some trouble with my mailbox on 12th Street I'm having people write me there, at least for the time being.

. . . .

December 16, 1979

Dear Barbara—

[. . .] I loved your account of the trip to Florida. The story of the sparkplug-changing incident took me back to the time I traveled through France with some mad English people in an antique French taxi, which kept breaking down along the way and drawing crowds of spectators, a few of them helpful, most of them inclined to jeer with that kind of superiority that is a specialty of the French. The owners of the creature, which went by the name of Felix, had a passion for examining the innards of old cars, and seemed happiest whenever they detected something wrong with the way he sounded, meaning we had to stop while they consulted over what the trouble might be. The more I hear about Joanie, the more admiring I am—and this goes for Hal, who at this moment is trying to install a piece of weather-stripping along a window that has been letting in drafts for years, and which the handyman declined to repair. (While I think of it, I should mention that after my mailbox on 12th Street was broken into and a couple of checks stolen, I'm giving the above address to a select few, as the place to reach me at least for the time being.) Some day, do you think she'll settle down long enough to write her memoirs?

Your comments on the irony of getting so simple-minded a thing accepted by a scholarly publication are the same as my own reaction. I don't know to this day why they took it; I've sent them various others I myself consider more suitable, from time to time, but no luck. I'll put in a thing or two written just lately, concerned with the scene from Hal's apartment window. The other night we were jolted by the noise of what I immediately knew was a bomb. It had gone off just outside the Soviet Embassy, two blocks up, and blew out (or in) about half the windows in the apartment house opposite; and though we weren't quite determined enough to know what had happened to venture outside, we were able to count the number of ambulances, police vans, and unmarked vehicles (the kind with the red light on the roof, and the siren for emergencies) that went by, and pretty much figured out what must have happened. Another neighborhood development—I don't think I've written you about this—is that a townhouse just down the block has been bought by Richard Nixon! A couple of co-op apartment buildings had refused to take him; but this time the only protest (if that is what it was) consisted of a lone figure in a jailbird suit, wearing a Nixon mask, with a suitcase beside him, who appeared a couple of times on the corner of Lexington and 65th. Most people went by without a look, but Hal and I went up to him laughing, whereupon the figure put on an imploring pose and said "Please forgive me," to which I said *I* wouldn't until he paid his taxes. The other day I went by when a couple of men were polishing up the brass on the knocker. Aha, I thought, Nixon retainers—until I got close enough to hear one of them saying " . . . guilty as sin." There are some rather phony-looking Christmas wreaths in the windows there now, but I'm not sure it means anybody has moved in. On the other hand, it may mean that we'll have them right there, within jeering distance, for Christmas! We wonder what we've done to deserve *this*. The *New Yorker* this week had a properly indignant piece in the Talk of the Town, quoting that terrible man as saying, "no one ever lives in New York; they stay in New York and work in New York"—whereas his heart will "always be in California." So what is he working up to now, one wonders. The Talk of the Town writer goes on, "If I had a few moments eye to eye with the ex-President, I would resist the temptation to grab his lapels but I would, very firmly, state the case, as follows: Watch it, Buster. You want to move your base of operations here—fine. We didn't stop Reverend Moon and we won't stop you.

But be warned: Play by the rules, be neighborly, stand back and let the other passengers off, try to show a little enthusiasm for the local sports franchises, don't smoke in the elevators, act nice, lay off the malicious gossip, and we will too." Well, maybe we will. I'll let you know if there are any interesting developments.

To think that your classmates would be so defensive as to take umbrage at anything less than the rah-rah tone of a cheering section! But I suppose those class letters must be regarded as largely a holdover of same. How depressing. Which reminds me that my nephew David—who's now making a sort of go in New York as a violinist, thanks for the nonce to CETA funding—went to Grinnell, and when I went to his graduation one of his roommates, an honor student, prize-winner for poetry, and so on—for whatever reason couldn't bring himself to appear at the ceremony at all. Later, over a kind of picnic in the ramshackle house where they were both living, I met him and we became instant friends. Not long afterward he took off for Israel, where he's lived ever since, and from which he writes fascinating letters that sound like a translation, he's now so immersed in speaking Hebrew. He's put in his obligatory two years of military service and lately gotten married. When he first told his classmates he was thinking of going to Israel (being from a secular Jewish family, he wanted to find out where his roots were) the leftists, of whom he was one, were horrified. I suppose they'd be even more horrified now that he's become a Talmudic scholar, but I find the whole thing thrilling and touching at once. There is, of course, no word of what he's done in the alumni news.

Speaking of orthodoxy, later today I'm going to celebrate Hanukkah with Hal's parents—first such holiday doings I've ever been invited to. There was a small flurry a while back when his father got it into his head that I might be persuaded to convert, and then they could have a proper daughter-in-law; but they have since been set straight on that, or so Hal says. They're dear people anyhow. [. . .]
Love,
Amy

. . . .

January 24, 1980
Dear Barbara—
Who wouldn't be a mite of a Scrooge under the circumstances? It is odd how misfortunes of that sort seem to arrive in clusters—last spring, for example, the week when I had *my* wallet lifted, for the first time (and I was

more indignant than anything else, and more with myself than with the perpetrator, whose cleverness I had to admire) was also the week when somebody broke into my mailbox and, as it turned out, stole a couple of checks. Which episode, followed by another breaking-in during the fall, has led to my gradually edging my correspondence in Hal's direction, for all that I have absolutely no plans for relinquishing my apartment or the legal address thereunto entailed. Letters to the above address do tend to get to me more quickly, these days.

I can also share your dismay over the jaywalking pedestrian. In Maine a couple of summers ago, a kid on a skateboard suddenly darted into the road just as we came over a little rise—and it was just after sunset, to make things scarier. We weren't going very fast, and Hal managed with great presence of mind to veer around him, but the shaken feeling at what might have happened took—as you observe—a while to get over.

Anyhow, here's to cheerier times in 1980. Before I forget to mention it, I had a nice letter from Jean Dimond London, of Grinnell class of '43, who had seen something about my getting into print in the alumni magazine and felt moved to send her felicitations. Unlike most old-grad recollections, which make me cringe, hers were on an identifiable wavelength, which is the more remarkable since we hadn't known each other at all well. I remember her as extremely pretty and voluptuous, and thus (I supposed) invulnerable to all my own perpetual anxieties and unrequited yearnings—but that's how wrong one can be. Anyhow, she now lives in Palo Alto but for years had a job in the government. Did you know her at all?

The *New Yorker* has taken another poem (which I called "Artifacts," but they want another title—I can't remember whether it was one I sent you or not), and Howard Moss, the poetry editor, came to dinner. It was just a few days after he'd been to the White House, where he found the President charming, Rosalynn less so. For one thing, the President let it be known that he reads Browning. There wasn't an awful lot of name-dropping during the evening here—it having been billed as an evening of Mozart, we put on a recording of *Così fan tutte* and listened almost as much as we talked—but he did tell us about Elizabeth Bowen, with whom he was friendly, and who invited him to Bowen's Court. He had gone to graduate school at Columbia about the same time I did, and found it just as uninspiring.

They're painting in the house down the block, and the moving-in (Nixon's, you know) is said to be imminent, and I realize how unreal the whole prospect still is. I can imagine taking some other route on runs to Central Park, to avoid the spot. A couple of times, incidentally, I've run two miles without being totally incapacitated. It does seem that running has become part of my way of life, and I do credit it with more energy than I used to have for getting things done—though part of the credit no doubt goes to being around Hal, and another part to continued pleasant working circumstances. Last night there was a party to celebrate having lived through the Heartbook—I think I wrote you something about the tribulations connected with that one—not, you understand, a party to promote it or anything, just a party. My boss brought champagne, and some people turned up, including the typesetter, whom I'd never seen before. The book looks awful, in my opinion, but it's useful and may even make money. I'm close to the end of *Daniel Deronda*, which I started reading back in the fall but never really got into until during the holidays—a real stunner—and have begun reading, of all things, *The Interpretation of Dreams*. My inclination to do that dates, I believe, to hearing Harold Bloom, the Yale critic and a classmate of Hal's at Cornell, say that the two great works of literature in this century were it and *Remembrance of Things Past*. So far, it's more entertaining than I expected.

Hal is grading exams. Recklessly, he assigned his class to decide a case the Supreme Court was in the midst of deliberating. The decision came down earlier this week. I haven't heard whether the students are concurring or dissenting. Anyhow, he sends his best.
Love,
Amy

. . . .

Good Friday 1980
Dear Rimsa—
[. . .] Howard Moss did come to dinner and was very pleasant company. He is somewhat pudgy without being fat, with a massive head and a benign look, behind glasses. One of his longtime friends is James Merrill, whom he calls "Jimmy," and who even in middle age would fit the description of the ultra-elegant young men in the audience at the Y (I heard him read at a memorial for Elizabeth Bishop, as I may have mentioned). The character of that audience has changed, it seems. The young men look mainly scruffy, and have beards, and there are lots of young women, and a fair amount of feminist swagger among the older ones. As for Anthony Hecht himself, the reports I've gotten suggest that he's developed

into more of a *mensch*: according to my friend at the *Atlantic,* whose best friend studied with him at Harvard, he was of the generous kind whose main concern is to encourage the writing of good poetry. I got the same kind of report from a friend of mine from politicking days—a maverick lawyer who now spends his time writing, who went to one of those workshops at Bread Loaf, and who said the one person on the staff who struck him as genuinely friendly was Anthony Hecht. He's still a formalist, but I don't find him cold (I can't remember reading anything of his until lately). Howard Moss seems to have been in graduate school at Columbia around the same time I was, and he found it just as uncongenial—the one person he remembered favorably was William York Tindall, the Yeats specialist who also wrote a funny book about D. H. Lawrence. Precisely my reaction. Besides "Artifacts" (now retitled "Salvage"—I'll enclose a copy), the *New Yorker* has just lately bought another one on the light side, called "Exmoor"—but the real breakthrough is that that same week, *Poetry* finally came through—they're going to publish "Balms." And the *Kenyon Review,* which in its second incarnation I find the most interesting of the literary quarterlies I've seen, is taking a weightier piece, "Or Consider Prometheus."

Please don't feel apologetic about sending *The Alexandria Quartet.* Durrell is one of those people who repay rereading. Do you know his travel books? I've just finished re-reading *Bitter Lemons,* which is wonderful. If you don't have it, let me know—I can get a paperback from Dutton with no trouble. I read *The Women's Room* a year or so back and found it devastating. Like you, I have no wish for grandchildren or any other aspect of marriage. But I feel compelled to add that in my experience not every male is quite as warped and disappointing as Marilyn French makes them out to be. Hal (whose last name is Korn) being one exception, and my nephew (whose first name is David) quite possibly another. CETA, the source of funds for the orchestra he plays in, is short for Comprehensive Employment Training Act, whose funds are going to shrink under the budget-cutters' axe, and when that happens David's regular income from that source will end. In the meantime, since the government is in effect his boss, he'll be going to Washington with his orchestra on the 10th, to play for the Department of Labor and at the White House ("Hail to the Chief" and maybe something else, maybe not). The music column of the *New Yorker,* early in February, had a nice section on CETA and the Orchestra of New York, as the group is known. If you can find it, you'll have a better idea of what the project is all about. [. . .]

Love,
Amy

. . . .

Corea, Maine 04624

June 1, 1980
Dear Mary Jo—
Yes, here we are in Maine once again, and I'm in my old spot on the sun-
porch with its view of water, islands and lighthouse, and in some ways it's
as though we'd always been here—though in fact there have been some al-
terations, including a fancy new bathroom where the spare room once was,
and that will take some getting used to. There is still spare sleeping space,
happily, and we do hope you and Brad will indeed come. The Fourth of
July weekend would be just fine, and of course we're all the more eager to
have you as our guests, knowing that you really are GOING TO JAPAN.
One does need to put in capitals, as you observe. For one thing, I feel that
it's absolutely necessary to show you the cormorants-in-their-element hereabouts, since I believe watching cormorants trained to behave as the aquatic equivalent of falcons is a big thing in Japan. We also, for the moment,
have a loon in our (aquatic) back yard. And then there's the sundew bog,
with its fine stand of pitcher plants. Yes, there is a Greyhound bus, the one
that goes to Nova Scotia and is presumably the route taken by Elizabeth
Bishop when the moose was encountered. The stop nearest us is Goulds-
boro, and as of last summer anyhow it left Boston late at night and got in
around breakfast time. There are also planes—the one to Bar Harbor is the
closest to us—but the bus stop is actually only six or eight miles from us.
   I somehow believed all along that you would be going to Japan, but
that doesn't make it any the less awesome to contemplate. To think of
those public baths! (Laurence Lieberman wrote a poem describing the
scene; what I didn't realize was that it was so entirely, inescapably part of
the fabric of things.)
   Meanwhile, I'm likewise awed by the Merrill ouija-board-poems project,
and await with real suspense the outcome of your researches. Much as I admire James Merrill for what he does with language, I have to confess being
put off by the idea of the ouija board, and to remaining just a bit dubious
after hearing him read the other week from *Divine Comedies*. He was introduced by Frederick Turner of the *Kenyon Review* as "the most civilized man
in the world," and since that may be true, it's probably fitting that he should

do what he does—write companionably of friends living or dead, along with the creatures of his own imagination, as though they were all parts of one big masque, for private performance. But I've read so little of him after all, that I'm hardly entitled to that much of an opinion.

The readings, anyhow, were probably the best, and undoubtedly the most exhilarating, I ever went to. Trude [poet Gjertrud Schnackenberg]— who so perfectly fitted your description that we had no trouble picking her out beforehand—had real presence, and I'm still haunted by the poem she read about finding the jawbone of a raccoon, as though I'd been in that kitchen, with the stars outside so tiny. I could also see, meeting her, how shy she is—a kind of shyness that must have been intensified by the circumstances. Hal had never been to a poetry reading before, except the one time I read in a back room at a pub, and that hardly counts,— on the supposition that he needed to *see* the words. He was so pleased to discover that it wasn't so that he came with me to the second evening of readings, when Walcott, Merrill and Hecht read their poetry and Doctorow read a story. A high-powered foursome, all impressive; we liked Hecht best of all, and I was sorry that he didn't turn up at the cocktail party on the third evening, or at least not while I was there. I took my friend Phoebe, and there was no one there (besides Trude) whom either of us knew except as a face; but it occurred to me afterward that if Anthony Hecht had been there, I might have been bold enough to introduce myself by way of mentioning Brad! I might also have ventured to speak to Frederick Turner of the KR—except that I'd just gotten a brief note rejecting everything I sent him (including both "The Dahlia Gardens" and "Rain at Bellagio") as "lacking passion." I was, as you may suppose, quite crushed. That will teach me to put any trust in the flattering words of editors—I even halfway wondered whether, after all, it wasn't my own flattering words about his editorial that made him look kindly on the thing he did take. One thing is clear—one is not going to be rewarded for showing any ambition, if there is the slightest doubt about whether or not it has succeeded—in which event one must expect to be punished.

I keep wondering whether you've heard from KR yet. And Howard Moss. I do hope for good news.

Hearing Brodsky read his poem on the Thames at Chelsea got me thinking about London, and a few days later the enclosed was the result. Originally it was called "Hazards of Foreign Travel"—but then, with revision, that began to seem too obvious. What do you think? [The poem ultimately became "A Hairline Fracture" in *The Kingfisher*.]

It's a relief that you could make more sense of the triptych in its revised condition. I hadn't thought about all those commas in the first Darwin stanza—but now that I look, I can see that you're right. I'm less sure about "looking like waste," but am going to think some more. Thank you, once again, for all the help of your close attention.

I've brought along not only the letters of Flannery O'Connor but also *The Voyage of the Beagle*—which, I'm almost ashamed to say, I'd never read more than snatches of before, but which turns out to be wonderful. Maybe it's better not to have read it until now. We plan also to read some poetry aloud—Anthony Hecht and Elizabeth Bishop are on hand, and the paperback Palgrave belonging to the owners was waiting, left where we'd be sure to find it. And just as the air here makes breathing something entirely new, so the silence makes listening to music all the better. We're having a feast of Beethoven, including Brendel playing the piano concertos, and some quartets we hardly knew before. Choosing and packing the records to be brought takes more time—and begins sooner—than any other part of getting ready. [. . .]
Love,
Amy

. . . .

Corea, Maine 04624

June 9, 1980
Dear Mary Jo—
Your action-packed letter arrived today, and I hasten to assure you that Hal and I are both delighted to hear the news that you and Brad are GETTING MARRIED. Brad's bursting into laughter at unexpected moments sounds to both of us like the best kind of sign. As for your sleepless nights, I hardly see how it could be otherwise—but hope you're getting some respite. I have them up here occasionally. My favorite forestalling remedy is hot milk immediately before retiring. Our exercise guru says the calcium is supposed to calm one down, and it does seem to work somehow. We'll certainly hope we can be at the wedding—especially since everything about the plans sounds just right. I'm not, I may add, even surprised; I somehow had a feeling it would work out this way, just as I had that you would indeed be GOING TO JAPAN.

Great news that you'll be coming up here meanwhile! I hope I won't have built up the surroundings too insufferably—you'll find nothing spectacular at first look, but the kind of place that grows on one. I made my first trip to the bog and the Inner Bar today—the Outer Bar was barely passable, but I decided not to chance it this time—and found the first of the arethusa in bloom, the season's crop of pitcher plants in the button-bud stage, and sundews just beginning to show themselves. I realize now that they don't become a whole blazing carpet until late July, which was when I first saw them—and even then the vision in retrospect was just that: the poem was written six months afterward. But you know how *that* is. Today there was a small falcon just outside the window—the first really good look I've ever had at a falcon of any kind. There is a whole flock of cedar waxwings, which look as though they'd been invented by a Japanese watercolorist; I hope they'll still be around for you to see. The lilacs are just blooming (which is mentioned in the tire-urns poem) to give you an idea of that incredible pastel. What's going on in the bog right now is that cloudberries are in bloom—locally referred to as hayth-berries. They're pure white, like some first-communion version of a primrose or a buttercup, with a pair of claws uncurling into leaves that, once opened, reveal the plant for what it really is, a kind of raspberry. I wonder if there would have been any of those in Nova Scotia. They're yellow tinged with red, and taste, amazingly, like baked apples.

I was sorry about all those magazines. I know how it feels to get that kind of letter—I got one from *Field*, with record speed. Editors sure are inscrutable—present company (let's hope) excepted. To be quite accurate, what Turner of KR said was "lacks the passion of your best stuff"—though what stuff he was referring to, other than the one thing he took, who knows? I'm consoled that you saw something in "A Hairline Fracture." Do please let me know if you have any thoughts about a title.

And if that one is sad, wait till you see what's coming with this letter for being *really* sad. It's something I'd been thinking about off and on for months—parts of it for years—and am somewhat surprised that it finally found a shape for itself. There will probably still be changes. The last phrase was originally a little different, and I'm not sure whether I've gotten it right yet. Anyhow, the poetry factory seems to have gotten into operation once again. Just yesterday I finished a draft of a narrative poem—unsad, but also about England, and three pages long. Today I did a draft of one, at last, directly inspired by the scene up here. I've discovered a place on the rocks outside where it's possible to write, and while I was out there working on project number two, this one came along in the nudging form of notes along the margin.

We've been reading Wordsworth aloud, if you can imagine. It started out with my reading Hal the J. K. Stephen parody of the sonnet on the subjugation of Switzerland (I think), which is one of the funniest such things I've ever read—and from there went on to others. I forget about Wordsworth for months and even years, and then realize what a total affinity I feel with the way he thought about things, for all that he seems to have had no sense of humor. Those political sonnets sound as timely now as anything anybody is writing, and are a reminder that in politics things never look very good, really. [. . .]

Love,
Amy

. . . .

Corea, Maine

June 18, 1980

Dear Barbara—

[. . .] Thus far, I'm not turning out new things with quite the dispatch of last summer, though I like to think what I'm doing is an improvement. I'll enclose a copy of something that was finished just before we came up here. The idea came to me as a result of going to hear Joseph Brodsky, the emigré Russian poet, read at an NYU affair. One of the poems had to do with the Thames at Chelsea, and its mention of various scenes in London reminded me of when Hal and I were there four years ago—having, as it happens, a terrible time. Things got better once we got out of London, but I was frightened half out of my wits. I originally called my poem "Hazards of Foreign Travel" to suggest that the situation proved only temporary; do you think that's a preferable title?—The NYU affair had to do with the revived *Kenyon Review*, and I got an invitation presumably because I'm now a contributor—I mean they took one thing of mine, though they've since turned down others in a crushingly offhand way. There were two evenings of readings and then a cocktail party. Hal refused the party, but was persuaded to go with me to the readings, which were quite exhilarating: besides Brodsky, they included Galway Kinnell, James Merrill, Derek Walcott, E. L. Doctorow (not a poet, but reading a sort of prose poem) and—best of all—Anthony Hecht. Hal had thought before that readings were not for him, but has now revised that opinion. The cocktail party was something of a bore—not many people, perhaps because the security was so tight (you had your name checked off a list), or maybe because of an Academy of American Poets do that was going on at the same time, or I don't know what. I took my friend Phoebe, who knows literary people, and we found nobody it seemed really urgent to talk to, though we recognized various faces. I'd halfway supposed Howard

Moss of the *New Yorker* would be there, but he wasn't. He's just taken two more poems—which brings the total in the works there to five. I hardly believe it. No telling when any of them will appear. [. . .]

Love,

Amy

. . . .

September 18, 1980

Dear Barbara—

[. . .] The latest literary development is a letter from Howard Moss at the *New Yorker*, saying that they're taking *two* out of a batch of three things I craftily sent him over the Labor Day weekend, so that they seem to have been near the top of the pile when he came back after a summer in the country—"The Kingfisher" and "Beethoven in Mid-America." They want another title for the latter, but I guess that can be managed. Also, he said that Helen Vendler (very big critic, new book out lately) had asked him who I was. There is something to be said for having no academic connections, maybe, people are annoyed enough to be curious. [. . .]

Love,

Amy

. . . .

October 25, 1980

Dear Robert [Quint]—

It's a day of slashing rain in New York, after a succession of mild full days that kept me from really believing the summer was over—which means that an appalling length of time has gone by since your letter arrived, with the diary entries I'd feared might have been lost. I'm greatly moved by what you say—most of all the entry about the struggle to *hear*, in a life without cease-fire. I believe something similar about that special interior rhythm, and being bathed in music from the stereo, day after day, only strengthens the conviction. Perhaps, given time for reflection, you'll find this can be developed further. Maybe it will have to be in Hebrew, after all—but in any event I can imagine how difficult it must be to deal in another language with experiences that are totally outside that language.

I can also understand your being drawn to a life according to rule. Yes, I did go through one of those conversion experiences—prepared for, I think now, as much by the esthetic side of Christianity, the paintings in European churches, the music of the liturgy, as by anything doctrinal—

and landed in an extremely liturgical Episcopalian congregation, where for a while I was happy to be, simply because my personal affairs had come unhinged and I was grateful for the grand predictability of the liturgical year. I even wondered for a while about joining a religious order, and spent some time in various convents. One of my best friends over the years has been a nun in an English Benedictine community, where she is very happy. She is one of the few people from that time to whom I still feel close. It's twenty years this autumn since she took up the contemplative life; in fact, I was with her in Italy when she left to begin it. Last fall I wrote a long poem about that weekend; I'll send a copy, on the chance that some of it will suggest my feelings about the whole question. I've often thought of your immersion in the Talmud as not unlike the Benedictines' immersion in silence—an opportunity to *hear* what the noise of everything else drowns out.

The noise of everything else is as bad as ever, this election year. I have no enthusiasm for anyone running for President, but will vote for Carter as less frightening than Reagan. I understand that there are Jews who think Reagan has more sympathy for Israel than Carter—but this doesn't seem likely, since Reagan's closest associates include oil company executives whose closest associates, in turn, are sure to include a lot of Arabs. For what it's worth, I'll pass along David Schoenbrun's observation that whatever happens, U.S. Policy toward Israel can't change much—Israel being the one democracy and the one friend we have in the Middle East, more truly now than ever, with all the turmoil in the Moslem countries. The one candidate I've really cared about this time is a young environmentalist who took on my loathsome Congressman in the Democratic primary (said Congressman being John Murphy, a friend of Somoza in Nicaragua, the late Shah, and assorted other shady characters). David got to know him better than I do, and became one of a small group of mainstays in his campaign while he was occupying my Village apartment and I was off in Maine; as so often happens, alas, he lost.

David has moved into an apartment in Washington Heights, on a sublet from another musician. He's managing fairly well, though these aren't good times for musicians, and has been sounding quite cheerful. A few weeks back, I had a pleasant evening with him and one of his friends from the summers he spent in Alberta—one Ralph Oberhaldt, who has been a forest ranger, then went to law school, and was now in New York for the first time, on his way to Oxford for a year as a Rhodes Scholar, and who had a sense of history, and of proportion in things, that's rare at any age but especially in anyone under thirty-five.

Just about a month ago I went out to Iowa, for a short visit with my sister—the only member of the immediate family I have there any more. I actually went through Grinnell on the bus, but the station has been moved to the very edge of town, so even less of the campus is visible from it now. There had been a drought, so the cornfields were browner than usual at that time of year, but even so I found the countryside beautiful in its own peculiar, amorphous and elusive way. I've been puzzling my head over the nature of that landscape for years, and have just lately begun writing about what it means. And it now occurs to me that possibly the reason I've been drawn to the ocean for as long as I can remember has to do with the nature of the prairie—"half sea half land," as Charles Olson calls it—which over the eons has so often been under water, and unlike most other parts of the continent has never once been lifted and folded under again. Rather than archeological, in other words, it may be that roots I have there are *geological.* Which might explain, also, why it's so hard for a Midwesterner to find out who he or she is.

And which might even explain the attraction of the church, as a definite structure with a deep history, as well as my eventual disenchantment with it. That disenchantment was precipitated by the Vietnam war. My question concerning that met with so much frightened, authoritarian rigidity that after a while I lost confidence in the figures I'd looked up to, and no longer felt at home. I'd asked of the institution more, I suppose, than any institution can be expected to offer. But that doesn't mean that the deeper configurations of reality that are represented by Christianity, as they are by all the great religions, have any less meaning for me. The Hammarskjold haiku (coal into diamonds) is wonderful, and fits in with the metaphors of geology that are preoccupying me these days. Thanks so much for sharing it with me.

Along with the weekend-in-Italy poem, I'll send a copy of another one that has appeared in the *Kenyon Review.* I don't believe I'd sent it to you before: anyway, it deals with another of my preoccupations, the short history of the human love affair with hydrocarbon.
With best wishes ever,
Amy

. . . .

October 18, 1981
Dear Barbara—
It begins to be a good while since your letter came with all the details

about Guam, which entertained me greatly. I don't know exactly where the time has gone, except that there has been a fair amount of rushing about. For one thing, there was Lana Turner and her memoirs, which I'd thought I was finished with. It's too tedious a tale to be gone into, but my boss flew out to Hollywood the other day to deal with her directly, and this time I think I may have seen the last of the project, aside from doing a little blurb for the Dutton catalog. There are now the New School lectures by David Schoenbrun, which means a set of notes to be delivered each week for the next month or so. And in the midst of it all, guess what? There was this invitation to go out and do a Poetry Reading at Kenyon College! The event took place just a week ago today, and it turned into a sort of cliffhanger— for the reason that just before I was to leave for Ohio I began catching cold, and by Sunday evening it had turned into laryngitis. I had imagined various calamities beforehand, such as not getting there at all, or getting scared to death, or having six people show up. What happened, I concluded as a believer in Nemesis, was that I'd simply told a few too many people. So what to do? In the end I had my student hostess read one poem, and the co-editor of the *Kenyon Review* who also entertained me read a couple of others. For the rest, I produced a sort of stage whisper—and it's just possible that everybody paid closer attention than if I'd been in normal voice. I got more laughs than I'd thought possible, and some spontaneous rounds of applause after the longer, more somber poems. Fred Turner, the *Kenyon Review* editor, told me I'd turned into a legend right on the spot. There must have been between thirty and forty people altogether—more than I'd been led to expect, since the student coordinator had assured me that the crowd, unfortunately, wouldn't be large, and I had said that was just fine with me. From among them there materialized a woman who grew up in my home town—metamorphosed from a fluffy, ruffly, ethereal little girl who gave solo piano recitals to a close-cropped, well-tailored type I would never have recognized—and a brother of my Massachusetts godchild, who appeared without any prompting (since I never got around to letting his mother and sister know). And there were some darling young people who sort of hovered around afterward. The evening before the reading there was a dinner, and on the morning before I had brunch with my student hostess, who showed me the grave of John Crowe Ransom and brought me some of her own poems, which I read in the midst of the graveyard and which turned out to be lovely, and then we went for a long walk out into the country, talking all the way despite my resolve to try to save my voice. In the afternoon I had tea at Fred Turner's house, also out in the country—

in fact Gambier really isn't a town, and the post office is right on the campus—and met his wife Mei Lin, an inscrutably lovely woman who I was told is Japanese, but that can't be, and who anyhow speaks with an impeccable educated-British accent, and their two little boys, and a couple of Canadian anthropologists who were their house guests. The conversation was an education in itself. Mei Lin phoned a singer for advice about the laryngitis, and provided a solution of equal parts of table salt and baking soda in lukewarm water, which I kept getting up to gargle; it did help a little. Fred Turner is a great enthusiast, interested in just about everything; he'd already sent me his epic poem, and I brought back with me a published collection of poems and another collection that's still in manuscript. His co-editor is on sabbatical and I didn't see him, but I got a little of the story of how they came to revive the *Kenyon Review*—to counteract a prevailing tendency in literary magazines that they agreed was all wrong. Such energy! They've taken two more poems of mine, by the way (and the *New Yorker*, the *New Republic*, and the *Nation* have all come through with acceptances just lately).

In the meantime, inspired by I. F. Stone's example—he started learning classical Greek at the age of seventy-one, so that he could find out just what happened to democracy back in those days, by reading Thucydides—I've signed up for a Greek course that meets on Saturdays, from 9:15 to after 1:00 p.m., at The New School. It was an impulse, and I'm still a bit astonished that I actually did it, but the course will have been worth while even if I'm not reading Euripides by the end of it. The instructor is absolutely top-notch, and it's as elite a collection of people as I could expect to be part of, ranging from college-age to a retired doctor (I think) who uses a magnifying glass. It's hard, and we're covering two or three textbook lessons at each session. But I'm already getting an idea of the sound, which is part of what I had in mind. [. . .]

Love,

Amy

. . . .

December 26, 1981

Dear Rimsa—

Your Christmas parcel is a real feast, in every sense of the word. I really look forward to cooking from the two cookbooks, since vegetarian dishes are more and more what I really prefer—and Paul Goodman, whom I have long admired, must have had one of the most original minds of the century. I've already dipped into the essays, none of which I've read before so far as I can remember, and am eager for more. Thank you very much—also for the desk calendar, the only one I've ever seen that takes account of the weather, which arrived just a few days ago.

I'd intended to send off some kind of greeting before the holiday, but there have been more than the usual disruptions this year. I don't remember whether I wrote you that my brother Richard, the Minnesota one, had come down with acute leukemia around the end of February. He was very ill for some weeks; after drastic chemotherapy the leukemia went into remission for several months, but just before Thanksgiving he phoned to say that he was given maybe months, maybe weeks to live. I went out early in December, and saw him while he was still at a home. He died on the 13th. You can understand that I've found myself rather behind—the more since I had a call for jury duty these last two weeks. But that's now over, and for the first time in a good while I feel as though I had time, finally, to catch up on writing and correspondence. I can't remember just when I wrote last—though I did send off a couple of magazines with me in them not long ago. Was it before I signed up for the Greek course, I wonder? Anyhow, it has turned out to be thrilling though formidably difficult. We plunged right into Xenophon—in snatches, that is—and have more recently been confronted with some passages from Plato, as well as from the Gospels, Pindar, Aeschylus, and Simonides, among others. The teacher—a moonlighting Sarah Lawrence professor— has the learning and the imagination to bring the entire scene alive, and almost every minute he is striking flint with some new insight, historical or etymological. The other unlikely development this past fall was being invited to give a poetry reading at Kenyon College. It turned out to be a delightful place, in hilly country with huge oaks; John Crowe Ransom's grave is right in the middle of the campus, and I paid a visit to it with my student hostess, a poet herself, who showed me her work and took me on a long ramble into the countryside. I had tea with Fred Turner, one of the co-editors of the *Kenyon Review*, and his fascinating wife Mei Lin, who must be Chinese but has a flawless upperclass English accent, and their Canadian houseguests, a couple of anthropologists; the conversation was all over the place and very lively, as you can imagine. My situation was that I had caught cold, it had begun turning into laryngitis, and with the reading only a few hours away, I wasn't sure I'd have any voice left. Mei Lin got on the phone to a singer, and produced a mixture of equal parts of table salt and baking soda in tepid water, to be gargled every few minutes. It helped more than all the other remedies I'd tried, but not very much. I would have been more frantic if the weather hadn't been so idyllic and everyone there so friendly. As it turned out, I managed a stage whisper, whose effect was that people had to listen very closely to hear anything, and so came closer to hearing everything. They laughed at my jokes, and applauded the more ambitious pieces—I suppose partly out of relief that I'd gotten through another one. I now have an invitation to read to a high school class in suburban Connecticut, which in a way makes me uneasier than Kenyon did; high school kids are harder to get to than a college audience.

Howard Moss came to brunch not long ago, with my nephew and some other musicians. He had a heart attack early in the year, and is much thinner than he was, but seemed cheerful enough. He's on a salt-free diet, and my solution to the problem was a couple of vegetarian dishes spiced with green chilis and ginger on the one hand, and cinnamon-clove-cardamom-coriander etcetera, with a yoghurt-coconut base, on the other—plus fresh pineapple, plus some marvelous dates that had just arrived from California for dessert. I still haven't persuaded Hal that a meatless diet is possible, but I keep trying. [. . .]

Love,

Amy

. . . .

February 1, 1982

Dear Mary Jo—

[. . .] I must delay no longer before I let you know how beholden I am to you for your comments on the essay—you've picked up just the kind of thing that needs picking up, where I halfway knew I'd slipped a little but wasn't quite alert—or sharp—enough to do anything about it. As for what Jonathan Holden thinks about closure-vs.-music, I wish I knew; it appears that he didn't when he wrote that sentence, but perhaps he is working his way toward a position of some kind. Fred Turner likes the essay, but hasn't given it the kind of reading you have. He says, by the way, that they will run all four of the still unpublished poems of mine they have in the summer issue! So aside from "The Dahlia Gardens" and a couple of other things, just about everything in the book will have seen print by the time it comes out. "The Dahlia Gardens" is a real problem. I wrote you, I think, about what Sydney Lea said—and he's as sympathetic an editor as one could hope for, once you get his attention. It occurs to me that aside from its being so long, people shy away from it because (a) they don't really know what I'm talking about and (b) they don't *want* to know about it. Which leads me to conclude that some sort of explanatory note may be necessary. In fact, I've about decided to do a real Marianne Moore number and annotate my book. I asked Alice Quinn about this, and without hesitation she said she was all for it. So I've done a set of notes (there may still be others) which I'm sending for your comments. They have been great fun to do, I must say.

As you'll gather, I've now met Alice Quinn. Originally we were to spend the day going over the manuscript [of *The Kingfisher*], but on the appointed day she hadn't gotten to it, so we just talked for a couple of hours. She is very pleasant and encouraging, but I came away feeling even more disorganized than I thought I was—if you see what I mean. What I like is the acid-free paper, and the understanding implicit in it that one is indeed publishing for posterity. So I suppose everything is going to be all right, though I do wonder how the book is ever going to be ready to come out next January. Oh yes, another thing that came up (before I've even seen a contract, or heard a mention of same) is what might go on the jacket. When I mentioned that I thought of the title poem as a piece of verbal cloisonné, Alice Quinn immediately said, "Oh, do you suppose we could find a piece of cloisonné with a kingfisher in it?" I rather doubt it, but now it occurs to me to wonder whether you might come across something like that in Kyoto. If you ever do, I'd love to know. [. . .]
Love,
Amy

. . . .

February 1, 1982
Dear Helen Vendler—
It was a delightful surprise to receive your letter. Though I'm not a teacher myself, I know what the pressures must be—so I hope you won't feel obliged to reply to this one. But I did want to say, quite aside from thanking you for your generous words about my own work, how much it meant to me to hear of your experience in reading Keats's copy of *Paradise Lost*. I'd just been immersed in the W. J. Bate biography, and had in fact done a draft of a poem about Keats at Margate, when your letter arrived. So you can imagine how eager I am to know whether you may be writing about the Keats P.L. one day soon—or perhaps even an entire book on Keats? If so, and if it's uncommitted, there would be a great deal of interest in it at

E. P. Dutton, where I'm a part-time editor; John Macrae III, the publisher, is a great admirer of yours. The address is 2 Park Avenue, if you're inclined to write him directly.

I'm happy to report what I've just learned—that Knopf will be publishing my collection of poems (to be entitled *The Kingfisher*) early next year. Meanwhile, I'll be looking for more of your criticism in print, and going back to what I already have of it.

Gratefully,

Amy Clampitt

. . . .

February 19, 1982

Dear Mary Jo—

[. . .] I forget whether I mentioned it, but I've begun reading Homer! It's at Hunter, which couldn't be more conveniently located—though getting admitted and then registering was a large bureaucratic drag. I've now been to two sessions. Three of the people in last term's class have also signed up, which makes it quite cozy. The instructor, whose name I still don't know, isn't quite the marvel Professor Seigel was, but he is just as lively and enthusiastic. We've plunged right into the *Iliad* , and to my own amazement I'd gotten the four lines I was asked to translate aloud just about right—which *never* happened with Thucydides or even Plato, in the other class. Homer really is easier to figure out, though I'm having to look up just about everything and the Ionic endings differ a good deal from the Attic. And I've already come across one of those ringing lines that can't be translated: because the sound is so integral to the meaning. I'd never seen *polyphloìsboio* before, but since it was next to *thalassès*, it of course had to be the sound of the ocean. I haven't even looked at any translation to see what anybody has invented it; I suppose it's something like "loud-roaring." I don't know whether it's possible to convey the peculiar excitement that goes with all this; it's like arriving in a place you'd dreamed of all your life. Whereas I would suppose that getting inside the Japanese language is more like arriving in a place you couldn't believe existed—as in fact you've demonstrated with "Japanese Characters." I know just what you mean about Brad's discovering new little knots; Hal does the same thing every now and then, so it must be in the nature of the function of best-friend-and-severest. I've just reread the poem, and found it (even in that early version) more wonderful than I remembered. I don't know whether I mentioned this before, but the "grammar reversing like a velvet nap" somehow linked up in my head with the way the hummingbird's ruby throat seems to reverse to black when the light changes, and eventually may account for the "unreversed, irrevocable dark" in my fisherman elegy. Who knows whether I would have thought of it at all otherwise? It's awesome to think of how many things I've picked up that way without even realizing it!

No, *Harper's* never took anything of mine either. The first time I tried, I got a small handwritten note from Hayden Carruth saying not now, but try again; when I tried again, everything came back with a standard rejection slip. I was about to get myself organized to send off "The Dahlia Gardens" when I took a look at the current masthead, and found this: "UNSOLICITED MANUSCRIPTS cannot be considered or returned unless accompanied by a stamped, self-addressed envelope. *Harper's* does not publish unsolicited fiction or poetry." So much for that. This issue has a poem by Joyce Carol Oates. There is evidently no poetry editor at all. In short, the situation resembles the one confronting an aspiring actor: You can't get into a real production without being a member of Equity, and you can't become a member of Equity without having appeared in a real production. I'm so annoyed by this announcement of policy that I'm going to write a letter for Hal to sign, in response to a renewal notice, giving it as his reason for not renewing his subscription. He subscribes to both *TNR* and the *Atlantic Monthly* because I've been represented in them. By the way, there was a long but not terribly interesting article in the *New York Times Magazine*, lately, all about Zuckerman and how Robert Manning got fired and is suing, and the hiring of Whitworth and what he is or is not likely to do with the magazine. It may be that I didn't find it of much interest because of everything I already knew about the place thanks to you.

I must have mentioned that *Alice in Wonderland* has been my favorite book—if anything so totally *sui generis* can be so designated—for as long as I can remember. I almost believe I was already reading it before I went to school—but that is, I suppose, simply because I can't remember when I first did read it. *Little Men* was the first of the Alcott books I read—even though, as I may have mentioned, my sister Beth and I both got our names by way of *Little Women* . I'd be a bit anxious about going back to either, though what you say does reassure me. I have to admit being entranced with *Heidi*, the first time round.

I can see that planning for your eventual re-entry into these parts can't be otherwise than a large bafflement. In a small way, I feel that about going to Maine in the summer—one complication being that Professor Seigel's summer Greek play-reading course begins around the middle of June and runs until the beginning of August, and I can't bear to think of missing that—even though the particular play hasn't yet been decided on (availability of texts being a perennial problem for anything he might assign; he mentioned the *Bacchae* as a possibility). But I'm not complaining about anything really, as I imagine you're not; I simply regard myself, in spite of everything, as one of the fortunate people who happen to be around.

Love,

Amy

. . . .

April 3, 1982

Dear Helen Vendler—

Your letter of nearly a month ago gave me such pleasure that it ought to have had an immediate reply; I can only plead all sorts of obstacles and distractions that have slowed down correspondence. But now I must delay no longer in letting you know that the Guggenheim fellowship did indeed come through—and the credit is truly all yours, since without your encouragement I wouldn't have thought of applying. This is supposedly confidential until the 9th; but I'm more concerned now that you should learn the news from me, with my admiring thanks once again, before you hear it from any other source.

I'm all the more eager for your Keats book, and can imagine the excitement of discovering those Dryden references. I must admit that I haven't read Dryden at all, but clearly I am going to have to. Just now I haven't been reading much except—with great excitement and wonder— the *Iliad* in Greek. I didn't know any classical Greek at all until this past fall, when on an impulse I signed up for an intensive class with a wonderful man, Sam Seigel, at The New School, and having been guided through Attic grammar, with his encouragement several of the survivors signed up for a Homer course at Hunter College, and in about eight weeks we've somehow gotten through nearly five hundred lines. You can imagine that I think of Keats every time I come to another especially resonant line; the pathos is all but overwhelming. I'm sending the poem I mentioned; it was written before I began reading Homer, but hasn't been sent anywhere— in fact I've only just now (being an inveterate reviser) gotten a version finished enough to think of sending out. I don't know how much it may come through, and I don't know that it's even important—but the original impulse to write it, as nearly as I can recall, came out of my inland childhood, electrified by discovering that K.'d been mesmerized by the sight of a barley field in Hampstead.

And here I haven't thanked you yet for offering to read, review and write a blurb for *The Kingfisher*. Alice Quinn at Knopf will be sending you a copy of the manuscript, if she hasn't already done so. And just to round out the picture, I'm sending you a couple of little books—one privately published several years ago, mainly because someone I knew had gone into the business of fine printing, the other a little workshop project to which the author is more or less incidental. I offer them with some diffidence, since I expect you will not approve of some things, in the earlier book especially. One does write differently in isolation, as I was then. It *is* good to have readers! [. . .]
With grateful best wishes,
Amy Clampitt

. . . .

May 14, 1982
Dear Rimsa—
The Liddell and Scott, and your letter and the Keats sestina, all arrived safely, and to great delight and astonishment. The sestina is very touching, quite aside from the fiendish difficulty of the form. I'd never ventured it, or more than thought of doing so, until last summer, when after many revisions I managed one—and then, amazed that it was possible at all, after many revisions once again, produced a second one. They're both going to be in the summer issue of the *Kenyon Review*, along with two other, longer poems—concerning which the cartoon you sent is more apt than you could have known: The *really* long one of those two, which runs to six typewritten pages, had already been turned down once out there, but last fall when I read it to the Kenyon poetry society, the editor who was sitting next to me said, "Send it again"—and this time, sure enough, they took it. There's more: when I'd read a little thing called "Sunday Music"—which saw the light of day, finally, in *Poetry Northwest*, which I believe I sent you—same editor said, "Send that one too"—to which my answer was, "I already did." That one apparently hadn't got past the first reader. So you never know—and the moral of that would seem to be that you ought not to give up on sending your own work out, either.

As for the Liddell and Scott, it has been put to good use without delay. There is a vocabulary section in the back of my Homer textbook, but it can be cryptic and/or just plain lacking. We did finish the first book of the *Iliad*, and have been working on a passage from the sixth book, about Hector's farewell to Andromache and Astyanax. Last fall, our wonderful Professor Seigel, in telling us about lexicons, mentioned the joke about Little Liddell, Middle Liddell, and Great Scott—and also who Liddell was the father of. In fact, this spring there was an exhibition of Lewis Carroll memorabilia at the Morgan Library, which (since it's just up the street from Dutton offices) I actually got to. One thing that struck me, so that I wonder that I hadn't thought of it before, was how much the Mad Hatter looks like Bertrand Russell, or vice versa.

Your house-painting project sounds so formidable that I really shouldn't feel the dread I do over having *somebody else* repaint my 12th Street apartment, including the closet—all a part of the flurry of repairs and tidying up in connection with the landlord's plan to offer it up as a co-op. I've just taken everything out of the closet for the first time since I moved in, so far as I can remember. What needs to be done in the way of replastering is nothing less than horrific. What *will* be done remains to be seen. If I didn't have elsewhere to flee to, I'd be frantic. As it is, here I am writing you a letter not only to thank you but also to wish you a happy birthday. A parcel is on its way; I hope it will have arrived in time, and that the magazines have gotten there by now.

Love,

Amy

. . . .

June 20, 1982

Dear Helen Vendler—

Thank you so much for your letter, and for your willingness to read and comment on the manuscript, and above all what you said about the samphire-gatherers. It had never occurred to me to connect that image with the Hopkins poem, for all my long acquaintance with it; but now that you're pointed it out, I can't doubt the connection, and it makes the whole thing just that much richer. I've gone on thinking about Keats, and will send along two more poems that concern him—one directly, the other indirectly. I may have mentioned that I've been trying to learn classical Greek; I'll never be very good at it, but the Homer class was one of the great experiences of my life, and the sonnet (as you'll gather) is a tribute to it. I've just begun a summer course in which we're reading *The Persians* of Aeschylus. Between all this and the work I've committed myself to before the Guggenheim officially begins, on July 1, I haven't had as much time to write poetry as I would otherwise; but the effort does seem worth making.

In keeping with your comment on the notes to *The Kingfisher*, I've already cut out some of the more personal observations in a few of them: to "Marginal Employment" and I forget just which others. If you should happen to have noted any that look especially superfluous, I'd of course be grateful to you for pointing them out—but please don't feel obliged in the slightest. It may be that I've overdone the notion, which arose out of having discovered that some informal explanation to people hearing the poems read aloud did seem to be enlightening—and then expanded the idea into a lot of glosses à la Marianne Moore, since my editor seemed to like the idea.

Gratefully yours,

Amy Clampitt

. . . .

June 21, 1982

Dear Barbara—

[. . .] We did join the big anti-nuke march a week ago Saturday, with a nice mongrel crew that included some old friends of Hal's from out of town, a crusading pediatrician, my nephew David's violin teacher (who must be close to eighty but is still full of life), but not David himself (he was playing quartets out in East Hampton), and an old friend of mine from the publishing business. Somebody bought one of those plastic headpieces that are the newest fad and that were being sold in great numbers along the march, and put it on my head. So there I was, adorned with giggling pinwheels, when somebody I didn't even recognize came up and said, "Are you Amy Clampitt? Have you seen Alice Quinn?"—Alice Quinn being my editor at Knopf, and I hadn't seen her, thank goodness. She's probably no more than thirty, and nice as can be. The other week I had one of those legendary publishing lunches with her and another Knopf poet, name of Marie Ponsot—an almost exact contemporary of mine, the great difference in our careers being that she married an improvident artist (whom she's now divorced) and had seven children! We found so much to talk about that long after the sole Veronique and strawberries were gone, and the second round of coffee had been poured, and there was almost nobody else left in the restaurant, we were still at it. I staggered home so overstimulated that I had to go to bed to recover.

The Mountain does sound like a fine place—though I don't know it from the movie, I've read various glowing accounts of all those birds and flowering trees. I hope the sprained ankle is mended by now. Oh yes, I do know about that out-of-the-mainstream feeling. I get it in just about every situation where I don't know anybody—and Hal and I have discovered that we get it in group situations where we do know people, and we still can't think of anything to make lively conversation about. And since Hal is naturally the sort people tend to seek out, I conclude that most people must react the same way to group situations generally.

Love,

Amy

. . . .

Corea, Maine 04624

August 8, 1982

Dear Helen—

The souvenir of Copenhagen arrived just the other day, and the thought of being thought of there, in that very particular connection, is so touching that only first names can any longer be appropriate. Though I've never been to Copenhagen myself I of course knew about the Little Mermaid being there in the harbor—but it somehow never struck me before how powerfully she must figure in the minds of all kinds of people. It also set me thinking about Andersen himself in Italy, and realized it's a thing to be looked into. Thank you ever and ever so much, too, for your generous words about *The Kingfisher*. As you know, nothing can be more satisfying than to know that one's work has given pleasure—the more so when it's to one whose judgment one holds in something like awe (though that isn't quite the word when so much positive enjoyment goes with it). I'm eagerly looking forward to the Keats book, and in the meantime I'm also greatly beholden for your comments on "Keats at Teignmouth." They're totally right and will be incorporated as soon as I get down to the business of writing and revising again.

As you'll note from the address, I've finally gotten away from New York, after a somewhat frantic effort to wind up various items of unfinished business so as to settle down to the serious business of being a Guggenheim Fellow. Now that I'm here, and for that purpose, I discover that I'm more than a little scared. I've never had quite such luxury in the time-to-do-nothing-but-write department before. It's a little like stage fright. Even opening up the typewriter entailed a minor struggle. But there are more ideas concerning Keats for which I have some notes, and which I hope to get to shortly. This is the town where I've spent some time in past summers—though we're in a different house, this time with a view onto the inlet where the lobster boats are anchored, with the profile of the Outer Bar island in the distance. I'll be here until around the end of August; later in the fall I expect to go to Iowa and other points west, and in the spring to England.

Your observation about the image of poppies twined with wheat in the Autumn ode is proof to me that you're wrong about poets not needing critics—that, and the absence of any seed falling into the earth to be resurrected. I'm especially eager now to read what you have to say about all this. For me, the image of poppies is a bit sinister because of associations with Mycenae; when I was there, they had just about finished blooming, and the fallen petals were black, like old bloodstains. I suppose this was lurking behind that line in the Teignmouth poem. Anyhow, it is salutary to be reminded of one's own departures in the process of re-imagining, whether legitimate or otherwise. My thanks once again.
Ever,
Amy

. . . .

Des Moines, Iowa

October 17, 1982
Dear Barbara—
Your letter caught up with me out here just yesterday—though Hal had read it to me over the phone—and it just so happens that I have access to this typewriter, though you must expect some wrong keys being hit. It's a Coronamatic and just a bit more newfangled than I can cope with without practice. But here goes anyhow. It was so exciting to hear about the three-act play and the goat manuscript. I do hope I'll finally get a look at both, once I'm back in New York. As you'll have gathered, I've been moving around. Left there on the 23rd of September, stayed several days in St. Cloud, Minnesota, with my sister-in-law, had twenty-four hours in Minneapolis, which I decided might just be the one truly civilized city in the U.S.—a really delightful, urban-and-woodsy metropolis at once rational and open, with lakes and little waterfalls and benches to sit and contemplate them from; and they have these sophisticated counterculture health-food bars at the Y, where you can eat for next to nothing (dig—tabouleh

salad, very peppy-tasting, with what must have been little green chilis: why, I only discovered them myself a year or so ago—and that a *Y*—you get the reaction of the Easterner who supposes the cuisine will be lagging by a light year or two, even if tasty, or be untasty in the effort to seem up to date—but Minneapolis knocked all that out of me). My niece who works there had gotten tickets to the symphony, with Yo-Yo Ma as soloist. And I spent a couple of hours before that, discovering the Pop art treasures of the Walker art gallery. The Guthrie theater is next door; I didn't go inside but got a notion of what a great place it is.

Anyhow, from Minneapolis I caught a bus to Greeley, Colorado, to visit my friend Doris, who teaches out there, and she and her husband drove me up into the mountains, and we had a picnic and admired the aspens, and saw mountain bluebirds, which are bluer than blue, and waited for the elk to bugle after the sun went down. They didn't bugle, but I had a few glimpses of them through binoculars. We also got up early and drove up into range country, near the Wyoming border, and saw and heard about ten thousand meadowlarks. And the weather was gorgeous, and I headed east toward Lincoln, Neb., and stayed overnight there, and then caught another bus that (with various switches and layovers) got me to Dallas. It was raining when I arrived, and the cousin who met me drove me out into one of those fast-growing bedroom exurbs where they have a brand-new house, designed by themselves, nestled in among native river oaks and yaupon holly, with a patio where we had breakfast next morning, and a barbecue that night. For a while I was alone in that carpeted, opulent, pale brick ranch-type showplace, with a brown marquisette shower curtain held back by silk ropes in the bathroom that was mine alone. Well, I'm making it sound more pretentious than it really is; but there is something about leaving a Greyhound bus terminal and taking a leisurely bath in such a place, totally still, with the rain dripping softly outside, where you've hardly even got your bearings yet, but you're a guest there! Dallas itself is a monument to seeing who can put up a glassier, tonier-colored, mirror-plated skyscraper; not much class at all that I could see, but out where my cousins live it's another matter. I had a wonderfully relaxed and leisurely time of it, and saw a lot of that unbelievable ornithological enterprise the scissortailed flycatcher. There was supposed to be a neighborhood roadrunner (ornithological enterprise, nonflight department), but like the bugling of the elk it was not to be on display.

Anyhow, since last Monday I've been in Iowa, based here in Des Moines but hopping about and having the greatest time I could ever have imagined for myself. It began with Grinnell, where some prodding by Margaret Matlack Kiesel, out there, and my editor in New York, a poetry reading had been arranged for last Tuesday. They sent a car for me in Des Moines, both to and from, and I had dinner in what used to be the Nollens' house, where I worked my sophomore year as a waitress and door-opening parlor maid—sitting now, if you please, flanked by the new (very young) president of the college and his young wife, both of them graduates years after me. Joe and Bea Mills Wall were also there, and a couple of other faculty members. After that Margaret Kiesel, who'd invited me to stay with her, had some people over, including Henry Alden—who retired as librarian a few years back but still lives here and hardly looks any older. And after they'd all left, Margaret and I sat around for a while longer, talking about I don't know what all. She's a cousin of George and David Matlack, who were special friends of mine, David especially, and she brought me up to date on them (David is now married to a third wife, I learn). But in a way the most astonishing thing of all was that there had been a little news story in the *Des Moines Register* about the reading, and an aunt of mine had seen it, and she and a neighbor had driven down to hear me! I had to stand at a lectern and use a microphone (instead of sitting down as I've managed to do elsewhere), and for a second or two I wasn't sure I would make it; but since then I've been astonished at my own aplomb. On Friday, just the day before yesterday—though I can hardly believe it was so recent—I went to Iowa State and did the same thing—only there, I also had a writing class to entertain in some way, and found that I could wing it fairly well—but then the instructor was right there, and we'd just had lunch and discovered that we were kindred spirits. At the reading itself, who should appear but a woman whom I hadn't seen since high school, but who'd seen a little news story in the campus paper and decided to come. The next morning she took me out to breakfast and then drove me back to Des Moines, and we had the most amazing time catching up on people we'd both known. I mean I listened while she filled me in. She'd served a term in the state legislature, and our political views coincided so perfectly that we hardly needed to say anything, except that it was all such fun. The people I stayed overnight with were just as serendipitous—both native New Yorkers, both on the faculty after living at Oak Ridge and in Geneva, and very happy to be where they are. They have a son who's a poet and a daughter who sounds remarkably like Joanie—whom of course I told them all about or as much as I was able to. The audience at the reading was rather subdued but perfectly attentive—and after Lorraine and her husband had taken me out to dinner in an opulent place, where the food was actually quite good, at the edge of Ames next door to a new sports-and-theater complex, with a view out over open country—after that, there was a party at their house and I met more darling young English-department types than I had time to keep straight. Do you know what? Out here, they *love Keats*! Now I'm about to go back to my actual hometown and see how that feels; then to Iowa City, Dubuque and Detroit where there is a Knopf poet, Ed Hirsch, who also went to Grinnell (??? coincidence) on account of whom I'm going to read at Wayne State. More when I'm at a more manageable typewriter.

Love,

Amy

. . . .

December 21, 1982

Dear Barbara—

It was great to hear that you're working on a *second* play—and I'm the more impressed given that I've not seen the first! I do hope to, one of these days. And oh my, what a lot of puzzlements you have to contend with— I mean the divorce and Social Security and options to retire or not. Do let me know how it all comes out.

I guess I haven't written since I got back here—on the first of November, just in time to vote. Aside from writing, of which there has been some, it's hard to account for where the time has gone, except that I do seem to have been perpetually either busy or distracted. And just now, not half an hour ago, my editor phoned to say that the very first, hand-bound copies of *The Kingfisher* have just come in. There have been almost daily phone calls from down there lately, and what to me sometimes feels like a whirl of social engagements. I mean, one night last week Alice, my editor, came to have dinner with Hal and me, and the next day I had lunch with her and the editor of the *New England Review*, with whom I've been carrying on a somewhat cantankerous correspondence. Nice man, though. A few weeks back Ed Hirsch was in town—Grinnell '72, went there to play football, discovered Keats and Shelley, decided to become a poet, and in fact did. I met him in Detroit, where he now lives, and we got to be friends almost instantly—a dear, almost bashful, full of enthusiasm and *very* bright, the main connection being that Knopf published *his* book, *For the Sleepwalkers*. He's evidently an insomniac, and there was a poem of his on the subject in the *New Yorker* a month or so ago (and another more recently, on fall in Detroit). Anyhow, he came to New York to do a poetry reading, and there was a party for him that Hal and I went to, and later Ed and I had lunch and went on talking about Keats and Shelley—*and* Wallace Stevens, whom he inexplicably (to me) also loves. He has a doll of a wife, who is just as nice, and while I was in Detroit I had dinner with them and another poet named Daniel Hughes who back about a year and a half ago wrote me my first real rave fan letter, and *his* wife. They turned out to have all sorts of connections with people I know, so there was great excitement. I hadn't known until then that he was a poet, but he has since sent me a book of his which I loved. So you'll gather the kind of excitement I've gotten into. The book is going to be *very* pretty; you'll see, I hope fairly shortly, but anyhow as soon as I can manage to get one off to you. Among other developments, I'm going to do a reading, in the upstairs room of a bookstore, on February 8—my first real public one in New York, though last month I did talk to a couple of classes at Friends Seminary, where my friend Phoebe's daughter goes, and read a few things in the process. I'm a bit scared of high school kids—more than of college students, really—but these were bright kids who really *read*, and who had a surprising amount to say.

I've just finished reading the Ian Hamilton biography of Robert Lowell—an appalling document in many ways. And I've been rereading Hart Crane, and reading Allen Ginsberg (*Howl*) for the first time. Also Galway Kinnell's *Book of Nightmares*. [. . .]
Love,
Amy

. . . .

January 24, 1983
Dear Rimsa—
[. . .] Helen Vendler is a critic who is now doing (has in fact finished) a book on the odes of Keats; she was also responsible for my applying for (and being given, I rather suppose) the Guggenheim fellowship. I still haven't met her, but hope to soon. She wrote an essay on how Keats' ode "To Autumn" influenced Wallace Stevens (it came out in a collection called *Part of Nature, Part of Us*), which is one big reason I began thinking about Keats myself. [. . .] Did you see, by the way, that Richard Wilbur has a wonderful new poem in the *New Yorker?* I haven't yet met *him*, but I did meet May Swenson the other day—very pleasant, plain-spoken, and comfortable—and she is coming to the *Kingfisher* party, which is to be on February 3. No telling who else will appear—at least no telling until I run through the

RSVPs, which Knopf is taking care of. Hal and I (or more precisely the Guggenheim Foundation) are paying for it, though; as a policy Knopf doesn't favor launching poets with parties, though my editor does her best to circumvent said policy. Yes, I'll need some help in keeping my head in the midst of all this (which I still attribute mainly to Helen Vendler—literary people are such sheep, they mainly don't know what to think, or even what to *read*, until somebody like her tells them), but Hal has promised to look after the matter, and has done pretty well so far—at least I hope so. This coming Saturday we're to have dinner with Ben Sonnenberg, the editor of *Grand Street*, and I'm looking forward to that. But what I'm really looking forward to is having things settle down enough to I can get back to reading Homer—thanks once again to you!
Love,
Amy

. . . .

February 13, 1983
Dear Rimsa—
Obedient to your injunction, and before I forget what I still remember, about the party: First of all, a sample invitation, which was Knopf's contribution, Hal having offered to foot part of the bill, the rest of which I can deduct from my taxable income as expenses (imagine!). So it really wasn't a literary party. The usual critics etcetera were invited, but such affairs can't be much fun for them, and I can't think I would have found them much fun either. Howard Moss came—but I think of him as a friend, not a literary type—and so did May Swenson and her delightful housemate (I think), a juvenile author named Zan Knudson, and Laurie Colwin and Ann Arensberg, who are fiction writers whom I've gotten to know lately; also a pair of poets named J. D. (Sandy) McClatchy and Alfred Corn, who are friends of James Merrill's, and who had invited me recently to have tea with them in the latter's apartment, or more precisely James Merrill's *mother's* apartment, where they're staying temporarily. They're both extremely good-looking, sociable, and fun to talk to—and I now think of them as friends rather than literary figures. Sandy is maybe better known as a critic, and told me he has written a review of my book for *Poetry*. Oh yes, Marilyn Hacker came. She looked totally unlike my idea of her—she affects to be a complete butch, though my editor thinks it's largely a pose, for political effect or something. I signed a book for her (very flattering to be asked) but we didn't have a real conversation. Oh

yes, David Schoenbrun, whom I've worked for on and off as a free-lance since 1967, came, bringing a bunch of roses, and soon had a gathering of admirers (so I'm told—I saw him only on his arrival and as he was leaving). My brother and his wife came down from Boston, and just about everyone else was an old friend from one or another period of my life— about a hundred people altogether. That was what was fun—all the various groups and constellations getting reassembled. My editor had sent a bouquet of freesias, anemones, stock and delphinium earlier in the day, and a friend brought more freesias (my favorite winter flower, because of the fragrance). The catering was wonderful—a hunch about the two young women just setting up in business proved correct. There were little watercress and cucumber sandwiches, freshly made Italian and other bread that got broken up by degrees, even more beautiful basketfuls of vegetables, boiled new potatoes stuffed with sour cream and caviar (???), and (my favorite item) melon balls on skewers, with one blue bead of blueberry at the tip, also passed repeatedly. Did I tell you about the house? It belongs to Hunter [College] now, but was originally Sara Delano Roosevelt's; she shared it for a time with Franklin and Eleanor—a mansion with two entrances, but with a common drawing room on the second floor, where the party was—with space to expand into and sit down, in a library and another smaller sitting room facing the street. In a corner of the big drawing room, overlooking a garden, there was George Gershwin's piano. Getting people out at the end—when the waiters' time ran out—was the hardest thing, but was managed. Laurie Colwin sent me a postcard afterward with a picture of a cat on it, with "Looking for a Sea Mouse" written in at the bottom, to say what fun she'd had. She's the author, most recently, of "Family Happiness," and a very funny woman. After much discussion, it was decided to have somebody from the Gotham Book Mart on hand so that people who wanted to buy books could—and I'm told she sold something like three hundred dollars' worth, some of which I autographed, though at one point I threw up my hands and called a temporary halt— I'd run out of whatever it takes to think of inscriptions. Well, I think that about covers everything. Several people told me they'd never been to a publishing party quite like it. So I guess it was a success though Everybody did not come.

I forget whether I mentioned that just five days later I was scheduled to give a poetry reading at Books & Co., along with Howard Moss reading Elizabeth Bishop in honor of her birthday. Anyhow, for a while in between I was afraid (having caught cold for the first time in months and months) that I might be going to lose my voice. So I spent a couple of days mainly in bed, mainly reading Alice Munro (a *New Yorker* short-story writer I like a lot, and a Knopf author whose new book comes out shortly), and forestalled the laryngitis. The room at Books & Co. was filled, and I didn't lose my voice, and afterward Alice Quinn, my editor, and Nina Bourne, another Knopf editor and a perfect darling, took me to dinner at an Italian restaurant. The next day I had lunch with Richard Howard, who'd introduced me, and about whom I'd been a bit uneasy. He is very nice, for all my misgivings, and I came away with a beautiful nineteenth-century limited edition of Keats. He's mainly known as a translator (Baudelaire most recently), but also has poems in the *New Yorker* now and then. He is, as Alice says, a Mandarin. Oh yes, and I did meet Helen Vendler, very briefly, before all these other events. I'm to see her again in Boston this week—I'm going to give more readings (providing the snowstorm we had this weekend has been dug out of sufficiently for people to get around) at the U. of Massachusetts's Boston branch, Wellesley, Wheaton, and finally at the Unitarian Church in Wayland, where my brother lives.

I think that's about everything about my own doings. [. . .] I'm still embroiled with the awful 12th Street landlord who intends to turn our poor little walkup building into a co-op, and sometimes I think I simply can't cope. But it may be that the worst of that situation is over.
Love,
Amy

. . . .

March 13, 1983
Dear Helen—
It's hard to believe so much time has gone by since I saw you, and I intended to have written before now if only to say again how much honored I was to have you at the reading, and to thank you again for the lift back to Wayland. (I do hope the drive back presented no more confusions!) Anyhow, I have finally revised the four last poems in the Keats sequence, and here they are. You'll see that I've proceeded pretty much in accord with your comments back in January. I'm especially indebted to you for pointing out the loose ends of syntax in the Isle of Wight poem, and also the false notes there and elsewhere. What has been beyond my power (so far, anyhow) to rectify is the scanting of the Autumn ode.

You'll see that I've made a gesture in that direction toward the end of the Winchester poem. Although I think I understand what troubles you, and although I continued to be awed by your argument with each rereading, my own preoccupations somehow can't be made to take proper notice— i.e., the preoccupation with finding (or, if need be, inventing) links between Keats the English poet and the new world his brother went off to live in; which must be what causes me to connect that roar as if of earthly fire with rocketry, and thus with a leap into the twentieth century— violation of the context though I must admit it is. I can only beg your indulgence, and assure you once again of my gratitude. You'll see that I've agreed with you about "the rest is silence": I think I halfway knew it wouldn't do, but needed to be told. I hope the solution (for which I'm indebted to one of your suggestions) will seem right to you—and that you'll let me know if it doesn't. The same applies to the new final stanza in the Epilogue. [In her earlier letter to Clampitt, making recommendations, suggestions, and otherwise commenting on the sequence called "Voyages: a Homage to John Keats," which later appeared in *What the Light Was Like*, Vendler objected to the use of "the rest is silence" as the last line in "Winchester: The Autumn Equinox," about Keats's stay in that city in September, 1819, and his composition there of the ode "To Autumn." Clampitt willingly acceded; the final line, emended and improved, is "The rest / is posthumous."]

I forget whether I mentioned that *Grand Street* will be carrying the first two poems of the sequence in its spring issue. (There has been a policy decision there not to run the dedication line for the Margate poem; but I hope to include it, with your permission, when there's a book.) More recently, Ben Sonnenberg at *Grand Street* has asked for three others in the sequence—the Hampstead, Isle of Wight, and Winchester ones. With the Elgin Marbles one appearing in the *Kenyon Review* for spring, and Chichester in (I think) the winter issue of *New England Review*, that leaves only the epilogue. I'm sending it to Howard Moss, though it's so full of allusions I'm not sure even I think it's right for the *New Yorker*.

I forget, also, whether I mentioned that I'm going to England—in fact, my friend and I now have our tickets about the QE2, sailing on April 16. My first objective while I'm over there is the Lake District, where I've never been; but I also have it in mind to follow George Eliot and Virginia Woolf around a little—not to mention John Keats himself. I did visit the house in Hampstead years and years ago, and have never forgotten the effect it had on me then. And as you can imagine, I'm looking forward with great eagerness to the book on the Odes.

Ever gratefully,

Amy

. . . .

28 Radnor Walk
London, SW3 4BN

May 4, 1983

Dear Helen—

Reading over your letter of a month ago, I realize you'll be in Berkeley just now. But it seemed imperative to write you with no more delay in any event, since just today I've made the pilgrimage to Hampstead—Well Walk first, and a ploughman's lunch in the pub at what was No. 30, where an almost churchlike stillness prevailed, as I was almost the only customer, and a tabby cat was on the threshold as I came out, and then along the edge of the Heath, where I saw my first robin and heard innumerable black-birds, and surreptitiously collected a couple of stray spears of just-opening bluebells; then to Keats Grove, where I spent the half hour before the house reopened after lunch in the public library, reading in the Bate biography of Coleridge about the encounter at Highgate and his complaint about the nightingales that kept him awake there, and finally the house itself. It's all of thirty years since I first saw it, and the whole day was magical. The weather has been mostly rainy (which I don't mind; when I was in London last, seven years ago, there was such a drought that the bright sunshine seemed unnatural), and it's dripping outside now; but for most of the several hours I spent in Hampstead, there was the feel of an English spring, with just enough sunshine for it to seem miraculous.

I can't tell you how pleased I am that the revised Keats poems seem right to you. And I must delay no longer in letting you know that they are to appear as a chapbook—Joe Freedman, who was responsible for the ty-pography of *The Kingfisher*, and who has a small press of his own, is plan-ning a small edition—a matter of three hundred or so copies, with a much smaller number to be printed on special paper and bound in leather, or maybe not leather. It is sure to be beautiful, since I know nobody more exacting when it comes to book design. What I also must delay no longer in saying is that I would like to dedicate the entire chapbook to you. As I may have mentioned, there is a dedication of the Elgin Marbles poem to Frederick Turner, and that will stand; but that the sequence as a whole should bear your name is absolutely fitting, if small recompense for the many ways I shall always be in your debt.

I've just finished reading Robert Gittings' biography, from which I learned so much that I'm somewhat appalled by my own ignorance—for which all the same I'm grateful, since I might not have dared write anything of my own if I'd been *less* ignorant. I dare say I'll feel the same way, only more so, about you on the odes, to which I look forward more and more eagerly. I do hope you'll have some respite in the meantime from the demands on your time. My own sloth since we arrived seems almost sinful, but perhaps has served its purpose. We go to Stratford this weekend; I've never been there, idiotic as it may sound, but that idiocy must go on no longer.
Ever,
Amy

. . . .

28 Radnor Walk
London, SW3 4BN

May 10, 1983
Dear Ed—
What a pleasure to reread your letter here in London, where Hal and I have been for just over three weeks now, and where I'm finally beginning to catch up on correspondence—and what fun to imagine you among the cornfields of Iowa, and on the Grinnell campus, now once again so vivid in my own imagination! We're staying in a small house on a quiet street in the middle of Chelsea, with its intensely private spaces (such as our own little garden), so utterly opposite to the sense of exposure that for me is essentially Midwestern. I can't begin to thank you properly for the generous things you have to say about *The Kingfisher* and also the Keats sequence. I'm turning over in my mind your objection to the recurrence of "he wrote"—in which you may be quite right, though my thought was simply to identify particular lines as Keats's own. Certainly I can't fail to take seriously anything you may have to say, above all on a subject so sacred to us both, and I'm grateful.

Though we were both so exhausted by weeks of turmoil in New York, before we finally got here, that much of our time has been spent doing nothing but read, sleep, and enjoy feeling so much at home abroad, we've made an excursion to Stratford, and from there into George Eliot country. But no excursion is likely to equal the day I spent in Hampstead, where I felt truly as though I had arrived in the middle of the nineteenth

century. I'd just finished reading the Gittings biography, from which I learned so much that it may be just as well that I hadn't read it before plunging into my own attempt on the subject—as Henry James said of his own *données*. Also, it meant just that much more. I'm now beginning to reacquaint myself with Coleridge—the meeting he had with Keats on the way to Highgate having become a point of departure—and I'm still mulling over the suddenly vivid meaning of Keats's notion that he might after all become a journalist, in the excitement over the Peterloo massacre—that fit of liberal enthusiasm which apparently never quite goes out of date. Tomorrow I'm planning to head for the Lake District, and from there to Scotland, to meet some poets in Dundee with whom I've corresponded—and in June it's my thought to spend two or three weeks in northern Greece. [. . .]
With much affection,
Amy

. . . .

Corea, Maine 04624

August 7, 1983
Dear Craig—
Your letter arrived while I was still in New York, and I had an opportunity to talk with Alice Quinn about it before I left. That said, let me assure you that even as the subject of your criticism, I found it admirable, and in all but a couple of instances I'm ready not only to accept but indeed to concur with your judgment. "The Cormorant in Its Element" and "Exmoor," for example, would not have been included in the first place if it hadn't been for other people's liking them immoderately, so that I tended to forget my own original opinion. Similarly, "The Dakota," "Amaranth and Moly," "Dancers Exercising," "Remembering Greece," and "The Local Genius" can be dropped without great regret on my part. I'm somewhat more reluctant about "Triptych"—but since you are very possibly correct in your reservations, I am not prepared to make a case for keeping it. The one poem I find myself wanting to hold onto despite your reservations, out of sheer fondness on my own part, is "Sunday Music." One reason for this may be that it's as much a statement on the subject of poetry as of the music it purports to describe, and is thus of more importance, from my own point of view, than it would otherwise be. Would you accordingly reconsider? I *would* be grateful, as of course I am anyway.

About the division of the book into sections I have no very strong views. It seems to have become customary, over here, to divide even the slimmest book of poems into sections, and for one as long as my original book it made more sense than it would for one of approximately eighty pages. So I'm content to leave this matter to your editorial judgment. I see I haven't mentioned specifically your wish to drop the entire final section—which does make sense, and though I suppose I'm a bit defensive on the matter of this reaching for larger significance, I'm agreeable to it.

About "Beethoven, Opus 111", and your wish to do away with the opening section: here I do have trouble. In my own defense, I can say that that section did receive the particular praise of the extremely curmudgeonly teacher of the pianist to whom the poem is dedicated—and in any event I can't see my way to doing without such an opening. I don't know where I was when the rule was handed down against writing of music in such terms—I'd never heard of it until a couple of reviewers of my book brought it up, both going on (as it happens) to say that in this instance the tabooed device seemed to work. The point made by the musical curmudgeon was, anyhow, that too much has been made elsewhere of the ethereal ending and not enough of the cantankerous opening of the sonata. Well, there I rest my case. I will give some thought to "the stranglehold of reasons nations," as you ask; I know it has a queer sound, but the queerness has seemed right to me. Still, I will think about it.

I have now a revision to propose. It occurs in "Rain at Bellagio." As I think I may have mentioned, after I saw you I was to pay a visit to the Benedictine abbey that is briefly described in the poem, and where my longtime friend is a member of the community. Though a bit uneasy about having the poem in print to begin with, she has gracefully reconciled herself to the situation. But its being included in an English edition raises another problem, which is connected entirely (if my understanding is correct) with one stanza in the 7th section, beginning "And will she be free to leave if she should wish to?" and ending " . . . what what they call *formation* amounts to." My friend's reason for dismay is not herself but any possible offense that might be given to the community, which she says would be quickly identified by anyone who had ever heard of it. Having been a guest there several times, I have reason of my own to wish to avoid offense, quite aside from my friend's wishes. I have not written to her, proposing something like the following as a substitute:

. . .

addressed to an abbess.

To *try her vocation*, as it seems the phrase goes.
As a nun. In an enclosed community.

Why in the world . . . ?

One might have said by way of a response (but did not)
that living under vows, affianced to a higher poverty,
might likewise be an exercise in living well.

I'll let you know when I have a reply. In the meantime, I hope you will
have no objection to a revision such as this.

And I'd like to say again what a happy occasion meeting you and others there turned out to be, and how greatly honored I am that you should wish to publish *The Kingfisher*, in whatever form.
Sincerely yours,
Amy

. . . .

October 28, 1983
Dear Rimsa—
No, no more job at Dutton. There has been something of an upheaval there, and by the time my leave of absence was to have ended, Jack Macrae, who'd hired me, had gone to Holt, Rinehart. And no more Guggenheim. I'd been a bit spoiled by not thinking about paychecks, but thus far I'm not starving—in fact, I'm at least breaking even, mainly (believe it or not) by going around giving poetry readings. Can you imagine—in a couple of weeks I'm going to give one at Harvard? This is Helen Vendler's doing. She knows now, by the way, about her mistake concerning that bus trip—and is duly apologetic. The thing is, she drives a car and takes planes. I finally met her, early in the year, after having corresponded for a while. She is stout and Irish, and doesn't look a bit like a literary critic, or put on any airs whatsoever.

I'll put in a clipping that still somewhat amazes me, and may interest you, about an Auden memorial I was somehow asked to take part in. I think Richard Howard, who is a critic as much as he is a poet, may have made up the list, but don't know for sure. Anyhow, I found myself sitting on the stage next to Joseph Brodsky, who recited his selection from memory, and got a storm of applause. I was pretty scared, but did not trip on the mike wire or spill my water glass or lose my place on the page. I read "Voltaire at Ferney," and got a small ripple of laughter (I mean *friendly* laughter) before I really intended to. Beforehand I met Anthony Hecht for the first time (as you'll gather, he's grown gray and a bit stouter). John

Ashbery arrived at the very last moment and I never actually met him; and I was too shy to introduce myself to Christopher Isherwood, as I heard Howard Moss doing in a nice courtly way. But I found it rather nice to be coupled in the news story with Alfred Corn, the youngest poet there and by far the best-looking, as well as friendly in a subdued sort of way.

I heard a lot of Ashbery gossip, as it happens, earlier this month, when I found myself in Milwaukee for a week as a writer-in-residence—one of my predecessors in that slot having been Ashbery himself. Another one was Grace Paley, who had clearly made a great hit, and I acquired a certain amount of prestige by being able to say that I'd been in *jail* with Grace Paley, back in the anti-Vietnam War days. One Ashbery story was of the writing class (to which I was also brought) in which, on his being asked to comment on the student work that had just been read, it was discovered that he was sound asleep! One of my several hosts in Milwaukee was an Irish poet, James Liddy, who is the permanent poet-in-residence, and he had more drunken-Ashbery stories. I hadn't known before that he had that trouble. He is said to have been quite ill in the last few months, and didn't look exactly cheerful that evening. [. . .]
Love,
Amy

. . . .

October 28, 1983
Dear Barbara—
[. . .] Yes, I do remember writing you from London. All kinds of things have been going on since. I was in Greece for three weeks. Faber & Faber made me an offer for a British edition of *The Kingfisher*, and a couple of editors there took me to lunch, and afterward I went back to their offices and met some more people—not quite on the spot where T. S. Eliot had charge, but not far from it, and still in Bloomsbury, with a little park full of roses just outside. Hereabouts, the book has gone into its fourth printing. I get all these fan letters, from the nicest people. On Monday a nice young man interviewed me over the radio. In a couple of weeks I'm going up to Cambridge and read to an audience at Harvard. A couple of nights ago I went to a party and met Kurt Vonnegut (who was very drunk, as I gather he tends to be, mumbling "Oh, old friend of mine," with obviously not a *clue* about who I might be), and discovered so many others I sort of knew that for once I didn't have to stand around feeling gauche. Last week there was this Auden memorial, as a result of which my

name and face appeared in the *New York Times*—I enclose a clipping to put it all in perspective. Though I've gotten used to reading my own stuff, I was pretty scared—the more since I was sitting next to Joseph Brodsky on the stage, and had to follow him in the reading. The morning afterward, I woke up with a real case of the horrors in the pit of the stomach, thinking I could never go through any such thing, ever again. Once I got over the stomach ache, fortunately, the horrors went away. Barbara, do you believe any of this? At the beginning of this month I spent a week in Milwaukee, as a momentary writer-in-residence. It turned out to be a lovely place, right on Lake Michigan, and a couple of mornings there was time to go running along the lakeshore. I was mostly kept busy, going from class to class, but they paid me well and I met some more lovely people, including three Irish poets, one of them bibulous and full of gossip, and a great teacher.

More to the point, on February 27 I'm going to be reading at the Library of Congress. That's a Monday, I believe. My young friends who were in Japan are now living down there, just a door or two from you—4701 Connecticut, to be exact—and Hal and I will be staying with them. They have a baby girl, Emily, born in July, whom I haven't yet seen. Brad Leithauser and Mary Jo Salter, their names are. They are special friends of Anthony Hecht, who is consultant on poetry to the Library of Congress, and whom I met for the first time at the Auden memorial. There is talk of a party of some sort, and in any event it's much too long since I saw you, so I do hope you'll mark that weekend on your calendar, as soon as you have a calendar for the dread year 1984—if there is a 1984, of course.
Love,
Amy

. . . .

December 14, 1983
Dear Rimsa—
A parcel arrived the other day, and is being kept for some kind of ceremonial opening. Meanwhile, here is a fairly new poem (to appear eventually in the *New Yorker*), by way of those New England regions through which my last letter so inscrutably passed. Bennington was my final appearance in a three-day swing—do I sound like a trouper?—that began at Harvard (with Helen Vendler to greet and introduce me), and proceeded to Boston University, where I was introduced by Rosanna Warren—

Robert Penn's daughter and herself a poet, and a perfectly darling young woman—and had dinner afterward with George Starbuck and his wife Kathy, who are two of the funniest people one could hope to know. Or did I mention him before?—he recently won the Marshall award for his *Argot Merchant Disaster,* and we now constitute a small mutual admiration society. Sylvia Plath knew him, and was a bit mean concerning him, in the days when he went around with Anne Sexton. I would love to hear him talk about those days, but doubt that I'll ever know him well enough. Helen Vendler took me for tea before the reading to a spot now called One Potato Two Potato, where she and Robert Lowell used to go, she told me, and he would pull out his latest poem to show her. More thrilling, though, was to be let into the Keats room at the Houghton Library, where I saw the actual letter in which he described Fanny Brawne—beautiful, elegant, silly, fashionable and strange (I see I've left out *graceful,* but never mind)—and those words leaped out at me; the letter begins (it's to his brother George and his wife, in America) with the news that their brother Tom is dead. In another display case I found the passport K. took with him on that sad trip to Italy. Adjoining it is an Emily Dickinson room, with a manuscript of a poem in that driving hand of hers—it scared me a little. At Bennington—where I had maybe the best audience ever, and met some students who were literally fascinating—I was shown Robert Frost landmarks and the house occupied by Bernard Malamud, who wasn't there. He was in fact in New York, and a couple of evenings ago I met him—we both read at a benefit for the *Columbia Literary Magazine,* with which I have no connection. There was no chance to converse with Malamud, who vanished before the program ended, but he is obviously a dear. Weirdly enough, from my own point of view, he read a piece having to do with Virginia Woolf—about whom, as you'll see, and won't be surprised to hear in any event, I've been thinking my own thoughts yet again. Fortunately I hadn't planned to read my own contribution on the subject—it would have been a bit of lèse majesté, I suspect, if I had. The other readers were a young novelist whose last name I never quite caught, who sounds like a New Yorker but writes about transplanted Cubans in somewhat the manner of *A Thousand Years of Solitude*—the author's name escapes me, but you'll know who I mean—and a playwright named Israel Horowitz; both good, the latter hilarious.

Further about John Ashbery: He has a poem in I think the November *Vanity Fair,* which I like especially; let me know if you don't find it, and I'll send you a copy. I mentioned this to Ben Sonnenberg, the editor of

Grand Street—I believe I wrote to you about meeting him the first time—when I went to have a drink with him not long ago, and the talk was all about poets he knows. He agreed, and said he had some new ones he'll be publishing that are also special, and he said Richard Howard had told him that when Ashbery read at the "Y" in October, he did so with great passion but then nearly fell off the stage. They seem to believe he is dying, and that the latest lyric burst is all part of the process. But I think he was believed to be desperately ill a year or so ago, and then rallied. Mainly, though, I'd gone to tell Ben about Greece. He lived there for a time, and knows all the places I saw. And now presumably, because of his own ailment (multiple sclerosis, which means he can't walk and some days doesn't feel well) he'll never go there again. But he is the most cheerful company imaginable.

You are sweet to suggest calling off the *New Yorker*. But no, it's a bargain compared with just about anything else these days, and anyhow the poetry department there has done so well by me lately that I'm more than solvent: along with the enclosed, they've taken two others, both somewhat longer, and will run them in a single batch. And just today I got two more (paying) invitations to appear for a reading or whatever. Did I tell you that I've also been asked to teach a course? And decided to chance it? It's just for two weeks, next July at Hofstra. Mostly I don't believe any of this.

Oh yes, about John Ashbery again—I gather that he is homosexual—I'm told he was in love with Frank O'Hara, and gives occasional signs of never having gotten over that, though O'Hara died twenty years ago. Which I guess is enough gossip, even if I knew any more. [. . .]
Love,
Amy

. . . .

September 17, 1984
Dear Helen—
Your letter was waiting for me on Friday when I came in from Williamsburg. Thus far I've been quite happy there. The apartment they give to the writer-in-residence is a less-than-ten-minute walk from the railway station, and a less-than-five-minute walk from the building where I have an office and teach my class. The campus seems to me as beautiful as any I ever saw, with its magnolia alleys and crape myrtle, its mockingbirds and cicadas,—and the notion of Jefferson going to classes right there in the Wren Building fills me with romantic amazement. People are friendly and

congenial, and my class is off to what feels like a good start: six young men (one a graduate student, and a bit older than the others, but likewise youthful and sweet) and two young women—who if perhaps not sophisticated are literate: when I asked what they'd been reading, the answer was Stevens, Merrill, Ammons, Peter Klappert (he was there in my spot once), Dickinson and Bishop! And the youngest member of the class is ahead of me in some respects—e.g. Ashbery. Their work doesn't suggest huge energies, but some of it is interesting. I'm having them read "Lycidas" (along with other poems on the fear of extinction, new and old—we've already touched on the theme in a couple of things in *A Wave*), which I'm told is hard to get youngsters to like, and am eager to see how they respond. I'm reading Gaston Bachelard on the poetics of space—a book I didn't know existed until a faculty member down there mentioned it in passing, and when I inquired, pulled it from his office shelf and lent it to me. Why, it's a book I'd been looking for all my life. Richard Howard, whom I saw yesterday, assured me he would have told me if I'd asked—but how could I have asked when I didn't know it existed?

Well, all right. The effort to keep muffling my birth date could, it seems, not have been kept up indefinitely. I have heard from two separate parties who found their way to New Providence, where there is a café (I've never been inside it, but have seen the outside; it was closed the day I was last there, two years ago) whose décor consists of composite graduating class pictures from the local high school—and have found mine among them, date and all; so a fib would hardly suffice. I was born June 15, 1920, and what above all I do not want is to find myself being asked to assure roomfuls of little old ladies that they can all be poets too! I gather that you've spoken with Patricia Morrisroe, the nice young woman who is writing me up for *New York* magazine, and who was especially happy over her conversation with you. I'd resisted being written up there for some of the same reasons (and others), but she seems to be talking with all the right people. As for my father's honorary degree: on the face of it, the reason was an autobiography he wrote (at my urging) and had privately printed; but I imagine the impetus came from the kind of shy eminence he'd arrived at in his later years as a Quaker activist: he went to Washington for an antiwar vigil of some kind, years before I thought of doing any such thing.

Thank you for liking "Venice Revisited." It was rewritten several times—but ending up on the moon came as a total surprise as I wrote it. The woman who set up the post was there from the beginning—she was in my mind from the minute I arrived in Venice last year. She didn't live in Iowa, by the way, but in North Dakota, on one of those homesteading tracts where you planted trees and when you'd planted enough of them the land was yours. My grandfather did that, and I remembered his telling about the woman. Quite possibly she was apocryphal; but if so, the force of the anecdote must have been his own perception of the region; otherwise I would never have heard of her. Iowa, though dreary to many sensibilities, was never totally treeless, or quite so arid or so unendingly windswept as the Dakotas. On the other hand, it's true that the reedbeds would be closer in appearance to the tall grass of the Iowa prairie than to the scrubbier one of the Dakota landscape.

What a thing to have seen Belfast. You evoke it for me as no one else has. I'm looking forward to the new Heaney book. He is one of the current poets whom I especially admire.

Ever gratefully—
Amy

. . . .

February 10, 1985
Dear Libby and Howard—
How nice to have some news, right from the spot! I remember that expedition to San Juan Bautista, and of course I remember Marian and Peggy, still not-very-big girls then. The thought of you and Barbara together does warm my heart. So here is the issue of *New York* Magazine with the portrait in full color. I'm not sure what to think of it, but it seems my own opinion is of little consequence when it comes to photographs—the ones I think are just too goofy-looking are the ones everyone else likes. Not to mention all those signs of age, which I still resist having to acknowledge. But in any event, you must not suppose that I would suppose any such thing about hearing from you after a lapse in our correspondence, and I can't begin to tell you how pleased I am that Barbara got you to sit down at the typewriter with her, so to speak. Will she have mentioned that I've been back to Grinnell, finally, after being terrified of doing any such thing for all these years? One of my nephews went there, and I got there for his graduation, but I hadn't actually stayed overnight until a couple of years ago—and then I stayed with Margaret Matlack Kiesel, whom I hadn't actually known, or don't remember knowing, but who is a slightly older cousin of the Matlack twins. We became friends instantly, and when I went back last May I stayed with her again, and she had a small gathering

that included Henry Alden (who looks remarkably unchanged) and Joe and Bea Mills Wall, who seem to me to have changed rather more. The word about David Matlack is that he's now married to a third wife, who is English, and they have a young daughter; in fact I've heard from him a couple of times lately. Less word of his brother George. I think I wrote Barbara about having lunch with Carl Neimeyer, with whom I was quite smitten as a sophomore, and who, again, seems hardly changed at all; he took me to an Italian place called Il Gattopardo, which seemed to be full of Mafia types making big deals, and I felt as though I'd momentarily entered a New York that one has only heard about. Lots of fun. Otherwise I could almost say that I don't go anywhere, which isn't true—only true about being here in New York, where Hal and I eat large quantities of take-out Chinese food instead of going to restaurants, and go out to a movie maybe once a year, and about that often to the theater (we did see both productions of the Royal Shakespeare Company not long ago), and the rest of the time look at old movies recorded on the VCR, or, in the best of times, read aloud to each other from Dickens—we're on *Martin Chuzzlewit* these days. . . . But what I started to say is that it isn't true that I never go anywhere any more, since in fact I've been to so many places in the last couple of years that I'm not sure I *live* anywhere at all: commuting to Williamsburg since September, with side trips—last week to Washington and Lee, in the Blue Ridge region, for a less-than-twenty-four-hour overnight visit; next week for a couple of days to Gainesville, Florida; next month for a few more days in Lake Charles, Louisiana, and from there northward to Grand Forks, North Dakota . . . and come next June, if all goes according to plan, Queen's College, Cambridge! Barbara may have told you what a ham I have become. What seems far less likely is the teaching part of it—last thing I ever thought I could do. I have just one class a week at William and Mary—fourteen young poets—and I still have a day of acute anxiety over each session. I'm learning as I go along, and there is a lot to be said for the experience, even though I'm not at all sure the writing of poetry can be taught. Anyhow, the campus at William and Mary is beautiful—deep magnolia alleys, crape myrtle and boxwood, a sunken garden, brick walls and Georgian architecture—and I've met several people on the faculty whom I really like a lot, and feel comfortable with. The beauty of it all is that I don't have to go to meetings, or worry about tenure. And I'm experiencing the South for the first time. Of course you both know a more Southerly South, much better than I know this bit of it. During Christmas week Hal and I took advantage of the five-room apartment they give the writer-in-residence, and had what turned out to be a genuine vacation—the temperature went up to eighty, and we explored plantation sites and had two picnics on the banks of the James, in addition to more social life than we usually bother with in New York.

My new book is coming out at the end of March, and I'll give you a copy. Which doesn't mean you have to *say* anything about it, you know. Just send me a postcard when the inclination strikes. I hope you're both thriving.

Love,

Amy

. . . .

25 John Street, Cambridge CB3 0DF

July 27, 1985

Dear Rimsa—

This is a very late thank-you for the Joan Didion books, which did arrive safely before we left for England. I read PLAY IT AS IT LAYS aboard the QE2, and am much indebted to you for introducing her to me as a novelist—I'd read only reviews and such of hers before. As a Hollywood novel, this seems to me to be in the same league as Nathanael West's DAY OF THE LOCUST. I don't know which one is sadder. But that seems to be the nature of movie people.

I'm sorry to have seemed not to answer your earlier queries. One, if I remember, had to do with Patricia Morrisroe. All I can tell you about her is that she's in her early thirties probably, and is on the staff of NEW YORK magazine—though when she phoned me first, well over a year ago, I believe she was simply a free lance. At that time I was dubious about being written up in NEW YORK, though I could see that she was conscientious and friendly. By the time we'd talked for several hours, I'd become very fond of her. She isn't especially literary, but the questions she asked were about the poetry, which she had obviously read with great intelligence, and that is how some of the more personal things got into the article—I'd originally said no, I just wasn't ready for that kind of exposure. And some things that got in weren't quite accurate, but by the time the checker got to me it wasn't possible to get everything straightened out.

About the new ownership of THE NEW YORKER: I don't have any notion, to tell you the truth, except that some staff people there seem to have been quite anxious; but when asked by outsiders what they thought (I haven't done this myself) they were noncommittal. Useless to speculate, so far as I'm concerned.

All of which seems a bit far away just now, in the wonderful serenity of the little house in which I now find myself. It was rented for the summer by the faculty member who became by best friend in Williamsburg [Tom Heacox], and who is over here for one of those study-abroad programs that all colleges now seem to have—the one at William and Mary just happens to be here in Cambridge, where I spent three days in mid-June. Tom wasn't here then, and Hal was still with me (he left for New York earlier this month), and we had rooms at Clare College, from which among other things we had a ringside seat for one of those garden parties one reads about, and it was just as described. An about-to-be-graduated student who aspires to arts journalism invited me to lunch, and did it very grandly, arriving dressed in pale blue and canary yellow, with umbrella in coordinated colors as well, and led me to the dining room of a hotel where the food wasn't very good, though pretentious, with the longest wine list I was ever invited to consider (I confessed to ignorance, and chose a Vouvray). But my host was really very bright and entertaining, and told me all sorts of stories of Cambridge undergraduate pranks, but mainly we talked about poetry. Also I met Seamus Heaney—we read on the same program, in fact, which meant that the hall was packed—and he was very cheerful and friendly, and invited me to come and see him in Dublin.

After that, anyhow, we went to London for a few days and another reading, and from there to Newcastle (likewise), then London again, then Chichester, where we have friends, and after Hal left I headed for Berlin, where an actor friend of mine (born there, with a U.S. passport—his name is Peter Kybart, and we traveled together on the Greek island of Thassos two years ago) had invited me to visit. Very interesting, and West Berlin is the greenest city imaginable—tens of thousands of linden trees—and I also spent a day in East Berlin, where there is a wonderful museum, and we also found the grave of Brecht in a shady, well-kept cemetery with lovely avenues of birch trees. From Berlin I went to Geneva, which was likewise new to me, and a bit too esplanadish to be my favorite kind of place; but I was staying with a bilingual French-American family who made it all great fun—took me to the castle of Chillon and to Voltaire's beautiful estate at Ferney, just across the French border, and then to the family chalet in the Haute-Savoie, where we went walking through mountain meadows covered with vivid alpine flowers. And of course we ate superlatively well—one goes to the market for the day's breakfast, which the morning I did it consisted not only of just-baked bread but a local cheese I'd never heard of, and the most enormously sweet fresh raspberries I ever tasted. And the café au lait was served in *bowls*, which somehow made it all the better. From there I went back to Geneva and caught a train for Amsterdam. I didn't see very much of it, since I'd been invited by a woman who lives outside it, in the midst of a nature preserve among the dunes—the most enormous and extensive dunes I ever saw, with vast beaches just beyond them. The house where I stayed had once been a hunting lodge, and was *also* vast. We walked in the dunes and did a little exploring by car, and I liked everything I saw exceedingly. My hostess spoke excellent English, and a friend of hers who gave us tea at his apartment in Amsterdam spoke it flawlessly. So I hardly learned a phrase of Dutch except "Spreekst U Engles?"

It's like coming home to be back in English-speaking territory. Though when I arrived there were other people in the house, I'm entirely alone just now—Tom has gone off to Stratford with a group of students, and the remaining guests left early this morning. It's very satisfying to do laundry and such mundane things in such circumstances, but my work is cut out for me—namely reading and rereading several hundred entries in the Arvon poetry competition which is the reason I'm still over here. A week from now, I meet with the two other judges, Craig Raine and Anne Stevenson, to thrash it out. We're to be closeted at a country house in Lancashire. Who knows what that will be like. [. . .]
Love,
Amy

. . . .

London, August 23, 1985

Dear Helen—
No, I'm not in Maine, but am spending the summer as even more of a nomad than usual. Your letter caught up with me in Cambridge just yesterday, and I'm really sorry about the pinched nerve and the nuisance of the surgery. The time I broke my wrist and lived six weeks with it in a cast still lived in my memory as more painful than any other period in my life—and a pinched nerve must be just that much worse. It's good to know that even with splints the pain is gone anyhow. And I'm more honored than I can quite say by your generosity about WHAT THE LIGHT WAS LIKE. What you say about Stevens and the imagination touched me especially, awed as I am by him and those longer poems, which I can get at only in bits—but then I find so much in the bits. A barnacle is what I sometimes think I really am, seizing on any passing thing that may be

tempting, but unequipped to deal with the whole of anything. Ideas do interest me, but I can't hold onto a whole idea long enough to understand it. A couple of weeks ago, in a conversation with some literary people (John Barnard, who did the little Keats edition and who turns out to be a friend of a friend, was one of them), I tried to ferret out the nature of Platonic Idealism, but I'm not sure I got any closer than before. Neo-Platonism I think I understand, but what a real Platonic Idea is I guess I'm destined not to get through my head.

Anyhow, I've been over here since mid-June, for the Cambridge poetry festival—where I met Seamus Heaney, in fact read on the same program with him, and that was a treat—and since then because of the Arvon competition, which I was flattered (or lured or something) into being one of the judges for. I found the entire process more interesting than I'd expected—and still don't know who the winner is, thanks to an ingenious safeguard against having anybody spill the beans. Craig Raine and Anne Stevenson were the other judges, and we got on quite amicably. I do hope we managed to pick someone hitherto unrecognized. The top six poems, with names finally, are to appear in this weekend's OBSERVER—but which one of the six actually gets the five thousand pounds, we won't know until September 11, when Ted Hughes is to be on hand to hand out the awards. So in the meantime I've been racketing about. My friend Hal was with me through June, and that was fun, but then he was obliged to go back to New York, and I made a little excursion to the Continent: Berlin, where I have friends, and then Geneva, and then a luxurious six days in dunelands outside Amsterdam, where a Dutch poet, Elly de Waard, had offered the hospitality of a onetime hunting lodge where she lives alone. I had the mornings largely to myself, and wrote two new poems without having planned to. I'll risk sending one, though it's still pretty rudimentary. My friends in Geneva took me to Chillon and Ferney, and then up into the Haute-Savoie where they have a chalet—and perhaps as much as the flower-filled mountain meadows and the view of Mont Blanc—yes, I know what you mean about the menacing aspect of the Alps—what I liked was going to the market in the little town of Samoens and choosing not only freshly baked bread but also a local cheese and some enormous, sweet local raspberries for that morning's breakfast. I'm intimidated by the French to a degree that I stay away from their country; but being taken into a French family under such circumstances was not intimidating (they're really bilingual, my original friend being an American who married a Frenchman and somehow lived through the process of adjustment, producing five children and adopting a Cambodian orphan along the way).

Back in England, I've gone on following Keatsian associations. Last weekend I stayed on Iona, where for one day the weather turned balmy, and I rode in an open boat to Staffa over water of glassy calm, and of a color I'd never seen before outside the Mediterranean. Reversing the route, I spent a night in Keswick, where the weather was baleful—a depressing place anyhow, I should think, but all the more so with hordes of the English on holiday wandering disconsolately from shop to shop. I got soaked, and there was a gale, but I didn't really mind since I had Keats and his getting soaked and not seeing Helvellyn to think of. I'm not a climber, but I did follow the side roads along the lower flank of Skiddaw, again thinking of him looking at it. I'm hoping to have a look at Burford Bridge, and if possible to stay there—perhaps also Margate, dreadful though I suppose it must be, and just possibly Teignmouth. The places I find I like best are the market towns, which go on being themselves and can be walked from one end to the other. Penrith, where I stayed before and after Keswick, was like that—a very handsome town, full of Wordsworth connections. I've become fascinated with Dorothy, and with her in mind I'm aiming next for Crewkerne, in Dorset, not far from which is Racedown, where she and William first set up a household. And then on the 13th of September I'm to board the QE2, and hope to begin collecting my thoughts.

I do hope the wrist is continuing to mend. Thank you again for making it possible to believe in a community of poets—in which you unquestionably figure; unquestionably and indispensably.

Ever yours,

Amy

. . . .

Winchester, September 7, 1985

Dear Helen—

[. . .] At the Burford Bridge Hotel, what they call the Keats Room turns out to be set up for business lunches (complete with coffee cups on the sideboard and fancy scratch pads labeled "Conference Notes"), and no one seemed to know, or care, what room Keats might actually have slept in. The hotel itself is showy and overpriced, though not unpleasant—just full of people for whom the view of Box Hill was (as a friend of mine put it) merely so much wallpaper. Box Hill itself is delightful in every way (a gathering of lepidopterists, the first I ever so identified by their nets and killing bottles, was to be seen at the top the afternoon I arrived), and would seem not much altered since Keats climbed it to look at the moon. I was very happy so long as I was on the open sward, a very steep one, or in the coves and undercrofts of shade under the beeches and yews and boxwoods.

Margate I didn't see, except passing through on my way to Broadstairs—itself a wonderfully intact Victorian resort, where I saw the room Dickens wrote in, and understood why he was partial to the place: a glimpse of a huge fun fair is what Margate offers, along with the English equivalent of Disney World.

Ah, but Winchester! It's all here, as though no time had passed since September 1819—the redbreast (lots of them, still vocal, in the hedgerows and the trees along the river), the swallows, the gnat swarms and the light, variable wind. The weather is uncannily as he described it—the more uncannily since it has rained so much that even when the rain stops people can't stop *talking* about it. And what he said about this being the pleasantest town he was ever in, I am ready to concur with—and I'm almost ready to say that it displaces Oxford as the city I think I would be happiest to settle down in for a while. This is hard to pin down, except that it has to do with the abundance of footpaths, which are much used by people walking their dogs, and of meadows where whole families are to be seen picnicking; but also with a very ancient and handsome High Street, wide enough to be used as a genuine thoroughfare, where this afternoon I discovered a company of morris dancers happily cavorting in scarlet hose with belled and beribboned garters, and funny hats of various descriptions. Having by chance gotten into conversation with a local lady, who wondered why so many of them were bearded and wore glasses, and asked one of them who happened to be passing (the answer: morris men tend to be individualists and above average in intelligence, and so it follows, etcetera etcetera), I then found myself brought into the conversation, and the morris man kissed me—it's that kind of place, though in three days that's the only conversation I've had with anyone. But I have somehow the feeling that even the indigent live in more comfort and dignity than in most other places. Perhaps this is an illusion fostered by my expedition this evening to the mysterious and venerable Hospital of St. Cross, which is reached by the loveliest of all the footpaths, through the water meadows along the Itchen. It seems to be a kind of monastery, but it is also clearly Church of England, with a Norman church of a massive and stolid grandeur that I find more moving than the cathedral, though it is also very grand inside. The window of my hotel room looks out onto a garden where a very old, propped-up apple tree is full of fruit, a fact which the condition of the trunk renders cheerfully improbable.

Last week, before I went to Broadstairs, I spent a few days at the Angli-can Benedictine abbey where my Bellagio friend is a nun—and she lent me a book from the communal shelves, called JOHN KEATS: THE DISIN-TERESTED HEART, by one Sister Thekla, who is an Orthodox nun but has some connection with the people at the abbey. I found it quite absorb-ing. Her concern was not so much with the poetry in itself as with the philosophical attitudes implicit or explicit in it, and the thoroughness of her knowledge of the poems, line by line, was (for me) quite humbling. I have said more than once that perhaps what really interested me most about Keats wasn't the poetry in itself but the person who wrote it—and here was a *scholarly* book by someone who feels that way. Have you seen it, by any chance, or heard of the author? More recently, it seems, she has done a book on George Herbert—and as I was leaving, the Reverend Mother passed along a spare copy of it as a present. I'm saving it for a propitious time, when I feel better able to deal with Herbert than I do just now. So many people whose taste I respect love him that I felt a need to fill in what is thus far a gap in my reading. If you don't know it either (Sr. Thekla's book that is), I would be happy to pass it along to you in due course.
With thanks once again, and best wishes always—
Amy

P.S.
September 9. Another thing about Winchester: real bookstores, several of them.

But what I wanted mainly to add has to do with that little joke of a thing about the hickory grove—namely that, as I recall, the notion of the way sea-sons exclude one another, even to the thinking of one in the midst of an-other, was encouraged, if not in fact given leave to be written of, by what you say on the subject in your essay on Stevens, to which you already know I am so very greatly indebted. For that, thank you yet again. I'm in London now, finding the proximity of the National Gallery the enduring chief at-traction, but looking forward to the Jonathan Miller RIGOLETTO (very controversial, I gather), which happily is on this evening, three minutes' walk away. I leave for New York on Friday, and am looking forward to that.

. . . .

December 19, 1985
Dear Barbara—
[. . .] Hal went with me, aboard the QE2, and from Southampton we

traveled by taxi all the way to Cambridge, and thus were delivered at the very gates (huge, wrought iron, closed at midnight) of Clare College, where we stayed. It was already dark, and raining. Students passing under umbrellas. Dim masses of trees. A gas fire in the guest suite. A New Zealand poet staying across the hall, with whom we shared a makeshift breakfast the next morning. Garden parties on the greensward, next afternoon. Tea at a place called Auntie's, featuring scones with gobs and jam and whipped cream. At the poetry festival, Seamus Heaney recognized and greeted me before I could introduce myself. We read on the same program—which guaranteed a full house—and the BBC was there, recording it all, and a week or so a bit of my segment, with me in my Library of Congress red dress, it was broadcast—or so I'm told; haven't seen it myself. Very friendly audience. Afterward, we had savory waffles (that is, stuff like ratatouille instead of ice cream) with an American poet, and suddenly realized it was nearly midnight. A mile's walk to Clare. Gates shut, no sign of anybody at the porter's lodge. Eventually a figure appeared out of the darkness; we asked whether he could tell us what to do, and he said "Follow me"—and after many turnings through back tunnels, arrived at our own door. An undergraduate took me to lunch at a tony hotel overlooking the Cam, with not very good food but a vast wine list to order from, and told me a lot of Brideshead-Revisited tales of student life at Cambridge. But I still like Oxford better. Hal and I spent a day there, being entertained by my Faber editor, Craig Raine, and his wife, Lee, who is a grandniece of Boris Pasternak and a tutor at Oxford—she came home to lunch in gown and hood, to see about her youngest who is about a year old. A gorgeous, goldenhaired, voluptuous beauty under all the academic regalia. We were taken to Garsington, a country house where the Bloomsbury crowd used to gather now owned by an OPEC millionaire, and sat in the hammock in the garden, contemplating the pool where the likes of D.H. Lawrence and Aldous Huxley once strolled. The most thrilling thing we did altogether, though, was to spend Saturday at the theater in London—a version of several medieval Mystery plays combined, and called simply *The Mysteries*, done by the National Theater, a venerable repertory group. The Nativity at 11, then lunch and a stroll, then the Passion at 3, then more strolling, along the Thames Embankment with views of Westminster and Houses of Parliament. Then dinner with an English friend, and then at 8, Doomsday. It was the most thrilling thing either of us had ever been to, though it's hard to describe the effect it had. Working-class clothing and North Country accents (the York and Wake-

field cycles were the main ones it was based on). If you know the sheep-stealing episode (which we didn't) from the Second Shepherd's Play, you have an idea of the comic side anyhow. After that we visited my friends at Chichester, on the Sussex coast, and then Hal sailed back to New York and I caught a train to the continent where I spent three weeks, visiting people in Berlin, Geneva and the dune country outside Amsterdam. Then back to Cambridge where a friend from Williamsburg had rented a house so he could entertain people, and where I settled in to try to sift out some likely winners from the huge mound of manuscripts I found waiting. At the beginning of August there was a weekend in a country house in Lancashire when, surrounded by all the amenities (including two cats named Pushkin and Koshka, who sat on our laps in the midst of everything) the three of us who were to judge the contest made our choices. Whether we came near choosing the best poems I'm not at all sure. But it wasn't the knock-down-and-drag-out I'd been afraid of. Great relief to have it over. Then I wandered around England and Scotland, tramping through the countryside, for another month before the prize-giving ceremony, where I shook the hand of Ted Hughes, the Poet Laureate, and met some nice people. Got back to New York just three months ago, and am not sure I can account for myself very well since then—except that I did go to St. Louis and from there to Des Moines and from Des Moines to Grinnell for an overnight visit, and after that visited some old aunts, one of whom is now ninety-three and still lives by herself, even drives her own car, though not for any great distance. Hal and I are spending Christmas quietly in New York. Let me know the news, which I'm sure there is bound to be more of. And merry Christmas!
Love,
Amy

. . . .

317 South Pleasant Street
Amherst, Massachusetts 01002

April 17, 1987
Dear Barbara [Blay]—
[. . .] [Hal and I] continue to be separated a bit more than would be ideal, but he has been here for some idyllic stretches of a week of more, and if all goes according to plan, will be back here soon. I'd thought I had arranged for a less strenuous schedule this spring than the fall one was—but things haven't worked out that way, or at least so it seems to

me at this moment, with more student works to be pondered than I ever had at one time before, and various little excursions here and there (introducing Seamus Heaney for a New York audience; talking about Marianne Moore in Philadelphia; and so on). The expeditions can be fun, and often I've met some delightful people, so I'm not really complaining.— Also, my new book is out—a copy will be on its way to you today. To mark the event, I gave a party, here in Amherst—more than a hundred people, including colleagues, students, and a fair number from farther away. Hal was here, and three other friends from New York also stayed overnight. People did seem to be having a good time, and it was nice to have the house filled with flowers and people. There are flowers in my back garden as well, and on sunny days I've done such rudimentary things as clear the last autumn's leaves from the flowerbeds. There have been snowdrops, daffodils are blooming now, and the violets just beginning. What I really look forward to is the lilacs—a towering hedge of them on two sides of the house, which should be blooming in a couple of weeks.

As for the teaching itself—I have another writing class, a totally different group from last semester's, with a couple of somewhat unruly people whom I like but who make some less boisterous souls unhappy; I haven't yet succeeded in mediating their differences, so I suppose I never shall. The other course is less worrying: The Language of the Stage, it's called, most of the students are husky young men, and what we mainly do is read plays aloud. The other day we even pushed furniture aside and did a sort of staging of *Waiting for Godot*. I'm learning a lot, though I come away from each session as exhausted as though I'd done all the parts myself! [. . .]
Love—and thanks yet again—
Amy

. . . .

August 24, 1987
Dear Barbara—
A couple of weeks ago I went up to Franconia, New Hampshire for one of those writers' gatherings, and was on the point of writing you a postcard, to at least prove my good intentions—only I never quite laid hands on the postcard. My goodness, it has been a long time. So I'm the more honored to have a letter. Yes, we did go to Maine, but only for two weeks at the end of June. I spent most of the time not doing much, which I like to think was by way of recuperating from my year of making like a professor. I did manage to come down with a ferocious summer cold after classes and wind-up operations were over at Amherst. What wasn't yet

over was an appearance at Harvard, as this year's Phi Beta Kappa poet—along with Alfred Kazin, who was this year's orator. Very venerable tradition, dating back to something like 1792, these literary exercises. I should add that although the likes of Emerson were represented, many of the participants are now totally forgotten. Anyhow, I was running a temperature when I got off the bus, caught a subway and found my way across Harvard Yard to the Faculty Club, where I had dinner with the Kazins and a couple of Harvard people. There were moments when it seemed to me that Harvard being full of itself was just too much—but the occasion was saved by Mr. Kazin, who went to City College and, though extremely courteous, was clearly not to be overimpressed by all those traditions. The Literary Exercises, so called, took place next day, and a nice touch was being greeted by William Alfred, he of "Hogan's Goat." I had met him back in the winter, and it was nice to be remembered. So then I found myself in a procession, launched by uniformed fife-and-drummers, in which I walked side by side with President Derek Bok himself—there is a snapshot to prove it, with me beaming all over and looking perfectly healthy. In fact, the reading went quite well, and I got through the reception afterward, and things wound up merrily in a café called the Algiers, with three graduate assistants whose attitude toward Harvard, or maybe toward academia on the whole, bordered on the derisive. Then I caught the Boston subway back to the bus station, and the bus back to Amherst, where I phoned Hal in New York—he had been laid low by the same cold, or its twin, or he would have been there—and crawled into bed. As a result of my then condition, all the things I had planned to do in the way of final get-togethers up there came to naught. We went to Maine, drove back to Amherst to collect my belongings, and here we've been since the beginning of July.

No, I still haven't even begun that play I keep talking about. I've thought about it, and I think I know more than I did about playwriting in a general way, but writing poems seems safer. Not that I've formally abandoned the notion. As I must have mentioned, during the second semester I taught a course called The Language of the Stage, for which I auditioned and rejected a lot of plays (the likes of Tennessee Williams, for instance) because I didn't think the language was interesting enough. Most of the ones who made it (I mean, not counting Shakespeare—we read "Troilus and Cressida" and "The Tempest") turned out to be Irish. Wilde, Congreve and Sheridan (both at least quasi-Irish), Yeats, Synge, Beckett. One play by Albee, "The Zoo Story." Three by David Mamet, who is clearly not Irish, but whose language is certainly interesting. We read " Dream on Monkey Mountain" by Derek Walcott and also "Raisin in the Sun." A good deal of time in class was spent reading things aloud. We staged "Waiting for Godot," sort of—I mean I brought in props, including four pieces of headgear. We wound up with Dylan Thomas's radio play, "Under Milk Wood." All those Irish writers meant inevitably that I got sidetracked into the history of relations between Ireland and England, and I'm still thinking about them: I just finished doing a review of Seamus Heaney's soon-to-be-published new book, THE HAW LANTERN, which is full of what he calls the Matter of Ireland. Very grim stuff.

It would be very nice to visit you sometime. I don't know that part of Florida at all. My next expedition—I leave on Labor Day—is in Lake Charles, Louisiana, where I've been before, and then in Houston, where there are people I know, and after that Los Angeles. All by train. Well, you know what that's like. [. . .]

Love,

Amy

. . . .

December 14, 1987

Dear Rimsa—

The parcel—I mean the parcel from you—arrived, with a wonderful promptness, and is waiting to be opened at the magical moment. You are the most faithful of all my old-time friends at remembering Christmas and birthdays, and I'm touched and grateful. I can't be sure when I wrote you last, or what I said then. Anyhow, I'm back in New York, somewhat settled although not quite reconciled to this increasingly awful and nerve-racking metropolis after a year in New England. A little over a month ago I went up to Vermont for four days of what I just heard somebody refer to as a dog-and-pony show: a way I rather like of characterizing whatever it was I did, along with a novelist and the arts council coordinator (himself a poet) who drove us around. We went to Rutland, St. Johnsbury and Putney, as well as Montpelier, where I stayed in what must have been the bridal suite of a hotel that wouldn't have seemed like much except for the view I had, in two directions, of the delectable little Greek-revival state-house and the wooded hills that surround it. There is, besides the state government, a cooking school in the vicinity, and as a result the restaurants are exceptionally good; there is an excellent bookstore, and anyhow

the region is crawling with poets. Our threesome got on so well that it was a real grief to go our separate ways. I was ready to settle in Montpelier for an indefinite stay. New York has truly become a place without either soul or manners. There are moments of savoring what it can be—such as earlier this month, when I gave a reading in the grandest setting yet: a small auditorium at the Morgan Library (upstairs from the main exhibition rooms), with an overflow audience consisting partly of directors of the library and the Academy of American Poets, who appeared in black tie, and a fair number of friends of mine, who mainly didn't. I did buy a new dress (having heard that somebody who planned to be in the audience had bought one, it suddenly seemed incumbent—but it wasn't an evening one), and beforehand I found myself having dinner at the Colony Club with the black-tie crowd, sitting next to a Viscount, no less, and there was a limousine at the door to deliver me and Seamus Heaney, who introduced me to the audience, to the door of the Morgan. Having been seen emerging from a limousine in those circumstances, and having it reported to friends in other parts, is a bit peculiar. But I did have fun. There was a party afterward in some of the grander rooms of the Morgan, where I'd never been before. Seamus Heaney is a genuinely good person, and said nice things. Well, it's been downhill since then. I caught cold, and am behind on everything. I have written a play. Did I tell you about my notion of a play on the life of Dorothy Wordsworth? Maybe not, since I don't think I quite believed I'd ever do it. But William Wordsworth's great-great grandson, an actor named Richard Wordsworth, was in town back in October, reading from the works of William, Dorothy and their friends; and then came a really superlative exhibition at the New York Public Library, on Wordsworth and Romanticism, and in the midst of all this I found myself writing dialogue. There are some problems, you won't be surprised to hear, that may mean it can't be staged: it seems I was envisioning a film all along, with scenery. Even so, I don't regret having done it. [. . .]
Love,
Amy

. . . .

May 9, 1988
Dear John,
Where to begin? I am such an impossible correspondent, I don't deserve to hear from anybody—much less be offered a tape of *Nixon in China*,

which we didn't see, and if it's not too late, of course we would be greatly beholden. We're pleased that you like *Emilia,* and will try to provide
further tidbits to amuse you. How delightful to hear of the Logan grant.
I'm eager to see the essay when it's convenient.

One thing I mustn't forget is that a couple of weekends ago I was in
Portland, Maine, for one of those writers' gatherings, and there I met André Dubus, who captivated everyone. I'm not sure whether you've met
him or just spoken over the phone; anyhow, when I discovered that he
was born in Lake Charles, I naturally mentioned you, and then we talked
about Cajun food. You'll know about his being crippled in the worst kind
of highway accident. His spirit in the face of all that is wonderful. I had-
n't know his work at all, but am now catching up, and have become a devoted fan of the writer as well as the person. I stayed with Ken Rosen, a
poet whose work was also new to me, and have now become a fan of his
as well. He is like nobody, but I couldn't help thinking of *your* work as I
read his, simply because you're likewise so totally yourself.

Before I got up there, my travels took me variously to points south—
Charleston and Greenville, South Carolina in March, then Tallahassee
and Savannah a month later. Southern audiences so seem naturally easier
to reach than they are up here. (I appeared at Furman University and
Florida State; the historic places were stopovers. Savannah is marvelous.)
And now Hal and I are beginning to plan a stay in Europe. We're expecting to sail on the QE2 on June 12 and spend a couple of weeks in England before going to Leyden, where he's to be on the faculty of a legal sem-
inar. Then we have the last two weeks in July free; we haven't settled
where we'll be before sailing back on the first of August. Are you by any
chance going abroad yourselves? Buying a house in the south of France,
even? When you wrote earlier, you said you were thinking about it.

Meanwhile, I can report that we were invited to have lunch with Lord
Eccles and his wife Mary, at the farm she owns in the horse country near
Somerville, New Jersey. I'm so ignorant of the world of collectors that I had
no idea what was in store for us: she (who was Mary Hyde, widow of Donald Hyde, until just four years ago) is a very big Johnson collector—not
only books but also the Reynolds portrait of Johnson as an infant, and several of Mrs. Thrale as well as of Thrale himself, and of Piozzi. What I saw
were mainly things connected with Wordsworth, Southey, Sir Gerge Beau-
mont, people like that; also an original typescript of *The Importance of Being Earnest* with Wilde's own notations. And we made a tour of the barns
(it's a sheep farm) and the greenhouses. I'd met the Eccles the night I read

at the Morgan Library and was seen getting out of the limousine. If anything, such experiences only confirm me in my bohemian ways; but I won't deny that they're fun, in extreme moderation if you know what I mean.

Here is the third version of my play, to be read only when you have the leisure to do so. It goes with love to all, and best from Hal, too.
Ever,
Amy

. . . .

May 13, 1988
Dear Rimsa—
A small token by way of a birthday remembrance went off the other day, and I now realize that I haven't written since the beginning of the year. It's hard to make an accounting of where the time has gone, except to say that no, I have no plans for writing an autobiography, though I have been trying to write a poem about my grandfather, the one who read Emerson. The play about Dorothy Wordsworth has gone through a third revision— I'll let you know when and if it ever gets aired anywhere, but in the meantime I can say that her life was, if not outwardly dramatic, full of dramatic tensions and conflicts: such as her being too greatly moved to go to her brother's wedding, and he married her best friend! Years later, Wordsworth himself couldn't manage to go to the wedding of his daughter Dora (named for his sister). As now constituted, this is what the play turns on. Besides which, Dorothy lost her mind in her later years— though not her memory; she would recite poems, mainly her brother's, at great length. I'm thinking about all this just now because Hal and I are planning to go to England in just a month (we have space on the QE2 for June 12), and a major item on the list is a stay in Grasmere, which he's never seen. The occasion of this trip is that Hal will be taking part in a legal conference at Leyden, and I'm just tagging along.

There has been some traveling over here in the meantime. Not quite a month ago I was in Tallahassee for a writers' conference, and I saw amaryllises in bloom all over the place—so now I know what you mean. I was also taken to a place called Wakulla Springs, where I saw all the alligators I'll need for the rest of my life, but also lots of wood ducks, anhingas, herons and (a rare one, this) limpkins, with chicks. On the way back I made a stopover in Savannah, where the azaleas had finished blooming but which was still just about the most romantically beautiful place I've seen, in this country anyhow. Some weeks before that, I went up to South Hadley, Massachusetts, where Joseph Brodsky teaches during the spring term, and where there was a celebration in honor of his winning the Nobel Prize. Quite a number of poets were on hand, and Brodsky himself was looking affable—though *I'm* still terrified of him. One thing that came out during the proceedings is that he is partial to cats. I can even report that I heard a distinct Meow as he approached the buffet table. I would have been more puzzled than I was if I hadn't just learned, from his essay on his parents, that he and his father were in the habit of conversing in this fashion, particularly when meat was in prospect. Also, one of his pet names for his mother was "Keesa," which I gather is a cat word. The most fun, for me, was seeing a number of my students from last year. Before that excursion, I "did" a strenuous circuit of Ohio colleges, winding up over the border in Louisville—another place that looks very attractive. Among other things, I was shown the grave of George Keats and the house associated with Fitzgerald's stay there, which was eventually to find its way into *The Great Gatsby*. [. . .]

Love,
Amy

. . . .

September 6, 1988
Dear Barbara—
Oh, to think of you traipsing (as you put it—and so would I) about London, makes me happy, but also eager for details. The above is where Hal and I stayed, for several days in June and again in the latter part of July—I think I may have mentioned it before. I'll have to admit that we resorted to the snack-in-the-room trick a good deal of the time. Dollars certainly don't go very far around there. Anyhow, the Jubilee is smack in the middle of the theater district, and one great treat was being able to go *on foot*, as we did four times in less than a week! *Les Liaisons Dangereuses* was about two minutes away, *Uncle Vanya* maybe as much as twenty minutes, a new show called *Greek* (Oedipus updated, with a wonderful yenta of a Sphinx) and the Festival Ballet at the Coliseum each less than ten minutes' walk from our funny little walkup of a pied-à-terre. (Which was still alarmingly pricey—but you'll know all about that.) All fairly heady stuff. So was taking the train to Glyndebourne, to see a new opera, the name of whose composer I keep forgetting, but the librettist for which is my friend and Faber editor, Craig Raine—it's called *The Electrification of the Soviet Union*, and is based on a story by Pasternak, and is not your usual Glynde-

bourne fare—anyhow, Craig went down with us, and instead of picnicking on the lawn, in view of the Sussex downs and their complement of grazing cattle, we had supper with him and the leading singer, and we also got to wander around backstage and smell all those backstage smells, and get the feel of the whole thing; and then afterward there is the train ride back to Victoria, talking poetry and opera the whole way. Another heady trip was taking the train to Oxford, just for the day, to have lunch, for the first time ever, *inside an Oxford College.* The company was very good—an American who's a tutor there invited me—and the food much better than I'd dared expect, and the atmosphere: well, the college was Brasenose, and a feature of the view from the tutors' lounge is the Radcliffe Camera, one of my most favorite pieces of architecture in the world. And I found my way back to the station without having to ask, and caught my train with two minutes to spare, and felt very very worldly. Also one evening, in the midst of all those snacks-in-the-room, we were picked up by a driver named Whiting, who took us to a house directly across from where John Gielgud lives, not far from the Houses of Parliament, where we had champagne with (get this) a member of the House of Lords! Or maybe I mentioned him; his name is David Eccles, he's married to an American, and they're both book collectors. While we had champagne, he showed me his three first editions of *The Waste Land,* among other things; and then we went out to dinner at a place called Odin's, where we dined very well, though I couldn't do justice to the wines.

But the part I likes best was tramping around outside London, in Wordsworth-and-Coleridge territory in Somerset, and then later in the environs of Grasmere. Looking back on it, I'm amazed at myself for being so carefree. Toward the end of our stay, I went to spend a weekend with the family of a young friend in Tunbridge Wells, and the high point of that visit was a morning spent tramping in what turned out to be Pooh country—A. A. Milne's house was pointed out as we went by it—in the company of a niece (of the young friend) who came equipped with a kite. The weather was exceedingly skittish, shifting from sunshine to sudden downpour in a trice a couple of times over, and I found myself sheltering under head-high bracken and gorse bushes in a most Pooh-like fashion. There were also various expeditions to look at English country houses, of which the supply is even more inexhaustible than I'd supposed. And there were the two weeks we spent in Leyden, living in the prettiest apartment imaginable, with a view of a canal with houseboats and barges and a windmill beside a drawbridge. Hal was teaching a course in American law to

European students, who turned out to be charming. I joined them for lunch a number of times, and Hal was completely in his element. I also went to visit my Dutch friend who lives in the dunes to the north of Amsterdam. And I made a two-day visit to a friend in Geneva. I wonder how nearly our paths came to crossing? [. . .]

On Saturday I'm to take a train for St. Louis, for a three-week stay on the campus of Washington University, one of those visiting-writer things, winding up with a three-day celebration of T. S. Eliot's hundredth birthday. Or maybe I mentioned that project. Since we got back from Europe I seem to have spent most of my accounted-for time trying to get my mind around him, and in particular around the "Game of Chess" sequence in *The Waste Land*, which I'm to read there and talk around for ten minutes or so. In November I'm to be in Washington for another reading at the Library of Congress, along with May Swenson and Mona Van Duyn: it's to honor a great benefactor of poets named Marie Bullock, who died a couple of years ago. Otherwise I'm staying pretty much in the vicinity for the foreseeable future. [. . .]

Love,

Amy

. . . .

October 24, 1988

Dear John and Carol and Dafydd—

It's bad enough not to have written a real letter in all this time (I *hope* a postcard I *think* I sent from somewhere abroad did reach you). But not to have thanked you for *Nixon in China* is plain ingratitude. When it arrived, before we left for England, the VCR had broken down irreparably. It had in fact to be replaced, and that didn't happen until around the beginning of September. So I finally had my evening with the opera more than a month ago, just before heading for St. Louis for a three-week stay. Thus far I've seen it just that once, but I can well understand your own repeated viewings. I found it quite enthralling, and if I weren't so hopeless as a correspondent I'd have let you know without all these weeks of not writing.

St. Louis was lots of fun. I'd been asked originally to be there for a T. S. Eliot centenary, the last weekend in September. Then I was invited to spend three weeks before that as a visiting professor, meeting mainly with poets in the MFA program at Washington U. I'd no sooner gotten a library I.D. card and proceeded to the stacks than a familiar face emerged from a corridor: John Griffin, whom I'd met at McNeese just a year before! I saw him a couple of times, and he appeared to be well—he's in the regular graduate program, but I gather has some prospects for his poems' coming out as a book. The Eliot celebration was illuminating if inconclusive. I'd spent several weeks boning up—though all I had to do was to read the Game Chess sequence from *The Waste Land* and do ten minutes' worth of comment—and the more I read, the less I knew what to think, except that *The Waste Land* must be more influential than any other poem written in the twentieth century, and not all for the good either. Anyhow, the evening when six of us poets did our thing was more thrilling than I'd expected. I sat next to Richard Wilbur at dinner beforehand, and we agreed that it's much more nervous-making to be reading another poet than to do one's own work. He read *Ash Wednesday*, and made it into something glorious—which is far from inevitable (the other evening I heard Susan Sontag read it, here in New York, and much as I revere her, and truly she is to be revered, it turned into a bit of a drag). I don't know that we ever traded the least smidgen of a view on T. S. E., and am wondering what you think.

I was very happy to have the postcard from France. Besides a month, all told, in various English places, we lived for two weeks in an apartment in Leyden—as all-of-a-piece as place as one is likely to be a visitor in. The Dutch are exemplary in many ways, and pretty living quarters is one of those ways. I never actually got to Amsterdam, though I did spent a day with my friend who has a house among the dunes outside it. Hal was doing a two-week course on American law at the ancient university there, and I had fun meeting the students, who were from all over the continent. I made a short trip to visit a friend in Geneva, and got into France for a couple of hours—long enough to have lunch in an out-of-the-way little café and to realize that there truly is no place like France when it comes to that department. [. . .]
Love,
Amy

P.S.
I've been working on a piece for an anthology on the New Testament, which brought me a bit up to date on where Biblical scholarship is at, and also on the millenarian wing. Do you know *The Rapture*, by Hal Lindsay? Well, I'd never heard of him until a few weeks ago, and it seems he's one of the best-selling authors ever. How about that? Puts one in one's place, it does.

April 3, 1989

Dear David Lehman—

First of all, thank you very much for the copy of "Twenty Questions," which is as charmingly produced as it is a pleasure to read. I can only wish that my happiness in reading it extended to the bulk of the work you have sent. That I can't say so is not your fault. Certainly there is much fine work there. But I have gone about reading it with a growing conviction that I am just not up to the job of putting together an anthology of the year's best poetry. I hesitated to begin with about accepting, and when I agreed it was, I now realize, without thinking through what troubled me in the first place.

I suppose everyone who is asked to be a judge of poems on any occasion whatever must feel something of what now troubles me so acutely. I have just groaned my way through yet another batch of contest entries, struggling (and hardly managing) to discover some shreds of poetic merit. Every time I do that, I am ready to swear off ever judging another contest—and maybe one of these days I'll do exactly that. Once in a while, asked for a jacket blurb, I have found the exercise of looking for particular qualities in a manuscript, and finding the phrases to convey some inkling of what those qualities may be, an illuminating and valuable one. What I do not find illuminating or valuable is having to say, This is the best. I find myself executing any number of rhetorical feints and dodges in order to avoid superlatives. Who can say what is best? All I see out there is anarchy. Even when some implicit common standard might have been expected, I keep stumbling up against intractable disagreement. One responds to a piece of work, or else one doesn't. Sometimes, in my own experience, not responding means simply drawing a blank. I have biases, as everyone does, and perhaps a greater share than many people; but more troublesome still, for the purpose at hand, are the blind spots—of which I begin to fear that I have a very great many. For a fair amount of what is being published these days, I simply discover no point of entry. I used—to take just one example—to think I understood what Jorie Graham was about, and on the whole to like it; but now I can't even speak of like or dislike: I simply do not *hear* what is happening. Being thus deaf to so much that is generally well regarded clearly means that I cannot do properly what I too rashly agreed to do—to make a selection that is genuinely eclectic and that at the same time represents my own taste. In the circumstances, to stand up and draw a ring around a collection of seventy-five poems labeled "best of the year"—even if it is understood that "best" is no more than shorthand for "what I think I like best, more or less"—this, I have concluded, is something I can't do because I am just not tough enough. I have looked at John Ashbery's selection, and it seems genuinely and conscientiously eclectic. I dare say that Donald Hall, with his long experience, has managed the task equally well and in his own way. But as a newcomer to being known at all, I simply can't muster the necessary assurance even to begin. There must be someone out there who will be as happy to assume the responsibility as I shall be to be excused from it. I do hope that you will excuse me, and can only begin to say how sorry I am to have put you to so much trouble. The poems are being returned separately, with my heartfelt apologies.

Sincerely yours—

Amy Clampitt

. . . .

December 1, 1989

Dear Barbara—

Well, imagine *that* coincidence! I wasn't at all sure anybody was going to read that review, and so I'm greatly honored that it was not only read but sent on to another reader. It was fun to do (though the book was a bore), and entailed getting a start at reading *Clarissa*, which I'd never taken even a peep at before. Anyhow, I've been aware of being a worse correspondent even than usual, so there is some kind of neat paradox at work here. One reason, or excuse, for this latest lapse is being preoccupied with looking after Hal over the past several months. He's feeling pretty much himself again by now, but it's been a long haul, beginning with a lymphoma that turned up in a routine physical just about a year ago, which meant six months of chemotherapy, which he weathered fairly well, without being hospitalized or missing more than a few classes. But no sooner were those six months of chemo over than he came down with a ferocious case of what turned out to be Legionnaires' Disease, picked up from who knows whose air-conditioning system. He was delirious, on and off, for days, and the just over two weeks he spent in the hospital were one long nightmare of nobody being in charge. The one good thing about it all was Vivian, whom I had the luck to hire as what's called a companion—a nurse's aide in other words—and who became our great friend and benefactor: one of the world's great life-enhancers, who of course is vastly underpaid and variously exploited but who is so marvelously equipped with energy and good sense that she just soars above the disagreeableness of things. We had her with us for a couple of days after Hal came home, and her horror over the condition of the apartment (books and records all over the floor, dust everywhere, et cetera et cetera: "*What a mess!*" was her indelible response, though she *had* been warned) led to action. For one thing, she found us Joyce, another Jamaican powerhouse, who comes three Mondays out of three to keep the dust down and many, many other things. For another, we acquired two new bookcases, the clutter came up off the floor, out of the boxes and onto the shelves or into closets, and though shabby by now, the place is cheerful again. But all this domesticity takes hold to an extent that it can interfere with just about everything else, including writing (though not reading; we've gotten back into the almost nightly reading aloud, and when Hall was too weak to do much else, it expanded into the daytime). I did manage, before the pneumonia crisis, to turn in a manuscript to my editor, and there will be a new book, called *Westward,* coming out sometime in late March. The play is still vegetating. A scene from it has just come out in a "little" magazine, and I'll send a copy so you can have an idea. The more I think about it, the more I conclude that I've got to start over. The Poets' Theatre people were encouraging enough, and such pleasant people to deal with, that I hope to get at it one of these days. [. . .]

Love,

Amy

. . . .

February 15, 1990

Dear Dorothy [Blake]—

It was good to hear from you, as it was to see you at Dr. Traube's memorial. I am just so sorry to hear about your depressed state since then. One might say that in the circumstances it is hardly surprising—but the truth is, I suppose, that bereavement is always a surprise, for which one simply can't be prepared. Do please accept my sympathy.

I have read and reread the poems in your folder, always with much interest, as well as concern for the dark view of experience I find there. It is a challenge to discover—or perhaps *invent* is a better word—a form that will in some way give legitimacy to one's own state of mind, particularly when that state is a despondent one. This at any rate is the challenge I seem to perceive your having set for yourself. Finding a form is, as I see it, the main problem when it comes to writing poetry. As I believe I may have said to you—I know I did to Dr. Traube, anyhow—I have always been doubtful about whether finding that form is a thing that can be

taught. When I find myself in the position of facing a class in writing poetry, I am more and more inclined to fall back on assigning strict verse
forms as an exercise: an account of the Superbowl game in the manner of
"The Rape of the Lock" is one example. You might suppose that nothing
could be more conventional than the heroic couplets of Alexander Pope.
I may have thought so myself once, but now I'm not so sure. Perhaps the
most inhibiting conventions are those that go unrecognized for what they
are. I believe (and in this I could be entirely wrong; in any event the matter is debatable) that I see something of this here and there in your work:
the prevalence of very short lines, the occasional device of ending a line in
mid-syllable, the not infrequent absence of a completely predicated sentence. No that there is any rule against such things, the point being rather
that if it once appeared daring to align a poem vertically on the page, or
to break a word open by way of enjambment, or to conclude without once
introducing a verb—as it did, perhaps, when the work of E. E. Cummings
first appeared—well, to imitate those who have imitated what was once
just a bit daring is another thing entirely. The same applies, I would say,
to the use of repetition. Just lately (I can't remember where, alas) I came
across the suggestion that mechanical, triphammer-like repetitions got
into poetry as an acknowledgment that triphammer-like rhythms had
overtaken the rhythms, say, of the minuet and the sarabande. In the same
way one might argue that rock music is such an acknowledgment, and
therefore inescapable. I myself refuse to go along with any notion that
rock music is the only real thing—and in the same way, it seems to me
that poetry has other ways to go than in the way of least resistance.

Your evident knowledge of music suggests to me what way you yourself
might go. "Prelude #1" seems to me to touch on possibilities that could be
developed more fully. "In the Staccato Vein" does likewise (with one quib-
ble: can a *vein* be thought of as *staccato*?). The longer line you use there
seems to me to suggest some possibilities yet to be realized. "Sadness in Col-
or and Sound" interested me in particular because of the way it ends: "I cry
in the key of small 'd,' the saddest of all sounds." (You'll note by inference
that I myself would not break this statement into quite so many lines.) The
unexpectedness of this is what made it, for me, genuinely poetic.

Thinking about the pleasure that conclusion gave me, it occurred to me
that you might consider writing an entire sequence on the states of feeling
associated with musical keys. Where it might lead I haven't the expertise to
predict—but unpredictability is, I think, to some degree necessary to any
successful poem. "Art inhabits the country between chaos and cliché": so

says Barbara Herrnstein Smith in a book, *Poetic Closure*, which I recently came across and would like to suggest as perhaps of some interest. That conclusion of hers follows this observation: "As we read a poem we are continuously subjected to small surprises and disappointment as the developing lines evade or contradict our expectations." In other words, something has to *happen* in a poem. It won't with every single thing one tries to write. Some effects are bound to be in the nature of experiments (not to mention those that simply go nowhere). But there is nothing wrong or reprehensible about the effort in itself. I commend you for tackling the Rilke sonnet—precisely because Rilke must be one of the most difficult of all poets to make sense of in English. I think you might profitably go on with that experiment, setting yourself the ultimate goal of a rendering that is musical in its own right, regardless of phrase-by-phrase fidelity to the original. An *exact* translation, it seems to me, is so nearly impossible as to amount to a contradiction in terms. There is a lot of debate about this, but it shouldn't deter you from trying your hand at it further.

In general, I would recommend that you break free of the vertical free-verse format more often in favor of longer lines and completed sentences. It's no more than a hunch, but I think that paradoxically you might find yourself freer to wander, to be various and surprising, than by adhering to what is after all (as I'm arguing anyhow) a convention, rather than an aid to originality of expression. Try writing a villanelle, for example. I've never managed to write one I was happy with, but that doesn't mean the practice was worthless. It might even be fun. And the more fun you can take in writing, the better it is likely to be. That's my guess anyhow.

I can't be sure any of this is what you've hoped for, or that it will be of any use. But it goes with my own heartfelt concern for you personally. I'm not the best of correspondents; but if you're inclined to send more poems, I'll do my best to respond.

Yours sincerely—

Amy

. . . .

February 20, 1990

Dear Jennifer Snodgrass—

In answer to your query, here are some of my thoughts about the novels of George Eliot:

During my most impressionable years, in college and after, the New-Critical notion of a work of literature as a self-contained artifact was pretty overwhelming. Looking back, though, I see a part of me that never really went along with that notion. I could agree that the literal facts of a writer's career were largely irrelevant when it came to aesthetic values. But there are other values to be found. I've just come across this, for example, in a review by Robert B. Adams (of a book by M. H. Abrams, among others):

> Viewing the art-object—the painting on the wall, the poem on the printed page—as an object-in-itself, to be judged by purely aesthetic standards, is a relatively recent habit of mind. . . . There may be values in the work, including those of direct, didactic statement, that the artist did not intend us to overlook . . . (*New York Review of Books*, March 1, 1990)

In the same vein is the very title of a new book, *The Didactic Muse*, by Willard Spiegelman, who goes so far as to suggest that "In the panorama of literary culture, it increasingly appears that modernism was an aberration." The subject of this book is the presence of instruction in contemporary poetry. And if poetry, with its undeniably large aesthetic component, is to be seen as a vehicle of instruction, how much truer must that be of the novel?

That is what I had in mind when I referred to George Eliot as a friend and guide. Reading a work of fiction, one is invariably trying on someone else's version of experience, and in so doing is engaging in vicarious behavior. Rachel Brownstein's *Becoming a Heroine: Reading about Women in Novels* is in part an account of that process. George Eliot, not surprisingly, is one of the novelists she writes about. As it happens, about ten years ago I found myself reading and rereading George Eliot's work, and making notes from it. Some of those passages found their way into poems about George Eliot, as a woman and a writer, which appear in my book *Archaic Figure*. One that didn't, from *The Mill on the Floss*, suggests something about what I kept finding:

> "She has some trouble or other at heart," he thought. "Poor child! she looks as if she might turn out to be one of—
>
> 'The souls by nature pitch'd too high,
>   By suffering plung'd too low.'"

This could well be a characterization of Mary Ann Evans herself—or so I was persuaded by a reading of Gordon Haight's marvelous biography. What I kept discovering in the novels, at any rate, was a powerful stratum of repressed poetry. It is acknowledged by the famous passage from

Middlemarch, about hearing the grass grow and the squirrel's heart beat (alluded to near the beginning of "The Prairie," and in an earlier poem of mine called "The August Darks"). And it is what must have been in Virginia Woolf's mind when she wrote in *The Common Reader*, referring to George Eliot's heroines, that "The ancient consciousness of women, charged with suffering and sensibility, and for many ages dumb, seems, in them, to have brimmed and overflowed." (I chose that passage as an epigraph to *Archaic Figure*.)

All of which will suggest something of the affinity I, as a poet, came to feel with George Eliot the novelist, and by a very slight extension, with Mary Ann Evans as a woman. I have found it illuminating to discover traces of the living woman in such fictions as Hetty Sorel in *Adam Bede*, Maggie Tulliver in *The Mill on the Floss*, and Gwendolen Harleth in *Daniel Deronda*—and by an extension of that woman's imaginative sympathy, Gregory Cass in *Silas Marner*, the Reverend Mr. Casaubon and even the unfortunate Bulstrode in *Middlemarch*, among many others. In asserting that the circumstances of the author's own life have such relevance, I am at least in distinguished company. Did not Samuel Johnson, that most formidable of English critics, write of the *lives* of the poets? "Petrarch was a real lover," he observed in his Life of Cowley; whereas of this latter poet "we are told . . . that, whatever he may talk of his own inflammability, and the variety of characters by which his heart was divided, he in reality was in love but once, and then never had resolution to tell his passion." Having argued that "the basis of all excellence is truth: he that professes love ought to feel its power," Dr. Johnson concluded that Cowley's real-life diffidence "cannot but abate, in some measure, the reader's esteem for the work and the author."

This does, as I've mentioned, fly in the face of the canon of the New Critics, with its disdain for any concern with the author's circumstances. But writers are all to some degree conscious of being lonely people; they crave a company they do not always find except in the vicarious company of those whose imaginative power has electrified their own. What I would be interested in exploring is certain narrative junctures, nodes of intensity that seem to emerge from some hidden sources in the author's own psyche and are part of what makes for great literature. To trace those junctures would entail a good deal of rereading, and I can't be sure in advance what might emerge. But the prospect excites me.

Sincerely yours,

Amy Clampitt

. . . .

November 20, 1991

Dear Eileen Berry—

You will have heard some weeks ago that you are one of the poets with whom I expect to be working in January at the Atlantic Center for the Arts. I write now to say how much I look forward to that experience, and to set down a few preliminary thoughts about how we might proceed. The work of a poet being as it is, much of your time will presumably be devoted to it in the solitude of your own quarters. I do not, in other words, envision such a thing as a daily workshop—or even a weekly one, as that term is generally understood.

Nevertheless, there is much to be gained from occasional gatherings, as well as from individual conferences. I would expect to schedule one meeting a week with each of the ten participants—leaving open the possibility of other, impromptu conferences now and then—and beyond this, a weekly session of the entire group as well, perhaps on Thursday afternoon. (It's my inclination to leave all mornings free for individual work.)

At these group sessions, those who wished to bring work for discussion would be free to do so; but whatever may develop in that particular direction, I would expect to concentrate less on the particular work in progress than on problems of craft. Just now, for example, I have found myself mulling over the contraries of spontaneity and withholding, of the cryptic as opposed to the discursive approach to language—opposite tendencies that have all had their place in the making of poems that somehow "work." You mentioned in your account of yourself a tension between the long tradition of English poetry and current American practice. Perhaps you can bring your experience with that tension to the rest of us in a way that will be helpful to us all.

I hope you will also come prepared to tell us about a particular writer whose work has had special meaning for you. Stanley Kunitz is one you mention, among others, whose influence on you I would be interested in hearing about. This sharing of enthusiasms might take place at a preliminary get-acquainted session, perhaps on the afternoon of January 6. If you are inclined to write to me about any of this meanwhile, I'd be not only pleased but grateful.

With Best Wishes,

Amy Clampitt

. . . .

Corea, Maine 04624

June 19, 1992

Dear Rimsa—

Your birthday parcel arrived safely a bit before we headed up this way. The sun dress is dear, whatever the size, and I'm indebted to you for extending my acquaintance with Barbara Pym—the *merciless* Barbara Pym in this instance. My impression of her thus far was derived from her account of some very different people—Anglican clergymen and their fluttery admirers, in a book whose title I've now forgotten, though the characters are with me still, as I dare say Leonora Eyre and company will be. Thank you, once again, very much.

As it turns out, my birthday was marked by some unexpected news—the announcement of this year's MacArthur Foundation grants, with my name among them. Not having picked up on various phone messages, I knew nothing of it until the next day, when the phone up here started ringing. Before I'd quite got that much through my head, there was a message from a producer on Ted Koppel's Nightline—a very nice man, whose wife is a poet—about a program featuring Joseph Brodsky and his notion that poetry might thrive, or anyhow do better, from being sold in supermarkets. At one point there were wild plans to send a video crew out here, for the purpose of taping a two-minute cameo of me reading something or other. I'd actually decided on "that time of year thou mayst in me behold," as the best I could do in the cause of poetry, when the final call came, and (quite to my relief) the invasion of the sound bites was off. From all I can gather (I went to sleep long before the show was aired), nothing came of any of these pipe-dreams—including Brodsky himself. Or perhaps there are options. Hal looked at the set for long enough at the appointed hour to conclude that it was all about the U.S. Open, no poets anywhere in sight.

But—as our actor friend, who was with us through the excitement, observed—that's showbiz. In any case, the grant is real. I hope you'll help me celebrate, and extend your own birthday observances, with the enclosed.

It's wonderful here, as always. We've watched a harbor seal swimming between the bar islands. There are bald eagles about, and one came near enough yesterday as to be unmistakable—that white helmet, those deep black wingbeats. A few nights ago I stayed awake watching almost continuous lightning, and listening to the huge reverberations that follow unendingly out over the water. The next evening I watched the full moon rising behind the porcupine crest of one of the bar islands, turning from

rose-color to gold to white and laying down a trail across the water. I've been writing and reading—among other things, the new biography of Jean Stafford, whom I knew very slightly, by Ann Hulbert, which is remarkably good; and *Les Misérables*, which Hal and I are reading aloud to each other in the evenings. It's generally cool enough for a fire of birch logs on the stone hearth that is the center of gravity except when something like a moonrise preempts everything. [. . .]
Love,
Amy

. . . .

July 2, 1992
Dear Family—
We're back from Maine, after much turmoil—and the apartment here having finally been painted in our absence, turmoil is what we're still in. Bit by bit, things are getting back into place, but the books and records that made the whole prospect such a nightmare are still mostly in boxes and *dozens* of shopping bags. The thing about apartment living that maddens us is having no attic or cellar to stow things in. Well. That situation, in a manner of speaking, seems to be about to change. Part of the turmoil just now has to do with what Hal and I have just done: WE HAVE BOUGHT A HOUSE! More precisely, we've made an offer and it has been accepted, but of course there turn out to be some hitches, having to do with zoning and variances, which a lawyer is dealing with (we hope) at this very moment. [. . .]

In the meantime, there has been quite a lot of excitement. Over a month ago now—though for some reason it doesn't seem all that long— I caught a bus up to Portland for the Bowdoin commencement, where I did have a perfectly delightful time. That was largely because of L & J's [brother Larry and his wife Jeanne] having paved the way, so to speak (actually, the honorary degree was a total surprise to them). And anyhow there seem to be an unusual number of pleasant people on that campus and in the town. During the procession across the campus, a faculty member who teaches ornithology turned to me and said, "Hear that? Rose-breasted grosbeak singing up there." (You all know—a robin with a cold.) It was that kind of atmosphere. The other honorees turned out to be especially congenial (a Maine painter, Katherine Porter; Franklyn Jenifer, who is president of Howard University; and James Michener, the novelist, who is eighty- five but as sharp as he turned out to be friendly). We all had a fine time at lunch after the degree-giving was over. The weather was glorious though unseasonably warm. Lilacs were in bloom. Bobolinks were singing in the meadow. The next day turned cold and rainy, but by then I was on my way back to New York—to begin to get organized for driving back that way the next weekend. We stopped on the way with our friends in Lenox, Mass.—a couple we met at Bellagio a year ago, whom we've since gotten to know very well and had a lot of fun with. We'd already been toying with the notion of some day looking for a house up there—but might never have gotten around to more than talking about it, up until the morning the news finally came through (since I hadn't gotten around to returning a call that would have tipped me off) about this-here MacArthur award. It was a call from Karen [Chase] in Lenox, all excited, that finally got me to return that call—and the man who made it turned out to have connections in South Bristol, and didn't wonder at all about not returning calls when you're on the coast of Maine. I'll enclose a piece that came out of a long telephone conversation with a reporter in Bangor, who got it pretty much the way I told it, so far as I can remember.

Anyhow, we drove back by way of Lenox, where in the meantime Karen had been out with a real estate agent she knows, screening possible houses. The one we think we're buying sits on a little over half an acre, in a very grassy and bucolic section, within (brisk, uphill) walking distance of the center of Lenox. It's not huge, but has a couple of spare bedrooms. Tanglewood is about fifteen minutes away. If all goes well, we'll hope to be issuing invitations to visit within a year or so. We have no plans to move out of New York completely—just to have a place to go to on weekends and in the summer, and eventually to retire into. About Maine, we can't imagine that we'd stop going there altogether. All this is very, very contingent, but exciting.

About the MacArthur Foundation—it was set up by a Chicago banker and his wife to avoid having all the money they'd made go to the IRS, and every year or so a batch of thirty or forty people are awarded a nice chunk, to arrive over a five-year period, with absolutely no strings attached. The only other poet this time round is named Irving Feldman, and probably no better known than I am. Twyla Tharp, the dancer, was one, and so was the first black woman mayor of a Southern town, Unita Blackwell. An ecologist and geologist named Geerat Vermeij, who studies marine life and is a professor at the University of California, and has been blind since the age of three (he relies on touch for his researches) is another. My favorite is Wes Jackson, who founded the Land Institute out in Kansas, and whose birthday turns out to be the same as mine. You'll gather that the list tends to be a bit offbeat. Very nice company to be in. Oh yes, Barbara Fields, the historian you may have seen on the TV series about the Civil War, is another I'm especially pleased to associated with.

This does seem to be a year of windfalls. A couple of months ago there came an invitation—which is what Jeanne was referring to—to spend a semester on the campus at Smith, as the first Grace Hazard Conkling Poet in Residence. I'll teach one course, and there is a nice stipend attached.
Love,
Amy

. . . .

September 16, 1992

Martha Hamilton-Phillips
Tercentenary Commission
The College of William and Mary
P. O. Box 8795
Williamsburg, Virginia 23187–8795

Dear Martha:
Your letters, of the 6th and the 8th, reached me yesterday, and I have now had time to consider what my response should be.

I knew, when I agreed to the challenge of writing a verse commemoration of the tercentenary of William and Mary, that I was taking a risk. It was only because of my great affection for the place, and the happiness I experienced there, that I would ever have considered the project. It was, of course, a risk taken equally by the planners of the celebration. How could they know what any poet might end up doing?

For my part, I assumed that whatever I eventually produced would be either accepted or rejected outright. That assumption turns out to be wrong. Rather, it would be appear, it has been found prudent to not quite do either one or the other. I won't deny that the real import of your letter of the 8th, with its copious praise and assurances of affection, along with its diplomatic concern over appropriate context, other examples of my work, and warmer weather, took a while to register. But to postpone the public reading of a commissioned work until a month or more after the date being commemorated would be the same as postponing a commencement oration until after the graduates had gone home.

Accordingly, to spare myself and everyone else that particular form of embarrassment, I write now to ask to be released from the agreement I signed on July 28, and at the same time to release the College of William and Mary from any and all agreements to pay, publish, or entertain me in connection with the proposed commission. I ask only that any copies of "Matoaka" still in your possession be returned to me.

I have offered the only kind of poem I could honestly write. I am sorry that no one at so distinguished an institution of higher learning has seen fit to reply in kind.

Yours sincerely,
Amy Clampitt

. . . .

January 10, 1993
Dear Rimsa—

[. . .] About the *New Yorker*—I *hate* just about every one of Tina Brown's innovations, which strike me as ugly and pointless. I haven't met her, and have really no wish to. I never met Mr. Shawn either, and wish I had. I do know his son Wallace, the actor and playwright, who is one of the most delightfully unpretentious people one could hope to meet. I would never have met *him*, either, if it hadn't been that several years ago in London, a rather pushy young English friend (Cambridge-educated, aspires to be a critic) took me to see *Aunt Dan and Lemon* at the Royal Court, after (as I recall) I'd taken him to dinner somewhere. He proposed going backstage, and though reluctantly, I agreed. I'd been wrong, as it turned out; Wallace Shawn was delighted, and has remembered the occasion every time we've happened to meet. The last time was at a gathering of Chinese poets at the public library in Chinatown; when he saw me looking for a taxi afterward, he lent me ten dollars to make sure I had enough to get home on. He is, aside from his personal friendliness, a very funny man onstage. But when his father died I was really grieved. It's as though a whole world had come to an end. And though he was too polite to be anything but a well-wisher to Tina Brown, I think too that the latest developments could very well have hastened his death. One reason Hal and I had begun thinking of a house away from New York is that the place has become so crass—what's happened to the *New Yorker* being just one symptom. Of course there are still good things in it—such as the account of the NAS [National Audubon Society] headquarters—which I haven't seen, but hope to. I haven't been yet to the Matisse show, which out-of-towners are coming to visit in droves. And there's not much time. Thank you again, and Happy 1993!

Love,
Amy

. . . .

June 21, 1993
Dear George [Bradley],

Not that I was ever an exemplary correspondent, but this response to your presence in Cambridge, and the generous letter that followed, is egregiously overdue. There is a tiresome excuse—namely that a couple of months ago, after all kinds of tests, I landed in a hospital for some rather massive surgery, followed by chemotherapy (with more of same to follow). For a time I was too weak to hold a book and, almost, to follow the words on the page—though I had the marvelous lifeline of being read to: the letters of Diana Cooper and Evelyn Waugh, of all people, and more recently a new biography of Ottoline Morrell. So I'm working up a new period. Garsington! I was actually there once, swinging in the hammock outside the manor with the redoubtable Craig Raine. I've been deprived of country life myself, but tomorrow we go to Lenox, finally, equipped with a Diana Cooperish Italian straw hat. [. . .]

Ever,
Amy

. . . .

November 9, 1993
Dear Philip—

A very long time ago, Hal taped the CD you sent, with a small bonus at the end: a Samuel Barber song as recorded by his research assistant, Ellen Paltiel—a most extraordinary young woman who has a very nice mezzo voice, but decided that she'd rather be a top-notch lawyer than anything less than a diva. It's my fault that it has taken all this time to get it moving your way. I've been feeling a good deal stronger than when you were here, after a really rough seventh round of chemotherapy. Now everything is up in the air; since something nobody quite understands happened to the radiologist's interpretation of the latest CAT scan, the time seemed to have come for a second opinion, which now sends me (or rather next week it does) to a Dr. Hoskins at Sloan-Kettering, for a whole new consultation and look at the records. I must say that I'd begun to feel just well enough, between treatments, to be impatient with any more treatment at all. In the meantime, I've begun going out a little, and tonight I do a half-hour reading at a gallery in SoHo. Hal has bought me a spectacular feathered hat for the occasion, and various friends—including Vivian—have promised to be there. I managed a ten-minute reading at the 92nd Street Y a month ago, and more recently took part in a marathon Scandinavian Poetry Festival, along with dozens of others from here and there. What I really enjoyed was reading the English translation of a Swedish-language poet named Karl-Erik Bergman. He comes from Aland (pronounced Oland), a group of islands in the Baltic Sea which have been shuttled from Sweden to Finland to the Russians and back to Finland, and thus (I gather) have no strong allegiance to any place but their own. Anyhow, Mr. Bergman couldn't have been more delightful; he is a fisherman, and his poetry made me think a lot of the coast of Maine. We had a chance to confer a little— he speaks excellent English, but has trouble understanding it as spoken over here—and actually made changes in the translation before we went on. I must say that we seem to have been, as a team, something of a hit— applause for both Swedish and English for every single poem! Here's a sample, and you'll see why:

> It happens that I long to be gone
> when I see the wild geese move on in September.
> But as yet
> it isn't clear to me
> where I want to go.
> Actually it's irrelevant,
> as I lack wings.

Aside from that little project, I seem to have spent a good deal of my time lately on a translation project of sorts—doing a version of the part of Ovid's *Metamorphoses* that concerns Jason and Medea, beginning with the voyage of the Argo for the golden fleece. I'd been asked some time ago if I'd be interested, then halfway forgot about it until a reminder came, back in September. I managed to type and send it off last week.

We've been once more to the house in Lenox, taking along a load of books from the apartment on 12th Street. The rest of the belongings I decided to hang onto—not too many, but still a small truckload—went up there a week or so later. So Twelfth Street is finally altogether a thing of the past. We had a great time up there—glorious weather, and with that great air to breathe I felt really quite well. I hope it won't be too long before you can see the inside as well as the outside of the house.

Hal is well though a bit frantically busy. We both send our best. How are you all?

Love,

Amy

. . . .

December 9, 1993

Dear Sister Mary John—

It was a great satisfaction to have your letter, with its account of what is being done and thought of at the Abbey—and I like to think that under more usual circumstances it would have had an immediate response. I do want to say that what you say of monasticism being a kind of hidden glue of society—those are your words, as you may remember—is very much what I think, and I feel quite sure that I'm not alone in doing so. For one thing, there is my friend Kathleen Norris, of whose Benedictine connections I've written you from time to time. Earlier this year, she published a book called *Dakota: A Spiritual Geography*, in which solitude and community are the principal themes, and the response by reviewers (and I hope readers, of whom there must be a fair number, given the attention it got) suggests hardly less than a yearning for that kind of life. I will send you a copy, so that you or someone there can see what Kathleen is thinking about.

As for current unusual circumstances—my own correspondence has been pretty largely disrupted by my having been really ill. I'd begun a series of medical tests when I wrote you, as I recall, as a result of which at the end of April I found myself in hospital for what turned out to be ovarian cancer, which meant drastic surgery and a series of returns for chemotherapy. I've been feeling livelier in recent weeks, but must go back in tomorrow for what's called a laparoscopy—a look-see because it seems the only way to find out about certain blurry little readings by way of a C/T scan. With luck, I'll be out again in a day or two. All this has kept me from the house in Lenox except for three relatively short visits, in June, August, and October. Those were heavenly. I've read a lot (and been read to), and done some writing, mostly things I'd been commissioned to do. My friends have been wonderfully attentive—including a wonderful Jamaican nurse's aide named Vivian, who was my daytime companion in

the hospital and came nearly every day for several weeks after I got home; we even took her to Lenox with us the first time. She happens to be a wonderful cook, but above all else she is one of those great people who make one feel better just by being there. Hal is well. I can't but consider myself generally lucky in spite of everything. A gift to Oxfam America for their project in Haiti has gone off in behalf of the Community. My very best to all, and very much love always—
Amy

P.S.
The apartment on 12th Street, herewith commemorated [the letter is written on the back of a sheet containing the poem "A Catalpa Tree on West Twelfth Street," printed below], has been relinquished, and books, etc. still remaining have gone to the house in Lenox.

"A CATALPA TREE ON WEST TWELFTH STREET"

While the sun stops, or
seems to, to define a term
for the interminable,
the human aspect, here
in the West Village, spindles
to a mutilated dazzle—

niched shards of solitude
embedded in these brownstone
walkups such that the Hudson
at the foot of Twelfth Street
might be a thing that's
done with mirrors: definition

by deracination—grunge,
hip-hop, Chinese takeout,
co-ops—while the globe's
elixir caters, year by year,
to the resurgence of this
climbing tentpole, frilled and stippled

yet again with bloom
to greet the solstice:

What year was it it over-
took the fire escape? The
roof's its next objective.
Will posterity (if there

is any) pause to regret
such layerings of shade,
their cadenced crests' trans-
valuation of decay, the dust
and perfume of an all
too terminable process?

. . . .

February 1, 1994
Dear Barbara,
No, I have not graduated to anything resembling a computer. Rather, it
would appear, I have regressed, and can only pray to be legible—or illeg-
ible seldom enough to give you at least an inkling. [. . .]

Things since [last March] haven't been so cheerful. I'd been feeling not
well for some weeks, and it got worse, and at the end of April I had myself carved open to deal with what turns out to be ovarian cancer, followed
by what is now going into a second round—or I guess I mean a second *series*—of chemotherapy. Very educational. I've just begun to cope for myself, and with the help of enterprising friends. In fact, I couldn't have been
luckier in the friends who've rallied round, with flowers, visits, phone
calls, and offers to shop or visit a library. And Hal is just so comfy to be
domiciled with . . . the *hours* he has spent reading aloud, book after book
of letters or biography, novel after novel—we're now on *Le Père Goriot*—
are not to be totted up. There were weeks when I was too feeble to hold
a book, and he was my lifeline. I'm stronger now but there are periodic re-
gressions interspersed with being able to go out and Make an Appearance
fortified by some fantastic piece of millinery (since I have lost all my hair),
the latest being a velvet beret with coq feathers. People come to me, total
strangers, to say they love it—it's *that* outrageous. The most recent of
these forays has been a trip to Toronto for the Modern Language Association's annual convention, to read a small paper on Edgar Allan Poe that
someone had asked me to do. (Good poet or bad poet or what? I concluded, mostly *bad* poet but a serious one all the same—and wouldn't it
be interesting to think of him in connection with Emily Dickinson, an-

other isolated phenomenon?) That was between Christmas and New Year's, and we traveled from our hideaway in the Berkshires, where we spent something like two and a half weeks, blissfully. We seem to have cast our lots with the New England winter mode—it snowed and snowed, and sometimes the thermometer goes down to zero, but the thermostat works, there are snug storm windows (and a caretaker to put them up for us, along with a man to plow the drive whenever it snows again), and a fireplace that we sit by to read aloud or just beam at each other, and there is also my own little studio—first time in my life, a studio that's mine and not borrowed for the nonce—which looks out on an expanse of New England meadow, with animal tracks to puzzle over every morning, and squirrels to be observed at their food-gathering, a thing I'd never watched before, so that one might be in the back wilderness, though in fact there are next-door neighbors a few steps to the left and right. And a couple of miles off there are Karen and Paul whom we met in Italy and who have since become our close friends, and who led us to this house that is now ours. Karen and I have bonded over trips to second-hand furniture stores, out of which the house is piece by piece being furnished, with now and then a foray into pricier regions. My studio now has a *Turkey carpet*!!!! (shades of my own Dorothy Wordsworth's house-furnishing)—or more precisely a kilim in hot colors, along with a nineteenth-century cherry wood table by way of a desk, and a chair that turns out to be Jacobean—if one believes the dealer, and all that carving persuaded me he was to be believed. A very cheerful room, where I wrote two new poems before we were obliged to head back for New York. I hadn't been sure there were any poems left in me—though there is a *book*, just about to be published, any day now, of things written over the past two or three years, and you will be receiving a copy before very long. Meanwhile, my apologies for reverting to handwriting—the latest round of chemo has left me too shaky to deal with the typewriter, ever. [. . .]
Love,
Amy

. . . .

April 8, 1994
Dear Eileen,
Sorry to have been so slow about my book—but here it finally is. In the meantime, I've been not too far from your vicinity: a friend brought me to Key West (we took the train to Fort Lauderdale, where we rented a car),

and we had a delicious few days of exploring, eating fish, and absorbing the wonderful light and air. I've read Wallace Stevens aloud, and had a look at the outside of the house where Elizabeth Bishop lived. Yes, I saw the letters in the *New Yorker*—only a few, which make one eager to read the rest.

Now I'm back in New York, where the climate feels like a set back. I go back into hospital on Monday, for a third round of the new chemotherapy—but anyhow I've had a reprieve. The main effect has been to leave me very tired—but still hopeful, I look forward to the house in the Berkshires.

As for "checkers"—they can be exasperating—but I'd guess they're too unimaginative to be inclined to point out what *isn't* there. Editors are just as exasperating, most of the time. Good for you for keeping at them—and I do look forward to more about the child in the cold.
Love,
Amy

. . . .

POSTSCRIPT

September 5, 1994
Dear Barbara [Blay] and Joan [Goom],
I'm writing you partly as Amy's surrogate, partly on my own. She has been fighting ovarian cancer the last year and a half and has been over the summer very ill, increasingly so, and now too weak to write. I went up to Lenox for nearly a month in August to help her and Hal out. One of my tasks was the correspondence. I was fortunately there when your lovely spoon arrived, and so can tell you at first hand how delighted she and Hal were with it and the thoughts that sent it, and so convey their thanks to you.

Amy has not long to live, days, a few weeks. She's at home, essentially starving to death with no big pain, only occasional discomfort. Her situation is lovely: she lies downstairs in a hospital bed looking out over a long receding landscape of green lawn (the back lawns of several houses) and trees; in the foreground is a busy bird feeder, and a cat occasionally ambles, or stalks, by. Her care is wonderful—the local nurses—and Hal is bearing up. I left because I was staying in the house of friends who were on vacation and wanted me to take over their guardianship of Amy and Hal. So sad as the occasion is, Amy couldn't be in better hands and is slipping away easily and peacefully. There will be a gathering of family and friends afterward, informal, some of us speaking and/or reading, with her ashes to go in a spreading tree in the back yard.

I know this will be a shock and sad for you, but hope the details will give you both a sense of things. Amy is so fond of you both. Hal has a leave from Columbia and will be in Lenox through the fall.

I think often of those weeks I spent in England in 1989 and seeing you both, your welcome of me on Amy's behalf.

Affectionately,

Phoebe [Hoss]

* * *

Amy Clampitt died, at home in Lenox, overlooking the green and active expanse of her backyard, on September 10, 1994. Her ashes were buried beneath a beech tree there. Harold Korn, professor of law at Columbia University, her companion of twenty-five years and her husband of three months, survived her by almost seven years.

Index

Absolution, emotional reality of, 82

Academic life: challenges of teaching poetry, 246, 247, 249, 271–72; in Milwaukee, 244; poetry conference planning, 276; at Smith College, 280; and tour of school in Lincoln, 110; at University of Massachusetts, 258–61; at Washington University, 267–68

Acropolis in Athens, 139

Adams, Robert M., 274

Adviser, Clampitt as: for brother Philip, 10, 25, 36, 91–92; on free will, 40; and women vs. men on conflict, 189–90

Aesthetics of ritual, *see* Ritual, aesthetics of

Age, Amy's feelings about, 247

Agents, literary, 7, 143

"Agreeable Monsters" (Clampitt), 197

Alcott, Louisa May, 223

Alden, Henry, 231, 249

Alfred, William, 260

Algeciras, Spain, 113

Alice in Wonderland (Carroll), 223

Allen, Robert P., 75

All God's Dangers (Rosengarten), 171

Altar, mythological origins of, 81–82

American Poetry Review, 209

American Scholar, 195

Ammons, A. R., 173

Amsterdam, 252, 253

Anger, Amy's struggles with, 59–62, 158, 160–61

Anglican (Episcopal) Church: attraction to, xii, xv, 58–59, 60, 214–15; disenchantment with, 151, 215; and experiences missed in Iowa, 109; process of joining, 64, 65–67, 69–71; vs. Quaker sensibility, 107; ritual experiences, 75–82, 104; *see also* Nuns

Anglophile, Amy as, 3, 4, 25, 35, 179

Antaeus, 197

Antinuclear protests, 198, 227

Apartment on West 12th Street: attachment to, 106–7, 206; birdwatching at, 104–5, 150; conversion to co-op, 236; death of neighbor at, 92–93; moving out of, 283–84; refurbishing of, 98, 171, 226; subletting of, 103, 105

Aquinas, St. Thomas, 16

Archaic Figure (Clampitt), 274

Arensberg, Ann, 234

Aristotle, 77

Arrests and jail time adventures, 159,
162–63, 168–69
Art and artists: Amy on, 15–16; and
Audubon Society, 75; Brancusi sculpture
show, 45; Cloisters tapestries, 49–50;
complexity of, 6; Redouté (painter), 18;
see also Marcasiano, Peter
Arvon poetry competition, 252, 253
Ashbery, John, 243, 245–46
Asolo, Italy, 122
Assisi, Italy, 120
Atlantic, xi, 193, 195
"At the Welfare Hearings" (Clampitt),
167–68
Auden, W. H., 90, 242, 243–44
Audubon Society: beginnings of job with,
7–8; and bird people, 74–75; and bird-
watching, 63–64, 109; book review work
for, 127–28; gossip about, 143; job-leaving
considerations, 91; job stress crisis, 84–88;
novel-writing sabbatical from, 98–99;
parties at, 18–19; resignation from, 100,
103; working life at, xii, 12, 33
Augustine, Saint, 26, 68–69
Aunt Dan and Lemon (Shawn), 281
Awe, definition of, 22–23
Azores, 113

Bachelard, Gaston, 247
Bailey, Mabel, 68
Balanchine, George, 187, 194
The Ballad of Baby Doe (opera), 94
Ballet, Amy's fondness for, 4, 94, 144, 187,
194–95, 197
"Balms" (Clampitt), 208
Banton, Vivian, 270–71, 284–85
Baudelaire, Charles, 29
BBC recording of poetry reading, 257
Becoming a Heroine: Reading about Women
in Novels (Brownstein), 274
"Beethoven, Opus III" (Clampitt), 241
Bellagio, Italy, 115–16
Bellow, Saul, 178
Bells, church, 107–8
Bereavement, Amy on, 271
Berenson, Bernard, 15
Bereny, Dorothy, 135–36
Bergman, Karl-Erik, 283
Bergson, Henri, 40
Berkeley, California, 129
Berlin, Germany, 251
Berry, Eileen, xxi

The Best American Poetry, xvii, 269–70
Bible, Amy on, 5, 71, 79
Binder, Peter, 112
Biography and correspondence, ix–x
Birdwatching: and bird researchers at
Audubon library, 8, 74–75; in Central
Park, 20, 25, 28–29, 32, 41, 63–64; in
Dallas area, 230; in England, 238, 255; in
Iowa, 108–9; in Maine, 209, 212; near
apartment, 104–5, 150; and respect for
nature, 16; sparrow's home near Fifth
Avenue, 62–63
Bishop, Elizabeth, 180, 185, 201, 288
Bitter Lemons (Durrell), 208
Black and Brown Caucus, 150–51, 152
Blake, Dorothy, xxi, 271
Blay, Barbara, xxi
Bloom, Harold, 207
Bok, Derek, 260
Bolshoi Ballet, 94, 144
Bombing of Soviet Embassy (1979), 204
Bonjour Tristesse (Sagan), 29
Book of Nightmares (Kinnell), 233
Book research work, see Editorial/research
jobs
Bookstores, Amy's fondness for, 33–34,
106–7, 256
Boston, Massachusetts, 236, 242, 244–45,
260
Boston University, 244–45
Bourne, Nina, 236
Bowdoin College, 278
Bowen, Elizabeth, 206
Box Hill in England, 254–55
Boyajian, Cecile Starr, 21–22
Bradley, George, xxi
Brancusi sculpture show, 45
Braudel, Fernand, 178
Braverman, Libby, xxi
Britain, Great, see England
Broadstairs, England, 255
Brodsky, Joseph, 213, 242, 244, 265, 277
Brontë, Emily, 45, 53
Brown, Tina, 281
Brownstein, Rachel, 274
Buckley, William F., 30–31
Burford Bridge Hotel, 254

California, 129
Calvinism, Amy on, 22
Cambridge, England, 250–51, 253, 257
Camus, Albert, 158

Cancer: Amy's ovarian, 282–83, 284–85, 286, 288–89; Hal's lymphoma, 270

Cannes, France, 115

Canvassing for Democratic vote, 145, 147

Careers, *see* Audubon Society; Editorial/research jobs; Writing career

Carlyle, Thomas, 34

Carroll, Lewis, ix, 223, 226

Carruth, Hayden, 223

Carson, Rachel, 55

Carter, Jimmy, 206

Carter, Rosalynn, 206

"A Catalpa Tree on West Twelfth Street" (Clampitt), 285–86

Central Park: birdwatching in, 20, 25, 28–29, 32, 41, 63–64; as escape from city life, 32–33; free Shakespeare performances in, 97, 128–29, 192–93

CETA (Comprehensive Employment Training Act), 208

Chase, Karen, 279

Chepstow, England/Wales, 123–27

La Chinoise (Godard), 146

Churches: in Assisi, 120; in Bellagio, 117; Greek Orthodox, 132, 133; music in, 50, 52, 58–59, 78–79, 95; NYC vs. Midwest, 107–8; power struggles in Iowa, 56; in Wales, 125–26; *see also* Religion

Church of the Epiphany, NYC, 151

Clampitt, Amy: biographical sketch, x, xi–xii, xiv–xv; and dealing with anger, 59–62, 158, 160–61; as defined by literature, xv; gratitude attitude, xix, 5, 10, 224, 285; last illness and death of, 282–89; nonconformity of, 33, 38–39, 42–43, 88–89; overview of character, xix; self-analysis, 23–25, 39, 195–96, 252–53

Clampitt, Beth (sister), xiv, 100–101, 103, 111

Clampitt, David (nephew), 176, 202–3, 205, 208, 215

Clampitt, Frank (grandfather), xiv

Clampitt, Holly (niece), 176

Clampitt, Larry (brother), xiv, 278

Clampitt, Pauline (mother), 101, 169, 176, 182, 197, 198

Clampitt, Philip (brother), xxi, 10, 25, 36, 57, 91–92

Clampitt, Richard (brother), 219

Clampitt, Roy J. (father), xiv, 56–57, 166, 169, 247

Clapp, Sara and Steve, 168

Clare College, 257

Clarissa (Richardson), 270

Clark, Barbara (McClenon), xiii, xxi

Clark, Ramsey, 163–64

Classical music, *see* Music

Class reunion, 166–67

The Cloisters, 46, 49–50

The Cloud of Unknowing, 92

Coleridge, Samuel Taylor, xi, 240

Colorado trips, 154, 230

Columbia University, 206, 208

Colwin, Laurie, 234, 235

The Common Reader (Woolf), 275

Communism, 202

Community of St. John Baptist, 91, 111

Company vs. solitude, *see* Solitude vs. company

Comprehensive Employment Training Act (CETA), 208

Confession, value of, 82

Confessions (Augustine), 26, 68–69

Conflict of interest, human relations as, 11, 12, 17–18, 23–24

Conservatism, Amy's flirtation with, 29–30

Conventionality vs. personal growth, 23–25

Convent life, visiting, 91, 111, 127–28, 215, 256

Cooking and cuisine: Amy's recipes, 172–73; and entertaining guests, 148, 170, 183, 841 in Minnesota, 229–30; Swiss, 251–52; vegetarian, 218, 220

Coppelia (ballet), 4

Corn, Alfred, 234, 243

"The Cove" (Clampitt), 193

Creation vs. evolution, 32

Creative Evolution (Bergson), 40

Crime in NYC, Amy as victim of, 205–6

Critics, discovery of Clampitt, xi; *see also* Vendler, Helen

Cummings, e. e., 173–74, 272

Cynicism vs. disillusionment about love, 44

"The Dahlia Gardens" (Clampitt), 220–21

Daily trivia as Clampitt theme, xviii; *see also* Observation, Amy's powers of; Weather

Dakota: A Spiritual Geography (Norris), 284

Dallas, Texas, 230

Dance: and Amy's natural rhythm, 184; ballet, 4, 94, 144, 187, 194–95, 197; as metaphor for life, 194

Dance Theatre of Harlem, 187

Daniel Deronda (Eliot, G.), 207

Dante Alighieri, 14, 15, 54, 64

Darwin, Charles, ix, 32
Day of the Locust (West), 250
Delos, Greece, 141–42
Delphi, Greece, 140–41
Democratic convention (1968), 147–48
Depression: Amy on, 91–92; Amy's holiday, 153, 183
Des Moines, Iowa, 101, 106
Dickens, Charles, 177, 181, 188–89, 200, 249, 255
Dickey, James, xi
Dickinson, Emily, xi, 245, 286–87
The Didactic Muse (Spiegelman), 274
Discipline, religious, 76–77
Disillusionment vs. cynicism about love, 44
Doctors, Amy's skepticism about, 76–77, 86
Dogma, religious, 5, 55
Dominance as driving force in relationships, 11, 12, 17–18, 23–24
Don Quixote (ballet), 144
The Dream of a Common Language (Rich), 197
Dubus, André, 263
Durrell, Lawrence, 208
Dutton publishing house, Clampitt's work at: boss's role in poetry publication, 188, 190; editing projects, 181, 182; employment arrangement, 178, 199; end of job relationship, 242; Lana Turner memoir, 217; manuscript reading, 197; overview of, xii

Easter celebrations, 82
Ebenezer Welsh Presbyterian Church, 125–26
Eccles, Lady Mary, 263–64
Eccles, Lord David, 263–64, 266
Eckelberry, Don, 74–75
"The Edge of the Hurricane" (Clampitt), 201
Editorial/research jobs: author relations on long project, 193; Christmas rush on, 177, 189; environmental position paper, 156–57; Franklin project, 169, 176; indexing and editing project, 169; overview of, xii; for Schoenbrun, 145, 176, 217; as source of income, 171; *see also* Dutton publishing house, Clampitt's work at
Eichelbaum, Stanley, 63
Eisenhower, Dwight David, 28
Elections and political views, 72–74, 110–11, 145–49, 215

The Electrification of the Soviet Union (opera), 265–66
Eliot, George, xi, 188, 197, 200, 207
Eliot, T. S., 17, 70, 267, 268
Emerson, Ralph Waldo, 37
Emotions, Amy on, *see* Feelings
England: Amy's love for, 3, 4, 25, 35, 179; and nature, 9–10, 238, 255; 1960s trip, 142; 1980s trips, 237–40, 250–58, 265–66
English literature, Amy's love for, 53–54
Environmentalism, 156–57, 187–88
Epidauros, Greece, 142
Epiphany, Church of the, NYC, 151
Episcopal Church, *see* Anglican (Episcopal) Church
Essays, Amy's, 220
Essential nature vs. free will, 39–40
European sojourns: conference trip with Harold, 264; on France, 203, 253; Germany, 251; Greece, 131–42; Italy, 95–96, 102–3, 112–23, 135–38; lessons from, 40; loss of desire for travel, 166; memories of youthful, 51–52, 95–96, 102–3, 107–8; The Netherlands, 252, 253, 266–67, 268; plans for in 1970s, 176–77; Switzerland, 251–52; *see also* England
Evil, reality of, 60
Evolution vs. creation, 32
Exercise program, 190, 191, 194, 195, 197, 207
"Existential Choice" (Clampitt), 169
"Exmoor" (Clampitt), 208

Façade (ballet), 4
Faith, role of, 62, 69–70, 74
Fame, period of, *see* Recognition, public
Family events: father's academic honors, 166; parents' deaths, 169, 198; parents' golden anniversary, 153–54; reunions in Iowa, 105–6, 130–31, 182; sister Beth's mental illness, 100–2; visits to brothers and their families, 127, 176, 229–30; *see also individual family members*
Family opinion, Amy's sensitivities to, 91
Farb, Peter, 177
Fashion and clothing: during final illness, 283, 286; in 1950s, 3, 31, 82; in 1960s, 143, 152; in 1970s, 170–71
Fear: Amy's loss of, 52, 53; as primary obstacle to happiness, 83; as root of all evil, 57; of thinking for oneself, 28; vs. ultimate benevolence of deity, 82

Feelings: Amy on anger, 59–62, 158, 160–61; and Amy's response to art/literature, 6–7, 50; and appeal of religion, 61–62; as central to successful writing, 35; happiness as self-generated, 42–43, 49, 58; importance of expressing, 5, 11; sorrow and joy dichotomy, 93–94; and truth, 17; virtues of emotional pain, 11–12, 22, 44, 58

Feldman, Irving, 279

Fields, Barbara, 280

Firebird (ballet), 4

Fitness program, 190, 191, 194, 195, 197, 207

Fitzgerald, F. Scott, 13, 83–84

Fleurs du Mal (Baudelaire), 29

Florence, Italy, 118, 120

Flye, Fr., 104, 105

Forms and styles, literary, see Styles and forms, literary

Fox, George, 62

France, Amy on, 203, 253

Francis of Assisi, Saint, 5, 120

Freedman, Joe, 238

Free love, 11

Free will, Amy on, 14, 39–40, 54

Friendships, see Personal relationships

Frost, Robert, 245

Funerals, apartment neighbor's, 92–93

Funiculare railway in Naples, 136–38

Gabriel, Dan, x

Gandhi, Mahatma, 11

Gene (apartment neighbor), death of, 92–93

Generations and interaction with hippies, 146, 147, 157, 163–64

Germany, 251

Ghost-writing job, 130–31

Gibraltar, 113, 133–34

Ginsberg, Allen, 173–74, 233

Gittings, Robert, 239, 240

God and Man at Yale (Buckley), 30–31

Goodman, Joe, 5, 6, 20–21, 58–59, 90–91, 94

Goodman, Paul, 218–19

Good works vs. prayer, 66

Grace, interpersonal role of, 61

Graham, Jorie, 269

Grand Canyon, 129–30

Grand Street, 237

Gratitude, Amy's attitude of, xix, 5, 10, 224, 285

Great Britain, see England

The Great Gatsby (Fitzgerald), 13, 83–84

Greece: mythology of, 143–44, 145, 222; trip to, 131–42

Greek language: ambitions to learn, 26; coursework in, 218, 219, 222, 224, 226–27; learning on voyage, 131–32, 133; translation project, 283

Greek Orthodox Church, 132, 133

Greene, Graham, 67

The Greening of America (Reich), 163

Gregory, Dick, 149

Griffin, John, 267–68

Grinnell College, 166, 200, 215, 248–49

Guggenheim Fellowship, 224, 227, 228

Guggenheim Museum, 45

Guide to Bird Finding West of the Mississippi (Pettingill), 20

Hacker, Marilyn, 234

"A Hairline Fracture" (Clampitt), 210, 212

Hamilton-Phillips, Martha, xvii, xxi

Hampstead, England, 238, 239–40

Happiness as self-generated, 42–43, 49, 58

Harper's, 223

Harvard University, 242, 260

The Haw Lantern (Heaney), 261

Heacox, Tom, 251

Health issues: colds and such, 8–9, 46, 196–97, 260; for Hal, 270; knee problems, 36–37; laryngitis and poetry readings, 217, 219–20, 235–36; and Lenten privations, 76–77; ovarian cancer, 282–83, 284–85, 286, 288–89

Heaney, Seamus, 248, 251, 253, 257, 261, 262

Hecht, Anthony, 207–8, 213, 242–43, 244

Herbert, George, 256

Hippies, working with, 146, 147, 157, 163–64

Hirsch, Edward, xxi, 232–33

History, holistic fabric of, 16–17

History of England (Trevelyan), 34

Holden, Jonathan, 220

Holy Week experiences, 76–82

Homeric epics, 222

Homosexuality, early views on, 14

Honors, Amy's, see Recognition, public

Hopkins, Gerard Manley, xi, 202

Horowitz, Israel, 245

Hospital of St. Cross, 255

Hoss, Phoebe, xii, xiv, xxi, 27, 289

House in Lenox, 278–79, 283–84, 287

Housing crises in NYC, 97, 157–59, 161–63, 167

Howard, Richard, 236, 242, 247

Howl (Ginsberg), 233
Hughes, Daniel, 233
Hughes, Ted, 258
The Human Equation (Farb), 177
Human nature, observations on: bird
    people, 8, 74–75; and difficulties of
    personal transformation, 22; and inev-
    itability of human progress, 54; self-
    acceptance needs, 84; on stupidity, 26–
    28; *see also* People watching; Personal
    relationships
Humboldt's Gift (Bellow), 178
Humility and gifts of religion, 66
Hungary, Soviet invasion of, 72

I, Claudius (Graves), 57
Ideas Have Consequences (Weaver), 29
Iliad (Homer), 222, 226
Illnesses, *see* Health issues
Illuminations (ballet), 4
Immortality, Amy on, 69
Incredible String Band, 152
Independence of mind, importance of, 12,
    28, 30–31
Inferno (Dante), 14, 15
Inflation, price, 156, 171
Intellect, Amy on, 36, 66
The Interpretation of Dreams (Freud), 207
Intuition: as decision-making method,
    88–89; feminine origins of, 55; impor-
    tance of, 17; and inspiration, 52–53; and
    listening, 71; vs. scientific knowledge,
    69–70
Iona, Island of, 254
Iowa: loss of family home, 176; memories
    of, 26; nature in, 20, 107, 127, 215, 248;
    plans for moving to, 101, 103; post-fame
    visits, 215, 230–32; temporary residence
    in, 106–10; *see also* Family events
Iowa City, Iowa, 107
Ischia, Island of, 135
Isherwood, Christopher, 243
Isolation vs. community, *see* Solitude vs.
    company
Israel, on U.S. policy toward, 215
Israel in Egypt (Handel oratorio), 94
The Isthmus (Clampitt), x
Italy, 95–96, 102–3, 112–23, 135–38

Jackson, Wes, 279–80
Jail time adventures, 159, 162–63, 168–69
James, Henry, 34, 54

James, William, 58
"Japanese Characters" (Salter), 222–23
Jersey Meadows poem, 190
Jogging program, 190, 191, 194, 195, 197,
    207
John Keats, the Disinterested Heart (Sister
    Thekla), 256
Johnson, Charles, 3
Johnson, Samuel, 275
Journal writing, Amy on, 52, 61, 76
Judaism, 196, 205, 215
Judging of poetry, Amy on, 252, 253, 258,
    269–70

Kansas City, 109
Kazin, Alfred, 260
Keats, George, 265
Keats, John: correspondence of, 245; as
    inspiration, x–xi, xix, 224; literary pro-
    duction of, ix; and philosophy, 256;
    poems on, xxi, 226, 228, 233, 236–37, 238;
    possible book about, 221–22; reintroduc-
    tion to, 51; visit to haunts of, 238, 254–55
"Keats at Teignmouth" (Clampitt), 228
Kennan, George, 145
Kennedy, John F., 111
Kenyon Review, 208, 210, 213, 216, 218, 225
Keswick, England, 254
Key West, trip to, 287–88
Kiesel, Margaret Matlack, 231, 248–49
The Kingfisher (Clampitt): and Amy's
    response to success, xvi; arrangement of
    poems in, 240–42; British edition, 243;
    launching party for, 185–86, 232–35;
    publication process, 221, 225, 227
Kinkead, Eugene, 63
Kinnell, Galway, 233
Kipnis, Igor, 170
Kissinger, Henry, xvii, xxi, 164
Kitchen, Paddy, 202
Knopf publishing house, 43, 222, 234
Knudson, Zan, 234
Korn, Harold: and Amy's illness and death,
    288, 289; Amy's missing of, 166; appreci-
    ation of poetry readings, 210; caring for
    Amy, 197, 286; European conference trip,
    264; first mention, 148; illness of, 270;
    Jewish background of, 205; joys of being
    with, 152, 207; lack of correspondence to,
    xiii; as life partner, xii, 170; perfectionism
    of, 193–94; and reading aloud tradition,
    xvi, 212–13, 249, 271, 278, 286; relation-

ship background, 172; relationship issues, 160–61, 189–90; teaching duties, 207; virtues of, 208

Kybart, Peter, 251

Laden, Henry, 166
Lake Como, Italy, 115
Landscape as theme, *see* Nature
Langer, Suzanne, 10, 17
Language, power of, 55
Language of the Stage course, 260–61
Lansdowne, Fenwick, 75
Lawrence, D. H., 25–26, 26
Lea, Sydney, 220
Le Gallais, M., 18–19
Legionnaires' disease, 270
Lehman, David, xxi
Leithauser, Brad, 211, 244
Lenox, Massachusetts, 278–79, 283–84, 287
Lent and Easter experiences, 75–82
"Letters from Jerusalem" (Clampitt), 196, 203
Letters to Young Churches (Phillips), 89–90
Letter writing: collection composition, xi, xii–xviii; demise of, ix; editor's method, xx–xxi; summary of Amy's themes, xviii–xix
Leyden, The Netherlands, 266–67, 268
Liberalism, Amy's, 149; *see also* Politics
Liberals, Amy on, 31
Librarian, Amy as reference, *see* Audubon Society
Library of Congress, readings at, 244
Liddy, James, 243
Lieberman, Laurence, 209
Life: importance of natural, 15–16; living vs. intellectual observation of, 55–56
A Life I Did Not Plan (Clampitt, R.), xiv
Lindsay, Hal, 268
Lindsay, John, 153, 163
Lisbon, Portugal, 133
Literary life and literature: on Audubon Society research papers, 33; on English literature, 53–54; on George Eliot, 273–75; on Henry James, 34; on literary people, 68, 199–200, 234; literature vs. life, 42; and reading life, 40–41, 68; on Salinger, 35; on *Wuthering Heights,* 53
Little Men (Alcott), 223
Little Women (Alcott), 223
Logic, inadequacies of, 17
London, England, 239, 251, 257–58, 265

London, Jean Dimond, 206
Loneliness, Amy on, 12, 38–39, 42–43
The Lonely Crowd (Riesman), 38
Los Angeles, California, 129
Love, Amy on, 22–23, 67, 70; *see also* Romances
Lowell, Robert, 185, 245
Lucia di Lammermoor (opera), 163
Luxembourg, visiting dignitaries from, 18–19

MacArthur Foundation grant, 277, 279–80
McCarthy, Eugene, 145–49
McCarthy, Joseph, 18, 26–28
Macaulay, Thomas Babington, 34
McClatchy, J. D. (Sandy), 234
Machiavelli, Niccolo, 16
Macrae, John III, 222, 242
Maine sojourns, 174, 180–81, 209–10, 211–14, 228–29, 277–78
Malamud, Bernard, 245
Mansfield, Katherine, 52
Marcasiano, Peter: beauties of friendship with, 50–52; deep conflict with, 59–62; initial meeting in Paris, 26; loss of relationship, 64–65; as Mary Russel's friend, 45; nature of relationship, xiii; personality of, 36; reconciliation with, 70
March Against Death, 151
Marjorie Morningstar (Wouk), 44
Marriage, Amy on, xii
Marshall, Anne (Sr. Mary John), xxi, 108, 117
Marshall, John, 115
Matlack, David, 231, 249
Matlack, George, 231
"Matoaka" (Clampitt), xvii, 281
Maundy Thursday, 79–80
Mayer, Milton, 56–57
The Maze Maker (Ayrton), 145
The Mediterranean (Braudel), 178
Mediterranean voyages, 112–23, 131–40
Men, Amy on, 208
Mental illness, sister Beth's, 100–1, 103; *see also* Psychoanalysis
Merrill, James, 209
Messina, Italy, 138
Metamorphoses (Ovid), 283
Michel, Rimsa, xxi, 261
Middlemarch (Eliot, G.), 188, 274–75
Millett, Kate, 163
The Mill on the Floss (Eliot, G.), 274

Milne, A. A., 266
Milton, John, 104
Milwaukee, Wisconsin, 244
Les Miserables (Hugo), 278
Mitchell, Arthur, 187
Monastic life, Amy on, 81, 215, 284; *see also* Nuns
Money and finances, Amy on, 5–6, 39
Monica, Countess de la Salle: Amy's replacement of, 84–85; on artists, 59; dislike of title, 20; on evolution vs. religion, 32; inheritance of, 103; on Suez Canal crisis, 73; support for Amy, 60
Montpelier, Vermont, 261–62
Moore, Fr., 71
Moral philosophy, 13–15, 23–24, 29–30, 76, 77
Moratorium movement, 150
Morgan Library, 262
Morralé, Fr., 69, 70–71, 119
Morrisroe, Patricia, 247, 250
Moses, Robert, 97
Moss, Howard: Amy's first meeting with, 200–1; on Columbia University, 208; dinner with Amy, 206, 207; health problems of, 220; at *Kingfisher* launch party, 185–86, 234; on monotony of manner in poetry, 190; and publication of Amy's poetry, xi, 214
Multitudes, Multitudes (Clampitt), x, 199, 200
Mumford, Lewis, 167
Murphy, John, 215
Music: appreciation of, 6–7, 50, 186–87; church, 50, 52, 58–59, 78–79, 95; concerts/operas attended, 31, 90–91, 94, 97, 152, 163, 170, 186, 256, 265–66, 267; David Clampitt's career in, 202–3, 205; employment issues for musicians, 215; government support for orchestral, 208; listening to classical, 206, 211, 214; and local friends, 20–21; on ocean liners, 112; as poetic metaphor, 272; recorder playing, 111, 117, 130; singing at parties, 13; Welsh singing, 124–26; *see also* Dance
The Mysteries (play), 257–58
Mysticism and stillness before unknown, 22–23
The Myth of Sisyphus (Camus), 158
Mythology: altar origins, 81–82; Amy's love of Greek, 143–44, 145, 222; and Gatsby as mythological character, 13; and Greek sightseeing, 138, 139

Naples, Italy, 114–15, 135–38
Nation, 218
The Natural History of Selborne (White), 9
Nature: in Colorado, 230; in England, 9–10, 238, 255; enjoyment of, xii, 9–10, 56; and environmentalism, 156–57, 187–88; far northeast, 174; and importance of outdoor time, 32–33, 46; in Iowa, 20, 107, 127, 215, 248; Italian landscape, 120; at Lenox house, 287; loss of in city life, 48; in Maine, 182, 211–12, 277–78; in Massachusetts garden, 259; and Pennsylvania countryside, 93; Peter's appreciation of, 51; roses, 19; seasonal observations, 76; in southern U.S., 264; and spirituality, 15–16, 33; spring in NYC, 190, 191; as theme in writing, xviii; Welsh countryside, 124; *see also* Birdwatching; Weather
Nauplia, Greece, 141
Naxos, Greece, 142
Neimeyer, Carl, 249
The Netherlands, 252, 253, 266–67, 268
New Criticism, Amy's critique of, 275
Newport, Wales, 124–26
New Republic, 218
The New School, 217, 218, 224
Newspapers, confusion of, 27
New Testament anthology, contribution to, 268
New York City: Amy's love of, 6, 106; anxieties of, 261; crime in, 205–6; housing crises in, 97, 157–59, 161–63, 167; increased dangers of, 140; loss of character, 262, 281–82; Nixon's residence in, 204–5; poetry readings in, 235–36, 262, 283; politics in, 96–97; slices of life in, 34, 47–48; vs. small town life, 107–8; theater in, 4, 178, 250, 281; water supply problems, 3; *see also* Apartment on West 12th Street; Central Park; Weather
New York City Ballet, 4, 187
The New Yorker: and income boost for Amy, 246; minor contributions to, 31–32; on Nixon's NYC residence, 204–5; Our Man Stanley, 63; ownership changes, 250, 281; publication of Amy's poetry, xi, 185–86, 188, 190, 192, 193, 195, 200–201, 208, 214; style of poetry for, 237
New York Magazine profile, 247, 248, 250

New York Public Library, 178
New York Times, 72, 169, 244
Nineteenth century as Amy's inspiration,
    x–xi, xviii, 14
Nixon, Richard, townhouse of, 204–5,
    206–7
Nixon in China (opera), 267
Nominalism, 29
Nonconformity, Amy's, 33, 38–39, 42–43,
    88–89
Norris, Kathleen, 284
Novel writing: break from Audubon Society
    for, 98–99; crisis vs. job, 86–88; in Iowa,
    109; mid-1960s, 142, 143; progress of, 5,
    29, 128; publishing frustrations with, 5, 7,
    35–36, 43, 48–49, 111–12, 143
Nuns: Amy's impressions of, 71, 80–81, 215;
    convent visits, 91, 111, 127–28, 215, 256

Oberhaldt, Ralph, 215
Observation, Amy's powers of: at
    Cambridge University, 257; on Iowa,
    107; Italian memories, 96; natural color
    contrasts, 33; NYC life, 33–34, 47–48;
    on small-city Minnesota, 229–30; on
    Winchester, 255; see also Nature; People
    watching
Ocean voyages, 112–23, 131–40
O'Connor, Flannery, 211
O'Dwyer, Paul, 148
O'Hara, Frank, 246
Olson, Charles, 215
Olympia, Greece, 141
On the Trail of Vanishing Birds (Allen), 75
Operas, 31, 94, 163, 256, 265–66, 267
Optimism, Amy's, 5, 10, 224, 285
"Or Consider Prometheus" (Clampitt), 208
Origin of Species (Darwin), 32
Our Man Stanley (New Yorker), 63
Ovid, 283
Oxford University, 257, 266
Oxford University Press, xi–xii, 38

Pacifism, Amy on, 11, 12
Padua, Italy, 121–22
Pain, emotional, virtues of, 11–12, 22, 44, 58
Paley, Grace, 198, 243
Palma, Spain, 113–14
"Palm Sunday" (Clampitt), 179–80
Palm Sunday experience, 78–79
Papp, Joseph, 97, 129
Paradise Lost (Milton), 5

Paradiso (Dante), 64
Parties and social life, see Social life and
    parties
Past vs. present, living in, 40, 70, 71
Paul, Saint, 89–90
Pavia, Italy, 116
Peale, Norman Vincent, 83
Penguin poem, 193
Penrith, England, 254
Pentagon of Power (Mumford), 167
People watching: in arrests for protesting,
    159; in Greece, 141; and Italian green-
    grocer, 34; in Italy, 136–37, 138; in Maine,
    181; on ocean voyages, 112–14, 134; at
    parties in NYC, 179
Performance in front of audiences:
    enjoyment of, 198, 199, 220, 249; Iowa
    experience, 231–32; overcoming of shy-
    ness in, 167, 184, 185
Personal relationships: Amy's privacy on,
    xiii; conflict of interest as basis for, 11, 12,
    17–18, 23–24; with father, 56–57; on fine
    line between love and hate, 65; on friend-
    ships with women, 44–45; generosity of
    friends, 8–9; with Mary Russel, 56; psy-
    choanalysis affect on, 21–22; truthfulness
    in, 161; and virtues of emotional pain,
    11–12, 44, 58; youthful romances, 24, 42,
    67; see also Korn, Harold; Marcasiano,
    Peter
Petrement, Simone, 179
Pettingill, Olin Sewall, 20
Phi Beta Kappa poet, Amy as, 260
Philadelphia, Pennsylvania, 93
Philosophy: Amy's comprehension
    difficulties with, 10, 253; and Keats, 256;
    on Machiavelli, 16–17; moral, 13–15,
    23–24, 29–30, 76, 77; nominalism, 29
Philosophy in a New Key (Langer), 10
Pirsig, Robert, 173
Plath, Sylvia, 167, 245
Play It As It Lays (Didion), 250
The Play of Daniel (church pageant), 90
Playwright, Amy as, 260, 262, 264, 271
Poe, Edgar Allan, 286
Poetic Closure (Smith), 273
Poetry, 208
Poetry and poets: Amy's attraction to, 51;
    Amy's late entry into poetry, xv; on
    Anthony Hecht, 207–8; cultural revival
    of, xvii; dance themes, 187, 195; on Dylan
    Thomas, 47; forms and styles, 63, 225,

237, 271–73; and George Eliot's novels, 274–75; Howard Moss on, 190; inspirations, x–xi, 29, 52–53, 149, 185, 196, 203, 241–42; on James Merrill, 209–10; judging of, 252, 253, 258, 269–70; and Keats, 221–22, 224–25, 226, 228, 233, 236–37, 238; during last illness, 287; letters to up-and-coming poets, 271–75, 276; on meetings with poets, 227–28, 232–35, 242–43, 245, 260, 263; on modernism in, 174; personal transformation and poet's birth, 53–56; Peter's rejection of Amy's poem, 65; pride in accomplishment, 59; production levels, 203, 212, 213, 220–21, 253; and reading of Bible aloud, 71; sharing with other poets, 199–200; on subjectivity of appreciation, 269–70; teaching of poetry, 246, 247, 249, 271–72; Vermont as mecca for poets, 261–62; virtues of reading aloud, 47; William and Mary commission, 280–81; workshop in poetry, 182; see also Publishing of work; Readings, poetry

Poetry Northwest, 225

Politics: Amy's dedication to, xi, xii, xv, xvii; anti-McCarthyism, 26–28; anti-nuclear protests, 198, 227; anti-Vietnam War protests, 144–45, 147, 150–52, 154–56, 159, 164–66, 168–69, 171–72; in church power struggles, 56; and disillusionment with Anglican Church, 150–51, 152, 215; and elections, 72–74, 110–11, 145–49, 215; and function of art in culture, 6; lack of long view in, 202; NYC, 96–97, 150, 153, 157–59, 161–63, 167; and pacifism, 11; Quaker roots of activism, xvii; reading of conservative ideas, 29–30, 31

Ponsot, Marie, 227–28

Poor People's Campaign, 146–47

Portrait of the Artist as a Young Dog (Thomas), 47

Prayer, uses of, 60, 61, 66, 68–69, 87

Present vs. past, living in, 40, 70, 71

Presidential elections, 72, 110–11, 145–49, 215

Private property and Amy's politics, 30, 31

Prose vs. poetry style, xviii–xix; see also Novel writing

Prostitutes, life of, 165

Protestantism, Amy's critique of, 66, 77, 87

Psychoanalysis: conflicted feelings about, 13–15, 21–22, 37, 83; and Philip's depression, 91–92; and religion, 66, 69

Publishing business, Amy on, 38, 176, 223, 242; see also Editorial/research jobs

Publishing of work: book collections, 221, 222, 225, 227, 234, 240–42; frustrations with novels, 5, 7, 35–36, 43, 48–49, 111–12, 143; and life vs. literature, 42; loss of desire for, 68; poetry in magazines, 169, 185–86, 188, 190, 192, 193, 195, 197, 200–201, 206, 208, 214, 216, 218, 225; possibilities for poems, 55; on rejection notices, 212

Purgatorio (Dante), 16

Pym, Barbara, 277

Quakerism: Amy's commentary on, 71–72; and family history, xiv; vs. high Anglican church, 107; and political activism, xvii; and simple life, xvi, xix

Quinn, Alice, 221, 225, 227, 236, 240

Quint, Robert, xxi, 201–2, 205, 214

Radcliffe Camera, 266

"Rain at Bellagio" (Clampitt), 241–42

Raine, Craig, xxi, 253, 257, 265–66

Ransom, John Crowe, 217, 219

The Rapture (Lindsay), 268

Ravenna, Italy, 121

Reader, Amy as: ancient Greek authors, 144; and attention to style, 68; biographies, 202; and books as reflections of personality, 56–57; on Camus, 158; childhood favorites, 223; and holistic fabric of history, 16–17; natural world, 9–10; 1950s choices, 5, 10, 13, 29–30, 38, 89–90; 1970s choices, 171, 173, 178, 180, 197; 1980s choices, 207, 208, 211, 219, 233, 239; and old bookshops, 33–34; overview, xv–xvi; on personal growth through reading, 40–41; reading aloud tradition, xvi, 177, 181, 188–89, 200, 212–13, 249, 271, 278, 286; tiresomeness of books, 46; and trading of books with friends, 26

Readings, poetry: after-parties, 6–7, 213, 217–18; in Boston, 244–45, 260; cultural revival of, xvii, xviii; in England, 251, 257; first performances, 182–83, 184, 185; at Kenyon College, 217, 219–20, 225; for Kingfisher launch, 233; at Library of Congress, 244; in NYC, 198, 235–36, 262, 283; and other poets, 209–10, 213; payment for, 242

Recognition, public: Amy's attitude toward, xvi–xviii; correspondence from old associates, 206; fan letters, 243; honorary degree at Bowdoin College, 278; in Iowa, 231–32; Phi Beta Kappa honor, 260; William and Mary commission, 281; *see also* Performance in front of audiences; Readings, poetry

Recorder, playing of, 111, 117, 130

The Red and the Black (Stendhal), 26

Redouté, Pierre-Joseph, 18

The Red Shoes (ballet), 4

Reference librarian work, *see* Audubon Society

Reform Democratic club, 145, 163

Reich, Charles, 163

Relationships, *see* Personal relationships

Religion: Amy's attraction to, 5, 58–59, 60, 61–62, 214–15; art and music in, 50; on Augustine, 68–69; dogma vs. doctrine, 55; and intuitive knowing of faith, 17; Judaism, 196, 205, 215; Protestantism's shortcomings, 66, 77, 87; Quakerism, xiv, xvi, xvii, xix, 71–72, 107; Roman Catholicism, 66, 77, 117, 120; and seasonal rituals at churches, 75–76; spirituality in nature, 15–16, 33; as subject of first inspired poem, 53; and suffering as path to growth, 22; virtues of, 61–62, 66, 86–87; *see also* Anglican (Episcopal) Church

Reviewer, Amy as book, 127–28, 270

Rich, Adrienne, 197

Riesman, David, 14, 38

Rigoletto (opera), 256

Rilke, Rainer Maria, 273

Ritual, aesthetics of: Amy's fondness for, 49–50, 58, 71, 78–82, 104, 109; Assisi commemoration, 120; general appeal of, 214–15; Greek Orthodox, 133; and importance of funerals, 93

Roman Catholicism, 66, 77, 117, 120

Romances: clues to Amy's lovers, xiii–xiv; in Greece, 141–42; and life lessons, 24, 42, 44; and ocean voyage courting rituals, 112, 113–14; youthful, 24, 42, 44, 67; *see also* Korn, Harold

Rome, Italy, 117–19

Rosen, Ken, 263

Der Rosenkavalier (opera), 31

Rovere, Richard, 26–27

Russel, Mary, xiii–xiv, xxi, 45, 73, 95–96, 102

Saint Augustine, 26, 68–69

Saint Cloud, Minnesota, 175–76, 229–30

Saint Francis of Assisi, 5, 120

Saint John Baptist, Community of, 91, 111

Saint Louis, Missouri, 267–68

Saint Luke in the Fields, Church of, NYC, 64

Saint Mark's Church, NYC, 150–51, 152

Saint Paul, 89–90

Saint Paul's Church, Manhattan, 79

Saint Thomas Aquinas, 16, 77

Salinger, J. D., 35

Salter, Mary Jo: Amy's analysis of "Japanese Characters," 222–23; as Amy's correspondent, xxi, 199–200; birth of child, 244; discovery of Amy, xi; marriage of, 211; publishing progress, 210

"Salvage" (Clampitt), 208

Salzburg, Austria, 122–23

Samos, Greece, 142

Santa Fe, New Mexico, 130

Santayana, George, 40

Savannah, Georgia, 264

Scandinavian Poetry Festival, 283

The Scarlet Letter (Hawthorne), 68

Schnackenberg, Gjertrud, 210

Schoenbrun, David, 145, 176, 217, 235

Schulman, Grace, 201

Scientific approach, drawbacks of, 69

Scribner's publishing house, 43

Seigel, Sam, 224, 226

Self-acceptance, human need for, 84

Self-analysis, Amy's, 23–25, 39, 195–96, 252–53

Self-interest and fear of independent thought, 28

Self-righteousness, Amy on, 66

Sestina form of poetry, 225

Sewing, 4, 46–47

Sexton, Anne, 245

Sexuality as sin, 13–14

Shakespeare, William, 44

Shakespearean plays in Central Park, 41, 97, 128–29, 192–93

Shawn, Wallace, 281

Shearer, Moira, 4

Shelley, Percy Bysshe, 44

Sicily, 138

Silas Marner (Eliot, G.), 200

Sills, Beverly, 163

Simone Weil: A Life (Petrement), 179

Simple life, Amy's comfort with, xvi, xix, 5–6, 39

Sin and need for moral compass, 13–14

Sister Mary John (née Anne Marshall), xxi, 108, 117
Sister Thekla, 256
Sleeplessness, Amy on, 211
Smith, Barbara Herrnstein, 273
Snodgrass, Jennifer, xxi
Social life and parties: at Audubon Society, 18–19; for book launchings, 185–86, 232–35, 259; on European sojourns, 112, 115–17, 132, 133, 134–35; excessive singing at, 13; with Goodmans, 6–7, 91; holiday season, 153, 169–70, 183, 184; hosting of, 207; in Kansas City, 109; and Mary Russel, 45; and Monica's new-found wealth, 103; as moral imperative, 76; and music appreciation, 6, 186–87; and NYC scene, 36, 95, 103, 179; original ambitions for, 23–24; politically related, 148; postpoetry reading, 6–7, 213, 217–18; and real vs. superficial conversation, 35; see also Cooking and cuisine; People watching
Society, Amy on, 19–20, 24–25
Solitude vs. company: and Amy's dedication to reading, xvi; and Amy's family environment, xiv; human need for both, 36; and loneliness, 12, 38–39; solitude as sin of self-indulgence, 76, 91; and talking to self, 13; for writers, xi, 228, 275, 284
Somerset, England, 266
Sonnenberg, Ben, 234, 237, 245–46
Sons and Lovers (Lawrence), 26
Sontag, Susan, 268
Soul on Ice (Cleaver), 162
South, observations on the, 249–50, 263
Soviet Embassy bombing (1979), 204
Space exploration, 15
Spain as stop-off on way to Italy, 113–14
Specialization, inevitability of, 40–41
Sphere (Ammons), 173
Spiegelman, Willard, 274
Spirituality: Amy's expanded, 216; dogma vs. spiritual feeling, 5; first poem as expression of, 54–55; and nature, 15–16, 33; necessity of transcendent reality, 29–30, 31; spirit as more real than matter, 74; summation of Amy's Anglican, 69–70; see also Religion
Squatters' movement in NYC, 157–59, 161–63, 167

Staffa, Scotland, 254
Starbuck, George and Kathy, 245
Stendhal (Henri-Marie Beyle), 26
Stephen, J. K., 212–13
Stevens, Wallace, xix, 233, 288
Stevenson, Adlai, 72
Stevenson, Anne, 253
Stone, I. F., 218
Strand, Mark, 182
Stromboli, Island of, 138
Styles and forms, literary: Amy's, x–xi, xviii–xix, 36, 200; Amy's attention to as reader, 68; New Yorker's preferred poetry style, 237; poetic forms, 63, 225, 273; and poetry-writing challenges, 271–72
Suburbia, Amy on, 175–76, 230
Suez Canal crisis (1956), 73
Suffering as gateway to growth, 11–12, 22, 24–25
"Sunday Music" (Clampitt), 225, 240
"The Sun Underfoot Among the Sundews" (Clampitt), 186
Swenson, May, 233, 234
Switzerland visit, 251–52

The Taming of the Shrew (Shakespeare), 192–93
Teaching profession, critique of, 38; see also Academic life
Telepathic experiences, 69
Terza rima poem, 63
Theater: Amy as playwright, 260, 262, 264, 271; in Central Park, 41, 97, 128–29, 192–93; in England, 256, 257–58, 265–66; in NYC, 4, 178, 250, 281; religious, 90, 257–58; student staging of Waiting for Godot, 259, 261
Thekla, Sr., 256
The Lonely Crowd (Riesman), 14
Thesiger, Wilfred, 197
Thomas, Dylan, 47–48
Thoreau, Henry David, 54
"The Tides" (Clampitt), 195
Tinbergen, Niko, 20
Tindall, William York, 208
Tintern Abbey, 123–24
Tortoise story, 9–10
Toynbee, Arnold J., 5, 58
Transformation, personal, Amy on, 22, 37, 50, 53–56, 64
Translation projects, 283

Travel, Amy's love of, xvi; *see also individual destinations*
Travel sketches writing idea, 143–44
Trevelyan, G. M., 34
The True Believer (Hoffer), 18
Truth, Amy on, 6, 17, 161
Turner, Frederick: on Amy's essay, 220; on Amy's poetry reading performance, 217; Amy's reluctance to meet, 210; dedication of poem to, 238; hosting of Amy, 218, 219; on James Merrill, 209
Turner, Lana, 217
Turner, Mei Lin, 218, 219
12th Street apartment, *see* Apartment on West 12th Street
Tyrrell, Arthur, 111

United Kingdom, *see* England
University of Massachusetts, 258–61

Varieties of Religious Experience (James), 58
Vendler, Helen: Amy's regard for, 234; comments on Amy's work, 226–27; as correspondent, xxi; initial interest in Amy's poetry, xi, 214; Keats book by, 221–22, 233; meetings with, 236, 245; support for Amy, 224–25, 242; surgery of, 252
"Venice Revisited" (Clampitt), 247–48
Vermont, 261–62
Vesuvius, Mount, 135
Vietnam War: and disenchantment with church, 150–51, 152, 215; letter to Kissinger, 164–66; protests against, 144–45, 147, 150–52, 154–56, 159, 164–66, 168–69, 171–72
Village Independent Democrats, xii
Villanelle as exercise in poetry writing, 273
Villa Serbelloni, Bellagio, Italy, 115–16
Vocation, Amy on, xiv–xv, 84–88, 99
"Voltaire at Ferney" (Clampitt), 242
Vonnegut, Kurt, 243
Vosburgh, John, 143
Voting, Amy on, 72
The Voyage of the Beagle (Darwin), 211
"Voyages: A Homage to John Keats" (Clampitt), xxi, 236–37

Waard, Ely de, 253
Waiting for Godot (Beckett), staging of, 259, 261

Wakulla Springs, Tennessee, 264
Wales and Welsh singing, 123–27
Wall, Bea Mills, 249
Wall, Joe, 166, 249
Warren, Rosanna, 244–45
Washington, DC, 154–56, 157
Washington Square Park, 97, 150
Washington University, St. Louis, Missouri, 267–68
The Waste Land (Eliot, T. S.), 267, 268
Wayne State University, 232
Weather: and birds in Central Park, 20, 28–29; in England, 238, 254, 255; foggy NYC, 62; in Iowa, 109, 197; in Italy, 119; on ocean liners, 112; rainy NYC, 214; spring in NYC, 75–76, 79, 127; summer in NYC, 97–98, 100, 103; as theme in letter writing, xviii; winter in NYC, 32, 53, 54, 189
Weaver, Richard M., 29
Weed, Fr., 87
Weil, Simone, 179
West, Nathanael, 250
Weston, Edward, 197
West 12th Street apartment, *see* Apartment on West 12th Street
What the Light Was Like (Clampitt), 237, 252
White, Gilbert, 9–10
Whitman, Walt, xi
Wilbur, Richard, 233, 268
William and Mary College, xvii, 246–47, 249, 280–81
Williams, William Carlos, 200
Winchester, England, 254–55
The Wings of the Dove (James, H.), 34
Wittgenstein, Ludwig, 110
Women: Amy on gender relations, 189–90, 208; difficulties in friendships with, 44–45; and feminine origins of intuition, 55; in George Eliot's novels, 274–75
The Women's Room (Durrell), 208
Wood, John, xxi
Woolf, Virginia, xvi, 245, 275
Wordsworth, Dorothy, xi, 254, 262, 264
Wordsworth, Richard, 262
Wordsworth, William, xi, 212–13, 264
Wouk, Herman, 44
Writer-in-residence positions, *see* Academic life

Writing career: confidence in style, 36; and distractions of NYC social scene, 103; essays, 220; ghost-writing, 130–31; jobs as interfering with, 86–88, 91; vs. love of living, 49; naturalness of for Amy, 98–99, 106; *see also* Novel writing; Poetry and poets; Styles and forms, literary

Wuthering Heights (Brontë), 45, 53

Zen and the Art of Motorcycle Maintenance (Pirsig), 173